Economics

4th edition

A student's guide

John Beardshaw
David Brewster
Paul Cormack
Andrew Ross

Dedicated to John Beardshaw 1943–1995

Pearson Education Limited
Edinburgh Gate
Harlow
Essex CM20 2JE
England

and Associated Companies throughout the world

Visit us on the World Wide Web at:
http://www.pearsoneduc.com

Fourth edition 1998

ISBN 0 582 303486

British Library Cataloguing-in-Publication Data

A catalogue record for this book is available from the British Library

Library of Congress Cataloging-in-Publication Data are available

Set in Sabon by 30
Produced by Pearson Education Asia Pte Ltd.
Printed in Singapore (COS)

10 9 8 7 6 5 4 3
04 03 02 01 00

Contents

SECTION III
The theory of distribution

SECTION VIII
Problems and policies

Preface

Today there is a wider range of excellent economics textbooks to choose from than ever before. It is natural therefore for students to ask 'which is the best?' Well, although John Beardshaw was flattered when the third edition of his famous textbook was the 'winner' of a comparative review of economic textbooks, he stressed that economic theory itself tells us that league tables are not necessarily a useful approach to making choices. For whereas economics tells us that competition through product differentiation can be wasteful, it also identifies that a monopoly may be a bad thing, not only because of the lack of price competition, but also because a monopolist is unlikely to cater for the range of characteristics desired by different consumers.

As with all textbook authors worth their salt, John was demonstrating that even quite elementary economics can be used to cast new light on everyday questions. Indeed, economic analysis is at its most useful when it reveals the essential issues at stake and hence the 'real' judgements and questions that must be addressed in actual decision making. Put simply, John saw that the product differentiation in the market for economics texts had increased overall student welfare and that hence students should use the recommended books which best suit their own needs and preferences.

That said, not all texts are good examples of their kind. Like consumers in other markets where knowledge is imperfect, students will not be familiar with the products on offer and are likely to make the wrong initial choices. Teachers therefore have the difficult task of recommending the correct learning resources for their students. Obviously, a text which is difficult to understand, irrelevant to the syllabus and inaccurate is unambiguously a bad text. Good characteristics, however, tend to be more conditional. The teacher must consider the suitability of various resources for particular courses and students.

There are the theoretically rigorous introductory texts for students who are intending to become economists. In effect they are introductions to econometrics without the mathematics and their 'scientific' approach must be part of the toolkit of anyone who wishes to study modern economics in depth. Some are truly excellent for the purpose and have become acknowledged classics selling well over a million copies. Nevertheless, for many students new to the subject, particularly at 'sub' degree level, they can appear unworldly, arid and difficult to get to grips with. In the jargon of educationalists, these books emphasise 'propositional' knowledge. For many students they are simply hard to swallow in terms of complexity and level of abstraction. At worst students may become so desperate that they engage in meaningless rote learning.

At the 'other end' of the product range there are the texts which have an almost magazine like format. They invite the student to interact with the world around them and hence 'discover' the underlying principles involved in ways which build on their own experiences. These texts can motivate students by their lively approach and by engaging the reader's own thought processes in helping to understand the world they see around them. Educationalists may say that they emphasise 'reflexive' learning. For many students, however, such texts can be frustratingly without structure. Emphasising activity rather than exposition, bits of economic analysis can suddenly appear in them rather like rabbits from a hat. In the absence of an explanation as to where such tools of analysis come from, the student may struggle to re-invent the wheel. At worst the student may come to be content with an impressionistic and disjointed form of shallow learning.

Perhaps the above descriptions are rather unfair caricatures, but they serve to identify the purpose of this book. In the preface to the third edition John Beardshaw states that it is the 'chief objective' of this book to 'bridge the gap' between these two types of texts. Judging by the popularity of the book John got it right. This edition aims to build on this success. To the extent that it retains its well established traditional strengths, it is more 'scholarly' than other more 'light-hearted' approaches. To the extent that it has utilised findings from recent research in teaching and learning, it is more worldly, digestible and interactive than other more complex and 'didactic' approaches.

What is new?

This edition further embraces and develops an 'active learning' approach to teaching and learning, but it avoids the mistake of confusing active learning with simply providing a set of resources for activities. The book is therefore packed with ***student activities, questions*** and ***data response*** exercises, but it is also unashamedly a textbook which seeks to provide the student with a structured and graduated ladder to understanding.

Admittedly, written text is a limited medium for interactivity, but this edition seeks to avoid the misconceptions which so frequently block understanding by pointing out the most ***common student misunderstandings*** as it goes along. The authors would be delighted to hear of other examples of such common misunderstandings, for this technique of addressing them at source is proving to be an extremely powerful aid to teaching and learning.

One feature missing from this edition are the quotations at the heading of each chapter. Although section quotes are included, it was a difficult decision to remove them from the chapter headings as many readers clearly derived pleasure from them. It was felt, however, to be uneconomical with space to retain these along with the addition of ***learning outcomes*** at the beginning of each chapter. Learning outcomes could not be omitted as they assist in making explicit what students are expected to achieve and hence are part of an active learning approach. The limits set on interactivity by written text again prevents these from being assessed learning outcomes in the strict use of the term, but they are more effective as direction signposts than quotations. Nevertheless, it is sad to see the passing of the previous tradition.

With his usual prescience, John Beardshaw wrote in the preface of the third edition, 'We have a greater need than ever to understand the problems which face us in the capitalist and mixed economies in which we live. We need to do more than simply place our faith in a uniformed belief in the magic of the "market place".' Today there are few who would disagree with John's emphasis. The experience of recurring recessions in the 'mature' Western economies, the recent turbulence in many 'Tiger' economies, the severe problems of transition faced by the former Soviet bloc countries and the new uncertainties of globalisation all highlight the inadequacy of a narrow equilibrium analysis approach. Within the necessary confines of the syllabus, this book continues to be deliberately more pluralist than most comparable texts and welcomes the resurgence of a more balanced approach elsewhere.

In accordance with this more pluralistic approach, and in addition to extensive updating and rewriting, this edition has important new features. At John's insistence, there is a new chapter which gives an intuitive account of John Maynard Keynes' fundamental insights free from the imposed constraints and distortions of equilibrium aggregate demand and supply analysis. Students will find this an easier approach to understanding the recent resurgence of Keynesian ideas. There is also far more applied economics with which to demonstrate the complexity of the real world and the problematic nature of applying abstract theory, for example in the case studies on privatisation and transport. The section on the theory of the firm relates to realistic market conditions and is not simply the traditional elements of disembodied value theory 'disguised' as an analysis of the firm. The challenge of 'green economics' and the application of economic analysis to environmental issues are both well represented. The essential insights of non-mainstream thinkers such as Friedman, Galbraith, Marshall, Hayek, Keynes, Kalecki, Schumpeter and Marx are referred to, hopefully with a lightness of touch which informs and broadens understanding by making the student aware that there are alternative ways of looking at the economic problem.

In the extensive rewriting, much attention has been given to reworking any exposition which fell short of the book's usual standard of clarity. Simplifications have been made to fit the new syllabuses better, e.g., the use of the 'Keynesian-Cross' has been reduced and simplified. Superfluous text has been trimmed out and much new material has been added. Mistakes have been corrected (no doubt a few new ones slipped by!). Data has been updated and simplified. More recent sources for data response questions have been added while the most useful of the original ones have been preserved. A systematic framework of learning objectives, integrated exposition and application, student activities and the highlighting of common misunderstandings, followed by summary, question and data response has emerged and we have attempted to apply this consistently where compatible with the particular task in hand.

Some issues of syllabus and coherence of content remain unresolved. For example, how much mathematical technique is it useful to introduce? How far should important but marginal syllabus topics such as demography and development be covered? Can the distinction between the short-run and the long-run of the firm be adequately represented without going too deeply into the much criticised 'geometry' of cost curves? To what extent should distinctions between schools of thought be developed? We don't think anyone really has definitive answers, but we look forward in anticipation to the usual correspondence!

How to use this book

Any textbook standing alone is an inadequate resource, even with the further reading listed at the back of this book. Education is intrinsically about a dialogue of minds, and so access to a good teacher is indispensable. There are, however, a wide range of other resources for the student to use independently. Indeed, students are unlikely to do well unless they themselves keep up to date and attempt to apply what they have learnt to new situations. Fortunately, students are today surrounded by an embarrassment of riches. There are many informative newspapers and periodicals full of examples of economics in action. In addition to this radio and television usually provide a stream of well-informed reporting. For many students there is now the additional access to the wealth of information provided by CD ROMs and the Internet.

As far as this book is concerned, a graduated approach to learning has been adopted. The first part of the book deals with the fundamentals of the subject and its basic vocabulary; as such it could form the basis of an introductory course. The remaining parts then develop the main areas of the subject. It is well recognised, however, that a problem endemic to economics is that it often appears difficult to appreciate parts of the subject without understanding the whole. In an attempt to cope with this difficulty copious use is made of cross-referencing. It is hoped that the summaries and questions at the end of the chapters may act both as a revision aid (a method of checking progress against the learning outcomes) and as a method of reinforcing essential ideas.

In conclusion

We hope that this edition is a worthy extension of the approach developed by John Beardshaw. Reviewers commissioned to give expert feedback on the drafts were enthusiastic, one was positively ecstatic but another didn't like it at all. For a book which seeks to occupy a distinctive market position this is a promising start, but obviously the most important judgement is your own. Economics profoundly affects all our lives and seeks to explain some of the most powerful forces of the human world. Whatever book you use or recommend, we would like to emphasise that studying economics should be interesting. If students are not finding it so then something is wrong. Unless you can find out what it is, motivation is likely to wane and potential will not be fulfilled. This book does require effort as few would argue that economics is easy! We hope that this edition helps makes studying economics interesting and successful for many more students.

David Brewster
Paul Cormack
Andrew Ross

Authors

John Beardshaw

John Beardshaw graduated from the London School of Economics and taught at colleges in and around London before becoming Senior Tutor in Banking Studies and Lecturer in charge of Economics at Southgate College. John maintained his regular teaching throughout a career which included authorship, examining and awards moderation, consultancy for a major merchant bank and a highly successful series of intensive revision courses for A-level students.

He began writing on economics with the intention of producing a book for students which was both comprehensive and comprehensible. Since his first and very successful publication in the late 1970s, he went on to write other well received textbooks, workbooks and articles on economics. This work brought him international recognition as a leading author in his field.

David Brewster

David Brewster has taught economics at Thames Valley University for over twenty years. He has written a number of articles in the field of industrial economics and has recently published '*Business Economics: Decision Making and the Firm*' (Dryden Press). He has also been a visiting Professor at California State University, Fullerton.

Paul Cormack

Paul Cormack is Senior Lecturer at Thames Valley University where he has taught economics for the past twenty years. Prior to teaching at degree level he had experience in teaching to A-level in two London schools. He studied economics at Hull University and Leicester University.

Andy Ross

Andy Ross was working as a telephone engineer when he returned to education at Southgate College as a mature student. He then studied as an undergraduate and graduate at the London School of Economics and as a post graduate at Birkbeck College London. He was awarded a distinction for the teaching Certificate of Education from Garnett College and taught A-level economics for five years before entering higher education. Since then he has held the post of Head of the Department of Economics and Head of the School of European and International Studies. Andy is currently the Director of the College of Undergraduate Studies at Thames Valley University.

Acknowledgements

Gratitude goes to Andreas Kyriacou, of Thames Valley University, for his major contribution to this edition in updating and rewriting the section on International Economics. Thanks also to Ross Parker for his research in locating and updating the many statistics used, with the cooperation of the British Library of Political and Economic Science. Thanks also to Clive Wilson in the Learning Resource Centre of Thames Valley University.

A particular thank you is given to Denise Beardshaw who read the entire manuscript and contributed comments and advice.

Acknowledgement must also be given for Malcolm Cummings, Chris Faux and David Palfreman for their contributions to previous editions.

Permission has been sought from the many newspapers and statistical sources used and these are noted as appropriate, but if any have been inadvertently overlooked, the publishers will be pleased to make the necessary arrangement at the first opportunity.

Appreciation also for the support, guidance, tolerance and patience of the team at Addison Wesley Longman; especially Paula Harris, Anna Herbert, Lee Hodder and Christian Turner.

As usual, the authors accept responsibility for any mistakes or shortcomings.

part I

Introduction

SECTION I Economics and the economy: an overview

SECTION 1 Economics and the economy: an overview

'It is not from the benevolence of the butcher, the brewer or the baker that we expect our dinner, but from their regard to their own self interest.'

Adam Smith

1 Introduction: what is economics about?

Learning outcomes

At the end of this chapter you will be able to:

- State what economists mean by the term **economic problem** and be able to use this idea to give a definition of economics.
- Explain the importance of **economics** for the current and future well-being of humankind.
- Describe and criticise the **scientific method** in relation to the work of economists.
- Define the term **price mechanism** and contrast **market** and **planned economies** as approaches to dealing with the economic problem.

The subject matter of economics

Students who can relate economics to the world around them will find it a fascinating subject. This should be easy for you to do, for examples of economic forces at work are all around you and are constantly in the media. This book will help you to recognise and analyse these powerful forces that affect us all.

There is something of interest in economics for almost everyone. This is because it is a very wide-ranging subject. Economics looks at people and production; markets and institutions; enterprise and exploitation; individual behaviour and social relations; scarcity and choice; prosperity and poverty; power and free trade; national economies and globalisation; efficiency and waste; crisis and growth; inequality and welfare; rent and reward; the creation and destruction of resources; the environment and the prospects for the economic future of humankind. It is a dynamic subject which studies changes in the economy and which itself changes as new ideas, and old ones, battle for influence.

Although there is much that economists will agree on there are also vast differences between different groups, or *schools*, of economists. They disagree as to what are the important areas of study, the scope and nature of the subject itself, as well as more technical matters such as the accuracy and interpretation of economic data. This is also true of the natural sciences such as physics at their frontiers of knowledge, but economics is made more involving for the student as its debates are so often the subject of intense media and political interest. Indeed, economics is seen to be so important to our lives that few people refrain from offering their views on economic matters regardless of their own training or lack of expertise in the subject! Economics cannot provide a set of ready-made answers, but you will be better informed on completion of this book and will have a had an insight into how exciting the study of economics can be.

Defining economics

As you might have suspected by now, a single definition of economics is unlikely to cover all its aspects. And yet, economics is as old as the human race. When some cave-dweller went out to hunt while others remained to defend the fire, or when skins were traded for flint axes, we had economics. But economics as an academic discipline is relatively new: the first major book on economics, Adam Smith's *The Wealth of Nations*, was published in 1776. Since that time the subject has developed rapidly and there are now many branches of it, such as microeconomics, international economics and econometrics, as well as many competing schools of thought.

Economics can help explain many of the changes we see around us. Recent examples include the collapse of the Soviet Bloc, privatisation, concepts of a stakeholder economy, the globalisation of products, the increase in paid female employment and part-time employment, increased inequality, rising participation in education, increased road congestion, urban decay and homelessness. But although most people are aware of economic forces affecting their lives few could define economics.

Most definitions of economics focus on ***scarcity*** and ***choice***. Virtually everything is scarce, not just diamonds or oil but also bread and water. How can we say this? The answer is that one only has to look around the world to realise that there are not enough resources to give people all they want. It is not only the very poor who feel deprived; even the relatively well-off seem to want more. Thus when we use the word scarcity we mean that:

All resources are scarce in the sense that there are not enough to satisfy fully everyone's wants. For the individual and humankind it seems that wants exceed means.

Common misunderstanding
Scarce should not be confused with 'rare'.

We can therefore say that resources are limited both in rich countries and poor countries. The focus for much of economics is to evaluate the choices that exist for the use of these resources. Thus we have another characteristic of economics: it is concerned with choice. Thus we could define economics as:

The human science which studies the relationship between scarce resources and the various uses which compete for these resources.

The central economic problem

There are many economic problems which we encounter every day – poverty, inflation, unemployment, etc. However, if we use the term economic problem we are referring to the overall problem of the scarcity of resources. Each society is faced with this, be it people still living a Stone Age life in New Guinea, people in the Commonwealth of Independent States, the USA, Poland or Argentina. Each society has to choose how to make the best use of scarce resources. The American Nobel Prize winner Paul Samuelson said that every economic society has to answer three fundamental questions: 'What?', 'How?' and 'For whom?'

What? What goods are to be produced with the scarce resources – clothes, food, cars, submarines, television sets, etc.?

How? Given that we have basic resources of labour, land, etc., how should we combine them to produce the goods and services which we want?

For whom? Once we have produced goods and services we then have to decide how to distribute them among the people in the economy.

STUDENT ACTIVITY 1.1

Read a newspaper to find an example of any economic concern of the day, e.g. inflation or unemployment. Explain why it is part of *the* economic problem of scarcity and choice and how it affects the questions of what, how and for whom.

Economic goods and services

All the things which people want, goods and services, are lumped together by economists and termed ***economic goods.***

Economic goods are those which are scarce in relation to the demand for them.

As such this definition encompasses almost all the resources in the world: not to be an economic good a resource would have to be not scarce.

About the only thing which fits happily into this category is air. But even a good in natural abundance could be made scarce if someone were able to establish property rights over it and hence restrict its supply.

STUDENT ACTIVITY 1.2

Make a list of things which are currently free. Describe ways in which a charge might be set by someone who owned all of the free good. Is it true that a price could be set for all the things you have listed? In the light of this explain why a price can be set for most things.

Wealth and welfare

An early definition of economics was that it is the study of wealth. By wealth the economist means all the real physical assets which make up our standard of living – clothes, houses, food, roads, schools, hospitals, cars, oil tankers, etc. One of the primary concerns of economics is to increase the wealth of a society, i.e. to increase the stock of economic goods. However, in addition to wealth we must also consider welfare. The concept of welfare is concerned with the whole state of well-being. Thus it is concerned not only with more economic goods but also with public health, hours of work, law and order, and so on. It is not difficult to see that it would be possible to increase the level of wealth in a society while decreasing its level of welfare. For example, if everyone were to work 50 per cent longer per day the country's wealth would be increased, but it is doubtful if its welfare would, because people would be overtired, their health would suffer, and so on.

Modern economics has tried to take account not only of the output of economic goods but also of economic 'bads' such as pollution. The wealth/welfare connection is thus a complex aspect of the subject.

Wealth and money

Economics is not just about money as many people think. Indeed we could have an economy without money. Also, if we consider economics to be the study of wealth, it is at once obvious that we could print twice as much money without altering the real wealth of the economy. The subject matter of economics is therefore much broader than the study of money.

Common misunderstanding

People often think money is wealth and has value itself. In fact, it is merely paper or metal, or even bank deposits which have no physical form at all! Money is just a claim to wealth. Nevertheless, changes in the quantity of money circulating in the economy could affect behaviour and hence change the outcomes of the central questions of the economic problem. Thus, although economics is not directly concerned with money as wealth, its effects on the outcomes of the central economic questions are studied by economists.

Methodology in economics

Consider the following two statements:

a) The death penalty reduces the number of murders.

b) Murderers deserve to die.

Which statement attempts to state a fact and which is a value judgement? You may agree or not agree with the first statement, but it asserts a relationship which may be investigated through investigating statistical evidence. For example, the murder rate may be compared under regimes which do and do not have capital punishment. If such evidence clearly points one way or the other, investigators may agree on whether the relationship exists or not even though they disagree over the second statement. In contrast, the second statement expresses a personal belief, or value judgement, about what ought to happen to murderers – it could not be disproved by any amount of statistical evidence.

Statement a) is called a ***positive statement*** and statement b) is called a ***normative statement***:

Positive statements concern what is, was, or will be and hence depend on facts. Normative statements concern what ought to be and hence depend on value judgements as to what is good or bad.

Unfortunately, even positive statements are usually difficult to prove or disprove as evidence is often incomplete, conflicting, or capable of being interpreted in different ways.

For example, consider the statement: 'Trade unions are the cause of inflation because in pushing up wage costs they also push up the price of the goods.'

This assertion has in fact been extensively investigated, but there is no consensus of opinion. Even where an apparent relation between trade union power and rising prices seems to have been statistically established, this has not settled the debate. One problem is that there is no clear-cut way of measuring union power, so how would we know which of the various possible measures is 'correct'? Another problem is that of the direction of causation. For example, are unions pushing up prices or merely attempting to keep pace with prices that are already rising? Even if unions succeed in pushing up wages and prices in one market will this not cause prices to fall in other markets? Moreover, trade unions are just one part of an economic system which itself might be the cause of industrial conflict and wage/price spiralling – is it a value judgement to single out unions for the blame? You will not have to study economics for long before realising:

Debates over the truth of positive statements in economics are seldom settled by looking at the facts because the facts are rarely simple and rather than 'speaking for themselves' have to be interpreted.

Does this mean that the investigation of issues by economists is pointless? No! The issues involved are just too important to be left to politicians and the 'layperson'. Even if disagreement cannot be eliminated, it can be reduced and the areas of disagreement clarified through rigorous investigation of the facts as seen from varying viewpoints.

Scientific method

Some economists say they attempt to test economic ideas scientifically, but how is this done? Scientific method begins with the formulation of a theory about behaviour. For example, we may put forward the idea that the demand for a good is determined by its price. On the basis of this we may reason that as the price is increased, demand goes down, while if the price is decreased the demand will go up. This then gives us a hypothesis which can be tested on observed behaviour. This testing of ideas on the evidence is known as ***empiricism***. Having made our observations we may then:

a) confirm our theory;
b) reject it;
c) amend it in the light of the evidence.

This process is shown in diagrammatic form in Fig. 1.1.

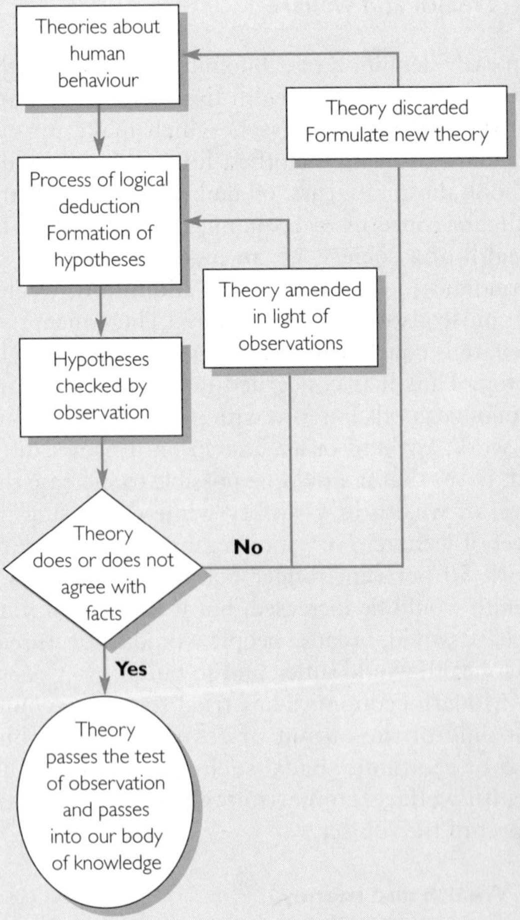

Fig. 1.1 **The scientific testing of theories**

STUDENT ACTIVITY 1.3

Try to explain what consumers are trying to achieve when they go shopping. This needs to be a very general theory which applies to most consumers and to most things which consumers may buy. Obviously there will be exceptions to the rule. Think about how your own behaviour matches up to this theory. Does your own behaviour or that of others contradict your theory? Later in this book you will read how economists have developed theories to explain consumer behaviour. Make a note to compare your theory with these.

Ceteris paribus

This is the Latin expression which means all other things remaining constant. This is an essential component of scientific method. In physics, for example, if we wished to test the effects of heat upon a body we would not simultaneously change the pressure, altitude, etc. It is the same in economics; if, for example, we wish to examine the effect of price on demand we do not simultaneously change incomes, tastes, etc. Therefore, when formulating economic principles, we are usually careful to state that such and such will happen, *ceteris paribus*. This principle presents particular problems in the social sciences because, whereas in the natural sciences we can undertake laboratory experiments, this is not possible where human society is concerned – we cannot command all social factors except one to stand still. This does not mean, however, that we have to abandon scientific method; rather, we should work harder to refine it in relation to the subject.

Human behaviour

It can be argued that since economics is concerned with human behaviour, it is impossible to reach any firm conclusions. This may be so if we consider the behaviour of one person, since human beings are unpredictable and may react in opposite ways to the same stimulus. However, while individuals are unpredictable, people in large numbers are not. If, for example, we increase people's income it is possible that any particular individual may or may not spend more. However, if we examine what happens to a million people as their income increases it is possible to conclude that, overall, their expenditure will increase. Thus, examining a large number of people's behaviour allows us to take advantage of the law of large numbers. This law predicts that the random behaviour of one person in a large group will be offset by the random behaviour of another, so that we are able to make predictions about the behaviour of the group as a whole.

Dissenting schools of thought

So far this chapter has tended to outline the ***mainstream*** or orthodox view of economics which gained almost total dominance after the Second World War and which still dominates economic syllabuses. This approach has emphasised a model of 'scientific economics' with its emphasis on the testing of positive statements by reference to, supposedly, value-free empirical data. But many of the century's most influential economists, such as Keynes and Hayek, have rejected this methodology. There are deep philosophical considerations here, but the student of economics soon comes to realise that the subject is inherently controversial. Many economists have come to accept that it is misleading to present these controversies in economics as debates between experts over purely technical matters. Increasingly there is a recognition that economics is a value-laden subject.

Such is the level of controversy in economics that there is a case for introducing the subject as competing schools of thought rather than a single discipline. Indeed, a more rounded view of a problem can often be gained by considering arguments from various schools of thought, and examiners do give credit for this. Those who reject the notion that mainstream economics is scientific and value free often prefer the original term of 'political economy' to 'economics'. Political economists take the view that an economist *necessarily* interprets theories and empirical data through a political perspective. It must be realised that there is a distinction between bias and dishonesty. In an honest and tolerant world bias should be confessed without shame or loss of argument; dishonesty will be hidden as it would destroy all credibility if discovered.

The syllabuses to which this book is directed do not demand a detailed knowledge of alternatives to the mainstream approach and this book does not pretend to give a proper airing to them. Nevertheless, wider arguments are included where appropriate. The major alternatives to the mainstream (or neo-classical synthesis) approach mentioned in this book are the ***Austrian***, ***post-Keynesian*** and ***Marxian*** schools of thought. After completing this book you should return to this chapter, and the exercises at its end, when these terms will mean something to you. In the meantime you will find that there is much to learn from the mainstream approach. Mainstream economics is studied by all economists, not only because it is the dominant school of thought but also because it provides many insights into the economic forces at work in the world. Also it is a route to understanding the writings of modern political economists from the 'right' and the 'left' of the political spectrum.

Different answers to the same questions

We stated earlier in this chapter that each society has to answer three fundamental economic questions: 'What?', 'How?' and 'For whom?' While there are a million variations on answers to these questions, when we look around the world we find that there are only a limited number of ways in which societies have set about answering them. We will now examine these briefly.

Tradition and hierarchy

For most of human history the 'What?', 'How?' and 'For whom?' have been solved by the twin forces of tradition and rulers. To illustrate this let us consider feudal society. What crop should be planted and how should it be grown? The answer is that the same crops were always planted and always grown in the same manner. The decisions that could not be taken by tradition were taken by command. The king or the lord of the manor simply ordered people what to do. The 'For whom?' question was answered in a similar manner, with the nobility taking most of the wealth, leaving a bare minimum for the rest.

It is easy to scoff at feudal society, but it should be remembered that this form of organisation lasted for hundreds of years, while our own system has lasted for a relatively short period of time and is now under great strain.

Free enterprise and the price mechanism

The feudal society we have described was largely a non-monetary society; people did not work for wages but merely to produce their food. They did not pay rent for their land; instead they worked for so many days in the lord's fields. Money was used only for the relatively small percentage of things which the local economy could not produce. However, over a period of several hundred years this changed and there was a monetisation of the economy: people grew food not to eat but to sell; labourers worked for wages; rent was paid for land; taxes were paid to the king. Thus was developed the ***price mechanism***.

Thus, everything – houses, labour, food, land, etc. – came to have its market price, and it was through the workings of market prices that the 'What?', 'How?' and 'For whom?' decisions were taken. There were no central committees organising shoe production or regulating wages, but this resulted not in chaos but order. People, by being willing to spend money, signalled to producers what it was they wished to be produced. The 'How?' question was answered because one producer had to compete with others to supply the market; if that producer could not produce as cheaply as possible then custom would be lost to competitors. The 'For whom?' question was answered by the fact that anyone who had the money and was willing to spend it could receive the goods produced.

A price mechanism is a system where the economic decisions in the economy are reached through the workings of the market: changes in the relative scarcity of

goods and services are reflected in changes in prices and these price changes produce incentives for producers to reallocate available resources towards reducing market shortages and surpluses.

The study of the price system forms much of the subject matter of economics and, hence, of this book. It should be said, however, that the free market, or free enterprise system, as envisaged by the classical economists such as Adam Smith and Alfred Marshall, has been much modified by the growth of large monopolistic businesses and unions. It would probably be more accurate today to describe the market system as capitalism rather than free enterprise.

Capitalism refers to the private ownership of the means of production.

Collectivism, command and planning

In the twentieth century in many countries there grew up, or was imposed, an alternative to capitalism known as collectivism.

Collectivism is the system whereby economic decisions are taken collectively by planning committees and implemented through the direction of collectively owned resources, either centrally or at local level.

Under this system planning committees are appointed and they provide the answers to our three central questions. Thus committees take the decision on whether, for example, more cars or more tractors should be produced. They solve the 'How?' problem by directing labour and other resources into certain areas of production and, at the end of the day, they decide the 'For whom?' problem not by pricing but by allotting goods and services on the grounds of social and political priorities.

From 1989 the former Soviet Bloc countries made dramatic shifts from a centrally planned systems towards the system of a market-based price mechanism. This involved large-scale ***privatisation***, i.e. the transfer of state-owned industries to private ownership (see also Chapter 26). A large part of the reason for this change was the failure of the planned system to cope effectively with the problems of 'What?', 'How?' and 'For whom?'

What. Unlike the workings of a smoothly operating price mechanism as we shall examine in Chapter 5, in a planned economy resources do not automatically move to eliminate shortages and surpluses. The amount of information that planners would need to collect as to wants and resources is immense – it often took months or even years to respond to shortages and surpluses because of bureaucracy and lack of information. Thus there were many farcical examples of tractors being produced even though there were no tyres for them, shortages of toilet paper, surpluses of black and white TVs, while, sometimes tragically, harvests rotted for want of transport and storage facilities.

How. Factory managers were concerned solely with meeting the output targets that had been set by the central planners. The waste of resources in production and the quality of the finished products were of secondary importance to them. The result was wasted resources, severe pollution and poor quality products.

For whom. The distribution of products and of incomes was largely set centrally. In the Soviet Union basic foodstuffs and housing were available to all, but the cost of this high basic security was a lack of consumer goods and luxuries. The material standard of living was below that of the richer market economies. The control of incomes and overproduction of basics led to bread being so cheap it was fed to cattle even though consumers had no meat. Workers had little incentive to move to new jobs or attempt to improve their income; the result was often a lack of incentive and a drab way of life.

The mixed economy

By a mixed economy we mean one in which some economic decisions are taken by the market mechanism and some collectively. In fact all real economies have a mixture of such collective or state ownership and private ownership. (Although, more recently, many nations have used the state to direct rather than own resources; see Chapter 26.)

All economies are mixed to some extent; even in Stalinist Russia some free markets remained while, at the same time, predominantly capitalist nations such as the USA took some economic decisions collectively, e.g. the provision of national defence.

When we use the term mixed economy it is usually applied to economies where there is a significant component of both collectivism and free enterprise.

Despite the wave of privatisation in the UK and elsewhere, significant economic decisions are still taken collectively. Education, health care, defence and social security remain in the collectivist section of the economy. In the UK 40 per cent of all expenditure is undertaken by the state. In countries such as the Netherlands and Sweden over 60 per cent of the economy is state directed.

Perhaps our classifications need revision. It is possible that the nature of some industries predisposes them to collectivist decision making while others remain in free enterprise. The Canadian economist John Kenneth Galbraith, for example, sees great similarities between the way decisions are taken in state planning committees and the way in which the modern large business corporation takes decisions.

The end of history?

Friedrich von Hayek (1899–1992), perhaps the century's greatest champion of capitalism, died with the satisfaction of believing he had lived just long enough to see his prophecy of the collapse of communist collectivism come true. Indeed, many economists and politicians believe that the collapse of the Soviet system is decisive proof of the superiority of capitalism over communism. Some philosophers have even called it the 'end of history' with the final victory going to capitalism.

As we noted above, however, facts are seldom so straightforward. (We ignore here the 'communists' who were simply terrorists, such as in some parts of South-East Asia.) But we should recognise that not only did the Soviet Union have severe economic problems, it was also an oppressive and corrupt regime. There was little freedom to express discontent in the performance of the planners or the economy, bribery was rife and there was little scope for reform from within the system. Its leaders also used a high percentage of resources to build up arms and the military to deter the West and to suppress any opposition; this added to the effects of inefficiency and corruption in leaving less resources to provide consumer goods.

In fact, the transition from communism to capitalism was immediately followed by enormous falls in output of up to 30 per cent, from which many of the former Soviet countries have not yet recovered. This has caused immense hardships and disillusionment, particularly among the older Russians who remember the comparative stability and basic security of the former system. Also, in contrast, China allowed the private sector to grow up around an industrial core which was kept under state control. China, despite only limited political changes, has been one of the world's fastest growing economies for more than a decade. In any case:

Accepting the efficiency of market systems and the obvious wealth creation of capitalism, the collapse of the Soviet Union does not prove the superiority of completely free market capitalism over the mixed economy.

Conclusion: why study economics?

In this final section of the chapter is a plea to avoid the OBE, the One Big Explanation for the economy. We have all met people who will tell us 'the whole trouble with the economy is trade unions', 'the whole trouble with the economy is management', 'there is only one thing which causes inflation', and so on. If you just glance through the pages of this book you will see that economics is a vast and often complex subject and many of the problems are, as yet, imperfectly understood. This should only encourage our wish to study and so to understand.

We study economics in the belief that through understanding we will be able to increase the welfare of society, and with the conviction that knowledge is better than opinion, analysis better than supposition. What we understand about economics is terribly important; it influences us all. We can put this need no better than it was put in 1936 by John Maynard Keynes in the closing words of one of the most influential economics books of the century, *The General Theory of Employment, Interest and Money:*

> The ideas of economists and political philosophers, both when they are right and when they are wrong, are more powerful than is commonly understood. Indeed the world is ruled by little else. Practical men, who believe themselves to be quite exempt from any intellectual influences, are usually the slaves of some defunct economist.

Summary

1 Economics is the human science which studies the relationship between scarce resources and the various uses which compete for these resources.
2 All economic societies have to answer three fundamental questions: 'What shall be produced?', 'How shall it be produced?' and 'For whom shall it be produced?'
3 Wealth is the stock of physical assets while welfare is the general state of well-being.
4 It is difficult to arrive at 'pure' economic decisions since the economic problems are closely bound up with political, moral, sociological and other problems.
5 Mainstream economics lays great emphasis on separating positive from normative problems.
6 There are four main categories of economic society: those run by
   a) tradition and hierarchy;
   b) the market mechanism;
   c) collectivism and planning; and
   d) a mixture of the other methods, i.e. the mixed economy.
7 The collapse of the Soviet Union highlights the strengths of the price mechanism but does not prove the superiority of pure capitalism over a mixed economy.

Questions

1 Comment upon the economic aspects of sport, leisure, religion, transport, television and education.
2 List five economic goods whose production also involves economic 'bads'.
3 Why do economists disagree?
4 Make positive and normative statements about:
   a) the distribution of income;
   b) inflation;
   c) industrial relations;
   d) health care.
5 Discuss the emotive content in the following terms: free enterprise; communism; trade unions; hard work; monopolies; gambling and money lending.
6 Give two examples of goods or services provided by the state-owned public sector.
7 What criteria would you use for assessing the effectiveness of an economic society? Are they all positive or are some normative?
8 Why have you chosen to study economics?

Data response A
Defining economics

Read the following statements carefully. They are all concerned with the subject matter of economics and economic society and about the study of economics.

> The great object of the political economy of every country, is to increase the riches and power of that country.
>
> **Adam Smith** *The Wealth of Nations*

> The history of all hitherto existing society is the history of class struggles. Freeman and slave, patrician and plebian, lord and serf, guild master and journeyman, in a word, oppressor and oppressed, stood in constant opposition to each other, carried on an uninterrupted, now hidden, now open fight, a fight that each time ended, either in a revolutionary reconstitution of society at large, or in the common ruin of the contending classes.
>
> **Karl Marx** and **Friedrich Engels** *The Communist Manifesto*

> The science of Political Economy as we have it in England may be defined as the science of the business, such as business is in large productive and trading communities.
>
> **Walter Bagehot** *Economic Studies*

> Economics is a study of mankind in the ordinary business of life.
>
> **Alfred Marshall** *Principles of Economics*

> Economic life is an organisation of producers to satisfy the wants of consumers.
>
> **John Hicks** *The Social Framework*

Economics is a science which studies human behaviour as a relationship between ends and scarce means which have alternative uses.

Lionel Robbins *An Essay on the Nature and Significance of Economic Science*

The economist's value judgements doubtless influence the subjects he works on and perhaps also at times the conclusions he reaches. . . . Yet this does not alter the fundamental point that, in principle there are no value judgements in economics.

Milton Friedman *Value Judgements in Economics*

Debates between economists are not just technical arguments among practitioners but often reflect philosophical and ideological positions which are not always made explicit.

Sam Aaronovitch *Radical Economics*

Less than a century ago a treatise on economics began with a sentence such as, 'Economics is a study of mankind in the ordinary business of life'. Today it will often begin, 'This unavoidably lengthy treatise is devoted to an examination of an economy in which the second derivatives of the utility function possess a finite number of discontinuities. To keep the problem manageable, I assume that each individual consumes only two goods, and dies after one Robertsonian week. Only elementary mathematical tools such as topology will be employed, incessantly.'

George J. Stigler *The Intellectual and the Market Place*

'Do you have anything on economics?' asked a colleague in his local bookshop. 'Over there', replied the assistant, 'beyond fiction.'

Anonymous. Quoted in *Financial Times* 9 November 1981

Having studied these statements, say which of the statements you consider is the best description of economic society and the study of economics. Explain the reasons for your choice as fully as possible. You should also explain your reasons for rejecting the other statements.

(All the above statements, including the last one, have something important to say about economics. If you are only just starting to study the subject you may find understanding them and explaining what they mean difficult. However, if you have read the first chapter you should be able to make some sense of them. This would be a very good exercise to return to at the end of your studies.)

2 Mathematical techniques in economics

Learning outcomes

After studying this chapter you will be able to:

- Assess critically the presentation of data.
- Understand and interpret index numbers.
- Use basic algebraic techniques as an alternative route to understanding economics.
- Distinguish between correlation and causation.

How to use this chapter

This chapter has been placed near the beginning of the book for ease of reference. You do not need to study all of it before learning economics. Treat it as a reference chapter that you can always go back to if you need some help with mathematical techniques.

A number of basic mathematical techniques are used in economics at this level: interpreting graphs and statistics; averages and distribution; using percentages and indices; basic algebra; visual interpretation of correlation. You do not need all these skills immediately. For some syllabuses, some of the skills are not necessary at all. The book is written in such a way that most of the algebra can be avoided if you are seriously allergic to it. However, maths is a useful avenue of understanding in economics, alongside words, statistics and graphs. Use it as an extra language and consider it to be an opportunity rather than a threat!

The use and abuse of statistics

Numbers often appear to have a magical authority about them. Politicians and economists produce statistics to 'prove' their case. However, we must treat figures with caution for three reasons. First, there may be inaccuracies in the compilation of data and, second, figures can be 'presented' in such a way as to distort them. This does not mean that we abandon statistics. It means that we need to study them more carefully in order to appreciate what they really do mean. Third, the compilation of statistics usually reflects a particular way of looking at a problem and thus they seldom speak for themselves.

We will first consider the visual presentation of data.

Visual deception

The choice of scale in graphs can be deceptive. Figure 2.1 is taken from Chapter 10. Both graphs show the same information but because of the different scales used, a very different impression is gained from (a) than from (b).

Figure 2.2 shows a graph as it might appear in a newspaper. This gives an extremely misleading impression but is typical of the way statistics are presented in the media. The vertical axis, as you see, does not start at zero but at 500 and the gap in the horizontal axis with the graph plunging through it gives the impression that the figures have broken some sort of barrier when, in fact, none exists.

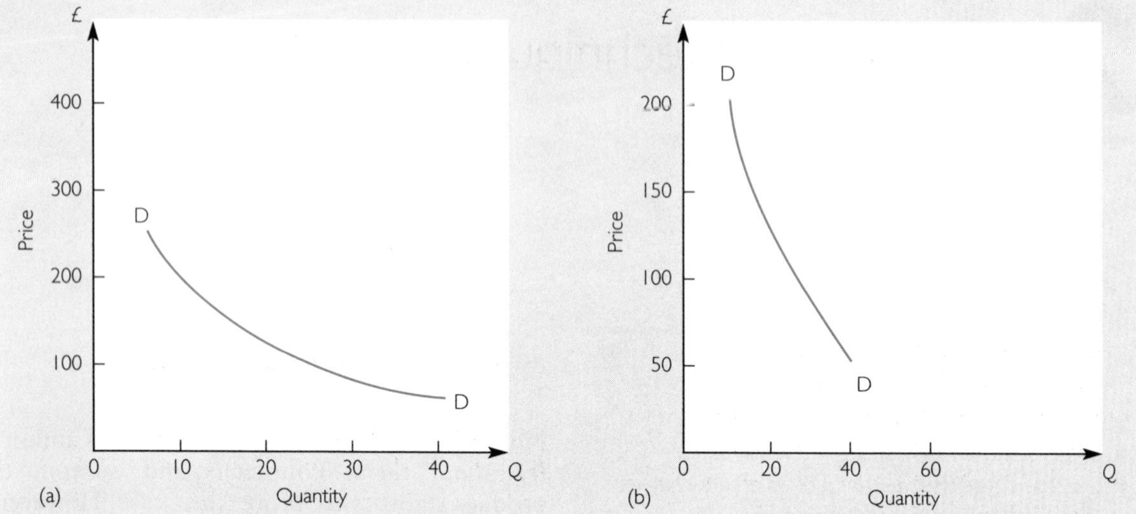

***Fig. 2.1* Deceptive calibrations on graphs**

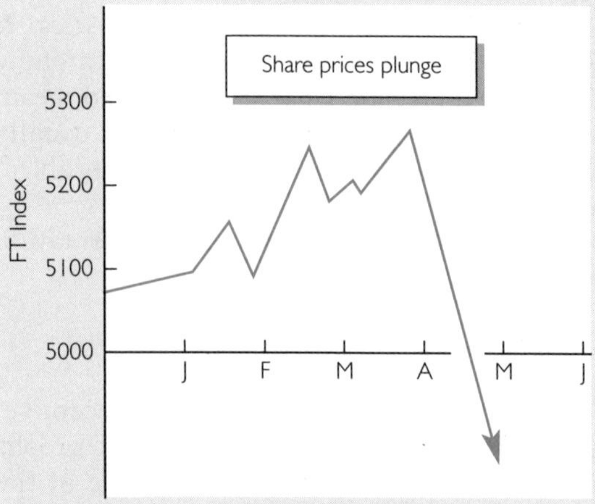

***Fig. 2.2* Visual deception**
The graph of share prices gives a misleading impression of the magnitude of changes in the index of share prices in the first six months of the year.

Numerical deception

Consider the following two statements:

> In the last four years annual government borrowing has grown by no less than £25 billion.
>
> In the last four years annual government borrowing has shrunk from 6 per cent of the national income to 5 per cent of the national income.

Which of the statements is correct? The answer is that they both may be, if national income has been growing faster than government borrowing. The first statement suggests government borrowing is in crisis, while the second one suggests it is being brought under control. Each statement emphasises the viewpoint of the writer.

Averages and distribution

Most people are familiar with the idea of an ***average***, or to use the correct name, an ***arithmetic mean***. Table 2.1 shows figures for the GDP (national income) of various countries. You can see that the average figure (GDP divided by population) gives a very different impression of the economies involved than the aggregate figure for GDP. However, the average figure can also be misleading. Does the fact that GDP per head in the United Arab Emirates was nearly three times as high as that of the UK mean that the typical citizen there enjoys a living standard three times as high as the average Briton? No! This is not the case because we also need to know about the ***distribution*** of income in the two countries.

Table 2.1 Population and income (1988)

Country	Population (millions)	GDP ($m)	GDP/head ($)
Nigeria	110.1	31 929	290
India	815.6	277 304	340
Malaysia	16.9	32 786	1 940
Greece	10.0	48 000	4 800
Singapore	2.6	23 582	9 070
UK	57.1	73 145	12 810
United Arab Emirates	1.5	23 655	15 770
West Germany	61.3	1 132 824	18 480
USA	246.3	4 886 592	19 840
Japan	122.6	2 577 052	21 020

Source: *World Development Report*, IBRD

Means and medians

Means can be very misleading. For example, in many countries the bulk of the national income is enjoyed by very few of the population. The mean income would therefore give us a very poor idea of the income of the average family. We therefore have another measure of the 'average' which is termed the ***median***. The median is the middle number, i.e. the one which is half-way between the highest and the lowest in the sample. Suppose that we lined up all the people in the country in order of income and then selected the person half-way down the line. This person's income would be the median. Thus, one-half of the line of people would have a larger income and the other half a smaller income.

The median is nearly always smaller than the mean. This is because the people earning less than median income mainly earn only a little less than the median income. A reasonably large number of those earning above the median earn substantially more than the median income. This pulls the mean above the median. It follows that the total of incomes for the poorer half of any community must be smaller than that of the richer half. With an understanding of these two measures of average you should now be able to make sense of statements like 'the majority of people earn less than average'!

The mode

Another measure of the 'average' exists and this is termed the ***mode***. The mode is the most commonly occurring figure in the sample. We can further explain these concepts by taking a numerical example. Table 2.2 shows the distribution of annual incomes in a community of 51 households. The total income for the community is £650 000 so that this gives an arithmetic mean of £12 745 per household. The most commonly occurring level of income, however, is 7001–£10 000 and this therefore is the mode. As there are 51 households in the community the median income is that of the 26th household, which is £9307. These figures are presented graphically in Fig. 2.3 (b). You can see that the mode is the highest point of the distribution curve, whilst the median and mean are displaced to the right. This is referred to as ***skewedness***. By comparison, Fig. 2.3 (a) shows how the curve would look if the distribution were ***normal*** i.e. evenly distributed on each side of the mean.

The existence of these various measures of the average should warn us to treat statistics with care. The mode or the median may give a much better idea of the typical unit in a sample than does the arithmetic mean.

Table 2.2 Distribution of household incomes

Number of households	Annual income (£)
1	less than 3 000
3	3 001–4 000
5	4 001–5 000
7	5 001–7 000
13	7 001–10 000
12	10 001–15 000
7	15 001–25 000
2	25 001–50 000
1	more than 50 000
Total 51	650 000

STUDENT ACTIVITY 2.1

Given the following incomes, work out the mean, the mode and the median:

120; 150; 150; 200; 300; 400; 500.

Is the distribution skewed?

Indices

What is an index number?

Index numbers or indices are another commonly used statistical technique in economics. An index is a method of expressing the change of a number of variables through the movement of one number. The technique consists of selecting a base, which is given the value of 100, and then expressing all subsequent changes as a movement of this number. This is most easily explained by taking the change in just one variable. Say, for example, that we consider the output of cars in the economy (see Table 2.3). If year 1 is adopted as the base, then this is given the value of 100. In year 2 production is 15 per cent higher and therefore the index becomes 115, and so on. The table records a fall in production in year 4 below the level of year 1, and so the index number is less than 100. As you can see in Table 2.3, it is rather easier to judge the magnitude of the changes by looking at the index number than by looking at the output figures.

Table 2.3 Index of car production

Year	Output of cars	Index number
1	1 502 304	100
2	1 727 609	115
3	1 906 003	127
4	1 400 005	93
5	1 679 294	112
6	1 699 024	113

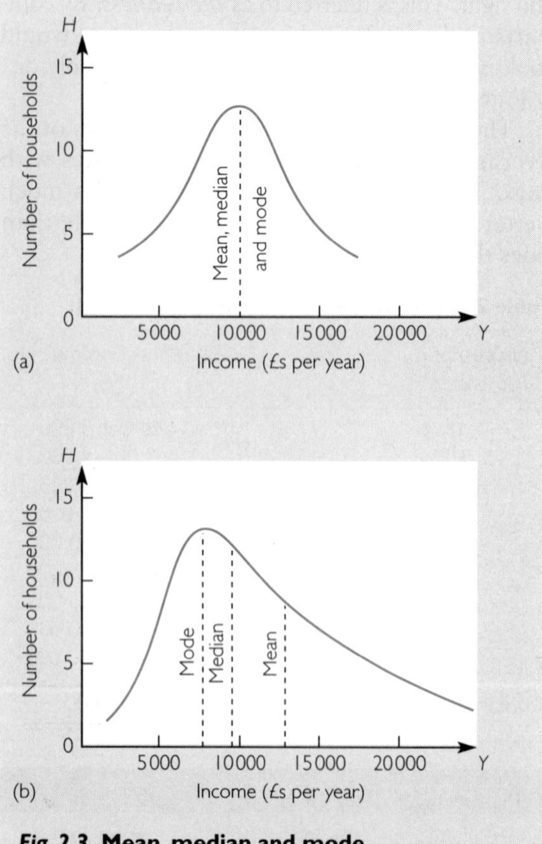

***Fig. 2.3* Mean, median and mode**
(a) Perfectly even distribution; the mean, median and the mode coincide.
(b) A 'skewed' distribution.

Weighting

Index numbers are usually used to measure the movement of many things simultaneously. In our example so far we have used the output of just one commodity, cars. However, if we wished to compile an index of all industrial production the output of many different commodities would have to be measured.

When we have to consider a number of factors simultaneously, we have to assign to them some measure of their relative importance. This is referred to as ***weighting***. Table 2.4 gives a simpli-

Table 2.4 Weighting an index

Industry (1)	Index of output, year 1 (2)	Index of output, year 2 (3)	Weight (no. of people) employed) (4)	Year 2 index multiplied by weight ((3) × (4)) (5)
A	100	115	2	230
B	100	90	7	630
C	100	95	9	855
D	100	120	2	240
E	100	110	3	330
Total	500	530	23	2 285
Index	100	106	–	99

fied example of how this may be done. Here we are concerned with five industries. In year 1 each industry's output has an index of 100, but in year 2 industry A's output has risen to 115, while that of industry B has fallen to 90, and so on. If we then add up the five index numbers in column (3) and average them out by dividing by five, we see that the index number for year 2 is 106. However, this could be misleading since industry B might be more important than industry C.

How, therefore, do we decide whether the 15 per cent rise in industry A is more significant than the 10 per cent fall in industry B? As a measure of their relative importance we have taken the number of people they employ, and this is shown in column (4). To weight the index we now multiply the index number by the weight. This gives a value of 230 for industry A and 630 for industry B, and so on. When this has been done we total the figures in column (5) and divide by the sum of the weights. Thus we arrive at an overall index number of 99 for year 2.

Thus the unweighted index made it appear that industrial output overall had risen, while the weighted index shows that it has fallen. This is because the rises in output were in the industries which employed few people, while the industries which employed more experienced falls in output.

Price indices

The most frequently used index is that which measures prices, the retail price index (RPI). In this we have to combine the movements in prices of thousands of different commodities. This is described in detail in Chapter 36. The weighting technique, however, is exactly as described above.

Common misunderstanding

It is assumed that you understand what a percentage is, but one feature of percentages often causes problems in economics and that is the **base** *on which the percentage is calculated. If a person earns £100 a week and gets an increase of 10 per cent then their income rises to £110. Many people assume that if their income falls by 10 per cent the following year, then their income will return to £100. This is not the case because 10 per cent of £110 is £11. Their income would fall to £99. This is because we have changed the base on which the percentage is calculated from £100 to £110.*

Rebasing an index

It may be the case that you are presented with index numbers but the base year chosen is not appropriate to your needs. For example, the index is based on 1989 but you wish to show it with reference to the current year (or another one).

In Table 2.5 we show an index which is based on 1989, but we would prefer it to be based on 1993. The method is to take the index for each year shown and to divide it by the index number of the year chosen for the rebasing. Thus we obtain:

$$\frac{\text{Old base year}}{\text{Required base year}} \times \frac{100}{1} =$$

New index with required year = 100

Can you complete the calculations for the remaining years in Table 2.5?

Table 2.5 **Rebasing an index**

Year	Index	Calculation	New index 1993 = 100
1989	100.0		
1990	138.2		
1991	147.3		
1992	182.7		
1993	186.2		
1994	170.6	170.6/186.2 × 100 =	91.6
1995	186.2	186.2/186.2 × 100 =	100.0
1996	200.7	200.7/186.2 × 100 =	107.8
1997	210.6		
1998	233.3		

Algebra

Some people develop an allergy to algebra when studying maths. A few simple techniques are a great help in understanding economic theory. Some of the more difficult algebra discussed below is simply an alternative route to understanding graphs which you may prefer to understand at a verbal, visual or numerical level. If you really find algebra a problem, use these alternative routes to understanding.

Symbols

We make use of ***symbols*** in economics. In so doing we are adopting a kind of shorthand. The symbols are common to most economics books so that once they are learnt they should help us to speed up our writing on the subject. Typical examples of such symbols are:

Y = income
Q = output or quantity
S = savings

Unfortunately, arrays of symbols in texts can look forbidding but the student should remember that they are not in themselves mathematical, just ***abbreviations***.

Functions

We will often find that the magnitude of one factor is affected by another. For example, the demand for a good is affected by its price. In mathematical terms we could say that demand is a ***function*** of price. This can be written as:

$$Q = f(P)$$

where Q is the quantity demanded and P the price.

Often the value of the factor we are considering will be affected by several variables. These we can add to the function. Thus, for example:

$$Q = f(P, Y, P_1 \ldots P_{n-1})$$

This tells us that demand is a function of the price of the commodity (P), consumers' income (Y) and the price of other commodities (P_n, P_{n-1}).

Writing things in this fashion is, again, just a form of shorthand because no values have been ascribed to P, Y, etc. Once we put in values, we obtain one of two kinds of function.

a) ***Linear functions.*** This is where, if we plotted the figures as a graph, we would obtain a straight line. For example, consider the function:

$$C = 0.8Y$$

where C is total consumer spending and Y is income. This expression tells us that consumption is always 0.8 (80 per cent) of income. This would produce a straight line graph.

Common misunderstanding

Many students are unable to relate decimals to percentages and believe they are talking about completely different things. As the example above shows, you can turn a decimal into a percentage by moving the decimal point two places to the right. If there aren't two places put some extra zeros in: 0.8 is the same as 0.80; adding a zero is adding nothing!

b) ***Non-linear functions.*** Any function which does not give a straight line when plotted as a graph is a non-linear function. Students up to GCE A level economics will not be required to handle non-linear functions in examinations.

The economist makes extensive use of graphs. These are both an illustration and a means of analysis. Once again the practised economist will tell you that they are also a form of shorthand and a method by which often complex relationships can be reduced to a few lines on a page.

Graphs are a method of showing the relationship of one variable to another. On the horizontal (or x) axis of the graph we place the ***independent variable***, and on the vertical (or y) axis we place the ***dependent variable***.

Consider the following figures:

Year	Sales of product Z (thousands/year)
1993	5
1994	10
1995	12
1996	7
1997	14

Which is the independent variable? Obviously, in this case, it is time (the year) since that depends upon no other factor, whereas the quantity of sales depends upon the year we are considering. Thus if we plot these figures on a graph we obtain Fig. 2.4.

The graph in Fig. 2.4 shows only positive values on the x and y axes. However, it is possible to have graphs with negative values, in which case the axes (or coordinates) would be as shown in Fig. 2.5. We will come across such graphs. Figure 17.2 (Chapter 17) shows negative values for y when we plot the marginal revenue of a business, and Fig. 5.8 (Chapter 5) shows negative values for x.

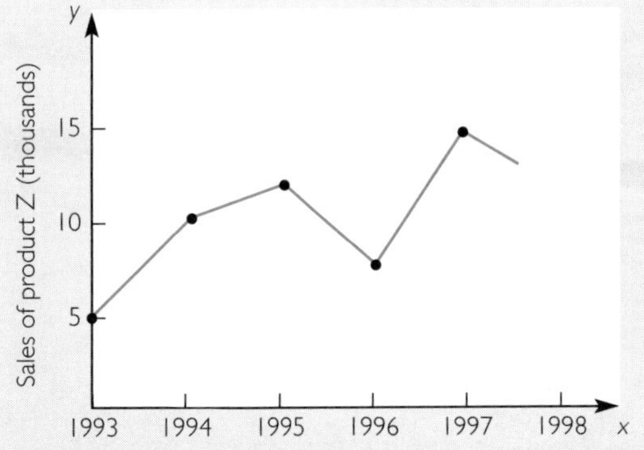

Fig. 2.4 **The dependent variable**
The independent variable (time) is plotted on the *x* axis and the dependent variable (sales of Z) on the *y* axis.

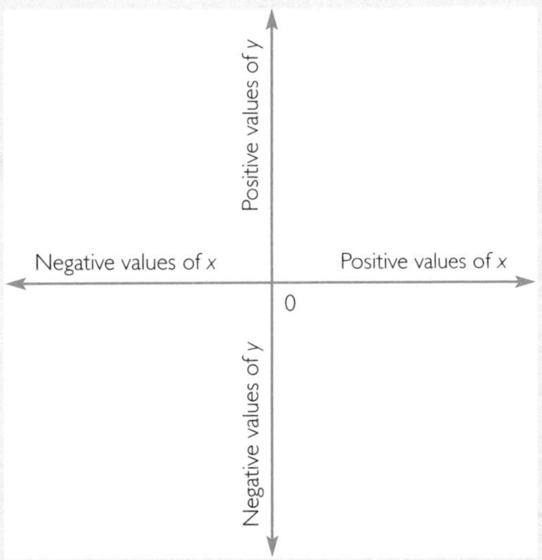

Fig. 2.5 **Plotting positive and negative values of *x* and *y***

Equations and graphs

If we have the equation for two related variables, such as the quantity of a good supplied and its price, then we can plot a graph to show them. Suppose we have the equation:

$$P = 2Q$$

Then in order to plot the graph we have to ask ourselves what if the value of Q were 1, what if it were 2, and so on? Knowing that Q is always half the value of P, we would obtain the figures in Table 2.6.

Table 2.6 **Values of *P* and *Q* (1)**

Values of Q (x)	*Values of P (y)*
1	2
2	4
3	6
4	8
5	10

What type of unit must we assign to P and Q? That need not concern us at the moment. We can simply have them as one unit of P or two units of P and so on. We can decide later whether we are talking about pennies or kilograms or tonnes.

If we plot the figures in Table 2.6, we obtain the graph in Fig. 2.6. The graph slopes upwards from left to right. This is said to be a ***positive slope*** since as the value of P increases so does the value of Q.

The graph we have drawn is an example of a ***supply curve***. In plotting it we have departed from mathematical convention because Q has been placed on the x axis. However, it is, strictly speaking, the dependent variable because the quantity supplied depends upon the price and so should go on the y axis. The reason for plotting it as we have is that when economists such as Alfred Marshall first began to plot supply and demand curves, they plotted them in this way. If they were plotted as they should be they would appear very unfamiliar to economists. We will therefore adhere to this convention for demand and supply curves. However, elsewhere we keep to the correct mathematical convention.

Suppose that we have a function which is:

$$P = 10 - Q$$

Now what happens if we ask ourselves the question, what is the value of P if Q is 1? We obtain the result that P must be 9. If we continue for other values of Q then we obtain the figures in Table 2.7. If these figures are plotted as a graph, as in Fig. 2.7, we see that this produces a downward-sloping line. This is referred to as a ***negative slope*** since as the value of Q increases, the value of P decreases.

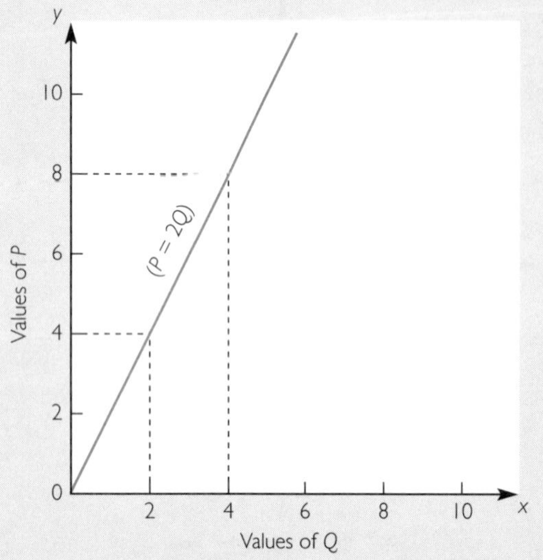

Fig. 2.6 **The slope of line given by the equation: P = 2Q**

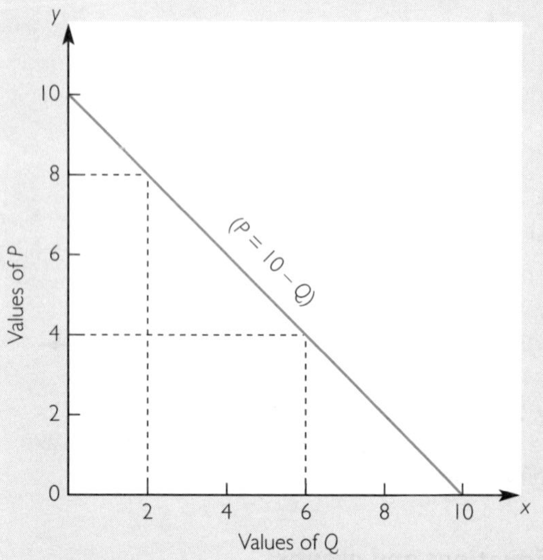

Fig. 2.7 **The slope of a line given by the equation P = 10 – Q**

Table 2.7 **Values of P and Q (2)**

Values of Q (x)	*Values of P (y)*
2	8
4	6
6	4
8	2
10	0

Problem solving

The graph we have constructed above is a ***demand curve***, showing the quantity of a product which is demanded at various prices. Suppose that we ask ourselves the question, at what price will quantity demanded be equal to the quantity supplied? We can answer this by using the ***simultaneous equation*** technique.

We have the values:

$$P = 2Q \text{(supply)} \qquad (1)$$

and:

$$P = 10 - Q \text{(demand)} \qquad (2)$$

We can find where the price (P) for demand and supply will be the same by substituting the value for P in equation (1) into equation (2):

$$2Q = 10 - Q \qquad (3)$$

If we move all the Q to one side of the equation and the numbers to the other, we obtain:

$$3Q = 10 \qquad (4)$$

Thus:

$$Q = 3\tfrac{1}{3} \qquad (5)$$

To obtain the value for P we now need only insert the value of Q into expression (1) and we obtain:

$$P = 2 \times 3\tfrac{1}{3}$$
$$P = 6\tfrac{2}{3}$$

We can check that this result is correct by doing a similar exercise with expression (2):

$$P = 10 - 3\tfrac{1}{3}$$
$$P = 6\tfrac{2}{3}$$

Thus the quantity is the same for both supply and demand when price equals $6\tfrac{2}{3}$. You can check that this is so by superimposing Fig. 2.6 on Fig. 2.7. You will see that this is the point where the two curves intersect. The student who is unsure about this analysis should now attempt the relevant questions at the end of the chapter. It is important to master this, because questions are set on it.

The approach we have adopted here might be criticised as being too specific to one set of problems (demand and supply). Many books prefer to conduct this analysis in purely abstract terms of x and y. We have adopted the price and quantity approach because this is the most usual area for problems. However, the student should remember that the algebra can be applied to any linear functions.

Statistics

Correlation

Correlation exists when there is a connection between two variables. We establish the existence of a correlation by collecting information.

Figure 2.8 shows two scatter diagrams. Both diagrams show information about the same group of 20 male adults. Figure 2.8 (a) depicts the relationship between income and expenditure while Fig. 2.8 (b) shows the relationship between income and height. It is clear that there is a possible correlation between income and expenditure, but none between income and height.

Regression

To measure the relationship between two variables when correlation appears to exist, we need to indulge in a regression analysis. How this is done is illustrated in Fig. 2.9. Here we have drawn two regression lines. This has been done visually to obtain a line of best fit. Visually they both may appear sound, but if we wish to find the best regression line then we must obtain the so-called line of least squares. This is done by drawing a line from each of the dots to the regression lines A and B. We then measure the length of each line and square it. Then the total of these squares is found for the two regression lines. The regression line with the smaller total is the better fit. In this case it is line B. You will not be required to undertake regression analysis yourself, but it is useful to know what it is.

The slope of the regression line now tells us the regression coefficient of the two variables.

In our example we have shown the regression of expenditure on income. This could be, for example:

$$E = 0.6Y$$

telling us that expenditure (E) is 0.6 of income (Y).

Correlation and causation

The fact that there appears to be a correlation between two variables does not prove that one causes the other. Two major problems exist.

a) *Wrong-way causation.* It is a proven fact that in the cities of northern Germany there is a

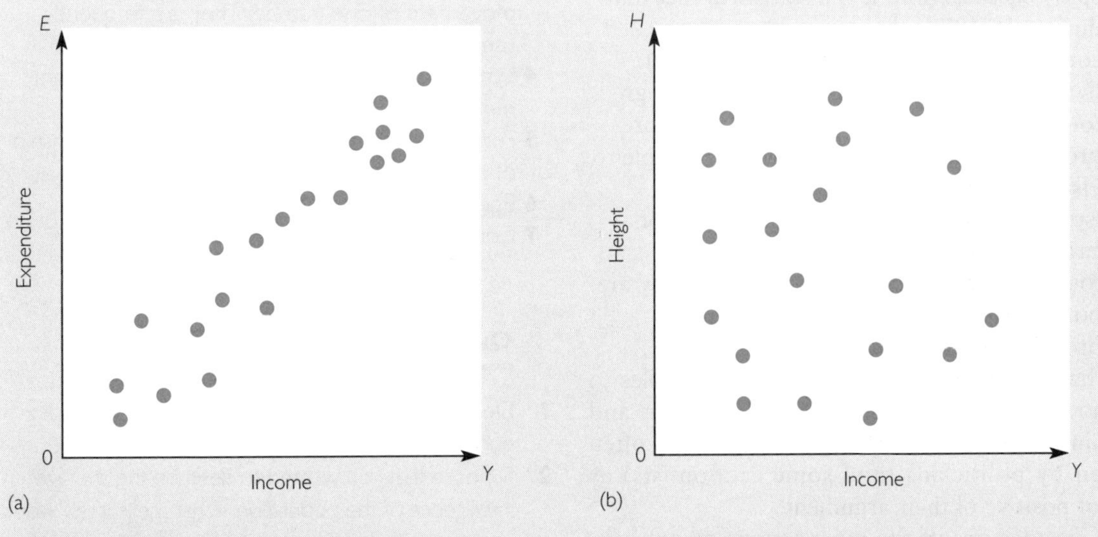

***Fig. 2.8* Scatter diagram**
(a) This shows a possible correlation between the income of the 20 persons in the sample and their expenditure.
(b) There is no correlation between income and height.

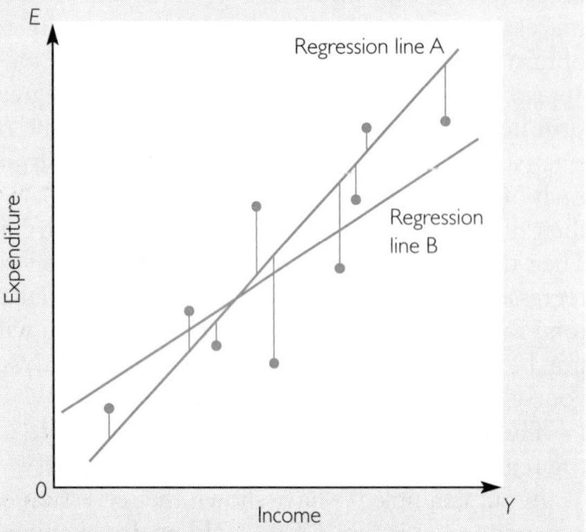

***Fig. 2.9* Least squares**
The line of best fit is the one which has the smallest total of the squares of the distances of the dots from it.

correlation between the number of babies born and the number of storks' nests. Should this then be taken as proof that storks do indeed bring babies? The causation is, of course, the wrong way round. Cities that have more children have more houses and, therefore, more chimneys for storks to build their nests in.

b) *Spurious causation.* It is a statistical fact that during the 1970s there was a positive correlation between the rise in the cost of living in London and the number of foreign tourists visiting the city. Does this therefore prove that rising prices caused more people to visit London? Here the correlation is 'spurious' because increased prices do not cause increased tourism, and increased tourism does not cause rising prices. They are both the result of more fundamental broader-ranging phenomena.

We have used here rather humorous examples to illustrate the problem, but it is a very serious and common error in the subject. Correlation is often taken by politicians (and some economists) as proof positive of their argument.

Consider one of the most serious of our economic problems, inflation. One can demonstrate a close correlation between inflation and the rise in wages. Politicians are therefore often heard to say, 'We all know that rising wages cause inflation.' Is this a true correlation? Is it a wrong-way causation or is it a spurious correlation? At the same time we can show a strong positive correlation between increases in the money stock and rising prices. Some politicians (often the same ones) therefore state with equal confidence, 'Increases in the money supply cause inflation.' A moment's reflection will tell you that if it is increased wages which are the cause of inflation it cannot at the same time be increases in the money stock.

It would be presumptuous of us to suggest a glib answer to the above problem, being, as it is, one of the most thorny in modern economics, but we hope by the end of the book to have shed some light on the issue. Suffice it to say that correlation is not causation. In addition to correlation, we need an explanation of why one factor relates to another.

Summary

1 Numerical and statistical information can be used both to inform and deceive.
2 There are several types of 'average'. These are the mean, the median and the mode.
3 Index numbers are a method of expressing the change in a number of variables through the movement of one number. They are frequently used to measure such things as the price level.
4 Symbols are used in economics as a convenient means of abbreviation.
5 Functions can be used to express the relationship of one variable to another.
6 Equations can be translated to draw graphs.
7 Correlation in a graph does not imply causation.

Questions

1 Define the following: mean; median; mode; index numbers; correlation.
2 Suppose that you wanted to describe the 'average' intelligence of the population. What measure(s) would you use and why? If instead you wanted to describe the average ownership of wealth in the economy, how would your choice of measure differ and why?

3 Construct a graph which is calculated to deceive someone, e.g. showing changes in the exchange rate in the last 12 months.
4 Re-read the section on numerical deception and then explain how the same information could lead to the two seemingly contradictory statements.
5 Describe how an index might be compiled to measure prices.
6 Construct a graph and on it draw the line which would illustrate the following functions: $y = 3x$ and $y = 10 - x$. State the value of x and y where the two lines intersect.
7 Construct a graph to illustrate the following function:

$$y = 4 + \frac{5}{x}$$

8 In the following situations, determine the points at which x and y are equal, i.e. where the graphs would intersect.
   a) $y = 1 + 3x$
      $y = 25 - x$
   b) $y = 20 + 5x$
      $y = 100 - x$
   c) $y = 10 + x$
      $y = 2x - 4$

Data response A
Index numbers

Study the information in the table below, and then attempt the questions which follow.

	1981	*1986*	*1991*	*1995*
Bus prices	100	139	198	252
Rail prices	100	137	201	246
Petrol & oil prices	100	145	156	203
RPI (all prices)	100	137	185	208

Adapted from *Social Trends* 1996

1 Which form of transport, car, bus or rail, has gone up by most in the period? Which has gone up least? How do you expect this to affect demand for each type of transport?
2 Compare the period 1981–6 and 1991–5. In which period has public transport become relatively more competitive than the car?

Data response B
Rebasing an index

The data below on bus prices is not collected for calendar years. Although 1992 = 100, it is difficult to see what is happening. Rebase the index to find out how much more bus prices have been rising than general prices (RPI) between 1993–4 and 1995–6; 1992 = 100.

	Bus prices	*RPI*
1992–3	101.3	100.4
1993–4	105.9	102.2
1994–5	110.9	105.0
1995–6	116.0	108.4

Adapted from the *Annual Abstract of Statistics* 1997

Data response C
Maps and models

Study carefully the maps shown in Fig. 2.10. These both show areas of London around the King's Cross area; one is an extract from the Streetfinder map and the other is based on the Underground map.

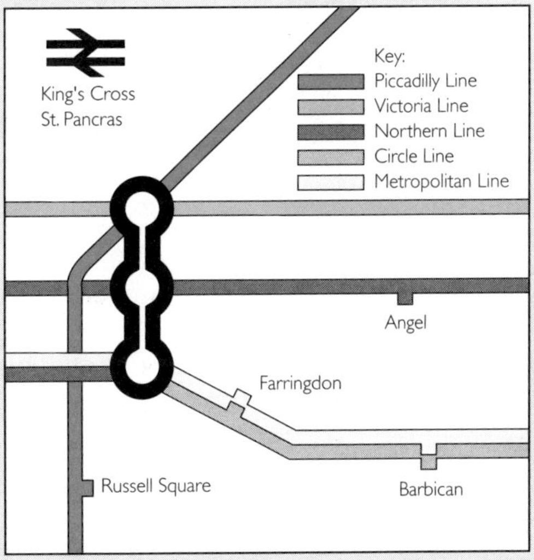

Fig. 2.10 (a)

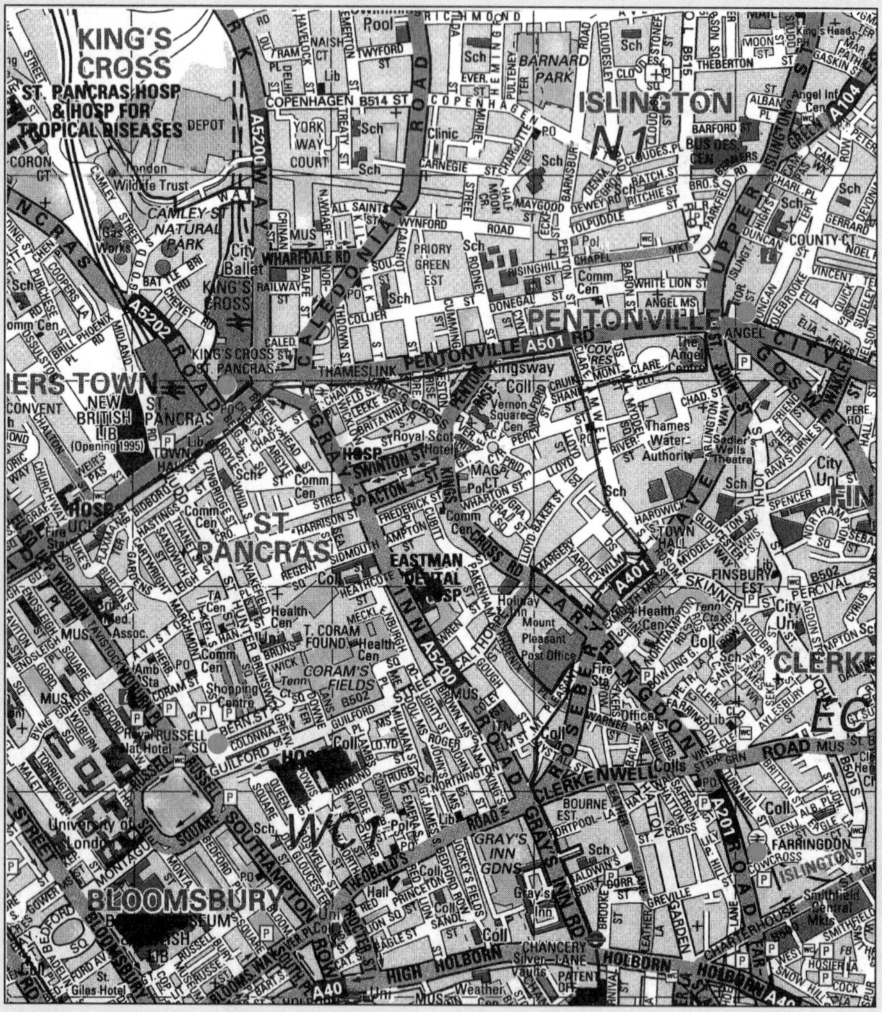

Fig. 2.10 (b)

1 a) What means of presenting information is used in the two illustrations?

b) How would the producer of the illustrations go about presenting the information?

c) In what ways can these presentations be seen as 'model building'?

2 Explain as fully as possible what the use of models is in economics.

3 The economic problem: resources scarcity and choice

Learning outcomes

At the end of this chapter you will be able to:

- Distinguish between needs and wants.
- Understand the consequences of scarcity of resources.
- Identify the effects on costs of expanding output in the short run and in the long run.
- Calculate the opportunity cost of an economic activity.

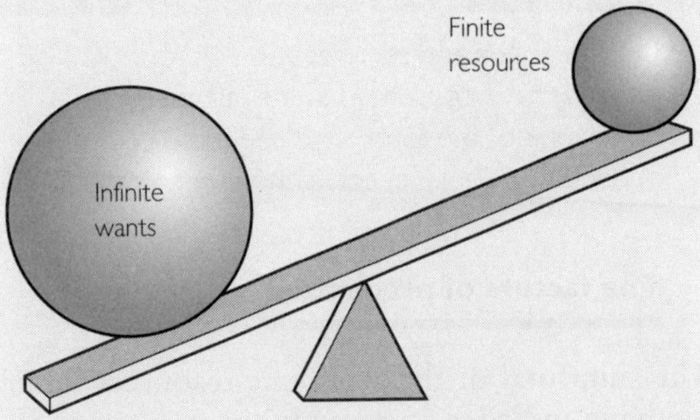

Fig. 3.1 **The economic problem: finite resources and infinite wants**

Wants and needs

We saw in Chapter 1 that the fundamental economic problem is the scarcity of all resources. Therefore all economic decisions involve choice in terms of what to produce, how to produce it and who will receive the output thus produced. We must now turn to another aspect of the economic problem – the ***insatiability*** of human wants.

Finite resources and insatiable wants

It is literally impossible to satisfy human wants because as one economic want is satisfied another appears to be created. We may liken this to a see-saw with, on the one hand, the finite resources of the world, while on the other hand are infinite wants (see Fig. 3.1). It may be possible to satisfy human needs, so that we could say, for example, a person needs three shirts, two pairs of shoes, good health care, etc., but this is not the same thing as human wants. If we give people enough to eat then they appear to want better or different foods; if we give them enough to wear then they want more fashionable clothes, and so on. Thus, in this sense, the economic problem is insoluble. There have always been a few people who reject this materialistic view, e.g. monks and nuns. In the late twentieth century supporters of 'Green' politics question whether the view of 'more is better' is a desirable or sustainable goal.

Conspicuous consumption

The problem of insatiability of human wants has been the subject of much thought in economics. The great American economist Thorstein Veblen (1857–1929), in his book *The Theory of the Leisure Class*, first described what is termed ***conspicuous consumption***. This refers to the tendency of those above the subsistence level, i.e. the 'leisure class', to be concerned mainly with impressing others through standards of living, taste and dress.

In more recent times Professor Galbraith has also pointed out that in most advanced industrial economies most people have gone beyond the level of physical necessity. Consumers may be observed to flit from one purchase to another in response to pressures of fashion and advertising. These arguments still do not apply to the poor of the world.

Whether it is a matter of need or want, decisions have to be made in the economy about what to produce, how to produce, and which factors of production to use in each industry.

STUDENT ACTIVITY 3.1

List the goods and services you (or your parents) have consumed in the last week under one of the following headings:
a) needs b) wants c) conspicuous consumption

The factors of production

The sum total of the economic resources which we have in order to provide for our economic wants are termed the *factors of production*. Traditionally, economists have classified these under four headings. They are:

a) labour
b) land
c) capital
d) enterprise

The first two are termed primary factors since they are not the result of the economic process; they are, so to speak, what we have to start with. The secondary factors, however, are a consequence of an economic system.

Labour

Labour may be defined as the exercise of human mental and physical effort in the production of goods and services.

Included in this definition is all the labour which people undertake for reward, in the form of either wages and salaries or income from self-employment. There is a problem with labour which is undertaken without payment. Housework, gardening and decoration are often undertaken by the owners of a house, and this is clearly labour because we would have to pay workers to do this work if we did not do it ourselves. This kind of work is not included in measures of the size of the economy because it cannot be easily valued, having no price. This problem is discussed in more detail in Chapter 7.

In more technical terms the working population constitutes the supply of labour. This is discussed in Chapter 4.

Land

Land may be defined as all the free gifts of nature.

As such, land constitutes the space in which to organise economic activity and the resources provided by nature. Thus, included within the definition are all mineral resources, climate, soil fertility, etc. The sea, since it is a resource for both fishing and mineral exploitation, would also fall within the definition of land. The economist, therefore, uses the word ***land*** in a special way.

In practice it may be very difficult to separate land from other factors of production such as capital but, theoretically, it has two unique features which distinguish it.

First, it is fixed in supply. Since, as we saw above, the sea is included in the definition, we are thus talking about the whole of the planet, and it is obvious that we can never acquire more land in this sense. Indeed, environmentalists emphasise how economic growth is using up the planet's resources. This issue is discussed further in Chapter 27.

Second, land has no cost of production. The individual who is trying to rent a piece of land may have to pay a great deal of money, but it never cost society as a whole anything to produce land. This last point may seem rather abstract but forms an important component of some political ideologies such as Marxism.

Capital

We define capital as the stock of wealth existing at any one time. As such, capital consists of all the real physical assets of society. An alternative formulation would be:

Capital is all those goods which are used in the production of further wealth.

Capital can be divided into ***fixed*** capital, which is such things as buildings, roads, machinery, etc., and ***working***, or circulating, capital which consists of stocks of raw materials and semi-manufactured goods. The distinction is that fixed capital continues through many rounds of production while working capital is used up in one round; for example, a machine for canning beans would be fixed capital, while stocks of beans to go into the cans would be circulating capital.

As stated previously, capital is a secondary factor of production, which means that it is a result of the economic system. Capital has been created by individuals forgoing current consumption, i.e. people have refrained from consuming all their wealth immediately and have saved resources which can then be used in the production of further wealth. Suppose we consider a very simple economy in which the individual's wealth consists entirely of potatoes. If the individual is able to refrain from consuming all the potatoes, these may be planted and, thus, produce more wealth in the future. From this example it can be seen that a capital good is defined, not from what it is, but from what it does, i.e. in our example the potato is a capital good if it is used in the production of more potatoes.

Education as capital

One of the purposes of education is to increase the skills and therefore the productivity of labour. The higher wages paid to workers with higher levels of education are thought to reflect this increased productivity.

Enterprise

Some economists have cast doubt on whether enterprise is a separate factor of production. However, we still have to explain the vital role fulfilled by the ***entrepreneur***. Enterprise fulfils two vital functions:

a) It hires and combines the other factors of production.
b) It takes a ***risk*** by producing goods in anticipation of demand.

It may be fairly easy to identify the role of the entrepreneur in a small business. However, in a large business the entrepreneurial function will be split up between many managers and departments, as well as being shared with the shareholders of the business. Despite the difficulties involved in identifying the entrepreneur, the role of enterprise is clearly vital to the economic process since it is the decision-making factor. It therefore provides an important tool in our understanding of how businesses work. In recent years there has been great political stress on the importance of 'the enterprise culture' in promoting economic progress. This emphasis has not lessened with the election of the Labour government in 1997, which claims to be 'business friendly'.

Factor incomes

The various incomes which the factors receive can also be termed ***factor rewards*** or factor returns. Labour receives ***wages and salaries***, land earns ***rent***, capital earns ***interest*** and enterprise earns ***profit***. In practice it is difficult to separate them precisely; for example, the 'rent' of a building is actually the rent for the land plus the interest on the capital, which is the building itself.

STUDENT ACTIVITY 3.2

Using either a train or a bus journey as your example, identify which resources used can be categorised as land, labour, capital and enterprise. Carry out the same exercise for your school/college/university.

The division of labour

Specialisation

The expression ***division of labour*** refers to the dividing up of economic tasks into specialisations. Thus few workers these days produce the whole commodity but undertake only particular parts of the production process. This process lies at the very heart of the modern exchange economy. The enormous advantages of the division of labour were recognised early by Adam Smith and he illustrated them by the use of, what is now possibly, the most famous example in economics – pin making. *In The Wealth of Nations* he described pin making thus:

> One man draws out the wire, another straights it, a third cuts it, a fourth points it, a fifth grinds it; to make the head requires two or three distinct operations, to put it on is another peculiar business, to whiten the pin is another, it is even a trade by itself to put them into paper.

The resulting increase in output is phenomenal.

It is important to grasp the significance of this idea of ***specialisation***. It is not necessary that any new technique be invented; the specialisation itself will result in increases in production. The ultimate extension of the principle is that of the specialisation of nations, which is the basis of the theory of international trade.

Advantages of the division of labour

a) *Increase in skill and dexterity*. 'Practice makes perfect', as the saying goes; the constant repetition of tasks means that they can be done more expertly. The authors can report that their typing speeds have improved as a result of writing this book!

b) *Time saving*. If a person has to do many different tasks then a considerable period of time is taken between operations. Time can also be saved in the training of people. If, for example, a person has to be trained as an engineer, this takes many years, but a person can quickly be trained to fulfil one operation in the engineering process.

c) *Individual aptitudes*. Division of labour allows people to do what they are best at. Some people are physically very strong, while others have good mental aptitudes. With division of labour there is a greater chance that people will be able to concentrate on those things at which they are best.

d) *Use of machinery*. As tasks become subdivided it becomes worthwhile using machinery, which is a further saving of effort. For example, consider wine production: if production is only a few hundred bottles then specialist bottling equipment is hardly justified; but if we are thinking of specialising in bottling tens of thousands of bottles, then it becomes worthwhile to use a specialist machine to do this.

e) *Managerial control*. Some economists have argued that the division of labour, in breaking down processes into separate tasks, allows managers to monitor workers more closely. Moreover, operatives on a production line are more easily coerced than craftpersons, who can withhold information from managers and cannot be so easily replaced.

Disadvantages of the division of labour

Economic life without division of labour is inconceivable. Thus when we speak of its disadvantages it should be realised that these are not arguments against specialisation but, rather, problems associated with it.

a) *Interdependency*. Specialisation inevitably means that one is dependent upon other people. In the UK today we are dependent for our food upon people thousands of miles away and beyond our control.

b) *Dislocation*. Because of interdependency the possibilities for dislocation are very great. For example, a strike by a key group of workers such as miners can bring the whole country to a halt.

c) *Unemployment*. Specialisation means that for many people their training and experience is narrow. This can mean that if that skill is no longer required it may be difficult for the person to find alternative work.

d) *Alienation*. This refers to the estrangement many workers feel from their work. If, for example, a person's job is simply to tighten wheel nuts on a car production line, it is understandable that they should feel bored or even hostile towards the work. This may have repercussions on labour relations and productivity. Some manufacturers such as Volvo have undertaken job enrichment schemes, putting division of labour into reverse, as it were, in order that people may have more varied tasks.

The alienation of the workforce is a major part of Marxist sociology. The capitalist would reply that although jobs may be dull, working hours are made shorter and leisure is enriched by greater wealth. However, alienation is not a problem that should be ignored, either at work or in society in general.

Economies of scale

Economies of scale exist when the expansion of a firm or industry allows the product to be produced at a lower unit cost. As such, economies of scale are an aspect of the division of labour. Economies of scale are possible only if there is sufficient demand for the product. For example, we would hardly expect to find scale economies in the production of artificial limbs, because there simply are not enough of them demanded. As Adam Smith put it, 'the extent of division of labour is limited by the size of the market'. Economies of scale cannot be achieved quickly because large-scale investment in capital (factories, machinery, etc.) is necessary to achieve them. The achievement of economies of scale is therefore a long-run objective.

Internal and external economies of scale

Internal economies of scale are those obtained within one organisation, while ***external*** economies are those which are gained when a number of organisations group together in an area. Industries such as chemicals and cars provide good examples of internal economies, where the industry is dominated by a few large organisations. Historically, the most famous example of external economies of scale was the cotton industry in Lancashire, where many hundreds of businesses concentrated in a small area made up the industry. A more up-to-date example might be the grouping of firms offering specialist financial services in the City of London.

Types of internal economy

a) *Indivisibilities.* These may occur when a large firm is able to take advantage of an industrial process which cannot be reproduced on a small scale. There is a 'lumpiness' about output which means a minimum size is necessary to use current technology. For example, many of the modern colour printing processes are not available on a small scale.
b) *Increased dimensions.* In some cases it is simply a case of bigger is better. For example, an engine which is twice as powerful does not cost twice as much to build or use twice as much material. This is partly due to area–volume relationships. As a rule of thumb engineers use the ***law of two-thirds***, which states that as the volume of a container (pipe, ship, plane) is doubled, its surface area is increased by only two-thirds. The surface area determines how much it costs to construct, while the volume determines its output. Doubling the volume of a ship doubles its ability to carry cargo, but only increases its construction costs by about two-thirds. Hence large ships are much more efficient than small ships. This explains the development of massive oil tankers and bulk cargo carriers. Jumbo jets (e.g. Boeing 747s) are also an example of this principle.
c) *Economies of linked processes.* Technical economies are also sometimes gained by linking processes together, e.g. in the iron and steel industry where iron and steel production is carried out by the same plant, thus saving both transport and fuel costs.
d) *Commercial.* A large-scale organisation may be able to make fuller use of sales and distribution facilities than a small-scale one. For example, a company with a large transport fleet will probably be able to ensure that it transports mainly full loads, whereas a small business may have to hire transport or despatch part-loads. A large firm may also be able to use its commercial power to obtain preferential rates for raw materials and transport. This is usually known as ***bulk buying***.
e) *Organisational.* As a firm becomes larger, the day-to-day organisation can be delegated to office staff, leaving managers free to concentrate on the important tasks. When a firm is large

enough to have a management staff they will be able to specialise in different functions such as accounting, law and market research.

f) *Financial.* Large organisations often find it cheaper and easier to borrow money than small ones as banks are less worried that they might go out of business.

g) *Risk bearing.* All firms run risks, but risks taken in large numbers become more predictable. In addition to this, if an organisation is so large as to be a monopoly, this considerably reduces its commercial risks.

h) *Overhead processes.* For some products very large overhead costs or processes must be undertaken to develop a product, e.g. an aeroplane. Clearly if more units of the product are made, the development costs attributed to each unit will fall.

i) *Diversification.* Most economies of scale are concerned with specialisation and concentration. However, as a firm becomes very large it may be able to safeguard its position by diversifying its products, processes, markets and the location of production.

j) *Economies of common multiples.* For any product we consider, the various processes which are needed to produce it may not have the same optimal scale of production. For example, a large blast furnace may produce 75 tonnes of pig iron but a steel furnace may be able to handle only 30 tonnes; we would thus need more than one steel furnace for every blast furnace. In fact the smallest optimal size for the whole process is the lowest common multiple of the individual processes involved. In our steelmaking example this would give us a plant consisting of two blast furnaces and five steel furnaces:

2×75 tonnes = 150 tonnes
5×30 tonnes = 150 tonnes

Thus the smallest optimal size is 150 tonnes.

Types of external economy

a) *Economies of concentration.* When a number of firms in the same industry band together in an area they can derive a great deal of mutual advantage from one another. Advantages might include a pool of skilled workers, a better infrastructure (such as transport, specialised warehousing, banking, etc.) and the stimulation of improvements. The lack of such external economies is a serious handicap to less developed countries.

b) *Economies of information.* Under this heading we could consider the setting up of specialist research facilities and the publication of specialist journals.

c) *Economies of disintegration.* This refers to the splitting off or ***subcontracting*** of specialist processes. A simple example is to be seen in the high street of most towns where there are specialist photocopying firms.

It should be stressed that what are external economies at one time may be internal at another. To use the last example, small firms may not be able to justify the cost of a sophisticated photocopier, but as they expand there may be enough work to allow them to purchase their own machine.

Efficiency and economies of scale

Where an economy of scale leads to a fall in unit costs because less resources are used to produce a unit of a commodity, this is economically beneficial to society. If, for example, a large furnace uses less fuel per tonne of steel produced than a small one, then society benefits through a more efficient use of scarce fuel resources. It is possible, however, for a firm to achieve economies through such things as bulk buying, where its buying power is used to bargain for a lower price. This benefits the firm because its costs will be lower, but it does not benefit society since no saving of resources is involved.

Diseconomies of scale

Diseconomies of scale occur when the size of a business becomes so large that, rather than decreasing, the unit cost of production actually becomes greater. Diseconomies of scale usually flow from administrative rather than technical problems.

a) *Bureaucracy.* As an organisation becomes larger there is a tendency for it to become more ***bureaucratic***. Decisions can no longer be made quickly at the local level but must follow centrally laid-down procedures or be referred up to higher levels of management. This may lead to a loss of ***flexibility***.

b) *Loss of control*. Large organisations often find it more difficult to monitor effectively the performance of their workers. ***Industrial relations*** can also deteriorate with a large workforce and a management which seems remote and anonymous.

Optimal plant and company size

Achieving the best size of business is not simply a question of getting bigger, but of attaining the optimal size of business or plant.

The typical size of plant will vary greatly from industry to industry. In capital-intensive industries such as chemicals the typical unit may be very large, but in an industry like catering the optimum size of a restaurant is quickly reached and, beyond this, diseconomies may set in. If a restaurant business wishes to expand, it does so by opening new branches (e.g. McDonald's, Burger King) in other locations.

Economies of scale and returns to scale

Confusion frequently arises between economies of scale and ***returns to scale***. Economies of scale reduce the unit cost of production as the scale of production increases; returns to scale are concerned with physical input and output relationships. If, for example, the input of factors of production were to increase by 100 per cent but output were to increase by 150 per cent, we would be said to be experiencing increasing returns to scale. Conversely, if inputs were to be increased by 100 per cent but output were to increase by less than this, then we would be experiencing decreasing returns to scale.

Increasing returns to scale should result in decreasing costs. However, it does not follow that every economy of scale which reduces costs is a result of a return to scale. To take the most obvious example, bulk buying may be a cost economy to the business but it does not involve returns to scale since no change in the input/output relationship is involved.

New technology

Improvements in technology are obviously of fundamental importance to the economy. We have learnt that improved technology brings improved productivity and is therefore beneficial. However, the impact of the new technology of microprocessors is likely to be so massive that it is worthwhile considering this as a constraint upon the economy.

The silicon chip has unleashed such power to process information and control activity and functions of all kinds that it is virtually impossible to foretell where it will lead. Fax machines can now transmit letters without the need for the postman; microprocessor-controlled lathes can undertake the most precise and complex of engineering tasks; robots can assemble electrical components; the Internet allows access to worldwide information and communication for the cost of a local phone call. The full potential of this ***information technology*** revolution has not been reached and it seems likely that it will have a more significant effect on the way we live than the original industrial revolution.

Many people view the technology with alarm, seeing it purely as a method of making workers redundant. What will the future hold, though? Will microprocessors free us from the drudgery of work and create a new Utopia, or will they create vast wealth for those who are able to exploit them, and unemployment for millions of others?

Economic history tells us that vast leaps in technology have been made before, as in the industrial revolution. For example, within ten years of its invention each spinning jenny was able to replace 100 workers. In the wake of the industrial revolution there was poverty and misery for millions, but in the long run the expansion of the economy was able to provide employment for most (labour is after all our most valuable resource) and a higher standard of living. Thus we may see our present problems as those of adjustment, although we must also bear in mind that a return to full employment depends upon a renewed expansion of the economy.

Increasing costs and diminishing returns

We have been examining factors which help people to exploit the resources of the world. However, the basic law of economics is that of scarcity. We must now consider the factors which place constraints upon our exploitation of resources.

The law of diminishing returns

Why can we not grow all the world's food in one garden? A silly question perhaps, but it illustrates a very important principle. We can get a greater output from a garden of fixed size by working longer hours or adding more seeds, etc., but the extra output we obtain will rapidly diminish. Indeed, if we just go on dumping more and more seeds in the garden, total output may even go down.

The principle involved here is known as the *law of diminishing returns*. This law is one of the most important and fundamental principles involved in economics. We may state it thus:

If one factor of production is fixed in supply and successive units of a variable factor are added to it, the extra output derived from the employment of each successive unit of the variable factor must, after a time, decline.

We can illustrate this by the use of a simple numerical example. Suppose that the fixed factor of production is a farm (land). If no labour is employed there will be no output. Now let us see what happens if people are employed. Suppose that one person is employed in the first year, two in the second, and so on. Table 3.1 shows the resulting output from the various combinations of the factors. The first person results in 2000 tonnes of produce. When two people are employed output rises to 5000 tonnes, so that the second person has resulted in 3000 extra tonnes being produced. However, after this, diminishing returns set in and the employment of a third person result in only 2000 tonnes more being produced, while a fourth person adds just 1000 tonnes to production. Were a fifth person to be employed there would be no extra output at all.

***Table 3.1* The law of diminishing returns**

Number of people employed	*Total output (tonnes)*	*Extra output added by each additional unit of labour*
0	0	
		2000
1	2000	
		3000
2	5000	
		2000
3	7000	
		1000
4	8000	
		0
5	8000	

The law of diminishing returns comes about because each successive unit of the variable factor has less of the fixed factor to work with.

The law of diminishing returns may be offset by improvements in technology, but it cannot be repealed.

The short run and the long run

At any particular time any business must have at least one of the factors of production in fixed supply. For example, the buildings which a firm uses cannot be expanded overnight, so that if the firm wants to obtain more output it must use more of the variable factors such as labour.

The period of time in which at least one factor is fixed in supply is defined as the ***short run***. Given time, all the factors may be varied, i.e. new buildings can be constructed, more land acquired, etc. The period of time in which all factors may be varied and in which firms may enter or leave the industry is defined as the ***long run***. The length of time involved will vary from business to business. Obviously it will take much longer for an oil refinery to vary its fixed factors by constructing a new refinery than it would, for example, for a farmer to rent more land.

The law of diminishing returns is thus a short-run phenomenon because, by definition, it is concerned with a situation in which at least one factor is fixed in supply.

STUDENT ACTIVITY 3.3

Which of the following are examples of
a) economies of scale
b) returns to scale
c) the law of diminishing returns?
(i) Congestion on the roads during the rush hour.
(ii) Very large 'supertankers'.
(iii) Lower rates of interest payable by larger companies on their loans from the bank.
(iv) The fall in price of personal computers over the last decade.
(v) The need to apply more and more fertilisers to agricultural land to maintain its productivity.

The law of increasing costs

The law of diminishing returns concerns what happens to output if one factor remains fixed; the ***law of increasing costs*** examines what happens to production, and therefore to costs, as all factors of production are increased.

Let us imagine we are faced with the choice which Hermann Goering gave the German people in 1936: we can produce either guns or butter. Table 3.2 shows a list of alternative possibilities.

Table 3.2 **Increasing costs: a production possibility schedule**

Possibility	*Guns (thousands)*	*Butter (millions of kg)*
A	15	0
B	14	5
C	10	10
D	5	14
E	0	15

If we start at possibility C, where we are producing 10 000 guns and 10 million kg of butter, and then try to produce more guns, this involves switching resources from farming to industry. To reach possibility B we have had to give up 5 million kg of butter to gain 4000 guns. If we want still more guns, to reach possibility A we have to give up 5 million kg of butter to gain only 1000 guns. Thus the cost of guns in terms of butter has risen sharply.

It would also work the other way. If we started from possibility C and tried to increase our output of butter, the cost in terms of guns not produced would become greater and greater. Figure 3.2 shows this graphically. As we move to either end of the production possibility boundary (or frontier) we can see that it is necessary to give up a greater distance on one axis to gain a smaller distance on the other axis. Why should this be? It is because, as we concentrate more and more resources on the output of a particular commodity, the resources we use become less and less suitable. For example, if we tried to produce more and more butter we would, inevitably, be forced to graze cows on land which is more and more unsuitable.

Opportunity cost

Limited resources have alternative uses; for example, the bricks and labour we use to build a house could have been used to build a factory or

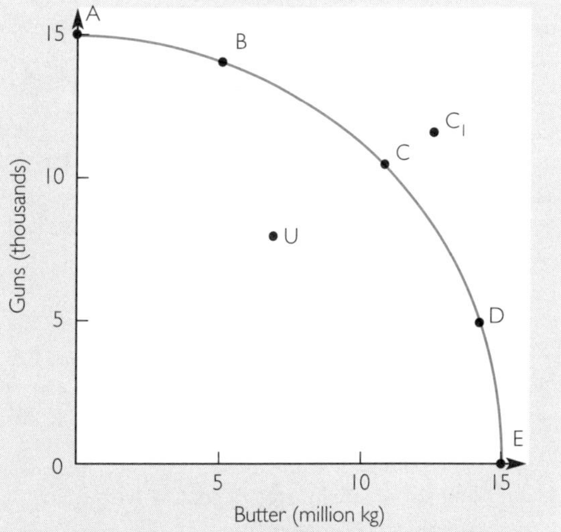

Fig. 3.2 **Production possibility boundary**
Society can attain any combination of guns and butter on line AE or any combination within it such as U, but is unable to attain a position beyond line AE such as C_1.

a hospital. Thus the cost of any produce may be looked at in terms of other opportunities forgone. In the example of guns and butter used above, any movement along the production possibility line tells us the ***opportunity cost*** of guns in terms of butter or vice versa.

Opportunity cost calculations often come up with different answers according to the viewpoint taken. For instance, if a person is unemployed what is the opportunity cost of them taking a job? From the viewpoint of the individual, leisure time must be given up, so there is a positive opportunity cost. From the point of view of the economy as a whole, the labour was previously unproductive, so opportunity cost is zero. From the point of view of the government, they no longer have to pay unemployment benefit, and their tax revenues will rise as the individual earns income. In this section it is the opportunity cost to the economy as a whole which is being considered.

STUDENT ACTIVITY 3.4

What is the opportunity cost to a) society and b) yourself of undertaking your present course of study? Choose from the following list of items to be included in each case:

a) Your leisure time.
b) Your income if you had a job instead.
c) Your output if you had a job instead.
d) The cost of producing your education.
e) Any fees or other expenses which you pay because of your course.
f) The increase in productivity that will result from your education.
g) The increase in your income which will result from your education.
h) The cost to your parents of supporting you financially.
i) The money you are able to earn in the holidays.
j) The social advantages of mixing with many people of your own age.

The production possibility boundary

If we plot the figures in Table 3.2 as a graph we obtain Fig. 3.2. This is termed a production possibility boundary (or frontier) because it shows the limit of what it is possible to produce with present resources. Society may attain any point on the line, such as point C, or, through the unemployment or inefficient use of resources, any point within the frontier, such as U.

However, point C_1 is unattainable at present. Point C_1 may become attainable as the production possibility shifts rightwards as a result of economic growth and improvements in technology.

You will note that the line is bowed outwards (concave to the origin). This is because of the law of increasing costs. A few moments experimenting with a ruler on the graph will show you that the rate of exchange of guns for butter, or vice versa, worsens continually as we move up or down the line. This is the typical shape for a production possibility boundary.

Three possibilities for a line

To check that you have understood this idea let us consider the three possibilities for the shape of the production possibility line. These are illustrated in Fig. 3.3. In Fig. 3.3 (a), as we move down the vertical axis each 20 units of *Y* given up gains smaller and smaller amounts of *X*. Moving from position A to position B we give up 20 units of *Y* but gain 50 units of *X*. However, as we move from position B to position C, a further 20 units of *Y* given up now gains us only 22 units of *X*. The ratio of exchange continues to deteriorate until the last 20 units of *Y* given up gains only three units of *X*. Review your understanding of this principle by considering it in reverse, i.e. as we move from point F to point E it costs only three units of *X* given up to gain 20 units of *Y*, but moving from position B to position A involves giving up 50 units of *X* to gain 20 units of *Y*. Thus the ratio of exchange of *X* for *Y* (or *Y* for *X*) deteriorates whichever way we move along a line which is concave to the origin of the graph. Such a line illustrates increasing costs (or diminishing returns).

In Fig. 3.3 (b) we show a constant cost case, i.e. that product *X* can be exchanged for product *Y* at a constant rate. You will find various applications of such a line in this book. (See Figs 39.1 and 39.3.)

If we look at a line which is bowed inwards (convex to the origin) this shows increasing

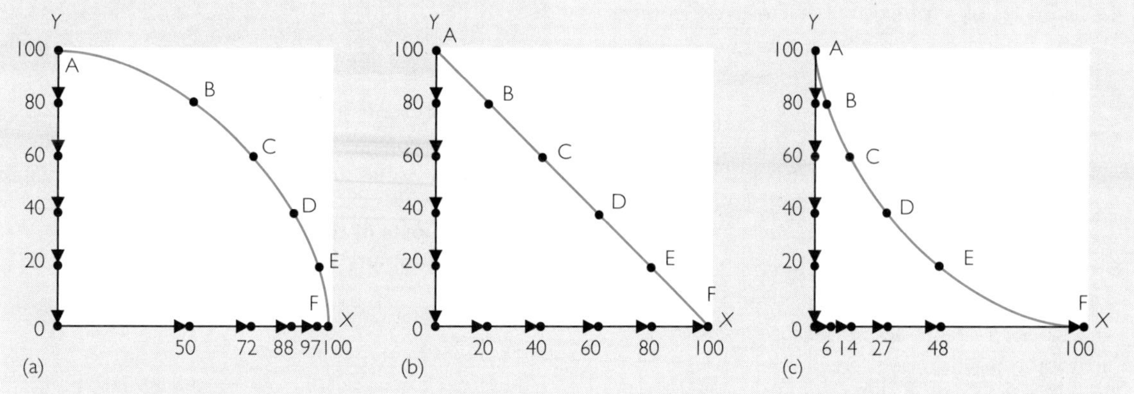

***Fig. 3.3* Three possibilities for a line**

returns (or decreasing costs), i.e. the ratio of exchange of *X* for *Y* (or *Y* for *X*) gets better as we move towards the ends of the line. In Fig. 3.3 (c) moving from position A to position B involves giving up 20 units of *Y* to gain six units of *X* but the next 20 units of *Y* given up gains eight units of *X* and so on until the last 20 units of *Y* given up gains us 52 units of *X*. This could come about if, for example, specialising in *X* allowed us to gain more and more economies of scale. Again check your understanding of the principle by moving the other way along the line and seeing that the ratio of exchange of *Y* for *X* also improves, i.e. the first 20 units of *Y* cost us 52 units of *X* given up but the next 20 only 21 and so on. As we have stated above, a production possibility line is most likely to be concave, but we shall encounter various applications of these properties of lines throughout the book.

Production and choice

This chapter has dealt with the question of production rather than choice. A choice has to be made in the real economy between alternative products. There will be many more than the two products presented in the simplified production possibility curve, but the question to be answered will be the same: what combination of products should be produced? We have dealt with the first piece of information we need to answer this question: what is the opportunity cost of producing a good at each level of output? On its own this will not be enough information; we also need to know the consumers' preferences.

Choice and the economist

The student can be forgiven for finding the principles in this chapter contradictory; increasing costs, for example, seem to contradict economies of scale. However, economies of scale do not go on for ever and eventually there is likely to come a point where costs start to rise. When looked at from the very large scale of the whole economy, the law of increasing costs is likely to hold. However, some economies have been very successful by concentrating heavily in a few areas of industry: for example, Japan has concentrated heavily on cars, motorbikes and electronic goods, while much of the west coast of the USA concentrates on producing aircraft, films and information technology.

Summary

1. The economic problem is that of infinite human wants but only limited resources with which to fulfil them.
2. Economic resources are traditionally divided into the four factors of production: labour, land, capital and enterprise.
3. Division of labour is the subdivision of the economic process into specialist tasks. The resultant increase in output is the basis of economic prosperity.

4 Economies of scale exist when the production of a product in large numbers allows its unit cost to be decreased. There are both external and internal economies of scale.
5 The law of diminishing returns states that if one factor is fixed in supply, but more and more units of a variable factor are employed, the resultant extra output will decrease.
6 The law of increasing costs is encountered when one type of production is expanded at the cost of others. It comes about because less suitable resources have to be used.
7 The production possibility line shows all the combinations of products which it is possible to produce with a given quantity of resources.

Questions

1 Define increasing costs, returns to scale and the law of diminishing returns.
2 Evaluate the extent to which the disadvantages of division of labour outweigh the advantages.
3 Show the effect upon society's production possibility line in Fig. 3.2 if technological improvements increased productivity in the production of guns but not of butter.
4 If in a given situation the quantity of land could be increased but labour could not, would the law of diminishing returns still operate? Explain your answer.
5 Assess the extent to which each of the following products is affected by available economies of scale: petroleum; milk; electricity; cars; frozen peas; coal; luxury yachts.
6 Evaluate the role which prices play in helping to answer the economic problem.
7 Consider the opportunity cost of:
   a) Leaving school at 16.
   b) Spending 5 percent of GDP on defence.
   c) Building a fifth terminal at London Heathrow airport.
   d) The construction of the Newbury bypass.

Data response A
Costs and choice

Table 3.3 presents information for the JSB Audiomax Speaker Company, showing how the cost of producing loudspeakers varies with the output produced per week.

***Table 3.3* Costs of the JSB Audiomax Speaker Company**

Units of output produced per week	*Total costs of production (£)*
1009	85 025
1998	110014
3004	130010
4014	160 002
4997	209 889
6011	280015
7003	370 000
7990	479917

1 From this information construct a graph to show how the cost of producing a loudspeaker (*unit* or *average cost*) varies with the quantity of loudspeakers produced each week.
2 State the range of output over which the company experiences:
   a) increasing returns to scale;
   b) decreasing returns to scale.
3 What is the most productively efficient level of output for JSB?
4 Distinguish between economies of scale and returns to scale.
5 What economies of scale are likely to be available to JSB?

Data response B
Growth, wages and poverty

Read the following passage which is taken from the *World Development Report* of 1990.

Growth, real wages, and poverty: the United Kingdom and the United States, 1770 to 1920

The history of the *industrial revolution* in the United Kingdom and the United States suggests links among growth, real wages, and poverty. In both countries development in the early phase of the revolution was *capital-intensive*. Since at the same time the labour supply was increasing, the *real wages* of unskilled workers grew slowly, and economic growth had only a small effect on poverty. After about 1820 in the United Kingdom and 1880 in the United States, however, real wages began to rise, and poverty began to decline.

Britain's industrial revolution began around 1770, but until 1820 real wages barely increased. In the first twenty years of the nineteenth century the earnings of adult male unskilled workers grew at just 0.2 per cent a year. The next fifty years saw a much faster and steadier increase at 1.7 per cent a year. After about 1840 the GDP of the United States grew significantly faster than that of the United Kingdom at a comparable stage, but real wages for urban unskilled labour increased by less than 0.2 per cent a year between 1845 and 1880. Then, as in the United Kingdom, they accelerated and grew by 1.3 per cent a year for the next 40 years.

In both countries technological advances initially favoured capital-intensive and *skill-intensive industry* over labour-intensive agriculture. Slow growth in labour demand coincided with dramatic population growth to restrict the growth of real wages. Several decades after the start of the industrial revolution, technological progress in farming led to a more *balanced pattern of growth*, and the labour-saving bias of early industrialisation gave way to a neutral or labour-intensive bias. Lower birthrates and stricter immigration laws slowed population growth, and real wages increased at a faster rate.

In the United Kingdom pauperism declined after 1840. The most reliable data for the United States, from records in New York State, suggest that poverty increased up to 1865, when 8 per cent of the population was receiving local relief. After that, poverty declined until the end of the century. In both countries growth in the real wages of unskilled labour reduced the incidence of poverty.

Answer the following questions.

1 Explain the terms in italics.
2 If population increased rapidly what would you expect to happen to the level of real wages? Explain what principle is at work in this situation.
3 Construct a production possibility curve to illustrate what would happen if technology increased rapidly in industry but not in agriculture.
4 State the conditions necessary for there to be an increase in population accompanied by growth in real wages.
5 Poverty is still a world-wide problem. Do the developments described in the article have any lessons for poor countries today? Explain your answer.

4 Demography

Learning outcomes

At the end of this chapter you will be able to:

- Account for the widespread concern about the trend in world population growth over the last 200 years.
- List the factors influencing population growth and family size in different countries and understand the economic implications of changes in the structure of a country's population.
- Define the terms birth and death rate, dependency ratio, working population and 'optimum' population size.

The statistical study of the characteristics of populations is called ***demography*** and hence is the title of this chapter. The economic consequences of demographic changes are of increasing concern in both rich and poor countries and will figure more and more in the economic debates to come and hence economics syllabuses. This chapter is in acknowledgement of the importance of the topic. We shall look at aspects of world and international demography and then focus on the demography of the UK.

World population

The population explosion

Since the eighteenth century the world has undergone a population explosion. The impact of the population explosion on all aspects of human life – economic, legal, social and political – is immense. For the firm it provides one of its essential resources, labour, as well as the markets for its goods and services. Government organisations must also base their plans on their estimates of changes in the future population. Although it would appear that population growth has stabilised in many Western countries, the continuing growth of world population poses some of the most important global questions for the future.

What is meant by the population explosion is demonstrated graphically by Fig. 4.1. It can be seen from this graph that estimated world population was 300 million in AD 1000 and that this slowly rose to around 728 million in AD 1750. Population then began to rise much more quickly. This means that population will have risen over 20-fold in the last 1000 years, having been almost static for the previous 20 000 years of human history. Moreover, the majority of this growth will have taken place in 100 years. Although figures for the rate of population increase show some signs of slowing, they nonetheless indicate very great potential for growth. In mid 1996 the world population was 5815 million and the US Census Bureau projected a world population of 9400 million by 2050.

T. R. Malthus (1766–1834)

Accurate population figures for the UK start with the first census of 1801. Three years earlier Malthus published the first major work on population. This was entitled *An Essay on the Principle of Population as it Affects the Future Improvement of Society*. Malthus had noted the quickening growth of the UK population and was also aware of the principle of diminishing returns as expounded by Adam Smith and other political economists. Malthus wrote that:

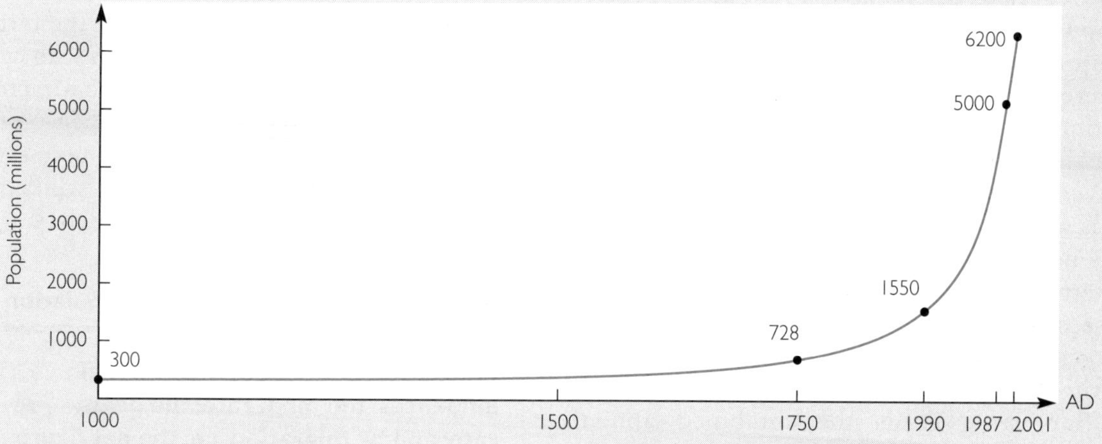

Fig. 4.1 **The population explosion**

> Population when unchecked, increases in a geometrical ratio [1, 2, 4, 8, 16, etc.]. Subsistence increases only in an arithmetical ratio [1, 2, 3, 4, etc.]. A slight acquaintance with numbers will show the immensity of the first power in comparison with the second.

STUDENT ACTIVITY 4.1

To see what Malthus meant by the differences in the 'powers' of the ratios, extend the above geometrical and arithmetical series for another 20 steps and compare the difference between them.

Since the amount of land on the planet is fixed, this would mean that there would be less and less food to feed each person. This would continue until population growth was halted by 'positive checks' of 'war, pestilence and famine'. This would give more food per person so that population would increase again, thus causing positive checks to set in again, and so on. Thus, the gloomy forecast of Malthus was that world population would forever fluctuate around the point where most of it is on the point of starving to death. This is termed a ***subsistence equilibrium*** and featured in the work of ***classical*** economists such as David Ricardo.

For a number of reasons these pessimistic forecasts did not come true in the UK. Through technological improvements, industry and agriculture became more productive, the New World and Australia provided room for expansion, and, towards the end of the nineteenth century, parents in the UK began to limit the size of their families. Moreover, there is a debate in economic history as to whether population growth stimulated economic growth or vice versa.

When one looks at the enormous spread of poverty, especially in Africa in recent years, one might be forgiven for thinking that Malthus was only too right. But estimates of a world population consistent with ***sustainable economic development*** vary enormously (see Chapter 27 for a discussion of sustainable growth). Some neo-Malthusians place it at 12 000 million, some at far less than the current population! The 'technological optimists' argue that just as Malthus underestimated the capacity of technology to provide, so the neo-Malthusians and pessimistic ecologists will be proved wrong.

There are very few observers who do not predict major crises at some point in the next millennium if current world population growth rates continue.

The rich and the poor

There is a growing disparity between the rich areas of the world and the poor. In both proportional and aggregate terms, the poor are poorer than they have ever been before. Population growth may provide one of the major clues as to why this is so. The United Nation's *Human Development Report* in 1996 estimated that 70 countries have average incomes less than they were in 1980. Many have had their problems compounded by wars. It is also the case that many of these countries are now also burdened with large amounts of international debt. But other observers emphasise other factors such as trade barriers and income inequality. For example, the UN report estimated that the wealth of the world's 358 billionaires exceeds the combined annual incomes of countries which are home to nearly half the world's people.

Asia (excluding the former USSR), South America and Africa together occupy about 55 per cent of the land surface of the Earth and have about 70 per cent of its population, whereas Europe, North America and Australasia occupy 45 per cent of the Earth and have only 30 per cent of the population. By the end of the century it is likely that the first of these two areas will have 80 per cent of the population and the second only 20 per cent. Obviously the poorer areas will need enormous advances in agricultural and industrial techniques to cope with this rise, but most of the expertise and the capital is possessed by the richer countries. The problems of developing countries are further discussed in Chapter 46.

It is because of these considerations that many people believe that a large fall in the birth rate in the poor nations is the only way out of this cycle of poverty for them. In response to some bigoted remarks that poverty is caused by overbreeding, reducing the birth rate is easier said than done. For example, in poor countries it is more difficult to fund welfare states. Hence, for the individual family, children are often required as extra income and as a protection against loss of income through sickness and old age. There can thus be a vicious circle of poverty and a high birth rate for the country as a whole. Some research, however, suggests that enhancing the economic status of women in relation to paid employment can substantially reduce the birth rate. In some countries this would clash with cultural attitudes. Such attitudes may be a factor and are studied by sociologists and hence not covered in this book. But any funding necessary to break out of such circles of poverty will have to be found by the poor countries themselves.

Factors influencing the size of population

Population is affected by three main influences: the birth rate; the death rate; and by migration, i.e. the net figure derived from immigration and emigration.

This is illustrated in Fig. 4.2.

Birth rate

Birth rates are usually expressed as a rate per thousand of the population.

This is sometimes called a crude birth rate since it simply records the number of live births, no allowance being made for infant mortality or other circumstances.

Table 4.1 gives figures for the birth rate for various countries.

Death rate

Death rates are normally expressed as the number of people in the country that died in a year per thousand of the population.

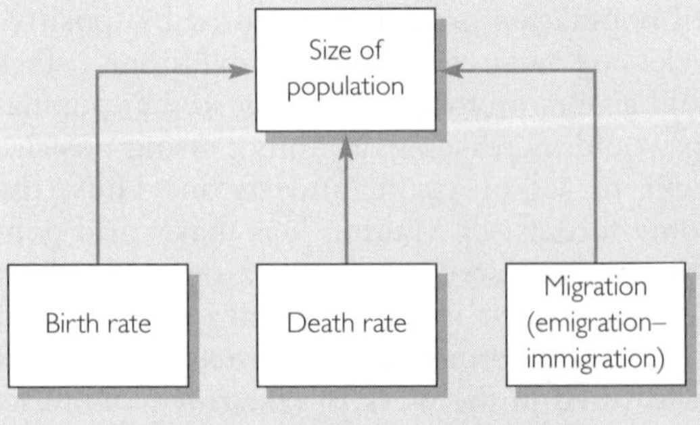

Fig. 4.2 **Factors influencing population**

***Table 4.1* Birth rates, selected countries**

Country	*Crude birth rate per 1000 of population*	
	1970	*1993*
Ethiopia	50	48
India	39	29
Kenya	53	36
Mexico	43	27
Malaysia	36	28
Ireland	22	15
Singapore	23	16
UK	16	13
France	17	13
Germany	13	10
USA	17	16

Source: *World Development Report*, IBRD, 1995

This is sometimes called the crude death rate because it takes no account of the age of the person at death; they could be 3 months old or 90 years. Table 4.2 shows death rates for various countries.

***Table 4.2* Death rates, selected countries**

Country	*Crude death rate per 1000 of population*	
	1970	*1993*
Ethiopia	24	18
India	16	10
Kenya	18	9
Mexico	10	5
Malaysia	9	5
Ireland	11	9
Singapore	5	6
UK	12	11
France	11	10
Germany	12	11
USA	9	9

Source: *World Development Report*, IBRD, 1995

Rate of natural increase

A way of presenting the change in population can be arrived at by comparing the birth rate with the death rate; this gives a simple measure of the rate of natural increase or decrease.

This can be illustrated by superimposing one bar diagram on another. Figure 4.3 does this for both the UK and Malaysia. As you can see there was virtually no growth of population in the UK in 1995, with a rate of natural increase of only 2 per thousand per year, but in Malaysia the rate was 23 per thousand (although this has fallen from 30 per thousand in 1988). Table 4.3 shows population growth rates for various selected countries.

Infant mortality

It is often misleading to speak of the average expectation of life, since for much of human history most people have died at a very early age. A measure of this exists, known as infant mortality. This records the number of deaths of children under the age of 12 months expressed as a number per thousand of children in this age group. Historically this was very significant in the UK. In the early eighteenth century over half of the children born died before the age of

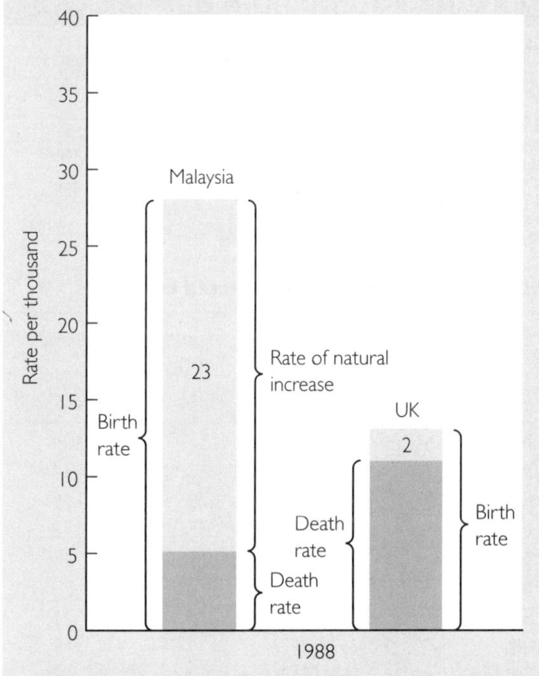

***Fig. 4.3* Rates of natural increase in population**
The rate for Malaysia is 23 per thousand (2.3%) whereas the rate for UK is only 2 per thousand (0.2%).
Source: *World Development Report*, IBRD 1996

Table 4.3 **Growth of population, selected countries**

Country	*Average annual growth of population percentage 1980–93*
Kenya	3.3
India	2.0
Ghana	3.3
Mexico	2.3
Malaysia	2.5
Ireland	0.3
Singapore	1.1
UK	0.2
USA	1.0

Source: *World Development Report*, IBRD

1 year and four out of five died before the age of 5. In 1951 the rate of infant mortality in the UK was 311 and by 1988 this had fallen to 9. The lowest rate in the world is enjoyed by Japan, at only 4 per thousand.

STUDENT ACTIVITY 4.2

Table 4.4 gives infant mortality rates for various countries. Use the table to calculate the difference in the percentage of children dying before their first birthday in Mali and compare this with Japan. What factors could account for this vast difference?

Table 4.4 **Infant mortality, selected countries**

Country	*Infant mortality per 1000 live births* 1993	1970
Mali	157	204
India	80	137
Ghana	79	111
Mexico	35	72
Malaysia	13	45
Ireland	7	20
Singapore	6	21
UK	7	18
France	7	18
Germany	6	22
USA	9	20
Japan	4	14

Source: *World Development Report*, IBRD

Migration

If immigration is compared with emigration, a figure of net outflow or inflow of migrants is arrived at.

In terms of the overall size of population, migration has not been a significant factor for the UK.

However, countries such as the USA and Australia have, effectively, been peopled by immigration. On the other hand, Ireland has on occasions experienced falls in its population because of emigration.

At the end of the Second World War 10 million people were displaced following the Holocaust. People fled from Eastern to Western Europe and many Jews left Europe to found the state of Israel. The problem of displaced people continues: the United Nations High Commission for Refugees had more than 20 million people on its books in 1991. We have all seen pictures of the displaced and starving on our television screens. These are all forms of migration.

More significant has been the migration of people for economic reasons, i.e. leaving poor countries to seek better conditions in the richer nations. Many of the advanced countries have used immigrants (both legal and illegal) as a source of cheap labour. Germany drew on East Germany before the Berlin Wall was erected – and following that on immigrants from Turkey and Yugoslavia. France drew on its former North African colonies while the UK drew on Asia and the Caribbean. The USA had a large inflow from Mexico and other Latin American countries.

Although gaining population through immigration the UK also experienced emigration. Many people left the UK after the Second World War to begin new lives in Australia, New Zealand and South Africa. This meant that the net migration figure for the UK was relatively small. As you can see in Fig. 4.4, there have been three periods when the UK was a net gainer by migration (lower part of graph). The period in the 1930s is explained by two factors: by people returning home because of the world-wide depression; and the large flow of refugees from Nazi Germany in the 1930s.

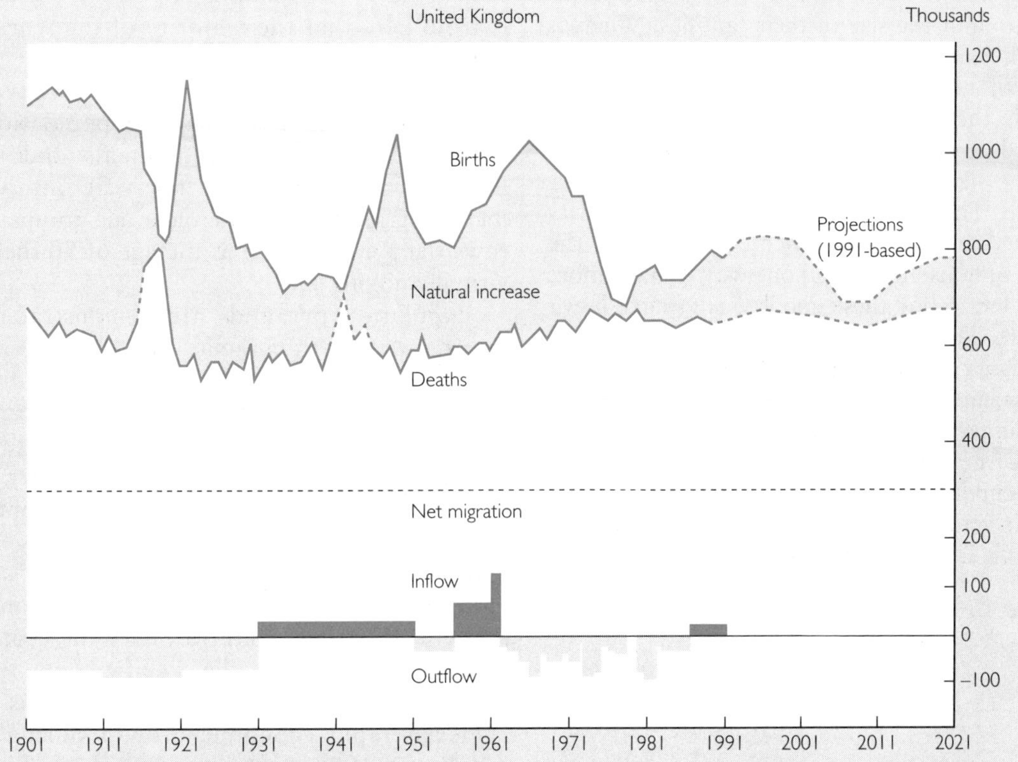

Fig. 4.4 **Population changes and projections**
Sources: Office of Population Censuses and Surveys; Government Actuary's Department

Successive waves of immigrants from the New Commonwealth countries account for the inflow in the 1950s and 1960s. The net gain in the late 1980s was due more to a decrease in the number of people emigrating than to an upturn in immigration. Although the net figure is relatively small, the swap of a considerable number of ethnic Britons for those from other ethnic, religious and cultural backgrounds has posed some social and political problems, e.g. in education.

For much of the period since the Second World War there has been a shortage of labour and immigrants have played a vital role in helping to deal with this.

The growth of the UK population

Table 4.5 lists the growth in the population of England, Wales and Scotland.

Table 4.5 **Population growth (thousands) in England, Wales and Scotland**

Year	*Population*	*Percentage increase per decade*
1801	10 501	–
1871	26 072	13.9
1911	40 891	11.5
1941 (estimate)	46 605	4.3
1951	48 854	4.8
1961	51 380	5.2
1971	54 388	5.9
1981	54 815	0.8
1991	56 207	2.5
1994	56 753	1.0

Source: Annual Abstract of Statistics, 1996

The decline in the size of the family

In the UK after 1870 the expectation of life continued to increase. Therefore reasons for the decrease in the rate of population growth are to be found in the birth rate. It was from this time on that people began to limit the size of their families. Whereas children had been a source of income, people began to take a different economic attitude towards them. Parents began to want higher standards for their children and realised that limiting the size of their family would make this possible. The new age of Victorian prosperity presented many goods which competed for the income of households, and one way to have more income left to buy these goods was to have fewer children. Later, the increases in the age of compulsory schooling and the increase in employment opportunities for women, combined with the persisting traditional role of women as direct carer, further increased the ***opportunity cost*** of children. It would appear that the smaller family is here to stay in richer developed countries such as the UK (see Table 4.6).

Table 4.6 **Crude birth rates, UK**

Year	Crude birth rate	Year	Crude birth rate
1911	24.6	1976	12.0
1932	16.3	1979	13.1
1942	15.0	1981	13.0
1951	15.9	1983	12.8
1956	16.1	1985	13.3
1961	17.9	1987	13.6
1964	18.8	1989	13.6
1971	16.1	1993	13.0

The structure of the UK population

When we come to analyse population structure we can split it up by age, sex, occupation and geographical distribution.

The age and sex distribution of the population

This refers to the number of people of each sex in each age group. The most important divisions are 0–14, 15–64 and 65 and over. The relative size of the 15–64 group is important because it is from here that the majority of the working population is drawn.

Both age and sex distribution in society can be presented as a 'pyramid'. The population is divided between male and female and then between age groups at five-year intervals. Increasing mortality in the older age groups narrows the pyramid until at the age of 90 there is virtually no one left.

Population pyramids are demonstrated in Fig. 4.5. A smooth pyramid would be associated with countries where there is a substantial difference between the birth rate and the death rate. This is illustrated in Fig. 4.5 (a) and 4.5 (b) by the UK at the end of the nineteenth century and by Bangladesh in the 1980s. You should contrast these pyramids with those of the UK and modern Malaysia. The UK was the world's first industrialised nation and hence has been one of the world's richest countries over the century. Malaysia is one of the Pacific rim 'tiger' economies which, from poor country status, has achieved rapid economic growth during the 1980s and 1990s and hence greatly improved overall living standards.

When the birth rate and the death rate are close together, then relatively small changes in the birth rate can bring about large changes in the age structure of the population. This is shown for the UK in 1995 by Fig. 4.5 (c). The fall in the birth rate between 1964 and 1977 accounts for the narrowing of the pyramid in the 20–24 age group. This produced a drastic fall in the number of school leavers during the 1990s. The reduced percentage of young workers is part of what is known as the ***demographic time-bomb***. This is examined below and in the data response question at the end of this chapter.

Geographical distribution

The UK has an overall density of population of 2379 per km^2. This is one of the highest in the

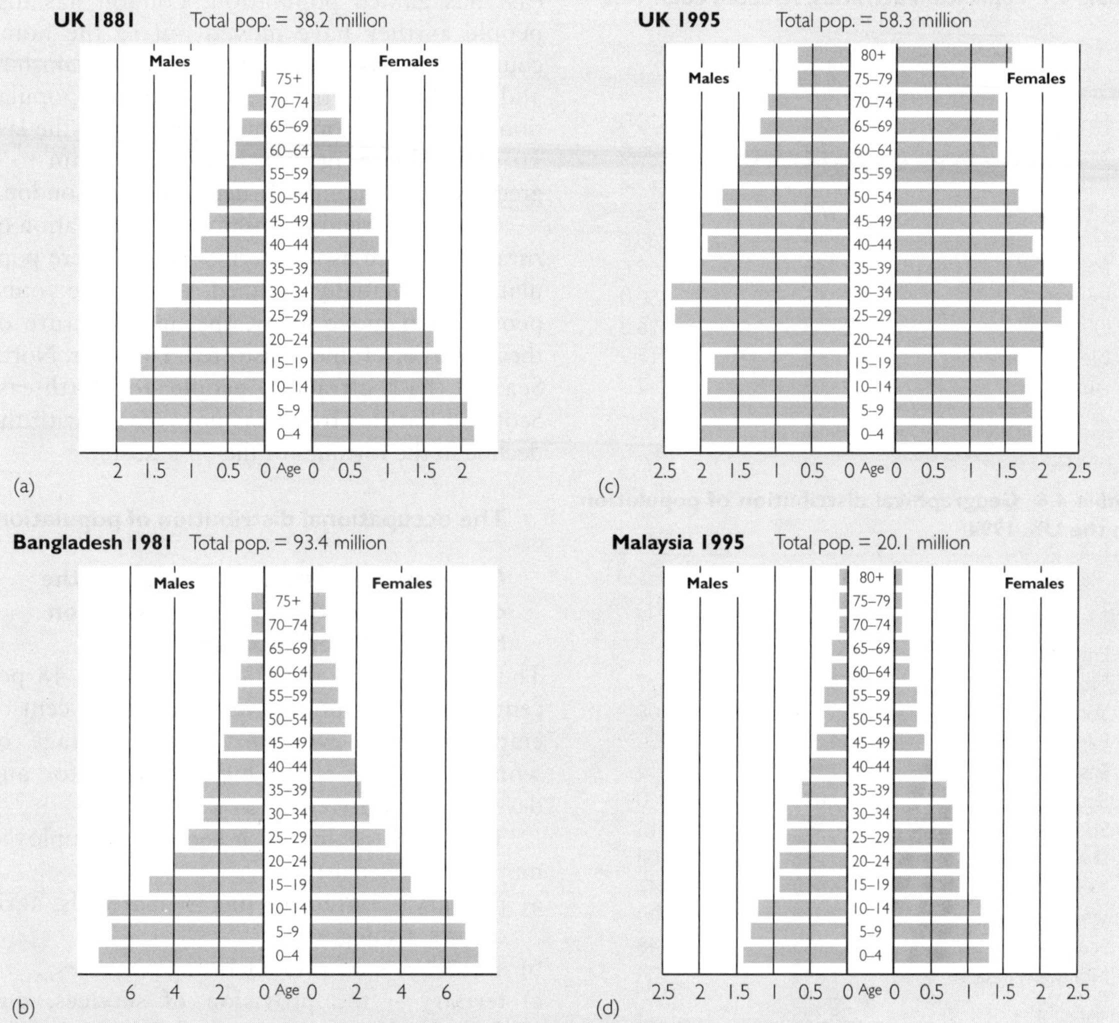

***Fig. 4.5* Population pyramids: population by sex and age (all figures millions)**
Sources: (a) and (b) Office of Population Censuses and Surveys; United Nations; (c) and (d) *The Sex, Age and Distribution of the World's Populations*, 1994 Revisions, United Nations.

world. Population densities for selected countries are presented in Table 4.7.

Despite the high density of population in the UK there are great regional disparities and the distribution is not static. Table 4.8 presents the regional distribution of the population in 1994 and also the figures for net variation in the regions for the years 1981 to 1994.

The population is predominantly urban. In England and Wales only 20 per cent of the people live in rural areas, in Scotland it is 28 per cent and in Northern Ireland 45 per cent. The majority of the urban population is concentrated in the major conurbations, i.e. Greater London, the West Midlands, south-east Lancashire, Merseyside, West Yorkshire, Tyneside and

Table 4.7 Population densities, selected countries

Country	Population (millions) mid 1993	Population per km²
Hong Kong	5.8	5800.0
Singapore	2.8	2800.0
India	898.2	273.2
UK	57.9	236.3
Ghana	16.4	68.6
Malaysia	19.0	57.6
Ireland	3.5	50.0
USA	257.8	26.3
New Zealand	3.5	12.9
Australia	17.6	2.3

Source: *World Development Report*, IBRD

Table 4.8 Geographical distribution of population in the UK, 1994

Region	Population (thousands)	Variation 1981–94
England		
North	3 100	–17
Yorkshire & Humberside	5 026	108
East Midlands	4 103	250
East Anglia	2 106	212
South East	17 871	860
South West	4 796	415
West Midlands	5 295	108
North West	6 412	–47
Wales	2 913	100
Scotland	5 132	–48
Northern Ireland	1 642	104
Total UK	58 395	

Source: *Annual Abstract of Statistics*, 1996

Clydeside. With the exception of London, the basis for these conurbations was the old staple industries of the nineteenth century, which were in turn dependent upon coal. The twentieth century has seen the relative decline of these industries and the emergence of new industries. The new industries, however, have grown up mainly in the Midlands and the south-east of England. This has meant that population has grown more rapidly in these areas.

Another feature of recent years has been the decay of inner cities. Thus, although the south-east has gained population, London has lost people as they have moved out to the home counties such as Hertfordshire, Buckinghamshire and Berkshire. In these home counties, population has grown more than 30 per cent in the last 20 years. These people, however, remain to a great extent economically dependent on London.

A separate trend has been the depopulation of rural areas such as northern Scotland. Here population has actually declined. As it is the young people who move away, the age structure of these areas is left most distorted. However, North Sea oil had attracted people to north-east Scotland but this trend has now ceased with the decline in the fortunes of the oil industry.

The occupational distribution of population

Occupational distribution refers to the distribution of the working population between different occupations.

The workforce in the UK in 1996 was 48 per cent of the total population and 50 per cent of employees were women. The percentage of women working is the highest figure for any developed country.

The industries in which people are employed may be classified as:

a) primary – extraction of raw materials, agriculture, fishing, etc;
b) secondary – all manufacturing processes;
c) tertiary – the provision of services, e.g. finance, education, the Civil Service and the armed forces.

As a rule a poor or 'underdeveloped' economy would have a large percentage of its total population working and concentrated mainly in primary industries. An 'advanced' or developed economy would have a smaller percentage working population with a larger tertiary sector. In the UK the tertiary sector represents about two-thirds of the working population. The proportion of the population which is available for work is affected by demographic factors such as the age structure of the population and by other factors such as society's attitude to women working, the school leaving age and the retirement age (see below).

Over the last 100 years there has been a sharp decrease in the percentage of people employed in agriculture, forestry and fishing. The UK now has one of the smallest percentages employed in these occupations of any country. Domestic servants also used to be very important, but they have now almost entirely disappeared (although recent increases in income inequality did see a small revival of this occupation). There have been large increases in those employed in commerce, the professional services, public administration, manufacturing and the armed forces. This was caused by the industrialisation of society and rising real incomes which have given people money to spend on a wider range of goods and services. The growing complexity of society also increased the numbers of those engaged in administration. This is also associated with the rise in the influence of the state in economic and social life (see also Chapter 29).

In recent years there have been dramatic changes in the occupational distribution of population. The percentage of those employed in manufacturing has dropped dramatically. This is associated with the deindustrialisation of the economy and also the depression in manufacturing industries brought about by imports. There was some increase in the number involved in primary industries because of North Sea oil although the output has since fallen off. Overall there is a marked trend to a reliance on tertiary industries, the growth areas being financial and professional services. Tourism is also now a major industry.

Demographic constraints

Consequences of the changes in the size and structure of population

If the population is increasing in size then, other things being equal, there is less land and other resources available per head. In the short term this could lead to a tendency to import more goods, thus worsening the balance of payments. On the other hand there would be an increasing domestic market for goods, which could lead to increasing economies of scale, profits for investment and a spur for new products. Indeed, in the nineteenth century the UK's population growth was accompanied by great technological improvements. Thus increasing population was attended by increasing prosperity (see also the data response question at the end of this chapter).

A declining population would, other things being equal, lead to more resources being available per head. It is possible, however, that lacking the stimulus of population growth there would be less incentive to improve technology. This could have an adverse effect on the long-term prospects of the economy.

The structure of any given population size is also of economic significance. For example, if overall the population was becoming 'younger' then there would be a smaller dependent population of old people, and a changing pattern of consumption away from geriatric hospitals and the like to a greater demand for schools, pop records, etc. In addition, a younger population might be more flexible and dynamic and more able to take advantage of technological change. There would also be a greater mobility of labour, both occupational and geographical. The increased number of young workers to retired persons could also increase the overall income per head. To examine this it is useful to define more accurately the terms ***working population*** and ***dependency ratio***.

The working population (or workforce) comprises all those people between the ages of 16 and 65 (60 for women) who are working or available for work, and thus includes the registered unemployed.

Also included in the figure are those over 65 who are still working. However, housewives not otherwise employed, those living off private means and those unable to work, e.g. the chronically sick, the insane and those in prison, are excluded from the definition of the working population.

The dependency ratio is the number of persons outside of a nation's working population as a percentage of the number of people within the working population i.e. the average number of dependants per potential worker:

Dependency ratio = Numbers outside working population/Working population

It is also important to note that a low dependency ratio does not, of itself, guarantee greater prosperity. For all to share, there have to be mechanisms whereby current output is transferred from workers to dependants. A skills shortage and ***structural unemployment*** could mean the potential of the workforce is not being utilised. The dependency ratio could also be misleading if a larger number of people go on to higher education or there is a rise in the number of the very old (since they make the greatest demand on welfare services), although it is envisaged that hospital activity for the very old will decline continuously until the end of the century. This picture is complicated by the increasing cost of medical services as improved knowledge makes new techniques available.

It is commonly supposed that the dependency ratio, or welfare burden (the ratio of the dependent population to the working population), has been steadily increasing in the UK. This was true up to the 1970s but then, owing to a combination of circumstances, the welfare burden actually fell up to the late 1980s. This was because the rise in the number of old people was more than offset by the fall in the number of children following the fall in the birth rate. Of more significance has been the lack of school leavers entering the workforce during the 1990s. In 1986 there were 6.2 million people aged between 16 and 24 in the UK workforce. In 1991 there were about 5.7 million and the figure for 1996 is only 4.9 million. It is unlikely that the recent rise in the birth rate will reverse this trend, and there are concerns being raised among ***OECD*** countries at the possible serious economic consequences of an ***ageing population*** during the first half of the twenty-first century.

The dependency ratio is often expressed as its inverse, the ***support ratio***. But to highlight the effects of an ageing population, this is often taken to be the number of persons of working age as a proportion of the number of persons of pensionable age. Figure 4.6 shows that, on this basis, the support ratio for the UK has been falling consistently for the latter half of the twentieth century. This has raised fears that the welfare needs of the increased numbers of the retired, e.g. medical care and pensions, will place an unacceptable burden on those of working age. Figure 4.7 puts this trend in an international context and these issues are explored further in the data response questions at the end of this chapter.

The optimum population

The concept of the optimum population

The optimum population has been defined as that size and structure of population which is most conducive to the betterment of the wealth and welfare of a society.

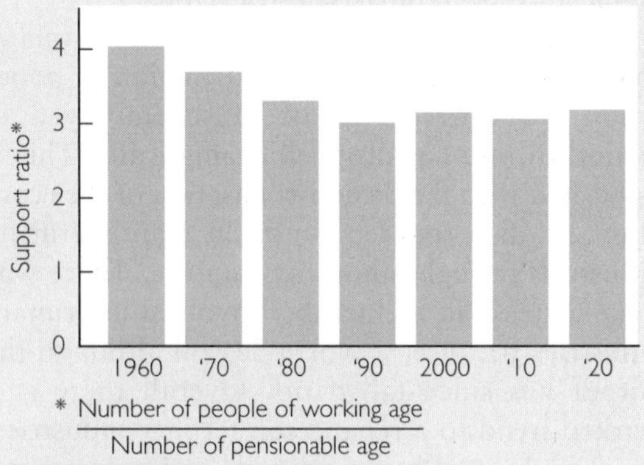

Fig. 4.6 **UK support ratio**
Source: Government Actuary's projections

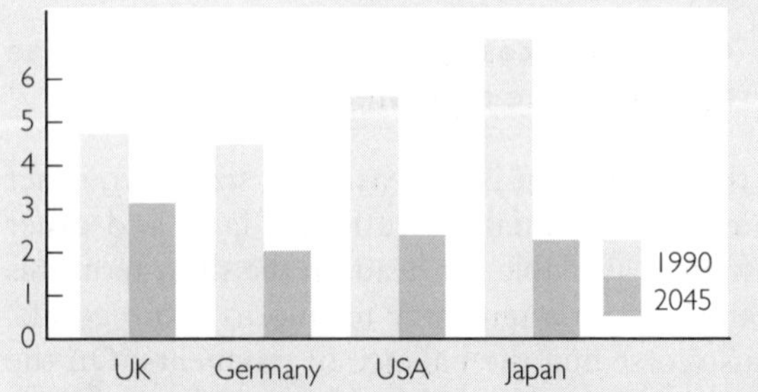

Fig. 4.7 **International support ratio**
Source: OECD projections

If a population is too small in relation to resources, underpopulation exists; if it is too large, a country is suffering from overpopulation. However, it is very difficult to quantify these ideas. The most obvious measure to consider is the GNP per capita of a country. We saw that for some countries in the world GNP per capita has indeed been declining. But there are no simple rules about the relationship of people and the availability of resources. Singapore has turned the seeming disadvantage of overpopulation into an advantage by industrialisation. Conversely, New Zealand has turned the apparent disadvantage of underpopulation to its advantage through agriculture. The idea of optimum population must, therefore, also depend upon the level of technology, the amount of capital per head and the ability of a population to adapt to change.

We cannot, therefore, state the optimum population as anything as simple as so many people per square kilometre. Optimum levels of population are therefore not comparable from one country to another. What is right for an industrial country is not right for an agricultural one. Neither is the optimum level static. Two centuries ago the UK would have been disastrously overpopulated with 57 million people, but technical change and capitalisation have proceeded at a rate sufficient to ensure that national income has gone up faster than population.

Diminishing returns

We can relate the concept of optimum population to the law of diminishing returns (see page 32). If we assume that all other things remain constant, it would follow that, as the population of a country grows and grows, there must come a point at which diminishing returns set in. This is illustrated in Fig. 4.8. Thus we have defined optimum population as that size of population where average output per person is greatest.

However, other things may not remain constant. If we allow for improving technology or the discovery of new resources, then the optimum level of population will rise. The peak of the curve in Fig. 4.8 will move to the right.

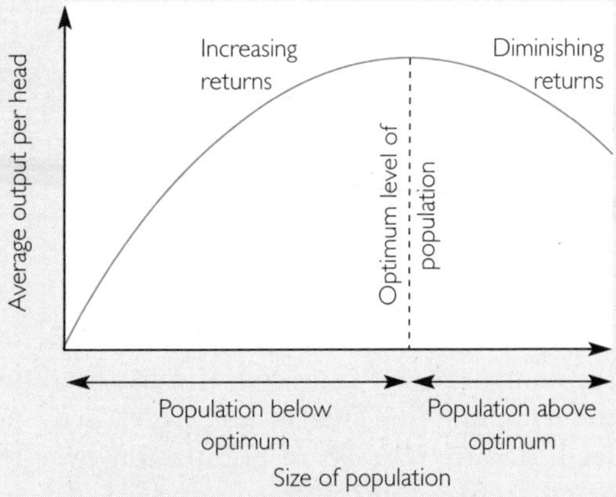

Fig. 4.8 **The growth of population and diminishing returns**

On the other hand, we must recognise that if improvements in technology only offset diminishing returns, there is a constant need to improve technology if we are to prevent the onset of falling productivity. When we consider diminishing returns on a global scale in the light of the continuing explosion of population, it is easy to appreciate the concern many authorities feel that Malthus's predictions may yet come true.

Environmental concerns

The measures we have attempted to use for optimum population are fraught with difficulties. The idea of average output per head is very hard to quantify. In addition to this we should be aware that GNP per head is not a direct measure of the standard of living, so it does not follow that if GNP per head increases the average standard of living is improving (see page 91).

On a broader scale there is increasing concern about the effect of increasing population upon the global environment. Finite resources such as oil, copper, tin, etc., are rapidly becoming depleted and there is no way in which they can be replaced. Renewable resources such as fishstocks and timber are being despoiled at a frightening rate. In addition to these very serious concerns, even if we are able to keep economic production increasing, we are also accelerating the problems of pollution of the environment. Thus, although our level of wealth increases, the level of welfare may decline. Groups such as Greenpeace might, therefore, give a very different definition of optimum population from that given by most economists.

Is the UK overpopulated?

It is a common fallacy to believe that, since the UK is comparatively crowded, it must therefore be overpopulated. This is not necessarily so. Indeed, despite the rise in population over the last two centuries, the average standard of living has continued to improve. It would seem unlikely therefore that the UK is, as yet, overpopulated. However, it might also be worth bearing in mind that there is practically zero population growth in the UK and other West European countries. Some commentators fear that this may have an adverse effect on the economy, i.e. it might lose the spur to economic growth and the dynamism that population growth provides.

Summary

1 The population explosion is one of the most significant factors in the human history of the last 200 years and gives rise to concern about adverse economic and environmental consequences.
2 The overall size of a nation's population is influenced by the birth rate, the death rate and the level of migration.
3 The birth rate is influenced by the age of marriage, the number of marriages, economic expectations and the opportunity cost of children, and the availability of contraception and abortion.
4 The UK population grew rapidly up to 1870. After this the rate of increase slowed until 1945. The growth of population accelerated after 1945 but was almost static in the 1970s and is increasing slightly in the 1990s.
5 The age and sex distribution of population can be shown in a population pyramid. The UK population is concentrated in the major conurbations. The occupational distribution of the UK population is characterised by the decline of manufacturing industries and the rise of tertiary industries.
6 For most of this century the dependent population in the UK has been increasing, but this will not be so significant during the last years of the century. The support ratio will decrease, however, during the first half of the twenty-first century.
7 The optimum level of population may be defined as that size and structure of population which is most conducive to the betterment of its wealth and welfare. In practice, this raises many questions which make the concept difficult to apply.

Questions

1 Describe the factors which have influenced the average size of family in the UK since 1945.
2 Discuss the view that the size of population is not as significant as its age, sex and geographical distribution.
3 Explain the problems involved in making forecasts of future population.
4 Consider the figures in Table 4.9 and then comment upon the relationship between the density of population and the level of prosperity.

***Table 4.9* Population and prosperity, selected countries**

Country	*Population (millions)*	*Area (1000 km²)*	*GNP per capita ($)*	*Growth of GDP 1980–93*	*Average annual growth of population 1980–93*
India	898.2	3288	300	5.2	2.0
Ghana	16.4	239	430	3.5	3.3
Brazil	156.5	8512	2930	2.1	2.0
Malaysia	19.0	330	3140	6.2	2.5
Mexico	90.0	1958	3610	1.6	2.3
Ireland	3.5	70	13000	3.8	0.3
UK	57.9	245	18060	2.5	0.2
Singapore	2.8	1	19850	6.9	1.1
UAE	1.8	84	21430	0.3	4.4
France	57.5	552	22490	2.1	0.5
Germany	80.7	357	23560	2.6*	0.2
USA	257.8	9809	24740	2.7	1.0
Japan	124.5	378	31490	4.0	0.5

*Data refers to West Germany before unification
Source: World Development Report, IBRD 1995

5 List the problems involved in defining the optimum level of population.
6 Having studied the figures in Table 4.8, describe as fully as possible the reasons for the discrepancies between the regions.
7 To what extent do you think that the ideas of Malthus are relevant to current world problems?
8 How might changes in population affect the standard of living in a country?

Data response A
Population and prosperity

Study the figures contained in Table 4.9

1 Identify which country:
   a) has the greatest density of population;
   b) has the least density of population;
   c) experienced the greatest percentage growth in population;
   d) experienced the smallest percentage growth in population;
   e) experienced the greatest percentage growth in GNP per capita;
   f) experienced the smallest growth in GNP per capita;
2 On the basis of these figures comment on the relationship between density of population and the level of prosperity.
3 Using these figures as illustration comment on the concept of the optimum population.
4 What other information would be useful in order to arrive at answers to questions 2 and 3 and why?

Data response B
Demographic time bomb?

Read and contrast the two newspaper articles from the *Guardian*. Then answer the following questions:

1 Use the definition of the economic problem used by economists to explain why a shift from state to privately funded pensions may not provide a solution to supporting an increased number of retired persons.
2 What is the role of labour productivity in supporting an increased ratio of dependants and how might this be influenced by private versus state funding for pensions?
3 What are the factors considered in each article which have led to pessimism in one and optimism in the other?

Poverty awaits those who fail to save up for their retirement

State's role

An old age lived in poverty is set to become the reality for a large number of pensioners over the coming decades.

First, as the state pension is uprated each year in line with prices, rather than incomes, the basic pension is declining steadily relative to average earnings – ignoring the reality that, as the standard of living rises, so does society's view of what is an acceptable standard for the poor.

Unemployment has been above two million for most of the past 15 years and more individuals coming to retirement will have experienced at least some period out of work.

There is greater inequality of earnings in work, and short-term contracts and job mobility are increasingly prevalent. There is a growing risk that an increasing proportion of the population will have been unable to contribute to an employer's or personal pension sufficiently to lift them away from dependency on the state pension for an important part of their income.

And others, more able to make their own provision, have yet to wake up to the reality of the falling value of the state pension and the need for increased private provision to realise the standard of living in retirement which they expect.

Put simply, if nothing is done there will be two out-

Continue on page 52

comes. First, inequality of income in old age will become more marked – continuing a trend already apparent in the 1980s. Second, means testing will increase as more pensioners depend on income support.

But it would be unrealistic to propose that the link to earnings can simply be restored, because this would require a much higher level of National Insurance contributions. Moreover, much of the benefit of the linkage to earnings would accrue to those who are already able to achieve a good level of pension provision outside the state scheme.

So it is questionable whether a universal scheme will still be appropriate as the number of pensioners rises. The main argument against any change from the universal principle is that the incentive to provide for old age is much reduced if entitlement to state pension becomes means tested.

Against this, however, it has to be recognised that disincentives to save will in any case affect more people as dependence on income support grows. And a cynical view might be that there will always be some incentive to save, as there is always suspicion that the state will renege on its promises.

A reform which challenges the universal entitlement with the aim of raising the floor for pensioner incomes therefore seems inevitable. An alternative future in which inequality of income for those of working age is extended into old age is an uncomfortable one.

Source: The Guardian

Britain has the advantage when it comes to state pension provision

Getting old

Fears that an ageing population threatens a pensions funding crisis are misplaced because the situation is not nearly as bad as most people think.

First, if the standard of living of the retired were to rise in real terms, but fall slightly compared to that of the employed, the cost burden should remain the same as now. This is because the increased burden would in part be paid for from the increase in productivity of the employed. Who gets how much of the increased resources that result from productivity gains is simply a political problem.

Second, the difficulty for other countries is far greater than that faced by the UK. We have already been through it in the last 30 years: our population is more aged than that of most developed countries. This should give us an advantage, in competitive terms, in the coming years.

Much of this is a matter of demographics. The conventional measure of the burden of pensioners is the old age dependency ratio. Whereas the old age dependency ratio in the UK is now around 30 per cent – or 30 pensioners for every 100 people of working age – it was 27 per cent in 1970. It is expected to show little change in the years to 2010 and, because the retirement age for women then increases to 65, should still be at around the same level in 2020, before drifting up thereafter.

In Japan the level of old age dependency is only 17 per cent and the OECD expects it to rise to 33 per cent by 2010. In most European countries other than the UK the expected increase between now and 2010 is between 5 per cent and 10 per cent. The UK's expected rise of only 2 per cent looks very small by comparison.

The question then is the extent to which our children, the future earners, will have to forgo the living standards they expect so that we, the pensioners of the future, can enjoy the pensions we consider we have earned (let alone paying for the costs for long-term care in old age).

One suggestion is to move to a system in which people save for their old age (a funded system) rather than paying for existing pensioners (a pay-as-you-go, or PAYG, system). The UK currently has a bit of both: a basic pension provided by the state on a PAYG basis alongside private provision, including both personal and occupational pension schemes.

But the distinction is in some ways a false one. The resources bought with pensions always come out of current production, even when pension payments are funded. So the expected situation for the basic state pension gives us a broad indication of the overall challenge.

And the situation turns out to be less stark than might have been expected. If the state pension were maintained at its present level – rather than rising in line with average earnings – then the rise in productivity of the employed expected would be more than sufficient to pay for it.

Indeed, if changes in the basic pension were indexed to the change in the Retail Prices Index during the years to 2050, then the combined National Insurance Contributions (NICs) rates for both employees and employers, currently 18 per cent, would fall to 14 per cent in spite of the expected rise in the pensioner ratio.

Source: The Guardian

5 The basis of the market economy

Learning outcomes

After reading this chapter you will be able to:

- Relate the concept of marginal utility to decisions by consumers.
- List factors which will affect the producer's decision to supply.
- Predict how the market will respond to disequilibrium positions.
- Identify areas in which the market system may not meet social objectives.

The price system

Micro- and macroeconomics

Owing largely to the work of the great economist John Maynard Keynes, it has been customary to divide economic theory into ***microeconomics*** and ***macroeconomics***. As its name implies microeconomics is concerned with small parts of the economy and the interrelationships between these parts, while macroeconomics is concerned with the behaviour of broad aggregates affecting the whole economy. A microeconomic topic therefore might be explaining movements of the prices of shoes or whether there has been under-investment in manufacturing *vis-á-vis* the service sector. Macroeconomic topics come under the four headings of ***inflation***, ***unemployment***, ***the balance of payments*** and ***growth***.

Obviously, macroeconomic explanations are not necessarily separate from microeconomic explanations, e.g. the growth of the economy is most likely to have been affected by the allocation of investment funds across the various sectors of the economy; unemployment will be affected by the decline and rise of individual industries. But the fundamental reason for a distinction being made is the notion that broad aggregates might behave differently from the way that is predicted by theories based on observing the behaviour of individual markets. For example, a cut in wages in one industry may make it profitable for employers in that industry to employ more workers, but Keynes suggested that a cut in wages across the economy as a whole might reduce the aggregate demand for goods and services, hence forcing all employers to cut back on production and hence workers.

Since the late 1960s, there has been a reaction to the macro/micro distinction; ***monetarists*** and ***neo-classicists*** in particular have attempted to explain all economic phenomena in terms of theories based upon explanations of how individual markets function, i.e. microeconomic theory.

Common misunderstanding

You should be aware that the 'big/small' distinction often made between macro- and microeconomics is misleading, because there is a branch of microeconomics known as ***general equilibrium theory*** *which tries to describe how a market economy as a whole would operate. General equilibrium is considered to be a microeconomic topic in that it studies the allocation of resources as determined by relative prices. It ignores the problems associated with the* ***disequilibrium*** *of* ***aggregate*** *supply and demand which gives rise to macroeconomic considerations. As monetarists and neo-classicists* *do not feel there is any particular problem with such aggregate disequilibrium it follows that they do not place much stress on the macro/micro distinction. To them much of macroeconomics is simply 'bad' microeconomics.*

In this chapter we will concern ourselves with the essentials of the price mechanism which forms the nub of microeconomic theory. At the end of the chapter we will consider general equilibrium theory further.

Assumptions about human behaviour

In examining the functioning of the price system we are not dealing with abstract forces but with people. It is therefore necessary to set out the assumptions we make about human behaviour.

First, we assume that people are maximisers: they try to gain as much wealth or pleasure as possible.

Those things for which people strive, be they goods, services or leisure, are said to give ***utility***. Perhaps in a true socialist state people would strive for the greatest good for all, but this is not generally true of our society. In saying this we are implying that people are primarily economic creatures. If political, religious or aesthetic motives overcame people's acquisitive instincts then most of our theories about markets and production would begin to break down. By and large, however, the picture of acquisitive society seems to hold true.

In addition to this we also assume that people are rational.

They will stop to consider which course of action will give them the greatest utility for the least cost. This somewhat unlovely portrait of humankind is not a suggestion of how people should be but an observation of how they are! Of course not everyone behaves like this all the time, but it is sufficiently close to the truth to act as a model of human behaviour which will yield useful predictions. Milton Friedman argued that the purpose of economic theory was to ***predict*** rather than ***explain*** or ***describe*** human behaviour. Friedman is helped by the ***law of large numbers*** which points out that although individuals may act irrationally and inconsistently, these aberrations will cancel each other out if we are dealing with a large enough sample of people.

We also assume that people are competitive. This is different from acquisitiveness, for it implies that people want to do better than other people. We can also see from this that people are ***individualistic***. In a competitive society such as ours, not only are people forced to compete but also the good working of the system depends upon their doing so.

In addition to assuming that people generally compete to gain as much utility as they can, we also assume that they do not like work. Work is said to have ***disutility*** and therefore people have to be paid to encourage them to undertake it. There are people who do like work, but, in general, if people were offered the same money for shorter hours of work they would accept it.

The price system

When we speak of the ***price system*** we mean situations where the vital economic decisions are taken through the medium of prices. A market price is the result of the interaction between the consumers' demand for a good and the supply of that product by producers. However, in order to produce goods the producers must have used factors of production. Ultimately all factors in the economy are owned by consumers, so that the producers must buy the use of these factors from consumers. There are therefore, in addition to markets for products, markets for the factors of production. This is illustrated in Fig. 5.1. This shows the critical importance of prices as the connecting, or communicating, mechanism between consumers and producers.

Consumer sovereignty

In the price system it is sometimes said that 'the consumer is king', meaning that a consumer decides what is to be produced by being willing to spend money on those particular goods. Rather than ***consumer sovereignty***, it is probably more accurate to say that there is a joint sovereignty between the consumer and the producer, because the producer's behaviour and objectives will also have great influence on the market.

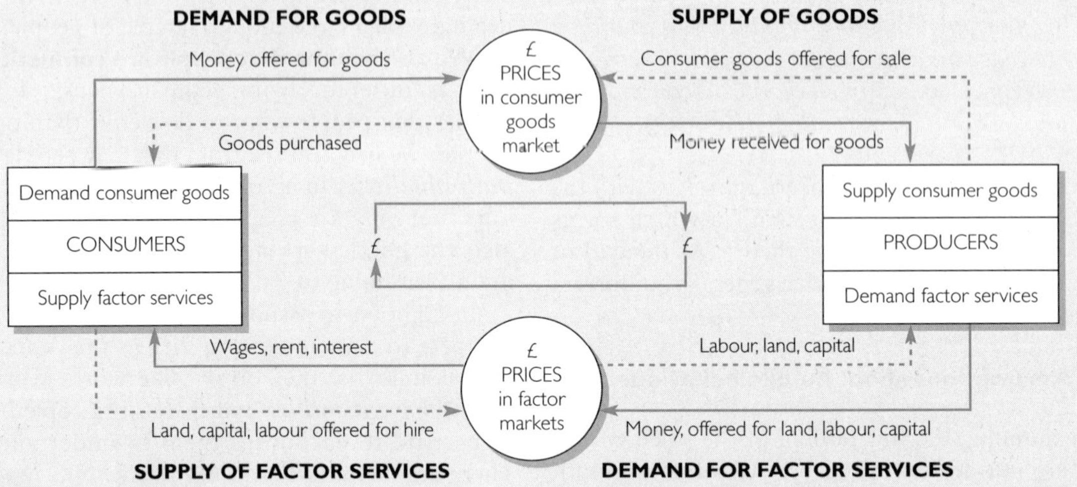

***Fig. 5.1* The price system**
The prices of consumer goods and services are determined by the interaction of consumer demand and supply from producers. Similarly, the price of factors of production is determined by the interaction of producers' demand for factor services and the supply of factors of protection from consumers.

The price system is also said, by some people, to be democratic in that every day consumers 'vote' for what they want to be produced by spending their money. Although to some extent this is true, it is considerably modified by the fact that money 'votes' in the economy are unevenly distributed. Thus those with a high income have more 'voting' power than those who are poor.

Market prices

Much of economics is concerned with the behaviour of market prices. Many criticisms can be made of prices as a method of allocating goods and services, but before we can assess the strengths and weaknesses of the price system we must understand its functioning. We will therefore examine the demand and supply of goods and then the formation of market prices.

Demand

Market demand

The demand for a commodity is the quantity of the good which is purchased over a specific of period of time at a certain price. Thus there are three elements to demand: price, quantity and time. This is the effective demand for a good, i.e. the desire to buy the good, backed by the ability to do so – it is no use considering a person's demand for a product if they do not have the money to realise it.

We may distinguish between ***ex ante*** demand and ***ex post*** demand. *Ex ante* demand is the quantity consumers will wish to demand at a particular price, while *ex post* demand is the amount they actually succeed in buying. The difference between the two may be brought about, for example, by a deficiency of supply in the market (see the section below on excess demand).

Ceteris paribus, it is usually the case that as the price of the commodity is lowered, so a greater quantity will be demanded. A formal analysis of the reasons for this is contained in Chapter 9. However, at this point we may consider the relevance of the ***law of diminishing marginal utility***.

Utility defined

We have used the word ***utility*** several times. This is another word which economists use in a special sense. It simply means the ***satisfaction*** which people derive from consuming goods or services. However, a good does not have to be 'useful' in the conventional sense; for example, cigarettes possess utility to the smoker even though they are harmful.

Marginal utility

The law of diminishing marginal utility states that:

Other things being constant, as more and more units of a commodity are consumed the additional satisfaction, or utility, derived from the consumption of each successive unit will decrease.

For example, if you have nothing to drink all day, the utility of a glass of water would be very high indeed and in consequence you would be willing to pay a high price for it. However, as you proceeded to drink a second, third and fourth glass of water the extra utility derived from each would become less. In this case you might have been willing to pay a great deal for the first glass of water but, as you continue to consume, the price you would be willing to pay would decrease because you would be deriving a smaller utility from each successive glass. This helps to clear up the puzzle of why we are willing to pay so little for bread, which is a necessity, and so much for diamonds, which have little practical value. The answer is that we have so much bread that the extra utility derived from another loaf is small, whereas we have so few diamonds that each one has a high marginal utility. Thus this principle helps to explain why more of a good is demanded at a lower price. The extra sales come from existing buyers, who buy more, and new buyers, who could not afford, or who did not think the good as worth buying at, the higher price.

When thinking about the law, it is important to consider the ***time period*** over which decisions are made, since this may vary according to the nature of the commodity. For example, if we are considering food, a person who has not had a meal for several hours will place a high value on food. They will then not require another meal immediately, but after several hours will be equally willing to buy another meal. If, on the other hand, we consider a product such as a car, if a person has just bought a new car it will be a long time before they are willing to buy other one.

An important exception to the law occurs in the case of ***addiction***. For example, smokers may find that the more they smoke, the more they want to smoke. The product need not necessarily be narcotic; for example, the avid philatelist may find a growing compulsion for stamp collecting. In the case of very rich individuals who still obsessively work to increase their wealth instead of taking leisure, the 'drug' may be power. This kind of behaviour is sometimes referred to as ***monomania*** since the individual pursues one activity to the detriment of all others.

STUDENT ACTIVITY 5.1

If the price of chocolate bars falls, persuading you to purchase more bars in any given week, which of the following would be true?

a) Total utility from eating chocolate bars is falling as you eat more of them.
b) Your marginal utility from the extra chocolate bars is less than from your first chocolate bar of the week.
c) You are heartily sick of chocolate bars and never want to eat another in your life.

The demand curve

The data in Table 5.1 is a hypothetical demand schedule for commodity X. It illustrates the first law of demand.

All other things remaining constant, more of a good will be demanded at a lower price.

Table 5.1 **Demand schedule for commodity X**

	Price of commodity X (£/kg)	*Quantity of X demanded (kg/week)*
A	5	110
B	4	120
C	3	150
D	2	200
E	1	250

Such information is usually expressed as a graph called a demand curve. As you can see in Fig. 5.2, the graph marked DD slopes downwards from left to right; this is almost invariably the case. The relationship between price and the quantity demanded is an ***inverse relationship*** since as price goes down the quantity demanded goes up. If the price is lowered from £3 per kg to £2 per kg, then the quantity demanded grows from 150 kg to 200 kg per week. This can be shown as a movement down the existing demand curve from C to D. This is termed an extension of demand. Conversely, if the price of X were raised then this could be shown as a movement up the curve, which is termed a contraction of demand. An extension or contraction of demand is brought about by a change in the price of the commodity under consideration *and by nothing else.*

An increase in demand

Suppose that the product X was wheat, and there was a failure of the potato crop. People would then wish to buy more wheat, even though the price of wheat had not fallen. This is shown as a shift of the demand curve to the right. In Fig. 5.3 this is the move from DD to D_1D_1: as a result of this, at the price of £3, a quantity of 150 kg is demanded instead of 100, as we have moved from point C to C_1. A movement of the demand curve in this manner is termed an increase in demand. If the curve were to move leftwards, for example from D_1D_1 to DD, this would be termed a decrease. An increase or decrease in demand is brought about by a factor *other than change in the price* of the commodity under consideration.

It is important not to confuse an ***increase in demand*** with an ***extension of demand.*** An extension of demand (sometimes referred to as increase in the quantity demanded) is brought about by a fall in the price of the product, whereas an increase in demand is brought about by a change in any other factor affecting demand except the price of the product.

Total revenue

The ***total revenue*** is the total sales receipts in a market at a particular price. In Table 5.1 you can see that if the price were £3 per kg the quantity demanded would be 150 kg per week. Consequently the total revenue would be £450. Thus we can say that:

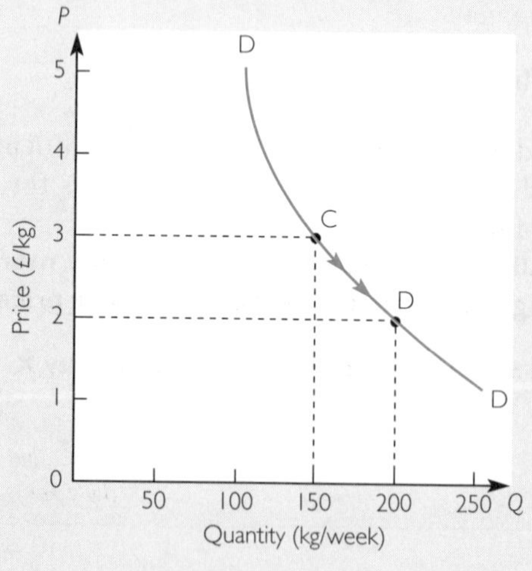

Fig. 5.2 **A demand curve**
A fall in the price of X from £3 to £2 per kg increases the quantity demanded from 150 to 200 kg/week.

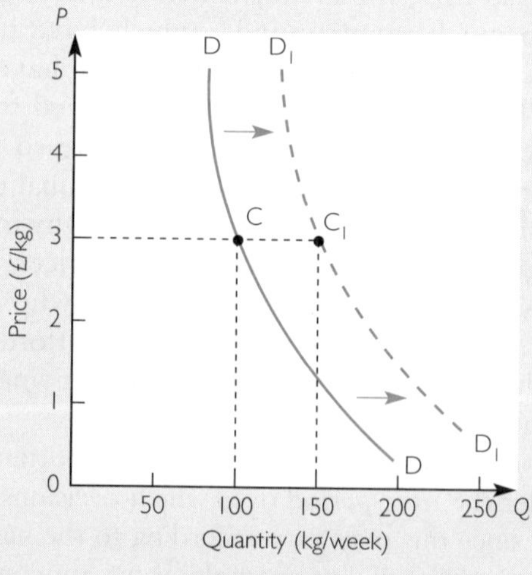

Fig. 5.3 **An increase in demand**
The shift of the curve from DD to D_1D_1 shows that more is demanded at every price, e.g. demand at £3/kg increases from 100 to 150 kg/week.

Total revenue (TR) = Price (P) × Quantity (Q)

If the price were lowered to £2 the total revenue ($P \times Q$) would be £400. You can see in Fig. 5.2 that the total revenue can be represented as a rectangle drawn under the demand curve (represented by the dashed lines).

STUDENT ACTIVITY 5.2

There is an increase in the demand for cars brought about by increased levels of employment and income as the economy comes out of the recession. Draw a diagram to show what has happened to the demand curve. If price remains the same, what will happen to the total revenue of the car companies?

Supply

The supply curve

We will now turn to the other side of the market, which is *supply*.

By supply we mean the quantity of a commodity that suppliers will wish to supply at a particular price.

This is illustrated by Table 5.2. As you can see, the higher the price is, the greater the quantity the supplier will wish to supply. If the price decreases there will come a price (£1) at which suppliers are not willing to supply because they cannot make a profit at this point.

As with demand, we can plot the supply information as a graph. This is illustrated in Fig. 5.4. As you can see the supply curve slopes upwards from left to right. This is a direct relationship, i.e. as price goes up the quantity supplied will go up. If the price increases from £2 per kg to £3 per kg, then the quantity suppliers are willing to supply goes up from 90 kg to 150 kg. As with the demand curve, this movement along the supply curve from D to C in called an ***extension of supply***. A movement down the curve would be called a ***contraction of supply***. As with demand, an extension or contraction is brought about by a change of the price of the commodity under consideration – *and nothing else*.

The first principle of supply is that, all other things remaining constant, a greater quantity will be supplied at a higher price.

The reason for this is that at a higher quantity, increased costs can be incurred. We have already dealt in Chapter 3 with two principles – ***the law of diminishing returns*** and ***the principle of increasing costs*** – both of which would suggest that costs increase with supply. Suppliers will need a higher price to persuade them to increase their production, if they are to make a profit on this extra production. This argument is examined in more detail in Chapter 16.

Table 5.2 **Supply schedule for commodity X**

	Price of commodity X (£/kg)	*Quantity of X suppliers will wish to supply (kg/week)*
A	5	240
B	4	200
C	3	150
D	2	90
E	1	0

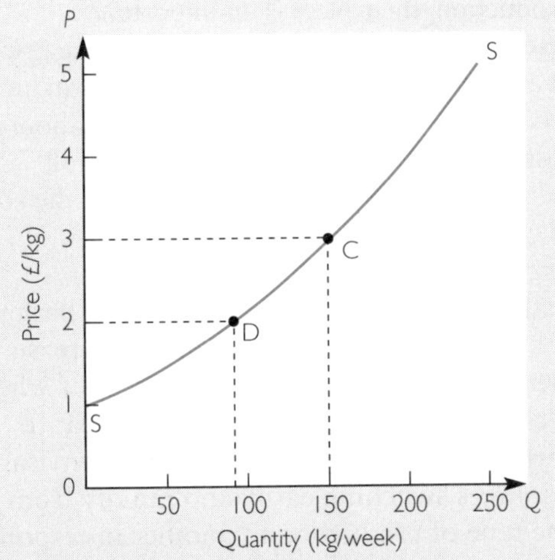

Fig. 5.4 **A supply curve**
An increase in the price of X from £2 to £3 per kg causes the quantity supplied to increase from 90 to 150 kg/week.

Common misunderstanding

When asked why more is supplied at a higher price, students frequently reply 'because increased profits can be made'. This you can now see is not so. Suppliers need the incentive of higher prices because costs are rising.

The determinants of supply

Progress can be made in understanding the supply side of the economy by simply listing the factors which can influence the supply of a commodity.

a) *Price*. The most important determinant of supply is price. As we have just seen, a change in price will cause a movement up or down the supply curve. The remaining determinants of supply can be termed the ***conditions of supply***. A change in the conditions of supply causes an increase or decrease in supply, shifting the supply curve leftwards or rightwards. For example, suppose that the product we are considering is tomatoes; then very bad weather would have the effect of decreasing the supply. In Fig. 5.5 you can see that this has the effect of shifting the supply curve leftwards. Conversely, unexpectedly good growing weather would shift the curve rightwards.

b) *Price of factors of production*. Since output is produced by combining the factors of production, their price is an important determinant of supply. An increase in the price of a factor will increase the costs of a firm and this shifts the supply curve leftwards. Labour costs (wages) tend to rise in periods of full employment. Interest rate rises increase the cost of capital purchased by loans.

c) *The price of other commodities*. If, for example, there is a rise in the price of barley but not of wheat, this will tend to decrease the supply (shift the curve leftwards) of wheat because farmers will switch from wheat to barley production. Economic theory envisages resources switching easily and rapidly from one type of production to another in response to price changes. In practice, though, this may be a slow and often painful process.

d) *Technology*. Changes in the level of technology also affect supply. An improvement in technology allows us to produce more goods with less factors of production. This would therefore have the effect of shifting the supply curve to the right. This has been well illustrated in recent years by the effect of microchip technology upon the supply of such things as pocket calculators, watches and personal computers.

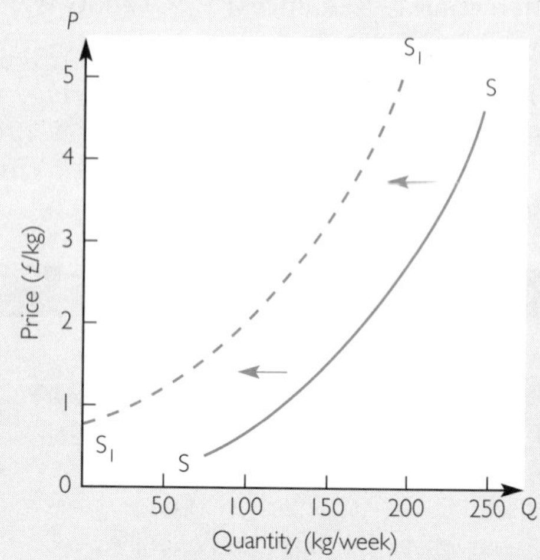

Fig. 5.5 **A decrease in supply**
The shift of the supply curve leftwards from SS to S_1S_1 shows that less is supplied at every price.

e) *Tastes of producers*. In theory suppliers are perfectly rational beings interested only in obtaining the highest return for their efforts. However, producers may have preferences and be willing to tolerate lower returns if, for example, they find the business stimulating or worthwhile or socially prestigious. Conversely, producers may avoid unpleasant lines of work.

f) *Entry and exit from the industry*. In the short run new firms will not be able to enter the industry because it takes time to set up production. In the long run firms may enter or leave the industry in response to the profitability of the industry. A good example of this is provided by North Sea oil. UK oil costs four or five times as much to extract as Saudi Arabian oil. The low prices of the 1950s and early 1960s would certainly not have allowed the UK to extract the oil profitably, but as the price rocketed in the 1970s it became profitable to produce oil.

g) *Exogenous factors*. Supply can be affected by conditions outside market forces. Perhaps the most obvious example of this would be the weather.

STUDENT ACTIVITY 5.3

Explain what would happen to the supply curve for pencils if the following changes took place:
a) the cost of wood rises;
b) the wages of workers in the pencil industry are increased;
c) a new machine is introduced which makes it cheaper to insert the lead down the middle of the pencil.

Regressive supply curves

Supply curves usually slope upwards from left to right. Sometimes, however, they change direction, as in Fig. 5.6, and are said to become ***regressive***; this might be the case with the supply of labour where there may be a high leisure preference. In coal-mining, for example, where the job is extremely unpleasant, it has often been noticed that as wage rates have been increased miners have worked shorter hours. This is because instead of taking the increased wage rate in money the miners are taking it in increased leisure. There has been a noticeable long-term historical trend for hours of work to be reduced as countries become richer.

A similar effect may be observed in some undeveloped peasant economies where producers have a static view of the income that they require. In these circumstances a rise in the price of the crop they produce causes them to grow less because they can now obtain the same income from a smaller crop.

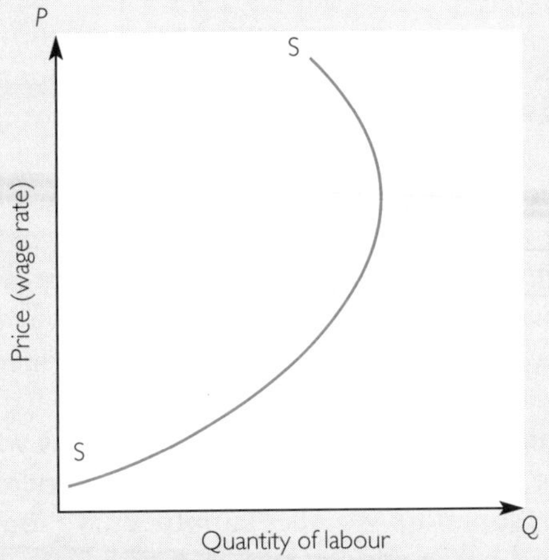

***Fig. 5.6* A regressive supply curve**
As the wage rate continues to rise, people eventually work shorter hours, preferring to take the improvement in wages as increased leisure rather than increased income.

Equilibrium prices

The formation of an equilibrium price

We shall now combine our analysis of demand and supply to show how a competitive market price is determined. Table 5.3 combines the demand and supply schedules. The motives of consumers and producers are different in that the consumer wishes to buy cheaply while the supplier wishes to obtain the highest price possible. Let us examine how these differences are reconciled.

***Table 5.3* The determination of the equilibrium price**

	Price commodity X (£/kg)	Quantity demanded of X (kg/week)	Quantity supplied of X (kg/week)	Pressure on price
A	5	110	240	Downward
B	4	120	200	Downward
C	3	150	150	Neutral
D	2	200	90	Upward
E	1	250	0	Upward

If, for example, we examine row A in Table 5.3, here the price is £5 per kg and 240 kg will be supplied per week. However, at this price consumers are willing to buy only 110 kg. As unsold stocks of goods begin to pile up, suppliers will be forced to reduce their prices to try to get rid of the surplus. There is a downward pressure on prices. Conversely, if we examine row D, where the price is £2 per kg, suppliers are willing to supply only 90 kg per week but consumers are trying to buy 200 kg per week. There are therefore many disappointed customers, and producers realise that they can raise their prices. There is thus an upward pressure on price. If we continue the process we can see that there is only one price at which there is neither upward nor downward pressure on price. This is termed the ***equilibrium price***.

The equilibrium price is the price at which the wishes of buyers and sellers coincide.

If we superimpose the supply curve on the demand curve we can see, in Fig. 5.7, that the equilibrium price occurs where the two curves cross. The surplus of supply and the shortage of supply at any other price can be shown as the gap between the two curves. The arrows in Fig. 5.7 show the equilibrium forces which are at work pushing the price towards the equilibrium.

Equilibrium prices ration out the scarce supply of goods and services. There are no great queues of people demanding the best cuts of meat at butchers; a price of £10 per kg for fillet steak ensures that only the rich or those who derive great utility from beefsteak buy the meat. Neither are there vast unsold stocks of meat at the butchers, the equilibrium price having balanced the demand and supply. It might be argued that the price mechanism is socially unjust, but if we do away with price as the rationing mechanism we only have to put something else, perhaps equally unacceptable, in its place.

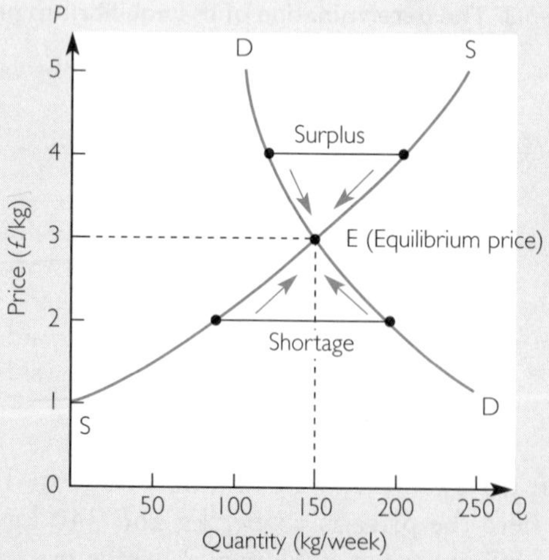

Fig. 5.7 The equilibrium price
At the price of £3/kg the quantity which is offered for sale is equal to the quantity people are willing to buy at that price.

Excess demand and supply

If the price is above the equilibrium more will be supplied than is demanded, this surplus of supply over demand being termed ***excess supply***. Conversely, if the price is below the equilibrium this will result in a situation of ***excess demand***. For example, in Table 5.3, if the price is £2 per kg, then 200 kg per week is demanded but only 90 kg is supplied and there is therefore an excess demand of 110 kg per week. It is possible to plot a graph which plots the excess demand function at all prices (having just one graph which combines both the demand and supply curves is more convenient for such things as computer modelling). This is done in Fig. 5.8. The graph crosses the vertical axis at the equilibrium price; at higher prices the graph shows that there is negative excess demand (usually termed excess supply) and at lower prices there is positive excess demand.

Shifts in demand and supply

If there is an increase in demand this will cause a shift to a new equilibrium price. This is illustrated in Fig. 5.9 (a). Similarly, in Fig. 5.9 (b) you can see the effect of a decrease in supply upon the equilibrium price.

The problems associated with changes in equilibrium price are discussed at greater length in Chapter 11.

If there is a change in the equilibrium price and quantity this brings about a reallocation of resources. For example, let us consider the increase in demand shown in Fig. 5.9 (a). Suppose that this shows an increased preference for tomatoes. The increase in demand raises the price of tomatoes and this encourages more people to produce them so that resources are switched away from other forms of market gardening and into tomato pro-

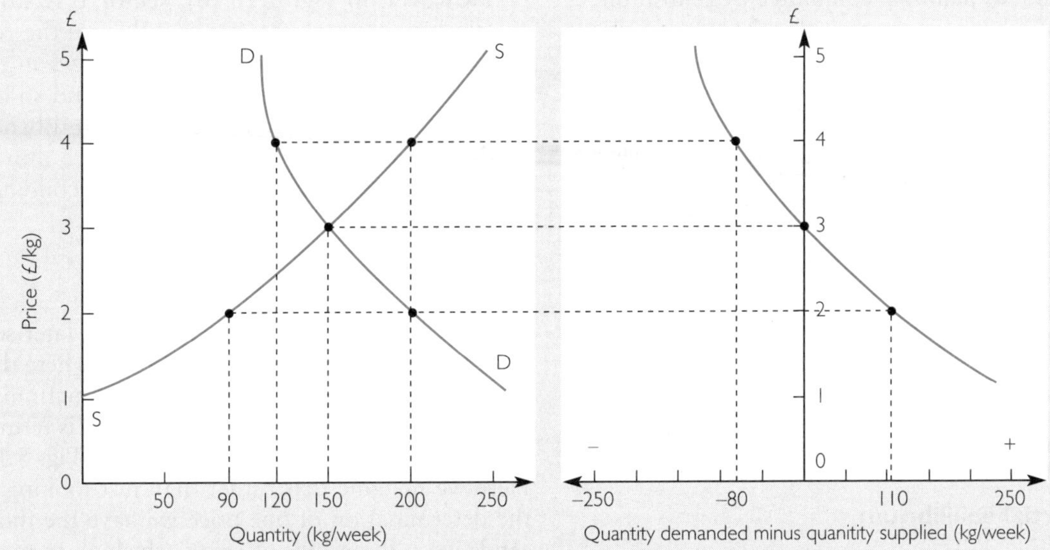

Fig. 5.8 **The excess demand curve**

If the quantity supplied is subtracted from the quantity demanded it gives the excess demand function, e.g. at a price of £4/kg 120 kg are demanded but 200 kg are supplied, giving a negative excess demand (excess supply) of 80 kg.

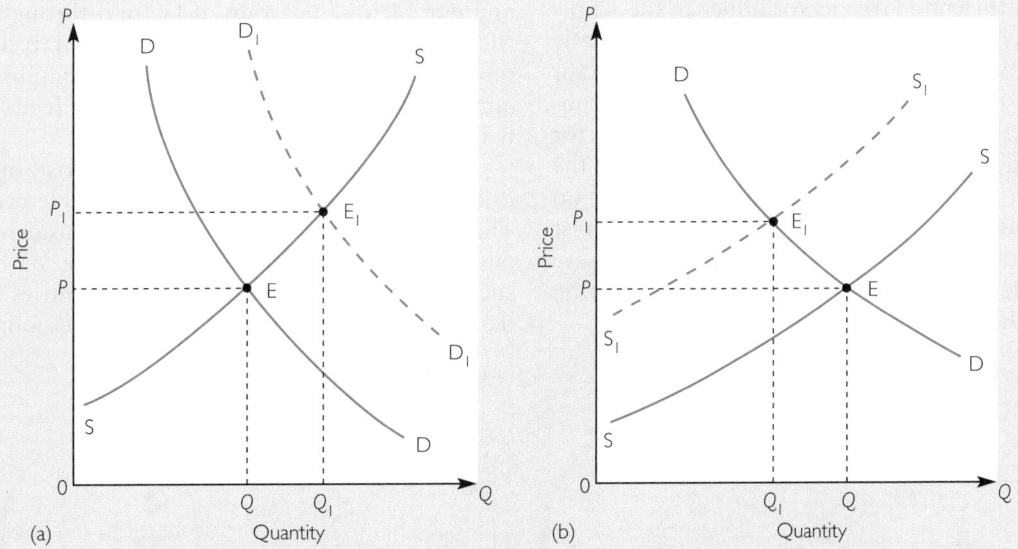

Fig. 5.9 **Changes in the equilibrium**

A shift of either the demand or the supply curve creates a new equilibrium price.

(a) An increase in demand gives a higher price and a greater quantity.

(b) A decrease in supply gives a higher price and lower quantity.

duction. No planning committee or central direction has been necessary; this has come about simply as a result of the change in price.

STUDENT ACTIVITY 5.4

Cup final tickets often change hands at substantially above the official price. What does this tell you about equilibrium in this market? Draw a diagram to show the situation. Why are the official prices of cup final tickets not increased to remedy this situation?

Partial and general equilibrium

Partial equilibrium

The analysis we have been using so far in this chapter is termed ***partial equilibrium*** analysis. It is termed partial because it only deals with one small part of the economy, e.g. the price of shoes. It is important to realise that this type of analysis is possible only when the sector we are studying is *not* sufficiently large as to influence the whole economy. Figure 5.10 attempts a diagrammatic explanation of this point. In Fig. 5.10 (a), sector A is not big enough to affect the rest of the economy, so that, for example, a rise in price in sector A does not affect the general level of prices in the rest of the economy and therefore there is no appreciable 'feedback' to sector A from the rest of the economy as a result of this change. We are thus able to keep our *ceteris paribus* assumption of all other things remaining constant.

However, in Fig. 5.10 (b), sector B is sufficiently large that changes in it influence the rest of the economy and that induced changes in the economy then 'feed back' to sector B and so on. Under these circumstances partial equilibrium analysis is no longer possible. We have moved from partial microeconomics to macroeconomics and a new type of analysis is needed.

General equilibrium

Macroeconomic analysis is dealt with in later sections in the book. However, we may note here that a microeconomic explanation of the functioning of the whole of the economy exists. This is termed ***general equilibrium*** and is illustrated in Fig. 5.11. Here we imagine that rather than just looking at the determination of one price we have the thousands upon thousands of prices which go to make up the economy. Prices are thus ***interdependent***.

An example of the general equilibrium analysis might be the interrelationship of fuel markets This would involve looking at coal-mining, oil tankers, electricity prices, gas exploration and so on, and tracing the ramifications of a change in any one factor (or group of factors) throughout the economy. General equilibrium analysis is much more complicated than partial equilibrium analysis because the possibility of feedback between sectors now exists.

This effect was illustrated by the rise in oil prices in 1978. OPEC attempted to double prices. The price of a barrel of oil might be considered a microeconomic phenomenon; however, oil was such an important product to most countries that the price rise was sufficient to push their economies

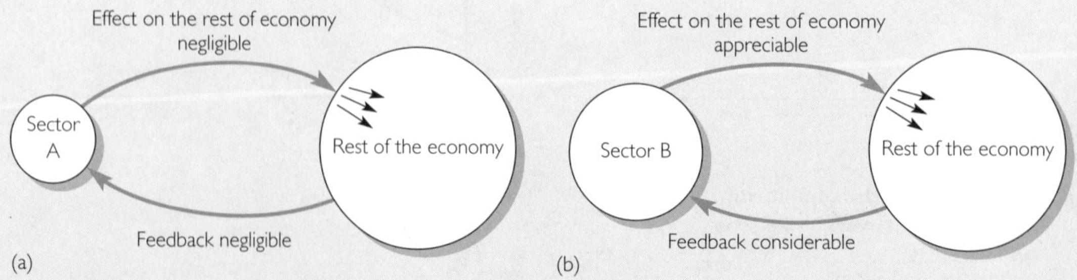

***Fig. 5.10* Partial equilibrium analysis**
Partial equilibrium is possible in (a) where we may assume ceteris paribus, but feedback effects make it impossible in (b).

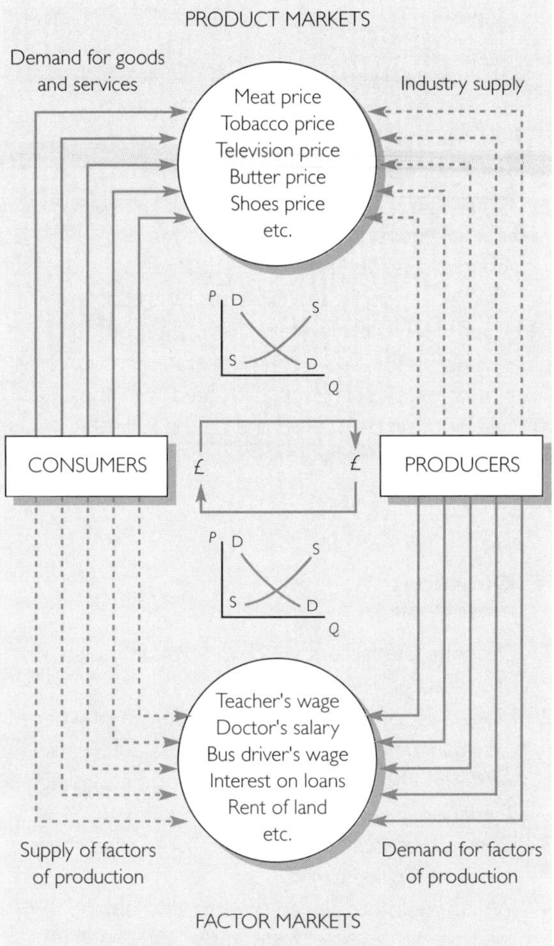

***Fig. 5.11* General equilibrium analysis**

into depression. Thus a microeconomic phenomenon became a macroeconomic one.

The credit for the invention of general equilibrium analysis is usually given to the French economist Leon Walras (1830). However, the development of it had to wait for the use of matrix algebra, which was the work of Wassily Leontief (1906–).

The price system assessed

The price system provides an answer to the fundamental problem of any economic society. Through prices the economy decides what to produce, i.e. anything people are willing to spend money on that can be produced profitably. We have also seen that how things are produced is also dependent on prices, since it involves producers buying the services of the factors of production in factor markets. The income generated in these factor markets also determines who will have the money to buy the goods which are produced.

The price system is also automatic in its operation and is self-regulating when changes occur in the economy. Whether or not this produces the best possible use and distribution of resources is one of the most important topics in economics. We will attempt to answer this question in Section IV of the book.

For the time being we will consider briefly some of the major problems associated with the operation of an economy through the price system. A fuller treatment of this must wait until we have considered all the aspects of the market.

The distribution of income

A serious problem associated with the market system is that income is very unevenly divided among the population. In theory people's income is determined by demand and supply in the factor markets. If the market does not work properly and a person's labour is not demanded even though they are willing to work, then they will be very poor. Other people may be able to command much larger incomes because they have a position of monopoly in the market place, or can take advantage of other people's ignorance to make very large sums of money. A person's income is also influenced by inheritance. Such are the inequalities in income that nearly all governments are forced to intervene in markets to alleviate the worst excesses. For example, the provision of old-age pensions in the UK is necessary to avoid mass poverty among the old, and benefit for those who are unemployed is also necessary.

Dangerous products

A minor interference with the market system that is forced on nearly all governments is the regulation of dangerous products. Thus, for example, governments may forbid the sale of arms or dangerous drugs.

Competition

The picture of the economy we have been developing in this chapter depends upon there being competition between suppliers. This, said Adam Smith, along with the 'invisible hand' of self-interest, leads to an optimum allocation of resources. But the invisible hand will not work if there is not free competition. When we turn to examine the economy we find that there are many monopolies and restrictions upon trade.

> A monopoly [said Smith] granted either to an individual or a trading company has the same effect as secret in trade or manufactures. The monopoly – by keeping the market constantly understocked, never supplying the effectual demand, sell their commodities much above the natural price, and raise emoluments, whether they consist in wages or profit, greatly above their natural rate.

Despite these reservations we continue to study the market because it provides a model by which we can judge the economic success of the real world.

Summary

1 The price system is a method of operating the economy through the medium of market prices.
2 The first law of demand tells us that, *ceteris paribus*, more of a product is demanded at a lower price.
3 The law of diminishing marginal utility states that, *ceteris paribus*, as more and more of a commodity is consumed the extra utility derived declines.
4 A change in price, *ceteris paribus*, causes an extension or contraction of demand, while a change in any other determinant causes an increase or decrease of demand.
5 The first principle of supply is that, *ceteris paribus*, a greater quantity is supplied at a higher price because at a higher price increased costs can be incurred.
6 An increase or decrease in supply is caused by a change in one of the conditions of supply.
7 The determinants of supply are price (the price of factors of production and the price of other commodities) the state of technology, the tastes of producers, and other exogenous factors.
8 The equilibrium price is the price at which the wishes of buyers and sellers coincide.
9 At any price other than the equilibrium there is either upward or downward pressure on price caused by either excess demand or excess supply.
10 Partial equilibrium analysis is possible only when there are no 'feedback' effects between the sector being considered and the rest of the economy.
11 Our view of the price system as a method of achieving the optimum allocation of resources is modified by problems associated with the distribution of income and by the lack of competition in the economy.

Questions

1 Describe the factors which determine the supply of wheat.
2 Make a list of as many cases as you can of where the government intervenes with the automatic working of the price system, e.g. food and drugs legislation.
3 Describe precisely how excess supply in a market causes the price to fall.
4 What would happen to the market demand for steak as the result of each of the following?
   a) An increase in the average income per head.
   b) An increase in the size of population.
   c) Increased advertising for lamb and pork.
   d) An increase in the price of lamb.
   e) A decrease in the price of pork.
5 What would happen to the equilibrium price and quantity of butter if:
   a) the price of margarine increased?
   b) the cost of producing butter increased?
6 Discuss the problems associated with using the price mechanism as a way to deal with:
   a) the allocation of university places;
   b) traffic problems in cities.
7 Explain the difference between partial equilibrium and general equilibrium analysis.
8 'When some people are very wealthy while others are poor, the whole notion of consumer

sovereignty in a market economy is misleading and prejudicial.' Discuss.

9 St Thomas Aquinas in the thirteenth century wrote: 'To sell a thing for more than it's worth or to buy it for less than it's worth, is in itself unjust and unlawful.' Discuss the problems which might be associated with the application of this view to a modern economy.

10 'If the price mechanism did not exist it would be necessary to invent it.' Discuss.

11 For the mathematically minded: suppose that a demand curve is given by the equation $y = 1000 - x$ and the supply curve by the equation $y = 100 + 2x$.
   a) What will be the equilibrium price?
   b) What is the excess demand or supply if the price is: (i) 900; (ii) 400?
   c) Devise an equation for the excess demand function based on the demand and supply schedules in this example.
   (Remember y = price and x = quantity.)

Data response A
Equilibrium prices

The following figures give the demand and supply schedules for product Z.

Price of Z (£/kg)	*Quantity demanded of Z (kg/week)*	*Quantity supplied of Z (kg/week)*
9	100	800
7	300	600
5	500	400
3	700	200
1	900	0

From these figures:
   a) Draw the demand and supply curves.
   b) Determine and state the equilibrium price.
   c) what is the excess demand or supply if the price is: (i) £7 per kg; (ii) £2 per kg?
   d) Suppose that demand were now to increase by 50 per cent at every price. Draw the new demand curve and determine the new equilibrium price.
   e) From the original figures, construct the excess demand function.
   f) From the original demand curve calculate the total revenue to be gained from the sale of product Z at £1, £2, £3, etc. Then plot this information on a graph, putting total revenue on the vertical axis and quantity on the horizontal axis. State the quantity at which total revenue is maximised.

Data response B
Economists and the market

People of the same trade seldom meet together, even for merriment and diversion, but the conversation ends up in a conspiracy against the public, or in some contrivance to raise prices.

Adam Smith *The Wealth of Nations*

Fundamentally, there are only two ways of co-ordinating the economic activities of millions. One is central direction involving the use of coercion – the technique of the army and the modern totalitarian state. The other is voluntary cooperation of individuals – the technique of the market place.

Milton Friedman *Capitalism and Freedom*

1 Both Smith and Friedman are great advocates of free market economics. Analyse these seemingly contradictory statements.

2 For what reasons do modern states find it necessary to interfere in the 'voluntary cooperation' of the market place?

3 To what extent do you consider that the collapse of many East European economies is a vindication of Friedman's view?

6 The role of government in the economy: the mixed economy

Learning outcomes

At the end of this chapter you will be able to:

- Identify the various roles of the government in the economy.
- Explain the main ideas of economists who have influenced thinking in this question.
- Relate growth of government involvement in the economy to both economic ideas and events in history.

What is a mixed economy?

The twentieth century has been the century of government involvement in the economy. As we move into the twenty-first century, around the world, governments have been trying to withdraw from that role.

In its most dramatic form this can be seen in the collapse of communism in Russia and Eastern Europe in the late 1980s. In China, the communists have retained control, but have enthusiastically embraced the market. Japan and the USA always had a lower involvement of government in the economy and this has not changed. The new 'tiger' economies of the Far East, such as Malaysia and Singapore, have developed using the private sector. In Western Europe, following the lead taken by the UK from 1979 onwards under Mrs Thatcher's Conservative government, the state has withdrawn from many activities, mainly by the process of privatisation. Despite these efforts, levels of government spending have remained obstinately high and these economies can still be referred to as mixed economies.

As we saw in the first chapter, all economies of the world can be said to be 'mixed' to a greater or lesser degree. However, we usually reserve the term 'mixed' for those economies where there is both a large element of a market economy, together with a significant degree of state control. It is thus a term which can still be applied to most of the countries of Western Europe. It is important to see why the government continues to have a role in the economy. To explore this question we will look at a brief history of the development of the mixed economy in the UK. We will also look at the economists who have influenced ideas on the role of the state in the economy.

STUDENT ACTIVITY 6.1

List the main goods and services provided by the state. Which of them are paid for by the consumer using prices rather than taxes? Which of them can also be provided by the market?

The origins of the mixed economy

The decline of the free market

The economy of the UK in the nineteenth century was one in which people and organisations were in a state of unfettered competition. It was believed that the economy would operate best if the government did not intervene in it.

Such beliefs were based on the writings of the Scottish economist and moral philosopher Adam Smith (1723–90), who argued that competition was the best regulator of the economy. The belief that internal and external trade should be left to regulate itself became known by the French expression *laissez-faire* – which roughly translates as 'leave to do'.

Adam Smith saw the economy as made up of millions of individuals and small businesses guided by the invisible hand of the market. He observed at first hand the world's first industrial revolution in the UK of the late eighteenth century and saw the benefits which the market could bring.

> Every individual endeavours to employ his capital so that its produce may be of greatest value. He generally neither intends to promote the public interest, nor knows how he is promoting it. He intends only his own security, only his own gain. And he is led in this by an invisible hand to promote an end which was no part of his intention. By pursuing his own interest he frequently promotes that of society more effectively than when he really intends to promote it.

To Smith, therefore, the economy was a self-regulating structure. For this to happen properly he believed that government should interfere in the economy as little as possible, for interference disturbed the mechanism of the market.

Common misunderstanding

It is often thought that free competition is the 'natural' state of the economy. This is not so: it is almost entirely a nineteenth-century phenomenon. Before this time monarchs felt free to regulate the economy as they saw fit. On the other hand, in the twentieth century the economy is dominated by the government and by giant business organisations. Only in a few sectors of the economy could free competition be said to exist today.

In his book *The Wealth of Nations,* Smith argued that the many taxes and regulations which surrounded the commerce of the country hindered its growth. Business organisations should be free to pursue profit, restricted only by the competition of other business organisations. From about 1815 onwards government began to pursue this policy. The UK, already a wealthy country, grew wealthier still. The success of industries such as textiles and iron appeared to prove the wisdom of Adam Smith. Belief in the 'free market' system became the dominant economic ideology. This was confirmed towards the end of the century when the British economist Alfred Marshall formalised Smith's ideas in the laws of supply and demand that you have already studied in Chapter 5 and will go on to study further in Section II.

As the nineteenth century progressed, however, it became apparent that the free market system had three major defects.

a) Although efficient at producing some products such as food and clothing, the free market system failed to produce effectively things such as sanitation or education.
b) Competition could easily disappear and give way to monopoly, as occurred with the railways.
c) Competition has winners but it also has losers. Society has to find some way of helping the losers – the incompetent, the sick and the unemployed. It was to combat these three problems that the state began to intervene in the economy.

In the case of a) the government did not take a conscious decision to depart from *laissez-faire* philosophy; rather, action was forced upon it by the severity of the problems. This is well illustrated by the 1848 Public Health Act. In this case cholera epidemics forced the government to promote better drainage and sanitation. In the case of b) there was a more conscious effort to regulate monopolies. This may be illustrated by the measures, which began as early as 1840, to regulate the activities of railway companies. Lastly, with 'one man, one vote' being achieved in the 1870s in the UK, and women being given the vote in the 1920s, government came under pressure to help all people in society. In the case of c) above, real changes in policy had to wait for the twentieth century, although ***the welfare state*** did have humble beginnings in the late nineteenth century. Its development and subsequent problems are discussed later in this chapter and in Chapters 29 and 30.
Thus the nineteenth century presents a picture of governments believing in a free

market economy but gradually being forced to regulate its most serious excesses.

1914–39: war and recession

For many economists, the writings of John Maynard Keynes (1883–1946) are the most important contribution to economic thinking in the twentieth century.

Despite the fact that during the 1930s the economy was patently not self-regulating, Keynes realised that the ideas of classical economics were still doughty opponents. In 1934 he wrote:

> The strength of the self-adjusting school depends on its having behind it almost the whole body of economic thinking and doctrine of the past 100 years. This is a formidable power. It is the product of acute minds and has persuaded and convinced the great majority of the intelligent and disinterested persons who have studied it. It has vast prestige and a more far reaching influence than is obvious. For it lies behind the education and habitual modes of thought not only of economists, but of banks and businessmen and civil servants and politicians of all parties.

Keynes was English and worked for many years at Cambridge University. His views on the economy, however, appeared so radical at the time that they were not accepted by governments in the 1930s.

Demand management

In his most famous book, *The General Theory of Employment, Interest and Money* (1936), Keynes analysed the workings of the economy and put forward his solution to unemployment.

Keynes maintained that it was not the demand for individual resources which was important but the level of total (aggregate) demand in the economy.

He said that a fall in the level of demand would lead to overproduction; this would lead to the accumulation of stocks (inventories) and, as this happened, people would be thrown out of work. The unemployed would lose their purchasing power and therefore the level of demand would sink still further, and so on. Cutting wages, advocated by the conventional wisdom of the time, would not therefore cure unemployment; it would make it worse by further reducing the purchasing power of the workers.

Since it would appear that the economy was no longer self-regulating, there was a clear case for government intervention. Keynes's solution was that, if there was a shortfall in demand in the economy, the government should make it up by public spending. In order to do this the government would have to spend beyond its means (a budget deficit). In the 1930s this solution was not acceptable. As Galbraith has written: 'To spend money to create jobs seemed profligate; to urge a budget deficit as a good thing seemed insane.' It took the Second World War to bring Keynes's ideas into the operation of government policy.

Socialism

Keynes was a 'conservative revolutionary': his concern was to show how the capitalist system could be better managed. The fact that Keynes argued for government intervention in the economy does not make him a socialist. In fact it can be argued that capitalist economies using Keynesian policies in the period 1945–70 enjoyed a period of unprecedented growth and low unemployment. It appeared that Keynes had helped capitalist economies to overcome their problems.

Socialists are those who believe that the means of production should be publicly owned. The idea of socialism is often associated with the nineteenth-century German philosopher and economist, Karl Marx. Marx shared one idea with Keynes: that capitalist economies suffer periodic crises of unemployment. Unlike Keynes, Marx was pessimistic about the ability of capitalism to solve this problem and believed that capitalism would eventually collapse and be replaced as a result of a revolution by socialism. His thinking was influenced by the poverty of the working class in the mid nineteenth century.

Ironically, in the late twentieth century, it is the socialist economies that have collapsed in Eastern Europe, to be replaced by capitalism!

In Western Europe a non-revolutionary constitutional form of socialism emerged. The two main strands were the further development of the welfare state, and the nationalisation of industries with monopoly power, such as rail, electricity, gas and telecommunications. Socialist thinking in the UK probably owes more to Sidney and Beatrice Webb and other great Fabian socialists than to Marx and Lenin. The UK prime minister, Harold Wilson, once remarked that 'British socialism owed more to Methodism than Marxism'.

The effect of the Second World War

From the outset of the Second World War the government took over the direction of the economy: industries were taken over, labour was directed, food was rationed. The UK could be said to have had a ***centrally planned economy***. The realisation spread that the government could intervene successfully in the economy. Keynes's ideas at last came to be accepted. Both the major political parties during the war committed themselves to the maintenance of a high and stable level of employment once peace was achieved. This was to be achieved by Keynesian techniques of the management of the level of aggregate demand. The fact that it was a Labour government which was elected in 1945 meant that an element of socialism was also introduced into the economy.

The welfare state

You do not have to be a socialist to believe that everyone is entitled to education, health services and social security. The origins of the welfare state can be traced back to Lloyd George and the Liberal party at the beginning of the twentieth century, but in its modern form was designed by the Beveridge Report of 1942.

This recommended a national health scheme for 'every citizen without exception, without remuneration limit and without an economic barrier'. Beveridge also stated that the basis for comprehensive social security must be the certainty of a continuing high level of employment. A White Paper, Employment Policy, which embodied this idea, was published in 1944 and accepted by both the major political parties. Subsequently, full employment was to become a first priority for all governments. The wheel had come full circle from the workhouses of 1834 which were designed to be so unpleasant that they would force people to find work. The age of *laissez-faire* had passed away.

The components of the mixed economy

What emerged from this period of Labour government was an economy which was a compound of socialist ideas, Keynesian demand management and capitalism. It was truly a mixed economy. The main components of the mixed economy were:

a) A free enterprise sector, where economic decisions are taken through the workings of the market.
b) Government intervention in the economy through spending, taxes and regulations.
c) Public ownership of some industries especially where there was monopoly.
d) The welfare state providing free education and health care plus a contributory scheme of state insurance providing sick benefit, unemployment benefit and an old-age pension.

In this list a) constitutes the private sector of the economy whilst b) to d) are the public sector. (See Data response A at the end of this chapter for recent trends in public spending.)

The monetarist counter-revolution

During the 1970s many Western economies were faced with the dual pressures of rising inflation and rising unemployment. There were two oil crises during the decade, in 1973–4 when the oil cartel OPEC raised oil prices four-fold and in 1979 when they were doubled again. This pushed most economies into unemployment, inflation and balance of payments deficit simultaneously, and slowed growth rates. Keynesian demand management policies seemed powerless to deal with these problems. Some economists came to believe that Keynes's ideas were flawed and that control of the money supply and a return to free market economics was the only way to restore the economy. The popular name, at the time, for these economists was ***monetarists*** but the counter-revolution was much wider than monetarism. It might be better to refer to those advocating a return to market values as the ***neo-classicists*** or ***new classicists***.

The foremost advocate of these ideas was the American economist Milton Friedman who was successful in persuading governments to adopt monetarist rather than Keynesian policies. The Austrian economist Friedrich Hayek was probably more influential with Mrs Thatcher's government since he persuaded her that she should attempt to 'roll back the frontiers of the state'. There followed a period of privatisation of all the industries nationalised by the Labour party in the late 1940s, shifting the UK substantially towards the capitalist end of the socialist–capitalist spectrum. The welfare state has been retained, but efforts have been made to make it more market oriented. Efforts to reduce the share of the economy accounted for by public expenditure have proved more difficult.

Common misunderstanding

Most people believe that the Conservative government from 1979 onwards reduced public expenditure. This is not the case for many of their years in office and in 1994–5 public expenditure was $42\frac{1}{2}$ per cent of gross domestic product (a measure of national income; see next chapter), exactly the same level as in 1979–80.

Markets and globalisation

The 1980s and 1990s have given time for the return to the market to be evaluated, and while there are clearly many benefits in terms of lower prices and better services from some privatised industries, there have also been problems in terms of two major recessions (in the early 1980s and early 1990s) with unemployment rising to 3 million in the UK on both occasions. Home ownership has risen spectacularly, but the collapse in the value of houses has left many people with debts greater than the value of their houses. Income distribution has widened with the better-off doing disproportionately well under the system. These problems have meant that reservations about the market have grown again. George Soros, the financier and currency speculator, claimed (1997) that with the demise of communism, the greatest enemy of the open society was the invasion of the market into too many aspects of life. Will Hutton, in his influential book *The State We're In*, wrote:

> The overall judgement on the market experiment must be at best mixed, at worst negative. The economy has been taken on a ferocious switchback ride; a period of deep recession in the early eighties, then an unsustainable boom and then a second chronic recession ... it has made the business sector understandably cautious about undertaking new investment. In area after area implementation of the market principle ... has failed to benefit the community.

At the same time the spectacular growth of the tiger economies of South Korea, Taiwan, Singapore and Malaysia has provided a major challenge to the competitiveness of many European economies. With the massive Chinese population ready to follow in their footsteps, there is no doubt that Europe and the USA are in for a period of fierce competition. Increasingly ***multinational companies*** move jobs around the world, looking for the most competitive workforce. This globalisation of the world economy reduces the power of individual governments to control events. Is involvement in the global market place the only way to defend jobs and create growth? Is the welfare state affordable under these circumstances? These are questions with which any future government has to grapple.

STUDENT ACTIVITY 6.2

What were the historical events which are associated with the following economic ideas and institutions?

a) Adam Smith and the invisible hand of the market.
b) The welfare state.
c) Keynesian interventionism and demand management.
d) The monetarist counter-revolution.
e) The new classical advocacy of a return to the market.

The stabilisation role: management of the economy

In the remaining sections of this chapter we will consider the various ways in which the government intervenes in the UK economy. We will be using the categories invented by the American public finance economist Richard Musgrave. He argued that governments intervened in the economy for three principal reasons: the stabilisation, the allocative role and the distributive role.

The objectives of economic policy

Whatever political party is in power, four main objectives of policy are pursued:

a) Control of inflation.
b) Reduction of unemployment.
c) Promotion of economic growth.
d) Attainment of a favourable balance of payments.

These objectives are not in dispute; they are concerned with the 'good housekeeping' of the economy. Different governments may, however, place different degrees of importance on individual objectives. Thus, for example, a Labour government might place a higher priority on reducing unemployment while the Conservatives might emphasise the control of inflation. In addition to these generally agreed objectives, more 'political' economic policies might be pursued, such as the redistribution of income.

There are five areas of action in which the government can pursue its economic policies: fiscal policy, monetary policy, direct intervention, supply side policy, and international relations (particularly in Europe).

Fiscal policy

The term fiscal policy is used to describe the regulation of the economy through government taxes and spending.

The most important aspect of this is the overall relationship between taxes and spending. If the government spends more money in a year than it collects in taxes, the situation is referred to as ***a budget deficit***. A deficit has an expansionary, or inflationary, effect upon the economy. Conversely, a situation where the government collects more in taxes than it spends is referred to as ***a budget surplus***. A surplus has a restraining, or deflationary, effect upon the economy. Keynesians believe that fiscal policy is more effective than monetary policy (see separate section below).

If the government spends more money than it collects in taxes, so that it is in deficit, the budget is financed by borrowing. The amount of money which the government may be forced to borrow in a year is referred to as ***the public sector borrowing requirement (PSBR)***. In the 1970s the PSBR became very large and governments since then have tried to restrain its growth. Borrowing would increase the total amount of money which the government owed to the individuals and institutions in the economy. The total amount of outstanding government debt stretching all the way back to 1694 is known as the National Debt. In the late 1980s the government was actually able to reduce the size of the National Debt. In this case it became possible to talk about public sector debt repayment (PSDR) but the National Debt grew again during the recession of the early 1990s. Fiscal policy is discussed in more detail in Chapters 31 and 43.

Monetary policy

Monetary policy is the regulation of the economy through the control of the quantity of money available and through the price of money, i.e. the rate of interest borrowers will have to pay.

Expanding the quantity of money and lowering the rate of interest should stimulate spending in the economy and is thus expansionary, or inflationary. Conversely, restricting the quantity of money and raising the rate of interest should have a restraining, or deflationary, effect upon the economy. Monetarists believe that monetary policy is more effective than fiscal policy.

It might be thought that, because the government controls the printing of banknotes, it is easy for it to control the quantity of money. This, however, is not so because most spending in the economy is not done with banknotes but with bank deposits. The amount of this 'cheque money' is determined by the banking system and can only be affected indirectly by the government. The government does, however, have a great effect upon the rate of interest because all other interest rates in the economy tend to move in line with the rates of interest set by the Bank of England. The government also affects interest rates since it is the biggest borrower in the economy. Monetary policy is discussed in more detail in Chapters 37 and 43.

Direct intervention

This expression is used to describe the many different ways in which the government, through legislation, spending or sanctions, tries to impose its economic policy directly upon the economy. Both fiscal and monetary policy are attempts to create conditions in the economy which will cause industry and people to react in a way which is in line with the government's wishes. Direct intervention, on the other hand, seeks to impose the government's will directly upon the economy, leaving people no choice. A good example of this would be the imposition of the statutory prices and incomes policies of the 1960s and 1970s, where the government controlled the increase of wages and in some cases prices. Government action to control wages directly has been limited to public sector employees in the 1980s and 1990s.

Supply side policy

Critics of Keynesian policy have argued that it concentrates too much on the demand side of the economy. Monetarists have also been criticised in this way since they are trying to manipulate the demand side of the economy too, but using monetary instead of fiscal policy. A distinct group of economists called supply-siders have been calling for government policy to concentrate on improving the supply side of the economy. The early advocates of this kind of policy concentrated on cutting taxes to encourage people to work hard and start up businesses. Reduction of the government's regulation and bureaucratic control of businesses has also been put forward as a way of encouraging enterprise and reducing costs.

Not all supply side policies concentrate on reducing the role of government. More recently, the need to improve the UK's performance in international league tables of education has led to more government expenditure on education. Education can be regarded as a supply side policy because it improves the quality of labour being offered to the market place.

Managing the open economy

It has become more difficult for both Keynesians and monetarists to manage the economy as it has become more 'open'. A progressively larger proportion of output is exported. A progressively larger proportion of consumption is imported.

Increasingly governments are dealing not with national firms but international firms which can choose which country to invest in. The exchange rate has become a more significant policy instrument as this process has gathered pace. This globalisation of the economy brings with it many benefits in terms of cheaper and better products, but also less control for individual governments. If the European economies recover more slowly than the UK economy from the recession of the early 1990s, this slows down the UK economy's recovery too because the UK cannot export as much to them. This has led to greater international cooperation, particularly within Europe.

The European Union (EU)

The EU began life as the European Community in 1957. After being rejected for membership in the 1960s, the UK finally joined in 1973. The EU is expanding fast and now has 15 members, with countries from the former East European Bloc queueing up to join. EU regulations replace those of individual member states in many areas of policy. Since the Maastricht Treaty of 1992, the EU has been moving towards a single market with a single currency. The EU is not a state, nor even yet a union of states like the USA, but it may be that this is the direction in which it is going.

STUDENT ACTIVITY 6.3

Categorise each of the following policies as fiscal, monetary, supply side or international (some policies might fall into more than one category!):

a) A cut in income tax.
b) An increase in interest rates.
c) The Maastricht Treaty.
d) Privatising the rail industry.
e) Putting a pay freeze on public sector workers.

The allocative role: provision of goods and services

Privatisation has substantially reduced the number of goods and services provided by the state, but there are still quite a large number of services which remain in state hands even after the nationalised industries have been sold off. These services have one thing in common: they are for one reason or another difficult or unsuitable for provision through the market. Defence, roads, health, education, law and order are provided by the state in almost every country to some extent.

These services are not, of course, free, since we pay for them indirectly through taxes and insurance schemes. Some are controlled directly by central government, e.g. defence and motorway construction, while in other cases the service may be decided upon by central government but administered by local government, e.g. local education authority schools. Services such as street lighting and refuse collection may be entirely controlled by local authorities. On the other hand, services may be provided by bodies set up by the government but which are not regarded as either central or local government bodies. An example of these are health authorities and trusts. Such bodies are termed *Quangos* (quasi-autonomous non-governmental organisations). The operation of these organisations is discussed more fully in Chapter 29.

Public goods and services

Public goods are those where consumption of the product by one person does not diminish the consumption by others.

The classic example of this is that of a lighthouse, where the fact that the light guides one ship does not detract from its ability to guide others. More significantly in the modern economy, such things as defence, street lighting, law and order, and roads are considered to be public goods. It is difficult to charge people for services which, once provided for one person, are immediately available to everyone! Parts of the road system can be charged for: bridges, tunnels and motorways have limited entry and exit points. It is more difficult to imagine a pricing system for the road system as a whole, although new technology may provide this soon (see Chapter 28).

External benefits and costs

Some services benefit people other than those purchasing them. Communicable diseases are best treated or they will affect others. An unhealthy workforce is not so productive; this may also affect the shareholders of the companies for which they work. Education increases people's potential productivity which may result in higher economic growth from which everyone benefits. These arguments are sufficient to suggest that the state should at least subsidise these activities. Further arguments that the state should be more involved are presented below. The state also intervenes to reduce ***external costs*** such as pollution from industry. These issues are discussed further in Chapters 25 and 27.

Merit goods and services

These are products which are allocated to the members of the public, not according to the consumers' preferences but according to the paternalistic judgements of the government.

Thus, for example, state-financed education is given to everyone as a right between the ages of 5 and 16 irrespective of their willingness or ability to pay. It is assumed that everyone has a need for education, however poor. Choice is removed from this market and education is compulsory. Health services may be concerned to change people's behaviour rather than meet their demands. Improved diet, giving up smoking and other drugs are questions of health promotion decided upon by governments or professionals.

The state and monopoly power

Many major industries in the UK were at one time nationalised. In most cases these industries had a degree of monopoly power (e.g. gas, electricity, telecommunications) and the idea of nationalisation was to protect the consumer from exploitation. These industries, and their subsequent privatisation, form the subject of a separate chapter in the book (see Chapter 26). After privatisation the government has continued to influence how these industries operate, but by regulation rather than ownership. A more general discussion of the question of regulating monopoly power is found in Chapter 18.

STUDENT ACTIVITY 6.4

Put arguments for and against the following being in the public sector. Try to use the following terms in your arguments: merit good, public good, external benefits and costs, monopoly.

a) school education
b) healthcare
c) higher education
d) roads
e) police
f) defence
g) electricity

The distributive role: transfer payments

Table 6.1 shows that the largest single item on the list of public expenditure is social security. This heading covers old-age pensions, unemployment benefit, sickness benefit, and family income support to those on inadequate incomes. These payments are known as transfer payments, since they are not in return for productive work, but simply transfer income from taxpayers to the groups of people receiving benefit. The government now takes responsibility for the poor and disadvantaged in our society, but other groups have taken this responsibility in the past. The family, the church and charities still continue to take some responsibility, but the twentieth century has seen the state shoulder the largest part of this burden. The number of pensioners is rising and the number of unemployed has remained obstinately high in recent years, so this is a commitment which the government cannot easily avoid.

Some services which are provided free, like education and health, can be regarded as redistribution in kind, providing a higher level of service in these two areas than the individuals would have been able to provide themselves. This raises an additional argument for these two services to be provided through the public sector. Consumers are at liberty to choose to pay for their education and health through the private sector.

Table 6.1 **Functional government expenditure (£bn)**

	1986	*1991*	*1996*
Defence	19.1	23.2	23.0
Public order	6.8	12.9	15.4
Education	19.3	29.4	39.1
Health	19.2	31.2	43.2
Social security	49.9	73.8	107.0
Housing/amenities	8.1	8.7	9.5
Transport	3.7	6.7	8.4
Debt interest	20.6	21.6	33.4
Other	15.7	20.9	27.2
Total government expenditure	162.4	228.4	306.2
GDP at market prices	384.8	575.7	742.3

Source: ONS *National Income and Expenditure 'Blue Book'*, August 1997

The prospect for the mixed economy

We can look at the prospect for the mixed economy in political, economic or technological terms. Considering the economic point of view first, the central problem is the failure of Keynesian management of the economy. Keynes's analysis centred on the macroeconomy and was based on the short-term management of demand.

This worked reasonably well until the 1960s but since that time there has been a conspicuous failure to solve the twin

problems of inflation and unemployment. In recent years governments have tried supply side policies, trying to encourage potential growth wherever it can be found in the economy.

Economic policy, however, must function within the political framework. In practice this gives the consumers very little economic choice. However detailed the manifesto is on which a government is elected, it will only roughly approximate to the wishes of even its own supporters. Politics also places another constraint upon the mixed economy. At least once every five years the government must seek re-election. It is possible to argue that any major economic policy should last for much longer than this and that therefore the real welfare of the country is being subjected to the government of the day's desire to ensure re-election. Thus politicians are led to ask themselves what most people want, while the economist would maintain that the correct question should be 'what do people want most?'

The election of the Thatcher government in 1979 was to have a radical effect upon the development of the mixed economy. The government was strongly opposed to all forms of collectivism and economic interventionism.

This led to a return to market-centred economics and to the round of privatisations. From 1988 onwards market-based reforms of the welfare state that stopped short of privatisation were introduced. The process of privatisation and reform of the welfare state continued with John Major's government in the 1990s. The shape of the economy in 1997 was profoundly different from that of 1979.

A third factor shaping the economy which may be independent of political and economic ideology is technology. It is obvious that technology, and in particular the revolution in microprocessing, is having a very profound effect upon our lives. There are many people, however, who believe that the revolution in technology has also brought about a revolution in the economic order and created a new decision-making process. Foremost among the advocates of this point of view is Professor J. K. Galbraith.

Galbraith maintains that power has passed from company directors, shareholders, trade unionists, voters and even the government to the ***technostructure***. It is argued that in all advanced states power actually rests with those who have the high level of skill and information which is necessary to operate in a large corporation or government department. While this is probably an extreme point of view, it cannot be doubted that the new technology, particularly that of the silicon chip, is transforming our lives.

Despite the changes wrought by the Conservative governments of the 1980s and 1990s the UK economy is still a mixed economy with the public sector accounting for over 40 per cent of GDP.

The UK mixed economy has shifted substantially towards capitalism and away from collectivism, but not without difficulties and controversy. In addition to this it has to cope with the rising power of multinational corporations and the new tiger economies of the Far East.

STUDENT ACTIVITY 6.5

Create a list of areas of the economy that the government intervenes in which you think it should move out of, or be less involved in. Do the same for areas where you think it should be more involved.

Summary

1. Despite a belief in *laissez-faire*, governments of the nineteenth century were forced to intervene in the economy.
2. Classical economics proved unable to explain or cure the mass unemployment of the 1920s and 1930s.
3. Keynes's insights into the workings of the economy revolutionised the subject.
4. The Labour government of 1945 was largely responsible for the shape of the economy for the subsequent 30 years.
5. The mixed economy is a compound of *laissez-faire*, government management, public ownership and welfare state.

6 The government controls the economy through fiscal policy, monetary policy, direct intervention, supply side policy and international relations.
7 A profound change of direction came about in the 1980s and 1990s through privatisation and measures to make the economy more market orientated.
8 In the late twentieth century the mixed economy faces new problems, in particular globalisation and the power of multinational business. The role of the state is once more a subject of great political controversy.
9 Economic policies can be categorised as Keynesian, monetarist or supply side.

Questions

1. Attempt to categorise each of the following as merit goods, public goods, goods with external benefits or costs, or private goods:
   a) roads
   b) dental care
   c) electricity
   d) rail travel
   e) libraries
   f) toothpaste
   g) lighthouses
   h) chocolate bars.
2. Distinguish between monetarists and Keynesians in relation to intervention in the economy.
3. Why do governments have to take notice of events in the rest of the world economy when formulating their policy?
4. Distinguish between the allocative, distributive and stabilisation roles of state intervention.
5. Explain why all economies are really mixed economies.

Data response A
Public expenditure analysis

Using the figures in Table 6.1 (page 76), answer the following questions:

1. Express each category of expenditure as a percentage of total government expenditure in that year.
2. Which categories of public expenditure have been growing fastest as a percentage of total public expenditure?
3. What has been happening to public expenditure as a percentage of GDP at market prices?
4. Which of the categories of public expenditure in Table 6.1 are in the public sector for which of the following reasons:
   a) They are public goods.
   b) There are external costs and benefits.
   c) There is a redistribution of income.

7 National income

Learning outcomes

At the end of this chapter you will be able to:

- State and account for the construction of the various measures of a country's national income and refer to official statistics to update these figures.
- Use national income statistics for international comparison purposes without reaching unwarranted conclusions.

We have seen already that micro- and macroeconomics are different approaches to the study of the economy. Macroeconomics is concerned with aggregate economic phenomena and processes. National income gives us a measure of those aggregates. In this chapter we will outline the main components of national income and consider some of the difficulties involved in measuring it. This is done in detail so that you will be able to understand the official statistics in the *National Income and Expenditure 'Blue Book'*, *Economic Trends*, *Annual Abstract of Statistics* or the *Monthly Digest*. A firm understanding is vital for anyone who wishes to refer to and use the national accounts. These accounts provide a rich source of information on the economy but their use is not without potential pitfalls. It is fair to say, however, that only a broad understanding is required for most introductory economics. In Section V we go beyond the accounting procedures and examine the factors that actually determine the size of national income.

The circular flow of national income

The national product

National product is a term we use to describe the total of all the output of goods and services produced in an economy over a specific period of time. As this output is the real income of the economy for the period, national product is also known as national income.

STUDENT ACTIVITY 7.1

Suppose the output of a country in a year consists of 10 000 hairgrips, 2000 toothbrushes, 5 million kilowatts of electricity, 18 luxury motor cars, 500 basic motor cars, 4000 hours of solicitors' advice, 8000 hours of housework, 5000 ball bearings, 400 tonnes of steel, 2590 tyres, 70 tonnes of pollutant gases, 5000 hours of entertainment, 6000 hours of gardening, 16 kilometres of egg noodle, 3000 cardboard boxes and 4000 sausages. The economy also exports 50 cars and imports 40 motorcycles. How might you go about producing a single measure for the output or real income of this economy? What problems will arise in this exercise? Make a list of the problems you have identified and tick them off as you read through this chapter.

There are several different measures of national product, the most commonly used being ***gross domestic product (GDP)***, ***gross national product (GNP)*** and ***net national product (NNP)***. In the UK the data relating to national income is collected together in ***national accounts*** prepared by the Office of National Statistics (formerly the Central Statistical Office). This annual publication is more commonly called the 'Blue Book'. Most countries use similar measurements; quarterly summaries for the leading 24 industrialised nations can be found in the OECD *Economic Outlook*.

The national product (or national income) is a flow with respect to time. Its size is of vital importance to the well-being of society because such things as employment and the standard of living are closely related to it.

The first problem you will have encountered in Student activity 7.1 is that to aggregate all the various outputs of the economy by counting or weighing them would be nonsensical. No doubt you realised that the best weights to use in aggregating these disparate outputs would be to use prices.

Common misunderstanding

The monetary measures of national income can suggest that it is the flow of money that is the focus of measurement. It is important to bear in mind that it is the flow of output of goods and services that the national income accountant is actually trying to measure.

The circular flow

To understand the various measures of national product it is necessary to understand the nature of the macroeconomy. Figure 7.1 illustrates a simple view of the economy in which there is no foreign trade and no government intervention. Here we see two of the main sectors of the macroeconomy, households and firms. These sectors are identified not by who they are but by what they do, i.e. firms produce while households consume. Everyone in the economy must belong to a 'household' since everyone must consume. The households also own the factors of production. In order to produce, firms must buy factor services from households. In return for the factor services, firms pay households wages, rent, interest and profit. The size of these payments will give us the cost of producing and therefore the value of the national product.

This payment for factor services is known as income and is usually abbreviated to the letter *Y* (the letter *I* is reserved for investment). We shall see later that this corresponds to the GDP measure of national product.

It should be clear that income is derived from the expenditure of others, e.g. when you buy something your expenditure becomes the income of the shopkeeper. In other words, for any given period the amount spent must be identically equal to the amount received as income. Thus, as we have included profits in the factor payments, it can be seen that we could also arrive at national product by measuring the total amount of money spent on producing it. Hence, if we totalled all consumers' expenditure (*C*) on the right-hand side of Fig. 7.1 it should be equal to all the factor incomes on the left-hand side. We can conclude:

There are (at least) two methods of measuring the national product: by measuring either national income or national expenditure.

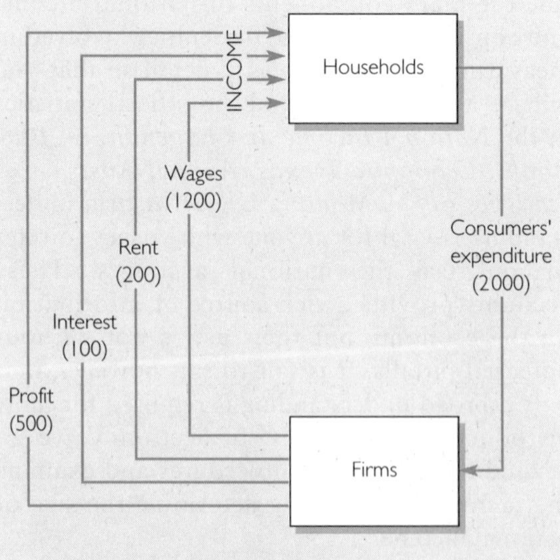

***Fig. 7.1* The circular flow of income**
National income is the same total as consumers' expenditure.

If we return to Fig. 7.1 again it should be obvious why this view of the economy is often referred to as the circular flow of income. Firms receive money from households which they then pay out as wages etc. This income is spent creating more income for firms and so on. Everyone's income is someone else's expenditure. This is the basic identity used by national income accountants:

Expenditure (E) ≡ Income (Y)

Two methods of measurement

A simple example will show the similarity of this two-fold method of measuring national product to the double-entry book-keeping used by accountants. Table 7.1 shows a simplified balance sheet for a farm. The profit reverts to the farmer as householder, i.e. it is the farmer's income. It is then spent in the same way as other factor incomes.

Table 7.1 **Balance sheet of a farm**

Sales (consumer's expenditure)		*Costs (factor income)*	
Sales of wheat	£1000	Wages	£600
		Rent	100
		Interest	50
		Profit	250
Total	£1000	Total	£1000

If the economy consisted just of 2 million such farms then we could arrive at the national product by aggregating (i.e. summing) all their balance sheets. This has been done in Table 7.2.

Table 7.2 **National product**

Sales (consumer's expenditure)		*Costs (factor incomes)*	
Sales of wheat (2m × £1000)	£2000m	Wages (2m × £600)	£1200m
		Rent (2m × £100)	200m
		Interest (2m × £50)	100m
		Profit (2m × £250)	500m
National expenditure	£2000m	National income	£2000m

Thus we can see that the two sides of the balance sheet give two different ways of arriving at the same measure for national product, and we have confirmed that:

National income = National expenditure

When we come to look at the actual statistics for the national product we shall see that both these measures are used. A third measure of national product exists and this is arrived at by totalling the ***value added*** by each industry in the country.

A third measure

Many products must go through several stages of production before they reach their *final* form. Consider a product such as bread: first, we must produce wheat; this must then be ground into flour; the flour must be baked into bread; and finally the product must be sold to the customer. The total value of bread to the national product will be its *final* selling price. The expenditure method of calculating national product involves totalling all expenditure on final products. Bread is obviously a final product because it is consumed and disappears from the economy. However, many intermediate products are bought and sold and if we examine their value we can determine the value added to the economy by each industry and we also arrive at another measure of national product, which is termed ***national output.***

When calculating the national product by the output method it is important to avoid ***double counting***. Let us pursue our bread example a little farther. The farmer produces wheat by employing the factors of production – land, labour, etc. The wheat is then sold for £1000. The miller then ***adds value*** to it by milling it and sells it for £1300. What is the value to the economy of the miller's contribution? It is £1300 minus the £1000 paid for the wheat.

Therefore, if we wish to calculate the value added to the economy by an industry we arrive at it by taking the value of its output and subtracting the cost of the raw materials or intermediate products it had to buy in order to produce its output. Thus:

The value added by an industry is the factor services it has applied to the

product. The payment for these services – wages, rent, interest and profit – returns to the households as income.

Table 7.3 illustrates a value-added method of calculating the national product.

Table 7.3 **The value-added method**

Type of industry	*Value of output*	*Cost of intermediate goods*	*Value added (factor services)*
Farming	£1000	0	£1000
Milling	1300	£1000	300
Baking	2000	1300	700
Retailing	2500[(a)]	2000	500
	£6800	£4300	£2500[(b)]

(a) National product by final expenditure method
(b) National product by value-added method

The stages of production

Figure 7.2 uses the same example of bread making to show that all three methods of calculating the national income can be reconciled. The value of the national product can be shown as the expenditure by households of £2500 on bread. The same figure can be arrived at by totalling the value added by each of the four stages of production. The national product can also be measured as the flows of income to households in return for the factor services. The national product is a monetary measure of the output (in our example, bread) produced in the economy over a certain period. We can now see that there are three methods of arriving at a measure of the same thing. Thus we can write:

National income = National expenditure = National output

The components of national income

So far we have been considering a very simple economy which produces only consumer goods and has no government intervention and no foreign trade. However, all these things must be included in the actual calculation of national income or product. We will consider each of these in turn.

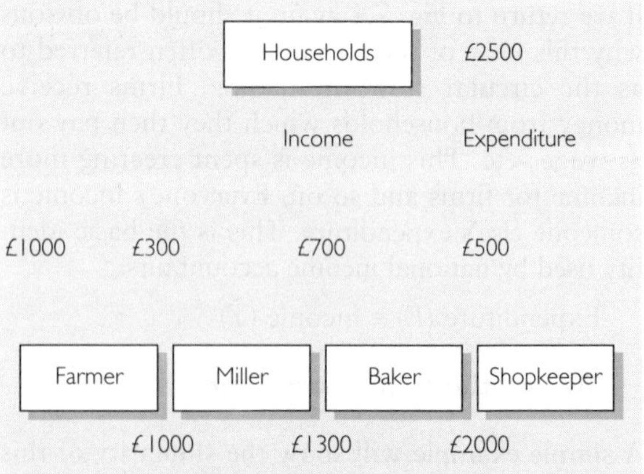

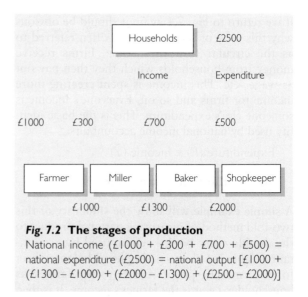

Fig. 7.2 **The stages of production**
National income (£1000 + £300 + £700 + £500) = national expenditure (£2500) = national output [£1000 + (£1300 – £1000) + (£2000 – £1300) + (£2500 – £2000)]

Capital goods

In order to produce consumer goods we need capital goods in the form of buildings, machines and stocks. Therefore an economy must produce not only consumer goods (*C*) but also investment, or capital, goods (*I*). We count both consumer goods and investment goods as part of the gross national product (GNP). Although we may not actually consume factories or machines, if our stock of them increases then the economy has become wealthier because we have a greater ability to produce wealth. We therefore need to count investment goods as part of the national product. From this we can see that national product is going to include the output of consumer goods plus investment goods (*C* + *I*).

Final goods

When we are calculating the national product we therefore need to include all ***final goods***. For example, bread is a final good because it is not made into anything else, but is consumed, i.e. it is wanted for its own sake. Conversely, although bakers' ovens are final goods because they are not made into anything else, they are included as investment (I) because they are used to produce bread rather than wanted for their own sake. Stocks of raw materials or intermediate goods, may also enter into the evaluation of the national product. If at the end of the year our stocks of raw materials etc. are greater than at the beginning of the year then we have obviously become wealthier. Therefore we include in the calculation of the national product the ***value of the physical increase*** in our stocks. (Stocks are also often referred to as ***inventories***.)

Gross and net output

The output of capital goods in any particular period is referred to as ***capital formation***. Capital goods may be either ***fixed capital***, such as buildings and machinery, or ***circulating capital*** in the form of stocks of raw materials and intermediate goods. In national income accounts these two items are considered separately. The output of buildings and machinery is shown as ***gross domestic fixed capital formation***. The change in circulating capital is recorded as the ***value of physical increase in stocks and work in progress*** (this may be either a positive or negative value depending upon whether inventories have increased or decreased during the year).

If we consider capital goods such as roads, buildings and machinery, it is obvious that as we use them they wear out. Therefore every year we must produce a certain amount of capital goods simply to replace those which are wearing out. The output of all capital goods during the year might therefore be referred to as ***gross capital formation***. However, when we have made allowances for the wearing out of capital we arrive at a figure known as ***net capital formation***. The allowance made for the wearing out or depreciation of capital is known as ***capital consumption***.

There are therefore two measures of the national product. If we simply count up the output of all final products – both consumer goods and investment goods – we will arrive at a measure which is known as gross national product (GNP), but if we make an allowance for capital consumption then we arrive at a measure known as net national product (NNP).

STUDENT ACTIVITY 7.2

Assume an economy with a capital stock of 100 machines, a depreciation rate of 10 per cent a year and a steady level of investment of 10 machines a year. Demonstrate that using net national product as the measure of the economy's output would avoid the double counting of investment goods and the consumption goods that they produce.

The government and the national product

We have so far considered expenditure by households on consumer goods, as well as the expenditure on capital goods. However, the largest single consumer of all types of goods is the government. Therefore, when we are calculating national expenditure, as well as consumer spending (C) and private investment spending (I), we add all government expenditure on goods and services (G), so that the total demand for goods and services will now be $C + I + G$.

Included within government expenditure are such things as the cost of new schools and the salaries of school teachers and the people in the armed services, and the cost of tanks and guns. In short, it is the wages of all government employees plus goods (medicines, paper, roads, etc.) which the government buys from the private sector.

This does not, however, include *all* government spending. We do not include items such as expenditure on old-age pensions or sickness benefits. These are termed ***transfer payments***. The reason for this is that these are not payments for current productive services and therefore are deemed to have nothing to do with the creation of the national product in the current year.

Figure 7.3 shows the proportions of total domestic expenditure which the various components of national expenditure represent. You will note that, despite efforts by Mrs Thatcher's government, the proportion represented by government expenditure has tended to increase over the years.

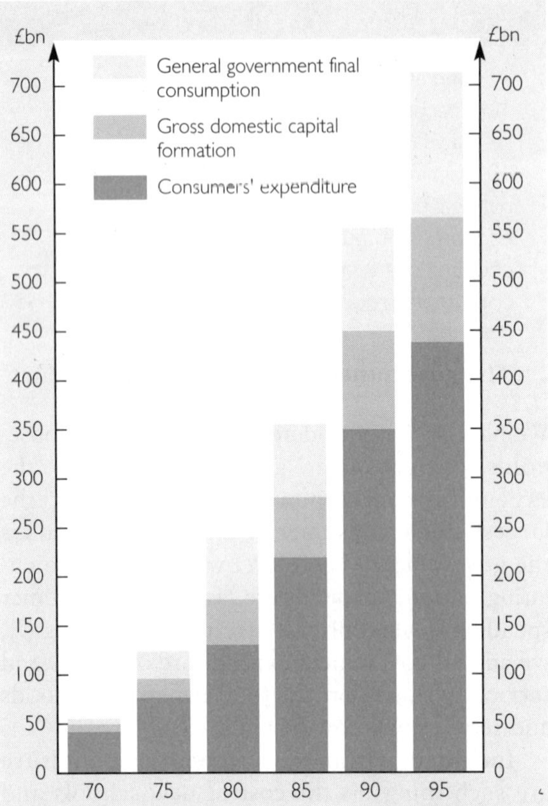

***Fig. 7.3* The consumption of total domestic expenditure (at current market prices)**

Foreign trade and the national product

So far the economy we have considered has been a ***closed economy***. The UK, however, is an ***open economy***, i.e. one which trades with the rest of the world. Of all countries in the world the UK is one of the most dependent on foreign trade. The UK imports (M) and exports (X) roughly one-third of its gross domestic product (X = 28 per cent and M = 29 per cent of GDP in 1995).

The sale of UK goods and services abroad creates income for people in the UK and we therefore include that in our calculation of the national product. On the other hand, much of what is spent in the UK is expenditure on imported goods and services which creates income for people overseas. This is therefore subtracted from the national product. When we have done this we can arrive at a full statement for all the components of the national product, which is:

$$Y = C + I + G + (X - M)$$

It will be obvious from this that the overall size of the national product can be either increased or decreased by the net effect of foreign trade. However, although foreign trade is enormously important, the import and export of goods and services are usually roughly equivalent, so that the net effect of foreign trade has only a small effect on the overall size of the national product. It has been the tendency of the UK and most other industrialised economies for a greater and greater proportion of the national product to be exported and imported.

Common misunderstanding

It is a common fallacy that it is only the export of goods which earns money for the country. In fact, the sale of services such as banking, insurance and tourism is also a major source of overseas income for the UK.

National income accounts

We have already seen that the value of the national product can be arrived at in three different ways. In this section we shall consider how these three different methods are actually presented in the national income accounts.

National expenditure method

Table 7.4 shows the expenditure calculation. It is the method which most clearly shows the components of national income as we have explained them.

a) *Consumers' expenditure*. This includes all consumers' expenditure on goods and services, except for the purchase of new houses which is included in gross fixed capital formation.
b) *General government final consumption*. This includes all current expenditure by central and local government on goods and services including the wages and salaries of government employees.

***Table 7.4* Gross national product, GDP and national income of the UK by category of expenditure, 1995**

Item		*£m*
Consumers' expenditure	(C)	447 247
General government final consumption	(G)	149 474
Gross domestic fixed capital formation	(I)	105 385
Value of physical increase in stocks and work in progress	(I)	3851
Exports	(X)	197 600
less imports	(M)	–203 086
Statistical discrepancy		419
GDP at market prices		700 890
Factor cost adjustments		
less taxes on expenditure		– 103 597
plus subsidies		6966
GDP at factor cost		604 259
Net property income from abroad		9572
GNP		613 831
less capital consumption		– 72 884
National income, i.e. NNP		540 947

Source: UK National Accounts

STUDENT ACTIVITY 7.3

Consumers' expenditure includes an imputed rent for owner-occupied dwellings. Why do you think this is done? (Hint: Think what would happen to national expenditure if all householders suddenly decided to sell their houses and pay rent.)

c) *Gross fixed capital formation.* This is expenditure on fixed assets (buildings, machinery, vehicles, etc.) either for replacing or adding to the stock of existing fixed assets. This is the major part of the investment which takes place in the economy.

d) *The value of physical increases in stocks and work in progress.* As explained previously we include in the calculation of the national product the change in the *quantity* of stocks, or inventories, during the course of the year. This may be either a positive or a negative figure. As you can see in Table 7.4, in 1995 it was plus £3851 million.

e) *Exports and imports.* Exports are part of the output of the economy and payment is received for them from abroad; hence they should be included. Conversely, much of the final expenditure is on imported goods and we therefore subtract spending on imports as they are not spending on domestic output. Having done this we arrive at a measure known as gross domestic product at market prices.

f) *Statistical discrepancy.* As we have explained there are three measures of national product, all of which should bring us to the same figure. However, all the methods are subject to some inaccuracy because of the enormousness of the task and the speed with which figures must be produced. In the hope of arriving at a more accurate answer an average estimate is produced by looking at the estimates for income and expenditure. The statistical discrepancy is, therefore, actually a measure of how much each measure differs from the average estimate.

g) *Gross domestic product (GDP).* The gross domestic product at market prices is the value of the national product (net of foreign trade) in terms of money actually spent. This, however, is misleading since the price of many articles includes taxes on expenditure or subsidies. Therefore in order to obtain the value of the national product in terms of the resources used to produce it we must make factor cost adjustments. In order to do this we must subtract the taxes on expenditure levied by the government and add on the amount of subsidies. When this has been done we arrive at a figure known as ***gross domestic product at factor cost.*** This is the most commonly used measure of national product and you will see that it appears in all three modes of measurement.

h) *Gross national product (GNP).* The GDP represents the extent to which resources (or factors) are used in the economy. National product, however, can be affected by rent, profit, interest and dividends paid to, or received from, overseas. This is shown in Table 7.4 as ***net property income from abroad.*** This figure may be either positive or negative. When this has been taken into account we arrive at the gross national product at factor cost.

i) *Net national product (NNP).* As previously explained the capital stock of a country wears out. Part of the gross fixed capital formation is therefore to replace worn-out capital and is referred to as capital consumption. When this has been subtracted we arrive at a figure known as the net national product.

Thus, summarising the above, we can say that:

$$Y = C + I + G + (X - M)$$

National income method

Table 7.5 illustrates the second method by which national product is measured.

Table 7.5 **Gross domestic product of the UK by category of income, 1995**

Item	*£m*
Income from employment	377 895
Income from self-employment	67 685
Gross trading profits of companies, corporations and government enterprises	96 274
Rent	62 758
Adjustments	
Imputed change for consumption of non-trading capital	4729
less stock appreciation	– 4902
Statistical discrepancy	– 180
GDP at factor cost	604 259

Source: UK National Accounts

Here you can see that income from all different sources is totalled and then adjustments are made to ensure it is measuring the same output as the expenditure method.

The imputed charge for the consumption of non-trading capital is, as with the expenditure method, principally the imputed rent for owner-occupied houses. The entry for ***stock appreciation*** is not equivalent, however, to the ***value of physical increase in stocks and work in progress*** of the expenditure method. Although not sold yet, the factors of production responsible for the increase in stocks will have been paid and already included therefore as value added in the income method. In fact, the stock appreciation adjustment is made as goods held in stocks throughout the year may appreciate in value because of price increases. To include this increase would exaggerate their value (in terms of factor cost).

When the GDP has been calculated by the income method it may be compared with the GDP average estimate to produce the statistical discrepancy. Mathematically, adjusting for this discrepancy produces the same figure for GDP at factor cost as for the expenditure method. By making the same adjustments as in Table 7.4 we would then arrive at the same figures for GNP and NNP as before.

Personal income

Not all the income in the economy is received by individuals; some is earned by companies but not distributed and some is received by government. A measure of ***personal income*** is arrived at by totalling income before tax from all sources, including transfer payments such as national insurance benefits. However, much of this personal income is subject to tax. If income taxes and national insurance contributions are taken away we arrive at a measure known as ***personal disposable income*** (PDI). In 1994 personal disposable income was £472 574 million compared with GDP of £579 177 million.

Personal disposable income is a significant measure. It will be watched by retailers as an indicator of likely spending. It is also important to individuals since it will determine how much money they have left in their pockets to spend. Disposable income is divided between consumer spending and saving. In 1994 £44 490 million was saved from disposable income.

National output method

The final method by which national product is calculated is to total the contributions made by the various sectors (industries) of the economy. This is illustrated in Table 7.6. Until recently the largest contribution came from manufacturing, but the relative contribution of manufacturing has declined as service industries have grown in importance and manufacturing has suffered from low investment and periods of high exchange rates for pounds sterling.

Table 7.6 **Gross domestic product of the UK by category of income, 1995**

Item	*£m*
Agriculture, forestry and fishing	11 953
Mining and quarrying incl. oil and gas extraction	14 594
Manufacturing	134 100
Electricity, gas and water supply	15 821
Construction	32 461
Wholesale and retail trade; repairs; hotels and restaurants	86 421
Transport, storage and communication	50 856
Financial intermediation, real estate, renting and business activities	158 192
Public admin., national defence and compulsory social security	39 150
Education, health and social work	72 972
Other services including sewage and refuse disposal	23 255
less stock appreciation	– 4902
less adjustment for financial services	– 30 794
Statistical discrepancy	–180
Gross domestic product	604 259

Source: UK National Accounts

When calculating the GDP in this manner it is necessary to avoid double counting. To do this only the value added by each business should be included (see pages 81–2); for example, the value of the steel in motor vehicles should not be included if it has already been counted in the steel industry. In Table 7.6 the figures for the various sectors are shown before allowance has been made for their net interest payment to the financial sector. This is allowed for in the entry listed as the ***adjustment for financial services***. After this and the statistical discrepancy have been allowed for we arrive at the GDP at factor cost. By then making adjustments for net property income from abroad and for capital consumption we can arrive at the GNP and the NNP.

Common misunderstandings

a) The various measures of the national product give us a tally of the nation's income for a year. However, this does not measure the nation's wealth. The nation has a great stock of capital goods. This stock of national capital is the sum total of everything that has been preserved from all that has been produced throughout our economic history. Interestingly, perhaps the greatest asset of modern economies is the skill and education of the workforce. This is called 'human capital' but is not included in measures of net capital stock owing to the difficulty of measurement.

b) If we were assessing someone's wealth, one of the first things we would look at is how much money they had and also whether they owned stocks and shares. However, these are excluded from the calculation of national wealth. Why? The answer is because we have already counted them in the form of real wealth such as buildings and machines. Money and other financial assets are only claims upon wealth and hence are simply paper certificates of ownership. Similarly, varying the amount of money in the economy does not directly make it any richer or poorer.

Problems and international comparisons

In this section of the chapter we consider some of the difficulties that arise when we attempt to take any measure of the national product as a guide to the standard of living. We will also look at problems associated with comparing the national product of one country with that of another.

Inflation and the GDP deflator

Remember that the national income accountant is attempting to measure a flow of real output. Thus a major problem faced when comparing one year's national product with another is that of inflation. If, for example, the national product were to grow by 10 per cent, but at the same time there was inflation of 10 per cent, then in real terms the national product would not have grown at all.

It is useful to have a measure of real national product in ***constant cost terms***, which can be calculated by ***deflating*** the figures by the amount of inflation that has taken place. We usually measure inflation by means of index numbers. The best-known index is the retail price index (RPI). This is, however, not an appropriate measure for the purpose of deflating the national product because it measures only consumers' expenditure and, as we have seen, the national product also includes expenditure on investment and expenditure by the government. Therefore a more complex index is needed and this is termed the ***GDP deflator***.

Let us consider an example. The GDP in current prices was £306.8 in 1985 and £438.8 in 1989. The GDP deflator for these years was 100.0 (base year) and 123.6 respectively. This therefore gives the overall price inflation for the components of GDP between these years as 23.6 per cent. To express the GDP in constant price terms we divide by the deflator and multiply by 100. Thus we obtain:

$$1985 = \frac{£306.8}{100} \times 100 = £306.8 \text{ bn}$$

$$1989 = \frac{£438.8}{123.6} \times 100 = £355 \text{ bn}$$

Thus, the 'real value' of the GDP in 1989 was £355.0 billion in terms of 1985 prices, rather than its current price value of £438.8 billion. Put another way, the real value of the GDP increased by 15.7 per cent between 1985 and 1989 while its monetary value increased by 43 per cent. There are tables in the *National Income and Expenditure 'Blue Book'* which have already applied the deflator in this way and hence show GDP at constant prices.

STUDENT ACTIVITY 7.4

The following figures give index numbers for GDP at current market prices and at 1990 market prices:

	1985	*1990*	*1995*
GDP at current prices	65	100	127
GDP at 1990 prices	85	100	106

Sketch a graph of these index numbers. Now explain why GDP at current prices is lower than GDP at 1990 prices before 1990, and higher than GDP at 1990 prices after 1995.

Satisfy yourself that you can explain the following conclusion that is often useful in answering data-response-type questions:

When the general price level is rising (i.e. inflation) national income at current prices will be growing faster than the real growth of GDP at constant prices.

National income per head

Table 7.7 shows the national income of various countries in 1993. You can see that the USA had by far the highest national income with a GNP of $6378 billion. The picture is modified, however, when the number of people in a country is taken into account.

Table 7.7 **GNP and GNP per capita, 1993**

Country	*GNP ($bn)*	*GNP per capita ($)*
USA	6378	24740
Germany	1901	23560
Japan	3921	31490
UK	1046	18060

Source: World Development Report, IBRD 1995

To produce a figure for GNP per head (known as per capita), national income is divided by the country's population.

The last column of Table 7.7 shows that when this is done it can be seen that the average income of Japan is actually higher than the average income of the USA. This effect is even starker between poor countries and richer countries. For example, although India has a far higher GNP than Singapore, in 1993 the GNP per capita of India was only $300 compared with Singapore's $19850.

GNP per capita is more useful for international comparisons of living standards than GNP.

The distribution of income

Although national income per head gives us a good basis for comparison between countries, this too may be a misleading guide to the standard of living because income may be very unevenly distributed within the country. India, as we saw, had a per capita income of only $300 per year, but income is also unevenly distributed, with a few rich people and millions of poor.

Table 7.8 shows the distribution of income in the UK before housing costs. You can see that in 1992 the richest 20 per cent of the population received 41 per cent of the income. In fact during the 1980s and 1990s the move towards more non-interventionist policies saw the share of the rich in the UK increase significantly while that of the lowest income families fell; this was a sharp reversal of the trend since the Second World War towards a more even distribution of income.

***Table 7.8* Distribution of income in the UK before housing costs**

Family income by rank	*Percentage of national income*		*Cumulative percentage*	
	1987	*1992*	*1987*	*1992*
Lowest fifth	8.9	7	8.9	7
Second fifth	12.9	12	21.8	19
Third fifth	16.9	17	38.7	36
Fourth fifth	22.2	23	60.9	59
Highest fifth	39.1	41	100.0	100

Source: *Social Trends*

Government expenditure

As we have seen, government expenditure is a major component of the GDP. Table 7.9 gives government expenditure for selected nations. It may seem strange that there are such large percentage differences between countries with similar living standards. Sweden and Switzerland are often regarded as having the highest living standards within the OECD area. The differences in government expenditure can partly be explained by their different approaches to problems. In Sweden and the Netherlands, for example, there is heavy government expenditure on transfer payments such as old-age pensions and sickness benefits, whereas in the USA and Switzerland they are mainly paid for on an individual basis.

The type of government expenditure affects living standards. In many poor countries the uneven distribution of income is further compounded by excessive government expenditure on arms. Expenditure on defence brings no immediate improvement to living standards whereas expenditure on hospitals does.

***Table 7.9* Total outlays of government as a percentage of GNP, 1990**

Country	%
OECD Nations	
Switzerland	29.9
Japan	32.9
USA	36.1
UK	40.9
Germany	45.1
France	49.7
Italy	51.7
Netherlands	56.1
Sweden	60.1
Others	
Malaysia	33.3
Singapore	35.0

Source: OECD and IBRD

Non-monetary transactions

National income accounts measure those transactions where money changes hands. This may omit activities which are economically beneficial. Housework, for example, contributes much to our economy, but most of this effort is not measured as it is done by householders themselves. Conversely, if householders suddenly decided to pay for a housekeeper the value of national income would increase, although there would be no 'real' difference in the output of housework.

This problem assumes more significant dimensions if there is a substantial amount of subsistence agriculture in the economy, i.e. people producing and consuming their own food. In an advanced economy the effect of people growing their own food is insignificant. However, many less developed economies find it necessary to add a significant proportion to their national income calculations to allow for this. In Kenya, for example, 25 per cent is added to the national income to allow for subsistence agriculture in the economy. This is termed the ***non-monetary sector***.

Tax evasion

Many transactions may go unrecorded because people are seeking to evade taxes.

For example, people may 'moonlight' by doing a second job which they do not declare. Payments made in cash are particularly easy to hide from the tax authorities. Because of this, such illegal unrecorded earnings are known as the 'cash economy' (or 'black economy'). People who are receiving social security/welfare payments may hide occasional earnings. Some groups of prostitutes oppose 'legalisation' as this could mean paying taxes. Obviously, it is impossible to be precise, but some estimates place a value on these transactions equal to 8 per cent of the UK GDP. Figure 7.4 shows estimates that have been produced for various countries.

Leisure

Leisure is also a complicating factor when we are trying to assess or compare living standards.

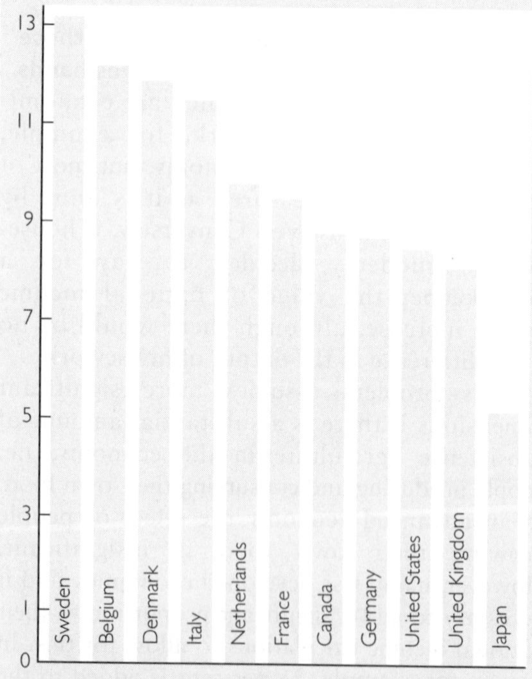

***Fig. 7.4* Estimates of 'black economy' as percentage of GDP**
Source: ISTAT 1990

If the GDP were to remain constant but the average working week were to decline then we could say that the quality of life had improved, even though this would not show up in the GDP figures.

Variations in the working week between different countries complicate comparisons. For example, the GDP per head of the USA is approximately 50 per cent higher than that of the UK, but the working week is shorter in the USA. Thus the disparity in standards is greater than it appears. Similarly, a survey published in 1991 demonstrated that male full-time workers in the UK worked longer hours than in any other EC country.

We might also consider the proportion of the population which works. In the UK almost 50 per cent of the population are in the working population. This is the highest figure in the EU and much higher than in the USA. However, in a less developed country the proportion of the population working would be even higher.

Regrettable necessities

In addition to defence spending, other expenditures might be seen as necessary rather than being wanted for their own sake. The argument is similar to that of final and intermediate goods and the double-counting problem, i.e. ultimately a final good is included as national income as it is wanted for its own sake.

Examples of regrettable necessities may include such expenditures as defence, policing, heating in very cold climates, health care and commuting.

The problem with this concept for the economist is to know when to stop regarding outputs as necessities. Perhaps most of what we consume is simply some form of compensation for an unsatisfying and stressful production process and the lack of the sense of belonging and support that used to be derived from a more community-based lifestyle. Taking this argument to extremes could lead to a claim that national income is zero! This is absurd, but using such arguments the eminent welfare economist E. J. Mishan seriously suggested that real economic growth for rich countries has actually been negative for many years!

Difficulties in international comparisons

In addition to the problems caused by the distribution of income, non-monetary transactions and differing effects of government expenditure, particular problems for international comparisons are caused by 'distortion' due to exchange rates.

In this chapter we have made comparisons in US dollars. Until 1971 the value of the dollar was fixed and was therefore a useful common unit of account. All national income figures could be converted at the existing rate of exchange. However, at the moment most countries' exchange rates float, i.e. their values change from day to day. Thus as exchange rates move against the dollar the estimates for per capita income as measured in dollars also change. For example, in 1988 GNP per capita for Japan was $21 020 and thus more than the $19 840 for the USA, but if the same figures for GNP are measured in dollars at 1990 exchange rates, the figure for Japan becomes $18 658, i.e. less than that for the USA.

When we are considering a large number of nations, each of whose exchange rates is varying, the possibilities for inaccuracy are multiplied. Many of the former Eastern Bloc countries used to quote wildly unrealistic exchange rates thus making comparison almost impossible.

National income and welfare

The problems considered above should persuade us to treat measures of national income cautiously. We should also guard against equating increases in wealth with increases in welfare. We have already noted that factors such as the distribution of income may modify our view of the standard of living in a country. However, to gain a fuller appreciation of the standard of life in a nation we should consider such things as the expectation of life, the crime rate, political stability, the standard of health care, etc.

We must also remember that producing more economic 'goods' such as cars is likely also to give rise to more economic 'bads' such as pollution, congestion and the destruction of the natural environment.

From time to time, attempts have been made to arrive at an alternative measure of the national product which takes into account both the unseen 'pluses', such as leisure, and the 'minuses', such as pollution. The most notable contribution came from Nordhaus and Tobin in their work *Is Growth Obsolete?* They put forward a new measure termed a ***measure of economic welfare*** (MEW). Their measure indicated that welfare has advanced much less rapidly than gross domestic product.

This chapter has listed many problems in attempting to use GNP as a measure of welfare. As with most areas of economic debate, however, there are arguments and evidence both ways. Arguments which suggest that GNP is a useful proxy for improvements in welfare are as follows. First, there is a strong political demand for both more private consumption and better public services. These simultaneous demands can only be achieved on a long term if there is economic growth. Second, even if the old saying 'you cannot buy happiness' is true, there is little hard evidence to suggest that the growth of GNP makes people *less* happy. Indeed, in the short term a growth in GNP may well make people feel better-off even if they subsequently adjust their expectations to this new level of income or are dissatisfied with other aspects of life. Third, the excitement of catching up or overtaking other countries can (some would say sadly) be a source of great national pride and satisfaction.

In 1984 *The Economist* published a survey it had conducted in which it had attempted to rank 23 countries in order of their desirability as places to live and work. The survey included many quantifiable measures such as infant mortality, climate, number of doctors per thousand people and so on? However, it also asked people to rank their preferences, e.g. would they put good health care above political stability, low taxes above adequate defence and so on? This was done 'blind' so that respondents did not know which countries they were considering. The results of the survey are shown in Fig. 7.5. The right-hand column shows *The Economist* ranking and the left-hand column the ranking in order of GDP per capita.

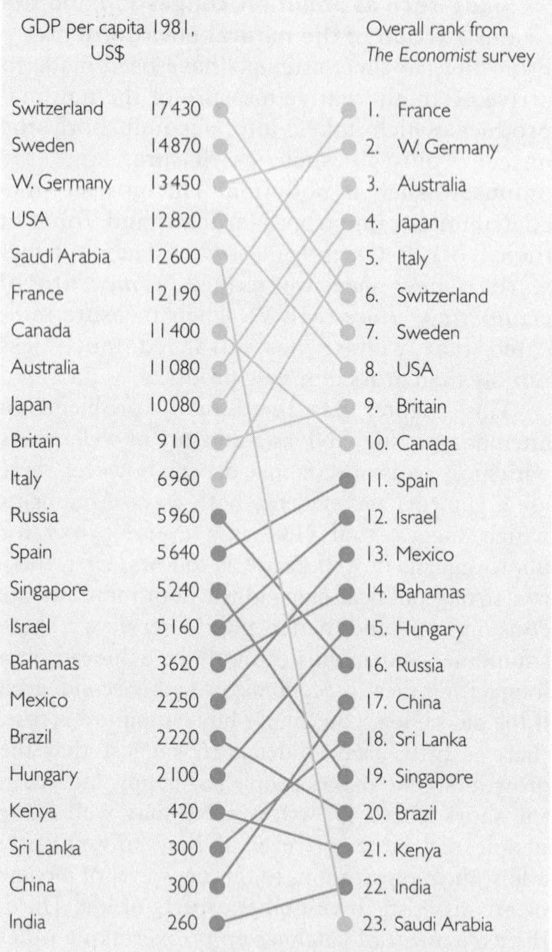

Fig. 7.5 Two measures of the standard of living

The interesting point to emerge from this survey is that, with one notable exception, the ranking produced by the survey did not differ widely from the GDP per capita ranking. As you can see from Fig. 7.5 the top 10 in *The Economist* ranking could all be found in the first 11 in the GDP per capita ranking.

We conclude from this that there are arguments for and against the equating of GNP with welfare. Nevertheless, growth in national income *does* at least record the growth of production capacity within a country. As long as all the shortcomings are borne in mind, the vast majority of economists (and politicians) would regard GDP per capita as at least a reasonable place to start an assessment of a country's living standards.

Summary

1. National income is a measure of the output of goods and services produced, distributed and consumed over a given period of time.
2. Income, expenditure and output are different methods of measuring the same entity.
3. Capital goods form part of the national product. An allowance must be made for depreciation and this is termed capital consumption.
4. Government expenditure and the net figure from foreign trade also form part of the national product.
5. The components of national product may be summarised as:

$$Y = C + I + G + (X - M)$$

6. National expenditure at factor cost is the total of all expenditure on final goods plus any change in the volume of stocks less taxes on expenditure plus subsidies.
7. National income is the total of all incomes excluding transfer payments and stock appreciation.
8. When calculating the national output care must be taken that there is no double counting, i.e. only the value added by each industry should be included.
9. Changes in the 'real' value of national product can be arrived at by using the GNP deflator.
10. Problems are caused in the interpretation of national income accounts and its use as a measure of welfare by:
    a) size of population;
    b) distribution of income;
    c) government expenditure;
    d) non-monetary transactions;
    e) tax evasion;
    f) leisure;
    g) expenditure on regrettable necessities;
    h) the production of economic 'bads' such as pollution.

Questions

1. $Y = C + I + G + (X - M)$. Give the precise names of all the terms in this formula.
2. Distinguish between gross and net investment.

Why is the level of net investment so important? Why is money not considered capital?

3 Distinguish between wealth and income.

4 Many people are turning to 'do-it-yourself' for household improvements. Does the GDP (which includes the cost of DIY components) therefore over- or underestimate the 'true' value of the national product?

5 In 1987 Subtopia had a GDP of $7750 million which had risen to $21 000 million by 1997. Over the same period the GDP deflator rose from 100 to 250. Meanwhile, population had also increased from 54.2 million to 58.7 million. What was the change in the real GDP per capita in Subtopia over this period?

6 Imagine that a simple economy produces nothing but wheat. Total output is 1000 tonnes at a price of £50 per tonne. What is the value of the GDP for the economy? Suppose that output rises to 11 000 tonnes but the price falls to £42 per tonne. Devise a 'deflator index' which will demonstrate the real change in GDP.

7 Suppose that Germany has a population of 77 million and a GDP of DM1250 billion, whereas the UK has a GDP of £244 billion and a population of 56 million. The exchange rate is £1 = DM3. Compare their relative prosperity. What other information would be useful in order to assess the standard of living in the two countries?

8 Explain how it is possible for the standard of living to improve in a society if there is no increase in the real GDP.

9 List and evaluate the factors that you consider important in determining the level of welfare in a society.

10 Why are transfer payments not included in national income? Give a counter-argument for taking account of some transfer payments in measuring output.

11 To what extent does gross national product provide a reliable measure of a nation's standard of living?

Data response A
National income accounts

Table 7.10 presents all the figures necessary for the calculation of the gross national product by the expenditure method. It also contains some figures relevant only to other methods of calculation.

1 Prepare a statement of national product by the expenditure method. This should show:
   a) GDP at market prices;
   b) GDP at factor cost;
   c) GNP at factor cost;
   d) Net national product.

Table 7.10 **Figures for the calculation of GNP**

National income accounts	*£m*
Imputed charge for the consumption of non-trading capital	230
Value of physical increase in stocks and work in progress	+461
Gross trading profits of companies	4750
Exports of goods and services	6614
Adjustments for financial services	249
Net property income from abroad	+450
Consumers' expenditure	23 120
Subsidies	571
Capital consumption	3000
Stock appreciation	+507
Imports of goods and services	6972
General government final consumption	6011
Gross domestic fixed capital formation	6630
Total domestic expenditure	36222
Taxes on expenditure	4922

2 Discuss the difficulties involved in compliling national income accounts.

3 What information other than national income data would be useful in attempting to assess the standard of living in a country?

Data respogse B
Health, wealth and happiness

Read the following two articles. The first is taken from the *Daily Mail* of 25 May 1991 and the second from the *Daily Telegraph* of 23 May 1991. Both are based on the Human Development Reports of the United Nations for succeeding years. (You will find other sections of the book useful in answering the questions.)

Britain's top ten spot for the quality of life

Jackl Davis,
Consumer Affairs Correspondent

The quality of life in Britain is tenth best in the world and better than in West Germany and America, according to a United Nations report.

Japan tops the list, followed by Sweden and Switzerland, while West Germany is two places behind the UK and the US is in 19th position. Niger in west central Africa is in last place.

The report was compiled by a group of leading economists from around the world led by the former finance minister of Pakistan, Mahbub ul Haq.

Its authors say the index is most useful for measuring differences between developing countries, because levels of purchasing power, literacy and life expectancy in most industrialised countries are well above basic levels.

Industrialised countries tend to cluster together, with only five years' difference in life expectancy and four per cent difference in literacy rates among the 19 highest ranked countries, says the report.

Literacy

The index shows Britain – with a life expectancy of 76, a 99 per cent literacy rate and real national wealth per head of population of £7,347 – in tenth place, but little separates it from the top country, Japan.

The report points out that there is no automatic link between a country's wealth and its people's well-being. America's real national wealth per head of population is £10,547, the highest of the top 20 countries, but it comes only 19th in the index.

The report's authors say America's low ranking is explained by the large number of different ethnic communities in its population, with lower health, nutritional and education levels than average.

'The USA is not one society, but several societies. For instance, among the black community in Harlem and New York the life expectancy is just 46 years, lower than Bangladesh and Africa and 30 years lower than the national average in the USA,' said Mr ul Haq.

West Germany's large population of immigrant Turkish workers, with much lower standards of living than average, helps push it below Britain on the index.

'It is also partly because Germany has devoted far less to human development levels and social security systems,' added Mr ul Haq.

He said Japan's place at the top of the index was achieved not only because of its huge economic success, but also because it is virtually a one-race nation with no ethnic minorities, due to a strict immigration policy.

The Soviet Union is in a lowly 26th place on the index. Its life expectancy of only 70, real national wealth per head of population of £3,592, and a much higher than average level of military spending combine to put it below regimes including East Germany and Czechoslovakia.

Modest

The report shows that high levels of human development can be achieved at even modest income levels, so long as people are placed at the centre of policies. But in some Third World countries money is poured into the military at the expense of basic necessities, with soldiers outnumbering physicians eight -to-one and the ratio of soldiers to teachers is as high as five-to-one.

Military expenditure in developing countries has increased three times as fast as in industrialised nations over the last 30 years, and in some of the poorest countries, military spending is two to three times larger than their spending on education and health.

But Costa Rica, which abolished its army in 1948, ranks 28th in the index with a life expectancy of 75 years, a literacy rate of 93 per cent and its national wealth per head of population of £2,251. The report says most developing countries could do more for their people by cutting military spending, inefficient state enterprises, unnecessary government controls and social subsidies which benefit the rich.

But is says significant progress has been made in developing countries in the last 30 years, with life expectancy up from 46 to 62 years, adult literacy up from 43 per cent to more than 60 per cent, a halving of child mortality rates and nutrition levels up by 20 per cent.

* *Human Development Report 1990, published for the UN Development Programme by the Oxford University Press.*

How we were judged

The list produced by the United Nations Development Programme ranks 130 countries according to a human development index. This goes much further than previous studies which concentrated on a country's wealth. The index combines factors such as life expectancy, adult literacy and purchasing power into a simple measure to show how economic growth translates into human well-being.

Source: *Daily Mail*, 25 May 1991

Britain lags in league of happiness

Clare Hargreaves

Britain is the eleventh most developed country in the world, but in some ways one of the unhappiest, with the highest divorce rate and one of the largest proportion of prisoners in Europe, according to a United Nations report published yesterday.

In terms of basic freedom, such as the right to hold multiparty elections, press freedom and the right to travel and assemble, Britain ranks only sixteenth, well below Scandinavian countries, France, Germany and the United States. Iraq comes bottom.

The findings are contained in a Human Development Report produced by the New York-based United Nations Development Programme. To reach their conclusions, the authors drew up two indexes: a Human Development Index and a Human Freedom Index.

The Human Development Index, which surveys 160 countries, is based on 'quality of life' variables such as life expectancy and adult literacy, as well as on basic purchasing power.

The Human Freedom Index, a new device based on 1985 data from 88 countries, uses indicators endorsed by a number of international treaties such as the UN Universal Declaration of Human Rights.

Britain was found to have the highest proportion of prisoners in Western Europe, with 98 people in every 100,000 in jail. It also has the highest rate of broken marriages in Europe, with $4\frac{1}{2}$ per cent of people over 25 divorced.

In 1989 more than 400,000 people in Britain were officially classified as homeless. of which 196,000 were children. An estimated 120,000 were living in bed and breakfast hotels, half of which were unfit for habitation.

In Western industrial countries about 100 million people live below the poverty line. In the United States more than 13 per cent of the population have an annual income below the poverty line.

In terms of human development, Japan comes top, with Sierra Leone ranked bottom. Britain has slipped one place since last year.

Development in the Third World has improved during the past three decades, with average life expectancy up by 16 years and adult literacy by 40 per cent. But a quarter of the developing world's inhabitants still lack basic necessities. For example:

- ☐ More than one billion people live in absolute poverty.
- ☐ About 180 million children, one in three, suffer from serious malnutrition.
- ☐ One and a half billion people are deprived of primary health care and nearly three million children die each year from immunisable diseases.

Continue on page 96

☐ About a billion adults cannot read or write.

Countries which have high levels of human development also rank high in human freedom.

There are some exceptions, such as Botswana and Senegal, which rank fairly high in human freedom but low in human development.

Conversely, countries such as Chile and South Africa, which rank high in development, lacked many freedoms in 1985 when the survey was carried out.

The real cause of human neglect is often a lack of political commitment rather than of financial resources.

Source: *Daily Telegraph*, 23 May 1991

Human development index		*Human freedom index*	
Top 10	*Bottom 10*	*Top 10*	*Bottom 10*
1. Japan	151. G-Bissau	1. Sweden	79. Pakistan
2. Canada	152. Chad	2. Denmark	80. Zaire
3. Iceland	153. Djibouti	3. Holland	81. Bulgaria
4. Sweden	154. B Faso	4. Finland	82. USSR
5. Switzerland	155. Niger	5. N Zealand	83. S Africa
6. Norway	156. Mali	6. Austria	84. China
7. America	157. Afghanistan	7. Norway	85. Ethiopia
8. Holland	158. Guinea	8. France	86. Romania
9. Australia	159. Gambia	9. Germany	87. Libya
10. France	160. S Leone	10. Belgium	88. Iraq
Britain is 11th in the table		Britain is 16th in the list	

Source: The Human Development Report 1991, Oxford University Press

1 What factors do you consider to be the best indicators of the standard of living and why?
2 In evaluating the relative positions of different nations (especially the wealthy) why is the exchange rate so crucial?
3 The two articles relate to much the same period (the 1980s). How and why do they manage to come to such apparently differing conclusions?

part 2
The microeconomic system

SECTION II Markets and price

SECTION II Markets and prices

'We must look at the price system as a mechanism for communicating information if we want to understand its real function.'

Friedrich August von Hayek

'Now Maple were Sam's Mon-o-po-ly; That means it were all 'is to cut. And nobody else 'adn't got none; So 'e asked Noah three ha'pence a foot.'

Marriott Edgar for Stanley Holloway

8 The price system

Learning outcomes

At the end of this chapter you will be able to:

- Choose the right kind of economic model to answer different types of question.
- Understand the difference between microeconomic and macroeconomic problems.

The first part of this book was a general survey of some of the important areas of the subject. We now commence our detailed study of economics. In the next three sections we will be concerned with the study of microeconomics. This is primarily an analysis of how markets work. The remaining four sections of the book in Part 3, then deal with macroeconomic topics.

The circular flow compared with the price system

It is tempting to try to reconcile the micro- and macroeconomic views of the subject. Figure 8.1 recapitulates the view of the price system as put forward in Chapter 5 and the circular flow of income from Chapter 7. With some slight amendments to the nomenclature, the two can apparently be made compatible. Indeed this is done in some textbooks. This, however, is misleading since the two views tell us different things about the economy. In the price system diagram you can see that the 'arrows' of demand and supply collide to form market prices and factor prices. This view of the economy is helpful in explaining how the price of a product is determined, as well as how the relative prices of products are determined and how they change; for example, it tells us how the price of carrots might change as a result of a change in the price of cauliflowers. However, it has little to tell us about how the general level of all prices is determined. For this we must turn to the macro view.

In the circular flow diagram we see a dynamic, i.e. moving, view of the economy. Here expenditure gives rise to income and income gives rise to expenditure, which are passed round in an endless flow. There is no clash of opposing forces as in the price system view.

Which view is correct? The answer is that neither presents a totally satisfactory picture of all aspects of the economy. The price system view is good for explaining some aspects and the circular flow view for others.

The circular flow view of the economy is the work of Keynes and his followers from the 1930s. The price system view is that developed by the classical economists from Adam Smith onwards. There is an unfortunate tendency for economists (and politicians) to take up entrenched positions and insist that one view of the economy is superior to all others. This is mistaken because, at present, no one theory can fully explain all that occurs in an economy.

Students should look at all theories and use those parts of them which can be proved to be reasonable. This has, in fact, been the basis of mainstream economics since the Second World War. The blending of the old ideas of the classicists and the ideas of Keynesians has been termed ***the neo-classical synthesis***.

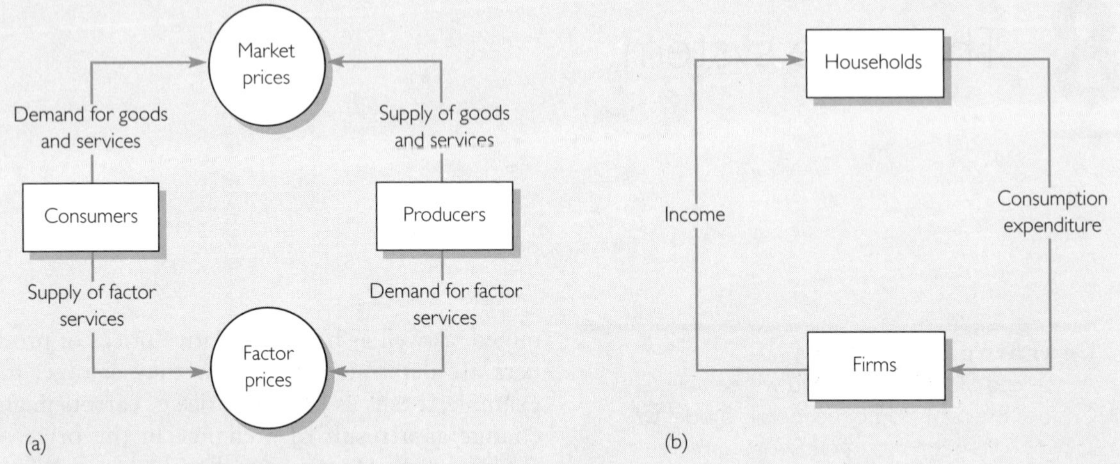

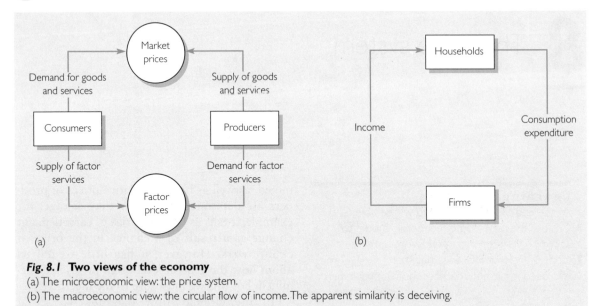

Fig. 8.1 **Two views of the economy**
(a) The microeconomic view: the price system.
(b) The macroeconomic view: the circular flow of income. The apparent similarity is deceiving.

STUDENT ACTIVITY 8.1

Identify each of the problems below as mainly microeconomic or macroeconomic in character (some may have a degree of both!).

1. Why did the rate of inflation rise in 1990?
2. What effect did the falling rates of interest have on investment and savings in 1996?
3. Why did the value of the pound against the Deutschmark rise dramatically between 1996 and 1997?
4. Why is the price of organic vegetables higher than ordinary vegetables?
5. How do schools reduce costs when government spending cutbacks reduce their budgets?

You should try to answer questions 4 and 5 in particular.

Market prices and factor prices

As we now continue to study the workings of the price system it should be remembered that it explains not only the price of consumer goods and services, such as food or cars, but also the price of factors of production. In Fig. 8.2 you can see that the price of a product (chocolate) can be treated in just the same way as the price of a factor (wages). Therefore as we study the price system we are looking at an explanation, not just of how the price of certain things is formed but how the price of everything in the economy is determined.

Why study the market?

We study the market because it provides answers to the three fundamental questions of economic society: 'What?', 'How?' and 'For whom?' With all the shortcomings it is still the most complete explanation of how economic society functions. It offers an explanation of not only consumers' behaviour but also that of businesses as well.

When it comes to assessing the market system we shall see that there are two different problems. First, there are those which are concerned with influences within the system itself. Thus, for example, we can demonstrate how imperfections in markets, such as the existence of monopoly, lead to an inefficient use of resources and a loss of 'welfare'. In this respect the price system is most important in giving us a reference standard by which we can judge economic efficiency. Second, there are the ***normative*** questions which

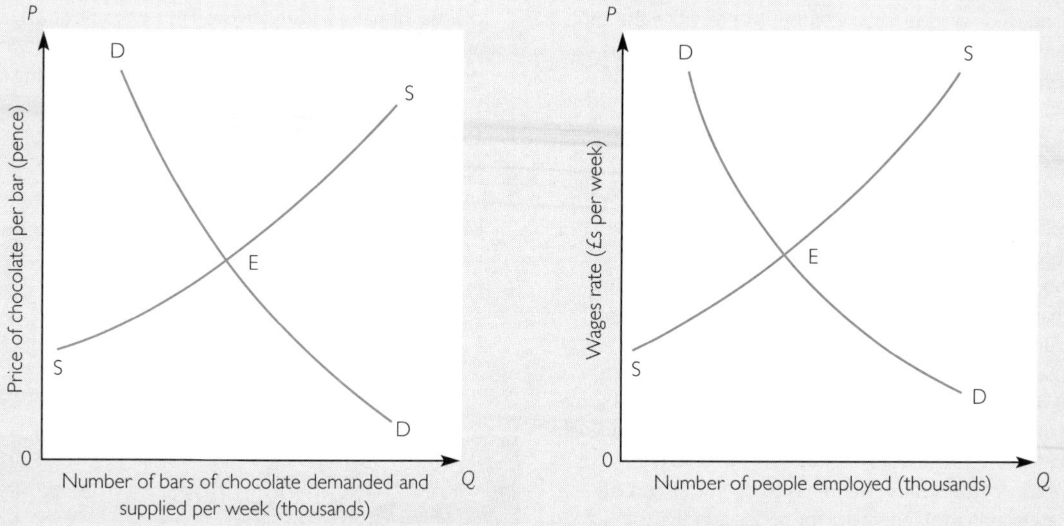

Fig. 8.2 **The price of a product can be treated in the same way as the price of a factor**

lie outside the system. Two of these have already been considered. There is the distribution of wealth and income, both of which, as we have seen, are very unevenly distributed; the theory of the price system has nothing to say about this. There is also the problem that the price system does not seem terribly good at providing such items as defence and education. Once again we are here concerned with society making ***normative judgements*** about what ought to be provided. These problems form the subject of Section IV of the book, where we consider modern welfare economics.

Summary

1 The price system and the circular flow present alternative views of the economy, neither of which is completely satisfactory.
2 The price system attempts to explain the price of all things in the economy.
3 The price system gives not only an explanation of the economy but also a measure of its efficiency.
4 The main areas of shortcoming in the price system form the subject matter of modern welfare economics.

Questions

1 What questions is microeconomics trying to answer; which questions are better left to macroeconomics to answer?
2 Give examples of normative microeconomic questions.
3 Give four examples of how governments interfere in the price system.

Data response A
Micro- and macroeconomics

Read the following passage, which is taken from Heilbroner and Thurow's *The Economic Problem*. Then attempt the questions which follow.

What is **microeconomics**, as contrasted with macroeconomics? Why do we study it separately, instead of joining the two together in a unified study of the operation of the economy as a whole?

The answer is that we study economics from two different perspectives because we need two different approaches to the economic world to understand two different kinds of problems we find in that world. Both micro- and macroeconomics are relevant for the study of **how we produce and how we distribute wealth**. The difference is that one approach, as we saw in our discussion of Adam Smith emphasises the total production or distribution of the system, while the other – as Smith's treatise also made clear – concerns the composition of output and the determination of individual incomes within that total flow.

The fact that we need two approaches to illuminate the movement of the economy as a whole and the currents within the economy does not mean that we will not constantly be using the same concepts, such as supply and demand or the laws of production, in both inquiries. Rather, it reflects the fact that the problems characteristic of micro- or macroeconomics become blurred when we use the approach of one to examine the other.

The fallacy of composition is also involved here: some truths at the micro level are untruths at the macro level and vice versa. Take, for example, the problem of inflation. Obviously, inflation has to do with the relation between the total demand for goods and the total supply of goods. Inflation has often been described as 'too much money chasing too few goods'. This problem lends itself naturally to an analysis that begins with the aggregative approach to demand, such as that implicit in national income, or an aggregative conception of supply, suggested by **gross national output**. But it is very hard to grasp the problem of inflation if we begin at the other end of the scale, where we concentrate on the production of particular goods or the demands of particular individuals or groups of individuals. To put it differently, microeconomics will help us understand why prices rise in, say, the market for beef or wheat, cars or houses, but it is less helpful in explaining why prices rise in all markets simultaneously.

Economists thus use two lenses to study the economy: one to see the actions and interactions of its individual participants; one to see the economy in a bigger scale. Neither perspective by itself is sufficient. In particular, a view through the macro lens does not tell us much about the process of allocating resources to various uses or distributing income within an economic society. Macroeconomics, as we will see, is interested in the size of total output, but it throws almost no analytical light on whether that output consists of Cadillacs or Chevrolets, or of bread or cake. So, too, macroeconomics is interested in the size of total incomes, but it does not explain why income is divided in such unequal shares.

At the same time, microeconomics by itself is inadequate. It tells us a great deal about Chevrolets and Cadillacs, bread and cake, but it does not tell us whether total income and output will be large or small. Yet there is clearly some relation between the proportions of Cadillacs to Chevrolets or cake to bread and the level of wealth that a society enjoys. Thus we cannot fully analyse the motives of microeconomic behaviour without taking into account the macroeconomic setting for that behaviour.

1 Explain the terms printed in bold type as fully as possible.
2 What factors would affect the output of bread? What different factors would affect total output in the economy?
3 What factors would affect the price of bread? What different factors would affect the rate of inflation?

Data response B
A recent history of intervention

Study the following passage, written soon after the Labour government's election in 1997, and then answer the questions based on it.

The history of the Conservative government of the UK from 1979 to 1997 is a story of the reduction of the role of the state. This statement is true of production for the entire period as the government progressively privatised almost every nationalised industry. As the state divested itself of road haulage, telecommunications, gas, airline, electricity and rail industries, it became progressively more careful to ensure that competition existed in these industries. From about 1988 onwards it turned its attention to the welfare state. In the cases of health and education, it was not considered appropriate to return them to the private sector because equity and equality of opportunity are considered more important than a consumer's ability to pay in these services. This did not stop them from introducing market principles in these areas, by creating competition between schools and between hospitals, and making the money follow pupils and patients to the successful organisations. Where competition was not possible franchises or tendering processes were introduced. Hospital laundry and catering, local authority refuse collection, and even rail services were organised on a franchise basis. The market was introduced in every possible way in every nook and cranny of the public sector.

The same cannot be said for the economy as a whole in the latter half of this period. In the first major recession of this period of government, the doctrinaire monetarist government of Mrs Thatcher continued to try and reduce state spending and balance the budget. When the scourge of recession returned in the early nineties Mr

Major's government used fiscal policy to help the economy to recover. Intervention was back on the agenda.

With the accession of Mr Blair's Labour government in 1997, the market seems set to remain the government's favourite solution to economic problems. With no renationalisation being mooted at present, and an attachment to flexible labour markets, it seems as though there has been no fundamental change in the attitude of government towards the market in the immediate period after the election. Minor reforms are in the pipeline, however. The proposal for a minimum wage, the reform of the internal market in the NHS and a major review of environmental policy are all due in 1998. This suggests the government does not believe that the market is a panacea for all ills. State intervention is beginning slowly to reassert itself, although at present it is lacking in self-confidence.

1 Which of the Conservative government's policies can be thought of as microeconomics and which as macroeconomics?
2 Why were education and health not considered suitable for the private sector?
3 In what ways has the Labour government shifted back towards state intervention?
4 How can you create competition without privatisation?

9 Demand and utility

Learning outcomes

At the end of this chapter you will be able to:

- Distinguish between normal, inferior and Giffen goods.
- Separate the income and substitution effects of a price change.
- List some reservations about utility theory.
- Understand the principle of consumer equilibrium.

Market demand and individual demand

In this chapter we will complete our look at the theory of demand. The first part of the chapter deals with the fundamentals of ***market demand***; it is extremely important for the student to understand these. In the remainder of the chapter we look at the theory of ***individual demand***. There is no incompatibility between the two, since market demand is made up of the demands of all the individuals in the market. The market demand curve can be seen as a horizontal summation of individual demand curves. This is illustrated in Fig. 9.1.

Determinants of demand

The first law of demand – again

We have so far examined market demand and stated that it is the total quantity of a product which is demanded at a particular price over a given period of time. The first law of demand tells us that, *ceteris paribus*, a greater quantity will be demanded if the price is lowered. This is the most important determinant of demand; the

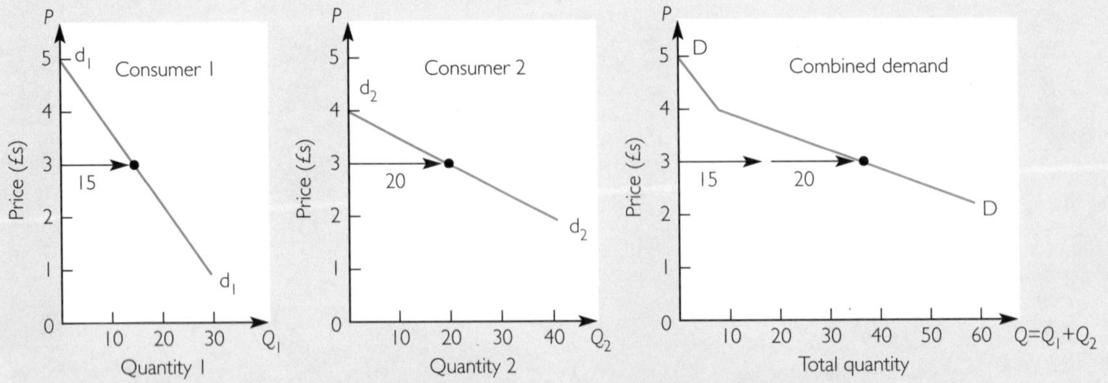

Fig. 9.1 **The market demand curve is a horizontal summation of individual demand curves**
At any price, e.g. £3, we add the quantities demanded by each consumer to produce the market demand.

determinants of demand other than price are referred to as the conditions of demand.

There are a number of exceptions to the first law of demand, i.e. situations when a fall in the price of a good actually causes people to buy less of it, or a rise in price causes them to buy more.

a) *Snob goods*. With some expensive items, e.g. a Rolls-Royce, or Chanel perfume, the consumer may buy the commodity *because* it is expensive. The price is part of the attraction of the article and a rise in price may render it more attractive.
b) *Speculative demand*. This is where purchasers believe that a change in price is the herald of further price changes. On a stock exchange, for example, a rise in the price of a share often tempts people to buy it and vice versa. The housing market also can be seen to work like this, particularly during price booms and slumps.
c) *Giffen goods*. Sir Robert Giffen, a nineteenth-century statistician and economist, noticed that a fall in the price of bread caused the labouring classes to buy less bread and vice versa. Giffen saw this as a refutation of the first law of demand. It is now recognised as an exception rather than a refutation. A more detailed discussion of the Giffen good is left until after some key concepts have been developed, but Student activity 9.1 provides a practical example.

STUDENT ACTIVITY 9.1

As a poverty-stricken student you have devised the following simple rules for your shopping because you promised your father you wouldn't go into debt. Your weekly income of £50 is mostly accounted for by £35 rent and £5 for the electricity and gas meter that you share. The remaining £10 is spent on food. You buy four loaves of bread and a tub of margarine each week because you are addicted to toast. It is not possible for you to live without eating two chocolate bars a week (there is no such thing as one chocolate bar). You always eat a kilo of sausages because you promised your mother that you'd keep up your protein intake. She also insisted on vegetables for vitamins, so you always buy four kilos of vegetables. You prefer carrots and cauliflower but if it has to be potatoes, it has to be potatoes. If there is any money left it goes on chocolate. Using the prices below work out your shopping list. Recalculate it if the price of potatoes falls to 25p a kilo. Have potatoes followed the 'law of demand'?

	Price
Loaf of bread	50p
Tub of margarine	£1
Kilo of potatoes	50p
Kilo of sausages	£2.50
Chocolate bar	25p
Carrots	£1
Cauliflower	£1

Income

Since ***effective demand*** is the desire to buy a good backed by the ability to do so, it is obvious that there must be a relationship between the demand for a firm's product and the consumer's purchasing power. Purchasing power is usually closely linked to income. The nature of the relationship between income and demand will depend upon the type of product considered and the level of consumers' income. Under normal circumstances a rise in income is hardly likely to send most consumers out to buy more bread, whereas it might cause them to buy a new car.

***Ceteris paribus*, if the demand for a commodity increases as income increases it is said to be a normal good.**

In Fig. 9.2 line (a) represents the income demand curve for ***normal goods***. As you can see, demand rises continuously with income. However, the graph tends to flatten out at higher levels of income because people will not want more and more cars and more and more swimming pools, etc. For some normal goods the income demand curve will flatten very quickly as people reach their desired level of consumption of, say, fresh vegetables.

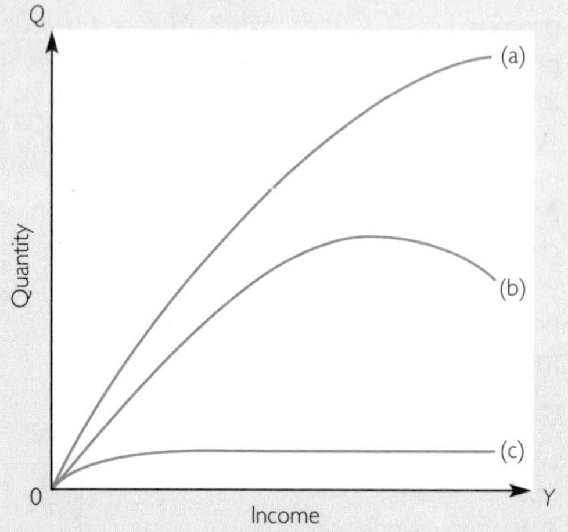

***Fig. 9.2* Income and demand**
(a) Normal goods, (b) Inferior goods, (c) Inexpensive foodstuff, e.g. salt.

With a small number of products, usually inexpensive foodstuffs such as salt, the demand tends to remain constant at all but the very lowest levels of income. The income demand curve for such products is shown by line (c) in Fig. 9.2.

Inferior goods

The final possibility, line (b) in Fig. 9.2, is that demand will decline as income increases. Such products are termed inferior goods and may be defined as follows:

> ***Ceteris paribus*, if, as income rises, the demand for a product goes down it is said to be an inferior good.**

The effect may be observed with products such as bread and potatoes. At low levels of income people will tend to consume large amounts of these products but, as their incomes rise, they will buy other foods – more meat, fish, fruit, etc. – and thus require less bread and potatoes.

You should note that the demand for inferior goods behaves like the demand for normal goods at lower levels of income. All ***inferior goods*** start out as normal goods and become inferior only as income continues to rise. For example, cotton sheets might be considered inferior if, as you become very wealthy, you substitute silk sheets. In other words the goods are not intrinsically inferior, but become inferior as income rises. In different periods of history, different products will be inferior as income rises over time.

The price of other goods

The demand for all goods is interrelated in the sense that they all compete for consumers' limited income. This relationship is obviously too generalised to be measured, but there are two particular interrelationships of demand which may be quantified: where goods are ***substitutes*** one for another, or where they are ***complementary***. Examples of substitute commodities would be tea and coffee, or butter and margarine. Complementary products are demanded jointly, for instance cars and petrol, or strawberries and cream. In all these cases there is a relationship between the price of one commodity and the demand for the other. This is illustrated in Fig. 9.3. In Fig. 9.3 (a) you can see that as the price of cars is lowered so the demand for petrol increases, whereas in Fig. 9.3 (b) as the price of butter increases so the demand for margarine increases.

In the case of the determinants of demand we have discussed above – price, income and the price of other goods – the relationships are quantifiable and we have been able to illustrate them with graphs. In the next chapter we will place precise mathematical values upon these relationships. However, many factors which influence demand are not so readily quantifiable. Some of these are considered below.

Other factors influencing demand

a) *Tastes, habits and customs*. These are extremely important as most people tend to continue their habits of eating etc. A change in taste in favour of a commodity causes an increase in demand.
b) *Changes in population*. Demand is influenced both by the overall size of the population and by the age, sex and geographical distribution. If the proportion of children rises in a society, more education will be demanded.
c) *Seasonal factors*. The demand for many products such as clothing, food and power is influenced by the season.

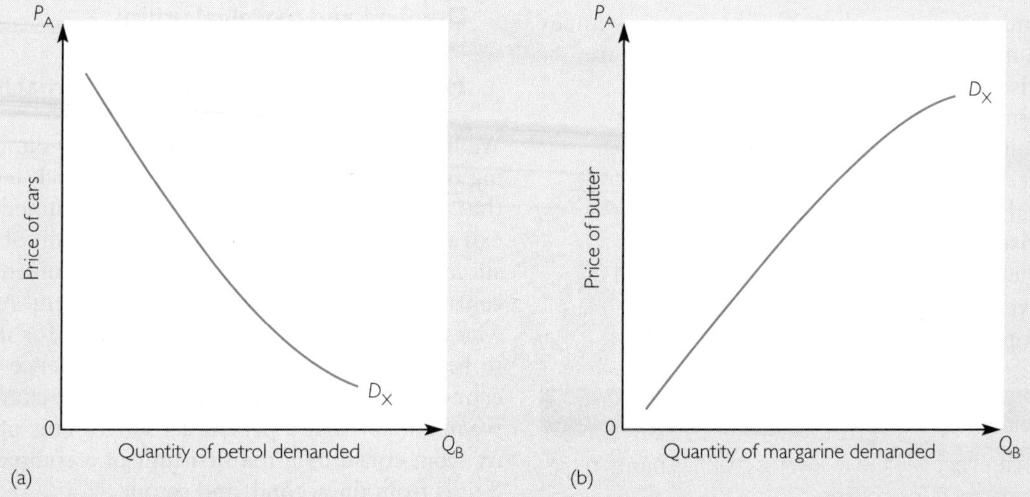

Fig. 9.3 **The price of other goods determines demand**
(a) Complements. A fall in the price of cars increases the demand for petrol.
(b) Substitutes. A rise in the price of butter causes an increase in the demand for margarine.

d) *The distribution of income.* It is not only the level of income which influences demand but also the distribution of income. A more even distribution of income, for example, might increase the demand for hi-fi equipment but decrease the demand for luxury yachts.

e) *Advertising.* A successful advertising campaign obviously increases the demand for a product, but may also be designed to emphasise the characteristics of a product which make it different from its substitutes. This idea is explored further in the next chapter on elasticity. Informative advertising may actually make the market mechanism work better by giving consumers the information they need to make the best purchasing decisions. Persuasive advertising uses people's emotions (envy, greed, sexual attraction, machismo, pride) rather than information to shift their expenditure.

STUDENT ACTIVITY 9.2

Taking current newspaper, magazine or television adverts as your example, decide whether the advert is mainly informative or persuasive.

f) *Government influences.* The government influences demand by legislation.
The government has made it compulsory to fit seat belts in school minibuses, which obviously increases the demand for them.
The government has restricted the purchase and use of certain types of guns, thus reducing the demand for them.

Common misunderstanding

Students are often tempted to say that supply is a determinant of demand; this is not so. Supply influences demand only via the price of a commodity. Similarly, indirect taxes such as VAT are not a demand but a supply influence since they affect the cost of production (see Chapter 11).

An increase in demand

A change in the price of a commodity can be shown to result in a movement up or down the demand curve. However, if we change one of the conditions of demand this will cause an increase or decrease in demand which can be shown as a movement to the right, or left, of the whole demand curve. Figure 9.4 shows an increase in demand for commodity X. The circumstances which might have caused such an increase are:

a) a rise in consumers' income if X is a normal good;
b) a fall in consumers' income if X is an inferior good;
c) a fall in the price of a complement;
d) a rise in the price of a substitute;
e) other circumstances such as a successful advertising campaign which change people's tastes.

STUDENT ACTIVITY 9.3

What effect will the following changes have on the demand for coffee?

a) An increase in people's income due to economic growth.
b) A fall in the price of tea.
c) An increase in the price of milk and cream.
d) A government health report suggesting that too much coffee is bad for your heart.
e) An increase in the price of beer.

Did you decide that coffee was an inferior or a normal good? What did you think were its close substitutes and complements?

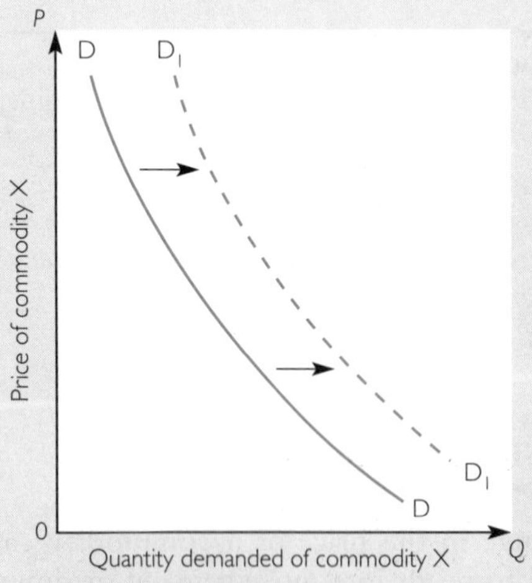

Fig. 9.4 **An increase in demand**
This is brought about by a change in the conditions of demand, *not* by a fall in the price of commodity X.

Demand and marginal utility

Marginal utility or cardinalist approach

We have already encountered the law of diminishing marginal utility (see Chapter 5), which tells us that as more of a commodity is consumed, the extra utility derived from the consumption of each successive unit becomes smaller. In the nineteenth century many economists, among them Alfred Marshall, believed that it was possible for utility to be measured in ***cardinal numbers***. Hence these economists are termed cardinalists. For example, we might say that a person derives 10 utils of utility from consuming the first unit of a commodity, 8 utils from the second, and so on.

No objective method of measuring the satisfaction that consumers enjoy from goods has ever been devised. It does, however, accord with subjective experience that different satisfaction is gained from consuming different goods. We can therefore learn something by following this approach a little further.

Equimarginal utility

Table 9.1 gives some hypothetical figures showing the total and marginal utility derived by a consumer from consumption of product X. Consuming 1 unit of X gives 15 utils of satisfaction, consuming 2 units gives 25 utils, and so on. The figures for marginal utility decline as each successive unit is consumed. If the consumer goes on consuming more and more units, eventually we see that the sixth unit yields no extra satisfaction at all, and, should a seventh unit be consumed, total utility actually decreases so that marginal utility becomes negative. Negative utility is referred to as disutility.

If we assume that consumers are utility maximisers, i.e. they wish to obtain as much utility as they can then, subject to no other constraints, the consumer in Table 9.1 would consume 5 units of X, where total utility is greatest. However, we must now consider two complicating factors:

a) The consumer's income is limited.
b) The consumer must distribute expenditure between many different commodities.

Table 9.1 Diminishing marginal utility

Units of X consumed	*Total utility (utils)*	*Marginal utility (utils)*
0	0	
1	15	15
2	25	10
3	33	8
4	38	5
5	40	2
6	40	0
7	39	−1

Assume that the consumer has a choice between two products, X and Y. If X and Y both cost £1 each, and the consumer has £1 to spend, then, obviously, the commodity which yields the greater utility will be bought. If we were to apply this principle to each successive unit of the consumer's spending, we could conclude that utility will be maximised when income has been allocated in such a way that the utility derived from one extra pound's worth of X is equal to the utility derived from the consumption of one extra pound's worth of Y. If this condition is not fulfilled then the consumer could obviously increase the total utility derived by switching expenditure from X to Y or vice versa. For example, a consumer would not spend a pound more on vegetables if it was considered that the same pound spent on meat would give more satisfaction, or in the reverse situation would not spend a pound extra on meat (or nuts if you are a vegetarian) if the consumer considered that the same pound spent on vegetables would yield greater satisfaction. This fits in with the common phrase used when people are deciding whether to buy something: 'is it good value for money?'

The extra satisfaction derived from the consumption of one more unit of X is its marginal utility which we can write as MU_X and that of Y as MU_Y, etc. We must also consider the relative price of X and Y which we can write as P_X and P_Y. We can then see that the ***utility-maximising condition*** is fulfilled when:

$$\frac{MU_X}{P_X} = \frac{MU_Y}{P_Y}$$

Any number of commodities may then be added to the equation. Table 9.2 gives hypothetical marginal utility figures for a consumer who wishes to distribute expenditure of £44 between three commodities, X, Y and Z.

Table 9.2 Equimarginal utility

Kg consumed	*Marginal utility derived from each kg of:* X (£8/kg)	Y (£4/kg)	Z (£2/kg)
1	72	60	64
2	48	44	56
3	40	32	40
4	36	24	28
5	32	20	16
6	20	8	12
7	12	4	8

In order to maximise utility, the consumer must distribute available income so that:

$$\frac{MU_X}{P_X} = \frac{MU_Y}{P_Y} = \frac{MU_Z}{P_Z}$$

By studying the table you can see that this yields a selection where the consumer buys 2 kg of X, 4 kg of Y and 6 kg of Z. Hence:

$$\frac{48}{8} = \frac{24}{4} = \frac{12}{2}$$

If the consumer wishes to spend all the £44 it is impossible to distribute it any other way which would yield greater total utility. You can check this by totalling the marginal utilities for various other combinations.

This theorem, which we may term the concept of ***equimarginal utilities***, should be carefully studied by the student, for it frequently forms the basis of data response or multiple choice questions.

STUDENT ACTIVITY 9.4

An individual derives the utility in Table 9.3 from consuming different quantities of three products: cheese, lamb and steak. The consumer lives in an ideal climate where it is only necessary to consume food in order to live. If this worries you, assume you make your own clothing.

Table 9.3 **Marginal utility**

Kilos	*Cheese*		*Lamb*		*Steak*	
	MU	*MU/P*	*MU*	*MU/P*	*MU*	*MU/P*
1	44		45		75	
2	30		36		60	
3	22		33		57	
4	20		31		55	
5	19		30		54	

(Hint: It is neccesary to calculate values for the second column in each case in order to work out consumer equilibrium.)

What will the individual's consumption be if:

a) The price in pounds per kilo is cheese 2; lamb 3; steak 5; and income is £35?
b) All the conditions in a) apply except the price of steak rises to £6 per kilo? Which is a better substitute for steak, lamb or cheese? Is steak consumption very sensitive to price for this income group?
c) All the conditions in a) apply except income falls to £12. Are all the products normal goods? Which products rise most strongly with income?
d) Could you construct an individual demand curve using this information?

If you are vegetarian substitute honey and nuts for lamb and steak. If you are a vegan, you could use soya, nuts and apples. Students are not recommended to follow the diet suggested by this exercise.

The demand curve

The marginal utility approach gives us a rationalisation of the demand curve. Suppose that, starting from a condition of equilibrium, the price of X falls relative to Y. We now have a condition where the utility from the last penny spent on X will be greater than the utility from the last penny spent on Y. Mathematically this can be written as:

$$\frac{MU_X}{P_X} > \frac{MU_Y}{P_Y}$$

In order to restore the equilibrium the consumer will buy more of X (and less of Y), thus reducing the marginal utility of X. The consumer will continue substituting X for Y until equilibrium is achieved. Thus we have attained the normal demand relationship that, other things being equal, as the price of X falls, more of it is bought. We have therefore a normal downward-sloping demand curve. The demand curve we have derived is the individual's demand curve for a product. The market demand curve can then be obtained by aggregating all the individual demand curves.

Income effects and substitution effects

When Marshall invented the demand curve he knew that there was one small logical flaw in its construction. When a price falls, there are two separate effects which change the quantity demanded. First there is the ***substitution effect*** which results in the consumer substituting one product for another as relative prices change. For instance, as the price of coffee goes up, some people may switch to drinking more tea. The second effect is the ***income effect.*** When a price goes down it increases the ***real value*** of people's income. They can buy all the goods they previously bought but now they will have a small amount of money left over with which they can buy something else. This is where the logical problem arises: when we originally constructed our demand curves we assumed that all other things except price remained equal (or *ceteris paribus*). You will be able to see now that this is not the case. When a price change occurs, consumers' real income changes. Money or ***nominal income*** can remain the same, but ***real income*** can change if prices change. Real income is what you can buy with your money income. Most people experience this difference when there is inflation. If their money income remains the same but prices in the economy are going up, then they will feel worse off because their real income is going down. They will be able to buy less with their money.

Marshall assumed that in most cases the income effect is so small that it can be safely ignored. There are some cases, however, where it is large enough to make a considerable difference. One is the case of Giffen goods, discussed in the next section. The income effect is also very important in the argument about tax rates and work incentives discussed in Chapter 30.

Giffen goods

The Giffen paradox referred to above can now be explained in more detail. Two conditions must be met for a good to be a Giffen good. First, the product concerned must be an inferior good and, second, it must be a product on which the household spends the major portion of its budget. In the case Giffen observed, as the price of bread declined this freed a proportion of the family income which was immediately spent on other foods, to vary the diet. Thus less bread was needed. As the price of bread increased again the family had to revert to living entirely on bread. In technical terms, the Giffen paradox occurs in the demand for inferior goods when the income effect outweighs the substitution effect.

Market demand and consumers' surplus

Common misunderstanding

After studying the relationship between demand and utility, students often believe that price is equal to marginal utility. This cannot be the case because both are measured on different scales: price is measured in money, while utility is measured (subjectively) in utils. A review of this chapter will show that price is proportional *to marginal utility. It is important to remember that this is only true for the last unit of a product purchased.*

In Fig. 9.5 £300 represents the market price of video cassette recorders, of which 100 000 are sold. However, the graph indicates that at £500 some 20 000 people would still have been willing to buy. Thus we must presume that they consider that they would receive at least £500 of utility from the recorder. Similarly, 40 000 would have been willing to pay £400. However, they all pay the market price of £300. The people who were willing to pay more could thus be said to be receiving extra utility for which they have not had to pay. It is only the 100 000th customer who has equated utility derived with the price.

Thus all the area above the price line and below the demand curve is surplus utility derived by consumers but not paid for. This is referred to as a ***consumers' surplus***.

Consumer surplus is the amount consumers would be willing to pay over and above what they actually have to pay in the market.

This again may seem a rather abstract concept, but as we shall see it has important implications for monopoly pricing (see Chapter 18) and public sector decision making (see Chapter 29). A similar analysis also occurs in the theory of production (see Chapter 20).

Objections to utility theory

Theories based on utility place a great emphasis upon rationality and the search for utility maximisation. This is often hard to accord with observed behaviour. How many of your friends are completely rational? How many of your decisions to buy goods lack calm rational calculation?

Arguments that consumers are not in fact rational beings can in part be countered by the law of large numbers and 'as-if' methodology, first discussed in Chapter 3. If the purpose of demand

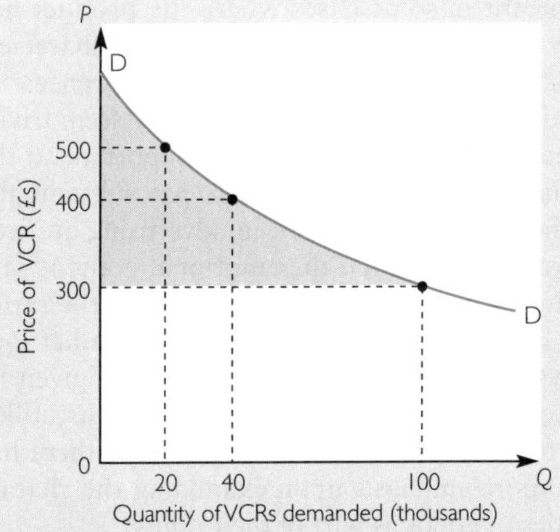

***Fig. 9.5* Consumer's surplus**

The shaded area represents utility which consumers receive but do not pay for.

theory is to *explain* consumers' behaviour, then the theory will not always succeed. If on the other hand the purpose of the theory is to *predict* then the law of large numbers will result in the inconsistencies and irrationalities of individuals often cancelling out when aggregated at the level of the market. As long as people behave collectively 'as if' they were rational utility-maximising individuals, then demand theory will yield useful predictions.

The discipline of marketing is related to economics and comes up with different explanations of consumer behaviour, concentrating on what the firm can do to change demand for its product. Advertising can change people's tastes as well as give them more information. Distribution strategies can make the product more accessible to its target market. Product design and packaging can make the product more attractive to the consumer. Even the location on the supermarket shelves can affect sales. These ideas are not necessarily in conflict with traditional economic theory, since economics assumes that the consumer has full information about and access to the products. Many marketing strategies are just making sure this is the case. Informative advertising is also covered by this argument, but persuasive advertising is an attempt by the firm to manipulate the consumer rather than satisfy the consumer's preferences. The details of product design are important in some cases where the product has many different possible combinations of characteristics. For example, the minor differences in brands of washing powder which may seem trivial to the logical economist may be important to the consumer, who is often willing to pay substantially for them. Those who work in advertising are well aware that it is often the emotional content of a product which is more important than the rational. This does not necessarily contradict our analysis since the emotional satisfaction given by the consumption of a product is part of its utility. It is for this reason that in recent years there has been more emphasis upon examining the characteristics of goods as part of their utility.

We have now concluded our look at the theory of demand. Next we turn to the measurement of demand and supply and the analysis of market changes.

Summary

1. The market demand curve is a horizontal summation of individuals' demand curves.
2. Price is the prime determinant of demand and is the basis of the first law of demand.
3. There are three exceptions to the first law of demand:
   a) goods demanded for their price;
   b) where there is an expectation of a further change in price;
   c) Giffen goods.
4. The conditions of demand are the income of consumers, the price of other goods and other non-quantifiable factors such as advertising and consumers' tastes.
5. The marginal utility (or cardinalist) approach to demand maintains that the consumer maximises utility when the marginal utility of product A divided by its price is equated with the marginal utility of product B divided by its price, and so on.
6. The consumers' surplus is the extra utility enjoyed by consumers which they do not pay for.
7. The assumption of a rational utility-maximising consumer may not describe human beings exactly, but it can be used successfully to predict their behaviour.

Questions

1. Examine the factors which determine the demand for:
   a) summer holidays;
   b) public transport.
2. Explain Giffen's paradox and state under what conditions you would expect to find it in today's world.
3. List the following commodities in order of their responsiveness to increases in income: colour televisions; petrol; wine; cigarettes; potatoes; beef; holiday travel; salt.

Appendix

Indifference curve analysis

The indifference curve approach to consumer theory is placed in an appendix, since it is not required by many syllabuses. The relationship between utility and demand has been adequately covered in the chapter so far, but indifference curve analysis provides a logically more precise analysis of the issues discussed above.

The ordinalist approach

The marginal utility approach is subject to the major criticism that we have never found a satisfactory way of quantifying utility. In the 1930s a group of economists, including Sir John Hicks and Sir Roy Allen, came to believe that cardinal measurement of utility was not necessary. They argued that consumer behaviour could be explained with ***ordinal numbers*** (i.e. is first, second, third and so on). This is because, it is argued, individuals are able to ***rank their preferences***, saying that they would prefer this bundle of goods to that bundle of goods and so on. Finite measurement of utility therefore becomes unnecessary and it is sufficient simply to place in order consumers' preferences. To explain this we must investigate indifference curves.

Indifference curves

In order to explain indifference curves we will again make the simplifying assumption that the consumer buys only two goods, X and Y. Table 9.4 gives a number of combinations of X and Y which the consumer considers to give equal satisfaction; for example, combination C of 8X and 20Y is thought to yield the same satisfaction as D where 12X and 10Y are consumed. The consumer is thus said to be indifferent as to which combination the consumer has – hence the name given to this type of analysis. Figure 9.6 gives a graphical representation of the figures in Table 9.4. Before proceeding any further with the analysis we must pause to consider several important features of indifference curves.

Table 9.4 An indifference schedule

Combination	*Units of X*	*Units of Y*
A	0	50
B	4	32
C	8	20
D	12	10
E	16	4
F	20	0

a) *Indifference curves slope downwards from left to right.* Since we assume that consumers are rational then we must conclude that if consumers give up some of X they will want more of Y. This will therefore imply a negative, or inverse, slope for the indifference curve. This is illustrated in Fig. 9.6. If the curve were to slope upwards from left to right, this would imply that as a consumer gave up some of X the consumer could only keep the level of utility constant by also giving up some of Y! This is clearly nonsense because it is illogical to assume that consumption of less of both goods can leave total utility undiminished.

b) Indifference curves are ***convex to the origin.*** You will notice in Fig. 9.6 that the indifference curve bends inwards towards the origin. This is because, as consumers give up more of X, they want relatively more and more of Y to compensate them.

c) *The marginal rate of substitution.* As noted above the consumer requires more of X in return for Y (or vice versa) as the consumer moves along the indifference curve. In other

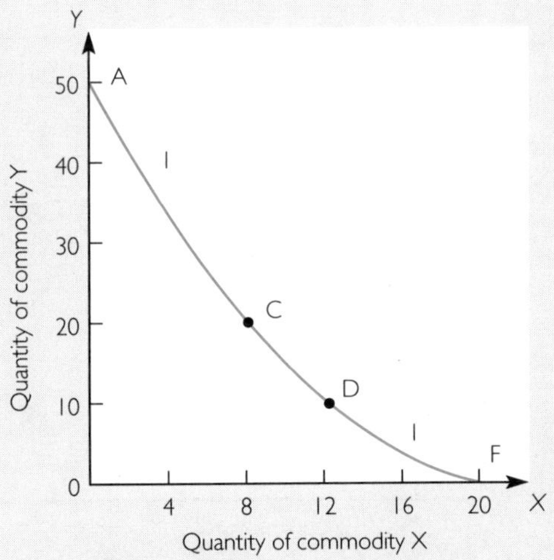

Fig. 9.6 An indifference curve
At each point on the indifference curve the consumer believes that the same amount of utility is received.

words the rate of exchange of X for Y changes along the whole length of the curve.

The rate at which a consumer is willing to exchange one unit of one product for units of another is termed the marginal rate of substitution. It is given by the slope of the indifference curve.

As indifference curves are drawn convex to the origin the slope of the curve diminishes as we move up or down any curve (this was first illustrated in Fig. 3.3 in Chapter 3), i.e. a diminishing marginal rate of substitution is assumed. Some textbooks incorrectly state that this is due to diminishing marginal utility. Such an error demonstrates a lack of knowledge of the development of economic thought and is clearly nonsense for, as we have seen, diminishing marginal utility assumes cardinal utility whereas indifference analysis assumes only ordinality.

d) *An indifference map*. If we construct another indifference curve to the right of the original one (see Fig. 9.7) this must show a situation where the consumer derives greater total utility, since for each point on the new curve the consumer is receiving more of both X and Y than the range NM on the old curve. We can say that:

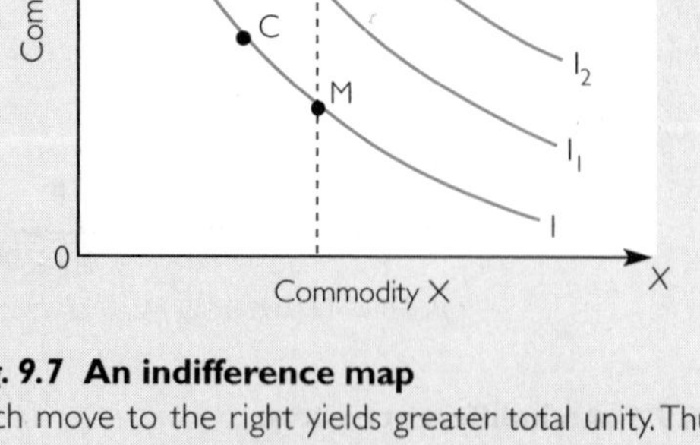

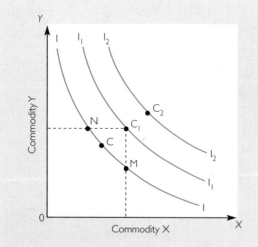

***Fig. 9.7* An indifference map**

Each move to the right yields greater total unity. Thus C_1 gives more utility than C and so on. It is possible to construct an infinite number of curves.

Any movement of the indifference curve to the right is a movement to greater total utility.

Thus in Fig. 9.7 point C_1 must yield more utility than point C, and so on. We are here at the heart of the ordinalist approach; we do not need to know how much utility the consumer obtains on indifference curve I to know that more is obtained on curve I_1 and more still on I_2. A series of indifference curves such as those in Fig. 9.7 is known as an indifference map.

e) *An infinite number of curves*. Given a consumer's scale of preferences, it is possible to construct any number of indifference curves on the indifference map. In each case a rightward shift gives more utility.

f) *Indifference curves never cross*. It would be logically absurd for indifference curves to cross since this would imply that a consumer was equally happy with, for example, two combinations of X and Y, both of which have the same quantity of X but different quantities of Y.

The budget line

The indifference curve shows us consumers' preferences but it does not show us the situation in the market place. Here the consumer is constrained by income and by the prices of X and Y. They can both be shown by a budget line. Suppose that product X costs £5 per unit and product Y £2 per unit and that the consumer's income is £100.

A budget line shows all the combinations of two products which can be purchased with a given level of income. The slope of the line shows the relative prices of the two goods.

In Fig. 9.8 you can see that the budget line AF stretches from 50 units of Y to 20 units of X. Thus X exchanges for Y at a rate of 2.5:1 which is their relative prices. The consumer is able to attain any point on the line, such as point C, or any point within the line, such as point U, where less than all of the budget is spent. However, given the constraint of an income of £100 it is not possible to obtain any combination of X and Y to the right of the budget line.

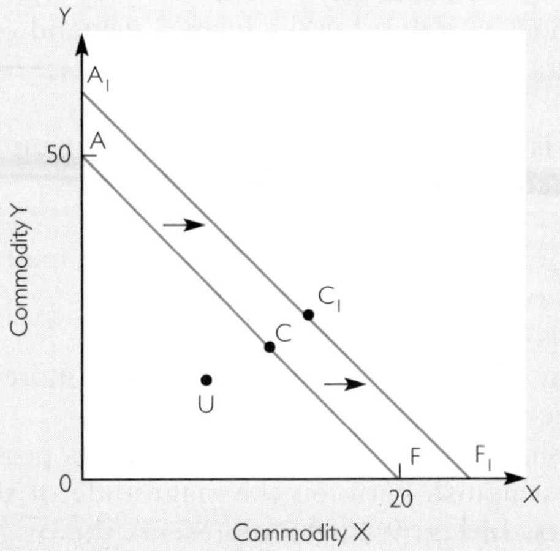

***Fig. 9.8* The budget line**
A budget of £100 and prices for Y of £2/unit and for X of £5/unit gives a budget line AF, showing the ratio of prices of 1:2:5. The consumer can attain any position on the line, e.g. C, or within it, e.g. U. Line A_1F_1 shows an increase in the budget.

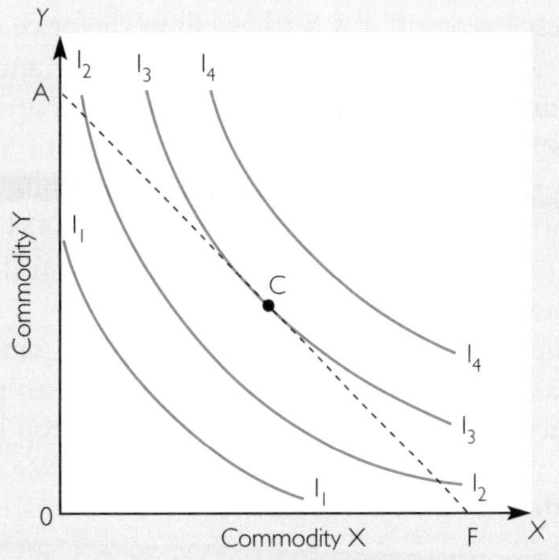

***Fig. 9.9* The consumer equilibrium**
The consumer obtains maximum utility from a budget of AF by choosing the combination of X and Y represented by C, where the marginal rate of substitution is equal to the relative prices of X and Y.

The line A_1F_1 shows the effect of an increase in income on the budget line. The whole line moves rightwards, showing that more of both X and Y may be consumed. Thus point C_1, which lies on the line A_1F_1, is unobtainable if the budget is limited to £100.

Consumer equilibrium

To demonstrate the consumer's equilibrium, i.e. the point at which the consumer maximises utility with a given budget, we need to combine the indifference map and the budget line. In Fig. 9.9 you can see that the consumer's equilibrium is at point C. This is because, with the budget line AF, it is the indifference curve the farthest to the right that can be reached. At this point the indifference curve I_3 is just tangential to the budget line.

Can we be sure that the indifference curve will be tangential to the budget line? Yes, because we have already shown that there can be an infinite number of indifference curves on an indifference map and therefore one of them must just touch the budget line without cutting it, i.e. be at a tangent to it.

Geometry tells us that when a tangent touches a straight line their slopes, at that point, are equal. Now in our model the budget line represents relative prices and the slope of the indifference curve the marginal rate of substitution. Thus we can conclude that:

The consumer's utility maximisation equilibrium occurs when relative prices are equal to the marginal rate of substitution.

Applications of indifference curve analysis

Having derived the consumer's equilibrium we can now use this to explain more fully the demand effects which we examined in the earlier part of this chapter.

The price–consumption line

Suppose that the consumer's budget is fixed and there are only two goods to choose from. Figure 9.10 shows us what happens as the price of X falls relative to Y. The original situation is shown by budget line AF where the consumer's equilibrium is at point C. As the price of X falls so the budget line pivots to AG and the consumer's equilibrium now changes to C_1. A further fall in the price of X relative to Y moves the budget line to AH and the consumer's equilibrium to C_2. Thus as the price of X has fallen relative to Y, so consumption of Y has fallen from OR to OS and then to OT, while consumption of X has grown from OC to OM and then to ON. These changes can be broken down into substitution and income effects.

The dashed line which joins points C, C_1 and C_2 shows how consumption alters in relation to price changes and is known as a price–consumption line.

Effect of a rise in income

We saw in Fig. 9.8 that the effect of an increase in income is to shift the budget line outwards. This being the case, it can be seen in Fig. 9.11 that as the budget line shifts outwards so the consumer moves to indifference curves further and further to the right. Thus as the budget line has shifted from AF to A_1F_1, and the equilibrium has changed from C to C_1, a further increase to A_2F_2 shifts the equilibrium C_2. Thus the effect of an increase in income is to increase the demand for both Y and X, provided that they are both normal goods. This accords with what we said earlier in the chapter; you can see that Fig. 9.11 provides evidence for the income demand curve illustrated in Fig. 9.2 (a).

Distinguishing between substitution and income effects

As the price of a product falls people may buy more of it for two reasons.

a) It is cheaper (substitution effect).
b) The fall in price in effect leaves them more income to spend (income effect).

By using indifference curve analysis it is possible to distinguish between the magnitude of these effects. In Fig. 9.12 AF represents the original budget line and C the original equilibrium. The shift of the budget line to AG shows the effect of a fall in the price of X. As you can see this moves the consumer to a new equilibrium C_2 on indifference curve I_2; this means that the consumption of X increases from OM to OM_1. But how much of this increase is due to the fall in price and how much to the income effect of the fall in price making the consumer better off? In order to distinguish the two we project a new budget line

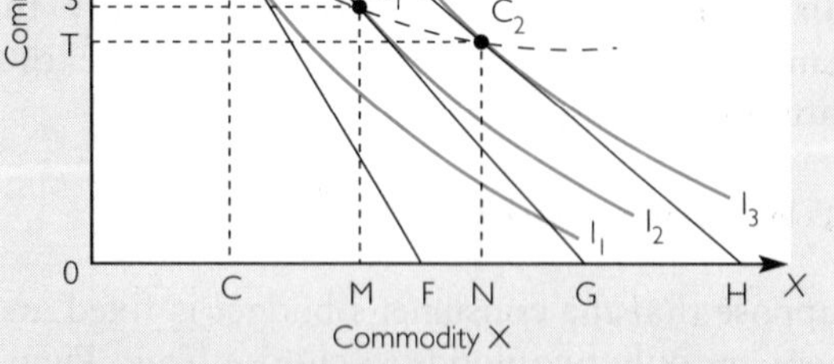

Fig. 9.10 The price effect
As the price of X falls, the budget line shifts from AF to AG to AH and the consumer shifts from C to C_1 and C_2, substituting X and Y. CC_1C_2 is the price–consumption line.

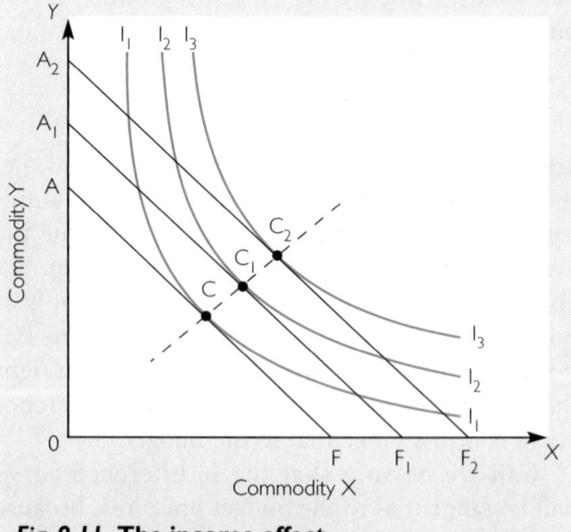

Fig. 9.11 The income effect
A rise in the consumer's income shifts the budget line outwards and equilibrium shifts from C to C_1 to C_2 as more of both X and Y are consumed. Line CC_1C_2 is the income–consumption line.

A_1F_1 which is parallel to AG and tangential to the original indifference curve I_1. Remember, the fall in price increases the real income of consumers by leaving more money to spend. The line we have drawn, A_1F_1, shows the new relative prices of X and Y but at the original indifference curve or satisfaction level. This will tell us how much of X the consumer would have bought at that price if real income had not been increased.

It can be seen that at equilibrium C_1, OZ units of X would have been consumed. Thus the increase MZ is due to the substitution effect, while the rest of the increase in consumption at C_2, i.e. ZM_1, is due to the income effect alone.

Derivation of the demand curve

We can now use indifference curves to show how an individual's demand curve is derived. The upper portion of Fig. 9.13 shows the effect of a price change similar to that in Fig. 9.10. In this case we can see that the price–consumption line shows how demand for X grows as its price falls relative to Y. The lower portion of Fig. 9.13 plots the price of X against the demand for it. If we correlate quantities of X demanded along the price–consumption line with the various prices on the demand curve we can see that we derive a normal downward-sloping demand curve. Thus as price has fallen from OA to OB to OC, so demand has expanded from OL to OM to ON.

As we concluded with marginal utility analysis, so we may also conclude here: if we can derive an individual's demand curve we can also derive a market demand curve by aggregating all the individual demand curves.

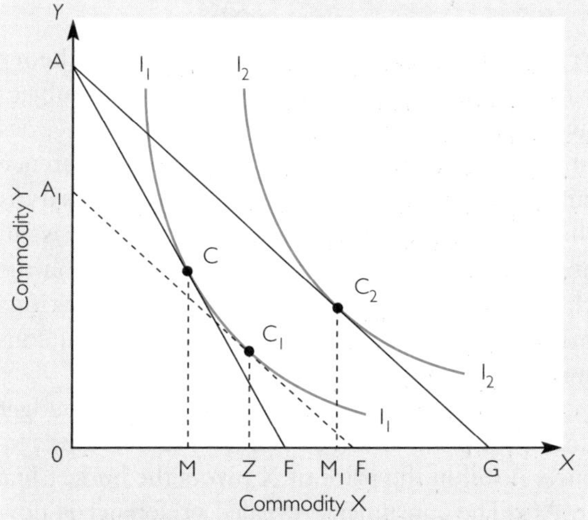

Fig. 9.12 **Separating income and substitution effects**

Increase in demand, MZ, is due to substitution effect and ZM_1 to income effect. This is determined by projecting a hypothetical budget line A_1F_1 which is parallel to the new budget line AG and tangential to the original indifference line I_1.

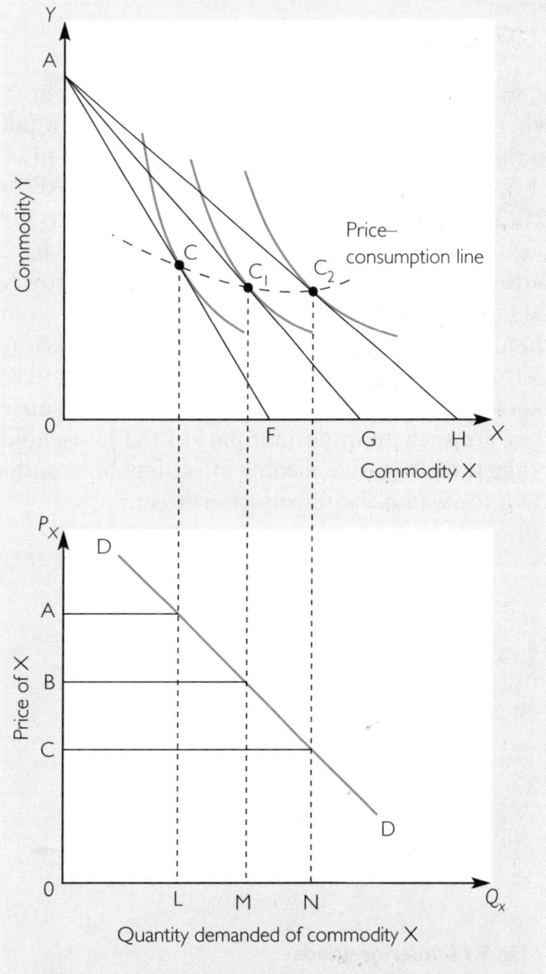

Fig. 9.13 **The derivation of the individual demand curve**

Inferior goods

We have demonstrated that a rise in a consumer's income will lead to an increase in demand. However, market observations tell us that this is not always so. In the case of inferior goods demand actually goes down as a result of an increase in income. The inferior goods phenomenon is due to the income effect and not to the substitution effect. In Fig. 9.14 you can observe that, as a result of the particular shape of the indifference curves, as the budget line has shifted outwards from AF to A_1F_1 the consumer's equilibrium has changed from C to C_1 involving a fall in the demand for X from OM to OM_1.

Giffen goods – again

It will be recalled that Giffen goods are those where a fall in the price of the good causes a fall in the demand. Figure 9.15 shows the fall in price of X by pivoting out the budget line from AF to AG and then to AH. As can be seen, owing to the peculiar shape of the indifference curves where Giffen goods are concerned, the demand for X does not expand but falls from OM to OM_1 and then to OM_2. This has come about because as Giffen goods are inferior there is a negative income effect as their price falls, and because they are such an important part of the household budget, the negative income effect has been sufficient to swamp the substitution effect.

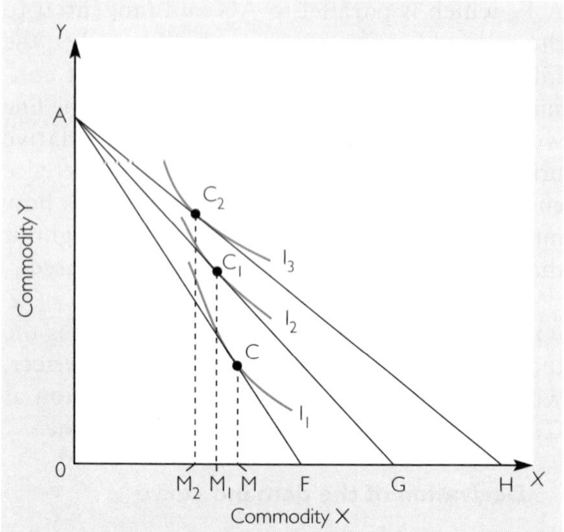

***Fig. 9.15* Giffen goods**
The fall in the price of X is shown by the line pivoting outwards from AF to AG to AH, but instead of demand for X expanding it contracts from OM to OM_1 to OM_2.

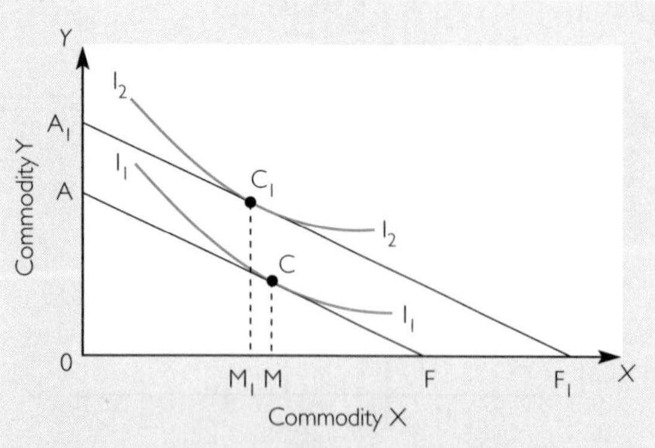

***Fig. 9.14* Inferior goods**
The increase in income shifts the budget line from AF to A_1F_1 but decrease the demand for X from OM to OM_1.

Revealed preference theory

Professor Paul Samuelson developed a theory which was designed to do away with the subjective element which is implicit in the utility theories of both the marginal utility and the indifference curve approach. The only assumption necessary is that the consumer behaves rationally. It is an analysis of consumer behaviour based only on the choices actually made by consumers in various price–income situations. Thus it is based on consumers' revealed preferences.

In Fig. 9.16 AF represents the original budget line, with point E the consumer's revealed preference. A fall in the price of X pivots the budget line to AG. The consumer's revealed preference is now for the combination of X and Y represented by E_1. We can analyse this change by projecting a new budget line, parallel to AG and running through the original equilibrium E; that is, we have projected a set of circumstances where the individual is not able to consume more than was originally consumed but is on a budget line reflecting the new price. The consumer would then have to

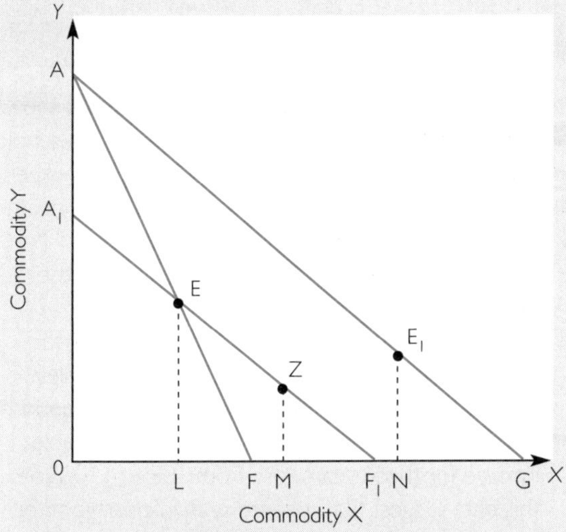

Fig. 9.16 **Revealed preference**
A fall in the price of commodity X pivots the budget line from AF to AG, The consumer moves from E to E_1. Of the increase, LN, in demand, LM may be attributed to the price effect and MN to the income effect.

choose some combination along the line A_1F_1. It would be illogical to choose a combination to the left of E, i.e. along the part of the line A_1E, since this combination was available before the price fell. Logically, therefore, the consumer would choose some point to the right, e.g. Z. We are therefore able to attribute the increase in the demand for X of LM to the substitution effect alone, while the remaining increase in demand of MN to the new revealed preference of E_1 must be due to the income effect. This analysis can then be extended to derive a demand curve for product X. We are thus able to analyse the effects of changes in price and incomes without reference to measures of utility or indifference curves.

Space precludes a fuller treatment of this theory; the interested reader should consult one of the more advanced texts on the subject.

Appendix summary

1 The indifference curve (or ordinalist) approach maintains that the consumer maximises utility when a person's marginal rate of substitution is equated with the relative price of products.
2 Indifference curve analysis can be used to explain price and income effects and to demonstrate the derivation of the demand curve.
3 Revealed preference theory is an attempt to explain consumers' behaviour without having to measure utility.

Appendix questions

1 Assume that a family has a weekly budget of £240 and a choice of only two goods which cost respectively £12 and £8.
   a) Construct the family's budget line.
   b) Show the effect of the price of the good which costs £12 increasing to £20.
   c) In the original situation show the effect of the family's budget increasing to £360.
2 If one wished to avoid the subjective element involved in the marginal utility approach and indifference curve analysis, how could one justify the first law of demand, including the explanation of both the price effect and the income effect?
3 Study Fig. 9.13 which shows the derivation of a normal demand curve and then show how the perverse demand curve for Giffen goods can be derived from Fig. 9.15.
4 Describe and explain the equilibrium condition of a consumer when faced with a given income and relative prices. Starting from the equilibrium, how would the consumer respond to:
   a) A rise in the price of one good?
   b) A rise in the level of prices while the consumer's income remained constant?

Data response A Maximising utility

Study the total utility figures given in Table 9.5 and then answer the following questions.

1 Assume that a poor family has a budget of £10, all of which it intends to spend, but only cheese is available. How many kilograms of cheese will be

Table 9.5 Total utility schedules

Kg consumed	Cheese (£2/kg)	Fish (£4/kg)	Meat (£5/kg)
1	7	8	16
2	13	16	29
3	17	21	41
4	20.5	25	51
5	22	28.5	59
6	25	31.25	65
7	26	33.5	68

bought and why? Calculate the consumer's surplus under these conditions.

2 A richer family has a budget of £34 and a choice of all three commodities. Explain how the family will allocate its expenditure between the three commodities, assuming that it wishes to spend all of its budget. (Hint: Remember the consumer equilibrium condition under the cardinalist approach.)

3 Do you notice anything unusual about the utility schedule for cheese? Explain your answer.

Data response B
Consumers' expenditure

Study the information contained in Fig. 9.17. This shows the indices of the sales of various categories of household goods and services. It also shows total consumers' expenditure. All figures are in real terms, but of course income was growing strongly over the period as a whole.

1 Describe the pattern of expenditure which the graph shows.

2 Which of the selected goods are normal goods?

3 Suppose that in 1978 the index for tobacco sales was 100 whereas in 1979 it was 97. Further suppose that the index for consumers' personal disposable income for those years rose from 108 to 110. Does this data suggest that tobacco is an inferior good or could the data be explained in some other way?

4 What would be the effect on the index for tobacco if the Chancellor were to increase significantly the tax on cigarettes?

5 What reasons account for the large increases in the index of sales of durable goods?

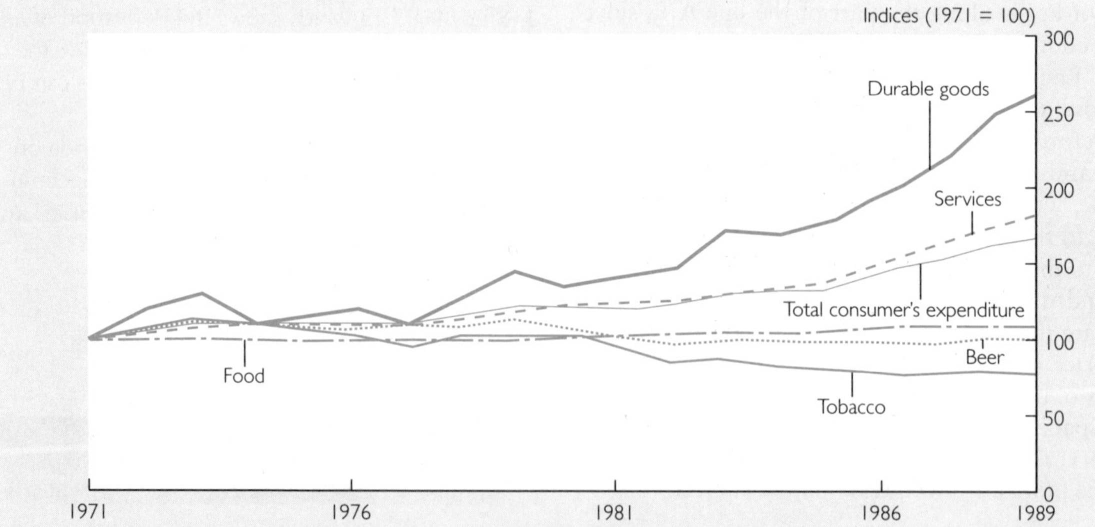

Fig. 9.17 UK consumers' expenditure at constant prices: by selected item

10 Elasticities of demand and supply

Learning outcomes

At the end of this chapter you will be able to:

- Calculate a range of elasticities from data.
- Understand the implications for a firm's pricing policy of different elasticity values.
- Use intuitive methods for estimating elasticity of demand.
- Predict which goods will grow in demand terms over time using income elasticity.
- Understand the relationship between elasticity and time for both supply and demand.

Introduction

In previous chapters we have considered how demand and supply determine prices. The first law of demand, for example, tells us that if we lower the price of a commodity, other things being equal, a greater quantity will be demanded. In this chapter we seek to measure and quantify those changes.

Everyone is familiar with the idea that if there is a glut of a commodity its price usually falls. As long ago as the seventeenth century Gregory King, the English writer on population, noted that when there was a good harvest not only did prices fall but farmers appeared to earn less. In other words bad harvests seemed to be better for farmers (see Chapter 12). King, without knowing it, was commenting on an application of the principle of elasticity of demand.

Elasticity of demand

Elasticity of demand defined

There are several different types of elasticity. The most important is elasticity of demand, which can also be termed the price elasticity of demand and is sometimes abbreviated to PED. We may define it thus:

> **Price elasticity of demand measures the degree of responsiveness of the quantity demanded of a commodity to changes in its price.**

It is worthwhile remembering this definition since it can be readily adapted to give the definition for any other type of elasticity. Responsiveness is measured by comparing the percentage change in the price with the resultant percentage change in the quantity demanded. This is best explained by taking a numerical example. Two very different demand curves are shown in Fig. 10.1. In both cases the price has been cut by the same amount, from £10 to £5, but this has had very different effects upon the quantity demanded. In (a) the quantity demanded has expanded a great deal, from 100 units to 300 units, but in (b) the demand has grown only from 100 units to 125. Thus the same percentage cut in the price has resulted in different percentage changes in the quantity demanded. Diagram (a) is said to illustrate an **elastic** demand because it is responsive to price changes, whereas diagram (b) illustrates an **inelas-**

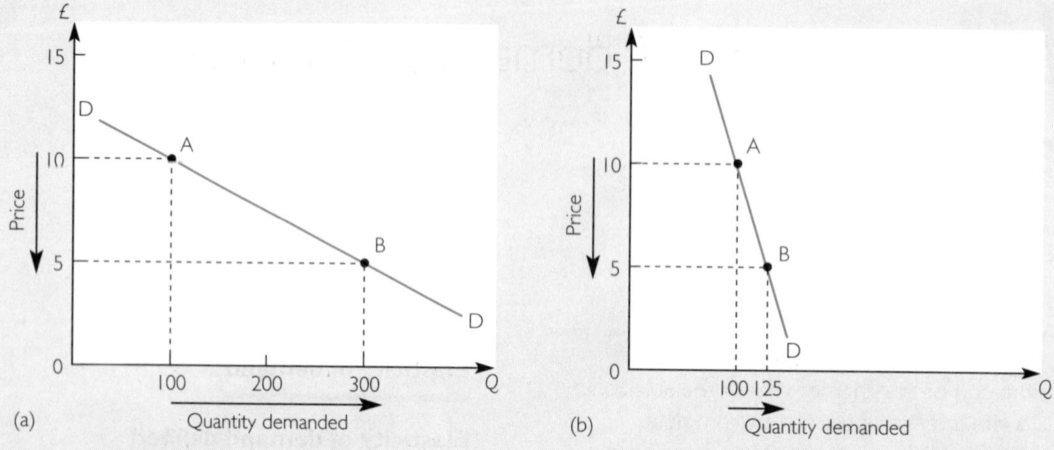

Fig. 10.1 **Elastic and inelastic demand**
(a) Responsive (elastic) demand. (b) Unresponsive (inelastic) demand.

tic demand because it is relatively unresponsive to price changes. Which category of elasticity the demand for a product falls into depends upon the product we are considering. A 50 per cent drop in the price of salt, for example, would hardly send everyone dashing out to the shops, but a 50 per cent drop in the price of cars might well have people queueing at the showrooms. Remember:

It is the demand which is elastic or inelastic, not the product.

Elasticity of demand and total revenue

Elasticity can also be defined and categorised by the effect of a price change on the total revenue of the firm. There are three categories of elasticity of demand: elastic, inelastic and unitary. Which category any particular demand falls into depends upon the relative percentage changes in price and quantity demanded and the resultant effect upon the total revenue.

a) *Elastic demand*

Demand is elastic when a percentage cut in price brings about a greater percentage expansion in demand so as to increase total revenue.

The relationship between elasticity and total revenue is illustrated in Fig. 10.2. Total revenue, as explained in Chapter 5, is calculated by multiplying the price of the commodity by the quantity demanded. In diagram (a) of Fig. 10.2 a reduction in price from £5 to £3 increases total revenue from £500 to £900. The shaded rectangle A shows the revenue that has been given up by lowering the price, but you can see that this is greatly outweighed by the shaded rectangle B, which is the extra revenue gained from increased sales. This, therefore, is an elastic demand because, as the price is lowered, total revenue increases.

It should be noted that this process works in reverse. With an elastic demand, a price increase results in a loss of revenue. You should check this for yourself by raising price from £3 to £5 in Fig 10.2 (a) and seeing what happens to revenue.

b) *Inelastic demand*

Demand is inelastic when a percentage cut in price brings about a smaller percentage expansion in demand so as to decrease total revenue.

In diagram (b) a reduction in price from £100 to £50 results in total revenue declining from £400 to £250. This is because the demand is inelastic. As with elastic demand, this relationship works in reverse. An increase in price will raise total revenue.

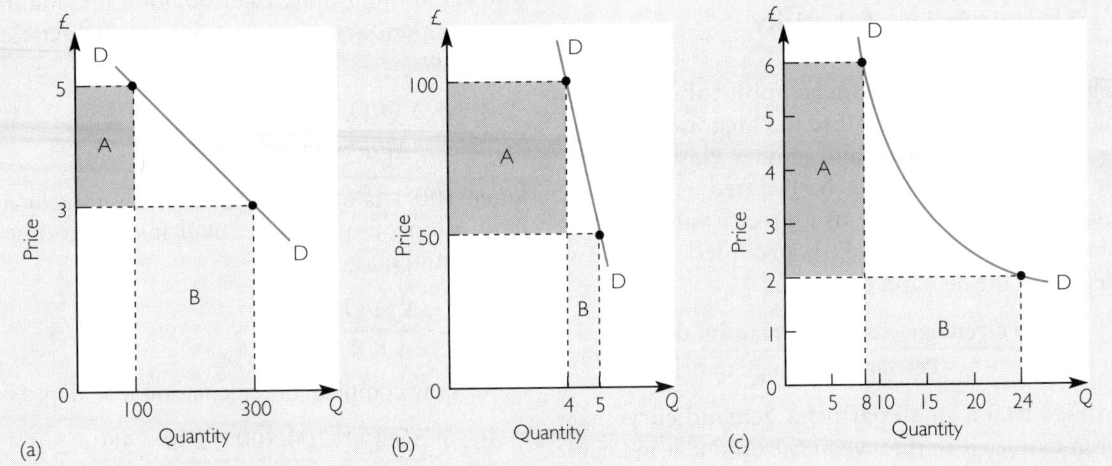

***Fig. 10.2* Elasticities of demand and total revenues**
(a) Elastic demand. Total revenue increases as price falls.
(b) Inelastic demand. Total revenue decreases as price falls.
(c) Unitary demand. Total revenue remains constant whatever happens to price.

c) *Unitary elasticity*

Demand has unitary elasticity when a percentage cut in price brings about an exactly equal expansion of demand so as to leave total revenue unchanged.

In diagram (c) the cut in price is exactly matched by the increase in quantity and therefore, although the price has fallen from £6 to £2, the total revenue remains constant at £48. Area A is exactly equal to area B. We therefore have unitary elasticity of demand. If you check the other points on the demand curve in diagram (c) you will discover that whatever is done to price, the total revenue remains the same. A graph such as this is called a rectangular hyperbola. The curve has the property that any rectangle drawn under it has a constant area (the area represents total revenue).

Elasticity and the firm's decision making

Pricing with an inelastic demand curve

If a firm faces an inelastic demand curve, then pushing up price will always increase revenue. Raising price will reduce output so costs must be falling at the same time. With revenue rising and costs falling, profits must go up. Checking the logic in reverse, it is always a mistake to lower price if facing an inelastic demand curve, because revenue will fall and costs will rise with output. Profits must, therefore, decline.

Pricing with an elastic demand curve

The firm has a more difficult decision if facing an elastic demand curve. The firm knows it can increase its revenue by lowering price, but this will also increase output and therefore costs. The question is, which has gone up more, revenue or costs? The firm needs to know more about its costs and this decision is discussed in more detail in Chapter 15.

Common misunderstanding

If you look back over Figs 10.1 and 10.2 you will see that the elastic demand curves tended to be rather flat whereas the inelastic curves were steep. The appearance of the curves, however, can be most deceptive. In Fig. 2.1 (see page 14) you will see that both demand curves show the same information: one is steep and the other is rather flat simply because the scales have changed. (As a convention, textbooks do use steep-looking curves to depict inelastic demand, and flatter ones for elastic demand.)

The calculation of elasticity

The effect of price changes upon total revenue has given us only three broad categories of elasticity: elastic, inelastic and unitary elasticity. The definition can, however, be restated as a mathematical formula to give us a precise value for the elasticity of demand (E_D), provided we know details of the demand curve:

$$E_D = \frac{\text{Percentage change in quantity demanded}}{\text{Percentage change in price}}$$

In Fig. 10.3 a small part of a demand curve has been extracted so that we may examine it in detail and use this formula to calculate the value of elasticity. In moving from point A to point B on the demand curve the price has fallen from £400 to £350. To calculate this as a percentage we take the original price (P) of £400 and divide it into the change in price (ΔP) of £50 which we are considering, and then multiply the result by 100:

$$\text{Percentage change in price} = \frac{\Delta P}{P} \times \frac{100}{1}$$

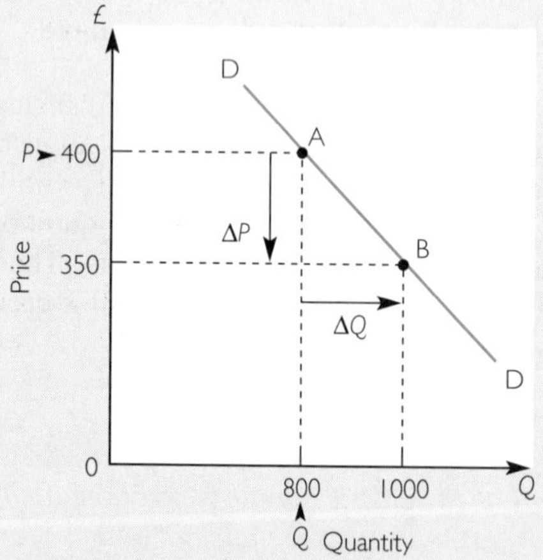

Fig. 10.3 **The coefficient of elasticity of demand**
As price falls from £400 to £350 the quantity demanded expands from 800 to 1000. Thus the original P = £400 and ΔP = £150, while Q = 800 and $\Delta Q = 200$:

$$E_D = \frac{200/800}{50/400} = 2$$

The same thing must then be done for quantity. We can then arrange the formula for elasticity as follows:

$$E_D = \frac{\Delta Q/Q \times 100/1}{\Delta P/P \times 100/1}$$

Since 100/1 is common to both numerator and denominator we may cancel it out, giving us the formula:

$$E_D = \frac{\Delta Q/Q}{\Delta P/P}$$

Let us now complete the calculation from Fig. 10.3:

$$E_D = \frac{\Delta Q/Q}{\Delta P/P} = \frac{200/800}{50/400} = \frac{200}{800} \times \frac{400}{50} = 2$$

In this example we have a value of two for elasticity. It is simply stated as a number and is independent of the units used to measure price and quantity. For price elasticity of demand, the value will always be negative because if price goes up then quantity goes down and vice versa. It is customary in introductory texts to drop the minus sign and present the elasticity as a positive number as above.

Ranges of elasticity values

Common misunderstanding
When looking at Fig. 10.3 it might be thought that the value of elasticity is the value of the slope of the demand curve. This is not so. What is being measured is not the slope of the curve but the relative movements along the axes. This is yet another warning not to be deceived by the appearance of the curve.

There are two cases, however, when the slope of the curve does tell us the value of elasticity. These are shown in Fig. 10.4. In diagram (a) the demand curve is horizontal, showing that consumers are willing to buy any amount at this price, but a price of even one penny higher would result in no sales at all. This is termed an infinite (or perfectly) elastic demand and the value of elasticity is infinity. In diagram (b) it would appear that consumers will buy exactly the same amount of the product whatever the price. There is therefore no responsiveness of demand to price changes. This is termed a

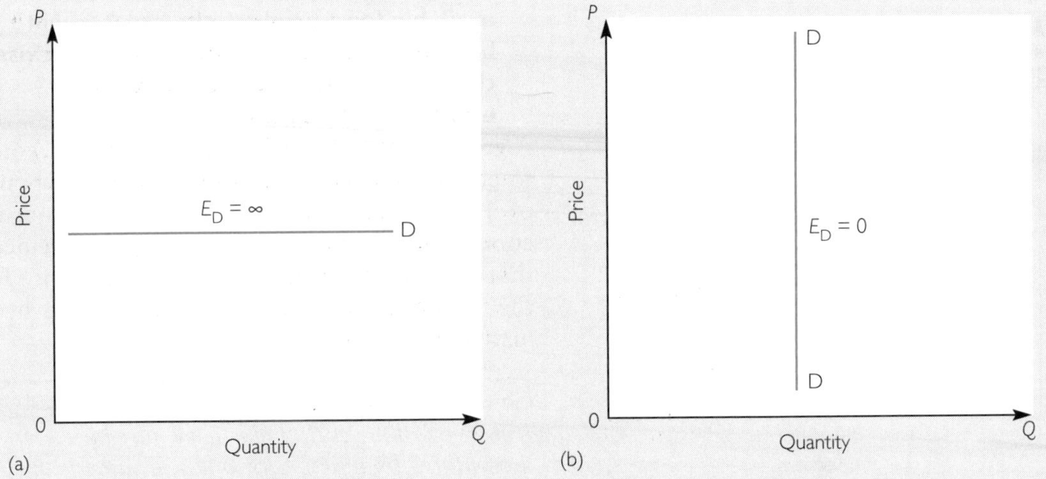

Fig. 10.4 **(a) Infinitely (perfectly) elastic demand. (b) Totally (perfectly) inelastic demand**

totally (or perfectly) inelastic demand and the value of elasticity is zero.

For the in-between case of unitary demand, which results in constant revenue whatever the price, the value of elasticity is one.

Having considered these three extreme cases we can state the boundaries of the values of the different categories of elasticity.

a) ***If elasticity is greater than one but less than infinity then demand is elastic.***
b) ***If elasticity is exactly equal to one then demand has unitary elasticity.***
c) ***If elasticity is less than one but greater than zero then demand is inelastic.***

STUDENT ACTIVITY 10.1

The only real way of making sure you understand elasticity is to do some calculations yourself. Use the information in Table 10.1 to calculate elasticity. Start at the top price of 10 and work your way down to zero. You need not calculate every price on the way, but make sure you calculate elasticities in the elastic and inelastic sections of the demand curve as illustrated in Fig. 10.5

Notes on your calculations:

1 Don't worry if some values are infinity or zero. This should happen at the top and bottom of the demand curve.

2 Notice that elasticity varies continuously along this (or any other) straight line demand curve.

3 An increase (+) in price will cause a fall (–) in quantity and, conversely, a decrease (–) in price will cause a rise (+) in quantity. If we divide the change of quantity by the change in price the value of the answer must always be negative. In introductory texts on economics it is traditional to ignore this negative sign and elasticity is quoted as a positive number.

Table 10.1 **A demand schedule**

	Price of commodity (£/kg) (1)	*Quantity demanded (kg/week) (2)*	*Total revenue (£) (3)*	*Category of elasticity (4)*
A	10	0	0	
B	9	10	90	
C	8	20	160	Elastic
D	7	30	210	
E	6	40	240	
F	5	50	250	Unitary
G	4	60	240	
H	3	70	210	
I	2	80	160	Inelastic
J	1	90	90	
K	0	100	0	

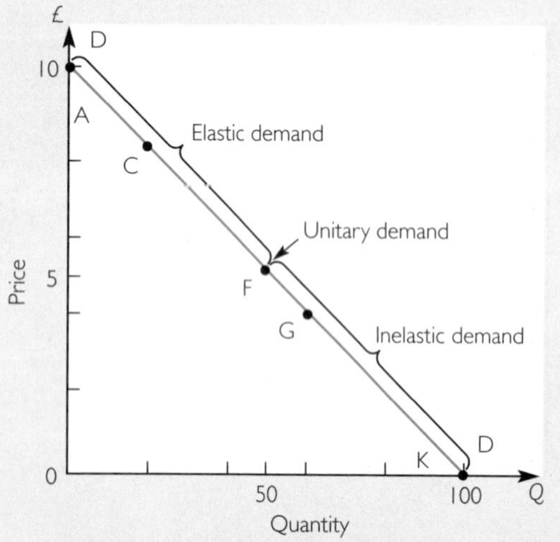

Fig. 10.5 **One demand curve can have all three elasticities**

The value of elasticity decreases from infinity at point A through unity at point F to zero at point K.

Factors determining elasticity

Although we know how to measure elasticity we have not yet discussed the reasons why some demands are elastic and others not so. Why is it, for example, that the demand for wheat is very inelastic while the demand for cakes, which are made from wheat, is much more elastic? Understanding the factors lying behind elasticity is very useful, because frequently there is insufficient information in the real world to know exactly where a demand curve lies. Intuitive estimates of elasticity are therefore useful to entrepreneurs.

Ease of substitution

This is by far the most important determinant of elasticity. If we consider food, for example, we will find that food as a whole has a very inelastic demand, but when we consider any particular food, e.g. cream cakes, we will find that the elasticity of demand is much greater. This is because, while we can find no substitute for food, we can always substitute one type of food for another. In general we can conclude that:

The greater the number of substitutes available for a product, the greater will be its elasticity of demand. Also the closer the substitutes are the greater the elasticity of demand.

A great deal of advertising expenditure is devoted to persuading consumers that a particular brand of a product is significantly different from its competitors. If the consumer can be convinced that other brands are not a good substitute for the product, then its demand will have been made more inelastic.

Common misunderstanding

It may be thought that elasticity may be determined by whether or not a product is a necessity. To some extent this is true. The 'bare necessities' do tend to have low elasticities of demand. However, this can be a misleading idea because what is a luxury to one person may be a necessity to another. Tobacco, for example, can hardly be considered a 'necessity' and yet to many people it is, because there is no substitute available. The idea of necessity determining elasticity is also further undermined when we discover that demand for many luxury goods, e.g. diamonds, is relatively inelastic. It is not therefore the 'expensiveness' which determines elasticity, but the availability of substitutes. For instance, when the international oil cartel OPEC more than trebled oil prices in 1973–4 and doubled them again in 1979, demand did not fall dramatically. There is no real substitute for petrol, but there is a substitute for oil in generating electricity. Coal or gas can be burnt instead to generate electricity, but it took time to convert power stations from one fuel to the other.

The proportion of incomes spent on the product

If the price of a box of matches were to rise by 50 per cent, for example from 2p to 3p, it would discourage very few buyers because such an amount is a minute proportion of their income. However, if the price of a car were to rise from £6000 to £9000 it would have an enormous effect upon sales, even though it would be the same percentage increase.

We can state this principle as:

The greater the proportion of income which the price of the product represents the greater its elasticity of demand will tend to be.

If we apply this principle to individual consumers it will be clear that those with high incomes may be less sensitive to changes in the price of products than those with low incomes. Similarly, if we consider the growth in national income over the years it is apparent that products which seemed expensive luxuries some years ago, e.g. colour televisions, are now regarded by many as 'necessities'. This is partly because the product now represents a much smaller proportion of their income.

Time

The period of time we are considering also plays a role in shaping the demand curve. In general the longer the period of time, the more elastic the demand curve. This is due to a number of different factors. First, people make many purchases as a matter of habit and do not change their spending habits immediately. Second, even if they are willing to reconsider their spending patterns, it may take time to find an acceptable alternative. Third, consumers may be locked into a particular technology. If the price of electricity rises sharply, people cannot immediately switch to gas if they have electric cookers. Since buying gas cookers is expensive they will probably wait until it is time to replace their electric cooker before switching fuels. This principle we may state as:

Following a change in price, elasticity of demand will tend to be greater in the long term than the short term.

Whether or not this is a noticeable effect will depend upon whether or not consumers discover adequate substitutes.

Addiction

Where a product is habit forming, e.g. cigarettes or alcohol, this will tend to reduce its elasticity of demand. In extreme cases of addiction, such as with heroin or crack, a person's income is no longer a constraint on the price that can be charged. If drug addicts run out of money, then they will steal in order to maintain their habit.

Complementary goods

Although we treat products as separate, they are often used in a complementary way. For instance, car tyres are only demanded for use with cars. When goods are complementary in this way, they are said to be 'jointly demanded'. If the price of tyres goes up by 10 per cent then demand for tyres will not be significantly changed. Although tyre prices have risen by a significant amount, they are only a small part of the cost of motoring, so the price of the composite good 'motoring' will have risen by only a very small percentage. This idea can be stated as follows:

Where a good is jointly demanded with another good, its elasticity of demand will tend to be lower. The smaller is the expenditure on such a product as a proportion of total expenditure on the composite good, the more inelastic is the demand.

STUDENT ACTIVITY 10.2

Use the intuitive approach for estimating elasticity outlined above to arrive at a range of elasticity for the following products:

1 Carrots
2 Vegetables
3 Petrol
4 Bread
5 Cigarettes
6 Chocolate
7 A brand of chocolate e.g. Mars bars
8 Replacement windscreen wipers

Arc elasticity and point elasticity

The content of this section is a little more technical than the rest of the chapter, and not absolutely necessary to the understanding of the concept of elasticity. If you prefer, you can skip this section and move on to the section on income elasticity of demand. This section is, however, useful in getting around some of the mathematical problems that can be encountered in calculating elasticity.

Problems with the percentage method

The percentage method of calculating elasticity which we have developed is given by the formula:

$$E_D = \frac{\Delta Q/Q}{\Delta P/P}$$

For the discussion below it is helpful to rearrange the terms of the equation as follows:

$$E_D = \frac{\Delta Q}{Q} \times \frac{P}{\Delta P} = \frac{\Delta Q}{\Delta P} \times \frac{P}{Q}$$

As will be discussed in the section on point elasticity below, this gives the right answer for straight line demand curves. It does not work for curved demand curves, however. If looked at as a way of estimating elasticity of demand *between* two points, it appears to give contradictory answers even with straight line demand curves. To check that this is so, perform the calculations in Student activity 10.3.

STUDENT ACTIVITY 10.3

In Student activity 10.1 you were asked to calculate elasticity of demand moving down the demand curve. Recalculate some of the elasticity values from Table 10.1 but move up the demand curve instead of down it. You should get different values from those you calculated in Student activity 10.1. As you move up from a price of 7 to 8, you will get a different value from moving down from a price of 8 to 7, although it is the same stretch of the demand curve.

The reason why different values are found depending on whether the calculation moves up or down the demand curve is that values for P and Q are determined by the starting point of the calculation. Different values for P and Q will be used according to whether we start at the top or the bottom of a section of the demand curve.

If we have a curved demand curve there is an additional problem. If we look at a small section of the demand curve, a different value for $\Delta Q/\Delta P$ is found than if we look at a longer stretch. This is illustrated in Fig. 10.6 which shows the demand curve from the data in Table 10.2.

Table 10.2 Calculating elasticity

P	Q	P/Q	dQ/dP	E_D
0	100	0	20	0
1	81	$\frac{1}{81}$	18	
2	64		16	
3	49		14	
4	36		12	
5	25		10	
6	16		8	
7	9		6	$4\frac{2}{3}$
8	4		4	
9	1		2	

If we calculate the elasticity of demand using the percentage method of a decrease in price from 7 to 3 then the result is:

$$E_D = \frac{\Delta Q}{\Delta P} \times \frac{P}{Q} = \frac{40}{4} \times \frac{7}{9} = \frac{70}{9} = 7\frac{7}{9}$$

The answer we get from reducing price from 7 to 6, using a shorter section or 'arc' of the demand curve, is closer to the true value of $4\frac{2}{3}$ (which is calculated in the section on point elasticity below):

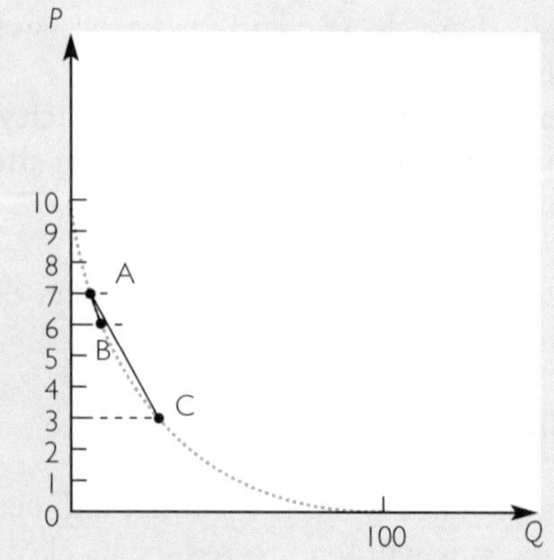

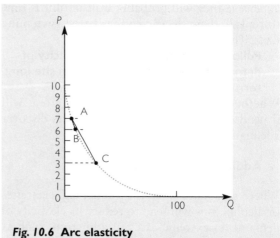

Fig. 10.6 Arc elasticity

$$E_D = \frac{\Delta Q}{\Delta P} \times \frac{P}{Q} = \frac{7}{1} \times \frac{7}{9} = \frac{49}{9} = 5\tfrac{4}{9}$$

The inaccuracy of the answer is minimised by considering as small a change as possible. If we are able to consider the slope of the curve at one spot we will obtain a value known as point elasticity. Before moving on to this, we can make improvements to our estimate by using 'arc elasticity'.

Arc elasticity is the average value of elasticity over a segment of the curve, while point elasticity is the value at any one point on the curve.

The formula for arc elasticity is the same as for the percentage method except that an average of the values of P and Q at either end of the arc of the demand curve is used. This means that the same value for elasticity is found whether moving up or down the demand curve. The formula is given below together with a calculation of its value between a price of 7 and 6 on the demand curve in Fig. 10.6:

$$E_D = \frac{\Delta Q}{\Delta P} \times \frac{(P_1 + P_2)/2}{(Q_1 + Q_2)/2} = \frac{7}{1} \times \frac{6.5}{12.5} = 3\tfrac{16}{25}$$

This value is between the correct value of $4\tfrac{2}{3}$ at a price of 7 and the correct value of 3 at a price of 6. We must now go on to see how the correct value can be calculated.

The point elasticity formula

In order to calculate E_D for point elasticity we need to use some simple calculus. It was noted in the section on arc elasticity that as the arc of the demand curve being considered was shortened, the result got closer to the true value. In calculus, when the value of ΔQ gets close to zero, $\Delta Q/\Delta P$ becomes dQ/dP, the first derivative of Q with respect to P. This is in fact the inverse of the slope of the demand curve:

$$E_D = \frac{P}{Q} \times \frac{dQ}{dP}$$

The ratio dQ/dP is the derivative of quantity with respect to price, while P and Q are price and quantity at the point where we wish to measure elasticity. In geometric terms the chord AC in Fig. 10.6 is first shortened to AB and ultimately, when ΔQ equals zero, it becomes the tangent DE.

In order to calculate dQ/dP we must have the equation of the demand curve. The data in Table 10.2 have been calculated from the following formula:

$$Q = 100 - 20P + P^2$$

When differentiated with respect to P this gives a value of:

$$dQ/dP = -20 + 2P$$

If we apply this formula to the example used in Fig. 10.6 for the price of £7 and a quantity of 9 then we can calculate the precise value of elasticity at that point as:

$$E_D = \frac{P}{Q} \times \frac{dQ}{dP} = \frac{7}{9} \times (-6) = -4\tfrac{2}{3}$$

STUDENT ACTIVITY 10.4

Use the data in Table 10.2 to calculate the value of point elasticity at other points along the demand curve. Identify the elastic and the inelastic range of the demand curve.

Straight line demand curves and point elasticity

If we are considering straight line demand curves, the percentage method of calculating elasticity will give an absolutely accurate answer. This is because dQ/dP, the inverse of the slope of the demand curve, will be the same at every point along the demand curve and will be equal to $\Delta Q/\Delta P$. The percentage method appears to be measuring the elasticity for a move along a stretch of the demand curve, but in fact gives the right answer for point elasticity.

Finally, we have spent a good deal of time examining price elasticity of demand. This is because it is an important and, at times, a complex topic. However, having examined it in detail, we will find that we can deal easily and quickly with the other types of elasticity as they all involve similar techniques.

It is important to understand the difference between the percentage method and arc and point elasticity. However, you will not be required to calculate point elasticity unless you go on to higher-level theoretical economics. In general, if you are asked to calculate the value of elasticity of demand, apply the percentage formula.

The main points of price elasticity of demand are summarised in Table 10.3.

Income elasticity of demand

Income elasticity defined

In the previous chapter we saw how the demand for a product has several determinants. The most important of these is price, and so far in this chapter we have been concerned with how demand alters in response to price changes. Another determinant of demand is income (*Y*). The response of demand to changes in income may also be measured.

Income elasticity of demand measures the degree of responsiveness of the quantity demanded of a product to changes in income.

The value of income elasticity can be calculated by the following formula:

$$E_Y = \frac{\text{Percentage change in quantity demanded}}{\text{Percentage change in income}}$$

In the same way as price income elasticity of demand, this formula can be reduced to:

$$E_Y = \frac{\Delta Q/Q}{\Delta Y/Y} = \frac{\Delta Q}{\Delta Y} \times \frac{Y}{Q}$$

where *Y* is income.

Categories of income elasticity

As was explained in the previous chapter, demand might increase or decrease in response to a rise in income, depending upon whether the product we are considering is a normal good or an inferior good. The demand for normal goods increases with income and so these are both positive movements; consequently the value of income elasticity will be positive. With inferior goods, as income rises demand falls and the value is therefore negative. A third possibility exists, which is that demand will remain constant as income rises. In this case there is said to be zero income elasticity. These possibilities are illustrated in Fig. 10.7. (You will note in Fig. 10.7 that quantity demanded is on the vertical axis and income on the horizontal axis. This is because we have returned to the correct mathematical procedure of placing the dependent variable on the vertical axis (see pages 18–19).

You will recall that price elasticity of demand is always negative but that we usually omit the sign. Income elasticity can be either positive or negative and it is therefore very important to include the sign (+ or –) when stating its value. Positive income elasticity can still fall into the three categories of elastic, inelastic and unitary. The possibilities are summarised in Table 10.4.

Table 10.3 **Elasticities of demand**

Category	*Value*	*Characteristics*
Perfectly inelastic	$E_D = 0$	Quantity demanded remains constant as price changes
Inelastic	$0<E_D<1$	Proportionate change in quantity is less than proportionate change in price
Unitary	$E_D = 1$	Proportionate change in quantity is the same as proportionate change in price
Elastic	$1<E_D<\infty$	Proportionate change in quantity is greater than proportionate change in price
Perfectly elastic	$E_D = \infty$	Any amount will be bought at a certain price but none at any higher price

Table 10.4 **Income elasticities**

Category	*Value*	*Characteristics*
Negative income elasticity	$E_Y<0$	Demand decreases as income rises
Zero income elasticity	$E_Y = 0$	Demand does not change as income rises or falls
Income elasticity	$0<E_Y<1$	Demand rises by a smaller proportion than income
Unit income elasticity	$E_Y = 1$	Demand rises by exactly the same proportion as income
Income elasticity	$1<E_Y<\infty$	Demand rises by a greater proportion than income

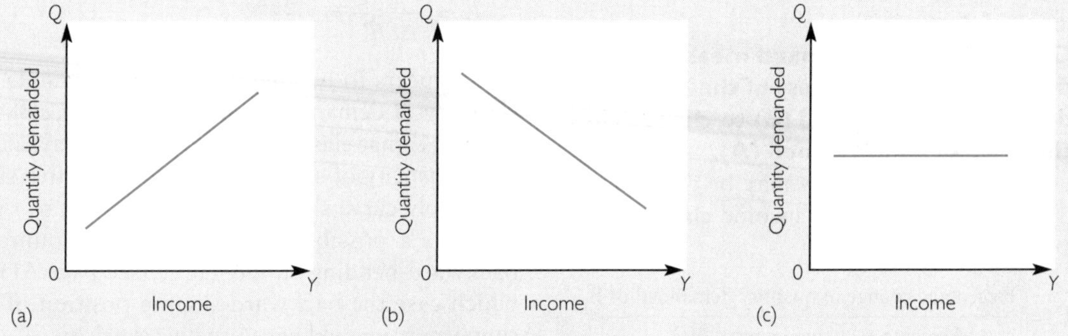

***Fig. 10.7* Income elasticities: three possibilities**
(a) Positive income elasticity as demand increases with income, e.g. colour television sets.
(b) Negative income elasticity as demand falls with income, e.g. potatoes.
(c) Zero income elasticity; demand remains constant as income rises, e.g. salt.

When we examined elasticity of demand we discovered that one demand curve might have all three categories of elasticity. This is also so with income elasticity of demand. Consider a product like potatoes. If an economy is very poor then as income rises people will be pleased to eat more potatoes and therefore potatoes will be a normal good. As income continues to rise and people buy other types of food to supplement their diet, the demand for potatoes remains constant and there is therefore zero income elasticity. As the economy becomes richer people consume such quantities of meat and other vegetables that they need less potatoes. There will now be negative income elasticity of demand for potatoes. This is illustrated in Fig. 10.8.

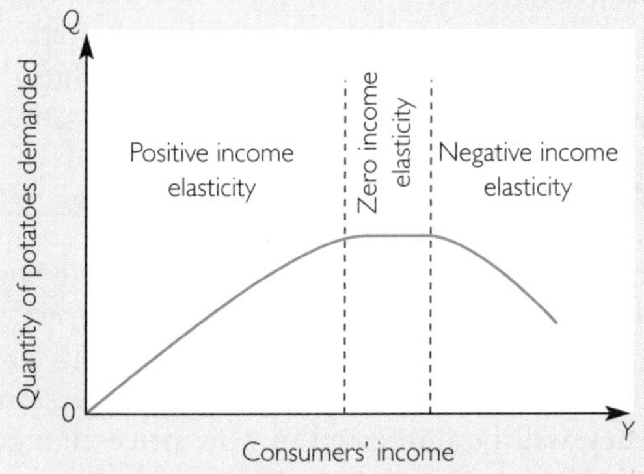

***Fig. 10.8* The demand for potatoes may have all three types of income elasticity**

The importance of income elasticity

Economic growth increases the income of a country and this is generally considered to be a good thing. However, for those engaged in the production of goods with negative income elasticities, this will mean a declining demand for their product. Even when we consider products with positive income elasticities, there is a great variability of response. For example, with commodities such as food and clothing, although demand may rise with income, it might not rise fast enough to offset improvements in productivity, so that the result may still be unemployment for some in the industry. The booming industries tend to be those making products which have highly income elastic demands such as personal computers, video games and personal phones. A downturn in national income, however, may well mean a rapid decline in the demand for these types of goods.

Income elasticity therefore has a most important effect upon resource allocation. We should not be surprised to find that the prosperous areas of the economy are often those associated with products which have a high income elasticity. In recession the opposite will be true.

Cross elasticity of demand

The demand for many products is affected by the price of other products. Where this relationship can be measured we may express it as the cross elasticity of demand.

Cross elasticity of demand measures the degree of responsiveness of the quantity demanded of one good (B) to changes in the price of another good (A).

The value of cross elasticity may be calculated in the same way as price and income elasticity. The formula is:

$$E_x = \frac{\text{Percentage change in quantity demanded of B}}{\text{Percentage change in price of A}}$$

This we may write as:

$$E_x = \frac{\Delta Q_B/Q_B}{\Delta P_A/P_A} = \frac{\Delta Q_B}{\Delta P_A} \times \frac{P_A}{Q_B}$$

In the case of complementary goods, such as cars and petrol, a fall in the price of one will bring about an increase in the demand for the other. Thus we are considering a cut in price (–) bringing about a rise in demand (+). This therefore means that for complements, E_x is negative. Conversely, substitute goods such as butter and margarine might be expected to have a positive E_x because a rise in price of one (+) will bring about a rise in the demand for the other (+) as was discussed in Chapter 9.

The value of E_x may vary from minus infinity to plus infinity. Goods which are close complements or substitutes will tend to exhibit a high cross elasticity of demand. Conversely, when there is little or no relationship between goods then E_x will be near to zero.

Elasticity of supply

Elasticity of supply defined

Much of what we have said about elasticity of demand will hold true for elasticity of supply. Indeed the definition is very similar. Elasticity of supply measures the degree of responsiveness of quantity supplied to changes in price.

The value of elasticity of supply can be calculated by the formula:

$$E_S = \frac{\text{Percentage change in the quantity supplied}}{\text{Percentage change in price}}$$

This may be written as:

$$E_S = \frac{\Delta Q/Q}{\Delta P/P} = \frac{\Delta Q}{\Delta P} \times \frac{P}{Q}$$

This appears to be identical with the formula for elasticity of demand. However, you will recall (see page 124) that elasticity of demand is always negative. Elasticity of supply, however, is positive since the supply curve slopes upwards from left to right. There is a possibility that we may encounter a backward-bending supply curve (see page 61), in which case the backward-sloping position of the supply curve would have negative elasticity.

Supply curves

When we examined demand curves we discovered that it was dangerous to infer the value of elasticity from the slope of the curve. With supply, however, things are much easier. Any straight line supply curve that meets the vertical axis will be elastic and its value will lie between one and infinity. A straight line supply curve that meets the horizontal axis will be inelastic and its value will lie between zero and one. Any straight line supply curve through the origin will have unitary elasticity.

Thus in Fig. 10.9 both S_1 and S_2 have unitary elasticity. (This is because at any point on the supply curve P, Q and ΔP, ΔQ form similar triangles with the supply curve.) This you may confirm by experimenting with curves of different slopes. Supply curves of more complex shapes pose similar problems to demand curves. The category of elasticity of supply at any point on a supply curve may be judged by drawing a tangent to the point of the curve we wish to know about. If the tangent hits the vertical axis then supply is elastic at that point. If it hits the horizontal axis, as in Fig. 10.10, then it is inelastic.

The importance of elasticity of supply

Business organisations, the government and public corporations all take a keen interest in elasticity of demand and are interested in its precise measurement. This is not hard to understand for they will be interested in how price changes affect their revenues. However, no conclusions about total revenue can be arrived at from the supply curve. The precise measurement of E_S is, therefore, of less interest.

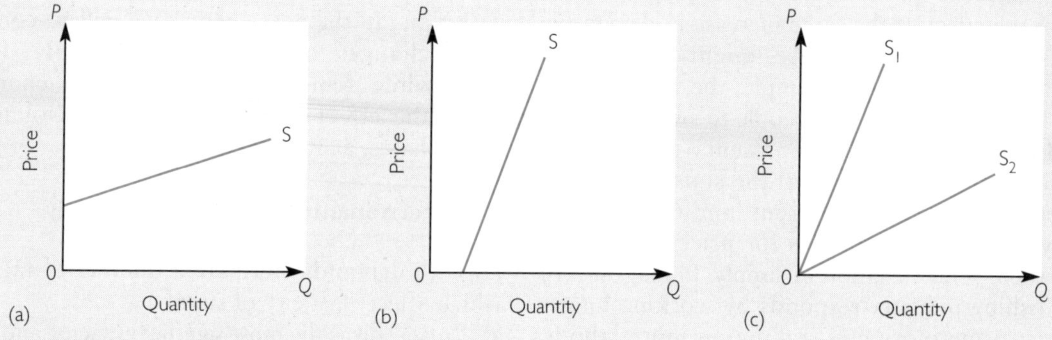

***Fig. 10.9* Elasticity of supply**
(a) Elastic. (b) Inelastic. (c) Unitary.

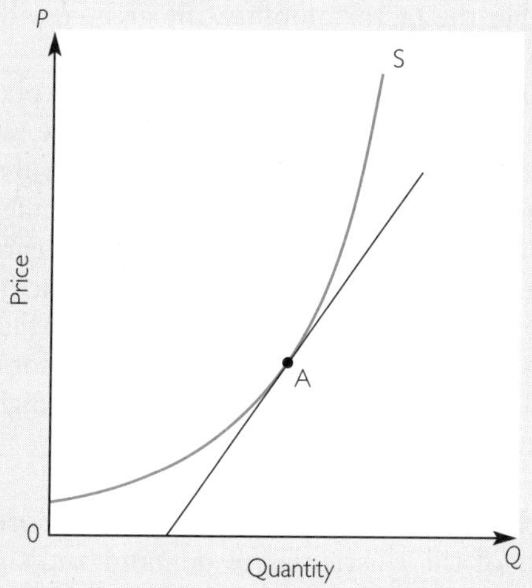

***Fig. 10.10* Elasticity of supply**
The elasticity of supply at point A can be judged from a tangent drawn to the curve at that point.

Although we have dealt with elasticity of supply only briefly here, it should not be thought that it is unimportant. Indeed, since the long-run shape of the supply curve is dependent upon the costs of production, it can be readily appreciated that its slope is of the utmost importance. In later chapters, when we come to consider costs and the theory of production, we will be investigating the factors which shape the supply curve.

Periods of supply

Elasticity of supply increases with time as producers have longer to adjust to changes in demand. Alfred Marshall maintained that there were three periods of supply – the momentary, short-run and long-run periods – defined as follows:

a) *Momentary*. In the momentary period supply is fixed and E_S is zero.
b) *Short run*. In the short run supply can be varied with the limit of the present fixed assets (buildings, machines, etc.).
c) *Long run*. In the long run all factors may be varied and firms may enter or leave the industry.

Suppose we consider an increase in the demand for candles as a result of a strike in the electricity supply industry. In the momentary period we have only whatever stocks of candles already exist in shops. In the short run the existing candle factories can work longer hours, take on more labour, etc. If the increase in demand for candles were to be permanent, then in the long run more candle factories could be built. The effect of periods of supply on costs is discussed in Chapter 15.

Periods of supply and the equilibrium price

If we accept the Marshallian periods of supply then we should be able to observe them in their effect on equilibrium price. Figure 10.11 follows Marshall's analysis. Suppose that the diagram represents the market for fresh fish. In each diagram the effect of the same increase in demand is considered. This increase might have been brought about by, for example, the BSE crisis in the beef industry causing people to switch to fish.

In each diagram E represents the original equilibrium. In diagram (a) the supply of fish is fixed at whatever the present landings are. The only response therefore is for price to rise (E_1) but there is no variation in supply. In diagram (b) the fishing industry responds by working longer hours, using more nets, taking on more labour, etc. The price falls from the momentary high of E_1 to E_2 as there is some expansion of supply. Diagram (c) shows what happens if there is a long-term increase in demand. Now in response to the increase in demand the industry is able to build more boats (vary the fixed costs) and new businesses enter the industry. The result is that the price falls to E_3 and considerably more is supplied. It was Marshall's contention that E_3 would be higher than E, i.e. that the supply curve is upward sloping. Marshall assumed that the industry had already benefited from economies of scale and that any expansion of the industry, in relation to others, would cause it to suffer from increasing costs (see pages 33–4). Since S_L is more elastic than S_M or S_S we may conclude that:

Elasticity of supply tends to increase with time.

It should not be thought that the equilibrium price leaps from E_1 to E_2. More usually it is a gradual process as elasticity of supply increases with time. In the next chapter we will be considering changes in demand and supply. It is worthwhile remembering that when changes occur the effect may be possible to isolate in three phases, as we have seen here.

Determinants of elasticity of supply

As with demand, there are a number of factors which affect elasticity of supply:

a) *Time*. This is the most significant factor and we have seen how elasticity increases with time.
b) *Factor mobility*. The ease with which factors of production can be moved from one use to another will affect elasticity of supply. The higher the factor mobility, the greater will be the elasticity.
c) *Natural constraints*. The natural world places restrictions upon supply. If, for example, we wish to produce more vintage wine it will take years of maturing before it becomes vintage.
d) *Risk taking*. The more willing entrepreneurs are to take risks the greater will be the elasticity of supply. This will be partly influenced by the system of incentives in the economy. If, for example, marginal rates of tax are very high this may reduce the elasticity of supply.

This chapter has concentrated on the theoretical aspects of the elasticities of demand and supply. You will find, however, that it is a concept which

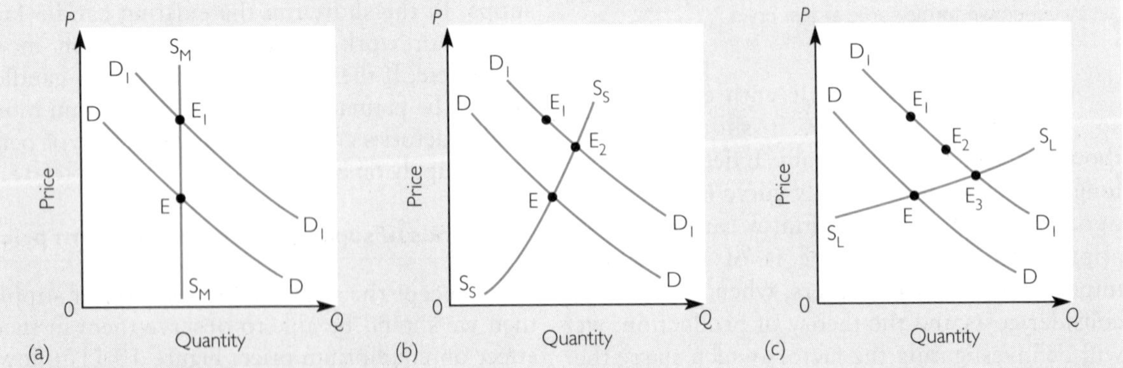

Fig. 10.11 Periods of supply
(a) Momentary period. (b) Short-run period. (c) Long-run period.

has widespread uses. It can be applied to exports and imports to assess the effects of depreciation in the currency. The Chancellor of the Exchequer will be concerned with it in determining the level of indirect taxes, and of course firms are vitally concerned with it in their price and output policy. You will find references to it throughout the book and especially in the next two chapters; therefore make sure you have understood this chapter thoroughly.

Summary

1 Elasticity of demand measures the responsiveness of quantity demanded to changes in price. Demand may be elastic, inelastic or unitary depending upon whether a cut in price raises, lowers or leaves total revenue unchanged.
2 Any value of elasticity is arrived at by dividing the percentage change in the quantity demanded (or supplied) by the percentage change in the determinant which brought it about (price, income, price of other goods).
3 Elasticity of demand is primarily determined by the ease of substitution.
4 Elasticity measured along a segment of a curve is referred to as arc elasticity while elasticity measured at one spot on a curve is point elasticity.
5 Income elasticity measures the responsiveness of demand to changes in income and may be positive, negative or zero, depending upon whether quantity demanded goes up, goes down or remains constant as income increases.
6 Cross elasticity measures the responsiveness of the quantity demanded of one good to changes in the price of another. It may be either positive or negative depending upon whether the two products considered are substitutes or complements.
7 Elasticity of supply may be elastic, inelastic or unitary depending upon whether, following a price rise, the quantity supplied rises by a greater, smaller or equal percentage.
8 Elasticity of supply increases with time. This can be analysed in Marshall's three supply periods: momentary, short run and long run.

Questions

1 Explain the factors which determine elasticity of supply.
2 Compare and contrast the responsiveness of demand of primary products and manufactured products with respect to changes in price and changes in income.
3 Explain how OPEC exploited its knowledge of the elasticity of demand for oil. Evaluate the success of its policy.
4 Explain how the value of price elasticity of demand will affect the success of the following actions.
   a) Cinema owners increase the price of admission in order to increase their receipts.
   b) London Transport reduces underground train fares to attract more customers and increase its receipts.
5 Consider the following information:

	1971	*1981*	*1986*	*1991*	*1994*
Disposable income at constant prices (1990 prices)	46.6	58.5	85.5	99.9	104.7
Cigarette sales (millions)	136	121	101	98	86

Are cigarettes inferior goods? Justify your answer. If you were asked to account for the observed variation in cigarette sales, what additional information would help you?
6 Examine the effect that elasticity of demand would have on government tax revenues if the government [illegible] increase the tax on:
   a) alcohol;
   b) video [illegible]
7 If we have [illegible]
that the [illegible]

$P =$ [illegible]

and su[illegible]

P [illegible]

wha[illegible]
the[illegible]

Data response A
BEEBOP trainers

The information in Table 10.5 represents the demand and supply for BEEBOP trainers.

Table 10.5

Price per pair (£)	*Quantity of trainers pairs/week* Supplied	Demanded
50.00	20 000	1 250
42.50	16 250	3 125
35.00	12 500	5 000
27.50	8 750	6 875
17.50	3 750	9 375
12.50	1 250	10 625
10.00	0	11 250

From this information:

1 Determine the equilibrium price and quantity of BEEBOP trainers.
2 Calculate the coefficients of the elasticity of demand (E_D) and supply (E_S) at the equilibrium price.
3 What would be the new equilibrium price if demand were to increase by 50 per cent at every price?
4 Why would it be useful to the owners of BEEBOP to know the elasticity of demand for their product? In what other circumstances is knowledge of the value of elasticity of demand likely to prove useful?
5 What does elasticity of demand tell us about the relative power of consumers, sellers and producers in given market situations?

Data response B
Alcoholic elasticities

Study the statistical estimates of elasticities for alcoholic drinks in Australia in Table 10.6 (the negative elasticities on the diagonal are own price elasticities; all other price elasticities are cross price elasticities).

Table 10.6 **Elasticities for beer, wine and spirits in Australia**

Product	*Price elasticities* Beer	*Wine*	*Spirits*	*Income elasticities*
1956–7				
Beer	–0.10	0.03	0.07	0.71
Wine	0.26	–0.57	0.31	1.11
Spirits	0.34	0.17	–0.52	2.34
1976–7				
Beer	–0.12	0.03	0.08	0.82
Wine	0.12	–0.27	0.15	0.51
Spirits	0.35	0.17	–0.52	2.34

Source: Clements and Johnson (1983)

1 Which drink has the most elastic demand, and which the most inelastic? Did this position change between 1956–7 and 1976–7?
2 Rank the drinks in terms of where you would expect to see the fastest growth in demand in each of the two periods studied.
3 Is wine or spirits a better substitute for beer?
4 If the spirits industry put up its prices by 10 per cent, what would be the expected reduction in quantity demanded? By how much would its revenues change? Would the beer industry or the wine industry benefit most from this price increase?

11 Markets in movement

Learning outcomes

After reading this chapter you will be able to:

- Predict the consequences of government intervention in the market.
- Identify markets that are likely to be unstable.
- Recognise the shortcomings of supply and demand analysis.
- Analyse areas of conflict between markets and government objectives.

In previous chapters we have examined the factors which shape demand and supply curves and the formation of equilibrium prices. We will now go on to analyse how changes in demand and supply affect market prices. We will start by recalling some important points.

Some important ideas reviewed

Here we will give a brief summary of some of the fundamentals established in previous chapters. It is necessary that you fully understand these ideas before proceeding with the rest of this chapter.

Equilibrium price

This occurs where the demand curve cuts the supply curve and is the point at which the wishes of buyers and sellers coincide. Equilibrium prices also have an important allocative and distributive function in a free enterprise economy, helping us to answer the 'What?', 'How?' and 'For whom?' questions. An equilibrium price, however, is not permanent; it lasts only so long as the forces which produced it persist. A change in the conditions of demand or supply will bring about a new equilibrium price.

Ceteris paribus

It is possible to reach any conclusions only so long as we keep the rule of considering only one change at a time. Most statements in microeconomics should be prefaced with the phrase 'all other things remaining constant' or *ceteris paribus*.

Changes in demand and supply

It is important to distinguish between changes in the quantity demanded or supplied, and changes in demand and supply. For example, lowering the price of a good will bring about a rise in the quantity demanded; it will not create a new demand curve. In Fig. 11.1 (a) this is seen as a movement along the existing demand curve from A to B. This is termed an extension of demand. However, if, for example, there is a rise in income such that more is demanded at each price than before, this shifts the demand curve to the right as a new demand is created. This is termed an increase in demand. These principles hold true for supply as well.

A movement along an existing supply curve is termed an extension or contraction of supply and a shift to a new supply curve is termed an increase or decrease in supply. Thus in Fig. 11.1 diagrams (a) and (c) represent changes in the quantity demanded or supplied while (b) and (d) represent changes in demand and supply.

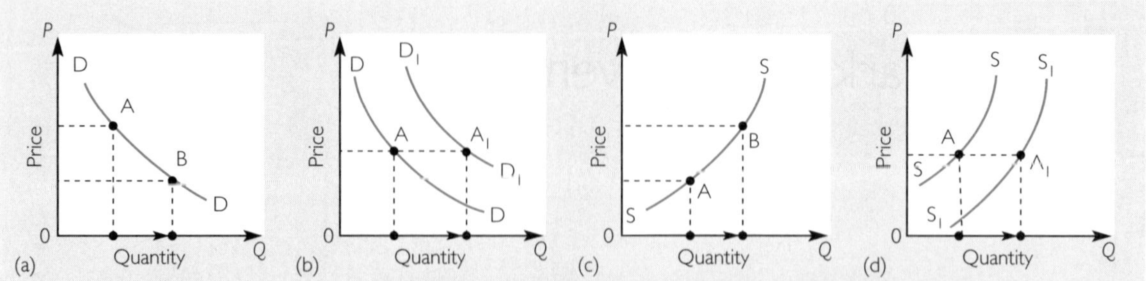

***Fig. 11.1* Changes in quantity demanded or supplied versus changes in demand or supply**
In (a) and (c) a change in the price of the commodity causes a change in the quantity demanded or supplied.
In (b) and (d) a change in the willingness or ability to demand or supply brings about a new demand or supply such that a different quantity may be demanded or supplied at the same price.

Elasticity

The extent to which the quantity demanded or supplied changes in response to changes in price may vary enormously depending upon the elasticity of demand or supply.

Changes in market price

Four possibilities for change

If we consider all the possible changes in demand and supply it will be apparent that only four basic movements in the equilibrium are possible. These are illustrated in Fig. 11.2.

Other things being equal, an increase in demand will bring about an extension of supply so that more is supplied at a higher price (Fig. 11.2 (a)). A decrease in demand leads to a contraction of supply, with less bought at a lower price (Fig. 11.2 (b)). Conversely, an increase in supply causes an extension of demand so that more is demanded at a lower price (Fig. 11.2 (c)); and a decrease in supply causes a contraction of demand so that less is bought at a higher price (Fig. 11.2 (d)).

STUDENT ACTIVITY 11.1

If you refer back to the determinants of demand and supply you will see what factors might have brought about these changes. Can you match the following four examples with

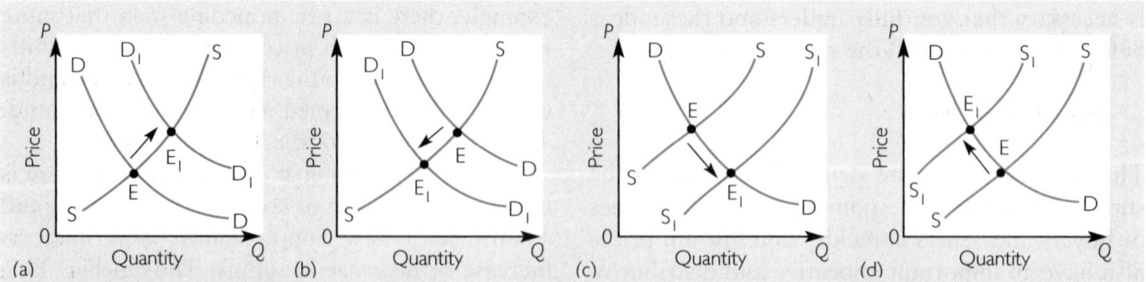

***Fig. 11.2* Changes in the equilibrium**
(a) Increase in demand results in more being bought at a higher price.
(b) Decrease in demand results in a smaller quantity being brought at a lower price.
(c) Increase in supply results in more being supplied at a lower price.
(d) Decrease in supply results in less being supplied at a higher price.

the correct diagrams in Fig. 11.2? Which diagram shows the effect on the market for:

1 computers, of improvements in silicon chips;
2 tomatoes, of an exceptionally poor summer;
3 beefsteak, of a rise in consumers' incomes;
4 potatoes, of a rise in consumers' incomes?

You should have got: 1 (c); 2 (d); 3 (a); 4 (b). (Remember that potatoes are usually considered an inferior good.)

Common misunderstanding

A mistaken argument is often advanced which goes something like this. 'If supply increases (Fig. 11.2 (c)) the price will fall, but if the price falls then more will be demanded. This rise in demand will then put up the price, increased price will cause less to be demanded and so on. Therefore it is impossible to say what the effect of the original increase in supply will be.'

This argument confuses changes in supply and demand with movements along supply and demand curves. The original increase in supply does not cause demand to change. For example, technological advance means that many more pocket calculators can be supplied very cheaply. This does not alter the conditions of demand. It does not, for example, increase people's incomes. Instead it means that the suppliers of pocket calculators have many more to sell and this they do by lowering the price. This causes a greater quantity to be demanded. If there is no further change a new equilibrium will have been reached, with more calculators bought at a lower price.

Complex changes

We were only able to reach any firm conclusions in the analysis above because we stuck to the rule of *ceteris paribus*, i.e. of considering only one change at a time. It is, of course, possible – even likely – that more than one factor may vary at a given point in time. Suppose, for example, that there is a large rise in the demand for apples because of a successful advertising campaign to promote them. This is followed by an unexpected bumper crop of apples. What will be the final effect upon the equilibrium price? (See Fig. 11.3.)

If you study Fig. 11.3 you will see that both diagrams could illustrate the example we have

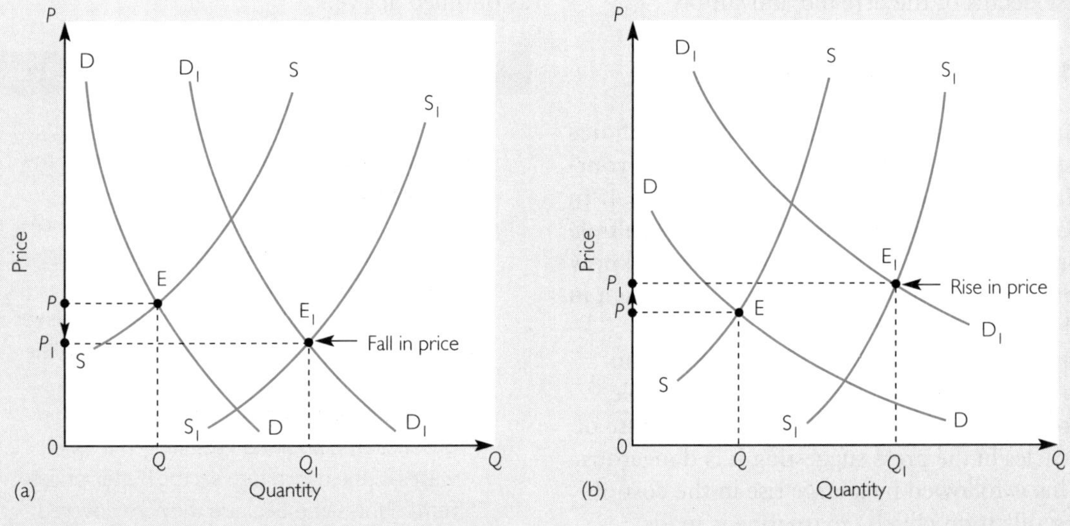

***Fig. 11.3* Complex shifts in demand and supply**

In both cases there is an increase in demand and supply, but in (a) this results in a lower equilibrium price and in (b) a higher equilibrium price. This is because of the different magnitudes of shifts in demand and supply.

just mentioned. However, although the quantity demanded and supplied increases in both cases, in Fig. 11.3 (a) the price falls while in Fig. 11.3 (b) it rises.

When multiple shifts in demand and supply curves are considered it is impossible to reach any firm conclusion about the effect on the equilibrium price unless the precise magnitudes of the changes are known.

This conclusion has important consequences for anyone undertaking an examination in economics.

Suppose you are asked to consider the effect of a number of changes in the demand and supply of a particular product. It is obvious from Fig. 11.3 that no firm conclusion can be reached unless both changes move in the same direction; for example, an increase in supply coupled with a decrease in demand will definitely lower the equilibrium price. What is the solution? The answer is to explain one change at a time. In the examples used above, for instance, first explain the effect of an increase in demand and draw a diagram to illustrate it. Then explain the effect of the increase in supply and draw another diagram to illustrate this. Always keep to the rule of explaining one thing at a time unless you have precise details of the demand and supply.

Multiple choice examinations

If your examination contains a multiple choice element it is quite likely that you may find yourself faced with a diagram similar to Fig. 11.4. In this case we can answer questions about multiple changes in demand and supply because we know the precise magnitude of them (they are shown in the diagram). Suppose the question were:

> Figure 11.4 shows the original equilibrium price of margarine. However, many people are discouraged from eating butter because of articles in the press suggesting it is dangerous. This is followed by a large rise in the cost of the oils from which margarine is made. What will be the new equilibrium price? A? B? C? D? E?

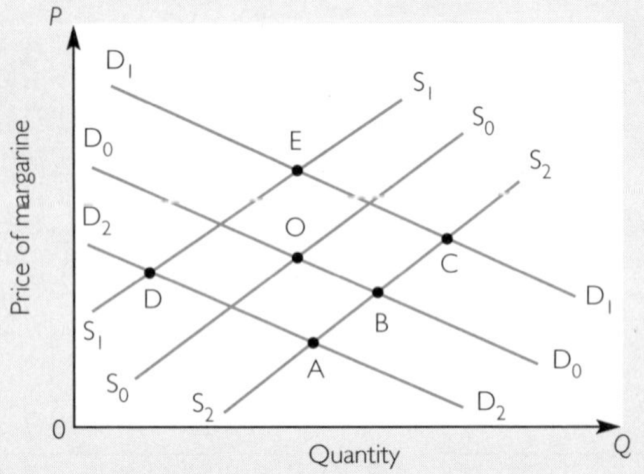

***Fig. 11.4* Multiple shifts in demand and supply**

The best way to answer the questions is to locate position O and then ignore the other DD and SS curves. Then follow the question one step at a time. The articles in the press will decrease the demand for butter and thus increase the demand for margarine; we are thus at the intersection of S_0S_0 with D_1D_1. The increase in the cost of oils will decrease the supply of margarine. Thus we will move to point E, which is the correct answer.

If there are more questions on the same diagram always remember to return to the original equilibrium O. Then follow the same procedure as outlined above.

STUDENT ACTIVITY 11.2

Using Fig. 11.4 and starting again at O, what will be the new equilibrium position in each of the following cases?

a) There is a massive increase in the price of bread, but the EU decides to subsidise margarine production.
b) New evidence suggests that butter is healthier for you after all, and crop failures push up the price of margarine's constituents.
c) The wages council covering agricultural production is abolished resulting in a fall in wages in the agriculture sector. Butter prices remain the same because they are covered by an EU price guarantee scheme. The economy as a whole is going into recession.

The effect of time on prices

Time lags

Supply often takes some time to respond to changes in demand. This ***time lag*** will vary depending upon the product we are considering. We may distinguish between two types of response:

a) *One-period time lag*. This is associated with agricultural products, where the supply in one period is dependent upon what the price was in the previous period. Say, for example, that there is an increase in demand for barley. This will cause the price to rise, but there will be no immediate response from supply; it will have to wait until more barley has been planted and grown. Then at the next harvest there will be a sudden response to the previous year's increase in price. The period need not be a year; if the product we were considering was timber it might take a good deal longer to grow more trees.

b) *Distributed time lag*. This is associated with manufactured goods. For example, if there is an increase in the demand for cars then manufacturers can respond to this by using their factories more intensively. However, if this does not satisfy the demand then supplying more will have to wait upon the building of new factories. The response is thus more complex and distributed over time.

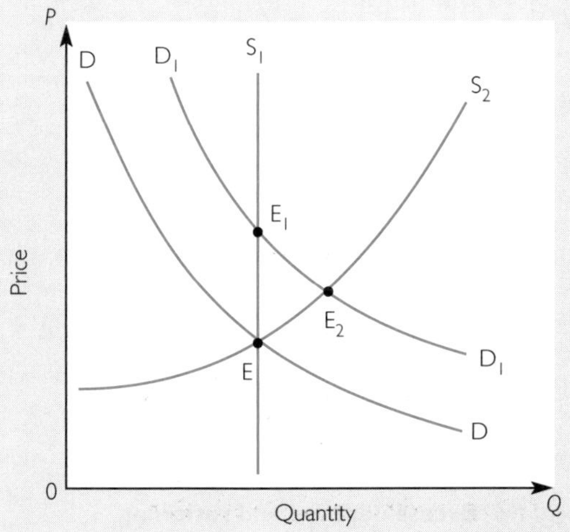

***Fig. 11.5* The effect of time on the equilibrium price**

Time lags and prices

It is easiest to consider one-period time lags. A possible effect is shown in Fig. 11.5. Suppose that the diagram illustrates the demand and supply of barley. The move from DD to D_1D_1 shows the effect of an increase in the demand for barley. However, at the time of harvest the supply of barley is absolutely fixed and can be represented by the vertical supply curve S_1. The only response of the market, therefore, is for the price to rise to E_1, but there is no change in supply. Seeing the increase in demand, however, farmers plant more barley and so next year there is more supplied and we arrive at E_2. The extra supply in year 2 has thus been called forth by the high price in year 1.

This is a development of the idea of elasticity of supply explained in Chapter 10. The further implications of this are discussed at the end of this chapter.

Government interference with equilibrium prices

The problem

We have seen that prices fulfil an ***allocating function*** in distributing scarce goods between different users or consumers. Income, however, is unevenly distributed so that although goods may be readily available people may not be able to buy them. If these goods are the essentials of life it is very hard for a democratic government not to interfere. Suppose, for example, rents are extremely high so that people cannot afford housing. The government could build more houses; this, however, is very expensive. It is very tempting for the government, therefore, to think that it can get round the problem by freezing the rent of houses below the equilibrium price. It is the object of this section to show that such interferences, almost invariably, have some undesirable side effects.

Any price artificially imposed by law may be termed a ***flat price***. Where the authorities stipulate a maximum price for a commodity this may be termed a ***ceiling price*** and where a minimum price is stipulated this is termed a ***price floor***.

The objectives

Governments do not just freeze prices at a low level; they sometimes maintain them at artificially high levels. It is possible for a government to be fixing some prices too high and others too low at the same time. This is because it has different objectives of policy:

a) *Cheapness*. It may be the objective of the government to keep the price of a product at a level at which it can be afforded by most people, e.g. housing or food.
b) *The maintenance of incomes*. The government may want to keep the incomes of producers at a higher level than that which would be produced by market prices. This is often true of farm incomes.
c) *Price stability*. If there is a wide variation in the price of produce from year to year, e.g. agricultural products, the government may wish to iron out these variations in the interests of both producers and consumers.

Ceiling prices

Governments in many countries have often interfered in the economy to fix the price of a commodity below the equilibrium. Good examples of this are to be found in wartime. In the UK during the Second World War almost everything was in very short supply. If the price of a basic commodity such as meat or eggs had been left to find its own level it would have been very high and beyond the means of many people. In Fig. 11.6 this is shown as price OT. A ceiling price is shown as OR. At this price consumers will wish to buy ON but suppliers who were willing to supply OM when the price was OT are now willing to supply only OL. There is therefore an excess demand of LN. Thus price is failing to fulfil its ***rationing function*** and some other method will have to be used. This might lead to long queues outside butchers' shops or to butchers serving only their regular customers. This often happened in Russia and the other former communist states, where prices were kept low despite chronic deficiencies of supply. This meant that other rationing measures had to be put in place such as allowing meat to be sold on only one day of the week, thus limiting demand.

Three examples of intervention in the market are considered below:

a) *Wartime controls*. During the Second World War the UK adopted a system of rationing. This meant that in addition to the price, customers also had to have a coupon issued by the government which entitled them to so many ounces of meat per week. Therefore, in effect, a new money-plus-coupon price had been created. Demand could be effectively decreased to equate with supply by regulating the issue of coupons. In Fig. 11.6 this is shown by the new demand curve D_1 and thus an equilibrium, of sorts, was arrived at. This system still had drawbacks; for example, a coupon entitled a person to a number of ounces of meat per week but it did not specify the quality of the meat.

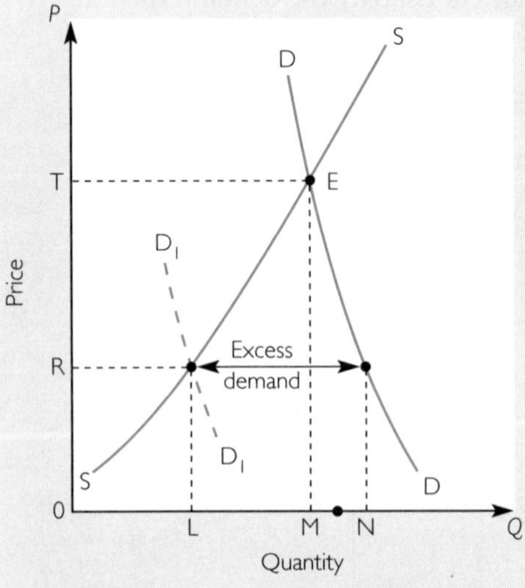

***Fig. 11.6* Excess demand and rationing**
The price set below the equilibrium brings about excess demand of LN. D_1 shows an artificial equilibrium created by the imposition of rationing.

b) *Rent control.* Such interference has not been limited to wartime. In the UK there has been rent control since the First World War. Rather than providing cheap accommodation for all, this had made it very difficult for many people to rent accommodation. Landlords have sold houses rather than let them at low rents and sitting tenants have clung to their accommodation. Thus rent control has had the opposite effect from that which was intended. Similar controls in France discouraged building between 1914 and 1948. Rent controls in the UK led to massive ***distortions*** in the housing market. They were, for example, one of the reasons for the high level of owner occupation. The Conservative government abolished most of the remaining controls in 1988. Although this return to market economics got rid of distortions in the market, it did not solve the problem of how to house the poorest people in society who ended up in unsatisfactory bed and breakfast accommodation.

c) *Interest.* In the Middle Ages charging interest on money was condemned by the church as the sin of usury, and since the sixteenth century many countries have placed a ceiling on the interest that can be charged. The best example of this in recent years has been regulation in the USA, which was intended to give cheap loans and mortgages to people. The drawback was that it also frequently created a shortage of funds for these purposes. The USA began to phase out restrictions on interest charges in 1981. Once again it is often the poorest people who suffer when the market is allowed to work without interference because only less reputable lenders, sometimes known as 'loan sharks', are willing to lend to them.

Price floors

If the government establishes a floor below which prices may not fall, and this price is above the equilibrium, then excess supply will be created. This is illustrated in Fig. 11.7. Here the price has been fixed at OT and this has caused demand to contract from OM to OL. However, at the higher price suppliers wish to sell more and supply expands to ON. The excess supply is shown as line AB.

We will consider three examples of this:

a) *Agricultural prices.* In the USA and in Europe governments frequently set guaranteed high prices for agricultural products in order to protect the incomes of farmers. The Common Agricultural Policy (CAP) of the EU does this and Europeans are familiar with the excess supply it creates in the form of 'butter mountains' and 'wine lakes' (see Chapter 12). It also results in high prices for the consumer, once again creating problems for the poorest people in society.

b) *Minimum wages.* Where wages are very low a government may try to improve the lot of workers by insisting on a minimum wage. This may, however, have the effect of encouraging employers to employ fewer people and instead substitute other factors of production. Thus the workers that remain in employment are better off but others may have lost their jobs. This is illustrated in Fig. 11.7. Here the diagram shows that not only are fewer people employed but also the possibility that the total amount of money paid in wages has declined. If OT is the

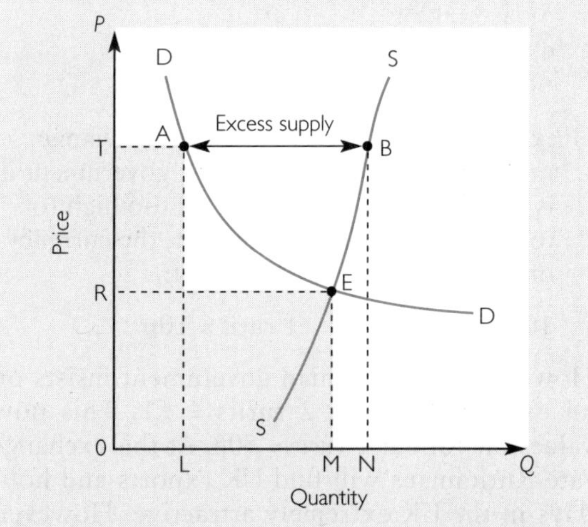

***Fig. 11.7* Excess supply and a price floor**

minimum wage then the total amount paid in wages is OTAL, whereas at the lower wage rate of OR the amount paid is OREM.

In the USA, Milton Friedman has argued that minimum wage regulations have significantly reduced the employment of young black people and have depressed the total paid in wages, as in Fig. 11.7. In the UK, on the other hand, the Wages Councils Act 1969 was passed to set minimum wage levels in a variety of industries, such as agriculture and catering, where wages were low. At one time wages councils were laying down the minimum wage levels for 3 million workers. The Conservative government, however, followed Milton Friedman's argument and set about dismantling many of the wages councils during the 1980s, believing that this would enlarge employment. The consequences of the Labour government's introduction of a minimum wage have yet to be seen. We will return to this argument in a macroeconomic context in Chapter 43.

STUDENT ACTIVITY 11.3

What do you think would be the consequence of imposing a standard minimum wage on the following groups of workers?

a) machinists in the clothing industry
b) cleaners in the NHS
c) school leavers of 16
d) accountants
e) part-time Saturday jobs

c) *Exchange rates.* Where the value (exchange rate) of a currency is fixed by a government it is possible for its price to be set too high (or too low). Suppose that the rurit, the currency of Ruritania, has a real value of:

10 rurits = £1 or 1 rurit = 10p

However, the Ruritanian government insists on an exchange rate of 2 rurits = £1. This now values the rurit at 1 rurit = 50p. At this exchange rate Ruritanians will find UK exports and holidays in the UK extremely attractive. However, they will not find anyone willing to sell them pounds at this rate unless they are sufficiently desperate for Ruritanian goods to pay five times their true value. Thus commerce between the two countries will be all but impossible.

Many of the former communist states of Eastern Europe insisted on rates as unrealistic as the one described above. Thus, their citizens found it very difficult, or impossible, to obtain pounds or dollars to buy imports or to travel abroad. Foreign currency earnings came from tourists who were willing to pay the unrealistic exchange rate in order to visit the country. Exports and imports had to be arranged by special agreements with foreign governments or companies. The difficulties of attempting to move to a realistic exchange rate led to the almost total collapse of the rouble (see Data reponse B at the end of the chapter).

Black markets

Whenever a government intervenes to fix a price too high or too low, it means that there is another price at which both buyers and sellers are willing to trade. Such fiat prices thus tend to bring so-called ***black markets*** into being, as people begin to make illegal arrangements to circumvent the government price.

During rationing in the Second World War there were active black markets in the USA, the UK and occupied Europe. Rent control had led to potential tenants making payments to landlords for 'furniture and fittings' or as 'key money' in order to obtain a tenancy. In the USA ceilings on interest payments frequently led banks to offer other inducements to attract accounts. Potential depositors were often offered gifts to open an account, the gifts varying from electric toasters to, on one occasion, a Rolls-Royce. The reader may be more familiar with the black market in tickets for Wimbledon or the FA Cup Final.

When we turn to prices set too high we find comparable attempts at circumvention. Anyone who has visited a communist country will be aware of the efforts of residents to buy foreign currency at black market rates. Wages set too high can also cause difficulties; for example, people are often employed illegally thus not only receiving a low wage but also defrauding the government of income tax. Employers also get round legislation by employing outworkers. The rates of pay for such work are often incredibly low. The artificially high prices of the CAP often mean that the EU itself has to make arrangements to dispose of the excess supply. An example of this was the sale of cut-price butter to the former USSR.

Not all these are black markets in the accepted sense, but they do illustrate the difficulties caused by interfering with equilibrium prices.

STUDENT ACTIVITY 11.4

You are working in a government department which has been asked to look at the way in which FA Cup Final tickets are distributed. The options which you have been asked to look at are:

1 Leave the system to the open market with no intervention from the government or the FA.
2 Offer tickets at a rate lower than the market rate only to supporters of the two clubs in the final and sell any that are left on the open market.
3 Offer a limited number of tickets to the supporters of both teams and further tickets to supporters of other football teams. Offer the same controlled price to everyone.

Advise the government which is the best system. Can you think of any alternative systems? What black market activity is likely to occur in each case?

Price stabilisation

Agricultural products are often subject to unplanned variations in supply, i.e. because of the influence of such things as the weather and diseases the actual output in any particular year may be greater or smaller than that which farmers planned. If we consider a product with a relatively inelastic demand, such as wheat, then comparatively small variations in supply may cause large variations in the price. This is illustrated in Fig. 11.8. S_0 represents the planned supply, with farmers happy to produce 20 million tonnes of wheat at £260 per tonne. A bad harvest might decrease the supply to S_2 while a good one might increase it to S_1. High prices in bad years might suit farmers but might cause distress or even famine to consumers. Although consumers might be delighted with low prices in good years, these prices might result in bankruptcy for many farmers. In extreme cases the price may fall so low that it does not even cover harvesting and distribution costs and the crops may be ploughed back into the soil.

It would seem desirable, therefore, to attempt to stabilise prices and incomes. This could be done by a producers' cooperative or by a government agency. Suppose that we have the situation represented by S_1 in Fig. 11.8, with supply totalling 25 million tonnes. If an agency were to buy up 5 million tonnes and store them, this would drive up the price to £260 per tonne. Suppose that in the subsequent year the crop was very poor so that now only 15 million tonnes is produced. By releasing 5 million tonnes from store the agency can keep the price down to £260 per tonne, thus bringing stability and order to the situation.

This policy is not easy to implement because it is difficult to determine the correct price for a product and to be certain in any year how much to build up or to release. Nevertheless many such schemes have been tried. (This subject is developed in the next chapter.)

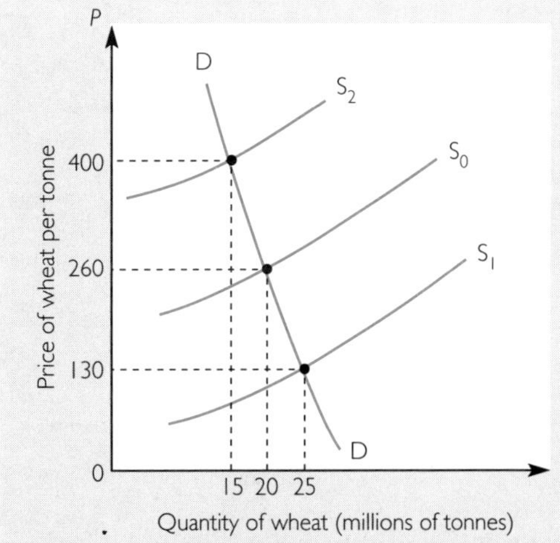

***Fig. 11.8* Price and income stabilisation**

Taxes and subsidies

Types of tax

Taxes fall into two main groups, direct and indirect. ***Direct taxes*** are those which are levied directly on people's incomes, the most important being income tax. ***Indirect taxes*** are those which are levied on expenditure. We are here concerned only with expenditure or outlay taxes and their effect upon demand and supply. (Taxes are more fully discussed in Chapter 30.)

The two most important indirect taxes in the UK are ***value-added tax*** (VAT) and ***excise duty***. VAT is an *ad valorem* (by value) tax, i.e. it is levied as a percentage of the selling price of the commodity. Excise duty is a specific (or unit) tax which is levied per unit of the commodity, irrespective of its price; for example, the same excise duty is levied per litre of wine irrespective of whether it is ordinary table wine or the finest vintage.

VAT is levied on most goods, with only a few essentials being exempt from it. Excise duty is levied mainly on alcohol, tobacco and petrol (hydrocarbon oils). VAT is levied after excise duty and consequently the purchaser may end up paying a tax on a tax. Thus products such as petrol have both a specific and an *ad valorem* tax on them.

The effect of a tax

If we wish to demonstrate the effect of a tax upon the demand and supply situation, this is done by moving the supply curve vertically upwards by the amount of the tax. The tax may be regarded as a cost of production. The producer has to pay rent and wages and now must also pay the tax to the government. The effect of indirect taxes is shown in Fig. 11.9.

In diagram (a) £1 specific tax has raised the supply curve from S to S_1. You can see that the new supply curve is £1 above the old curve at every point. In diagram (b) the effect of a 50 per cent *ad valorem* tax is shown and you can see that the new supply curve diverges from the old one as the tax increases with price.

The incidence of a tax

If we use the phrase 'the ***incidence*** of taxation' this means who the tax falls upon. The ***formal*** (or legal) incidence of a tax is upon the person who is legally responsible for paying it. In the

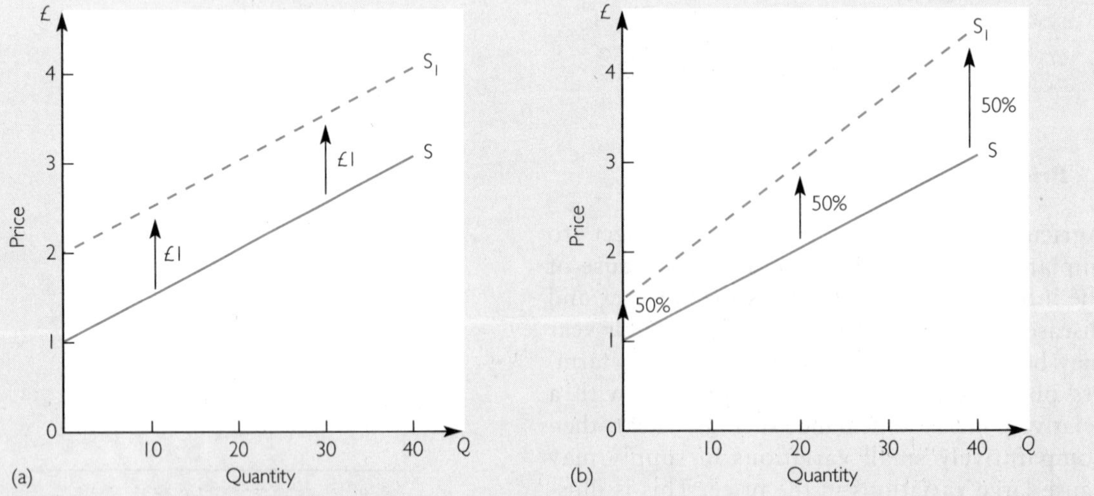

Fig. 11.9 Taxes and the supply curve
(a) This shows the effect of a £1 specific tax, while (b) shows the effect of a 50 per cent *ad valorem* tax.

case of alcohol, for example, this is the producer or importer. It is possible, however, that some or all of the tax may be passed on to the consumer, in which case the incidence is said to be shifted so that the actual incidence (or ***burden***) of the tax is wholly or partly upon the consumer.

It is often thought by the consumer that if the government places a tax upon a commodity the price of that commodity will immediately rise by the amount of the tax. This is usually not so. Consider what might happen if a tax of £1 per bottle were placed on wine. If the price were to be put up by £1 consumers would immediately begin to look for substitutes such as beer, spirits or soft drinks. The wine merchants, being worried about their sales, might well reduce their prices. In other words they have absorbed part of the tax. Thus the incidence has been distributed between the producers and consumers of wine.

This situation is analysed in Fig. 11.10. Here you can see that the original price of a bottle of wine was £2.50 and that 25 000 bottles were sold. The imposition of a £1 tax might be expected to raise the price to £3.50. This you can see is not so; the new equilibrium price is £3.10 and the quantity sold is 21 000 bottles. The price to the consumer has thus risen by 60p. The price the producer receives is now £3.10 but £1 of this must be given to the government, so the producer is effectively receiving only £2.10, i.e. 40p less than previously. Thus the incidence of the tax is 60 per cent to the consumer and 40 per cent to the producer. In Fig. 11.10 BC is paid by the consumer and CD by the producer.

The extent to which the tax is passed on to the consumer will be determined by the elasticity of demand and supply – the more inelastic the demand the greater will be the incidence upon the consumer. Consider what would happen in Fig. 11.10 if the demand curve were vertical. The price would rise to £3.50 and all the tax would be passed on to the consumer. The more elastic is the demand the less the producer will be able to pass on the tax.

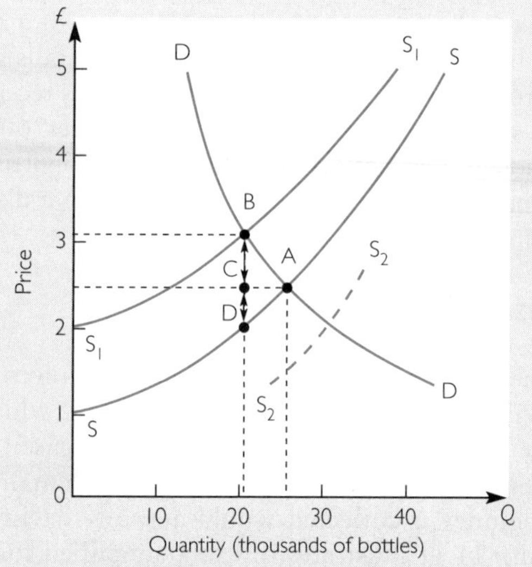

***Fig. 11.10* The effect of a £1 specific tax**
The original equilibrium is at A, with price £2.50 per bottle and 25 000 bottles sold. After the imposition of a £1 tax the new equilibrium price is £3.10 and the quantity sold is 21 000 bottles. S_2 shows the effect of £1 per unit subsidy.

STUDENT ACTIVITY 11.5

a) Can you determine the amount of revenue the government will receive from wine sales in Fig. 11.10?
b) Would you expect the incidence of a tax on each of the following products to be more on the producer or more on the consumer?
   (i) petrol
   (ii) carrots
   (iii) chocolate

Subsidies

The government sometimes subsidises a product by giving an amount of money to the producers for each unit they sell. This was the case with many agricultural products in the UK before its entry into the EU. The benefit of the subsidy will be split between the producer and the consumer. The division will, once again, depend upon the elasticity of demand. In Fig. 11.10 S_2 shows the effect of a £1 per unit subsidy. In this case the price falls to approximately £2.10 so that the consumer is receiving 40p of the subsidy and the producer 60p. Although subsidies may be regarded as supporting an inefficient industry they do not result in a disequilibrium (see also Chapter 12).

Government tax revenues

If the government is trying to raise more revenue it will increase taxes on those products which have inelastic demands. If it were to increase the tax on those products with elastic demands the money it collected would actually decline. Figure 11.11 illustrates this in a simplified form by omitting the supply curves. In diagram (a) you can see that if the tax is increased from £10 a unit to £20 a unit, tax revenue increases from £100 to £180, but in (b) the same increase in the tax causes revenue to fall from £30 to £20.

It would follow, therefore, that if a government wanted to increase its tax revenue from those products with elastic demands it would do best to lower the tax. This point was well illustrated when the nineteenth-century UK prime minister Robert Peel reduced the import duties on many commodities and thereby considerably increased the revenues of the exchequer.

Problems with demand and supply analysis

In these last two sections of the chapter we will examine some of the shortcomings of demand and supply analysis and suggest some ways in which these might be remedied. It is necessary for the reader to be aware of these problems, but a thorough study of them belongs in a more advanced course of economics.

Comparative statics

The demand and supply analysis which we have developed so far has been concerned with the formation of an equilibrium price. Any change in the market condition has then moved us to a new equilibrium. For example, the analysis predicts

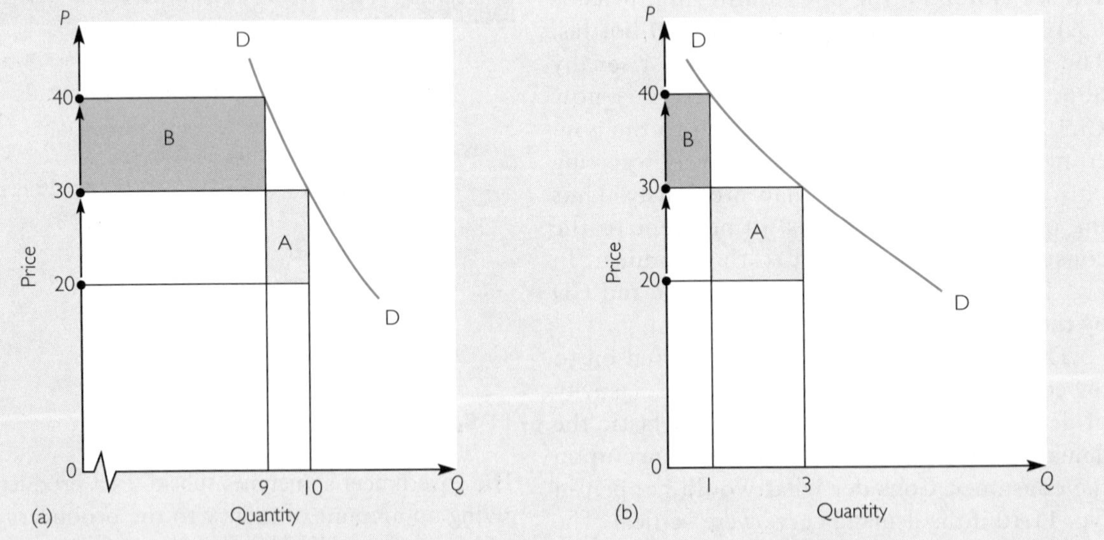

***Fig. 11.11* Revenue from an indirect tax**
(a) Inelastic demand. (b) Elastic demand. B is the revenue gained by raising the tax and A the revenue lost. Only if B is greater than A will increasing the tax be worthwhile.

that an increase in supply will lead to a new equilibrium at a lower price with a greater quantity supplied (see Fig. 11.2 (c). We arrive at this conclusion by comparing one static equilibrium with another. This method of analysis is therefore termed ***comparative statics***.

It has already been pointed out in this chapter that a time element may enter into the formation of prices (see page 141). This being the case, we need a theory which will explain the movement of prices with respect to time. Such a study is termed dynamic analysis. We may indeed find when we use ***dynamic analysis*** that a market may never be in a state of equilibrium. This does not mean, however, that we shall abandon comparative static analysis. Comparative statics is a useful way to explain changes in market and is the basis of our understanding of the forces involved, i.e. its predictions are often correct.

Ceteris paribus – again

It has been emphasised throughout this section of the book that we can only reach any firm conclusions if we hold all other things constant and just consider the influence of one factor at a time. A moment's reflection will tell us, however, that in the real world all other things are not constant; in reality the demand for a particular product will be the result of the influence of price, incomes, tastes, the price of other goods and dozens of other factors all acting upon prices simultaneously. If we were to be limited to our comparative static analysis we should perhaps end up with a situation like Fig. 11.4, with both demand and supply curves shifting upwards and downwards simultaneously. Thus if we wish to enter the real world of economic measurement and forecasting we must have a method of analysis which allows us to combine all these factors together but nevertheless allows us to identify the separate influence of each factor.

Multiple correlation

A demand curve expresses the correlation between the quantity demanded and the price of the product (correlation was explained in Chapter 2). We may say that demand is a function of, i.e. depends upon, price and this we can write as:

$$D = f(P)$$

It is necessary, however, to consider not just one correlation but many. Thus demand will become a function of all the variables which influence it:

$$D = f(P, Y, T, ...)$$

where P is the price of the commodity, Y is consumers' income and T is consumers' tastes, and we would have to continue for all the other factors which might influence demand. The same could then be done for supply. It at once becomes apparent that this is a complex task.

The astute reader, however, will have noticed that we have already quantified some of these variables. For example, we know the nature of the relationship between demand and income and can measure this as the coefficient of income elasticity. The problem, however, is further complicated by the influence of such things as taste and quality upon price. The quality of a product is extremely difficult to quantify but it is undoubtedly important and some allowance for the effect of changes in quality upon demand must therefore be made.

Exogenous and endogenous variables

The factors which influence price can be divided between ***exogenous*** and ***endogenous***. Endogenous variables are those which are explained within the theory; for example, the explanation of how changes of price affect demand is within the theory of demand. Exogenous factors are those which are outside the theory. For example, the weather certainly affects the demand for ice cream and as such we must take account of it; however, it is an exogenous variable because, although it affects the demand for ice cream, it is itself unaffected by it.

An exogenous variable which frequently upsets calculations and forecasts is war. Most of the forecasts of the early 1970s proved very inaccurate because they could not foresee the Arab–Israeli conflict of 1973. Inflation may also be regarded as an exogenous variable. If, for example, we are trying to predict the price of a product next year, the estimate of the rate of inflation will be an important factor, but the rate of inflation is determined outside the model of the market for one commodity that we are analysing. (This would not be so if we were constructing a macroeconomic model of an economy for government policy purposes. In this case the rate of inflation would be internal to the model of the whole economy and would thus be endogenous.)

It might be thought from what has been said that the price of a commodity is affected by everything else in the world. There may be, for example, a remote connection between the price of ball point pens and the demand for ice cream. However, it is so slight that we can ignore it. By selecting the factors which have a significant effect upon the market we are considering we will be able to build a model of how that market works.

Towards a dynamic theory of market prices

The cobweb theorem

We may develop a simple dynamic theory of market price by considering the ***cobweb theorem***. Let us return to the problem depicted in Fig. 11.5 where we considered the effect of time lags. We would normally say that supply is a function of price, which we could write as:

$$S = f(P_t)$$

where t is the time period we are considering. However, it has been pointed out that for some products, especially agricultural ones, it is the price in the previous period which determines the supply. For example, farmers will look at this year's price in determining how much barley to plant for next year. Thus we can write:

$$S_t = f(P_t - 1)$$

i.e. the supply in the period we are considering (S_t) is a function of the price in the previous period ($P_t - 1$).

Let us consider the effect this might have upon the market situation. Examine Fig. 11.12, where P and Q represent the equilibrium situation for the market for barley. Suppose in year 1 that for some reason the crop is less than intended, so that supply is Q_1(A). This will mean that the price is P_1. You can see that at this price farmers would wish to supply Q_2 (B) and are therefore encouraged to plant this much for year 2. You can see, however, that an output of Q_2 can be sold only for a price of P_2 and so the price falls to this level (C). The low price discourages farmers from planting barley and so they only produce Q_3 in the following year and there is thus a deficiency of supply which drives the price up to P_3. The high price of P_3 encourages farmers to overproduce, and so on. You can see from the graph how the cobweb theorem gets its name.

Thus when we introduce a time lag into the situation we may introduce ***instability*** into the system, or even permanent disequilibrium. Figure 11.12 illustrates a diverging or unstable cobweb. This is brought about because the slope of the supply curve is less than (flatter than) the slope of the demand curve. Other possibilities are illustrated in Fig. 11.13. In diagram (a) you can see a converging or stable cobweb. In this situation any disequilibrium will reduce and, other things being equal, an equilibrium price will eventually be reached. This is brought about when the slope of the supply curve is greater than (steeper than) the slope of the demand curve.

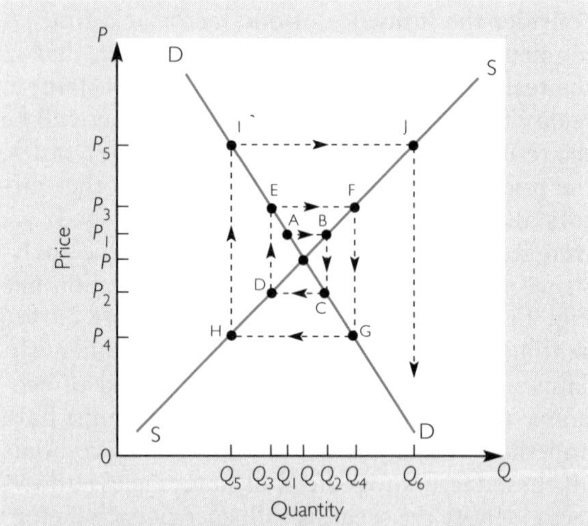

***Fig. 11.12* An unstable or diverging cobweb**

The supply in one time period, e.g. Q_3, is determined by the price in the previous period i.e. P_2. Thus:

$$S_t = f(P_{t-1})$$

For example:

$$Q_3 = f(P_2)$$

Diagram (b) illustrates what may happen with more complex curves. Here we see what are termed non-linear oscillations. The oscillations finally stabilise when the absolute slopes of the DD and SS curves are equal. If the price and quantity continue to fluctuate around the box indicated by the solid rectangle in Fig. 11.13 (b), then we would be experiencing persistent oscillations.

These predictions may appear fanciful but were in fact developed from Professor Ezekiel's observations of the 'corn–hogs cycle' in the USA. In this, a low price of corn caused farmers to switch to hogs (pigs) so that corn became dear and hogs cheap. This caused farmers to revert to corn and so on. The inherent instability of some agricultural markets is one of the reasons why governments intervene to aid farmers.

Factors modifying the cobweb

There are a number of factors which modify the extent of oscillations in the market associated with the cobweb theorem:

a) Producers learn from experience and thus do not vary their behaviour to the full extent predicted by the theory.
b) We have examined only one-period time lags. Distributed time lags (discussed earlier in the chapter), on the other hand, will modify the cobweb.
c) The cobweb depends upon actual supply equalling planned supply. ***Unplanned variations*** in supply can occur, particularly in the agricultural industry. These will further modify the cobweb, either diminishing or increasing its effect.
d) Prices may be inflexible, in which case prices may change too slowly to bring about significant changes in supply.

Having considered all these points, we may still conclude that some markets are inherently unstable.

Market prices – a postscript

This chapter completes the overview of the price system. It is not necessary for our purposes to develop the theory of demand any further, but we must go on to consider supply in much more detail. Before doing this we will pause to evaluate some of the features of market prices.

Market prices are efficient

Competitive markets are said to produce what people want *efficiently* (the precise meaning of

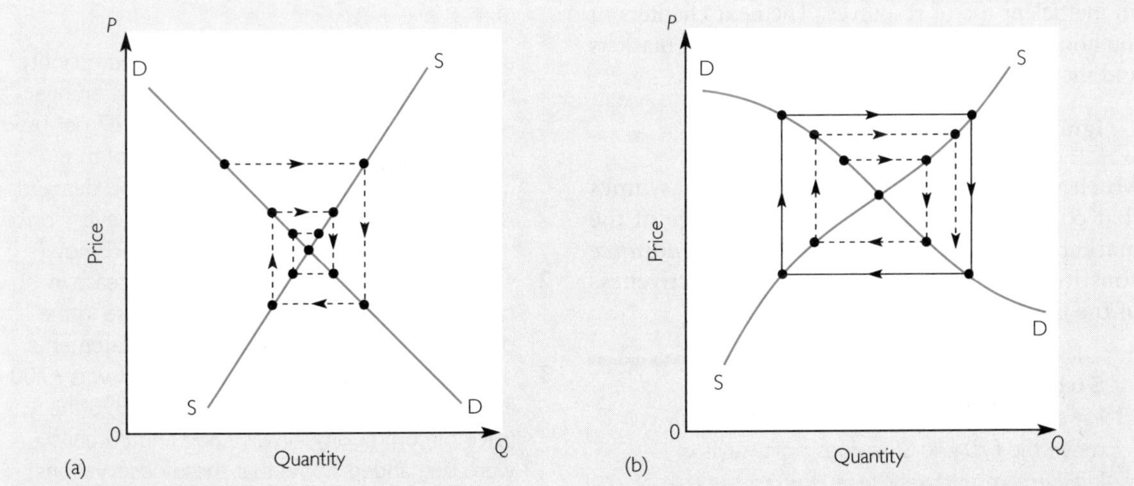

***Fig. 11.13* Other cobwebs**
(a) A stable or converging cobweb. (b) A cobweb with non-linear oscillations.

this term is explored in Chapter 24) and cheaply. However, we must remember that income is unevenly distributed and the price system will do nothing to redress these inequalities. In addition we must remember that an 'efficient' price system may, if unchecked, also result in such problems as pollution (see Chapter 27).

The system is automatic

Much is often made of the fact that supply decisions seem to happen automatically and that adjustments to changing demand conditions happen without central coordinating bodies. We should be careful not to equate 'automatic' with 'good'. Some rivers flood automatically every year but few people suggest that we do nothing about this; in a similar way it may sometimes be necessary to regulate the 'automatic' price mechanism. It can be said that interferences with the price mechanism often lead to undesirable side effects, but the social or political reasons for intervening in markets may outweigh the economic disadvantages.

Monopoly interferences

It is one of the basic assumptions of the market system that there are a large number of suppliers competing with one another. In many industries today this is not the case. The existence of a ***monopoly*** in an industry may result in high prices and an inefficient use of resources. The next chapters of the book go on to consider the structure of markets and the effects of monopolistic interferences.

Ignorance

Much of demand and supply analysis assumes that consumers have a ***perfect knowledge*** of the market. In practice this is not so and ***ignorance*** constitutes a major criticism of the effectiveness of the market mechanism.

Summary

1 Increases or decreases in demand or supply will move the DD and SS curves rightwards or leftwards respectively. If we keep to the rule of *ceteris paribus* there are then only four basic changes which occur in the equilibrium.
2 Time may affect the ability of supply to respond to changes in demand.
3 Any government interference with equilibrium prices is likely to have undesirable side effects which often lead to the opposite result from that desired by the government.
4 The incidence of an indirect tax will be determined by the elasticity of demand and supply for the product.
5 The shortcomings of demand and supply analysis place limitations upon its usefulness.
6 The cobweb theorem predicts constant disequilibrium for some markets.

Questions

1 The following information concerns the demand and supply of oranges.

Price (£/box)	*Quantity demanded (boxes/week)*	*Quantity supplied (boxes/week)*
8	500	1700
7	800	1200
6	1100	700
5	1400	200
4	1700	0

a) Determine the equilibrium price and quantity.
b) As part of the CAP support system orange growers are guaranteed a price of £7 per box. What are the likely consequences of this?
c) Suppose that in the original situation demand were to increase by 50 per cent at every price. What would be the equilibrium price now?

2 'A decrease in demand leads to a decrease in price.' 'A decrease in price leads to a rise in the quantity demanded.' Reconcile these statements.

3 In July 1997 the price of commodity X was £700 and 60 units were demanded. In July 1998 the price of commodity X was £800 and 80 units were demanded. Show that these observations are consistent with demand and supply analysis.

4 The following information is known about the elasticities of demand of three products X, Y and

Z. For X $E_D = 2$, for Y $E_D = 1$ and for Z $E_D = 0.75$. Each bears a sales tax of 15 per cent. Last year the tax revenues were as follows: product X = £200 million; product Y = £100 million; and product Z = £300 million. This year the government wishes to raise its total revenue from the sales tax on these products to £700 million. What advice would you give the government?

5 Why is the price of some agricultural products inherently unstable?

6 Contrast the incidence of a commodity tax imposed in the market for peaches with that of a similar tax in the market for potatoes.

7 Product K has linear demand and supply curves such that DD = Y = 10 – X and SS = Y = 1 + 2X. Further suppose that $S_t = f(P_t - 1)$. If the quantity produced in period 2 were to be $O_S = 1$, what would be the price and quantity supplied of product K in period 3?

Data response A
Football pricing

Study the following passage and then answer the questions below.

The concern over safety at football matches has resulted in all-seater stadiums in the Premier League. The effect of this change has been to substantially reduce the number of fans who can get into the stadium, as people take up more space sitting down than they do standing up.

The more civilised atmosphere that results from all-seater stadiums, together with the major efforts of the police and clubs to stamp out football hooliganism, has resulted in a widening of the appeal of the game. More 'middle class' fans are spending Saturday afternoon at the football ground, and the proportion of women fans has risen to 25% at some clubs. This civilisation of the game has reached its ultimate stage with the development of corporate hospitality, with major companies reserving some of the best seats to entertain their clients.

The top clubs are taking advantage of this situation to raise their prices. Increasingly, they are now public limited companies floated on the stock exchange with a responsibility to their shareholders to provide a good return on their investment. Even with the higher prices, the clubs are able to regularly fill their stadiums.

Inevitably these changes have brought some resentment from traditional fans, often from a more working class culture, with incomes to match. One wonders whether the high prices will deter poorer parents from taking their children to see their teams on a regular basis. Who knows what effect this might have on the inspiration of the next generation? We may see the cost of such developments in the quality of our footballers in decades to come.

1 Depict the changes that have taken place in terms of a supply and demand diagram.

2 What intervention in the market place would be necessary to help younger, poorer fans see their teams?

3 Is it in the interest of the clubs themselves to introduce such policies or does the government need to take action?

4 Should football clubs operate as profit-maximising companies responsive to their shareholders, or local institutions responsive to their fans? Is there necessarily any conflict between these two alternatives?

Data response B
Rouble devalued by Soviet Union

Read the following article by Jonathan Steele which appeared in the *Guardian* on 26 October 1989.

Answer the following questions:

1 With the aid of demand and supply diagrams explain the existence of a black market in foreign currency in the Soviet Union prior to the changes mentioned in the article.

2 Assume that the exchange rate before the devaluation was 60 kopeks to the dollar and also assume that the new rate of 6 roubles 26 kopeks is the correct exchange rate. Demonstrate the proposed changes with the aid of a diagram.

3 What is the effect of the change in the value of the rouble for

a) the standard of living in the USSR, and

b) value for money for tourists visiting the USSR?

Rouble devalued by Soviet Union

The Soviet Union has dropped the rouble to one-tenth of its previous value against the dollar in some transactions, in a sweeping attempt to defeat the flourishing black market.

The massive devaluation, which comes into effect on November 1 is a blow to Soviet citizens who need hard currency to go abroad.

It is not yet clear how it will benefit tourists coming in or the resident foreign community.

A terse four-paragraph notice from the official news-agency, Tass, said that the USSR State Bank had taken the decision 'to serve Soviet and foreign citizens'. But the notice made no further reference to visiting or resident foreigners.

Soviet citizens going abroad will have to pay 6 roubles 28 kopeks for a dollar, instead of the 60 to 65 kopeks that they pay at the moment.

They used to be allowed to get up to $200 at the favourably high rate of the rouble.

With so many Soviet citizens travelling abroad since President Gorbachev started his reform programme, there has been a serious drain on the country's hard currency reserves.

The new rate makes foreign travel more of a luxury and will soak up more of the population's spare cash.

For foreigners holding hard currency, the official rate was absurd, as a brief commentary in the government newspaper *Izvestia*, accepted last night.

'If a businessman could unofficially get 10 000 roubles for $1000 instead of 600 roubles at the official rate, the temptation to change on the black market was too high,' the newspaper said.

The devaluation was a 'more than decisive measure' against the black market, it added.

Senior officials at the State Bank were unavailable for comment last night, but it was assumed that the new exchange rate would work for cash transactions for foreigners as well as for Soviet citizens.

It was not clear whether it would change the system whereby foreigners have to make certain purchases in roubles, exchanged at the present high rate, such as hotel rooms and rents. Nor is it clear how it affects foreign trade. Tass said that two rates for the rouble would apply in future.

'The rouble's special rate will be published monthly, along with the official rate of the USSR State Bank, in the newspaper *Izvestia*, before the two rates come into force,' Tass said.

The devaluation is a partial step towards the full convertibility of the rouble which President Gorbachev has put forward as his eventual goal.

It is the first official admission that the present exchange rate was unrealistic.

Source: The Guardian, 26 October 1989

12 Agricultural prices: a case study

Learning outcomes

After reading this chapter you will be able to:

- Understand how intervention in agriculture can result in surpluses.
- Compare the effects of price support and subsidy.
- Identify the objectives of agricultural intervention.

Introduction

The structure of the chapter

This chapter is treated as a case study in much the same way as the case-based chapters in Section IV. The chapter follows the same style, with student activities being placed at the end of the case. There is no data response as the chapter as a whole should be treated as a data response article.

Interventionist policies

In this chapter we look at the application of demand and supply theory to agriculture. Agriculture has been called the UK's most successful industry: output and productivity have boomed since the Second World War. This has been achieved by extremely ***interventionist*** policies on the part of the government; the average Briton supports farmers through artificially high prices and through taxes.

The UK policy is now decided in Brussels. The role of the Common Agricultural Policy (CAP) is an area of vigorous political debate. The budget for the CAP is larger than all other EU expenditures put together and is a constant cause of argument. On the international scene there have been disputes between the EU and other World Trade Organisation (WTO) members. The USA and many of the poorer members of the WTO have often argued that the EU is unfairly subsidising agriculture and ***discriminating*** against their exports. Farming practices are also a subject of disagreement; for example, many of the 'Green' lobbies maintain that the use of fertilisers and other modern aspects of agriculture are damaging the environment.

It is, perhaps, a curious paradox that agriculture is the economist's most used example of the market place. We use it to illustrate shifts in demand and supply and all the workings of the free market system. But no market is so interfered with as agriculture. Governments, not only in the UK but in most other nations, constantly interfere to regulate and manipulate production and farm incomes. In many nations the quantity of next year's crop is as likely to be affected by government policy as it is by market forces and the weather.

The UK system of subsidy after 1947

Farming's privileged status can be traced back to the Agriculture Act 1947. The experience of two world wars had taught the UK the danger of being over-reliant on imported foodstuffs. Agriculture was therefore supported by government grants for improvements, tax relief, fixed prices for milk and ***'deficiency' payments*** on many products to bring prices up to a guaranteed level and enable farmers to compete with imports. The detail of the schemes need not concern us, but we can say that the main effect was a heavy ***subsidisation*** of farm prices. The effect of this is shown in Fig. 12.1. Here you can see that, although 'inefficient' farmers are being propped up, no disequilibrium is created because the lower price brought about by the subsidy encourages consumers to buy more. The price before subsidy was OG and the quantity demanded was q_1. After the subsidy, the price has fallen to OD, and the quantity demanded has been extended to q_2. This form of support, as well as helping farm incomes, also benefits the consumer because some of the subsidy comes back to the taxpayer by way of lower prices. This particularly benefits ***low-income groups***, to whom the price of food is very important (see also Chapter 11). The cost of this kind of policy is quite high, shown by the shaded area ABCD in Fig. 12.1. It is clear that not all this cost comes back to the consumer, and in Fig. 12.2 the savings from buying the same amount of food as was bought prior to the subsidy is only GEFD. On the other hand consumers also decide to buy more agricultural products to the value of FCq_2q_1. This extra consumption is not necessarily a good thing, as the market is being ***distorted*** away from the consumers' true preferences by a manipulation of costs. The idea of market distortion is explored more fully in Section IV.

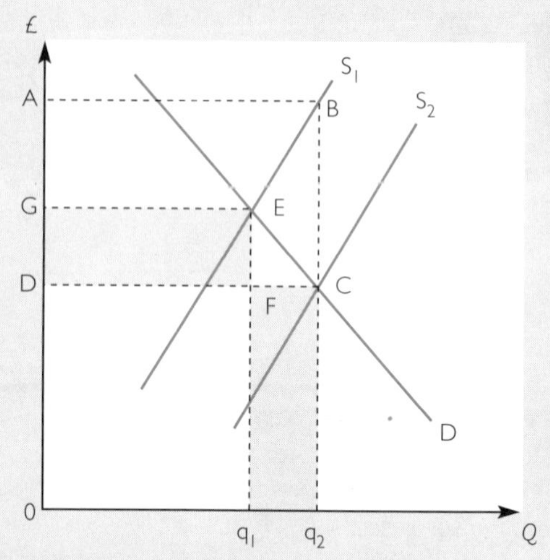

Fig. 12.2 **The benefit to the consumers of subsidising agriculture**

The Common Agricultural Policy (CAP)

When the UK joined the EC the subsidy system just described was replaced by ***guaranteed high prices*** and a stable ***import levy*** to keep cheap non-EC food out of Europe. This situation is illustrated in Fig. 12.3. Transitional arrangements were made to protect the UK's traditional suppliers, particularly New Zealand. The farmers' incomes are supported by artificially high prices instead of subsidies. The consumer is worse off because of these higher prices. It is argued that this is offset by lower taxes to sup-

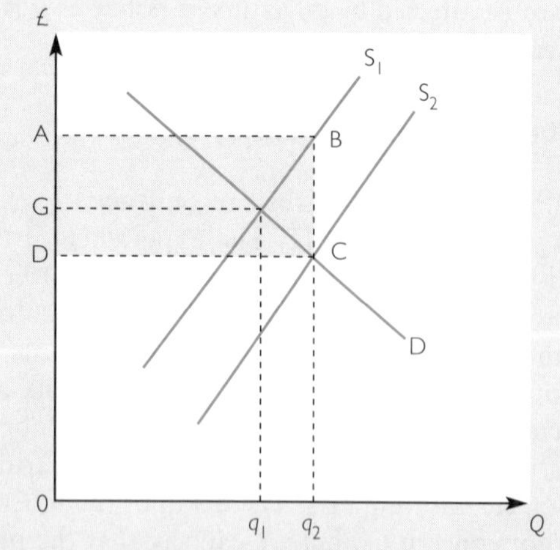

Fig. 12.1 **The cost of subsidising an agricultural product**

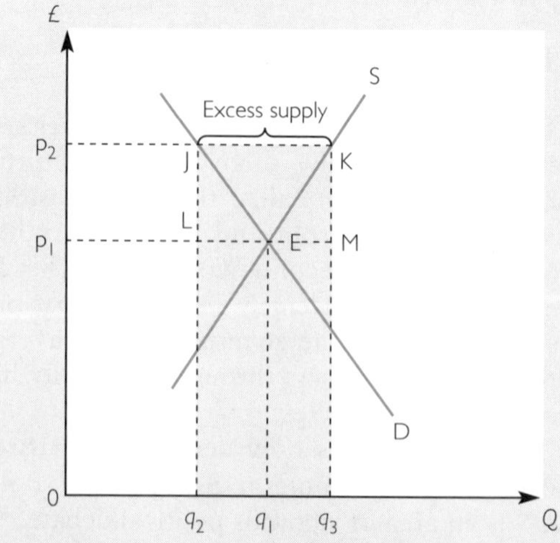

Fig. 12.3 **the cost of imposing floor prices in agriculture**

port the scheme because there are no expensive subsidies. The main problem with the CAP is its tendency to create a disequilibrium of ***excess supply***, this excess supply being familiar to us as the butter mountain, the wine lake, etc. This situation is illustrated in Fig. 12.3. Point E is the original equilibrium with a market price of p_1 and an output of q_1. The CAP guaranteed-prices policy raises the price to p_2. This contracts demand to q_2 but expands supply to q_3. CAP intervention agencies are then forced to buy up the excess supply of q_2q_3. The EU is thus committed to additional expenditure of the shaded area q_2 JKq_3. Of course, some surplus of agricultural products in storage is an advantage, acting as a buffer against poor harvests. It is only when these stocks become excessive that there is a problem.

What shall we do with the surplus?

The argument put forward in the previous paragraph (that the CAP is cheaper to the taxpayer than a subsidy-based system) has a weakness. What does the EU do with the excess supply? The hope that the uncertainties of agricultural production would result in surplus years being balanced out by years of shortage was not borne out by experience. Mountains of butter and beef, and a lake of wine, all grew in the 1970s and 1980s. Theoretically the EU could sell the excess output on world markets at a price of p_1, making a loss of p_1p_2 for each unit sold. The cost of the system would then be reduced to area JKML in Fig. 12.3. The problem with this solution is that it breaks international agreements about trade. Selling a product abroad below the domestic price is known as ***dumping***. Offloading large surpluses on world markets could depress the world price for certain products, reducing the incomes of farmers in poorer countries. It can also be argued that the resources used to produce food that no one eats could be better employed producing goods that are in demand. The costs of storing excessive surpluses must also be included as a waste of resources.

The surpluses have mainly been dealt with in the following ways:

a) Sale to old-age pensioners at a reduced price. This is a form of price discrimination (see Chapter 18) but clearly benefits poorer sections of society.
b) Sale to non-market economies. Considerable quantities of butter were sold to the former USSR (Russia). Since these economies were not part of the world market system, selling them the surpluses did not have much effect on world prices. Most of these countries have now become capitalist, so this solution is decreasingly available.
c) Downgrading the product, e.g. turning wine into vinegar.

Features of the agriculture industry

Problems for the UK

Farming in the UK is different from that in most of Western Europe. There are a number of reasons for this:

a) *Climate*. The UK's cool, damp climate favours barley and pasture but rules out crops such as olives, tobacco, vines and maize – all products which feature largely in the CAP budget.
b) *Land*. The UK has much of the poor quality hill grazing in the EU and in consequence rears almost 50 per cent of the EU sheep.
c) *Land ownership*. The UK has a large average size of farm, three times as large as the average French farm and four times as large as the average German farm. There are two main reasons for this. First, there is the custom of primogeniture in the UK, i.e. a system whereby the first-born inherits the whole of the property, in contrast to the system of gavelkind where property is automatically divided up between the surviving relatives. This tends to make UK farms larger and larger and European ones smaller and smaller. Second, many UK small farmers were driven from the land by cheap food imported from Britain's former empire.
d) *Workforce*. In the UK only 1.6 per cent of the workforce are employed in agriculture. This is not only the smallest percentage in the EU; it

is the smallest in the world. This compares with 5.3 per cent in West Germany, 10.9 per cent in Italy and 28.5 per cent in Greece. In view of all these differences there is little wonder that the CAP often seems ill attuned to the UK's needs. Other countries are likely to put a greater emphasis on the maintenance of farming incomes because the farming 'lobby' is a larger percentage of the electorate.

e) *Population density*. The UK has one of the higher population densities of the EU, approximately twice that of France, although less than Belgium and the Netherlands. Agricultural self-sufficiency is more difficult as a result, particularly as many of the less populated areas in Scotland and Wales are mountainous.

Productivity growth

Since the Second World War there have been spectacular increases in the productivity of the UK's agriculture, in terms of output per hectare and output per worker. There are a number of reasons for this:

a) *Breeding*. Better varieties of crops and improved livestock have resulted in large increases in productivity. Since 1947 the average yield of wheat has risen from 2.4 tonnes to 6.7 (1989) tonnes per hectare.
b) *Mechanisation*. In 1947, 700 000 people were employed in agriculture in the UK, compared with 307 000 in 1990. This is largely the result of mechanisation, attributable not so much to more machines as to more powerful machines.
c) *Fertilisers and sprays*. The use of fertilisers and pest control agents is thought to account for about 30 per cent of the increased productivity.
d) *Improvements*. The most significant improvement has been improved drainage, but in addition to this there are better buildings etc.
e) *Innovations*. The introduction of new crops, e.g. rape seed, and of new methods, e.g. zero grazing (keeping livestock indoors all year), has also increased productivity.

Against these spectacular rises in productivity must be set concerns about the environment particularly arising from ***intensive farming***. The environment lobby argues that the destructive effects of new farming methods upon the countryside should be taken into account when deciding on farming policy. Here there is clearly a divergence between private and public costs and benefits. The welfare economist would argue that the negative externalities of farming are one of the contributory causes of overproduction (see Chapter 25).

Instability in agricultural markets

As we have already seen, prices in markets for agricultural products are inherently unstable because of ***unplanned*** variations in supply. This is deemed to be undesirable both to producers and consumers. Governments therefore usually intervene in agricultural markets, with the object of ***stabilising*** both farm incomes and consumer prices. However, complete price stabilisation would lead farmers' incomes to vary directly with output, making them high in bumper years and low in times of bad harvest. This is the complete opposite of the normal state of affairs.

Common misunderstanding

People often believe that a good harvest must be good for farmers and a poor harvest will result in problems for them. This is the complete opposite of the case. Because of the inelasticity of demand for agricultural products, farmers' incomes usually vary inversely with output.

A sensible scheme will therefore probably aim not at total stability but rather at limiting fluctuations in prices and incomes. This will be difficult to achieve in practice because of the following:

a) *Imperfect knowledge*. The government does not possess perfect knowledge about the shape of the consumers' demand curve, or about the absolute state of supply at any particular moment. Much estimation would therefore be involved.
b) *Political pressure*. In most European countries farmers are a strong ***political lobby*** and there is therefore great pressure to set the target price and income too high. This results in the

government holding greater and greater surpluses of products and the scheme costing a great deal of money. What has been said about the CAP above will bear testimony to the strength of this argument.

c) *The vagaries of climate.* In recent years different parts of Europe have suffered from drought and floods. There is concern that the climate is becoming more unstable, possibly as a result of global warming (see Chapter 27).

Recent developments in policy

Pressure for reform of the CAP has come from WTO, the USA and also from the UK whose pattern of agriculture contrasts with that of many of its EU partners. The EU also faced internal pressure to restrain spending on the CAP in order to reduce the size of the CAP budget (see Table 12.1). The existence of persistent surpluses has also been something of an embarrassment to the EU.

***Table 12.1* CAP appropriations by sector (items over 1 billion ECU)**

	Billion ECU 1993	Billion ECU 1997 (budget)
Arable crops (including land withdrawal)	10.6	16.2
Sugar	2.2	1.8
Olive oil	2.5	2.2
Tobacco	1.7	1.0
Milk/milk products	5.2	3.6
Beef and veal	4.0	7.5
Sheep/goats	1.8	2.0
Other	6.6	6.5
Total	34.6	40.8

Source: Adapted from data in the *General Report on the Activities of the EU*, 1996.

Set-aside

One solution to the problem of excess supply has been the introduction of ***set-aside***. This is a policy where farmers are literally paid not to produce on 15 per cent of their land. The cost of this payment is offset because the excess supply problem has been reduced. The warehousing costs and the losses made on sales of old surpluses are therefore avoided. The policy is illustrated in Fig. 12.4. It can be seen that production has been reduced by q_2q_3 resulting in the elimination of the surplus, while retaining the high price which guarantees income to the farmer on the land which is farmed. The farmer also receives income from the EU for the land which is not used from the set-aside fund. This policy was successful in reducing surpluses. EU stocks of cereal fell from 27 million tonnes in May 1993 to only 7 million tonnes in May 1995. The butter mountain was reduced to a sixth of its former size and the beef mountain virtually eliminated during this period. Because of the set-aside payments, however, the CAP budget continued to grow.

The environmental impact of this policy has good and bad aspects. The land that lies fallow attracts wildlife that might not have survived on farming land. On the other hand, there are pressures to farm the remaining land even more intensively with the bad side-effects of fertilisers, insecticides, removal of hedgerows, etc. Environmentalists argue that policies to encourage ***less intensive*** farming using ***organic*** methods would be better. The set-aside policy illustrated in Fig. 12.4 demonstrates that prices remain high for the consumer.

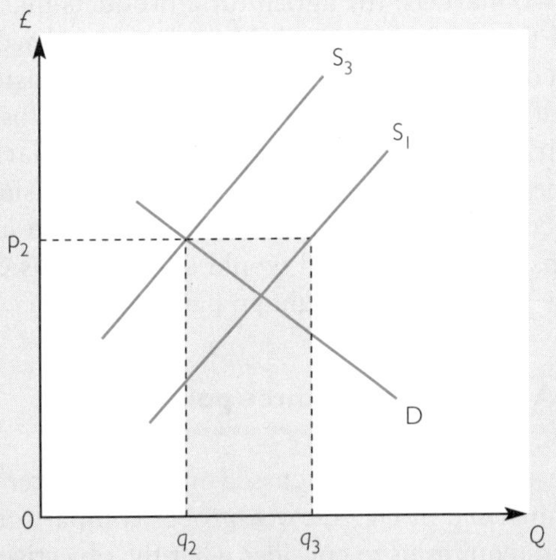

***Fig. 12.4* The effect of set-aside on agriculture surpluses**

EU expansion

The opening of negotiations with Poland, Hungary, the Czech Republic, Estonia, Slovenia and Cyprus will create problems for the CAP because the income of these countries and their agricultural efficiency is so far below that of existing members. In July of 1997 the EU launched plans to shift the emphasis away from price support and set-aside and towards ***targeted*** support for those farmers in greatest need of additional income. It remains to be seen whether this shift away from price support and towards income support will reduce the overall CAP budget of some £27 billion (1997). The accession of new states brings concerns that the budget may actually increase further unless the subsidies are better targeted at those who need them.

It is argued that the main effect of subsidies going to efficient farmers is to increase the value of agricultural land. This process is known as ***capitalisation***, where a subsidy or tax on a product is transferred into the capital values. Farmers appear not to be making very excessive profits, but that is because the cost of acquiring the land is set against profits. If the increased value of the land was regarded as a ***capital gain*** rather than a cost, it can be seen that removal of subsidies would not necessarily result in lower profits, but simply in lower land prices. The farmer is clearly in two markets: the agricultural products market, and the market for land. Holders of land would of course make capital losses when subsidies were removed, but they would make this loss in their role as speculators in the land market, rather than producers in the agriculture business. Of course some farmers who had taken on large loans to purchase land would suffer serious cash flow problems and might go bankrupt.

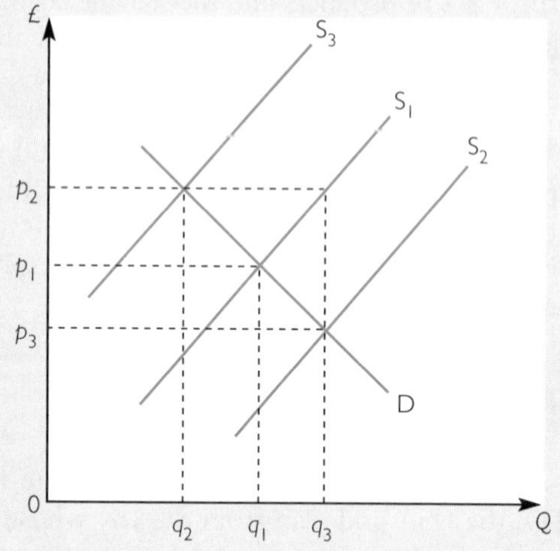

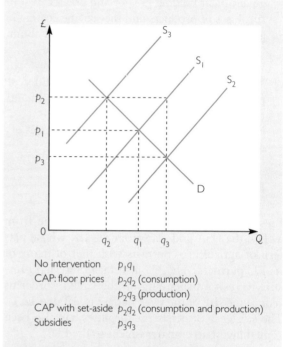

No intervention	p_1q_1
CAP: floor prices	p_2q_2 (consumption)
	p_2q_3 (production)
CAP with set-aside	p_2q_2 (consumption and production)
Subsidies	p_3q_3

***Fig. 12.5* A comparison of three policies**

A comparison of three polices

The three policies discussed in this chapter are summarised in Fig. 12.5. A proper comparison of them requires us to consider what the objectives of EU policy might be in intervening in the agricultural market. Since the EU is not a government, but is composed of many countries, it is also necessary to consider what conflicts of interest there might be between different countries.

Policy objectives

a) To stabilise agricultural prices. Political pressures to stabilise them at too high a level are a problem for this policy goal.
b) To maintain farmers' incomes which are under pressure from world competition. Obviously this is an objective which will interest countries with large, low-income, farming communities.
c) To maintain rural communities. Many European countries experienced industrialisation and urbanisation later than the UK and are concerned to maintain a viable rural community.
d) To increase efficiency in farming in order to compete with the rest of the world, and to reduce the size of the CAP budget.
e) To farm in a way which is friendly towards the environment.

f) To achieve overall self-sufficiency in agriculture in the EU.
g) To provide the population with affordable food in sufficient quantity.

Not all of these possible policy objectives are necessarily achievable at the same time. Different countries will put a higher priority on different objectives. EU policy making will therefore have a strong political component as countries fight for their own interest.

Non-intervention

Non-intervention results in a price of p_1q_1. Farmers' incomes in all but the most efficient cases will be pulled down towards those in poorer countries who compete in world agricultural markets. Marginal farmers will leave the industry and the EU will fail to be self-sufficient in agriculture. A large balance of payments deficit may develop in this sector. These consequences make this an unlikely policy option.

Subsidy

This results in p_3q_3 which allows farmers to compete in world markets and gives consumers low prices and plentiful food. The subsidy is costly to the taxpayer and can be interpreted by other countries as protectionist. In order to prevent the farmer leaving the industry as described in the previous section, it is necessary to set subsidies at a reasonably high level.

Price floor

This results in p_2q_2 (consumption) and p_2q_3 (production), the difference between the two being surplus production which is difficult to dispose of. Once again protectionist, but this time with high prices and lower consumption than the subsidy case.

Set-aside

The same consumption result as in the price floor case but this time with the surpluses removed. It is possibly more costly than a price floor because of the set-aside payments. It can be argued that the set-aside payments should be targeted at lower-income farmers to limit the cost of such a policy.

STUDENT ACTIVITY 12.1

1 Which of the objectives listed above do you think are in the interests of the UK?
2 How would the priorities of countries like Ireland or France differ from those of the UK?
3 Which of the policies described above would be in the interests of each of these countries?
4 Explain how the expansion of the EU eastwards is likely to affect the size of the CAP budget. What policies would you advocate to contain this expansion of the budget?
5 If the bulk of the CAP budget is targeted towards low-income, small, inefficient farmers, how can we make sure that these farmers have an incentive to become more efficient?
6 Design a policy towards agriculture that has, as its highest priority, a concern for the environment.
7 Indicate on Fig. 12.5 the following:
   a) The cost of a price floor if the excess supply cannot be sold.
   b) The cost of a price floor if the surplus can be sold at world market prices.
   c) The benefit to the consumer in lower prices if a subsidy policy is used.
   d) The cost to the taxpayer in the case of a subsidy.
   e) The amount of agricultural production reduced by the set-aside policy.
8 Show using diagrams what the effect of introducing price ceilings in agriculture would be at a level below the market clearing price. Would the objective of providing people with cheap, plentiful food be achieved?
9 What are the advantages to a country of being self-sufficient in food?.

Summary

1 UK agriculture has been supported since the Second World War. This support mainly took the form of price subsidies, in contrast with the CAP system of guaranteed high prices.

2 The pattern of agriculture and land ownership in the UK is very different from much of the rest of the EU, which has created friction with other member states.

3 Productivity has increased greatly in terms of output per hectare and output per worker. However, there are environmental concerns about 'industrial' farming techniques.

4 Agricultural markets are inherently unstable so that governments usually intervene to stabilise prices and farm incomes.

5 Agricultural policy is complicated by imperfect knowledge, political pressure and administrative costs.

6 The choice of policy will depend on the objectives of the government.

13 The business organisation: its type, size and location

Learning outcomes

At the end of this chapter you will be able to:

- Distinguish between the main types of business organisation.
- Understand the concepts of market and aggregate concentration ratios.
- Recognise the different types of mergers.
- Identify the reasons for the survival of small firms and appreciate the significance of multinational firms.
- Appreciate the factors that determine the location of industry and the government influences thereon.

Types of business organisation

There are many different types of business organisation, all of which trade goods and services in exchange for money. In this chapter we shall deal with those business organisations that operate in the *private sector* and which, we shall assume, exist mainly with the intention of ***maximising profits***. Thus, public corporations, like the Post Office, that operate in the ***public sector*** and which do not exist primarily to maximise their profits are temporarily excluded from the analysis (see Chapter 20).

Plants, firms and industries

The ***plant*** or ***establishment*** is the unit of production in industry: it can be a factory, a shop, a farm, a hotel or any economic unit that carries on its business at one geographic location.

The firm is the unit of ownership and control.

A firm may consist of just one plant or establishment, in which case it is referred to as ***single plant.*** However, many large firms are likely to comprise a number of plants: they are ***multiplant.*** We can make the distinction between plants and firms clearer by taking an example: Ford UK is a firm but it controls 16 different plants in the UK, such as at Dagenham and Bridgend.

An industry is all the firms concerned with a particular line of production.

The government's latest (1992) Standard Industrial Classification (*sic*) divides industries into 17 sections (some of which are split into subsections) and then into 60 industrial divisions (which are further broken down into groups and classes). The main sections are shown below:

A Agriculture, Hunting and Forestry
B Fishing
C Mining and Quarrying
D Manufacturing
E Electricity, Gas and Water Supply
F Construction
G Wholesale and Retail Trade; Repair of Motor Vehicles, Motorcycles and Personal and Household Goods
H Hotels and Restaurants
I Transport, Storage and Communication
J Financial Intermediation
K Real Estate, Renting and Business Activity
L Public Administration and Defence; Compulsory Social Security
M Education
N Health and Social Work
O Other Community, Social and Personal Service Activities
P Private Households
Q Extra-Territorial Organisations and Bodies

Thus, section D is manufacturing, subsection DB denotes the manufacture of textiles and textile products and division 17 is the manufacturing of textiles alone.

The SIC groupings are according to the production processes used rather than the substitutability of their products for consumers. This characteristic can be seen at the broadest level of aggregation, sections. Hotels and rented accommodation can be viewed as substitutes in terms of the demand created by local authority tenancies and by lengthy business trips. However, hotels are listed in section H and rented accommodation in section K of SIC(92). This is a problem if instead of looking at the industry share of a firm the economist wishes to focus on its market share.

An industry is defined in terms of close substitutability in production, whereas a market is defined in terms of close substitutability of consumption.

Substitutability in consumption is measured by cross elasticity of demand (see Chapter 10): the higher the (positive) value of cross price elasticity the greater the degree of substitutability. The problem for the economist is that economic theory does not tell us the value of the elasticity at which we can assume that products are in separate markets. Moreover, data on cross elasticities are not usually available. Industries are also difficult to define rigorously as one firm may operate in more than one industry. However, despite these definitional problems and the differences between the two terms, markets and industries, they are often used interchangeably.

STUDENT ACTIVITY 13.1

Can you think of any other examples of products that are considered substitutes by consumers, yet may be classified as belonging to different industries? Refer to SIC(92) if possible.

Classification of firms

There are many ways in which we might classify firms: for example, we could do it by size. However, the most important distinction as far as the economist is concerned is the type of competition under which a firm operates, and this forms a major portion of this part of the book. Before turning to this aspect, though, we must first look at the ***legal forms of business***. As a prelude to this we will look at the development of the modern business organisation.

The development of the business organisation

As society evolved from feudalism to *laissez-faire* and then to capitalism, so the forms of business organisations evolved. The earliest forms were the sole trader and the partnership. The joint stock company did not become common until the nineteenth century, although its origins can be found much earlier in the ***commercial revolution*** of the sixteenth and seventeenth centuries. During this period the capitalist system of production became well established, i.e. a system where there was a separation of functions between the capital-providing employer on the one hand and the wage-earning worker on the other.

The joint stock form of organisation developed not from industry but from foreign trade. In order to raise the necessary capital and spread the risk of early trading ventures a company form of organisation was adopted. The ***joint stock company,*** which had a continuous existence and was run by a board of directors and owned by its shareholders, became much more popular. The most important of these early companies was the East India Company. This was founded in 1600 and became a joint stock company in 1660.

Limited liability (see page 167) was first introduced in 1662 but it was granted to only three companies. Dealings in shares took place from the beginning but the first stock exchange was not established until 1778. By this time there was a flourishing capital and insurance market centred on a number of coffee houses in the city of London. The most famous of these was Lloyd's. A great speculative boom known as the South Sea Bubble ruined many people and caused the passing of the Bubble Act 1720. This made it illegal to form a company without a Royal Charter and effectively hindered the development of companies for many years.

The importance of the joint stock company and the need to raise large capital sums received a massive boost during the ***industrial revolution*** that occupied most of the second half of the eigtheenth and the first half of the ninteenth centuries. The demand for British manufacturing goods in overseas markets and a spate of technical innovations, especially the creation of steam power, produced the necessary conditions for the rapid development of large-scale manufacturing industry. The building of canals (from 1761 onwards) required vast amounts of capital. In the nineteenth century the building of railways involved hundreds of joint stock companies and by 1848 their quoted share capital was over £200 million. The development of joint stock banking in the UK dates from 1826.

Throughout the nineteenth century the family business remained the dominant form of organisation in industry. It is interesting to note that at this time, when industry and commerce were finding it necessary to adopt the joint stock form of organisation, the government was also finding it impossible *not* to interfere in the economy; just as the sophistication of industry and commerce needed regulation through company legislation, so the increasingly complex urban world demanded government intervention to ensure adequate drainage, street lighting, education, etc.

Much of the organisation of institutions which evolved at this time, such as hospitals and schools, was modelled on factories. These forms have survived the ***scientific revolution*** of the twentieth century. We are now on the threshold of great changes in our economy which will be brought about by the ***microprocessor revolution***. If we are tempted to cling to the forms of organisation of the past it should be recalled that they originated in the need to exploit large steam engines as a source of power.

Legal forms of firms

The sole trader

A sole trader is a business organisation where one person is in business on their own, providing the capital, taking the profit and standing the losses themselves.

Typical areas of commercial activity for the sole trader are retailing and building, i.e. activities which are not usually capital intensive. Sole traders are often wrongly termed 'one-man businesses'. Sole traders are indeed *owned* by one person but the business may *employ* many people.

Limits are placed on the growth of a sole trader's activities by two main constraints. First, finance: economic growth depends largely on the availability of capital to invest in the business, and sole traders are limited to what can be provided from their own resources or raised from banks, etc. Second, organisation: one person has only limited ability to exercise effective control over and take responsibility for an organisation. As a business grows, a larger and more complicated business organisation will generally replace the sole trader.

The sole trader is in a potentially vulnerable financial position. The profits may all accrue to one person but so do the losses, and many sole traders are made bankrupt each year.

Limited capital resources often make the sole trader particularly vulnerable, not only to sustained competition from large business units but also to bad capital investments, e.g. a grocer opening a delicatessen in an area which turns out to prefer more mundane food or the introduction of a restaurant in an area where a number of others already exist.

It can be argued, however, that a sole trader is able to weather a short reduction in consumer spending far better than a large business unit. The sole trader can adapt quickly to the level of demand and, if necessary, can make personal economies until business improves.

Sole traders remain the most common business unit in the UK and they are the backbone of the business structure on which the country depends, although, in terms of capital and labour resources employed, sole traders are of limited importance. Nonetheless, in recent years there has been a substantial increase in the number of sole traders partly as a result of the government encouragement of the 'enterprise culture'. Since the late 1970s the UK has had the fastest rate of growth of self-employment (the self-employed usually operate as sole traders) of any major industrial country. However, there has also been a record number of bankruptcies. Some of the reasons for the failure of sole traders are listed below:

a) Lack of capital to invest in new premises, equipment and materials.
b) Lack of expertise in every aspect of the business resulting in inefficiency, e.g. the sole traders may be good at selling but bad at administration.
c) Lack of advice and guidance about the operations of the business – consultancy is usually too expensive to be considered.
d) Competition from chain stores and other larger business units which are able to benefit from various economies of scale.
e) Increased overheads resulting from bureaucratic functions imposed by law, e.g. VAT collection, which sole traders are often disinclined and ill-equipped to perform (this is less quantifiable as a reason but still important).
f) Interest rates that were extremely high in the late 1980s and early 1990s. Since many businesses relied heavily on borrowed money this, therefore, put up their costs substantially. This occurred at a time when sales were considerably down because of recession in the economy.

Yet sole traders survive and even flourish. As a business organisation they offer attractive advantages when compared with others. The initial capital investment may be very small and the legal formalities involved are minimal. In sharp contrast to joint stock companies, they offer financial secrecy and the 'personal touch'(a subjective but often important factor). Sole traders are also able to alter their activities to adapt to the market without legal formality or major organisational problems.

Excluding the legal point just mentioned all these factors could apply equally to any ***small business*** whatever its legal form. The reasons for the continued existence of small business are discussed at the end of this chapter.

Partnerships

The Partnership Act 1890 defines a partnership as 'the relation which subsists between persons carrying on a business in common with a view of profit'.

Many partnerships are very formal organisations, such as a large firm of solicitors or accountants, but two people running a stall in a local Sunday market would almost certainly be in partnership with each other and subject to the same legal rules as a firm of city solicitors with an annual turnover that may run into millions of pounds.

Two or more persons in partnership can combine their resources and, in theory, form an economically more efficient business unit, producing a better return on the capital invested. In most cases each partner has unlimited liability and is responsible for any debts of the business without limit. A rare form of this type of enterprise is the limited partnership in which sleeping partners, who take no part in the management of the business, have limited liability.

The maximum number of members possible in most partnership is fixed by law at 20. The professional partnerships that are allowed to exceed this number – solicitors, accountants and members of a recognised stock exchange – are often organisations of some size, with considerable capital resources and offering economies of scale and the benefits of specialisation. It is unusual, however, to find a trading partnership consisting of more than five or six partners, for corporate status as a company with limited liability is usually more attractive.

Quite apart from the rules of professional bodies, which usually prohibit their members from forming a company, a partnership is a business organisation generally more suited to professional people in business together than to manufacturers or traders. In the former, the risk of financial failure is less of a disadvantage. For all but the small trading ventures, or where there are particular reasons for trading as a partnership, registration as a company with limited liability is usually preferred.

The joint stock company

A joint stock company may be described as an organisation consisting of persons who contribute money to a common stock, which is employed in some trade or business, and who share the profit or loss

arising. This common stock is the capital of the company and the persons who contribute to it are its members. The proportion of capital to which each member is entitled is their share.

The need for more capital explains both the development of partnerships and, later, the development of joint stock companies. As soon as it became possible to do so, many partnerships chose to become registered joint stock companies with limited liability. Today, in terms of capital and labour resources employed, the joint stock company is the dominant form of business organisation.

The principle of limited liability is extremely important to a company. Limited liability means that an investor's liability to debt is limited to the extent of their shareholding.

Thus, for example, if you own 100 £1 shares in a company, in the event of it becoming insolvent, then the most you can lose is the £100 originally invested. This encourages investment because it limits the risk investors take to the amount they have actually invested. It is possible for even very large companies to go bankrupt, as we saw with the failure of Polly Peck in 1990. At the time Polly Peck was in the *Financial Times* top 100 companies. Without limited liability, it is likely that none but the safest business venture would ever attract large-scale investment. In particular, the institutional investors, such as life assurance companies and pension funds, would not hazard their vast funds in any speculative venture and would invest only in the gilt-edged market (government securities).

Public and private companies

To the outsider the most obvious distinction between ***public and private limited companies*** is that a public limited company has the letters PLC after its name as, for example, Marks and Spencer PLC, while private limited companies have the abbreviation Ltd after their name. A public limited company may own subsidiaries which are private limited companies. When one company owns and controls others it is often referred to as a ***holding company***.

Legally speaking, a public company is a company limited by shares (or guarantee) which has been registered as a public company with the Registrar of Companies. It has two or more members and can invite the general public to subscribe for its shares or debentures. A private company is any company which does not satisfy the requirements for a public company. In common with a public company it has two or more members.

Thus the essential distinction between a public and a private company is that the former may offer its shares or debentures to the public while the latter cannot. It is a criminal offence to invite the general public to subscribe for shares or debentures in a private company.

The private company at present is in some respects a transitional step between the partnership and the public company; typically it is a family business. In common with a public limited company, it possesses the advantage of limited liability, but in common with a partnership it has the disadvantage of only being able to call upon the capital resources of its members (supplemented by possible loans from its bank). Since public companies can offer their shares to the public – the shares of many (but certainly not all) public companies are quoted on the stock exchange – they are able to raise considerable sums of money to finance large-scale operations.

A private company used to be limited to a membership of 50, was unable to invite the public to subscribe for its shares and had by its articles to restrict the right to transfer its shares, e.g. only to existing shareholders. These restrictions on membership and transfer of shares no longer exist. This means that private companies have the prospect of growth and development previously open only to public companies. Non-public share offers, e.g. through business contacts or bankers, are now possible. As a result, some private companies, like Amstrad and Virgin, can become extremely large organisations, although in terms of capital public companies usually dwarf private companies; public companies have also been responsible for the immense growth in investment this century. The typical public company can carry on such diverse activities as manufacture cars, give overdrafts or sell insurance – in other words, there is no such thing as a 'typical' public company.

Common misunderstanding

A public limited company is not part of the public sector, nor is it owned by the public at large. It operates in the private sector and is owned by those people who have purchased its shares, the shareholders.

Consumer and worker cooperatives

A consumer cooperative is a registered retail business that is owned essentially by the people who shop there and who wish to make a minimum deposit on a share in the organisation.

Each shareholder has a vote at the annual meeting, where a committee to run the business is elected. Profits (having allowed for taxes and investments) used to be distributed to members in proportion to the value of their purchases, but this policy has now mainly been superseded by the issue of trading stamps that can then be used in exchange for goods in the retail outlets.

Consumer cooperatives originated in the UK in the mid nineteenth century, but their numbers have fallen quite dramatically in the last 20 to 30 years as increasingly people pefer to shop in the large stores operated by the main supermarket chains.

A worker cooperative is a registered form of business that is owned and controlled by some or all of its employees, who share any profits.

Worker cooperatives originated over a hundred years ago and then declined in popularity. Recently their numbers have revived as workers have taken over businesses threatened with closure, although these new organisations have met with a mixed degree of success.

STUDENT ACTIVITY 13.2

Give examples of the different legal forms of business enterprise in your area. State which you think is the most common type of organisation and which has the most local impact.

The size of firms

Of the estimated 3 million business units in the UK, the vast majority (probably over 90 per cent of all business units) are classified as ***very small firms***, each having less than 10 employees. Most of these busineses are sole traders, although they may also comprise some partnerships. These firms tend to be more labour intensive than firms in general, evidence of which can be seen by the fact that they account for approximately 26 per cent of total employment in the economy but only 13 per cent of total sales revenue. Such very small concerns occur in all industrial sectors, especially services; they are particularly prevalent in the construction, hotel and catering and distributive industries.

Manufacturing firms tend, on average, to be larger than businesses in other sectors of the economy because they have a higher degree of capital intensity. ***Small firms***, each employing less than 100 people, predominate numerically, comprising over 96 per cent of all manufacturing firms, yet they are only responsible for a quarter of manufacturing employment and a fifth of manufacturing output.

There is a high concentration of production in the sense that large firms in manufacturing, each of which has more than 5000 employees, number less than 100 individual enterprises but account for almost 30 per cent of manufacturing employment and over 34 per cent of output in the sector.

Concentration of production

The degree of concentration of production can be measured in two ways, or to be more precise, at two levels:

a) *The market or seller concentration ratio.*

This measures the share of employment or output of the largest few firms in a market or industry.

Thus, the five-firm concentration ratio measures the share of a market taken by the five largest firms. Manufacturing industries are usually the most highly concentrated: the five largest firms in the tobacco industry are responsible for over 99 per cent of total output, in iron and steel production the equivalent figure is 96 per cent, for motor vehicles 82 per cent, in the supply of domestic electrical goods 56 per cent and for pharmaceuticals 48 per cent. There is also evidence of increasing concentration of production in service industries like food retailing and in financial services, such as banking and insurance.

High concentration is associated with a high degree of market or monopoly power on the part of the largest firms in an industry.

The degree of market concentration grew rapidly in many manufacturing industries in the 1950s and 1960s, mainly as a result of the high level of merger activity. Since then, on average, market concentration has remained fairly stable. However, the level of concentration in many industries in the UK is reckoned to be higher than in most other industrial economies.

Concentration ratios refer only to domestic output; therefore, they overestimate the extent of concentration in a market where there is a significant amount of competition from imports. In industries like motor vehicles and consumer electronics, however, the domestic suppliers may import finished products from their overseas branches and resell them in the home market; in these circumstances concentration ratios underestimate the degree of concentration in a market. They also understate the true level of concentration where local or regional monopolies exist, as in food retailing. People usually only shop for food locally; the market comprises a fairly narrow area which is dominated by two or three of the large supermarket chains.

b) *The aggregate concentration ratio.*

This measures the share of total employment or output contributed by the largest firms in the whole economy, or in large sectors of it.

The 100 largest manufacturing firms in the UK account for about 38 per cent of total manufacturing output. As is the case with market concentration, aggregate concentration in the UK increased quite rapidly until the late 1960s, since when the level has stabilised or even fallen.

Common misunderstanding:

Concentration ratios are sometimes confused with the actual or absolute size of firms (i.e. the actual number of employees or level of sales revenue), whereas in fact they measure their relative size (i.e. size relative to the market or to the sector as a whole). It may be possible for firms which are quite small in terms of their numbers of employees to hold a significant amount of market power (and hence for there to be a high degree of market concentration). This can be the case in services like catering and dry cleaning where the market is considered very localised, such as a small town; two or three small firms may dominate such a market. However, in most manufacturing industries large relative size is also equated with large absolute size.

In the UK any increase in absolute firm size that is implicit in rises in concentration has occurred more by firms taking over or merging with other firms and thus acquiring more plants than through increases in the average size of plant. Before we discuss mergers and takeovers in more detail, there are two other issues worth examining in connection with the size of firms: first, the basis for and the impact of the multinational firm; and second, the reasons for the survival of the small firm.

Multinational firms

The size of the firm and the economic power that it can wield is taken to its extreme in the case of the multinational corporation (MNC). This is a firm that has production facilities (i.e. plants that it owns and controls) in more than one country.

In setting up these plants or subsidiaries the MNC engages in ***foreign direct investment*** (FDI). MNCs invest abroad for a variety of reasons: to gain access to raw materials and to markets, to avoid trade barriers, to take advantage of lower labour costs and to exploit their technological and organisational advantages (such as superior managerial skills) over local firms. The largest MNCs (e.g. Shell, Ford, General Motors, IBM, Nestlé and Unilever) have subsidiaries worldwide and exercise enormous economic power by being able to transfer resources across virtually any national boundary.

The capital resources, technological knowledge and jobs that MNCs can bring to an economy create intense competition among national governments (as well as among regional authorities within countries) to try to attract these firms to their areas through the offer of various financial inducements. Whether such financial incentives are entirely warranted can depend upon the nature of the inward investment. For example, many of the Japanese car-producing and consumer electronic plants set up in Western Europe prior to the creation of the single market in the EU in 1993 are essentially assembly operations with relatively little local content. In this sense they are 'footloose'and are not dependent on particular locational advantages. The initial inflow of funds has a positive impact on the capital account of the balance of payments (see Chapter 40) and new jobs are created. However, there are also future outflows of profits and managerial royalties to consider and any export earnings on sales from the plant may have to be weighed against the import of components from the home country (i.e. Japanese) suppliers.

The continuation of the small business

Despite the fact that both national and international business is dominated by the large firm, the small firm remains the most popular form of business enterprise.

There are various reasons for its survival:

a) *Limited economies of scale*. In some industries, such as agriculture, only limited economies of scale can be gained. However, small firms may still exist in industries where there are considerable economies of scale, as you may see by considering the remaining points in this list.
b) *'Being one's own boss'*. Entrepreneurs may accept smaller profit for the social prestige of working for themselves or the possibility of making a profit in the future.
c) *Goodwill*. A small business may survive on a fund of goodwill where its customers might tolerate higher prices for a more personal service.
d) *Banding together*. Independent businesses may band together to gain the advantages of bulk buying while still retaining their independence. This is so in the UK grocery chains such as Spar and Wavy-Line.
e) *Specialist services or products*. Businesses may gain a market niche by providing specialist products for particular market segments, e.g. many small car manufacturers exist making specialist sports cars.
f) *Subcontracting*. Since the 1980s there has been a trend in many countries, notably the UK and the USA, for greater flexibility in production. One method of achieving this, so it is claimed, is by large firms subcontracting what are regarded as peripheral activities, such as design, marketing, accounting services and even basic research, to smaller concerns.

Professor Galbraith in his book *Economics and the Public Purpose* suggests two more reasons for the survival of the small firm. First, he says: 'There are limits to the toil that can be demanded in the large firm, but the small businessman is at liberty to exploit himself and in this role he can be a severe taskmaster.' He goes on to suggest that some industries are particularly suited to this kind of discipline which 'rewards diligence and punishes sloth' and he singles out agriculture, suggesting that this is one reason it adapts badly to socialism. The second reason he gives is that as society fulfils its more fundamental economic needs, people begin to demand aesthetic satisfaction from products, thus creating a role for the artist in the economic process, e.g. interior design.

STUDENT ACTIVITY 13.3

Examine some small firms in your area and suggest reasons for their continued existence.

Mergers and takeovers

Firms can grow in size in one of two ways:

a) through ***internal growth***, by investing in new plant and equipment; and
b) ***externally***, through mergers and takeovers.

A ***merger*** refers to the combination of two (or more) firms to form a new legal entity. A ***takeover*** occurs when one company buys out another; if this happens without the consent of the acquired company's management it is known as a ***hostile takeover***. The two terms, mergers and takeovers, are often used interchangeably, as they will be here, although there are obvious distinctions between them.

There are three main types of merger:

a) *A horizontal merger*, or horizontal integration, occurs when two firms in the same industry and that are at a similar stage of production combine. For example, if an oil company which already owned a string of petrol stations were to take over another competitive chain, this would be horizontal integration.
b) *A vertical merger*, or vertical integration, is a combination of two firms at different stages of production in the same industry. Vertical integration can either involve a firm expanding *backwards* towards its sources of supply or *forwards* towards its markets. For example, an oil company which bought oil wells would be engaging in backwards integration, while if it purchased filling stations this would be forward integration.

   It is possible for a firm to undertake both horizontal and vertical integration. Figure 13.1 illustrates the case of an oil company which is vertically integrated from its ownership of oil wells to its control of filling stations and is horizontally integrated by controlling several chains of filling stations.
c) *A conglomerate merger*, or conglomerate integration, refers to the combination of two firms with no obvious common link between them. In the UK, GEC, Hanson and Trafalgar House are examples of conglomerates that have expanded largely by acquiring companies in non-related industries.

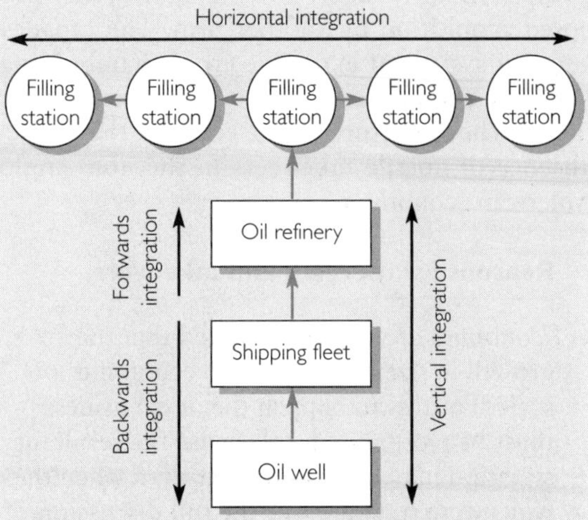

***Fig. 13.1* Vertical and horizontal integration**

Mergers usually occur in waves, with periodic increases in activity.

In the UK there have been three such merger waves this century: in the 1920s, during the late 1960s and early 1970s, and in the mid to late 1980s. There has also been a significant rise in merger activity since the mid 1990s. There is no satisfactory explanation for these sudden bursts of activity, although each wave has coincided with peaks in share prices. In the two earliest waves horizontal mergers activity were by far the most popular form of acquisition. In the wave during the 1980s conglomerate deals predominated, comprising over half of all mergers. Large companies, hitherto immune from takeover, also became more prone to acquisition during this merger wave.

British and American firms have traditionally been regarded as the most merger active, both at home and in other countries, and they continue to be so. There is evidence of increased levels of merger activity in other West European economies and in Japan, although the acquired companies usually tend to be smaller. This is because there are fewer companies whose shares are freely tradable on the stock markets of these countries compared with the UK and the USA. In many other West European economies firms are able to issue shares to friendly third parties, such as family board members and banks with whom the companies have long-established ties; these groups would be likely to vote against any proposed acquisition by another firm. The Japanese *keiretsu* system of extensive cross-shareholdings between companies restricts takeover activity there. These features also explain the virtual absence of hostile takeovers in the non-Anglo-American economies.

Reasons for mergers and takeovers

a) *Economies of scale.* It is argued that the growth in size should lead to economies of scale. For this to happen the new business must be reorganised, otherwise the resultant situation may be less efficient than when the firms were separate (see the full discussion of economies of scale on page 29).

b) *Market domination.* One of the most frequent motives for horizontal mergers is simply to dominate the market and thus be able to reap the advantages of monopoly power.

c) *Reduced uncertainty.* Mergers can reduce uncertainty in a variety of ways. A horizontal merger can reduce uncertainty through the acquisition of a rival; the fewer the rivals, the less the uncertainty concerning their actions. A vertical merger is often undertaken to establish a more secure source of supply of raw materials and components or to maintain the quality of the finished product in retail outlets.

   Diversification into different product areas via conglomerate merger activity spreads a firm's risks. By avoiding the uncertainty of 'having all one's eggs in one basket' a firm may be able to offset periodic declines in sales in one of its products against increases in sales elsewhere. BAT (British American Tobacco) has diversified into hotels, frozen foods and many other lines to protect itself against the risk of a decline in tobacco sales.

d) *For growth.* Mergers provide a quicker, and sometimes cheaper, form of growth than via internal expansion. This may be a particularly important motive for mergers if the managers of a firm are more interested in growth than in profits as an objective (see Chapter 14). The increased size that results from growth may also make the firm less vulnerable to takeover by other firms.

e) *Asset stripping.* This occurs when a company is taken over with the object of closing all or part of it down so that its assets may be realised. This can occur when a company's real assets (land, capital equipment, etc.) have a greater value than its stock market valuation. Asset stripping has often been criticised, especially when a going concern has been closed down. In strict economic terms, however, asset stripping amounts to a more productive use of resources.

The success of mergers and takeovers

To determine if mergers are successful it is first necessary to define success. If it is defined in terms of improved profitability (resulting, say, from lower costs due to economies of scale and/or from increased market power), then the evidence suggests that most mergers are not very successful: many merged firms have proved to be no more profitable, and sometimes less profitable, than had the individual firms remained separate. This applies particularly to horizontal mergers. On the other hand, some conglomerates have grown quite rapidly and successfully through merger activity. In general, however, the evidence on the performance of merged firms is fairly disappointing: there is no evidence that, on balance, the best-run and presumably therefore the most profitable companies naturally acquire the least profitable ones, thus leading to an overall improvement in efficiency. Since there is also no evidence of a downward trend in merger activity, it has to be concluded that many mergers are undertaken with insufficient prior knowledge or appraisal of potential targets by the acquiring firms.

STUDENT ACTIVITY 13.4

Find examples of recent mergers from the financial press and state which type of merger you think they represent (note: some mergers may belong to more than one category).

The location of industry

There are many factors which affect the attractiveness of a location for a firm. These are examined below in two groups: those occurring spontaneously in the economy; and those engineered by the government. We might imagine that organisations weigh all the possible advantages and disadvantages carefully and site their business so as to minimise their costs. It is doubtful whether this is ever totally the case; historical accident might well play a big part in location. For example, William Morris started car manufacture in Oxford because that is where his cycle shop was. Equally, business people tend to be gregarious and will often site their organisation where there are lots of others. However, no one will begin a business or site a new factory without considering some of the following factors.

Spontaneous factors

a) *Raw materials*. Extractive industries must locate where the raw materials are, and this may in turn attract other industries, e.g. the iron and steel industry was attracted to coalfields and engineering industries were then often attracted to the same location. Thus around Glasgow there were the Lanark coalfield, an iron and steel industry and shipbuilding. Today, when many raw materials are imported, industries frequently locate at or nearby ports.

b) *Power*. The woollen industry moved to the West Riding of Yorkshire to take advantage of the water power from Pennine streams. In the nineteenth century most industries were dependent upon coal as a source of power. Since coal was expensive to transport, they tended to locate on coalfields. Today, most industries use electricity or nuclear power, which is readily available anywhere in the country. This means that the availability of power is not an important locational influence today. An exception to this is the aluminium industry, which uses vast quantities of electric power. The industry is therefore centred in countries where there is lots of cheap hydroelectric power, such as Canada and Norway.

c) *Transport*. Historically, transport was a vital locational influence. Water transport was the only cheap and reliable means of transporting heavy loads. Most industries, therefore, tended to locate near rivers or the coast. Canals and, later, railways allowed industry to spread to other locations. Today, access to good transport facilities is still a locational influence. This is illustrated by the town of Warrington in Cheshire, which experienced a renaissance in its industrial fortunes partly as a result of standing at the intersection of three main motorways.

Max Weber, a famous economic historian and sociologist, developed a theory of the location of industry. Weber maintained that industrialists would try to minimise their transport costs. This means that if a commodity ***lost weight*** during manufacture the industry would tend to locate near the raw materials, whereas if it ***gained weight*** during manufacture it would tend to locate near the market. Steel is an example of a commodity which loses weight during manufacture. To manufacture steel near the market would mean transporting several tonnes of raw materials but selling only 1 tonne of finished product. Brewing is an industry in which the product gains weight during manufacture. It is therefore more economical to transport the hops, barley and sugar to the market, where water is added and the brewing takes place. Traditionally, brewing was a widely dispersed industry, although in recent years it has become more centralised. Weber's theory is modified by the value of the commodity. Whisky, for example, is so expensive that transport costs are only a small percentage of the price and are therefore not a locational influence.

d) *Markets*. Service industries such as catering, entertainment and professional services have nearly always had to locate near their markets. In the twentieth century many industries initially located with respect to markets. Goods which are fragile and expensive to transport, such as furniture and electrical goods, may be better produced near where they are to be sold; however, the globalisation of production, with many industries now dominated by large multinational firms, means that this factor is far less significant as a locational force than it once was.

e) *Labour*. The existence of a pool of highly skilled labour may be a locational influence but, increasingly, manual skills can be replaced by automated machinery. An exception to this may be 'footloose' industries. Since they are not dependent upon other specific locational influences they may therefore be attracted to cheap labour.

f) *Industrial inertia*. This is the tendency of an industry to continue to locate itself in an area when the factors which originally located the industry there have ceased to operate. An example of this would be the steel industry in Sheffield, although this may be explained, partly, by external economies of scale and the existence of skilled labour.

g) *Special local circumstances*. Such things as climate or topography may affect the location of an industry. The oil terminal at Milford Haven is located there because of the deep-water anchorage available. A further example is provided by the market gardening industry in the Isles of Scilly, located there to take advantage of the early spring.

h) *'Sunrise' industries*. This is the term given to industries such as computer software which are associated with the 'new technology'. They could be regarded as 'footloose' industries since they are relatively free from apparent locational constraints. However, many of them have become concentrated in the so-called 'M4 corridor' which is the area either side of the M4, stretching from Slough towards Bristol. Reasons that have been suggested for this, apart from the natural gregariousness of business people, are the good communications and, more importantly, the fact that, freed from other obvious constraints, business people have opted to live and work in the pleasant environment of Berkshire and Oxfordshire.

Government influences and the location of industry

The old staple industries, such as iron and steel, shipbuilding and coal-mining, have been in decline for most of this century. They tended to be heavily concentrated in the coal-mining areas. The operation of free market economics seemed powerless to alleviate the consequent economic distress of these areas. This meant that from the 1930s, the government brought in more and more measures to try to attract industry to these areas. We used to explain things in terms of the decline of the old staple industries and the rise of the new industries such as motor vehicles, electronics and chemicals. However, since the 1970s some of these 'new' industries have been in decline, or at least have not been experiencing any significant growth in sales, so that previously prosperous areas such as the West Midlands themselves became areas of industrial dereliction during the depression of the early 1980s. Subsequently, as the economy moved into a further recession in the early 1990s, yet more such industries and areas experienced difficulties. A good example of this is the recession in the financial services industries in London and the south-east.

Over the years since the Second World War governments of both the major parties built up such an armoury of legislative controls and financial inducements that government came to be one of the most important influences upon the location of industry. By the early 1990s many of the controls and incentives had disappeared. Nevertheless, some controls and incentives did remain, provided by both the British government and the EU. We will now consider the most important of these.

a) *Financial incentives*. Financial incentives to encourage organisations to move to depressed areas started with the Special Areas Act 1934. After the Second World War various Acts increased regional assistance. The Industry Act 1972 designated large areas of the country as Special Development Areas (SDAs), Development Areas (DAs) and Intermediate Areas (IAs), all of which qualified for financial assistance.

Successive Conservative governments in the 1980s and early 1990s drastically reduced both the amount of regional aid and the extent of the areas which could receive aid, although Northern Ireland continued to receive considerable assistance. At present there are two types of Assisted Area that qualify for regional aid, ***Development Areas*** and ***Intermediate Areas***, the distinction between Development Areas and Special Development Areas having been dropped in 1984. The situation is illustrated in Fig. 13.2.

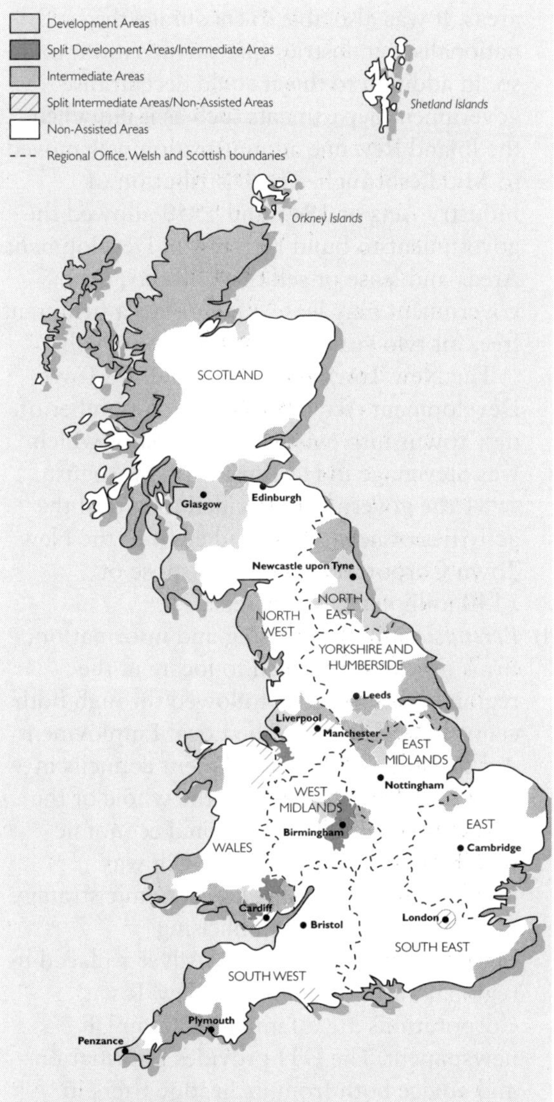

***Fig. 13.2* The Assisted Areas**
Development Areas and Intermediate Areas as defined by DTI at August 1993.

Figure 13.3 traces the decline in regional assistance.

The reasons for the decrease in regional assistance were the government's disinclination to intervene in the economy, stemming from its belief that market forces are the best way to ensure a healthy economy, and its desire to cut public expenditure.

In 1988 Regional Development Grants (RDGs), available to manufacturing and some service projects that created or increased capacity in Assisted Areas, were replaced by discretionary Regional Selective Assistance (RSA). The latter focused more on helping new firms to set up in Assisted Areas rather than on aiding the more traditional industries in those areas. RSA is available to both manufacturing and service firms that create or safeguard jobs and benefit the local economy. Small firms (defined in this instance as those employing less than 25 people) in Assisted Areas can apply for Regional Enterprise Grants (REGs) to aid investment and innovation.

A development in 1980 was the introduction of Enterprise Zones. These are small areas of inner cities, averaging in size approximately 150 hectares. Currently there are 30 such zones in existence in the UK. Firms setting up in Enterprise Zones get a stream of incentives for their first 10 years of operation: no rates;

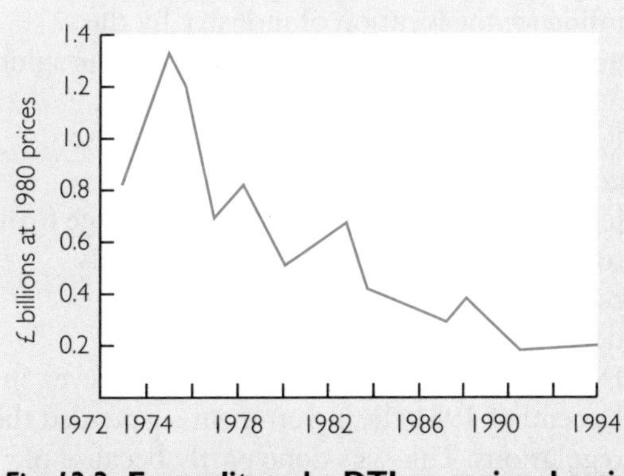

***Fig. 13.3* Expenditure by DTI on regional assistance – constant prices**

100 per cent capital allowances on all commercial and industrial property; and generally less bureaucracy and fewer planning regulations. Another development in the 1980s was the creation of a number of Urban Development Corporations (UDCs). These virtually independent bodies have freedom from many planning constraints together with tax privileges. The most famous of these is the Docklands Development Corporation, which is associated with the 'yuppiefication' of London's docklands.

In 1988 the Action for Cities Programme was launched, which was aimed at coordinating government policy on the inner cities and at encouraging private investment. In 1994 this was largely replaced by the Single Regeneration Budget (SRB) under the control of the Department of the Environment.

The EU makes some funds available from the European Regional Development Fund (ERDF), which is part of the broader EU Structural Funds. In principle, EU financial assistance is supposed to be additional to help given by national governments, but often the DTI has deducted the amount of any ERDF grant from any assistance it may have given.

Whether interventionism works or whether free market forces are more effective, there can be no doubt that in the 1990s massive regional disparities still existed in the UK.

(See Data response A at the end of this chapter.)

b) *Legislative controls*. The government can influence the location of industry by the negative method of forbidding or discouraging new building where it does not want it. Between 1947 and 1974 successive governments created a whole series of legislative controls designed to encourage firms to move to SDAs and DAs. The controls required all new industrial or office developments first to obtain Industrial Development Certificates (IDCs). However, in December 1981 the government suspended the regulations. This was done partly because of the government's desire to reduce the role of government intervention in the economy and partly because of the need to facilitate development of all kinds in an effort to alleviate unemployment.

Thus, to all intents and purposes, planning regulations are the same throughout the country. The exceptions are Enterprise Zones and the Urban Development Corporations, where regulations are less strict.

c) *Direct intervention*. The government can place orders for goods and services in development areas. It was also able to encourage the nationalised industries (pre-privatisation) to do so. In addition to this it could decentralise government departments such as it did when the Inland Revenue administration was moved to Middlesbrough. The Distribution of Industry Acts of 1945 and 1950 allowed the government to build factories in Development Areas and lease or sell them. Today, the government may lease a factory to a firm, rent free, for two years if it creates enough jobs.

The New Towns Act 1946 and the Town Development Act 1952 brought a number of new towns into existence, the first of which was Stevenage in Hertfordshire. In August 1981 the government decided to curtail the activities of new towns and eight of the New Town Corporations had to dispose of £140 million of their assets.

d) *Persuasion*. By advertising and information, firms may be persuaded to locate in the regions. This policy is followed through both centrally and locally. The Local Employment Act of 1960 set up development councils in depressed regions. In 1965 the whole of the UK was covered by 11 regional economic planning councils, each of which was responsible for devising an economic strategy for its region and for publicising opportunities in the region. Adverts placed by regional authorities and by New Town Corporations are a familiar sight in UK newspapers. The DTI provides information and advice both from its headquarters in London and from its regional offices.

An assessment of regional policy is included in Chapter 45.

Summary

1 The firm is the unit of ownership and control in industry. It is usually assumed that all businesses in the private sector seek to maximise their profits.
2 The main types of business are sole traders, partnerships, joint stock companies and cooperatives. Sole traders are the most numerous, but there is a significant concentration of production in the hands of a relatively few large firms.
3 Takeovers and mergers are common in the UK and have contributed significantly towards the increased concentration of production, although many mergers do not appear to be particularly successful.
4 Multinational firms dominate international production. Firms invest abroad for a variety of reasons and many countries compete to attract them to their shores.
5 Despite the concentration of production, many small businesses survive.
6 Location of industry is influenced by spontaneous factors such as markets and communications as well as by government policy.

Questions

1 Account for the continued existence of so many small firms.
2 What are the advantages and disadvantages of sole proprietorship as a method of owning and running a business?
3 Examine and evaluate the factors that influence a firm in the choice of a new site.
4 Distinguish between market and aggregate concentration. Account for the growth in the concentration of production in the UK.
5 For what reason do mergers and takeovers take place? Discuss whether they are in the public interest.
6 Account for the fact that, despite the concentration of production in UK industry, the average size of plant remains relatively small.
7 Why do firms invest in production facilities abroad? Discuss why countries compete to attract such investments.
8 'The advantages of large-scale production will lead to the elimination of all small firms.' Discuss.

Data response A
The north–south divide

Study the article on pages 178–9 which is taken from *The Economist* of 28 September 1996.

Answer the following questions.

1 Discuss the changes in regional unemployment rates that have taken place in the UK in the last 20 years.
2 Average incomes per head have increased by 20 per cent since 1979. Does the north–south divide really matter?
3 Why do firms tend to cluster in the south of the country?
4 Discuss the potential problems for the south of such an agglomeration of industry.
5 Examine why regional rankings of unemployment rates in the UK have stayed largely unchanged since 1918.
6 Given the continued existence of the north–south divide, discuss the implications for government regional policy.

Data response B
The urge to merge

Read the article on pages 180–1 (taken from the *Guardian* of 28 June 1991) which is included to indicate the problems of mergers, and then attempt the following questions.

1 For what reasons may mergers and takeovers take place?
2 Are mergers successful?
3 The article states that not all mergers, not even successful ones, result in increased economic efficiency. How might increased profits accrue to an enlarged business if not from increased efficiency?
4 In recent years a great deal of attention has been given to the process of expanding share ownership. What reasons does the article suggest for distrusting this process?
5 What is meant by the term 'asset stripping'? Discuss whether it is in the public interest.

Return of the North–South gap

During the boom of the late 1980s, it became fashionable to describe a Britain divided into two nations: the loadsamoney South and the Bugger-all-money North, in Harry Enfield's uncryptic words. The recession of 1990–92, which hit the South disproportionately hard, silenced such talk. Indeed, the thought spread that the 1980s were an aberration, and that future economic growth would be spread more evenly throughout the land. Now, with another consumer boom taking hold, it seems that the gulf between the rich South and the poor North is starting to widen again, and that it may go on widening for years to come.

The extent of the North–South divide, past or future, should not be overstated. In every region of Britain, average incomes per head have risen by a least 20% since 1979. There have long been pockets of wealth north of Birmingham to match anything in the Home Counties. The three local-authority districts in Britain with the lowest average incomes per head are in London. Some southern areas receive regional aid: Cornwall has had assisted-area status for more that 15 years. Even so, the North–South distinction matters.

Chart 1 shows the difference between unemployment in selected British regions and the national average rate (excluding Northern Ireland). The highest rate of joblessness over the past 20 years has been in the North of England, and the other above-average regions are all from the northern half of the country. The South (comprising the regions of south-east and south-west England, East Anglia and the east Midlands) had below-average unemployment. In the 1980s, the gap between the highest and lowest jobless rates soared from 2–3% to 6–8%, then fell to 4% in the recent recession.

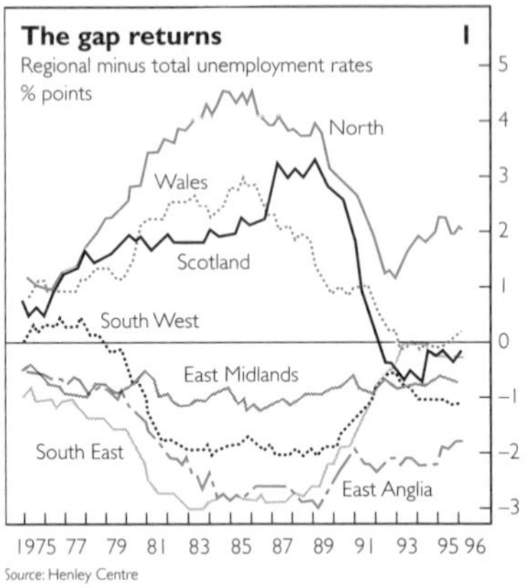

That four-percentage-point gap suggests that rumours of the death of the North–South divide in the 1990s were exaggerated. So do aggregate measures of prosperity: average GDP per head in the South is now £10,069; it is £8,448 in the North. The South's per capita consumer spending beats the North's by £7,544 to £6,412.

Does this matter? The answer depends largely on whether the gap is self-correcting or permanent. After all, simple theories of supply and demand would suggest that firms will move to areas of low wages and high unemployment, to take advantage of cheaper labour and surplus workers, or that workers will move away from such areas to where more and better-paid jobs exist. Both movements should narrow the gap. At first glance, this seems to be what has helped to narrow the unemployment differentials since the late 1980s.

However, this optimistic interpretation is challenged in "Planning for local Change", a study of the British economy published on September 27th by the Henley Centre, a firm of economic forecasters. It concludes that the narrowing of the gap during the 1990–92 recession, far from being the start of a permanent structural shift in favour of the North, was a temporary correction resulting from the bursting of the late 1980s' housing and consumption bubble, which was biggest in the South.

With that correction now complete, the South is likely to grow faster once again, says the study. Indeed, the gap between the highest and lowest regional jobless rates has grown from four percentage points to five since 1992. And, as chart 2 shows, although manufacturing jobs have been lost equally in both North and South during the post-1992 recovery, the South has been leading the way in creating new service-sector jobs, as it did in the 1980s.

According to one of the report's authors, Paul Williams, an economist at the Henley Centre, rather than moving to areas where wages are lowest, firms tend to cluster together in the more competitive bits of the country. The South is better represented in those service industries which are likely to create the most wealth over the next few years: telecoms, computers and financial services.

Some leading economists, such as America's Paul Krugman, argue that, although regional disparities may grow in the short run, congestion costs will limit, and then reverse, the process of agglomeration in the long run. Mr Williams disputes this, arguing instead that the South's competitive edge comes from its superior ability –

from a greater pool of educated workers and better access to finance, among other things – to move rapidly into whatever economic activity has the highest value added at any given moment.

The North produces the lion's share of manufacturing output, but the manufacturing that does take place in the South has a far higher value per tonne. When service firms have shifted away from congested parts of the South, they have tended to move first to less congested parts of the same region. There have been a number of well-publicised moves to the North, but most of these were of back-office, low value-added activities. High value-creating activity remains largely southern-based: 60% of venture-capital investment in Britain goes to south-east England alone.

The beautiful South

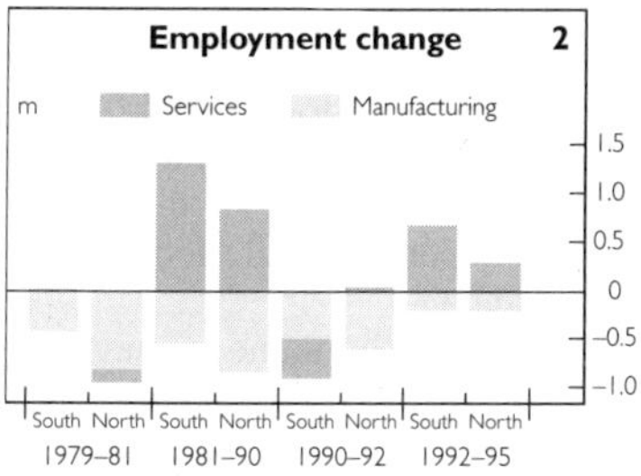

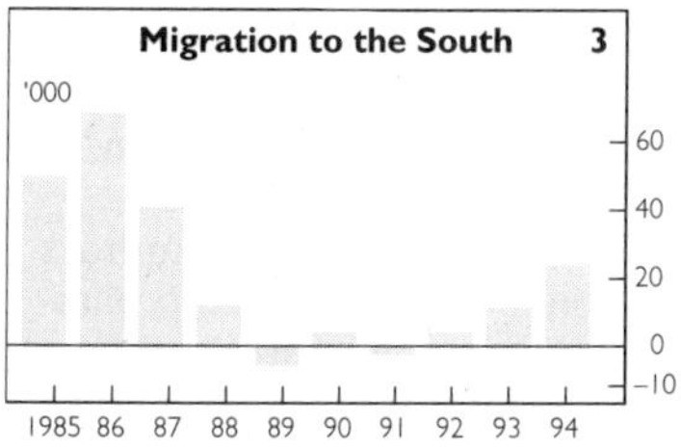

Source: Henley Centre

In America, although some states have enjoyed consistently faster economic growth than others during the past half-century, the average rate of unemployment in each state has tended to stay close to the national average. Any deviations from the national average have mostly vanished within a few years, as the jobless moved to where the work was.

In Britain however, regional differences have persisted. Incredibly, the regional ranking of unemployment rates has barely changed since 1918. Migration has been relatively modest, although a southwards drift has recently restarted (chart 3). Moreover, movement is mostly by skilled, non-manual workers. As a result, there is little regional disparity in non-manual unemployment rates, but there are huge differences in manual joblessness. There are several plausible reasons why the less-skilled stay put: it is hard for council tenants to move around the country, and property costs more in the South. But the perverse result is that, by offering an escape route to poorer regions' most valuable people, labour mobility exacerbates rather than ameliorates the North–South divide.

If the divide does grow ever wider, it is likely to increase demand for more active regional policies to correct the imbalance. In fact, the government already transfers huge amounts northwards through the tax and social-security systems. "Financing Regional Government in Britain", a recent study by the Institute for Fiscal Studies, an independent research group, calculated how much tax each region would have to levy to pay for its own public spending. It found that, using 1993–94 data (the latest available), the basic rate of income tax would have to rise to 41% in Wales, 38% in Scotland and 32% in the North of England, compared with 24% now. (There would have to be similar increases in the top rate of tax.) People in the south-east and south-west would enjoy a tax cut, to 18.5% and 22.6% respectively.

This complicates current demands for regional government in Scotland, Wales and northern England. Genuine autonomy in these areas would cost locals a fortune in higher taxes. But perhaps the oddest feature of British politics is the lack of interest in regional autonomy in southern England, which has much to gain by loosening ties with the rest of the country. Many people in Italy's wealthy north voted for the independence-minded Northern League. So where is Britain's Southern League?

Source: The Economist, 28 September 1996

Why British industry must overcome the urge to merge

Outlook
Roger Cowe

TAKEOVERS are bad for you – that's official – unless you are a shareholder in a company being bid for.

A worthy body of academics and quasi-academics takes this as a starting point for their deliberations on how to depress the urge to merge which proves irresistible to so many British and American managers.*

Mergers and takeovers do not create wealth (except for the bankers and lawyers involved) but simply transfer ownership of assets. 'Unless these assets are employed more efficiently by their new owners than they were before,' the authors comment, 'then nothing will have been gained while real resources will have been wasted in the process of transfer, especially in contested bids.'

Of course the argument used by every bidder, no doubt including Lord Hanson if he ever makes his long awaited bid for ICI, is that they know better than the existing owners how to get the most out of the target company's assets.

The evidence, such as it is, suggests that they are wrong as often as they are right. Individual cases do not prove the general point, but this week's example of Beazer attempting to dig itself out of a takeover-induced hole is the latest in a long line of late-1980's bids which have subsequently proved disastrous to the winning side.

Saatchi & Saatchi, Blue Arrow, Brent Walker, British & Commonwealth, and News Corporation are all in that line.

Economic performance

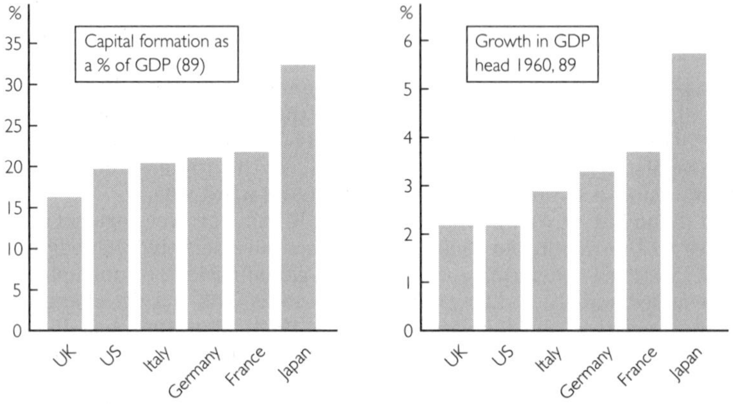

Moving from the specific to the general, the macro-economic evidence, shown in the chart, links poorly performing countries such as the US and UK with a high incidence of takeovers. This is, of course, not conclusive. Nobody can know how the UK and US economies would have performed if the rate of takeovers had been the same as in Japan and Germany.

Similarly, nobody can know how a company which has been taken over would have performed if it had remained independent. And since companies are not yet required to disclose takeover profits separately, nobody knows how much the profit of companies like Hanson comes from their acquisition activity. So we cannot tell how they would have performed without those takeovers.

The evidence – including the judgements of company directors who have made takeovers – is not encouraging, however. As the authors say, the evidence does not support the belief that mergers are generally beneficial.

'Assessment of company performance before and after takeovers provides no concrete evidence that takeovers are predominantly 'successful'. . . There is no evidence to suggest that takeovers have a positive effect on overall economic performance.'

This is not the same as saying that takeovers should be banned, or that takeovers are bad. The authors accept that some are justified and work well for all concerned and for the economy as a whole. But they disdain detailed consideration of individual examples.

The reason is that the authors are economists, concerned primarily with creating an economic environment that might discourage another takeover boom when the next stock market surge pushes up share prices once again to a level which makes share-based bids more worthwhile than now.

A valiant aim. It might put a virtual end to the merger and acquisition industry, but the British economy could probably stand that shock to the system. Unfortunately the aim is deflected by an obsession with small entrepreneurs.

Proposals for discouraging takeover activity are therefore

concerned more with expanding share ownership and encouraging owner-managers, mainly through the tax system and including the abolition of corporation tax.

It is difficult to see how this has much bearing on a potential Hanson bid for ICI. Indeed, it is difficult to see how directors of companies as large as Hanson and ICI can be expected to own a significant portion of their companies' shares. One per cent of ICI shares would cost £8.9 million at current prices.

It is also difficult to see how spreading the ownership of shares in such companies would help the scrutiny of their directors' actions. Surely an institution such as the Prudential owning three per cent of ICI, has more chance of influencing its strategy than 27,000 shareholders each owning £1,000 worth of shares.

But, at least a learned investigation has knocked on the head the notion that takeovers are good for anybody but those in the M&A industry that make them happen.

**Corporate takeovers and the public interest*, Alan Peacock and Graham Bannock, Aberdeen University Press.*

Source: *The Guardian*, 28 June 1991

14 Competition, profits and other objectives

Learning outcomes

After studying this chapter you will be able to:

- Understand the significance of the profit-maximising objective.
- Distinguish between the different types of competition.
- Understand the nature of barriers to entry.
- Appreciate the distinctions between both normal and abnormal profit and implicit and explicit costs.
- Have a knowledge of the alternative theories of the firm.

Supply

Earlier in this part of the book we gave considerable attention to the theory of demand. We must now turn to the other side of the market, that is to say, to supply.

This part of economics is sometimes called the ***theory of the firm***. The firm is the unit of supply, so that if we are able to explain the behaviour of one firm we may explain the behaviour of market supply by aggregating all firms' supply.

> **In the same way that the market demand curve is a horizontal summation of individual demand curves, so market supply is the horizontal summation of firms' supply curves.**

In Fig. 14.1 we envisage a market which is supplied by two groups of firms, A and B. At a price of £4 per unit group A supplies 60 units and group B 80 units, whereas at a price of £2 A would supply 20 units and B 30 units. If we total the amount supplied at each price we obtain the market supply, i.e. 140 units at £4 and 50 units at £2.

Profit maximisation

One of the basic assumptions on which the whole theory of business behaviour is based is that firms will seek to maximise their profits, i.e. they not only attempt to make a profit but attempt to make the last penny of profit possible. At the end of the chapter we are going to suggest some modifications to this view, although it is generally accepted that no other comprehensive explanation of the behaviour of firms has been put forward and certainly no other that stands up well to the rigours of empirical testing and benefits from widespread supportive evidence. Thus, we will find that whatever type of competition we consider, profit maximisation can be regarded as a unifying principle.

Types of competition

When the economist classifies types of firms it is usually with respect to the type of competition under which they exist. At one extreme we have perfect competition, which represents the theoretically optimal degree of competition between firms, while at the other extreme we have monopoly, where the firm is synonymous with the industry and there is no competition at all.

Figure 14.2 gives a diagrammatic representation of the possibilities. We have inserted a gap in the line between perfect competition and all other types since perfect competition is only a theoretical possibility. Economists refer to these as different types of ***market structure***. The structure of a market is indicated by those characteristics that determine the ***conduct*** of firms or how they

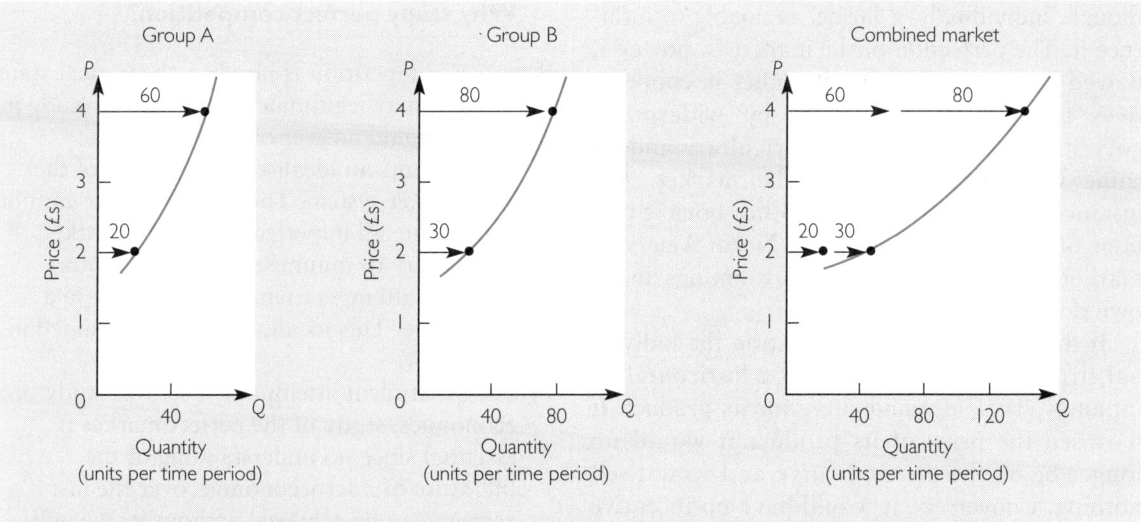

Fig. 14.1 **Group A's and group B's supply curves combine to make the market supply curve**

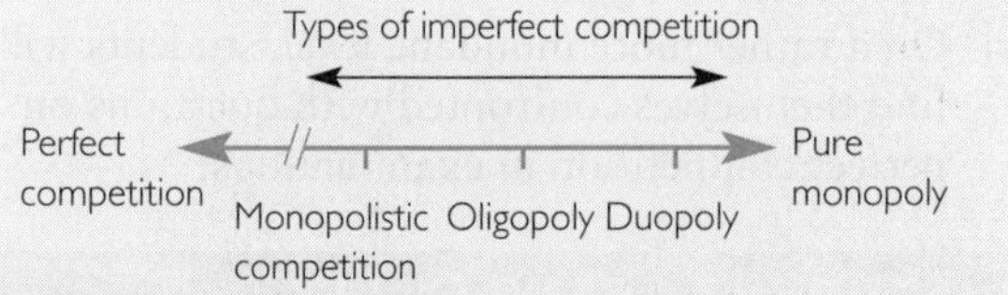

Fig. 14.2 **Types of competition**

behave (i.e. their pricing policies) and ultimately their levels of *performance* (e.g. their profitability). The key structural characteristics of a market are the number and relative size of firms in a market (i.e. the level of market concentration), the extent of the freedom that firms have to enter and leave a market and the nature of the product (i.e. the degree of similarity between the products of the various firms in a market).

Perfect competition

In perfect competition firms are price-takers, i.e. they have no power to affect the market price, although they can sell all they want to at this prevailing price.

For a state of perfect competition to exist in an industry the following conditions have to exist:

a) A large number of buyers and sellers of the commodity.
b) Freedom of entry and exit to the market for both buyers and sellers.
c) Homogeneity of product, i.e all goods being sold have to be identical, and are perfect substitutes.
d) Perfect knowledge of the market on the part of both the buyers and sellers.

STUDENT ACTIVITY 14.1

Explain why each of the above assumptions is necessary for price-taking to exist.

It is obvious that all these conditions cannot exist in one market at once. There are, however, close approximations to perfect competition, e.g. the sale of wheat on the commodity market in Canada. In this situation there are thousands of sellers and ultimately millions of buyers and it is relatively easy for farmers to enter or leave the market by switching crops; as far as homogeneity is concerned, once graded, one tonne of wheat is regarded as identical with another. In addition to this, when wheat is sold on the commodity market both sides have a good knowledge of the market and it appears to the farmers that they can sell all they want at the market price even though, individually, a farmer is unable to influence it. The perfection of the market is, however, flawed by farmers banding together in cooperatives to control the supply, by widespread government intervention in agriculture and by some very large buyers in the market. For instance, in recent years the CIS has bought millions of tonnes of wheat on the North American market to make good the shortcomings in its own domestic output.

If there were perfect competition the individual firm would *appear* to face a horizontal or infinitely elastic demand curve for its product. If it raised the price of its product it would no longer be on the demand curve and would sell nothing. Conversely, it would have no incentive to lower its prices since it appears to be able to sell any amount it likes at the market price. The organisation is thus a ***price-taker*** and its only decision, therefore, is how much to produce (see Fig. 14.3). The price may of course change from day to day, as it does in the case of wheat, but to the farmer the demand curve always appears horizontal. The industry demand curve will remain a normal downward-sloping one; indeed the world demand curve for wheat is fairly inelastic, large changes in price bringing only relatively small changes in demand.

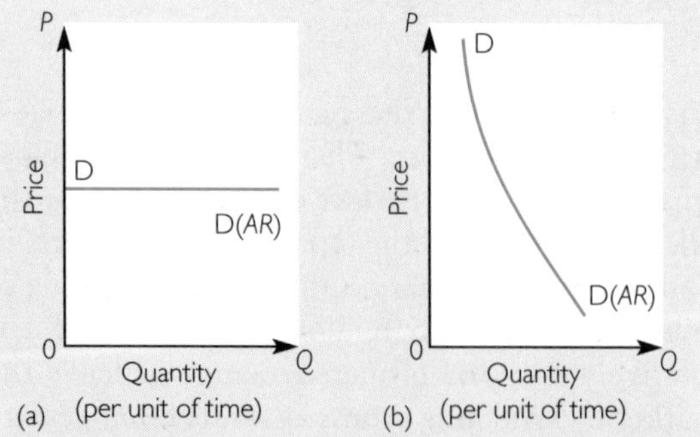

***Fig. 14.3* The demand curve under perfect competition**

(a) The demand curve for the individual firm's product.

(b) The industry demand curve. Note: In the theory of the firm the demand curve is usually labelled *AR* (average revenue).

Why study perfect competition?

If perfect competition is purely a theoretical state the student may legitimately ask why we study it. To this we could answer on three grounds:

a) It represents an idealised functioning of the free market system. Thus, although we cannot elimininate all imperfections in the market, we may try to minimise them, as a motor engineer attempts to minimise friction in a car engine. This idealised view is examined in Section IV.
b) For the student attempting a serious study of economics, study of the perfect market is essential since no understanding of the literature of microeconomics over the last century can be achieved without it. We will also see that perfect competition is vital to the neo-classical view of the macroeconomy (see Chapter 34).
c) On a rather more mundane level, students will find themselves confronted with questions on perfect competition in examinations!

STUDENT ACTIVITY 14.2

Can you think of any other market situations that may approximate to perfect competition?

Imperfect competition

We will now turn to look at imperfect markets. All markets are to a greater or lesser extent imperfect. This is not an ethical judgement on the organisations which make up the markets. There is nothing morally reprehensible about being an imperfect competitor; indeed this is the 'normal' state of affairs. It could be the case, however, that firms contrive imperfections with the object of maximising their profits to the detriment of the consumer.

In imperfectly competitive markets firms are price-makers; they have the power to determine their own prices.

The main influence on whether firms can set their own prices is the degree of ***product differentiation*** that exists in a market. This is the extent to which similar products are perceived to be different by consumers; the differences may be due to actual physical differences in, say, quality or they may be the result of advertising and policies to develop a particular brand image. Jeans may vary in quality according to their manufacturer, but some makes also have a particular brand image perpetuated through advertising; Levis, for example, are associated with durability and a certain tough, 'macho' image as well as being regarded as a prime fashion article.

In other words, the products in imperfect markets are not perfect substitutes for each other.

As a result, all imperfect competitors share the characteristic that the demand curve for their individual firm's product slopes downward, i.e. if the firm raises its prices it will not lose all its customers as it would under perfect competition. Conversely, it can sell more of the product by lowering its prices.

In addition to this it can be affected by the action of its competitors. In Fig. 14.4, for example, the decrease in demand DD to D_1D_1 could have been brought about by a competitor lowering prices. If, for example, Ford were to drop the prices of its cars by 5 per cent it would probably bring about a fairly substantial decrease in demand for cars produced by other manufacturers. This would not be so in the case of perfect competition. If, for example, Farmer Jones were to cut the price of wheat by 5 per cent it would scarcely affect the sales of the thousands of other farmers who make up the market.

Imperfectly competitive markets are also characterised by imperfect information: firms may be unsure of how their rivals are going to behave in any situation and consumers are unlikely to possess enough information to distinguish adequately between the products of all the firms in a market. Furthermore, firms in imperfectly competitive markets are unlikely to be completely free to enter or leave it.

It is possible to distinguish several types of imperfect competition. These distinctions arise chiefly out of the level of market concentration, the degree of product differentiation and the ease with which firms can enter (or leave) a market. The latter depends on the extent of barriers to entry (and exit) to and from a market.

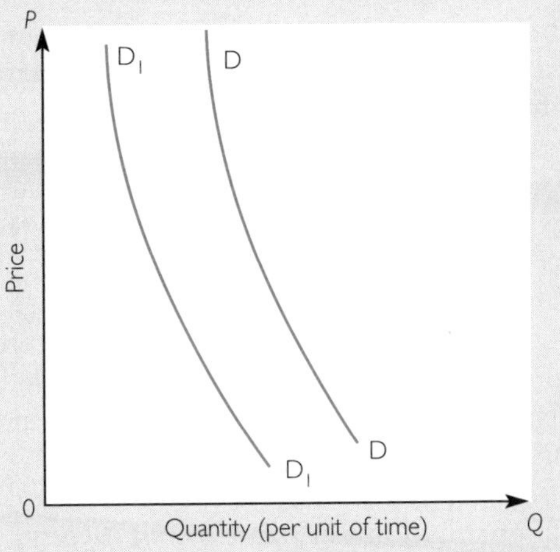

***Fig. 14.4* The demand curve for an individual firm's product under imperfect competition**
The firm has some choice over price and output, but can also be affected by competitors. The decrease in demand from DD to D_1D_1 could have been brought about by a fall in the price of a competitor's product.

Barriers to entry and exit

Barriers to entry, hardly surprisingly, make it difficult for new firms to enter a market; in such circumstances the established firms, or incumbents, may be able to charge a higher price and make more profit than if entry to the market was relatively easy.

The main barriers to entry are:

a) *Economies of scale*. When there are significant economies of scale in an industry (see Chapter 3), only a few firms may be able to supply the market efficiently, i.e. at lowest possible cost. A new firm trying to enter on a relatively small scale would face higher unit costs than the incumbents and hence would find it difficult to survive. In the extreme case, where unit costs continue to fall beyond the level of market demand, just one firm can benefit from economies of scale; a ***natural monopoly*** exists.

b) *Capital requirements*. Many manufacturing industries employ capital-intensive production techniques; a large capital outlay, a potential obstacle to entry, is required to begin production. The problem is compounded if, as in many consumer goods industries, an expensive advertising campaign is required or, as for example in pharmaceuticals, a large-scale R&D programme is necessary. Evidence suggests that capital requirments, along with the relevant technical knowledge, represent the greatest obstacle to entry in many industries.
c) *Product differentiation*. Product differentitation can create ***brand loyalty***, whereby consumers associate good quality with a particular brand name (such as the St Michael brand of Marks and Spencer) and are therefore loyal to it in their purchases. To overcome brand loyalty a new firm may have to spend more on advertising than the incumbents. Established firms may also make it difficult for new firms to enter a market by each supplying several brands; such ***brand proliferation*** occurs among beers and lagers, breakfast cereals, cigarettes and soaps and detergents.
d) *Lower unit costs*. Incumbents may have lower unit costs than potential entrants for a variety of reasons: knowledge of operating in the industry may give them favoured access to managerial talent, suppliers and superior locations; ***patent rights*** give firms the right to supply a product for a specified number of years.
e) *Pricing policies*. Incumbents may engage in ***limit pricing*** if their costs are lower than those of the new entrant. Instead of trying to maximise their own short-run profits the incumbents may eliminate the potential for profits on the part of the entrant by charging a price only up to the level of the new firm's costs.
f) *Legal restrictions*. Patent rights represent one form of legal restriction on firms selling certain products. In addition, in the UK the Post Office has the legal right to be the sole supplier of letter deliveries under £1. Licences are required to sell alcohol (whether on or off the premises). Legal permission is required to supply banking services, although the deregulation of the financial services market in the1980s means that firms in the industry are now freer to sell other financial products (e.g. banks can sell mortgages and life insurance).
g) *Sunk costs*. These are costs that cannot be recovered once a firm leaves an industry. Specialist capital equipment often falls into this category, as does most marketing costs, like advertising. Firms are unable to recoup these costs. These act as ***barriers to exit*** for incumbents given the large capital outlays involved. They also represent barriers to entry for new firms, which may be reluctant to enter an industry if faced with the prospect of substantial sunk costs should they not be successful.

Barriers to entry can be divided into structural barriers, which tend to occur naturally in an industry. They include capital requirements and economies of scale. There are also behavioural or strategic barriers, the result of intentional decisions by the incumbents.

Limit pricing is an example of the latter. Product differentiation, however, may be categorised as either type: most consumer goods are naturally prone to a certain level of advertising in order to inform the public about the products, although established firms in these industries may also advertise with the express intent of raising costs for potential entrants. Incumbents can also use excess capacity, R&D expenditure and predatory pricing as intentional actions to ward off would-be entrants, although this is a controversial area and is hotly disputed by industrial economists.

Traditionally, it has been assumed that barriers to entry are fairly extensive in many industries, especially in manufacturing. The Austrian school views barriers to entry as rather less formidable: most, it is assumed, can be overcome over time. Legal barriers are regarded as the most effective obstacles to entry according to the Austrian view and are also thought to be the most likely to persist.

Monopoly

Monopoly lies at the opposite end of the competitive 'spectrum' to perfect competition. It literally means a situation where there is only one seller of a commodity, although in practice a dominant firm may be able to exert a considerable amount of monopoly power with far less than 100 per cent of the market.

Legally speaking, an organisation may be treated as a monopoly under the Fair Trading Act 1973 if it has more than 25 per cent of the market. In principle, for a monoply to exist there should also be no close substitutes for the firm's product. However, in most cases a certain amount of competition is likely to occur with other similar products. Thus, the railways compete with other forms of transportation, such as road, air and even sea. The Post Office is in competition with firms such as DHL and Federal Express for parcel deliveries.

The monopoly power of a firm is partly determined by the size of its regional market. Thus, if a village has a single hairdressing salon it will have some monopoly power, since customers will not wish to travel far to get their hair done.

Oligopoly

The word oligopoly, like monopoly, is derived from the Greek and means a situation where there are only a few sellers of a commodity.

In other words, there is a high degree of seller concentration. 'Few' is never strictly defined, but can mean anything from two to, say, 10 firms. The situation where just two firms dominate a market is known as a *duopoly* and is regarded as a special case. In a few instances, such as cement, steel and aluminium production, oligopolists produce virtually identical products and compete in terms of prices; they are referred to as *perfect oligopolies*. However, in most cases oligopolies are characterised by a high degree of product differentiation and little price competition and are known as *imperfect oligopolies*. Many manufacturing industries in the UK can be classified as oligopolies: motor vehicles, electrical goods, confectionery, glass manufacture, pharmaceuticals and so on. A growing number of service markets, e.g. banking and insurance and food retailing, are also dominated by a few, large sellers. Tobacco and soaps and detergents are examples of duopolies.

Monopolistic competition

When there are a large number of sellers producing a similar but differentiated product, then a state of monopolistic competition is said to exist.

Thus, seller concentration is quite low and the products tend to be fairly close substitutes. Such a market is also characterised by the frequent entry and exit of firms. It is called monopolistic competition because, owing to imperfections in the market, each organisation has a small degree of monopoly power.

Examples of monopolistically competitive markets are more likely to be found in the service sector: estate agents, dry cleaners, restaurants and various forms of retailing. However, as noted previously, in a small town one or two individual sellers may possess considerable market power. The various types of competition are summarised in Table 14.1.

It is paradoxical that under perfect competition very little competition is visible since there is no advertising and promotion of products, whereas under all types of imperfect competition rivalry between firms is only too obvious. Even firms with significant market power advertise. Tate and Lyle, for example, which has a large share of the market for cane sugar production, not only promotes its product but extols the virtues of free competition. It is a case, as Professor Galbraith wrote in *The Affluent Society*, of competition being advocated 'by those who have most successfully eliminated it'.

STUDENT ACTIVITY 14.3

List as many industries as you can and categorise them according to the type of competition that you think prevails.

***Table 14.1* Different market forms**

Type of competition	*Number of producers and degree of product differentiation*	*Barriers to entry*	*Influence of the firm over prices*
Perfect competition	Many producers, homogeneous products	None	None
Imperfect competition:			
Monopoly	Single producer no close substitutes	Very likely	Considerable
Oligopoly	Few dominant producers	Likely	Considerable
Perfect	Homogenous products		
Imperfect	High degree of product differentiation		
Monopolistic competition	Many producers, product differentiation	Very low	Fairly small

Profits

Normal and abnormal profits

At its simplest, profits are the difference between total revenue (*TR*) and total costs (*TC*). However, economists have a concept of ***normal profit***:

Normal profit is the minimum amount of profit which is necessary to keep the firm in the industry.

It is obvious that the firm must pay for the labour it uses, pay rent for its site and pay for its raw materials. It must also pay for the capital that it uses: the owners of the business must be rewarded or they will not consider it worthwhile supplying the necessary financial capital. We may thus regard some profit as a legitimate cost of the business. We therefore include this in the costs of the business; this is because if profits fall below a certain level it will no longer be considered worthwhile producing the product and the owners of capital will transfer their money elsewhere. Thus:

Normal profit represents the opportunity cost of supplying capital to a business. Any profit in excess of this is termed abnormal profit (or, sometimes, pure, excess or supernormal profit). When there is relative freedom of entry to the industry, as in perfect competition or monopolistic competition, any abnormal profit will attract new firms into the industry.

However, with monopoly or oligopoly, barriers to entry are likely to exist and any abnormal profit may persist.

The concept of normal profit is an essential tool in explaining the behaviour of a firm. What the normal level of profit is may vary both from industry to industry and even between firms within an industry. Some investments, or some lines of business, are more risky than others. What sort of investment people undertake depends on their attitude towards risk: the more risky the investment, the higher the expected return or level of normal profit. Shareholders in a company that has a secure position in an established market are likely to be content with a lower, but more certain, return on their investments than are the suppliers of capital to a business that is, say, introducing a new product into a relatively volatile or uncertain market, such as fashion or films.

Implicit and explicit costs

In arriving at a calculation of profit a firm needs to consider both explicit and implicit costs. These are both measured in terms of their opportunity costs. For resources *not owned* by the firm their opportunity costs are simply the prices the firm has to pay for their use. Thus, explicit costs are those which the firm is contracted to pay, such as wages, rates, electricity, etc. In the case of resources *owned* by the firm their costs are implicit; they are what the resources could earn in their next best alternative use. For example, suppose a firm owns the site on which it operates; the economist would argue that in addition to its wages bill, its electricity bill, etc., the firm should pay itself the market rent for the site, otherwise it is making an uneconomic use of its resources because it is conceivable that it could do better by closing down and renting the site to someone else. We are thus once again speaking of the concept of opportunity cost.

An example may make the point clearer. Some years ago Lyons had 'Corner House' cafés on many of the most prominent sites in London. These appeared to be making a profit. However, Lyons discovered that if it were to close the cafés, dispose of the sites and invest the money gained it could make more than its present level of profit. Lyons had been ignoring the implicit costs of its business. Having considered these costs Lyons decided to sell off many of these sites and London lost some of its most familiar landmarks.

Common misunderstanding

Normal profit is not part of profit in the accounting sense. It is actually regarded as a cost of production. It is the minimum reward necessary for the owners of the business to continue supplying the necessary capital, given the risks involved. Thus, normal profit represents the implicit costs of ownership.

Alternative objectives

While we shall assume that profit maximisation remains the key objective of the firm, whatever the level of competition, alternative theories postulating different objectives have been advanced from time to time.

The managerial theories of the firm that originated in the 1950s and 1960s refer particularly to large firms in which, it is assumed, there is a divorce between ownership and control.

Shareholders, the owners of the firm, are interested in maximising profits, while the managers, it is argued, have other objectives from which they obtain prestige, power and increased monetary rewards. Thus, William Baumol suggested that the prime objective of management is to maximise sales revenue, while Robin Marris postulated that the main managerial aim is to maximise the rate of growth of the firm; managerial salaries and prestige are thought to be more closely associated with sales and the size of the firm than with profit alone. Oliver Williamson put forward a more general model in which managerial interests are met by the optimisation of a utility function comprising salaries, the number of subordinates, fringe benefits, such as plush offices and company cars, and control over a firm's resources.

In each model the firm is expected to achieve a certain level of profits in order to provide the shareholders with an acceptable return on their investments. This reduces the risk of them selling their shares and so lessens the threat of takeover. The profit also helps to provide the necessary funds for capital investment purposes.

Another theory of the firm developed in the 1960s was the ***behavioural model***, mainly associated with H. A. Simon. The firm is seen as a coalition of interest groups, including managers, shareholders, employees, customers and suppliers. Each group has goals and these may conflict. However, since each group has limited knowledge of the firm's operations and of the aims of the other groups, a coalition of interests results. ***Satisficing*** rather than maximising behaviour ensues: a satisfactory level of sales, profits, wages or quality of product is sought. Each goal takes the form of an ***aspiration level***, which changes if targets are not met or if there is a change of emphasis (a larger market share, say, to counteract the growth of a competitor) by coalition members.

Both the managerial and behavioural theories incorporate the concept of 'organisational slack'. Where there is a lack of competition members of the firm may receive payments over and above what is required for the continued existence of the organisation; in other words, a firm is likely to produce at above minimum cost.

Slack can accrue to any member of a firm, but managers are thought to be in the best position to receive such payments, which can take the form of higher salaries and fringe benefits or reduced effort.

Small firms may also have non-profit-maximising objectives. In the previous chapter it was noted that one of the prime reasons for the continued existence of the small concern is the desire to be one's own boss; once this desire is met entrepreneurs may be content with a relatively quiet life and the achievement of a satisfactory level of profit.

Consumer cooperatives are supposed to be mainly concerned with satisfying the interests of their customers, while worker cooperatives may have a particular concern for protecting jobs.

Summary

1 The theory of the firm is the basis of the theory of supply, since if we are able to explain the behaviour of the firm we can then explain the operation of industry supply.
2 The traditional theory of the firm is based on the profit maximisation hypothesis.
3 Perfect competition represents the ideal functioning of the market system. The two most important conditions of perfect competition are that:
   a) no individual buyer or seller can influence market price;
   b) there is freedom of entry and exit to the industry.
4 The main types of imperfect competition are monopoly, oligopoly and monopolistic competition. All firms operating under these conditions have some control over the market price.
5 The principal types of barriers to entry are economies of scale, capital requirements, product differentiation, lower unit costs, pricing policies, legal restictions and sunk costs, the last of which is also the main barrier to exit. Barriers to entry are most likely to feature in monopoly and oligopoly markets.
6 Normal profit is the minimum amount of profit which is necessary to keep a firm in an industry; it varies with the degree of risk in a market.
7 There are alternative theories of the firm that assume non-profit-maximising objectives. However, profit remains an important feature of any theory.

Questions

1 Contrast perfect competition and monopoly as market forms. Discuss whether one is superior to the other from society's point of view.
2 Evaluate the profit maximisation hypothesis. Examine the role of the profit motive in alternative theories of the firm.
3 If the government imposes a price ceiling on a product (see page 142) does that make the firms that sell the product price-takers, regardless of whether or not they are perfect competitors? Give reasons for your answer.
4 List five products you have bought in the last week. Assuming that they were not bought from perfect competitors how did the supplier compete for your business with other rival suppliers?
5 Outline the main barriers to entry. Discuss whether they are likely to occur naturally in an industry or are more the result of the deliberate actions of the incumbents.
6 Explain what is meant by implicit and explicit costs. How is it possible for a firm to be making an accounting 'profit' but an economic loss?

Data response A
Barriers to entry

Read the following passage and study Table 14.2.

> The traditional view of the degree of profit in economic theory is associated with market structure, that is to say the degree of competition existing in an industry. Monopoly, for example, may experience profits above the normal because other firms are excluded from competition. When firms set out to exclude other firms there are said to be barriers to entry. In theory profits should be lower when there is a great deal of competition. Concentration ratios show us how much of an industry is accounted for by, say, the largest three or five firms. An attempt to relate the degree of competition through barriers to entry to profitability is indicated in the table.

Answer the following questions.

1 What do you understand by the term 'barriers to entry'? How do barriers to entry arise? Assess the importance of barriers to entry for the following industries:

Table 14.2 Rates of return for 15 concentrated industries

Barriers to entry	*Rate of return (%)* 1970–80	1980–88
Very high	15.2	12.3
Substantial	11.2	9.0
Low	12.1	10.1
Average	13.0	10.5

Source: Datastream

a) motor vehicle production;
b) the manufacture of video cassette recorders;
c) fresh fruit and vegetables;
d) aircraft construction;
e) plumbing services.

2 Explain what is meant by the concept of normal profit.

3 Based on the information contained in the table, does there appear to be any relationship between barriers to entry and performance and how has the relationship changed in recent years?

4 What reasons do you think there are for the overall decline in performance shown in the table?

5 What action might a government take to reduce barriers to entry?

Data response B Market structures

Market structures can be divided into four main types: perfect competition, monopoly, monopolistic competition and oligopoly (including duopoly). Each type has particular characteristics which are summarised in Table 14.1. State which of the following features belong to which category (some may belong to more than one):

a) Firms are price-takers.
b) Firms are price-makers.
c) Barriers to entry exist.
d) There are many sellers, each selling a differentiated product.
e) A few large firms supply most of the market.
f) Two firms dominate a localised market.
g) Economies of scale occur beyond the level of market demand.
h) The market exhibits a high level of seller concentration.
i) Firms sell homogeneous products.
j) It is relatively easy to enter and leave the industry.

Data response C Implicit costs

A person decides to set up a travel business and invests £200 000 of their own money, which could have earned 10 per cent p.a. in a high-interest building society account. The person could also have earned £20 000 p.a. working for somebody else. In the first year of operation the business has sales revenues of £145 000; its costs of production total £120 000. Calculate:

a) The level of profit according to an accountant.
b) The level of profit according to an economist.

Discuss the reasons for any difference.

15 Costs in the short run and the long run

Learning outcomes

At the end of this chapter you will be able to:

- Distinguish between the terms the short run and the long run.
- Understand the concepts of total costs, fixed costs, variable costs and average costs.
- Account for the nature of long-run average costs in theory and practice.
- Understand the concept of marginal cost and appreciate the relationship between marginal cost and average cost.
- Explain the effects of changes in fixed costs and variable costs.

We have seen that there are different kinds of competition, but no matter what market conditions a firm operates under its cost structures will be similar. Thus the cost structures which we investigate in this chapter apply to all types of competition, from perfect competition to monopoly.

Imperfections of competition may affect the cost structure in two ways. First, monopolisation of a market may make economies of scale available to the firm which are not available to competitive firms. Second, the opposite may also be true, i.e. monopoly may protect inefficient cost structures. We will consider these possibilities in Chapter 18.

It is convenient to split up the costs of the business organisation in various ways because is allows us to understand its behaviour more fully. The firm itself will analyse its own cost structures in order to try to improve its performance.

We will consider costs under three main headings: total costs; average costs; and marginal costs.

Total costs (*TC*)

Total costs (*TC*) are the costs of all the resources necessary to produce any particular level of output.

Total costs *always rise with output*. This is because obtaining more output must always require more input. Thus, no matter what the scale of production, obtaining another unit of output must involve, say, the input of some raw materials or labour, no matter how small the amount, so that a greater output must always involve a greater total cost.

We can obtain a better understanding of total costs by splitting them into their two main components: fixed costs and variable costs.

Fixed costs (*FC*)

Fixed costs (*FC*) are those costs which do not alter with output in the short run.

They are derived from fixed factors of production.

Fixed costs usually comprise such things as hiring plant and equipment, the interest on borrowed capital, insurance costs, property taxes, most managerial and administrative expenses, depreciation costs (that depend on the ageing of fixed assets) and an advertising campaign that runs for a set period. These costs will exist (and remain constant) whether the business is producing as much as possible or nothing at all. If a business wishes to expand beyond the capacity of its present fixed assets, then it must build or acquire new premises, capital, equipment, etc. The period of time necessary for it to do this is said to be the ***long-run*** period.

Variable costs (*VC*)

As a firm produces more output, so it needs more labour, raw materials, power, etc. The cost of these factors which *vary with output* is termed variable costs. Examples include most wage costs, raw material expenses, heating and lighting, depreciation costs (that are associated with the use of the capital equipment) and sales commissions.

Variable costs (*VC*) are those which vary with output. Variable costs are zero when output is zero and rise directly with output.

Thus, total cost comprises *fixed costs* and *variable costs*. This we can state as:

$TC = FC + VC$

This is illustrated in Table 15.1, where you can see that whatever the level of output, fixed costs remain constant at £116 per week. If there is no output there is no variable cost, but as output increases, so do variable costs.

Table 15.1 **Total costs, fixed costs and variables costs**

Output units per week, Q	*Total costs, TC (£)*	*Fixed costs, FC (£)*	*Variable costs, VC (£)*
0	116	116	0
1	140	116	24
2	160	116	44
3			60
4	200	116	
5	240	116	124
6	296	116	180
7			252
8	456	116	

STUDENT ACTIVITY 15.1

You can test your understanding of the concepts by filling in the blanks in Table 15.1. The answers may be checked with Table 15.2.

The figures in Table 15.1 are illustrated in Fig. 15.1. Here you can see that fixed costs are constant whatever the level of output in the short run. Variable costs are zero when output is zero and rise with output. The *TC* curve is obtained by aggregating the *FC* and *VC* curves.

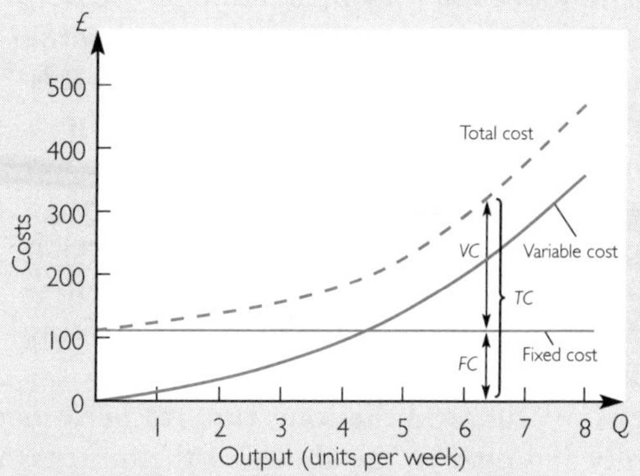

Fig. 15.1 **Total costs are fixed costs plus variable costs**

Why does the *VC* curve (and thus the *TC* curve) begin to rise more rapidly at higher levels of output? The reason for this is that after a certain output, the business has passed its most efficient use of its fixed assets (buildings etc.) and ***diminishing returns*** begin to set in.

Figure 15.2 illustrates the effect of a change in fixed cost in the long run. As plant size is expanded, this causes a shift from one level of total cost to another. Thus:

In the long run all costs are variable.

Digression 1: the short run and the long run

We have already defined the short run and long run in Chapter 3, but it is useful here to restate the definitions in terms of the costs of the firm.

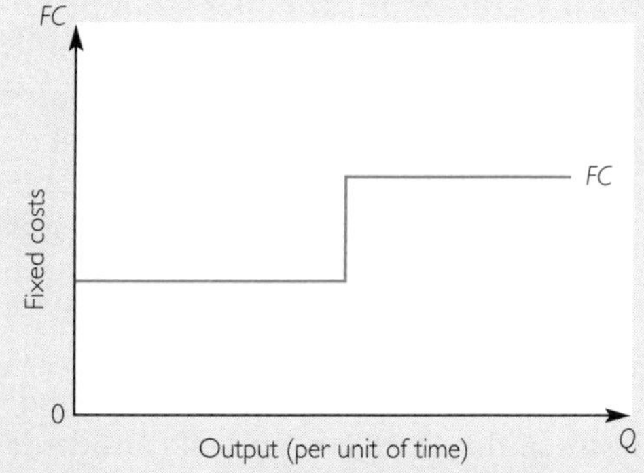

Fig. 15.2 **Fixed costs in the long run**
The increase in fixed cost as the firm expands its capacity in the long run causes a 'kink' in the curve.

The short run may be defined as the period during which output may be varied within the limits of the present fixed assets. It is not possible for new firms to enter the industry or for existing firms to leave it.

The long run may be defined as the period in which all factors of production and hence all costs are variable and new firms may enter the industry or existing firms leave it.

The short run and the long run are ***periods of supply*** and refer to the ability of the business to vary its behaviour within the market. They are *not* chronological periods of time, e.g. we *cannot* say the short run period is, say, six months. How long the supply period is will depend upon the industry. In the motor vehicle industry, for example, the short run may extend for a very long time, e.g. five to ten years for the business to vary its fixed assets, i.e. build a new plant or re-equip an existing one, while in the retail trade it may be possible for a business to acquire new premises in a relatively short time, e.g. six months.

Common misunderstanding

The relationship between the terms the short run and the long run and precise periods of time needs to be made completely clear. While the short run may extend for quite a long period, the long run may actually only be a very brief amount of time. At any one time a firm is almost bound to have some fixed factors of production, such as plant and equipment; hence, it is almost permanently in a short-run position. At the time the firm makes the long-run decision to invest in a new plant it is in a short-run situation; it remains in that position until the new plant is up and running. Then it will be in a new short-run situation.

Throughout most of this chapter we shall be concerned with the behaviour of costs and of businesses in the *short run*; we will consider later how their behaviour might be modified in the *long run*. Therefore, unless it is clearly stated otherwise, you may assume that we are talking about the short run.

Digression 2: short-run shut-down conditions

Suppose that a business is running at a loss. Obviously in the long run it will go out of business, but what is the best policy in the short run? Will it make a smaller loss if it stays open so long as there is still some money coming in, or is it best to close down immediately?

The answer to this conundrum lies in the *variable costs*.

So long as the revenue the business is getting in is greater than the variable costs, it is worth its while staying open in the short run because it will make a smaller loss than it would do by closing immediately.

However, if the revenue it is earning from selling its product is less than its variable costs, then it will make a smaller loss by closing immediately.

Ultimately, though, in the long run all costs must be covered if the business is to remain in the industry.

Let us consider the case of an apple grower. The cost of planting the trees and of renting the land could be regarded as fixed costs, since the farmer can shed them only by going out of business. Other costs, such as harvesting the crop and transporting it to the market, will vary with output and can therefore be described as variable costs. This being the case, it is apparent that if the price of apples were low the apple grower could not recover all the costs, but would still continue to sell apples in the short run if variable costs could be covered. In other words, if the money from the sale is greater than the costs of picking and selling the apples, it would appear that in the short run the grower will produce and ignore fixed costs.

Conversely, if the cost of harvesting, transport, etc., were greater than sales revenue, the apple grower would be better off closing down immediately and saving the variable costs.

Common misunderstanding

A firm does not need to recover all its costs in the short run in order to stay in production. It is worthwhile remaining open as long as revenue covers its variable costs, since the fixed costs have to be paid anyway. Thus, a firm makes a smaller loss by staying open than by closing down.

You can check your understanding of this point by trying Data response B at the end of this chapter.

Average (or unit) cost (*AC*)

Three types of average cost

Average cost (*AC*) is the total cost divided by the number of units of the commodity produced.

This can be expressed as:

$$AC = \frac{\text{Total cost}}{\text{Output}} = \frac{TC}{Q}$$

As we have already seen that total costs can be divided into fixed costs and variable costs, it would follow that average cost can be divided in the same way:

$$\text{Average fixed costs} = \frac{\text{Fixed costs}}{\text{Output}}$$

$$AFC = \frac{FC}{Q}$$

and:

$$\text{Average variable costs} = \frac{\text{Variable costs}}{\text{Output}}$$

$$AVC = \frac{VC}{Q}$$

It would therefore follow that:

$AFC + AVC = ATC$ (average total costs)

Using the same figures as in Table 15.1, we may illustrate these various concepts. It should be apparent to the student that we can calculate all these various figures once we have the total cost schedule (see Table 15.2).

AFC declines continuously with output in the short run as fixed costs are spread over a greater and greater number of units of output. Whether *AVC* increases or decreases depends upon the rate at which total cost is increasing. We can arrive at *ATC* either by adding *AFC* and *AVC* or by dividing total cost by output. We can also verify the fact that:

$$AFC + AVC = ATC$$

For example, if the output is 5 units per week, then *AVC* is £24.80 while *AFC* is £23.20, thus giving *ATC* as £48.00.

Figure 15.3 shows *AFC*, *AVC* and *ATC* plotted graphically. You can see that AFC slopes downwards continuously and is ***asymptotic*** to the axis, i.e. it gets nearer and nearer to the horizontal axis but never touches it. The *AVC* curve at first falls and later rises owing to the effects of diminishing returns.

The most important curve, as far as we are concerned, is the *ATC* curve. This, you will see, is an elongated U-shape. This is always so in the short run. *ATC* always starts at infinity and then falls rapidly as the fixed costs are spread over more and more units. It continues to fall until the point of ***optimum efficiency*** or ***optimum capacity*** is reached (output of 5). Average costs then begin to rise as diminishing returns set in and the increase in *AVC* outweighs the fall in *AFC*.

***Table 15.2* The costs of the firm**

Output units per week, Q	Total costs, TC (£)	Fixed costs, FC (£)	Variable costs, VC (£)	Average fixed costs, FC ÷ Q = AFC (£)	Average variable costs, VC ÷ Q = AVC (£)	Average total costs, AFC + AVC = ATC (£)
0	116	116	0	∞	–	∞
1	140	116	24	116.00	24.00	140.00
2	160	116	44	58.00	22.00	80.00
3	176	116	60	38.60	20.00	58.60
4	200	116	84	29.00	21.00	50.00
5	240	116	124	23.20	24.80	48.00
6	296	116	180	19.30	30.00	49.30
7	368	116	252	16.60	36.00	52.60
8	456	116	340	14.50	42.50	57.00

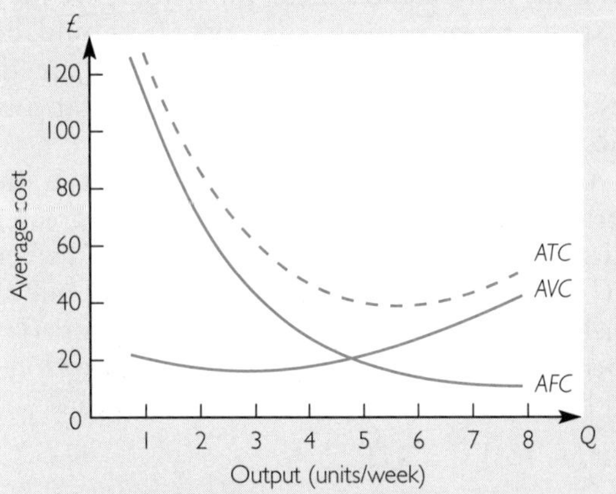

Fig. 15.3 **Average costs**
Average total cost is average variable cost plus average fixed cost.

Economically speaking, therefore, the best output is 5 (in our example) because here the article is being produced at the ***lowest unit costs***. If output were to be any greater or any less then unit costs would rise. It should also be noted that, as average fixed costs gets progressively smaller, the distance between the *AVC* and *ATC* curves narrows. This can be confirmed from Table 15.2 and Fig. 15.3.

The efficiency of a business can be judged by the extent to which it is managing to minimise its unit costs. This is an important point which we will return to later.

Shut-down conditions – again

If we return to the section above on short-run shut-down conditions, we can re-examine the principles involved in terms of average cost. We stated the principle that the firm should continue to operate in the short run so long as it covers its variable costs. If, for example, the variable costs of the business were £68 per week and output were 400 units, then the business would have to recover at least 17 pence per unit to stay in business, i.e. £68/400. This we can now recognise as the average variable costs (*AVC*) of production. Thus we can restate the short-run condition as:

> **The firm will continue to produce in the short run so long as the price of the product is above *AVC*.**

If you are in doubt about this, then re-read this section carefully and attempt Data response B at the end of the chapter. It is important to understand this principle because it is a necessary component of the theory of the firm.

STUDENT ACTIVITY 15.2

The manager of a small 20-room hotel in a seaside resort reckons he can charge an average of £15 per room per night during the off-peak season. Total fixed costs off-peak are estimated as £60 000. Variable costs sum to £7500 over a 30-day period. Should the hotel remain open?

Average costs in the long run

It has already been stated that the average cost curve is U-shaped in the short run because of the law of diminishing returns. In the long run, however, the fixed factors of production can be increased to get round this problem.

What effect does this have on costs?

If the business has already exploited all the possible technical economies of scale, then all it can do is build an additional factory which will reproduce the cost structures of the first. However if, as the market grows, the business is able to build bigger plants which exploit more economies of scale then this will have a beneficial effect upon costs.

In Fig. 15.4 SAC_A is the original short-run average cost curve of the business. As demand expands the business finds it possible to build larger plants which are able to benefit from more economies of scale. Thus it arrives at SAC_D. SAC_M represents a repeat of the process with a larger scale of production.

Exactly what size of plant a firm should choose to produce a certain output is an extremely important decision. For example, if the firm decides to produce output OQ it chooses the plant size that gives the lowest unit cost for that particular level of output. This is SAC_D, yielding unit costs of OC. SAC_D represents the plant size that can produce OQ most efficiently. Note that

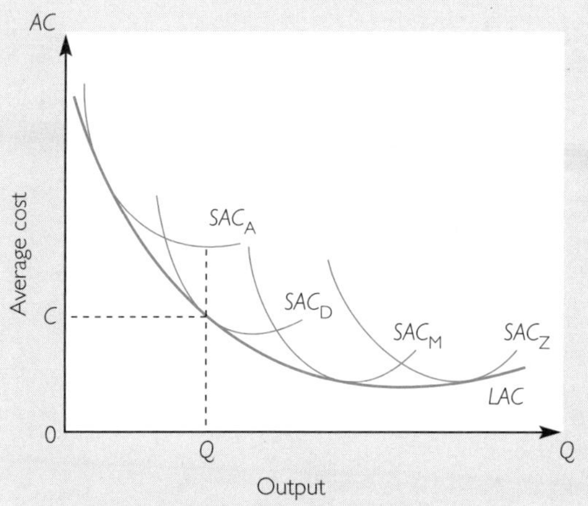

***Fig. 15.4* Smooth envelope curve**
SAC_A to SAC_Z represent an indefinite number of short-run average cost curves created as plant size is increased. *LAC* is the long-run average cost curve (smooth envelope) which is tangential to the *SAC* curves. Both *SAC* and *LAC* are U-shaped.

OQ could be produced by operating a smaller plant, SAC_A, at optimum capacity (i.e. at its lowest point). However, it is better that the firm ***underutilises*** the larger plant, SAC_D, than operates the smaller plant at its lowest point. Such a process continues until all available economies of scale have been exhausted. Beyond this level of output successive *SAC* curves, such as SAC_Z, lie higher and to the right owing to the existence of diseconomies of scale. Increased size adds to bureaucracy and leads to control loss. In addition, highly specialised labour can create repetitive work. Both can have the effect of reducing productivity and raising unit costs. In these circumstances (i.e. where diseconomies of scale exist) it is preferable for a firm to ***overutilise*** a smaller plant than to operate a larger plant at its most efficient level.

Every plant size, or level of fixed input, is represented by an *SAC* curve; each *SAC* curve is tangent to the long-run average cost curve. The *LAC* curve is often referred to as the envelope curve of all the *SAC* curves. It shows the minimum attainable unit cost for each and every level of output.

The curve we have produced is known as a smooth envelope curve. It is drawn on the assumption that there are an infinite number of choices of plant size between SAC_A and SAC_D, and so on, so that we obtain a smooth transition in long-run average costs (*LAC*). If on the other hand there were only a limited number of choices of size of plant, this would tend to make the *LAC* curve more irregular. This is shown in Fig. 15.5.

We saw above that diminishing returns to scale mean that short-run average costs will eventually increase as output expands. Alfred Marshall also assumed that the long-run average cost curve is U-shaped. This implies that expanding firms will always eventually hit diseconomies of scale.

In practice, evidence suggests that, in those industries investigated, economies of scale exist but diseconomies of scale either do not or are outweighed by economies of scale. In other words, the *LAC* curve is more L-shaped than U-shaped.

A summary of the main evidence for the UK and the EU is given in Table 15.3. The table shows the minimum efficient scale (MES) as a percentage of output in various industries in the UK and the EU.

MES is defined as that level of output where the *LAC* curve first reaches its

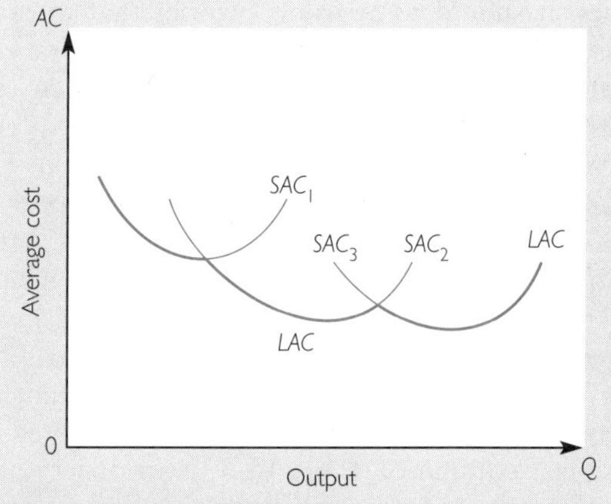

***Fig. 15.5* Long-run average cost**
SAC_1 to SAC_3 represent three possible sizes of plant. The *LAC* curve is still an envelope of these curves but is no longer smooth.

Table 15.3 Evidence of economies of scale in selected manufacturing industries in the UK and the EU

Industry	*MES (% UK output)*	*MES (% EU output)*	*Rise in costs (%) at one-thrid MES*
Beer	12	3	5
Cigarettes	24	6	2.2
Oil refining	14	2.6	4
Integrated steel	72	9.8	10
Cement	10	1	26
Petrochemicals	23	2.8	19
Paint	7	2	4.4
Ball bearings	20	2	8–10
Televisions	40	9	15
Refrigerators	85	11	6.5
Glass bottles	5	0.5	11
Washing machines	57	10	7.5
Bricks	1	0.2	25*
Nylon and acrylic	4	1	9.5–12*
Cylinder blocks	3	0.3	10*
Tyres	17	3	5*

* The percentage increase in costs for bricks, nylon, cylinder blocks and tyres is at one-half MES

Source: Pratten (1989) *The Cost of Non-Europe*, Vol. 2 (Luxembourg: Office for Official Publications of the European Communities)

minimum point, or where all economies of scale have been fully utilised.

Thus, in Fig. 15.6 MES is given by OQ. As can be seen MES varies considerably between industries. It should come as no surprise that in each case MES represents a much greater share of UK output than for the EU as a whole, given the latter's much larger market size. In most of the investigations MES is less than 5 per cent of EU output, suggesting that the market can support at least 20 plants. For the UK alone, however, MES is above 10 per cent in most cases, and often substantially so, implying that only a relatively small number of plants can survive in each industry.

The other method of assessing the extent of economies of scale in an industry, as indicated in the last column of Table 15.3, is to observe by how much unit costs increase at a certain percentage of MES output. In the majority of instances the cost disadvantage for plants at a third (or a half) MES is only around 10 per cent; smaller plants do not incur a large cost penalty.

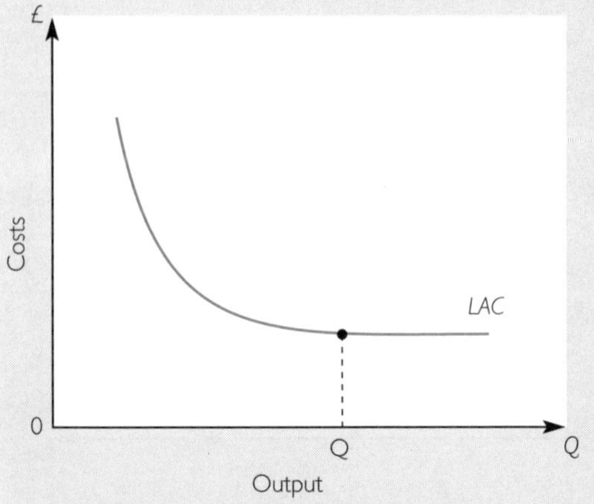

Fig. 15.6 The MES level of output
This is where the *LAC* curve first reaches its minimum point.

The evidence gives rather contradictory signals about the extent of economies of scale. The data in the table suggests that they are quite extensive in most industries, especially when the UK alone is considered, while the information in the last column implies that they may be rather less so. The general conclusion is that, while economies of scale occur in most industries, they do not preclude smaller units from surviving.

STUDENT ACTIVITY 15.3

Study the data in Table 15.3 and state in which industries you think economies of scale are most or least significant and why.

Marginal cost (*MC*)

Marginal cost defined

Marginal cost (*MC*) may be defined as the cost of producing one more (or less) unit of a commodity.

Like all the other costs we have considered marginal cost may be calculated from the total cost schedule. We arrive at marginal cost by subtracting the total costs of adjacent outputs. We may illustrate this by using the same total cost figures we have used throughout this chapter. In Table 15.4 you can see that it is the cost involved in moving from one level of output to the next. The figure is therefore plotted half-way between the two outputs. Hence if we produce 6 units the total cost is £296, whereas if we produce 7 units total cost rises to £368. The cost involved in producing 7 units is therefore £72. This is shown not at 6 or 7, but half-way between.

Table 15.4 **The marginal cost schedule**

Output units per week, Q	*Total costs, TC (£)*	*Marginal cost, MC (£)*
0	116	
1	140	24
2	160	20
3	176	16
4	200	24
5	240	40
6	296	56
7	368	72
8	456	88

The marginal cost curve

When we come to plot the marginal cost curve some particular problems are involved. Since the marginal cost is the cost of moving *between* two levels of output, it is plotted as a horizontal straight line between these outputs. Thus, in Fig. 15.7 (a), for example, the cost of moving from an output of 6 units per week to 7 units per week is £72. Marginal cost is therefore plotted as a horizontal line between these outputs. When this is done we end up with a graph looking like a step-ladder. If we wish to represent marginal cost as a smooth curve, this can be done by joining up the midpoints of each step. This is done in Fig. 15.7 (b).

The step-ladder graph and the smooth curve represent two different concepts of marginal cost. The step-ladder shows that costs move in ***finite*** steps from one output to the next, whereas the smooth *MC* curve suggests that costs are infinitely variable between outputs. Thus we would see the marginal cost of producing 1.1 units, 1.2 units, 1.3 units and so on. The step-ladder therefore shows ***discrete*** data and the smooth curve ***continuous*** data. These conditions apply to all

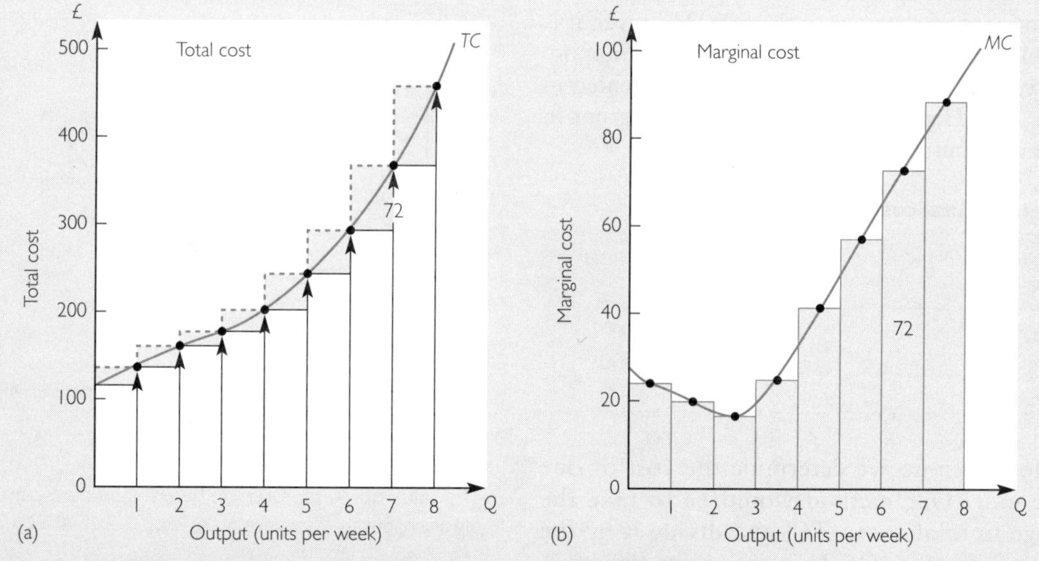

Fig. 15.7 **Total cost and marginal cost output of 6 units/week to 7**
Marginal cost is the difference between successive levels of total cost, e.g. the cost of moving from an output of 6 units/week to 7 units/week is £72. You can see that the distance in (a) corresponds to the same distance in (b). Thus the value of the shaded areas in both diagrams is equal.

marginal figures. It is increasingly becoming the practice in economics texts to adopt the discrete data approach at this level of the subject. However, it is usually more convenient to adopt the continuous data approach, and this we shall do for most purposes.

The shape of the *MC* curve

You will see in Fig. 15.7 (b) that the *MC* curve at first falls and then rises, presenting a similar U-shape to the *AC* curve. This is because the same principles of diminishing returns apply to marginal cost in the short run as they do to all the other cost structures. As we shall see in subsequent chapters, the firm is almost invariably concerned with the levels of output where marginal cost is rising. The student should not be surprised therefore if sometimes economic texts present marginal cost as continuously upward-sloping lines.

The mathematics of marginal cost

This section may be omitted without impairing your understanding of subsequent chapters.

The method of calculating marginal costs which we have used is quite adequate for the purpose of explaining the behaviour of the firm. However, it is possible to envisage further complications. Suppose that we have figures for total costs as presented in Table 15.5. Here we have output increasing not in single units but in 50 units.

Table 15.5 **Total cost schedule**

Output, units per week, Q	*Total costs (£)*
350	12 500
400	13 500
450	15 000

How then do we determine the cost of one more unit? One method would be to take the change in total costs (*TC*) and divide it by the change in output (*Q*). Thus, using the figures in Table 15.5, if output increases from 350 to 400 per week, we would obtain the calculation:

$$MC = \frac{TC}{Q}$$
$$= \frac{£1000}{50}$$
$$= £20$$

This, however, is only an approximation because it gives the average increase per unit between 350 and 400 units per week. It would therefore be better to refer to it as the ***average incremental cost*** (*AIC*) rather than marginal cost (*MC*). The figures in Table 15.5, if plotted as a graph, would give a curved line for *MC* so that its value would vary all the way from 350 units to 400 units, i.e. *MC* would be different at each level of output – 300, 301, 302, etc.

This can be better understood by considering Fig. 15.8. In measuring *MC* we have so far taken a method which depends upon comparing distance XY with distance YX_1. That is to say, if XY represents an increase in output of 1 unit then YX_1 is the resulting increase in total cost, i.e. the *MC*. It would be mathematically more precise to define *MC* as the slope of the *TC* curve at any particular point; that is:

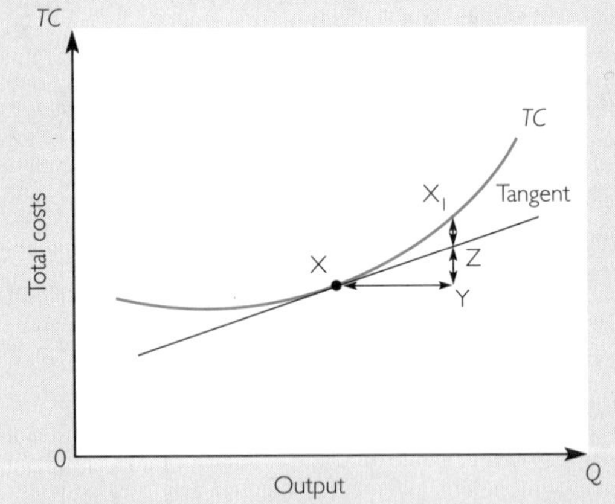

Fig. 15.8 **Marginal cost**
The value of *MC* at X can be determined by constructing a tangent to the curve at X. Thus:

$$MC = \frac{XY}{YZ}$$

$$MC = \frac{d(TC)}{dQ}$$

which the mathematically minded will recognise as the way of saying that:

Marginal cost is the first derivative of cost with respect to output.

That is to say, it is the change in cost associated with an infinitesimally small movement along the *TC* curve. In Fig. 15.8 we can demonstrate this by the construction of a tangent to the *TC* curve at the point we wish to measure. Then the value *MC* at point X is:

$$MC = \frac{XY}{YZ}$$

By turning our stepped *MC* curve into a smoothed-out one we are in fact making an approximation to the correct mathematical way of calculating *MC*.

Average cost and marginal cost

The relationship between *MC* and *AC*

In Fig. 15.9 we have brought together the figures for *MC* and those for *AC*. A most important point is revealed:

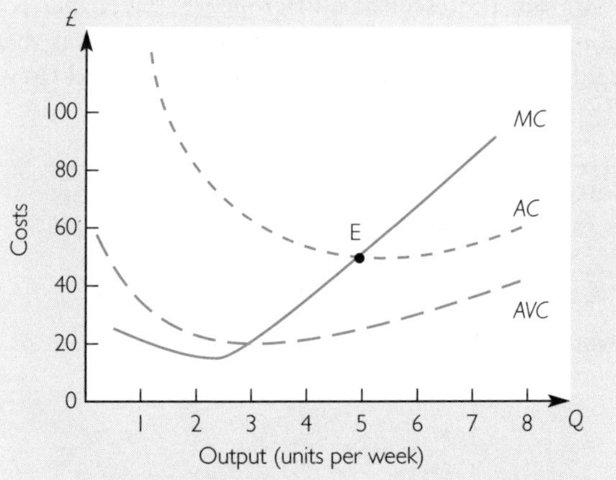

***Fig. 15.9* Marginal cost and average cost**
The *MC* curve cuts the *AC* curve at point E, which is the lowest point of average cost.

The *MC* curve cuts the *AC* curve at the lowest point of *AC*.

As you can see in Fig. 15.9, this occurs at an output of 5 units per week. You can also see that *MC* cuts the lowest point of the *AVC* curve.

Why does this relationship occur? The reasons are mathematical rather than economic and the explanation is this. So long as *MC* is less than *AC*, then it will draw *AC* down towards it, but as soon as *MC* is greater than *AC* then it will pull up the *AC* curve. Thus, the *MC* curve must go through the bottom point of the *AC* curve. This applies to both the short-run and the long-run situations.

This principle applies to the relationship between any marginal and average figure. Consider the following example.

A batsman in the county cricket championship has an average score of 25 runs after 10 innings. In the next match (*marginal*) he scores 13 runs. What happens to his average? It falls because the marginal score is below the average. In the next match he scores 18. Although his marginal score has risen, his average is still brought down because the marginal is still less than the average. However, were he to score 30 in the next match, the marginal score, now being greater than the average, would pull up the average.

The student should also note that the same principle applies to the marks or grades awarded on school or college courses!

A change in fixed costs

Suppose that a firm's fixed costs were to increase – for example, its rent might be doubled – but its variable costs were to remain unchanged. What effect would this have upon the cost structures? The answer to this question is found in Fig. 15.10. The marginal cost is not affected because it shows the change in cost associated with increasing output. Therefore:

Marginal cost is unaffected by fixed cost.

The average cost, however, is increased at every level of output so that it shifts upwards from AC_1 to AC_2. You will note that the *MC* curve cuts both *AC* curves at their lowest points.

A change in variable costs

In Table 15.6 we have doubled the level of variable costs at each level of output. As you can see

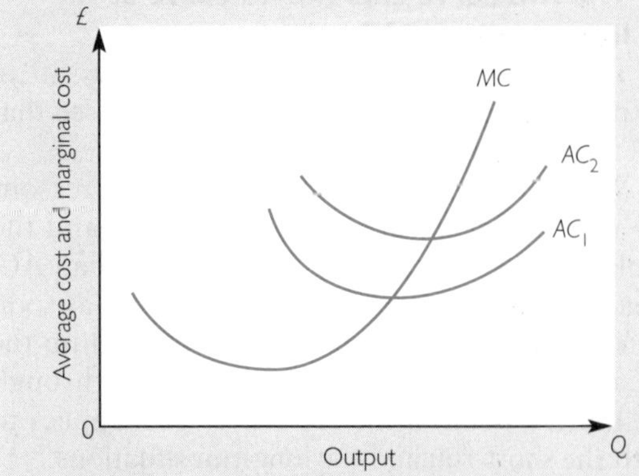

***Fig. 15.10* An increase in fixed costs**
If fixed costs are increased but variable costs are not, then the *MC* curve is unaffected by the *AC* curve moving upwards from AC_1 to AC_2.

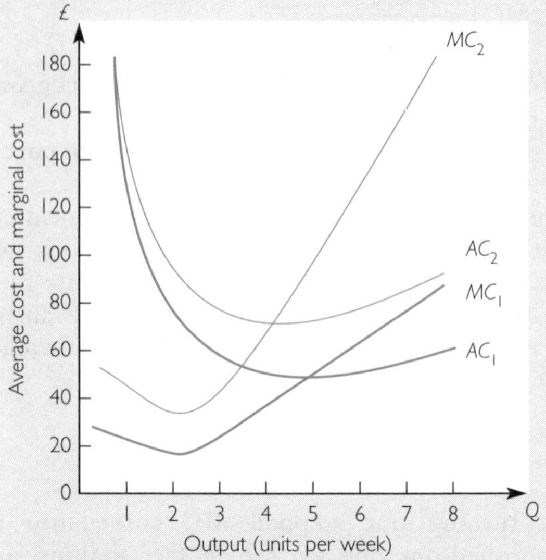

***Fig. 15.11* A change in variable costs**
Both the *MC* and the *AC* curves shift upwards as a result of the increase in variable costs.

this affects both the average cost and the marginal cost. In Fig. 15.11 you can see that both the *AC* and *MC* curves have shifted upwards as a result of the change. The intersection of *MC* and *AC* is now *at a lower level of output*. Once again you can see that *MC* cuts *AC* at its lowest point.

As we shall see in subsequent chapters, there will be consequences for the output policy of firms as a result of these changes in cost structures.

Conclusion

We have now all but completed our examination of the costs of the firm; it only remains in the next section of the book to demonstrate the relationship between cost and diminishing returns. As has already been stated, we may treat the cost structures of the firm as being governed by the same principles no matter what type of competition the firm operates under. It will therefore be obvious to the astute reader that the differences must lie on the demand side. We will therefore conclude this chapter by restating the essential difference between perfect competition and imperfect competition. This is that under perfect competition the firm's demand curve

***Table 15.6* The effect of an increase in variable costs**

Output units per week, Q	*Original total cost, TC_1 (£)*	*New total cost, TC_2 (£)*	*Original average cost, AC_1 (£)*	*New average cost, AC_2 (£)*	*Original marginal cost, MC_1 (£)*	*New marginal cost, MC_2 (£)*
0	116	116	∞	∞		
1	140	164	140	164	24	48
2	160	204	80	102	20	40
3	176	236	58.6	78.6	16	32
4	200	284	50.0	71.0	24	48
5	240	364	48.0	72.8	40	80
6	296	476	49.3	79.3	56	112
7	368	620	52.6	88.6	72	144
8	456	796	57.0	99.5	88	176

is horizontal, while under all types of imperfect competition the firm's demand curve is downward sloping. This is illustrated in Fig. 15.12. The difference in behaviour thus stems from the relationship of these demand curves with the cost curves. Marginal revenue (*MR*) is explained in Chapter 17.

Summary

1 Total costs (*TC*) comprise fixed costs (*FC*) and variable costs (*VC*). Fixed costs are fixed in the short run, while variable costs start at zero and increase with output.

2 A firm will stay in business in the short run so long as it is recovering its variable costs. In the long run all costs must be covered.

3 Average (unit) cost (*AC*) is total cost divided by output. It may be divided into average fixed cost (*AFC*) and average variable cost (*AVC*). Thus:

$$ATC = AFC + AVC$$

4 The *AC* curve is U-shaped in the short run because of diminishing returns. In the long run the *AC* curve will also be U-shaped because of economies and diseconomies of scale.

5 In practice it has been discovered that economies of scale occur in most industries that have been investigated, whereas diseconomies are less likely to exist; hence the long-run average cost curve is actually more L-shaped.

6 Marginal cost (*MC*) is the cost of producing one more unit of a commodity. Mathematically it can be defined as the first derivative of cost with respect to output.

7 The *MC* curve is plotted in a special incremental manner.

8 The *MC* curve always intersects with the *AC* curve at the lowest point of *AC*.

9 A change in fixed costs will affect *AC* but not *MC*, whereas a change in variable costs will affect both *AC* and *MC*.

10 The cost structures of the firm are the same irrespective of the type of competition. The differences in firms' behaviour originate from the differences in the demand curves, which are a result of the market conditions.

Questions

1 Of the following list – wages, managerial salaries, rent, heating and lighting, sales commissions, raw materials, interest and depreciation – which are fixed

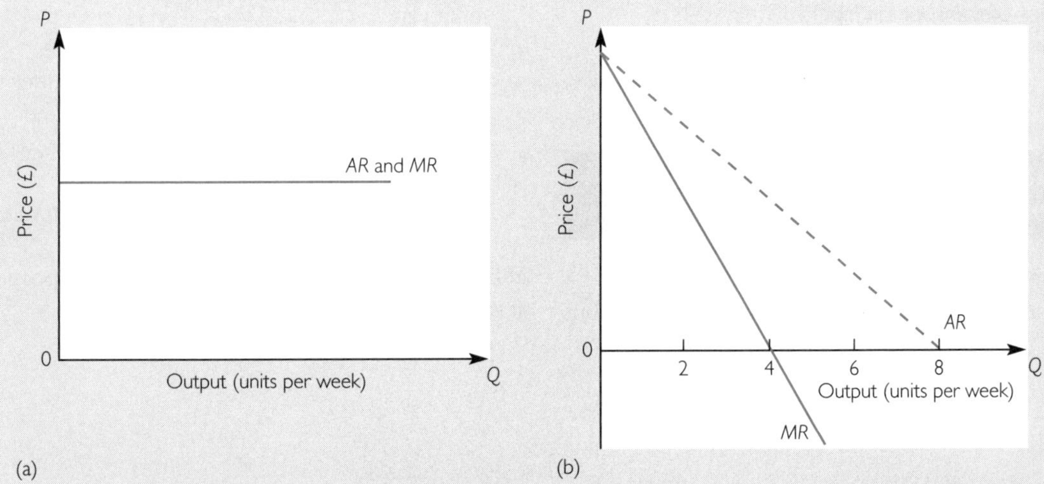

***Fig. 15.12* (a) Perfect and (b) imperfect competition**
The difference is that under perfect competition the firm's demand curve is horizontal while under imperfect competition it is downward sloping.

costs and which are variable? How will the answer vary between the short run and the long run?

2 Define *MC*, *AC*, *AFC* and *AVC*. Explain the shape and relationship of the *AC* and *MC* curves.

3 Consider how *AC* will vary in the long run in theory and in practice.

4 In an industry the MES level of output forms a significant share of total output, yet the cost disadvantage for smaller plants is fairly small. What does this say about the extent of economies of scale in the industry?

5 If an industry experienced neither economies of scale nor diseconomies of scale, how would this affect the long-run average cost curve? Draw a diagram based on Figs 15.4 and 15.5 to illustrate your answer.

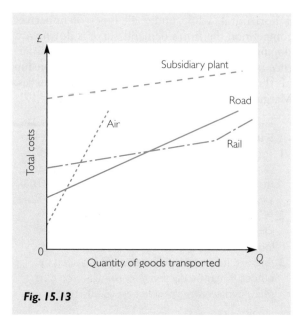

Data response A
Costs of transport

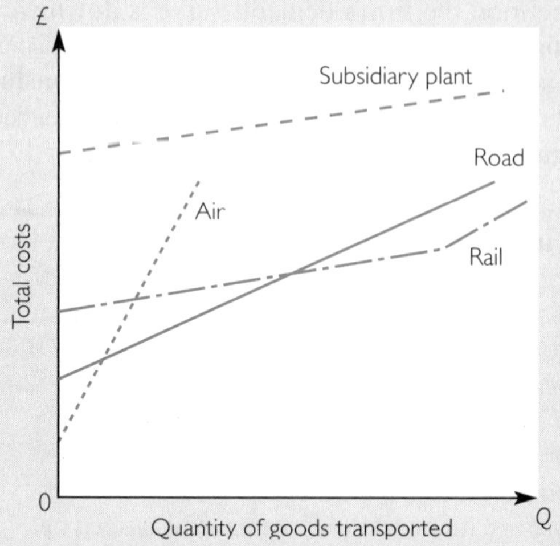

Fig. 15.13

Study the information in Fig. 15.13. The line for subsidiary plant relates to the cost of setting up a branch near to the market.

Now answer the following questions:

1 Use the information in Fig. 15.13 to comment on:
   a) fixed costs;
   b) variable costs;
   c) marginal cost.

2 Which types of products are most suitable to the modes of transport in Fig. 15.13?

3 For what reasons do you think that Japanese firms have chosen to locate manufacturing bases in the UK?

Data response B
Short-run shut-down conditions

Suppose that a farmer is able to rent an orchard at a cost of £1000 per year and other fixed costs amount to a further £100 per week. Itinerant labour to pick the apples can be hired at a wage of £120 per week and each labourer can pick 600 dozen apples per week. Other variable costs such as packaging and transport amount to 6 pence per dozen. Under these conditions:

1 What is the minimum price per dozen that the apple grower would be willing to accept in the short run?

2 Suppose that the apple grower employs five workers for five weeks picking apples to gather the complete harvest. Assuming that all costs and productivities stay the same as stated above, what is the minimum price per dozen the apple grower will look for to remain in the industry in the long run?

In both cases explain your answer as fully as possible. Illustrate your answers with a diagram.

16 Competitive supply

Learning outcomes

After studying this chapter you will be able to:

- Distinguish between the short-run and the long-run equilibrium positions of the competitive firm.
- Understand the derivation of the supply curve in perfect competition.
- Appreciate the significance of a perfectly competitive environment for an optimum allocation of resources.

Having examined the cost structures of the business, we can now turn to look at how a firm's price and output policy is determined. In this chapter we consider market behaviour under conditions of perfect competition. It should be remembered that the guiding principle of the business is ***profit maximisation***. We can therefore say that the firm will be in equilibrium if it is maximising its profits.

The best profit output

Output and profit in the short run

Under perfect competition the firm is a price-taker, i.e. it has no control over the market price. It can only sell or not sell at that price (see page 183). Therefore, in trying to maximise its profits, the firm has no pricing decision to make; it can only choose the output which it thinks most advantageous. For example, in a freely competitive market a farmer could choose how much wheat to plant but could not control the price at which it would be sold when harvested.

The best profit position for any business in perfect competition would be where it equated the price of the product with its marginal cost (*MC*).

If the cost of producing one more unit (*MC*) is less than the revenue the producer obtains for selling it, i.e. the price, then profit can be increased by producing and selling that unit. Even when *MC* is rising, so long as it is less than the price, the firm will go on producing because it is gaining ***extra profit***.

It does not matter if the extra profit is only small, it is nevertheless an ***addition to profit*** and, if the firm is out to maximise profits, it will wish to receive this. This is illustrated in Fig. 16.1, where the most profitable output is OM. If the business produced a smaller output (OL), then the cost of producing a unit (*MC*) is less than the revenue received from selling it (*P*). The business could therefore increase its profits by expanding output. The shaded area represents the extra profit available to the producer as output expands. At point E (output OM) there is no more extra profit to be gained. If the firm were to produce a large output (ON), then the cost of producing that unit (*MC*) would be greater than revenue from selling it (*P*) and the producer could increase profits by contracting output back towards OM. Thus the output at which *MC* = *P* is an ***equilibrium position***, i.e. the one at which the firm will be happy to remain if it is allowed to.

Let us look again at our example from the last chapter where we considered the apple grower. Suppose that the orchard owner has produced a crop of apples. The grower now has to harvest them and send them to market. Since apples are highly perishable they will continue to be sent to market while the extra cost (*MC*)

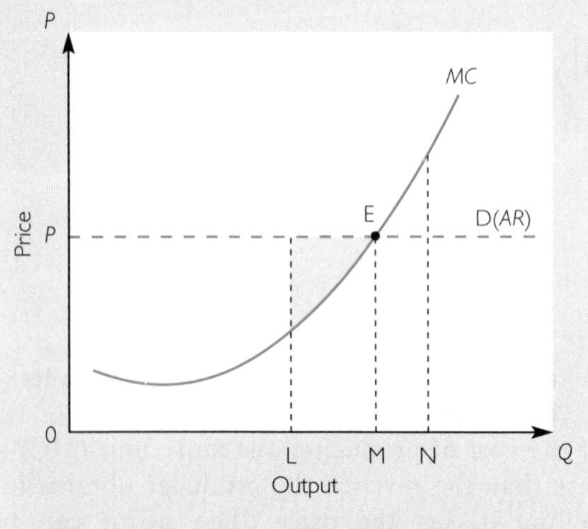

***Fig. 16.1* Perfect competition in the short run**
The firm produces the output at which $MC = P$

incurred in doing so (labour, transport, etc.) is less than the money received for selling them (P). As soon as the cost of getting them to market is greater than the money received for them the grower will cease to do so, even if it means leaving the apples to rot.

You will notice in Fig. 16.1 that we have not included the AC curve. This is because it is not necessary in the short run to demonstrate how much or how little profit the firm is making to be able to conclude that it is the best profit possible. We have already seen that a firm may produce in the short run, even if it is making a loss, so long as it is covering its variable costs.

Therefore we can conclude that so long as price is above *AVC* a perfectly competitive business will maximise its profits or (which is the same thing) minimise its losses by producing the output at which *MC* = *P*.

We shall see in the next chapter that under perfect competition price can be equated with marginal revenue (MR). Thus we could restate the proposition as $MC = MR$. This then becomes the profit maximisation position for all types of competition.

Common misunderstanding

Profit is not *maximised where* MR *(or the competitive price) exceeds* MC; *a firm could gain more profit by expanding its output. Profit is maximised at the level of output where* MC = MR *(or, in the perfectly competitive case, where* MC = P*). At this point all available profit has been obtained; no extra can be gained. Should* MR *(which equals price in perfect competition) be less than* MC *it would pay the firm to reduce its level of output.*

The long-run equilibrium

Although a business might produce at a loss in the short run, in the long run all costs must be covered. In order to consider the long-run situation we must bring average cost into the picture.

Before doing this it will be useful if we list some of the main points established so far. Check that you fully understand them before proceeding any further.

a) Under perfect competition there is a freedom of entry and exit to the market.
b) $MC = MR$ is the profit maximisation output.
c) MC cuts AC at the lowest point of AC.
d) At below normal profit, firms will leave the industry; if profit is above normal new firms will be attracted into the industry.

Since the MC curve cuts the AC curve at the lowest point on AC it follows that this intersection must occur at a level which is higher, lower or equal to price. These three possibilities are shown on Fig. 16.2. In situation (a) the ATC curve dips down below the AR curve and the business is making ***abnormal profit***. Remember that normal profit is included in the costs of the firm. Thus any positive gap between ATC and AR must be abnormal profit. In the long run the abnormal profit attracts new firms into the industry and the profit is competed away. Therefore (a) cannot be a long-run position.

In situation (b) the ATC is at all points above AR and therefore there is no output at which the business can make a profit. It may remain in business in the short run so long as price (AR) is above AVC, but in the long run it will close down. Therefore (b) cannot be a long-run position either.

In situation (c) the ATC is tangential to the AR curve. Thus the firm exists making just normal profit but no abnormal profit. The firm may there-

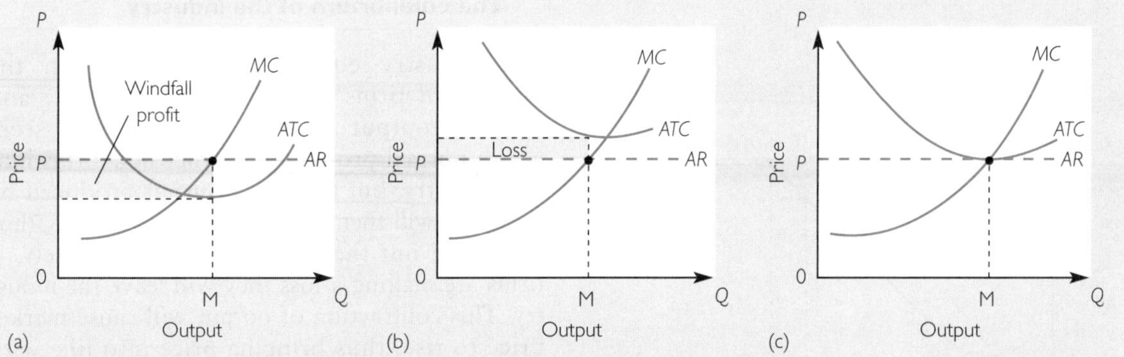

***Fig. 16.2* The long-run equilibrium of the firm under perfect competition**
(a) Windfall profits attract new firms to the industry. This lowers price and eliminates the abnormal profits. (b) The firm is making a loss and in the long run will leave the industry. (c) The firm is just recovering normal profit. This is the long-run equilibrium where: $MC = P = AR = AC$.

fore continue in this position since it is not making enough profit to attract other firms to compete that profit away. Hence (c) is the long-run equilibrium position of the business operating under conditions of perfect competition. We may conclude, therefore, that under perfect competition the long-run equilibrium for the business is where:

$$MC = P = AC = AR$$

The average business is hardly likely to look at the process in this way. Profit maximisation is arrived at by practical knowledge of the business and by trial and error. The concepts of marginal cost, average revenue, etc., allow us to generalise the principles that are common to all businesses. Although business people may not be familiar with words like 'marginal revenue', they are nevertheless used to the practice of making small variations in output and price to achieve the best results. Thus, they are using a marginal technique to maximise their profits.

STUDENT ACTIVITY 16.1

Imagine that you are running a business and that your objective is to maximise its profits. Decide what information you would need to be able do this and whether you think such information is available to you. If you think that some information is not available, would it still be possible to achieve your objective?

The supply curve

The firm's supply curve

Having demonstrated the equilibrium of the firm we will now go on to consider the derivation of the supply curve.

It will be recalled that the supply curve shows how supply varies in response to changes in price. No matter how the market price changes, the demand curve always appears to be a horizontal line to the individual firm under perfect competition. Therefore as price goes up or down the firm always tries to equate price with marginal cost in order to maximise its profits. In Fig. 16.3 as price increases from OP_1 to OP_2 to OP_3 the firm expands output from OM_1 to OM_2 to OM_3. This, therefore, shows how the firm varies output in response to changes in price; in other words it is a supply curve. Thus we may conclude that:

Under perfect competition the firm's *MC* curve, above *AVC*, is its supply curve.

Industry supply

If we can explain the firm's supply curve then we can explain the industry supply curve since, as we saw at the beginning of Chapter 14, the industry supply curve is the horizontal summation of individual firms' supply curves.

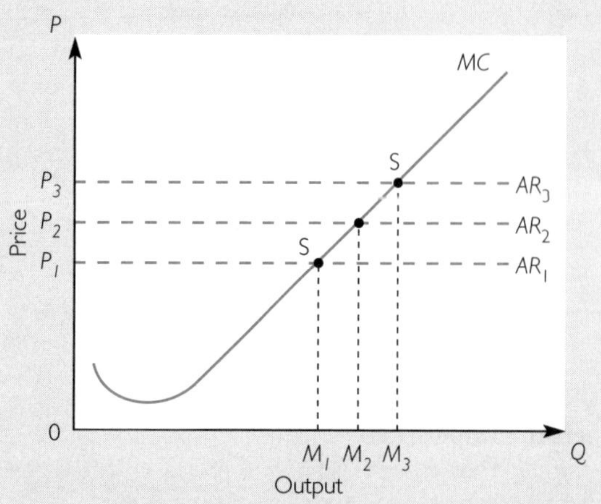

Fig. 16.3 **Under perfect competition the firm's *MC* curve is its supply curve**
As price rises from OP_1 to OP_2 to OP_3, so the firm expands output from OM_1 to OM_2 to OM_3, in each case equating *MC* with *P*. Thus SS is the supply curve.

A change in supply

Figure 16.4 illustrates a shift in the supply curve; this would be brought about by a change in the ***conditions of supply***. Thus, for example, the leftward shift in the supply curve could have been brought about by an increase in the costs of production.

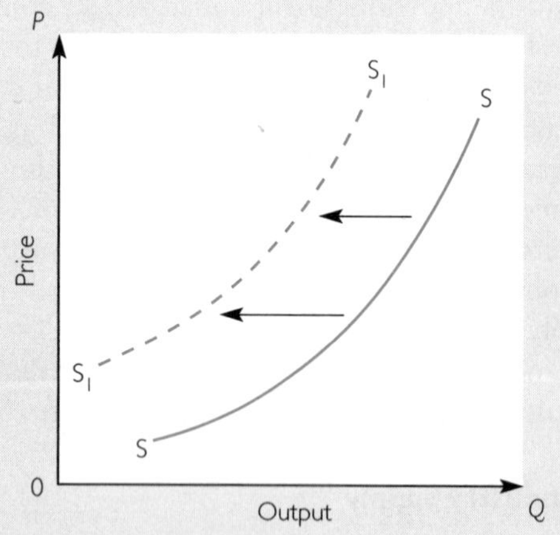

Fig. 16.4 **A change in supply**
The leftwards shift of the SS curve is the result of change in one of the conditions of supply, e.g. a rise in costs

The equilibrium of the industry

The industry equilibrium occurs when the number of firms in the industry is stable and industry output is stable. As we have seen, above-normal profits will attract new firms into the industry, but the extra output produced by the firms will then depress the market price, thus squeezing out the excess profit. Conversely, if firms are making a loss they will leave the industry. This contraction of output will cause market price to rise, thus bringing price into line with average costs. Figure 16.5 shows the relationship between industry supply and individual firm's supply. If price is OT then this attracts new firms into the industry and shifts the supply curve rightwards, whereas if price is OR firms are leaving the industry, thus shifting the supply curve leftwards. It can be seen that the industry equilibrium price OS corresponds with the price at which the firm is just recovering normal profit.

It should not be thought that the equilibrium for the industry represents a static situation. The equilibrium may be the long-run result of a situation where different firms are constantly entering and leaving the industry, but overall the situation is stable.

STUDENT ACTIVITY 16.2

State what effect the following would have on the market supply curve for wheat: a) a rise in the wages of farm-workers; b) the introduction of a new, high-productivity strain of wheat; c) a rise in the price of wheat on the international market; d) poor weather conditions; e) a and b together.

The optimality of perfect competition

The optimum allocation of resources

The importance of the idea of perfect competition is that it represents, to many economists, the ideal working of the free market system. The fundamental problem of any economy, it will be remembered, is to make the best use of scarce

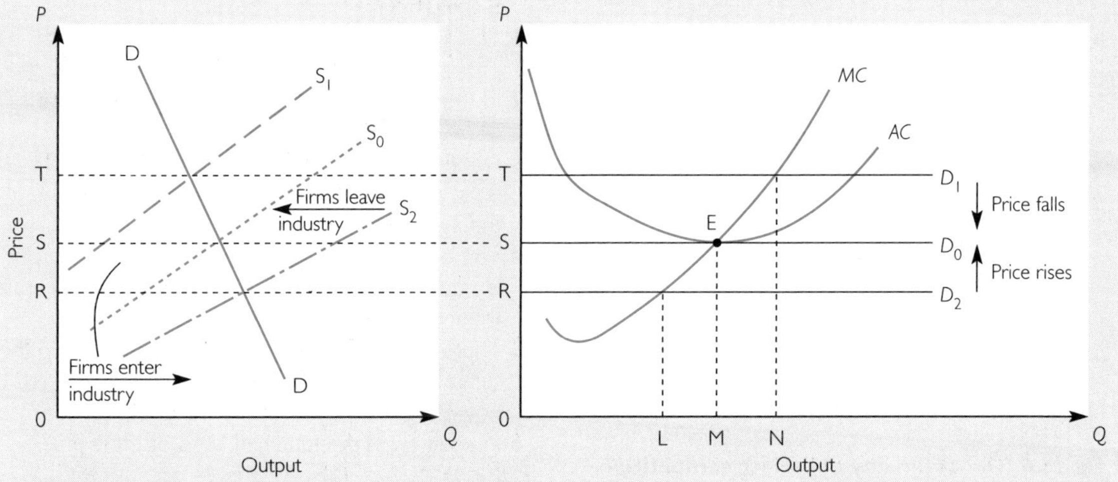

Fig. 16.5 **Industry equilibrium and firm's equilibrium**
If industry price is OT then abnormal profits attract new firms and supply increases from S_1 to S_0 and price falls to S. If industry price is OR firms leave the industry and the supply curve shifts from S_2 to S_0. Industry equilibrium is where S_0 intersects with industry demand curve DD, corresponding to long-run equilibrium for the firm at OM. Note: Industry demand curve is downward sloping but it always appears horizontal to the firm; thus at price OT the firm's demand curve is D_1, at price OS it is D_0, and so on.

resources. If we look at the model of perfect competition we will see how it relates to this.

An individual will purchase a product until the marginal utility from the last unit purchased is equal to its price; at that point no further consumer surplus can be gained from buying the good. The marginal utility curve is the basis of the demand curve when expressed in monetary terms (see Chapter 9).

In perfect competition $MC = P$ for any level of output. Since $MC = P$, then:

Marginal utility equals marginal cost. This is a welfare-maximising equilibrium position for the individual.

At lower output levels the consumer values any additional unit purchased more than its marginal cost, i.e. $MC < P$, and output should be increased. At higher output levels the individual places a lower value on an additional unit purchased relative to its marginal cost, i.e. $MC > P$; less should be produced. By the aggregation of individual marginal utility (*MU*) and *MC* curves it would be possible to demonstrate the welfare-maximising equilibrium for the whole industry.

In addition, in its long-run equilibrium the firm is producing where $MC = AC$, i.e. at the bottom of the *AC* curve. At this point output costs, i.e. the quantity of resources needed to produce a unit of the commodity, are minimised. Looking at Fig. 16.6 you can see that if the firm produced a greater or smaller output the cost of producing a unit would rise. In the long-run equilibrium, therefore, the firm is making an optimum use of its resources. If every firm in the economy operated under these conditions it would follow that there would be an optimum allocation of resources (since $MC = P$) and every commodity would be produced at a minimum unit cost. Indeed all firms would be producing to consumers' demand curves and therefore not only would the goods be produced at a minimum cost but they would also be the goods which people wanted.

It has already been seen that this view of the economy is subject to two major criticisms. First, that the commodities which people are willing to pay for may not be the goods which are most useful to society, and, second, that income in the economy may be unevenly distributed, meaning

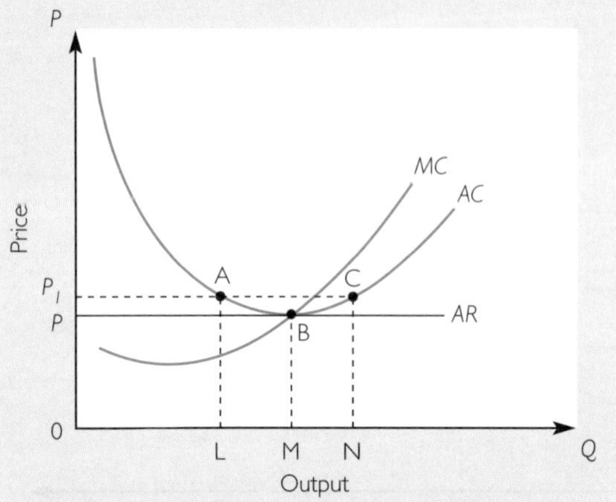

Fig. 16.6 The optimality of perfect competition
The long-run equilibrium is at output OM, which corresponds to the lowest unit cost at point B on the AC curve. At any other output, greater or smaller, the unit cost is higher, as at points A and C on the AC curve.

that an efficient system may not be socially just (see Chapter 5).

Competition is, however, also important as a political idea. When right-wing parties advocate increasing the amount of free competition in the economy it is in the belief that this will lead to a more efficient use of resources. Even trade unions have advocated 'free competition' in wage bargaining. Free competition in our economy is something of a myth, in that markets often tend to be dominated by large organisations with a great deal of monopoly power. In the same way, in some industries 'free collective bargaining' is dominated by large unions, although the power of the unions generally has declined in recent years. Imperfections in the market are the rule rather than 'free and unfettered competition'. The importance of the model of perfect competition is not that it is attainable but that it gives us a measure with which to assess the imperfections of competition.

Summary

1 The firm under perfect competition maximises its profits by producing the output at which $MC = P$.
2 In the long run the firm's equilibrium is where $MC = P = AR = AC$.
3 Under perfect competition the firm's supply curve is its MC curve and the industry supply curve is the aggregation of individual firms' MC curves.
4 The equilibrium for the industry is where output is stable, the number of firms is stable and overall the industry is making normal profit.
5 There is an optimum allocation of resources in the sense that the marginal utilities of consumers are equated with the marginal costs of production.
6 In addition, in the long run firms operate at the bottom of their AC curves; output costs are minimised.

Questions

1 'Perfect competition is an ideal state that is unattainable; it has no practical relevance.' Discuss this statement.
2 Explain the 'welfare connotations' of perfect competition.
3 How will a firm's long-run equilibrium differ from its short-run equilibrium under conditions of competitive supply?
4 Contrast the effects on the equilibrium of a competitive firm of a change in its fixed costs with those of a change in its variable costs.
5 The figures below give the revenue, output and costs of a firm. From this information construct the firm's short-run supply curve. Explain how you establish your answer.
6 A firm's MC curve is given by the function:

$$y(MC) = 10 + 2x$$

If the firm is operating under conditions of perfect competition and the market price is 20, what will be the profit maximisation output?

Output	*0*	*1*	*2*	*3*	*4*	*5*	*6*	*7*	*8*
Total revenue (£)	0	300	600	900	1200	1500	1800	2100	2400
Total costs (£)	580	700	800	880	1000	1200	1480	1840	2280

Data response A
The Puckboat Company

The following table gives the total cost schedule for Puckboat, a small business making fibreglass dinghies.

Costs of the Puckboat Company

Output of dinghies per week	*Total costs (£)*
0	1160
1	1400
2	1600
3	1760
4	2000
5	2400
6	2960
7	3680
8	4560

1 Calculate Puckboat's average and marginal cost schedules.
2 Assuming that Puckboat is able to sell any quantity of dinghies at a price of £480, construct a graph to show the firm's average cost, marginal cost and marginal revenue.
3 Determine the profit maximisation output for this firm.
4 Consider the long-run effects upon Puckboat of the following price changes, assuming that its cost structure remains unaltered.:
   a) Price falls to £320.
   b) Price increases to £640.
   In both cases explain your answer as fully as possible.
5 What alternative policy strategies might Puckboat have to that of profit maximisation?
6 What extra information would Puckboat need in order to pursue each of these 'alternative policies'?

Data response B
The liberal point of view

Read the following passage which extols the merits of the free market.

In a society where the sheer quantity of information necessary for the co-ordination of the immense number of projects and individual actions is dispersed amongst a large number of individual personalities and surpasses the ability of any individual brain to comprehend, it is the mechanism of the market which allows each of us, and society as a whole, to benefit from the sum total of information, understanding and knowledge in a way which is beyond the capability of any other system of economic organisation.

To put it another way, the superiority of the market mechanism is that it allows us to bring about an optimal distribution of resources, without a full comprehension of all the information and understanding which is scattered throughout society, and without the procedures which must be prescribed under any other economic system. This characteristic, according to Hayek, allows us to bring about the best co-ordination and thus the best coherence and effectiveness of all decisions and actions of each individual.

It is fundamental to the nature of the market that the knowledge of the things necessary for the well running of a complex society is atomistic and dispersed, because it is founded on the principle that *'each person is free to utilise all the knowledge available, even if it is incomplete, to interact with his environment according to his own designs'*, the mechanism of the free market is that which experience has shown to be the most effective at resolving the problems of the mobilisation, communication and accumulation of knowledge.

Henri Lepage *Les Cahiers Français*
(Translated by John Beardshaw)

Answer the following questions:
1 Explain as fully as possible the assumptions on which this liberal view of the market economy is based.
2 With the aid of a diagram(s) explain how perfect competition brings about an optimal distribution of resources.
3 What are the shortcomings of the market system?
(With all these questions you may find it useful to refresh your knowledge of the views of Adam Smith.)

17 Price and output under imperfect competition

Learning outcomes

At the end of this chapter you will be able to:

- Explain the techniques for profit maximisation.
- Understand the concept of marginal revenue and account for its relationship with price elasticity of demand.
- Identify the equilibrium positions of the monopolist and the monopolistic competitor.
- Appreciate the notion of oligopolistic interdependence.
- Discuss the kinked demand curve model as an explanation of oligopolistic behaviour and be aware of its limitations as a general model.
- Account for oligopolistic price collusion and appreciate the significance of non-price competition.
- Recognise the prevalence of mark-up pricing.
- Outline the limitations of alternative theories of the firm.
- Explain the concept of a contestable market.

Perfect and imperfect competition

Perfect and imperfect markets compared

Having considered perfect markets we will now turn to imperfect ones.

An imperfect market is simply one in which one or more of the assumptions of perfect competition does not hold true.

You will recall that the assumptions of perfect competition appeared very unrealistic and, indeed, very few real-life industries even approximate to perfect competition.

In practice virtually all markets deviate from the conditions of perfect competition and hence are imperfectly competitive.

Rejecting perfect competition as a description of how actual markets operate does not mean it is of no importance as a theoretical model. As we have seen, perfect competition provides the conditions under which we can construct a supply curve; it is important to realise that:

A supply curve assumes that firms are responding to a price which is given to them, i.e. beyond their control.

In imperfect competition firms typically decide and set the price themselves. Hence, although demand and supply analysis often provides useful predictions about market behaviour it can be a misleading analysis if applied to imperfect competitive markets.

We shall also see in Part 4 of this book that perfect competition is also an important assumption in welfare economics. The problem for the economist is that, when looking for a model of the way firms behave in an imperfect competitive world, there are many models to choose from. We will state at the outset that there is no consensus as to which of these alternative approaches is the most useful. Nevertheless, the range of models provides an array of analytic tools from which the economist may choose as seems appropriate to understanding a particular industry.

You will recall that under perfect competition a firm which raises its price will immediately lose all its customers to its competitors. Hence, the demand curve facing the individual firm in perfect competition is horizontal. In imperfect competition such price competition is less fierce because there are fewer competitors for customers to turn to and/or the products of firms are not identical and hence consumers may have a preference for a particular firm's product. This means that a firm which raises its price will lose some but not all of its customers, and hence the demand curve facing the firm is downward sloping. The ability to recognise that a firm facing a downward-sloping demand curve signifies imperfect competition is often called for in economics examinations.

The 'traditional' theory of monopoly

This model is often said to apply to the situation where there is just one firm in an industry, i.e. the monopolist is the sole seller of the product. We shall see that this definition of monopoly is too simplistic (see below). But for now it should be appreciated that even complete freedom from competition does not mean the firm can sell any amount at any price it wishes.

Common misunderstanding

It is incorrect to say that a monopolist will always charge the highest price it can. Even within a market a higher price will mean that some consumers can afford to buy less or are induced to switch their purchasing power to other markets. In short, a monopolist faces a downward-sloping demand curve.

We will now reconsider profit maximisation in the case of such a firm and compare this with profit maximisation under perfect competition.

Profit-maximising techniques

Analysis using total revenue and total cost

We can demonstrate profit maximisation most easily by simply subtracting total cost from total revenue at all levels of output. This is done in Table 17.1. Here we have used the same total cost schedule as in Chapter 15. The total revenue schedule is derived from the downward-sloping demand curve for the firm's product. As you can see, in this example, the business maximises its profits at an output of 4 units per week where it makes a profit of £184 per week. You will notice that this is *not* the output at which revenue is maximised; this occurs at the output of 5 units per week. We will see the reason for this as we work through the chapter.

***Table 17.1* Profit maximisation using total cost and total revenue schedules**

Output, units per week Q	*Total revenue, TR (£)*	*Total cost, TC (£)*	*Total profit, TP (£)*
0	0	116	−116
1	144	140	+4
2	256	160	+96
3	336	176	+160
4	384	200	+184
5	400	240	+160
6	384	296	+88
7	336	368	−32
8	256	456	−200

Figure 17.1 presents the information from Table 17.1 in graphical form. Total profit (*TP*) is the gap between the total cost curve and the total revenue curve. From the graphs you can see that the firm can make abnormal profits anywhere between the output of 1 unit per week up to an output of about 7 units per week.

While profit is increasing the *TC* and *TR* curves must be diverging, while as profit is decreasing *TC* and *TR* must be converging. Therefore, when profit is maximised the two curves will be neither diverging nor converging, i.e. they will be parallel to each other. At the same output the *TP* curve will be at its maximum and its slope will be zero, since at that point profit will be neither rising nor falling.

We will return to total cost and total revenue curves later when we consider ***mark-up pricing***, but now we will turn to the more usual way of presenting profit maximisation, which is through the marginal and average cost structures.

Marginal revenue

In order to explain the behaviour of the firm we must introduce the concept of marginal revenue (*MR*):

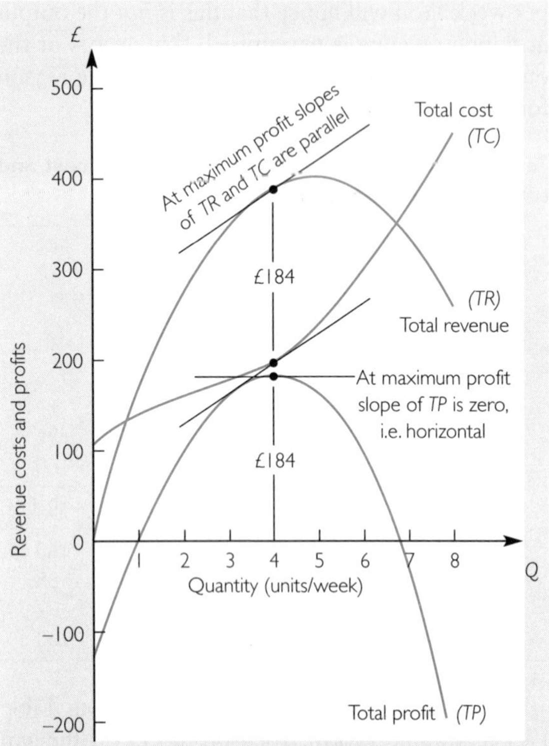

***Fig. 17.1* Total profit can be seen as either the gap between *TR* and *TC*, or the height of the *TP* curve**

Note: The total profit does not occur where *TR* is at its greatest.

Marginal revenue is the change to total revenue from the sale of one more unit of a commodity.

Suppose for example that a firm was selling 4 units a week at £10 each. Then the total revenue would be £40, but, since this is imperfect competition, if it wishes to sell more it must lower its prices. Therefore, for example, selling 5 units a week may involve dropping the price to £9, in which case the total revenue will now be £45. Thus the change to the firm's total revenue as a result of selling one more unit is £5. This is termed the marginal revenue.

In order to sell more the imperfect competitor must, as we have seen, lower the price. If, for example, sales are 50 units per week at a price of £10 and sales are increased to 51 units by lowering the price to £9, then not only does the firm lose money on the 51st unit but also all the preceding units now all have to be priced at £9. Thus total revenue decreases from £500 to £459, giving a marginal revenue of minus £41. (For the extra £9 sales revenue gained from the 51st unit the firm has sacrificed £1 on the preceding 50 units; thus $MR = (£9 - £50) = -£41$.) Whether or not marginal revenue is positive or negative depends upon whether the gain in revenue from extra sales is greater or smaller than the loss on preceding units. This depends upon which part of a firm's demand curve schedule we are considering.

***Table 17.2* Marginal revenue**

	Output, Q (units/week)	*Average revenue, P (£/unit)*	*Total revenue, P × Q (TR)*	*Marginal revenue, $TR_n - TR_{n-1}$ (MR)*
A	0	160	0	
B	1	144	144	144
C	2	128	256	112
D	3	112	336	80
E	4	96	384	48
F	5	80	400	16
G	6	64	384	−16
H	7	48	336	−48
I	8	32	256	−80
J	9	16	144	−112
K	10	0	0	−144

Table 17.2 gives a demand schedule, a total revenue schedule and, in the last column, the marginal revenue schedule. The marginal revenue can now be seen as the difference between adjacent total revenues. You can see that as price is lowered, total revenue increases until point F in the table and then begins to decrease because the increase in sales is now no longer great enough to offset the fall in price. Thus after point F marginal revenue becomes negative.

Figure 17.2 presents the information for demand and marginal revenue in graphical form. Note that once again the *MR* curve is plotted in a special manner, as was marginal cost. The mathematical relationship between *AR* and *MR* means that the *MR* curve descends at twice the rate of the *AR* curve. Thus you can see that the *AR*

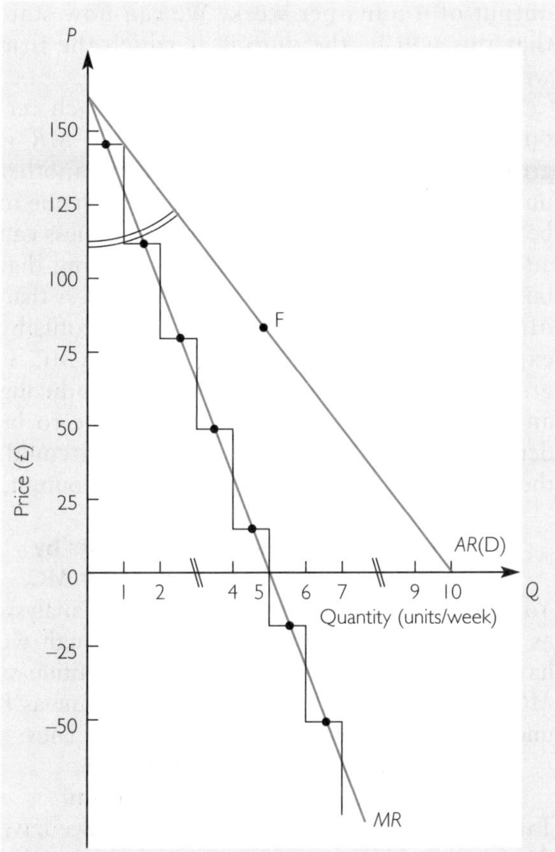

Fig. 17.2 **Marginal revenue**
The *MR* curve descends at twice the rate of the *AR* curve, bisecting the quantity axis.

curve meets the quantity axis at 10 units per week while the *MR* cuts the quantity axis at 5 units per week. This can also be seen in Table 17.2, where you can see that average revenue descends in amounts of £16, i.e. £160, £144, £128, etc., while the marginal revenue descends in amounts of £32, i.e. £144, £112, £80, etc. This relationship holds good so long as we have a linear function for *AR*, i.e. the demand curve is a straight line. If the *AR* curve is non-linear (curved) then the relationship becomes more complex. When drawing sketch graphs to illustrate examination answers the student should remember this relationship between *AR* and *MR*; a carelessly drawn graph will show the examiner that you do not appreciate the concepts involved.

Marginal revenue and elasticity

If we examine point F on the *AR* curve in Fig. 17.2 we will find that it is when demand is unitary. How can we say this with such certainty? It is because *MR* is zero at that point. As we descend the demand curve towards point F then the total revenue is increasing; therefore demand must be elastic. Below point F, as price is lowered total revenue decreases and therefore demand must be inelastic. Therefore at point F total revenue must be neither rising nor falling, i.e. it must be constant and thus elasticity must be unitary. You can check this by calculating E_D at F:

$$E_D = \frac{1}{5} \times \frac{80}{16} = 1$$

Thus we can conclude that:

Demand is elastic when *MR* is positive, inelastic when *MR* is negative and unitary when *MR* is zero.

Marginal revenue and perfect competition

Why did we not consider *MR* when discussing perfect competition? The answer is that, under perfect competition, price and marginal revenue are the same thing. This is because the price is constant so that the firm can sell more without lowering its price. There is thus no loss on preceding units as sales expand; each extra unit sold results in the same addition to total revenue. This is illustrated in Table 17.3, where you can see that *MR* and *AR*(*P*) are both £5. Thus, when we come to draw the *MR* curve for perfect competition it coincides with the *AR* curve as shown in Fig. 17.3 (a). The short-run

Table 17.3 **Marginal revenue under perfect competition**

Output, Q (units/week)	*Average revenue, AR (£/unit)*	*Total revenue, TR (P × Q)*	*Marginal revenue, MR* ($TR_n - TR_{n-1}$)
0	5	0	
			5
1	5	5	
			5
2	5	10	
			5
3	5	15	
			5
4	5	20	
			5
5	5	25	

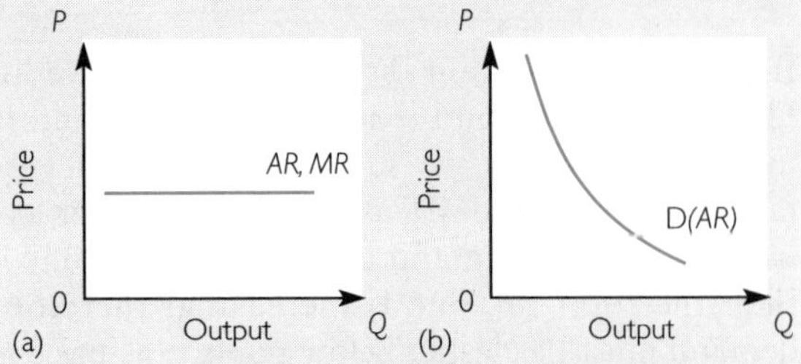

Fig. 17.3 **The marginal revenue curve**
(a) Perfect competition. *MR* and *AR* curves coincide because price is constant.
(b) The industry demand curve remains downward sloping, thus the *MR* curve would look like that in Fig. 17.2.

equilibrium condition for the firm under perfect competition, which you will recall is:

$$MC = P$$

can now be restated as:

$$MC = MR$$

and the long-run equilibrium as:

$$MC = MR = AC = AR$$

The short-run equilibrium of the firm: marginal analysis method

If we draw the *MR* and *MC* curves on one graph we can see that they cross exactly at an output of 4 units per week. We can now state that this will be the output at which the firm will maximise its profits.

How are we able to say this with such certainty? The explanation is this. While *MR* is greater than *MC* the cost of producing another unit of the commodity is less than the revenue to be gained from selling it, so that the business can add to its profits by producing and selling that unit. This remains true so long as *MC* is *less* than *MR*. Thus the business will increase its profits by expanding its output. However, once *MC* is *greater* than *MR* then the cost of producing another unit is greater than the revenue to be derived from selling it and the business could, therefore, increase its profit by contracting output.

We can conclude, therefore, that:

The business will maximise its profits by producing the output at which *MR* = *MC*.

You will see that this is essentially the same analysis as for perfect competition because although we have stated the condition for perfect competition as $MC = P$, we now realise that *MR* is the same as *P* under perfect competition (see Chapter 16). Thus:

***MC* = *MR* is the profit maximisation condition for all types of competition.**

Table 17.4 shows us all the information we have developed in this chapter. You can see from the table that the business does indeed maximise its profits at an output of 4 units per week, and this is where $MR = MC$. This is confirmed in Fig. 17.4 where the information in Table 17.4 is presented graphically.

Table 17.4 **Costs, revenues and profits under imperfect competition**

	Output, Q (units/week)	*Average revenue, P (£/unit)*	*Total revenue, TR (P × Q)*	*Total cost, TC (£)*	*Total profit, TP (TR – TC)*	*Marginal cost, MC* $(TC_n - TC_{n-1})$	*Marginal revenue, MR* $(TR_n - TR_{n-1})$	*Average cost, AC (TC/Q)*
A	0	160	0	116	–116			∞
						24	144	
B	1	144	144	140	+4			140
						20	112	
C	2	128	256	160	+96			80
						16	80	
D	3	112	336	176	+160			58.6
						24	48	
E	4	96	384	200	+184	MC = MR		50
						40	16	
F	5	80	400	240	+160			48
						56	–16	
G	6	64	384	296	+88			49.3
						72	–48	
H	7	48	336	368	–32			52.6
						88	–80	
I	8	32	256	456	–200			57

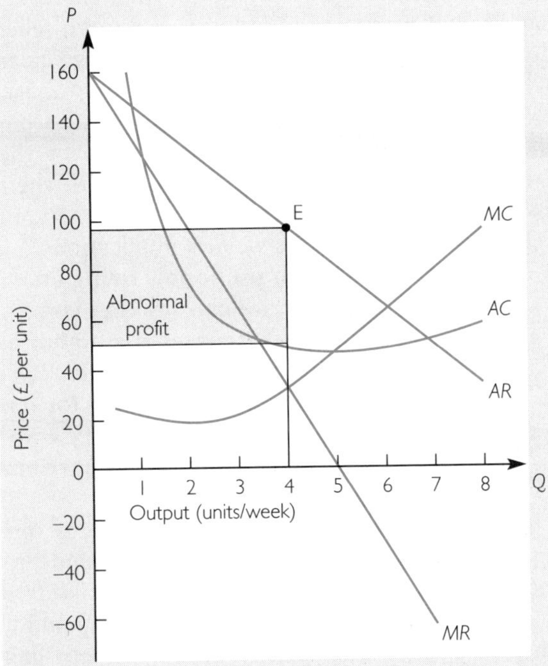

Fig. 17.4 **The equilibrium price and output of the firm under imperfect competition in the short run**

Profit is maximised at an output of 4 units and a price of £96, i.e where:

$MR = MC$

and:

Profit = $(AR - AC) \times Q = £184$

The shaded rectangle represents abnormal profit. At an output of 4 units per week *AR* (price) is £96 and average cost (*AC*) is £50. The difference between the two (£46) is profit and the firm has made this profit on 4 units. We could express this as:

$$\begin{aligned} TP &= (AR \times AC) \times Q \\ &= (£96 - £50) \times 4 \\ &= £184 \end{aligned}$$

Alternatively it could be expressed as:

$$\begin{aligned} TP &= TR - TC \\ &= (AR \times Q) - (AC \times Q) \\ &= (£96 \times 4) - (£50 \times 4) \\ &= £184 \end{aligned}$$

The mathematically minded will realise that the 'contribution' to total profit can also be calculated by summing all *MR*s at the output of four and subtracting the summation of all the *MC*s at that output. To calculate actual profit, fixed costs must also be subtracted from this contribution, that is:

Total profit = Sum of all *MR*s – Sum of the *MC*s – Fixed cost

or:

$$TP = \Sigma MR - \Sigma MC - FC$$

You will recall from Chapter 14 that normal profit is included in the cost of the business. Therefore, the profit discussed above is all ***abnormal profit*** (also called ***excess profit*** or ***monopoly profit***), i.e. all this profit could be eliminated without forcing the business to leave the industry. How has this abnormal profit been made? The answer is by selling a restricted output at a higher price, i.e. in comparison with perfect competition the monopolist (or any imperfectly competitive firm) has raised the price by ***contriving scarcity***.

The equilibrium of the monopolist

This contrived scarcity can be seen in Table 17.4 and Fig. 17.4. For the monopolist *MR* is less than price and hence profits are maximised where $MR = MC$ at an output of 4 units and a price of £96. For firms in perfect competition *MR* = price and hence output will be increased until $MC = P$ at 6 units of output and a price of £64. Thus, a standard criticism of monopoly is that it tends to restrict output and raise prices to consumers. In fact such welfare aspects of monopoly turn out to be more complicated than this and are considered in the next chapter.

STUDENT ACTIVITY 17.1

Can you think of any circumstances under which a monopolist may actually charge a lower price than, say that which operates in a perfectly competitive industry?

The traditional textbook model of monopoly assumes that there is a sole seller of a particular product, which is usually protected by high barriers to entry. In this case there is no one, therefore, able to compete for the monopolist's abnormal profit and, if there were, they would find it difficult to enter such a market. Thus in the traditional theory of monopoly the long-run equilibrium is like the short-run one, i.e. unlike perfect competition abnormal profits are not competed away in the long run. For many examination questions the assumptions of a sole seller and long-run abnormal profits are the distinguishing features of monopoly; in practice it is more accurate to consider degrees of monopoly.

The degree of monopoly

As noted in Chapter 14 the traditional view of monopoly as described above is rather simplistic.

In practice, a firm can exert considerable market power with far less than 100 per cent of the market.

In most instances a monopolist is likely to be in competition with firms selling similar products. Furthermore, the breadth of definition of a market must be arbitrary. Thus, the market share of a firm depends on how broadly we choose to define the market. The broader the range of products included as part of the market (or the wider its geographic limitations), the smaller will any firm's market share appear to be, i.e. the market concentration ratio (see Chapter 13) is inversely related to the level of product (or geographic) aggregation.

Industrial economists often use the definitions of industries employed in Standard Industrial Classifications to assess the degree of monopoly power. However, as noted in Chapter 13, industries are not necessarily the same as markets and both concepts can be difficult to define and measure with any accuracy.

There is also the question of how long we can assume a relative absence of competition to persist. High profitability may result eventually in new entry or the introduction of more products which are partial substitutes. Indeed, if high profits have hastened the development of a product or new competition (or, if the development of a new product or process led to the establishment of the monopoly in the first place), then the monopoly may be judged to have been beneficial. The Austrian school of economics emphasises precisely these dynamic benefits of monopoly profit. In fact, while some evidence points towards a positive relationship between the degree of seller concentration and profitability, not all studies support the notion that the average level of profits in an industry rises with seller concentration. It is also not entirely clear whether the higher profits, should they exist, stem from increased monopoly power or from the greater efficiency (i.e. lower costs) of the largest firms in a market compared with their smaller rivals. Such considerations blur the concept of monopoly and its welfare implications.

In short, rather than monopoly being an 'either or' situation, we can say that the degree of monopoly increases the higher a firm's industry and market share; the lower the price elasticity of demand for its product; the lower the cross elasticity with other products; and the higher the barriers to new entry.

These determinants are not independent of one another and, in addition, firms may collude to increase the effective degree of monopoly (see below). Michael Kalecki, the great Polish economist, and some modern economists such as K. Cowling have suggested that we can expect the mark-up of a firm's price above its unit variable cost to reflect the degree of monopoly (see Fig. 17.5).

Common misunderstanding

Monopoly is not necessarily a 'bad thing'. Most firms with monopoly power are likely to face

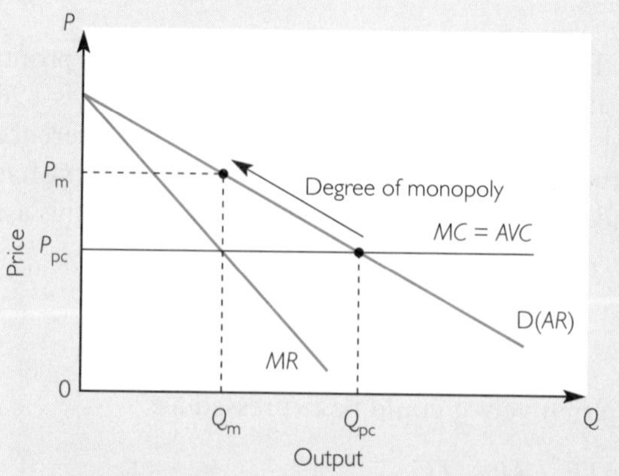

Fig. 17.5 Price and the degree of monopoly
In a perfect market, price and output are P_{pc} and Q_{pc}. The greater the degree of monopoly the nearer the firm moves towards situation P_m, Q_m.

competition from rival products, although the extent of competition may be quite limited. Monopolists are able to restrict output and raise prices, but, by the same token, monopolists may benefit from lower costs of production compared with those in perfectly competitive conditions. Evidence cannot say with complete accuracy whether lower costs or greater market power are more of a determinant of profitability in highly concentrated industries.

The equilibrium of the monopolistically competitive firm

This model was developed independently by E. H. Chamberlin and J. Robinson in the 1930s as a response to the inadequacies of perfect competition and traditional monopoly theory.

These economists had noted that in most industries firms tend to differentiate their products either by actual differences or by perceived differences such as brand names.

Monopolistic competition differs from the assumptions of perfect competition in that, although a large number of firms are assumed, firms differentiate their products from competitors.

Thus, as there are no perfect substitutes, firms again face a downward-sloping demand curve. But the model is like perfect competition and different from monopoly in that there is relative freedom of entry to the industry; hence no abnormal profits can persist in the long run.

If one business is seen to be making high profits in a situation where there are lots of competitors in an imperfect market, other businesses will be encouraged to enter that line of production and compete the profit away because there is something close to freedom of entry and exit to the market. This is illustrated in Fig. 17.6.

In (a) abnormal profits are being made. Since there is free entry to the market other businesses enter and compete this profit away. This occurs as the demand curves for the existing firms are shifted to the left by new firms attracting some customers by offering similar products. In (b), however, less than normal profits are being made; firms will thus leave the industry and the demand curves for the firms that remain will therefore be shifted to the right. Both (a) and (b) represent short-run equilibrium positions. The long-run equilibrium is (c), where firms are maximising profits by setting $MC = MR$ but the AC curve is tangential to the AR curve; thus firms are receiving only normal profits.

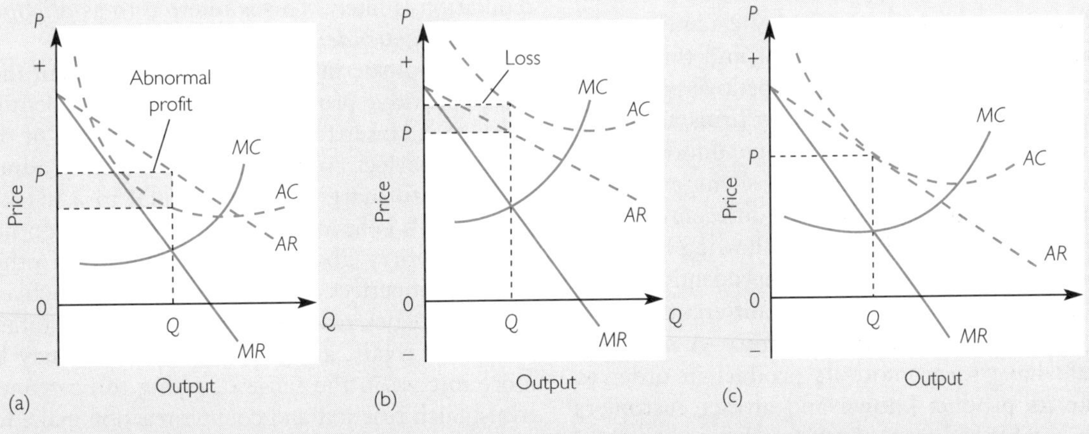

***Fig. 17.6* The price and output of the firm under monopolistic competition in the long run**

(a) The existence of abnormal profits attracts new firms to the industry, which lowers the price and eliminates the profit.

(b) The firm makes a loss at any level of output and in the long run will leave the industry.

(c) The long-run equilibrium, where the firm just recovers normal profit. AC is tangential to AR.

An example of this might be found in, say, the fashion industry. A manufacturer who accurately predicts a new fashion trend may enjoy monopoly profit until other firms copy the designs and the excess profit is competed away. Independent traders such as local newsagents may face similar market characteristics.

You will note in Fig. 17.6 (c) that, unlike perfect competition, the business does not produce at the lowest point of average cost. This is often regarded as a loss of welfare to the economy in that unit cost would be lower in perfect competition. Against this, however, should be put the greater variety to the consumer under monopolistic competition.

As with monopoly *MR* is less than price; hence, as profit maximising is assumed, *MC* is again below price in equilibrium. This would seem to imply a loss of welfare to society, but, as is always the case when the assumptions of perfect competition are relaxed, the welfare implications are muddied. This is because although *MC* is less than price (implying a less than Pareto-optimal output; see Chapter 24) and firms exhibit excess capacity there is also the benefit from greater product variety.

As with all other theories, the theory of monopolistic competition has weaknesses. For example, the assumptions of similar but differentiated products and independent profit maximisation by firms are inconsistent; in practice firms are acutely aware of the reactions from rival firms and this would lead to a far more complex competitive process. It might be countered that as many firms are in the industry changes by one firm go unnoticed by others, but then the model is silent as to the number of firms or the level of differentiation at which behaviour switches from allowing for interdependence to acting entirely independently.

The assumption of product differentiation is also at odds with freedom of entry. A new firm would have to promote its product in order to make its product known and attract customers from established firms. Such 'market penetration' costs could, as research strongly suggests, act as a barrier to entry. As with monopoly we also have the problem of determining the breadth of the industry. Even if it were possible to compile a complete list of cross price elasticities (which it is not), the model would still not tell us the numerical value of such elasticities that would allow inclusion of a firm's product as part of an industry's output – what exactly constitutes 'the same but different' assumption of product differentiation.

Since the degree of product substitutability, barriers to entry and long-run entry are ill defined, many economists do not feel that the model contributes anything above that offered by a broader treatment of monopoly, e.g. the notion of degrees of monopoly. It is significant, however, that Robinson later rejected the relevance of her model because of its reliance on marginal analysis and certain knowledge of demand and costs.

Oligopolistic competition

Oligopoly – the situation where the market is dominated by a few large firms – is hard to analyse. In perfect competition all firms are so small in relation to the total market that they can ignore changes in the behaviour of individual rivals. This simplifies the analysis as each firm can be assumed independently to maximise profit. But where there are a smaller number of firms in an industry, they will be affected by changes in one another's behaviour and hence retaliation is likely. This is referred to as ***oligopolistic interdependence***.

Oligopolistic interdependence may mean that the competitive process in imperfectly competitive markets is closer to the everyday meaning of the term. In perfect competition firms simply adjust output until marginal cost is equal to a market price which is beyond their control. They do not need to worry about any reactions from other firms. In imperfect competition firms may actively form strategies to gain a competitive advantage over their rivals, and hence competition may be more intense in the sense of trying to beat one's rivals. Such reaction and counter-reaction make for great complexity, all the more so since firms are very *uncertain* about rivals' reactions to changes in their competitive strategies. Thus, predicting the behaviour of the market becomes difficult.

The kinked demand model of oligopoly

This model was developed in 1939 by the economist P. M. Sweezy. It is often given prominence in textbooks although some A level examiners have recently stressed its weaknesses. The model assumes that an oligopolist will expect rival firms to follow any price decrease it makes but not follow any increase. Thus the elasticity of demand for the firm's product is much greater above the ruling price than below it, and hence there is a kink in the demand curve faced by the firm.

For straight line demand curves the marginal revenue line lies half-way between the demand curve and the vertical axis. It is thus easy to show that the kink in the demand curve implies a discontinuity, i.e. a sudden drop, in the marginal revenue curve of the firm (see Fig. 17.7).

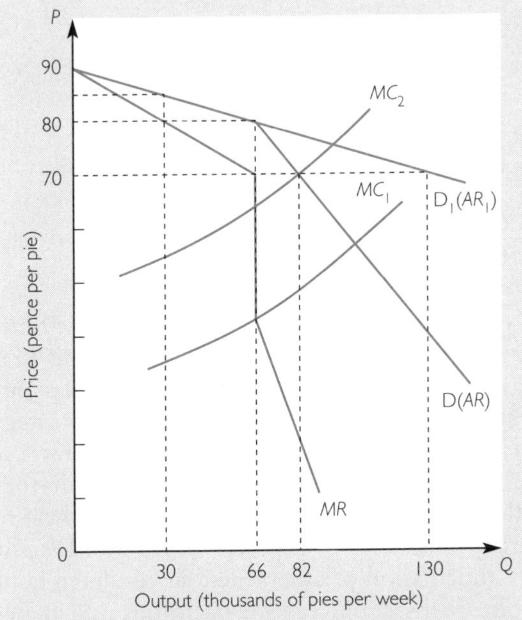

***Fig. 17.7* A 'kinked' oligopoly demand curve**
Assume Meaty is a firm selling meat pies in an oligopolistic market. Meaty's original price is 80p per pie. Meaty raises the price to 85p per pie and sales fall to 30 000. Meaty calculates that if it cuts its prices to 70p per pie sales will expand to 130 000 ($D_1(AR_1)$). However, the cut in price causes competitors to cut prices too and therefore, Meaty's sales are only 82 000. This causes a 'kink' in the demand curve and discontinuity in the *MR* curve.

Marginal cost could thus vary greatly but still pass through this discontinuity in marginal revenue. Equally, changes in market demand could shift demand curves in and out without affecting the height of the kink. In short, profit maximising at $MC = MR$ could leave price unaffected despite considerable fluctuations in costs and demand.

The model has been used to explain why prices appear to fluctuate less in oligopolistic markets than in competitive markets (oligopolistic prices are often said to be 'sticky'). The model has serious flaws, however: again it implies a knowledge of marginal costs and revenue not possessed by real firms; it is not clear that entrepreneurs hold such pessimistic expectations of the reactions of their competitors. But the greatest flaw is that the model does not explain price determination, i.e. it does not explain how the prevailing price was established in the first place or what happens when the price is eventually changed.

Collusion and price leadership

Rivalry usually results in lower profits than could be achieved through firms cooperating with one another.

Such cooperation to limit competition is known as ***collusion***, and many economists believe that this is often a more realistic assumption than rivalry. A more formal type of collusion would be a price- or output-fixing ring, known as a cartel, in which all firms coordinate their activities so as to maximise joint profits by behaving, in effect, as a monopolist. Such an arrangement is illegal in most countries, but a student should be aware of the term.

Probably the most famous cartel is OPEC, the Organisation for Petroleum Exporting Countries. Its power has reduced as non-OPEC oil supplies have increased, but it has survived because as an international organisation it transcends national laws. IATA, the International Air Transport Association, which fixes scheduled air fares, is another international cartel arrangement, although its power has also diminished as the growing deregulation of the world's airline markets has led to excess capacity in the industry. Despite their illegality cartels also persist within countries owing to their profit-raising potential for member firms. Recent examples in the UK have been found among betting shops and Cross-Channel ferries and in the glass, insurance, milk, roofing and sugar refining industries. In the EU cartels have been discovered in the steel, PVC and cement industries.

Collusion may take the form of price leadership where, instead of competing through price, firms accept one of their number in the industry as a price leader and simply keep their own prices in line with that firm's. Often the dominant firm takes the lead in setting prices. Thus, Ford usually acts as the price leader in the UK car industry and Thomsons in the holiday market.

Although these assumptions appear to sidestep the need to analyse oligopolistic interdependence, interdependence still arises if firms are closely related or if new entry is likely. Moreover, where collusion arises firms can improve their individual position still further by cheating on their 'partners'; hence, collusion has an inherent tendency to break up. Where joint profits are maximised arguments between firms can still arise as to how these profits should be shared. These considerations, together with the illegality of cartels and restrictive practices, suggest that collusion cannot always be assumed.

Price leadership is notoriously difficult to prove as firms will argue that simultaneous price changes are not the result of collusion but the need to respond quickly to changes in the market and the competitive threat of rivals.

Non-price competition

A common feature of oligopoly is the tendency to avoid competing through price and to use instead other forms of competition such as branding, advertising, competitions and free offers, after-sales services, etc. For example, a car manufacturer will realise that if it cuts the price of a particular model, rival manufacturers can respond almost immediately. If market demand is inelastic, such a price war might do little to expand the market and simply reduce the revenue earned by all the oligopolists. Instead, the firm might introduce a sun roof into the design of the car, or offer a CD player as standard equipment, knowing it may take some time for other firms to respond.

In the same way, oligopolistic firms might attempt to use ingenious advertising to steal advantage over competitors.

There is evidence that the advertising to sales ratio tends to be higher in oligopolistic industries than in industries with either a very low or very high seller concentration ratio.

The advantage of launching an advertising campaign is that it takes a long time (and a lot of expense) for rivals to react by launching a campaign of their own. It is estimated that it takes between £5 million and £7 million, for example, to advertise successfully a new brand of instant coffee.

STUDENT ACTIVITY 17.2

Can you think of other practical examples of how firms in oligopolistic industries may compete with each other?

Game theory

Game theory attempts to analyse the decision-making behaviour of rivals (players).

It is necessary to assume that players have a finite number of possible courses of action and that they know what the outcome of each possible strategy will be for any given retaliatory strategy played by rivals. The players then assume the worst for themselves in terms of the retaliatory action of rivals. Players thus choose the best of these pessimistically expected outcomes. Usually this anticipation of others' actions results in none of the firms achieving an optimum and hence there are welfare losses for the economy.

The realism of this approach has been questioned and game theory has been described as the 'Argentina' of economics in terms of the gap between potential and achievement. However, given the interdependence and uncertainty that characterises oligopoly, it has been suggested that game theory can provide some insights into oligopolistic behaviour.

Mark-up pricing

It was suggested previously that firms may price, not by using marginal rules (i.e. equating marginal cost and marginal revenue), but via some kind of mark-up procedure above unit variable costs (a technique also known as ***cost-plus pricing***). There is plenty of evidence from the UK and the USA that both small and large firms price in this way. The evidence dates back to a survey of oligopolistic firms undertaken in the 1930s by two British economists, R. Hall and C. Hitch: it was discovered that firms make an estimate of what unit (average) cost will be at the level of output at which they expect to operate (known as the ***normal level*** of capacity utilisation). A mark-up is then added to this to arrive at a price which covers costs and allows for profit.

According to this approach firms are more likely to adjust their outputs rather than their prices (as implied by the marginal rules) should a change in costs or demand occur.

In principle, therefore, prices would be expected to remain fairly stable or sticky. Since price stickiness is regarded as an important feature of oligopolies, the notion of mark-up pricing has often been closely associated with oligopolistic behaviour. Confirmation of price stickiness is revealed by the fact that, on average, firms change their prices only once or twice a year. They do not like to change prices too often because of the expense involved: current prices have to be checked and, if changes are thought necessary, price lists have to be altered. In addition, firms simply do not like starting price wars.

However, while mark-up pricing may be descriptively accurate of the pricing practices of many firms, this approach is not an analysis of price determination unless the magnitude of, and changes in, the mark-up are explained. In practice, despite the prevalence of cost-based pricing techniques, the main factor that determines price would seem to be market conditions (i.e. the level of demand). Evidence suggests that many oligopolistic firms set their prices at the highest level the market can bear; they are also likely to charge similar prices to their competitors.

Managerial and behavioural theories revisited

In Chapter 14 it was pointed out that firms may pursue objectives other than profit maximisation. However, the pursuit of profit remains an integral part of both managerial and behavioural theories of the firm. Managerial models deviate from the neo-classical assumption of profit maximisation but are similar in that the firm is regarded as attempting to maximise something, usually with the constraint that there is a minimum of profit which is necessary to prevent takeover and/or keep shareholders happy.

To an extent, the pursuit of growth, employees or sales revenue will coincide with profit making. The point of these models is that managers would be willing to trade off some of the firm's profit in order to get more of what they themselves want. Thus, a general representation of these models might be as shown in Fig. 17.8.

However, these models can be criticised. In particular, they do not address the important considerations of oligopolistic interdependence – each firm appears to pursue its managerially chosen ends oblivious of the reaction from rival firms. The evidence as to what is the most general goal of managers and firms is also inconclusive.

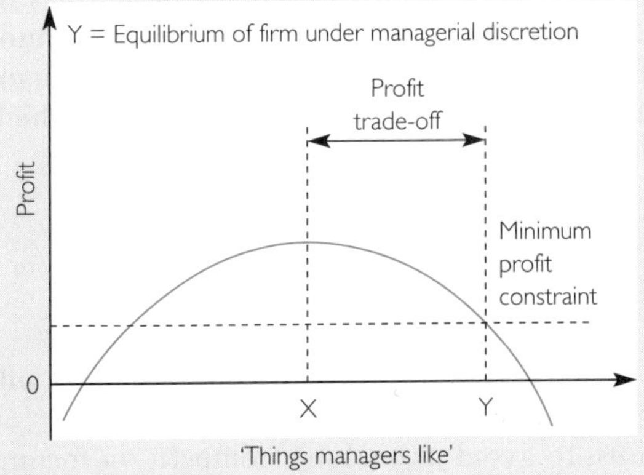

Fig. 17.8 **Managerial discretion**
In this graph profits are plotted against 'things managers like'. Profit maximisation is at X, but left to themselves, managers might go for position Y where the things they like are maximised.

It is often claimed that these models predict that price will be raised in the face of an increase in fixed costs in order to preserve the minimum profit constraint. As firms do appear to increase price with increases in fixed costs this is claimed as evidence in support of managerial theories. It has been shown, however, that the predictions of managerial theories vary substantially with minor alterations in their assumptions.

Another line of criticism has been to argue that in most cases the pursuit of managerial goals is ultimately furthered by increasing a firm's profit. For example, growth and sales revenue maximisation in the long run requires substantial investment and the funds for this, whether internally generated or borrowed, depend on the level of profits. Hence, a great deal of intricate analysis can be avoided, with little loss of accuracy, by simply assuming long-run profit maximisation in the first place! According to behavioural analysis limited knowledge and uncertainty combine to create satisficing rather than maximising behaviour; thus, only a 'satisfactory' market share or level of profit or sales revenue may be sought.

To anyone familiar with a large organisation the model is appealing as a description of the way decisions are reached. Again, however, the problem of oligopolistic interdependence is ignored. But by far the biggest problem is that, although in the short term predictable rules of thumb may be adhered to, the model cannot offer any predictions as to how price and quantity will change in response to events which require a new satisficing search.

Contestable markets

A contestable market is one in which if price is raised sufficiently new entrants will be attracted to the market.

Thus, to avoid unwelcome competition incumbent firms may hold price below the level at which short-run profits are maximised (i.e. at the limit price). Obviously, the extent to which price must be limited depends on barriers to entry; the greater these are the higher the price can be set without attracting new entrants.

A problem with limit price models is that barriers to entry are not easily measured. In particular, the extent to which advertising, excess capacity and the threat of predatory pricing by incumbent firms is and can be used to ward off would-be entrants is hotly disputed by industrial economists.

The theoretical extreme is a perfectly contestable market in which any profit at all immediately attracts new entry.

As incumbents can retaliate by lowering price to average cost, entrants will dash into the market in such a way only if they will suffer no sunk costs. Thus, in principle, there are no barriers to entry or exit, even in oligopolistic or monopolistic markets.

The model of perfectly contestable markets was used to justify airline deregulation in the USA in the early 1980s where 'capital on wings' could potentially be quickly rerouted to undercut incumbent airlines or to avoid loss-making routes. Research suggests, however, that actual competition has a far greater influence on price than potential competition and that very few industries have insignificant sunk costs, e.g. airport facilities and advertising constitute fixed costs in civil aviation. Incumbent airlines in the USA were able to overcome the threat of entry by investing in computerised reservation systems and undertaking large-scale marketing campaigns.

Conclusion

In this and the previous chapter we have seen that profit maximisation implies producing where $MC = MR$. In practice, firms may not attempt to maximise profits and there may be many reasons for the $MC = MR$ rule being of little guidance, e.g. uncertainty and the retaliation of competitors. Nevertheless, we have seen that there is a rich variety of theories which offer insights into actual firm behaviour even though no single model is entirely satisfactory. Having considered the theory of the firm we will continue in the next chapter to examine various ways in which imperfect competition manifests itself in the economy.

Summary

1 Profit maximisation occurs where there is the greatest possible positive difference between total revenue and total cost.
2 Marginal revenue is the change to total revenue as a result of the sale of one more unit of commodity.
3 Profit maximisation always occurs where marginal revenue is equal to marginal cost.
4 For the monopolist abnormal profits may persist in the long run.
5 The long-run equilibrium for the monopolistic competitor occurs where *AC* is tangential to *AR* and the firm is just receiving normal profit.
6 In the absence of collusion, oligopoly behaviour is complex and unpredictable.
7 Not only is formal collusion (i.e. a cartel) illegal, but it has a tendency to break up as firms have an incentive to cheat on one another.
8 Mark-up techniques are commonly used to calculate prices, although market conditions remain an important determinant of the actual prices charged.
9 There are many theories of the firm to choose. Profit maximisation is not always assumed. Each theory, however, has its particular strengths and weaknesses.
10 A perfectly contestable market is one in which there no barriers to entry or exit; it represents a theoretical extreme.

Questions

1 Discuss the alternatives that exist to the profit maximisation hypothesis.
2 Explain the relationship between *MR* and elasticity of demand. Examine the significance of a knowledge of this relationship for a firm.
3 Demonstrate that profit maximisation requires $MC = MR$. Can firms profit maximise?
4 'Profit maximisation occurs where the difference between *AC* and *AR* is at a maximum.' Discuss.
5 Compare and contrast the long-run equilibrium of the monopolistic competitor with that of the perfect competitor.
6 What explanations exist for oligopolistic behaviour? Discuss the prevalence of price and non-price competition in oligopolistic markets.
7 What are the strengths and weaknesses of the kinked demand theory of oligopoly?
8 Explain how the threat of new entry to the industry may affect the behaviour of a firm.
9 What factors might be taken into consideration in assessing the degree of monopoly in an industry? Explain how these factors are likely to affect prices set within the industry.
10 What is meant by mark-up pricing? To what extent do firms follow such a procedure in setting prices?

Data response A Maximising profits

The following is hypothetical data relating to a firm operating under conditions of imperfect competition in the short run.

Quantity, q	*Price, p*	*Average cost, AC*
0	400	∞
10	360	350
20	320	200
30	280	146.6
40	240	125
50	200	120
60	160	123.3
70	120	131.4
80	80	142.5

1 With the aid of this data and with a diagram demonstrate that the condition:

$$MR = MC$$

is the profit maximisation position for the firm.
2 If this firm is operating under conditions of monopolistic competition how will its equilibrium position alter in the long run?

The dates of general price increases by the largest three suppliers in the UK car market, 1986 to mid 1991

Year	*Ford*	*Rover*	*Vauxhall*
1986	1 January	15 February	14 January
	17 August	18 August	10 September
1987	4 anuary	12 January	5 January
	11 May	4 May	11 May
	17 August	1 September	24 August
1988	4 January	11 January	7 January
	16 May	16 May	16 May
	15 August	15 August	22 August
1989	3 January	1 January	3 January
	N/A	15 May	N/A
	14 August	14 August	21 August
1990	2 January	1 January	2 January
	1 May	26 June	8 May
	13 August	18 September	4 September
1991	21 January*	11 February	14 January
	N/A	1 July	N/A

* Except Granada/Scorpio models, where the date was 4 February

Source: Monoplies and Mergers Commission 1992, Report on New Cars, page 90

Data response B
Oligopoly pricing

Study the information in the table and answer the following questions:

1 What sort of market structure do you think exists in the UK car market?
2 What does the data suggest about the nature and extent of price competition in the industry?
3 Justify your answer to question 2.

18 Aspects of monopoly

Learning outcomes

At the end of this chapter you will be able to:

- Understand the rationale underlying competition policy.
- Outline the main sources of monopoly power.
- Describe the key features of the policies of the UK and the EU authorities towards monopolies, restrictive practices and mergers.
- Appreciate the problems involved in establishing a suitable pricing policy towards monopolies.
- Recognise the conditions for, and bases of, price discrimination.
- Discuss the techniques involved in establishing prices in different market segments.
- Describe the relative merits of monopoly for society.

Governments and monopoly

Most governments have a policy towards monopolies, which is usually referred to as ***competition policy***. There are two reasons for this.

First, governments recognise the misallocation of resources brought about by monopoly. Second, on the grounds of equity most governments feel obliged to have a policy to limit monopoly profits.

To some extent the government's attitude is determined by how the monopoly arose. We will therefore first consider the sources of monopoly.

The sources of monopoly

a) *Natural*. This arises out of the geographical conditions of supply. For example, South Africa has an almost complete monopoly of the Western world's supply of diamonds. Another example would be Schweppes's monopoly of Malvern water.
b) *Historical*. A business may have a monopoly because it was first in the field and no one else has the necessary know-how or customer goodwill. Lloyd's of London has a command of the insurance market that is largely based on historical factors.
c) *Capital size*. The supply of a commodity may involve the use of such a vast amount of capital equipment that new competitors are effectively excluded from entering the market. This is the case with the chemical industry.
d) *Technological*. Where there are many economies of scale to be gained it may be natural and advantageous for the market to be supplied by one or a few large companies. This would apply to the utilities, like gas and electricity supply and distribution.
e) *Legal*. The government may confer a monopoly upon a company. This may be the case when a business is granted a patent or copyright. The right to sole exploitation is given to encourage people to bring forward new ideas.
f) *Public*. Public corporations such as the Post Office frequently have monopolies. In the UK the Post Office has the monopoly right to deliver letters of up to £1 in value.
g) *Contrived*. When people discuss the evils of monopoly, it is not so much the above forms of monopolies they are thinking about as those that are deliberately contrived. Business organisation can contrive to exploit the market either by taking over, or driving out of

business, the other firms in the industry (***scale monopoly***) or by entering into an agreement with other business to control prices and output (***complex monopoly***, see below). It is this type of monopoly at which most legislation is aimed.

STUDENT ACTIVITY 18.1

Using the above list of sources of monopoly power, think of other examples for each category. Consider whether, besides the inherent drawbacks of monopoly, there may be any potential advantages for consumers in each case.

Possibilities for policy

There are three basic policies the government can adopt towards monopolies:

a) *Prohibition*. The formation of monopolies can be banned and existing monopolies broken up. This is more the attitude in the USA. 'Antitrust' legislation, as it is called, in the USA, dates back to the Sherman Act of 1890. However, very few monopolies are actually broken up nowadays. One exception was the telephone company, AT&T, which was divested of its local services in 1984. Thus, there are still a considerable number of monopolies in the USA. Legislation against actions 'in restraint of trade' has been more vigorously prosecuted against unions than against big business.
b) *Takeover*. The government can take over a monopoly and run it in the public interest. Although many industries and companies have been taken over by the government, it has not usually been done with the object of controlling a monopoly. As the chapter on the privatisation debate reveals the recent trend has been for firms and industries to be returned to the private sector rather than for them to be taken over by the government.
c) *Regulation*. The government can allow a monopoly to continue but pass legislation to make sure that it does not act 'against the public interest'. This is basically the attitude of the UK government as part of its competition policy.

The main legislation concerning monopolies in the UK is embodied in the Fair Trading Act 1973; this codified much previous legislation. The main agency for implementing government policy on competition is the Office of Fair Trading (OFT). Under the Fair Trading Act 1973 the Director-General of Fair Trading (DGFT) must keep commercial practices in the UK under review and collect information about them in order to discover monopoly situations and uncompetitive practices. Under the Restrictive Trade Practices Act 1976 the DGFT also has a major role in the regulation of restrictive trading agreements. The 1980 Competition Act allowed for the investigations of public sector monopolies.

Policy on monopolies

At its simplest a monopoly arises when one trading organisation supplies an entire market. This, however, is very rare and the Fair Trading Act 1973 defines

> a monopoly as being where one person, company or group of related companies supplies or acquires at least 25 per cent of the goods or services in question in the UK – this is a 'scale monopoly'. A 'complex monopoly' exists if at least 25 per cent of the goods or services of a particular description are supplied in the UK as a whole by two or more persons, unconnected companies or groups of companies who intentionally or otherwise conduct their affairs in such a way that they prevent, distort or restrict competition in the supply of goods or services, e.g. refusing to supply goods or services to particular customers.

Complex monopolies are far more common than scale monopolies, for there are many cases where particular industries are dominated by a small number of suppliers, each of whom holds a very large share of the market, e.g. the motor industry (four major suppliers) and detergents (two major suppliers).

The DGFT may refer what is considered to be a monopoly to the Monopolies and Mergers Commission (MMC) for investigation.

The main inherent dangers or costs of a monopoly, whether a pure monopoly or the more usual scale or complex monopolies, are restriction of output, price fixing, regulation of terms of supply and removal of consumers' choice and, most importantly, cost inefficiency. Additionally, free competition may be stifled by preventing competitors entering the market, and a monopolist may also use its monopsonistic buying powers to dictate terms to suppliers. The government uses the law to forbid or regulate these practices. Alternatively, there may be some benefits of monopoly power to consider, such as the advantages of achieving economies of scale and being able to spend more on research and development (R&D) (see below). The UK approach has tended to be fairly pragmatic or 'neutral'; in each case the costs are weighed against any prospective benefits before a decision is reached. However, very few cases are actually investigated (only an average of five p.a. between 1991 and 1994).

Restrictive practices

The Restrictive Trade Practices Act 1976 is concerned with any agreement or arrangement between suppliers of goods or services, including recommendations made by trade associations, which restrict competition. Examples include agreements between suppliers to charge the same prices, or to divide up the market and to trade on the same terms of business.

Such practices are unlawful and the object of the Act is to ensure that only such agreements, arrangements and recommendations as are in the public interest are allowed to continue. To achieve this, full details of 'registrable agreements' must be sent to the OFT for entry in a public register maintained by the DGFT. The DGFT then has the power to refer the practice to the Restrictive Practices Court to consider whether or not it is against the public interest. There are a number of grounds (often called 'gateways') on which the practice can be upheld as being in the public interest, e.g. showing that a restriction protects the public from injury or counterbalances market power elsewhere.

Under the Act the DGFT may instigate action for an injunction to restrain the continuance or repetition of the unlawful restrictive practice. A consumer directly affected by it may bring an action for damages. Well over a thousand restrictive agreements have been referred to the Court since its inception, although only a tiny minority have been upheld. For example, in 1991 price fixing by the suppliers of ready-mixed concrete was investigated and declared illegal. By this time many of the customers, including the National Health Service, had paid many millions of pounds in excess of the competitive price.

The power given to the DGFT, under the Competition Act 1980, to investigate and control the ***anticompetitive practices of single firms*** supplements the existing powers for investigation of monopolies and restrictive agreements among firms. The government's declared intention in the Act is to promote competition and efficiency in industry and commerce.

In 1994, for example, the MMC ruled that LRC's exclusive dealings with retailers to stock only the company's condoms were regarded as a barrier to new competition. The Price Commission has now been abolished by the Competition Act, but the Secretary of State for Trade and Industry retains the power to investigate prices which he or she considers to be 'of major public concern having regard to whether the supply, or acquisition, of goods or services in question is of general economic importance, or the price is of special significance to consumers'. There are no direct sanctions that can be taken in such a situation but it could be treated as an anticompetitive practice.

Resale price maintenance (RPM)

Resale price maintenance is the practice whereby manufacturers impose a fixed retail selling price on the retailers they supply. They enforce this by taking action against anyone who undercuts the price (or charges more).

The enforcement of minimum selling prices by manufacturers or distributors of goods, either individually or collectively, is illegal under the Resale Prices Act 1976 unless held to be in the public interest by the Restrictive Practices Court. At present only minimum prices for books has the Court's sanction, but a number of retailers are now undercutting recommended retail prices in this area. Any person adversely affected, or the DGFT, may take civil proceedings against those who seek to reimpose minimum resale prices.

Resale price maintenance poses an economic dilemma to governments. On the one hand consumers benefit, and efficient organisations are rewarded, by allowing free pricing of commodities. On the other, consumers can suffer because many small businesses will be unable to compete with large multiple retailers in price cutting and may be forced to close down or face insolvency, thereby reducing retail services to the public. A good example of what can happen is the decline of independent chemists since supermarkets have been allowed to sell patent medicines. Indiscriminate promotion of competition may have the effect of operating to the detriment of the very consumers it seeks to protect. On the other hand, an MMC report in 1997 found that the manufacturers of electrical goods fixed the prices of a wide range of their commodities (e.g. televisions, video recorders, washing machines and refrigerators) and enforced price discipline by restricting supplies to retailers who discount.

Common misunderstanding

Resale price maintenance, the imposition by manufacturers of fixed prices on retailers, may not be entirely detrimental for consumers. The number of outlets can be protected; firms can also compete in non-price terms, such as service and guarantees. However, prices are likely to be higher than they otherwise would be; competition may also be restricted as a result of the enforcement of the price-fixing arrangement.

The EU and monopoly

The EU has generally favoured a more free market Austrian approach towards monopolies than in the UK, in which profit is not taken as conclusive evidence of market power.

Article 85 of the Treaty of Rome 1957 prohibits all agreements between business organisations, decisions by trade associations and concerted practices which may affect trade between member states and which have as their object or effect the prevention, restriction or distortion of competition within the EU. Article 85 includes fixing, buying and/or selling prices or other terms of business, discriminating in favour of certain business organisations, thus giving them a competitive advantage, and sharing markets. If, for example, a manufacturer appointed a sole distributor of its products in each EU country, and each distributor agreed not to export to other EU countries, the 'common market' would be divided into 15 separate markets and competition among member states would be effectively distorted. Some practices may qualify for exemption if an agreement improves production or distribution or promotes innovation.

Article 86 declares that the establishment and abuse of a dominant position in the market structure is incompatible with the EU objectives, e.g. imposing buying or selling prices or other trading conditions which are unfair, limit production, markets or technological development to the prejudice of consumers. However, relatively few cases of market dominance are investigated – only 16 in 1994.

Policy on mergers

The Fair Trading Act 1973 covers mergers involving the acquisition of gross assets of more than £70 million or where a 'monopoly', i.e. 25 per cent or more of the relevant market in the UK or a substantial part of it, would be created or enhanced. Also included are situations where one company acquires the ability to control or materially influence another company without actually acquiring a controlling interest.

The DGFT is responsible for keeping a watchful eye on possible mergers within the Act, but the DGFT's role is only to advise the Secretary of State for Trade and Industry as to whether a reference should be made to the MMC; the DGFT may not make a reference directly. This contrasts with the DGFT's powers relating to monopolies. The Secretary of State has power under the 1973 Act to order that the merger shall not proceed or to regulate any identified adverse effects of a merger or proposed merger, e.g. the effect on labour relations.

Since the early 1980s successive Secretaries of State have referred mergers mainly on competition grounds.

Again, the approach is broadly neutral, at least in principle. Each reference is considered on its own merits and on the criterion of the 'public interest', the latter encompassing the maintenance and promotion of competition, consumer interest, effects on employment and, in some cases, the possibility of 'asset stripping', or tax avoidance. However, as with monopolies, very few cases are actually investigated. Since 1965, less than 3 per cent of eligible mergers have been referred to the MMC and less than 1 per cent have been declared against the public interest. The fact that most mergers in the UK are consequently regarded as being within the public interest may seem surprising given their relative lack of success (see Chapter 13).

The guiding principle behind UK legislation on monopolies, mergers and restrictive practices is that of 'the public interest'. Monopolies are not prohibited *per se* but only if they act against the public interest. The problem is that no one has defined adequately what the public interest is or established adequate criteria for assessing it.

The EU and mergers

EU legislation on mergers came into force in 1990. The regulations only apply to very large mergers that affect more than one member state. There are two qualifying rules:

a) the merging companies have a combined global turnover of over 5 billion ECU; and
b) at least two of the companies involved in the merger each have an EU-wide turnover of over 250 million ECU (as long as less than two-thirds of the business is in a single member state, otherwise national laws apply).

In 1994, 95 mergers were notified to the European Commission and six were investigated.

Pricing problems

Government policy on monopoly pricing

If a monopoly does exist and the government decides not to break it up but regulate prices in the public interest, what shall its policy on prices be? In the 'normal' monopoly situation, illustrated in Fig. 18.1, monopoly legislation could be aimed at making the monopolist produce at point F where $AC = AR$. At this point the price is OR and the output ON. All monopoly profits have been eliminated and the public is obtaining the largest output for the lowest price that is compatible with the monopolist remaining in the industry. Pure economic theory would suggest setting a price where $MC = P$ (called ***marginal cost pricing***), but as you can see in Fig. 18.1 this would result in the firm actually making a loss. There are also difficulties in determining MC accurately.

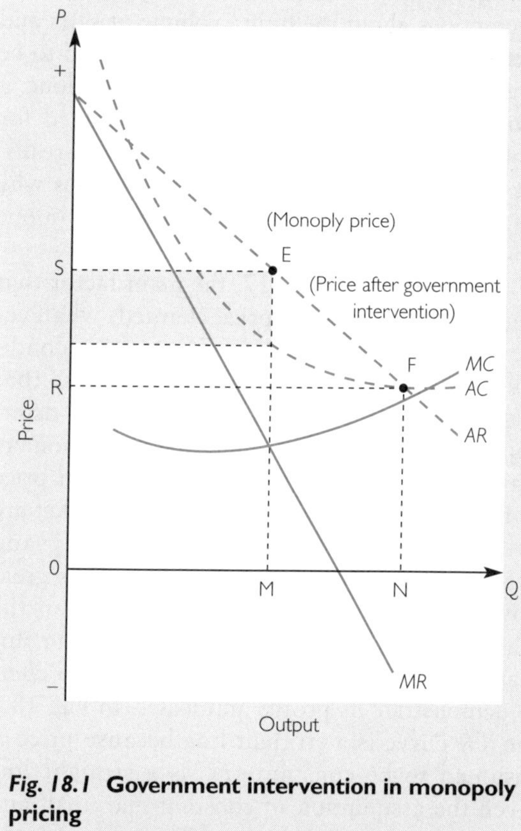

***Fig. 18.1* Government intervention in monopoly pricing**
The monopolist would choose to produce at point E, making maximum profit. Government policy aims to compel the monopolist to produce at point F where $AC = AR$, thus eliminating abnormal profit.

STUDENT ACTIVITY 18.2

In Fig. 18.1 explain a) why pricing at marginal costs would yield the 'best' solution from society's point of view and b) why pricing at this level would lead to a loss for the firm in question.

Mark-up pricing and break-even charts

Although an organisation's behaviour may be governed by concepts such as marginal revenue and marginal cost, in practice they may be very difficult to determine, especially when a large organisation is marketing a variety of products. In these circumstances they often try to base their prices on average or unit cost. To do this they must make assumptions about the future volume of sales and likely average cost (which is usually assumed to be constant) at that output. This having been done, a ***mark-up*** of, say, 10 per cent is then added for profit. This fascinating simple theory seems realistic, but stops tantalisingly short of telling us why the average mark up should be 40 per cent in one industry and 5 per cent in another.

As noted in Chapter 17, the main factor that seems to determine the price charged, whatever the pricing procedure adopted, is market conditions. The reader should take careful note that this is the way the organisation may try to determine the right price for itself, but the customers may or may not be willing to pay the right price or buy the right quantity. Prices in the market are still determined by the forces of supply and demand. The monopolist organisation has great power, of course, to impose its wishes on the market. If an organisation sets its price in this manner then we can draw up a ***break-even chart*** to demonstrate its profits and losses. In Fig. 18.2 the *TR* curve is a straight line because price is assumed to be constant; *TC* is a straight line given the assumption of constant marginal, and hence average variable, costs. This way of looking at profits is much closer to the accountants' view than most of the economists' ways of looking at the market.

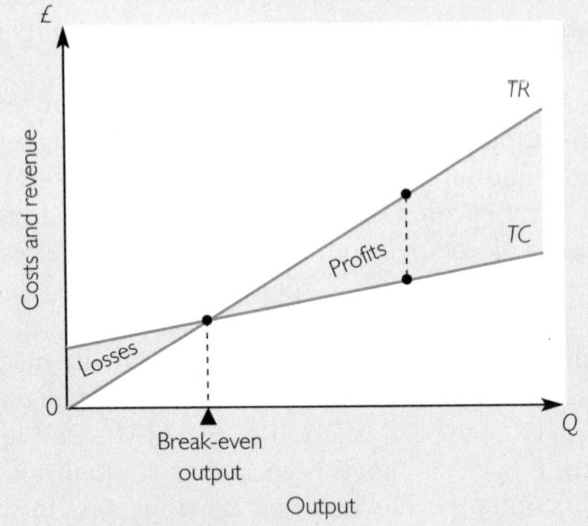

***Fig. 18.2* A break-even chart**
If the price is fixed then *TR* is a straight line. Profits or losses are the vertical distance between the two curves.

Discriminating monopoly

Discriminating monopoly (or price discrimination) is said to exist when different buyers or groups of buyers, in separate market segments, are charged two or more prices for the same product, for reasons not associated with differences in costs.

Thus, price discrimination exists when price differences do not reflect cost differences or when consumers are charged the same price despite cost differences.

The conditions for discriminating monopoly

Every producer knows that there are some consumers who are willing to pay more than the market price for the good. The consumers are therefore in receipt of utility they are not paying for and this is known as a ***consumers' surplus*** (see page 111). A monopolist may be able to eat into this surplus by charging some consumers higher prices than others. For price discrimination to be worthwhile two conditions must be fulfilled:

a) The monopolist must be able to separate the two markets or market segments in order to avoid the resale of the product from one group of consumers to another. This may be done geographically, by time or by income. The suppliers of personal services such as doctors and lawyers also often charge different prices for the same service.

b) The two or more market segments thus separated must have different elasticities of demand, otherwise the exercise would not be worthwhile.

Price discrimination enables a firm to achieve a higher revenue from a given level of sales (and thereby to obtain higher profits).

Common misunderstanding

It should not be presumed that price discrimination, despite enabling the monopolist to achieve greater profits from a given level of sales, automatically operates against the interests of the consumer. By opening up previously untapped markets, it can also lead to increased output.

Bases for price discrimination

It perhaps seems unlikely that consumers would willingly pay two different prices for the same product. However, this can happen if consumers are prevented from buying the cheaper product in some way, or if they are unaware that the difference exists. The main ways in which this is achieved are as follows:

a) *Geographical.* Goods are sold at different prices in different countries. This was illustrated in 1977 when the Distillers Company were ordered by the EU to cease selling the same brand of whisky at one price in the UK and at a higher price in the rest of the EU. (See also the example of car prices discussed below.)

b) *Time.* Some firms with monopoly power sell the same product at different prices at different times. Examples of this are off-peak electricity, weekend returns on the railways and 'stand-by' flights by British Airways.

c) *Income.* Firms may be able to sell their products at different prices to different groups of consumers depending on their levels of income. Thus, doctors and lawyers can charge higher rates to those with higher incomes, children may be charged lower rates than adults in cinemas and on aeroplanes, buses and trains, business passengers may pay more than other travellers and students can often obtain lower prices in restaurants or hairdressers.

d) *Dumping.* This is a variation on geographical discrimination, but in this case the manufacturer 'dumps' surplus output on foreign markets at below cost price. This often has the object of damaging foreign competition. The EU has often resorted to dumping to get rid of excess agricultural products.

STUDENT ACTIVITY 18.3

Demonstrate that dumping increases a firm's profits so long as the dumped goods are sold at more than *AVC*.

Car prices in the EU: a case study

Common misunderstanding

It is commonly supposed that car prices in the UK are higher than in the rest of the EU. However, the data in Table 18.1, admittedly based on a fairly small sample, does not seem to bear out such a hypothesis. The table shows the differences in the prices of selected cars in various national markets of the EU. Allowance has been made for different tax regimes, transport costs, etc. In fact, prices vary widely across the EU and not just between the UK and elsewhere; models can cost up to one-third more in some countries than in others. Such price differentials are way beyond the 12 per cent variation in prices permitted by the EU.

Despite the protestations put forward by the motor trade (differences in tax rates, exchange rates, transport costs, etc.), it is clear that there is extensive geographical price discrimination. The reason for this is that the car market in the EU is

Table 18.1 Car prices in the EU (cheapest = 100, 1 May 1994)

	Fiat Cinquecento 900 iE	Ford Mondeo 1.6 CLX	Honda Accord 2.0 LS	BMW 730i
Belgium	117.2	118.2	114.0	115.6
Britain	117.7	110.5	112.3	100.0
France	124.1	109.2	117.3	121.0
Germany	134.1	118.7	112.9	116.3
Holland	121.6	106.2	100.0	118.5
Ireland	122.0	101.2	107.9	111.2
Italy	107.9	110.0	103.4	107.7
Luxembourg	117.2	118.2	114.0	116.4
Portugal	111.0	110.4	na	na
Spain	100.0	100.0	105.0	113.7

* All figures quoted are free of tax; excludes Denmark and Greece
Source: European Commission, reprinted in *The Economist*, 27 August 1994

not truly competitive and the car manufacturers have been exempted from some of the effects of competition policy legislation. (See also Data response B at the end of the chapter.)

We will now proceed to demonstrate by the use of a hypothetical example why price discrimination benefits the manufacturer and how the marketing strategy is determined. Let us assume that the price for a particular make of car is higher in market A than in market B. Figure 18.3 shows the situation for a car manufacturer. The first diagram shows the situation in the combined market (A plus B). Given this situation the manufacturer would maximise profits by producing where $MR = MC$. This gives an output of 25 000 cars a month at a price of £6500 giving a total revenue of £162.5 million. However, from experience the manufacturer knows that consumers in market B are willing to pay more for this type of car and therefore sets the price at £7500 per car, and sells 10 000 per month, thus earning £75 million in home sales. In market A, however, there is more price competition and the price is dropped to £6250 to compete with other manufacturers. As a result of this the company sells 15 000 cars, bringing in a revenue of £93.75 million. Thus, as a result of this price discrimination total revenue

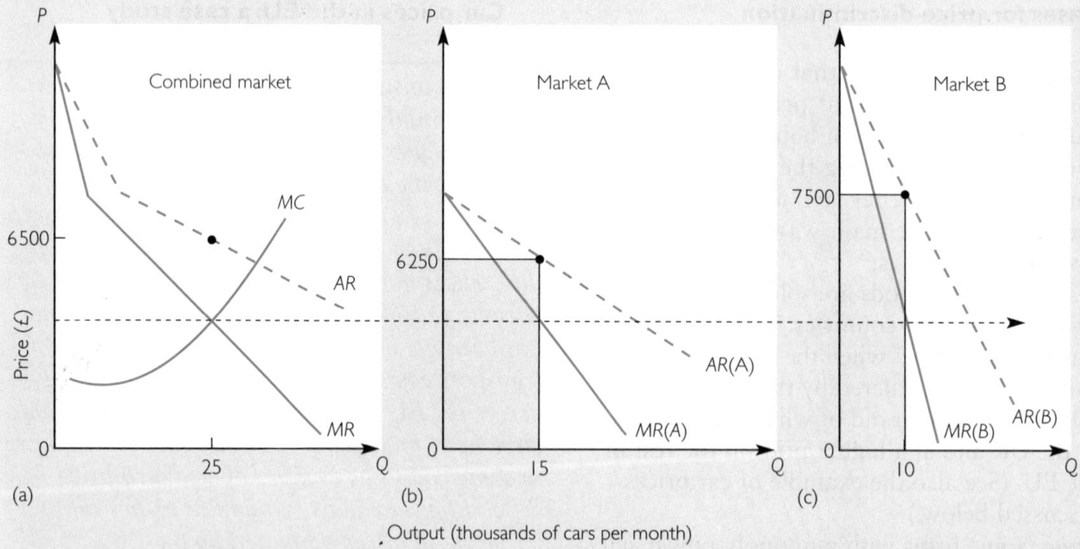

***Fig. 18.3* Discriminating monopoly**
(a) Combined market. (b) Market A (exports). (c) Market B (domestic). The discriminating monopolist divides output between two markets. In the combined market it equates combined *MR* with *MC*; this would give an output of 25 000 cars at a price of £6500 per car. However, by equating *MR* with *MC* in the separate markets it increases total revenue while keeping the same costs. In market A 15 000 cars are sold at £6250 (*TR* = £93.75m) and in market B the remaining 10 000 cars are sold at £7500 each (*TR* = £75m). This is an increase of £6.25m per month on the combined market price.

has increased by £6.25 million per month (£168.75 million – £162.5 million). This must all be extra profit because output, and therefore costs, are the same as in the combined market.

Figure 18.3 also shows the way in which the market strategy is determined. This is to take the level of *MC* at the *MC* = *MR* intersection in the combined market and then equate this level of *MC* with the *MR* in the separate markets. By then tracing this output to the demand (*AR*) curve the manufacturer is able to determine the best price to charge.

In practice the situation is more complicated. There are indirect taxes to consider, exchange rates and, often, many different markets. However, our analysis shows the principles underlying the practice. This applies to all types of price discrimination. Thus, when one is offered cheap 'Awaydays' on the railways, off-peak electricity or lower prices for children for certain products, it should be remembered that this is all part of a strategy by the producer to increase profits.

Monopoly assessed

In this section of the chapter we will consider the advantages and disadvantages of monopoly to the economy. We will first consider two advantages, those of economies of scale and of research and development, and then proceed to the disadvantages.

Economies of scale

In some industries, especially those involving a great deal of capital equipment such as chemicals and motor vehicles, it could be that the larger and more monopolistic a business organisation is the more it is able to take advantage of economies of scale.

In Fig. 18.4 the national market for cars is 2 million per year. In our example, the production is divided between two companies, Kruks and Toymota. Toymota has a bigger share of the market (1.1 million) and, because of the economies of scale to be gained, the long-run average cost (*LAC*) curve of the industry is downward sloping. This means that Toymota's average costs (£4000) are lower than Kruks' (£4800). In the price-conscious car market this means Toymota will sell even more cars, gaining a bigger share of the market and leaving Kruks with a smaller share and even higher costs. In this situation Kruks will eventually go out of business and Toymota will have a complete monopoly. This could be to the public's benefit if continuing economies of scale mean even cheaper cars.

The end result of such a situation, then, is monopoly or some form of oligopoly. This is very much the case in the motor industry, which is dominated by a small number of very large firms. Most medium-sized firms have tended to disappear, but a few companies producing a very small output of specialist cars still exist, e.g. Morgan and Lotus, because they are not so concerned about unit costs. As noted in Chapter 15, while economies of scale occur in most manufacturing industries, they do not preclude the survival of smaller firms.

In such an industry it would not be economic sense to break up the monopoly. Indeed, it has been observed that in the UK the government has sometimes promoted the formation of monopolies in these sorts of industry. In these circumstances the government's options are limited either to taking over the industry or to regulating its prices and output. Although the choices are very clear in theory, in practice it is often very difficult to acquire enough information to judge what is happening in an industry.

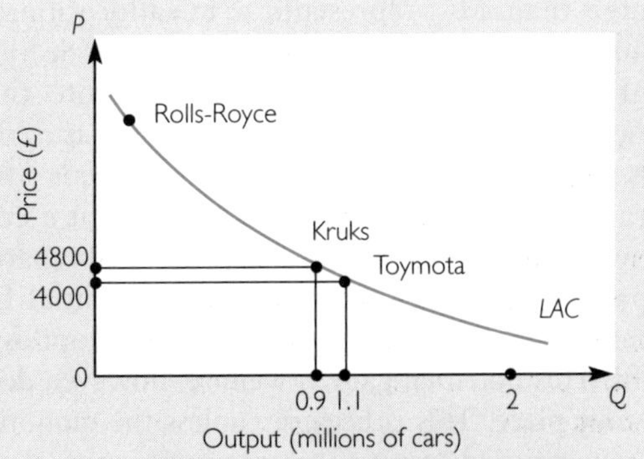

***Fig. 18.4* The flat-bottomed average cost curve**

Research and development (R&D)

It has been argued, most notably by Schumpeter (see below, in Chapter 23), that it is only the monopolist or the oligopolist that can provide the large sums of money necessary to provide for expensive research and development programmes. Keen price competition can cut profit margins and leave nothing for product development. As we shall see below, it can also be argued that monopoly leads to complacency and lack of development.

In fact, the evidence suggests that R&D spending increases up to a certain medium size of firm and moderate level of industry concentration; beyond these points R&D spending increases less than proportionately with increases in size or levels of concentration.

Redistribution of income

Monopoly brings about a redistribution of income from the consumer to the monopolist. If the consumers are selling their own goods or services in a competitive market then they will be receiving the marginal cost of doing so. The monopolist, however, receives a price above marginal cost and the monopoly rent so earned represents a transfer of income above what is economically necessary. The continued existence of monopolies, therefore, further worsens the unequal distribution of income in the economy.

Allocative inefficiency

The fact that the monopolist produces at a price greater than *MC* represents a misallocation of resources. This point is fully explained in Section IV. For the moment we can simply note that monopoly power has resulted in ***contrived scarcity***. This refers to the fact that, as price exceeds *MC*, extra units of output *could* be produced at a cost below that which the consumers would be prepared to pay. Thus, there seems to be the potential for increasing consumer surplus and the monopolist's profit. This potential gain in welfare, however, does not take place. This is because, unless the monopolist can price discriminate, producing the extra units would cause *MR* to fall below *MC* and hence reduce the monopolist's actual profit. In short, there seems to be an underproduction of the product concerned in that not enough of the nation's resources are being allocated to its production.

Lack of X-efficiency

X-efficiency is the term used to describe the minimisation of cost which occurs under conditions of competition.

It is argued that it is a necessary corollary of profit maximisation that a firm achieves X-efficiency. However, under conditions of monopoly or oligopoly the firm is protected from competition and may therefore not be under pressure to be X-efficient. Adopting the economist H. Leibenstein's terms the firm will be ***X-inefficient***. If this is so it will lead to an upward shift in the cost curves. Figure 18.5 shows an upward shift in the *MC* curve as a result of X-inefficiency, thus further worsening the adverse effects of monopoly. Measurement problems mean that evidence of the extent of X-inefficiency is fairly limited, but estimates suggest that it can be quite significant.

Conclusion

Economists since the time of Adam Smith have usually opposed monopoly. As we saw in Chapter 5 Adam Smith wrote:

> A monopoly by keeping the market constantly understocked, never supplying the effectual

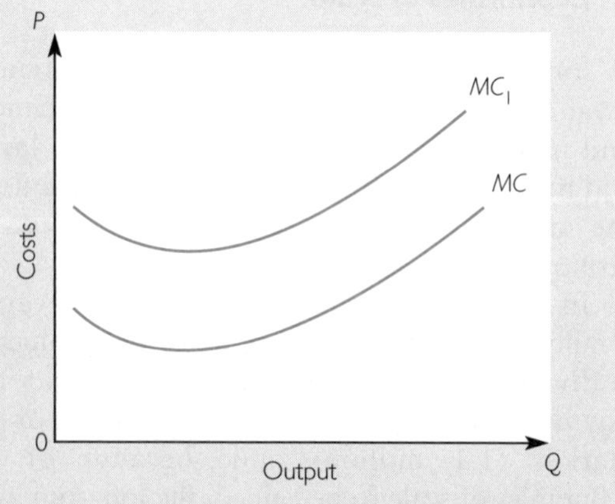

Fig. 18.5 **Increase in costs caused by X-inefficiency**

> demand, sell their commodities much above the natural price, and raise emoluments, whether they consist in wages or profit, greatly above their natural rate.

It should not be thought, therefore, that the modern capitalist state is the legatee of Smith; free enterprise, indeed, is the very antithesis of much that he argued for.

We have seen, however, that under certain circumstances monopoly can be both efficient and desirable. It would therefore seem sensible to say that we should take a pragmatic case study approach to the problem, weighing each situation on its merits. Against this it can be argued that full investigation of all monopoly practices would be very expensive. It must also be said that, despite the existence of much legislation on monopoly, there appears to be a general lack of effectiveness. The most cynical viewpoint on this is put forward by J. K. Galbraith, who argues that the purpose of competition policy is so that the government can be 'seen to be doing something' about monopoly. The state, however, is too wedded to the capitalist structure to actually want to do anything about it. Thus, it is argued, monopoly legislation is a propaganda exercise.

Summary

1 Government policy on monopoly is based on the idea that monopolies should not be 'against the public interest'. However, this concept is vague and ill defined.
2 The chief UK government agencies for competition policy are the Office of Fair Trading (OFT) and the Monopolies and Mergers Commission (MMC).
3 The EU Treaty of Rome prohibits most restrictive practices; the establishment and abuse of monopoly positions can also both be investigated.
4 Both the UK and the EU have policies towards mergers, although very few cases are actually investigated in either instance.
5 Government policy on monopoly prices could be aimed at getting the monopolist to produce where $P = MC$, but this is impossible if the firm is taking advantage of economies of scale.
6 Discriminating monopoly is a situation where a firm sells the same product at two (or more) different prices.
7 Arguments in favour of monopoly include economies of scale and support for research and development.
8 Arguments against monopoly include worsening the distribution of income, allocative inefficiency and the possibility of X-inefficiency.

Questions

1 What is the scope for price discrimination for the following:
   a) British Telecom (BT);
   b) a wheat farmer;
   c) the CAP;
   d) a doctor?
2 Examine the main bases for price discrimination. Discuss the relative merits of price discrimination from the points of view of both the producer and the consumer.
3 Discuss the problems involved in implementing a policy of marginal cost pricing for monopolies.
4 Describe the main features of competition policy. Evaluate its success.
5 'The tragedy of monopoly is not excessive profits. There may indeed be no profits at all, the high price being frittered away in small volume and inefficient production.' Discuss.
6 Discuss the view that breaking up monopolies would increase prices by increasing costs.
7 While the law [of competition] may be sometimes hard for the individual, it is best for the race, because it ensures the survival of the fittest in every department. We accept and welcome, therefore, as conditions to which we must accommodate ourselves, great inequality of environment, the concentration of business, industrial and commercial, in the hands of a few, and the law of competition between these as being not only beneficial, but essential for the future progress of the race.' Critically evaluate this statement by Andrew Carnegie, made in 1889.
8 Discuss the view, with reference to official policy, that company mergers are against the public interest.

Data response A
Compact discs sales

Figure 18.6 shows the situation of a record company under conditions of imperfect (monopolistic) competition.

1 Assess the extent to which a company producing and marketing compact discs can be said to be in a monopolistically competitive market.
2 Assuming that the record company wishes to maximise its profits, at what price and output would it choose to produce in this market?

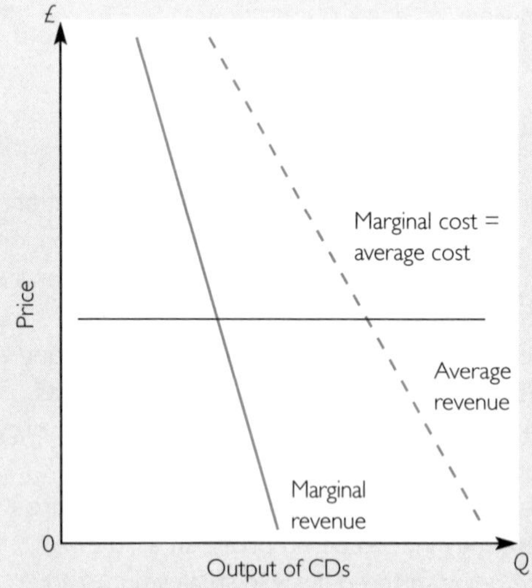

Fig. 18.6 **The producer of compact discs under conditions of monopolistic competition**

3 Consider the position of the artist who appears on the compact disc. Assuming that the artist is paid a fixed percentage of total sales revenue of the disc, which price and output would be most beneficial to the artist? If this objective were to be achieved, in what position would it leave the company?
4 What do you consider the attitude of the government should be if Fig. 18.6 is a true representation of the market?
5 You should have realised that the market conditions are greatly influenced by the existence of copyright laws. What would be the situation if these laws were to be repealed and would this be desirable from the public's point of view?

Data response B
Euro car prices

Read the following article taken from *The Economist* of 27 August 1994 and answer the following questions:

1 Describe the conditions which must exist for price discrimination such as that described in the article to be both possible and worthwhile to the businesses concerned.
2 Why do you think price differences have persisted after the introduction of the Single European Market in 1992?
3 Examine the view of the Chicago school that the best protection for the consumer is competition rather than consumer legislation.
4 How do firms determine the optimum prices at which to sell their products in the different markets under conditions of price discrimination?

Caveat emptor

Brussels

CONSUMERS are again being betrayed by the European Commission which is supposed to be patrolling the single market of the European Union. At the end of this month, Europe's car makers will get an early Christmas present from the commission: a draft regulation that would shield them from the full force of competition for another ten years from next July. A few days later, the 17 commissioners are due to publish their ideas on how small payments can best be sent from one country to another. Cynics predict that the methods will suit the banks more than their customers.

Under the single market, consumers are supposed to be able to shop where they want, including across national frontiers. In theory, that should narrow price differences across the whole of the EU.

Why, then, do cars cost anything up to one-third more in some countries than in others? According to the commission's latest figures, the pre-tax price of a Ford Mondeo – trumpeted by its maker as a world car – is 19% higher in Germany than in Spain; for the Fiat Cinquecento, the price difference between those two countries is 34%; the Honda Accord is 17% higher in France than in Holland.

The explanation is that the consumer – the single market or no – is still not really free to shop around. Since 1985 Europe's car makers have been exempted from the full rigour of the competition rules: they can insist that their dealers sell only their cars, and that garages use only their spare parts, which hampers arbitraging. And, in a "consensus" agreement with Japan, the Commission agreed in 1991 to continue the competition-reducing curbs on Japanese car imports (limited at the time to 3% of the market in France, 2.3% in Italy, 6.4% in Spain, 11% in Britain and 14% in Portugal) until the end of 1999.

All of which makes perfect sense to manufacturers. disingenuously citing both the need to preserve quality "for their customers" and the importance of their industry for employment. The new regulation will narrow the exemptions, but not enough to smooth out the anti-competitive price differences. The car makers will still happily shelter from competition.

Source: *The Economist*, 27 August 1994

SECTION III The theory of distribution

'The first man who, having fenced in a piece of land, said "This is mine," and found people naive enough to believe him, that man was the founder of civil society.'

Jean-Jacques Rousseau

19 The pricing of productive factors

Learning outcomes

At the end of this chapter will you be able to:

- Evaluate the theory of the distribution of income.
- Appreciate the notion of the derived demand for a factor.
- Account for the significance of the law of diminishing returns in distribution theory.
- Explain the concepts of the marginal physical product, the average physical product and the marginal revenue product of a factor.
- Recognise the importance of measures of productivity.
- Explain the derivation of the firm and industry demand curves for a factor.
- Account for the fact that the principles underlying resource utilisation are consistent with those supporting cost structures of the firm.
- Identify isoquants and isocosts.
- Recognise the least cost combination of factors.

Introduction

In this section of the book we wish to examine the use of the factors of production. In this chapter we will look at the general principles covering the use of resources and the factors which determine their price. In the subsequent chapters we will see how these general principles apply to each factor.

The theory of distribution

Let us return for a moment to the fundamentals of the subject. Economics must answer the 'What?', 'How?' and 'For whom?' questions in society. In this section we will be completing our explanation of the 'How?' and 'For whom?' questions in a market economy. As we examine the theory of production, this will explain how and why firms use the factors of production, but in doing so it will also explain how the factor incomes – wages, rent, interest and profit – are determined. We will thus be explaining the 'For whom?' question, because it is income which will determine people's ability to buy goods. This is termed the ***theory of distribution*** since it attempts to explain how income is distributed between the factors of production.

The derived demand for the factors of production

When a firm demands a factor of production it is said to be a derived demand, i.e. the factor is not demanded for itself but for the use to which it can be put.

If we examine the demand for such things as bread, these are wanted for *direct* consumption. If, however, a company demands labour it is because it wants to produce something which it can eventually sell. The demand for labour is thus said to be *derived* from the demand for the final product.

Marginal distribution theory

The law of variable proportions

In order to explain the factors which determine the firm's demand for a factor of production we must turn once again to the law of diminishing returns.

The *production function* describes the relationship between output and the factors of production used to produce that output. In the short run the production decision is constrained by the fact that at least one factor is fixed in supply, while the other factors can be varied. For example, a firm will have a factory of a certain size or a farm of a certain area and to this fixed factor the business adds variable factors such as labour and power. Under these circumstances the firm will be affected by the law of diminishing returns, i.e. as the firm adds more and more of the variable factor, e.g. labour, to a constant amount of fixed factor, e.g. land, the extra output per person that this creates must, after a time, be successively reduced. This means that the relationship between the amount of resources used (inputs) and the amount of goods produced (output) will vary. For this reason when considering the diminishing returns in relation to the firm it is often termed the ***law of variable proportions*** or the ***law of non-proportional returns***.

The marginal physical product (*MPP*)

As factors of production are combined, in the short run various principles will emerge which will apply to any firm. These are best illustrated by taking a simple example. In Table 19.1 a farmer, whose land is fixed at 10 hectares in the short run, adds more and more units of the variable factor – labour – in order to produce a greater output of wheat. Obviously if no labour is used there will be no output. When 1 unit of labour is used the output of the farm works out at 12 tonnes of wheat per year. If two persons are used the output rises to 36 tonnes.

The average physical product (*APP*) per person has risen from 12 tonnes to 18 tonnes. This does not mean that the second person was more industrious than the first but rather that a 10 hectare farm was too big for one person to work and it runs more efficiently with two. The higher average product therefore applies to both workers. It may have been achieved through ***specialisation*** and ***division of labour***, impossible when there was only one worker.

As the employer continues to employ more workers so the total output continues to rise, but eventually the rate at which it increases starts to diminish. The third worker adds 34 tonnes per year to the output, the fourth worker only 30 tonnes, the fifth adds only 20 tonnes per year, and so on. Eventually the seventh worker adds nothing more to total output, and if an eighth worker is employed total output actually falls. The amount added to the total output by each successive unit of labour is the ***marginal physical product*** (*MPP*). If we generalise this principle we could define it as:

The *MPP* is the change to the total output resulting from the employment of one more unit of a variable factor.

Table 19.1 **Marginal physical product and average physical product**

Number of people employed	Output of wheat, Q (tonnes/year)	Marginal physical product, MPP (tonnes/year)	Average physical product, APP (tonnes/year)
0	0		0
		12	
1	12		12
		24	
2	36		18
		34	
3	70		23.3
		30	
4	100		25
		20	
5	120		24
		10	
6	130		21.6
		0	
7	130		18.5
		–10	
8	120		15

STUDENT ACTIVITY 19.1

The number of people employed in a factory and the total output produced are as follows:

Number of people employed	Total output Q (units)	Marginal physical product, MPP	Average physical product, APP
0	0		
1	20		
2	44		
3	69		
4	87		
5	100		
6	106		
7	107		
8	106		
9	103		

Complete the figures for the *MPP* and *APP* of labour.

These figures are illustrated graphically in Fig. 19.1. The *MPP* curve rises as the benefits of division of labour make the utilisation of land more efficient. Between 2 and 3 units labour the curve reaches its highest point and then begins to decline as ***diminishing marginal returns*** set in. The *APP* curve also rises initially. ***Diminishing average returns*** occur between 4 and 5 units of labour; beyond this point the *APP* curve declines.

Diminishing returns come about because, as more labour is employed, each successive unit of labour has less of the fixed factor – land – to work with. If it were not for the law of diminishing returns we could supply the world's food from one farm simply by adding more and more labour to it. Obviously this is not possible.

The peak of the *MPP* curve indicates the optimum efficiency of the variable factor in terms of its marginal return. You will also see that the *MPP* curve goes through the top of the *APP* curve. This is always so, for the reasons described in Chapter 15. The intersection of the *APP* with the *MPP* tells us when the firm is at its optimum efficiency in terms of its average output or output per unit.

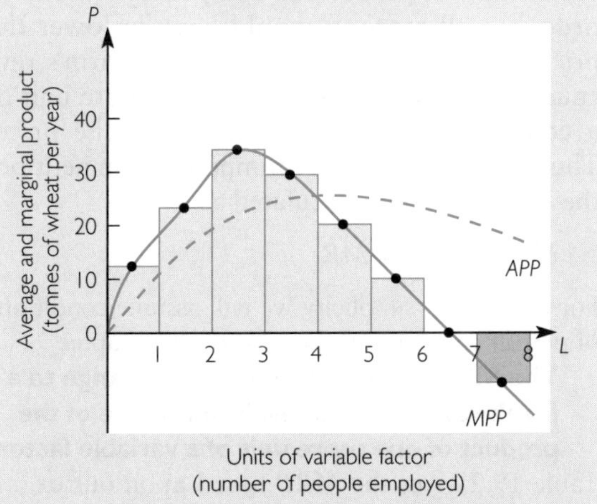

***Fig. 19.1* The marginal physical curve**
The *MPP* shows the amount of extra output produced by each additional unit of the variable factor. Note that the *MPP* curve goes through the highest point of the *APP* curve.

Common misunderstanding
The point of optimum efficiency of the variable factor in terms of either its marginal or average return is not necessarily the output the firm will choose. If, for example, the product we were considering was gold then it might be worthwhile running a very inefficient mine. Eventually, however, because of diminishing returns, MPP *may even become negative when total output falls. No business would be willing to employ more resources to get less output.*

Once again, because *MPP* is a marginal figure it must be plotted in a particular way. In Fig. 19.1 the columns represent ***discrete data*** for the *MPP*. We can turn this into ***continuous data*** by plotting *MPP* half-way between 1 and 2 persons, half-way between 2 and 3 persons and so on. This is shown by the black dots in Fig. 19.1. These can then be joined up to give the *MPP* curve.

Output goes on increasing while *MPP* is positive. Thus in our example total output is maximised (there is optimum utilisation of the fixed factor) when the sixth person is employed. If a seventh person is employed *MPP* becomes negative and total output therefore falls. The relationship between *MPP* and total output is shown in Fig. 19.2.

Production and productivity

Production denotes the total amount of a commodity produced by turning factors of production into output, whereas ***productivity*** is the amount of a commodity produced per unit of resources used. When a firm is improving its efficiency, productivity will be rising; that is, if, by better management, more efficient equipment or better use of labour, the firm manages to produce the same or a greater amount of product with a smaller amount of resources then it has increased its productivity. However, an increase in output does not necessarily imply an improvement in a firm's efficiency. If, on the other hand, the firm produces an increase in output but only at the expense of an even greater increase in resources then, despite the increase in output, its productivity has fallen.

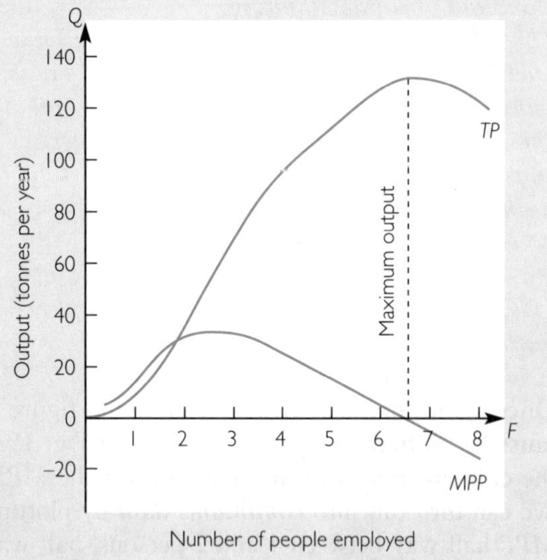

***Fig. 19.2* Marginal physical product and total product**

MPP is zero at the point where total product is maximised.

Common misunderstanding

A rise in total output need not involve an increase in productivity. It may be the result of an even greater increase in the firm's resources, in which case productivity will have fallen. Only when an increase in output is the result of a rise in output per person will a firm be more efficient.

Productivity may be difficult to measure. One of the most common methods is to take the total output and divide it by the number of workers to give ***labour productivity***. Another method, used in agriculture, is to express productivity as output per hectare (see the discussion of productivity in agriculture in Chapter 12). In the example we have been using, productivity is rising while the *APP* is rising and falling when the *APP* is falling. Productivity is vital to the economic welfare of both individual firms and the nation. It is only by becoming more efficient that we can hope to compete with other businesses or nations. We have considered here only a simple case involving two factors of production; other considerations, such as education and training to improve labour productivity and the level of technology that raises the productivity of capital equipment, are vital issues in productivity.

The marginal revenue product (*MRP*)

The marginal physical product is so called because it is measured in ***physical units*** such as tonnes of wheat or barrels of oil, depending upon what is being produced. It is more convenient, however, to express it in money terms. We can do this by examining how much money the *MPP* could have been sold for. For instance, in our example, if the fourth person employed adds 30 tonnes to output and each tonne can be sold for £750 then the ***marginal revenue product*** (*MRP*) is £22 500. Thus the *MRP* can be calculated as:

$$MRP = MPP \times P$$

where *P* is the price of the commodity being produced. However, this formula works only if the firm is producing under conditions of perfect competition, i.e. the firm can sell as much of the product as it likes without lowering the price and hence $P = MR$. (The *MRP* under perfectly competitive conditions is often referred to as the ***value of the marginal product***, or *VMP*). If, on the other hand, the firm was operating under conditions of imperfect competition then, in order to sell more, it would have to lower the price of the product; the change in a firm's revenue as the result of the sale of one more unit of a commodity, i.e. *MR*, is less than the price. Thus, under conditions of imperfect competition, the *MRP* would be calculated as:

$$MRP = MPP \times MR$$

For the sake of simplicity we will assume conditions of perfect competition for most of this chapter.

The *MRP* may be defined as the change to a firm's revenues as a result of the sale of the product of one more unit of a variable factor.

Table 19.2 gives the *MRP* based upon our example and assuming that wheat can be sold at a price of £750 per tonne.

If we plot the *MRP* schedule as a graph we will find that its shape is exactly that of the *MPP* but the units which are used on the vertical axis have now become pounds (see Fig. 19.3).

Table 19.2 **The marginal revenue product**

Number of people employed	*Marginal physical product, MPP (tonnes of wheat)*	*Price of wheat per tonne, P (£)*	*Marginal revenue product, MRP = MRP × P (£)*
0		750	
	12		9 000
1		750	
	24		18 000
2		750	
	34		25 500
3		750	
	30		22 500
4		750	
	20		15 000
5		750	
	10		7 500
6		750	
	0		0
7		750	
	–10		–7 500
8		750	

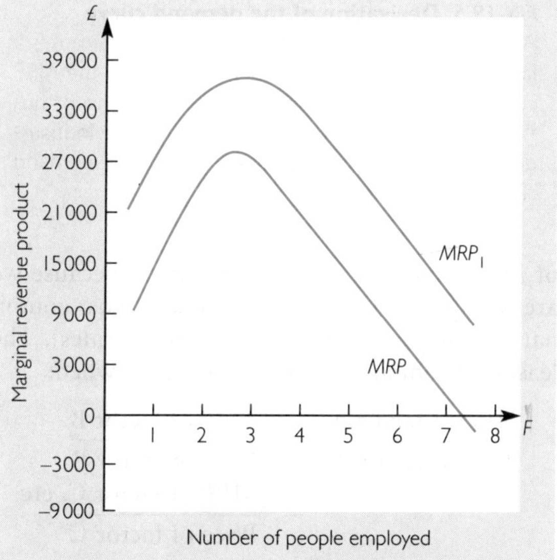

Fig. 19.3 **The marginal revenue product curve**
The shift from *MRP* to MRP_1 could be the result of an improvement in technology or an increase in the price of the product.

STUDENT ACTIVITY 19.2

Given a constant price per unit for the product of £800, calculate the *MRP* figures based on the information from Student activity 19.1.

The firm's demand for a factor

We calculate the *MRP* in order that we may explain the quantity of a factor of production which a firm will demand. This we will find is the quantity of the factor at which its *MRP* is equal to its price. If, for example, the *MRP* of a unit of labour were £25 500 per year and the cost of that unit of labour were £9000 per year, the business would obviously be £16 500 better off as a result of employing that unit of labour. If the *MRP* of the next unit of labour fell to £22 500, but the cost of it remained £9000, the firm would still employ that unit of the factor since it would be a further £13 500 better off. In other words the business will go on demanding a factor of production while the *MRP* of that factor is greater than the cost of employing it.

This is best understood graphically. In Fig. 19.4 if the wage rate were £11 250 per person, the best number of people for the firm to employ would be five. The cost of labour would be the area under the wage line, i.e. 5 × £11 250. The shaded area above the wage line and below the *MRP* curve would be the money the business would get back over and above the cost of employing the factor. The firm will always be best off by trying to obtain as much of this shaded area as possible. If, for example, the wage fell to as low as £3750 then the firm would employ six people, but if the wage rose to £18 750 it would be best off employing only four people. Thus:

> **The firm's *MRP* curve for a factor is its demand curve for that factor provided that the price of the commodity being produced remains fixed.**

The industry's demand for a factor

If we consider a fall in the price of the factor, this will have the effect of causing the firm to hire more of the variable factor. However, if all other firms in the industry do the same thing this will cause a rise in output and, therefore, a fall in the price of the product. As a result the *MRP* curve will shift leftwards. In Fig. 19.5 OT represents the original price of the factor and the quantity of the factor employed is OL where the price of the factor coin-

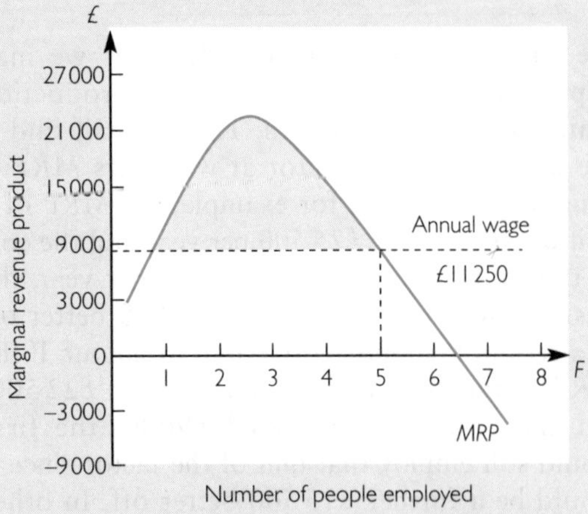

***Fig. 19.4* The marginal revenue product and wages**
The best number of workers for the firm to employ is five. This is where the marginal revenue product is equal to the wage rate.

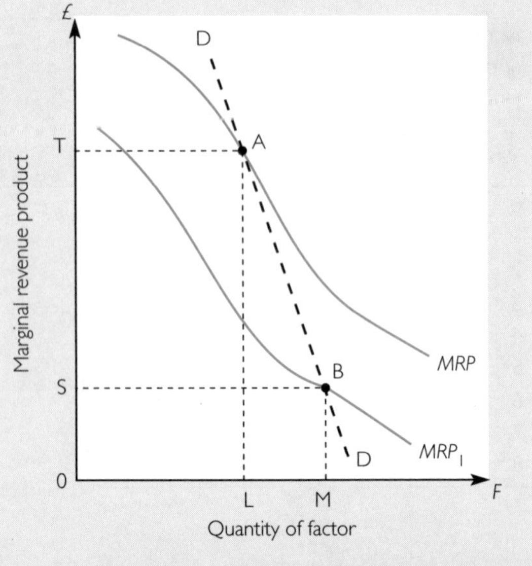

***Fig. 19.5* Derivation of the demand curve**
A fall in the price of the factor from OT to OS causes a fall in the price of the product, which shifts the *MRP* curve to MRP_1. The equilibrium shifts from A to B; thus AB is the demand curve for the firm. The industry demand curve is the horizontal sum of the demand curves of the individual firms.

cides with the original *MRP* curve. The leftward movement of the *MRP* curve to MRP_1 shows the effect of a fall in the price of the commodity. The price of the factor is now OS and the firm employs OM units of the factor. We have thus moved from point A on curve *MRP* to B on MRP_1. If we join up these points this gives the firm's demand curve for the factor, given the effect of a fall in the price of a factor on the price of the product. In these circumstances, the ***industry demand curve for a factor*** is the horizontal sum of the demand curves of the individual firms; this demand curve is therefore less elastic than the firm's demand curve.

The best factor combination

The profit maximisation equilibrium for a firm would be when the conditions of *MRP* = price of the factor have been fulfilled for each factor. Thus, it will be where:

MRP of factor A = Price of factor A

and:

MRP of factor B = Price of factor B

and so on.

If we wish to obtain the least cost combination of factors at any output we must abandon the use of *MRP*s and return to *MPP*s. This is because we are trying to explain simply the least cost combination without reference to revenues (sales). The least cost combination will be achieved when:

$$\frac{MPP \text{ of factor A}}{\text{Price of factor A}} = \frac{MPP \text{ of factor B}}{\text{Price of factor B}} = \frac{MPP \text{ of factor C, etc.}}{\text{Price of factor C}}$$

Thus, if MPP_B/P_B were greater than MPP_A/P_A then the firm could produce the same output at a lower cost by hiring more of A and less of B until equality was achieved.

The above conditions assume that all factors are variable and are thus long-run conditions. We will return to this at the end of the chapter.

The demand and supply curves for a factor

The *MRP* curve gives us a normal downward-sloping demand curve for factors of production, showing that more of a factor is demanded at a lower price. This is true both for the firm and for the industry. We have so far assumed that the supply curve is horizontal, i.e. that the firm could employ more of a factor without affecting its price. However, if an industry wished to employ more of a factor it is likely that it would have to pay more to attract the factor from other uses. We would thus have a normal upward-sloping supply curve. Therefore, we are able to analyse factor markets with the same tools of microeconomic analysis that we used for consumer goods markets.

STUDENT ACTIVITY 19.3

Identify those conditions that may cause the industry demand or supply curve for a factor to shift, either to the left or to the right.

Problems with the theory of distribution

The theory explains how the prices of factors of production are determined in competitive markets and thus how incomes are determined. However, there are a number of factors which distort the allocation of incomes:

a) *Non-homogeneity*. The theory assumes that all units of a factor are identical. This is not true, either of the quality of a factor or of the size of the units in which it is supplied.
b) *Immobility*. The theory assumes that factors of production can move about freely, both from industry to industry and area to area. In practice serious difficulties are attached to the free movement of factors.
c) *Inheritance*. Marginal distribution theory is also supposed to explain how the national income is distributed between the owners of the factors of production. However, in addition to income there is wealth, which may also be a source of income. In the UK, as in most other countries, the majority of wealth is obtained by inheritance and this is outside the operation of market forces.
d) *Political–legal*. The value of factors such as land is often determined by planning regulations, etc.
e) *Historical*. The value of factors such as land and labour can also be affected by historical factors such as industrial inertia.

These criticisms notwithstanding, marginal revenue theory is one of the best aids we have to understanding the cost structures of an organisation.

Resources and costs

In this section of the chapter we will demonstrate that the principles associated with the utilisation of resources, which we have just examined, are consistent with the cost structures of the firm which we examined in the previous section of the book.

The cost structures of the firm

So far the one cost we have been concerned with has been labour, and in our example we have assumed a wage rate of £11 250 per year. Let us assume that labour costs are the only variable costs of the firm and that fixed costs (land, capital, etc.) amount to £30 000 per year. This having been done, we are able to project the cost schedules shown in Table 19.3.

a) *Variable costs*. In Table 19.3 you can see that variable costs increase as the number of people employed increases. If one person is employed then variable costs are £11 250; if two people are employed this becomes £22 500, and so on.
b) *Average costs*. We calculate average costs as before by dividing total costs by output. Because the example we have been using in this chapter is based upon the number of people employed, the output increases in rather uneven amounts. Thus if two people are employed, then average costs (*ATC*) are calculated by dividing total costs by the output of 36; if three people are employed then the total costs are arrived at by dividing total costs by the output of 70, and so on. Similar calculations will produce the figures for average fixed costs (*AFC*) and average variable costs (*AVC*) shown in Table 19.3.
c) *Marginal costs*. It will be recalled that marginal cost is the cost of producing one more unit of a commodity. However, in our example here we are faced with the problem that output increases in uneven amounts as each additional unit of the variable factor is employed. We can get round this problem, though, by taking the increase in costs as each extra unit of variable

***Table 19.3* The cost structures of the firm**

Number of people employed	*Total output of wheat, Q (tonnes/ year)*	*Marginal physcial product, MPP (tonnes/ year)*	*Average product, APP (tonnes/ year)*	*Fixed costs, FC (£)*	*Variable costs, VC (£)*	*Total costs, TC (FC+VC)*	*Average fixed costs, AFC* (FC/Q)*	*Average variable costs, AVC* (VC/Q)*	*Marginal costs, MC* (ΔTC/ΔQ)*	*Average costs, AC* (TC/Q)*
0	0		0	30 000	0	30 000	∞	–		∞
		12							938	
1	12		12	30 000	11 250	41 250	2500	938		3438
		14							469	
2	36		18	30 000	22 500	52 500	833	625		1458
		34							331	
3	70		23.3	30 000	33 750	63 750	429	482		911
		30							375	
4	100		25	30 000	45 000	75 000	300	450		750
		20							563	
5	120		24	30 000	56 250	86 250	250	469		719
		10							1125	
6	130		21.6	30 000	67 500	97 500	231	519		750
		0							∞	
7	130		18.5	30 000	78 750	108 750	231	606		837
		−10							–	
8	120		15	30 000	90 000	120 000	–			–

* To nearest whole number.

factor is employed and dividing it by the number of extra units produced. For example, if the firm employs four people rather than three, then total cost rises from £63 750 to £75 000 and the output rises from 70 to 100 tonnes. Thus, we can obtain marginal cost (*MC*) by dividing the increase in total costs (ΔTC) by the increase in output (ΔQ); this gives us £11 250/30, which in turn gives the figure of £375 for marginal cost. (This method of calculating *MC* is also known as average incremental cost (*AIC*).) We have thus obtained an approximation for *MC* which is:

$$MC = \frac{\Delta TC}{\Delta Q}$$

When it comes to plotting these figures graphically we must plot *MC* half-way between the outputs we are considering. Thus, in the figures used above, the marginal cost of £375 would be plotted half-way between the output of 70 and 100 tonnes, i.e. at 85 tonnes.

STUDENT ACTIVITY 19.4

Given the information supplied in Student activities 19.1 and 19.2, coupled with the fact that fixed costs are £15 000 and the price of labour, the sole variable factor, is £12 000 per person per year, calculate the best profit level of output.

Cost curves

If we use the figures in Table 19.3 to construct average and marginal cost curves, we see that they all accord with the principles discussed in Chapter 15. Once again you can see that in Fig. 19.6 the marginal cost curve passes through the bottom of the average cost curves.

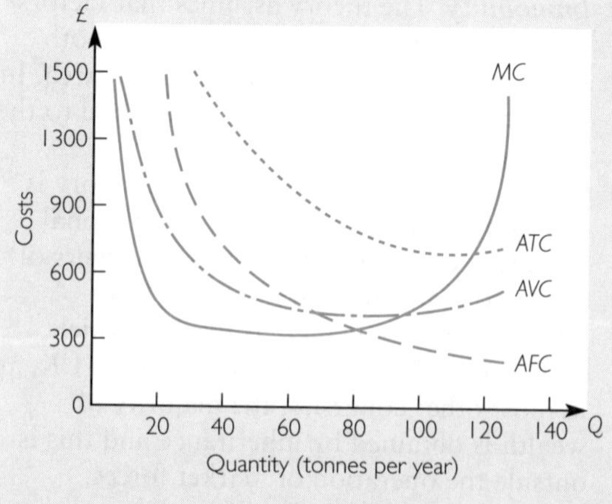

***Fig. 19.6* Cost curves of the firm**
Here:

ATC = AFC + AVC

and the marginal cost curve cuts through the lowest point of *ATC*, *AVC*.

Marginal cost and price

So far we have said the firm will try to equate the *MRP* of a factor with the cost of that factor. The *MRP*, however, depends upon the price at which the product can be sold. In Fig. 19.3 we assumed that the price of wheat was £750 per tonne and therefore we obtained an *MRP* curve by multiplying *MPP* by the price. We can then proceed to develop the cost structures of the firm based on these assumptions. In Table 19.4 we demonstrate the best profit output based on these same assumptions about costs and price. We also include in Table 19.4 the *MC* schedule.

Having obtained *MC* from the example we are able to use this to confirm the proposition in Chapter 16 that, assuming perfectly competitive conditions, the best profit output for the firm is the one at which *MC* = *P*. In Fig. 19.7 you can see that this occurs at the output of 120 tonnes, this being the same output at which *MRP* is equal to the price of the variable factor. Thus the analysis we have developed in this chapter is consistent with the analysis in Chapter 16.

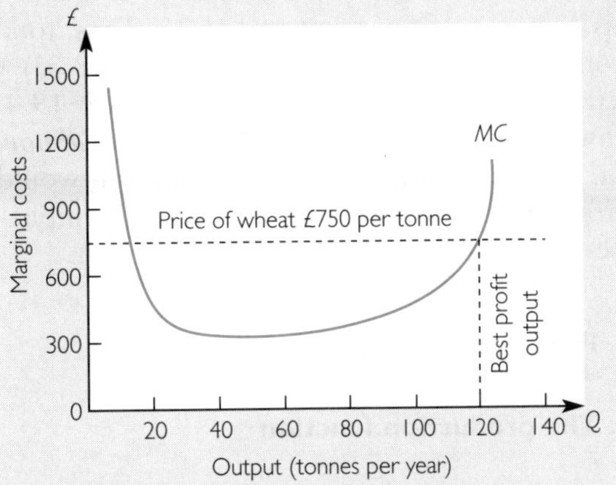

Fig. 19.7 **The best profit output**

As we have assumed so far in this chapter that there is perfect competition, then the price of £750 per tonne is also the marginal revenue (*MR*). This result therefore confirms the proposition that profit maximisation occurs where *MR* = *MC*.

At the output of 120 tonnes per year the firm makes a profit of £3750 per year. At this output

Table 19.4 **The best profit output of the firm**

Number of people employed	*Output of wheat, Q (tonnes/year)*	*Price of wheat, P (£/tonne)*	*Marginal revenue product, MRP (MRP × P)*	*Total revenue, TR (P × Q)*	*Total costs, TC (FC × VC)*	*Total profit, TP (TR – TC)*	*Marginal cost, MC* (ΔTC/ΔQ)*
0	0	750		0	30 000	–30 000	
			9 000				938
1	12	750		9 000	41 250	–32 250	
			18 000				469
2	36	750		27 000	52 500	–28 250	
			25 500				331
3	70	750		52 500	63 750	–11 250	
			21 500				375
4	100	750		75 000	75 000	0	
			15 000				563
5	120	750		90 000	86 250	3750	
			7500				1125
6	130	750		97 500	97 500	0	
			0				∞
7	130	750		97 500	108 750	–11 250	
			7500				–
8	120	750		90 000	120 000	–30 000	

* To nearest whole number

average costs are £718.75 and, since price is £750, this gives a profit per unit of £31.25. Thus, total profit is $TP = (AR - AC) \times Q = (750 - 718.75) \times 120 = £3750$, as confirmed in Table 19.4. However, it should be recalled that this is ***abnormal profit*** and, therefore, in the long run would attract new firms into the industry. This emphasises the fact that this is a short-run situation.

Production in the long run

The production function

Our example so far has mainly concerned the short run where at least one factor of production is fixed in supply. In the long run all costs may be varied. To illustrate the principles involved we will use just two factors of production, capital and labour.

It is possible for a firm to produce the same output using different combinations of capital and labour, i.e. labour may be substituted for capital or vice versa. Figure 19.8 shows a production function for product X. You can see that the output of 69 units of X can be produced by using 6 units of capital and 1 unit of labour, or 3 units of capital and 2 of labour, and so on. Similarly, an output of 98 units of X could be produced with various, greater, quantities of capital and labour.

If we move horizontally across the production function – for example, if we use 3 units of capital and then add successive units of labour – the gap between each successive level of output will give us the *MPP* of labour. Similarly, moving vertically would show the *MPP* of capital.

Isoquants

If the various combinations of factors of production which produce the same amount of output are plotted as a graph this produces an ***isoquant*** or ***equal product curve.*** In Fig. 19.9, IQ_1 plots the various combinations of capital–labour which would produce an output of 69 units of product X. Similarly, IQ_2 is the isoquant for the output of 98 units of X. A rightward movement of the isoquant shows a move to a higher level of production and the use of greater quantities of factors of production.

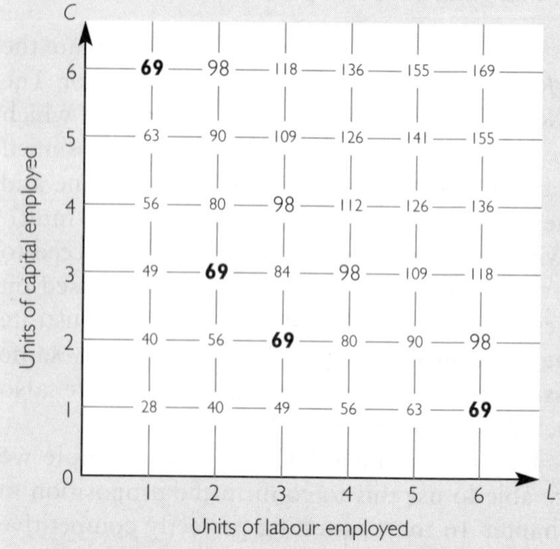

***Fig. 19.8* Production function**

This shows quantities of product X which can be produced by various combinations of labour and capital.

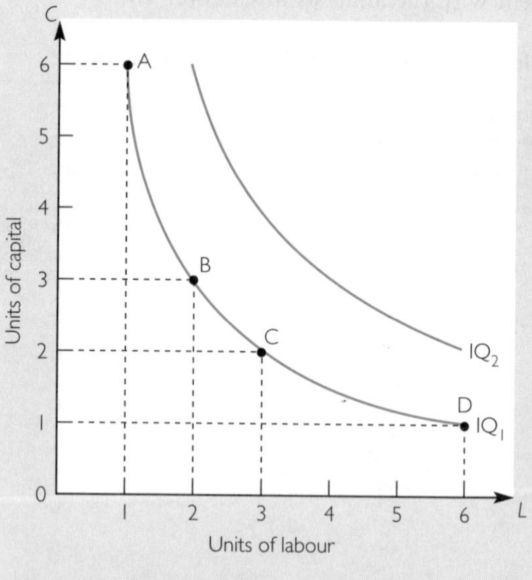

***Fig. 19.9* Isoquants**

Isoquants join the combinations of factors which would produce the same quantity of a product. IQ_1 gives the combinations which would produce 69 units of X and IQ_2 gives the combinations which would produce 98 units of X. A series of IQ curves is termed an isoquant map.

Theoretically we can construct any number of isoquants on the graph to produce an ***isoquant map***. The reader may notice here the similarity with indifference curves (see Chapter 9). What reason is to be found for the isoquant being a similar shape? The reason is that although capital can be substituted for labour or vice versa they are not perfect substitutes. Therefore as we substitute capital for labour, for example, it takes more and more units of capital to replace labour as capital becomes a less and less perfect substitute. In Fig. 19.9 if we move from point C to point B, 1 unit of labour can be replaced by 1 unit of capital, but if we move to point A then the next unit of labour given up requires 3 units of capital to replace it. In fact, the substitution ratio of one factor for another at any point on the curve is equivalent to the ratio of their respective marginal physical products.

STUDENT ACTIVITY 19.5

You can check that you understand this point by starting from point B in Fig. 19.9 and examining how the same thing happens in reverse as labour is substituted for capital.

The slope of the isoquant shows the substitution ratios of the factors of production.

Isocost lines

In Fig. 19.10, using the same axes, we can construct a graph to show the relative prices of the two factors of production. If, for example, capital costs £100 per unit per time period while labour costs £150 per unit, then a line drawn from 3 units of capital to 2 units of labour would show us all the combinations of capital and labour which could be bought for a cost of £300. Similarly, a line from 6 units of capital to 4 of labour would show combinations costing £600 and so on. The *isocost lines* stay parallel to one another so long as the relative prices of the two factors remain unchanged.

The slope of the isocost shows the ratio of the relative prices of the factors of production.

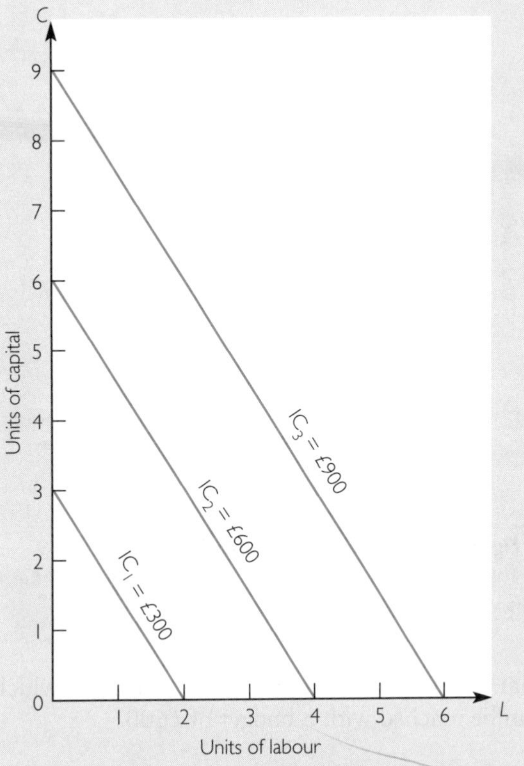

Fig. 19.10 **Isocosts**
Each isocost joins all the combinations of factors which can be bought with the same amount of money. The isocosts here are drawn on the assumption that capital costs £100 per unit and labour costs £150 per unit.

The least cost combination

If we combine the isocosts and the isoquants on one diagram we can demonstrate how a firm could achieve the least cost combination. This occurs when an isoquant is just tangential to an isocost. For example, if we wish to produce an output of 69 units of X then the cheapest cost at which this can be achieved is £600. This is illustrated in Fig. 19.11.

The least cost factor combination occurs where the rate of substitution is equal to the ratio of the relative prices of the factors of production.

We could explain this by saying either that it is the isocost nearest to the origin which can produce an output of 69 units or, alternatively,

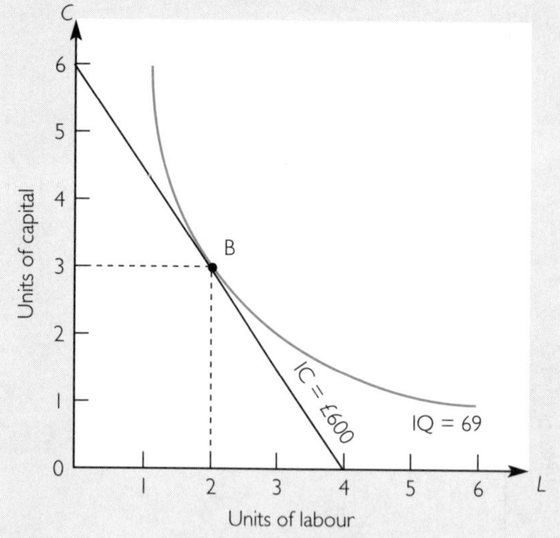

***Fig. 19.11* The least cost output**
The least cost output for the firm is at point B where the isoquant is tangential to the isocost line.

that it is the isoquant furthest to the right which can be reached with a budget of £600.

STUDENT ACTIVITY 19.6

You can confirm this by checking the cost of producing 69 units in Fig. 19.8. (You will see that all other combinations result in a higher cost.)

Given the fact that the slope of an isoquant is represented by the ratio of the marginal physical products of the two factors and that the slope of an isocost is given by the ratio of the relative factor prices, then the least cost factor combination occurs at the tangency point of an isoquant with an isocost, where:

$$\frac{MPP \text{ of factor A}}{MPP \text{ of factor B}} = \frac{\text{Price of factor A}}{\text{Price of factor B}}$$

Rearranging gives:

$$\frac{MPP \text{ of factor A}}{\text{Price of factor A}} = \frac{MPP \text{ of factor B}}{\text{Price of factor B}}$$

This is the equation for the best factor combination achieved earlier in the chapter.

Expansion path

If we undertook the same operation as above for various levels of expenditure, then we could achieve the cost minimisation expansion path for the firm. In Fig 19.12 this is line ABC.

Conclusions

In this chapter we have attempted to deal with the principles governing the use of the factors of production both in the short run and in the long run. These principles will be applied in the following chapters to each of the factors of production. There are, however, important tie-ups with earlier parts of the book, such as the theory of the firm. To check that you have understood the implications of the ideas in this chapter you are advised to work through the questions at the end.

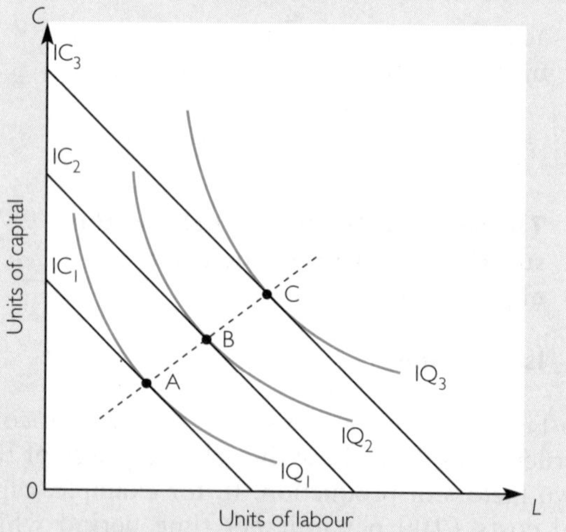

***Fig. 19.12* An expansion path**
As total expenditure increases from IC_1 to IC_2 to IC_3 the least cost combination shifts from A to B to C. Thus this is the expansion path for the firm.

Summary

1 The theory of distribution is concerned with the distribution of income between the factors of production.

2 The marginal physical product is the amount added to production from the employment of one more unit of a variable factor.
3 The marginal revenue product is the change to the firm's revenue from the sale of the marginal physical product.
4 The *MRP* curve of a factor is a firm's demand curve for that factor.
5 The industry demand curve is less elastic than the firm's demand curve for a factor.
6 The demand and supply of a factor can be analysed in a similar way to consumer demand and supply.
7 Marginal productivity theory can also be used to explain the cost structures of a firm.
8 An isoquant shows the various quantities of factors of production which are needed to produce the same quantity of a product.
9 An isocost shows all the combinations of a factor which can be used at a given level of cost.
10 The least cost combination for the firm is where the isoquant is tangential to the isocost, i.e. where the substitution ratio is equal to the relative prices of the factors of production.

Questions

1 The following data show the variation in output of product X as inputs of labour are increased.

Labour	1	2	3	4	5	6
Total product	5	15	24	28	30	30

a) Calculate the marginal and average physical products.
b) Plot these on a graph.
c) Indicate on the graph over what output there are increasing returns and over what output there are diminishing returns.

2 Redraft Table 19.4 assuming that fixed costs rise to £60 000, the wage rate increases to £18 000 and the price of wheat increases to £1200 per tonne. Determine the best profit output for the business.

3 What shortcomings are there to marginal distribution theory as an explanation for the distribution of income?

4 Examine Fig. 19.4. If Marxists were to look at this diagram they would argue that all the shaded area is the product of labour of which it is being deprived. Do you agree? Give reasons for your answer.

5 Computer technology should increase the *MRP* curve, thus increasing wages and employment. Reconcile this with the fact that the same technology replaces labour and creates unemployment.

6 Redraw Fig. 19.11 assuming that capital increases in cost to £200 per unit. If the firm still wishes to produce 69 units of X what would now be the least cost combination and why?

7 Use the production function in Fig. 19.8 to confirm the proposition that the least cost combination is where:

$$\frac{\textit{MPP}\text{ of labour}}{\text{Price of labour}} = \frac{\textit{MPP}\text{ of capital}}{\text{Price of capital}}$$

(Note: The answers may be slightly inaccurate owing to rounding the figures to whole numbers.)

8 Under what circumstances will a rise in wages lead to unemployment?

Data response A
The Eversharp Pencil Company

The data in the table refers to the Eversharp Pencil Company, which manufactures ballpoint pens. The company has premises and machinery which cost it £250 per week.

Productivity of Eversharp

Number of people employed	*Average product (pens/week)*
0	0
1	2500
2	2750
3	3500
4	4375
5	4500
6	4250
7	3785.8
8	3187.5

1 From this data calculate the marginal physical product (*MPP*) schedule of labour at Eversharp and plot it as a graph.

2 Suppose that Eversharp is able to sell any number of ballpoints it wishes to a distributor at a price of 10 pence each. Further suppose that Eversharp is able to employ workers at £200 per person per week. Calculate the marginal revenue product (*MRP*) schedule and, with the aid of a graph, determine how many workers Eversharp would wish to employ.

3 Assuming that Eversharp's only variable cost is labour determine the profit maximisation output.

4 Calculate the effects of doubling the wage rate to £400. Determine the number of people that Eversharp will now wish to employ and its profit maximisation output.

5 In question 4 it should be apparent that an increase in the wage rate would cause the business to contract both output and employment. Since the Second World War real wages have risen and, for most of the period, so have output and employment. Explain how this is possible. Your answer should also consider whether marginal revenue product theory has any relevance to the very high levels of unemployment since the late 1970s.

Data response B
How to bring technology to book

Read the following article on the shortcomings of accountancy procedures and then attempt the questions which follow.

Conventional accounting is ill-equipped to deal with modern manufacturing. Technology has left accounting behind and as a result managers are making important decisions about product mix and pricing on the basis of unreliable information.

This is the central thesis behind the work of Robert Kaplan at Harvard Business School. In a series of articles and books published in the latter half of the 1980s, Kaplan and other business academics popularised the idea of 'activity-based costing' – ABC – as a solution to the problem of old-fashioned accounting in a modern factory environment.

The UK's Chartered Institute of Management Accountants (CIMA) is poised to publish the results of a research project into three British companies which have adopted ABC. Two of the case studies by John Innes and Falconer Mitchell of the University of Edinburgh are manufacturers, but one is a large, long-established retail group with several hundred stores and a listing on the London Stock Exchange.

The idea behind ABC is that managers should take a rigorous look at the activities – such as materials-handling, number of orders, size of orders and so forth – which determine overhead costs. By becoming alert to the true 'cost-drivers' of a business, the manager is able to make better decisions about what products to make and how much to charge for them.

Vigorously marketed by squadrons of management consultants from the big accountancy firms, these ideas have been taken up by manufacturing businesses in the US and Europe. The third CIMA case study is unusual because it shows that an activity-based approach can work in an environment very different from that of an automated factory.

The identity of the company is not disclosed; the researchers call it Gamma. It has had a patchy profits record and the regular lurches into losses prompted a review of the company's cost structure.

Over 25 000 separate product lines are bought, distributed and sold by Gamma. Sale volumes are very high, and profitability is highly sensitive to the profit margin achieved on each product. A small change in the volume/margin mix could significantly affect its earnings per share and ultimately its share price.

The essential problem identified by the review was that there was no meaningful data on the cost of the individual product lines. The only information available to the managers was the buy-in cost of each product plus a fixed percentage add-on to cover overheads. Overhead allocation was thus determined solely by the product value, and not by other factors (such as size, weight and fragility) which might influence selling and distribution costs.

'It was obvious our product line costs weren't accurate,' Gamma's commercial manager told the researchers. 'Anyone with basic sense could see that. We needed our costs to reflect the work a product line caused us and the company facilities it used.'

Gamma has four types of cost: the buy-in price of the merchandise; distribution; storage; central overheads and finance charges. The project concentrated on distribution and storage. The aim was to identify the 'cost-drivers' – i.e. the factors which determined storage and distribution costs.

These were identified as: the recording of freight movements; unloading deliveries from suppliers at a central depot; storing suppliers' deliveries; selecting items to comply with store orders; checking orders and loading deliveries to the stores. 'It was clear that the cost associated with these activities varied considerably among Gamma's product lines,' the report says.

The two most important drivers were found to be the size or bulk of the package in which the individual products were contained and the extent to which it was necessary to break open the package when delivered. All the company's product lines were categorised into six classifications around the two drivers.

These classifications were then used as a basis for allocating labour costs from product to product. Occupational costs – such as rates, rent, light and depreciation – were allocated on the basis of the bulk (by cubic feet) of the package.

As a result of this exercise, managers for the first time had net margin figures available for each product line. 'The differences in product line profitability compared with gross margin ... were considerable and extensive. Many popular lines with highly satisfactory gross margins proved to be making net losses due to their high use of distribution and retail resources within Gamma.'

The information helped with management decisions. Those products with a high net margin and a high volume of sales could be considered for extra promotion and display; those with a high margin but low volume would get more advertising those selling in high volume but low net margin could be selected for internal cost reduction, price increases and reductions in promotion. Those products which sold in low quantities and at a low margin could be dropped.

The ABC exercise provided a number of other benefits for management. It increased the visibility of distribution costs and their links to individual products and, as a result, it was easier to identify cost-cutting measures. Management took steps to have suppliers reduce the size of packages, improve the accessibility of the merchandise, and to pack in sizes which removed the need for break-up.

'The danger in using ABC lies too readily in assuming that it provides a panacea which will solve all the problems associated with the provision of costing information to mangement,' the researchers conclude. 'It should be recognised that ABC is not a general purpose system ... suitable, without thought or modification, for use in all areas of control, performance, assessment and managerial decision-making.'

All three companies in this study were optimistic about the future of ABC. They were aware of its limitations but on balance felt that it was a valuable innovation. The Gamma case-study provides a rare example of how ABC can prove valuable in a non-manufacturing environment.

1 Briefly explain what is meant by activity-based costing (ABC).
2 What is the difference between 'the gross profit margin' and the 'net profit margin'?
3 Assess the extent to which the economist's ideas of marginal productivity are relevant to a firm such as Gamma.
4 The report identified several product problems, characters and solutions (see below):

   Explain what is meant by the terms used to describe the characteristics of products and the rationale behind the proposed policies (solutions).
5 Economists put great emphasis on the importance of marginal costs. Do the points raised in the article support this view? Explain your answer.

Characteristics	*Solutions*
High net margin and high sales volume	Extra promotion and display
High margin but low sales volume	More advertising
High sales volume but low net margin	Cost reductions, price increases and reduction in promotion
Low sales volume and low margin	Discontinue sales

20 The determination of wages

Learning outcomes

At the end of this chapter you will be able to:

- Determine the equilibrium wage rate and level of employment under competitive conditions.
- Assess the effect on employment of a monopolistic product market.
- Appreciate those factors that affect the total supply of labour.
- Account for the trade-off between work and leisure by an individual.
- Distinguish between geographic and occupational mobility.
- Understand the role of trade unions as monopolistic suppliers of labour.
- Appreciate those factors determining a union's bargaining strength.
- Outline the reasons underlying the fall in union membership and the decline in industrial action by unions.
- Recognise the effects on wages and employment of a monopsonistic buyer of labour.
- Explain the reasons for wage differentials.
- Understand the factors causing disequilibrium situations in labour markets.
- Outline the costs of job search for both employers and employees.

The determination of the wage rate and level of employment

Assuming competitive conditions

The wage rate will be determined by the interaction of the organisation's demand for labour and the supply of labour forthcoming.

In the previous chapter we saw that an organisation's demand for a factor of production is the marginal revenue product (*MRP*) curve of that factor. The supply of labour, you will remember, is determined by such things as the size and age distribution of the population (see Chapter 4). Without interference from the government or trade unions and assuming perfectly competitive conditions the wage rate and level of employment will be determined by the forces of demand and supply. This is illustrated in Fig. 20.1, in which the demand for and supply of labour curves for a particular industry have been summed from the demand curves of single firms on the one hand and from the supply curves of individuals on the other. Initially the ***equilibrium*** level of wages and employment settle at O*W* and OM respectively. The movement of the demand curve from DD to D_1D_1 leads to a rise in the equilibrium wage rate at OW_1 and an increase in the level of employment to OM_1.

STUDENT ACTIVITY 20.1

What factors may cause a rightward shift in the demand for labour curve, as in Fig. 20.1?

Employment and the monopolist

If a firm is the monopoly supplier of a product, then, as the monopolist sells more of the product, it will have to lower the price of the product. Thus the *MRP* for labour is determined by the formula:

$$MRP = MPP \times MR$$

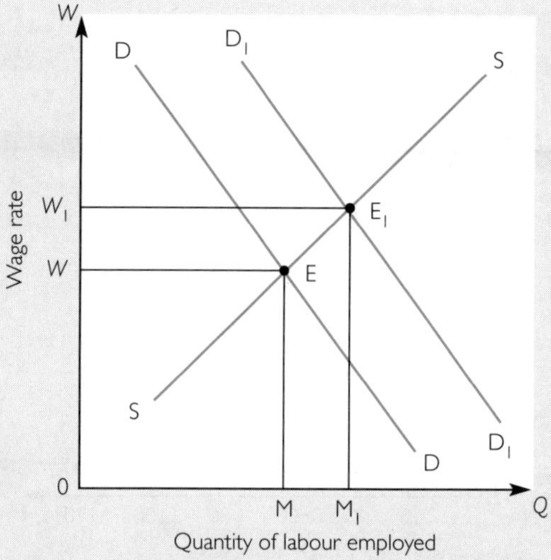

Fig. 20.1 **The determination of wage rate**
The original wage rate is OW at equilibrium E. The movement to E_1 and to a higher wage of OW_1 shows the effect of an increase in demand for labour.

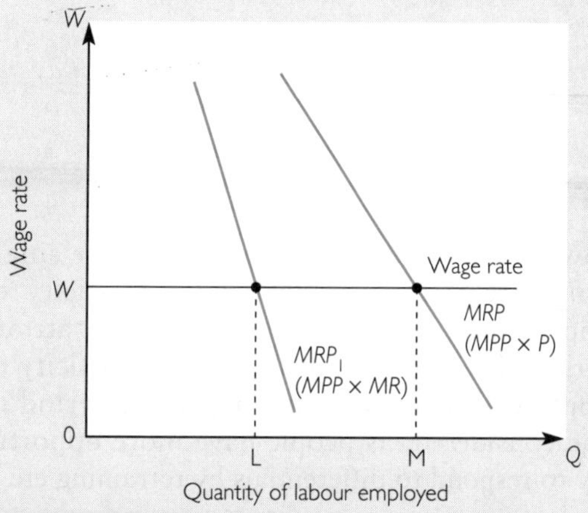

Fig. 20.2 **Employment and the monopolist**
Under perfect competition the business would employ OM units of labour, but under monopoly:

$MRP = MPP \times MR$

and therefore the monolpolist restricts employment to OL.

rather than:

$$MRP = MPP \times P$$

This is illustrated in Fig. 20.2. Thus curve *MRP* represents the firm's demand curve for labour as it would be under perfect competition and MRP_1 as it is under monopoly. We have here assumed that the wage rate remains constant. Thus we can see that the monopolist will choose to employ OL units of labour rather than OM as it would under conditions of competitive supply.

Under conditions of monopoly the employer will tend to restrict the employment of a factor.

This restriction of employment in the labour market is associated with the monopolist's restriction of supply of consumer goods. Both therefore distort the optimum allocation of resources (see Chapter 18).

The supply of labour

Total supply and industry supply

We examined the factors underlying the demand curve for a factor in some depth in the previous chapter, but we did not say much about the supply curve other than that it can be assumed that it is upward sloping. In this section we shall explore those factors determining the supply of labour in a little more detail.

The total supply of labour (the ***working population*** or ***workforce***) is determined primarily by non-economic factors such as the size of the population and its age and sex distribution (see Chapter 4). It may also be influenced by institutional factors such as the school leaving age and social attitudes to such things as women working (although this fact can now be safely taken for granted). In general, therefore, the total supply of labour is highly inelastic, although that is not to say that it may not be varied by exceptional circumstances, as was seen in the Second World War when many women went out to work.

In the last 20 years the main changes in the pattern of employment have been the steady decline in male full-time jobs and the fairly dramatic increase in female employment, especially part-time.

Common misunderstanding

The workforce does not simply consist of those in full-time jobs. It also consists of part-time workers as well as those registered as unemployed. The workforce comprises those of working age who are available for work; they are the economically active, whether employed or unemployed, in full-time occupations or in part-time positions.

However, if we consider an industry or single firm there is a great deal more elasticity of supply, since offering higher wages will attract workers from other industries. The elasticity of supply will be greater the longer the period of time considered, as people have more opportunity to respond to differentials by retraining etc.

The leisure preference

The supply of labour is also influenced by the length of the working week. Here we encounter the factor known as the ***leisure preference***. As real wages have risen over this century people have taken the opportunity not only to consume increased quantities of goods and services, but also to reduce the length of the working week. They have, therefore, consumed part of the income as increased leisure. The possibilities for the individual confronted with a rise in the wage rate are illustrated in Fig. 20.3. In the original situation the wage rate is £2.50 per hour. The various possibilities for the worker are, therefore, represented by the budget line TA. At T the worker enjoys 24 hours' leisure but no income, while at A the worker has an income of £60 per day but has to work 24 hours to earn it. Suppose that the worker chooses point E working 10 hours a day, i.e. 14 hours of leisure, and an income of £25. Now suppose that the wage rate doubles to £5 per hour, so that the worker's budget line is now TB. As a result of this, three possibilities confront the worker.

First, the worker may continue to work the same number of hours and therefore moves to point Y, so that income now increases to £50 per day. Second, the worker could choose to take some of the increase in more leisure and some as more income; for example, at point X income would rise to £40 per day and the working day decreases to 8 hours. The third possibility is that, in response to the higher wage rate, longer hours are worked; for example, at point Z the working day has increased to 12 hours and therefore the wage to £60.

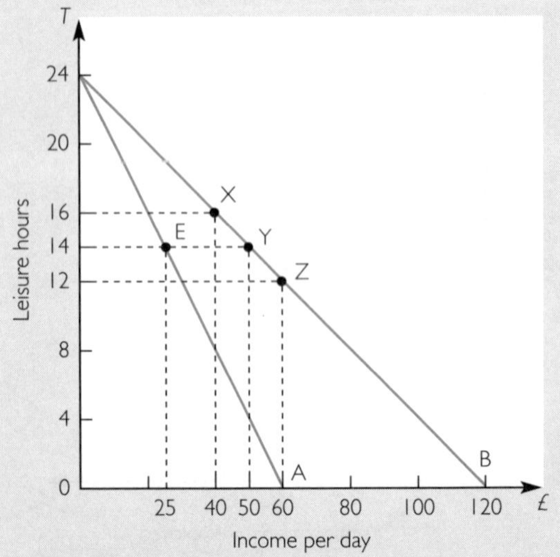

***Fig. 20.3* The leisure preference**
The increase in wages from £2.50/hour to £5.00/hour moves the budget line outwards from TA to TB. Originally the worker supplied 10 hours of work per day (point E). As a result of the increase in pay the worker may move to position X, Y or Z.

Historically, what seems to have happened is that workers have moved towards the position represented by X, i.e. a shorter working week. The possibility therefore exists for a ***perverse*** or ***backward-sloping supply curve for labour***, where increasing the wage rate (at least, beyond a certain level of real wage) causes less labour to be supplied. Some industries, such as coal-mining, where the work is extremely unpleasant, exhibit a very high leisure preference and, thus, effort has sometimes gone down as wages have gone up.

STUDENT ACTIVITY 20.2

Given the possibility of a perverse supply of labour curve, comment on the feasibility of cutting income taxes as an incentive to make people work harder.

Labour mobility

The supply of labour is also affected by labour mobility because the lack of mobility may restrict the supply of labour. Labour mobility is a key determinant of the elasticity of labour supply to a particular industry or type of job. There are two main types of mobility.

a) *Occupational mobility*. This refers to the ease with which people move from one type of job to another. If a person were to give up a job as a steel worker and become a teacher this would be an example of occupational mobility. This type of mobility is likely to be influenced by the amount of training required for a job, the reluctance of workers to change jobs, the restrictions on job entry placed by unions and professional associations and by the age of the person concerned.
b) *Geographical mobility*. This refers to the ease with which people move from a job in one area to a similar job in another area. This is restricted by the unwillingness of people to leave the social ties they may have in an area, by the difficulty of finding housing, the reluctance to disturb their children's education, the cost of moving and the lack of information about opportunities elsewhere in the economy. Surprisingly, in the past geographical mobility has tended to decrease as unemployment has risen because people have become unwilling to risk a new job in an unknown area.

Both types of mobility have tended to be low in the UK compared with a country like the USA. A higher level of mobility would reduce both the level of unemployment and also the differentials between wages. However, moves to make the UK labour market more *flexible* (see Chapter 45) are designed to raise labour mobility, especially occupational mobility, and reduce demarcation disputes (see below).

Trade unions and wages

Most labour markets are subject to imperfections. These may be both on the demand side (employers) or the supply side (employees). Improving productivity is one of the most certain ways of increasing wages, although there is little that trade unions can do about it *per se*. Trade unions may, of course, be involved in agreements with employers to increase productivity.

Trade unions therefore tend to work by affecting the supply of labour.

In so doing a trade union may act as a ***monopoly supplier*** of labour.

Restrictive labour practices

A most effective way for trade unions to increase their members' wages is to restrict the supply of labour to a particular occupation. This can be done by ***closed-shop*** practices, whereby all workers in an industry or occupation have to belong to a particular union. These are not always aimed at increasing wages but have certainly been used in the past for this purpose in some industries, e.g. printing and film making. The supply of labour to an occupation could also be limited by the enforcement of long apprenticeships or training periods. Another method is ***demarcation***, where particular tasks in a job may be done only by members of a particular union, e.g. plumbers not being allowed to do joiners' jobs in a particular factory. In the past demarcation or 'who does what' disputes have been a frequent cause of unrest in UK industrial relations and have affected a wide variety of industries such as shipbuilding and printing. In the late 1980s there was a demarcation dispute about the role of ambulance personnel and paramedics.

Figure 20.4 shows that the effect of restricting the supply of labour is to increase the wage rate from OW to OW_1. It also means that the quantity of labour employed declines from OM to OL. It is estimated that unionised workers receive ***wage premiums*** (i.e. union/non-union wage differentials between groups of similar workers) over their non-union counterparts of about 8–10 per cent in the UK (the estimate for the USA is higher, at between 10–25 per cent).

However, while some workers are receiving higher wages, other people may be unable to

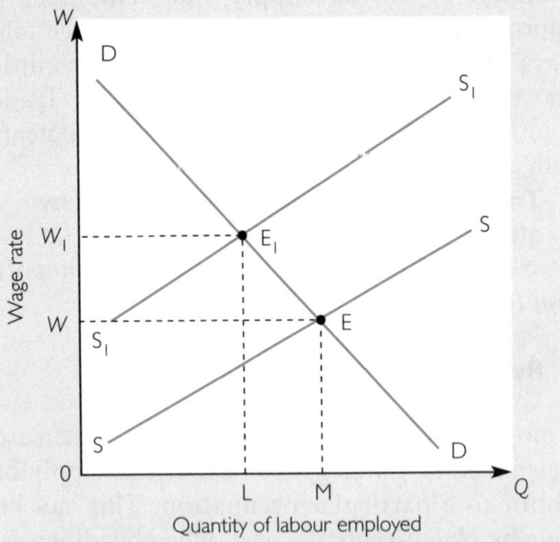

Fig. 20.4 **The effect of restrictive practices upon the wage rate**

By restriciting the supply of labour from SS to S_1S_1 the union is able to raise the wage rate from OW to OW_1, but the quantity of labour employed decreases from OM to OL.

obtain jobs. This kind of practice is not restricted to trade unions; the Inns of Court run a most effective closed shop which restricts the supply of labour to the Bar, thereby keeping out many young lawyers who might like to become practising barristers. This not only has the effect of driving up barristers' fees but also contributes to the delays which bedevil the administration of justice.

Collective bargaining

Working people learned long ago that to ask the employer individually for a wage rise was a good way to lose a job. Trade unions therefore negotiate on behalf of all their members and if agreement is not reached they may take action collectively to enforce their demands. The collective bargaining strength of a trade union varies enormously from industry to industry. Until the unsuccessful strike of 1985 the bargaining strength of coal-miners was regarded as great because there was almost 100 per cent membership of the National Union of Mineworkers, a strong community spirit and the possibility of bringing the country to a standstill. On the other hand, the bargaining strength of some workers in the UK is so poor that the government set up wages councils to determine minimum wage rates. However, the rising tide of unemployment in the 1980s weakened the bargaining power of most workers. Those protected by wages councils saw a further weakening of their position when the government set about restricting the activities of some wages councils and dismantling others. Most were abolished in 1993. Agriculture is the only industry now covered by any form of minimum wage legislation, the Agricultural Wages Boards setting minimum wages for various grades of workers.

Recently there has been a renewal of discussion on the topic of a ***national minimum wage***. The Labour government elected in 1997 has included such a proposal as part of its manifesto, although there is an ongoing debate about the level at which the minimum wage should be set. A minimum wage also forms part of the Social Charter of the EU, which the government signed in 1997. Whether or not such legislation could bring about an increase in wages for the lower paid or whether it would result in increased unemployment has been a subject of much dispute.

STUDENT ACTIVITY 20.3

Given perfectly competitive conditions, if a minimum wage was imposed above the equilibrium level, what factors are likely to influence any resulting job losses? (Figure 20.5 may help you to decide.)

Figure 20.5 illustrates three possibilities for collective bargaining. Which one occurs will depend upon the strength of the union. Here successful collective bargaining has raised the wage rate from OW to OW_1. As a result of this the employer would like to employ less labour (OL instead of OM); this is position A. However, the strength of the union may be such that it is able to insist that the organisation retains the same number of workers as before. This is position B,

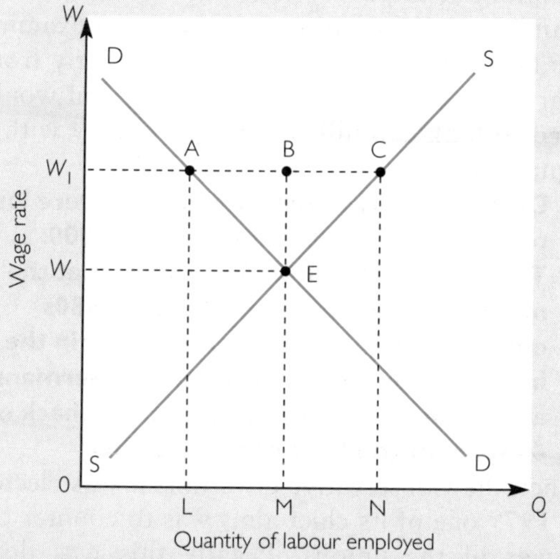

***Fig. 20.5* Collective bargaining and wages**
Collective bargaining raises the wage from the equilibrium level at OW to OW_1, thus creating a disequilibrium. The quantity of labour employed – OL, OM or ON – depends upon the bargaining power of the union.

where the wage rate is higher but the quantity of labour remains OM. As a result of increasing the wage rate more people would like to work for this organisation. In an extreme case the union may be able to insist that the organisation moves to position C where the wage rate is OW_1 and the quantity of labour employed is ON. If the organisation is pushed into this position it may be forced to close down since AC represents a surplus of labour which it would not choose to employ if it were not forced to do so.

Such ***feather-bedding*** and ***overmanning*** have occurred in a number of UK industries, such as newspaper printing, in the past, although the changed industrial relations climate and the effects of the general economic conditions noted below mean that such a scenario is now far less likely to occur.

Common misunderstanding

The establishment of a higher wage through collective bargaining, while quite possibly reducing employment, may not actually create as much unemployment as is first thought. If, in Fig. 20.5, the union negotiates a higher wage of OW_1, fewer people may be employed (i.e. position A). In these circumstances LN workers (i.e. the distance AC) comprise the excess supply of labour. Of these, LM workers were previously employed and therefore can be regarded as unemployed as a result of the higher wage rate. However, the remainder, MN workers, have been encouraged to enter the labour market because of the higher wage; it is not quite so obvious that they have become unemployed in consequence.

Economic factors affecting bargaining strength

The ability of a trade union to raise wages will be influenced not only by its collective bargaining strength but also by several economic factors, which are listed below:

a) *The elasticity of demand for the final product.* If the demand for the product for which labour is being used is highly inelastic, it will be relatively easy for the firm to pass increased wage costs on to the consumer. Conversely, an elastic demand will make it difficult to pass on increased costs and, thus, make it difficult for unions to obtain wage rises.
b) *The proportion of total costs which labour represents.* If labour costs make up a large proportion of total costs this will tend to make it more difficult for workers to obtain wage rises. On the other hand, if the labour costs are a small proportion of the organisation's costs and, more especially, if the worker's task is vital this will tend to make it easier to secure a wage rise. This is referred to by Professor Samuelson as 'the importance of being unimportant'.
c) *The ease of factor substitution.* If it is relatively easy to substitute another factor of production for labour, e.g. capital, this will mean that as unions demand more wages the business will employ fewer workers. In the UK since the Second World War, rising labour costs have encouraged employers to substitute capital for labour wherever possible, e.g. the microprocessor revolution.
d) *The level of profits.* If an organisation is making little or no profit then the effect of a rise in wages could well be to put it out of

business. Conversely, high profits would make it easier for unions to obtain higher wages and job security. High profits in some of the newly privatised industries, such as the utilities, have had the effect of stimulating wage claims.

e) *Macroeconomic influences*. The influences discussed so far are all microeconomic. However, wage bargaining can be influenced by the macroeconomy. First, the general state of the economy affects wage bargaining. If there is economic growth it is easier for unions to obtain wage rises and wage earners tend to capture a larger share of national income, although the reverse is true in times of economic recession and unemployment. Second, inflation influences wage claims. Inflation decreases the real value of wages and, therefore, stimulates demands for higher money wages. Whether wage earners are able to keep pace with inflation depends upon their relative bargaining power. Inflation may also make it easier to obtain higher money wages if the increased costs can easily be passed on as higher prices because of the inflationary climate.

If trade union activity were successful in the national sense it would increase the proportion of the national income going to wages. Nevertheless, despite all the struggles of trade unions, this is not so. The portion of national income going to wages and salaries now is not significantly different from 45 years ago, being 65 per cent of GNP in 1946, 67 per cent in 1961 and 63 per cent in 1995.

Industrial relations in the UK

The UK's record of industrial relations in the past has not been good compared with other industrialised economies. In particular, the economy has been bedevilled with strikes. However, this situation has changed dramatically since the mid to late 1980s.

The withdrawal of labour is the ultimate weapon unions possess. The word 'strike' is very emotive and many people believe that previously strikes have been the cause of the UK's economic difficulties. It is more likely, however, that rather than being a cause, strikes have been more a symptom of the UK's industrial malaise. Rather than expressing opinions it is better to examine the facts. Statistics on strikes vary greatly from year to year, but until the mid 1980s you would need to look carefully to find a country with a significantly worse record than the UK.

During 1979 29.5 million man-days were lost to strikes; in 1995 the total was 415 000. The dramatic fall in strikes meant that the number of days lost from the late 1980s onwards has been among the lowest in the industrialised world. However, the Germans and Japanese have been able to look back on 40 years of good industrial relations.

When the Conservative government was elected in 1979 one of its chief aims was to counter the power of the unions. Legally this was done through the Employment Acts of 1980, 1982, 1988 and 1990, the Trade Union Act of 1984, the Trade Union and Labour Relations Act of 1992 and the Trade Union and Employment Rights Act of 1993. The government saw these as redressing the balance after the privileges given to the unions by the Labour governments of the 1970s.

The 1980 Act made available public funds for secret ballots for such things as electing officers, calling or ending a strike or amending union rules. The Act also gave the Secretary of State wide-ranging power to issue codes of practice 'for the purpose of improving industrial relations'. The 1982 Act, among other things, provided for regular reviews of closed-shop agreements by secret ballot, brought legal immunities for trade unions into line with those of individuals and restricted the meaning of lawful disputes to those between workers and their employers, i.e. it made sympathetic strikes illegal.

The 1984 Trade Union Act made strike action lawful only if sanctioned by a secret ballot of members and it also placed strict limitations on actions such as secondary picketing. This Act also required that every voting member of a union's principal executive committee be (re-)elected by ballot at least every five years.

The 1988 Employment Act made it illegal to dismiss an employee for not wishing to join a union. It also made it unlawful for a union to take action to create or maintain a closed shop.

The 1990 Act made all secondary picketing illegal. It also gave any worker the right of complaint to an industrial tribunal if denied employment when not a member of a union.

The 1992 Act consolidated the earlier Acts into a single piece of legislation. The 1993 Act specified that all ballots in support of union action should be postal and gave individuals much greater freedom to join the union of their choice (therby virtually ending the notion of the closed shop).

Opinions differ as to whether this bout of legislation was an outright attack on trade unions or a much needed attempt to introduce sanity into industrial relations.

Certainly membership of unions has fallen sharply since the early 1980s: in 1980 52 per cent of the workforce belonged to unions, but by the mid 1990s this figure had fallen to about one-third of all workers. However, this decline in membership has had as much, if not more, to do with the shift in employment from the traditionally more unionised manufacturing sector into services and in the growth of part-time work than with the legislation.

There has been a similar fall in union membership in most other industrialised countries. At the same time there has been a corresponding fall in the proportion of workers covered by some form of collective agreement; the pay and conditions of 54 per cent of UK workers were so determined in 1992, compared with 71 per cent of workers in 1984.

The government argued that the intention of the legislation was to sweep away restrictive practices and in so doing allow free determination of wages and greater flexibility in the labour market generally. In this way it was hoped that industry would be able to compete successfully with countries such as Japan and Germany. Either coincidentally or as a result of government policy the economy had passed through a huge economic recession in the late 1970s and early 1980s; it did so again in the early 1990s. It was the general economic conditions as much as legislation which broke the grip of the unions. The very low level of strikes in the last decade has lent credence to the view that it was the effects of unemployment rather than legislation which resulted in the reduction in union membership and in the lack of disputes. However, the absence of strikes by itself does not mean that there are good industrial relations. More must be done to create a positive attitude of cooperation and trust between management and workforce if there is to be lasting improvement in economic performance.

It should also be noted that, while the wage premiums effect of unions has fallen in the UK since the mid 1980s, recent evidence has suggested that unionised workers have become more productive than their non-unionised counterparts. Thus, the ***efficiency-enhancing*** effects of unions may have become at least as significant as their monopolistic influences.

Monopsony in labour markets

Most labour markets are subject to imperfections. As noted earlier, these may be both on the demand side (employers) and the supply side (employees). We have considered the supply side situation above, i.e. that a trade union may act as a monopoly supplier of labour. If the trade union restricts the supply of labour, it is behaving in a classic monopolist fashion. However, as we have seen, unions may also act to protect jobs, thus departing from typical monopoly behaviour.

Wages and the monopsonist

A monopsony exists when there is only one buyer of a commodity.

This situation exists in labour markets, but much less so than before given the privatisation of many of the previously nationalised industries. Thus, British Rail used to be the sole employer of train drivers, but now more than 20 companies own the rail franchises and compete to employ railway workers; however, the Post Office remains the sole 'purchaser' of postal workers. Under these conditions the employer may influence the wage rate. In Fig. 20.6 SS shows the supply curve for labour. Under normal competitive conditions the equilibrium would, therefore, occur where the *MRP* (demand) curve for labour intersects with the supply curve (point E_1), i.e. at a wage rate of OB and a quantity of OM. However, if the monopsonist is a profit maximiser it will wish to equate the *MC* of the factor with the *MRP*. This gives an equilibrium point D. (Note that the *MC* of labour curve lies above the supply curve for labour; this is because when labour is expanded a higher wage is not just paid to the last person employed but to all existing workers). To attract this quantity of labour (OL) the monopsonist must pay a wage of only OA. Thus, the wage is less than that in the competitive market by the amount of AB and the quantity of labour employed is reduced by the amount LM. These conditions could apply to the monopsonic purchase of any factor, not just labour. Thus we can conclude that:

The monopsonist will tend to employ less of a factor and pay a lower price than in competitive markets.

This imperfection therefore also creates a distortion in the allocation of resources (see the discussion of Pareto optimality in Chapter 24).

The situation may be further complicated if the monopsonist employer is bargaining with a monopolist union (a situation called ***bilateral monopoly***) because under these circumstances the union may be able to prevent the employer moving to position E on the graph. Under these circumstances the income represented by area ACDE becomes a zone of bargaining between employer and union.

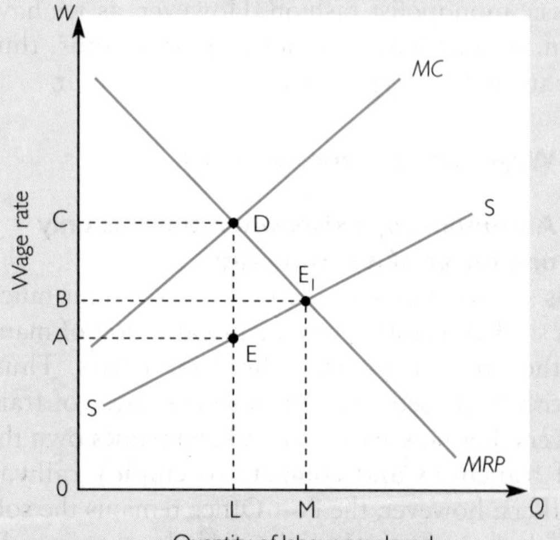

***Fig. 20.6* Wages and the monopsonist**
The profit maximisation equilibrium is where *MC* = *MRP*, i.e. employment of OL, but the business is obliged to pay a wage of only OA. This compares with the competitive wage of OB and employment of OM. Thus both wages and employment are lower under monopsony.

STUDENT ACTIVITY 20.4

List the factors that you think are likely to influence the bargaining outcome between a monopolist seller of labour (i.e. a trade union) and a monopsonist buyer of labour (i.e. the employer).

Differentials and disequilibriums

Wage differentials

In 1996 the highest paid 20 per cent of the population received 50 per cent of incomes whilst the lowest paid 20 per cent received only 2.6 per cent of incomes.

Taxes and social security payments narrow the gap between the richest and poorest sectors of society, but only slightly: in 1996 the respective shares of income after taxes and benefits were 43 per cent and 6.9 per cent.

STUDENT ACTIVITY 20.5

In fact, incomes are now much less equal than in 1979; then, the richest fifth of the population received 43 per cent of all earned income, while the poorest fifth were responsible for 2.4 per cent. Suggest reasons for this.

Some of the reasons for these widespread differences in income are listed below:

a) *Non-homogeneity*. Differences may exist in the workforce by way of natural abilities such as strength, intelligence and skill and also because of training and education.
b) *Non-monetary rewards*. Workers may receive benefits and payments in kind in addition to

their wages, e.g. company cars, cheap loans and mortgages. People may also be willing to work for the non-monetary rewards of a job such as social prestige or pleasant working conditions. Certain jobs such as nursing or teaching are thought to give non-pecuniary advantages to the worker by way of job satisfaction and therefore workers may tolerate lower wages (although this is probably less true now than in the past). On the other hand, people may have to be rewarded for working in unpleasant or hazardous conditions, like coal-miners or steeplejacks.

c) *Ignorance*. People may simply be unaware of the opportunities which exist elsewhere.
d) *Barriers to mobility*. As discussed above, barriers may exist to the geographical and occupational mobility of labour, either from the unwillingness of people to move from area to area or because of the restrictions placed on entry to certain jobs.
e) *Geographical considerations*. Certain areas are considered more desirable to live in than others. The so-called 'sunrise industries' such as computer software have tended to concentrate in areas which are considered geographically desirable. This, however, increases house prices etc. and therefore higher wages may be necessary. Many employees working in London and the south-east receive an additional 'living allowance' to compensate them for this very fact.

Having considered all these problems many economists would maintain that jobs and incomes are still determined by the ***principle of net advantage***, i.e. people will still choose their job and move job so as to achieve the greatest net advantage having considered both the pecuniary and non-pecuniary advantages of jobs.

Disequilibriums in the labour markets

It may be surprising that excess demand can exist in a labour market when there is general unemployment or that excess supply can exist when there is generally full employment. However, this is so and a number of factors which may account for this are listed below:

a) *Non-competing groups*. Since labour is a heterogeneous factor, excess supply in one sector may not influence another; for example, it is quite possible to have an excess supply of history teachers while experiencing a shortage of mathematics teachers.
b) *Rigidity of wages*. Although it may be possible to increase wages it is very hard to decrease them. Thus successful union pressure may raise wages, creating excess supply, but union bargaining strength may prevent employers from shedding labour (see Fig. 20.4)
c) *Internal promotions*. In many occupations people are recruited relatively young and untrained and then gain specialist training. As a result, ***internal labour markets*** are established for certain occupations and jobs. These usually require specific knowledge and training, are governed by established rules and procedures and are characterised by internal promotions and 'job ladders'. It thus becomes very difficult for someone outside to compete for the higher grades in such jobs; for example, it would be very unlikely that a person might switch into a senior post in education or local government if their experience is outside the industry, whatever their qualifications may be.
d) *Information costs*. Seeking a new job or new employee imposes costs on both the employee and the employer. The more senior the post, the more important these costs will tend to become. This point is developed below in search theory.

Search theory

This modern theory of labour markets maintains that both employers and employees will 'search' for the best bargain in the labour market. According to this theory the traditional marginal productivity approach ignores the cost of pay bargaining, information collection and labour mobility.

To the employer the cost of the search may include advertisements for suitable employees, interviewing costs and the costs of doing without the required labour in the interim period. The costs are likely to rise with seniority of the post. For the potential employee there is the opportunity cost of the search, i.e. doing without income until the right job has been found. High levels of unemployment may discourage the worker in the search.

Thus, differentials in incomes may be partly explained by the problems of job search.

Summary

1 The equilibrium wage rate is determined by the interaction of the firm's demand for labour and the supply of labour forthcoming.
2 A monopolist supplier of a product is likely to restrict employment of a factor.
3 The supply of labour as a whole is determined by non-economic factors. The supply of labour is also influenced by leisure preferences and labour mobility.
4 Trade unions attempt to affect wage rates both by restricting supply and by collective bargaining.
5 Factors which affect the bargaining strength of unions are elasticity of demand for the final product, the ease of factor substitution and the proportion of total cost which labour represents.
6 A monopsonist is likely to restrict both employment and payment.
7 The differentials which exist between wages are much greater than can be explained by marginal productivity theory.
8 Disequilibriums frequently occur in labour markets irrespective of the overall employment situation.

Questions

1 Examine the impact of a trade union's ability to raise wages above the equilibrium level in a perfectly competitive labour market. Outline the factors which influence a trade union's ability to raise wages.
2 Explain how wages are determined assuming perfectly competitive conditions. Discuss the factors which account for the differentials in wage rates.
3 'If unions succeed in raising real wages this will lead to less employment and ultimately a smaller total of wages.' Evaluate this statement. (Hint: Remember elasticity of demand.)
4 Discuss the factors that determine the total supply of labour. Explain why the supply of labour to a firm or an industry is much more elastic than the supply of labour as a whole.
5 Discuss the extent to which the industrial relations legislation of the 1980s and 1990s has been responsible for the decline in both trade union membership and industrial activity.
6 Identify and explain an example of:
   a) excess supply;
   b) excess demand in labour markets.
   Account for the existence of excess demand in conditions of high unemployment and excess supply when there is full employment.
7 To what extent do you consider unemployment to be an inevitable consequence of the introduction of new technology?
8 Why do accountants earn more than 'dustmen' (household refuse collectors) and yet many teachers earn less than some unskilled labourers on North Sea oil rigs?

Data response A Employment and unemployment

Study Figs. 20.7 and 20.8. These illustrate data relating to employment and unemployment in the UK.

Answer the following questions:

1 Say what is meant by the term the working population (or workforce). Estimate the size of the

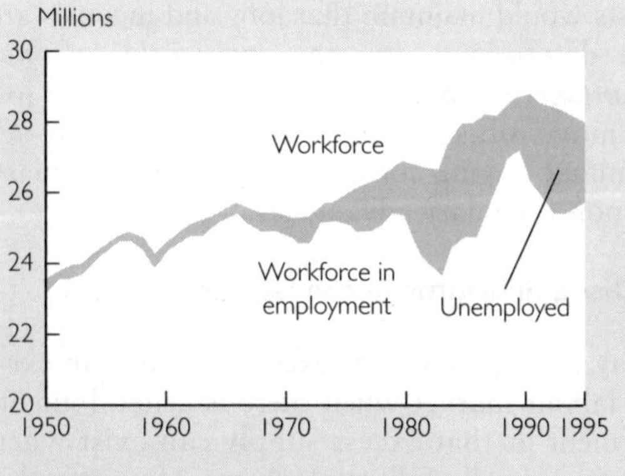

***Fig. 20.7* The workforce 1950–95**
Source: Economic Review, September 1996

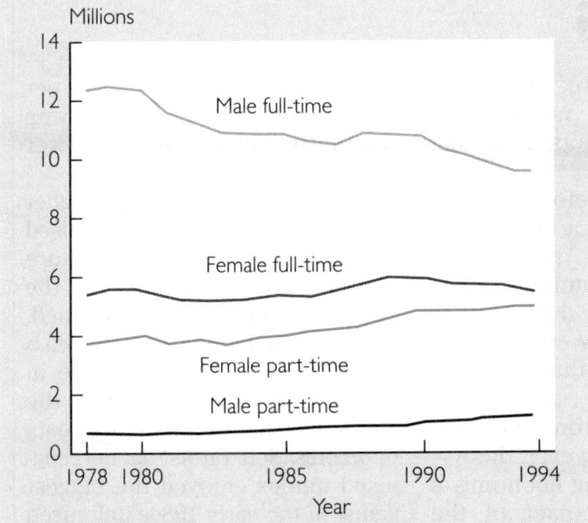

Fig. 20.8 **Employees in employment**
Source: Economic Review, September 1995

UK working population in:
a) 1950
b) 1995

2 Since 1978 the population of the UK has increased by 3.2 per cent, yet the workforce has increased by 5.4 per cent. Account for this discrepancy and assess the possible implications.

3 Account for the observed changes in the UK's employed labour force since 1978.

4 Women now outnumber men in the workforce, yet female pay still lags behind that of men. How do you account for this?

5 To what extent do you think the size of the employed labour force is an indicator of the level of economic activity in a country?

6 What effects are changes in the total supply of labour likely to have upon wages and employment?

Data response B
The decline of the unions

Read the following article from *The Economist* of 14 September 1996 and answer the questions which follow.

1 Outline those factors that may have been responsible for the decline in union power since the early 1980s, irrespective of any legislative changes.

2 Discuss the importance of strikes in broad macroeconomic terms (i.e. relative to GDP).

3 'Given the productivity-enhancing effects of unions, they are probably more likely to improve efficiency than act as monopolist suppliers of labour in the UK labour market of the 1990s.' Explain and discuss.

4 To what extent can it be said that the reduction in the power of the unions has reduced the 'natural' rate of unempoyment?

Bashing the unions

As Labour and the Tories out-tough each other with plans to further restrict trade-union "militancy", it is worth asking what has been achieved by the union reforms of the past 17 years

AS AN illustration of how much Britain has changed over the past couple of decades, look no further than the dramatic decline of the trade unions, which gathered this week in Blackpool for their annual conference. In the late 1970s, the unions lorded it over the Labour government, eventually bringing it down by engaging in a wave of strikes dubbed the "winter of discontent". Now, two high-profile strikes this summer in the public sector notwithstanding, the unions are feared by no one. Even Labour feels able to attack them, competing with the Tories in proposing new limits on union activity that would extend Tory changes to the law (all originally opposed by Labour) which have helped curb the unions since 1979. So what has the unions' decline meant for the economy? Are further legal changes really needed?

The Tories won power in 1979 believing that reducing trade-union power held the key to reviving Britain's economic fortunes. In a series of labour laws since 1980, unions were made liable for the actions of their members and easier to sue for damages when they called strikes illegally. Secondary picketing (the picketing of firms not directly involved in a dispute) and the closed shop (forcing employees in a firm or plant to join a union) were outlawed. Firms were allowed to withdraw recognition of a union. The power of union officials has been cut by giving more influence to individual union members, notably by requiring secret ballots to be held before striking.

These legal reforms went hand in hand with a collapse in union membership, from 13m in 1979 to 8m, and in militancy (see chart [next page]). during 1979, 29.5m man-days were lost to strikes. Last year, the total was 415,000. This may seem proof enough that the reforms have paid off handsomely. However, there is much debate among economists both about the impact of the decline of unions on the economy, and how far the Tory legal changes were responsible.

Even if the law had been left unchanged, other factors would have reduced unions' clout. Unemployment soared, making workers less willing to put their jobs at risk. It rose furthest in manufacturing which, outside the public sector, had a far greater union presence than other parts of the economy. Competition between firms increased. Job growth since 1979 has largely been in parts of the labour market where unions have been weakest: in part-time work, especially by women; in the service sector; in smaller firms; and in the South rather than in the North.

Even so, says David Metcalf, of the London School of Economics, the legal changes clearly had a significant impact. He calculates that they resulted in perhaps one-quarter of the decline in membership, and at least one-third of the reduction in union militancy.

Turning to the economic impact of the decline of the trade unions, the most obvious – less strikes – is arguably least important. As Mr Metcalf points out, in terms of their direct impact on GDP, strikes were never that significant: one day lost per worker per year in 1979, five minutes per worker now. What mattered was the inefficient balance of power they symbolised.

Bigger gains came from higher productivity and profits. Unionised firms raised productivity by more than non-unionised ones in the 1980s, as union power declined. Studies have found that between a quarter and a half of the rise in British labour productivity in the 1980s was due to the falling costs of unionisation. Firms that derecognised unions enjoyed the biggest gains. In the early 1980s unionised firms were almost 10% less likely to report above-average profits than non-unionised ones. By 1994 firms with closed shops were still less likely to outperform. But other unionised firms were no longer less likely to report above-average profits than non-unionised ones.

The reason for these gains was that, as union power ebbed, managers found it easier to restructure working practices and to hire and fire. This, rather than the reductions in job protection also pushed through by the Tories, was responsible for the creation of Britain's more flexible labour market. According to John Philpott of the Employment Policy Institute, an independent think-tank, job protection in Britain never amounted to much, unlike the ability of its unions to stop change.

Does the decline in union strength mean that Britain could now enjoy lower unemployment without inflation? In principle, a better match between the supply of labour and demand for it (made possible by greater flexibility) ought to mean that unemployment can now fall further without stirring up inflation than was the case in, say, the 1970s when the unions were stronger. Most economists think this "natural" rate of unemploy-

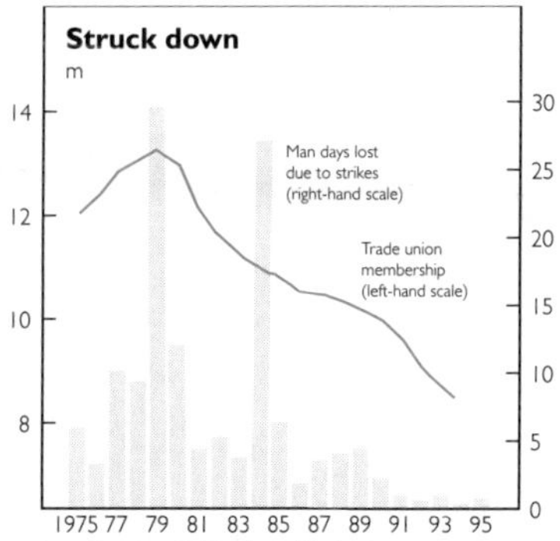

Source: Department for Education and Employment

ment is now lower, but opinions differ on how much lower.

Patrick Minford, an economist at Liverpool University, thinks that union reforms are one of the main reasons why unemployment could now fall to 3% of the workforce (from its current 7.5%) before inflation started to rise. But Julian Morgan, an economist at the National Institute of Economic and Social Research, reckons that weaker unions have had only a modest effect on unemployment. If the "natural" jobless rate has fallen, that owes more to social-security reforms and efforts to help the long-term unemployed. So far, lower unemployment has failed to ignite wage inflation, which is good news. Only time will tell how good.

So what need is there for further reform? The current proposals are aimed most at the public sector. There, unions are increasingly holding one-day strikes, so the Tories want to do away with the legal immunities of such strikes. Labour wants more use of conciliation and binding arbitration, and to extend the use of independent pay-review bodies. These ideas are worth considering, but are unlikely to achieve much while the state tries to achieve its broader public-spending goals by squeezing the pay of its own employees without any regard to merit.

Private-sector employers no longer fear the unions, however, and most have little interest in seeing them bashed by politicians. Instead, many firms might be happy to give unions a bigger role if unions became co-operative rather than hostile. This opens up intriguing possibilities. One, proposed by Demos, a think-tank, is for unions to evolve into "employee mutuals" – organisations which, to overcome job insecurity, become the long-term employer of members, hiring them out, often on short-term contracts, in the flexible labour market.

Source: *The Economist*, 14 September 1996

21 Rent

Learning outcomes

At the end of this chapter you will be able to:

- Distinguish between the terms 'rent', which is paid for the use of land alone, and 'economic rent', payable to all factors.
- Explain the concepts of economic rent and transfer earnings.
- Account for the proportions of earnings to a factor comprising either economic rent or transfer earnings.
- Explain the meaning of quasi-rent.
- Assess the problems involved in taxing rent incomes.

Economic rent and transfer earnings

Definitions of rent

The term rent has a wide usage in the economy. People speak of renting a car or renting a house. Economists, however, use the word in a much more specific fashion. There are in fact two concepts of rent which are in current use in economics:

a) *Rent*. This is the payment made for the use of ***land*** as defined in the economic sense. In practice, however, land is frequently 'mixed up' with other factors of production and it is difficult to ascertain precisely how much is being paid for the land and how much is being paid for the capital bound up with it.

b) *Economic rent*. This is the payment made to any factor of production over and above that which is necessary to keep the factor in its present use; for example, a soccer star may earn £10 000 per week because his special skills are in great demand. If his skills were not in great demand it is possible that he would be willing to work as a footballer for £500 per week, for there is little else he can do, in which case £9500 of the £10 000 is a kind of ***producer's surplus*** or ***rent of ability***, for it is not necessary to keep his skills in their present use. This payment can therefore be described as an ***economic rent***.

STUDENT ACTIVITY 21.1

Can you think of other examples of occupations where a high proportion of earnings represents economic rent?

Economic rent

Common misunderstanding

It is perhaps a little confusing that we have two different ideas, both called rent. The explanation of this is that the idea of economic rent, which we now apply to any factor of production, was an idea which was first put forward by David Ricardo with respect to land and it was only later applied to other factors.

In developing the idea Ricardo made two assumptions: first, that the supply of land is fixed; and, second, that land has only one use and that is growing food. If this were the case, the supply curve for land would be a vertical straight line as in Fig. 21.1.

The demand for land, or any other factor, is a derived demand, for it is demanded, not for itself,

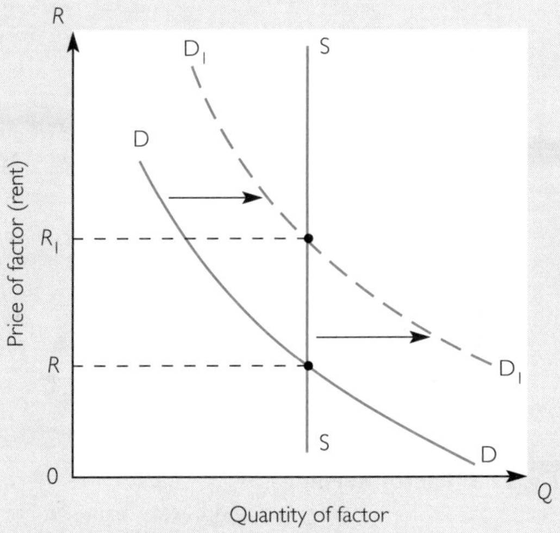

Fig. 21.1 **Economic rent**
All factor earnings are economic rent because, whatever happens to the price, the quantity supplied remains the same.

but for what can be produced with it. In Ricardo's time the demand for land was very high because Napoleon's Continental System had cut off European grain from the UK market. The result of this was that the landlords were able to charge very high rents for the land on which to grow grain. Ricardo argued that this did not create more land; landlords were receiving more money but not supplying anything more. Conversely, the demand for land might fall, in which case the rents would decrease but the supply of land would not. From this Ricardo concluded that rent fulfilled no purpose and was a producer's surplus.

Although Ricardo's assumptions are subject to criticism, he did manage to construct the theoretical extreme of the supply of a factor of production. In Fig. 21.1 you see that the supply curve is vertical (i.e. supply is totally inelastic) and that, therefore, the factor earning is determined by the demand curve. The increase in demand from DD to D_1D_1 increases the price but not the quantity of land. Theoretically, demand could decrease until the price (rent) were zero without the quantity supplied decreasing. Thus all the earnings made by this factor are over and above that which is necessary to keep it in its present use and are therefore economic rent.

Ricardo also argued that rent was ***barren*** since, however high rent was, it produced no more of the factor. To some extent this is true, but high rents do have the function of making us exploit scarce resources more sensibly. For example, when land was very cheap in the USA it was ruthlessly exploited. This resulted in the 'dust bowl'. High rents for land mean that farmers are anxious to preserve the fertility of land and look after it carefully.

Since the time of Ricardo his view of rent has been modified in two major ways:

a) It is now acknowledged that the supply of land is fixed only in the global sense. There is not a single market for land but different markets for building land, agricultural land, etc. Thus, in practice changes in the price of land for one use cause land to shift from use to use, creating some elasticity of supply.
b) We now apply the idea of economic rent to any factor of production. Thus we can repeat our definition that:

   Economic rent is the payment made to any factor of production over and above that which is necessary to keep it in its present use.

Transfer earnings

In practice if a factor's earnings decline there comes a time when that factor will transfer to some other use.

The payment which is necessary to keep a factor in its present use is described as transfer earnings.

If we assume that a firm is borrowing money and it is able to borrow all it wishes at 10 per cent but the bank is not willing to lend any at lower rates, then we could represent the supply curve for capital as a horizontal straight line (i.e. supply is perfectly elastic). In this case the whole of the 10 per cent interest payment could be regarded as being necessary to prevent capital transferring to another use. It is, thus, all transfer earnings. This is illustrated in Fig. 21.2.

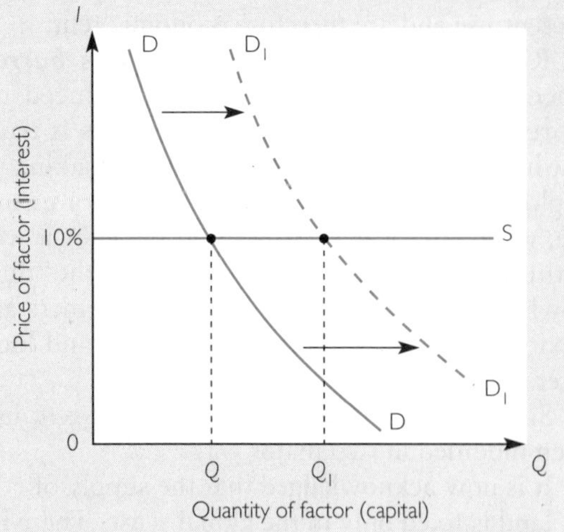

Fig. 21.2 **Transfer earnings**
All factor earnings are transfer earnings because, whatever the demand, the same price must be paid for the factor. If, for example, the firm offered less than 10 per cent for capital then the capital would all transfer to another use.

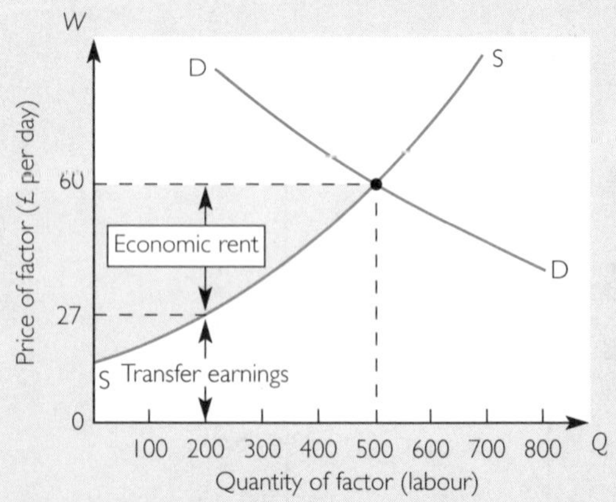

Fig. 21.3 **Factor earnings**
A composite of economic rent and transfer earnings. The wage is £60 and therefore the 200th worker's pay is £27 of transfer earnings and £33 of economic rent. The shaded area represents the economic rent of the entire workforce.

Separating economic rent and transfer earnings

The cases of pure economic rent and pure transfer earnings present the theoretical extremes of the concepts; in practice most factor earnings are a composite of the two. In Fig. 21.3 the firm requires a workforce of 500. In order to attract this many workers it must pay a wage of £60 a day per person. If we consider the 200th worker, however, it appears that this worker would have been willing to work for a wage of £27. This worker is, therefore, receiving £33 a day more than is necessary to keep the worker in the present employment. This is therefore economic rent. One could make a similar division of the workers' earnings until one reaches the 500th worker, where all of the £60 is necessary to attract this worker to the firm. Thus all the shaded area is economic rent while the area beneath it is transfer earnings.

Note that the relationship between economic rent and transfer earnings depends on the elasticity of supply of the factor in question. The more elastic the supply, the lower the proportion of earnings that comprises economic rent. Thus, in Fig. 21.1, where supply is totally inelastic, all factor earnings are economic rent, whereas in Fig. 21.2, given a perfectly elastic supply curve, all factor earnings are transfer earnings.

STUDENT ACTIVITY 21.2

Draw supply curves for occupations where a) most of the earnings comprise transfer earnings and b) most of the earnings consist of economic rent. Think of actual examples in each case.

Rent and profits

It is now possible to see the exact correspondence between the concepts of rent and profits. It may be recalled that we defined normal profit as that amount of profit which is necessary to keep a firm in the industry (page 188). This we may now align with our definition of transfer earnings. Similarly, we defined abnormal profit as any profit in excess of normal profit just as we have defined economic rent as any payment made to a factor over and above transfer earnings.

Quasi-rent

Whether or not a particular portion of a factor earning is considered to be economic rent or transfer earnings may sometimes depend upon the period of time we are considering.

Common misunderstanding

It is not true that what is regarded as economic rent to a factor will always remain so. What may be considered as economic rent in the short run, may be regarded as transfer earnings in the long run. If one considers a machine that is recovering £1500 a year above its operating cost, then in the short run (i.e. when supply is relatively inelastic and there is little alternative means of production) we could consider this as an economic rent since it is £1500 more than is necessary to keep capital in its present use. However, in the long run (given that supply is more elastic and alternative production methods may be considered) the machine must recover not only its operating cost but also its replacement cost if capital is going to remain in that use. If, for example, the replacement cost of this machine were £1500 per year then, in the long run, all the machine's earnings become transfer earnings.

Those earnings which are economic rent in the short run but transfer earnings in the long run are correctly termed quasi-rent.

The problem of rent incomes

The problem

Ever since Ricardo described rent as a surplus, people have been concerned with the potential social injustice of this. If we start from the proposition that land is fixed in supply then we may view the problem as one in which, as more and more people and capital, etc., are added to the fixed factor, there is an ever-increasing demand for land and, therefore, ever-increasing rents. As a result, more and more of the national product will accrue to the owners of the land but nothing more will be supplied in return for it. This forms an important plank of Marxist philosophy.

Henry George (1839–97)

Henry George has the distinction of writing the single most popular book ever written on economics, *Our Land and Land Policy*. George's central thesis was that poverty is caused by the monopolisation of land by the few who expropriate the product of working people. The solution, he suggested, was that rent should be confiscated by the government through a single tax on land. According to George no other taxes would be necessary.

The idea of the single tax was debated by famous economists such as Alfred Marshall and J. B. Clark. They concluded that the tax would have less adverse effects upon the allocation of resources than other taxes but the idea had three major shortcomings:

a) The tax would be unjust because, as we have explained, rent can be earned by other factors of production even though they escape the tax.
b) The tax would not produce enough revenue to replace all other taxes.
c) The tax would be impossible to administrate since, in practice, it is often impossible to separate land from other factors such as capital.

George himself died in 1897 during a campaign to become mayor of New York. However, an active Henry George Society still exists. It promotes his ideas, proving the enduring popularity of fiscal ideas suggesting that all the tax in the country should be paid by someone else.

Economic rent and taxes

It could be argued that economic rent is the subject of tax today, since high incomes are hit by higher rates of income tax. Thus, for example, the soccer star who is earning £500 000 a year, most of which the economist would describe as an economic rent, is likely to find a good proportion of it appropriated by the government in taxes. (However, since the top rate of income tax was gradually reduced in the 1980s and now stands at 40 per cent, a much lower proportion of the player's income goes in taxes than previously would have been the case.) There have, however, been specific attempts to tax economic rent, such as the Labour government's Development Land Tax Act of 1976, which was an attempt to tax profit made through the development (change of use) of land. The problem remains that of identifying rent and separating it from the other factor rewards for tax purposes.

The other alternative would be to nationalise land. The problem with this solution is that of destroying the price mechanism as a means of allocating scarce resources. Would a government be able to allocate land between different uses as efficiently as the market system?

Summary

1. Rent is the payment made for land.
2. Transfer earnings are the payment made to keep a factor in its present use and economic rent is any payment made in excess of this.
3. The amount of economic rent and the amount of transfer earnings in any factor payment depends upon the elasticity of supply of the factor.
4. The earnings which are economic rent in the short run, but transfer earnings in the long run, are correctly termed quasi-rent.
5. Because rent has been described as 'barren surplus' it has sometimes been the target for taxation schemes.

Questions

1. Explain why the rents in the City of London can be as high as £2000 per m^2 but may only be this much per square hectare for agricultural land in Lancashire.
2. Discuss the effect of a 50 per cent tax on all rent incomes from land in the UK. How would the effect differ if this tax were imposed only in Greater London?
3. Account for the fact that property values may be twice as high in Enterprise Zones as in immediately adjacent property.
4. Distinguish economic rent from transfer earnings. Discuss the relationship between elasticity of supply of a factor and economic rent.
5. Discuss the economic justification for taxing economic rent.

Data response A
Modern times, old trends

Read the following article from *The Economist* of 20 April 1996 and answer the questions which follow.

1. Discuss the impact of increased 'globalisation' in the late nineteenth century on relative factor prices in America and Europe.
2. To what extent can the changes in factor prices that occurred be explained by standard economic theory?
3. Discuss whether you think there were any changes in the division of factor earnings between economic rent and transfer earnings at this time.
4. Assess the possible impact of increased globalisation now on relative factor incomes.

Data response B
Surely not rent controls?

Read the following article taken from *The Economist* of 8 April, 1995 and answer the questions which follow.

1. 'The traditional view of rent controls is that they are socially undesirable because they reduce the amount of rented property available.' Explain and discuss.
2. Are housing markets perfectly competitive?
3. Discuss the effects of rent controls assuming a monopolistically competitive market for rented accommodation.
4. Are rent controls socially beneficial?

Modern times, old trends

Economic historians are studying the similarities between today's global economy and that of a century ago. What have they discovered?

According to their bent, journalists and politicians like either to enthuse or to rant about "globalisation". Some hail the greater ease with which capital and goods can move between countries as a cause of prosperity. Others rail against it, saying that it will impoverish workers in rich countries.

Economic historians, however, are a far less excitable bunch. Globalisation, they point out, is nothing new. The half-century or so before the first world war was similar to modern times, in that national economies became more closely linked. Declining transport costs made it cheaper to send goods across oceans. Migrants left Europe for the Americas and Australia in huge numbers. Investment poured from the Old World into the New.

In a paper published last year Jeffrey Williamson of Harvard University stressed another similarity: the convergence of wages among many countries now in the OECD.* Since the 1950s, the amount by which Americans' wages exceed Europeans' has shrunk markedly. In the same way, in the second half of the 19th century, European wage rates caught up on American ones (see chart), although the trend changed after about 1895. Within Europe, some smaller countries closed the gap with Britain, then the continent's leader. In 1870 Swedes' wages were about half of Britons'; by the first world war, they were ahead.

Then as now?

Real wage rates*, 1905 British wages = 100

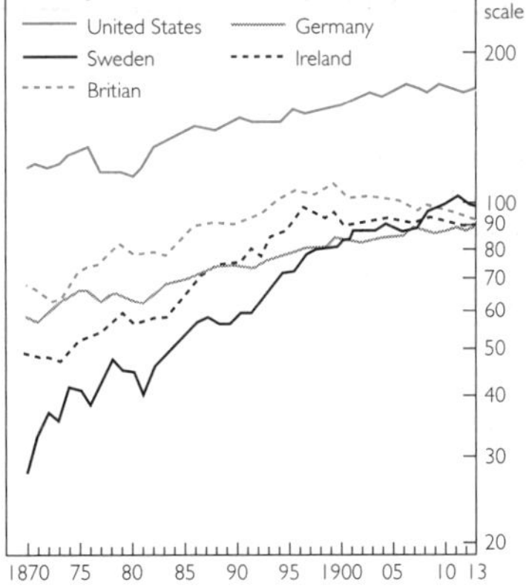

Source: J. Williamson

* Hourly rate of unskilled urban workers

The interwar years, however, were quite different. Not only did countries retreat behind tariff walls and curb immigration, thus reversing international economic integration, but, says Mr Williamson, the convergence of wage rates ceased and, in the late 1930s, was reversed.

Is there a link: does economic integration cause wage rates to converge? In principle, there could be other causes of convergence, such as improved education in lower-wage countries. In another recent paper, in which he draws on research jointly undertaken with other economic historians, Mr Williamson argues that, at least in the late 19th century, economic integration was the main cause.**

In part, integration happened through increased international trade – as a result, in particular, of a fall in transport costs. According to standard economic theory, this should have had two effects. First, the prices of internationally traded goods should have become more alike in different countries. Second, countries with relatively large amounts of land and little labour (such as America and Australia) should have specialised in producing agricultural goods; more crowded countries (ie, Europe) should have produced more labour-intensive goods.

This in turn should have increased the demand for relatively abundant factors of production in each country, raising their prices, and reduced the use of relatively scarce factors, lowering theirs. Thus the ratio of wages to land rents in America and Australia should have fallen; in Europe it should have risen. A study by Kevin O'Rourke of University College, Dublin, Alan Taylor of Northwestern University and Mr Williamson finds that this indeed happened.†

The authors estimate that between 1870 and 1913 the ratio of wages to rents in America fell by half, while Australia's ratio dropped by three-quarters; Britain's and Sweden's more than doubled, while Ireland's more than quintupled. Furthermore, the change in wage-rent ratios was smaller in European countries, such as France and Germany, in which protection remained high.

Standard theory explains much of the convergence of wages and rents between Britain and America, where the gap between national commodity prices narrowed greatly: between 1869-71 and 1911-13, for instance, the amount by which grain prices in Chicago exceeded those in Liverpool fell from 60% to 15%. But the theory is less useful for explaining, say, Sweden's catch-up on Britain:

Continued on page 278

* "The Evolution of Global Labour Markets since 1830: Background Evidence and Hypotheses". *Explorations in Economic History*. 1995

** "Globalisation, Convergence, and History". *Journal of Ecomomic History*. 1996

† "Factor Price Convergence in the Late Nineteenth Century". *International Economic Review*. 1996

commodity prices in the two countries converged only modestly, perhaps because Sweden increased tariffs in the 1880s.

Go west, young man

Emigration to America, which made labour scarcer at home, explains much of the relative increase in Swedish wages. The same goes for Ireland, where a huge wave of emigration began after the country's famine in the 1840s. With no emigration after 1870, says Mr Williamson, urban wage rates would have been lower by one-third in Ireland and one-eighth in Sweden in 1910.

By making labour more abundant, migration also held down wages in receiving countries. Had there been no immigration into America after 1870 and had it had no effect on American investment, reckons Mr Williamson, real wages in American cities would have been 34% higher than they actually were in 1910. But, he says, it is nonsense to assume that the capital stock did not respond. Immigration increased the return on investment; capital chased labour across the Atlantic. The result? Without immigration, wages would still have been higher in 1910 – but only by 9%.

That said, Messrs O'Rourke, Taylor and Williamson point out that the type of investment reinforced the effects of migration on wages and rents. In Europe, investment tended to economise on scarce land; in America, the emphasis was on saving labour.

Nonetheless, the prediction of standard theory – that global economic integration may hurt owners of a country's relatively scarce resources (American labour, European land) – is borne out by the evidence of the late 19th century. Today, rich countries' relatively scarce resource is low-skilled workers: there are many of them, but relatively fewer than in emerging nations. They may lose from globalisation. Mr Williamson muses that in the early 20th century such fears contributed to barriers to migration and trade, with dire results. Might it happen again?

Source: The Economist, 20 April 1996

Surely not rent controls?

The theories that have led some economists to argue that minimum-wage laws may be a good thing have led others to challenge a different, even more sacred, orthodoxy. Might rent controls actually makes sense?

In 1992 members of the American Economic Association were polled about their views to see whether economists agreed about anything. They did, which was surprising. Even more so was the idea that won most support – not the blessings of free trade or the incentive-destroying effects of high taxes, but a claim about the housing market. No fewer than 93.5% agreed that "a ceiling on rents reduces the quality and quantity of housing."

If the poll were repeated now, the figure would be lower. Just as a literature has appeared in the past few years attacking the view that minimum-wage laws destroy jobs, so revisionists have challenged the consensus against rent controls. Richard Arnott, a professor of economics at Boston College, surveys the arguments in the current *Journal of Economic Perspectives*.

The solidity of the old consensus owed a lot to the spectacular failure of controls at their most idiotic – in New York city. There, decades of frozen rents made apartments in many old buildings insanely cheap. This grossly distorted the market for housing discouraged maintenance, tied protected tenants to their apartments (Ed Koch refused to give up his rent-controlled apartment in exchange for the official mansion when he became mayor) and raised rents for everybody else. Strong controls introduced in Europe during the second world war also did harm wherever they were left in place too long, as in Britain.

All this the revisionists accept. Controls of that sort, they say, are the equivalent of setting an absurdly high minimum wage. However, they insist that "second-generation" rent controls, the equivalent of a cautiously low minimum wage, may not only keep rents down but also serve the cause of economic efficiency.

As Mr Arnott points out, the debates over minimum wages and rent controls are closely connected. In both cases, the traditional view was based on the assumption of perfect competition. In a world of many buyers and sellers, homogeneous workers and houses, full information, no uncertainty and so forth, the case against minimum-wage laws and rent controls stands: both kinds of control make economies worse off in the aggregate. In the real world, few if any of those assumptions hold. A theoretical case can generally be made for some kind of intervention to promote efficiency.

The rent-control revisionists concentrate on various market imperfections, all of them much analysed in other branches of eco-

Two models

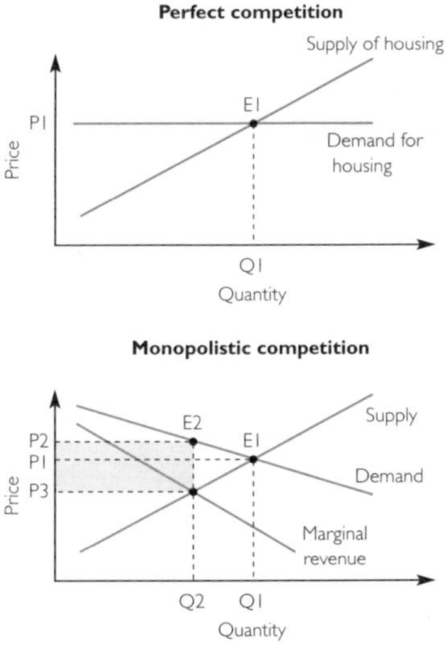

nomic theory. Applying these notions to the housing market, which is peculiar in several ways, is not straightforward. Of these ideas, monopolistic competition is perhaps the easiest case.

The argument is that the housing market is less competitive than it appears. Housing is heterogeneous, and people have idiosyncratic tastes. If a buyer likes a certain house he will be willing to pay a premium over houses of (apparently) identical quality. Instead of one broad market for housing, in other words, there are many thin ones. Landlords enjoy a measure of market power even though barriers to entry (usually regarded as necessary for monopolistic power) are low or absent. Landlords understand this and set prices higher than would be necessary, collectively, to clear the market.

The charts illustrate (in a dangerously simplified way) the choices facing each landlord. In the top panel, competition is perfect. If the landlord raises his price an iota over the market rate, he sells nothing: the demand curve is flat. So he accepts the point E1, where the price (ie, rent) is P1 and the quantity consumed is Q1.

In the lower panel, the landlord has monopolistic power: he faces a downward-sloping demand curve. He no longer maximises profit at E1, but at E2, where the extra (or marginal) revenue from letting one more house just equals the cost of supplying it. For the individual landlord, the result is a higher price (P2), a lower quantity consumed (Q2) and a monopolistic profit (shown by the shaded area). In the aggregate, the result is high rents together with simultaneous vacancies and homelessness. The latter is a feature of most real-world housing markets.

In principle, fixing the rent at P1 would prevent the landlord from exploiting his monopoly power. But if the rent should be fixed too low – ie, lower than P3 in the second panel – the supply of housing would be even lower than with unrestricted monopolistic landlords.

Going soft

How well have soft controls worked in practice? Since the 1970s many cities in Europe and America have introduced milder forms of rent control – either from scratch, or by liberalising existing, harsher systems. Rather than freezing rents, the new controls impose complicated formulae that restrain the rate of increase according to a variety of criteria.

These mild controls have certainly been less damaging than the hard controls of New York city and post-war Britain. That is unsurprising. The question is whether they have brought an economic benefit as compared with no controls. The evidence, though available by the ton, is inconclusive. Mild controls appear to have had little effect either way: their influence has proved econometrically imperceptible. Those who put the burden of proof for intervention on the state will see this as evidence against controls; those who believe that intervention is good unless proven to be bad will draw the opposite conclusion.

In a way, the whole argument is beside the point. Those who favour rent controls or minimum-wage laws do so not for reasons of efficiency, but because they want to redistribute income to the poor. That is a legitimate aim. So here is a proposition that 100% of economists and non-economists should agree to. Whatever the ability of rent and labour-market controls to promote efficiency, there are far simpler, fairer and more effective ways to raise the real incomes of the poor than trying, however cleverly, to micro-manage the markets for housing and labour.

Source: The Economist, 14 September 1996

22 Capital and interest

Learning outcomes

At the end of this chapter you will be able to:

- Distinguish between different types and forms of capital.
- Appreciate the nature and impact of capital formation.
- Understand the derivation of the net productivity of capital, determine the capitalised value of an asset and identify the marginal efficiency of capital.
- Distinguish between capital deepening and capital widening.
- Appreciate the relationship between the marginal efficiency of capital and the rate of interest.
- Explain the neo-classical determination of the rate of interest.
- Distinguish between real and nominal rates of interest.
- Appreciate the different methods of appraising investments.
- Recognise the significance of discounted cash flow techniques.
- Identify the main sources of funds for a firm.
- Understand the concepts of capital structure and capital gearing.
- Appreciate the different methods of calculating the return on a share.
- Understand the role and importance of the Stock Exchange.

Capital and capital formation

Types and forms of capital

When the economist uses the expression capital, it usually refers to the stock of ***capital*** (or ***producer***) ***goods***. As we saw in Chapter 3, the definition of a capital good arises not out of its intrinsic nature but out of the use to which it is put. For example, if we consider a commodity such as a potato, to the household it is a consumer good but if used by the farmer to plant for next year's crop then it is capital because it is being used in the production of further wealth. Similarly, a can of beans is a consumer good once it reaches the shopping basket but it is a producer good while still on the shelves of the supermarket since it is then still part of the capital of the business. There are some goods, such as oil tankers or tractors, which are invariably capital goods; this is because they are used only for the purpose of supplying other goods and services.

The term capital is also used to describe the ***legal forms*** by which ***wealth is owned***. Thus, for example, the real capital of Ford UK is the factories etc. it possesses; these are owned by shareholders and their shares represent the legal, or financial, claim upon that capital.

Thus the term capital is used in two senses, either to describe capital goods or to describe financial resources.

In this latter sense one may distinguish between invested finance (share capital in the case of a company) and the loaned finance (loan capital) of a firm. This is the way most people think of capital. These two legal forms tell us the way in which the organisation is owned and controlled.

Common misunderstanding

Shares, debentures, money, etc., are not real wealth but a legal claim upon it. It is capital goods that are the real wealth of a country. This distinction may not be important to the individual but it is vital to the economy as a whole. If the paper forms of capital were real wealth then the country could solve all its economic difficulties by printing more of them.

Capital formation

As we have already seen, capital goods are not necessarily different from consumer goods but, rather, are used for a different purpose. If, for example, we have a stock of potatoes then we can consume them all or consume some and then plant the others. In this way one hopes to have more potatoes next year. In the same way an organisation is faced with the choice of distributing all its profits or ***ploughing them back*** into the business in the hope that this will enable it to make even more profit in the future. This is the old familiar idea of 'no jam today for more jam tomorrow'. In other words capital is formed by doing without now and using the resources so freed to create more wealth in the future.

Capital is formed by forgoing current consumption and diverting these resources to the production of future wealth.

Figure 22.1 shows the possible effects of capital formation on growth. Line C shows the growth of consumption in an economy over a 50-year period with 15 per cent of income devoted to capital formation. At point K a change in the consumption pattern occurs and 20 per cent of income is now devoted to capital formation. Thus consumption is reduced to 80 per cent of income, i.e. people have a lower material standard of living. However, this creates a new consumption path (C_1) which has more rapid growth than before. At point L in year 20 consumption has now reached the level it would have been had not the extra capitalisation taken place. After this point line C_1 is above C, showing that a higher standard of living has been achieved. Thus the economy on path C_1 is able to reach point N, which is unobtainable for the economy on path C. The shaded area to the left of point L represents the extra current consumption forgone in order to obtain path C_1. The shaded area to the right of point L shows the extra consumption made possible.

International comparisons

The thing which separates the rich nations of the world from the poor is the possession of capital. Since capital is formed by going without now to produce more for the future, it is relatively easy for the richer nations to become even richer since they can forgo current consumption of some goods and still have a high standard of living. However, if a very poor country is living near subsistence level it is impossible for it to depress current living standards to form capital since this

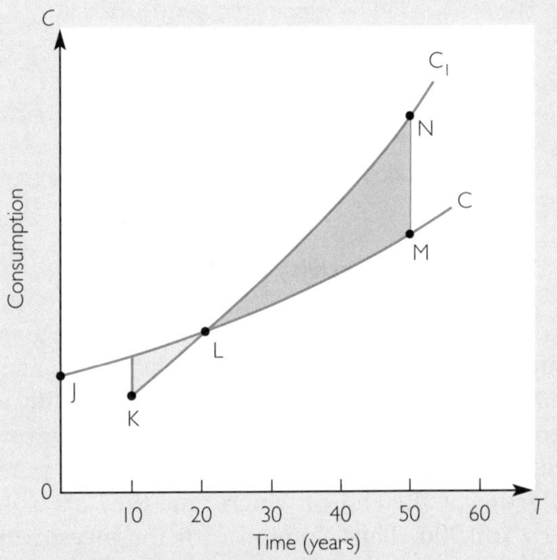

***Fig. 22.1* Capital formation**
Growth path C_1 shows the result of increased capital formation at point K.

would result in mass starvation. Imagine an economy which is so poor that everyone must spend all their time working in the fields to produce sufficient food just to keep them alive. Under these circumstances it will be impossible for the population to turn aside from agriculture to build roads or factories which might increase their living standards, since they will have nothing to live on while they do so. It is very difficult indeed for poor nations to break out of this cycle of poverty.

Even for a country such as the UK it is important to realise that we cannot hope to keep pace with our competitors while we are devoting less to capital formation than they are. For example, between 1980 and 1990 the share of investment in capital goods averaged 17.4 per cent of GDP for the UK, 17.7 per cent for the USA, 20.5 per cent for Germany and France, 21.5 per cent for Italy and 29.5 per cent for Japan. There has been some evidence of a catching-up process by the UK since the mid to late 1980s, although it still tends to lag behind most of the other countries in terms of the share of total output that is devoted to investment expenditure.

STUDENT ACTIVITY 22.1

Some so-called developing countries, such as India and Pakistan, tend to devote an equally large share of their resources to investment as do the main industrialised economies listed above. Why, though, may their investment spending be less in absolute terms?

The net productivity of capital

As with any other factor of production, a firm employs capital for the product which it creates. Imagine that the owner of a barren hillside in Scotland invests £200 000 of capital by planting and growing trees on it. The trees take 25 years to grow, at the end of which time they are sold for £500 000. Thus, in return for the investment the forester has received £300 000 or £12 000 per annum. This income resulting from the employment of capital is referred to as the ***net productivity of capital*** and is normally expressed as a percentage which, in our example, would be 6 per cent (£12 000 expressed as a percentage of £200 000). Firms are willing to pay for the use of capital, therefore, because it enables them to produce goods and services in the same way that the employment of labour does.

The return on capital is not expressed as an amount in monetary units but as a percentage per year of its capital value.

The capitalisation of an asset

The capitalised value of an asset is that value which would be placed on it at its existing level of earnings and current rates of interest.

The thing which determines the capital value of an asset is the income it produces. Suppose, for example, we have an asset which gives a fixed income per year of £500 for ever and that the prevailing rate of interest is 5 per cent. Then the present value (V) can be calculated from the formula:

$$V = \frac{A}{i}$$

where A is the amount of permanent receipt, e.g. £500, and i is the interest rate (in decimal terms), e.g. 0.05.

Thus in our example we would obtain the result:

$$V = \frac{£500}{0.05} = £10\,000$$

If the interest rate were 10 per cent and A remained £500, this would give a value of £5000, whereas an interest rate of $2\frac{1}{2}$ per cent would give a value of £20 000. In other words:

The value of an asset and the rate of interest are inversely proportional to each other.

STUDENT ACTIVITY 22.2

Calculate the capitalised value of an asset that pays an annual income of £1200 p.a. at an interest rate of 6 per cent. Calculate the capitalised value at an interest rate of 12 per cent.

The marginal efficiency of capital

Marginal efficiency of capital (*MEC*)

As we have seen, the output attributable to capital is referred to as the net productivity. This behaves in the same way as the returns to other factors; thus we see the same pattern of *APP* and *MPP*. Once again, with capital the terminology is a little different because we are measuring the output as a percentage rate of return. When the *MPP* is measured in this way we obtain a figure known as the marginal efficiency of capital (*MEC*).

The marginal efficiency of capital is the rate of return on the last unit of capital employed.

In fact, given that there is usually a monetary basis for the rate of return of capital (i.e. the income resulting from the employment of capital), the marginal efficiency of capital is probably better indicated by the *MRP* of capital. Figure 22.2 shows an *MEC* curve. This is arrived at by plotting the return from each additional unit of capital.

Common misunderstanding

Note that the MEC *curve is a stock concept; it does not actually refer to the flow of investment over time. The* MEC *curve relates the rate of return to the desired stock of capital at any point in time. It is the marginal efficiency of investment* MEI *curve that shows the relationship between the rate of interest and the actual rate of investment per time period; however, this is essentially a macroeconomic concept and is dealt with in Part 3.*

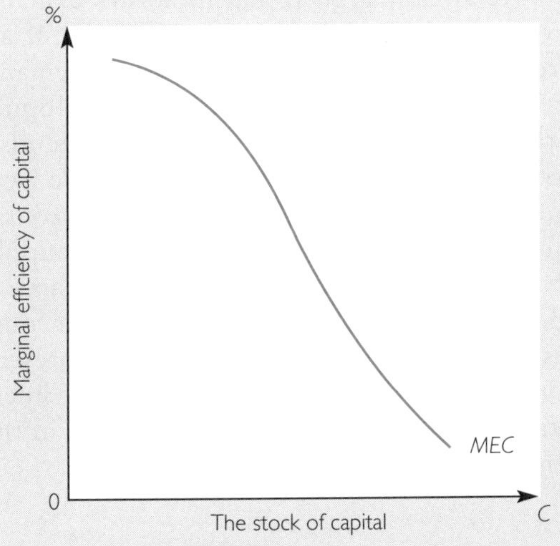

Fig. 22.2 **The marginal efficiency of capital**

Capital deepening and widening

The *MEC* curve is drawn on the usual assumption of *ceteris paribus*. If we continue with the assumption we can then explain the meaning of ***capital deepening*** and ***capital widening:***

a) *Capital deepening*. This refers to the accumulation of more capital in relation to the other factors of production. If, for example, a firm acquires more capital so that each worker has twice as much capital to work with, this would be an example of capital deepening; the capital/labour ratio has increased.
b) *Capital widening*. This refers to the accumulation of more capital without changing the proportions of factors of production. If, for example, a firm was to build a second factory which duplicated the system in its first factory, this would be an example of capital widening; the capital/labour ratio is unchanged.

It is capital deepening which accounts for the downward slope of the *MEC* curve. If we assume that technology is constant, as more and more capital is combined with a constant amount of other factors, then diminishing returns must be experienced.

MEC and the rate of interest

We measure the productivity of capital as a percentage rate so that we can compare it with the rate of interest, which is the price of borrowing capital. If we combine the two together we can explain the size of the capital stock at any point in time. If the *MEC* exceeds the cost of capital then firms will invest and so the stock of capital expands. In Fig. 22.3 the rate of interest is 10 per cent. If the existing stock of capital is OL then the stock of capital would be expanded to OM where the *MEC* is equated with the rate of interest (i). Conversely, if the stock of capital is ON then the tendency would be to contract the stock to OM. Thus the optimum stock of capital is where:

$$MEC = i$$

You should be able to recognise this as a variation on the $MRP = P$ statement of Chapter 19.

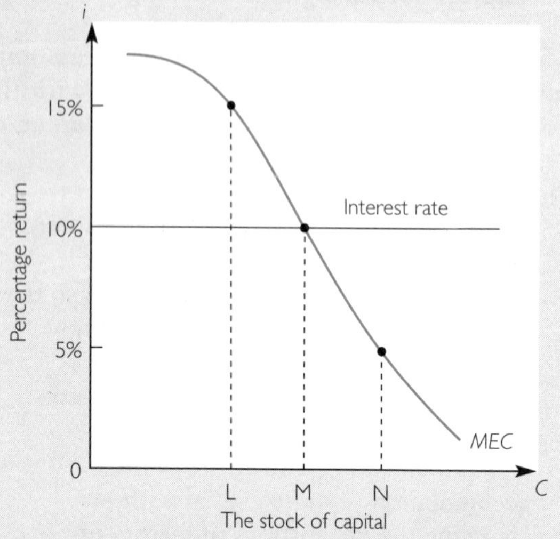

Fig. 22.3 **The marginal efficiency of capital and the rate of interest**
If the *MEC* is 15 per cent then the stock of capital will be expanded, whereas if the *MEC* is 5 per cent the stock of capital will be contracted.

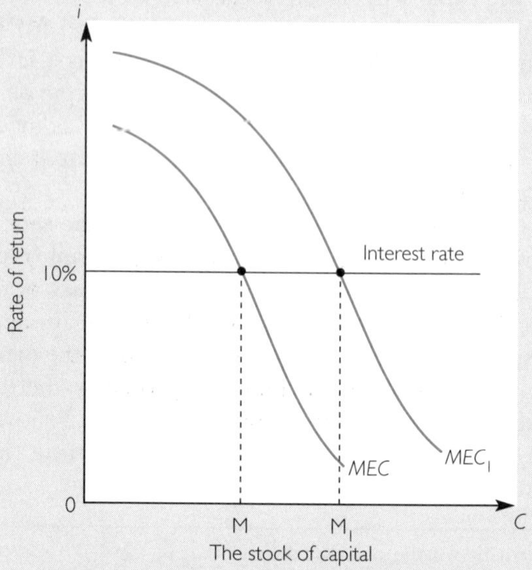

Fig. 22.4 **Interest, the marginal efficiency of capital and technology**
An increase in the level of technology causes the stock of capital to be expanded from OM to OM_1.

We could also examine the effect of changes in the rate of interest. *Ceteris paribus*, a fall in the rate of interest should cause the stock of capital to be expanded and a rise in the rate of interest should cause the stock to be contracted.

Thus the *MEC* curve could be described as the demand curve for capital.

Again you should be able to see how this fits in with the analysis in Chapter 19. It is only the terminology which is slightly different.

The *MEC* and technology

An improvement in technology within a firm would have the effect of shifting its *MEC* curve upwards as shown in Fig. 22.4. As you can see, if the rate of interest is 10 per cent then the shift of the *MEC* causes the stock of capital to expand. *Ceteris paribus*, the firm would be substituting capital for other factors.

The interest rate

The determination of the interest rate

We have already argued that the firm's demand curve for capital will be downward sloping. If we were to aggregate all the individual demand curves we would produce a downward-sloping market demand curve for capital (people also borrow more at lower rates of interest). We have taken the supply curve as being horizontal although we could argue that the total supply curve of capital will be upward sloping, since a higher rate of interest is one factor that encourages people to save more. Thus we can present the rate of interest as a price formed by the intersection of the demand and supply curves in the normal way. This is illustrated in Fig. 22.5.

This is the neo-classical theory of the interest rate. A fuller discussion is to be found in Chapter 38, when we also consider monetary theories of the rate of interest.

The real rate of interest

One way of looking at the rate of interest is to say that it is the payment made to lenders to compensate them for doing without their capital for a time. At the end of the period of the loan they receive the repayment of the capital as well as the interest. If there has been inflation, this will have decreased the value of the capital, so in order to obtain the ***real rate of interest*** we need to subtract from it the rate of inflation.

The real rate of interest is the difference (+ or –) between the nominal rate of interest and the rate of inflation.

Figure 22.6 shows the real rate of interest in recent years. As you can see in the early and mid 1970s the rate was negative. High nominal rates were often accompanied by negative real rates. In the 1980s the nominal rate declined but real rates increased substantially. Both the real rate of interest and the rate of inflation have declined in the 1990s.

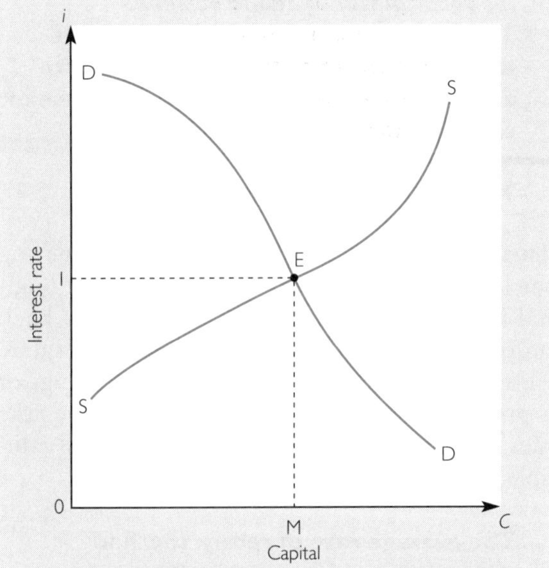

***Fig. 22.5* The determination of the rate of interest**

Reswitching

If the rate of interest falls then firms will 'switch' to more capital-intensive methods of production. This is the implication of the normal downward-sloping demand curve. However, Joan Robinson and Nicholas Kaldor of Cambridge (UK) argued that below a certain rate of interest 'reswitching' may occur into less capital-intensive means of production (see Fig. 22.7). This would be possible if the marginal product of capital were to start increasing again because this would mean that the

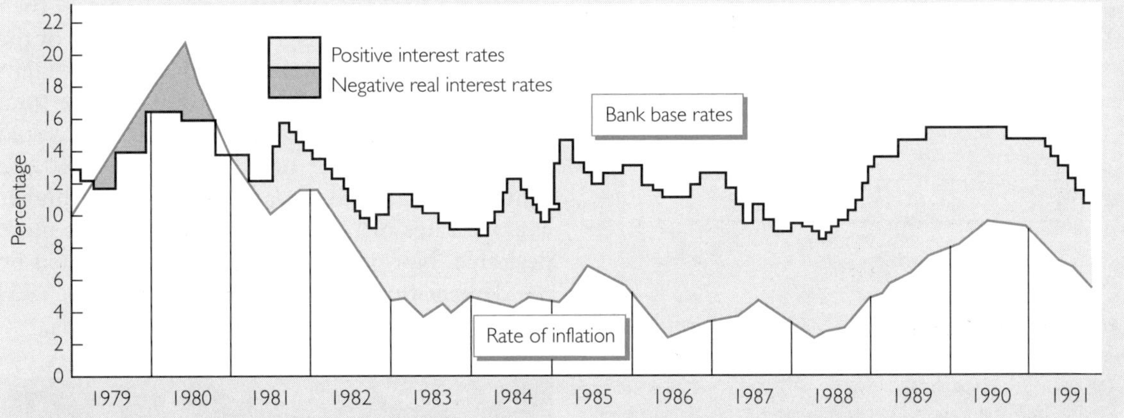

***Fig. 22.6* The real interest rate in the UK**

The real interest rate is the vertical distance between the two graphs. Negative real rates of interest occur when the rate of inflation is greater than the nominal rate of interest.

economy could provide a greater output with a smaller stock of capital. This may happen in less developed countries, where the acquisition of new capital stock leads to great increases in productivity as the country changes from one level of technology to another. This view has been disputed by R. Solow and P. Samuelson of Cambridge (Massachusetts) who have stuck to the neo-classical theory of the conventional downward-sloping demand curve. This disagreement has been referred to as the 'two Cambridges controversy'.

Appraising investments

Different techniques

When a firm comes to decide whether or not an investment is worthwhile, a number of different techniques can be used. Traditional methods of doing this use:

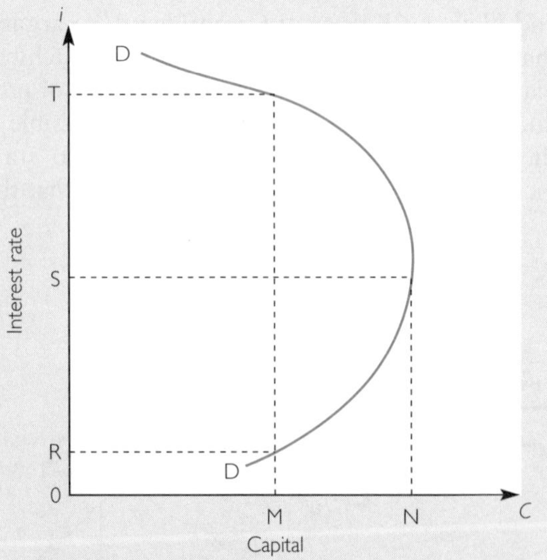

***Fig. 22.7* Reswitching**
As the interest rate falls from OT to OS, so the demand for capital expands from OM to ON. However, as the interest rate falls even further the economy 'reswitches' to less capital-intensive methods, so that at interest rate OR the demand for capital is same as it was at OT.

a) *the pay-back method*; and
b) *the average rate of return method.*

Although they are now regarded as old fashioned, a survey in the *Bank of England Quarterly Review* (August 1994) found that many firms, especially smaller companies, still used these techniques. The more modern methods use *discounted cash flow analysis*. These methods are:

a) *the net present value method*; and
b) *the internal rate of return method.*

The discounted methods appeal to the economist more because they take into account the opportunity cost of the use of capital funds.

The pay-back method

This method appraises projects by considering the length of time required to pay back the original investment. Thus, projects which pay back more quickly are regarded as more desirable. This method takes no account of the earnings of a project after pay-back, and it also ignores the fact that earnings in the future are not as valuable as present earnings

The average rate of return method

This method takes the total proceeds from a project over its entire life and divides this by the number of years of the project. This give the average annual income of the project. This is then expressed as a percentage of the capital cost of the project. Thus, for example, if an investment scheme had a total cost of £20 000 and the total proceeds over five years were £40 000, this would give annual proceeds of £8000 which is 40 per cent of the original outlay. Schemes with higher average rates of return are presumed to be more desirable. Not only is the method complicated by the depreciation of capital but also it can be used only to compare projects of identical lifespans.

STUDENT ACTIVITY 22.3

An investment project costs an initial £100 000 and has a lifespan of five years. The proceeds in each of the first two years are £30 000 and £40 000 in each of the final three years. Calculate a) the pay-back period and b) the average rate of return.

Discounted cash flow

Discounted cash flow is a method of appraising the value of an asset based upon the idea that the value depends upon when the income from it is to be received.

It is always better to receive money now rather than in the future. For example, £100 received now would produce £110 in a year's time if invested at 10 per cent, £121 in two years' time, £133.10 in three years, and so on. Conversely, we could obtain the present value of money by asking what amount of money today would be necessary to produce, say, £100 in a year's time, two years' time and so on. To do this we discount money by the 'market' rate of interest. Thus, for example, if £90.91 were invested at 10 per cent this would be worth £100 in a year's time, whereas £82.64 invested would be worth £100 in two years' time, and so on. This is illustrated in Table 22.1. In these circumstances, the £100 is the ***future return*** and £90.91, £82.64, etc., are the respective ***present values.***

Table 22.1 **Amounts of money invested needed to produce £100**

Net present value invested today	Produces				
	Today	*1 year from today*	*2 years from today*	*3 years from today*	*4 years from today*
£100.00 →	£100	£100	£100	£100	£100
£90.91					
£82.64					
£75.13					
£68.30					
etc.					

Rate of discount = 10%

Common misunderstanding

The need to discount future returns to secure their present values is not due to the effects of inflation. It is simply based on the passage of time and an acknowledgement of the fact that money can earn interest over time. All costs and revenues (or net returns) that accrue in the future have to be discounted backwards to the present time at an appropriate rate of interest; only then can they be compared with expenses incurred or with revenues received today.

Present discounted value

It is both possible and necessary to discount the future earnings of a project in order to make a truly viable asessment of its worth.

If, for example, a scheme produces an income of £2000 per year for five years and we assume an interest rate of 10 percent, then we could discover its present discounted value (PDV) as follows:

$$PDV = \underset{\text{Year 1}}{£1818.18} + \underset{\text{Year 2}}{£1652.89} + \underset{\text{Year 3}}{£1502.63} + \underset{\text{Year 4}}{£1366.03} + \underset{\text{Year 5}}{£1241.84}$$

$$PDV = £7581.57$$

This compares with the undiscounted earnings of:

$$5 \times £2000 = £10\,000$$

The discounted values for each year can be found by looking them up in tables. However, they may also be calculated (although not very easily) from the formula:

$$PDV = \frac{A}{(1+i)^t}$$

where A is the amount of earnings per year, i the rate of interest and t the number of years of the project.

Thus in our example above we could obtain the calculation:

$$PDV = \frac{£2000}{(1+0.1)} + \frac{£2000}{(1+0.1)^2} + \frac{£2000}{(1+0.1)^3} + \frac{£2000}{(1+0.1)^4} + \frac{£2000}{(1+0.1)^5}$$

This produces the value shown in the text above and therefore gives us:

$$PDV = £7581.57$$

Net present value method

Having obtained the present discounted value we can arrive at the net present

value by subtracting from it the initial cost of the investment.

Suppose that the scheme we have considered above had an original cost of £5000; then:

Net present value = £7581.57 – £5000 = £2581.57

The result is positive, which indicates that it is a profitable investment and worthwhile undertaking.

The internal rate of return method

This method seeks to find the rate of interest that will discount the proceeds from the project to the original cost.

If the internal rate of return is greater than the rate of interest paid for borrowing money, then the scheme is worthwhile. If in our example the capital cost were £5000, while the proceeds of the scheme were £2000 a year over five years, a rate of 28.5 per cent would discount this flow of proceeds to £5012. If we subtract this total from the initial cost of £5000 we obtain an answer of almost exactly zero. Thus 28.5 per cent is the internal rate of return. If this rate is higher than the rate of interest then the project is profitable.

STUDENT ACTIVITY 22.4

Taking the same investment project as in Student activity 22.3, calculate the net present value of the project at an interest rate of 10 per cent, where the present value of £1 at the end of year 1 equals £0.9091, at the end of year 2 equals £0.8264, at the end of year 3 equals £0.7513, at the end of year 4 equals £0.6830 and at the end of year 5 equals £0.6209. State whether you think the internal rate of return is likely to be just above or just below the rate of interest.

Financing the firm

Sources of finance

As we have seen, capital is formed through forgoing current consumption. Thus the source of capital funds is the savings of both private individuals and firms. We may divide the sources of funds into ***internal*** and ***external***. Internal funds are those generated by the firm itself while external funds are those obtained outside the firm. Internal finance (or ***ploughed-back profits***) is generally the most important source of funds to firms, although it has declined in importance in recent years. The sources of external finance are listed below:

a) *The capital market.* The firm can raise money by selling shares (equity) on the capital market or by the sale of debentures (fixed interest securities). The shares or debentures might be purchased by private individuals, pension funds, insurance companies or unit trusts. Table 22.2 shows the distribution of the ownership of shares between these various people and institutions. You will note the declining importance of the individual investor. The distribution of figures shows the remarkable rise in the importance of pension funds and insurance companies. However, this survey of ownership covers only those companies listed on the London Stock Exchange. The newly formed Unlisted Securities Market has been a big magnet for the private investor.

Table 22.2 **The ownership of company shares in the UK (%)**

	1963	*1975*	*1981*	*1989*	*1994*
Private individuals	54.0	37.5	28.2	20.6	20.3
Insurance companies	10.0	15.9	20.5	18.6	21.9
Pension funds	6.4	16.8	26.7	30.6	27.8
Trusts	1.3	4.1	3.6	7.5	8.8
Overseas investors	7.0	5.6	3.6	12.8	16.3
Other	21.3	20.1	17.4	9.9	4.9

Source: CSO

It may at first seem surprising that there has not been a more dramatic growth in the shareholding of private investors as a result of the government's privatisation programme during the 1980s. Several reasons can be advanced to explain this. First, the table shows the percentage of shares owned. Most of the new shareholders from privatisation had very small holdings (e.g. £500) which made very little difference to the overall picture. Second, the institutions such as insurance companies took major shareholdings in the privatised companies. Third, many of the new small shareholders promptly resold their shares to make capital gains.

These comments notwithstanding, the 1980s saw a dramatic increase in the *number* of private shareholders. At the end of the 1970s it was estimated that only 6 per cent of the population were shareholders whereas by 1992 estimates suggested that this figure had risen to 22 per cent.

b) *Banks*. UK banks do not buy shares in companies (such shares that they do own are usually limited to those of their subsidiaries). In other countries such as Germany and Japan, banks are much more significant shareholders. In the UK banks finance firms by giving loans or overdrafts. They are thus really helping to finance the working, or circulating, capital of the firm.
c) *The government*. During the 1970s the government became a significant shareholder in a number of firms, the shares being held by the National Enterprise Board. In the early 1980s the government was concerned to reduce the role of the government in industrial finance. However, some government finance is still important such as regional grants and subsidies; the farming industry, for example, is still heavily dependent upon government finance.
d) *Trade credit*. A traditional method of finance is simply to delay the payment of bills, thus in effect obtaining an interest-free loan. The granting of trade credit in this manner is an important sales technique to many firms.

Shares and debentures

As we have seen, companies may raise capital by the sale of shares or debentures. While both result in the same thing – finance for the company – there are a number of differences between them. Primarily, debentures are loan capital which acknowledge and secure loans to the company, while shares are evidence of part ownership of the company and part investment in it. Thus debenture-holders are a company's creditors while shareholders are its members. Debentures normally provide for repayment and they are usually secured by a mortgage over the property of the company; a shareholder's investment is completely repaid only if and when the company is wound up while solvent. Consequently, the latter involves greater ***risk***. An important commercial difference is that dividends on shares can be paid only out of profits and therefore presuppose a profitable year's trading, but the interest on debentures may be paid out of capital. Hence, a debenture-holder receives payment for the loan, irrespective of whether the company makes a profit or a loss.

Debentures are usually issued to raise temporary finance up to the limit specified in the company's articles of association. Debentures may be either ***redeemable*** or ***irredeemable***. The former are repayable at or after a specified date and they are usually issued when the need for finance is temporary or when interest rates are high and likely to fall. Conversely, the latter are not repayable until the company is wound up or it defaults on the payment of interest due. They will usually be issued when longer-term finance is required or when interest rates are low and likely to rise.

Many companies will also have overdrafts with their banks and these accommodate fluctuations in their 'cash flow'. The amount and duration of the overdraft will depend largely upon the reputation of the company. The directors of small companies often give their personal guarantee as security for the debt to the bank.

Types of shares

There are two main types of shares and they are distinguishable according to the voting rights and rights to receive dividends and repayment of capital which their holders enjoy:

a) *Preference shares*. The holders of preference shares receive a dividend in priority to other shareholders, but it is usually only a fixed rate dividend. Preference shares are presumed to be cumulative, i.e. if in any one year the dividend cannot be paid it is carried forward and added to the dividend for the following year, and so on. In many cases preference shareholders are also entitled to repayment of capital in priority to other shareholders should the company be wound up.

Preference shares do not normally give voting rights and their holders are not entitled to share in the surplus profits of the company unless they hold participating preference shares.

b) *Ordinary shares*. The precise rights of ordinary shareholders depend on a company's articles of association, but normally they are entitled to attend and vote at meetings and to receive a variable dividend according to, and from, the profits remaining after the preference shareholders have received their dividend. If the company is wound up they are entitled to share in the surplus assets after all debts have been discharged and shareholders repaid. Ordinary shares are the risk-bearing shares because they have the greatest potential for either profit or loss.

Capital gearing

As we have seen there are different types of both shares and loans. The make-up of the company's financial resources we refer to as its ***capital structure***. The proportion of loan capital to share capital in a company is referred to as the ***capital gearing*** of the company. If there is a small proportion of share capital to loan capital, the capital is said to be ***high geared*** because a small number of ordinary shares (giving voting rights) control a large amount of capital. Conversely, if the company's capital is mainly shares, with only a small proportion of loan capital, it is said to be ***low geared***. Generally speaking it is to the company's advantage to have at least some of its capital as loan capital since this gives two benefits:

a) *Reduced tax burden*. Since debt interest can be claimed against corporation tax this will reduce the amount of tax the company has to pay.

b) *Increased growth*. Because the company retains more of its earnings it will require a smaller cash sum to pay the rate of dividend on each share. This could result in more money being available for ploughing back into the company or it could be used to pay a higher dividend on each share. In the case of a successful gearing operation this can lead to spectacular results. The National Freight Corporation (NFC), which was privatised in 1981, was financed by a very high-geared operation. As a result of the success of the NFC its shareholders saw a 35-fold increase in the value of their shares in seven years.

However, it may be dangerous for a firm to have too large a proportion of loan stock if business is poor, since the interest on it must be paid, whereas with shares the firm can always reduce the dividend.

Calculating the return

To the economist the return on capital is interest, which is the return for lending money where ***no risk*** is involved. However, many investments involve risk and therefore the factor earnings will be a composite of both interest and profits. The person who buys shares is therefore both a capitalist and an entrepreneur.

Interest and dividends

Debentures have a fixed rate of interest, i.e. in return for a loan of £100 the debenture-holder will receive a guaranteed rate of interest. Some shares, e.g. preference shares, may have a stated income on them, but by and large their income will depend upon the ***dividend*** declared by the company. When the company has paid all its costs, including taxes, and after it has retained some profits to finance growth, it distributes the rest of its earnings as a dividend on the par (or face) value of each share. If a share is bought on the Stock Exchange it will almost certainly be at a price other than its par value, e.g. a £1 share may be bought for £2. This, however, will not affect its earning capacity. If, for example, the company has declared 10 per cent (or 10p) dividend per share then it is 10p that the owner of the share will receive. Since the investor paid £2 for it, the effective return is not 10 per cent but 5 per cent. This principle also applies to the return on debentures.

To the owner of the share, however, the important thing will be the effective earning of the share. Shareholders may obtain benefit from shares in two ways: first, from the dividends declared by the company; second, by selling the share for more than they paid for it. Since dividends vary from share to share and the price of a particular share may vary from day to day, various methods of expressing the share's earnings or potential earnings have been devised. This is so that the shares of one company may more easily be compared with the shares of a different company. The different ways of expressing this are considered below.

Yield

This gives a simple measure of the return capital expressed as a percentage of the share current market price. If, for example, a company declared that it would pay a dividend of 15 per cent on each £1 share in the company, but the current market price of each £1 share is £2.50, then the yield is not 15 per cent but 6 per cent. This can be worked out in the following manner:

$$\text{Yield} = \frac{\text{Par value} \times \text{Dividend}}{\text{Market price of share}}$$

In our example:

$$\text{Yield} = \frac{1.00 \times 15}{2.50} = 6 \text{ per cent}$$

Price/earnings (P/E) ratio

The yield of a share may not be a good guide to its earning capacity. The P/E ratio is the relationship between the market price of the share and total earnings, i.e. all profit, not just the declared dividend. The P/E ratio can be expressed as:

$$\text{P/E} = \frac{\text{Market price of share}}{\text{Earnings}}$$

If the company has a share capital of £500 000 and its total profits or earnings are £250 000, then its earnings are 50 per cent or 0.50. If the market price of the shares is £2.50 then the P/E ratio will be:

$$\text{P/E} = \frac{2.50}{0.50} = 5$$

This is a ratio, not a percentage.

Dividend cover

Since 1973 the complexities of corporation tax have made the calculation of the P/E ratio somewhat problematic. A new measure of the earnings of shares has arisen and that is dividend cover. This relates the net after-tax profits of the company to the declared dividend. If, for example, the profits of the company were £250 000 after tax had been paid, and £100 000 were distributed in dividends, then the dividend cover would be 2.5.

There are thus several ways of looking at the earnings of a company. Anyone contemplating the purchase of shares in a company should take care to look at the financial position of the company in as many different ways as possible.

STUDENT ACTIVITY 22.5

A firm pays a dividend of 10 per cent on each 50 pence share. The current market price per share is £1.50; the share capital is valued at £1 million. Annual profits come to £300 000. Calculate a) the yield and b) the price/earnings ratio.

The Stock Exchange

The Stock Exchange is not involved with the issue of shares; it is concerned only with the sale and transfer of 'second-hand' shares. Thus, when shares are bought on the Stock Exchange they do not bring money to the company concerned but to the shareholder who has sold them. The Stock Exchange is important to the new issue market, however, since the ease with which shares can be resold encourages people to invest as they know they can easily turn their shares back to cash. In addition, market makers may be members of the Stock Exchange and may sell the new shares they have recently acquired to other brokers on the Exchange.

In Stock Exchange jargon, those who speculate on rising markets are termed ***bulls***, those who speculate on a falling market are termed ***bears***, and those who speculate on new issues are called ***stags***.

The day of 27 October 1986 saw significant changes in the London Stock Exchange. Collectively these changes were known as the 'Big Bang'. The Stock Exchange changes were part of wider developments affecting financial institutions generally. The changes encompassed both the regulation of the Stock Exchange and the introduction of new technology. As far as the operation of the Stock Exchange was concerned the most important changes were:

a) *Dual capacity dealing*. Before October 1986 there was strict division between ***jobbers***, who had no contact with the public, and ***brokers*** who dealt with the public and made deals with the jobbers. After 1986 a member of the Exchange could undertake both jobs. This raised the problem of a possible conflict of interest. For example, a member of the Exchange might be ***making a market*** in a company's shares, i.e. buying and selling the shares, producing research information on the company, etc., while on the other hand, in their other capacity, be buying shares for customers who are members of the public. You could argue that such an Exchange member might not give unbiased advice to clients.
b) *Abolition of fixed commissions*. From 1912 onwards there was a fixed commission on all dealings. That is to say, whatever member of the Exchange a member of the public dealt with they would be charged the same percentage commission on all sales and purchases. This practice was abolished in October 1986. It was argued that this would lead to greater competition and lower commissions but on the other hand it was also argued that brokers might charge higher commissions to certain customers. This latter criticism was borne out when many brokers began to impose minimum fees on deals for small customers.
c) *The ownership of firms*. Up to 1986 stockbroking firms had to be owned by members of the Exchange. After this date it became possible for firms to be owned by outside businesses. This meant, in effect, that companies such as banks were able to take over stockbroking firms, thereby giving their customers direct access to the Exchange. As examples of this, Credit Suisse acquired Buckmaster & Moore, while Barclays acquired the jobbers Wedd Durlacher Mordaunt as well as the brokers de Zoete & Bevan.

Other changes came about as a result of the new technology. Instead of dealing face to face with one another firms were able to gain their information through electronic systems. ***Topic*** and ***Talisman*** were already in existence. October 1986 saw the introduction of ***SEAQ*** (the Stock Exchange Automated Quotation system). This is a composite screen network which shows the latest prices on a range of over 3500 domestic and international securities. These changes were, in themselves, sufficient to bring about the death of the 'floor' in a matter of months.

In May 1992 the Transfer and Automatic Registration of Uncertified Stock (***TAURUS***) system was due to be introduced. This would have allowed for the sale and purchase of stocks and shares without share certificates and brought about so-called 'paperless' dealing. However, the safeguards which had to be built into the system were possibly more bureaucratic than the old system. The TAURUS system was designed more for the convenience of large than small shareholders. In the end the problems involved in its setting up proved insurmountable and it was not introduced. A scaled-down substitute system, ***Crest***, was introduced in its place. Electronic trading was introduced in 1997.

In addition to the Stock Exchange there is now the USM (Unlisted Securities Market) which deals in the securities of companies too small to be quoted on the Exchange. Also established in 1986 was the ***third tier*** of dealings in even smaller companies.

Regulation and deregulation

The changes which have come about in the stock market were, in fact, introduced by the Stock Exchange itself. They were a result of the ***Parkinson–Goodison accord*** whereby than Stock Exchange agreed to reform itself rather than have reform imposed on it by the government. It was the Conservative government's (1979) intention to increase competition and to deregulate as many sectors of the economy as possible. However, the government also recognised the need to protect the interests of investors. It was with this in mind that the ***Financial Services Act 1986*** was passed. This established a regulatory framework, not only for the Stock Exchange but for all sectors of the financial services industry. The various bodies, such as FIMBRA, are made up chiefly of representatives of the various sectors of industry. Thus the guiding principle is essentially one of self-regulation.

With the need to report to regulatory bodies and stricter rules on the sale of services many people in the industry thought that the new regime was one of greater regulation rather than less. Figure 22.8 illustrates the pattern of regulation of the financial markets as established by the Financial Services Act. However, dissatisfaction with the large number of regulatory agencies led to proposals in 1997 for the absorption of the supervisory powers of the other bodies by the Securities and Investment Board (SIB), thus paving the way for the introduction of a single, unifying body to oversee the whole financial services sector.

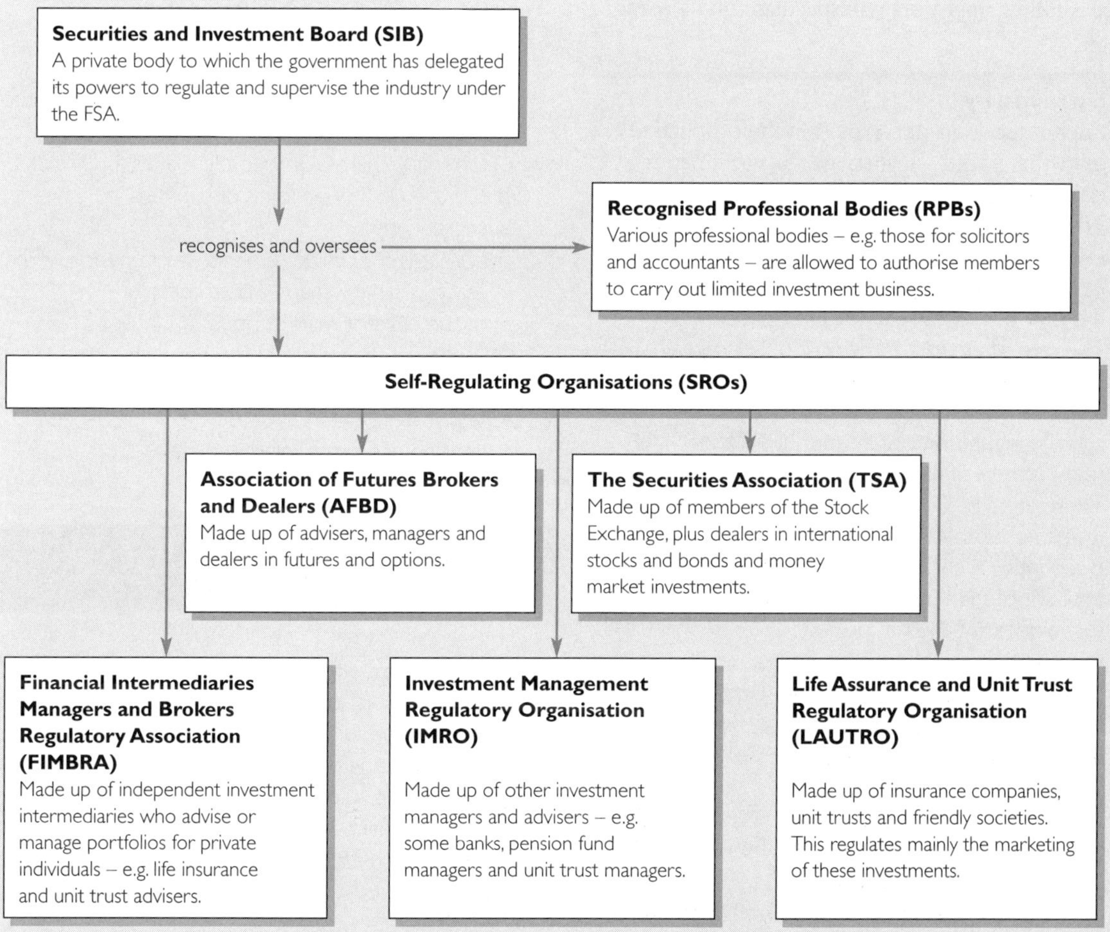

Fig. 22.8 **The regulation of financial markets**
The provisions of the Financial Services Act (FSA) 1986 established a pattern of self-regulation for the financial markets.

The crash in the market in October 1987 illustrated the dangers involved in stock market dealings. Commenting on the Stock Exchange Keynes said: 'When the capital development of a country becomes a by-product of the activities of a casino, the job is likely to be ill done.' Many people do indeed criticise the Stock Exchange for the speculation which goes on there, arguing that the changes in the price of shares often have little to do with the *real* economy. On the other hand, supporters of the Stock Exchange would claim that speculation *decreases* the fluctuations in the prices of shares. It is argued that if the price of a share is rising investors will speculate on its falling, thus decreasing the magnitude of the rise. Conversely, if a share's price is falling, investors will speculate on its rising.

Summary

1 Capital goods are those used in the production of further wealth. Financial capital is the paper claims upon the wealth of the country.
2 The marginal efficiency of capital (*MEC*) is the rate of return on the last unit of capital employed. The *MEC* relates the stock of capital to the rate of interest.
3 The rate of interest is the cost of borrowing capital or the reward recovered for lending it. The real rate of interest is obtained by subtracting the rate of inflation from the nominal rate of interest.
4 There are a number of techniques for appraising investment projects. Economists tend to favour discounting techniques because these take account of the time value of money. Two of these techniques are the net present value method and the internal rate of return method.
5 Companies raise finance by selling shares and by taking loans. The relationship between share capital and loan capital is known as capital gearing.
6 There are a number of methods of assessing the return on a share. These include the yield, the P/E ratio and the dividend cover.
7 The Stock Exchange is not directly involved in the raising of new capital but is important to it because it provides a way of selling shares once they have been bought.

Questions

1 What is the capitalised value of a bond with a permanent income of £500 per year if the interest rate is 15 per cent? Comment on the relationship between the value of an asset and the rate of interest.
2 Compare and contrast the traditional methods of investment appraisal with discounting techniques.
3 Explain the difference between capital deepening and capital widening; examine their significance for the shape of the *MEC* curve.
4 Distinguish between capital structure and capital gearing. State the advantages to a company of having its capital structure highly geared.
5 Umoco plc has a nominal share capital of £1 million. This is made up of 700 000 £1 preference shares which have a fixed maximum dividend of 8 per cent. There are also 300 000 £1 ordinary shares. Umoco plc makes a profit of £250 000 all of which is distributed to shareholders.
   a) What is the dividend per share in pence which each ordinary share would receive?
   b) If the current market price of Umoco's ordinary shares is £3.00, what is the yield on each ordinary share?
6 Assess the importance of the Stock Exchange in the raising of finance for companies.

Data response A
Accounts and capital

Table 22.3 presents financial data about Conabco Ltd. It shows the results of the year to 28 March 1997. At the time these results were published the company's share capital consisted of 25 million £1 ordinary shares and there had been no change in this for the two previous years. The current market value of the shares at 2 March 1997 was 749 pence.

Having studied the information attempt the following questions:

1 Calculate the yield, dividend cover and P/E ratio assuming that the price of each share remains at 749 pence.

Table 22.3 Conabco Ltd results at 22 March 1997

Turnover	248.7
Profit before taxation	27.0
Taxation	6.75
Profit after taxation	20.25
Dividends	8.9
Retained profit	11.35
Earnings per share	81 pence
Fixed assets	292.3
Net current assets	42.9
Term loans	335.2
	(33.7)
Represented by equity	301.5
Net assests per share	1206.0 pence
Dividends per share	Total
Inclusive of tax credit	47.5 pence
Net of tax	35.6 pence

2 Explain the term capital gearing and demonstrate whether Conabco is a high- or low-geared company.

3 Comment upon the financial position of Conabco. You should include an assessment of the present stock market valuation of the company, the likely effect of these figures upon that valuation and Conabco's vulnerability or otherwise to takeovers.

Data response B Investment appraisal techniques

Read the following article from the *Bank of England Quarterly Review* of August 1994, which summarises the results of a study undertaken by the Bank of England into the investment appraisal techniques used by 250 UK firms.

Answer the following questions:

1 Why do you think real rates of return are lower than nominal rates?

2 Explain why target rates may vary according to the investment project under consideration.

3 Comment on the importance of discounting techniques according to the study.

4 Explain why the pay-back method remains important.

The appraisal criteria used by firms

This section considers some of the underlying practical issues raised by the adjustment of investment criteria. To understand the process of adaptation to an environment of stable prices, it is necessary to consider both the kinds of investment appraisal criteria firms use and the role they give them in their investment decision-making,

Firms use a wide variety of criteria in their appraisal of investment opportunities. The Bank's inquiry revealed significant differences in appraisal techniques and in the rates of return that firms seek. Those using required real rates generally reported targets in the range of 7%–20%, and those using nominal rates targets in the range of 10%–25%. The average among firms targeting a real rate return was around 15% after tax; nominal targets averaged around 20%. (Given the nature of the inquiry, it would be inappropriate to draw any conclusions from the differential between these average nominal and real target rates of return.) Larger firms tended generally to employ lower target rates than smaller firms.

Other differences – for example, in the cost of capital faced by large and small firms – may partly explain the width of these ranges; the ranges may also reflect differences in the nature of the investments that firms tend to undertake. Nevertheless, the wide variance is an area that warrants further investigation. It would be interesting to assess the significance to the threshold level of firm size, status (eg whether the company is public or private) and other variables.

Within individual companies, target rates of return varied according to the nature of the investment project: its risk, its necessity for the firm and its size. For example, investment in manufacturing operations – where the returns are largely in the form of known cost savings – attracted lower target rates of return than 'riskier' investment in new product development. The difference in the threshold rates within a single company was as much as 10%. Some multinationals distinguished between investments undertaken in different countries, notably between those in Europe and the United States (where the required rates of return are often lower). In addition, a number of firms noted that a significant part of their recent capital expenditure had been on projects which offered no direct commercial return, such as compliance with environmental, and health and safety legislation.

The Bank's inquiry also showed that many firms used more than one criterion when assessing investment opportunities. The criteria used included: net present values; internal rates of return; accounting rates of return; payback periods and broader measures such as the return on capital employed.

Many used accountancy-based measures together with other techniques; this is not surprising given the importance accorded to accountancy practices in many areas of corporate decision-making. It is also not surprising to observe that larger firms tend to employ more sophisticated appraisal and capital-budgeting techniques.

70% of inquiry respondents reported that they made some use of net present values, but other techniques are also common, even in larger firms. Some 40% of firms surveyed used a payback criterion in one form or another; this kind of criterion was used mainly – but not exclusively – by the smaller companies in the sample. It was also notable that many of the firms that used payback criteria alongside other measures stressed the importance of payback rules at that time, ie they sought a target rate of return within a specified period.

Source: Bank of England Quarterly Bulletin, August 1994

23 Enterprise and profit

Learning outcomes

At the end of this chapter you will be able to:

- Appreciate the different views of the entrepreneurial function.
- Distinguish between the accountant's and the economist's views on profit.
- Understand the allocative role that profit plays in an economy.
- Identify profit as a return to innovation.
- Appreciate the relationship between profit and risk.
- Explain monopoly profit.
- Discuss the problems that control of profit represents for the government.

Enterprise

The importance of enterprise

Labour, capital and natural resources do not naturally form themselves into a wealth-making combination.

Someone must make the decisions – not only what to produce but also how and when to produce. The people who undertake this task are providing a very special service because they must, in so doing, take a risk.

In this chapter we discuss the nature of this risk and the consequence of taking it both successfully and unsuccessfully. Economists term this decision-taking and organisational factor ***enterprise*** and the person who supplies it is the ***entrepreneur***.

Some economists have doubted the existence of this separate factor of production – enterprise – and argued that it is just a special form of labour. However, if we do away with the idea we will still have to explain how economic decisions are taken. Having said this, we will find that, as with other factors such as land, it is difficult to identify pure enterprise because it is usually mixed up with other factors. For example, the person who invests in a company by buying shares will be acting as both entrepreneur and capitalist and the reward received will be a mixture of profit and interest.

The role of the entrepreneur

Common misunderstanding

The term 'the entrepreneur' should not necessarily be equated with the owner–manager of a company, although this was the traditional view of the entrepreneur's role. Today the capitalist might be a group of people (shareholders) who have invested money in a business but may have never visited it; alternatively, the capital could just as easily have come from the banks, from the government or from entrepreneurs themselves.

The entrepreneur's function, however, is to *organise* the business. In order to produce goods and services it is necessary for someone to take a risk by producing in ***anticipation of demand***, i.e. since it takes time to produce goods the entrepreneur must predict what the demand is going to be when the goods are produced. Entrepreneurs differ from the other people involved in the business in that the amount of money they make is ***uncertain***. The workers, the capitalists and the landlord will all have to be paid an agreed ***contractual amount*** if the business is not to go into liquidation. There is no way in which one can contract to make a profit, and if the entrepreneur is unlucky or unwise then there will be not a profit but a loss.

In organising production entrepreneurs carry out three main functions:

a) They buy or hire the resources, labour, raw materials, etc., which the business requires.
b) They combine the resources in such a way that goods are produced at the lowest cost.
c) They sell the products of the business in the most advantageous way possible.

We assume that the entrepreneurs will always try to maximise the profits of the business and also that they will act in a rational and sensible manner. These assumptions were discussed more fully in Section II of the book.

STUDENT ACTIVITY 23.1

Can you think of any modern-day entrepreneurs, some of whom may have founded large and successful companies?

The role of profit

Since goods must be produced in anticipation of demand, it is essential that someone takes the risk of doing this. In a mixed economy many production decisions are taken by the government, but there are still many more taken by private persons. Entrepreneurs do not act from a sense of public duty but out of a desire to make profit. Adam Smith argued that the 'invisible hand' of self-interest guided the economy to the best possible use of its resources. This was because, to produce profitability, the business would not only have to produce the goods which people wanted but also have to produce them at minimum cost in order to compete with its rivals. Profit acts not only as an incentive to encourage businesses to produce but also as an indicator. If, for example, profits are high in one particular line of business, this indicates that people want more of that good and encourages more firms to produce it. Also if one firm in an industry is making more profit than another this could indicate that its methods are more efficient, and the other firms will therefore have to emulate this greater efficiency or go out of business.

Schumpeter saw profit and economic development inextricably bound up with each other: 'Without development there is no profit, without profit no development. For the capitalist system it must be added that without profit there would be no accumulation of wealth.'

Thus profit acts as an ***incentive*** to firms to encourage them to take risks, as a ***measure of efficiency*** and as a ***spur*** to the introduction of new products and processes.

Joseph Alois Schumpeter (1883–1950)

We shall have cause to mention Joseph Schumpeter several times in this chapter. Schumpeter was an Austrian who fled to the USA in 1939, where he made his name as professor of economics at Harvard University. He is perhaps best known for his writing on monopolies. His most famous book, *Capitalism, Socialism and Democracy*, was published in 1942 and looked forward to the end of economic growth and capitalism. Despite being one of the most original thinkers of the twentieth century he has never attracted the following of other famous economists such as Keynes, with whom he shared his year of birth.

The entrepreneurial function

In a small firm it is easy to identify the entrepreneur; this may not be so in a large firm. While the board of directors may be the most obvious risk taker, many of the senior and middle management may have to take decisions which in a small firm would be considered the job of the entrepreneur. In a large firm, therefore, the ***entrepreneurial function*** may be spread among many people and be hard to identify. It may also be the case that when a large company is run entirely by managers and not by profit earners they may be less interested in maximising profits and more interested in such things as growth of the company and security. They may therefore act more as risk avoiders than risk takers. (See Chapter 14.)

When a company is in a monopoly position the profits it earns may owe more to dominance in the market than to any risk taking.

Schumpeter foresaw a day when economic progress may have proceeded so far that the entrepreneurial functions become redundant. What would be the result of this?

> A more or less stationary state would ensue. Capitalism being essentially an evolutionary process, would become atrophic. There would be nothing left for entrepreneurs to do. They would find themselves in much the same situation as generals would in a society perfectly sure of permanent peace. Profit, and along with profits the rate of interest, would converge toward zero. The bourgeois strata that live on profits and interest would tend to disappear. The management of industry and trade would become a matter of current consumption, and the personnel would unavoidably acquire the characteristics of a bureaucracy. Socialism of a very sober type would automatically come into being. Human energy would turn away from business. Other than economic pursuits would attract the brains and provide the adventure.

It should perhaps be pointed out that Keynes had a similar view of the future free from most economic wants when he wrote of the 'Economic possibilities for our grandchildren' in his *Essays on Persuasion*.

Achieving the best factor mix

It is the job of the entrepreneur to achieve the optimum combination of factors of production, i.e. to achieve the desired output for the least cost in relation to the demand for the commodity. We examined the principles underlying this in Chapter 19. This is essentially an economic problem rather than a technological one. One can produce a technically superb product such as a Rolls-Royce car and still go bankrupt. It is an economic problem because the supply, and hence the prices, of resources differ greatly from place to place. An English farmer who tried to grow wheat in a manner which is successful in Canada would rapidly come to grief, since in Canada land is plentiful and cheap whereas farming in the UK depends upon getting as much as possible out of a limited area.

Common misunderstanding

The fact that the relative supply and prices of resources vary from location to location and production decisions need to take account of this is a simple but commonly misunderstood point. Many projects in developing countries have come to grief because they have copied the techniques of advanced countries. In most of these countries labour is cheap and plentiful and it may be that the production technique should reflect this fact by using labour-intensive methods wherever possible.

There is no blueprint for the running of a firm because each commercial situation is unique. Two farms side by side will have to be run differently, just as two chemist shops in the same high street will have to be run differently. Therefore in every situation entrepreneurs have to work out that combination of resources which is economically correct. If they do it successfully they will be rewarded with profit – unsuccessfully and they will make a loss. Since they are responsible for production decisions you can see that entrepreneurs are one of the most vital cogs in the economic system.

STUDENT ACTIVITY 23.2

In Chapter 13 it was noted that the largest multinational firms can set up production facilities anywhere in the world. How might a multinational car producer divide its various production processes between developed and developing countries?

Different views of profit

The accountant's and the economist's views contrasted

To the accountant profit is essentially a residual figure, i.e. the money which is left over after all the expenses have been paid. Even so, one might talk of profits before tax or after tax, distributed or undistributed. In the previous chapter, for example, we saw that there is a difference between profit and dividends. To understand these figures fully requires a working knowledge of accounts and is beyond the scope of this book. We may say, however, that there are many judgemental elements at work in accounts. Accountancy is often regarded as an exact study but in arriving at a figure for profit the accountant will have to exercise judgement in ***estimating*** many figures in the accounts; for example, estimates will have to be made in arriving at figures for the value of stock, debts and assets. These calculations are made all the more difficult when the accountant must also estimate the effects of inflation. It is therefore possible for a company to have a healthy-looking balance sheet but be near to insolvency, or to appear to be making virtually no profit at all but be very sound.

It is possible that a firm owns some of the resources it uses; for example, it may have the freehold on its premises. In these circumstances it is essential to its effective running that these are costed and accounted for as if they were rented. This point is developed below.

It is possible for a business to make an accounting profit but an economic loss. This is perhaps best explained by taking a simple example. Imagine the case of a self-employed solicitor who works in premises he or she owns. At the end of the year the solicitor has made £50 000 above the running costs of the practice and therefore regards this as profit. The economist, however, will always enquire about the ***opportunity cost***, i.e. what else could have been done with the resources of capital, labour, etc? We may find on examination that the solicitor could have rented the building out for £10 000 per annum, that the capital involved would have earned £5000 interest if invested elsewhere and that £40 000 could have been earned working as a solicitor for the local council. Under these circumstances the solicitor could be £5000 per annum better off as a result of closing down the practice and placing the resources elsewhere. (See also Data response C at the end of Chapter 14.)

As we saw in Chapter 14, economists also have a view of the ***normal profit*** for a firm. You may recall that normal profit is that amount of profit which is just sufficient to keep a firm in an industry, i.e. even though a firm may be making a profit in accounting terms, if this is very small the entrepreneur will not consider it worthwhile and will close it down. The amount of profit which is considered normal will vary from industry to industry and area to area. Since this profit is necessary to keep the firm in business economists regard this as a legitimate cost of the business. Any profit in excess of normal profit is ***abnormal*** or ***supernormal*** profit.

The source of profit in a firm is an area where there are many different views. We will now move on to consider some of these.

Profits and the returns to other factors

As we saw above in our example of the solicitor, much of what is commonly called profit is in fact the ***implicit cost*** of other factors of production. Thus, for example, the owners of a corner shop might say they have made £40 000 profit but in fact £25 000 is payment for their own labour, £8000 is rent for the shop which they own, and so on. This principle can apply to any size of organisation.

The return to innovation

Schumpeter's view was that profit is the reward for bringing new products or processes to the market. This has a special name – ***innovation***. Innovation is the application of invention to industry. It is often the innovators who are remembered rather than the inventors, e.g. James Watt, George Stephenson and Guglielmo Marconi were all people who made a commercial success of already existing inventions. If someone is ***enterprising*** enough to bring in a new product or process and it is successful then they will for a time make a large profit. This will disappear after a while when competitors copy the process.

Recognising the importance of innovation the state rewards the entrepreneur with a limited legal monopoly of it in the form of ***a patent***. There are of course often many more unsuccessful inventors and innovators than successful ones.

STUDENT ACTIVITY 23.3

Explain the difference between invention and innovation. What innovations or inventions were the following responsible for?

a) Charles Babbage
b) Sir Henry Bessemer
c) Christopher Cockerell

Risks, uncertainty and profit

Frank H. Knight in his book *Risk, Uncertainty and Profit*, published in 1921, said that profit is the reward for a risk successfully taken. Profits therefore arise because the future is uncertain. This would certainly include the innovator's profit because this can be viewed as the reward for the risk of bringing in a new product.

To a certain extent all the factors of production may earn a profit from uncertainty. For example, when a young person decides to train as a lawyer they are taking a risk that society will later wish to buy their services. The person who trains as an engineer runs the risk that they might be replaced by an automated machine. We saw in the previous chapter how the payment made to a debenture-holder in a risky business contains an element of profit. In all these cases, if the risk is successfully taken then the person receives a reward, if unsuccessful a loss. In other words profit can be both positive and negative.

We might distinguish between:

a) a speculative risk, where a broker or similar person buys shares, bonds or commodities in expectation of a favourable change in their price;
b) an economic risk, where an entrepreneur anticipates the demand for goods and services and supplies the product to the market.

Businesses do not, of course, go around looking for 'risky' products. In fact they tend to try to avoid risk as much as possible. Indeed, many risks may be avoided by ***insurance,*** but so long as uncertainty remains in the world, someone, be it the entrepreneur or the state, will have to assume the risk of supplying goods to the market.

Monopoly profits

Where a company has reached a dominant position in the market, it may reap a rich reward without taking very much risk. However, it is not only entrepreneurs who might benefit from monopoly power. A trade union might use its monopoly power in a wage market to obtain a greater reward for its members. Similarly, any factor which is earning an ***economic rent*** could be regarded as making a monopoly profit.

We should distinguish, however, between the situation where a monopolist deliberately contrives a scarcity to drive up the price of the product and a situation where the scarcity occurs naturally.

Economists have traditionally condemned monopoly profits because they cause a distortion in the allocation of resources. Schumpeter, however, disagreed with this view. He maintained that monopolies, with their economies of scale and ability to innovate, are the handmaids of economic growth. As noted in Chapter 17 the Austrian school of economists have emphasised the dynamic benefits of monopoly profit, especially that resulting from entrepreneurial innovation.

The government and profits

The problem

Profits present special problems of control to the government. Although profits are a relatively small share of GDP (15.5 per cent in the UK in 1995), the government may have particular reasons for wishing to control them:

a) *Equity.* In times when the government may be urging restraint upon other factor incomes such as wages, it may find it expedient also to control profits.
b) *Monopoly profits.* Since monopoly profits are usually regarded as undesirable, the government may feel bound to do something about these.

It is arguable that control of profits is more desirable from the point of view of social justice than on straight economic grounds. It has been calculated that monopoly profits may account for only 2 to 3 per cent of GDP, so that redistribution of this would do little for other factor incomes. If we went along with Schumpeter's view, the taxing of monopoly profits may be positively harmful because it may restrict the innovative potential of monopolies on whom, he argues, rests the burden of technological change. It should be stated that this view is highly contentious. In the 1980s the then Conservative government, which was highly sympathetic to capitalists, nonetheless found it necessary to bring in special regulatory powers to control the monopoly profit-making potential of the newly privatised utilities, such as telecommunications, gas, water and electricity.

The control of profits

If a government decides to restrict profits there are two main ways by which it might do this:

a) *Price controls.* By forcibly holding down the price which a firm wishes to charge, the government can reduce or eliminate profit. There are two circumstances in which this might be the appropriate policy. First, the government might wish to do this as part of an incomes policy. To enlist the cooperation of trade unions in any incomes policy it will be necessary to have price restraint. Second, irrespective of prevailing economic conditions, price control is one of the best ways of dealing with monopoly profit. This is the method of control used by the respective agencies (e.g. Oftel, Ofgas, Ofwat, Offer) that are responsible for regulating the utilities.
b) *Taxation.* The government has a number of fiscal weapons which it uses, depending upon how the profits arise and how they are paid. The earnings of a company are taxed by ***corporation tax***. However, the firm will usually incur less tax if it ploughs profits back into the business rather than distributing them. On distribution the profits may also become subject to ***personal income tax***. Profits which are made from the sale of shares, commodities, property, etc., are taxed by ***capital gains tax***.

If we regard taxation as a method of dealing with abnormal profit we face the problem of identifying the amount of normal and abnormal profit in the profits of any particular company. This is difficult because, as we have seen, the rates of normal profit may differ significantly from one industry to another.

Furthermore, taxing monopoly profits does not alleviate the misallocation of resources involved in prices and output policy of the monopolist. Despite such problems, and for reasons of equity, the new Labour government of 1997 imposed a one-off ***'windfall' tax*** on the profits made by the utilities since privatisation.

The consequences of profit control

The control and taxation of profit present problems to any government. Although poor controls may be appropriate to a monopoly, and may be politically expedient, elsewhere they run the risk of forcing the firm into a loss and so driving it out of business. Since profits are the return to enterprise, high profits could be regarded as the reward to a very successful business. By removing this profit the government will take away the incentive for firms to seek new opportunities and to take new risks. Under these circumstances the removal of profits could have a disastrous effect upon the economy. Alternatively, the firm may find it possible to pass taxes on to consumers by way of higher prices, in which case the objective of the government will have been defeated. If the business is an exporter, high taxation may have the effect of making its products uncompetitive abroad.

Another problem of company taxation is that it encourages what Keynes termed 'the double bluff of capitalism'. This is where companies are not taxed on the profits which they plough back because capitalisation will be to the advantage of the economy. The ploughing back of profits will, however, lay the foundation for even larger profits in the future. Undistributed profits also improve the dividend cover, thus forcing up the price of shares and making capital gains for their owners.

Conclusion

Ricardo believed that profits would decline while wages are fixed at a subsistence level: wages are fixed while increased demand for land, because of population growth, forces up rents, therefore contracting profits. Marx also believed that profits must eventually decline, squeezed in the dialectic of materialism. We have also seen in this chapter that Schumpeter believed profit would disappear in the long run and the economy would stagnate.

None of these gloomy prophecies seems to have come true, nor are they likely to. Nonetheless, one of the crucial issues facing any modern economy is whether or not to expect continuous increases in employment, growth and profits.

Summary

1. Enterprise is the vital decision-making factor in the production process, deciding what, how and when to produce and when to take a risk by producing in anticipation of demand.
2. Profits fulfil a vital allocative function in the economy, redistributing resources from one use to another, rewarding efficiency and punishing inefficiency.
3. As with the other factors of production, it is very difficult to isolate pure enterprise.
4. The job of the entrepreneur involves achieving the best mix of the factors of production, i.e. the one which gives the desired output for the lowest cost.
5. The accountant's and the economist's view of profit differ. The economist has a view of normal profit which is counted as a cost of the business. This is not so in accountancy.
6. Profits may be the return to enterprise and innovation, to risk or to monopoly.
7. The control of profits presents particular difficulties for the government. On the grounds of equity, it can be argued that profit should be controlled but controlling profit may stifle enterprise.

Questions

1. What is meant by 'implicit' factor earnings? Compare this with other concepts of profits.
2. Discuss the arguments for and against taxing 'excess' profits.
3. Given the fact that monopoly profits only account for a relatively small proportion of GDP, there seems little point in controlling them. Do you agree?
4. A teacher spent several months of her spare time writing a book for which she subsequently received £2000 in royalties. She argues that, since her only costs were paper and typewriter ribbon, nearly all the £2000 could be regarded as profit. Do you agree? Give reasons for your answer.
5. The role of the entrepreneur and of risk taking is fundamental to a capitalist society. However, if we consider a communist state there appear to be no entrepreneurs. Is it therefore true to say that there are no economic risks in a communist state? If there are risks, who takes them and who benefits (or loses) from them?
6. Assess the importance of profit as an allocative mechanism in the capitalist system.
7. What does an economist mean by 'normal profit'? Explain why a firm's normal profit is unlikely to be the average rate of profit for the economy as a whole.

Data response A
Why the age of the inventor is over

Read the following article which was printed in the *Guardian* newspaper, 4 March 1988.

Answer the following questions:

1. What reasons does Professor Bell give for saying that the inventor now 'disappears from the horizon'?
2. What is meant by the term the 'post-industrial society'?
3. What is the role of invention and innovation in the creation of profit?
4. If Professor Bell's arguments are correct on the nature of research and its impact on post-industrial society, what are the implications for government policy towards profits, companies and the economy?

Data response B
'Health' warning for companies

Read the article on p. 305 taken from *The Financial Times* of 14 April 1997. Then attempt the questions that follow:

1. Explain why the 'health' of many companies still seems precarious, despite the relatively good prospects for the UK economy.
2. Comment on the possible impact of the 'windfall' tax on the utilities.

3 State which industries appear financially the strongest and which the weakest. Can you suggest any reasons for such differences?

4 Why might the financial performance of firms vary not just *between* industries, but also *within* industries?

Why the age of the inventor is over

Peter Large
Technology editor

THE INVENTOR is dead. Long live the pure scientist. That, according to a first-division futurologist, is one of the already established strands of post-industrial change.

Professor Daniel Bell, of Harvard, listed the evidence in a lecture at Salford University yesterday.

All the major industries of the industrial age – steel, electricity, the phone, even aviation – were created by 'talented tinkerers' who were clever with equipment but knew little, or cared less, about the science behind their ideas.

Alexander Graham Bell, one of the inventors of the phone, was a speech teacher who wanted to transmit amplified voice by wire to help the deaf.

Thomas Edison, who invented the long-lasting filament for the light bulb, the phonograph, and the motion picture, was a mathematical illiterate.

Marconi invented radio communication while knowing little about scientific work on radio waves.

And Bessemer, whose inventions led to stronger steel, knew equally little of what had been discovered about the properties of metal.

But the developments that underpin the post-industrial economy stem from science.

Einstein's work was the starting point for opto-electronics; Bohr's model of the hydrogen atom, constructed in 1912, was the key to today's solid-state physics and therefore to the microchip; Alan Turing's mathematical work in the 30s created computer science.

On the basis of that evidence Bell gets dogmatic. Theory now precedes artifice, he says. The inventor 'disappears from the horizon'.

There will always be innovation and new products, but fundamental innovation in theoretical knowledge – not just in physics but in biology or cognitive psychology – becomes 'the new principle of innovation in society'.

So much for the UK government's reduction in investment in pure science. On other fronts, too, Bell's conclusions are a refutation of most of the industrial-age thinking of Thatcherism. What he says about today's need for deeper education investment, about obsolete economics, about the logic of devolving more government power to local units, is not merely orthodox post-industrial thinking; it's what many nations are actually doing.

Bell's aphorism here is: 'The national state has become too small for the big problems of life and too big for the small problems.' Today's politics, he says, are increasingly ineffective in dealing with the tidal waves of the international economy. 'Coordination through economic summitry is only a charade.'

Equally, when political decisions are concentrated in a bureaucratic centre, the nation state is too big 'for the diversity and initiative of the varied local and regional units under its control'.

Post-industrial society, Bell says, is not a projection of existing trends. It is a new principle of social organisation, just as the industrial age replaced an agrarian way of life.

The change to activities based on information-processing and automation of production is producing a social way of life that becomes a 'game between people'. The old service jobs of the industrial age were auxiliary to industry – transport, real estate, utilities. The new ones are 'human' services – health, social services, professional help, analysis, design, programming.

Classical economics saw services as inherently unproductive. But education and health services contribute to the increased skills and strengths of a population.

Source: *The Guardian*, 4 March 1988

'Health' warning for companies

By Daniel Green

One in 14 listed UK companies will fail or have to be restructured in the next three years, according to a report published today by Syspas, a City-based risk evaluation consultancy.

But the finances of utility companies are so strong that the Labour party's proposed windfall tax "is unlikely to have any material effect upon the financial health of this sector", it says.

Syspas analyses profitability and balance sheets in published accounts – especially the proportion of short-term liabilities – to establish the risk of financial failure.

Its latest survey says that although the UK economy is doing well there is 'no improvement' in the health of UK companies.

Based on an analysis of 1,482 fully-listed companies and another 256 on the Alternative Investment Market, not only is the proportion of weak companies not improving but those already weak are not strengthening.

About 21 per cent of the companies had "profitability and/or balance sheets that have not yet been restored to financial health following the ravages of the past recession," said Mr Guenter Steinitz, Syspas's chief executive.

Of these, 110 companies are "expected to undergo major reconstruction or even fail before the millenium".

Sectors most at risk include extractive industries and smaller retailers. Many companies in mineral extraction, for example, lose money and rely on short-term funding of their fixed assets.

Tesco, Sainsbury, Asda and Safeway have steady profit margins of about 5.5 per cent but smaller rivals have seen margins fall from about 8 per cent to 2 per cent "with a consequent increase in the likelihood of financial distress".

The strongest industries are gas distribution, pharamaceuticals and telecommunications. "This is hardly surprising with profit margins of the water companies averaging 32 per cent," said Mr Steinitz.

Syspas says there is little difference in the financial health of fully-quoted companies and those on Aim.

Aim was established in June 1995 and, on average, the turnover of an Aim-quoted company is just 3 per cent of that of a fully-quoted company.

Aim-companies have average profit margins of 7 per cent, compared with 8 per cent for main market companies, but they are less dependent on short-term funding.

The Health of Corporate UK, Syspas, 11–13 Dowgate Hill, London EC4R 2SU.

Source: *Financial Times*, 14 April 1997

SECTION IV Applied microeconomics

'"Would you really tax General Motors for selling unsafe cars? Isn't that selling the right to destroy human life?" The economist thought for a moment and replied, "Surely it is better than giving that right free of charge."'

W. Baumol and W. Oates

24 An introduction to welfare economics

Learning outcomes

After reading this chapter you will be able to:

- Apply a precise criterion of efficiency to problems of production and allocation.
- Describe the conditions necessary for a market economy to be efficient.

Introduction

What is welfare economics about?

In Chapter 1 we saw that some economists believe it is possible to have a value-free economics. But whatever the philosopohical considerations of such a stance, economists are *inevitably* led to examine the questions of what ought to be done by the very nature of the problems they study. Economics is concerned with the problems of choice in the face of scarcity; it is vital to ask the question 'What would be the best use of existing resources?' (Making the best use of existing resources is of course what is meant by 'economising'!)

The notion of 'best' can only be defined by making normative judgements, i.e. subjectively. I might take it to mean that I have everything and you have nothing; you of course might define it differently. Nevertheless, it would seem absurd for the economist to reply 'I can offer no suggestions as to what might be considered the best allocation of resources.'

It is important, however, that the economist makes clear exactly what value judgements have been made and how economic decisions would be altered if different value judgements were made. In this way the economist can clarify the thinking of the final decision maker without claiming a monopoly of knowledge of what is morally right or wrong.

Welfare economists study both positive and normative questions. The notion of 'best' in economics involves considerations of both efficiency and equity.

Different schools of economists approach the welfare question from different perspectives. Mainstream economists use neo-classical economics to construct welfare criteria and analyse the welfare attributes of market economies. Inevitably, this imparts a bias towards seeing welfare in terms of maximising individual satisfaction in the face of scarcity rather than, say, achieving a contented or 'good' society. This is not to say one bias is better than the other, but in the following account of welfare economics you should be aware of the 'hidden' neo-classical perspective of emphasising the individual rather than the collective welfare.

The Pareto criterion

Production or technical efficiency

In neo-classical welfare economics, the term efficiency has a precise meaning. This was first formulated by Vilfredo Pareto (1848–1923), an Italian economist and philosopher. He gave a definition of efficiency which sought to separate questions of efficiency from those of equity. Accordingly, he argued that a change is only unambiguously better if no one loses from it. Such an improvement in which no one loses is called a ***Pareto improvement***. According to this criterion, if a situation exists in which it is possible to improve the welfare of someone without making anyone else worse off, then it cannot be efficient to leave the situation as it is. Therefore, inefficiency can be said to exist whenever there is an unexploited potential for a Pareto improvement. This reasoning led to Pareto's definition of efficiency which now underpins neo-classical welfare economics:

'Pareto efficiency' requires that it must not be possible to change the existing allocation of resources in such a way that someone is made better off and no one is made worse off.

This criterion is intended to guard against wasting opportunities for gaining more utility for some people out of existing resources at no expense in terms of lost utility to others.

STUDENT ACTIVITY 24.1

Think of a time when you have seen something which could be described as 'inefficient' (if you can't think of a situation imagine a plumber and a carpenter are forced to swap jobs). Now give examples of how, by removing the inefficiency, at least one person could benefit without anyone losing out. Satisfy yourself that the original situation therefore fails the Pareto criterion for efficiency and is therefore inefficient.

We can illustrate this idea of efficiency by referring back to the concept of an economy's production possibility function (see pages 30–5). In Fig. 24.1 we assume that, because of a misallocation of resources, e.g. land best suited to growing wheat is being used for barley production and vice versa, the economy is producing at point A in the diagram. Let us also accept that consumers always desire more of both wheat and barley, i.e. 'goods are good'. Now what can be said about point A in terms of the Pareto criterion? Clearly point A is not Pareto optimal, for, by changing the allocation of resources, it would be possible to have:

(i) more wheat and no less barley;
(ii) more of both wheat and barley;
(iii) more barley and no less wheat.

These three possibilities are shown in Fig. 24.1.

STUDENT ACTIVITY 24.2

You should now satisfy yourself that a move to anywhere in the shaded area would be a Pareto improvement compared with point A.

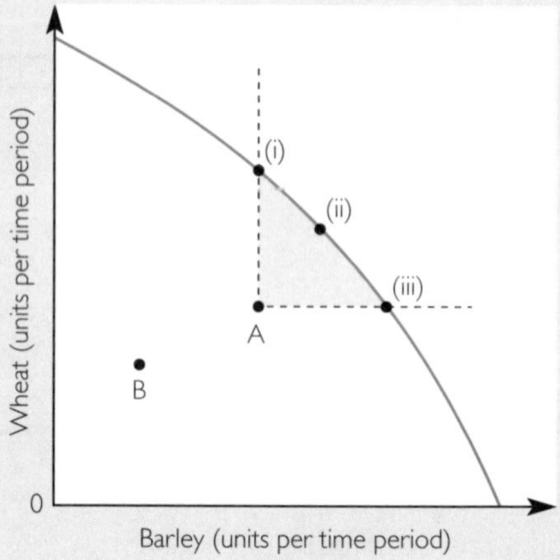

***Fig. 24.1* The Pareto criterion**

If, then, it is possible to have either more of one good and no less of another, or more of all goods, then it follows that it must be possible to distribute this extra output in such a way that all consumers are made better off or some consumers are made better off without other consumers being made worse off. This is simply because there is more to share out! If this is done a 'Pareto improvement' has been made. You should now be able to explain why a movement from B to A in the diagram also represents a Pareto improvement even though A itself is also an inefficient point.

Points on the production boundary are said to be production, or technically, efficient in that it is not possible to increase the output of one good without decreasing the output of another.

Common misunderstanding

Sometimes students write that a situation is efficient if it is possible to increase the welfare of someone without decreasing the welfare of another. Write out why this is incorrect before reading on. (Hint: Can a situation be efficient if a potential Pareto improvement has been ignored?)

Allocative efficiency

It is tempting for the student to think that points on the production boundary must represent

Pareto-efficient resource allocations. But this is not necessarily the case as another aspect of efficiency has also to be considered. Although such points *do* demonstrate that production is efficient, this does not ensure that the ***product mix*** is Pareto efficient, i.e. that resources are allocated in the right proportions to producing the various goods. As was the case with productive efficiency, ***allocative efficiency*** again requires that it must not be possible to change the existing product mix in such a way that someone is made better off and no one is made worse off (or, of course, everybody is made better off!). In fact at most points on the production boundary this possibility will arise!

Take for example the point in our wheat/barley example where the production possibility boundary crosses the horizontal axis, i.e. where the economy is producing nothing but barley. It seems most unlikely that consumers as a whole would not be prepared to sacrifice any of this barley in order to obtain some wheat (you might like to think of this as sacrificing some beer, which is made from barley, in order to obtain some bread to eat). If consumers are prepared to make this sacrifice then overall welfare, in the Pareto sense, could be increased by moving along the production boundary, sacrificing barley output in order to increase the output of wheat.

It turns out that the potential for such a Pareto improvement will in fact exist whenever consumers are prepared to accept, in return for the sacrifice of 1 unit of one good, an amount of another good which is less than the amount which the economy can in fact provide for that sacrifice. This is best explained by an example.

Suppose that consumers as a group are prepared to sacrifice 1 unit of barley in order to obtain 3 units of wheat, but that the economy's production possibility boundary is such that decreasing the output of barley by 1 unit would allow the output of wheat to increase by 4 units. It would thus be possible to use three of the four extra units of wheat to compensate consumers for their loss of barley and use the remaining unit of wheat to raise overall welfare, i.e. to bring about a Pareto improvement. Only when changes in the product mix can just compensate consumers, and no more, is it no longer worthwhile making further changes to the output mix. This could also be expressed by saying that it is no longer worthwhile moving further along the production possibility frontier. We will then have reached the Pareto-efficient product mix.

Allocative efficiency exists when it is not possible to bring about a Pareto improvement by changing the product mix.

STUDENT ACTIVITY 24.3

Draw a curved production possibility boundary as in Fig. 24.1. Use a ruler to approximate the slope of the line at a point near the vertical axis. Now do the same for a point near the horizontal axis and for a point half-way along the curve. For each of the points, write out in words the rate at which wheat would have to be given up in order to gain one more unit of barley. Now assuming that consumers are prepared to substitute barley for wheat at the rate given by the slope of the line at its centre, explain why a movement along the boundary towards the centre from the other two points would constitute a Pareto improvement. For Pareto efficiency what must the relationship be between the rate at which consumers are prepared to substitute barley for wheat and the rate at which it is possible to substitute barley for wheat in production?

When the slope of the production possibility boundary is equal to the rate at which consumers as a whole are just prepared to substitute one good for another then at this point there will be both technical (production) efficiency and allocative (product-mix) efficiency – both are needed for Pareto efficiency.

Efficiency and the free market

The price mechanism and Pareto optimality

We now turn to the important question of whether the allocation of resources as determined by a free market is Pareto efficient. Not surprisingly the answer is no. But it is possible to construct a set of highly unrealistic assumptions under which a free market economy would be Pareto efficient in equilibrium. Economic theory has demonstrated that under these assumptions (the first of which is that perfect competition exists in all markets!) the price mechanism would act automatically to bring about a Pareto-efficient allocation of resources, i.e.

Under certain conditions, which do not exist in the real world, a price mechanism would automatically bring about production/technical efficiency and allocative/product-mix efficiency.

You may now be asking: 'If Pareto optimality does not exist in the real world, nor will it ever be likely to exist, what is the point of studying it?' The answer is quite simply that unless we are aware of the conditions necessary for Pareto efficiency we will not be able to identify deviations from these conditions. Hence this unrealistic model can, perhaps, provide a useful point of departure for discussing reality.

STUDENT ACTIVITY 24.4

Think of a partner, relative or friend. Do you consider them to be perfect? (Unless perhaps you are entranced in the very first stages of romance.) You will obviously answer no – as we all fall short of being perfect. But how do we know something is less than perfect unless we compare it with something which is probably an unrealistic notion of perfect? Imagine your idea of a perfect person and then consider whether such a person is realistic.

The conditions for Pareto efficiency

The conditions under which a free market economy, functioning via the price mechanism, would produce a Pareto optimal allocation of resources are summarised in the *first optimality theorem* of modern welfare economics:

If, in all markets, there is perfect competition, no externalities and no market failure connected with uncertainty, then the resulting allocation of resources will be Pareto efficient.

(See Chapter 25 for a discussion of externalities such as pollution.)

Needless to say, the situation described by this theorem is not even an approximate description of reality. Nevertheless it is often used as a benchmark by economists with which real-world situations are compared.

STUDENT ACTIVITY 24.5

Before reading on, try to work out for yourself why monopolies, externalities such as pollution, and uncertainty might prevent a Pareto-efficient allocation of resources.

Pareto efficiency and perfect competition

If you have understood the chapter so far you will be able to grasp in an intuitive way why the conditions stated in the first optimality theorem will produce Pareto efficiency. Turning first to the question of production or technical efficiency, you should be able to use what you have learned from Chapter 16 to see that the assumption of perfect competition in all markets is sufficient to ensure this result. We can explain this by remembering that the model of perfect competition assumes that firms are profit maximisers and have perfect knowledge of production techniques and factor prices, and that all factors of production are perfectly mobile. Therefore firms will choose the least cost methods of production. In short, firms will hire those factors which are relatively most productive and will use the smallest possible quantity of these factors to produce any given output. This efficient use of factors of production and cost minimisation would ensure that, for any given level of resources, overall output is maximised. That is:

If there is perfect competition in all markets the economy will be operating on its production possibility frontier and will therefore be production (or 'technically') efficient.

Pareto efficiency and market equilibrium

You may recall from Chapter 9 that the theory of demand and supply in competitive markets depended on the assumptions of perfect competition. We saw above that the assumption of perfect competition will bring about production efficiency but you now know enough to understand why an economy composed of competitive markets could also automatically bring about allocative efficiency (ignoring problems of externalities and uncertainty). If there is both productive and allocative efficiency then the economy is Pareto efficient as a whole.

To explain how competitive markets bring about allocative/product-mix efficiency we need to give new interpretations to our familiar demand and supply curves.

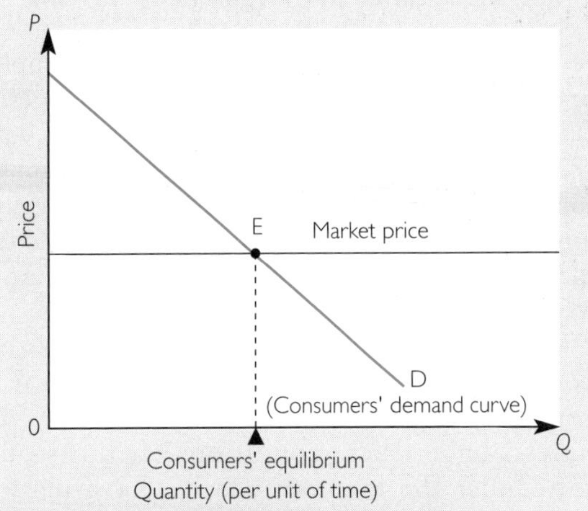

***Fig. 24.2* Marginal valuation of a product**
Point E is where the consumer's marginal valuation of the product is equal to the price of the product.

Social marginal benefit (*SMB*)

Under the conditions of perfect competition all consumers are faced with the same price for a product. We also know that consumers will continue to purchase extra units of this product so long as they place a higher monetary value on these units than the price they actually have to pay (this is the concept of consumer surplus, see Chapter 9). They will thus consume extra units of the product up to the point at which the monetary valuation they place on the marginal unit of consumption is equal to its price (see Fig. 24.2).

Thus when consumers are in equilibrium, the price of a product will reflect its marginal valuation by consumers (in monetary units). As this price is common to all consumers, it follows that *all* consumers will be attaching the same monetary valuation to their marginal unit of consumption. We will call this monetary valuation the ***social marginal benefit*** (*SMB*) of the marginal unit of output of the product concerned. The demand curve for a product, of course, shows how much of the product will be demanded at any market price. Hence by reading off the market price at a specific output, the demand curve automatically shows the social marginal valuation of the product at any level of output (see Fig. 24.3).

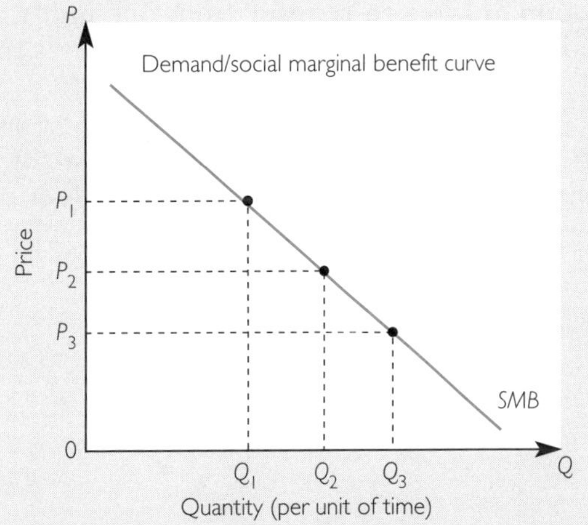

***Fig. 24.3* The social marginal benefit curve**

We can see that at an output of Q_1 the *SMB*, i.e. consumer valuation of the last unit sold, is equal to P_1. At Q_2 the *SMB* is equal to P_2, and so on. As might be expected, the demand curve for the product shows that the *SMB* of an extra unit falls as output increases.

If all markets in the economy are perfectly competitive (and there are no externalities or uncertainty) the demand curve is also the social marginal benefit curve.

The significance of marginal cost pricing

We now turn to the interpretation of the supply curve under the conditions of perfect competition. Recall that firms in perfect competition will produce up to the level of output at which marginal cost is equal to price. Hence, reading up from the quantity axis, the supply curve tells us what the marginal cost of production is at any level of output (see Fig. 24.4).

We can see that at Q_1 the marginal cost of production must be equal to P_1. What, however, is the significance of marginal cost for analysis under these conditions? It turns out that, under the assumptions we have made, marginal cost will measure the valuation by consumers of the alternative products forgone by increasing the output of the product concerned by 1 unit. We can explain this somewhat surprising result as follows. Recall that in perfect competition the factors of production are free to transfer from one industry to another. Now as marginal cost measures the payment to the factor services needed to produce the last unit of output: the cost of these extra factors, at the margin, must be just sufficient to induce these factors of production away from their best alternative employment.

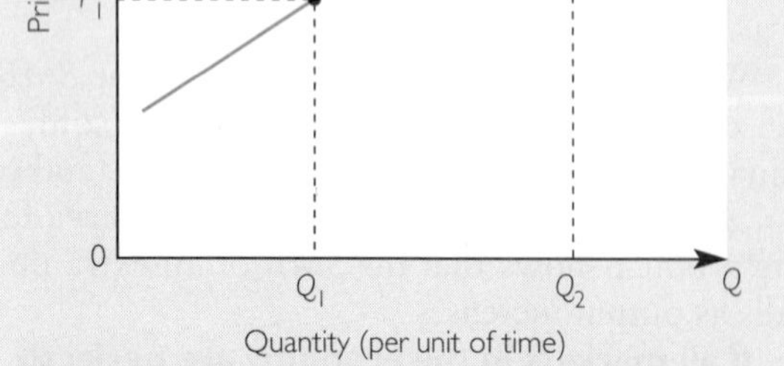

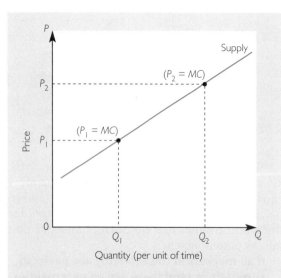

Fig. 24.4 **The supply curve is the marginal cost curve**

In short, the payment to these extra factors will equal the opportunity cost to these factors of forgoing their best alternative employment in another industry (another way of saying this is that these factors must be paid their transfer earnings; see Chapter 21). Hence if factors are perfectly mobile they must be paid, at the margin, the amount they could earn in their best alternative employment. However, the amount these extra factors could earn in an alternative industry will be equal to the amount that consumers would pay for the alternative products that could be produced by these factors, i.e. the valuation by consumers of the alternative products forgone. Hence we have the result that, under perfectly competitive conditions:

The marginal cost in one industry measures the valuation by consumers (in monetary terms) of the alternative products that are forgone by increasing the output of that industry by 1 unit. This valuation of alternatives forgone is the 'social marginal cost' (*SMC*).

STUDENT ACTIVITY 24.6

You should now work through the following sequence until you are satisfied that you understand why *MC* is also equal to *SMC*:

MC = Payment to extra factors required = What these factors could have earned in an alternative industry = Consumers' valuation of alternative products forgone = *SMC*

Let us now run through this new interpretation of the supply curve. The supply curve of an industry under perfect competition is represented by the marginal cost of that industry at any level of output. This marginal cost in turn measures the value to consumers of the alternative forgone, i.e. the *SMC*. We thus have the result:

If all markets in the economy are perfectly competitive (and there are no externalities or uncertainty) the supply curve is also the social marginal cost curve (Fig. 24.5).

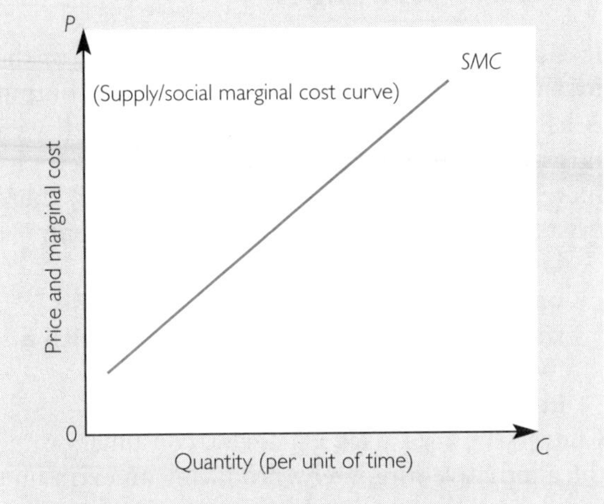

***Fig. 24.5* The social marginal cost curve**

The welfare significance of market equilibrium in a perfect market

The equilibrium price

From the previous section of this chapter we have derived the following results:

a) The price that consumers will pay for the last unit of output of a product is equal to the marginal valuation by consumers of the product concerned. This is known as the social marginal benefit of this unit of output and is shown by the demand curve for the product.

b) Marginal cost reflects what the factors used to produce the last unit of output could earn in their best alternative employment. These earnings in turn reflect the valuation by consumers of these alternative uses of factors. Hence marginal cost measures the valuation by consumers of the best alternative products forgone by increasing production by 1 unit. This valuation is called the social marginal cost (*SMC*).

c) Because firms in perfect competition will produce where price equals marginal cost the supply curve automatically shows the *SMC*.

We can now draw the following important conclusion for perfectly competitive markets:

When the market for a product is in equilibrium the last unit of a product bought is valued equally by consumers to the best alternative forgone by its production. There is thus an optimum balance between scarcity and want.

This is illustrated in Fig. 24.6.

The Pareto- or socially efficient level of output

It is now fairly easy to see why an equilibrium of output at which $SMC = SMB$ corresponds to a Pareto-efficient allocation of resources. We need only consider the points either side of the equilibrium level of output.

In Fig. 24.7 we can see that at Q_1 consumers value an extra unit of output more than the alternative that would be forgone by its production. The actual gain in welfare available to consumers and hence 'society' from the production of an extra unit at Q_1 is given, in monetary units, by $SMB - SMC$, i.e. the vertical distance between the demand and supply curve is the excess of consumer valuation of the extra unit over its marginal cost of production. The overall welfare loss associated with the output Q_1 can therefore be calculated, in monetary units, by summing the

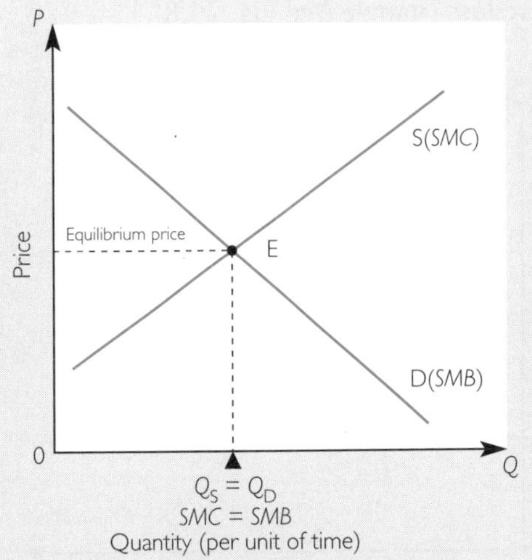

***Fig. 24.6* The socially efficient price**

This occurs where consumers' valuation of the best alternatives forgone by producing an extra unit (*SMC*) is equal to consumers' valuation of an extra unit of the commodity (*SMB*).

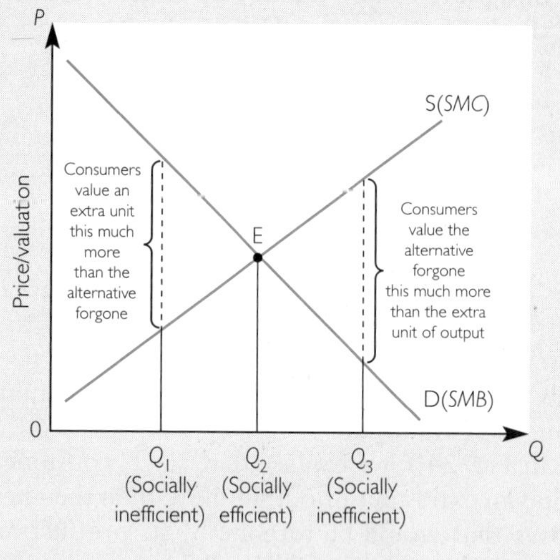

Fig. 24.7 **The social efficiency of the equilibrium price**

vertical distance between the supply and demand curve for all extra units up to the point at which the level of output is Pareto efficient. Thus the loss of welfare to society associated with the output being at Q_1 rather than the socially efficient output of Q_2 can be represented by a welfare loss triangle (see Fig. 24.8).

Welfare loss triangles

It can be seen that under the assumptions of the first optimality theorem, whenever actual output is below the market equilibrium the overall welfare of consumers could be increased by increasing the output of the product, i.e. there exists the potential for a Pareto improvement.

Under the assumptions of the first optimality theorem outputs below the market equilibrium are associated with a 'welfare loss' and hence a socially inefficient allocation of resources.

Conversely, at Q_3 (see Fig. 24.9), consumers value the alternative forgone by producing an extra unit more than they value that extra unit of output. There is therefore a welfare loss, as consumers would have preferred the alternative now forgone. The welfare loss associated with the production of this marginal unit can be measured in monetary units by the vertical distance between the demand and supply curve, i.e. *SMC* – *SMB*. As the overall welfare of consumers could be increased by decreasing the output of the product and diverting resources towards alternatives, it is clear that at outputs above the market equilibrium a potential Pareto improvement exists. The overall welfare loss associated with the output Q_3 can be calcu-

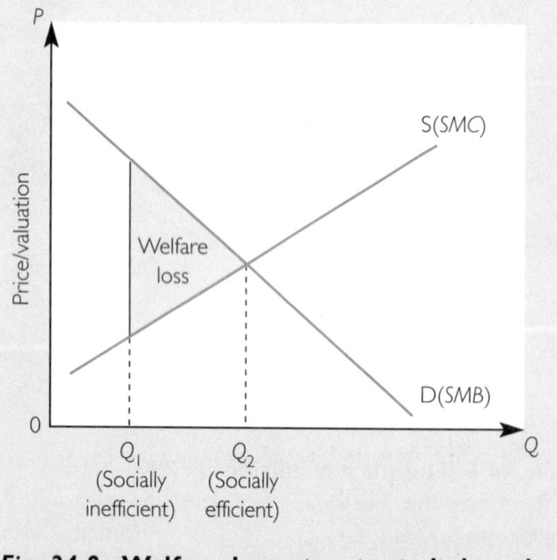

Fig. 24.8 **Welfare loss at outputs below the equilibrium**

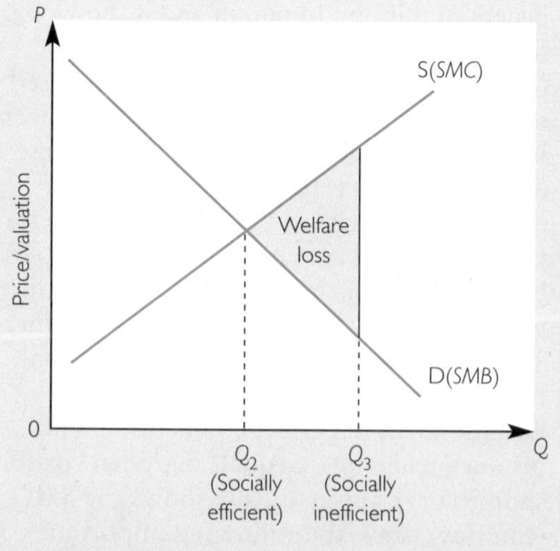

Fig. 24.9 **Welfare loss at outputs above the equilibrium**

lated by summing the vertical distance between the demand and supply curves for all units of output from Q_3 down to Q_2. Hence the loss of welfare to society associated with output being at Q_3 rather than the socially efficient output of Q_2 can again be represented by a welfare loss triangle. This is illustrated in Fig. 24.9.

Under the assumptions of the first optimality theorem, outputs above the market equilibrium are associated with a 'welfare loss' and hence a socially inefficient allocation of resources.

STUDENT ACTIVITY 24.7

Suppose a politician attempts to bribe the electorate by saying he will print enough money to buy everyone a new washing machine. Explain why the effect of this would tend to decrease the welfare of consumers rather than increase it.

Common misunderstanding

SMB = SMC *is often called the socially 'optimal' point and hence often regarded as unambiguously the 'best' level of output. But we were careful to note the individualistic nature of the Pareto criteria. The Pareto criterion says* nothing *about fairness. For example, the rich may cause a high demand for Rolls-Royce cars and their valuation exceeds their valuation of the alternatives. Conversely the poor may place a high marginal utility on food but lack the money to convert this want in to a monetary valuation and hence demand. In short, the rich have more money 'votes' as to how resources should be allocated. Redistributing income would tend to decrease the demand for Rolls-Royces and increase the demand for certain foodstuffs. Thus a new set of Pareto-efficient equilibriums will be established. Thus for every Pareto-efficient equilibrium there is a given income distribution.*

The 'invisible hand' theorem

The only point at which it is impossible to change the allocation of resources so as to bring about a Pareto improvement is Q_2. This is the level of output which would be arrived at through the operation of market forces! At this point want and scarcity are brought into balance and the gain, in monetary units, to consumers from the last unit of output is exactly matched by the cost in terms of alternative output forgone. This result that, subject to certain conditions, the equilibrium of an economy in which all markets operate under the conditions of perfect competition will be socially (i.e. Pareto) efficient, is known as the 'invisible hand' theorem. The name of the theorem reflects the belief of some writers that it is a rigorous statement of the ideas of Adam Smith (in Chapter 45 we look at an alternative interpretation of Smith's ideas by the Austrian school of economics).

For some this theorem is taken as a powerful argument in favour of a free market system. Others point out that the assumptions needed for the efficiency of free markets are so unrealistic that the theorem actually demonstrates that real-world markets are socially inefficient. Yet others argue that the theorem is totally abstract and therefore has no implications for real-world market systems. But, whether justified or not, the 'invisible hand' theorem, intuitively or rigorously stated, has had enormous influence in political and economic circles. Since the early 1980s it has often been called upon as part of the argument for a shift away from state intervention and a greater reliance on market forces both in the West and the East. For this reason alone it should be examined carefully, but such welfare economics is now also an important part of economics syllabuses. Its approach is developed and criticised in the rest of this section of the book.

Summary

1 Welfare economics is concerned with both positive and normative questions. The notion of best considers both efficiency and equity.
2 Pareto efficiency (often referred to as Pareto optimality) requires that it must not be possible to change the allocation of resources in such a way that someone is made better off and no one worse off.

3 Under certain rigorously stated conditions Pareto efficiency in both production (technical efficiency) and consumption (allocative efficiency) may be brought about by the price mechanism.

4 The first optimality theorem states that if in all markets there is perfect competition, no externalities and no market failure connected with uncertainty, then the resulting allocation of resources is Pareto efficient.

5 The social marginal benefit (*SMB*) is the monetary valuation of the marginal unit of consumption.

6 Social marginal cost (*SMC*) in one industry measures the valuation by consumers of the alternatives forgone by increasing the output of that industry by 1 unit.

7 Under the conditions stated, where the demand (*SMB*) curve intersects with the supply (*SMC*) curve, the resulting equilibrium price is Pareto optimal. Any other level of output involves a welfare loss.

8 When these conditions are met in all markets, there is said to be 'social' efficiency and this is often referred to less accurately as a socially 'optimum' allocation of resources. The conditions necessary for this result are described by the 'invisible hand' theorem.

Questions

1. Discuss the statement: 'Because of their special training economists are in a better position than politicians to decide which economic policies should be implemented.'
2. 'Economists are in agreement on the answers to positive questions; it is over normative issues that they disagree.' True or false?
3. Explain why Pareto efficiency is not necessarily the same thing as the 'best' situation.
4. Examine Fig. 24.10 and rank points A, B, C, D and E in terms of Pareto optimality. Is a complete ranking possible? If not why not?
5. Assume that an economy consists of three consumers and two industries. The production function is such that, at present output levels, an increase in the output of barley of 4 units requires

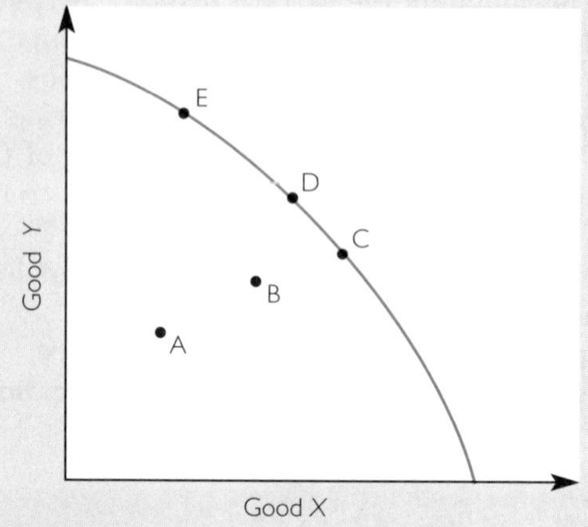

Fig. 24.10

a reduction in the output of wheat of 1 unit. The rates at which the consumers are prepared to exchange wheat for barley are given by the following table:

Consumer A is prepared to sacrifice 1 unit of wheat for 5 units of barley
Consumer B is prepared to sacrifice 1 unit of wheat for 3 units of barley
Consumer C is prepared to sacrifice 1 unit of wheat for 1 unit of barley

Demonstrate that this does not represent a Pareto-efficient product mix.

6. Assume that an economy has a fixed weekly output of milk and coal. This economy also has two groups of consumers, type A and type B. With the present distribution of output between consumers, group A consumers would be indifferent between a choice of 1 litre of milk and 5 kg of coal. Group B consumers, on the other hand, would be indifferent between a choice of 5 litres of milk and 1 kg of coal. Demonstrate that consumption is not Pareto efficient.
7. Assume that you are given the following information about a two-good, two-consumer economy. An increase in the production of oats of 1 tonne necessarily requires a reduction in the output of rye of 2 tonnes. If both consumers traded 1 tonne of oats for 2 tonnes of rye their levels of satisfaction would be unaltered. What can you say about the efficiency of the existing allocation of resources in this economy?

8 Consider the following two statements:

> This so-called perfect market economy constitutes the formal basis for propositions about the advantages of perfect competition. **P. Bohm**

> Once we have cleansed the impurities in impure value judgement by a rational debate, we are left with factual statements and pure value judgements between which there is indeed an irreconcilable gulf on anyone's interpretation of the concept of 'facts' and the concept of 'values'. **M. Blaug**

Attempt to reconcile these two statements.

9 Discuss the view that an unaided price mechanism ensures the best allocation of resources.

Data response A
Prices, output and welfare

Assume that there are two perfectly competitive industries, X and Y, and there is only one factor of production, labour. Labour has no non-monetary preference for working in either industry.

The marginal product of labour in industry X, at the present level of output, is one (*MPP* = 1).

Now attempt the following questions:

1 If the wage in industry X is £100, what is the marginal cost (*MC*) in industry X?

2 The marginal product of labour in industry Y is two (*MPP* = 2) and the price of a unit of Y is £50. Assuming equilibrium, show that the *MC* of industry X measures the valuation by consumers of the number of units of Y forgone by increasing the output of industry X by 1 unit. (Remember that in perfect competition the wage equals the labour's marginal product multiplied by price.)

3 Using the above information explain why the equilibrium is said to be socially efficient.

4 Demonstrate how the equilibrium would be likely to change if there were an increase in the price of product X.

5 Explain the loss of welfare if the production of product X involved the output of negative externalities.

25 Market failure

Learning outcomes

After reading this chapter you will be able to:

- Identify aspects of the real world which do not meet the efficiency criteria developed in the last chapter.
- Apply the tax/subsidy solutions to problems of externality.
- Identify products for which the market fails to exist.
- Recognise when criteria other than efficiency may be appropriate, such as paternalism or equity.

Causes of market failure

In the previous chapter we demonstrated that under certain conditions an economy that has perfect competition in all markets has equilibrium positions that are socially (or Pareto) efficient. The conditions necessary for this outcome were summarised in the first optimality theorem of modern welfare economics. We can thus gain insight into why efficiency is not achieved in real-life markets by examining the implications of deviations from the conditions assumed in this theorem. It is also necessary to consider the income distribution in society. Efficiency might not be enough on its own without a fair distribution of income.

Imperfect competition

Welfare loss under imperfect competition

A profit-maximising firm, operating under the conditions of monopoly or monopolistic competition, produces and sells the volume of output at which marginal cost and marginal revenue are equal. Equilibrium will thus occur with marginal cost being less than the market price. From the arguments of the previous chapter this implies social inefficiency, i.e. a loss of welfare to society. This is illustrated in Fig. 25.1, where the shaded area represents the welfare loss to society, with the firm producing output Q_1 rather than Q_2.

Common misunderstanding

It is often thought by students that monopoly pricing is inefficient because it results in high prices for consumers. This is not an efficiency problem in itself, but a separate problem of

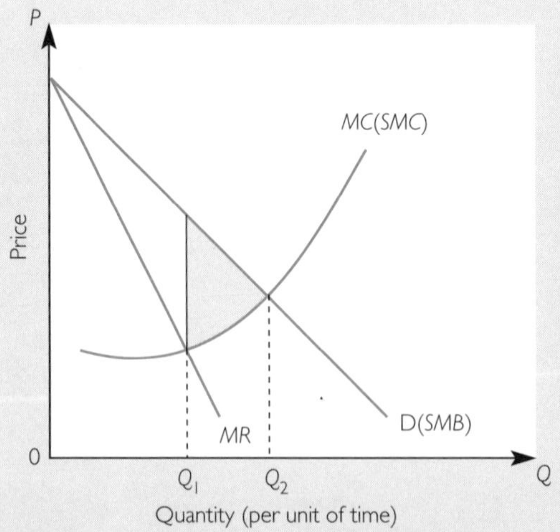

Fig. 25.1 **Welfare loss under imperfect competition**

Q_1 is the profit-maximising output, while Q_2 is the socially efficient output. The shaded area represents welfare loss at the profit maximisation equilibrium.

income distribution. The consumers' loss is the monopolist's gain. The inefficiency results from the misallocation of resources between industries, with too few resources going to the monopoly industry. Check back in Chapter 24 if you are unsure of this.

Cost inefficiencies

So far we have looked only at the loss of social welfare caused by price exceeding marginal cost. However, the lack of competition might also result in cost inefficiency. Firms which are, for various reasons, insulated from competition might have the potential to make very large profits and thus are not forced to minimise costs in order to match the prices of their competitors. In such situations firms may have discretion as to the objectives they pursue; for example, they may pursue managerial objectives (see Chapter 14). To the extent that costs are not minimised, this will result in a second kind of efficiency loss caused by unnecessarily high production costs. This welfare loss can again be represented diagrammatically.

In Fig. 25.2 the shaded area between the two marginal cost curves, up to Q_1, represents the social loss caused by the cost-inefficient production of Q_1 units of output. If, however, costs are reduced to MC_2 the socially efficient output becomes Q_2. Thus the shaded triangle between Q_1 and Q_2 would also be available as part of the total welfare gain to society. The whole of the shaded area therefore represents the welfare loss to society from the wasteful method of production.

Some, admittedly inconclusive, empirical evidence has suggested that the welfare loss from cost inefficiency in monopolies is far greater than that caused by underproduction. This has led some observers to state that underproduction due to monopoly pricing policy is of no practical significance. However, it has been pointed out by other observers that even a small welfare loss in the present will accumulate into a large long-term welfare loss if left uncorrected. It should also be pointed out that policies designed to decrease monopoly power through increased competition will tend to reduce both types of inefficiency. Government policy towards market power is discussed in Chapter 18.

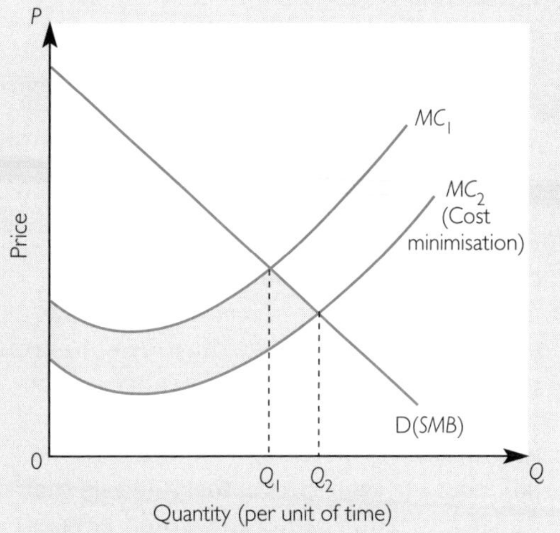

***Fig. 25.2* Cost inefficiency**

If monopoly protects inefficiencies then the cost curve is MC_1 instead of MC_2, which is where it would be under competitive conditions. Thus the shaded area represents the welfare loss to society.

Externalities

What are externalities?

Externalities are said to exist when the action of producers or consumers affects not only themselves but also third parties, other than through the normal workings of the price mechanism.

This is likely to result in allocative inefficiency because individuals normally consider only the private costs (the cost incurred by themselves) of their decisions. They largely ignore, or are unaware of, the wider social costs (the full opportunity cost to society) and benefits of their actions. External effects can be either positive or negative. For example, if one person is cured of a contagious disease this obviously gives benefit to others; hence the external effect is said to be positive. On the other hand, airports near residential areas are likely to have negative external effects because of the noise of aircraft taking off and landing.

We can categorise these 'spill-over' effects under four headings:

a) *Production on consumption.* A negative example of this would be the adverse effects of pollution on recreational areas. A positive externality could result from the warm-water discharge from many industrial cooling processes making rivers more attractive to bathers.
b) *Production on production.* A negative externality would result if the release of industrial waste into rivers decreased the catch of commercial fishermen. An important positive externality in this category is that arising from the use of non-patented inventions. As inventors would receive no payment for their efforts this suggests that under *laissez-faire* too little would be spent on research and development.
c) *Consumption on production.* Negative externalities might arise from the careless discarding of packaging on farm land. Alternatively, congestion caused by private motorists will increase the transportation costs of many firms. Positive externalities in this category are in principle possible, but in practice of little significance.
d) *Consumption on consumption.* Negative externalities include the unwelcome noise from radios and the congestion caused to other private road users of using one's own car. Positive externalities include neighbours enjoying the sight of each other's gardens and the fact that other people's possession of a telephone increases the utility of one's own telephone. A rather controversial negative externality in this category is that of envy (see page 25, conspicuous consumption). It is argued that status-orientated consumption by one consumer is likely to reduce the utility of others. However, it might conversely be argued that the copying of others' consumption is due to the information provided by this consumption. This latter argument suggests a positive rather than a negative externality, i.e. people are receiving free information.

It should be noted that the same spill-over effect can simultaneously have both positive and negative effects; for example, the smoke from oil refineries is beneficial to the cultivation of citrus fruits, but it can also be considered as undesirable pollution.

Pecuniary 'external effects'

Pecuniary 'external effects' are the effect of prices in one sector of the economy upon other sectors of the economy.

As we have seen, prices are determined by the interaction of all the economic 'units', i.e. producers and consumers, in the economy. Hence the act of demanding or supplying these units by one group will affect the prices faced by other groups. Although such changes can cause a redistribution of welfare among units, they are not a cause of allocative inefficiency. This is because such effects work *within* the price mechanism; they are not external to it and are therefore not ignored by profit- or utility-maximising decision makers. For example, if firms in one industry increase their demand for a particular factor of production, this is likely to raise the price of this factor of production. It is not a case of market inefficiency because it is the normal working of the price mechanism; the increased price of the factor of production merely reflects the fact that it is scarce in relation to the demand for the products it produces. Such price increases provide an incentive for producers to economise in the use of this factor and conveys to consumers the fact that to have more of one product they must, as a group, have less of another. It is exactly this type of consideration that brought about the efficient balance between wants and scarcity outlined in the previous chapter.

In view of the confusion between pecuniary externalities and true spill-over effects, it might be better to call the former 'price effects'. However, in a world of imperfect information pecuniary effects do have an importance as regards efficiency. For example, suppose that one entrepreneur found an ideal but remote location for a hydroelectric dam, but also finds that it would be uneconomical to transmit power to where it is in demand and decides not to go ahead with the project. Further suppose that a separate entrepreneur surveys the same area and finds that it is rich in deposits of bauxite (the ore from which aluminium is extracted). Aluminium smelting requires vast amounts of power, so this entrepreneur also decides not to go ahead with this project. It might thus be the case that if both projects were to go ahead the first entrepreneur would be able to sell electricity at a high enough price to make the dam profitable and the second entrepreneur would be able to buy electricity from the first entrepreneur at a low enough price to make the smelting of aluminium profitable. The essential point to realise here is that it is not the pecuniary effects themselves that are the cause of market failure; indeed they work in exactly the direction required. It is the lack of information and hence coordination between the entrepreneurs that results in inefficiency. We will return to the problem of market failure caused by incomplete information later in this chapter.

Negative externalities

Consider the soap industry, which, in a free market, would discharge waste products into the air and rivers. This is because owners of soap factories, if they are profit maximisers, will consider only their private costs and ignore the wider social costs of their activities. Indeed, if competition was fierce, they might be unable to incur the cost of purification or non-polluting disposal of their waste products and still match the price of their competitors. Where such negative externalities are present the price mechanism is likely to fail in bringing about a Pareto-efficient allocation of resources. This is because the cost to society in terms of the deterioration of the environment is unpriced by the price mechanism. Private profit makers are given the use of the environment free of charge. It is in this sense that such spill-over effects are external to the price mechanism. The cost to society of the use of this resource is not reflected in the private costs of the individual using it. Individuals are thus 'invited' to destroy these resources at zero price. No incentive is provided by the price mechanism to economise on the use of the environment and hence the price mechanism fails to bring about an efficient balance between the wants of society as a whole and the use of the scarce resources available to it.

Using the analysis we have developed we can again represent the welfare loss resulting from negative externalities in the form of a diagram. This is illustrated in Fig. 25.3. It is assumed in the diagram that the soap industry is perfectly competitive. The supply curve of the industry is thus the horizontal summation of the marginal cost curves of all the firms in the industry (see Chapter 16). This curve is represented by the private marginal cost curve (*PMC*) in the diagram. As firms in perfect competition will equate *MC* to price, the free market equilibrium output of the industry is thus Q_E. The social marginal cost (*SMC*) curve represents the full opportunity cost to society of an extra unit of soap production. *SMC* lies above *PMC* as *SMC* includes not only the cost to society in terms of forgone alternative marketed products, i.e. *PMC*, but also the loss to society in terms of the deterioration of the environment, i.e. the external marginal cost (*EMC*). *EMC* represents the loss in value corresponding to what consumers would have been prepared to pay to avoid this loss in utility from the environment associated with extra units of soap production. It can be seen that *SMB* equals *SMC* at Q_D units of output.

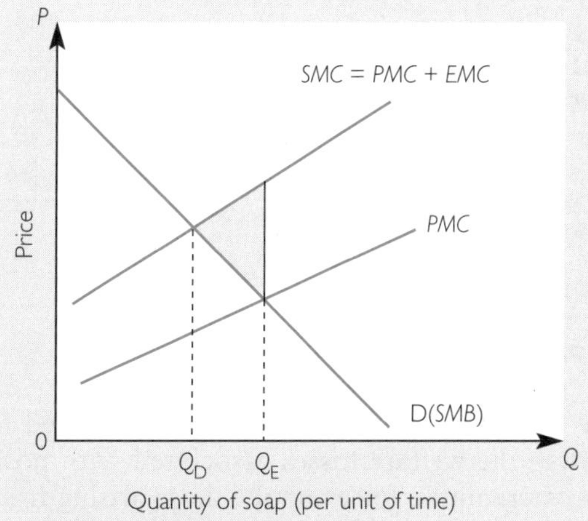

***Fig. 25.3* Negative externalities**
Q_E represents the profit-maximising equilibrium when firms in the industry are able to ignore external marginal costs (*EMC*). The socially efficient output is Q_D. Thus the shaded area represents the welfare loss to society at the profit-maximising equilibrium.

Thus in terms of social efficiency, as we have defined it above, there is an oversupply of the private good, soap. By summing the excess of *SMC* over *SMB* for the units between Q_D and Q_E we again arrive at a monetary measure of the welfare loss to society, i.e. the shaded triangle in the diagram.

Because of this overproduction of goods in cases of negative externality, economists have often suggested that the government should intervene in such markets to correct the situation. The Cambridge economist, A. Pigou, suggested that a tax on the private good should be introduced to reflect the cost of the externality. A full discussion of the possible range of policies follows in Chapters 26 and 27.

STUDENT ACTIVITY 25.1

Suppose that Fig. 25.3 represents the costs and benefits associated with flights from a particular airport. The costs are the noise suffered by local residents. The benefits are the willingness of passengers to pay for the flight. The government decides to put a tax on the airlines because of the externality they are producing. Consider the following consequences of this action:

1 What will happen to the number of flights?
2 What will happen to the price of flights?
3 Will the local residents be any better off as a result of this policy?
4 Should the tax revenue be used to compensate the local residents for the remaining level of noise?

Positive externalities

The same framework as above can be used to analyse the welfare losses associated with positive externalities; for example, those arising from medical care, attractive front gardens, telephone installations and inventions and innovations which can be copied without charge. We could proceed by representing social costs as being less than private costs. It is conceptually easier, however, to represent the positive externality by an upward shift of the marginal benefit curve. This indicates that the benefits of consumption include not only the benefits to the purchaser but also the benefits to those enjoying the positive spill-over effects of this consumption.

We have adopted this procedure in Fig. 25.4. Here the upward shift in the *SMB* curve represents the valuation of other residents of having their neighbours' property protected by fire alarms. It can be seen that when positive externalities exist there is a tendency for underproduction of the product in question, i.e. the Pareto-efficient output is greater than the equilibrium output that would occur in an 'uncorrected' free market. Pigou suggested that this situation could be corrected by giving a subsidy to the private good to reflect the external benefit arising from its consumption. Subsidies to public transport and higher education are good examples of this type of policy. Free provision of school education and health care in the UK also reflects the existence of positive externalities. In these cases the policies are also concerned with issues of equity which is discussed later in this chapter. Government policy in this area is discussed in more detail in Chapter 29.

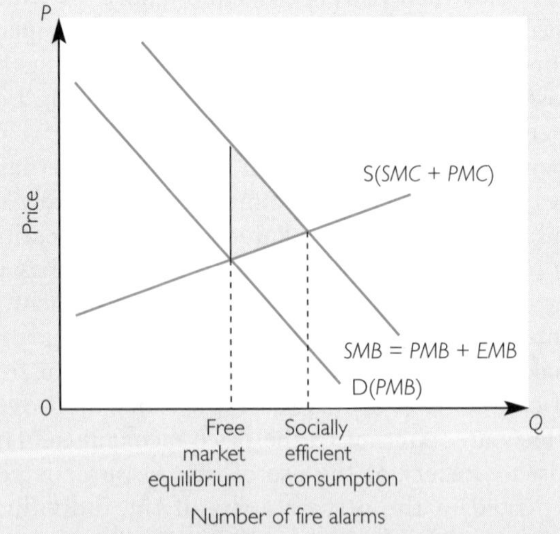

Fig. 25.4 **Positive externalities**
The existence of external marginal benefit (*EMB*) shifts the *SMB* curve to the right. The free market equilibrium is below the socially efficient level of consumption. The shaded area shows the welfare loss brought about by underproduction.

STUDENT ACTIVITY 25.2

Classify the following in terms of positive, negative and pecuniary externalities:

a) Smoke from a soap factory.
b) One firm in an industry sets up a training school for its workers.
c) A mine owner installs a powerful pump which lowers the water table in the area.
d) A driver makes a right turn on a busy road and causes a traffic jam.
e) A school leaver decides to go to university.
f) A home owner plants an attractive front garden.
g) A crop disease increases the price of bread.
h) Fred hits Bill.
i) A reduction in the number of people using buses results in higher prices.

Public goods

Definition of public goods

We have already mentioned public goods in Chapter 6. We will now define them more precisely.

Public goods are defined as products where, for any given output, consumption by additional consumers does not reduce the quantity consumed by existing consumers. Another way of putting this is that the marginal cost of production for an extra person is zero.

There are relatively few pure public goods: defence and lighthouses are the examples usually cited. In cases of pure public goods, it is not possible to think of individual consumption. Provision of public goods is for everyone or no one; either the country is defended against external aggression or it is not. An increase in population would not result in any increase in the cost of defence, but more people would be 'consuming' the good. Public goods are therefore said to be ***non-rival in consumption***. This contrasts sharply with purely private goods such as chocolate bars, where consumption by one person rules out the consumption of that chocolate bar by another person. Private goods are said to be ***rival in consumption***, which also implies positive marginal cost.

Indivisibility and collective consumption

There is another group of goods which appear to have the characteristics of a public good up to a certain level of consumption, but which then appear to become private goods. Uncongested roads, parks, swimming pools, buses and bridges can all take extra customers at virtually zero costs up to a capacity limit. Once they reach that capacity limit, however, marginal cost rises again, often very substantially. The cost of putting on an extra bus for one extra passenger, because the previous bus has filled up, is very high. When a road reaches its capacity, congestion results in extra costs. These fall on the motorists themselves in terms of wasted time and high car running costs at low speed. These are not cases of public goods, but instances of indivisibility in production. Production is 'lumpy' and can only be increased by large increments. If a congested two-lane motorway needs to be enlarged to meet increased demand, the only way to do it is to increase capacity by 50 per cent by adding a third lane. The term collective consumption or collective goods is used to describe these situations.

Public goods and property rights

A pure public good has the characteristics of non-rivalry in consumption, as discussed in the previous section. It also is characterised by ***non-excludability***. This means that, unlike private goods, it is difficult to create property rights over the product that can be enforced. If you buy a chocolate bar the property rights over it belong to you. If someone takes the chocolate bar from you by force, they have committed a crime (admittedly a fairly small one) and you could call on the police and the courts to *enforce* your property rights over the chocolate bar! The same arguments do not apply to public goods like defence. The best way to understand this is to imagine door-to-door defence sales people calling at your house, attempting to sell you some of the defence 'product'. After they have interested you in the idea of defending your country, if you are reasonably intelligent you will ask them if they are already producing this product. If they say yes, a selfish person will then say they are not interested in buying the product. This kind of behaviour is called ***free riding***. Since the person is already defended they have no interest in paying for the product. The consumers who have already paid for the provision of defence have no means of preventing such 'free rider' consumers from benefiting from their purchase. They have no enforceable property rights over the product because it is a public good.

Of course if everyone behaves in this selfish way there is a chance that the product will not be produced at all, even though there is considerable demand for it. There is a way around this problem adopted by most governments. Defence is usually provided through the government, not the market, and *citizens* pay compulsory taxes to finance it rather than *consumers* paying voluntary prices. This brings us to a third characteristic of public goods: **non-rejectability**. Some citizens may have a moral or religious objection to violence which leads them to be opposed to paying for the armed forces. Their objection may be more specific, e.g. opposition to the use of nuclear weapons. They will still have to pay taxes to finance these 'products' which they do not want.

The characteristic of non-rivalness in consumption implies zero marginal cost and therefore, for efficiency, a zero price. This makes public goods unattractive to private enterprise. The characteristic of non-excludability suggests that private enterprise would in any case find it extraordinarily difficult to persuade people to part with their money. Therefore not only is it impossible to charge for the consumption of public goods, it is also undesirable. These considerations obviously make public goods unsuitable for provision through the price mechanism. The characteristic of non-rejectability, however, also provides us with some objections against the provision of public goods by the state!

Collective action

It is possible to object that people are not as selfish as the above discussion of free riders suggests. In practice people act collectively in charities, voluntary social work, religious and political organisations, clubs and societies, trade unions, and youth organisations. The 'voluntary sector' is in fact quite a sizeable chunk of the economy! In the 1960s, Olson argued that small groups were more likely to be effective in setting up such collective action, because the benefits to an individual were quite large compared with the costs of setting up the necessary organisation. He argued that as groups got larger and larger, they became progressively more difficult to mobilise. Social incentives such as status, honours, embarrassment, or even intimidation, might be necessary to make larger organisations work effectively. However, he accepted that where people are motivated by ideology or faith, their beliefs are sometimes powerful enough to overcome their natural human selfishness.

The voluntary sector is clearly an interesting alternative to government provision for those who wish to reduce the role of the state. Olson's analysis suggests that the government will need to give the voluntary sector encouragement if it is to be a success. A fuller discussion of the role of the state is to be found in Chapters 6 and 29.

STUDENT ACTIVITY 25.3

The difficulty of collective action can be demonstrated by an experiment. Divide your class into groups of about five students (without the help of your teacher/lecturer). Each student should take responsibility for reading up, understanding and explaining one of the following concepts to fellow group members: non-excludability; free riders; non-rejectability: non-rivalness in consumption; indivisibility. Arrange to meet outside normal class time to exchange the information you have gained. At the end of the experiment check how many people refused to cooperate or did not turn up, and how many people listened to other students' explanations but had not done much work themselves (free riders). Remember, this is a small-group situation so you should have some success.

Public goods, efficiency and valuation

The *SMB* curve of public goods

Given all these difficulties, is it possible to decide on the Pareto-efficient level of output of a public good? It was thought too difficult until the American economist, Paul Samuelson, put forward a solution in the 1950s. Because all consumers of a public or collective good consume the same output, the social marginal benefit of such products is the vertical summation of all the individual consumers' private marginal benefits. As we shall see in Chapters 27 and 29, the estimation of these benefits poses difficult problems. However, we shall ignore these problems for now and assume that we can draw individual demand curves which measure the true willingness to pay of each individual consumer. This is shown in Fig. 25.5.

The Pareto-efficient output will have been reached when the aggregate valuation of the last unit is equal to the valuation of the best alternative forgone by its production. This is shown in Fig. 25.6, where the Pareto-efficient output of a public good is where the *SMC* curve cuts the *SMB* curve. It may appear to the alert reader that the idea of a positive *SMC* for a public good contradicts the idea of non-rivalness in consumption. Earlier in the chapter it was argued that the marginal cost of producing the good to an additional consumer is zero. The *SMC* does not measure the cost of providing the same level of defence to an extra person, but the cost of providing more defence to everyone. If the government buys additional fighter aircraft, the level of defence provision has been increased, and clearly the marginal cost of doing so amounts to several million pounds. When thinking about public goods, it is important to understand that there are two concepts of marginal cost. Samuelson appears to have solved the problem of the correct output levels of a public good in theory, but we are left with the problem of estimating people's willingness to pay.

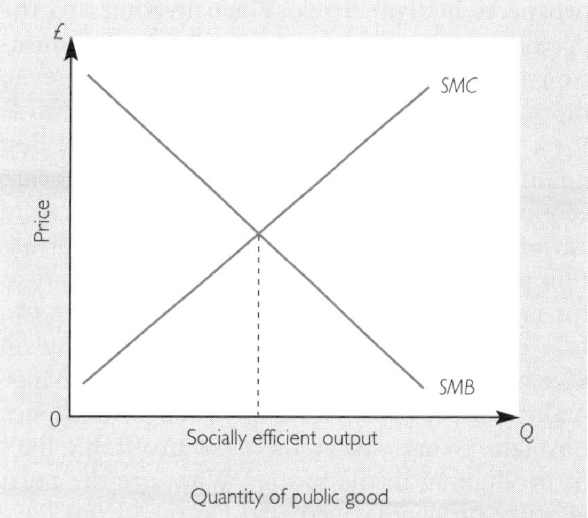

Fig. 25.6 **The socially efficient output of a public good**

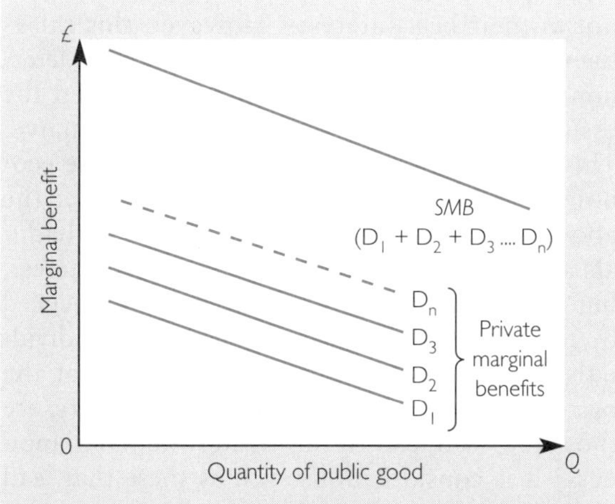

Fig. 25.5 **The social marginal benefit curve of a public good**

Imperfect knowledge

We now drop the last of the conditions assumed in the first optimality theorem, that of perfect information. Lack of information is probably the most apparent cause of market failure to consumers. We have all no doubt experienced frustration from our less than perfect knowledge of the prices on offer, the qualities and range of commodities on offer and our weakness in resisting persuasive advertising. As workers we also are forced to make decisions based on incomplete information regarding, for example, the wage rates on offer in an area, the jobs available in other areas, even other countries, and career prospects in rival firms. When it comes to the decision to invest in human capital, i.e. in education and training, the problems become even more acute. How are we to know our aptitude for a particular career? What exactly are the best qualifications? How are we to know how future economic changes will affect the prospects from various careers? Producers face similar information problems concerning available supply prices for labour, raw materials and capital. They too face uncertainty when it comes to deciding on investment projects, e.g. will technological change make present processes unprofitable and hence obsolete? What will be the most profitable lines of production in the future? What are the most effective productive methods? Do rival firms have information not possessed by one's own firm?

It is the cost of information which causes many economic decisions to be less than optimal, thus resulting in inefficiency. Information gathering involves inputs of resource and time. In principle it is an easy matter to define the optimum level of 'search'. Search should continue up until the point at which the marginal benefit from search is equal to the marginal cost. However, there is a logical problem here: how can the benefit from extra search be calculated unless the content of the resulting information is known? But if the content of the piece of information is known, there is no need to search for it! As with public goods the application of the $SMC = SMB$ condition raises more problems than it solves.

Merit goods

Problems of definition

We have so far defined merit goods as:

> **Those products or services which are not distributed through the price system but on the basis of merit or need.**

The concept of merit goods is somewhat controversial and is often confused with information and externality problems. Thus health care is often given as an example of a merit good. It is argued that consumers will not know in advance if they are going to need expensive health treatment and thus might underinvest in health insurance; as we have seen this can be analysed in terms of a lack of information. Alternatively, it is argued that health care benefits people other than just the recipient, and should therefore be subsidised. This analysis is essentially correct but is simply an application of the analysis above concerning positive externalities.

The essential reasons why health care and other products might be thought of as merit goods is the consideration that fully informed consumers might not be the best judge of what is best for them.

This of course immediately begs the question, 'Who is the best judge?' It is thus best to state that merit goods arise from a divergence between the values of society (as expressed through government) and the values of individuals. Hence smokers might be fully informed of the health risks to themselves yet society might feel obliged to act in a paternalistic manner by discouraging this activity through taxation. Tobacco, in this case, would be an example of a 'de-merit' good; drugs and pornography might be considered to be other examples. Products considered by governments to be undervalued by many citizens have included opera and art in general, libraries and milk.

Obviously where addiction is involved, e.g. as with a drug addict, consumers themselves might admit that their own immediate preferences are not in their best interests. However, this raises the very deep problems of free will and the determination of tastes. As sociologists point out the assumption of 'given tastes' is extremely naïve. This again emphasises that modern welfare economics is normative rather than positive; the above analysis implicitly assumes that individuals are the best judge of their own best interest, but individuals' tastes are bound to be influenced by the nature of the society in which the individuals live. How then can they be sure that the present goals, both of themselves and society, are those that will lead to the greatest human happiness? It is considerations such as these that lead some individuals to feel justified in overriding the preferences of others.

Merit goods and future generations

If we accept the definition of merit goods as arising from the fact that consumers might not be the best judges of what is best for themselves, we may see that this is allied to the problems of future generations. If people currently alive cannot take economic decisions in their own best interests, how should we evaluate the welfare of future generations? Investment and consumption decisions taken today often have effects extending far into the future, nuclear waste and indestructible plastics being obvious examples.

Some commentators have argued that advancing technology and economic growth will mean improved living standards. Hence economic decisions should be weighted in favour of existing generations. Other observers argue that pollution, the depletion of non-renewable resources and rapid world population growth will lead to crises. Hence economic decisions should be weighted in favour of the future rather than the present. The essential point for the analysis outlined in the previous chapter is that future generations, like animals and the destitute, have no money votes. Hence their preferences are ignored by the price mechanism. Society then might decide that policies which protect the interests of future generations are desirable, as the wishes of these generations cannot be directly reflected by their own 'money votes' or laws in the present.

Equity

Even given the attainment of Pareto efficiency, we cannot be sure that the outcome will be socially desirable. The initial distribution of wealth in society may result in a distribution of income with a few wealthy individuals at the top, and a large group of poor people at the bottom. If the labour market does not work well, there may be some people with no income at all without the assistance of charity or the welfare state. Even with a successful labour market, some people may be in this position because of an inability to work, due to sickness, disability, or old age. There is thus an argument for the state to intervene to help those in difficulties, by redistributing the incomes allocated by the market. Feelings of envy or injustice may also persuade politicians that money should be taken away from those who are very rich.

Conclusion

In this chapter we have outlined the reasons free markets will not, in practice, result in Pareto efficiency. Our conclusion must thus be that it is impossible for a *laissez-faire* market economy to attain a state of Pareto efficiency. In the next chapters we will examine how analysis might be used to design policies intended to help real economies reach a more efficient state. However, we will also note arguments which claim that the first optimality theorem does not provide a fruitful point of departure when it comes to policy formation. We will additionally examine the concept of 'the maximisation of social welfare'; as we can see this is a broader concept than efficiency, in that the former includes considerations of equity as well as efficiency.

Summary

1. The restriction of output involved in profit maximisation under imperfect competition brings about a welfare loss to society.
2. If monopolistic practices protect inefficient cost structures this also involves a welfare loss.
3. Externalities exist when the actions of producers or consumers affect third parties other than through the price mechanism.
4. Where changes in prices in one market influence other sectors of the economy this is said to be an external pecuniary effect, perhaps better described as 'price effect'.
5. Public goods are those where, at any given output, consumption by additional consumers does not reduce the quantity consumed by existing consumers. An example of this would be defence.
6. The socially efficient output of public goods is where the *SMB* curve intersects the *SMC* curve, but this is very difficult to determine.

7 Collective action by the voluntary sector is sometimes a viable alternative to intervention by the state to provide public goods. However, there are difficulties in mobilising collective action.
8 Imperfect knowledge is a major source of inefficiency in markets, both for consumers and producers.
9 Merit goods are normally defined as those distributed on the grounds of merit or need rather than by price. However, the essential reason goods such as health care are thought of as merit goods is the paternalistic consideration that fully informed consumers might not be the best judge of what is best for themselves.
10 Because of the problems caused by such things as externalities, ignorance and merit goods it is impossible for a fully *laissez-faire* economy to be socially efficient.
11 Even with an efficient price mechanism, problems

Questions

1 Demonstrate that if the monopolists were able to practise perfect price discrimination there would be no loss of welfare through inefficiency, i.e. output of the goods would be socially efficient (assume profit maximising behaviour). Explain why this situation might be held to conflict with equity considerations.
2 Assume that a monopolist equates *MR* and *MC* but does not minimise production costs. Draw a diagram indicating the total welfare loss to society resulting from inefficiency.
3 Discuss the view that not enough attention is given to the interest of future generations in taking economic decisions today. Give examples both for and against this argument.
4 Discuss the arguments for and against charging tuition fees for higher education.
5 Explain why collective action is observed to be the preferred solution in the following cases:
   a) trade unions
   b) Oxfam
   c) religious groups
   d) amateur football clubs.
6 Identify which of the terms on the left below are relevant to the industries on the right below:

a) Public good	1) Water
b) Externality	2) Defence
c) Monopoly	3) Education
d) Equity	4) Electricity
e) Collective action	5) Healthcare
f) Merit goods	6) Roads
g) Indivisibility	7) Rail

Data response A
Overcoming market failure

Study the following extract from *The Economist* of 17 February 1996 and then answer the following questions:

1 Give examples of how the market has overcome the problem of market failure in each of the following cases:
   a) monopoly
   b) external benefit
   c) public goods
2 Categorise each of the following according to the type of market failure that is involved:
   a) clean air
   b) law and order
   c) education
   d) defence
3 How can a lack of information create market failure? Which institutions can be seen as an attempt by the market to make the best use of limited information?

Schools brief

State and market

People are quick to assume that "market failure" justifies action by the government. This final brief in our series on economic fallacies argues for a strong presumption in favour of markets – not because they always work perfectly (they never do) but because the alternative is usually worse.

According to the central deduction of economic theory, under certain conditions markets allocate resources efficiently. "Efficiency" has a special meaning in this context. The theory says that markets will produce an outcome such that, given the economy's scarce resources, it is impossible to make anybody better-off without making somebody else worse-off.

Economic theory, in other words, offers a proof of Adam Smith's big idea. In a market economy, if certain conditions are met, an invisible hand guides countless apparently uncoordinated individuals to a result that is, in one plausible sense, the best that can be done.

In rich countries, markets are too familiar to attract attention. Yet a certain awe is appropriate. When Soviet planners visited a vegetable market in London during the early days of *perestroika*, they were impressed to find no queues, shortages, or mountains of spoiled and unwanted vegetables. They took their hosts aside and said: "We understand, you have to say it's all done by supply and demand. But can't you tell us what's really going on? Where are your planners, and what are their methods?"

The essence of the market mechanism is indeed captured by the supply-and-demand diagram shown in chart 1. The supply curve measures the cost to sellers, at any level of output, of selling one more unit of their good. As output grows, the law of diminishing returns forces this (or marginal) cost higher, so the supply curve slopes upwards. In the same way, the demand curve measures the benefit to consumers of consuming one more unit. As consumption grows, the benefit from extra consumption falls, so the demand curve slopes downwards.

At the place where the curves cross, a price is set such that demand equals supply. There, and only there, the benefit from consuming one more unit exactly matches the cost of producing it. If output were less, the benefit from consuming more would exceed the cost of producing it. If output were higher, the cost of producing the extra units would exceed the extra benefits. So the point where supply equals demand is "efficient".

The shaded area in chart 2 shows the "surplus" created by the market. The upper part is the consumers' surplus: the benefit from consumption (ie, the total area under the demand curve) less what consumers have to pay for it. In the same way, the lower part measures the producers' surplus: revenues received, less the cost of production (the area under the supply curve).

This gain in welfare is at its greatest if consumption and production happen where the lines cross. If, for some reason, consumption and production are less than that, the surplus is smaller and the economy suffers what economists call a deadweight loss, as shown in chart 3.

If production and consumption are more than the efficient amount, the same is true. Producers' surplus is smaller because the extra output has cost more to make than it brings in revenues; consumers' surplus is reduced because the extra consumption has cost buyers more than the benefits it brings. Again, as shown in chart 4, the economy suffers a deadweight loss.

Fine on paper

However, the conditions for market efficiency are extremely demanding – far too demanding ever to be met in the real world. The theory requires "perfect competition": there must be many buyers and sellers; goods from competing suppliers must be indistinguishable; buyers and sellers must be fully informed; and markets must be complete – that is, there must be markets not just for bread here and now, but for bread in any state of the world. (What is the price today for a loaf to be delivered in Timbuktu on the second Tuesday in December 2014 if it rains?)

In other words, market failure is pervasive. It comes in four main varieties:

- **Monopoly.** By reducing his sales, a monopolist can drive up the price of his good. His sales will fall but his profits will rise. Consumption and production are less than the efficient amount, causing a deadweight loss in welfare.
- **Public goods**. Some goods cannot be supplied by markets. If you refuse to pay for a new coat, the seller will refuse to supply you. If you refuse to pay for national defence, the "good" cannot easily be withheld. You might be tempted to let others pay. The same reasoning applies to other "non-excludable" goods such as law and order, clean air, and so on. Since private sellers cannot expect to recover the costs of producing such goods, they will fail to supply them.
- **Externalities.** Making some goods causes pollution: the cost is borne by people with no say in deciding how much to produce. Consuming some goods (education, anti-lock brakes) spreads benefits beyond the buyer; again, this will be ignored when the market decides how much to produce. In the case of "good" externalities, markets will supply too little; in the case of "bads", too much.

The price of failure

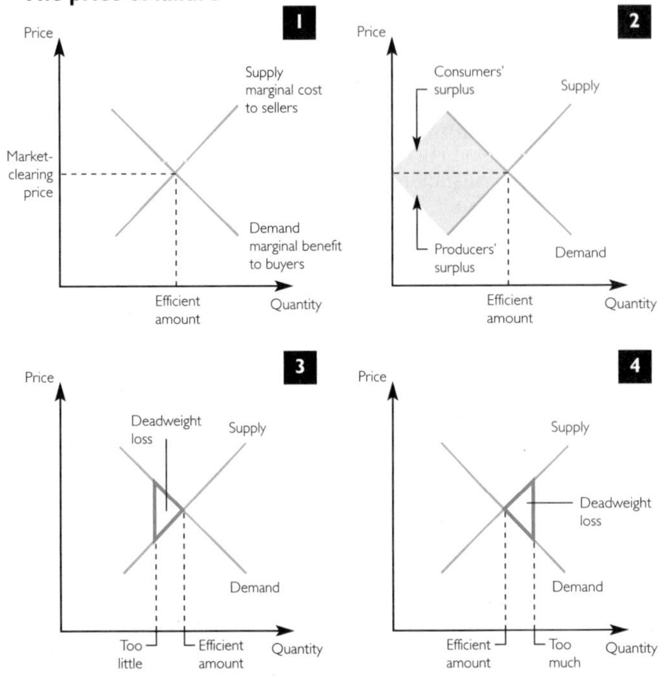

• **Information**. In some ways a special kind of externality, this deserves to be mentioned separately because of the emphasis placed upon it in recent economic theory. To see why information matters, consider the market for used cars. A buyer, lacking reliable information, may see the price as providing clues about a car's condition. This puts sellers in a quandary: if they cut prices, they may only convince people that their cars are rubbish.

The labour market, many economists belive, is another such "market for lemons". This may help to explain why it is so difficult for the unemployed to price themselves into work.

How harmful?

When markets fail, there is a case for intervention. But two questions need to be answered first. How much does market failure matter in practice? And can governments put the failure right? The rest of this article deals with the first question. For a brief response to the second, see the box on the next page.

Markets often correct their own failures. In other cases, an apparent failure does nobody any harm. In general, market failure matters less in practice than is often supposed.

Monopoly, for instance, may seem to preclude an efficient market. This is wrong. The mere fact of monopoly does not establish that any economic harm is being done. If a monopoly is protected from would-be competitors by high barriers to entry, it can raise its prices and earn excessive profits. If that happens, the monopoly is undeniably harmful. But if barriers to entry are low, lack of actual (as opposed to potential) competitors does not prove that the monopoly is damaging: the threat of competition may be enough to make it behave as though it were a competitive firm.

That is why economists are no longer so interested in concentration ratios (the output of an industry's biggest firm or firms as a proportion of the industry's total output). Judging whether markets are "contestable" – that is, whether barriers to entry are high – is thought to be more important.

Many economists would accept that Microsoft, for instance, is a near-monopolist in some parts of the personal-computer software business – yet would argue that the firm is doing no harm to consumers because its markets remain highly contestable. Because of that persistent threat of competition, the company prices its products keenly. In this and in other ways it behaves as though it were a smaller firm in a competitive market.

Suppose, on the other hand, that a "natural monopoly" (a firm not subject to the law of diminishing returns, whose costs fall indefinitely as it increases its output) is successfully collecting excessive profits. Then would-be competitors would spare no effort to make the market contestable, through innovation or by other means.

Telecommunications was once considered a natural monopoly. Today, thanks to new technology and deregulation, it is an intensely competitive business – and in many countries would be more so if not for remaining government restrictions. Economists used to see natural monopolies wherever they looked. Now, thanks mainly to innovation – inspired chiefly by the private pursuit of profit – these beasts are sighted much less often.

Economists have also changed their thinking on public goods. Almost all economists accept that there are such things: national defence and law and order remain the most straightforward examples. But it was once taken for granted that many other products also qualify (if not by being pure public goods, at least by having some of the relevant characteristics). This is no longer so.

The classical example of a public good is a lighthouse. Its services are both non-excludable and "non-rivalrous in consumption", meaning that extra ships can consume its output without the existing users having to consume less. This implies that lighthouses are a public good: only the state can provide them. Such a neat example, cited by economists from John Stuart Mill to Paul Samuelson – yet it is at odds with the facts.

As Ronald Coase pointed out in a celebrated paper, from the 17th century many of Britain's lighthouses were privately built and run. Payment to cover costs (and provide a profit) was extracted through fees collected in local ports. The government's role was confined to authorising this collection, exactly as a modern government might provide for a private road-builder to collect a toll.

On the face of it, television broadcasting is another pure public good – again, both non-excludable and non-rivalrous in consumption. Now, thanks to technology, it is straightforwardly excludable: satellite broadcasters collect a subscription, and in return provide a card that unscrambles their signal. With cable and pay-per-view, excludability works with even finer discrimination. And these market-strengthening innovations were not necessary for privately provided television to succeed, despite its public-good appearance. Non-excludable television was and is financed through advertising (another kind of innovation).

Fable of the bees

The same Ronald Coase who attacked the lighthouse myth is better known (and won a Nobel prize) for his work on externalities – the third species of market failure discussed earlier. He argued that, so long as property rights are clearly established, externalities will not cause an inefficient allocation of resources. In fact, few economists would agree: in many cases, unavoidably high costs will prevent the necessary transactions from taking place. Even so, Mr Coase's insight was fruitful. Markets find ways to take account of externalities – ways to "internalise" them, as economists say – more often than you might think.

Bees are to externalities as lighthouses are to public goods. For years they served as a favourite textbook example. Bee-keepers are not rewarded for the pollination services they provide to nearby plant-growers, so they and their bees must be inefficiently few in number. Again, however, the world proved cleverer than the textbooks. Steven Cheung studied the apple-growers of Washington state and discovered a long history of contracts between growers and bee-keepers. The supposed market failure had been effectively – and privately – dealt with.

As for lack of information, the final main source of market failure discussed earlier, here too economists have discovered all manner of private remedies. Recall the used-car example. An easy way round the difficulty is to buy from a seller with a good reputation (one worth protecting), or who offers guarantees. In ways such as this, the information gap can often be filled, albeit at a cost, and sometimes only partially.

More broadly, the new thinking on information in economics sees the institutions of capitalism largely as attempts to solve this very problem. The fact that firms, banks and other institutions exist, and are organised as they are, reflects society's efforts to make best use of scarce information.

Even on economic grounds (never mind other considerations), there is no tidy answer to the question of where the boundary between state and market should lie. Markets do fail – because of monopoly, public goods, externalities, lack of information and for other reasons. But, more than critics allow, markets find ways to mitigate the harm – and that is a task at which governments have often been strikingly unsuccessful.

All in all, a strong presumption in favour of markets seems wise. This is not because classical economic theory says so, but because experience seems to agree.

Source: *The Economist*, 17 February 1996

Imperfect government

The case for intervention in response to market failure requires not only that the failure is damaging but also that governments can do something about it. Just as the dangers of market failure are often exaggerated, so too are the skills of government. Intervention must overcome three formidable difficulties: the tendency of regulated firms to "capture" their regulators, weak incentives for efficiency within the public sector, and missing information (where markets lack it, governments are likely to lack it as well).

The regulation of monopolies is a telling example of capture. Most monopolies or near-monopolies are supported rather than curbed by regulation. For instance, the licensed professions – doctors, lawyers and so on – are among the world's best-defended monopolies. Rather than merely certifying the skills of people in such occupations, most governments make it illegal for unlicensed sellers to practice. The resulting monopoly is typically run by the licence-holders themselves.

In industry, too, regulation that begins as an attempt to control a monopoly often ends up defending it. America's Interstate Commerce Commission began as an agency to regulate railways, which arguably had monopoly power. In due course it extended its reach to trucking – partly to help the railways survive. In much of Europe, regulation of telecommunications has lately changed in the same way: from controlling to protecting.

The record of intervention is poor. Sometimes there is no choice, but history suggests that the burden of proof should lie with those who would extend the government's role.

26 The privatisation debate: nationalisation and privatisation

Learning outcomes

At the end of this chapter you will be able to:

- Describe the ways in which the former nationalised industries were structured and regulated after privatisation.
- Identify the problem of residual natural monopoly and methods used to deal with it.
- Understand the arguments for and against privatisation.
- Relate differences in regulation to differences in the nature of the industry being regulated.

How to use this chapter

This chapter is divided into case studies on the following issues:

Case study 26.1: Development of nationalised industries
Case study 26.2: Problems of nationalised industry control
Case study 26.3: The privatisation process
Case study 26.4: Privatisation and the introduction of competition
Case study 26.5: The regulation of privatised industries
Case study 26.6: Is privatisation a success?

These cases can be taken in any order but are better in the sequence you find them in. Case studies 26.1 and 26.2 on nationalisation may be omitted by those readers who are less interested in the historical perspective. However, understanding why the industries were originally nationalised is relevant to the problems they face as privatised industries, so study of these cases will bring benefits to the student of the privatised industries. Student activities are found at the end of each case as well as at the end of the chapter.

Introduction

What is privatisation?

Undoubtedly privatisation has been one of the most significant trends in economic and social policy in recent years. This has been the case not only in the UK but also in many other industrial nations. Perhaps the most dramatic and difficult privatisation process is taking place in former communist countries in Eastern Europe. At its simplest, privatisation means the denationalisation of state-controlled industries. Everyone understands that the sale of British Gas and British Telecom are examples of privatisation, but privatisation is much wider than this. It also includes the sale of council houses, the sale of the assets of the New Town Corporations and the contracting out of local-authority-controlled services such as refuse collection.

At a more fundamental level we can see privatisation as a piece of social economic engineering. It is aimed at reintroducing competition and free market economics to the centre of the economy. It is aimed at changing people's attitudes and bringing in what the Conservatives have termed the 'enterprise culture'. It is also aimed at widening the ownership of private property, in both the housing market and the Stock Exchange, developing a greater involvement in ***popular capitalism***.

What is a nationalised industry?

The term public corporations is used to describe industries that are owned by the state but are set up as separate organisations and run much like companies. Like companies, the public corporations are run by boards of directors who run the corporation on a day-to-day basis. The difference between a public corporation and a company quoted on the Stock Exchange is that the government is the only shareholder. The public corporation usually has a sponsoring department, whose minister is responsible for the long-term success of the industry, and who can, like the shareholders of a company, change the membership of the board if performance is unsatisfactory.

Occasionally, a nationalised industry will be run, not as a public corporation, but directly by a government department. This was the case with the GPO which was not set up as a separate public corporation, as the Post Office, until 1969.

By 1979 the state also owned some of the shares in a large number of businesses, such as BP and Amersham International. Such joint ownership may be termed mixed enterprise. Such businesses are only partly nationalised and are not usually referred to as nationalised industries.

It is useful to distinguish between the welfare state (reforms of which will be discussed in Chapters 29 and 30) and nationalised industries. The main distinction is that the nationalised industries sell their products in the market place like any other company, while the welfare state for the most part offers its services for free. There are a few grey areas in this distinction. Some services of the welfare state have charges, such as prescriptions for medicine, while some nationalised industries were deliberately subsidised, e.g. provincial branch lines of British Rail. Despite these examples, the distinction between the two is fairly clear and widely accepted.

When Margaret Thatcher came to power in 1979 the combined turnover of all public corporations amounted to £44 billion or 22.9 per cent of the gross domestic product. At the same time they employed 1 710 000 people and were responsible for 20 per cent of all investment in the economy. The great majority of these nationalised industries have now been privatised.

Case study 26.1
The development of the nationalised industries

It is often thought that nationalised industries are recent developments and the creation of socialist governments. This is not entirely the case. Indeed the Post Office, which has a claim to be the oldest nationalised industry, was set up in the time of Charles II in the sixteenth century.

The early nationalised industries

Nationalisation can be truly said to have started in the UK with the establishment of the Port of London Authority in 1908. The interwar period saw the creation of the Central Electricity Board (1926), the British Broadcasting Corporation (1926), the five London Passenger Transport Boards (1933) and the British Overseas Airways Corporation (1939).

The Labour nationalisations of 1945–51

The major nationalisations of this period included coal, transport (road freight, railways and canals) and electricity generation in 1947, gas in 1948 and iron and steel in 1951. Road freight transport (with the exception of the company BRS) and iron and steel were subsequently denationalised by the Conservative government in 1953. The nationalisations of this period created the bulk of nationalised industries.

The later nationalisations

The scope of nationalisation widened in the 1960s and 1970s. Iron and steel was renationalised in 1967, and aircraft construction and shipbuilding were nationalised in 1977. The GPO ceased to be a government department in 1969 and became, as the Post Office, a public corporation. This was subsequently divided into the Post Office and British Telecommunications in 1981.

Reasons for nationalisation

A socialist would consider the main reason for nationalisation to be control of the means of production, but someone who believes in capitalism may also argue for state ownership in some cases.

Economies of scale and natural monopoly

There are many industries which are best organised on a very large scale. In the extreme case, these economies of scale will result in monopoly creating a strong argument for state ownership, since the advantages of competition are not available and the consumer can easily be exploited. Some industries were thought to be **natural monopolies** because creating competition would result in the wasteful duplication of expensive infrastructure such as rail track, gas pipelines and electricity cables. In most such cases a network exists which transports the service to the customer. Rail, telecommunications, gas, electricity and water were all nationalised partly for this reason.

Lame ducks

A number of private sector companies were taken into public ownership in the 1970s which were clearly not monopolies, but which instead were major employers which faced bankruptcy. Rolls-Royce, the aircraft engine manufacturer, was rescued in this way by a Conservative government, and British Leyland, the car producer, by a Labour government. Such **lame ducks** can be nursed back to health by the state but are eventually returned to competition.

Capital expenditure

Some industries demand such major investment expenditure that it is argued that only the government is capable of providing the funds. This is particularly the case where large expenditure is associated with considerable risk. Some people argued that the Channel tunnel was too large and risky a project for the private sector to undertake. Its early financial performance with considerable annual losses may be seen as confirmation of this view. Such an argument was advanced to support the nationalisation of the iron and steel industry in 1967. It was also used to support the nationalisation of coal and the railways. In addition to capital expenditure, some industries demand large spending on research and development (e.g. atomic energy and aircraft).

Control of the economy

The nationalisation of industries may enable a government to pursue its economic policies on investment, employment and prices through the operation of the industries concerned. For example, it might hold down prices in the nationalised industries as a counter-inflationary measure as occurred in 1976 or, alternatively, invest to create employment in depressed areas of the economy.

Strategic reasons

The government might find it necessary to nationalise an industry considered vital for the defence of the country. Thus, for example, the aerospace industry in the UK was nationalised to keep it in existence. The defence implications of nuclear power were also a reason for ensuring that this was a nationalised industry. Key industries of less obvious strategic significance, such as iron and steel, coal and transport, might be seen as vital to the defence of the country in times of war.

Political reasons

The coal industry was neither a natural monopoly nor a lame duck when nationalised (although it later faced losses in the 1960s and 1980s when undercut by cheap oil and gas). Issues of safety and the preference of the workforce, together with its influence in the Labour party, may explain this nationalisation. The steel industry is a similar case. The Russian revolutionary leader, Lenin, once described such industries as the commanding heights of the economy, which might explain why socialists were keen to nationalise them.

Externalities

Many industries create negative externalities such as pollution, e.g. global warming from the output of carbon dioxide from electricity generation. Another example is commuter rail fares; these are effectively subsidised because if these customers switched to the roads, the resulting congestion would be unacceptable. It should be much easier to control these externalities in nationalised industries than in those under private ownership. However, the experience in many East European states might seem to contradict this. After the collapse of communism in Eastern Europe it became apparent that many governments had put industrialisation before the environment and health of the population in a way which would not have been acceptable in the West. Market solutions to the problem of externalities are discussed in Chapter 27.

Social costs and equity

Nationalised industries often produced essential goods and services such as heating, lighting and transport, which it was argued should be available to everyone in a civilised society, irrespective of income. Socially needy customers may benefit from preferential treatment. A nationalised industry may offer special low rates to customers such as old-age pensioners; free bus passes for old-age pensioners might be seen as an example of this. A product or service may be supplied to the public below cost price where this is considered beneficial. An example of this might be postal services supplied to the remoter parts of the country. These factors probably were not the most important when considering whether to nationalise an industry. However, the issues of equity and social costs were important in policy formation in the nationalised industries. They created problems when setting objectives for these industries (see the discussion on political interference below). These problems have not entirely disappeared after privatisation.

STUDENT ACTIVITY 26.1

In each of the following industries, indicate what part is a natural monopoly which must be either nationalised or regulated, and which parts are potentially competitive.

Rail, gas, electricity, telecommunications, coal, steel, car production, roads, the post office.

STUDENT ACTIVITY 26.2

Should the following products be considered as necessary for all citizens in a civilised society: housing, health, heating, food, local transport, education?

If you agree that any of these products should be available for everyone at a reasonable price, what policy (other than nationalisation) would make sure they are available for the poorest people in society?

STUDENT ACTIVITY 26.3

If a major industry is close to bankruptcy, what alternative does the government have to nationalisation as a solution to the 'lame duck' problem? Does it matter if the industry is taken over by a foreign multinational company? If there is no buyer for the industry and the output is replaced by imported goods, what is the effect on the balance of payments and the value of the pound?

Case study 26.2
Problems of the nationalised industries

Efficiency

Although it would not be desirable for nationalised industries to maximise their profits, it could be argued that the lack of the profit motive removes the spur to efficiency which private enterprises have. It is argued that nationalisation creates overlarge and overbureaucratic organisations which, therefore, suffer from diseconomies of scale.

The abuse of monopoly power

As argued above, many of the nationalised industries were nationalised because they were monopolies. This argument can also be used against nationalisation, however. It could be argued that a state monopoly is more disadvantageous to the consumer than a private one. This is because there is no higher authority to protect the consumer's interests. The consumer therefore has to tolerate the lack of choice and high prices associated with monopoly, with little hope of redress, although there were normally consumer consultative bodies. It is argued by some that the monopoly power of the nationalised industry may be used by trade unions to raise pay and protect jobs by creating restrictive practices. This can be the case even if, as in the case of British Coal, the industry was not a natural monopoly.

Common misunderstanding

Many of the nationalised industries were profitable

most of the time, and where this was not the case there was often good reason for the losses. For instance, British Rail made losses because it was not allowed to close down many of its loss-making provincial branch lines, as identified in the Beeching Report (1963) and the Serpell Report (1982). Instead, from 1974, the government paid British Rail an amount known as the ***public service obligation*** *(PSO) for keeping these services open. Some freight services, intercity and commuter lines into London broke even or better. Other services were kept open for reasons of social cost (congestion on the roads) and equity (access to a national transport network) as discussed above.*

In general it was the natural monopolies in industries like electricity, telecommunications and gas which were profitable. Of course it is not difficult for monopolies to make a profit, as was discussed in Chapter 18. Large losses were made by lame ducks, such as British Leyland, the car manufacturer. Coal, when faced with cheap oil, and steel, when there was world excess capacity and competing subsidies from other national governments, were also frequently loss making.

Political interference

The sound administration of nationalised industries is often undermined by politicians interfering in the industries' policies for short-term political gains. An example of this would be a ministerial order not to raise prices in an attempt to combat inflation. The National Economic Development Office (NEDO) Report of 1976 (into the performance of nationalised industries) argued that managers should be left with the day-to-day running of the industry, and that the ministers should only be allowed to interfere by setting the long-run strategy of the industry. This suggestion was never taken up as the Conservative party soon came to power and concentrated on privatisation as their main policy.

Conflicting objectives

Even if nationalised industries are left to meet the objectives set for them by politicians, there is a possibility that these objectives might conflict, or may be vaguely stated. White Papers (statements of government policy) were produced in 1961, 1967 and 1978 to clarify evolving policy towards the nationalised industries. The NEDO Report (1976) made useful comments about the problems of running these industries. The concerns of these documents can be discussed under the following headings:

a) break-even and cross-subsidisation
b) profit
c) pricing
d) decreasing cost industries
e) the 1978 White Paper

Break-even and cross-subsidisation

In 1948 the government required industries to meet the demand for their product at a reasonable price which would allow them to break even over a number of years. The idea of the break-even level of output is illustrated in Fig. 26.1. This overall equality of total revenue and total cost allowed for a large disparity between the cost of supplying any one individual and the price charged to this individual. For example, the cost of supplying a telephone line to a farmer in the Welsh mountains would obviously be higher than the cost of providing a telephone line to a business in London. However, the excess of cost over revenue in providing the telephone to the farmer could be met by the excess of revenue over cost in supplying the business in the

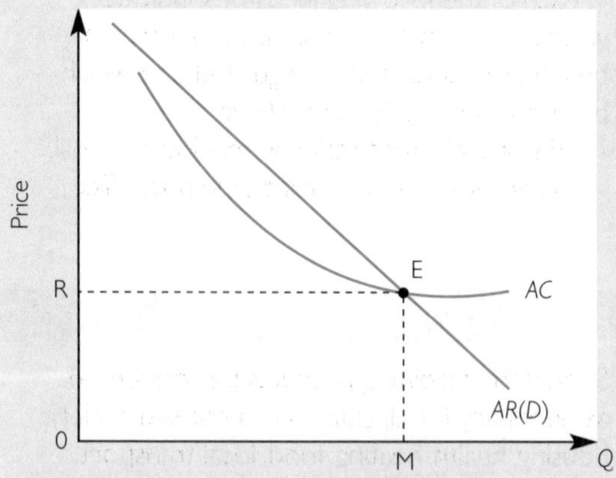

***Fig. 26.1* The break-even output**
This occurs where the *AC* curve cuts the *AR* curve at point E. Here:

$TR = TC$

cities. This cross-subsidisation among consumers was felt, by many observers, to be undesirable in that the cost to consumers did not always represent the full opportunity cost of the resources they enjoyed.

Profit

Studies of the nationalised industries in the 1950s discovered that the rate of return on capital was higher in the private sector than in the nationalised industries. As a result, the government's 1961 White Paper introduced financial targets for the nationalised industries, and as a consequence downgraded the social objectives. The financial targets were most often expressed as a rate of return on all assets employed by a particular industry. The prevailing market conditions were taken into account in setting these financial targets; hence the required rate of return laid down by the government varied from industry to industry, as well as from year to year. There is no reason why the financial target must always be positive. For example, in 1979–80 the financial target for British Shipbuilders was a maximum trading loss of £100 million.

Apart from asking the nationalised industries not to cross-subsidise, the 1961 White Paper gave no advice on how the financial return was to be achieved. Since many of the industries were monopolies, they could achieve the targets easily by raising their prices without having to consider reducing their costs. The 1967 White Paper retained the idea of financial targets but introduced a pricing method (marginal cost pricing) which was inconsistent with making profit, as will be discussed in the next section.

The 1978 White Paper tried to resolve the conflict between profits and social costs. It set a financial target in the form of a required rate of return on capital. It argued that any non-commercial objectives set by the government, such as providing services to remote regions of the country, should be paid for by the government.

Pricing

The 1967 White Paper introduced more explicit guidelines on pricing in nationalised industries. As an attempt to ensure an efficient allocation of resources, a policy of long-run marginal cost pricing was introduced. The prescriptions of modern welfare economics point to the adoption of marginal cost pricing, i.e. prices should be set at the level of marginal cost, as they are in perfect competition. The optimality of marginal cost pricing was described in Chapter 24, while its welfare implications are more fully discussed in Chapter 25. Attractive as this idea is, it is beset with difficulties.

There are practical difficulties in estimating marginal cost in practice. For example, in transport, vehicles are indivisible; thus the marginal cost of transporting an extra passenger is very close to zero. However, once the vehicle is full and a new vehicle must be laid on, the marginal cost is suddenly very high. There is obviously a problem in attributing increases in costs to individual passengers. Again, in integrated systems such as telecommunications the problem of identifying marginal cost arises. Cables are expensive to lay but relatively inexpensive to use. Also, each phone has access to equipment it may or may not use. It is thus difficult to attribute cost to users who enjoy a potential facility. The NEDO Report (1976) found that with the exception of the electricity industry, nationalised industries were not basing prices on marginal cost, and for the most part did not know what their marginal costs were.

Decreasing costs

There are further difficulties when the idea of marginal cost pricing is applied to decreasing cost industries. It is the case that many nationalised industries have large economies of scale which are thought to result in continuously decreasing average costs over the relevant range of output. This should result in a permanent financial deficit for such industries if marginal cost pricing were to be applied.

This is illustrated in Fig. 26.2. Here the marginal cost output would be OM at the price *OP*. This, however, is beyond the break-even output of OL and price of OP_1. This therefore results in a loss, which is shown by the shaded area in the diagram. It has been argued that OM still represents the best situation and that the resultant trading deficit should be financed by taxes. However, the taxes required may have disincentive effects (see Chapter 30) and be a cause of allocative inefficiency in the economy as a whole.

There are also some theoretical problems. The first of these is that the *MC* pricing rule is based on the assumption that costs have been minimised. Thus the policy of *MC* pricing must be accompanied by pressure to minimise costs in public enterprises. In the private sector this pressure might come from competition and the threat of insolvency or takeover. Although most

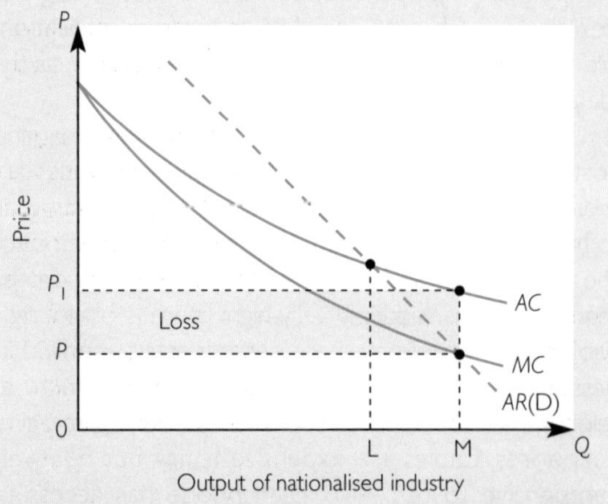

***Fig. 26.2* Marginal cost pricing and decreasing costs**

At $MC = P$ the output would be OM and the price OP, but since P is below AC this involves the loss indicated by the shaded areas.

nationalised industries did face competition in one form or another, it is generally agreed that the threat of closure was less strong in the public sector. One reason for this is that public enterprises often provide essential services. Another, often related, reason is that where the government itself is seen as the employer, closure would arouse much political opposition. Financial targets might be seen as a substitute for the **discipline of the market**, but it is difficult to devise acceptable sanctions in the event of these targets not being met. However, if costs are not minimised, *MC* pricing will not ensure a socially efficient allocation of resources.

The second theoretical problem is rather technical and comes under the heading of the theory of second best (see Chapter 24). Basically this theory demonstrates that setting price equal to marginal cost may not in fact improve efficiency if the conditions assumed in the first optimality theorem (see Chapter 24) do not hold for the rest of the economy.

The 1978 White Paper

This White Paper reintroduced financial targets as a key indicator. The target took the form of a required rate of return on capital. The principle of long-run *MC* pricing was relaxed and the requirement became one of prices being reasonably related to costs. The problem of social costs was dealt with by a proposal that the government should compensate the nationalised industry for any social objective that moved it away from its financial target objective. This was based on the PSO payment introduced in 1974 for British Rail to pay for provincial and other loss-making services. Just as it appeared that conflicts between the three objectives had been finally resolved, the election of Mrs Thatcher moved the agenda on from the control of nationalised industries to their sale.

STUDENT ACTIVITY 26.4

What are the problems of setting price equal to marginal cost in a natural monopoly? Which formerly nationalised industries would have suffered from this problem? How would a private sector company overcome the problem of loss making by adjusting their price? Would its solution to the problem be in the interests of the customer?

STUDENT ACTIVITY 26.5

Loss-making routes on the railways can sometimes be justified on the grounds of reduced congestion on the roads, or in terms of regional aid to depressed areas of the economy. Who should pay for this social benefit ?

a) Taxpayers at a national level.
b) Taxpayers at the local level.
c) Other customers on profit-making parts of the railway.
d) Road users (via petrol tax).

STUDENT ACTIVITY 26.6

Which of the following regulations should be applied to a nationalised electricity industry? Which of the criteria are consistent with each other?

a) Make a profit which produces a rate of return on capital equal to the average obtaining in the private sector.
b) Set price equal to marginal private cost.

c) Set price equal to marginal social cost.
d) Set price equal to average cost.
e) Charge the same price to all areas of the country even if it costs more to supply more remote or sparsely inhabited areas.

Case study 26.3
The privatisation process

The process of privatisation has been a continuous one since 1979. Not only have more and more industries been privatised, but also the approach to privatisation and the regulation, where necessary, of privatised industries have continuously evolved. Table 26.1 shows the dates and proceeds of the principal privatisations.

Table 26.1 The proceeds of privatisation

Organisation	*Date(s) of sale*	*Percentage sold*	*Amount raised (£bn)*
British Petroleum	1977, 1979, 1983, 1987	All	7.40
British Steel	1988	100	2.50
British Telecom	1984	50.2	3.90
	1991, 1993	49.8	9.65
Rolls-Royce	1987	100	1.08
British Gas	1986	100	5.40
National Freight	1982	100	0.05
Water	1989	100	5.3
British Aerospace	1981	51	0.15
	1985	49	0.36
British Airways	1987	100	0.90
British Airports Authority	1987	100	1.30
Electricity (distribution)	1990	100	5.18
Electricity (generation)	1991	100	2.10
Electricity (Scottish)	1991	100	2.90

Methods of privatisation

The objective of privatisation is to return state-run industries to private ownership, but this objective can be reached by many different methods. The three principal methods are management buy-out, share flotation and sale to another private company, but parts of an industry can be franchised or contracted out.

Management/employee buy-out

In this form of privatisation shares are offered to managers, workers or both. It differs from a workers cooperative in that the shares may not be held equally by all employees, and may be sold. The best example of this is the case of National Freight, a road freight business which was privatised in 1982. This form of privatisation is suitable for smaller companies in competitive markets.

Sale to private companies

British Leyland, the nationalised car producer, was sold to British Aerospace (itself a privatised company) in 1986. It was renamed The Rover Group and after a period of collaboration with the Japanese company Honda, it was sold on to the German car producer BMW. Prior to the sale of the company, the lorry section was sold to DAF trucks (a Dutch company) and Jaguar was sold to Ford.

Share flotation

The large public utilities have been sold by share flotation to the general public. These flotations differ from normal flotations in that the objective is not necessarily to obtain as much money as possible, but also to widen share ownership and thereby to promote the development of popular capitalism. This has been achieved by prioritising small applications for shares and limiting overseas applications. Care has been taken to encourage small share owners to apply by setting the offer price of the share in advance, rather than putting the shares out to tender. Critics of the privatisation process have argued that the shares were often underpriced with the shareholders gaining at the taxpayers' expense.

Franchising

Where part of an industry is run by a franchise, it is possible to simulate some of the characteristics of competition even in situations which appear to be monopolistic. Much of the franchising that has taken place has been in the welfare state or local authority services (e.g. the contracting out of laundry and catering services in the NHS; refuse collection and disposal). These aspects of franchising are discussed in Chapter 29. However, this form of privatisation has also been used in the transport industry. Although the track and rolling stock have passed into private ownership, the operation of the services is sold as a franchise. The franchise system is particularly useful in attracting firms to run loss-making parts of an industry, such as rural bus routes and provincial rail branch lines, where a negative bid would be expected.

Clearly the terms of the contract are very important so that the subcontracting company can be checked up on, and penalised if it is not fulfilling the terms of the contract. At the end of the agreed period of time, the contract is offered anew, and it is open to other companies to bid for it.

In the early 1990s the principle of competitive tendering was adopted for many government departments and local authority services. Under this arrangement, the existing department of the council could bid against outside companies to decide who should provide the service. This type of tendering was made compulsory for certain services. The idea was that even if the council retained the contract, the process would force its costs down.

STUDENT ACTIVITY 26.7

Imagine you have been asked to set up the franchise agreement for a privatised industry. What conditions would you require of the franchisee before granting the franchise in the case of each of the following?

a) A rail branch line in a provincial area.
b) A commuter rail route into London (or another major city).
c) Catering services for an NHS trust hospital.
d) Refuse collection for a local authority.
e) Cleaning services for your school or college.

STUDENT ACTIVITY 26.8

Which of the following considerations are most important when deciding on the right price for a privatisation share issue?

a) A price that will attract large numbers of ordinary citizens to apply for shares in the knowledge of a certain capital gain.
b) The maximum price that will give the tax-payer the largest return (even at the risk that a few shares might not initially be sold).
c) The maximum price that will ensure the sale of all the shares on offer.
d) A high price in return for the promise of lax regulation after privatisation.

STUDENT ACTIVITY 26.9

The government has a choice of privatising a nationalised industry by the following methods: a) share flotation; b) management buy-out; c) sale to a private company; d) franchising. Which do you think is most suitable in the case of:

(i) British Telecom	(ii) Jaguar Cars
(iii) Rover Group	(iv) Electricity
(v) Gas	(vi) Local water company
(vii) British Rail	(viii) Channel 4 TV?

Case study 26.4 Privatisation and the introduction of competition

Although many nationalised industries were monopolies, as the privatisation process continued new methods for introducing competition were invented. Some of these were more successful than others. Where the introduction of competition has been less successful, the government may need to regulate. This section discusses some of the competitive innovations by looking at a number of individual privatisations. The innovations are discussed under three headings:

a) Vertical disintegration
b) Local monopolies competing in the capital markets
c) Competition and new technology

Vertical disintegration

The large public utilities were mainly in a monopoly position before privatisation. The response of the government to this problem has evolved with successive privatisations. Earlier privatisations such as British Telecom and British Gas left the structure of the industry largely unchanged, and have relied on a mixture of regulation and protected competition to overcome the natural monopoly problem. With later privatisations the industries have been restructured extensively prior to privatisation. The objective has been to separate the natural monopoly from the potentially competitive parts of the industry.

Electricity

In the case of electricity, the industry in England and Wales was broken into three sectors based on different stages of production (see Figure 26.3). First, electricity generation at power stations is essentially competitive. Second, transmission of electricity from the power stations to different parts of the country takes place via the national grid. This system of pylons and high-voltage cable is a natural monopoly network. The distribution of electricity to homes and businesses is usually effected by underground cable in the UK. This is also a natural monopoly network. However, this is a local network, and had been organised on a local basis before privatisation. The local electricity boards were converted into Regional Electricity Companies (RECs) for different areas of the country (see Figure 26.4). The RECs were also allowed to enter the generation market, by producing up to 15 per cent of their own electricity.

The Scottish industry was vertically integrated, by contrast, with Scottish Power providing for the Lowlands, and Hydro for the Highlands. This does create two additional competitors in the generation industry. With National Power, PowerGen and Nuclear Electric this makes five major competitors. Imports of electricity from French generators, and competition from the RECs, mean that generation is slowly evolving from an oligopolistic to a more competitive market. The direct sale of electricity from generators to consumers also takes place to large companies, but this may be extended to ordinary consumers in the future. Transmission and distribution companies would be paid a regulated fee for transporting the electricity to the consumer.

Gas

Initially the gas industry was privatised as a single company, which was thought of as being in competition with electricity and other fuels. Criticism of the gas industry grew after privatisation, culminating in the loss of the charter mark in the early 1990s originally awarded to the company for good customer service. Monopolies and

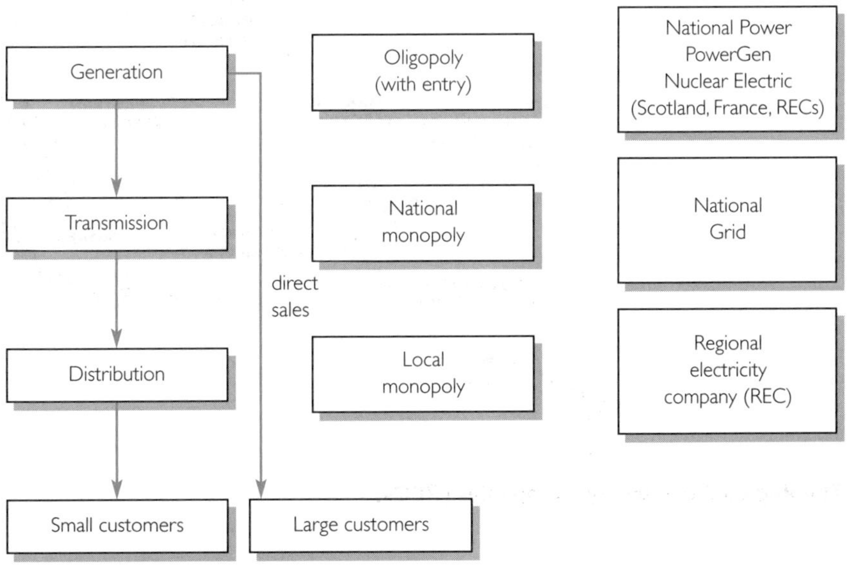

Figure 26.3 **The electricity industry in England and Wales**

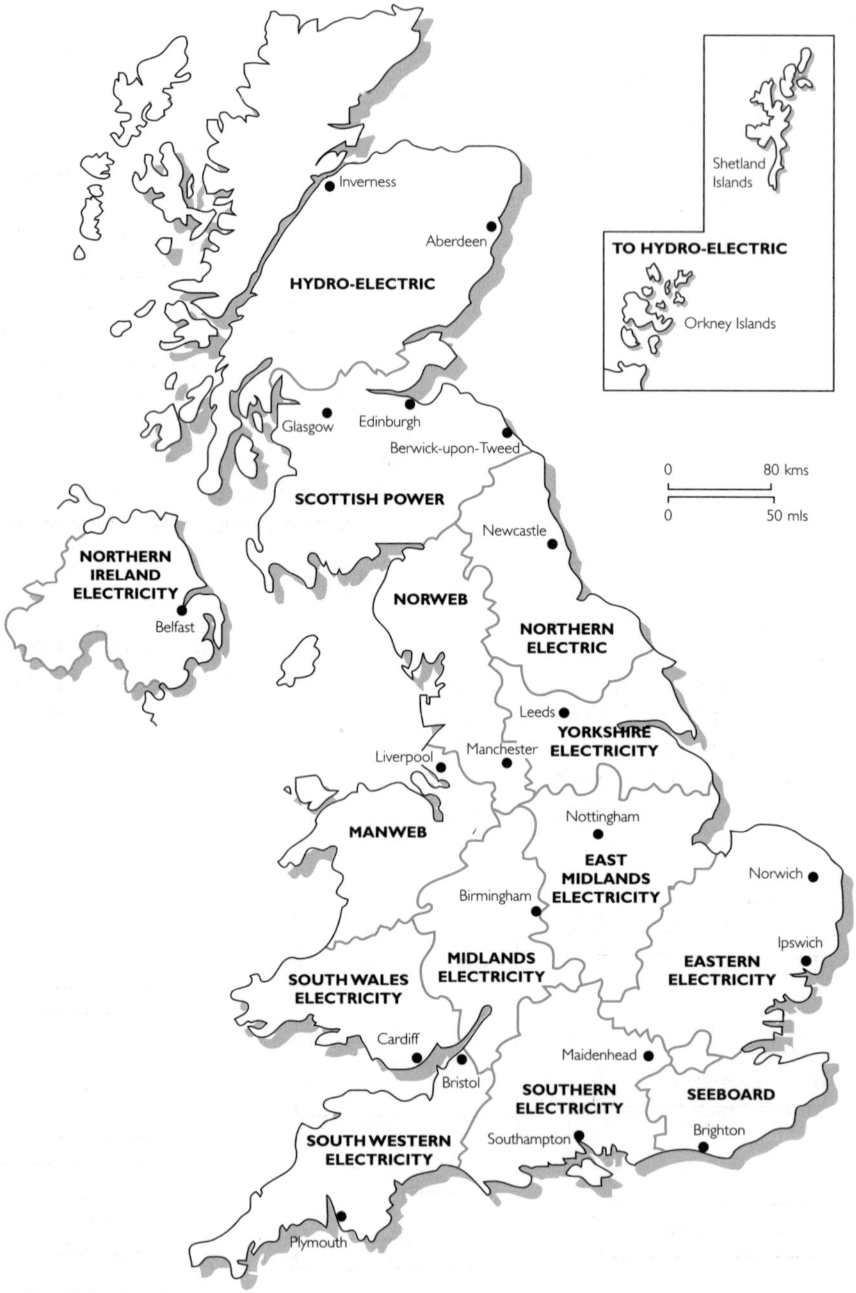

***Figure 26.4* The Regional Electricity Companies (RECs)**

Mergers Commission reports in 1988 and 1993 suggested that more competition needed to be injected into the industry. Reconsideration of the nature of the gas industry has resulted in more regulation to prevent the abuse of monopoly power. After its success in the electricity industry, the vertical disintegration of the industry is now seen as the way forward. The natural monopoly pipe network, Transco, is being separated from the competitive supply of gas. Competing gas suppliers, including British Gas Energy, can then lease the use of Transco's network to get gas supplies to the consumer.

Rail

The natural monopoly in this case is the system of railway tracks and the stations. A separate company, Railtrack, was set up to manage this side of the industry, and was privatised in 1996. The stock of trains was sold off to three companies which lease them back to operators of train services. The train services are operated by companies which have won a time-limited franchise for a part of the rail network. In the case of the rail network, there is a deliberate policy to increase competition as much as possible by vertical disintegration of the industry. This may create problems of coordination between different companies in the design of an integrated timetable and through-ticketing system. A passenger may use a number of different companies in the course of a long journey. The revenue from a single ticket for the journey must be distributed to the various companies. This distribution process will in itself cost money. This type of cost is referred to as the **transactions cost of setting up the market**, and must be set against any efficiency gains which arise from competition.

Local monopolies competing in the capital markets

Water and electricity distribution

Where vertical disintegration of industries is difficult to achieve, some degree of competition can occur if the industry can be split up into local natural monopolies. This is the strategy that has been adopted for electricity distribution and for the water industry. This is of course not competition from the consumer's point of view since the consumer has no choice but to accept the local supplier. It does, however, create competition in the capital markets, with less efficient companies vulnerable to takeover. Nobody suggests that this type of competition protects the consumer from poor service or overpricing, so considerable regulation is still required in these cases. If there were a national network of water pipes the water could be separated from the network as in the case of gas. However, the cost of transporting water long distances, sometimes against gravity, would be much greater than for gas.

Competition and new technology

British Telecom

In some cases, after privatisation, competition can be developed to the point where regulation is no longer necessary. New technology can sometimes change a market from being a natural monopoly to being naturally competitive. The introduction of relatively cheap fibre-optic cable to replace the old wire system of transmitting telephone calls, and the simultaneous development of mobile phones using radio technology, make a good case study of such a change.

Since its privatisation in 1984, British Telecom has been tightly regulated by price controls, which are discussed in more detail in the section on regulation below. This was necessary initially because of the strong monopoly position of the company. However, the more important action of the regulator (Oftel) was to protect the major new entrant, Mercury. Mercury was wholly owned by Cable and Wireless, itself a recently privatised company specialising in international telecommunications. The problem for a new company in telecommunications is that it does not have a country-wide network of cables. In order to connect customers, it needs to use the network of the dominant firm in the business, British Telecom. This put British Telecom in a very strong bargaining position with Mercury. Oftel protected Mercury by requiring British Telecom to carry Mercury's calls, and by regulating the price.

British Airways

The international air passenger market was highly regulated from 1919 to the late 1970s. It was decided by the Paris Convention in 1919 that the air space above a country belonged to that country. Since then, if an airline from one country wishes to carry passengers to another country, the two governments must first sign a **bilateral**

agreement. These agreements decide the terms under which airlines can carry passengers between the two countries. Most agreements signed between 1945 and 1975 were very restrictive in nature. In most cases each country could nominate only one airline to fly on each route, often known as the **flag carrier**. In addition only a limited number of airports were designated as **gate of entry** airports which could be used by airlines from other countries. The prices were largely determined by the International Airlines Trade Association (IATA). In some cases the two airlines on a route would operate a revenue pool, sharing the revenue irrespective of which airline the passengers chose to fly on.

This very uncompetitive state of affairs was challenged by President Carter of the USA in the late 1970s. Since then the bilateral agreements have become progressively more liberal, allowing for two airlines from each country for instance, and designating more airports in each country as international gate of entry airports. Prices are no longer determined by the trade association, IATA. This process of introducing more competition into the airline industry is known as deregulation. It occurred first on the North Atlantic route, particularly between the USA and the UK, and in the USA domestic airline market. It soon spread to other areas of the world where passenger air transport was a large-scale industry. By 1986 when BA was privatised, deregulation was widespread. Curiously enough, despite the Single European Market, deregulation was late to come to the EU. A number of nationalised airlines such as Air France and Iberian Airlines were still being heavily subsidised by their national governments in 1996.

The year after BA was privatised it swallowed up its major British rival, British Caledonian, leading to concerns that BA would have too much monopoly power. The growth of international competition because of deregulation has ensured that BA faces international competition. Indeed the development of such competition provides an argument for the expansion of BA so that it can achieve the economies of scale necessary to compete effectively with the giant American airlines in the world market.

There remain some elements of monopoly power in the airline industry. The ownership of **time slots** for take-off and landing at the major British airports based on past practice gives BA an advantage over new British rivals. The ownership of a computer reservation system (CRS) also gives any airline the potential for greater knowledge about customers' and rivals' behaviour.

Television

New technology in the form of satellite broadcasting, cable transmission, and digitisation of the original technology (terrestrial transmission), has led to an enormous increase in the number of competing channels on television. The BBC has had its licence extended and remains in the public sector but has to contend with a more competitive environment.

STUDENT ACTIVITY 26.10

If the government decides to privatise the post office consider whether:

a) it is possible to introduce competition
b) there are any benefits from vertical disintegration of the service
c) the telephone system and the internet are effective substitutes for the postal industry.

Case study 26.5
The regulation of privatised industries

It can be seen from the above discussion that although competition can be injected into many of the privatised industries, in many industries natural monopoly and market power remain a problem. For these areas it is necessary for the government to intervene by regulating the industry in order to protect the consumer from excessive price increases.

In most cases the problem of regulating privatised industries is monopoly. The main issues faced by the regulators are:

a) abnormal profit;
b) protecting new competition;
c) efficiency and costs.

Rate of return regulation

In the USA, where regulation was preferred to nationalisation, the rate of return on capital was the most common form of control on electricity and gas utilities to prevent them from earning excessive profits. A maximum rate of return on capital meant that the firms could not raise their prices too much. This long experience also led the Americans to notice the main drawback of this type of regulation. If the regulated firm is allowed to make a reasonably good return on capital, it has an incentive to over-invest. Each additional pound spent on capital increases their allowed profit. This unwanted consequence of rate of return regulation is called the Averch–Johnson effect after its discoverers.

RPI ± X

The method of regulation adopted in the UK, starting with British Telecom, is to control prices rather profits. The retail price index (RPI) gives the rate of inflation for the previous year. The privatised industry is allowed to increase its prices, on average, by the rate of inflation minus X. For instance, the initial figure for X in the case of British Telecom was 3 per cent. If the rate of inflation was 5 per cent this would mean that the company could only raise its prices by 2 per cent on average. However, a 2 per cent rate of inflation would mean that a reduction in price by, on average, I per cent would be required.

The permitted rate of increase is usually below the rate of inflation, but in one case, water, an RPI + X formula was used to enable water companies to raise the large sums of money needed to finance investment and meet EU water quality standards. Another variation on the theme occurs where there is a significant input price which is subject to market variations. In the case of electricity, coal, oil and gas, prices can significantly affect their costs. The solution in this case is to adopt an RPI – *X* + *Y* formula. The *Y* is to allow for changes in input prices and can itself be negative or positive, depending on whether input prices have fallen or risen.

The big question here is what determines *X*? Unfortunately, there is no easy answer to this question. Governments are trying to achieve a number of objectives with this single percentage figure and some of them are hard to quantify:

a) *Reduce abnormal profit* made by the firm. It might seem easy to calculate what the normal rate of profit is that firms should earn, but industries facing more risky environments expect a higher rate of return to compensate them for taking this risk. Unfortunately the assessment of the risk facing a firm is an uncertain and subjective business, unless you have a crystal ball which foretells the future.
b) *Reduce costs of production* by forcing out any inefficiency. Privatised industries usually have some inefficiency which can be 'squeezed out' by regulators. The difficulty is knowing how much fat an organisation has. In the case of British Telecom continual increases of the value of X failed to make much impression on its recorded profit (after allowing for redundancy payments) which remained obstinately around the £3 billion level in the early years.
c) Encourage the adoption of *new technology*. The cost-reducing effects of new technology are always hard to predict in advance.
d) *Reduce price* for the consumer. This objective will usually be achieved. However, since the formula is normally applied to a basket of prices representing the industry's product range, not all prices will come down by the same amount, and indeed some may actually rise as happened to domestic telephone customers in the early days of privatisation.

Is there a difference?

Some economists argue that there is no real difference between these two forms of regulation, because X gets adjusted upwards if the company continues to make a high profit (or rate of return). This certainly seems to be the case with British Telecom. When a value of 3 per cent for X failed to reduce profits, the regulator, Oftel, kept increasing its value until it reached 7.5 per cent. In this case, however, the potential competition in the telecommunications industry has acted as an additional incentive for British Telecom to reduce costs (see page 345).

Information problems

The problem faced by regulators is that they do not know enough about the industry they are regulating. This is because the best source of information is the industry itself. It is not in the interest of the industry being regulated to give useful information about itself, if the effect of that information would be tougher regulation and therefore lower profits. This situation is sometimes termed **regulatory capture**, where the industry being regulated is really in charge of the situation. Regulators sometimes have to impose tough price controls despite loud protests from the industry. This can be somewhat of a gamble by the regulator. If the industry did in fact have lots of potential for reducing costs by shaking out labour, or introducing new technology, then the tough price controls would have been justified. If on the other hand most of the potential for further cost reductions had been exhausted, then tough price controls would substantially reduce profits, and possibly investment as a result.

The windfall tax

The idea that some companies had been sold at below market price led the Labour government to introduce a **windfall tax** on certain privatised companies. This one-off tax was related to the capital gain that an investor would have made by buying at the privatisation price and then selling at the market price. Of course the new shareholders who actually sold their shares and made this capital gain will not bear this tax. It is the existing shareholders who will lose. Nevertheless the increase in share prices can be taken as a measure of the high profitability of the company and therefore can be taken as a **proxy** for excessive profits made by such companies. Concern expressed by the Labour party while in opposition about the so-called 'fat cat' directors of privatised firms who made enormous sums on share options and other deals, has faded away in government as there is no legal way in which this money can be recovered. The allegations, however, did contribute to the 'sleaze' factor used against the Conservatives in the election.

Competition: the best regulator

The best regulator is, of course, competition. Sometimes regulation is needed to create and protect this competition. The dominant position of British Telecom in the telecommunications market means that the most important long-term policy of the regulator is to protect new competition. This has been achieved by allowing access to British Telecom's network for the new entrant Mercury as explained earlier in the chapter. Ofgas, the gas industry regulator, has performed a similar task by requiring Transco to carry gas from many competing companies. Industrial users of electricity can also buy their electricity direct from a generating company, and the National Grid and REC are required to transmit the energy to the customer at a regulated price. This process of introducing competition into these very large former state monopolies can be an extremely slow process.

STUDENT ACTIVITY 26.11

A privatised industry is regulated by the formula RPI – X + Y, where X is the figure for efficiency gains and Y is a figure allowing for changes in input costs over which the industry has no control.

a) If the rate of inflation last year was 3 per cent and X is set at 5 per cent, while Y is set a 2 per cent, what will be the average increase in price allowed for the industry in the coming year?
b) If the industry has already decided to increase its price by 3 per cent on 40 per cent of its output, how must it change the prices on the remaining 60 per cent of its output?

STUDENT ACTIVITY 26.12

An industry is being controlled by rate of return regulation fixed at 10 per cent on the company's assets. Which of the following policies would increase the total profit which the company can earn?

a) Increased expenditure on capital.
b) Increases in prices.
c) Increased expenditure on perks for the management.

Which of the following policies would allow the company to raise its prices?

a) Increased expenditure on capital.
b) Increased expenditure on perks for the management.
c) Increased costs of raw materials.

STUDENT ACTIVITY 26.13

Which of the following parts of privatised industries still need price regulation?

a) Transco b) Gas supply companies c) Rover Group d) British Telecom e) Regional Electricity Companies f) National Grid g) A rail franchisee (passenger services)

Case study 26.6
Is privatisation a success?

Raising money and transferring wealth

At one level privatisation can be seen as a way of the government raising money and thus reducing the need for taxation. But more important than this are the ideological motives which underly the trend. At a superficial level we may view privatisation as a response to the supposed inefficiencies of nationalised industries.

Selling off publicly owned assets was likened by the ex prime minister Harold Macmillan to selling off the family silver. This is a mistaken understanding of the situation. The government does indeed receive wealth from the public which can be used to lower taxes and it is the case that such assets cannot be sold twice in order to increase revenues in subsequent years. However, what happens to the wealth of the nation? Nothing! The ownership of assets has just passed from the public sector to the private. It is only in the extent to which privatised assets are bought by foreigners that the net wealth of the country is affected. Of course, this argument also works in reverse if an industry is nationalised.

The political economy of the market

More fundamental than this is the belief that the price system is the most efficient way to run the economy and that the price system brings about an optimum allocation of resources. The classical economists, such as Adam Smith, argued that this optimality was brought about by the invisible hand of self-interest (i.e. everyone striving to maximise their own individual benefit) and was regulated by the forces of competition. Many twentieth-century economists have disagreed with this view. However, in recent years Milton Friedman and the Chicago school have argued for a return to classical values. According to this school of thought the market economy is essentially self-regulating and efficient. Problems in the economy such as inflation and unemployment are caused by state interference. Thus, in order to have a well-run economy it is essential to reduce the role of the state to a minimum so that the maximum percentage of the economy will be self-regulating. The idea that private enterprise results in more efficient use of resources is also part of the supply side view of economics.

The most influential school of thought in the UK privatisation process has been the Austrian school, particularly the writings of Hayek. This school of thought stresses the value of the market, not just as a way of meeting consumer preferences and driving down costs, but also as a source of innovation and investment funds. Abnormal profits may form the basis for investment in new technologies, research and development, and may be regarded as a good thing. It is the view of the Austrian economists (not all of whom are Austrian) that such monopoly power will be challenged in the long run.

Whatever view of privatisation is adopted, the fact remains that reversing the process is very difficult. The cost of renationalising these industries would be prohibitive and could only be achieved at the cost of raising tax rates. This has not been a popular policy proposal in recent elections. The alternative approach of political parties on the left is to concentrate on tighter regulation.

An extension of this argument is that the state sector of the economy has crowded out private investment. During the years of high government intervention there was a high demand upon the investment funds available, of which the state took a large proportion. It is argued by the free market school that the state will take investment decisions on non-economic grounds – for example, it may build coal-fired power stations to keep the miners happy, which will therefore lead to low-yielding investments. It is thus necessary to reduce the role of the state as investor and leave markets to allocate capital in the most efficient manner possible. This argument also helps to explain why the Conservative government thought it necessary to keep down the size of the PSBR and therefore not compete for available funds.

It is therefore necessary to see the events of recent years not simply as the selling off of state-controlled industries but as a fundamental shift in the way in which the economy is organised. Initially the sale of assets could be seen as merely a change of emphasis, but as the government extended the role of the market into the operation of the welfare state (as discussed in Chapter 29), it became clear that some of the basic principles which have ordered our society for the last 50 years have been called into question. The election of the Labour government in 1997 has not brought renationalisation with it; indeed further privatisation has not been ruled out.

Performance

One way of deciding whether the policy of privatisation has been a success is to examine the performance of the privatised industries. The results of studies into efficiency have been mixed. Studies of the nationalised industries suggest that they performed moderately well in terms of productivity growth in the 1950s and 1960s, but that they performed rather less well in the 1970s. Curiously enough, their profitability rose in the decade of privatisation, the 1980s! They seem to have done particularly well just before being privatised! Whether this is because the government was deliberately allowing profits to rise in order to get a good share price, or whether the prospect of private sector competition forced it to lower costs, is a matter of dispute.

Increased profitability can be achieved by a number of methods:

a) Wages can be reduced. This does not constitute an increase in productivity, but a redistribution of income. There is evidence that this occurred in some cases of bus and refuse collection privatisation.
b) New technology can reduce costs. A good example here is British Telecom where fibre-optic cables and computerised exchanges have revolutionised the technology of the industry. Prices have been driven down continuously in real terms since privatisation. A question that can be legitimately asked here is whether such changes would have occurred as extensively or as rapidly if the industry had remained nationalised. Is the increased productivity due to the privatisation, increased competition, or the new technology?
c) Market power can increase profits. Where industries have been privatised with relatively little competition, profits have been satisfactory but consumer relationships have not. British Gas lost its charter mark for consumer relations in the early 1990s. The performance of some of the water companies in maintaining supplies has been criticised (although to be fair to them rainfall fell in the mid 1990s). There was at one stage considerable criticism of the reliability of British Telecom public telephone call boxes, but the reliability improved dramatically when Oftel suggested that Mercury could take over provision.
d) Restrictive practices achieved under nationalisation can be removed. This can result in a substantial reduction in employment in these industries. Closure of loss-making parts of the business can also have a similar effect. Major changes of ths kind can create local unemployment which can take time to eradicate.

Ownership or competition?

A strong view emerging from studies of the privatised industries is that competition is more important than ownership in determining efficiency. Where it has not been possible to introduce competition, privatised industries have needed considerable regulation, and because of the information problems discussed above, this has not always been completely satisfactory. Where it has been possible to introduce competition, results have been better, although where the process of introducing competition has been slow there have been transitional problems. Because it is not always possible to introduce competition, there will always be an argument that nationalisation is still appropriate for some unavoidably monopoly industries.

STUDENT ACTIVITY 26.14

At the time of writing the Post Office had not been privatised. Competition exists in the parcels business for items above a £1 delivery price, but not for letters. If privatised, which sector would you advise a new company to enter?

a) An urban area with high population density.
b) A rural area in a remote part of the country.
c) Mass delivery for companies' 'junk mail'.

What effect will your entry into the market have on:

a) The revenues and costs of the Post Office?
b) Wages in the industry?
c) Numbers of deliveries in the day?
d) Prices of delivery in rural areas?

STUDENT ACTIVITY 26.15

Transco and the National Grid are natural monopolies where competition is not a sensible option. What are the advantages of privatising and regulating as opposed to nationalisation in such cases?

Summary

1 Industries were nationalised for reasons of monopoly power, social costs, strategic reasons and ideology.

2 There are problems in regulating the nationalised industries because of conflicting objectives: profit, allocative efficiency, social objectives and macroeconomic objectives.

3 Privatisation works best where there is competition. Sources of competition include vertical disintegration, new technologies, deregulation and capital market competition.

4 Regulation is still necessary where there is monopoly power, or in order to protect new entrants into the market.

5 Regulation of privatised industries suffers from shortage of information. Rate of return regulation may lead to overinvestment. RPI – X is initially good but difficult to set accurately.

6 There remains a debate about whether competition is more important than ownership.

27 The economics of the environment

Learning outcomes

At the end of this chapter you will be able to:

- Understand the relationship between the economy and the environment.
- Identify the alternative policies available and their appropriateness in different cases.
- Distinguish between renewable and non-renewable resources, and understand the arguments about recycling.
- Appreciate the problems of cooperation between countries and between generations.

Introduction

This chapter consists of case studies in the economics of the environment, which should be treated as data response articles. As a result there are no data response articles at the end. Student activities appear at the end of each case.

The impact of economic activity on the environment was not widely discussed until a group of academics known as the Club of Rome reported in the early 1970s that the planet faced pressures from the overuse of ***resources***, the growth of ***population*** and the increase in ***pollution***. These three issues are frequently interrelated. The contribution of economists in helping to solve the problems of the environment date back to Pigou and his concept of ***externality***. As discussed in Chapter 25:

An externality is a side effect of economic activity which affects people or companies not directly involved in that activity.

The usefulness of this concept is best illustrated by describing some of the most pressing environmental problems which result from economic activity. A minimum amount of understanding of the science behind these (usually chemical) problems allows us to trace the environmental problem back to its industrial source.

When looking at the case studies, you should distinguish between ***market instruments*** which affect price, such as taxes and subsidies, and ***regulations*** which affect technology or output directly.

Case study 27.1 Global warming

The scientific background

Global warming is a rise in the average temperature of the whole planet. The scientific theory which suggests that global warming will be a significant problem in the twenty-first century is known as the **greenhouse effect**. The sun's rays warm the earth during the day, but when this energy is reflected back into outer space it is trapped, much as energy in a greenhouse is trapped. The increase in the production of certain gases (since the industrial revolution started in the late eighteenth century) is responsible for this effect. Carbon dioxide, nitrous oxides, CFCs (see the case on ozone depletion below) and methane are the main gases responsible.

Some of the effects of global warming are beneficial. The agricultural productivity of more northerly countries such as the UK should improve and their climates could become more pleasant. However, other countries such as Ethiopia could suffer from increased **desertification** and problems of **famine**. Patterns of rainfall are likely to change. The greatest threat comes from the projected **rises in sea level**. Sea level will rise as warmer water expands, but more seriously, the polar ice-caps may start to melt. As a result, countries such as Bangladesh and Egypt with large populations in low-lying coastal river deltas will suffer. Much of the projected costs of global warming comes from the loss of agricultural production from these fertile areas, or from the cost of providing them with sea defences. It is also believed that the strength and frequency of hurricanes is related to seawater temperature in the tropics. There is uncertainty about many of the projected effects of global warming, but there is a possibility that the climate of the UK could become *colder*. If the Gulf Stream, which carries warm water to our shores, changes direction, our climate would become more like that of other North European countries.

The link with the economy

The main source of carbon dioxide is from the burning of coal, oil and gas. The main industries responsible for adding carbon dioxide to the atmosphere are electricity, gas and transport. These are industries which are vital to production and distribution in a developed economy. The lifestyle of consumers in the industrialised countries is also highly energy intensive. As more countries successfully **industrialise,** so the problem will worsen.

Transfrontier pollution

Global warming is an example of an externality which crosses frontiers. If individual countries attempt to deal with the problem on their own, much of the benefit will in fact go to other countries while the cost of reducing the pollution will fall on their own country. Where there is **transfrontier pollution**, progress can only be made if there is international agreement about common policy to be followed by all countries. Such agreements usually take the form of agreed targets for each country, and it is then up to each country to achieve that target in the way it thinks best. The Rio environmental summit in Brazil (1992) formed the basis of many such agreements. In the case of global warming, countries agreed to limit their output of carbon dioxide to 1990 levels by the year 2000. This may not seem like a very dramatic control policy, but it is set against the background of sharply increasing output levels in previous decades.

Intergenerational externality

The problem with global warming is that the predicted adverse effects are not expected to be very serious until well into the next century. Predictions of how much sea level will rise vary and there are even some scientists who remain sceptical about the whole thing. What we are faced with here is an external effect of **uncertain magnitude** occurring in the future. Figure 27.1 shows the range of temperature forecasts by the International Panel on Climate Change (IPCC) and compares these forecasts with historical evidence. The costs of reducing the externality are borne by the current generation, while the benefits will accrue to future generations. This situation is known as an **intergenerational externality**. This may explain the fairly conservative management policy being advocated at present. World environmental policy on global warming can best be described as holding carbon dioxide output levels steady while we check what the effects really are.

Sustainable development

The Brundtland Commission (1987) popularised the notion that when faced with intergenerational externalities of this kind, the right approach was to try to follow a path of **sustainable development.** Sustainable development means that we should try to achieve eco-

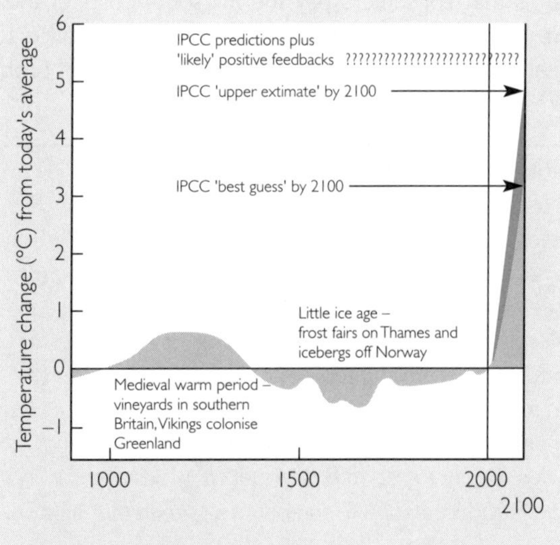

Fig. 27.1 **Global warming**

nomic growth in such a way as not to affect future generations adversely. This may be easier for developed nations than those undergoing a process of industrialisation. We can hardly complain if China or India attempt to achieve the same standard of living as in Europe, increasing their use of energy per capita to our levels. Clearly an extra 2 billion people consuming energy at that level is likely to have a major impact on global warming. The main problem with the idea of sustainable development is that optimists argue that there will be a **technical fix** for the problems as science progresses and that we need not worry too much. Pessimists would argue the opposite, so policy will depend upon attitudes towards the **uncertainty** of future events.

Policies

VAT on fuel

In 1993 the government introduced a VAT rate of 8 per cent on fuel, which had been previously zero rated. Plans to increase VAT to the standard rate (now 17.5 per cent) the following year had to be abandoned owing to strong political opposition. After its election in 1997, the Labour government announced its intention to reduce this tax to 5 per cent as soon as was prudent (this is the lowest rate of VAT that can be charged under EU regulations). In Chapter 25 we discussed Pigou's idea of imposing a tax equal to the value of the externality. The idea of such a tax is that consumers pay the full social costs of their energy consumption. The use of this form of taxation to deal with energy pollution runs into a number of problems which are discussed in the following sections.

Common misunderstanding

Most people believe that there was no tax on energy before the introduction of VAT on gas and electricity. This is not the case because of the way in which VAT works (see Chapter 30 for a fuller discussion). VAT is levied on the value of the output of companies at each stage of production. There is a rebate of the tax already charged on inputs from earlier stages in production. Inputs such as energy that did not themselves attract tax are taxed when they are used to produce other goods and services. The introduction of VAT on energy was therefore only on domestic energy, since industrial and commercial use of energy was already taxed in the way described in this paragraph.

Targeting the externality

Because the tax is on the private good rather than on the externality itself, it is not well **targeted**. The tax does not discriminate well between different sources of energy that have different effects on the environment. For instance, nuclear energy, although it may have other external effects, does not produce any carbon dioxide at all. Electricity production works by burning fossil fuels to create high-pressure steam, which turns turbines, which generate the electricity. Not all fuels produce the same amount of carbon dioxide per unit of energy produced. Gas is more environmentally efficient at producing energy, both when used directly and when used for generating electricity. It also has a lower sulphur content and is therefore also preferable because it produces less acid rain (see Case study 27.2). It is because there are a number of alternative energy technologies available that a tax on energy is badly targeted.

Incidence and equity

The demand for energy is very inelastic, so the reduction in consumption is small compared with the increase in tax (see Fig. 27.2). Most of the incidence of the tax will be on the consumer because of the inelasticity of demand. In addition to questions about the effectiveness of the tax in meeting its objectives, there is a problem of **equity**. The poorest people in society also spend the highest proportion of their income on energy. The elderly and families on low income with young children both need warmth in winter to stay well, so this is a matter for social concern. However, it can be argued that the government should concentrate on getting relative prices to reflect social costs properly, and then deal with problems of income distribution separately by increasing pensions and social security payments to poorer households, so that they can afford to maintain their energy consumption at an adequate level.

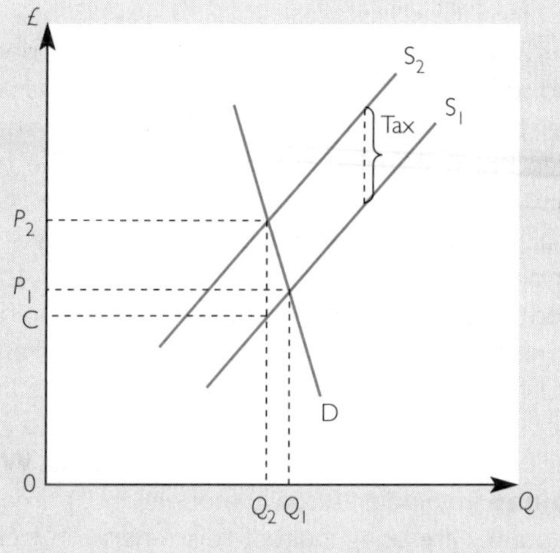

Fig. 27.2 **The incidence of a tax on domestic energy**

On the plus side it must be said that the absence of a tax on domestic energy consumption was encouraging excessive use of this energy by lowering its price relative to the prices of the majority of products which do attract VAT. Paradoxically, greater efficiency following the privatisation of the electricity industry will have the effect of lowering prices and increasing consumption! A further advantage of using VAT is that it is rebateable on exported goods, so it does not adversely affect the country's balance of payments. Finally, as noted below, higher energy prices may persuade people to take energy-saving measures.

The petrol tax escalator

The government decided to discourage use of the car by increasing the excise tax on petrol by 5 per cent a year in real terms. This process has been accelerated by the Labour government which made a further increase in petrol duty over and above the 5 per cent increase in its first budget. Once again this is a tax on a price inelastic product, so the reduction in demand is likely to be small as in the case of domestic energy illustrated in Fig. 27.2. However, this time the tax is much better targeted because the choice of fuels is limited. There will be an incentive for consumers to use more fuel-efficient means of transport. Unfortunately the high income elasticity of demand for transport will constantly be moving consumers in the opposite direction. This time the poorer people in society are likely to bear a smaller proportion of the costs because public transport is generally more fuel efficient per passenger carried.

Infrastructure

Decisions about investment in transport **infrastructure** can also affect carbon dioxide output. Public transport consumes less fuel than car transport. Building more roads reduces congestion and makes travelling on the roads more attractive. Any decision to curb the road-building programme must be accompanied by greater investment in **public transport**, possibly with greater **subsidies** if people are to be persuaded by lower prices to use it. Transport is fundamental to the operation of market economies because markets depend on the free movement of labour, goods and services. Other aspects of this problem area are discussed in Chapter 28.

Information technology

To the extent that information technology reduces the need for transport, by video conferencing, faxes, file transfers on the World-Wide web, e-mail, etc., it reduces the demand for energy and is environmentally beneficial. People are more able to work at home some of the time using a modem instead of a car. Information transmitted electronically is also less intensive in paper.

Subsidy for loft insulation

Energy-saving measures such as loft insulation and double glazing do pay for themselves eventually, but may cost a great deal of money. A universal subsidy was available in the 1970s when the oil crisis led the government to put a premium on saving energy and reducing expensive oil imports. In the 1990s this subsidy is limited to old-age pensioners. A tax on energy may have the result of persuading more people to take energy-saving measures. As part of its initiative to get younger people off unemployment benefit, the Labour government announced the setting up of environmental task groups to help with loft insulation, among other environmental tasks.

The carbon tax

Although not implemented, this has often been advocated as a good method of reducing carbon dioxide output. Instead of placing the tax on the private good, electricity, the tax is levied on **the carbon content** of the fossil fuel. This acts as an effective **proxy** for the real thing we wish to tax: carbon dioxide.

The recession

The recession of the early 1990s made it easier for the UK to meet its targets, since energy use is related to GDP. This is not a policy as such, and indeed it may persuade people that pollution control is going well. The economy recovered strongly in the mid 1990s leading to increased environmental problems and a need for stronger policy to help meet targets.

Nuclear power and the fossil fuel levy

Nuclear power does not use fossil fuel and creates no global warming effects. It seems, on the face of it, to be an ideal solution to the problem. Unfortunately, nuclear power has externalities of its own, both in terms of the low-level **radioactive waste** that nuclear power plants produce routinely, and the more dramatic **accidents** that sometimes occur. The relatively recent Chernobyl disaster has worried some people about the use of nuclear energy. Nevertheless the UK government initially subsidised the nuclear industry after the rest of the electricity industry had been privatised, by charging a levy on all fossil fuel (coal, oil, gas). This levy has now been phased out.

Operational and accidental pollution

It is helpful from the point of view of policy to make a distinction between pollution which occurs as a normal by-product of industrial activity (**operational pollution**) and **accidental pollution** when something goes wrong, as in the case of the accident at the Chernobyl nuclear power plant in the former Soviet Union. The production of carbon dioxide as a result of burning fossil fuels is clearly operational. Operational pollution can more frequently be dealt with by **market-based incentives**, whilst accidents nearly always require regulations to prevent frequent occurrence.

Renewable energy

The revenue from the fossil fuel levy was also used to subsidise renewable sources of energy, such as wind power, but only a small fraction of the total went on this kind of sustainable energy production. The fossil fuel levy was phased out with the privatisation of the nuclear industry in 1997. **Alternative energy** is the technology of the future, if global warming is to be tackled successfully. Unfortunately these technologies are mostly more expensive to produce at present. Most of them use the energy from the sun, directly or indirectly. Direct solar energy can be used to heat water or generate electricity using **solar cells. Wind turbines** in windier (usually mountainous) areas of the country are using indirect solar energy. In Iceland **geothermal** energy is used by pumping water down to hot parts of the earth's crust (which are near the surface), which then returns as steam to drive turbines. The most urgent need in the case of renewable technologies is research and development to drive down the costs of producing energy in this way. If significant progress can be made in reducing these costs, the hottest countries may become the natural location for energy-intensive industry.

Trees and the rainforests

Common misunderstanding

Many people believe that trees grow out of the soil. In fact they largely grow out of the air! Trees are mainly made of carbon which they obtain by 'breathing in' carbon dioxide from the air through their leaves, removing the carbon, and then 'breathing' out the oxygen through their leaves. This is very useful as human beings and other animals need this oxygen to live. It is also useful because it reduces the amount of carbon dioxide in the atmosphere, so growing trees reduces the greenhouse effect. The trees act as a ***carbon sink*** *effectively storing the carbon. All plants have this effect, but trees are the bulkiest and therefore the most effective store of carbon.*

There are many reasons for protecting the rainforests. They have a vast variety of animal and plant species which may be of medical value to humankind. Water evaporates from them and falls as much needed rainfall in more arid regions. They are the natural home of indigenous peoples. But most of all they are the world's biggest carbon sink. The argument about sustainable development arises again here (see earlier in the chapter). Europeans cut down their vast forests over a period of thousands of years as their populations grew and their economies developed. Are Europeans in a strong position to argue that tropical countries should not do the same? The tropical areas include some of the world's poorer countries (in Central Africa), but also some of the world's faster-growing developing countries such as Brazil and the 'Asian tiger' economies (Malaysia, Thailand, Indonesia). Cutting down trees in these forests is no problem in itself as long as they are replanted. If the trees are turned into wood products like furniture they will continue to act as a carbon store while new trees are growing. **Sustainably managed** rainforests used for commercial timber add to the carbon sink and are environmentally desirable.

Consumer information and self-interest

Some reduction in energy use can be achieved by more energy-efficient homes and vehicles. The introduction of official miles per gallon (mpg) figures for cars has helped consumers both to save money and help the environment. Energy use figures for washing machines and dishwashers have the same effect. Campaigns to persuade people to insulate their lofts, or install double glazing, will also save people money in the long run. This approach is known as **eco-labelling**.

STUDENT ACTIVITY 27.1

Undertake a survey of your school or college listing the areas where energy saving might be possible. List the measures you suggest in terms of rising expense. You can undertake a similar activity for your own home as an individual exercise.

STUDENT ACTIVITY 27.2

Which are the easiest policies to implement from the above list? What are the best ways of reducing carbon dioxide output from domestic heating and transport respectively? Which policies would have less impact on poorer people?

STUDENT ACTIVITY 27.3

Using Fig. 27.2, indicate how much of the incidence of the tax on domestic energy consumption is on the consumer and how much is on the producer.

Case study 27.2
Acid rain

Acid rain: the scientific background

Once again a little science is needed to understand the nature of this problem. Burning coal and oil produces sulphur dioxide (SO_2) and nitrogen oxides. When mixed with water vapour in the atmosphere these gases turn into sulphuric acid and nitric acid. When rain falls at some distance from the vehicle or power plant which caused the problem, the acidity of the rain corrodes buildings and makes the soil more acid. A more acid soil can reduce agricultural productivity and is thought to reduce growth in trees. Acid can build up in freshwater lakes eventually killing off fish. Once again, the culprits are the energy and transport industries.

Characteristics of the externality

Acid rain, like global warming, is a transfrontier pollution. Acid rain from the UK will often fall on Scandinavian countries because of prevailing south-westerly winds. It is also an operational pollutant because it is a side effect of normal production processes. Unlike global warming, it is not solely an intergenerational pollutant. Although the effects of acidification are passed on to later generations, it has an immediate impact on agricultural productivity, tree growth, and the erosion of buildings, although acidity does build up in the soil and in lakes. Although its effects are less serious than global warming, because they are more **immediate**, they have been taken more seriously.

Imports and exports

In the case of global warming, the externality was said to be a transfrontier pollutant because the whole planet could be affected by the actions of a single country. In the case of acid rain the effects are not global in this way, but rather the pollution is exported to a number of neighbouring countries. Which countries receive the pollution will depend on weather conditions at the time. Some of the acid rain which a country produces will of course fall locally in that country. Weather forecasters can keep track of the flow of air and rainfall and have produced information about which countries are polluting which. In Table 27.1 the imports and exports between some European countries are documented. The column under each country shows its 'exports' of acid rain to each of the countries on the left. The diagonal (top left to bottom right) shows how much acid rain is domestically produced for each country. Can you see why the Scandinavians have been so annoyed?

***Table 27.1* Importers and exporters of acid rain, thousands of tonnes of sulphur p.a. (1989)**

	Exporters			
Importers	*UK*	*France*	*Scandinavia*	*West Germany*
UK	571	14	0	15
France	43	332	0	40
Scandinavia	32	5	59	18
West Germany	45	69	0	330

Source: Adapted from EMEP data

Valuation

External costs are difficult to value because they do not pass through the market place, but are imposed on 'victims'. Where the costs are on other production processes, valuation is easier. It is possible to estimate the loss of timber or agricultural production as a result of acid rain. It is also possible to put a price on the damage caused to buildings and paintwork by the corrosive effects of acid rain. It is more difficult to put a value on consumption activities. If fishing is no longer possible because the fish have died as a result of rising acidity in Scandinavian lakes, how much is this worth? If landscapes are affected by dying trees, by how much is tourists' enjoyment reduced?

Stated preference

One way of obtaining values for external costs is to ask people directly how much they would be willing to pay for the pollution to be removed. There is a problem with this approach, because people are not actually asked to pay and the questions are hypothetical. People may be tempted to overstate their price because they think it may influence policy in their favour. This is known as **strategic bias.** There is a further problem in that people are not used to buying and selling pollution. It is argued that consumers need the experience of real markets to practise on before finally deciding what price to pay. Values obtained from questionnaires are therefore subject to **hypothetical market bias.** Careful design of questionnaires is necessary to try and avoid these biased answers and to cross-check for consistency. Strand (1981) found an average value of 800 Norwegian krone per person to reduce acid rain in Norway to levels that would allow freshwater fish to survive. It is likely that this value is understated because some respondents would think it was more appropriate for the British or Germans to pay for the clean-up since they were causing about half of the pollution (see Table 27.1). There is a confusion here between **values** (how much is a clean-up worth) and **value judgements** (who should pay for it). This example underlines some of the difficulties of the technique.

Revealed preference

An alternative approach is to infer from peoples' behaviour what value they place on an externality. In the case of acid rain a number of studies have been made on the relationship between air quality and house prices. The basis of these studies is that poor air quality will make a neighbourhood less desirable and this will be reflected in house prices. Differences in house prices for similar houses in different areas will reflect the value housebuyers put on the environment. In this way consumer preference is revealed. The main problem with studies of this sort is deciding what houses are similar. Consistent results from a number of studies suggest the values obtained are in fact fairly reliable. This method is also used to place a value on the noise around airports. This helps planners to decide where to put airports: too close to the city and noise costs rise; too far away and passengers' time costs rise. It has also been used to study the effects of sulphur pollution in the USA, with the results of several studies suggesting house prices fall by about 0.1 per cent for each 1 per cent increase in sulphur levels.

Optimal pollution

Placing a value on an externality makes deciding policy towards it easier. An economic assessment of the problem would involve comparing the costs of the externality with the costs of reducing that externality. This is illustrated in Fig. 27.3. The usual way of looking at an externality is as a social cost added to a private cost. Figure 27.3 takes a different approach. It looks at pollution as a good (or rather a bad) which is produced for which there is no market. Since no one wants pollution, benefits are achieved by moving from right to left on the diagram, by reducing pollution. The starting point is E_0, which is the **do nothing** situation. This is the outcome if there is no regulation or taxation of the polluter. As we move towards E_2, the optimal position, we start with the cheapest methods of reducing pollution, and as these are used up we gradually have to move on to more expensive methods.

Where the marginal costs of reducing the externality (*MRC*) exceed the marginal costs of the pollution itself (*MDC*), there is a net loss to society as a whole if the pollution is further reduced. This would be the case if we reduced pollution to level E_3. If on the other hand the marginal costs of pollution (*MDC*) are more than the costs of pollution reduction (*MRC*), then it makes sense to reduce the pollution further. This would be the case if we had only moved as far as E_1. The optimal level of pollution will be at point E_2 where the two costs are just equal at the margin.

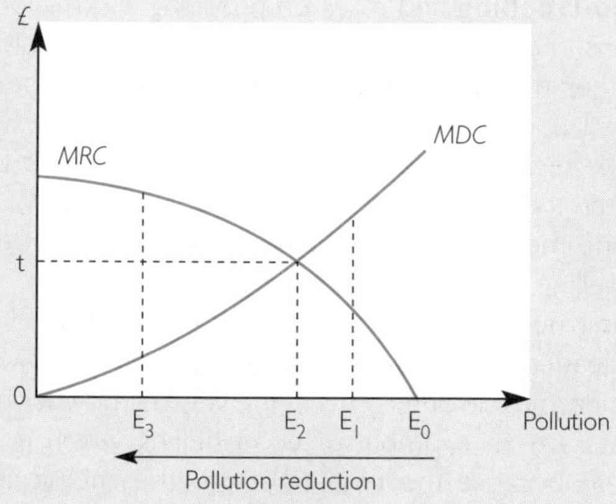

Fig. 27.3 **Optimal pollution**

Deep greens and light greens

Some people object that putting the two words 'optimal' and 'pollution' together in this way is a contradiction in terms. If all pollution is regarded as bad then should it not all be eliminated? The economist's answer to this viewpoint is that both the costs and benefits of pollution reduction should be considered. In the same way that economists are concerned with equilibrium and balance in the economic system, ecologists are also concerned with equilibrium and balance in ecological systems. If an economic activity is resulting in the breakdown of an ecological system, an ecologist is likely to object. Which of these two viewpoints is correct? The answer is that they both reflect different value judgements about what is important in the world. The economist's viewpoint only counts the costs and benefits which affect humankind. This approach is sometimes referred to as **anthropocentric** (centred on humankind) or **light green.** The ecological approach values all living systems and is sometimes referred to as **deep green** because it values the environment for itself, and not just for its value to humankind. You can hold either of these viewpoints, but if you are a deep green you must recognise that there are substantial economic costs of holding this position.

STUDENT ACTIVITY 27.4

From Table 27.1 calculate which countries are the largest net exporters and which are the largest net importers. Could the problem be solved by the importers paying the exporters not to produce the acid rain? Alternatively, should the exporters have to pay the importers for the damage they cause them? What does your answer say about who 'owns' the environment?

STUDENT ACTIVITY 27.5

The costs of pollution reduction using alternative technologies are shown in Table 27.2.

Using low-sulphur fuel oil results in less sulphur being burned with each tonne of oil in the power station. Flue gas desulphurisation involves putting an alkaline filter in the chimney of the power station which absorbs the sulphur, resulting in less of it reaching the atmosphere. Fluidised bed combustion is a technology which results in less of the sulphur being burned. You will notice that it is more expensive to put these technologies into old plant (retrofitting) rather than building them into new plant.

If the benefits of acid rain reduction are estimated to be \$500 per tonne of SO_2, which acid rain reduction technologies would be worthwhile implementing? In what order should they be implemented? Does your answer depend on whether you hold a deep green or light green point of view?

Table 27.2 **Estimates of reducing sulphur output (average of several studies)**

	Cost (\$) per tonne of SO_2 removed
Using low-sulphur fuel oil	600
Flue gas desulphurisation (FGD)	
New plant	300
Old plant	600
Fluidised bed combustion	
New plant	100
Old plant	2300

Case study 27.3
Ozone depletion

What does ozone do

The ozone layer is high in the earth's atmosphere and acts to deflect ultraviolet (UV) radiation away from the surface of the planet. Ozone is in fact a form of oxygen which has three atoms in each molecule (O_3) instead of the normal two (O_2) which we breathe at ground level. Ozone found at ground level is a pollutant which irritates the lungs. A group of chemicals known as **CFCs** (chlorofluorocarbons) have the effect of breaking down the ozone molecules. As a result, more UV radiation reaches ground level. The main harmful result to humankind is an increased incidence of skin cancer which is often fatal. Agricultural productivity might also be affected in the long run as radiation can affect growth. The main use of CFCs was as a propellant for aerosol spray cans and as a coolant for refrigerators and freezers.

Characteristics of the externality

This once again is a transfrontier externality. Although most CFC use has been in North America and Europe, the first measurable effect was the 'ozone hole' which has appeared over the Antarctic. Ozone thinning has also been detected in the northern hemisphere. The ozone layer does eventually recover but it is thought that this process might take up to 80 years. It is thus also an intergenerational externality. Since it is associated with the operation of a particular product, it is an operational externality.

Eco-labelling

Not all manufacturers had the ability to switch to alternative spray propellant technology immediately. Although CFCs have now been banned, there was an interval while the new technology was being introduced when reduction in output was dependent on the consumers' unwillingness to pollute the environment. Spray cans were labelled as 'ozone friendly' if they did not contain CFCs. This approach is known as **eco-labelling** and relies on providing information to consumers to help them make the right decision, rather than telling them what to do by introducing regulations. It works well as a transitional policy while new technology is being introduced. It works best when the issues are straightforward and simple for the consumer to understand. Another example of eco-labelling is lead-free petrol, although this was combined with a tax differential between leaded and unleaded petrol to encourage people to switch. Biodegradable detergents in the washing powder business are an example of eco-labelling which is less clear, because the time taken for the chemicals to degrade safely varies between different brands, and the consumer has no way of knowing what the acceptable period should be. This is perhaps an area where government regulation of environmental standards is needed to bolster simple eco-labelling.

Stock and flow pollutants

Until this point in the chapter, pollution that lasts well into the future has been referred to as 'intergenerational'. An alternative way of classifying pollutants is by deciding if they are **stock** or **flow** pollutants. As students of economics you should be aware of this distinction already: wealth is a stock while income is a flow; capital is a stock, while interest is a flow. In a sense most pollutants are a flow in that there is a steady flow of them into the environment. In some cases, however, these flows build up in the environment as stocks. Carbon dioxide builds up in the atmosphere making global warming gradually worse. Acidity of the soil as a result of acid rain can also build up over time. The ozone layer takes a long time to recover after CFCs have broken it down. On the other hand, some pollutants disappear almost as soon as they arrive. Noise from an aeroplane dies away. Many chemical smells are temporary. Oil pollution of the sea will eventually be dissipated (there are at least 90 organisms which eat oil!).

Certainty and uncertainty

Clearly, stock pollutants are more worrying in the long run, but there are sometimes scientific **uncertainties** about the nature of the environmental threat. Forecasting well into the future also brings with it uncertainties. The appearance of the ozone hole over the Antarctic confirmed scientific hypotheses and led to strict action by the world, and the development of the Montreal Protocol for phasing out CFCs. Because of the increased certainty that ozone depletion is taking place and is causing harmful effects, policy has been stricter in this area and international agreement has been easier to achieve.

Technology transfer

Although technologies which do not use CFCs exist for both aerosols and fridges, they are not necessarily easily accessible to less developed countries because of patents held by companies based in developed countries. As these countries industrialise they may use cheap polluting technology in their production techniques. The solution to this problem is to **transfer new technology** to developing countries by providing information, waiving patent fees, and giving technical assistance and training. Profit-making countries are unlikely to do this of their own accord, so government involvement would be necessary.

STUDENT ACTIVITY 27.6

Make a list of supermarket products which make environmental claims. Are they easily understood to the average consumer? Are they confirmed by any body other than the producers themselves? Which products would you purchase as a result of the information made available in this way?

Case study 27.4
Rubbish and recycling

The costs of rubbish

Industrial economies produce an enormous quantity of waste which must be disposed of in some way. The majority of waste is disposed of in landfill sites which are eventually covered in earth and returned to other uses. The costs of this process are:

a) the loss of land for agricultural and other purposes;
b) because of the 'chemical soup' in the tip, the land may be unsuitable for any other purpose for a long period after tipping has ceased and may cost a considerable amount of money to make safe at a later date;
c) the cost of the materials thrown away instead of being recycled, including the energy needed to replace materials like glass and aluminium;
d) the energy costs of transporting waste to distant landfill sites.

Policy

Refuse collection

Local authority collection is not a solution to the problem of waste but it prevents it from becoming a local nuisance. The service is frequently produced by private sector companies given the franchise by local authorities.

Recycling

There are four main products which are recycled: paper, glass, aluminium and plastic. In addition batteries are sometimes recycled because they contain heavy metals, and CFCs from fridges are recycled because of their impact on the ozone layer. The purpose of this recycling varies from material to material.

Biodegradability

A substance is said to be **biodegradable** if it quickly decomposes into environmentally beneficial substances. Paper and cardboard are biodegradable but are still recycled for three reasons. First, recycling reduces the demand for tree felling for raw materials. Second, it reduces the bulk of refuse considerably, much of which comes from cardboard packaging and newspapers. Third, biologically useful degraded materials are no use to anyone if mixed up with a lot of toxic materials. Plastics and glass are not biodegradable, and aluminium is not a very useful biological material.

Food waste and some garden waste can be turned into soil by **composting** in compost heaps in people's gardens.

Energy saving

Glass and aluminium production are both energy-intensive processes and considerable energy savings can be achieved by using recycled materials. The benefit of energy saving is not only the money saved; it is a contribution to the reduction of global warming (see Case study 27.1 above).

Rubbish tax

The introduction of a **tax on landfill** makes this way of disposing of rubbish less attractive. It is not a tax on the manufacturers who produce packaging, or directly on the households who throw it out. It falls on the refuse disposal firms who are presumably able to pass it on to the local authorities who pay for their services. Most of the disincentive effects therefore fall on these firms and local authorities rather than on households and manufacturers. It might be argued that making sure that manufacturers meet the cost of disposing of their products and packaging, as in Germany, might change the behaviour of those causing the problems, rather than concentrating on those who have to clear them up. Landfill tax can be avoided mainly by persuading households to recycle rather than throw out by providing separate collection services (paper and card) or local recycling centres. Indirectly, households may benefit from a lower council tax, but individual households may act selfishly if recycling costs them too much time or effort.

STUDENT ACTIVITY 27.7

Discover from your local authority what services are provided for recycling. In each case try find out how much effort has to made by the person or company providing waste for recycling. Use economic theory to explain why minimising this effort is likely to lead to more recycling.

Summary

1 Pollution can be dealt with by market instruments or regulation.
2 Transfrontier pollution requires international agreement before progress can be made.
3 Operational pollution is more likely to be dealt with by market instruments, although regulation will be used if zero or closely controlled emissions are required (e.g. CFCs and nuclear waste).
4 Accidental pollution is usually best dealt with by regulatory methods.
5 Eco-labelling works well for easily understood straightforward cases.
6 Intergenerational pollution requires us to develop in a sustainable way.
7 Stock pollutants such as carbon dioxide need monitoring because above a certain level serious consequences may result.
8 The certainty or uncertainty of the harmful effects will influence how seriously governments take any pollutant.

Questions

1. Why is global warming a problem? What are the best policies available to deal with it?
2. Why are international agreements needed to deal with transfrontier pollutants?
3. What is meant by optimal pollution? What information would you need to arrive at an estimate of what level of a pollutant is optimal? Why do 'deep green' environmentalists disagree with this idea?
4. In what way is sustainable development different from most industrialisation that has taken place in the twentieth century?
5. Explain why market instruments are often better for operational pollution, while regulation is more likely to succeed with accidental pollution.
6. What are the benefits of recycling materials?

28 Transport and the economy

Learning outcomes

At the end of this chapter you will be able to:

- Apply appropriate cost concepts and market structures to different transport situations.
- Recognise that different solutions are needed to solve the problem of congestion in different situations.
- Relate pricing to cost structure and market environment.

Introduction

This a case study chapter so the cases can be regarded as examples of data responses as well as giving an opportunity to apply economics in a new area.

The transport sector of the economy is important in both production (principally freight transport) and consumption (mainly passenger). It provides us with a rich range of economic problems to discuss. There are problems of ***monopoly*** (rail), ***deregulation*** (airlines), ***social cost*** (most transport), ***pricing*** (roads, rail, air), ***privatisation*** (rail). Although each of these ***modes*** of transport are separate they are often in competition with each other. The Channel tunnel has created strong competition not only for the Cross Channel ferries, but also for the airlines on the London–Paris and London–Brussels routes. The car, rail and bus compete in the commuter market. The social costs of transport include congestion, noise, global warming and acid rain, some of which have already been discussed in Chapter 27 on environmental policy. A few technical transport terms will be introduced as the need arises in this chapter, but the emphasis will be on the application of ideas you should already be familiar with. The chapter is presented as a series of case studies, each focusing on a different problem.

The case studies

Each of the case studies is designed to focus on particular problems in microeconomic policy. Each of them has current relevance, and as much as possible uses the student's experience of the world.

Case study 28.1 is concerned with a transport market where pricing is difficult: the road system. Rationing, investment, taxation, new technology and pricing of substitutes are considered. Concepts of public goods, externality, elasticity and peak load demand are applied to the problem.

Case study 28.2 looks at the problems of pricing on the railways. Problems discussed include joint costs, price discrimination and external benefits.

Case study 28.3 continues the study of the railway system by considering the ways in which competition and profit have been introduced into what was considered to be a declining monopoly. Problems of coordination, service quality and social costs are discussed.

Case study 28.4 extends many of the lessons learned in Case study 28.2 to the different competitive environment of the airline industry.

Case study 28.5 considers the problems for competition when one competitor (the Channel tunnel) cannot easily exit the industry.

Case study 28.1
Road congestion

The transport problem that most people are familiar with is **congestion:** sitting in queues of traffic sometimes for long periods of time. The existence of a queue usually means a situation of excess demand (see Chapter 11). The usual response of the market to a situation of excess demand is to raise price in the short run, and increase capacity if the problem persists in the long run. It is necessary to examine the special features of the road market which make this difficult to achieve.

Do roads have public good characteristics?

It is easy to find bits of the road system which have the characteristics of a **private good**. It is not difficult to set up charging systems for bridges and tunnels. In France and Italy, there also tolls on the motorways. The reason why these parts of the road system can be easily charged for is that there are limited entry and exit points where toll booths can be placed. This means that people can be **excluded** from using this part of the road network. Exclusion is an important characteristic of a private good. The time savings offered by bridges, tunnels or motorways will mean that many people are willing to pay to use that part of the road system.

This argument cannot be easily applied to the road system as a whole. If **tolls** are set up at regular intervals in the road network, then people will find routes that miss these tolls. Such a charging system would drive people off the main roads and onto the side roads in a bid to minimise their toll payment. This would create more congestion in the side roads and would in addition be socially undesirable for local residents. The only way to stop people from engaging in this kind of behaviour would be to set up toll points at every road intersection. While this might solve the problem of unemployment, it would be clearly too expensive and would in any case probably add to the problem of congestion that it is trying to solve. It appears that it is difficult to exclude people from the road system as a whole and that therefore the road system has some public good characteristics.

Pricing systems for the roads

Road users do pay for the road system, however, by a system of **taxes.** In the UK an annual road tax provides an entry price on to the road system (and allows the authorities to keep track of which vehicles are on the road so they can be regulated). Although it is difficult to price the road system, it is easy to put a tax on petrol which cars need to use the road system. The petrol tax system of charging for roads also has the advantage that car users pay in proportion to their use, and that heavier vehicles which take up more room and create more wear and tear on the road system will pay more. On top of this there is a built-in incentive to use more fuel-efficient vehicles. The system has to be run by the government because taxes rather than prices are being used, but it seems on the face of it to be a good pricing system.

Peak and off-peak demand

Two features of the transport market create problems for the tax system of pricing. First, demand is not regular over time. There is a strong **peak demand** in the morning 'rush hour' as people drive to work, and a similar problem in the evening as they return. On its own variation in demand need not matter. Christmas cards have a strong peak demand in December, but can be produced over a longer period and stored in a warehouse. Unfortunately, transport is not so easy to **store.** Road space not used in the afternoon cannot be stored and used in the evening!

In rail passenger transport a higher price is charged in the peak period, and a lower one in the **off-peak** period to encourage off-peak use and remove pressure on the system from the peak period (see Case study 28.2 below). This option is not available for the road system, because the 'pricing' is based on the petrol tax. Petrol bought in the off-peak period can be used in the peak period. The pricing system is not sensitive to the time and place of use of the road system.

Optimal road pricing

Economists have long been aware of this problem and many have advocated a **road pricing** solution. The analysis of the problem in terms of demand and costs is well established, but the technical solution has been missing. An early suggestion was to bury electronic devices in the road which would transmit a signal to a meter in each vehicle as it passed overhead, but this idea was rejected as being too expensive. The advent of the smart card may have solved the technical problem, since a smart card bought in advance and placed in the windscreen can be electronically 'zapped' on passing selected points on the road. The price could be raised at certain times of the day, when demand is at a peak. Trials are currently being conducted.

Congestion as an externality

It is possible to analyse the problem in terms of the **externality** concept. Motorists will decide whether or not to make a journey on the basis of their valuation of the benefits from the journey and their valuation of the alternatives forgone in terms of time and money for petrol and other variable costs. They will not consider, however, the additional cost imposed on others owing to increased congestion. This cost can be regarded as an external cost to the motorist, and one therefore which the motorist will not take into account when making decisions.

In Fig. 28.1 the average cost is the private cost which the motorist will take into account when deciding whether to make a journey or not. It will be flat up to the point where congestion begins at F_1. After this it will rise as more and more vehicles try to use the same limited road space. The cost to the individual motorist is less than the cost to society as a whole because when an extra motorist joins a congested road, other vehicles will also be slowed down as indicated by the steeper line *SMC* which diverges from *AC* after F_1. The demand curve measures the willingness to pay for using the road. As can be seen from Fig. 28.1 motorists are willing to pay up to F_3 where the demand curve cuts the *AC* curve. In thinking about this, you should realise that the motorist is both producer and consumer of the driving.

It is apparent that the social costs at this level of road use (bF_3) are greater than the 'price' that the motorist is paying (cF_3). The efficient level (see Chapter 24) is where price is equal to social marginal cost at F_2. In moving from F_3 to F_2, the lost benefits (acF_3F_2) are less than the reduced costs (abF_3F_2), leaving a net gain to society of the shaded area abc.

Using the same diagram, an investment solution can be illustrated. If the road space was increased, for instance by building a new road or increasing the number of lanes on an existing one, then congestion could be completely eliminated by providing enough

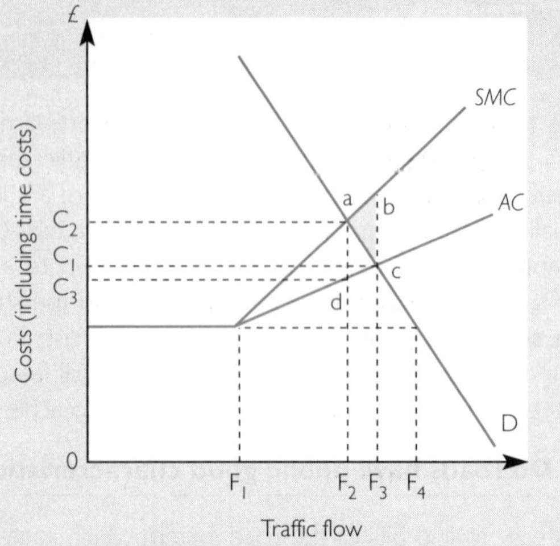

***Fig. 28.1* The costs of congestion**

capacity at F_4. The benefits of such a building programme would have to be set against the costs of road building and of course other social costs such as global warming and air pollution which were discussed in Chapter 27.

Other pricing solutions

Since the road pricing solution above has been technically infeasible until recently, practical pricing solutions have concentrated on reducing the prices of competing modes of transport such as rail and bus, rather than increasing the price of using the roads. This has often resulted in **subsidies.**

One of the main arguments for subsidising public transport has been to reduce congestion on the roads. Such arguments may become weaker if road pricing is successfully introduced, but it must be remembered that public transport is also more fuel efficient. The discussion in Chapter 27 on global warming noted that fuel use in transport is proving more difficult to contain than other fuel use.

Parking charges in central urban areas can also be used as a road pricing measure because, like petrol, parking is jointly consumed with road use. Drivers have to put the vehicle somewhere at the end of their journey. While this will not affect motorists who have access to private parking, on-street parking can be priced in this way. Special arrangements may have to be made to allow local residents parking rights where the housing stock does not have adequate off-street parking facilities. Through traffic is of course unaffected by this type of policy. **Park and ride** schemes encourage motorists to leave their vehicles on the edge of towns and travel in to the centre on subsidised public transport.

Rationing solutions

When **rationing** was first discussed in Chapter 11, it was suggested that it was most appropriate in situations of acute shortage, such as during famines, or in the immediate aftermath of war. It is also appropriate when the pricing system is not working well, as in the case of roads. Parking restrictions, such as the **yellow lines** and **red routes** used in the UK, ration the use of the road as a parking area by preventing parking on busy streets, or limiting it to off-peak periods. This reduces congestion by improving traffic flow. **Pedestrian-only zones** also ration the amount of road space available to the motorist. This solution is often used in medium-sized cities and large towns in association with an inner ring road as indicated in Fig. 28.2. Its main benefit is the separation of shoppers from traffic. It is a **zoning solution** to an externality problem. Sometimes the cheapest solution to an externality problem can be to separate the polluter from the polluted in this way, particularly if the externality is local. **Bus lanes** are also a good example of rationing. By giving priority to buses during the peak period, bus lanes speed up the buses and make them a more attractive alternative.

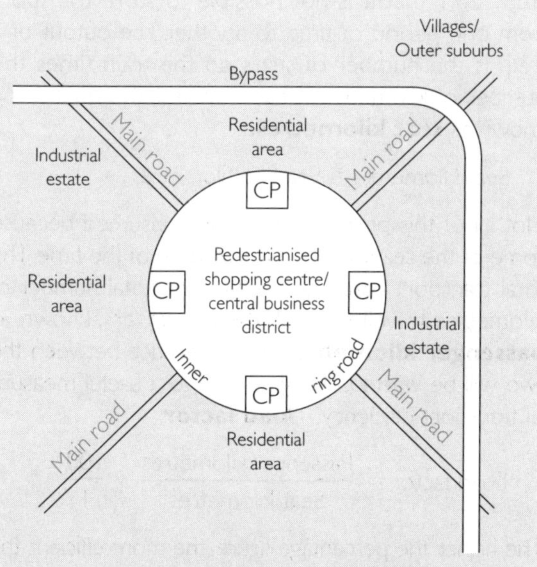

***Fig. 28.2* Zoning solutions to congestion**
CP = car park.

Investment solutions

Building additional roads to increase capacity in cities is difficult because roads already occupy about 25 per cent of the land available in the city. Further road building is difficult without displacing existing residents or facilities outwards. Expansion of the city in this way is only likely to increase demand for transport and make matters worse. Investment in city transport systems therefore often takes the form of public **transport infrastructure.** The Victoria and Jubilee Underground lines and the Docklands light railway in London; the Newcastle metro system; and new 'supertram' systems in Manchester and Sheffield are all good examples of major investments of this kind over the last few decades. Investment in computerised traffic management systems, to speed up traffic and prevent **gridlock,** try to make better use of the existing road system rather than to extend the volume of roads.

The construction of a **motorway network**, the upgrading of major roads to **dual carriageways** and the construction of **bypasses** round towns have been the major areas of road investment in the second half of the twentieth century. This investment programme is in a constant race to keep up with demand. The M25 around London was completed in 1986 but had to be upgraded from three to four lanes along its busiest sections in the early 1990s. This massive investment programme is justified by the demand forecasts of the Ministry of Transport, but its detractors argue that it is the building of the motorways that is inducing demand growth. The environmental arguments against traffic growth have been discussed already in Chapter 27. Policy is also influenced by the **freedom** that the car brings to individuals.

Conclusions

The car brings enormous freedom to consumers and greater flexibility than most forms of transport. Its development and use represents a large portion of economic growth in the second half of the twentieth century. On the other hand it also brings with it considerable social and environmental costs. Any policy has to balance these two considerations.

Given the complexity of the market it is unlikely that any one solution will be sufficient on its own. It is necessary to have a range of solutions to cover different aspects of the problem.

STUDENT ACTIVITY 28.1

Discuss the best solution to congestion caused by each of the following types of traffic:

a) Commuter traffic going into London (or your nearest major city).
b) Heavy goods vehicles travelling through cities, towns and villages on their way to ports or the Channel tunnel.
c) Cars on their way to the coast on a public holiday.
d) Heavy use by all vehicles of major motorways such as the M25 or M6.

STUDENT ACTIVITY 28.2

Rank all the possible policies discussed in the case study in terms of their impact on the environment. Put the policy which has the most beneficial effect on the environment at the top of the list.

STUDENT ACTIVITY 28.3

Identify the gainers and losers of each of the following policies to combat congestion:

a) Subsidising commuter trains into a city.
b) Introducing road pricing using the smart card system for peak traffic.
c) Building urban motorways.
d) Building bypasses round towns.
e) Using yellow lines on roads in residential areas around the central business district of towns.

STUDENT ACTIVITY 28.4

Using Fig. 28.1, work out the consequences of continuously rightward shifting demand curves for road space because of the high income elasticity of demand for private road transport.

Case study 28.2
Pricing in practice on the railways

Costs and indivisibilities

It is difficult to speak of the marginal cost of an extra rail user, because rail transport suffers from **indivisibilities.** An extra user of a rail service may impose virtually no additional costs on the railway if the train is not full. It is only if additional carriages or additional trains are required that substantial costs will result. It only makes sense to talk about reasonably large chunks of increased demand. There is a clear difference between the peak and off-peak, however. An additional chunk of demand in the peak period requires investment in new trains or carriages (rolling stock). In the off-peak period, however, it is a matter of making use of rolling stock already acquired for the peak. For this reason, revenue from off-peak demand only has to cover **variable costs** for there to be a **contribution** to profits. The capital costs should be attributed to the peak demand. This is one of the reasons for the difference in price between peak and off-peak journeys.

Load factor

Average costs will be affected by the proportion of seats which have been filled. It was noted in Case study 28.1 that it is not possible to store transport from one period of time to another. The output of a train is the number of seats on the train times the number of kilometres it has travelled, the total being known as **seat kilometres:**

$$\text{Seat kilometres} = \text{Seats} \times \text{Kilometres}$$

Not all of this production will be consumed because some of the seats will be empty some of the time. The total transport consumed will be the total number of kilometres travelled by all the passengers, known as **passenger kilometres**. Any difference between the two will be wasted. This gives rise to a useful measure of transport efficiency – **load factor**:

$$\text{Load factor} = \frac{\text{Passenger kilometres}}{\text{Seat kilometres}} \times \frac{100}{1}$$

The higher the percentage figure, the more efficient the mode of transport. Intercity services usually manage the highest load factor, followed by commuter trains (which are often nearly empty on the return journey) and then provincial services last. Peak transport will normally achieve a higher load factor than the off-peak.

Joint costs

A final notable feature of railway costs is the existence of **joint costs**. Trains using the same track must pay for that track between them. There is no logical justification for any particular distribution of these jointly consumed **track costs** between two different services. An intercity train and a provincial service will frequently use the same track and the way in which the track costs are allocated between them will substantially affect the profitability of both. This was not very important before privatisation, but now has become a real issue.

Markets and market structure

Each railway service faces its own unique market structure, depending on the modes it is competing with. Commuter services into major cities will enjoy a substantial degree of **monopoly power** as they are usually faster than the congested roads. Intercity services will compete with both the car and the long-distance coach. On the longer-haul services the speed of service will provide an advantage over the coach, but air transport will be a serious competitor. Ferries and airlines will provide competition for the Channel tunnel route. Provincial services, particularly in less populated parts of the country, will face competition from bus and cars operating on much less congested roads and may have insufficient demand to break even at any price – see Fig 28.3.

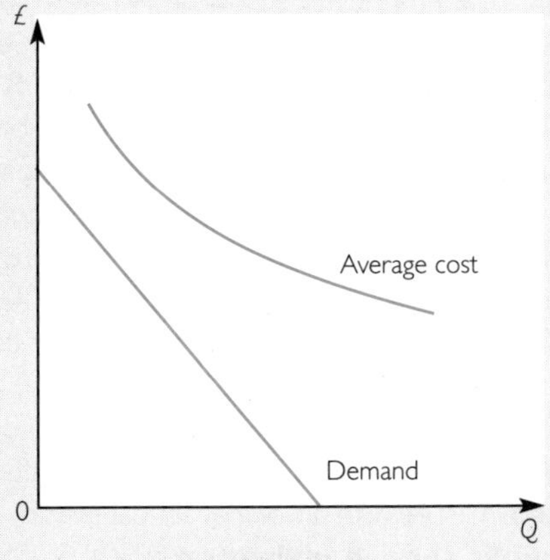

Fig. 28.3 **Inadequate demand**

For most services it will be possible to break the demand into different segments with different **elasticities.** Most estimates of commuter demand in the peak suggest a price elasticity between –0.2 and –0.4. The business traveller on intercity is also likely to have a more inelastic demand than the leisure traveller. Whole segments of the population can be identified who have lower elasticity of demand, such as young people and senior citizens. If methods can be found for the separation of these markets, then some degree of price discrimination can be practised (see Chapter 18).

Pricing

Railway pricing is difficult to analyse because there are two distinct reasons why peak fares should be higher than off-peak fares. In the discussion on costs above it was pointed out that only variable costs should be considered in the off-peak, while the peak travellers should be charged the capital costs. This is usually referred to as **peak load pricing.** Higher prices in the peak will persuade some passengers to postpone their journey to later in the day. This will reduce the pressure in the peak and allow the railway to operate more cheaply with less capacity and therefore lower capital costs.

The second reason for higher prices in the peak has to do with inelastic demand. The discussion of **price discrimination** in Chapter 18 shows that the three conditions for this pricing strategy are met. Where there is some degree of monopoly power, where demand segments have different elasticity, and where markets can be separated, then price discrimination is possible. In the commuter market demand is more inelastic in the peak, the railways have some degree of monopoly power, and the markets can be separated by making off-peak tickets valid only after 9.30 a.m.

On the other hand, there are three reasons why this price difference should be minimised. First, higher load factors in the peak reduce average costs. Second, discounts are offered to season ticket holders as a reward for loyalty and to discourage occasional car use. Third, lower fares in the peak reduce congestion on the roads. This last point requires specific **government intervention** since it will not be in the interests of a profit-making railway.

STUDENT ACTIVITY 28.5

Each student should select different destinations and collect as much information as possible about different fares to that destination. You should try to work out how much market power the railways have in transporting people to each destination and identify the competitors. Try to work out which of the factors influencing pricing have been most important for each destination.

STUDENT ACTIVITY 28.6

Railtrack decided to charge the same amount for use of the track for an intercity express as a provincial train. Both trains use the same length of track at approximately the same time of day. Has Railtrack maximised its profit?

STUDENT ACTIVITY 28.7

If passenger kilometres are 20 million and seat kilometres are 50 million what is the load factor? What pricing techniques can be used to increase it and thus push down average costs?

Case study 28.3 Privatising a loss-making monopoly

The railways are a monopoly in the sense that they have a monopoly over rail transport. This is true even after privatisation, although the monopolies have in most cases become local monopolies. There is no point in having a monopoly, however, if there is insufficient demand for your product, or if very good substitutes make the demand for your product elastic. In many cases it is better to think of railways as taking part in a very **competitive market in transport,** rather than having a monopoly. In some cases, however, the railways have retained some market power.

In the last decade of the nineteenth century, regulations had to be introduced to prevent the railways overcharging their customers. The rail system had an effective monopoly over much transport, facing only the horse, the canal barge and coastal shipping as competitors. It was able to use price discrimination (see Chapter 18) to maximise its revenue from freight, charging more for higher-value products. In the twentieth century the car, the bus and the lorry have taken over most of the railway's market, but there are still some areas where the railway system has a competitive advantage.

Good markets for rail

Because of the urban congestion discussed in Case study 28.1, the railways and Underground systems still have advantages for commuter journeys to work. Long-distance intercity journeys are also often faster than by car and more restful for the traveller. The train enables business travellers to work on the journey. The airlines are the main competitor with the train in this market, becoming more competitive as distance increases. The lorry has almost completely supplanted the train for **short-haul freight** transport and is usually more effective for small and medium consignments, but the railways retain some competitiveness on **long-haul routes**, particularly if one customer can provide a **train-load** of goods to transport.

A short history of closure: Beeching and Serpell

The car took off as a popular means of transport in the UK in the 1950s. This coincided with the early period of nationalisation of British Rail in 1947. It became clear that British Rail was unprofitable in the 1950s and the immediate response was a modernisation plan which began to replace steam by electric and diesel power. However, the **Beeching Report** (1963) argued that the only way to regain profitability was to reduce capacity radically by closing nearly half of the route distance. It was largely small branch lines that were closed, but local resistance to closure meant that the network was only reduced from 16 000 miles to 11 000 miles. The extent of the network at the time of the later Serpell Report is shown in Fig. 28.4.

The railways continued to make losses throughout the 1960s and early 1970s until this state of affairs was recognised in 1974 with an official annual subsidy known as the **public service obligation** (PSO). In 1982 the **Serpell Report** concluded that only the major intercity

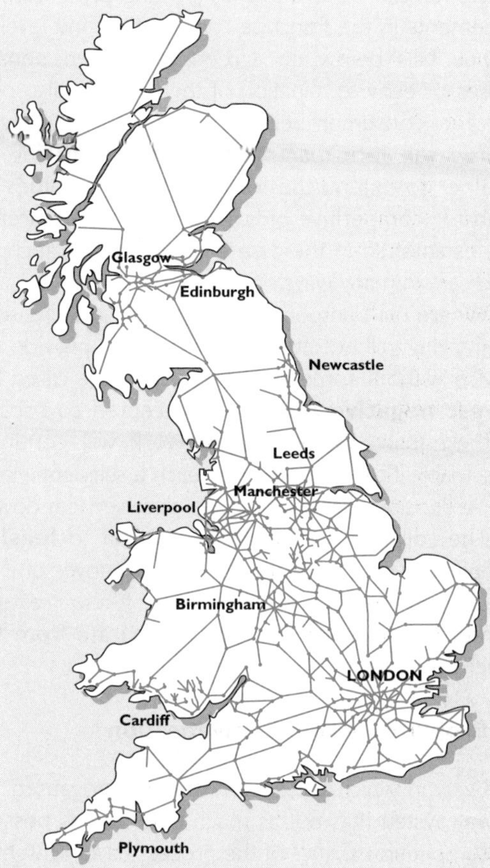

Fig. 28.4 **The network in 1980**
Source: Serpell Report, HMSO, 1982

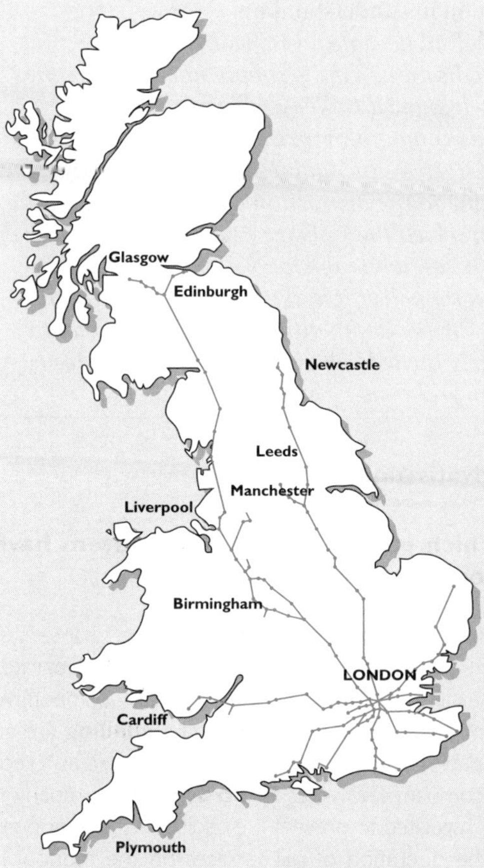

Fig. 28.5 **The profitable network**
Source: Serpell Report, HMSO, 1982

routes and a few commuter lines were profitable. The profitable network is shown in Fig. 28.5 which should be compared to Fig. 28.4. Freight and the remaining commuter lines could be run at a small loss, but the major loss-makers were the **provincial routes** to towns in the regions. The PSO was a payment to British Rail for carrying out this non-commercial part of its services.

Reasons for subsidising commuter routes have been discussed in the case study above about congestion. It may be the cheapest way of relieving congestion in some urban areas. The reasons for subsidising provincial routes has more to do with **access** to a national transport system for those without use of a car. The young, the elderly and the poor are the main groups who have generally less access to car transport. It can be seen that the PSO was a kind of **social policy** in the transport sector, keeping open routes which might be closed on purely commercial grounds.

As the Serpell Report rightly pointed out, this social policy might be more cheaply achieved by subsidising bus and coach transport instead. An additional argument for subsidising a rail link to a town and more importantly to a region is to generate local economic growth. If a region is not linked to the network, it may make attracting **inward investment** more difficult. One of the policy options put forward by the Serpell Report was that all towns which had a population over 25 000 should be connected to the rail network. This may seem a little arbitrary, but any size for the route network will be a compromise and involve subjective opinions.

Common misunderstanding

British Rail became a loss maker after nationalisation. This is simply not the case; the privately owned railways struggled with lorry and bus competition in the 1920s and 1930s and were largely unprofitable. Some of this may have been due to the depression of the 1930s, and the way in which the railways were forced to publish their prices, while the lorry owners were not. After nationalisation, the railways were faced with further competition from the car and any privately owned rail system would have faced similar problems.

Privatisation

Which parts of the railway system have monopoly power?

As with many of the later privatisations (see Chapter 26) British Rail has been privatised in a way that separates the natural monopoly from the potentially competitive parts of the industry. The **track** and **signalling** are an unavoidable monopoly that has been privatised as a separate company known as **Railtrack.** This company is heavily regulated to prevent it exploiting its market position. The operation of rail services on the monopoly track can be arranged in a more competitive way. In some cases, other modes will provide sufficient competition. Where rail services do not face strong competition from other modes, price regulation is necessary, particularly as, in the case of commuter routes, low prices may be desirable to reduce congestion.

Franchises

The provision of passenger services has been split into a large number of **franchises**. Each franchise operates a group of services for a fixed period of time after which the franchise must be renegotiated. This introduces an element of competition in two ways. First, the company which puts in the highest bid for the franchise will believe that it can operate the franchise most profitably. Initially, until the companies have experience of operating franchises, they may make mistakes in their estimation of profitability, but this should improve with experience. Exploitation of the consumer can be avoided by putting price control agreements in the franchise agreement. If the level of service falls below an agreed level, then penalty clauses or early termination of the franchise also protect the consumer. Second, the quality of service offered can form part of the decision making on whether to extend the franchise when it comes up again for competitive bids. This technique is already well established in the case of regional TV franchises which are in many ways similar.

Where rail transport is provided for social reasons, loss making will not attract companies to provide the service without some inducement. In these cases, the **lowest negative bid** will be accepted so subsidy of these parts of the rail network will continue. Presumably, if the negative bids reach a sufficiently large level, a decision might be made to close services down.

The rolling stock has been sold off to **leasing** companies. This enables the smooth handover of franchises from one company to another. It also creates a market in rolling stock which is separate from the franchisees' market in railway services.

Problems with rail privatisation

The way in which the government has privatised the railway system has put as much emphasis as possible on competition. Critics of the process have highlighted problems of coordination between different companies. The main problems of dividing up the railways into so many franchises are the following:

a) It becomes more difficult to create a coordinated timetable with connections between trains run by different franchises. Railtrack has been given this coordinating role.
b) Buying a ticket on a route that uses several different franchise companies requires coordination between them if a single ticket is to be issued. If this fails to happen, the passenger will pay for several short journeys instead of one long journey, probably at a higher price.
c) In the same way, methods must be found to continue with timetable and ticketing coordination between different modes of transport, such as bus and rail, which may have been easier when they were both in the public sector.
d) In the case study on railway costs above, the problem of joint costs was introduced. Where two

franchises use the same section of track, the question of who should pay for it arises. As was noted before, pricing can make a major difference to the apparent profitability of the two franchises. The marginal cost of using the track is low, but the average cost is quite high. Soon after Railtrack was set up this was illustrated in a dramatic way when rolling stock which needed servicing was sent by lorry because it was cheaper than the price asked for by Railtrack!

Alternative methods of privatisation

Two main alternative methods of privatising the railways were suggested. The railway could have been broken up into the old **regional** companies which existed before 1939. This would have improved coordination within the region but it would have left the regional company as a regulated monopoly. This goes against the principle used in most later privatisations (see Chapter 26) of separating the potentially competitive parts of the industry from the natural monopoly – in this case Railtrack. The other alternative would have been to separate British Rail into its constituent businesses: intercity, freight, commuter and provincial. This idea would still run into the problems of joint cost discussed above, but would have none of the advantages of the franchise system. As with the first idea, greater coordination would probably be achieved at the cost of reduced competition.

STUDENT ACTIVITY 28.8

You have been asked to bid for a rail franchise for the next five years. The franchise is for a small branch line (in reality franchises are much bigger than this). You are required to provide 10 passenger trains a day in each direction which can be accomplished by leasing one train. The following information has been provided to help you decide on your bid. Assume zero inflation in your calculations.

Current annual passenger kilometres	1 000 000
Regulated price per passenger kilometre	10p
Cost of leasing a train	£10 000
Variable costs per single train journey (fuel, labour)	£10
Payments to Railtrack per single journey	£5
Administrative costs	£20 000

A private survey you have commissioned suggests that passenger kilometres have been declining by 10 000 a year, but points out that this was during a recession and the economy is now growing strongly.

Submit your bids to your teacher/lecturer. Be prepared to justify your proposed bid.

STUDENT ACTIVITY 28.9

The Department of Transport has been asked by the Treasury to reduce its subsidy to the rail industry as part of its contribution to reducing public expenditure. As a civil servant in the department you have to prioritise the following proposals to achieve this objective. Assume each of them saves the same amount of money.

a) Close 1000 miles of provincial rail lines mainly in the north of Scotland, north and central Wales, Devon, Cornwall, Lincolnshire and Norfolk (if you are studying outside the UK choose areas of low population without much industry).
b) Increase franchise bids due for renewal by:
   (i) allowing higher prices on commuter routes;
   (ii) reducing frequency on off-peak and provincial services.

Case study 28.4 Air transport

The discussion of roads was about creating a market where one does not fully exist at the moment. The discussion on the railways was about replacing a state monopoly with a privatised, competitive system. In the case of air the emphasis is on the removal of **collusive** arrangements between airlines operating in the international market. As with rail, it is helpful to start with a discussion of costs, pricing and market structure so the reader is familiar with the details of the industry being studied.

Costs

The airlines have a very similar cost structure to the railways. Like the railways, they have indivisible units of output. You cannot fly with half a plane! This means that the marginal costs of a plane which is not full are very close to zero, while the average costs are quite high. As with all forms of transport, the product is not **storable** and so the question of load factor again becomes important. Raising load factor is an important way of reducing average costs.

The major difference in air transport is the way in which the costs of take-off and landing at airports influence costs, as illustrated in Fig. 28.6. These costs incurred at the airport can be thought of as **fixed costs** since no matter how long the flight, a plane will have to take off and land. The longer the flight the lower the **average fixed costs** of take-off and landing per passenger kilometre travelled. Since the variable costs of operating the plane at cruising speed are fairly constant, there are **economies of range.** The further the plane is flying, the lower its **average total costs** will be. The unit of output is the seat kilometre as discussed in Case study 28.2, but passenger kilometres are what bring in the revenue.

Of course if a European airline is flying to Sydney in Australia, it will usually break the journey in a number of places to take on extra passengers and fuel. It might stop in Dubai, Delhi and Singapore on the way. Each of the parts of the total journey is referred to a **stage**. Each stage involves one take-off and one landing, so economies of range refer to the individual stage lengths, not the whole route. Flights are divided into short haul, usually internal flights within a country, or between neighbouring countries; medium haul, across continents; and long haul, between continents.

Pricing

The main basis of pricing in the scheduled market is the separation of leisure and business traffic. At first sight this may be seen as a straightforward case of price discrimination with the higher prices being charged for the relatively inelastic business market and lower prices for the more elastic leisure market. As with the case of rail pricing considered above, the separation of the two markets is achieved by ticket conditions. Business travellers want the ability to book up to the last moment, and also to cancel if their plans change. The leisure market is separated out by the **APEX** (advanced passenger excursion) ticket which cannot be cancelled and must be bought some specified time in advance. Although this ticket is substantially cheaper, business travellers would not want its inflexibility. Last-minute purchase of **IPEX** tickets is also cheap because it enables airlines to fill empty seats. **Stand-by** tickets are available even more cheaply to travellers who are prepared to wait for a seat to be available.

APEX tickets also allow an airline to reduce its costs. These tickets are not available for all flights, but will be mainly directed towards the off-peak times of travel which are less popular with business travellers.

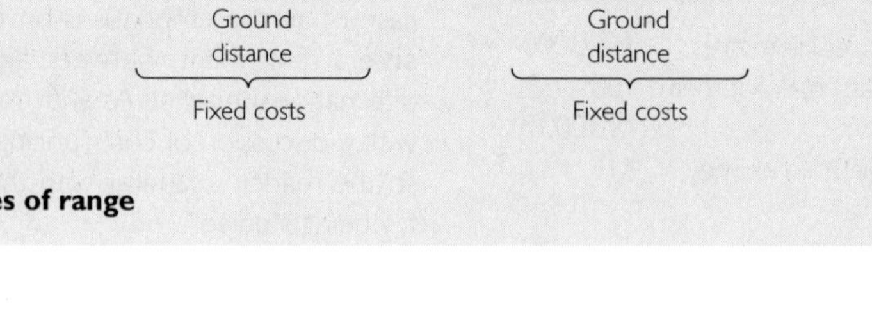

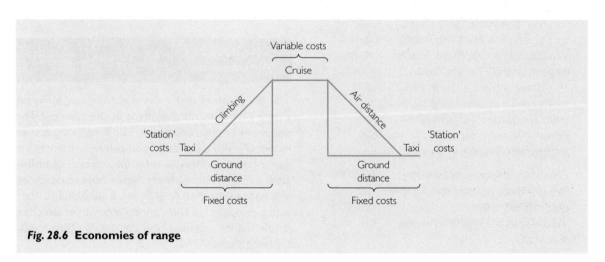

***Fig. 28.6* Economies of range**

This enables the airlines to increase their load factor, and so reduce their average costs. Different prices for different seasons also try to shift demand into flights where lower load factors are expected. The prices of airline tickets will also reflect the level of service offered. The three main service levels are economy, cabin class and first class with a progressively higher quality of service, comfort and leg-room.

As in the discussion of railway pricing, it can be seen that standard textbook models of pricing are useful in understanding what is happening, but real-world pricing will often be a mixture of different pricing strategies; in this case both demand-related and cost-related strategies are being followed. The view that price differences are not merely a question of price discrimination is confirmed by the fact that these pricing strategies have survived the introduction of greater competition in international air transport. Price discrimination should only occur where there is monopoly or collusive oligopoly.

Market structure: scheduled and charter

There is a major distinction between the **scheduled** market which is timetabled and open to bookings from all members of the public, and the **charter** market which mainly operates to take package tour holiday makers to their destination. In most cases there is vertical integration (see Chapter 13) in the charter market in that the charter airlines are often owned by package holiday companies. This means that competition is really between the holiday companies, not the charter airlines themselves.

The charter airlines have cost advantages over the scheduled airlines for two main reasons. First, they are usually able to plan their activities well in advance so that they achieve very high load factors. Second, they usually offer a lower level of service than the scheduled airlines, since they are not trying to attract business travellers.

Market structure: bilateral agreements and IATA

Scheduled airlines operating on international routes do so only with the permission of the governments of the countries in which they land. The Paris Convention of 1919 decided that the air space over a country belongs to that country and as a result a system of bilateral agreements between each pair of countries is necessary to give permission for airlines to overfly countries other than their own, and to land in their airports. Until the late 1970s, this resulted in most international routes being operated by the two **national flag carriers.** In many countries the flag-carrying airlines were nationalised and private sector airlines were mainly confined to the charter market, or a small secondary role.

Deregulation

The bilateral agreements varied a great deal in how much competition they allowed for. The most restrictive resulted in the airlines from each country operating almost as a single monopoly company, sharing costs and revenues. In all bilaterals, pricing was determined by the International Airlines Trade Association (IATA). The USA led the way in dismantling this restrictive system in the late 1970s and early 1980s. The first route to be partly deregulated was the North Atlantic route between the USA and Europe. After an initial successful period when prices fell and profits rose, a vicious price war ended with the bankruptcy of one operator (Laker) and massive losses for the others (PanAm, TWA and BA). After this experience, and the court case which followed it (settled out of court), airlines became more careful about starting price wars in case they were accused of anti-competitive practices. It should be noted that the term deregulation is a relative one. Even after deregulation, only two airlines from each country were allowed to fly on each route. Not all airports in each country were open to international traffic. This is a long way from an **open skies** policy.

A single European market in air transport?

Curiously, although most international air transport became more deregulated, European air transport remained heavily regulated. There were certain exceptions like the Anglo-Dutch bilateral agreement which was very liberal, but in general progress was slow. The coming of the European Single Market and the Maastricht Treaty meant that this had to be re-examined. Proposals for the development of a single air transport market met strong resistance and the policy was only in place in 1997. The reasons for resistance were as follows:

a) There was a sharp difference of culture between the largely privatised and profitable airlines of Northern Europe, and the largely subsidised and nationalised airlines of Southern Europe.
b) Airlines such as Air France and Greece's Olympic Airlines were granted extensions in order to get their finances in order. A competitive market cannot work if some of the competitors are in receipt of massive subsidies from their governments.
c) Traditional nationalised flag carriers were concerned about being taken over by the stronger privatised airlines. A reserve of nationalism remains associated with national airlines even in a single market!
d) There was a recognition that most airlines in Europe were not as large as their American and Far Eastern rivals and therefore did not benefit from the same **economies of scale**. This further fuelled nervousness about takeovers.

Further difficulties are expected when the policy is implemented because:

e) *Slots* at airports are in limited supply. A slot is a take-off or landing time at a given airport. With strong growth in demand there is a shortage of slots at the busiest of European airports. How should this limited supply be allocated? The most common method is **grandfathering**. This means that those who have always had slots continue to have slots. This makes it very difficult for new competition to break into an airport. The building of the fifth terminal at Heathrow and the second runway at Manchester are both attempts to increase capacity.
f) *Hubs* are airports that act as junctions for airline routes as illustrated in Fig. 28.7. They are the aviation equivalent of Crewe or Clapham junction on the railways. It is not economic for regular flights to take place between each pair of airports, so some airports, often because of geographical position, become **interline** centres where people change planes. Heathrow is the busiest hub in Europe, followed by Frankfurt. Airlines based at such airports have a competitive advantage.
g) *Cabotage*. The provisions of the single market in air transport include the right of airlines to compete on the internal routes of another country. BA could take passengers from Paris to Marseilles, for instance. This invasion of the domestic markets of other countries is likely to meet resistance.

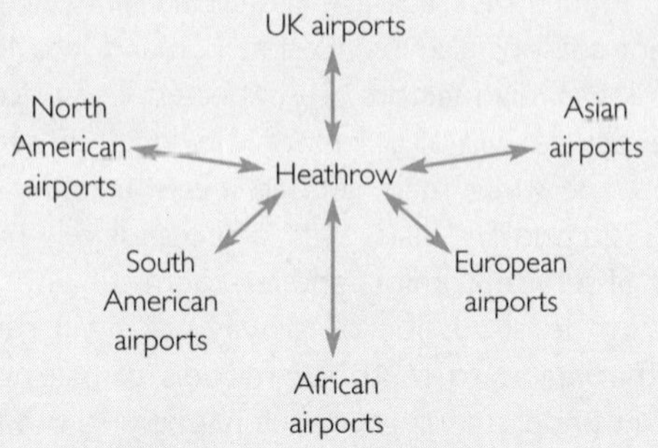

***Fig. 28.7* Heathrow as a hub airport**

STUDENT ACTIVITY 28.10

a) Which airlines do you think will benefit most from the deregulation of European air transport and which ones will have the most difficulty?
b) Do you think that it would be better to have lots of small airlines competing in Europe, or a few large ones to compete with other large world airlines?
c) Is it a good idea to increase airport capacity in Manchester and Heathrow in order to make them more effective as hub airports from the point of view of
   (i) the balance of payments
   (ii) UK employment
   (iii) local residents
   (iv) global warming?
   Which of these criteria is most important?

STUDENT ACTIVITY 28.11

You are working for a new airline which has started up with one aircraft with 200 seats and a single route. You have commissioned research that suggests the elasticity of demand is –0.4 for business traffic but –1.6 for leisure traffic at the current price of £100. Currently you are achieving 50% load factor split evenly between the business and leisure sectors.

a) Calculate the effect on revenue and load factor of a 10% increase in business prices and a 10% reduction in leisure prices.
b) What are the likely effects on cost and profits?
c) What pricing strategies can you use to separate business and leisure traffic?

Case study 28.5 The Channel crossing: intermodal competition

The ferries

The Channel crossing before the Channel tunnel was built was often used as a good example of an oligopolistic market. The crossing was dominated by Sealink (later taken over by Stena) and P&O European Ferries (formed by a merger in 1985) with small competition from the Sally line. The airlines provided effective competition for the business and weekend-break markets, but for the growing car tourism market and freight to the continent, the ferries were in a strong position. Demand growth was strong with the numbers of cars crossing doubling between 1985 and 1995.

The tunnel

The arrival of the Channel tunnel provided a competitor to both the airlines (from Eurostar) and the ferries (from LeShuttle) and has made substantial inroads into both markets. The usual behaviour of oligopolistic markets faced with entry is to engage in price wars either to establish market share in the case of the entrant, or to protect it in the case of the existing firms (see Chapter 17). As with the case of deregulation of air transport on the North Atlantic (see Case study 28.4 above), it was the new entrant who initiated the price war by nearly halving prices in 1995. The ferries had no choice but to respond to protect market share. They also considered merger in 1996 in order to rationalise and reduce costs. The western crossings of the Channel to ports like Cherbourg and Caen are less affected by the tunnel, because cars with destinations in the west of France would have a long way to drive after going through the tunnel.

Is the tunnel profitable?

The price war may have established the tunnel's market share (which in 1997 is roughly equal to that of the two main ferry operators put together) but it did nothing for its profitability. As with many large projects, the final cost of building the tunnel was almost twice the original estimate, and together with early operational losses, Eurotunnel ended up with debts of £8.5 billion. It has now started to cover operational costs and make small contributions towards debt interest, but it is clearly not going to be able to repay any of the capital in the near future. If you owe the bank £1000 you have a problem, but if you owe the bank £8.5 billion, the bank has a problem! Eurotunnel's creditors from banks and other financial institutions have taken the only sensible step and converted much of the debt into equity holdings with the hope of making a long-term return.

The impossibility of exit

The problem that the ferries face in this situation is the impossibility of the tunnel **exiting** the market. If Eurotunnel goes bankrupt, the tunnel will still exist and could be sold by the liquidator to a new business. It would then only have to cover its variable costs. The tunnel's costs are nearly all **sunk** costs and the variable costs are quite small by comparison.

The competitive response

The ferries have responded by introducing so-called superferries onto the route achieving economies of vessel size, faster turnarounds and a better quality service on board. The longer crossing time is being marketed as an advantage, allowing drivers to relax and take a break. The ferry is reconstructed as a resort in itself. Profits from duty-free sales have been eroded by competition from Eurotunnel and are due to be phased out in any case as a result of the single market. The *Herald of Free Enterprise* disaster of 1987 made some people concerned about ferry safety. The fire in the Channel tunnel has now worried some people about safety in the tunnel. The effect of these two events probably cancel each other out. There remains excess capacity on the route and the competitive position of the ferries must be much weakened. If the initial price war is over, and both sides accept the other is there to stay, a period of more sensible pricing may return profitability to the ferries and give the bankers some of their money back. For the consumer, who has enjoyed very low prices, the party may be over.

STUDENT ACTIVITY 28.12

a) Using the ideas developed in the other case studies, suggest ways in which the ferries could increase their load factors by offering special deals.
b) If prices rise, how could the government tell if the operators were simply using more sensible prices to cover their costs, or whether they were engaging in covert collusion to exploit the consumer?

Summary

1 The combination of non-storable outputs and peak and off-peak demand in transport industries results in considerable price variations.
2 Price differences between the peak and off-peak also allow transport to shift demand away from the peak and economise on capital expenditure.
3 Congestion can be dealt with by pricing, investment or rationing, or a combination of these three methods.
4 Subsidy of the railways has been continued after privatisation. This policy can be explained in terms of environmental objectives, congestion reduction and equity considerations.
5 Deregulation of European airlines is facing difficulty from loss-making nationalised airlines and 'ownership' of slots.
6 When considering competition, exit is as important as entry as in the case of the Channel tunnel.

29 Efficiency in the public sector

Learning outcomes

After reading this chapter you will be able to:

- Identify the main problems of public expenditure control.
- Explain the main market-oriented reforms of the public sector.
- Understand the difficulties of making decisions in the absence of the market.
- Recognise policy areas where there are trade-offs between equity and efficiency.

Introduction

Reasons for the public sector intervening in the economy were discussed in Chapter 6. If part of the economy is in the public sector, it should be produced in an ***efficient*** way. We do not necessarily have the market to fall back on as an automatic pressure towards efficiency. This chapter explores the way in which the public sector attempts to deal with the problem of efficiency and with conflicts with other ***objectives*** which the government may be trying to achieve.

As with other case study chapters, the cases can be treated as data response articles and there will be no further data responses at the end of the chapter. Student activities are to be found at the end of each case study.

Case study 29.1
The growth of public expenditure

The growth of public expenditure is a twentieth-century phenomenon. In the nineteenth century, the public sector accounted for 12 per cent, or less, of total national income (see Chapter 7). In the twentieth century we see a continuous increase until figures between 40 and 50 per cent become common in European countries. Figures for the USA and Japan are lower, but have also been growing. This case study explores the reason for this growth and the methods which have been used to control public expenditure growth.

Public expenditure is organised by a bureaucracy, the Civil Service, under the control of the government. This contrasts with the private sector which operates through the market. Recent reforms have tried to simulate the market in the public sector, particularly in education and health. The case studies in this chapter therefore try to look at the public sector from the point of view of microeconomics. The macroeconomic aspects of public expenditure are considered in Chapter 43.

Components of public expenditure

As can be seen from Table 29.1, the main components of public expenditure are pensions and benefits, defence, health, education, transport, and law and order. Benefits and transport are discussed in Chapters 30 and 28 respectively. These industries are not exclusively provided by the public sector. There are flourishing private sector schools and health care services. In some countries health care is provided mainly by the private sector (e.g. the USA). Defence and law and order are nearly universally provided by the public sector, although private security firms do exist to protect property. Pensions can also be provided through the private sector.

Reasons for growth in public expenditure

Common misunderstanding

Since it was the Conservative party's policy to

Table 29.1 Functional composition of general government expenditure in 1995 (£m)

Defence	23 154
Public order and safety	15 320
Education	38 330
Health	40 042
Social security	102 483
Debt interest	25 800
Transport	9 127
Other	49 652
Total	304 708

reduce public expenditure from 1979, most people assume this was achieved. In fact all it succeeded in doing was to prevent further growth, and in some years did not even succeed in doing this. Compare the figures for 1979–80 and 1995–6 in Table 29.2

Table 29.2 Growth of public expenditure as a percentage of GDP at market prices

1965–6	36½
1970–1	39½
1975–6	46¾
1979–80	42½
1985–6	43¼
1990–1	39
1995–6	42¼
1996–7	41¼

Income elasticity of demand

It is argued that the services which are naturally provided by the public sector also have high income elasticities of demand. The process by which this is turned into extra production is the political process rather than the market process. Governments which meet the voter–consumer's demand for more education and health tend to get elected. The idea that demand for public sector output tends to grow faster than the rest of the economy is called **Wagner's law** after its German inventor. It is for this reason that governments have been trying to shift some of this expenditure onto the consumers of public services. A good example is the shift away from grants to students in higher education and over to loans. The Dearing Report on Higher Education (1997) has recommended to the Labour government that students should also pay part of their tuition fees.

Demographic change

The age structure of the population has changed dramatically over the last century as people live longer (see Chapter 4). In the UK there was a surge in births immediately after the Second World War, known as the **baby boom**. The baby boom generation start to reach the age of 60 in the year 2005. Health care for elderly people is estimated to be up to six times as expensive as for young people. The number of people drawing the state pension will continue to rise over the next decade.

Efficiency in the public sector

Rising demand on its own need not lead to increasing expenditure. The massive rise in the demand for computers has been accompanied by a massive reduction in their price and an increase in their power because of rapid technical progress. It is argued that service industries find it more difficult to reduce their costs because it is more difficult to introduce assembly line techniques. In the health service, for instance, it is difficult to introduce technology to reduce the number of nurses per patient. In fact introducing more capital sometimes increases the demand for nurses (e.g. in intensive care wards). It may be difficult to reduce costs in services, but it is not impossible. In some services new technology has significantly reduced labour needs, e.g. banking. By contrast, labour-saving inventions in hairdressing are few and far between and basically there is still one hairdresser per customer.

Many of the industries in the public sector fall into the service industry category, so this problem makes reducing costs difficult. If increases in pay were only related to productivity increases then there would be less of a problem. If we wish to continue to persuade talented people to become teachers, doctors and nurses, then to attract them into these professions the state must pay them competitive wages.

The business cycle

When the economy is booming the ratio of public expenditure to GDP goes down. This is for two reasons. First, GDP is going up, and second, because spending on unemployment benefit is falling, public expenditure will be falling. For the opposite reasons, during a recession, the ratio will rise. When trying to judge the success of a government in reducing public expenditure, you should take into account the level of unemployment. The generally higher level of unemployment that has been experienced in Europe and North America in the 1980s and 1990s has contributed to the difficulty in reducing the percentage of GDP going to public expenditure.

Strategies for the control of public expenditure

The range of policies which have been used to control public expenditure is very wide, but policies can be grouped together:

a) *Privatisation* can reduce public expenditure if the privatised industry was making a loss when it was in the public sector. When industries were first privatised, the revenue gained was subtracted from public expenditure. It is now recognised that privatisation proceeds are a revenue, not a 'negative' expenditure. This kind of revenue does allow a one-off reduction in taxes, however. For a fuller discussion of privatisation, see Chapter 26.
b) *Price indexation.* By indexing pensions to prices rather than wages in the 1980s, the government ensured that pensions would grow more slowly than national income. This may keep public expenditure under control, but pensioners might not think it was such a good idea!
c) *Charges* can be introduced or increased for public services resulting in a lower net expenditure. The charges for prescriptions and dental treatment were increased under the Conservative administration, although free provision was retained for children, pensioners and low-income groups. In higher education the replacement of much of the student grant by loans has a similar effect as does the introduction of tuition fees, recommended by the Dearing Report.
d) *Cost reduction* in services provided have largely been achieved by the introduction of competition by various means. The development of an **internal market** within the public sector in education and health is discussed below in Case studies 29.2 and 29.3. **Compulsory competitive tendering** (CCT) has been introduced for many government departments and local government services. This means that the public sector bureaucracies have to compete with alternative bids from the private sector for the production of services.
e) *Means testing* can be introduced for services previously offered free. Care of the elderly in residential homes is offered free only if a person has less than £16 000 of assets (1997). Home help services are also means tested.

STUDENT ACTIVITY 29.1

Ask your teacher how it is possible to reduce the costs of your education without also reducing its quality. To what extent is it possible to substitute capital for labour by using technology? Should you be becoming more of an 'independent learner' so your teacher can teach more students? Should your teacher receive pay increases only when productivity has risen?

STUDENT ACTIVITY 29.2

How can the following expenditures be reduced by introducing charges?

a) dentistry
b) in-patient hospital treatment
c) school
d) pensions

Case study 29.2
The reform of the NHS: technical efficiency and transactions costs

Why is health care in the public sector?

In Chapter 6 the rationale for government involvement in the market was discussed in some detail.

Externality is one of the reasons for government involvement, both because people spread diseases if untreated and because an unhealthy population is unproductive. There are **equity** reasons for government involvement so that poor people can achieve a minimum standard of health. There are **paternalistic** reasons because richer people may wish to redistribute income to poorer people in this particular way. The market may not work well because of **ignorance** about health in the population, so the government may concentrate on **preventive medicine** and health education. It can be seen that there is no simple reason for the government to intervene, and different aspects of health care may have different reasons for government intervention. This is a complex area which you must think about carefully before jumping to conclusions.

It is also clear that if people have the money they may naturally wish to buy the best medical attention as quickly as possible. It is evident that there are services supplied to the patient in hospital which are clearly private goods and have little to do with health. The so-called **hotel services** of a hospital can be provided at many levels to satisfy the preferences and ability to pay of the consumer–patient. Food, accommodation, furnishing and entertainment are necessary in a hospital but are not part of health care.

The size of the NHS budget

In 1995, the NHS spent £40.8 billion, representing 13.4 per cent of government spending. The NHS was created in 1948 out of a mixture of private and local authority hospitals. The belief of its founders was that by providing free health care, people's health would improve and costs would be reduced. While this may be true when people are younger, the success of the health industry in keeping people alive until they reach old age has meant a considerable increase in expenditure. Elderly people are more costly to the NHS as they need more care for chronic conditions. The advance of medical technology has meant that many illnesses such as heart disease and cancer which afflict the elderly can be treated with expensive surgery or drugs and operations.

As the elderly represent an increasing proportion of the population, this means that expenditure on the health service has to keep rising constantly just to provide the same level of service to everyone. The important questions are how to keep costs under control and how to pay for the service.

How to pay for the service?

The private sector

In the private sector the method of payment is usually by insurance, where a person pays annually whether they need treatment or not. In the USA where health care is mainly private, this is the usual method of payment. It is not necessarily the case that such insurance will pay all costs and there may be a maximum payment for treatment in a particular year. It is of course more expensive to join such schemes as you become older, since the risk of expensive illnesses rises. What happens to poor people who cannot afford medical health insurance? In the USA there is a **safety net** of publicly provided medicine. The quality of service in this sector is obviously lower, otherwise people would not choose to pay for expensive private health insurance. The USA spends more on health care as a percentage of GDP than almost any other country. This could be partly explained in terms of the high income elasticity of demand for health care and the high US standard of living (Wagner's law). There is also a suspicion that because of ignorance on the part of the patients and fear of litigation on the part of the doctors that more is spent on health care than is strictly necessary. If a doctor making decisions about which is the right treatment for you is also likely to profit from your treatment, it is possible the doctor will sometimes take advantage of the situation, although one hopes this would not happen too often.

Public provision and private production

In Germany each person pays a proportion of their income tax for health care. If a person has no income they pay nothing. As their income rises they will pay more until a point comes where it would be cheaper for them to opt out of the system and pay for private health care insurance. In this case the government has effectively nationalised the insurance part of the health care system and introduced a pricing system based on **ability to pay** rather than **willingness to pay**. The **production** of health care could be in the private sector under such a system, but its **provision** can remain in the public sector.

Public subsidy

In France payment is made for certain types of health care, such as a visit to the doctor, and the patient is reimbursed by the government. In this system patients sometimes have to pay a proportion of the cost themselves. It is argued that if a good is free it will be overused (see Fig. 29.1). If a person has to pay something towards a visit to the doctor then they will not make visits which are trivial. Against this argument it is pointed out that people are often ignorant about the importance of symptoms that they may suffer from and may delay going to the doctor when an earlier appointment could have saved money and suffering by successful treatment of the disease in its early stages.

Bureaucratic control

The NHS in the UK before the recent reforms was organised in a bureaucratic way. Funds were channelled down from the government to Regional and Area Health Authorities which were responsible for delivering health care in their part of the country (see Fig. 29.2). Since the NHS is 'free at the point of use' there will be a tendency for demand to be very high (see Fig. 29.1). If price is not used to allocate resources in health care then rationing is likely. It is possible to imagine so many resources being put into health care

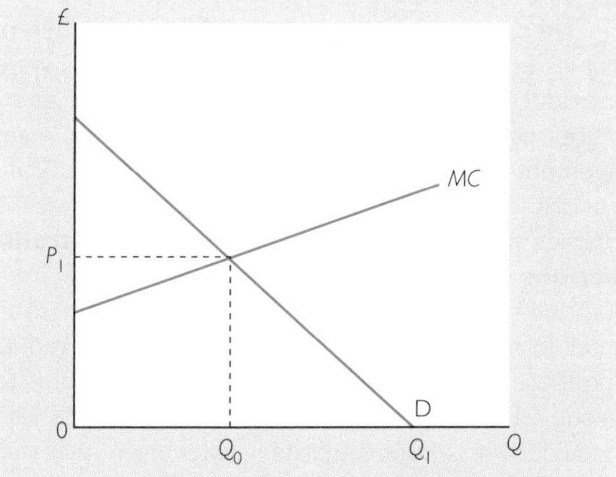

Fig. 29.1 **Excessive demand at zero price**

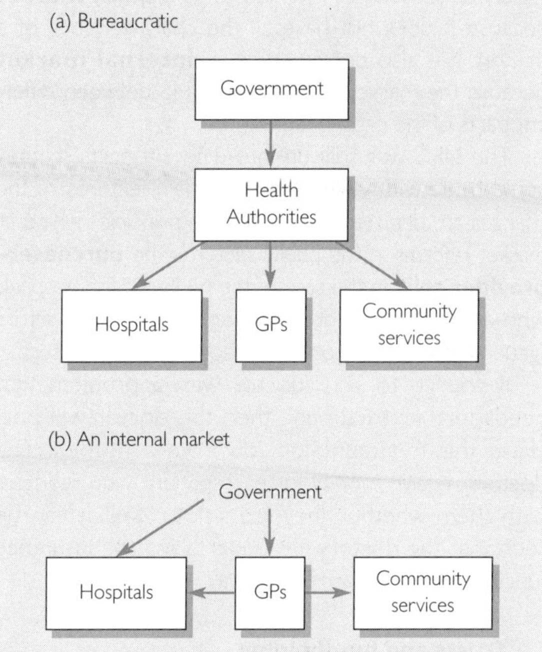

Fig. 29.2 **Changes in the organisation of the NHS**

by the government that all demands on it could be met, but this has never been the case since the NHS was set up. The NHS has always prioritised emergencies and serious illness.

As a result **waiting lists** have developed in non-urgent surgery and treatment. This is similar to a situation of excess demand because the price (set at zero) is below the market clearing price as indicated in Fig. 29.1. Health care is being **rationed** on the basis of **need** rather than **willingness to pay**. In effect doctors are taking the decision about who should be treated first rather than the market.

There is not only a problem of allocating resources between different types of medical expenditure; there is also the problem of how much should be put into the health care system as a whole. Total expenditure on the NHS has often been a major political issue in the UK.

The internal market

The idea of a market in the public sector was put forward in a White Paper in 1989 but was implemented in the early 1990s. It is not a market in the full sense since customers do not use their own money to buy services. It is sometimes referred to as a **quasi-market** because it does not have all the characteristics of a market. It is also described as an **internal market** because the market is inside the NHS between different parts of the organisation.

The NHS was split up into different parts so they could trade with each other. The main features of the changes are depicted in Fig 29.2. The principle behind all market reforms in the public sector is the **purchaser–provider split**. In the case of the NHS it is the hospitals who are largely the providers and the family doctors (general practitioners or GPs) who are the purchasers.

If you go to your doctor with a problem that needs further treatment, then the doctor will purchase this treatment for you from a hospital. The doctors receive money for each patient who registers with them whether they are sick or well. It can be seen that the doctors are undertaking the insurance function of health care in this way.

Trusts and fundholding

When the internal market started in 1990 not all hospitals **opted out** to become independent **trusts**, but gradually all hospitals have shifted to this status, sometimes grouped together, or linked with community services like district nursing and health visiting. The status of a trust is very different from a private company. It does not have shareholders and is not trying to maximise profits. It does have revenues and costs and will normally try to break even or reinvest any surplus. Unlike bureaucratic organisations in the public sector it will try to build up a small **reserve** to cushion it for times when it cannot break even. Like private companies it will face competition from other trusts for its services and doctors are able to choose the cheapest or the best service for different kinds of standard treatment. It is argued that people in a position of power within non-profit-making organisations may pay themselves a **rent** (see Chapter 21) in the form of high wages or advantageous conditions of employment.

The other main organisational reform of the internal market, GP **fundholding,** is organised differently. GPs have always been self-employed, so there was no need to set up trusts. GP practices are partnerships (see Chapter 13) which receive more income as more patients are registered. The main effect of the reforms was to transfer the funds allocated for treating patients in hospital from Health Authorities to GP practices. If GP practices do not spend all this money, they are allowed to spend any surplus on the surgery, but given the insurance function of fundholding, they are well advised to hold money in reserve in case their patients are less healthy the following year. Not all GP practices have elected to take fundholding status and patients from non-fundholding practices continue to have their hospital treatment funded by the local Health Authority.

Efficiency and transactions costs in the internal market

The central principle that the NHS should be **free at the point of use** has been retained but competition has replaced bureaucratic control. Competition should drive down costs or improve service quality. The question that arises is whether this has happened in practice. The problem is that treatments were not costed individually before the reforms, so comparison is difficult. One measure that has been used is the length of waiting lists. Targets to reduce waiting to less than a year were met, but it is questionable as to whether this is desirable. If the cost of keeping all waiting lists at less than one year is bringing non-urgent cases in earlier but delaying some more serious cases, then needs are not being prioritised correctly. There have been attempts to place hospitals in league tables but these have also run into some difficulties. An early study of heart treatment in Scotland put the most prestigious hospital at the bottom of the list. Since it had the most seriously ill patients, it had the highest death rate. This underlines the difficulty of making such comparisons.

There has been a reduction in the number of nurses employed in the NHS since the reforms were introduced, but this has been more than offset by increases in the number of administrative and management staff. Competition may well have reduced costs, but the costs of setting up and administering the market must also be taken into account. These **transactions costs** are the main drawback of the reforms. Labour suggestions for reforming the system soon after forming the government concentrate on reducing these transactions costs. The initial proposal is to group GPs into larger groups to set up contracts with providers. It is hoped that fewer administrative staff would be needed, thus releasing cash for more direct medical expenditure.

Equity and the internal market

A second undesirable by-product of the internal market was the advantage that fundholding GPs had in their dealings with hospitals. The waiting time for the patients of non-fundholding GPs was longer on average than for those of fundholding GPs. This was because the hospitals were keen to keep their new customers happy. The Labour government has instructed hospitals to end this inequitable practice. The early Labour moves against bureaucracy and inequity seem reasonable, but defenders of the reforms are concerned that competition will disappear.

Relationships between the public and private sectors

The largest provider of private medicine in the UK in 1996 was the NHS! This surprising answer takes us back to a much older debate about how the NHS is run. When asked about how he had persuaded the doctors to support the nationalisation of the health service, Beveridge is reputed to have said 'I stuffed their mouths with gold'. It certainly seems to be the case that consultants can quite happily combine their contract with the NHS and their private work, even undertaking both activities in one hospital in some cases. If there is a waiting list for an operation on the NHS, a patient can 'jump the queue' by becoming a private patient, and may even be operated on by the same doctor possibly in the same hospital. Waiting lists have never been a problem for those who can afford the treatment or insurance. It is therefore not true to say that before the internal market, the NHS always operated in an entirely equitable way. There is also evidence to suggest that more articulate, educated middle-class patients are better at 'working the system' to obtain second opinions, or to challenge unsatisfactory treatment. However bureaucratic a system may be, market forces have a habit of making themselves felt, particularly if it is a matter of life and death.

STUDENT ACTIVITY 29.3

Which of the following scenarios for the development of the health service do you think is preferable? Use the concepts of equity, efficiency and transactions costs in your answer.

a) A bureaucratically run health service; free at the point of use; owned by the state; where doctors cannot work for the private sector; with treatment prioritised solely by need.
b) A private sector backed up by a private insurance system with a lower-quality state safety net system.
c) An internal market primarily run by the state but with cooperative relationships with the private sector.

Case study 29.3
Markets in education: allocative efficiency

Opting out

The 1988 Education Reform Act (ERA) introduced the market into state education. Before the ERA, education was largely run by local government; a mixture of local democracy and local bureaucracy. After ERA schools could choose (provided they had the support of their parents) to opt out of local government control and receive funding directly from the Department for Education (later known as the Department for Education and Employment – DfEE). Initially such direct funding was more attractive, to encourage more schools to opt out. Funding was on a per student basis so that the more successful a school was in attracting 'customers', the more money it received. This principle of **formula funding** was later extended to all schools including those remaining under local authority control. All schools have been given much greater control of their own budget under a scheme known as the local management of schools (LMS).

Competition?

Schools now have to compete to attract customers in order to increase revenue. They have to manage their resources in order to keep costs under control. They can make a profit or a loss. Are they like firms in private sector competition? In some important respects they are. They are rewarded for successful operation of their 'businesses'. They can reinvest any surplus that they make. Successful schools are more likely to attract new investment if an expansion of capacity is needed. However, there are some important respects in which they are not like private companies:

a) They do not have shareholders and do not distribute profits.
b) They cannot usually take over other schools.
c) If a school gets into financial difficulty it is difficult for it to 'exit' the market because of its responsibility to its students. A change of management (headteacher) is more likely.
d) They have no control over pricing, but must accept the price set nationally (for opted out schools) or locally (for those remaining under local government control).

Choice?

For allocative efficiency to exist, the consumer must have **choice**. Is this the case with the market in the state schools system? Certainly there has been a big increase in the apparent choice of schools available to students, but there is a conflict between two government objectives. One objective is to reduce costs, which can be best achieved by getting rid of spare capacity and making sure every class is full. This can conflict with choice because successful schools have reduced the **spare capacity** which would allow them to accept extra students who want to attend them. Less successful schools may have spare capacity because students have not chosen to enrol with them.

Who chooses whom?

Where there is no spare capacity the schools will choose which students to accept. In the market place, the question of which consumer will buy the best products is usually settled by who is willing to pay the highest price. Could the problem of who should attend the best schools be solved in this way? There is a problem here with an equity concept, the idea of **equality of opportunity**. In practice, schools will tend to accept students who they believe will enhance their reputation. Systems designed to discover which students have the greatest potential, such as exams or interview, tend to be manipulated best by middle-class parents. The question of equality of opportunity therefore arises again. Even where there is 'comprehensivisation' of schools, local people tend to know which is the 'best' comprehensive to get into. They may even be willing to move house to get into the catchment area of the school. Temporary religious conversions have not been unknown!

Measuring success: the value-added debate

In order to help consumers choose the right school, the government has published league tables to show which ones are doing best. These league tables have largely been at A level and GCSE level but SAT results have also been published to show relative performance at younger ages. Critics of such league tables argue that they are not measuring the schools, but the students in them. Schools which select their students, or which recruit from an affluent middle-class area, are likely to do better than inner city schools recruiting from poor areas with high unemployment. This might sound like a suggestion that middle-class children are more intelligent than working-class children. Far from it; this view suggests that there is no difference in intelligence at birth, but the middle-class affluent environment will generally provide the motivation, advice and role model for a student to succeed. There will of course also be intelligent, self-motivated, successful working-class students, and rebellious, lazy, cerebrally challenged middle-class students.

Conclusion

Creating competition in schools does not automatically bring improvement to the school system as a whole. International comparisons of school students' abilities suggest that the UK competes well at the top end of the distribution, but our average students are doing less well than the average students of our competitors. Generating excellent schools at the top end will not necessarily help our competitiveness in world markets which depends on the abilities of the vast majority of our workforce. The question is whether the opting out system will drive the performance of all schools or just benefit the elite. The Labour government's first response on this question is to continue initially with league tables, but to be more pro-active in changing the culture of 'failing schools'. Money is being made available to reduce the class size of under 7 year olds to below 30. It remains to be seen whether this approach is more successful than that of their predecessors.

STUDENT ACTIVITY 29.4

a) What measures could be used to improve exam results in your school or college?
b) Study the results of the following two schools and put forward possible explanations for the differences. How could school A's results be improved?

Number of pupils achieving five A-C grades

School A *Inner city comprehensive*	*School B* *Suburban grammar school*
27%	95%

Case study 29.4 Problems of decision making in the public sector

The cases considered above indicate that the two criteria of equity and efficiency are sometimes in conflict with each other. The same thing has a tendency to happen in investment appraisal in the public sector. A **Pareto improvement** implies no one has lost, even though someone has gained. Unfortunately, most economic changes in the real world do hurt someone. It is sometimes theoretically possible for the gainers to compensate the losers and still be better off themselves, but this is rarely done in practice. If we were willing to undertake projects only if an actual Pareto improvement were to result, most major changes would not be considered.

Cost–benefit analysis

Definition

This branch of economics is the result of the practical application of modern welfare economics to public sector decision making. Put simply, it attempts to evaluate the social costs and benefits of proposed investment projects as a guide when deciding upon the desirability of these projects. Cost–benefit analysis (CBA) differs from ordinary investment appraisal in that the latter considers only private costs and benefits. In short, it is intended to enable the decision maker to choose between alternative projects on the basis of their potential contribution to social welfare.

E. J. Mishan, perhaps the leading authority on CBA, has summarised CBA concisely as follows:

> It transpires that the realisation of practically all proposed cost-benefit criteria ... implies a concept of social betterment that amounts to a **potential** Pareto improvement. The project in question, to be considered as economically feasible, must, that is, be capable of producing an excess of benefits such that everyone in society could, by costless redistribution of the gains, be made better off.

The Hicks–Kaldor criterion

To get around the problem that in practice gainers rarely compensate losers Kaldor and Hicks proposed that if the gainers could *in principle* compensate the losers and still enjoy a net increase in welfare then a project should still go ahead. This weaker test of the **potential** for a Pareto improvement is known as the Hicks–Kaldor criterion. This criterion has led to considerable controversy, particularly where the losers are the poorer people in society and there is a clear conflict with principles of equity. Suggestions have been made that the costs and benefits of poorer people should be given higher weights to reflect equity value judgements in society. No objective way has ever been found of arriving at such weights so these proposals have not usually been implemented. After a CBA has been undertaken, it must be remembered that there will still be gainers and losers, so a political dimension to the argument can be expected. Recent examples include the route of the high-speed Channel tunnel link with London, the acceptability of a fifth terminal at Heathrow airport or an additional runway at Manchester airport. It should be noted that towns in northern France vied with each other to have the high-speed rail link with Paris pass their way because of the employment it would bring.

The imperfection of the world

The major difficulty in attempting a CBA stems from the fact that, in a world where imperfect competition, externalities and ignorance abound, market price will not reflect the true social costs and benefits. The CBA thus estimates **shadow prices.** These are imputed prices which are intended to reflect more faithfully the true social costs and benefits of a project. For example, the value of the time saved by an individual following an improvement in transport facilities is often approximated using that person's average hourly wage for working drivers (leisure time is worth less). The Roskill Commission used the depreciation in house prices around Gatwick airport in estimating the negative value of noise around any proposed third London airport. The techniques for valuing costs and benefits which do not pass through the market place were discussed in Case study 27.2.

CBA in practice

CBA is quite expensive and is not used in many project appraisals because of difficulties in valuation. One area where it is still extensively used is in the assessment of road improvement schemes, using a Department of Transport computer programme called **COBA**. The main costs and benefits which are assessed other than the building of the road itself are time, vehicle operating costs and death or injury. The change to the road system is simulated based on known experience elsewhere. Injury is costed in terms of treatment costs and lost income. Death is costed as the present value of a person's expected stream of income plus an amount for grief of those left behind. This is clearly less than adequate, but supporters of this approach argue that it is better than having no value at all. Working time is costed at the wage rate because it is assumed that the value of a person's output is equal to their wage rate (see Chapter 20). The gross wage rate (wages plus the costs of employing a person such as employer's national insurance contribution) is used because this is the cost to the employer. Leisure time is valued at about 40 per cent as a result of stated preference and revealed preference studies. The value that people place on time can be inferred by their choice between slow, cheap modes of transport and fast, more expensive modes of transport. For instance, if a person can get to work by bus for £1 in 40 minutes, or by train for £2 in 20 minutes, the person choosing the train is in effect buying 20 minutes for £1. This choice is usually related to a person's income. Time is therefore a normal good with a positive income elasticity of demand.

The Newbury bypass

COBA found that the Newbury bypass gave a positive return on the investment needed, but large numbers of environmental campaigners had a different point of view. The problem is that COBA does not value everything. In particular it does not have room for estimates of global warming, or the possible value of sites of special scientific interest (SSSIs). Where it is not possible to place values on such damage, a separate environmental impact assessment (EIA) can be undertaken. Where COBA and the EIA conflict there remains the political problem of how to resolve them. The idea of sustainable development discussed in Chapter 27 may be of use here.

Criticisms of CBA and welfare economics

There are many criticisms of this field of economics, some of which are extremely technical. It is important, though, that all students of economics appreciate the controversial nature of much of economics. Hence we will examine some of the simpler, but nevertheless important, objections. It should also be borne in mind, when reading these, that CBA utilises the concepts of modern welfare economics and is thus subject to the same criticisms as that body of theory.

a) CBA identifies only potential Pareto improvement using the Kaldor–Hicks criterion; it does not stipulate that the project should go ahead if only gainers actually compensate losers, i.e. that an actual Pareto improvement should take place. There are therefore potential problems of equity.
b) The money values placed on intangibles such as the value of the environment are sometimes extremely speculative.
c) CBA often involves estimates of consumer surplus, but it can be shown that, unless extremely unlikely assumptions are made, conventional measures of consumer surplus will be inaccurate. A simple example of this is the commonly used assumption that demand curves are linear, i.e. straight lines. Since this is extremely unlikely, considerable inaccuracy results when changes in consumer surplus are estimated following large price changes. Indeed, one authority on CBA, I. M. D. Little, has gone so far as to suggest that consumer surplus is 'a totally useless theoretical toy'.

d) Welfare economics is ultimately normative and this led early on to criticisms from positivists who felt that normative issues should not be the concern of the economists.

e) Some economists feel that welfare economics concentrates on relatively insignificant welfare losses and ignores the far more important losses caused by cost inefficiency, e.g. in complacent monopolies (sometimes known as the 'X-inefficiency') and the loss of welfare caused by unemployment. This may be a valid criticism if the social returns to the development of welfare economics have been less than the social costs! However, it hardly seems fair to criticise a body of theory simply because it does not provide answers to all the questions one would like answered.

STUDENT ACTIVITY 29.5

A bypass is about to be built around a local town, city or village. Make up a list of who the gainers and losers would be of such a project. How would you assess the environmental impacts of such a road improvement?

Summary

1 There has been considerable growth in public expenditure as a percentage of GDP throughout the twentieth century.

2 The efforts of the conservative government from 1979–97 has resulted in, at best, a stabilisation of public expenditure as a percentage of GDP.

3 Factors which make the control of public expenditure difficult include the increasing proportion of older citizens in the population, and increasing demand for services such as health and education which are traditionally produced in the public sector.

4 The construction of internal markets, compulsory competitive tendering and franchising may have made contributions to increased efficiency.

5 The costs of setting up mechanisms which simulate the market must be set against any benefits which accrue.

6 The quasi-markets in health and education do not perfectly simulate the market and there are areas of concern.

7 In addition to efficiency, equity must be used as a criterion for most publicly provided services.

8 Although it is possible to make some progress in placing values on costs and benefits which do not pass through the market, in many cases there will be large areas of ignorance.

30 Taxes and benefits

Learning outcomes

After reading this chapter you will be able to:

- Explain the main forms of taxation.
- Understand the arguments about taxes and incentives.
- Identify shifts that have taken place in the tax system.

Structure of the chapter

This chapter is structured around an introduction to the tax system and four case studies of current issues in taxation. It is advisable to read the introductory section first in order that you are familiar with the ways in which the main taxes work and some basic concepts. Apart from that, the case studies are self-contained and can be taken in any order. Once again, they may be treated as data response articles. Student activities are to be found at the end of each case.

Introduction

Understanding the tax system

The tax system is a complicated system of laws which are updated and changed annually in the Chancellor's budget. The law on tax is frequently tested in the courts on questions of interpretation. The objective of this chapter is not to make you an expert on the tax system, but to show how taxation has an impact on the economy. In the course of understanding the impact on the economy, you will have to learn the basics of how the tax system works.

Taxation is studied for its effects on the whole economy (macroeconomics) and its effect on individuals, firms and markets (microeconomics). We have already studied the way in which taxes levied on the retailer may be passed on to the consumer in Chapter 11. We have also discussed its role in fiscal policy, and its possible effects on incentives in Chapter 6.

This chapter concentrates on the details of the taxes, recent changes in the system, and their microeconomic effects. The macroeconomic effects will be considered in Chapter 43. A case study approach is taken to focus on different aspects of the tax system, but first a familiarity with the whole tax system is needed.

Why is taxation necessary?

Taxation is needed to finance public expenditure. There are three other methods of financing public expenditure. One is by selling off publicly owned assets (privatisation, discussed in Chapter 26), but this has only financed a tiny proportion of public expenditure. There is a limit to this source of finance because eventually there will be no further assets to sell. Second, by borrowing (the public sector borrowing requirement is discussed in Chapter 43), but this is just putting off taxation into the future. The National Debt has never been repaid in full, but tax is needed to pay the interest on the National Debt. Third, public expenditure can be financed by direct charges to the users of the service, such as prescription charges for medicines prescribed by doctors in the National Health Service. This issue is discussed in Chapter 29.

The main taxes

The study of taxation is a whole subject in itself, and many people make a living out of keeping up to date with changes in the system and advising individuals and companies. What follows in this section is a very introductory description of the main taxes in use in the UK today. The rates of tax quoted are for 1997–8. It is possible to find the up-to-date rates and allowances for the current year by consulting *Tax Which?* or various tax guides published by newspapers and banks. The contribution of each tax to total tax revenue is shown in Table 30.1.

Table 30.1 **Tax revenue by source, 1996–7 estimated out-turn (£bn)**

Income tax	68.1	Air pass. duty	0.4
Corporation tax	26.1	Insurance premium tax	0.6
Petroleum revenue tax	1.7	Landfill tax	0.1
Capital gains	0.9	Customs duties and levies	2.2
Inheritance tax	1.6	Vehicle excise	4.3
Stamp duty	2.4	Oil royalties	0.7
VAT	47.5	Business rates	14.2
Fuel duties	17.4	Social security contributions	46.7
Tobacco	7.8	Council tax	9.9
Alcohol	5.7	Other	5.8
Betting and gaming	1.5	Total	265.6

Source: National Income and Expendiure 'Blue Book', August 1997

Direct taxes

Direct taxes are those which are levied on the income or earnings of an individual or an organisation. The basic rates can be found in Table 30.2. These are the most important revenue raisers for the government and can be considered under four headings.

a) *Taxes on income.* Before taxing an individual's personal income, personal and other allowances are first deducted. After these tax allowances have been deducted, what is left of a person's income is known as taxable income. For example, if a person had an income of £10 000 p.a. and allowances of £4045, taxable income would be £5955. The marginal rate of tax is the amount of tax a person would pay on each successive unit of taxable income. In 1997–8 a person paid 20 per cent on the first £4100 of taxable income and 23 per cent on the next £22 100 of taxable income. Only the reasonably well paid would pay the top rate of 40 per cent on taxable income above £26 100. Such a tax is said to be progressive because it takes proportionately more from people with higher incomes. This idea is illustrated in Fig. 30.1. The average rate of tax can be calculated by dividing gross income (income before tax) by actual tax paid and converting it into a percentage Marginal and average tax rates are perhaps best presented in an algebraic manner:

Table 30.2 **Top and basic tax rates: changes**

	1979 → 79	*86*	*87*	*88*	*96*	*97*
Top 83	60	60	60	40	40	40
Basic 33	30	29	27	25	24	23

$$\text{Marginal rate of tax} = \frac{\text{Increase in tax paid}}{\text{Increase in income}} \times \frac{100}{1}$$

or:

$$\text{Marginal rate of tax} = \Delta T / \Delta Y$$

The average rate of tax is:

$$\text{Average rate of tax} = \frac{\text{Total tax paid}}{\text{Total income}}$$

or:

$$\text{Average rate of tax} = T/Y$$

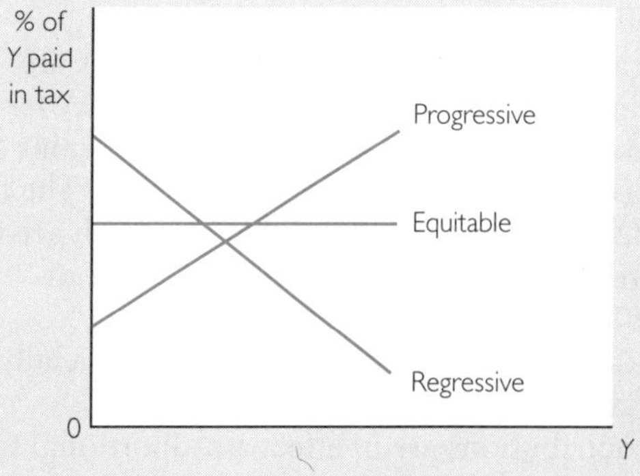

Fig. 30.1 **Tax revenue by source**

With progressive taxes it is the case that the marginal rate is higher than the average rate; that is:

$\Delta T/\Delta Y > T/Y$

b) *Corporation tax*. This is the tax which is levied on the profits of companies. In 1997–8 the rate of tax started at 23 per cent for small businesses in line with income tax. The main rate was 33 per cent. When taxpayers receive dividends from companies that have paid corporation tax, the Inland Revenue treats that income as already taxed at the standard income tax rate of 23 per cent. It can be seen therefore that, in effect, dividends from larger companies are taxed at a rate 10 per cent higher than other types of income. This is often justified because of the legal privileges granted to companies. The privilege of limited liability means that shareholders lose a maximum of the capital they put into the company if it should go bankrupt. On the other hand supply side economists argue that this higher rate of tax is a disincentive to investment, enterprise and risk taking.

   Corporation tax rates have moved down considerably from the 50 per cent rates which obtained in the 1970s. The new Labour government has shown a willingness to continue with this process. Tax revenues from corporation tax have increased, however, because allowances have been reduced. In the 1970s, industrial companies were allowed to set investment expenditure in the current year against profits before taxes were calculated.

c) *Taxes on capital*. Capital as such is not taxed, but tax is paid when capital is sold or transferred. The most important taxes are capital gains tax and inheritance tax. After a tax-free allowance of £6500, capital gains are taxed as a part of a person's income. The first £215 000 of a person's estate on death are tax free but after that a marginal tax rate of 40 per cent applies.

d) *National insurance*. Although not officially classed as a tax, national insurance contributions are in effect a proportional tax, i.e. it takes a constant percentage of income up to a ceiling of £465 a week, upon employer and employees alike. Originally contributions used to be a fixed rate 'stamp' and could be regarded as a price for an insurance service offered by the state rather than as a tax. While the standard rate of tax has been falling, national insurance contributions have been rising.

Indirect taxes

Indirect taxes are usually taxes on expenditure. They are so called because the tax is not directly on income, but on expenditure. For example, in the case of the duty on whisky it is the distiller who must pay the tax. The ***formal*** incidence of the tax is said to be on the distiller. The tax is then 'shifted' down the chain of distribution until the burden (or ***effective*** incidence) of the tax falls also upon the consumer. The determination of the incidence of tax is explained in Chapter 11.

These are the main forms of indirect tax in the UK:

a) *Customs and excise duty*. Customs duty may be levied on goods coming into the country but this only accounts for 1 per cent of government revenues. Excise duty is levied on a commodity, no matter where it is produced; it is a specific tax, i.e. it is levied per unit of the commodity irrespective of its price. The main duties are on tobacco, alcohol and petrol.

b) *Value-added tax (VAT)*. The most important of indirect taxes, VAT was first introduced in 1973 when it replaced purchase tax. VAT is an *ad valorem* tax, i.e. it is levied on the selling price of the commodity. There are currently three rates of VAT: zero, 5 and 17.5 per cent. Unlike purchase tax, which was only collected from retailers, it is collected from each stage of production. Each company pays VAT on the full selling price of its products, but can claim it back on its purchases from outside the firm. The difference between its sales and its purchases is ***value added***.

Taxes on expenditure are generally said to be regressive, i.e. they take a larger percentage of the incomes of the lower paid. The reason for this is that poorer people spend a higher proportion of their income. On the other hand, zero-rated or exempt goods like food and children's clothes form a higher proportion of poor people's budget. It can be seen that the actual average rate of tax paid will be different for everyone and will depend on their spending pattern.

Are some taxes really prices?

Other indirect taxes include car purchase tax, road fund and television licences, betting tax and stamp duty. It is sometimes argued that these taxes are really more like prices, paying for goods and services provided by the public sector, such as television and roads. The revenue from these taxes is not necessarily spent on the relevant industry, however. The Treasury rejected a link between tax revenue on a sector of the economy and the amount spent on it (known as ***hypothecation***). The last case of hypothecation – between road taxes and expenditure on roads – was abandoned in 1926.

STUDENT ACTIVITY 30.1

Using the tax rates and allowances in Table 30.3 calculate the total tax paid and the marginal and average rates of tax for a single person with an income of:
a) £10 000 b) £25 000 c) £40 000
Which income group has the lowest marginal rate of tax? Draw a graph to illustrate how progressive the system is (see Fig. 30.1).

How much do each of these people gain by getting married ? Is it worth it? (Note: Count national insurance contributions as a tax in your calculations.)

STUDENT ACTIVITY 30.2

An engineering company sells 1000 machines a year at £1000 each. Its purchases of raw materials are £300 000 a year and other expenditure (office supplies, telephone, computers, etc.) comes to £50 000. Its labour bill is £500 000 a year and a gross profit of £150 000 is achieved. What will its net value-added tax bill be after claiming back VAT on purchases?

Table 30.3 **Current tax rates**

Allowances		*1995–6*	*1996–7*	*1997–8*
Personal		3525	3765	4045
Married		1720*	1790*	1830*
Additional personal		1720*	1790*	1830*
Widow's bereavement		1720*	1790*	1830*
Age 65–74		4630	4910	5220
Married		2995*	3115*	3185*
75+		4800	5090	5400
Married		3035*	3155*	3200*
Blind	1200	1250	1280	
Bands	20%	0–3200	0–3900	0–4100
	25%	3201	(24%) 3901	(23%) 4101
		–24 300	–25 500	–26 100
	40%	24 301+	25 500+	26 100+
National insurance				
	2%		First £61	£62
			(3172)	
	10%		61–455	62–465
			(23 660)	
	0%		455+	465+
Inheritance	0%	0–154 000	0–200 000	0–215 000
	40%	154 000+	200 000+	215 000+
Capital gains	0%	0–6000	0–6300	6500
Above this, exemption allowance added to income for assessment under income tax				
Corporation tax				
Small companies		25%	24%	21%
Large companies		33%	33%	31%
MIRAS max. allowance				30 000
Rate of allowance				15%

* Relief at 15%

An outline of the cases

The cases

Case study 30.1 is concerned with the question: what should we tax? It uses the concepts of equity and efficiency, progressivity and regressivity.
Case study 30.2: Government policy has shifted the economy towards expenditure tax.
Case study 30.3 considers whether redistribution always creates disincentives. Government policy has abolished the higher rates of income tax, but are the highest tax

rates on the poor? It uses the concepts of income and substitution effects.
Case study 30.4 charts the reforms to local tax in the 1980s and 1990s. The benefit principle, mobility and capitalisation are concepts used here.

Case study 30.1
What makes a good tax?

Taxation is a controversial topic. There is disagreement about the purposes of taxes and what constitutes a good tax. More fundamentally there is argument about the effects of taxation upon the economy. The eigtheenth-century economist Adam Smith was the first to put forward a set of economic principles to guide policy makers.

The canons of taxation

Adam Smith laid down four **canons** (criteria) of taxation. Although taxes have changed a great deal the principles still remain good today. A good tax, said Smith, should have the following characteristics:

a) *Equitable.* A good tax should be based upon the ability to pay. Today, progressive income tax means that those with higher incomes pay not only a larger amount but also a greater proportion of their income in tax.
b) *Economical.* A good tax should not be expensive to administer and the greatest possible proportion of it should accrue to the government as revenue. In general, indirect taxes are cheaper to collect than direct taxes, but they are not, however, so equitable.
c) *Convenient.* This means that the method and frequency of the payment should be convenient to the taxpayer. The introduction of pay as you earn (PAYE) made income tax much easier to pay for most people.
d) *Certain.* The tax should be formulated so that taxpayers are certain of how much they have to pay and when. This information is widely available today, but is often poorly understood.

Modern economists would add to this list:

e) *Flexible.* A good taxation system should be readily adaptable to changing circumstances such as changing price levels. VAT goes up automatically as prices rise, but excise taxes do not.
f) *The benefit principle.* As government expenditure increasingly provides services for 'voter-consumers', it is argued that taxes should be regarded as a kind of price. If people receive the service then they should be paying the 'tax-price'. This principle is often in conflict with the idea of progressivity as will be seen in Case study 30.4 on local taxation.

The redistribution of income

All political parties subscribe to the view that the fiscal system should be used to **redistribute income.** A right-wing view might be that this should be just sufficient to redress the worst inequalities in the economy while left-wingers might wish to see something more drastic done to effect a fundamental shift from the rich to the poor. The redistribution of income is achieved by taking more tax from richer people and giving benefits to poorer people. The provision of free services like health and education also in effect redistributes income.

Progressivity, regressivity and equity

A progressive tax system is one where richer people pay a higher proportion of their income in tax. A good example of a progressive tax is income tax, as the tax rate goes up as income goes up. A regressive tax is one which results in richer people paying a smaller proportion of their income in tax. A good example of a regressive tax is the TV licence, or the poll tax (see Case study 30.4). When all taxpayers pay the same proportion of their income in tax, the system is said to be equitable. Taxes on expenditure come closest to being equitable. Rich people save a higher proportion of their income and avoid paying some expenditure tax in this way making it slightly regressive. On the other hand, poor people spend a higher proportion of their income on goods like food which is exempt from tax, which makes the tax more progressive. These three concepts were illustrated earlier in Fig. 30.1.

STUDENT ACTIVITY 30.3

Use Smith's canons of taxation to asses the following taxes:

a) income tax
b) VAT
c) TV licence
d) Excise duty on beer

Case study 30.2 The shift to expenditure taxation

The aspect of the economy which is being taxed is called a tax base. There are four tax bases: income; expenditure; wealth; and existence. The taxation of income is sometimes criticised for taxing what people put into the economy (their labour, capital, land, enterprise), rather than what they take out. A tax on expenditure is based on what people take out of the economy (goods and services). The taxation of income would appear to discourage people from supplying factors of production to the economy. It would also appear to discourage savings which are needed for investment. Both these disincentives form part of the supply side argument which was introduced in Chapter 6. The arguments about the supply of labour are discussed in Case study 30.3 below. The great advantage of taxing income is that it enables the government to achieve its aims on the redistribution of income.

One of the main changes which has taken place in the last 20 years is the shift away from the taxation of income and towards the taxation of expenditure. Income tax rates have been reduced, especially on higher incomes, and expenditure taxes have been increased, particularly VAT. The main changes that have taken place are discussed below.

Reduction in top income tax rates

Common misunderstanding

In 1979 the top marginal rate of tax on income was 83 per cent. This does not, of course, mean that 83 per cent of a person's income would be taken in tax (that would be an average rate of 83 per cent). The 83 per cent rate was only to be collected on taxable income above the 83p tax threshold. In addition, if more than a certain amount of the person's income was from investment (interest, dividends, etc.) then an investment income surcharge of 15 per cent was collected from this income. This meant that the top marginal rate of tax was effectively 98 per cent. There can be little doubt that such tax rates would create disincentives to work or invest. These rates were pointless in a different way, however. Anybody who earned that amount of money could also afford the best tax accountants to advise them on how to avoid paying such high rates of tax by using tax loopholes.

After their return to power in 1979, the Conservative government soon reduced the top rate of tax to 60 per cent and then reduced it further to 40 per cent in 1987. This is one of the lowest top rates of tax in the industrialised world.

Reduction in the standard rate of tax

The standard rate of tax was also gradually reduced from 33 per cent to 23 per cent in 1997, with a new initial 20 per cent band introduced in the 90s. This decrease in the standard rate was partly offset by increases in the national insurance contribution. The objective of the Conservatives was to widen the 20 per cent band sufficiently so that it could be regarded as the standard rate. The reductions of the top and standard rates of tax are shown in Table 30.3.

Common misunderstanding

It is commonly thought that, since the rate of tax on income has gone down considerably in the way described in the two sections above, tax as a whole has gone down. This is not the case because increases in other taxes have more than offset the reductions in income tax, as can be seen in Tables 30.2 and 30.3.

Increases in the rate of VAT

When the Conservatives came to power in 1979 there were two rates of VAT: 8 per cent on standard commodities and $12\frac{1}{2}$ per cent on luxury items. In 1980 a uniform rate of 15 per cent was introduced which was later raised to $17\frac{1}{2}$ per cent

Increases in the scope of VAT

The scope of a tax is the range of items on which it can be raised. Some categories of expenditure are exempt from VAT or are zero rated. A number of items have recently been included in the VAT net, most notably takeaway foods such as fish and chips and domestic fuels (electricity and gas). VAT on domestic fuel was introduced at the rate of 8 per cent. Although the plan was to impose the higher $17\frac{1}{2}$ per cent rate on domestic fuel, political pressure resulted in the rate staying at 8 per cent. Since its election the Labour government has reduced this rate to 5 per cent, the lowest that the EU would allow (once a country introduces VAT on a product, EU rules state that it cannot be removed). Food, books, children's clothing and newspapers remain free of VAT but future governments may tap these sources of revenue.

Cross-border shopping

Taxes on alcohol have been reduced recently because of cross-border shopping to France. This is a good example of the bizarre behaviour that a badly designed tax can encourage. British alcoholic products are shipped to Calais where they are sold to British residents who have crossed the Channel to buy them cheaply. The British residents then bring the alcohol back to the UK! Who gains from these extraordinary transactions? Well clearly the French government gains extra revenue as do the ferry companies, Eurotunnel and the entrepreneurs involved in shipping the products out and selling them in France. The British residents who visit France clearly do better than they would have done if they had bought their alcohol at home, but they have been inconvenienced by having to take such a long trip (unless they were going to France in any case). The clear loser is the UK government with a loss of tax revenue.

The double taxation of savings: TESSAs and PEPs

Advocates of expenditure tax argue that saving is taxed more heavily than consumption. This is because saving takes place from taxed income, and then the income from the savings (interest, dividends, etc.) is taxed again. To avoid this, tax-exempt special savings accounts (TESSAs) were introduced. Taxpayers were allowed to put a certain amount into TESSAs each year over a five-year period. Providing they did not touch the money until the end of the period they would not pay any tax on the interest. PEPs worked in a similar way but applied to savings used to buy shares, rather than savings in bank and building society accounts. In the case of PEPs, it was dividends and capital gains that were free from tax.

Investment income

Taxation on income from investment was eased in a number of other ways. The basic rate of 20 per cent was applied to all interest from bank and building society accounts in 1996. Indexation was introduced on capital gains. Capital gains tax is charged on any increase in the value of assets when they are sold (the house you live in is exempt). In periods of inflation the price of an asset may rise, but its value may not go up in real terms after allowing for inflation. In periods of inflation capital gains tax may be a tax on inflation, not on real increases in income. Indexation therefore improved the tax situation of people who put their savings in shares. Contributions to pension funds up to a certain percentage of income continue to be allowable against income tax and a tax-free lump sum can be paid in the year of retirement.

Bucking the trend: insurance

Two areas of savings have been treated more harshly since 1979. Premiums paid into an endowment life assurance policy used to be allowable against income tax. An endowment life assurance policy invests the policy holder's savings over an agreed number of years. At the end of the agreed period (or when the policy holder dies, whichever is the sooner) the policy holder receives a large lump sum or endowment. Since 1984 tax allowances have not been available for new endowment policies, although the old ones have continued to benefit. A rationale for this change is provided by the attitude to risk of the life assurance companies. Since they needed to provide a large lump sum some distance in the future to satisfy their customers, it was argued that they would tend to go for safe, low-risk investments. This may not be the best strategy for an entrepreneurial capitalist economy. The shift away from preferential tax treatment for life assurance can be justified on supply side grounds.

Housing

The tax advantages of owning a home have been reduced in the period since 1979. Home owners who are in the process of buying a house are allowed to set the interest on their loans against income for tax purposes. The extent to which they are able to do this has been severely cut back in recent years. First a ceiling of £25 000 was placed on such tax allowances. Home owners were able to set the interest on the first £25 000 of their mortgage against tax, but any borrowing above that level received no further tax exemption. This ceiling was raised only once, to £30 000, but has remained at that level ever since. At the time of its introduction this ceiling seemed quite high and the majority of mortgage holders continued to receive full tax exemption.

Inflation has gradually reduced the real value of the ceiling, so that now very few new mortgages are taken out under £30 000. The success of the Conservative government in curbing inflation in the early 1990s meant that the £30 000 ceiling was no longer being eroded away quickly in real terms. The government acted to cut tax exemption in another way. The rate at which the mortgage holder could claim exemption was progressively reduced to 15 per cent. Someone with a mortgage of £30 000 paying 10 per cent interest with a marginal tax rate of 40 per cent was entitled to a tax exemption of £1200 on the £3000 interest bill before the changes. After the changes the exemption had been reduced in value to £450! The Labour government has continued this trend with a further reduction to a 10 per cent tax exemption rate in their first budget in June 1997.

Common misunderstanding

It may seem odd that a government that claimed it wanted to create a 'property-owning democracy' should remove many of the financial benefits of home ownership. The answer can be found in the same supply side argument used in the previous section. Home ownership is not the kind of risky but potentially successful investment that a dynamic capitalist economy should concentrate on. It must be pointed out, however, that housing continues to receive favourable tax treatment. It is still the case that a person's first house is exempt from capital gains tax (a second house is regarded as a business venture with potential for rent). Some exemption of interest against tax remains. Housing also can be regarded as non-pecuniary income which escapes taxation. If you do not own a home you have to rent from a landlord. The rent you pay is regarded as part of the landlord's taxable income. If you own your own house you can be thought of as your own landlord, but the benefit of the house does not pass through the market, so you pay no tax on it.

The large increase in home ownership in the UK had nothing to do with the tax treatment of housing which became less favourable in the 1980s and 1990s, but had more to do with the subsidised sale of council houses, the house price boom of the mid 1980s and changes in attitudes. The collapse of house prices in the early 1990s left many people with mortgages larger than the value of their homes. This position of so-called 'negative equity' has made people a little more cautious.

Conclusion

It can be seen that most tax changes over the last 20 years have been shifting the balance of taxation towards an expenditure base and away from an income base. The two notable exceptions of housing and life insurance can be justified on supply side grounds. The reduction of high marginal tax rates may have had the benefit of reducing disincentive effects for top earners (see Case study 30.3) but also has made the tax system less progressive (see Case study 30.4). The changes have almost certainly made saving more attractive.

STUDENT ACTIVITY 30.4

Work out the value of tax relief in monetary and percentage terms on a mortgage of:
a) £10 000
b) £30 000
c) £60 000
Use curent mortgage interest rates.

STUDENT ACTIVITY 30.5

Explain how a rich person can avoid paying tax in ways which are not open to a poorer person.

Case study 30.3
Direct taxes: a disincentive to work?

Supply side economists argue that taxes, particularly taxes on income, are a disincentive to work effort. It is argued that if taxes are cut this will increase incentives because people will be receiving more for their efforts. Thus people will work harder. This will increase productivity and, as the economy expands, create more employment. There will, therefore, be a rise in the level of real national income. If this is the case then it is possible that a greater total amount of tax may be paid. This was the argument put forward by A. Laffer.

This argument was accepted by President Reagan in the early 1980s and by the UK Chancellor, Nigel Lawson, in the late 1980s, and was the basis of their tax-cutting budgets. The macroeconomic side of this argument is to be found in Chapter 43, but below we will explore some of the microeconomic arguments.

Income and substitution effects

It is important not to accept uncritically arguments of the kind used in the above section. It does seem intuitively correct that high taxes would make working less attractive as there is less take-home pay for each hour's work. On the other hand it can be argued that raising taxes would increase effort as people struggle to maintain their level of disposable income. They might not like higher taxes but, at the end of the month, they have to find the money to pay their mortgage, the electricity bill and so on and are thus forced to work harder.

These two arguments can be restated in terms of the **substitution effect** and the **income effect** explained in Chapter 10. Suppose that we look at the problem in terms of the 'cost' of leisure. If we raise the rate of tax then we reduce the opportunity cost of leisure, because an extra hour's leisure consumed costs less in terms of income forgone. If the substitution effect predominates people may, therefore, work less hard. They are, as it were, 'buying' more leisure because it is cheaper. The substitution effect is associated with the marginal tax rate since this is the tax rate which applies to the last unit of work effort.

Alternatively, we could argue that increasing taxes reduces people's income and we could, therefore, look at demand for leisure from the point of view of an income effect. As we know, *ceteris paribus*, if income decreases the demand for a normal good will decrease. If leisure is a normal good, then reducing take-home incomes by raising taxes will decrease the demand for leisure. In other words people will work harder. They are, in effect, 'buying' less leisure because they are poorer and cannot afford it. The income effect is associated with the average tax rate because it measures the percentage by which income has been reduced.

It appears that economic theory on its own cannot settle this question. If taxes are raised, what will happen to the total amount of effort supplied by the labour force will depend upon whether the income effect or the substitution effect is stronger. These alternatives are illustrated in Fig. 30.2. Empirical studies to determine which of the two effects is stronger is the only way forward.

Institutional constraints

Apart from the problem of whether people actually regard the situation in this light we have the problem as to whether they can vary their effort at will. For example, if you are a salaried worker then working 10 per cent harder (or less hard) probably has little or no effect upon your immediate wage packet, although it might increase your chances of promotion. If overtime is recognised and paid for, the fact that a person is willing to work overtime is no guarantee that it will be available. If trade unions have negotiated a standard working week (usually somewhere between 35 and 40 hours) then variation of work effort may be quite difficult in practice.

Evidence

We will consider microeconomic evidence in this chapter. The macroeconomic evidence represented by the Laffer curve is left to a discussion of the supply side economists in Chapter 43, since more macroeconomic theory is necessary before the student can fully appreciate the arguments involved. Needless to say, the supply siders believe that tax reduction will increase work effort.

a) *Interview evidence*. The balance of evidence from interviews is that there is a slight disincentive effect of higher taxation. The two classic studies quoted

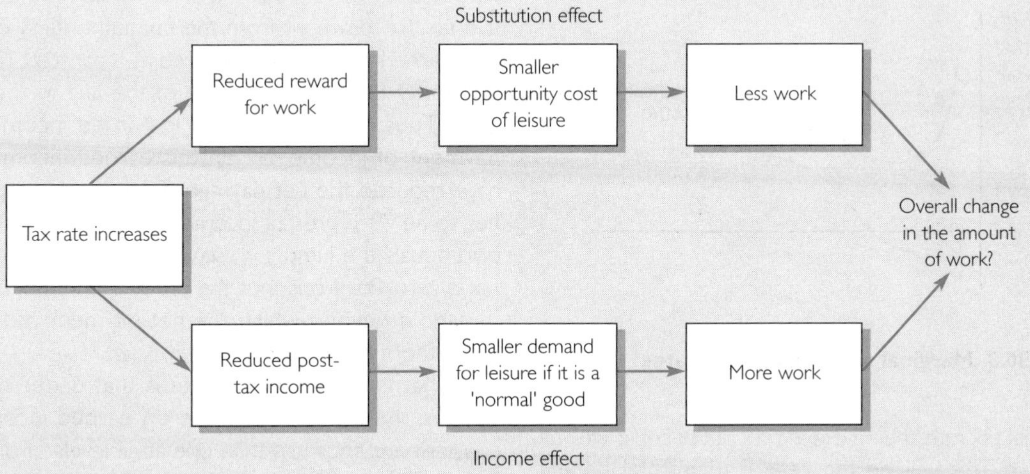

Fig. 30.2 **Income versus substitution effects – non-determinancy**
Raising taxes could cause some people to work harder and others to work less hard. The overall effect depends upon which predominates, the income effect or the substitution effect.

are Break (1956) and Fields and Stanbury (1968), but these results have been replicated subsequently. Both interviewed professional people (accountants and lawyers) who could vary their hours of work. It has been noted above that not all workers have this flexibility. Break found that 77 per cent of respondents reported no change in work effort when taxes were increased and only 13 per cent reported disincentive effects as against 10 per cent reporting incentive effects. Fields and Stanbury found slightly higher disincentive effects at 19 per cent with 11 per cent reporting incentive effects, but both studies find the majority of people unaffected.

b) *Statistical evidence.* Likewise, most microeconomic statistical studies have found inelastic labour supply curves when wages or taxes change. The only exception to this is the more elastic labour supply of married women. For those feminists among you, you should note that this is merely a report of how married women do behave, not how they should behave!

The rest of this debate is deferred to Chapter 43 when the Laffer curve is considered.

Tax reform

The poverty trap

One of the worst features of the fiscal system is the **poverty trap**. As Fig. 30.3 indicates the poorest people in the economy are the ones facing the highest marginal rates of tax. This is because the tax system and the benefit system overlap. A person who earns a small income may also receive benefit. Until the reforms of the social security system in 1988 marginal tax rates of more than 100 per cent were common. Marginal tax rates are not usually above 80 per cent on the poorest group in society now, but this still represents by far the highest marginal rate in the tax system.

The reason why the poorest people face such a high marginal rate of tax is because, as their incomes rise, so their benefit is withdrawn (**means tested**). If a person is losing 50 per cent of their benefit as their income rises and also paying the lower 20 per cent tax rate and national insurance contributions of 10 per cent, then they will face an effective marginal tax rate of 80 per cent. At the same time as facing such a high

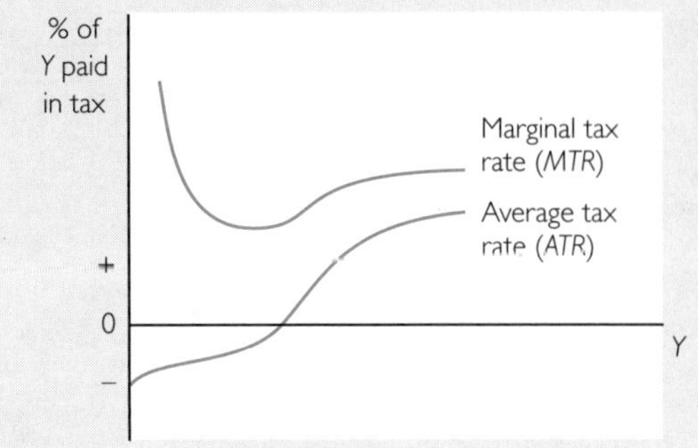

Fig. 30.3 **Marginal and average tax rates**

marginal tax rate, their average rate of tax could well be negative. This will be the case if their total benefit exceeds their total tax paid. It is easier to think about this if you regard a benefit as a negative tax.

Negative income tax

Under this system those above the threshold would pay positive income tax while those below it would receive payments (instead of receiving benefits from the Department of Health and Social Security, etc.). Such payments would thus be a **negative income tax.**

Negative income tax is illustrated in Fig. 30.4 In effect, under a negative income tax, everyone in the economy receives a lump sum of Og. Hence someone who had no earned income at all would have a negative tax (i.e. payment from the tax authorities) of Og. Any earned income is then taxed at a constant rate as shown by the constant slope of the line in the diagram. Thus, if Oa is received in earned income the payment of income tax on this earned income will have reduced the net payment from the tax authorities to ae. At a pre-tax income of Ob the income tax paid equals the lump sum so that the net payment of tax is zero. Point b is thus the break-even point or the threshold beyond which the net payment of tax to the authorities becomes positive.

What is important to note is that under such a scheme the marginal tax rate on earned income is constant and thus less than one at all levels of pre-tax income. Thus it always 'pays to work' and the poverty trap has been abolished. Moreover, it is claimed, the system would be cheaper to administer than means-tested flat-rate benefits and thus be more economical in accordance with Adam Smith's canons of taxation.

The major drawback of the negative income tax system is that it is, in effect, a universal benefit system, because everyone implicitly receives Og. This is of course why it works as a solution to the poverty trap – because there is no means-tested benefit. The drawback of universal benefit systems is their expense. If we do not target benefit to those who really need it, then public expenditure will be much higher and so will taxes. The other side of the dilemma is that if we do means test benefits we will create poverty trap disincentive effects.

This dilemma can be illustrated by asking: what would be an acceptable minimum income Og that we could pay someone who has no work and no income? If we give a conservative estimate of £60 and impose a tax rate of 25 per cent then the break-even level b will be £240. Negative income tax is always worked out relative to the break-even level. The amount of tax paid can be found in the following way:

$$T = t(Y - b)$$

Verbally, the tax paid (T) is the tax rate (t) times the difference between income (Y) and the break-even level of income (b).

The consequence of this is that no one earning less than £240 will pay any income tax! Indeed they will all be receiving some kind of benefit. People earning above £240 will have to pay higher rates of tax to

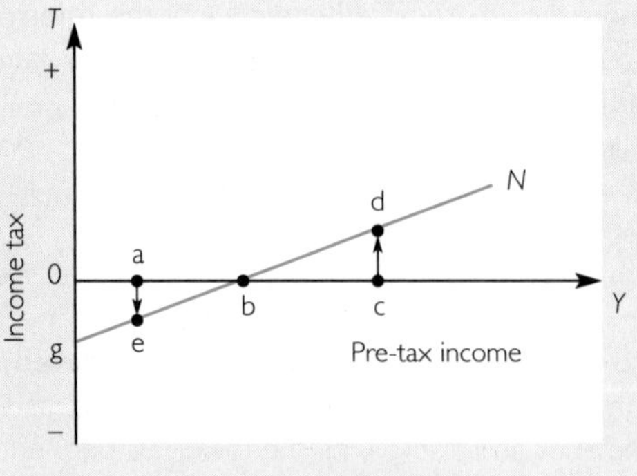

Fig. 30.4 **Negative income tax**
Line *N* represents a constant rate income tax and negative income tax. At the threshold b no tax is paid. Above the threshold at Oc the amount of tax paid is cd. Below the threshold at Oc negative income tax is received of ae.

pay for this. Is the result of eliminating the poverty trap the creation of disincentive effects elsewhere in the income distribution?

The minimum wage

Another way of looking at the problem of the poverty trap is to ask why people in employment need the assistance of the state. Employers who do not give their workers a **living wage** can be thought of as exploiting them. The Labour government has promised to introduce a **minimum wage**. The poverty trap and the benefits bill could be dealt with at the same time by such a policy. Are there any drawbacks to this one?

a) Opponents of the minimum wage argue that it would destroy jobs. The groups most likely to be affected in this way are low-paid workers competing with cheap imports from less developed countries, and young people with few skills and low productivity. It is likely that a cautiously low level will be set initially, possibly with a lower rate for young people.
b) If a person has a very large family then even a reasonable level of minimum wage will not provide them with enough. One possible solution to this is to upgrade child benefit so that family size is not an issue. The public expenditure consequences of such universal benefits have already been discussed, however. An alternative approach is to suggest that having such a large family on a low income is irresponsible, and refuse to give benefit to children above a certain number. This will tend to impact on the children rather than the parents and would incur the opposition of the Child Poverty Action Group.
c) The minimum wage helps those in full-time work, but those with part-time jobs may still run into poverty trap problems. The question of poverty, as opposed to the poverty trap, is discussed in Chapter 45.

STUDENT ACTIVITY 30.6

Conduct a survey among your parents and working friends to discover how they are likely to respond to increases in income tax rates.

STUDENT ACTIVITY 30.7

Explain the difference between the income effect and the substitution effect. Explain why leisure can be thought of as a good. Do you think it would be a normal good in your case?

Case study 30.4
Local taxation and autonomy

Local authority finances have been subject to great changes in recent years. The rating system for domestic property was changed into the community charge but opposition to this was so great that the government was forced to reconsider it. The council tax was introduced as a compromise.

Central government financial support for local authorities comes mainly in the form of the rate support grant. Pressure has been put upon local government to curtail its spending since 1976. This pressure became acute under the Conservative government after 1979. This led to local authorities raising a greater proportion of their revenue as rates. The reluctance, or inability, of local government to make cuts led to more and more draconian measures being taken by the central government. The so-called rate capping Act of 1984 was seen by many people not just as an attempt to control expenditure but also as an attack upon local autonomy.

The pattern of local authority expenditure is determined by the services for which it is responsible. The chief form of expenditure for most local authorities is on education, as this is administered at a local level. There is also localised expenditure on roads, social services and housing

Income and expenditure are the main sources of revenue for governments in modern economies, but wealth taxation is a much older form of taxation. For instance, peasants in the Middle Ages were often taxed on how many cattle they possessed. In capitalist societies, governments are concerned not to discourage the accumulation of capital which drives the economy. Wealth taxation occurs when wealth is handed over from one generation to the next (inheritance tax) and when assets are sold (capital gains tax). Another old form of tax is the poll tax, or head tax, paid equally by all people irrespective of economic position. It is effectively a tax on existence. When introduced by Richard III it resulted in a peasant revolt led by Wat Tyler, and had to be dropped. When introduced by Mrs Thatcher, it led to widespread protest and riots. Many people believe this was the issue which led to Mrs Thatcher's fall from power. Poll taxes create no economic disincentives, but have been very unpopular.

Rates

Rates were often criticised as being unfair because they were not related to the services a ratepayer receives from the local authority. This is a difficult argument to maintain since few taxes are related to services received. It was also argued that rates were unfair since they fell only on the head of the household. Thus if, for example, there were two identical houses in a borough but six people lived in one while only one person in the other, the household of six would pay only the same rates as the household of one.

Another criticism of the rating system came from the business community. Rates on business premises in fact raised more money than rates on housing. However, unless the business people happened to live in the same area as their company they got no say in how the money was spent since businesses do not have a vote.

The Conservative government of 1987 was committed to the reform, or abolition, of the rating system. Various proposals were put forward such as local income taxes or complete funding from central government. In the end the government opted for the community charge. Under this system all people over the age of 18 living in a local authority area paid the same amount of tax. It was for this reason that it became known as the poll tax because because one would pay tax simply as a result of being on the electoral register. The tax was largely unrelated to income or wealth although some relief was given to various categories of people such as full-time students.

The community charge (poll tax)

The community charge was introduced in Scotland in 1988 and in England and Wales in 1990. The domestic community charge was determined by the local authority. In addition to this there is an industrial rate which is set nationally. Local authority incomes continued to be supplemented by transfers from central government. Income from other sources continued with central government enforcing council house sales, making local authorities privatise leisure centres and so on.

The community charge was subject to much criticism. It certainly was a highly regressive tax which 'taxes a duke the same as a dustman'. It is hard to see how it accords with the accepted canons of taxation (see Case study 30.1). It proved to be both difficult and expensive to collect. This is because people are more mobile and numerous than houses. In the end the government decided to abolish it and bring in a new council tax. The new tax was to be a mixture of the old rating system, i.e. a tax on property, and a charge on all adults.

Throughout this time the rating system for business properties survived unchanged except for the important fact that it became set by central government. The uniform business rate, as it is known, suffered from problems of its own because property prices were so much higher in the south-east than in other parts of the country. Transitional relief had to be offered to businesses disadvantaged by this change.

The council tax

The council tax is based on the value of a person's house, not the rentable value as had been the case with rates. It is also capped at the top end so that a house of £500 000 pays the same as a house of £1 million. Houses are placed in value bands, but the taxation is regressive for two reasons. First, house prices do not rise as fast as income does, and second, the council tax does not rise directly in proportion to house values.

Conclusion

The government has had to go back to a system of taxing houses at the local level, because houses are not mobile, unlike people. The real problem with the poll tax was that people could avoid paying it by moving around frequently. There are also more people than houses and therefore more bills to send out. Ultimately it was its inequity which led to its demise.

STUDENT ACTIVITY 30.8

Find out your local council tax rates and work out if they are proportional to house prices.

Summary

1. Tax is needed to finance public expenditure.
2. Adam Smith laid down the four canons of taxation: that taxes should be equitable, economical, convenient and certain.
3. There has been a shift away from direct taxation towards indirect taxation over the last 20 years.
4. The progressivity of the income tax system, particularly at the top end, has been reduced over the last 20 years.
5. Evidence about the disincentives effects of income tax is mixed but is more persuasive at the top end of tax rates.
6. The shift from rates to the council tax reflects the increase in home ownership.
7. The poll tax failed because of inequity and collection costs.
8. Discussion of taxation revolves around its effect on efficiency, equity and economic growth.

part 3

Macroeconomics

SECTION V The determination of national income

SECTION V The determination of national income

'Who knows when some slight shock, disturbing the delicate balance between social order and thirsty aspiration, shall send the skyscrapers in our cities tumbling.'

Richard Wright

'Using official statistics to govern the country is like looking up today's trains in last year's timetable.'

Harold Macmillan

31 Keynesian macroeconomics

Learning outcomes

At the end of this chapter you will be able to:

- Provide a brief account of the social and economic events that Keynes was responding to.
- Give a definition of macroeconomics.
- Explain the elements of the debate between Keynes and the 'classical' economists and describe the fundamental insights of Keynes.
- Describe a sequence of possible events leading up to a Keynesian recession and how Keynesian policy could be used to end the recession.

The Keynesian revolution

When economists look at how the whole economy responds to changes, they are looking at how ***aggregates*** behave rather than at how individuals or individual markets behave. This approach owes much to the work of the UK Cambridge economist John Maynard Keynes (1883–1946). Keynes wrote one of the most influential of all books of the twentieth century, i.e. *The General Theory of Employment, Interest and Money* (1936). This book, usually called simply *The General Theory*, led to what is often described as the Keynesian 'revolution' in economics. Indeed, from the mid 1940s until the early 1970s Keynes's economics was the foundation stone of macroeconomic policy making in the UK and the USA and other Western countries.

Keynes argued that although the forces of supply and demand work very well to establish equilibrium in individual markets, the economy as a whole could experience periods of severe instability.

In particular, Keynes presented a convincing explanation of how a collapse in demand in the economy as a whole could throw millions of workers out of work and into chronic unemployment, even though they were eager to work. This was in stark contrast to the prevailing economic orthodoxy of the time which emphasised market equilibrium and which therefore had no convincing explanation for how such steep increases in mass unemployment could occur. Governments of the time thus believed that market forces should be left alone and relied on to eliminate unemployment unaided by government action. Controversially, Keynes argued passionately that governments should take a responsibility for restoring full employment at such times by deliberately regulating the overall, or ***aggregate***, level of demand in the economy. Indeed he went further than this and argued for

> A regime which deliberately aims at controlling and directing economic forces in the interests of social justice and social stability
>
> Keynes. *Essays in Persuasion*

The social and economic background to *The General Theory*

In order to understand the context and impact of Keynes's *General Theory* it is necessary to know something of the economic and political events of the times. Keynes was responding to the experience of the interwar depression in the Western economies which had seen unemployment reach levels as high as 25 per cent of the workforce. This had caused much accompanying misery, poverty and loss of dignity for millions of people. In the UK there was also widespread social unrest such as the general strike of 1926. Perhaps because free market capitalism appeared to be in crisis, working-class political and trade union movements were making great advances.

Although things were not nearly as dangerous as before the revolution in Russia of 1917, the upper and middle classes in Britain were shaken by these events. In the USA the Wall Street crash in 1929 saw the US stock market prices crash; many had their wealth, held in stocks and shares, wiped out. The Wall Street crash was followed by prolonged depression and this cast further doubt on the stability of capitalist economies. Back in the UK, it was clear that the soldiers of the First World War had not come home to the land 'fit for heroes' that they had been promised. Events such as the Jarrow hunger march troubled consciences across the country.

Many post-war politicians of all parties had their political outlook shaped by these events and these memories formed the backdrop for much subsequent policy making. Indeed, until Margaret Thatcher came to power in 1979, all governments after the Second World War explicitly accepted a responsibility for maintaining 'full employment'. Hence, although Keynes's ideas were not immediately adopted, and events were eventually overshadowed by the Second World War, the Great Depression of the interwar years led to a political climate in which many politicians and economists were looking for new ideas (particularly young ones wishing to upstage their tutors!).

In the period following the Second World War Keynes's ideas triumphed over the former emphasis on *laissez-faire* capitalism. His theories were interpreted and developed and became the mainstream orthodoxy of macroeconomics. Governments of all parties accepted an explicit responsibility for the maintenance of 'full employment'.

Common misunderstanding

Students sometimes confuse Keynes's ideas with socialism. Keynes was not a socialist. He was a wealthy and respected economist and mathematician from a well-established family. He was a well-known patron of the arts and a member of the 'smart' set of the day. He was a supporter of capitalism and wrote enthusiastically about how market forces brought the 'wonderful fruits of the world' to his table. In keeping with the English tradition of those supported largely by unearned income, he had a distaste for the 'vulgarity of trade'. Indeed, he dreamed of a time when economic necessity had been overcome and society would be dominated and ordered by a ruling class of cultured intellectuals. He was not a supporter of the common ownership of the means of production and certainly was not advocating a command system to replace market forces in order to achieve social and economic equality.

Macroeconomics

In macroeconomics we are concerned with the behaviour of broad aggregates in the economy, e.g. the total level of investment or the volume of employment for the economy as a whole.

In microeconomic theory we are concerned with such things as the determination of the relative wage rates of particular industries, whereas in macroeconomics we are concerned with the general level of wages in the economy. Similarly, a microeconomic view could be used to explain the determination of the relative prices of products, i.e. the price of one product in terms of other products, whereas in macroeconomics we are concerned with the general level of all prices in the economy. Keynes's *General Theory* clearly used a macroeconomic approach.

Keynes and the 'classics'

Most microeconomic theory revolves around the idea of self-regulating markets. The forces of demand and supply reconcile the disparate aims of producers and consumers through the medium of prices. The equilibrium price clears the market, so that there are no unplanned additions to stocks (excess supply) and also no consumers planning to buy at present prices but unable to find a seller (excess demand). It is possible to view the whole economy as being governed by relative prices. This microeconomic view, in which all markets clear, is the general equilibrium theory which we met in Chapter 5. Such ideas of supply and demand equilibrium form the foundations of neo-classical economics in which there is little distinction made between how individual markets function and how the economy as a whole behaves. Keynes argued that the aggregate economy cannot be analysed adequately using microeconomic analysis. Keynes was thus attacking the dominance of neo-classical economics and introducing a new macroeconomic approach for the analysis of economic aggregates.

In fact, early economists (e.g. Smith, Ricardo, Mill and Marx) had used very different approaches to that of neo-classical economics and today these writers would be described as the 'classical' economists. The classical economists used concepts based on social grouping or classes, e.g. workers, capitalists and landlords. They developed theories of instability and of the causes of crisis in capitalist economies. For example, Smith believed that the spread of more efficient techniques would eventually saturate markets so that economic expansion would eventually slow and then cease altogether. Ricardo also had a theory that capitalist expansion would reach a 'stationary state' which set an upper limit to the expansion of capitalism. All this is very different to the harmonious equilibriums of neo-classical economics.

Confusingly then, Keynes was *actually* criticising neo-classical economists and the economics which stemmed from the 1870s 'marginalist revolution' (e.g. Walras, Jevons, Menger and, later, Marshall and Pigou). These neo-classical economists emphasised how market forces act speedily to establish an equilibrium which is efficient and reflects a harmony of interest between freely trading individuals (see Chapters 24 and 25). Class and crisis did not feature in this analysis. Keynes, however, (with typical arrogance) lumped together all economists before him under the title of 'classical' economists.

The neo-classical economists put forward the view that the free enterprise economy will automatically reach an equilibrium where there is no voluntary unemployment.

In this analysis, any unemployment which exists can be only a temporary phenomenon. For example, if there were unemployment there would be an excess supply of labour; this would cause wages to fall and therefore employers would be more willing to employ labour; therefore unemployment would be cured (see Fig. 31.1) Such analysis was used to support *laissez-faire* economic policy and suggested that unemployment was in fact a voluntary condition and hence not really unemployment at all.

A Keynesian view

As explained above, the idea of a self-regulating economy became increasingly untenable during the 1930s when there was chronic mass unemployment. The (neo-)classical view was overturned by Keynes. He argued that equilibrium in the economy was determined by ***aggregate demand*** and ***aggregate supply***. Because these aggregates do not necessarily work in the same way as demand and supply in microeconomics, Keynes argued that it was possible for the economy to be in equilibrium when there was either unemployment or inflation.

According to Keynes the coincidence of the equilibrium level of national income with full employment is a matter of chance.

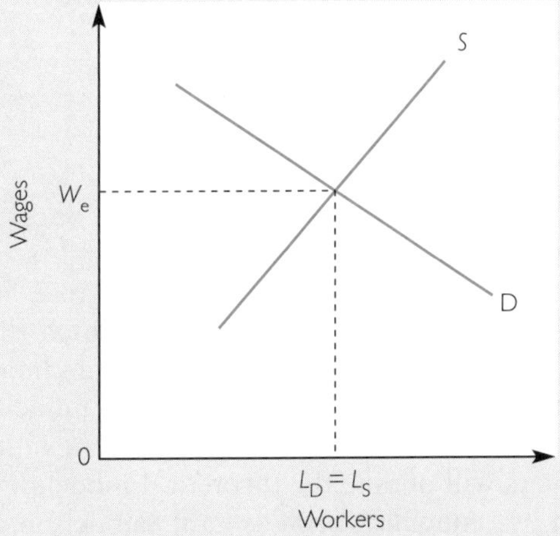

Fig. 31.1 **The (neo-)classical view of employment determination**
In neo-classical analysis the labour market works like any other. Wages adjust until demand equals supply, i.e. anyone who wants to work can.

For example, the neo-classicists argued that lower wages would create more demand for labour. Conversely, Keynes said that, since wages are the largest component of aggregate demand, lower wages would lead to a lower demand for goods. In the face of this falling demand firms would further reduce their demand for labour. Thus employment and production are pushed into a downward spiral.

Thus the equilibrium which results from aggregate demand and supply is not a market clearing equilibrium, i.e. it is possible for there to be unemployed resources, unplanned stocks of goods, or, conversely, excess demand in the form of inflation. If the government were to boost aggregate demand, say by cutting taxes, thereby giving consumers more spending power, retailers would notice a surge of new demand for their products. This would result in new orders being placed with the suppliers of goods and services. Sales and output would rise thereby increasing real national income. To produce this output more labour would be employed.

Keynes argued that since the economy is not self-regulating it is necessary for the government to intervene to regulate aggregate demand in order to ensure a satisfactory level of national income and employment

The fundamental ideas of Keynes

In *The General Theory* Keynes was concerned with putting across fundamental insights into how free market economies may lapse into depression. He suggested ways in which these could be worked into a macroeconomic model, but the technical development of such modelling was left for others to develop. The next four chapters will outline the theoretical model developed by economists such as Paul Samuelson and Sir John Hicks. This simple model became the orthodox way of teaching macroeconomics to whole generations of economists and is still the mainstay of most textbooks even though it has been extended to produce non-Keynesian conclusions. There are, however, many ***Keynesian fundamentalists*** who argue that these technical models do not adequately capture, or at worst distort, Keynes's original ideas. One such school of economists describes itself as ***Post-Keynesian*** (see Chapter 43).

The fundamental insights of Keynes concern uncertainty, expectations, the nature of money, time and movements in quantities rather than prices.

These ideas will now be explained briefly and then you will see how Keynes used them to explain how an economy could be plunged into a depression.

Uncertainty

Neo-classical economics assumes that economic agents possess a great deal of information. For example, firms in perfect competition have perfect knowledge about production techniques, demand, prices and costs. Likewise, consumers possess much information about their income and the relative prices of products. In stark contrast, Keynes emphasised that the real world is an uncertain place. For example, firms cannot be sure about the levels of future demand. Consumers do not know their future income. The risks of a sudden fall in demand or income are simply not known. Prices, costs, exchange rates and interest rates may change unexpectedly.

Uncertainty is everywhere in the real world and this is not well represented by stable demand and supply curves and diagrams of markets in equilibrium.

Expectations

If many things cannot be known with any certainty, then people are more likely to make decisions based on their expectations.

Expectations are often more important in determining behaviour than what might actually be happening.

This is often apparent in stock exchanges where the price movements of stocks and shares may reflect rumours or waves of optimism or pessimism without there being any real change in the underlying economy itself. Indeed, Keynes likened gambling on a stock exchange to betting on a beauty contest: it is not who you think is the most beautiful that matters but who you think most people will regard as most beautiful. In the same way, individual economic agents are likely to be affected by what they think others are thinking. For example, if entrepreneurs come to believe that consumers are going to cut back on spending they may stop investing in new production plants even though current demand is high. If consumers fear a future rise in unemployment they may reduce their spending even though their current income is high.

Keynes called these changes in expectations which have crowd effects changes in 'animal spirits'.

STUDENT ACTIVITY 31.1

Use back copies of newspapers with financial sections, or use a CD-ROM for the *Financial Times*, *Guardian* etc., to locate several articles on sudden or large movements in the prices of company shares as reflected in changes in the level of the 'Footsie' (the FT Stock Exchange Index which maps the prices of the shares of the 100 largest companies). List the reasons given for the changes in share prices and list those reasons that seem to reflect changes in expectations rather than real changes in the economy.

The nature of money

Keynes emphasised the role of money as a ***store of value*** Money does not have to be immediately spent, it can be kept as a store of value to finance future spending. This is because, other than in times of very high inflation, money is a relatively risk-free asset because it is the most ***liquid*** of all assets, i.e. it is the most directly 'spendable' asset one can have. It is relatively risk free because it is unique among assets in being the general ***medium of exchange***, i.e. it is what one generally uses to buy things. In contrast, houses are ***illiquid*** as turning them back into money requires an involved and lengthy selling procedure. Whereas the price of any one asset, such as shares, may fall and the owners may lose wealth before they are able to sell, money is unlikely to lose value suddenly against all things. Thus, by holding money rather than other assets the risk of the 'real' world can be avoided.

Other than in times of very high inflation, money is a relatively safe store of value in an otherwise uncertain world.

Time

In much of neo-classical analysis time is virtually ignored. For example, in a supply and demand diagram there is no account of how long it will take to reach an equilibrium. There is no account of how markets out of equilibrium move through time and what is happening to quantities supplied and demanded during market 'adjustment'. Keynes emphasised that in the real world adjustments *do* take time. Indeed, sometimes the periods are far too long for the *ceteris paribus* assumption to hold.

Keynesian demand and supply interdependence

In criticising the deceptive nature of *ceterus paribus* assumptions, Keynes stressed that quantities may change long before prices have made a full adjustment. For example, an unexpected fall in demand may see many firms unable to pay back the interest on loans and hence go out of business before an equilibrium is reached on the former supply curve. Thus in real time supply curves do not sit passively waiting for demand curves to move along them to a new equilibrium; they may themselves start shifting. Unlike the neo-classical demand and supply analysis you studied in Section II, in Keynesian analysis supply and demand may not be independent of each other. A fall in demand may result in a fall in supply also without prices falling! This is particularly likely with a general fall in demand, i.e. a decrease in aggregate demand. If this is the case the distinction between supply and demand as independent forces in the economy becomes less relevant. For example, supply may follow demand quite passively with quantities changing rather than prices. Although it has now become fashionable in textbooks to represent Keynes's ideas in demand and supply diagrams (see Chapter 35) this does rather distort his ideas.

In neo-classical economics prices adjust quickly to restore equilibrium. In Keynesian economics quantities supplied and demanded may change more quickly than prices. Hence the volume of output and employment may change greatly through time.

Keynesian recession and depression

We can now piece together the above ideas to present a Keynesian explanation as to how the level of economic activity may suddenly fall and then stay low in an economy. Suppose, for example, that a dip in company profits causes investors to expect a fall in the price of company shares. In order to avoid a loss in the value of their shares, shareholders may try to sell them before prices fall. But this selling of the shares may actually cause the price of shares to begin to fall. Confirmed in their expectations, investors attempt to increase their selling. If this process continues until there is panic selling the stock market may crash, i.e. share prices in general start to plummet.

As shares lose their value the wealth of shareholders is greatly reduced. Existing shareholders begin to cut back their consumption and companies find it harder to raise finance for investment as former investors either have less wealth or become more reluctant to part with it. Debtors who have lost wealth become unable to repay their debts and hence both creditors and debtors lose wealth. Again consumption and investment is reduced. Instead of money flowing around the economy as before people begin to hold on to their money, either as insurance again loss of income or to avoid the risks of investing in the real world.

Money is the refuge from uncertainty; liquidity preference is the desire to hold assets in as liquid a form as possible rather than risk investing in capital investment or spending in the face of an uncertain future income.

As investment and consumption fall so aggregate demand falls. Firms thus face a reduced demand for consumption and investment goods. Some firms may cut back on production. Some firms, especially those who have borrowed, become unable to cover their debts or operating costs and hence are wound up, either voluntarily or through legal action. Even firms which have strong financial reserves may be reluctant to invest in new capital investment when demand for their output is falling. In all such cases, however, investment is reduced and workers are laid off. This begins a second round of falling aggregate demand which ***multiplies*** the first falls in aggregate demand.

Faced with falling stock market prices, reduced investment and a rising level of unemployment and business bankruptcies, a wave of pessimism is likely to arise. As gloomy stories about the economy build up it appears riskier than ever to part with money.

A 'retreat into liquidity' may occur, i.e. people and firms hold money in 'idle' money balances rather than spend it or invest it in the real world.

As worsening expectations again multiply the fall in aggregate demand, the recession in the level of economic activity turns a 'collapse' of the economy into depression. The level of output is reduced and millions of previously hardworking people are thrown into unemployment.

STUDENT ACTIVITY 31.2

It is important to note that the initial cause of a reduction in aggregate demand and the sequence of events leading to up to economic recession and depression are not important. The point is that real changes and changes in expectations build up into a vicious circle of falling consumption and investment and rising unemployment and business failure. You should now work through a similar scenario for yourself. Start from an initial fall in confidence in the economy and work your story through to a full-blown depression. (Hint: If you are stuck as to how to begin the story, search back issues of newspapers, or use a CD-ROM, to locate an article on a change in the level of business confidence.)

Government-led recovery

In a Keynesian depression there is no single individual firm or consumer who can break the vicious circle. If workers had jobs they could spend and if consumers were spending firms could sell more and hence take on more workers. If more production were needed firms would begin to invest again and so take on more workers, and so on. But in a Keynesian depression the markets are stuck or 'jammed'. Consumers cannot spend because their income (or expected future income) is low. Firms will not invest because consumers are not even buying up what can be produced within current production capacity. The unemployed cannot get jobs because firms cannot sell and hence they do not need workers. Firms cannot sell because consumers cannot get jobs and hence cannot spend. The economy is thus stuck in depression.

The economist Ben Fine has likened Keynesian recession and depression to people walking round one behind the other in a circle. No one can go faster unless the one in front can also go faster. What is needed is a ringmaster who can crack a whip to speed everybody up simultaneously. Unlike most other economic agents, the government is big enough to act as this ringmaster.

If an individual consumer or firm attempted to increase aggregate demand their spending would be a drop in the ocean. The unemployed consumer could spend all his or her precious savings and see no effect in the job market. Equally, firms may make large capital investments and see no increase in consumption; hence they would fail to sell the extra output and get no return on their investment. The government, however, is different. It is in a position to pour massive amounts of spending into the economy through cutting taxes or increasing its own spending on public sector projects. If all else failed, Keynes argued, it could simply print money to pay the unemployed to dig holes and fill them in again if there was no other way to get money into the economy (Keynes was demonstrating the power of government here rather than making a serious policy suggestion!).

Government 'pump-priming' of the economy

In fact, Keynes suggested that large injections of spending into the economy by the government is unlikely to be necessary. Once the initial effects of increased government-generated spending were felt expectations would begin to pick up again. As consumers and firms began to 'feel good' about economic prospects consumption and investment would begin to rise in a 'virtuous circle'. Hence, in most cases governments would only have to start the process of recovery off, i.e. pump-prime the rise in aggregate demand. Indeed, in an extreme case simply the announcement that the government intended to 'reflate' the economy could spark of such a virtuous circle.

In Keynesian economics mere announcements by the Chancellor of the Exchequer might affect the real economy.

Keynesian trade-off between inflation and unemployment

As noted above, it is quantities rather than prices which adjust during Keynesian recessions. Output and employment fall while prices may fall only slowly, if at all. Conversely, when a return of confidence injects aggregate demand back into the economy employment and output may rise rapidly and hence aggregate demand begin to outpace aggregate supply. When this happens full employment or industrial plant capacity may set an upper limit to the expansion of supply even though demand continues to climb. Thus an excess of aggregate demand over aggregate supply will tend to push prices up. You should now satisfy yourself that you understand the next statement:

Elementary Keynesian theory suggests that there will be an inverse relationship between unemployment and inflation. As unemployment rises inflation will tend to fall or even become negative. When the economy expands output may rise at first but then prices will tend to increase more rapidly as economic capacity is exceeded. See Fig. 31.2.

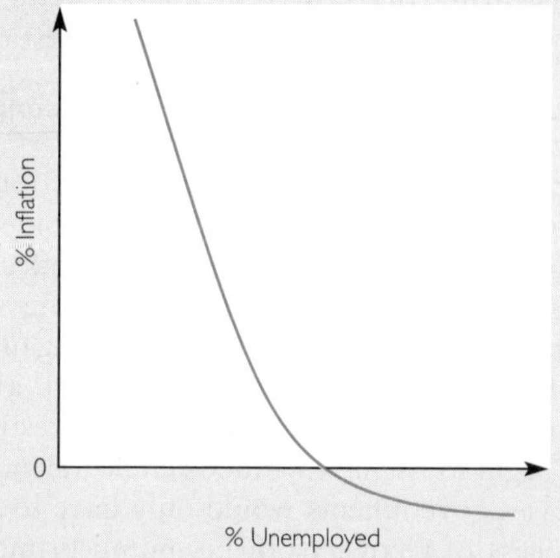

Fig. 31.2 **Keynesian trade-off between inflation and unemployment**

The revival of the neo-classical school

A gathering tide of opinion in economics during the 1960s and 1970s questioned the validity of Keynesian economics. In the USA this was associated with Milton Friedman of the Chicago Business School. The period from the 1950s to the early 1970s had seen a remarkably stable economy and very low unemployment. Perhaps this was not the result of Keynesian policies but in fact capitalist economies were stable after all! Friedman argued that it was a fundamental misunderstanding to believe that governments had to intervene and regulate aggregate demand. This excuse for government intervention had led to a rise in the proportion of government spending as a percentage of the whole economy. Margaret Thatcher later called this 'socialism through the back door'.

In the 1970s inflation and unemployment were rising simultaneously, which appeared to contradict elementary Keynesian theory. The worsening problems of inflation and unemployment and the arguments of Friedman led many politicians to support market-orientated policy prescriptions. These opinions became known as ***monetarism*** (see Chapter 38) because they advocated that governments should do little more than regulate the growth of the money supply. In the UK and USA these policies became associated with the governments of Margaret Thatcher and Ronald Reagan.

Monetarism is, in fact, just one branch of neo-classical economics. In the later 1980s some of the ideas of the monetarists themselves became discredited as it proved extremely difficult to define, let alone control, the money supply. It was also pointed out that the sudden rises in oil prices created by the Organisation of Petroleum Exporting Countries (OPEC) in the 1970s could explain increases in unemployment and inflation without any contradiction of Keynesian theories.

Governments began to take a less dogmatic and more pragmatic approach to macroeconomic policy. Keynesian ideas are now more likely to be used by governments than in the 1980s, but crude attempts to increase employment through boosting aggregate demand are no longer favoured because of the likely inflationary effects. The closer international links between national economies also limit one country's ability to regulate its own domestic demand. Today, a range of ***supply side*** as well as ***demand side*** measures are used and far more attention is now given to external effects such as the balance of trade with other countries and the movement of exchange rates. Nevertheless, Keynesian analysis is widely used by governments and economists today even if the policy prescriptions of Keynes have been greatly modified.

Summary

1 In his book *The General Theory*, Keynes was seeking a solution to the major economic problem of the time, i.e. mass unemployment.

2 Macroeconomics looks at how the economy as a whole and economic aggregates behave rather than using the analysis of individual markets.

3 Keynes was arguing against the economic orthodoxy that free market economies are inherently stable.

4 The fundamental insights of Keynes concern uncertainty, expectations, the nature of money, time and quantity adjustments rather than price movements.

5 Keynesian recessions can occur when pessimistic expectations cause a 'retreat into liquidity'.

6 Keynes argued that otherwise unstable economic forces could be corrected by adjusting government taxation and spending. This became the new orthodoxy of economics and government economic policies.

7 Simultaneously rising unemployment and inflation and the arguments of the monetarists led to a move away from crude Keynesian policies.

Questions

1. What did Keynes identify as an inherent weakness of free market economies and how did he think this could be corrected?
2. How did Keynes explain why the forces of supply and demand in the labour market would not eliminate unemployment?
3. Why was Keynes more concerned with aggregate demand than aggregate supply?
4. Collect evidence on the movements in several economic aggregates for the last 20 years. Does this evidence suggest that capitalist economies are inherently stable or unstable?
5. What difficulties may arise for governments in attempting to use taxation and expenditures to offset fluctuations in aggregate demand?
6. How might a Keynesian government go about tackling inflation?
7. To what extent do you think the government of the day is influenced by Keynesian economic policies?

Data response A
The 'feelgood factor'

Read the following article from the *Daily Mirror* of 30 June 1997 and then answer the questions:

1. Use Keynesian theory to explain the supposed link between the 'feelgood factor' and the rate of business failures.
2. What other explanations might there be for a simultaneous rise in the feelgood factor and a fall in the rate of business failure?

Feelgood factor boost for firms

By Kevin Relly

The number of businesses going bust has fallen to a seven-year low as the feel-good factor continues to boost the economy

Just 19,962 firms went under in the first six months of the year – the lowest total since 1990. It compares with 20,720 in the first half of 1996 and 32,448 in 1993 at the height of the recession.

But experts Dun and Bradstreet say there's still a long way to go to fall back to the 13,760 that crashed in the first half of 1990.

"These figures show that business failures are set on a downward trend," says analyst Philip Mellor.

"But the monthly toll of 3,000-plus is still far too high for comfort and companies need to look constantly over their shoulder."

Drop

The biggest drop came in the East Midlands with the number falling to 980 compared with 1,180 a year ago.

But the neighbouring West Midlands saw an increase in firms collapsing as did Wales.

Source: *Daily Mirror*, 30 June 1997

32 Consumption, savings and investment

Learning outcomes

At the end of this chapter you will be able to:

- Plot simple relationships between aggregate income and aggregate consumption.
- Calculate propensities to consume and save.
- List and explain the determinants of consumption, savings and investment.

Income and consumption

In order to build up a Keynesian model of the economy it is first necessary to know more about consumption, savings and investment. Consumers' expenditure (C) in the UK makes up the largest part of national expenditure, being roughly two-thirds of GDP. Consumption is therefore the most important determinant of the level of national income. Conversely, we shall see that the main determinant of consumption is the level of income. There is, therefore, a 'feedback mechanism' between the two which tends to cause consumption and income to rise together in a ***multiplier*** effect.

Components of consumption

As the country has become wealthier over the years, people have been able to afford a wider range of goods and services. The amount spent on non-durables such as food remains much more constant than that of durables such as cars. It is possible to see changes of demand of up to 25 per cent in a month for cars, whereas this is virtually inconceivable for food. These differing income elasticities for goods cause difficult aggregation problems for economic modelling. Keynes, however, used a very simple relationship whereby aggregate consumption increases in a straightforward way with income.

The consumption function

As income increases, *ceteris paribus*, so does consumption.

Figure 32.1 shows the amount of personal disposable income which has actually been consumed from 1938 to 1995. The 45° line on the

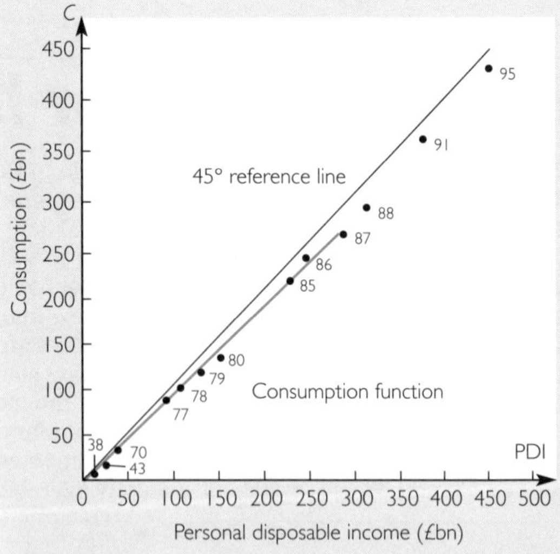

Fig. 32.1 **The consumption function**
This shows the amount of personal disposal income spent (consumed) in the UK in various years from 1938 to 1995. Most years are on or near the line of best fit. The relationship between consumption and income is termed the consumption function.

diagram shows what would happen if all income were consumed. The line of best fit shows that the proportion of income consumed remains reasonably stable from year to year. The relationship between consumption and income is referred to as the consumption function.

To explain the theory of national income we will use a simplified version of the consumption function based on hypothetical data. We will, for the present, ignore foreign trade and government intervention. The figures in Table 32.1 show consumption increasing with income. What is not consumed must be saved and therefore we can calculate savings as:

$$S = Y - C$$

***Table 32.1* A consumption function**

	National income, Y (£bn)	Planned consumption, C (£bn)	Planned savings, S (£bn)
A	0	30	–30
B	30	50	–20
C	60	70	–10
D	90	90	0
E	120	110	10
F	150	130	20
G	180	150	30
H	210	170	40
I	240	190	50
J	270	210	60
K	300	230	70

You can see that, at very low levels of income, consumption is actually greater than income so that savings are a negative figure. This is termed ***dissaving***. This is caused by consumers who have experienced recent falls in income running down their savings or borrowing. We can plot these figures graphically to obtain a picture similar to Fig. 32.1.

Figure 32.2 is constructed from the figures used in Table 32.1. The 45° line simply shows all the points of equality between the two axes; hence mathematically its value may be said to be $E = Y$.

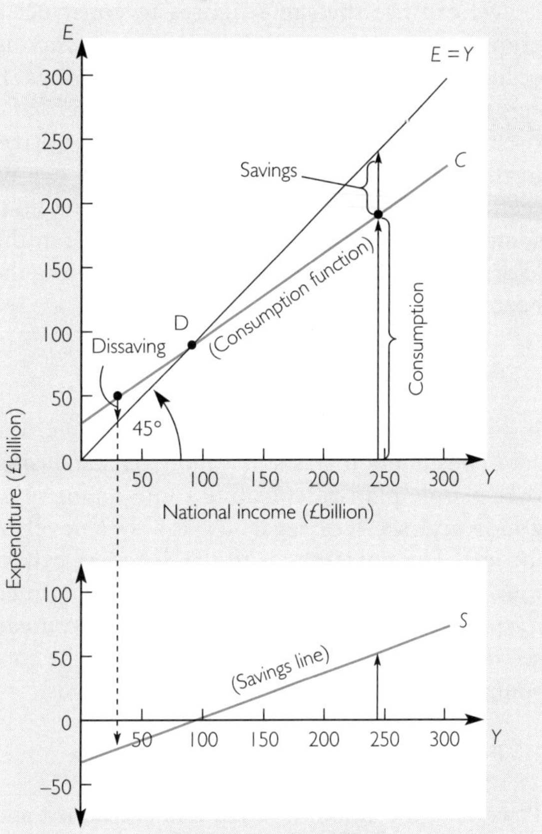

Fig. 32.2 **The consumption function and savings line**

STUDENT ACTIVITY 32.1

The 45° line will be significant later on for the model we are building. It is simply a construction line put there to aid analysis, but it is important that you understand how it works. Make sure you can see why a 45° line maps points on the graph where expenditure would equal income or sketch a graph to prove this.

The consumption function (C) passes through the 45° line at the level of income (£90bn) at which savings are zero. To the right of this point savings are positive while they are negative at lower levels of income.

We can use the same figures to construct a graph to show savings. Now where dissaving occurs the graph is below the horizontal axis. It cuts the axis at £90bn where savings are zero and rises above the axis as savings become positive. In the upper graph savings (or dissaving) can be seen as the vertical distance between the consumption function and the 45° line, while in the lower graph it is the distance above or below the horizontal axis.

Autonomous consumption

In Fig. 32.2 you can see that when income was zero consumption was still £30bn. This indicates that people plan to consume some quantity of goods and services regardless of their level of income. This corresponds to the dissaving behaviour we have already noted. It is termed ***autonomous consumption***. In Fig. 32.3 you can see that it is equal to the height at which the consumption function intersects the vertical axis.

Propensities to consume and to save

If we take the amounts saved and consumed and express them as proportions of income, we arrive at the ***propensities*** to consume and save.

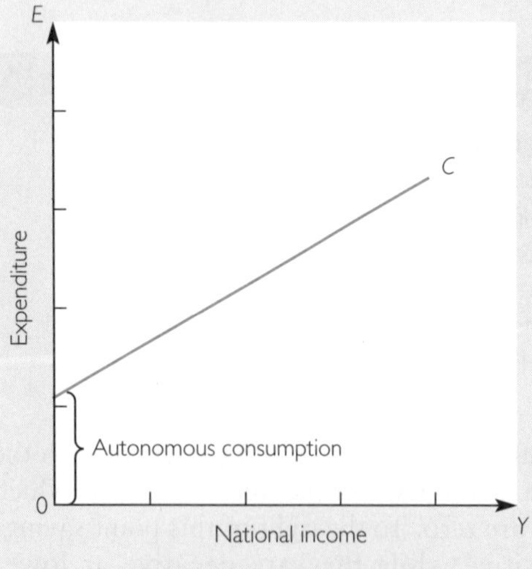

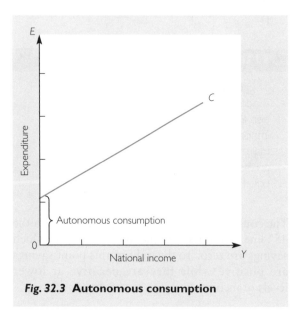

Fig. 32.3 **Autonomous consumption**

In Fig. 32.4 you can see that, of 100 units of income, 10 are saved and 90 are consumed. Thus 9/10 of income is consumed. This is termed the ***average propensity to consume*** (*APC*).

The average propensity to consume (*APC*) is the proportion of income devoted to consumption.

The *APC* is calculated as:

$$APC = C/Y$$

The average propensity to save (*APS*) is the proportion of income devoted to savings.

The *APS* is calculated as:

$$APS = S/Y$$

In the example used in Fig. 32.4 the *APS* is therefore 1/10. It therefore follows that:

$$APC + APS = 1$$

This is always so since 1, here, represents the whole of income, and the whole of income is either consumed or saved.

If national income were to increase, then a proportion of this increase would, similarly, be saved and the rest consumed. In Fig. 32.5 you can see that *Y* has been increased by 10 units and, of these 10 units, 4 have been saved and 6 consumed. You will note that in this particular case a smaller proportion of the additional income is consumed.

The marginal propensity to consume (*MPC*) is the proportion of any addition to income that is devoted to consumption.

The *MPC* may be calculated as the increase in consumption divided by the increase in income:

$$MPC = \Delta C/\Delta Y$$

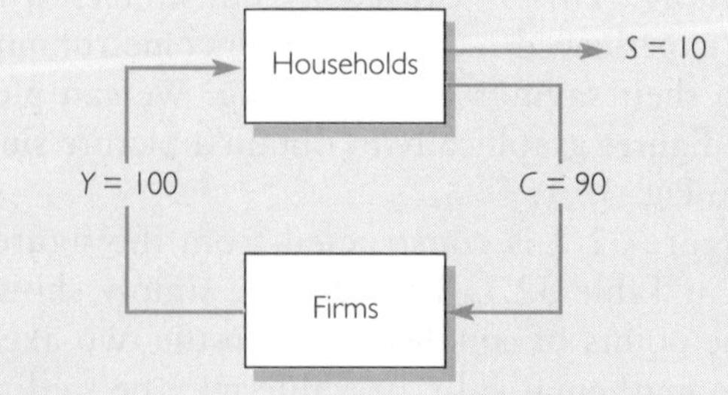

Fig. 32.4

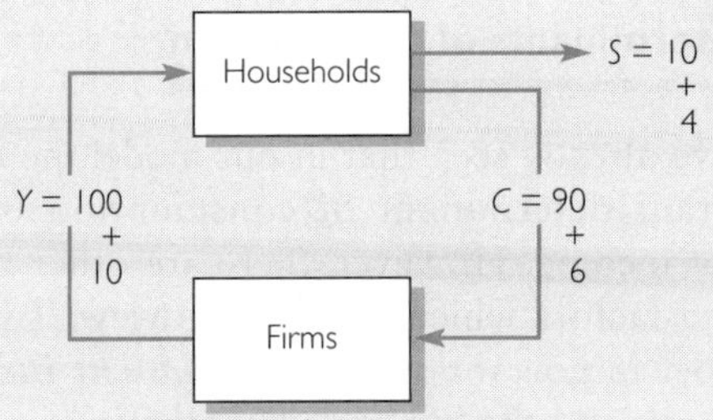

Fig. 32.5

In the example used in Fig. 32.5 it would be:

$MPC = 6/10$

The marginal propensity to save (*MPS*) is the proportion of any addition to income that is devoted to savings.

This could therefore be calculated as:

$MPS = \Delta S/\Delta Y$

In our example it would be:

$MPS = 4/10$

It also follows that:

$MPC + MPS = 1$

because, here, 1 represents the whole of the addition to income. In this theoretical model we assume that *APC* is greater than *MPC*. This is because a greater proportion of income is consumed at lower levels of income.

The *APC*, the *MPC* and the consumption function

Table 32.2 shows the value of the *APC* and *MPC* for various points on a consumption function. As you can see, the *MPC* remains constant as *Y* rises while the *APC* declines. This occurs wherever a consumption function is a straight line, as it is in this case. This may be confirmed by examining Fig. 32.6, which is drawn from these figures.

The *MPC* shows what happens to consumption as income rises. It can therefore be calculated as the slope of the consumption function between any two points. Since the slope of the consumption function is constant, the value

Table 32.2* The *APC* and the *MPC

	National income, Y (£bn)	*Planned consumption, C (£bn)*	*Average propensity to consume, APC*	*Marginal propensity to consume, MPC*
A	0	30	∞	0.66 B
30	50	1.67	0.66	
C	60	70	1.16	0.66
D	90	90	1.0	0.66
E	120	110	0.92	0.66
F	150	130	0.87	0.66
G	180	150	0.84	0.66
H	210	170	0.81	0.66
I	240	190	0.79	0.66
J	270	210	0.78	0.66
K	300	230	0.77	0.66

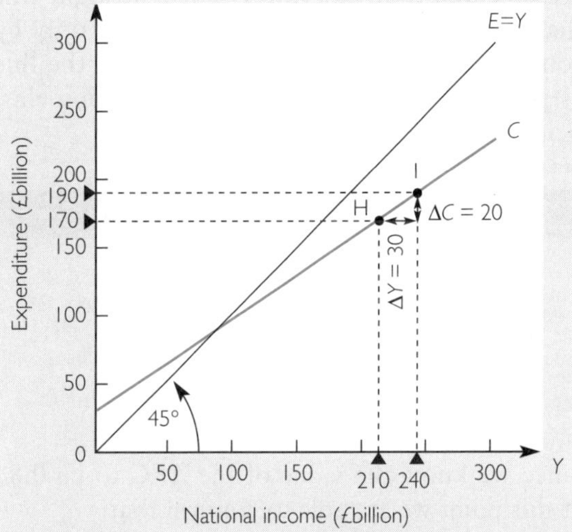

Fig. 32.6* The *APC* and the *MPC

The *APC* can be calculated from any point on the *C* line, e.g. at point H:

$$APC = \frac{170}{210}$$

whereas the *MPC* is the slope of the line between two points, e.g. between points H and I:

$$MPC = \frac{20}{30}$$

of the *MPC* is constant in this example. Examine the slope of the *C* line between points H and I and you will find that income increases by £30bn while consumption increases by £20bn. Therefore we have:

$$MPC = \Delta C/\Delta Y$$
$$MPC = 20/30$$
$$MPC = 0.66$$

The value of the *APC* can be taken from any point on the line. For example, at point H:

$$APC = C/Y = 170/210 = 0.81$$

We can therefore conclude that the coordinates at any point on a consumption function give us the value of the *APC*, while the slope between any two points will give us the value of the *MPC*. If we are calculating the value of the *MPC* and the consumption function is not a straight line then we will obtain an accurate answer only by considering as small a movement along the line as possible (cf. the problems of calculating elasticity in Chapter 10).

STUDENT ACTIVITY 32.2

A little work with the figures in Table 32.2 should enable you to calculate the *APS*. For example, satisfy yourself that at point H, *APS* = 0.19.

Since we know the value of the *APC* to be 0.81 at this point we are able to confirm that:

$$APS + APC = 1$$

This remains true even when the *APC* is greater than one because under these circumstances the value of the *APS* becomes negative.

STUDENT ACTIVITY 32.3

Confirm from Table 32.2 that *MPC* + *MPS* = 1.

Determinants of consumption

We have already seen that in our model the most important determinant of consumption is the level of income. However, there are other theories and factors which modify this view. Two of the most important are the ***permanent income hypothesis*** and ***the life-cycle hypothesis.***

The permanent income and life-cycle hypotheses

The hypothesis is that people, in the short run, hold an estimation of their permanent income level. If their income were suddenly to increase (or decrease) they would, in the short run, go on spending roughly the same amount because they regard the change as only temporary. Thus a cross-sectional analysis of household incomes would reveal much greater variations in short-term than in long-term propensities to consume.

The permanent income hypothesis is primarily associated with Milton Friedman. An alternative formulation is that of the life-cycle hypothesis formulated by Professors Modigliani, Ando and Brumberg. In the life-cycle hypothesis households are supposed to formulate their expenditure plans in relationship to their expected lifetimes' earnings.

Both formulations attempt to explain the observed variation of actual expenditure patterns from the predicted pattern if expenditure was entirely determined by disposable income levels. Modern econometric models of the economy usually divide consumption (*C*) into two components: one element is set to vary with the level of disposable income while the other element is not, i.e. it is regarded as autonomous income.

When we consider these theories it brings into question our original proposition that *APC* declines as income rises. We can now see, and observation confirms this, that consumption and savings may be subject to considerable fluctuation, at least in the short run. However, regarded in the long run, there is greater stability.

Other determinants

a) *The distribution of income.* Income remains very unequally distributed and different income groups have different *MPC*s. Understandably the *MPC* of lower-income groups tends to be much higher than that of the very rich. A movement to a more even distribution of income should therefore lead to a higher *MPC* for the economy as a whole.
b) *Consumers' expectations.* Consumers' spending now is influenced by their expectations of the future. Three main factors we might mention are their expectations of inflation, unemployment and income.
c) *Cost and availability of credit.* Since many goods, especially consumer durables, are bought with the aid of hire purchase or other forms of credit, the terms on which these are available and their cost must have an effect upon the level of consumer demand. A rise in general interest rates will thus tend to decrease consumption.
d) *Wealth and savings.* Since purchases can be made not only out of current income but also from consumers' assets and savings, the quantity of these can influence consumption. For example, those with savings may be more willing to maintain their level of consumption in the face of falling income. It is also argued that those with a cushion of savings are more willing to spend a greater proportion of their income.

Shifts and movements

If the level of national income increases then we would expect to see a movement along the consumption function to a higher level of consumption. Thus, a change in the level of income need have no effect upon the *MPC*. However, if one of the determinants of consumption changes, such as the availability of credit, this might be expected to lead to a change to a new level of consumption at the same level of income, so that we will have shifted to a new consumption function above or below the old one. We will also have moved to a different propensity to consume.

Savings

Savings are money not spent; they are a withdrawal from the circular flow of income. The most usual formulation of savings is that they are the proportion of personal disposable income that is not consumed. Thus, savings are seen as being undertaken only by households. However, as stated in the previous chapter, savings might be undertaken by firms and even by the government. For most of this section of the chapter we will concentrate on household savings; indeed it is the usual pattern for firms and government to be dissavers (borrowers) rather than savers. (See page 423 for other sectors of economy.)

Savings, income and consumption

We have examined the determinants of consumption and discovered that the most significant factor is the level of income. Since savings are defined as income not spent we have, therefore, considered the most significant influence upon savings. It would follow, therefore, that as income increases savings will tend to increase both as a total figure and as a proportion of income. There are, however, many other influences which can disturb this relationship.

Motives for saving

Given the income to do so, there are many reasons people save. The motives also are often not closely related to current economic circumstances although high rates of inflation or unemployment will alter people's saving habits.

Some of the most important motives are listed below.

a) *Deferred purchase.* This is saving up to buy something in the future such as a car, a house or a holiday.
b) *Contractual obligations.* The most significant form of contractual saving is life and pension assurance premiums. Contractual savings form a very significant share of all personal savings.
c) *Precautionary motives.* Most people will, if they can, put some money by for a 'rainy day'.

d) *Habits and customs*. Some people and societies save more than others out of habit. This is, internationally, an important determinant of savings.
e) *Age*. People tend to save and dissave at different times of their life. For example, many young people will be borrowing for house purchase while older people will be saving for their retirement.
f) *Taxation*. Saving may also be significantly affected by taxation policy towards savings. If, for example, people are able to gain tax relief on assurance premiums this will encourage them to save.
g) *Expectations*. As Keynes emphasised (see Chapter 31) expectations of the future economic situation can also be a significant factor.

Savings and the rate of interest

The view of the classical economists was that the amount of savings was determined by the rate of interest, i.e. a rise in the rate of interest would call forth more savings. However, as we have just seen, there are many non-economic reasons for saving. This was well demonstrated during the 1970s when, in many years, the real interest rate was negative but people saved significantly more!

The real interest rate is arrived at by subtracting the rate of inflation from the rate of interest.

Thus, if, for example, the interest rate was 10 per cent and inflation was running at 15 per cent, the real rate of interest would be –5 per cent; anyone who saved £100 would, at the end of the year, have purchasing power equal to only £95 in real terms. (See Chapter 7)

This is not to say that interest rates have no effect. High rates of interest may encourage savings while low rates will discourage them. It would appear, however, that other motives, such as deferred purchase and expectations, are more important. Differences in rates of interest between financial institutions, however, have a significant effect upon the type of savings which take place.

The savings ratio

A common measure of the amount of savings taking place is the ***savings ratio***. This is the amount of savings expressed as a percentage of personal disposable income (PDI). It is thus very similar to *APS* except that it is expressed as a percentage.

During the depression of the 1930s the savings ratio was very low as people had to draw on their savings to get by. In the USA in the same period the savings ratio was actually negative. During the Second World War the savings ratio shot up as people were encouraged to lend to the government to help the war effort. After the war the ratio returned to a more normal 45 per cent. During the 1960s the ratio gradually rose to 9.3 per cent in 1970. From 1973 onwards the ratio began a rapid rise to 14.2 per cent in 1980. However, by 1990 it had fallen back to 8.5 per cent.

This rise in the savings ratio in the UK during the 1970s is in need of some explanation. It may appear entirely consistent with the rapid rise in income during the 1970s, but this was mainly a rise in nominal income attributable to high rates of inflation. Apart from the early years of the decade real income was growing very slowly and in some years actually fell. We must also consider that high rates of inflation might be expected to discourage thrift since inflation devalues savings. Both these factors therefore argue against a rise in the savings ratio.

How then do we account for the observed increase in the savings ratio and decline in the *APC*? The following are given as possible reasons.

a) The volatility of incomes made people uncertain about their future incomes and therefore inclined to save more.
b) Unemployment also made people uncertain and more likely to increase their precautionary savings. Unspent redundancy money may also have increased savings.
c) Inflation also had an effect by increasing uncertainty. Because inflation devalues savings many people were led to save more to ensure that they had sufficient stocks of money wealth.

The fall in the savings ratio in the personal sector in the 1980s can be attributed to a number of factors:

a) The decline in inflation.
b) Younger people tend to save less and borrow more. During this period the proportion of people in their twenties and early thirties increased.
c) Privatisation meant that private individuals transferred money to the public sector in return for shares. Remember that the ownership of shares is not savings in the macroeconomics sense.
d) The high rates of inflation in the 1970s and early 1980s meant that, despite the large increase in the savings ratio as a proportion of nominal PDI, the real value of savings declined. Lower rates of inflation meant that despite lower savings ratios the value of real savings increased.
e) Some of the changes in household savings were offset by changes in business and public savings. For example, the proceeds from privatisation led to increased government savings.

Savings ratios differ considerably from country to country. In 1990, while the savings ratio in the UK was 8.6 per cent, in the USA it was only 4.6 per cent while in Japan it was 14.3 per cent. These differences, which are a result of the different structures and habits in the economy, result in considerable variation in the way industry is financed.

Discretionary and contractual savings

Personal savings may be divided into contractual savings and discretionary savings.

Contractual savings are those where a person contracts to save a certain amount per month. The most significant forms of contractual savings are life assurance and superannuation and pension schemes. Discretionary savings are all other forms of savings where people are not obliged to save a specific amount. The most significant forms of discretionary savings are building society deposits, bank deposits and lending to the government.

Figure 32.7 shows the trends in saving for the personal, business, overseas and public sectors since 1989.

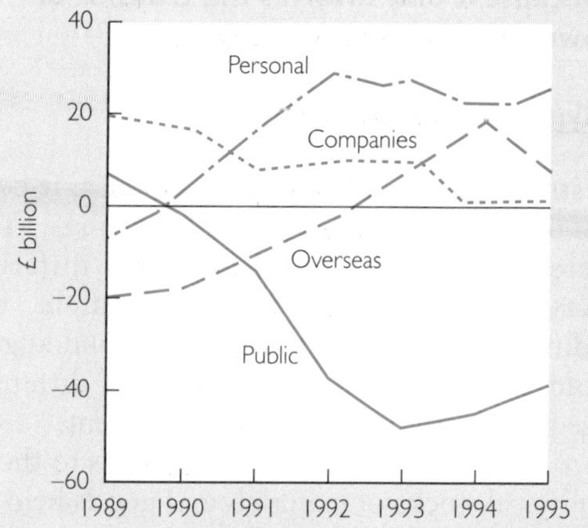

Fig. 32.7 **Financial balances**
Source: National Income and Expenditure 'Blue Book', 1997

STUDENT ACTIVITY 32.4

Explain why the financial balances shown in Fig. 32.7 must in total equal zero.

Other sectors of the economy

It is possible for sectors of the economy other than households to save; companies, for example, can save by not distributing all the profits. It is often the case that large surpluses in the personal sector are balanced by deficits in the other sectors. Overall the total of the surpluses will exactly match that of the deficits. This may be confirmed by examining Fig. 32.7.

Investment

Investment is both an important component and determinant of the level of national income. When we use the term investment in this context it refers exclusively to the acquisition of new physical capital such as buildings and machines. It is in this sense that we can describe investment as an addition, or an injection, to the circular flow of income.

'Investment' on the Stock Exchange, or in government bonds, is not investment as the term is used in macroeconomics

because it only involves the transfer of ownership of pieces of paper.

Types of investment

Investment is not a homogeneous mass; it consists of many different types of things. The different types of investment have differing effects upon the economy; for example, the building of a new oil terminal and the building of an old people's home will have very different consequences, though both are investment.

a) *Stocks (or inventories).* Net additions to the physical stocks of materials and goods held by businesses are counted as investment. They are the most volatile component of investment, being subject to change in response to changes or expected changes in the level of national income. It is possible for the change in stocks to be either positive or negative.
b) *Fixed capital.* All investment other than stocks is termed fixed capital formation. The 'Blue Book' divides fixed capital formation into the five categories shown in the right-hand column of Fig. 32.8. As you can see, construction of housing is included in investment even though it might be more accurate to describe houses as consumer durables. As was explained in Chapter 7, much investment is to replace worn-out capital. We would have to subtract capital consumption from gross fixed capital formation to give us the net addition to fixed capital stock of the country.

Savings and investment

As was explained in the previous chapter, national income accounting conventions ensure that realised saving will always equal realised investment. The equality between these two components is demonstrated in Fig. 32.8. The first column shows the gross savings carried on by different sectors of the economy. The investment is shown in the middle column. It will be noted that the savings column is exactly equal to the

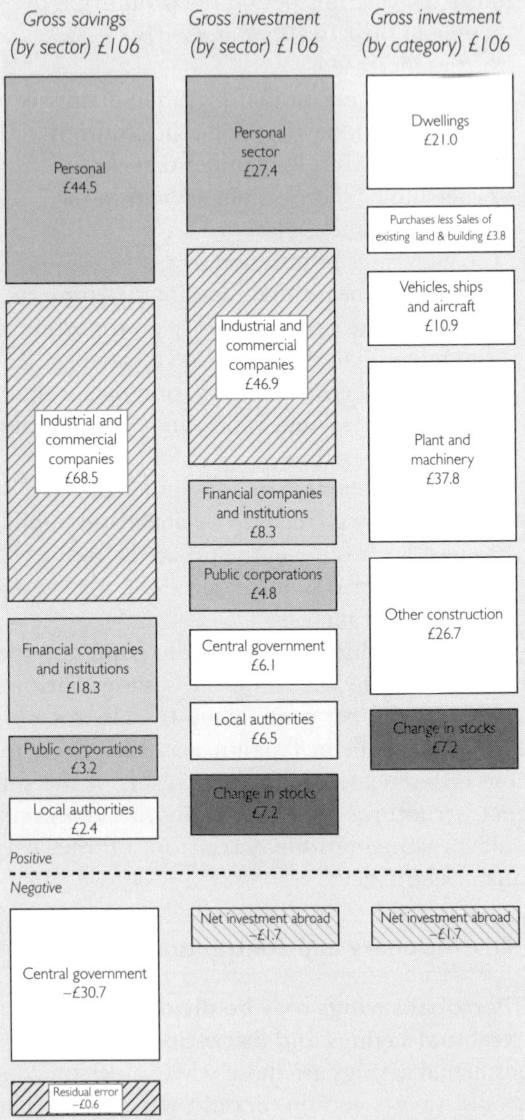

Fig. 32.8 **Savings and investments in the UK economy, 1995**
Gross savings are equal to gross fixed capital formation together with the value of the physical increase or decrease in stocks. Each column (+) and (−) totals £106bn. All figures in the diagram are in £bn.
Source: UK National Accounts, HMSO

investment column. It is possible for the change in stocks to be negative, in which case this would be referred to as destocking and would have to be subtracted from the total for investment. The item 'Net investment abroad' is equivalent to the overseas sector's financial deficit or surplus.

As you can see, most savings come from the personal sector (households) and from the industrial and commercial sector (firms). When we turn to the investment column it can be seen that the private sector (households and firms) is also responsible for the bulk of investment. The fluctuation in the volume of stocks brings savings and investment into equality. If, for example, savings were to increase suddenly, consumption would fall. This would mean that investment would be rising to keep pace with savings. If you are not sure of this point re-read Chapter 7.

Determinants of investment

Autonomous and induced investment

When we turn to look at the factors which determine investment it is useful to make a distinction between autonomous and induced investment. When we were looking at the determinants of savings we saw that an increase in the level of income was quite likely to induce an increase in saving. Thus the saving had been brought about by a variable (Y) within the model of the economy we are developing. Similarly, investment which is brought about by changes in the level of income may be termed ***induced investment***, i.e. investment which is brought about by a factor which is endogenous to (within) the theory. However, much investment is not brought about in this manner. Consider what might happen to a new invention, e.g. 3D television. It is quite likely that firms would go ahead and invest in such a development but there need have been no prior change in income or any other variable within our theory of the economy. Thus the investment would be brought about by something outside or exogenous to the system. Such investment may be termed autonomous.

We normally reserve the term induced investment for that investment associated with the ***accelerator principle***, i.e. the relationship between investment and the rate of change of aggregate demand. All other types of investment may be termed autonomous. In practice one may be very hard to disentangle from the other.

Investment and the rate of interest

A detailed discussion of individual investment decisions and the rate of interest is included in Chapter 22. Here we are concerned with the relationship between the rate of interest and the aggregate level of investment within the economy.

It seems reasonable to assume that firms make the decision to invest on the expectation of making a gain. This we may contrast with the decision to save where, as we saw earlier in the chapter, households will save even if it involves economic loss. Most decisions to invest involve borrowing money and there should therefore be some relationship between the cost of borrowing and the amount of investment taking place.

There is a relationship between the rate of interest and the capital stock which people will wish to hold. This is illustrated in Fig. 32.9, which shows an *MEC* (marginal efficiency of capital) curve. The *MEC* relates the desired stock of capital to the rate of return (yield) an addi-

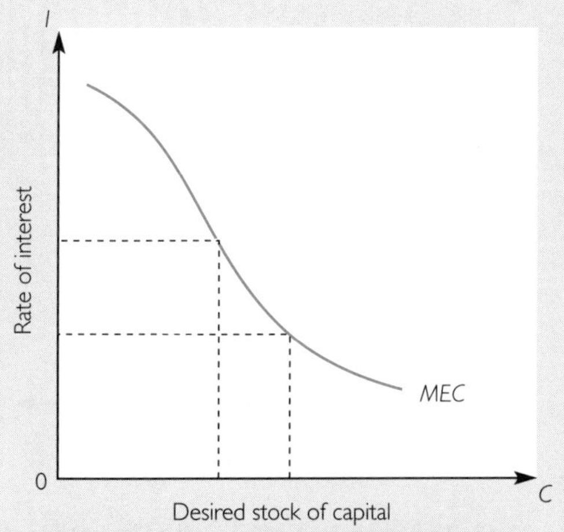

Fig. 32.9 **The marginal efficiency of capital**
A fall in the rate of interest increases the size of the desired stock of capital.

tional unit of capital will produce. The yield is related to the rate of interest. Suppose, for example, that a capital project were to yield 10 per cent; if the rate of interest were 12 per cent investors would not be interested in it. However, were interest to fall to 8 per cent, investors might wish to invest. The capital stock they desire would have increased.

Marginal efficiency of investment

While the *MEC* shows the relationship between the rate of interest and the *desired* stock of capital, the marginal efficiency of investment (*MEI*) shows the relationship between the rate of interest and the *actual* rate of investment per year.

MEC is concerned with a stock while MEI is concerned with a flow.

There will be important differences between the capital stock people desire and the capital investment that takes place. This is because there are physical constraints upon the construction of capital.

Figure 32.10 shows two possibilities for *MEI*. With both we show the effect of dropping the interest rate from 14 per cent to 7.5 per cent. If the curve is relatively flat (MEI_2) then the rate of investment increases substantially from £18bn to £30bn, but if the curve is steep (MEI_1) then there is only a small response and the rate of investment increases from £18bn to £21bn.

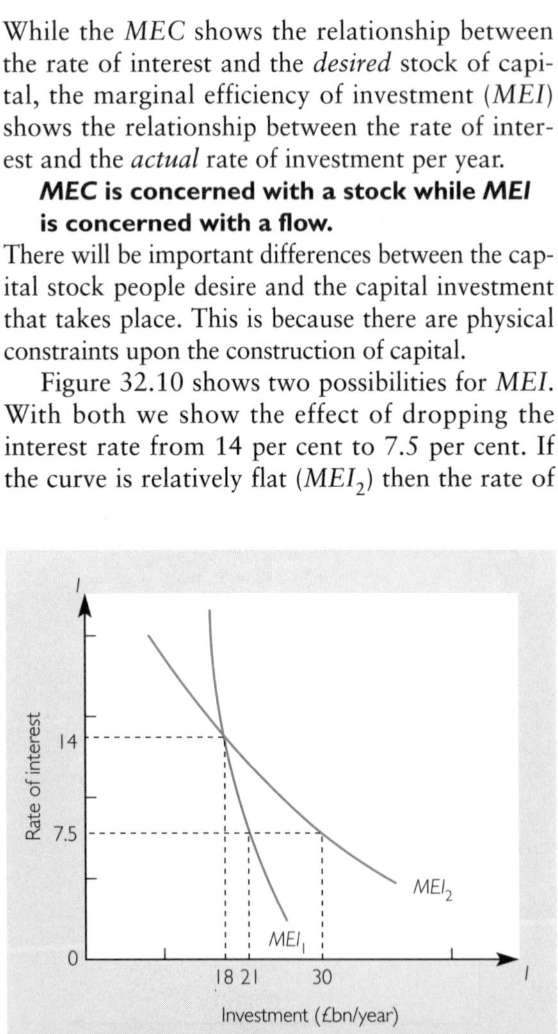

Fig. 32.10 **The marginal efficiency of investment**
A fall in the rate of interest brings about more investment; how much more depends on the slope of the *MEI* line.

The *MEI* reflects the inelasticity of investment.

It would be theoretically possible for the *MEI* line to be vertical, in which case there would be no relationship between investment and the rate of interest. This would be a very extreme view; most economists today believe that there is a relationship, even if it is difficult to plot. There are, however, other factors to consider

Business expectations

The classical view of investment was that if a scheme yielded 11 per cent and interest was 10 per cent, investment would take place. However, we cannot see into the future to be able to judge the profitability of a scheme with such accuracy, nor can we tell whether or not circumstances will change. Because investment decisions take time to accomplish, there may be a great deal of uncertainty about them. Thus what businesses expect to happen in the future is very important. If they are pessimistic about the future, low rates of interest will not encourage them to borrow, whereas if they are optimistic, high rates will not necessarily discourage them.

The level of income

A high level of national income appears to stimulate investment. One reason for this is that it has an effect upon business expectations, i.e. high levels of income tend to make businesses optimistic about the future. Second, a high level of income could mean high profits and therefore businesses have more funds with which to invest. This latter argument is presuming that ploughed-back profits are more significant than borrowed funds. While this has often been so, in recent years borrowed funds have assumed increasing importance.

There is much disagreement about whether or not the level of income determines the level of investment.

Many economists would reverse the causality of the relationship and say that high levels of investment cause high levels of income. Whichever way round it is, high levels of income are certainly associated with high levels of investment.

The government and investment

The government has a very significant effect upon investment, both indirectly through its policies and directly as the largest investor in the economy. Investment decisions by businesses are influenced by government taxation policies, which may give incentives to investments, and by monetary policy, which plays a significant role in determining interest rates.

There is evidence that public and private investment tend to counterbalance each other, public investment being high when private investment is low and vice versa. It can be argued that this is the government deliberately trying to stabilise the level of total investment, or, conversely, that public investment 'crowds out' private investment from time to time and thus depresses it.

Induced investment: the accelerator

We have already considered the level of income as a determinant of investment:

The accelerator theory maintains that the rate of change of national income will determine the level of new investment.

The accelerator hypothesis assumes that it is the size of the capital stock in relation to national income that is the object of decision making. In its simplest form the accelerator hypothesis assumes that firms seek to maintain a constant capital to output ratio. Investment is thus reduced to behaviour which seeks to change the capital–output ratio if it is not at the desired level.

The capital stock of the nation is several times greater than national income. We may say, therefore, that it takes several pounds of capital to produce £1 of output. For example, say that it takes £3 of capital to produce £1 of output (i.e. the capital–output ratio is 3:1). If total demand in the economy were to rise then, in order to meet the new demand, £3 of capital equipment would have to be built to meet each £1 of new demand. Conversely, if national income were to fall investment could possibly fall to zero if the capital stock is greater than that desired for that particular level of income.

The accelerator hypothesis predicts that it is the rate of change of income rather than its level which determines investment.

In the appendix to this chapter several possible offsetting factors are discussed which make the accelerator effect a matter of some dispute among economists. Nevertheless, although not invented by Keynes himself, the hypothesis accords with his view that the aggregate demand of the private sector is subject to fluctuations which can have a destabilising effect on the economy (see Chapters 33 and 34).

Postscript on investment

There are important theoretical differences between Keynes and the classical economists, and the monetarists and neo-classicists, about interest, investment and income. We cannot go into these fully until we have had a closer look at income determination and monetary theory. We may simply note here that the classicists placed a much greater importance on the rate of interest than we do today. As you have seen in this section of the chapter, we have argued that investment might also be determined by factors as diverse as government policy and expectations in general.

Summary

1 The consumption function is the relationship between consumption and income. Generally speaking the proportion of income consumed declines as income rises.
2 The *APS* and *APC* show the proportions of income which are devoted to savings and consumption respectively. The *MPS* and *MPC* show the proportions of any increase in income which are devoted to savings and consumption.
3 A rise in income will bring about a movement along the *C* line while a change in the other determinants of consumption will cause a shift to a new *C* line.
4 Saving is a withdrawal from the circular flow of income. It is related to the level of *Y* and is

motivated by a number of non-economic factors such as habit and age. There is no clearly defined relationship between S and the rate of interest; people will save even when real interest is negative. Savings may be divided into contractual and discretionary. Contractual savings are the more stable.

5 Savings may be undertaken by any sector of the economy. Overall there is a balance between the financial deficits and surpluses of the various sectors.
6 Investment is an injection to the circular flow of income and consists of additions to the real physical stock of capital. There is an equality between realised savings and realised investment.
7 Autonomous investment is determined by exogenous factors such as business expectations. Induced investment is brought about by the rate of change of *Y*.

Questions

1 What reasons can be advanced to explain the observed variations in the propensity to consume in Fig. 32.1? How do you think this diagram would differ if there were no inflation?
2 Does the information contained in Fig. 32.7 support the permanent income hypothesis? Give reasons for your answer.
3 We have spoken of induced and autonomous investment. How far would it be true to speak of induced and autonomous savings?
4 Consider Fig. 32.10. What would be the significance of a vertical *MEI* curve?
5 Prepare a table to compare the percentage of GDP devoted to gross fixed capital formation of four different countries with which you are familiar, e.g. the UK, the USA, Nigeria and Malaysia. Suggest reasons for the observed differences.
6 Examine the role of interest in determining savings and investment.
7 What factors determine investment in a modern economy?
8 What are the determinants of aggregate private investment and why is it likely to fluctuate?
9 In a closed economy with no government intervention:

$$C = 50 + 0.85Y$$

Autonomous investment is constant at 60 units. Induced investment is $I = 0.05Y$ for all levels of Y. At what level of Y will $S = I$? Suppose that autonomous investment were to increase to 80 units. At what level of Y would $S = I$?

Appendix: the accelerator

A model of the accelerator

To explain the working of the accelerator we will use the model of a very simplified economy. In this economy the initial capital stock is valued at £200m. When fully employed, this stock is just adequate to produce the £100m of goods which constitute the aggregate demand (*Y*) in the economy for a year, i.e. there is a capital–output ratio of 2:1, which means that a capital stock of £2 is necessary to produce a flow of output of £1. The capital in this economy has a life of five years and is replaced evenly so that a replacement investment of £40m per year is needed to maintain the capital stock.

Aggregate demand (*Y*)	Capital stock required
£100m	£200m
Replacement	Investment required net
£40m	0

Suppose now that aggregate demand were to rise by 20 per cent to £120m. This would mean that to meet this demand a capital stock of £240m is required. If demand were to be met the following year it would mean that the economy's demand for capital will now be £80m, i.e. £40m for replacement and £40m to meet the new demand. We can summarise it thus:

Aggregate demand (*Y*)	Capital required
£120m	£240
Replacement	Investment required net
£40m	£40m

Thus, between the first and second years a rise of 20 per cent in aggregate demand has brought about a 100 per cent rise in investment demand. This is an illustration of the accelerator principle.

The accelerator (a) is concerned with new (or net) investment demand. In our example £40m of the new investment is necessary to meet a rise in Y of £20m. This is because it takes £2 of capital equipment to produce £1 of output per year. From this we can derive a formula for the accelerator effect which is:

$$I_N = a\Delta Y$$

I_N is the new investment, a is the accelerator coefficient (the capital–output ratio, in this case 2) and ΔY is the change in income. Thus in our example we have:

$$I_N = 2 \times £20\text{m} \\ = £40\text{m}$$

To explain the accelerator more fully we need to follow our example through several time periods. This is done in Table 32.3.

Table 32.3 **A model of the economy (capital–output ratio = 2, capital is replaced over a five-year period)**

Year	*Aggregate demand, Y (£m)*	*Capital stock required (£m)*	*Replacement*	*Investment (£m) Net*	*Total*
(1)	*(2)*	*(3)*	*(4)*	*(5)*	*(6)*
1	100	200	40	–	40
2	120	240	40	40	80
3	130	260	40	20	60
4	140	280	40	20	60
5	120	240	–	–	–
6	120	240	40	–	40

Years 1 and 2 in Table 32.3 recapitulate our example. Now assume that in year 3 demand rises to £130m. The capital stock required is now £260m. Therefore there will be a demand for £20m of extra capital but the total demand for capital will have fallen. The capital demand is now £40m for replacement and £20m for new capital. The £40m of extra capital last year will not need replacing for a further five years. Therefore, although aggregate demand is still rising, capital demand has fallen. This is because when the rate of increase of aggregate demand falls, the absolute level of induced investment will decline. You can confirm this by applying the formula.

Further implications of the principle can be observed between years 3 and 4, where the demand for capital is constant because the rate of increase is the same as between years 2 and 3 (remember the increase is ΔY not $\Delta Y/Y$). Between years 4 and 5 aggregate demand drops from £140m to £120m and the capital stock required, therefore, decreases from £280m to £240m. What new investment is required?

If we apply the formula we get:

$$I_N = 2 \times (-£20\text{m}) \\ = -£40\text{m}$$

There is therefore no need to replace the £40m of capital stock which has worn out. In this case it has therefore completely eliminated the need for replacement investment.

Finally, in year 6 demand has stabilised at £120m. The formula predicts that there will be no demand for new capital. However, it is necessary to replace the £40m of capital stock which will have worn out.

The accelerator (*a*) links the rate of change of aggregate demand to the level of new investment demand.

Factors modifying the accelerator

When we look for evidence of the accelerator in the economy we do indeed find that fluctuations in the level of investment demand are significantly greater than those in aggregate demand. But:

a) they are much smaller fluctuations than those predicted by the theory;
b) it is very difficult to demonstrate any mathematical relationship between the two.

This does not necessarily mean that the theory is therefore wrong. It could be that a number of factors modify the accelerator and, therefore, mask the effect. Some of these are listed below:

a) *Businesses learn from experience.* This means that they are unlikely to double their capacity on the strength of one year's orders. Conversely, if demand is dropping, they might be willing to increase their inventories against a rise in demand in subsequent years.

b) *Capital–output ratios.* These are not as constant as suggested by our example. If demand rose it might be possible to obtain more output from the existing capital stock by varying other factors of production. For example, the workforce might undertake shift work or overtime to meet the extra demand.

c) *Depreciation.* The replacement of the capital stock may be a function of factors other than time. In our example it was assumed that capital wore out after five years. If there was an increase in demand it might be possible to continue using old capital equipment after was it planned to scrap it. Often the period over which capital is depreciated is an accounting convenience and does not correspond to the physical life of the capital. Conversely, capital may be obsolete before it has physically depreciated.

d) *Other investment.* It should be recalled that the accelerator applies only to net or new investment resulting from changes in Y. There are other forms of investment such as replacement investment and investment in new techniques.

e) *Time lag.* New capacity cannot be created immediately after a rise in demand, since plant and machinery take time to build. Also, the time lags will vary depending on the nature of the capital we are considering. We are thus concerned with a distributed time lag. Thus, much more sophisticated mathematics will be needed to measure the effects.

f) *Capacity.* The operation of the accelerator depends upon the economy being at or near full capacity, otherwise the new demand would be coped with by existing plants expanding their output. However, in apparent contradiction to this, there must be surplus resources (labour, land, etc.) with which to construct the capital equipment.

All these factors make it very difficult for us to observe the accelerator effect in any simple manner.

Questions on the accelerator

1 Draw up a table to show the annual percentage change in GDP and the annual percentage in gross fixed capital formation and net capital formation for each year in the last decade. Use this as information to argue a case for the existence of the accelerator.

2 Reconstruct Table 32.3 assuming that the capital–output ratio is now 3:1 (columns (1) and (2) will be unchanged).

Data response A
What determines consumption?

Study the figures in Table 32.4 relating to income, savings and inflation in the UK. The income figures refer to personal disposable income, i.e. the income of individuals after allowing for deduction of income tax and national insurance contributions. The savings referred to are those of the personal sector.

Table 32.4 **Income, savings and inflation in the UK**

Year	*Personal disposable income (£m)*	*Savings (£m)*	*Consumer price percentage change from previous year (%)*
1979	136 152	17 257	13.4
1980	160 735	22 405	18.0
1981	177 594	23 360	11.9
1982	192 614	23 609	8.6
1983	207 457	22 774	4.6
1984	223 092	26 264	5.0
1985	241 362	25 627	6.1
1986	263 448	23 516	3.4
1987	284 483	20 914	4.1
1988	315 787	19 304	4.9
1989	352 097	26 174	7.8
1990	378 325	30 798	9.4
1991	405 831	40 859	5.9
1992	434 854	53 139	3.8
1993	457 450	51 988	1.6
1994	472 574	44 490	2.5

Source: *UK National Accounts*, HMSO, *Monthly Digest of Statistics*, HMSO, and *Economics Trends Annual Supplement*,

1 Using graph paper, construct a consumption function for the UK economy based on this data.

2 Determine the marginal propensity to consume (*MPC*) and the average propensity to save (*APS*)

for the years 1980, 1985, 1989 and 1993. Explain how you arrived at your answers.

3 How would you account for the observed variations in the size of the APC?

4 What theories have been advanced to explain the determination of the level of consumption in an economy?

Data response B Savings–investment imbalances

1 Fully explain the headings in Table 32.5.

2 Explain the likely effects on the economy of:
   a) an increase in investment;
   b) an increase in savings.

3 In an open economy how may a deficit on the balance of payments current account be related to deficits or surpluses in the private sector of the economy?

Table 32.5 **National savings and investment (% of GDP)**

	National savings		*National investment*		*Growth of GDP % annual average*
	1970	*1993*	*1970*	*1993*	*1970 – 93*
UK	21	14	20	15	2.5
USA	18	15	18	16	2.7
Japan	40	33	39	30	4.0
Germany	30	22	28	22	5.6
France	27	20	27	18	2.1
Italy	28	20	27	17	2.2
Canada	24	18	22	18	2.6
OECD	22.1	20.7	22.9	21.3	2.9

Source: *World Development Report*, IBRD

4 Comment on the relationship between savings, investment and growth shown in Table 32.5.

33 The Keynesian aggregate model

Learning outcomes

At the end of this chapter you will be able to:

- Classify the various flows of expenditure and income around, into and out of the circular flow of income.
- Use a simple Keynesian circular flow model to identify equilibrium national income.

To explain the determination of economic aggregates, Keynes developed the 'circular flow of income' model as an alternative to the supply and demand model of microeconomics. You have already seen this model in Chapter 7 where Keynes's classification of aggregate expenditures (i.e. C, I, G and X) was utilised as a means of national income accounting. In this chapter the model of the circular flow of income will be used, not as a model for accounting for past income and expenditures, but as a simple model for *determining* expenditure and hence income. The model is far too basic and incomplete to be used for actual forecasting, but it is a simple model of income determination that was actually used for some 30 years to teach introductory macroeconomics to students and politicians alike.

It is important when reading this chapter not to lose sight of Keynes's fundamental insights of why aggregate demand might be unstable (see Chapter 31). Indeed, the rather mechanical and deterministic model of this chapter has been criticised as distorting Keynes's fundamental ideas. These mechanical representations have sometimes been called 'hydraulic models' as they appear to represent the behaviour of water flowing through pipes rather than the subtleties of human behaviour that Keynes appeared to be describing. The explicitly derogatory name 'bastardised' Keynesian has been used to cast doubt on the model's representation of Keynes's fundamental insights.

Many economists who regard themselves as Keynesians, however, are quite happy to use the model as a stepping stone to more complex economic modelling. Indeed, the economist and engineer A.W. Phillips, famous for the Phillips curve which showed a Keynesian-type trade-off between unemployment and inflation (see Chapter 44), actually built a real hydraulic Keynesian 'model' of the economy. It used coloured water and valves, and the water flowing around the various pipes was used to represent income flowing around the economy. The model has recently been reconstructed at the London School of Economics.

Goods and money

In Chapter 7 we saw that there were two sides to the national product: national income and national expenditure. We thus established that:

$$Y = C + I + G + (X - M)$$

We now wish to examine these components of national income more closely.

Figure 33.1 shows again the basic elements of the circular flow of income. Firms produce goods and services and households buy them. The components in the diagram are thus identified not by who they are but by what they do, i.e. firms produce while households consume.

In our simple view of the economy the households own all the factors of production and

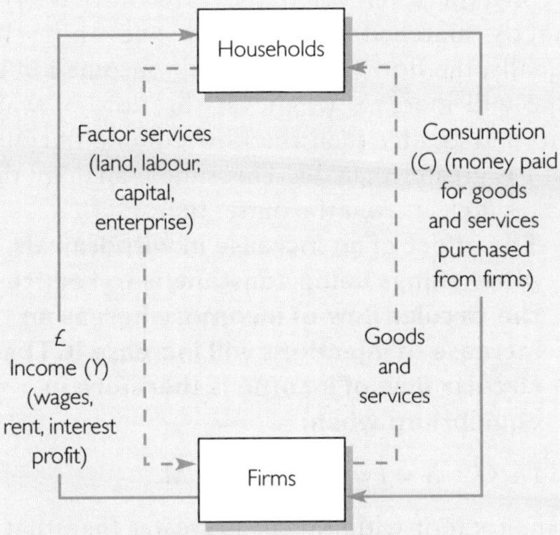

Fig. 33.1 **The flow of goods and money between households and firms**

hence all expenditure flows to firms are paid back out to households as payments for the use of the factors of production. In order to produce, the firms must hire factor services from households. On the other hand, households buy goods from firms in return for which they pay money. The money received by households is termed income (Y) and the money spent by households is termed consumption (C).

You can see in Fig. 33.1 that goods and factor services flow one way round the diagram while money flows the other way. Since there is always a flow in the opposite direction, it is convenient to simplify our future diagrams by leaving out the flow of goods and to show just money flows. We shall also use abbreviations wherever possible.

Withdrawals and injections

In Fig. 33.1 the value of consumption (C) equals the value of income (Y), i.e. all of income received in one period is directly spent in the next. It appears that there would be no tendency for the level of Y to change, in which case our economy could be said to be in equilibrium. Thus income in the first period is equal to the consumption of the next period. If consumption is the only form of expenditure then it follows that expenditure in this next period must be the same as this consumption. This expenditure, however, is all received by firms and all paid out again as income to factor payments. The model in Fig. 33.1 is simply a closed loop with nothing leaking out and nothing being put in from outside. The flow of expenditure and income continues to flow around the circular flow at a constant level. This can be written in simple notation (where t denotes the first time period and $t + 1$ the next time period and so on):

$$C_t = E_t \equiv Y_{t+1} = C_{t+1} = E_{t+1} \equiv Y_{t+2}$$

where ≡ indicates the national accounting identity described in Chapter 7.

However, there are various factors which cause money to be ***withdrawn***, or to 'leak', from the system and, conversely, there are also ***injections*** into it.

Withdrawals

A withdrawal (W) is any part of income that is not passed on within the circular flow.

Savings (S) are an example of a withdrawal. Savings may be undertaken either by households who do not spend all their income or by firms not distributing all their profits but retaining some to finance future development. Equally income taken by the government in taxes (T) may or may not be respent, and hence taxes are also a withdrawal. Lastly, income 'escapes' from a country's domestic circular flow through expenditure on imports (M). Hence the total withdrawals from a country's circular flow can be written:

$$W = S + T + M$$

Injections

An injection (J) is an expenditure which is not the consumption of domestic households, i.e. it comes from 'outside' of the circular flow of income.

The most obvious example of an injection is exports (X) because the income of the firm selling them comes not from domestic households but from overseas. Less obviously, if a firm produces investment (or capital) goods (I) and sells them to another firm, this is an injection because the flow of income and expenditure has been increased, even though this increase is not a result of extra spending by households. Lastly, government expenditure in the economy (G) may or may not have been financed by current taxation (e.g. it could be financed by past taxation, borrowing or even simply by printing new money). Government expenditure will therefore also be regarded as an injection.

The 'hydraulic' Keynesian model – an overview

In order to understand the dynamics of the simple Keynesian circular flow model it is useful to draw on the analogy with the volume of water flowing through pipes. This is illustrated in the 'cartoon' of Fig. 33.2.

It should be obvious from the cartoon that the flow of water in the circular pipe would be at a constant level when the flow into it (J) is exactly matched by the flow out of it (W). Equally, the flow of water (think 'income') in the pipe will increase whenever the flow of water into it is greater than the flow coming out of it, i.e. J is greater than W. This simple analogy thus makes it clear from the outset that:

The effect of an increase in withdrawals, other things being constant, is to reduce the circular flow of income, whereas an increase of injections will increase it. The circular flow of income is therefore in equilibrium when:

$$I + G + X = J = W = S + T + M$$

If the total of withdrawals is greater than that of injections, national income will contract. This is because the planned expenditure of the economy is insufficient to take up all the goods and services which the firms had planned to produce. Firms will therefore be faced with mounting stocks of unsold goods (inventories) and will cut back on their output, thereby reducing the income of households. (Remember: the costs of the firm are the income of the households.)

Conversely, if injections are greater than withdrawals the planned expenditure will be greater than the planned output of firms. Firms will therefore expand output and thereby raise the level of households' income.

If the total of all withdrawals (W) is equal to the total of injections (J) there will be no tendency for the level of national income to change and it is said to be in equilibrium. Thus the equilibrium condition for the economy is:

$$W = J$$

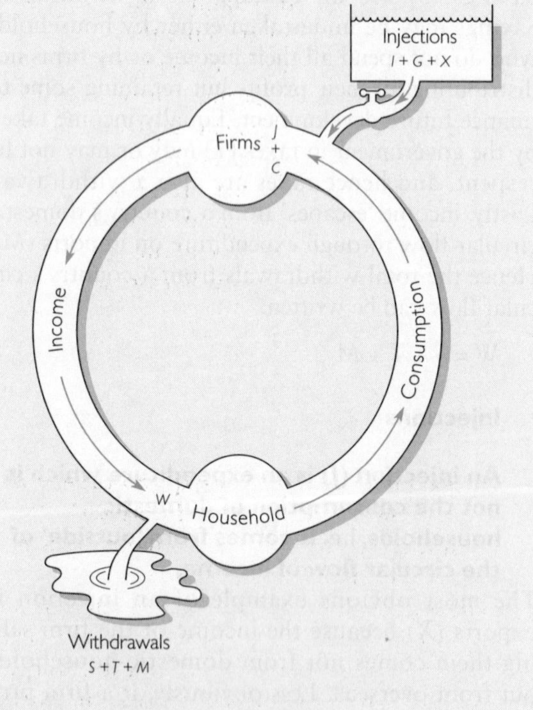

***Fig. 33.2* Circular flow model**

STUDENT ACTIVITY 33.1

You will also have noticed an emphasis in this section on the word planned. Another way of stating the equilibrium condition would be to say that it occurs when the planned expenditure is equal to the planned output. Within any one time period it is obvious that all expenditure is received as income and hence the two are identically equal. This is simply the national income accounting identity you saw in Chapter 7. Now use the t, $t + 1$, $t + 2$ notation used above to complete the sequence below and to satisfy yourself that, if there are withdrawals and injections, the income in one period is not necessarily equal to the expenditure of the next time period. By doing this you should also be able to demonstrate that when withdrawals equal injections the expenditure in the next time period will be equal to the income of the current period, i.e. the level of aggregate demand is in equilibrium when $W = J$ and this is the same thing as saying planned expenditure equals income.

$$\begin{array}{l} \nearrow W_{t+1} \\ Y_t \longrightarrow C_{t+1} \longrightarrow E_{t+1} \equiv Y_{t+2} \\ \qquad\qquad\quad J_{t+1} \nearrow \end{array}$$

Common misunderstanding

Students sometimes regard W = J *and planned* E = Y *as two separate equilibrium conditions. In the student activity above you will have identified that they are simply alternative ways of stating the same equilibrium condition.*

Components of national income

In this section we briefly recap on the various components of the circular flow and describe and define the various injections and withdrawals which constitute the components of national income to construct a simple model of the economy.

Savings (S) are defined as income not spent. Savings might be undertaken by either households or firms. With households, savings are simply the part of their income which they have not consumed. For firms, savings would consist of profits not distributed to shareholders. For the sake of simplicity in drawing the diagram we shall represent all savings as being undertaken by households.

Investment (I) is any addition to the real capital stock of the nation.

Investment therefore consists of the purchase of new capital equipment, the construction of new buildings and any additions to stocks. It is important to understand that investment is concerned with real capital goods and not with paper claims upon them. For example, purchase of shares on the Stock Exchange is not investment, as used in this sense, because all that has happened is that the ownership of pieces of paper has changed but there has been no real effect upon the economy.

The open economy

An economy which takes part in international trade, as all do, is described as an open economy. The sale and purchase of goods and services overseas introduce two more components into our model. Imports (M) are a withdrawal because the money paid for them 'leaks' out of the economy and, conversely, exports (X) are an injection because people overseas are now creating income for domestic households and firms.

STUDENT ACTIVITY 33.2

If imports are greater than exports the economy is said to have a trade deficit. Demonstrate that, other things being equal, this will cause the level of national income to fall. Conversely, if exports are greater than imports there is a trade surplus and again, other things being equal, you should be able to show that this will cause the level of national income to rise.

The government and the circular flow

Governments, both local and central, influence the circular flow of income. Taxes (T) are a withdrawal from the circular flow whereas government expenditure (G) is an injection. Taxes might be levied on personal incomes, on expenditure or upon firms, but it is easier to show them as simply being paid by households. This will not destroy the validity of the model.

Earlier in this chapter we stated Keynes's view that the government should intervene in the economy to regulate the level of economic activity. Keynes suggested that this should be done by varying the amount of government expenditure and taxes. Directing the economy in this manner by using the income and expenditure of the government's own budget (or rather that of the public sector) is termed ***fiscal policy***. If, for example, there was a deficiency of demand in the economy so that there was unemployment, the government could increase the level of aggregate demand by running a budget deficit, i.e. it could spend more than it collected in as taxes. Conversely, if the government wanted to reduce the level of national income it could withdraw more from the economy in taxes than it put in by way of government expenditure. This would be termed a budget surplus.

The equilibrium of national income

We have now completed our simple model of the macroeconomy. You can see in Fig. 33.3 that there are three withdrawals (W) consisting of:

$$W = S + M + T$$

and three injections (J) consisting of:

$$J = I + X + G$$

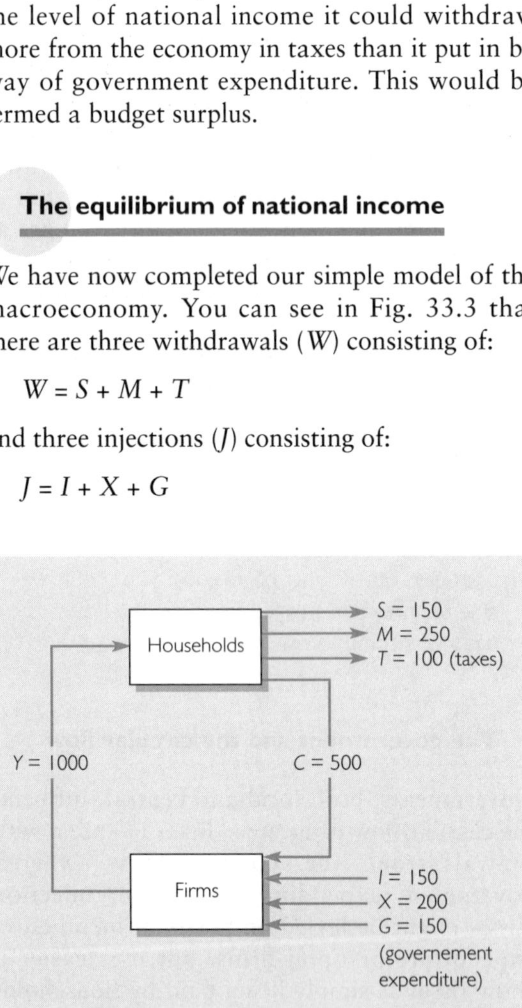

***Fig. 33.3* The complete model of the economy**
Taxes (T) are a withdrawal and government expenditure (G) an injection. This model of the economy is in equilibrium because the total of all withdrawal ($S + M + T$) is equal to the total of all injections ($I + X + G$).

The figures used in Fig. 33.3 indicate that the model is in equilibrium because withdraws are equal to injections. As you can see, it is not necessary for each withdrawal to be equal to the corresponding injection for an equilibrium to exist, only that the total of all withdrawals is equal to the total of all injections. Thus the equilibrium occurs when:

$$S + M + T = I + X + G$$

or:

$$W = J$$

or (equivalently):

$$\text{Planned } E = Y$$

It is worth restating that in Keynesian economics there is nothing necessarily desirable about an equilibrium level of national income. The significance of this is that our living standards, employment and well-being depend upon the level of national income and in Keynesian economics governments should not leave these things to chance. In contrast to neo-classical economics where there is less distinction between micro- and macroeconomics and a *laissez-faire* approach particularly at the macro level, Keynesian theory prescribes an ***interventionist*** role for governments at the macro level. Neo-classical economists believe that governments should pursue 'sound' financial policies which avoid inflations and should not try to influence unemployment and the level of output through macroeconomic policies. Such intervention, they believe, is unnecessary and could do as much harm as good and would present a temptation towards reckless policies based on short-term political objectives rather than long-term economic good. This different attitude towards the role of government is at the heart of the ideological differences between neo-classical and Keynesian economists.

A model of the economy

Assumptions

The economy is an extremely complex entity. Therefore, in order to advance our understanding and to make the construction of our model more straightforward, we will make general simplifying assumptions. Having developed a better understanding of the economy we will then drop these assumptions.

a) *Potential national income.* Although there is actually a gradual upward trend in UK national income of 2 to 2.5 per cent per annum, assume that at any time there is a fixed level of national income which corresponds to the full employment of all resources; this is given the symbol Y_F. Thus the level of actual national income Y may be less than but no greater than Y_F. If everyone in the economy were to start working overtime it would be possible to exceed the level of Y_F.
b) *Unemployment.* We assume that there is some unemployment of all factors of production. Thus it is possible to increase the level of Y by bringing these into employment.
c) *Constant prices.* For most of the time it is convenient to assume that there is no inflation (or deflation). In this way the changes in income which we are looking at are changes in real income.
d) *Technology.* We also assume that there are no significant changes in the level of technology such as would significantly alter the relationship between inputs and outputs.

Exogenous injections

Here we will make the assumption that injections are constant. Therefore in Fig. 33.4 injections (J) are represented as a horizontal straight line at £50bn, determined by exogenous factors (i.e. by influences outside of our model).

Withdrawals

It is to be expected that savings, imports and taxation all increase as income increases. Thus we shall assume, reasonably, that withdrawals increase with income.

Table 33.1 presents the data for a hypothetical economy. An equilibrium will be reached in this economy when planned withdrawals are equal to

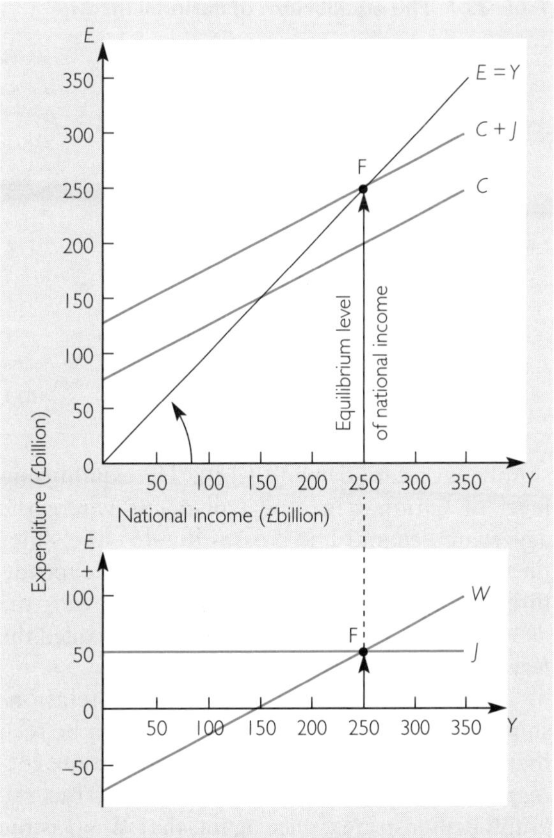

***Fig. 33.4* The equilibrium of national income**

injections. As can be seen from Table 33.1, this will occur at row F when national income is £250bn. Another way of looking at the equilibrium would be to say that it will occur when total expenditure (E) in the economy is equal to total income (Y). Total expenditure in this economy has two components: spending on consumer goods (C); and expenditure from injections (J). Thus total expenditure is $C + J$. In Table 33.1 it can be seen that total expenditure is equal to income at the level of £250bn, therefore confirming this as the equilibrium level of income.

Figure 33.4 gives a graphical representation of these figures. In the top graph the $C + J$ line shows the total of all expenditure in this economy. Since J is constant, the $C + J$ line will be parallel to the C line. This line shows the aggregate demand for this economy; this is termed aggregate monetary demand (*AMD*), total final expenditure (*TFE*) or

***Table 33.1* The equilibrium of national income**

	Level of national income, Y (£bn)	Planned consumption, C (£bn)	Planned withdrawals, W (£bn)	Autonomous injections, J (£bn)	Total expenditure, C + J = E (£bn)	Tendency of income to:
A	0	75	–75	50	125	
B	50	100	–50	50	150	
C	100	125	–25	50	175	↓
D	150	150	0	50	200	Expand
E	200	175	25	50	225	↓
F	250	200	50	50	250	Equilibrium
G	300	225	75	50	275	↑
H	350	250	100	50	300	Contract

simply aggregate demand (*AD*). The equilibrium level of national income will occur where the aggregate demand line crosses the 45° line, since the 45° line shows all the points at which expenditure is equal to income. This diagram showing the determination of the equilibrium is often called the ***Keynesian cross diagram.***

The lower graph demonstrates the relationship of withdrawals and injections. It can be seen that the equilibrium level of national income corresponds to the point at which $W = J$. Thus the graph demonstrates, once again, that $W = J$ is the equilibrium condition for the economy.

The nature of the equilibrium is illustrated in Fig. 33.5. Here, if the level of *Y* were below the equilibrium, e.g. OL, then *J* would exceed *W* by AR. Thus injections would be greater than withdrawals and *Y* would rise. Conversely, if *Y* were to be ON then *W* would exceed *J* by TG, so that withdrawals would now be greater than injections and *Y* would fall.

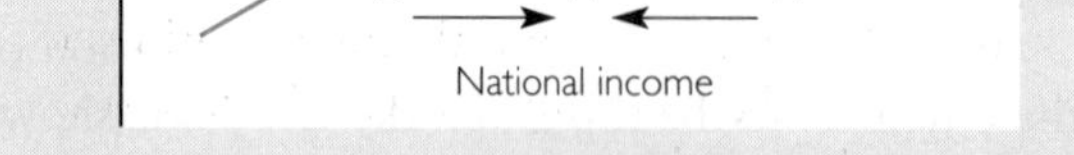

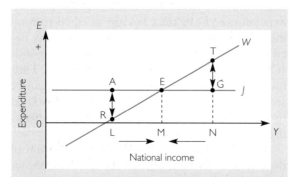

***Fig. 33.5* The reasons for equilibrium**
At income level OL, $J > W$ and therefore *Y* tends to rise. At income level ON, $W > J$ and therefore *Y* tends to fall. Therefore OM is the equilibrium level of *Y*, where $W = J$.

Conclusion

This chapter has explained the simple circular flow model used to explain Keynesian ideas. This model of equilibrium determination can also be represented as a Keynesian cross or 45° line diagram. The mechanics of the model are crude and have a close analogy to the flow of water in pipes whereby the level of flow is in equilibrium when the withdrawals (leakages) equal the flow of injections into the pipe. Doubts have therefore been expressed that the model adequately represents Keynes's ideas. Nevertheless, the majority of economists are happy to regard it as a stepping stone to more complex models (e.g. the Treasury model shown in Fig. 33.7).

Summary

1 The circular flow of income was used by Keynes as a simple model of national income determination.
2 Micro- and macroeconomics give us contrasting views of the economy.
3 A withdrawal is any part of income that is not passed on within the circular flow, whereas an injection is an addition to the circular flow which

does not come from the expenditure of domestic households.

4 The level of the flow of expenditures and income within the circular flow is affected and determined by changes in the balance between injections and withdrawals.

5 An equilibrium level of income is reached where withdrawals are equal to injections or, equivalently, when planned expenditure equals income.

6 Savings (*S*), imports (*M*) and taxes (*T*) are all withdrawals, whereas investment (*I*), exports (*X*) and government expenditure (*G*) are all injections.

7 An equilibrium level of income is reached where:

$$S + M + T = I + X + G$$

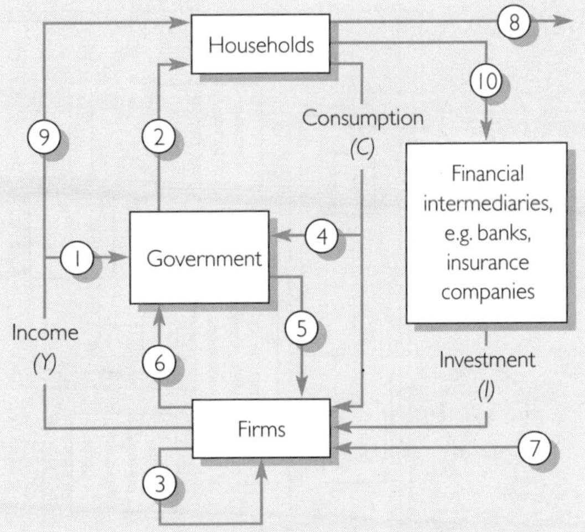

Fig. 33.6

Questions

1 What is meant by the circular flow of income?

2 Distinguish between microeconomics and macroeconomics.

3 'The economy is in equilibrium when expenditure equals income. In the National Accounts expenditure is always equal to income. Hence the economy is always in equilibrium!' Discuss.

4 In an economy with $C = 2 + 0.8\,Y$ and injections constant at 50 units at all levels of income. What would be the equilibrium level of national income?

5 Study Fig. 33.6 which presents a more complex picture of the circular flow. Try to match the following items with the numbered flow which best illustrates it.

a) Government payment of civil servants' salaries.
b) A UK householder's purchase of a Volkswagen.
c) Old-age pensioners' deposits in a building society.
d) A UK firm's sale of goods to a West African firm.
e) Income tax.
f) The government's purchase of arms from a munitions firm.
g) Disposable income.
h) A firm ploughing back profit by purchasing new equipment.
i) VAT.
j) Corporation tax.

Data response A
The Treasury model of the circular flow

Study Fig. 33.7 for a few minutes which is a diagrammatic representation of the links between the variables which make up the model used by the UK Treasury. You should be able to see that although this is a far more complex model than the model of this chapter, it still has the Keynesian elements of income and expenditure flows that have been described. Now go back to the diagram to answer the following questions:

1 Follow the arrows flowing *into* 'Total Final Expenditure' near the centre of the diagram and list the items of expenditure they represent. Classify these items according to the categories *C*, *I*, *G* and *X*.

2 List the elements which go to make up 'Total personal income' and explain the relationships shown between this and 'Real personal disposable income' and 'Consumers' expenditure'. Briefly, describe how these elements and relationships would complicate the consumption function of our simple model.

3 Check that the expenditure on the import of goods and services does not feed into the box showing 'Total Final Expenditure'. Why is this so? Trace through how an increase in expenditure on

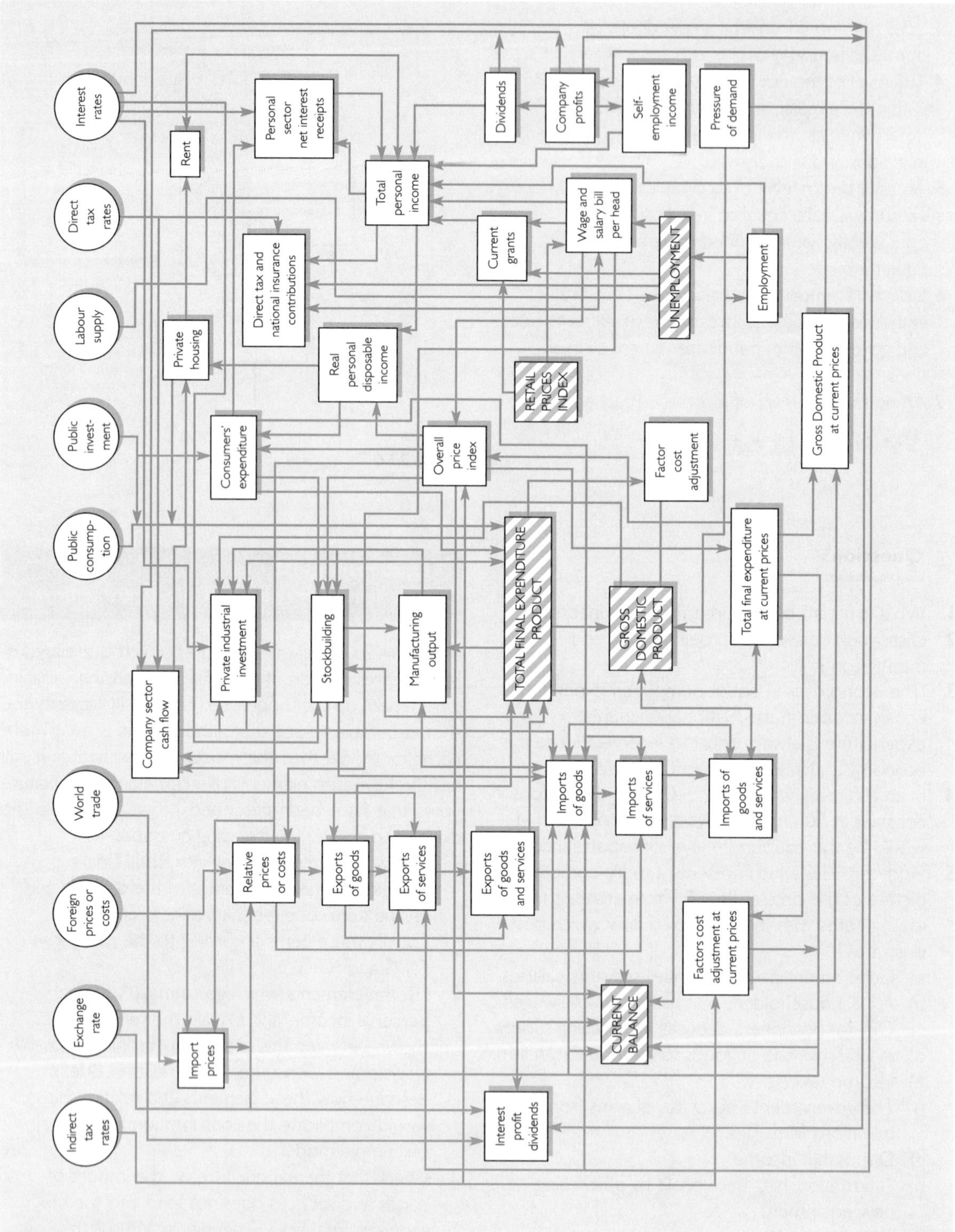

Fig. 33.7 The Treasury model of the economy

imports would lead to a reduction in 'Total Final Expenditure'. What exogenous influences might affect the 'Current Balance' and how would this in turn affect the level of domestic expenditure?

4 Make a list of all those boxes shown in the model which show items which do not appear in our simple model. Attempt to account for why they are included in the Treasury model of the 'real' economy and briefly explain how the simple model of this chapter could be extended to incorporate them.

34 Changes in aggregate demand: the multiplier

Learning outcomes

At the end of this chapter you will be able to:

- Define the multiplier and demonstrate its effect algebraically and diagrammatically.
- Explain and list reasons why the multiplier is modified and thus difficult to identify in real economies.

In the previous chapter we saw how equilibrium is determined in circular flow models of the economy. This chapter looks at changes in the level of equilibrium aggregate demand and hence national income. The ***multiplier concept*** is an important feature of such Keynesian modes. In Chapter 31 we saw that the multiplier has strong psychological aspects in that changes in the level of activity tend to be reinforced by changes in expectations. For example, as economic activity starts to increase economic agents may become more optimistic about economic prospects and hence firms increase investment and consumers spend more. Thus the pace of the recovery is greatly increased. Equally, small initial downturns in the economy may be greatly magnified as pessimistic expectations create a self-fulfilling prophecy of decreased aggregate spending and reduced economic activity.

Even in the absence of such expectations effects, the process of income determination in the circular flow will tend to magnify initial changes in aggregate demand. This is because initial changes in C, J or W affect subsequent rounds of spending in the circular flow. Thus there is a build-up of ***secondary effects*** which add to the initial effect. For example, a decrease in government spending on domestically produced weapons will see an initial fall in output and incomes from weapon production. But the laid-off workers will then in turn reduce their own spending on consumer goods. Thus in the local areas around the weapons factories shops, cinemas, licensed drinking places, etc., will be faced with reduced demand and perhaps lay off workers or reduce their payments. This further reduces demand and so on. Thus the initial effect on aggregate demand is multiplied by a reduction in the income of consumers and demand for consumer goods.

STUDENT ACTIVITY 34.1

Take a blank sheet of paper and write '8bn' on it in the currency of your choice, e.g. \$8bn. Now 'spend' this 8bn note on an imaginary item also of your choice. Income has thus increased in the item's industry by 8bn. Now suppose that all recipients of this money in the industry concerned spend half of what they receive (i.e. $MPC = 0.5$). You can 'model' this by tearing the sheet of paper in half and 'spending' one half, i.e. 4bn. Income has now increased by 8bn + 4bn = 12bn. But the process will not stop there; tear the sheet in half again and spend 2bn. Income has now risen overall by 8bn + 4bn + 2bn = 14bn. Continue this process to satisfy yourself that the stream of income will increase to a limit of 16bn, i.e. twice the initial 8bn injection. Thus an *MPC* of 0.5 has produced a multiplier coefficient of 2.

The multiplier defined

In Fig. 34.1, we show the effect of an increase in the level of injections. Injections have increased by £50bn from J to J_1 and this has the effect of raising the level of national income by £100bn. Thus £50bn of extra injections has brought about £100bn of extra income. This is a diagrammatic example of the multiplier principle. The numerical value of the change is known as the multiplier. The strength of the multiplier, or its coefficient, is given the symbol K. In our example the multiplier would be:

$$K = \Delta Y / \Delta J$$
$$= 100/50$$
$$= 2$$

In this case the multiplier is 2. This means that for every, say, extra £1 of investment that is injected into the economy national income will rise by £2. This effect can also work downwards, so that a decrease in investment would cause a multiple decrease in national income.

The multiplier principle is that a change in the level of injections (or withdrawals) brings about a relatively greater change in the level of national income.

The operation of the multiplier

The operation of the multiplier can be explained by taking a simple example. Assume that investment and savings are the only injection and withdrawal respectively. If a firm decides to construct a new building costing £1000, then the income of builders and the suppliers of the raw materials will rise by £1000.

However, the process does not stop there. If we assume that the recipients of the £1000 have a marginal propensity to consume of 2/3, they will spend £666.67 and save the rest. This spending creates extra income for another group of people. If we assume that they also have an *MPC* of 2/3, they will spend £444.44 of the £666.67 and save the rest. This process will continue, with each new round of spending being two-thirds of the previous round. Thus a long chain of extra income, extra consumption and extra saving is set up (see Table 34.1).

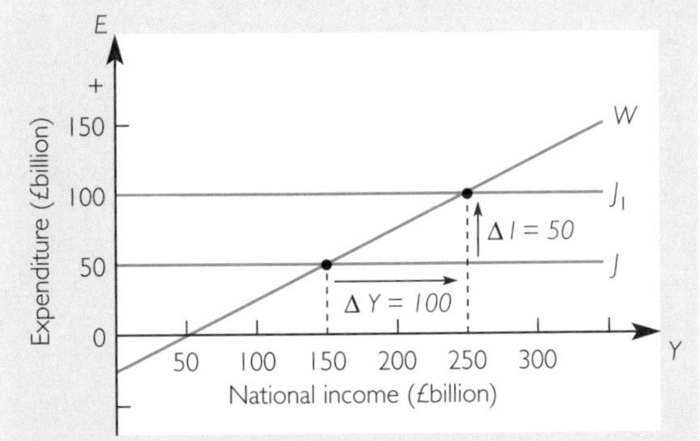

Fig 34.1 **The multiplier**
An increase in investment of £50bn has increased the equilibrium level of national income by £100bn.

Table 34.1 **A simple example of the multiplier at work**

	Increase in income, ΔY (£)	*Increase in consumption, ΔC (£)*	*Increase in savings, ΔS (£)*
1st recipients	1000	666.67	333.33
	+	+	+
2nd recipients	666.67	444.44	222.23
	+	+	+
3rd recipients	444.44	296.30	148.14
	+	+	+
4th recipients	296.30	197.53	98.77
	+	+	+
5th recipients	197.53	131.69	65.84
	+	+	+
	.	.	.
	.	.	.
	.	.	.
Total	ΔY=£3000	ΔC=£2000	ΔS=£1000

The process will come to a halt when the additions to savings total £1000. This is because the change in savings (ΔS) is now equal to the original change in investment (ΔI) and, therefore, the economy is returned to equilibrium because $S = I$ once again. At this point the additions to income total £3000. Thus £1000 extra investment has created a £3000 rise in income; therefore, in this case, the value of the multiplier is 3.

Temporary and permanent changes

For the change in the equilibrium level of national income to be permanent it is necessary that the increase in investment is also permanent. If in our example (see Table 34.1) the £1000 of investment were an isolated example, it would create a 'bulge' in national income of £3000 and then the equilibrium would return to its previous level. On the other hand, if £1000 of investment were undertaken in each time period, it would cause a permanent increase in the equilibrium level of national income of £3000. This is illustrated in Fig. 34.2

The multiplier formula

As we have seen, the size of the multiplier is governed by the *MPC*. In our example we saw that additions to income were generated in the following series:

$$Y = £1000 + £666.67 + £444.44 + £296.30 \ldots$$

because the *MPC* was 2/3 and therefore two-thirds of all income received was passed on to create income for someone else. However, if the *MPC* were larger, say 9/10, then the same increase in investment would yield:

$$Y = £1000 + £900 + £810 + £729 \ldots$$

If we followed each series we would find that each successive round of extra income would get smaller and smaller but never quite reach zero. Fortunately such a series is well known in mathematics and is termed a ***geometric progression***. Its value is given by the formula:

$$\frac{1}{1 - r}$$

where r is the value of the common ratio. In the case of the multiplier the common ratio is the *MPC* so that we obtain:

$$K = \frac{1}{1 - MPC}$$

If, therefore, the *MPC* were 2/3 we would obtain:

$$K = \frac{1}{1 - \frac{2}{3}} = 3$$

whereas if the value of the *MPC* were 9/10 we would obtain:

$$K = \frac{1}{1 - \frac{9}{10}} = 10$$

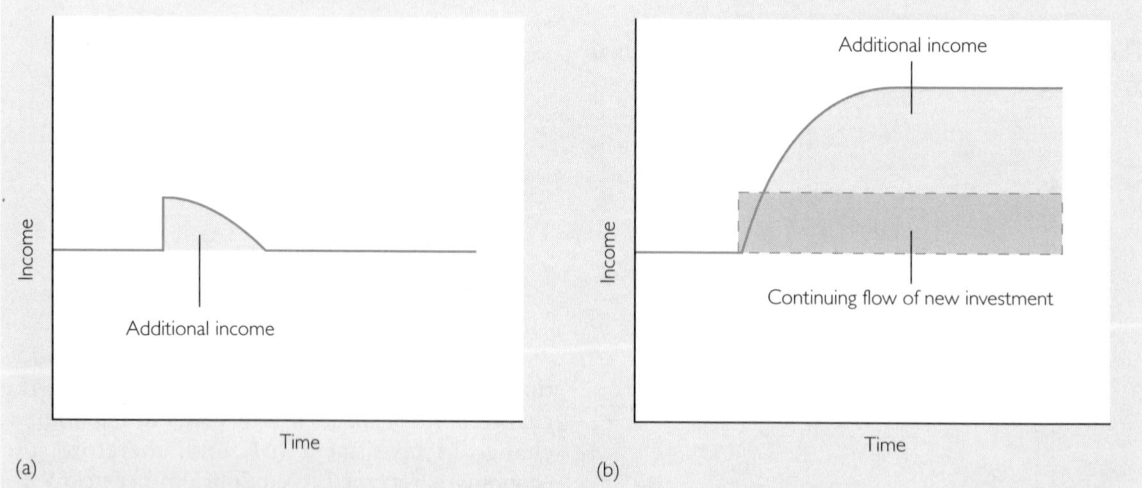

***Fig. 34.2* Effects of investment**
(a) The effect of a single act of investment of £1000. (b) The shift to a higher equilibrium level of income caused by a continuous flow of new investment of £1000. Here the value of the multiplier is 3.

The larger the *MPC* the larger the multiplier will be.

If in fact the *MPC* were to be one the value of the multiplier would be infinity. However, if everything were consumed there could be no investment anyway, so this is only a theoretical possibility.

STUDENT ACTIVITY 34.2 (optional)

If you enjoy simple algebra, you should be able to derive the formula for the multiplier for yourself from the following equations of our simple model.

$Y = E$ The equilibrium condition

$E = C + J$ The components of aggregate expenditure

$C = a + bY$ A Keynesian consumption function, where a is autonomous consumption and b is the *MPC*

Substitute to get:

$$Y = a + bY + J$$

Thus:

$$Y = \frac{1}{1 - MPC(a + J)}$$

and therefore:

$$\Delta Y = \frac{1}{1 - MPC} \Delta J$$

or:

$$\Delta Y = K\Delta J$$

Equilibrium and the multiplier

In our simple representation, as all extra income is either consumed or withdrawn, we can write:

$$MPC + MPW = 1$$

where *MPW* is the ***marginal propensity to withdraw.*** In more complex models the derivation of *MPC* is complicated by the distinction between *MPC* from gross income and *MPC* from personal disposable income. Here we abstract from such complications by simply assuming that *MPC* refers to the proportion of *gross* income passed on in the circular flow by way of consumption.

It follows in our model that $1 - MPC = MPW$, and thus we could also write the formula for the multiplier as:

$$K = \frac{1}{MPW}$$

Thus, if we know the value of *MPW* we can predict the effect of a change in injections upon national income. The effect will be the change in injections multiplied by *K*, which we can write as:

$$\Delta Y = K \times \Delta J$$

or as:

$$\Delta Y = \frac{1}{MPW} \times \Delta J$$

To determine the overall *MPW* we must total all the other propensities to withdraw. That is:

$$K = \frac{1}{MPS + MPT + MPM}$$

where $MPW = MPS + MPT + MPM$ and *MPS* is the marginal propensity to save, *MPT* is the marginal propensity of taxation and *MPM* is the marginal propensity to import.

If, for example, $MPS = 0.1$, $MPT = 0.15$ and $MPM = 0.25$ then:

$$K = \frac{1}{0.1 + 0.15 + 0.25}$$

$$= \frac{1}{0.5}$$

$$= 2$$

Thus any permanent increase in investment (*I*), government spending (*G*) or exports (*X*) would lead to a permanent increase in the level of equilibrium national income of twice this amount. For example, an increase in government spending of £1 million would lead to an eventual increase in equilibrium national income of £2 million.

Modifying factors

The multiplier of the simple Keynesian model is far more difficult to identify for a real economy. Partly this is because of the following factors:

a) *Different MPCs*. Different sections of the population will have different propensities to consume. For example, the poor may have higher *MPC*s than the rich. The great Polish economist Michael Kalecki (who had in fact already developed similar models to Keynes but who did not get the acknowledgement he deserved) distinguished between the *MPC* of those who earned wages/salaries and those who live off unearned income. He showed that these differences in *MPC* mean that income distribution can greatly affect the value of the multipliers and hence equilibrium national income.
b) *Progressive taxes*. Because of the progressive nature of taxation, any rise in income will tend to increase the proportion paid in tax and hence tend to reduce the multiplier.
c) *Inflation*. Increases in expenditure may be absorbed by price increases rather than increases in output (see Chapter 44). Thus output will not increase by as much as aggregate demand. Price increases may also affect people's real wealth and thus change their level of consumption.
d) *Type of investment*. Different types of investment will have different multiplier effects. For example, extra spending on defence will have a different effect from spending on house building because of the different *MPC*s of the recipients and the different ratio of imported to domestically produced parts and materials. Because of the bulky nature of building materials most will come from domestic producers and hence the multiplier will tend to be larger than for expenditure on manufactured products where many of the components may be imported.
e) *Endogenous investment*. What would happen if we dropped the assumption that investment is exogenous/autonomous? Suppose that investment were to increase with income. This is shown by the upward-sloping injections function in Fig. 34.3 (b). This would therefore magnify the multiplier effect as injections could now increase with income. This is also illustrated in Fig. 34.3 (b).
f) *Time lags*. The various rounds of spending which cause the multiplier take time to build up. Thus the strength of the multiplier may not be seen for some time. This can cause difficulties for the timing of government macroeconomic policies.
g) *Expectations*. We have already noted that in Keynesian economics expectations may greatly add to or reduce other effects.

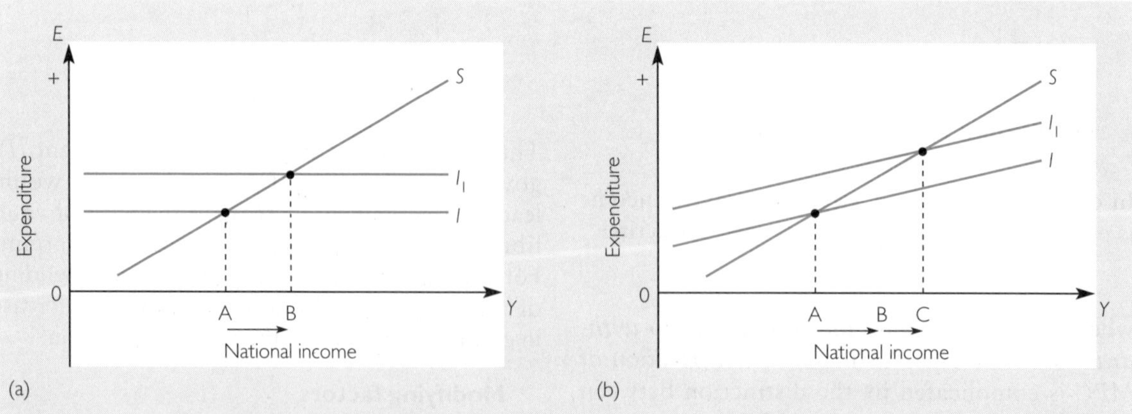

Fig. 34.3 **The multiplier and non-autonomous investment**
If investment is constant (a) then the increase in *I* increases Y from OA to OB. However, if investment increases with income (b) then the same increase in *I* increases Y from OA to OC.

STUDENT ACTIVITY 34.3

Keynes asserted that it could be possible for an increase in the level of planned savings to lead to a fall in the level of actual savings. This he called 'the paradox of thrift'. To explore this possibility, assume that the only injection and withdrawal are investment and savings respectively. It should be clear that an increase in the level of planned savings can be represented by a vertical shift upwards of the withdrawals function, i.e. more saving is planned than before for each level of potential income. Now refer to Fig. 34.3 to draw diagrams demonstrating that when injections are constant savings will fall back to their former level and that they could actually decrease if investment is non-autonomous!

Conclusion

In this and the previous chapter we have explained the usual textbook Keynesian model which was the mainstay of macroeconomics teaching for some 30 years. Basically, it is a theory of aggregate demand determination. We have hardly mentioned aggregate supply other than to suggest that it adjusts passively to increases in aggregate demand up until the point of full employment. Indeed, this was essentially the assumption made by Keynes. It is incorrect, however, to say he ignored aggregate supply. Unless there were significant changes in costs or physical supplies of materials, he simply did not think aggregate supply mattered very much as a force in the economy until full employment is neared. Thus supply followed demand more or less passively and was not an independent force which had to be reconciled with demand through price adjustments. As he was explaining economic depressions rather than inflationary booms he thus tended to suppress the effects of aggregate supply in his analysis.

In the next chapter you will see how aggregate supply can be incorporated into the analysis. But we should also note that as this textbook model is being built up the fundamentals of Keynes's ideas seem harder to discern. For example, the multiplier effects of Chapter 31 were based more on changes in expectations and unjamming of 'jammed' markets than on the size of the mathematical coefficient *MPC*. Post-Keynesians point out that equilibriums and stable functions seem at odds with Keynes's emphasis on instability and uncertainty. Nevertheless, the majority of economists use such simple models of aggregate demand determination as part of more complex models incorporating many additional influences on demand and supply.

Summary

1 An increase in planned consumption or injections will, *ceteris paribus*, tend to increase aggregate demand. An increase in planned savings or other withdrawals will, *ceteris paribus*, decrease aggregate demand.

2 Any initial change in spending results in a larger change in the level of *Y* as a result of the multiplier effect.

3 The size of the multiplier is determined by the *MPC* and can be calculated from the formula:

$$K = \frac{1}{1 - MPC} \text{ or } \frac{1}{MPW}$$

4 *MPW* consists of *MPS*, *MPT* and *MPM*.

5 In more complete models the calculation of *MPC* and *MPW* becomes more complex, as does the determination of injections when the influences on them are incorporated into the model.

6 In the real world the multiplier is difficult to identify and may change as income levels change.

7 There is a periodicity in the determination of national income such that the output in one period creates the income in the next period. The periodicity may be complicated by the existence of time lags in the economy

Questions

1 List the components of injections to, and withdrawals from, the circular flow of income.

2 Give a brief explanation of the multiplier in the following terms:

a) common sense
b) arithmetical
c) graphical

3 How might the multiplier and the accelerator combine to cause fluctuations in national income and what might set the limits to these fluctuations?

4 What policies might a Keynesian government take to eliminate:
a) Unemployment?
b) Inflation?

5 List the factors which complicate the identification of the multiplier for 'real' economies.

6 What might happen to the aggregate demand function when it exceeds income at the point of full employment?

7 Assume:

$$C = 40 + \tfrac{2}{3}XY$$

and injections are constant at 50.

Confirm that $Y = 270$ when the economy is in equilibrium. Increase J by 1 and confirm that Y increases by 3. What is the value of the multiplier and why?

Data response A Plotting the equilibrium

Complete the following table for a hypothetical economy (all figures £bn). Assume that the consumption function is a straight line and that investment is constant at all levels of income.

Y	*C*	*S*	*I*	*APC*	*MPC*
0	25		25		
100	100				
200					
300					
400					
500					

1 From this data, draw a graph of the consumption function and of aggregate demand. Underneath this graph draw another to show savings and investment. Demonstrate the relationship between the two graphs.

2 What is the equilibrium level of national income? Show it clearly on the graph.

3 Now assume that *I* increases by £25bn. What will be the new equilibrium level of national income?

4 Explain the principle that is at work in moving from the first to the second equilibrium.

5 This is a model of a closed economy with no government intervention. What would be the situation if these assumptions were dropped?

Data response B The multiplier

The following table shows the allocation of gross national income:

Gross national income	£276 000m
Direct taxes	£ 24 000m
Retained profits	£ 18 000m
Personal disposable income	£234 000m
Personal savings	£ 20 000m
Indirect taxes	£ 40 000m
Imports	£ 8 100m
Domestic consumption at factor cost	£165 000m

Assuming that additional income would be allocated in the same proportions as above:

1 Calculate the marginal propensity to consume.

2 Using your figure for *MPC*, calculate the value of the multiplier.

3 a) What factors determine the value of the multiplier in such a way that its value is decreased as these factors increase?
b) Show the values of these factors and show how they can be used to calculate the value of the multiplier.

4 a) If output adjusted instaneously to changes in demand, what would be the change in real GNP following an increase in government expenditure of £100m?
b) Is it likely that the increase in government expenditure would cause this increase in the volume of output in the real world?

35 Aggregate demand and supply analysis

Learning outcomes

At the end of this chapter you will be able to:

- Give a descriptive account of the derivation of aggregate demand and supply curves.
- Conduct simple analysis of macroeconomic changes using aggregate demand and supply diagrams.
- Criticise the model as a complete explanation of economic fluctuations.

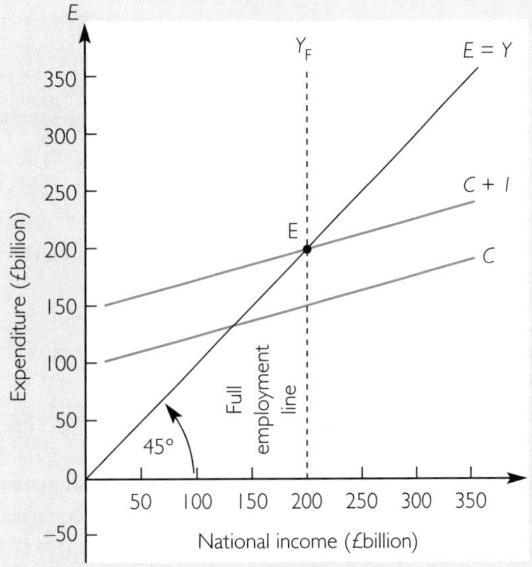

***Fig. 35.1* The full employment line**

Here the equilibrium level of national income coincides with the full employment line. However, this need not be so.

The aggregate demand and supply curve approach

As we saw in Chapter 33, Keynes put forward the circular flow model as an alternative to the supply and demand model of microeconomics. Nevertheless, it has become fashionable to represent macroeconomic interactions in terms of aggregate supply and demand diagrams. Not so long ago textbooks dealt only with the demand-determined Keynesian macro models we have developed in the previous chapters. Thus national income and output would expand passively with increases in aggregate demand until full employment is reached. The full employment equilibrium in this approach can be shown using the Keynesian cross diagram as in Fig. 35.1.

Although this allowed a very simple representation of Keynes's ideas it did lead to the supply side of the economy being virtually ignored in introductory textbooks. It is important, however, that supply conditions are considered.

Indeed, without incorporating aggregate supply as an independent force in the model it is difficult to show the various modern neo-classical theories such as ***monetarism*** and ***new classical*** and explain their policy prescriptions which were influential in the 1980s and 1990s. These modern neo-classical models were part of a revival of the non-interventionist *laissez-faire* political movement. They reversed the emphasis of Keynes back to pre-Keynesian models.

In contrast to supply behaving passively, in pre-Keynesian models it is aggregate demand which adjusts more or less passively to supply-determined levels of output and employment.

These supply-side-determined models are examined in Chapter 38. Between these two extremes there can be various balances between the strength of aggregate demand and aggregate supply in the macroeconomy. We shall also note the limitations of, and issues raised by, the practice of representing macroeconomic adjustment in terms of supply and demand diagrams.

Common misunderstanding

To the student who has read through the micro sections of a textbook the aggregate demand and supply curve diagrams will look deceptively familiar. It is all too easy to engage in the geometrical moving of lines in order to find new 'equilibrium' points of intersection. But unless you are aware of the theoretical underpinning of such curves you are doing little more than moving a ruler across a page.

It is important that you always think about what lies behind these curves and to realise that different schools of thought may offer alternative interpretations and approaches. For now we note that:

Aggregate demand and supply analysis tends to impart a neo-classical bias.

For example, strictly speaking, supply curves imply that firms and consumers are price takers as in perfect competition (see Chapter 16). This is not an assumption that all economists are happy with. Nevertheless, so useful and convenient is this approach that economists of virtually all persuasions will employ it from time to time! Moreover, the concept of a supply curve can be 'stretched' in order to represent different theories, but it must be said that such an approach can sometimes distort rather than elucidate the perspective of some schools of thought, e.g. ***monopoly capitalism theorists*** (see pages 218 and 625).

The derivation of the aggregate demand curve

The derivation of the aggregate demand curve in neo-classical and Keynesian models is fairly straightforward. As the level of prices falls the *real* money supply is expanded. That is:

$$\text{Prices} \downarrow \Rightarrow \frac{\text{Money supply (fixed)}}{\text{Prices}} \uparrow \Rightarrow \text{Real money supply} \uparrow$$

For example, halving the general level of prices would double the real purchasing power of a constant nominal money supply.

STUDENT ACTIVITY 35.1

To understand the concept of the real money supply, take the highest-value monetary note from your pocket (if you are a student you may need to borrow one!). Now, think of a favourite item that you buy regularly. Divide the nominal (or face) value of the note by the price of the item to calculate the 'real' value of the note in terms of the number of items it can buy. It is immediately obvious that if the price of the item were halved the value of the note would double and vice versa. For the economy as a whole an index of prices (e.g. the GNP deflator) must be used to measure movements in the level of prices. Official statistics do show various measures of money as deflated by various price indices to calculate the real money supply. See Chapter 36 for examples.

An increase in the real money supply will tend to increase the volume of aggregate demand at the lower price level. For example, the increase in the real money supply will tend to reduce the cost of borrowing money (i.e. the interest rate) and thus expenditure on consumer durables and investment by firms may increase. The precise monetary ***transmission mechanism*** may vary (see pages 521–2) but the end result of this expansion is an extension of demand for the output of the economy. Depending on the exchange rate regime, the demand for exports may also increase as the domestic price level falls relative to foreign markets. In addition there might be a decrease in the demand for imports as domestically produced goods become cheaper. Therefore:

We assume the aggregate demand curve to be downward sloping.

This means that, bearing in mind any multiplier effects, the lower the price level the greater will be the volume of goods and services demanded in the economy. The end result shown in Fig. 35.2

looks like a normal demand curve, but is drawn using an index of the overall price level and plots the aggregate demand for goods and services in the economy as a whole.

The derivation of the aggregate supply curve

The shape of the aggregate supply curve depends crucially on the assumptions we make. In neo-classical schools perfect competition is assumed. Thus the labour market clears at the level of employment which corresponds to profit maximisation (see Chapter 19). That is:

$$W = MPP \times P$$

or in real terms:

$$\text{Real wage} = W/P = MPP$$

i.e. for the economy as a whole, labour will be employed up until the point at which the real wage (W/P) of the marginal worker is equal to the worker's marginal physical product (MPP).

To understand the idea that the level of employment is determined by the real wage, assume that there is only one output of the economy. Thus workers produce and are paid in the same commodity. We could assume it to be any such commodity, say 'fudge' (i.e. the soft, sweet toffee) or any other item that you may prefer. If the price of a unit of fudge were £5 and the money wage were £20 per week, then the real wage would be 4 units of fudge. Thus, assuming diminishing marginal physical product, it would be profitable for employers to employ workers whose *MPP* exceeded 4 units of fudge but not those extra workers for which *MPP* falls below 4. If the price of fudge were to rise to, say, £10, then the real wage will have fallen to 2 units of fudge. Thus at the previous level of employment the marginal worker will be producing 4 units of fudge but be receiving only 2 units in wages. It therefore becomes profitable for employers to take on more workers up until the point at which the *MPP* of labour falls to 2. This relationship between the real wage and the level of aggregate employment is shown in the top half of Fig. 35.3.

In the short run the stock of capital (and land) is fixed; hence Fig. 35.3 shows that each level of employment will also correspond to a

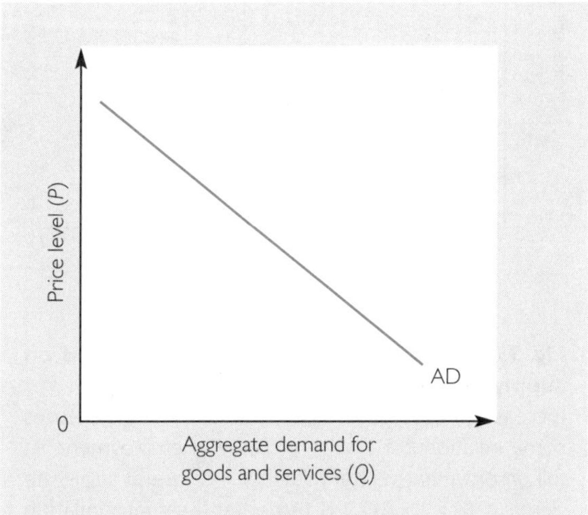

Fig. 35.2 **The aggregate demand curve**

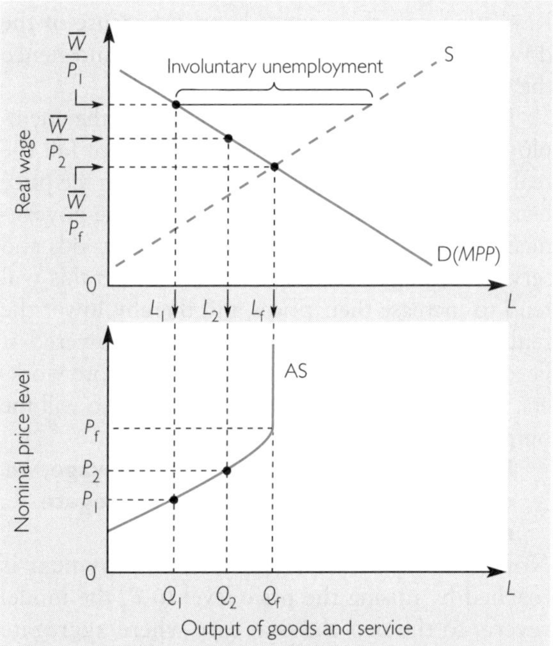

Fig. 35.3 **The aggregate supply curve**
At price level P_1, lower the real wage and more labour is employed (L_2). At price level P_f full employment is reached and the supply curve becomes vertical.

definite level of output. We shall now trace out such a relation.

A (neo-)Keynesian view of the aggregate supply curve

Keynesians assume that money wages are downwardly sticky perhaps because of institutional rigidities, such as past contracts, or union resistance. In the absence of inflation in the prices of goods and services the real wage might thus be 'stuck' at too high a level for the labour market to clear. This is illustrated in the top half of Fig. 35.3. The assumption that money wages will not decrease is indicated by the bar over the symbol for money wage, i.e. $\overline{W}$.

It can be seen that at a price level of P_1, the real wage is above the equilibrium. Thus employers are prepared to employ only L_1 of labour and there is an excess supply of labour, i.e. involuntary unemployment. In neo-classical models this excess supply would simply force down money wages until the equilibrium real wage is reached. In this Keynesian case this cannot happen because of the downward stickiness of money wages and hence the involuntary employment can persist.

Figure 35.3 also shows the solution to the unemployment. Although money wages will not fall the real wage can be lowered by an increase in the price level of goods and services. Hence, if the government increases the aggregate demand for goods and services through fiscal or monetary means this will tend to increase their prices and thereby lower the real wage. As the real wage is thus lowered it becomes profitable for firms to employ more workers. As the level of employment increases so will the output of goods and services. Thus:

For any given value of the money wage, we can derive an upward-sloping aggregate supply curve.

Notice, however, that once full employment is reached by raising the price level to P_f the model reverts to the neo-classical case where aggregate supply is fixed. This is because there is nothing to prevent an *increase* in the money wage. Hence any further increase in the price level tending to produce excess demand in the labour market would simply cause money wages to increase so as to hold the real wage and the level of employment and output constant.

STUDENT ACTIVITY 35.2

In neo-classical economics the labour market is regarded as working in the same way as any other market. Hence, wages are fully flexible and will adjust with market forces until the real wage is in equilibrium. Refer to Fig. 35.3 to demonstrate that the neo-classical (in macroeconomics this is often called the 'new classical' school) aggregate supply curve will be vertical.

In Fig. 35.4 we show aggregate demand and supply based on neo-Keynesian sticky money wage assumptions.

Post-Keynesians emphasise uncertainty, expectations and dynamic movements through time in their analysis and hence make little use of equilibrium aggregate demand and supply analysis.

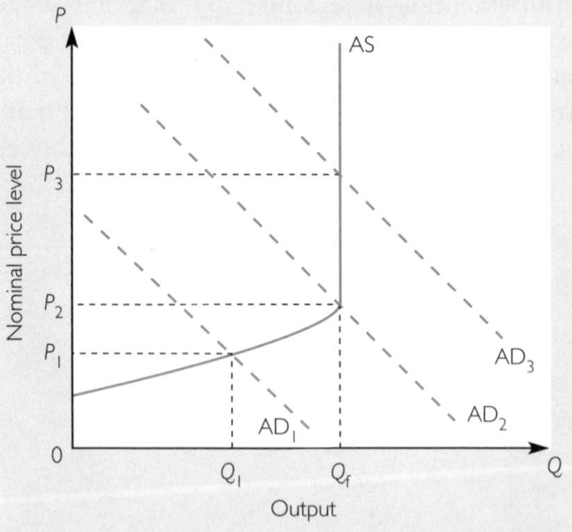

Fig. 35.4 **Neo-Keynesian aggregate demand on supply analysis**

Increase in aggregate demand (AD_1 to AD_2) causes some inflation but a large increase in employment. At full employment (Q_f) any further increase in aggregate demand (e.g. to AD_3) is turned entirely into inflation with no rise in output or employment.

Neo-Keynesians use the same sort of demand and supply approach as neo-classical economists but emphasise that markets do not move smoothly towards market clearing.

Neo-Keynesians emphasise sticky prices and restricted elasticities which prevent rapid market clearing.

The post-Keynesian view is often shown by a completely flat aggregate supply curve as post-Keynesians regard aggregate supply as adjusting passively to demand and set at a level determined by historical and institutional processes.

Let us return to the upward-sloping 'sticky money wage' aggregate supply associated with neo-Keynesians as shown in Fig. 35.4. As can be seen, increasing aggregate demand from AD_1 to AD_2 results in a mild inflation of the price level and a substantial increase in output (and employment). But once full employment has been reached a further increase in aggregate demand to AD_3 will be absorbed wholly by an increase in the price level as there is no increase in output.

A neo-Keynesian recession

A common fear among Keynesians is that money wages will begin to rise before full employment is reached, e.g. as union strength increases with the developing shortages of labour, or as bottlenecks in labour markets begin to develop causing employers to bid against each other for the remaining supply of labour. You should now work out the result that this wage inflation will cause the AS curve to shift upwards with increases in AD. Thus government attempts to lower the real wage by reflating the economy might be thwarted. For this reason neo-Keynesians (and some post-Keynesians) are usually also keen advocates of incomes policies.

Incomes policies attempt to prevent wages rising in the face of increasing aggregate demand and are thus intended to increase the expansionary effects on output of increases in aggregate demand by reducing the effects on inflation.

Some writers, as well as the post-Keynesians, have challenged the neo-Keynesian interpretation of Keynes's work which identifies downwardly rigid money wages as the critical assumption in Keynes's theory of macro unemployment. If this were the sole reason that Keynes had given for the persistence of unemployment we could hardly speak of a Keynesian 'revolution' in economics. As the Swedish economist Axel Leijonhufvud wrote in his paper 'Keynes and the Classics':

> Any pre-Keynesian economist, asked to explain the phenomenon of persistent unemployment, would automatically have started with the assertion that its proximate cause must lie in too high wages that refuse to come down.

Some Keynesian economists, including the post-Keynesians, have thus focused on Keynes's distinction between ***nominal*** and ***effective demand*** as holding the key to his analysis. Thus it may be the case that even if the real wage is at the level at which the labour market could nominally clear, the effective demand for labour is constrained by lack of demand in the markets for goods and services. This is illustrated in Fig. 35.5. In this diagram the real wage *is* at the level which would cause the labour market to clear in neo-classical analysis. In Keynesian analysis, however, a distinction is drawn between this nominal demand for labour and the effective demand for labour as constrained by conditions in the goods market shown in the top half of Fig. 35.5.

In Fig. 35.5, we can see that the level of aggregate demand (AD_1), as determined in the Keynesian cross diagram, is insufficient to purchase the level of output associated with full employment (L_f) in the labour market. Thus the effective demand for labour is *actually* set by the level of aggregate demand equilibrium at Q_1. Employers will not employ workers past this level, for whatever the potential profit suggested by wages and prices there can be no profit in producing goods and services that no one will actually buy!

This interpretation clearly breaks with the assertion that unemployment is caused by too high a level of the real wage. In this interpretation the 'prices are right' for full employment as it would nominally be profitable for firms to employ all the labour wishing to work. This does not happen, however, as it is profitable to employ the labour only if the products so produced can be sold.

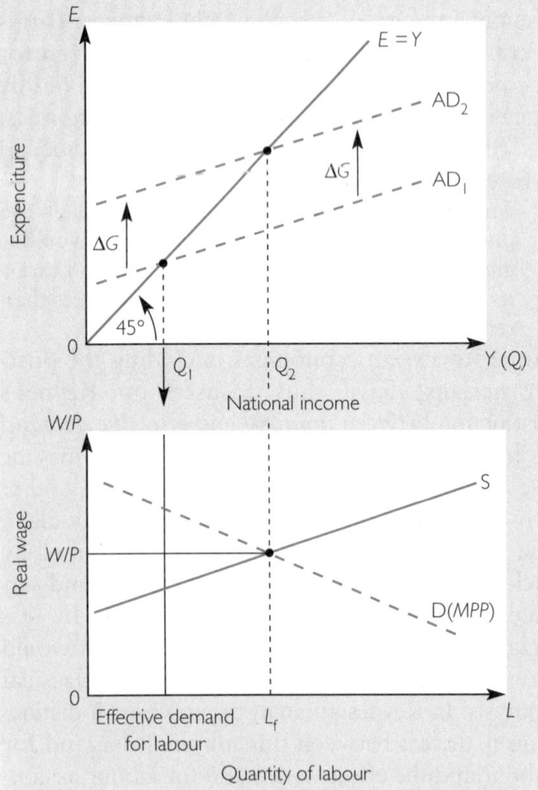

Fig. 35.5 **Curing a Keynesian recession**
Lack of effective demand keeps employment below the full employment equilibrium. This is cured by an increase in government expenditure (ΔG) increasing the level of aggregate demand.

If the produce of labour cannot be sold because of lack of aggregate demand it is not profitable to employ labour whatever the level of the real wage.

STUDENT ACTIVITY 35.3

Adapt Fig. 35.5 to show that if a lack of aggregate demand for goods and services is the problem, a fall in wages could actually worsen unemployment, i.e. a reduction in the spending power of workers might further reduce aggregate demand thereby further constraining effective demand in the labour market.

Curing the recession

As is so often the case the analysis of a problem suggests the cure. In Fig. 35.5 we can see how an increase in government expenditure could lift the constraint of effective demand in the labour market by increasing the demand for goods and services.

The upper part of the diagram is the familiar Keynesian cross/45° diagram in which an increase in government injections has increased the demand for goods and services. The lower part shows that this allows the profitable employment of more workers even if the real wage remains at the same level. Once full employment is reached the model again reverts to the neo-classical vertical AS case, i.e. further increases in aggregate demand will simply cause prices and wages to increase in equal proportion.

The above interpretation of increases in aggregate demand, acting to lift constraints on the quantity of goods that can be sold and consequently the amount of labour employed, implies an AS curve as shown in Fig. 35.6.

As can be seen, in this interpretation, increases in AD can increase output until full employment is reached without the need for any price changes or reduction in the real wage.

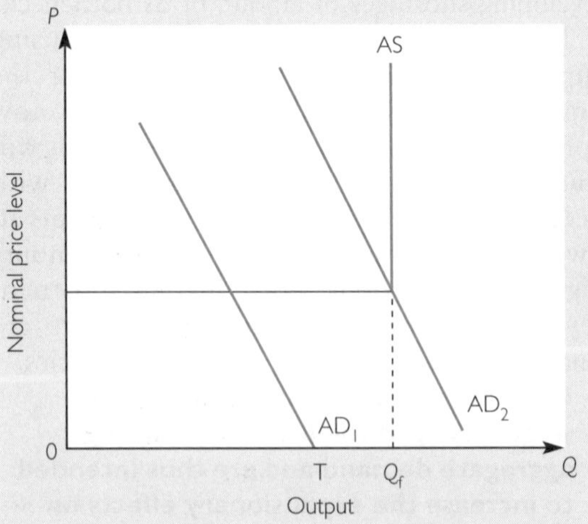

Fig. 35.6 **A Keynesian aggregate supply**
An extreme view would allow increases in aggregate demand to increase output, without inflation until full employment is reached.

A neo-classical view

The transmission mechanism

We have seen that in macroeconomic representations of neo-classical economics (e.g. the new classical school) the aggregate supply curve is vertical. If we stick to the assumption of perfectly competitive markets for goods and services and flexible wages there is a monetarist rebuttal to the Keynesian assertion that a lack of AD can for ever prevent full employment being reached. If markets are perfectly competitive the lack of effective demand as compared with the level of aggregate supply would cause a persistent downward pressure on prices. Thus, given a constant nominal money supply, the real supply of money will be constantly increasing. The neo-classical monetarist school argues that eventually this increase in the real money supply must 'spill over' into extra spending. This supposed transmission mechanism is explained in more detail on page 522. This will cause AD to increase until eventually full employment is again reached.

The Pigou effect

The increase in consumption due to increased real money balances described above is known as the ***real money balances effect*** or the 'Pigou effect' after the economist who used it to challenge Keynes's assertion in *The General Theory* that the economy could remain permanently at less than full employment. Many Keynesian economists have responded by accepting its validity as a theoretical solution but insisted that the process would take far too long for policy purposes and hence that the increase in aggregate demand would have to be 'artificially' hastened by government-induced reflation.

The debate between Keynesians and neo-classical economists over the Pigou effect relates to the time the effect would take to cure unemployment.

The effect of pricing policies

If we drop the assumption of perfectly competitive markets the Pigou effect loses much of its persuasiveness to the effect that a free market capitalist economy is ultimately self-correcting.

Neo-Keynesians point out that it has been known for a long time that most firms are not engaged in marginal cost pricing but in fact set their price according to a pre-determined mark-up on average cost.

Such pricing practices were examined in Chapter 17. Now, much empirical evidence also suggests that average cost is fairly constant for most firms over a wide range of output. Thus reality may not consist of firms moving up their marginal cost curves in response to increased prices, but instead firms may use some 'rule of thumb' mark-up pricing formula and then sell as much as they can at this price.

Figure 35.7 shows the effect of such mark-up pricing practice. The figure shows that increases in demand may be met by firms increasing their output in response to increased sales without any upward pressure on prices.

STUDENT ACTIVITY 35.4

Taken literally, neo-classical theory suggests that firms will refuse to sell more output at the same price when the point at which $MC = MR$ is reached. Think about your experiences as a consumer and consider which theory of the firm, neo-classical or (neo-)Keynesian, best describes your experiences. Is descriptive accuracy necessarily the most important feature for comparison?

Similarly, firms may respond to decreases in aggregate demand by cutting back output without any change in price. Thus, unlike in perfect competition, there is not necessarily a tendency for prices to fall as aggregate demand falls. If, following depressed sales, firms competed with one another for increased sales, then the real money supply might again be increased, leading ultimately to a real balance effect. But, particularly in highly concentrated markets, firms may resist the temptation to cut prices for fear of precipitating a self-defeating price war. (See discussion of oligopoly behaviour in Chapter 17.)

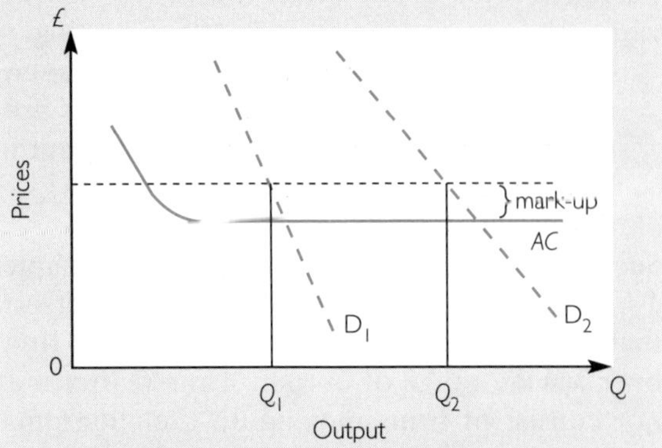

Fig. 35.7 **The effect of mark-up pricing**
The existence of a flat-bottomed *AC* curve and mark-up pricing policies means large changes in demand have no effect upon price. This means that excess capacity can exist without affecting prices. Thus the market might not be self-correcting.

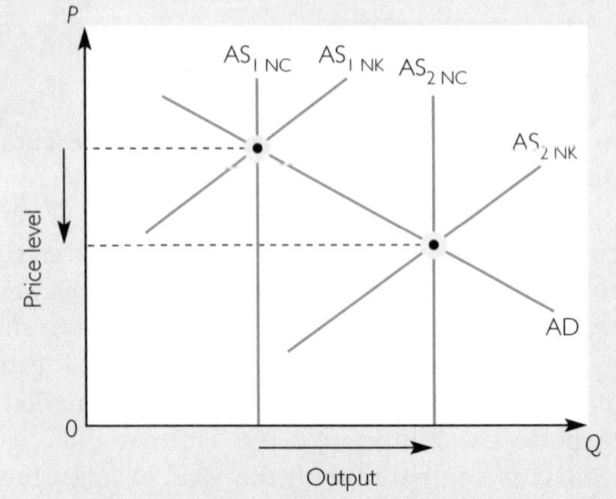

Fig. 35.8 **Successful supply side policy**
For neo-classical economists (NC) inflation is reduced and the natural level of output/employment increased. For neo-Keynesian (NK) economists the inflation output/employment trade-off is improved. For both schools equilibrium output is increased and prices lowered.

Mark-up pricing can also be used to explain why the aggregate supply curve might begin to slope, and increase in slope, as full employment is approached. For example, as firms near their maximum potential output production might become less efficient causing average costs to rise. Alternatively, as resources become more fully utilised input costs might rise, again causing unit costs to increase. In either case the increase in unit cost will be passed on as a price rise if a constant mark-up is maintained.

Shifting the aggregate supply curve rightwards

In both the neo-classical and neo-Keynesian views, anything which increases labour productivity or the incentive to work will shift the aggregate supply curve to the right. Neo-classical economists will think of a vertical aggregate supply curve shifting as the ***natural rate*** of output increases. Neo-Keynesians will show an upward-sloping aggregate supply curve shifting and improving the inflation output/employment trade-off. In both schools such a shift will tend to lower inflation and increase output (see Fig. 35.8).

Common misunderstanding
Students sometimes think that because the price level is almost always rising (i.e. there is always some inflation) aggregate demand must permanently be exceeding aggregate supply. More complex models, however, take account of this persistent tendency for inflation (e.g. see Chapter 44). Thus a rightward shift of the aggregate supply curve can be considered to reduce *inflation rather than actually cause the price level to fall.*

Labour market supply side measures associated with the neo-classical schools are examined in more detail in Chapter 45. These measures include reduced welfare payments, reduced taxation, reduced trade union power and the abolition of wage floors. These policies are often advocated by those who believe that government intervention in the economy should be as little as possible. They see obstacles to the operation of the free market as being the root cause of disappointing economic performance.

The interventionist policies associated with the left of the political spectrum in the UK, however, have also increasingly been couched in terms of supply side economics. Such analysts point out that the evidence on the effects of 'free market' supply measures is inconclusive. They believe that the major effects of such policies have been an increase in poverty and the deterioration of working conditions. Keynesians continue to maintain that significant increases in employment and economic forces can be achieved, so it is argued, only by intervention in the economy and changes to the structure of the economy.

Interventionist policies suggested to shift the aggregate supply have included increased provision and subsidisation of education and training. This has recently been given strong emphasis in the UK by the Prime Minister, Tony Blair. This might directly increase labour productivity but its effects may be long term. Another way to increase productivity might be to increase the level of investment by deliberately directing resources towards it, e.g. by tax allowances and grants. Left-wing analysts also criticise the financial markets of the UK for maintaining very high levels of overseas investment and would take measures to redirect this investment towards UK manufacturing. By increasing investment, labour productivity would be raised and UK industry made more competitive. But should the investment decisions of private individuals be interfered with?

STUDENT ACTIVITY 35.5

Draw the effects on aggregate supply of an increase in wage pressure or a loss of industrial capacity. What will be the effect on employment and inflation?

Objections to aggregate supply and demand analysis

We have seen that the slope of the aggregate supply can be used to represent neo-classical and neo-Keynesian views. But economists from both the *laissez-faire* Austrian school and the interventionist post-Keynesian school would challenge the usefulness of aggregate demand and supply analysis. Although at near opposite ends of the political spectrum both of these schools feel that it is misleading to represent the economy in terms of equilibriums. In particular they point out that equilibrium ignores uncertainty and the dynamics of the economy with the passage of time.

For example, an economist looking at aggregate demand and supply diagrams might attempt to reduce inflation by decreasing aggregate demand so as to intersect the aggregate supply curve at a lower level of prices. But this might instead result in a collapse of investment as expectations are adjusted to a downturn in the economy. This collapse of investment in turn means demand is sharply reduced still further. As industrial capacity, job skills and investment in new technology are lost the economy becomes trapped in a downward cycle. If an attempt is made to reflate the economy by restoring aggregate demand the economy is unable to respond quickly by restoring industrial output; hence inflation and imports surge upwards. Instead of a mere adjustment of demand the attempt to reduce inflation has permanently damaged the performance of the economy and made it even more difficult to control inflation!

STUDENT ACTIVITY 35.6

Attempt to draw the effects of the analysis of the preceding paragraph using aggregate demand and supply curve diagrams.

Conclusion

Enough has now been said for the reader to appreciate that there is more than one interpretation of aggregate demand and supply diagrams and hence they should not be used unthinkingly. Nevertheless they can provide a convenient way of demonstrating likely macroeconomic interactions. For example, a reduction in the cost of an important raw material can be expected to increase aggregate supply, thereby causing an increase in output and a reduction in the price level.

Summary

1 For many years macroeconomic analysis focused on aggregate demand, following the work of Keynes. The neo-classical school has moved the emphasis to aggregate supply.

2 Deceptively simple aggregate demand and supply curves should be treated with caution. Many assumptions may be used when constructing them, such as that of perfect competition.
3 A fall in the level of prices causes the real money supply to increase, which results in an extension of demand for the output of the economy. Thus the aggregate demand curve is downward sloping. This relationship may be reinforced by changes in imports and exports.
4 The neo-classical view is that the aggregate supply curve is vertical as the real wage adjusts to maintain equilibrium in the labour market.
5 The neo-Keynesian view is that the aggregate supply curve slopes upwards until full employment is reached, when it becomes vertical.
6 Post-Keynesians follow Keynes in emphasising the constraint on employment set by the level of demand in the goods and service market. For such economists the aggregate 'supply' curve may be flat over a wide range.
7 Neo-Keynesians argue for the need for governments to increase the level of aggregate demand to cure unemployment. The neo-classical view is that this causes inflation, not employment.
8 Neo-classicists argue that any lack of effective demand causes prices to fall and thus an increase in real money balances. This causes an increase in demand and eliminates the unemployment. This is sometimes termed the Pigou effect. Keynesians believe the effect would take too long to restore full employment for practical relevance.
9 Uncertainty, imperfections of competition and oligopolistic pricing policies may interfere with the attainment of full employment equilibriums.
10 Supply side improvements can be represented by a rightward shift of the aggregate supply curve.

Questions

1 Demonstrate how the aggregate supply curve may be derived from the demand curve for labour.
2 Contrast the different views of the shape of the aggregate supply curve.
3 Discuss the view that the macroeconomy is essentially self-regulating.
4 How may persistent unemployment arise in the macroeconomy according to the neo-Keynesian school of thought?
5 What is the real money balances (or Pigou) effect?
6 Contrast neo-classical and neo-Keynesian views on policies to reduce unemployment.
7 Use aggregate demand and supply curves to demonstrate how inflation occurs.
8 If the Treasury were to fill old bottles with banknotes, bury them at suitable depths in disused coalmines which were then filled up to the surface with town rubbish, and leave it to private enterprise on well-tried principles of laissez-faire to dig the notes up again ... there need be no more unemployment and with the help of the repercussions, the real income of the community, and its capital also, would probably become a good deal greater than it actually is.
Do you agree with this statement taken from Keynes's *General Theory*? Give reasons for your answer.
9 'Supply-siders argue that if the poor have more they work less but if the rich have more they work harder.' To what extent is this statement a fair representation of the arguments of supply side economists?

Data response A The effects of a maximum working week

Read the following extract from the *Daily Mail* of 28 August 1997 and then answer the questions that follow:

1 To what extent could there ever be said to be full employment in an economy where the working week is artificially constrained?
2 Accepting the definition of a full-time job as a 35 hour week, what would be the effect on the full employment level of output in a Keynesian cross/45° diagram?
3 Show the effect on an upward-sloping aggregate supply curve of a tax surcharge on workers' extra hours and an obligatory reduction of hours without a proportionate reduction in salary. Explain you answer.
4 What might be the effect on the aggregate demand curve of increased marginal taxation and a shorter working week with a less than proportionate reduction in salary? Explain your answer.
5 What would be the overall effect of the changes in questions 2, 3 and 4 above on (where the overall change is indeterminate explain why this is so):
   a) output
   b) employment
   c) the price level?

Data response B
Money, expectations and markets

Read the following extract from the *Observer* of 31 August 1997 and then answer the questions that follow:

1 To what extent might past experience of changes in the economy affect and modify current behaviour?
2 Explain the importance of the distinction between 'private' and 'external' logic, as described in the article, to Keynesian economics.
3 Link fluctuations in money markets to changes in aggregate demand.
4 Use the article and aggregate demand and supply analysis to suggest how a deliberate attempt to reduce inflation could lead to an unintended recession.
5 'The volatility of markets is as much an argument against government macro-economic intervention as it is for it.' Explain and discuss.

The French put a tax on hard work

From Peter Shard in Paris

French workers face paying extra tax if they work too hard.

Under extraordinary proposals being drafted by Lionel Jospin's Socialist government, anyone labouring more than 39 hours a week will automatically pay an income tax surcharge and more on national insurance.

The plan has been formulated because M Jospin wants to cut the working week to 35 hours to create more jobs. From next year, workers doing official overtime beyond the current working week of 39 hours will have to pay a tax surcharge on their extra hours.

From 2000, all salaried employees will be liable to pay the extra tax for every hour a week they work above 39, even if it is part of their normal work and not overtime.

The plans are contained in a leaked document prepared for employment minister Martine Aubry.

By law, all French companies have to register employees' hours. Most workers are said to be in favour of the shorter week even if it means earning less. They believe it is a way of helping to persuade companies to take on more employees on shorter working weeks, although the trade unions and bosses are sceptical.

Confederation of industry spokesperson Jean Gandois denounced what he called this 'massive obligatory reduction of hours without a cut in salary which will seriously harm the competitiveness of our businesses.'

Small firms would be particularly hard hit, Small Businesses Confederation president Lucien Rebuffel warned.

'The reduction in the working week is impracticable because of the way specialised jobs and functions are divided up,' he said.

Louis Viannet, leader of the Communist-backed CGT union, insisted that workers must not be made to suffer. 'This measure must take effect comprehensively and quickly without any reduction in salary' he said. And he warned: 'If the bosses maintain their opposition, there is going to be conflict.'

Source: *Observer*, 31 August 1997

Money: A Telling Lore

Are buyers and sellers rational people, creating a nice balance between supply and demand? Theorists think they are, but real life is different, says Dorothy Rowe.

Money isn't real. It may be a very important means whereby we maintain our sense of identity, but it isn't real. It's simply a set of ideas, some of which we share with other people and some which are our own. We might both agree that this piece of metal is a £1 coin, but is it a lot or a little to pay for a pint of milk? Value is in the eye of the beholder.

If you want to understand why the market does what it does we need to understand ourselves; that is, our own private logic. Nothing pleases me more than when I find some scientific research that supports my theories, especially my theory that to understand why people behave as they do we need to discover each person's private logic.

Research reported by the Guardian recently did just that. Here, researchers used artificial-life methods to create computer software working as 'robotraders' to examine classic market theory.

Classic market theory, or the competitive equilibrium model, assumes buyers and sellers behave rationally and thus, in a free market, produce an equilibrium between supply and demand. In real life, markets might produce some thing like an equilibrium but they also produce much volatility, bubbles and crashes – events that classic theory finds difficult to explain.

Economists, like psychologists, have always been strong on theory. Again like psychologists, they have steadfastly ignored what real people actually do, because real people ruin theories. Some people might do what the theory predicts, but many won't. Instead of asking why this happens, economists and psychologists, since the beginning of their disciplines in the nineteenth century, have seen their task as being that of scientists, of uncovering the orthodox truths that are immanent in nature. In the search for such universal laws, what individuals think is irrelevant.

For psychologists, no word implied such complete rejection and scorn as 'subjective'. The ideal of science towards which they strove was physics, but in such striving they managed to overlook Heisenberg who, in describing his Uncertainty Principle in 1927, said the experimenter was always part of the experiment.

What this means in terms of theory is that the particular theory a person creates or espouses may or may not reflect the real world but will always reflect the individual personal meanings created by those who hold it.

In psychology and economics, theories are never proved or disproved. They simply come into and fall out of fashion.

Freud's theories used to be all the rage while Jung's were seen as the product of an unworldly nutter. Now Freud is deplored or ignored while Jung is extremely popular. In economics, Maynard Keynes went out of fashion and Milton Friedman came in, but now he is on the wane and Keynes is becoming increasingly fashionable.

By ignoring the essence of how we live our lives – the personal meanings we each create – economists and psychologists have developed theories about the world and the people in it from which all sense of personal experience has been removed.

Psychologists have developed models that represent us as being nothing but puppets manipulated by the strings of behaviourist stimulus-response, or of genes, or of unconscious drives. Economists, wrote Paul Ormerod (an economist who is extremely critical of classical economics), 'see the world as a machine – a very complicated one, but nevertheless a machine, whose workings can be understood by putting together carefully and meticulously its components parts'.

'The behaviour of the system as a whole,' he continued 'can be deduced from a simple aggregation of these components. A lever pulled in a certain part of a machine with a certain strength will have regular and predictable outcomes elsewhere in the machine.'

The Science Museum now houses a model of such a machine made by Bill Phillips, an engineer turned economist. This wonderful contraption has levers to pull, buttons to press, sluice gates and liquids of different colours which, representing economic forces, would rush around the system's tubes.

Such economic machines were not assumed to be thinking. Computers might not think for themselves but they can contain software that simulates thought. This is what the robotrader computers did or, at least, these were models of how their makers, the computer programmers, thought people thought.

They gave their robotraders the ability to adapt to market conditions by using learning algorithms that allow them to try out different buying and selling strategies to optimise their portfolios.

They each reacted individually to events, using the trading rules with which they had been programmed. These rules corresponded to what we can call shared, public logic. However, these robotraders also had a kind of private logic.

We all share a public logic, but each of us has his or her own private logic, which is the set of conclusions we have drawn from our individual experience. No two people ever have the same experience, so no two people ever see any thing in exactly the same way.

The robotraders' programmers created a kind of private logic for their robotraders by running a genetic algorithm, a technique that created a kind of Darwinian evolution in the software, cross-breeding sections of the code to create new strings, some of which then made changes in the external logic rules.

We human beings do this all the time. Your mother might have laid down the rule; 'On your way to school, cross the road only at pedestrian crossings'. You then change that rule to; ' Use a pedestrian crossing only when mother can see you'. Your changed rule is part of your private logic. We use private logic continuously. These robotraders could do so only when the researchers used the genetic algorithm. The researchers ran their experiment 25 times, involving each time some 250,000 trades.

The results were clear. Under certain conditions the efficient market of classic theory emerged. Under other conditions the market that emerged was just like real life – lots of activity, prices bubbling up and then crashing down, the kind of market that pension-fund managers and market-watchers find so hard to predict.

And what were these different conditions? The classic market emerged when the robotraders were using only their external logic, but when the genetic algorithms were used frequently this private logic produced a market very close to real life.

This is a simple scientific replication of what goes on all the time in real life.

In dealing with money, as in dealing with every aspect of our lives, we use both the shared, external logic, which is contained Aristotelian logic, scientific method and laws, mathematics and agreed rules and laws; and our own private, individual logic of the structure of meaning, which gives our sense of identity.

Source: *Daily Mail*, 28 August 1997

SECTION VI Money, prices and national income

'Money is a good servant but a bad master.'

Oxford Dictionary of English Proverbs

36 Money and prices

Learning outcomes

After reading this chapter you will be able to:

- Distinguish between different measures of the money supply.
- Use the characteristics and functions of money to determine how well various assets can perform as money.
- Compare different measures of inflation.
- Understand the link between money and inflation.

Introduction

Monetary economics

In this section of the book we will concern ourselves with money. We will look at monetary theory, at institutions which are concerned with the creation and transmission of money and at the monetary policy of the government. Together these subjects constitute the branch of the subject known as monetary economics. Not only is monetary economics an important branch of the subject, it is one of the most controversial areas of modern economics.

In this chapter we shall explain the nature and functions of money in a modern society, as well as the concept of the price level.

The importance of money

'Money', said Geoffrey Crowther, 'is a veil thrown over the working of the economic system'. Money may indeed obscure some of the workings of the ***real economy*** but it also facilitates its working. It would be impossible for a complex society to function without money. However, money does more than facilitate the working of the economy; it may also be a powerful influence upon the real economic variables such as consumption, investment, foreign trade and employment. Monetary economics has much to tell us about how changes in the demand, supply and price of money influence the economy.

The development of money

The origins of money

The word money derives from the Latin *moneta* – the first Roman coinage was minted at the temple of Juno Moneta in 344BC. Before coinage, various objects such as cattle, pigs' teeth and cowrie shells had been used as money. Such forms of money are termed ***commodity money*** and they are not confined to ancient societies; for example, when the currency collapsed in Germany in 1945, commodity money in the form of cigarettes and coffee took its place.

For most of its history money has taken the form of coins made of precious metal. This kind of money had ***intrinsic*** value. Many of the units of modern money recall their origin in amounts of precious metal; for example, the pound sterling was originally the Roman pound (12 ounces) of silver. Hence the symbol £ derives from the letter L standing for *libra*, the Latin for a pound. Similarly, dollars were originally one-ounce pieces of silver (the origin of the $ symbol is obscure; it probably derives from the figure 8 on old Spanish 'pieces of eight', which had the same value as a dollar).

From coins to banknotes

Both paper money and modern banking practice originated from the activities of goldsmiths. Goldsmiths used to accept deposits of gold coins and precious objects for safe keeping, in return for which a receipt would be issued which was, in effect, a ***promissory note*** (a promise to pay the bearer). As time went by these notes began to be passed around in settlement of debts, acting as banknotes do today. Goldsmiths also discovered that they did not need to keep all the gold they had on deposit in their vaults because, at any particular time, only a small percentage of their customers would want their gold back. Thus they discovered that they could lend out, say, 90 per cent of their deposits, keeping only 10 per cent to meet the demands of their depositors. This relationship of cash (assets) retained to total deposits (liabilities) is known as the ***cash ratio***.

Let us now consider what happened to the gold which the goldsmith re-lent. This was used by borrowers to pay bills and the recipient would then redeposit it with the same or another goldsmith. This goldsmith issued a promissory note for the deposit and then re-lent 90 per cent of the new deposit of gold. The process would then be repeated with the redeposit of more gold and the writing of more promissory notes. The limit to this process was that the goldsmiths always had to keep, say, 10 per cent of their assets in gold. This would mean that if the goldsmiths kept to a 10 per cent ratio, each £1 of gold could secure a further £9 in promissory notes. Thus, the banker, for this is what the goldsmith had become by this time, could be said to have created money.

The completion of this process came in the 1680s when Francis Childs became the first banker to print banknotes. Today the process of credit creation lies at the heart of our money supply. Originally the gold had intrinsic value and the paper money was issued on the faith in the bank. Any currency issued that was not fully backed by gold was called a ***fiduciary issue***. Today banks create credit in the form of deposits against the security of Bank of England notes in the same manner that the old banks created banknotes on the security of gold.

Common misunderstanding

Most people do not question whether money is valuable. They know from their experience that the system works. Today, however, it can be seen that the whole edifice of money rests on ***confidence*** *in the banking system, since all notes are now fiduciary issue. The creation of credit is kept under control by the Bank of England since it issues the banknotes and is responsible for supervising the banks. If you examine a banknote you will see it has written on the side with the Queen's head on it: 'I promise to pay the bearer on demand the sum of five (ten or twenty) pounds.' What would happen if you took a banknote to the Bank of England and asked them to keep their promise? They would exchange it for another banknote of the same value!*

Credit creation

A single-bank system

Let us imagine there is only one bank with which everyone in the country does business. This bank has initial deposits of £10 000 in cash so that its balance sheet would be:

Liabilities (£)	*Assets (£)*
Deposits 10 000	Cash 10 000

The bank knows from experience, however, that only a tenth of its deposits will be demanded in cash at any particular time and so it is able to lend out £9000 at interest. The people who borrow this money spend it. The shopkeepers etc. who receive this money then put it into the bank and the bank finds that the £9000 it has lent out has been redeposited. This could be described as a created deposit. It is then able to repeat this process, lending out nine-tenths of this £9000 and retaining £900. The £8100 it has lent out will find its way back to the bank again, whereupon it can once more lend out nine-tenths, and so on. This is illustrated in Table 36.1.

Thus at the end of the process, with total cash of £10 000 in the system and a cash ratio of 10 per cent, the bank is able to make loans

Table 36.1 Deposit creation in a single-bank system with a 10 per cent cash ratio

	Liabilities (£) (Deposits)		*Loans and advances*		*Assets (£) Cash retained*	
Created deposits	Initial deposit	10 000	1st loan	9 000	1/10 of deposit retained	1 000
	1st redeposit	9 000	2nd loan	8 100	1/10 of redeposit retained	900
	2nd redeposit	8 100	3rd loan	7 290	1/10 of redeposit retained	810
	3rd redeposit	7 290	4th loan	6 561	1/10 of redeposit retained	729
		.		.		
		.		.		.
		.		.		.
	The maximum possible creation of deposits occurs when					
		.		.		.
		.		.		.
		.		.		
	Liabilities =	£100 000	Assets =	£90 000	+	£10 000

amounting to £90 000. Although many more deposits have been created, you will see that everything balances out because the bank still has the necessary one-tenth of its assets in cash to meet its liabilities. You can also see that each horizontal line in Table 36.1 balances assets against liabilities and, therefore, at no stage are accounting principles infringed. The bank's balance sheet at the end of the process would appear as:

Liabilities(£)		*Assets(£)*	
Initial deposits	10 000	Cash	10 000
Created deposits	90 000	Loans and advances	90 000
	£100 000		£100 000

Note that the bank itself cannot distinguish between its initial deposits and created deposits.

The bank multiplier

The limit to credit creation in this manner is given by the formula:

$$D = \frac{1}{r} \times C$$

where D is the amount of bank deposits, r is the cash ratio and C is the cash held by banks. Thus, in our example we would get:

$$D = \frac{1}{0.1} \times £10\,000 = £100\,000$$

The value of the expression $1/r$ is known as the bank or ***credit creation multiplier***. It shows the relationship between the cash (or reserve assets) retained against total liabilities. In this example the cash ratio is 10 per cent, so the bank multiplier would be 10. However, if the cash ratio were dropped to 5 per cent the multiplier would be 20, whereas if it were raised to 20 per cent it would be only 5.

The effect of any additional deposit of cash into the system upon the level of deposits can be given by the formula:

$$\Delta D = \frac{1}{r} \times \Delta C$$

where ΔD is the effect upon total deposits as the result of a change in cash deposits, ΔC. Note also that there would be a comparable multiple contraction in deposits if cash were lost from the system.

STUDENT ACTIVITY 36.1

In a very small economy with only one bank, what will be the maximum value of deposits the bank can create if the bank holds £100 in cash, and the cash ratio is 10 per cent? What would happen to the maximum value of deposits if
a) the cash ratio were changed to 20 per cent
b) the bank's holdings of cash rise by £10?

A multibank system

If we consider a system in which there are many banks, credit creation will go on in the same manner except that money which is loaned out may find its way into a bank other than the one which made it. This is illustrated below, where we assume that there are two banks in the system. Here we have raised the cash ratio to 12.5 per cent, partly to guard against the possibility of deposits being lost to the other bank(s) or leaking out of the banking system altogether. The initial £10 000 of deposits is divided equally between the two banks, and with a cash ratio of 12.5 per cent they are able to create deposits of seven times this amount:

Bank X

Liabilities (£)		*Assets (£)*	
Initial deposits	5 000	Cash	5 000
Created deposits	35 000	Loans and advances	35 000
	£40 000		£40 000

Bank Y

Liabilities (£)		*Assets (£)*	
Initial deposits	5 000	Cash	5 000
Created deposits	35 000	Loans and advances	35 000
	£40 000		£40 000

Thus, the initial £10 000 is used to support £80 000 of liabilities.

STUDENT ACTIVITY 36.2

What would happen in this situation if account holders in bank X made payments to account holders in bank Y of £2000? Bank X's liabilities would be reduced by £2000 and bank Y's would be increased by £2000. To balance this out bank X would be obliged to make a payment of £2000 to bank Y in cash (in the real world they would make this adjustment through the bank's accounts at the Bank of England). Draw up the banks' balance sheets at the end of these transactions. What has happened to the two banks' cash ratios? What will each bank now try to do to maximise credit creation within the cash ratio constraint? Could bank X be patient and expect some payments in the opposite direction in the next period of time? Will these uncertainties about shifting account balances make banks a little more cautious about credit creation?

Cash ratios and the control of the money supply

The cash ratio was abolished in the UK in 1971 and was replaced by a 12.5 per cent reserve assets ratio, although the clearing banks were expected to keep 1.5 per cent of their assets in cash at the Bank of England. In August 1981 this reserve assets ratio was itself abolished. From this date all banks were required to keep the equivalent of 0.5 per cent (reduced to 0.35 per cent in 1992) of their eligible liabilities in cash at the Bank of England. This is held in non-operational accounts, i.e. the banks may not use this cash. The object of these non-operational, non-interest-bearing accounts is to supply the Bank with funds. In addition to this money, banks have to keep cash at the Bank for the purpose of settling interbank indebtedness (clearing of cheques). Although there is now no cash or reserve assets ratio, banks still need to keep a minimum level of cash and liquid assets, i.e. assets that can quickly be turned into cash in order to meet their obligations on a day-to-day basis. The Bank has laid down guidelines for banks to assess the ***prudent*** proportion of liquid assets which they need. The asset cover varies according to the kind of deposits (liabilities) the bank has accepted. Thus it is not possible, at present, to state this as a simple ratio.

The functions and attributes of money

We have not as yet defined money. So far we have suggested that coins, banknotes and bank deposits are money. Whether an asset is regarded as money or not depends not so much on what it is but upon what it does.

Money can be defined as anything which is readily acceptable in settlement of a debt.

Thus we have a functional definition of money. For any asset to be considered as money it must fulfil the four functions discussed below. The different forms of money do not all fulfil the functions equally well.

The functions of money

a) *Medium of exchange.* Money facilitates the exchange of goods and services in the economy. Workers accept money for their wages because they know that money can be exchanged for all the different things they will need.

   If there were not money, then exchange would have to take place by barter. For barter to be possible there must be a ***double coincidence of wants***. For example, if you have chickens but wish to acquire shoes, you must find someone who has shoes which they wish to exchange for chickens. The difficulties of barter will limit the possibilities of exchange and thus inhibit the growth of an economy. This situation was summed up by the classical economists when they said that, rather than a coincidence of wants, there was likely to be a want of coincidence.

b) *Unit of account.* Money is a means by which we can measure the disparate things which make up the economy. Thus, barrels of oil, suits of clothes, visits to the cinema, houses and furniture can all be given a common measure which allows us to compare them and to aggregate their value.

   It could be argued that there are many things which cannot be given a price. For example, you might possess mementoes of your family or friends which you value highly but which the economist would say were economically worthless. At this stage you might be tempted to agree with Oscar Wilde and say, 'What is a cynic? A man who knows the price of everything and the value of nothing.' The economist, however, is commenting on the exchange value of things within the economy, not the sentimental value which a person may put upon their possessions.

c) *Store of value.* For a variety of reasons, people may wish to put aside some of their current income and save it for the future. Money presents the most useful way of doing this. If, for example, a person were saving for their old age, it would be impossible to put to one side all the physical things – food, clothing, fuel, etc. – which they would require, apart from the fact that their needs may change. Money, however, allows them to buy anything they require.

   In times of high inflation the value of money is eroded and people may turn to real assets such as property. The value of physical assets is, however, also uncertain, in addition to which they may deteriorate physically, which money will not.

d) *Standard of deferred payment.* Many contracts involve future payment, e.g. hire purchase, mortgages and long-term construction works. Any contract with a time element in it would be very difficult if there were not a commonly agreed means of payment. The future being uncertain, creditors know that all their economic needs can be satisfied with money.

Inflation and the functions of money

Inflation adversely affects the functions of money but it does not affect them all equally. Inflation would have to become very rapid before money became unacceptable as a medium of exchange; for example, when the rate of inflation in the UK was above 20 per cent in the 1970s, shopkeepers showed no disinclination to accept money. Even in the hyperinflation in Germany in 1923, money was still used.

The unit of account function is affected by inflation since it becomes more difficult to compare values over time. For example, we may know that the GDP increased from £44.1 billion in 1970 to £438 billion in 1989, but how much of this was real increase and how much due to inflation? It requires statistical manipulation to deflate the figures and separate the ***real*** change from the ***nominal***. In fact, in the figures used above, the nominal increase of almost nine-fold in GDP is reduced to only 37 per cent in real terms when the effects of inflation have been discounted.

The effect of inflation on the store of value function is to reduce the value of people's savings. This is especially so when ***real rates of interest*** are negative, as they were in several years in the 1970s. The real rate of interest is the ***nominal rate of interest*** minus the rate of inflation (this is an approximation but works well for low values). If the nominal rate of interest is 5 per cent and the rate of inflation is 8 per cent then the real rate of interest is minus 3 per cent. If the rate of interest is not even making up for the rate of inflation then even after interest has been added in, the value of a saver's capital will have fallen in real terms. When real interest rates are negative, the effect of inflation can be, paradoxically, to increase savings as people attempt to maintain the real value of their wealth. This effect was observed in the 1970s. Inflation did, however, encourage people to search for substitute methods of preserving the value of their assets, such as purchasing gold, property or even works of art. In order to encourage people to save in times of inflation, the government introduced ***index-linked*** financial assets such as 'granny bonds'.

Inflation also affects the standard of deferred payment function. Businesses, for example, may be unwilling to become creditors over long periods of time when they fear a decline in the value of money. Alternatively, special clauses may have to be written into contracts to take account of inflation. On the other side of the coin, people will become more willing to borrow money when they believe that the real burden of the debt will be reduced by inflation.

Inflation may also have an international effect upon the currency. High rates of inflation will make the currency less acceptable internationally and therefore cause adverse effects upon the exchange rate.

The characteristics of money

We have seen that money fulfils four functions and also that many different things have functioned as money. Here we will consider what characteristics an asset should have to function as money.

a) *Acceptability*. The most important attribute of money is that it is readily acceptable.
b) *Durability*. Money should not wear out quickly. This is a problem which may affect paper money and to a lesser extent coins. The chief form of money in a modern society, which is bank deposits, suffers no physical depreciation whatsoever as it exists only as numbers on a page, or digits in a computer.
c) *Homogeneity*. It is desirable that money should be uniform. Imagine, for example, that a country's money stock consisted of £1 gold coins, but that some coins contained 1 gram of gold and others 2 grams. What would happen? People would hoard the 2 gram coins but trade with the 1 gram coins. Thus, part of the money supply would disappear. This is an illustration of ***Gresham's law***, that 'bad money drives out good'. Most forms of commodity money will suffer from Gresham's law.
d) *Divisibility*. Another of the disadvantages of commodity money, such as camels' or pigs' teeth, is that they cannot be divided into smaller units. Modern notes and coins allow us to arrive at almost any permutation of divisibility.
e) *Portability*. Commodity money and even coins suffer from the disadvantage that they may be difficult to transport. A modern bank deposit, however, may be transmitted electronically from one place to another.
f) *Stability of value*. It is highly desirable that money should retain its value. In the past this

was achieved by tying monetary value to something which was in relatively stable supply, such as gold. It is one of the most serious defects of modern money that it may be affected by inflation. The hyperinflation in Germany in 1923, for example, made the mark worthless.

g) *Difficult to counterfeit.* Once a society uses money which has only exchange value and not intrinsic value, it is essential that the possibilities for fraud and counterfeit be kept to a minimum.
h) *Scarcity.* If a commodity used as money is readily available in the environment, there are likely to be distortions in economic activity. For instance, if leaves from trees were the main form of currency, the most lucrative economic activity would be the defoliation of trees (or for those with a longer view, planting trees). This may seem a bizarre example, but the gold rushes in North America in the nineteenth century are an essentially similar phenomenon.

A cashless society?

In today's society we are seeing ever more sophisticated ways of paying for goods and services. Following cheques we have seen the arrival of direct debits, standing orders and credit cards. The late 1980s brought the introduction of EFTPOS (Electronic Funds Transfer at Point Of Sale). Under this system a customer presents the shop with a card which is fed into a machine which automatically debits the amount of the sale from the customer's bank account. It is possible to envisage a future in which there is no need for cash. Cash transactions today account for only a small percentage of the total value of sales, but cash is still used for a large number of small transactions. It is unlikely that cash will be replaced for minor day-to-day transactions such as for slot machines, bus fares and small purchases. The cost of making a payment by card is usually borne by the retailer and is therefore not noticed by the consumer. It is this cost which makes small transactions unviable by card at present.

It seems unlikely that we shall see the end of cash, but the cheque system has declined in relative importance as people switch to credit and debit cards.

STUDENT ACTIVITY 36.3

1 Assess each of the following possible assets usable as money in terms of the functions and characteristics described above.
a) premium bonds b) national lottery tickets c) daffodil bulbs d) Smarties
e) unshelled nuts f) snooker balls

2 If the rate of inflation is 10 per cent, what will the real rate of interest be for each of the following nominal rates of interest?
a) 5 per cent b) 10 per cent c) 15 per cent

Measuring the money supply

As we have seen, the vast majority of the number of transactions take place in cash, but in terms of the amount of money spent the most significant form of money is bank deposits. People have deposits of money in a bank which are only fractionally backed by cash but they are quite happy to write and accept cheques which transfer the ownership of these deposits from one person to another.

Common misunderstanding

Because people use cheques to transfer money in this way, there is a common belief that the cheques themselves are money. However, this is not the case. We could print more or less cheques without making any difference to the money supply. The money supply consists of bank deposits. Thus, when we come to try to measure the stock of money in a country, we will find that it is made up of cash and bank deposits.

Changes in definitions

There was much interest in the money supply during the 1980s by the Conservative government, which originally placed great faith in monetarism. (Monetarists place a great deal of emphasis on control of the money supply – see Chapter 38.) Changes in the financial world and the effort to try to find a 'true' measure of the money supply led to several different measures of the money stock being introduced. In 1987 the Bank of England introduced new definitions of the broader definitions of the money stock. In 1990 definitions were changed again and the Bank of England ceased publication of some of the measures of money stock. There are several measures of the money stock because there are different types of bank account.

Narrow money

Most countries of the world have two measures of the money stock: broad money supply and narrow money supply. Narrow money consists of all the purchasing power that is immediately available for spending. In the UK two narrow measures are currently published. The first, M_0 (or monetary base), consists of notes and coins in circulation and the commercial banks' deposits of cash at the Bank of England. This is shown in Table 36.2.

Table 36.2 **M_0 seasonally unadjusted, June 1997**

Money stock	*£m*
Notes and coin in circulation outside the Bank of England	25 257
Bankers' operational deposits with the Bank of England	177
M_0 (wide monetary base)	25 434

Source: Financial Statistics, August 1997

The other measure M_2 consists of notes and coins in circulation and the NIB (Non-Interest Bearing) bank deposits – principally current accounts. Also in the M_2 definition are the other interest-bearing retail deposits of banks and the retail deposits of building societies, although in recent years many of the larger building societies have become banks. Retail deposits are the deposits of the private sector which can be withdrawn easily. Since all this money is readily available for spending it is sometimes referred to as the 'transactions balance' (see Fig. 36.2).

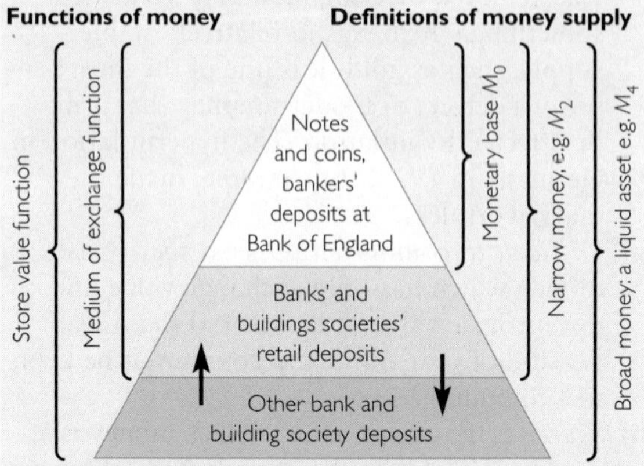

Fig. 36.1 **Concepts of the money supply**
Cash, i.e. notes and coins, are at the apex of the money supply. Similar relationships exist for all countries. Certain deposits may be moved in definitions of the money supply from time to time.

Any bank deposit which can be withdrawn on demand without incurring a (loss of) interest penalty is referred to as a ***sight deposit***.

Despite some differences in definitions from country to country, similar concepts apply to measures of the money stock(s). These may be seen as relating to the functions of money. This idea is illustrated in Fig. 36.1.

The old M_1, NIB M_1 and M_3 measures are no longer published by the Bank of England. M_1 is no longer published because it did not contain building society retail deposits. As building societies have come to operate much like banks in the 1980s with cheque books and debit cards, the Bank argued that M_1 was misleading. The Bank ceased publication of M_3 in 1989 following the Abbey National Building Society becoming a bank. Since M_3 did not contain building society deposits, it appeared that there had been a enormous increase in the M_3 supply. The M_2 measure is shown in Table 36.3.

The broad measure of the money supply includes most bank deposits (both sight and time), most building society deposits and some money market deposits such as CDs (Certificates of Deposit). The M_4 definition of the broad money supply is shown in Table 36.4.

***Table 36.3* M_2 seasonally unadjusted, June 1997**

Money stock	*£m*
Notes and coin	21 540
NIB bank deposits	38 857
IB bank deposits in M_2	295 661
Building society deposits in M_2	126 946
M_2	483 004

Source: *Financial Statistics*, August 1997

***Table 36.4* M_4 seasonally unadjusted, June 1997**

Money stock	*£m*
M_2 (see Table 36.3)	483 004
Bank wholesale deposits (incl. CDs)	235 329
Building society wholesale deposits in (incl. CDs)	10 263
	728 597

Source: *Financial Statistics*, August 1997

The changes in definitions, and suspension of the publication of some of them, reflect the arguments about what constitutes money. The reader may well ask which is the correct definition. The answer is that the various measures reflect different concepts of money and different definitions may be useful for different purposes. The M_4 definition might be said to be equivalent to the monetarist definition of money being anything which is the 'temporary abode of purchasing power'. Keynesians tend to prefer narrower definitions of the money supply.

Figure 36.2 shows the various definitions of the money supply and how they relate to one another. It shows both the measures which are published and those which are not. The factors determining the size of money stocks are discussed in Chapter 37.

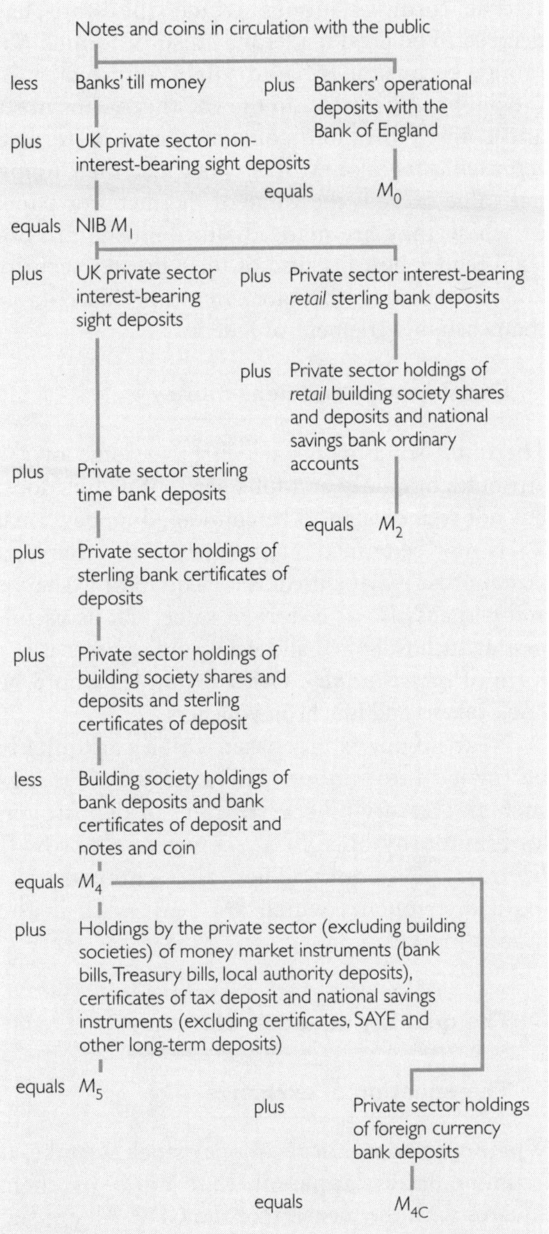

***Fig. 36.2* How the definitions of the money supply relate to one another**

Legal tender

Legal tender is anything which must be accepted in settlement of a debt. In the UK, Bank of England notes have been legal tender since 1833. The notes issued by Scottish and Northern Ireland banks are also legal tender. Royal Mint coins are legal tender too, but the law places limits on the quantities of coin which a creditor is forced to accept. Thus, for example, a creditor can refuse to accept payment of a £1000 debt entirely in 1p coins.

The form of money which the state has decreed to be legal tender may also be termed ***fiat*** money because it is based solely on the faith of the public in its value. In the UK this means notes and coins. Notes and coins may also be termed ***representative*** money; this is because their nominal value exceeds the value of the metal or paper of which they are made. Bank deposits are not legal tender but, because of their greater security and convenience, they are often more acceptable than cash in settlement of a debt.

Quasi-money and near money

There are some assets which have some of the attributes of money and fulfil some of its functions, but not well enough to be considered money. Such assets may be termed quasi-money. For example, a postal order may be used as a medium of exchange and perhaps also as a store of value, but its usefulness as such is limited and we would say that it is a form of ***quasi-money***. Other examples would be book tokens and luncheon vouchers.

Near money is any asset which can quickly be turned into money. This consists of things such as Treasury bills, certificates of deposit and local authority bills. Near money assets provide ***liquidity*** for banks. They also comprise the main instruments which are dealt with in the money markets.

The quantity equation of money

The equation of exchange

Whatever measure of the money stock we take, it is immediately apparent that none of them equates with the measure of the GDP. All are significantly smaller. This is hardly surprising since each unit of the money supply may be used several times during a year. The number of times that a unit of currency changes hands in a given time period (usually a year) is referred to as the ***velocity of circulation*** (V).

Consider Fig. 36.3. Here we see a simple economy made up of four individuals, A, B, C and D. As in a real economy, each makes their living by selling goods and services to others. Thus, B is producing the goods which A wants, A is producing the goods which D wants, and so on. In each case the value of the goods concerned is £1. Therefore the total value of all the goods exchanged is £4. However, it would be necessary to have a money stock (M) of only £1 because A could pay this to B who in turn uses it to pay C and so on. Thus the value of the total income generated is £4.

This is because income is a flow of money with respect to time, while the amount of money is a stock. An analogy might be a central heating system: the amount of water in the system is the stock, which is constantly being circulated around; the quantity of water passing through any particular part of the system is the flow. The stock may remain constant while the flow becomes greater, or smaller, as the system is speeded up, or slowed down. Similarly, the amount of money in an economy does not depend solely upon the stock of money but also upon how quickly it is used. The total value of money changing hands to finance transactions can be calculated as the ***stock*** of money (M) multiplied by the velocity of circulation (V). Algebraically this can be represented as:

$$M \times V$$

In the above example this would be £1 × 4 = £4. It is possible to arrive at the same figure by taking the general or ***average price level*** (P), in our example £1, and multiplying it by the ***number of transactions*** (T), in our example 4. This would give the same figure of £4. Thus we can derive the formula:

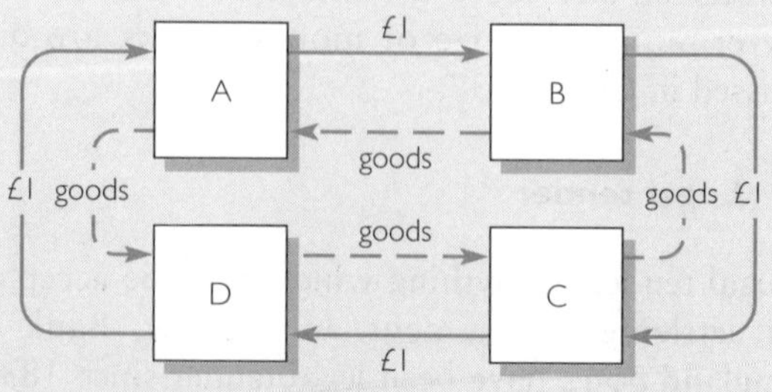

Fig. 36.3 Velocity of circulation

$M \times V = P \times T$

This is sometimes known as the quantity equation or, more properly, the equation of exchange. It was first developed by the American economist Irving Fisher.

On the left-hand side we have the total value of money changing hands in a given time period, and on the right-hand side, the total value of the transactions in the same time period. The two sides have to be equal to each other as a matter of logic. Every time there is a sale or transaction, it will be equal in value to the money changing hands. What is true of each transaction will also be true in aggregate.

The velocity of circulation

Let us consider another simplified economy. Suppose that the following is a summary of all the transactions in one time period:

2 shirts sold @ £10	£20
6 pairs of shoes sold @ £5	£30
10 loaves sold @ £1	£10
2 coats sold @ £20	£40
Total value of all transactions	£100

If the money stock is £25, we can then determine the values of the other components in the quantity equation. Since there are 20 transactions in the time period and the total value of these transactions is £100, it follows that the average price of each transaction is £5:

$$\underset{(M)}{£25} \times \underset{(V)}{4} = \underset{(P)}{£5} \times \underset{(T)}{20}$$

The value of V is difficult to measure directly, and must be calculated from the other three values.

The equation of exchange and GDP

In order to relate the equation of exchange to GDP, it is necessary to consider only ***final*** transactions. The distinction between ***intermediate*** transactions and final transactions was first made in Chapter 7. Intermediate transactions are excluded from GDP because they would result in double counting. In order to relate the exchange equation to GDP, it must be amended so as to cover only final transactions. The letter Y is used to refer to the ***number*** of final transactions. The equation is rewritten as:

$M \times V = P \times Y$

It is important to note that we are using the letter Y in a slightly different way than in the rest of the book, where it is used to denote national income. It should also be noted that the average price level (P) now also relates only to final products and not intermediate products. This is the version of the price level as used in standard measures of inflation.

Since GDP is equal to the number of final transactions times their average price ($P \times Y$), it is now possible to restate the equation:

$M \times V = \text{GDP}$

and therefore:

$V = \text{GDP}/M$

The values for the velocity of circulation are given for recent years in Fig. 36.4. The values for M_0 velocity have been rising while those for M_4 have been falling. This implies that M_4 has been rising faster than M_0 and that there is a shift out of cash and into cheque or card methods of payment.

STUDENT ACTIVITY 36.4

a) If national income is £900bn per annum, M_4 is £600bn, and M_0 is £30bn, calculate the velocity of circulation for each definiton of the money supply.
b) If $M = 100$; $P = 1$ and $T = 200$, what is the velocity of circulation? What will happen to P if M is doubled and V and T remain the same?

The concept of the general price level

Purchasing power

As we have seen, money is a unit of account and as such we can use it to measure the value of goods and services in the economy. We must now consider how we measure the value of money.

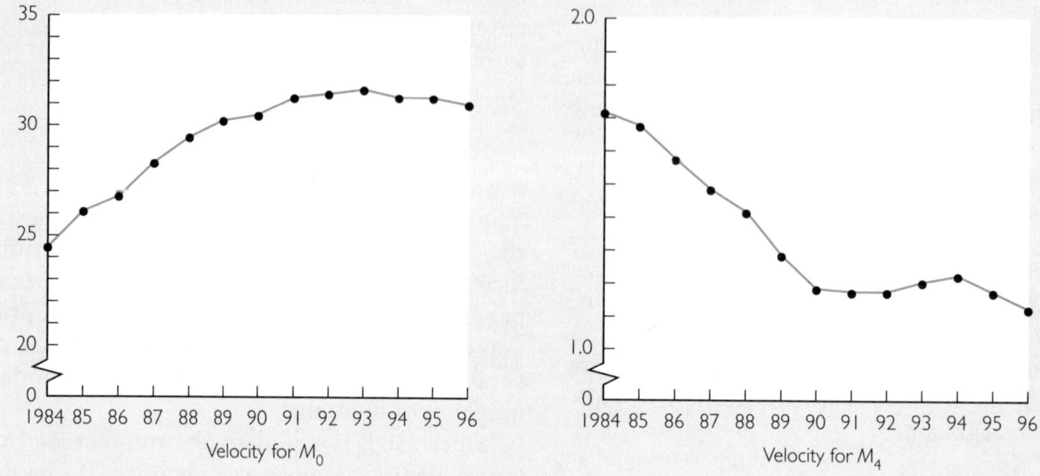

***Fig. 36.4* The velocity of circulation for M_0 annd M_4**

The value of money is determined by its purchasing power. The relative prices of goods and services are always changing but this may not imply any change in the value of money. However, if there is a rise in the general level of prices, so that the value of money declines, we have inflation. Conversely, if the general level of prices were to fall, so that the value of money increased, we would be experiencing deflation. Although an accurate measure of changes in purchasing power over long periods is virtually impossible, Fig. 36.5 gives a general idea of what has happened to the value of the pound this century. As you can see, in 1991 it would take £1 to purchase what would have cost only 1.75 pence in 1900 or, put another way, prices rose nearly 60-fold over this period. During 1997, this value will fall below 1.5 pence. However, Fig. 36.5 also shows the deflation of the interwar period when the value of money increased by some 70 per cent between 1920 and 1935.

Measures of the price level

A measure of the general price level is arrived at by monitoring the price of many individual commodities and combining them together in one index number. By then looking at the rise or fall in the index we are able to see how prices change and consequently how the value of money alters. In the UK, the main indicator of annual changes in the level of consumer prices is the general index of retail prices (RPI), but there are numerous other price indices. These include the wholesale prices index, export prices index, agricultural prices index, pensioner prices index, the consumer expenditure deflator and the taxes and prices index (TPI).

The index of retail prices (RPI)

The construction of an index number was discussed in Chapter 2. Table 36.5 shows the RPI at five yearly intervals from 1950. The index has been adjusted so that 1985 is equal to 100. It can be seen that after relatively low rates in the 1950s and 1960s, inflation took off in the 1970s with prices almost doubling every five years. Inflation settled down in the 1980s, but did not fall back to

***Table 36.5* RPI at five-year intervals, 1950–90**

Year	*% increase over five years*	*RPI*
1950		8.8
	31.8	
1955		11.6
	13.8	
1960		13.2
	18.9	
1965		15.7
	24.8	
1970		19.6
	84.2	
1975		36.1
	95.8	
1980		70.7
	41.4	
1985		100
	33.3	
1990		133.3

Source: ONS *Economic Trends Annual Supplement* 1996

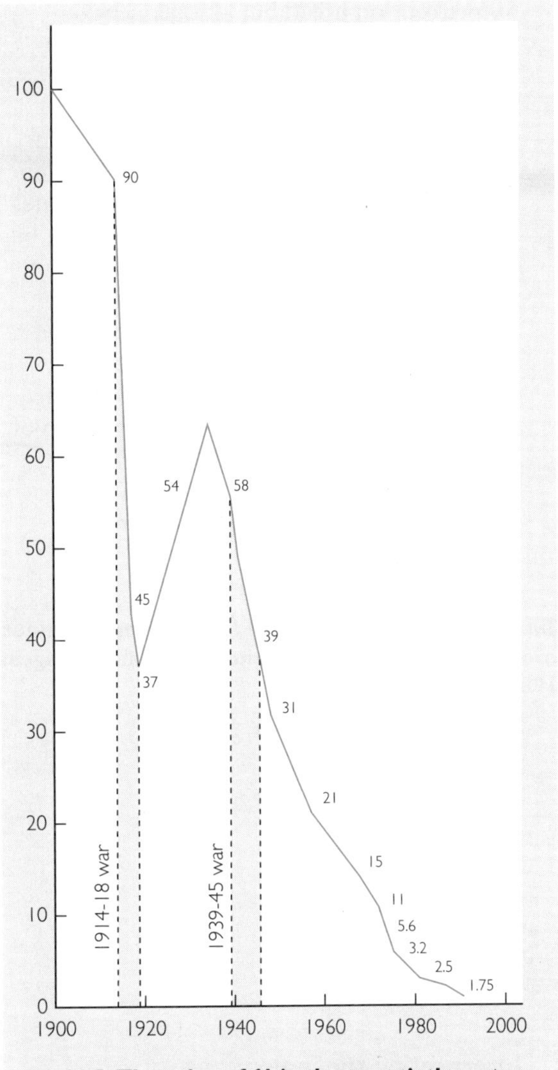

***Fig. 36.5* The value of £1 in the twentieth century**

the levels found in the 1950s and 1960s. Recent performance in the 1990s is discussed later.

To compile an index which gives an accurate reflection of the change in all retail prices is obviously a difficult and complex task. In constructing the index three questions must necessarily be answered.

1 *Who?* Who is the index thought to be relevant to? In the case of the RPI it is supposed to reflect price changes for the vast mass of the population but it is not relevant for those on very high or very low incomes.
2 *What?* We must also make decisions as to which goods are to be included – in fact, over 130 000 separate price quotations on a specified Tuesday near the middle of each month. Commodities sampled are divided into 14 main groups and 85 subgroups.
3 *Weight?* The many different commodities must be allotted an importance, or weight, in the index. A 10 per cent rise in the price of bread would have a very different effect upon the average household from the effect of the same percentage rise in the price of cars.

Calculating the index

The process of calculating an index was discussed in Chapter 2, but is revised below using the simple economy used to illustrate the velocity of circulation earlier in the chapter. The first three columns in Table 36.6 showing price, quantity and expenditure represent the starting point in the economy. The fourth column shows the weight given to each category of expenditure, which is proportional to expenditure. After a period of time a new set of prices develops which are given in the fifth column and calculated as a percentage change in the sixth column. The effect of each price change on the index can be found by multiplying the percentage rise in price by its weight in the index. To find the overall level of inflation, add these effects up. You will notice from the table that some of the price changes may be negative. To simplify this example, we have assumed that changes in relative price have no effect on quantity consumed, and that the economy has not grown. Of course, in the real world neither of these assumptions will apply, but it does enable us to cross-check that in the final

***Table 36.6* Calculating the RPI**

	P_1	Q	E	Weight	New price	% change	Effect on index	New exp.
Shirts	£10	2	£20	0.2	£11	10	+2%	£22
Shoes	£5	6	£30	0.3	£6	20	+ 6%	£36
Loaves	£1	10	£10	0.1	£1.50	50	+ 5%	£15
Coats	£20	2	£40	0.4	£15	–25	–10%	£30
Total value			£100	1.0			+3%	£103

column expenditure on the same quantity of products has indeed gone up by 3 per cent as calculated by the method described above. If the index was set at 100 at the beginning of the period, then it will have risen to 103 after the price changes.

Problems associated with the RPI

Having compiled the index, there are problems associated with the interpretation of the figures.

a) *Time*. Because the compilation of the series has been varied from time to time, and because the weighting has changed significantly, comparisons of prices over many years are difficult. This is well illustrated by the change in the value of weights in Table 36.8 (see page 480). The weights themselves give a picture of the social history of the twentieth century with major shifts away from the necessities of life towards leisure products.
b) *Quality changes*. As time goes by the quality of products will change, either improving or worsening, but this will not be reflected in the index. For example, television sets are now generally much better than they were some years ago, but only the change in their price will appear in the index. On the other hand some products have built-in obsolescence and don't last as well as in previous years.
c) *Taxes and benefits*. Changes in indirect taxes such as VAT will be shown in the RPI since they affect prices; changes in direct taxes, however, will not affect the index. Similarly, government price subsidies will influence the index whereas changes in social security benefits will not. Indeed it was partly these limitations which led to the introduction of the TPI (Taxes and Prices Index).
d) *Minorities*. While giving a generally good impression of how prices have changed for the mass of the population, the RPI will not be a good guide to how the cost of living has changed for groups whose spending patterns differ greatly from the norm. Examples of such groups are the very rich, the very poor and those with large families. A close look at Table 36.6 will reveal that inflation was 50 per cent on bread but –25 per cent on coats. Poor people are likely to be facing a higher inflation rate than rich people in situations like this.
e) *Mortgage interest* payments are included in the RPI, but this results in perverse behaviour of the index. Governments raise interest rates to discourage spending and curb inflation, but this policy increases inflation because the rate of interest is also a price. Some economists argue that interest rates should be excluded from the index. The RPI without the mortgage element is often referred to as the ***underlying*** rate of inflation. A comparison of the two measures is found in Table 36.7 which shows considerable variation, particularly at times of high interest rates such as the early 1990s.

Table 36.7 **A comparison of RPI with and without mortgage interest payments (annual averages; 1987 = 100)**

	RPI	*% change on previous year*	*RPI excl. mortgage payments index*	*% change on previous years*
1992	138.5	3.7	135.1	4.3
1993	140.7	1.6	139.0	2.9
1994	144.1	2.4	141.3	1.7
1995	149.1	3.5	144.5	2.3
1996	152.7	2.4	148.2	2.6

Source: ONS *Economic Trends*, July 1997

Interpreting the index

If the RPI increases from 100 to 103, it is obvious that prices have risen 3 per cent. However, high rates of inflation quickly make it difficult to see annual rates of inflation. For example, from 1979 to 1980 the RPI increased from 223.5 to 263.7 (1974 = 100). Some minor mathematics is necessary to see that this is an annual rate of inflation of 18 per cent. This has meant that in recent years it has become common practice to express prices as X per cent higher than 12 months previously rather than giving the index number.

Common misunderstanding

It is commonly assumed that to arrive at an equivalent annual rate from a monthly rate it is necessary to multiply the monthly rate by 12. High rates of inflation have also encouraged the projection of monthly rates into such ***annualised rates****. If inflation were to be 1.5 per cent for the last month many people would argue that if this rate of inflation continued all year then the annual rate would be 18 per cent. In fact the correct answer is 19.6 per cent because we have to use the* ***compound interest*** *formula. Similarly, if prices rose by 5 per cent a month this would give an annual rate of inflation of 79.6 per cent, not 60 per cent.*

The problem of interpreting inflation data is further complicated by the fact that some sources use the average index value for the year (see Table 36.7) while others use the year end (see Table 36.9). The situation is further complicated by the use of different base years in different tables.

STUDENT ACTIVITY 36.5

From the following data work out the annual rates of inflation:

RPI

Year 1 100	Year 2 110
Year 3 115.5	Year 4 127.05

The development of the RPI

The first index of prices compiled by the UK government was the cost of living index. This was introduced in 1914 and continued until 1947. It was designed to measure the costs of maintaining living standards of working-class households. From 1947 to 1956 the interim index of retail prices was similarly angled towards lower-income households. In 1956 the index of retail prices was introduced, and was supposed to reflect changes in prices for the average household.

In 1962 the general index of retail prices (RPI) was introduced. The next major revision of this was in 1974. There is a need to change the index from time to time, partly because with inflation the index number becomes so large, and partly because the composition of the 'basket' of goods in the index changes so greatly. For example, goods such as video cassette recorders were not even in existence when the index of 1974 was compiled.

Although it is difficult to make meaningful comparisons of prices over long periods of time because the weighting changes so much, we have attempted to do so in Fig. 36.5 which shows the decrease in the purchasing power of the pound during this century.

The weighting of the RPI

The weights for the indexes mentioned above are given in Table 36.8. A profound change has come over the measurement since the first cost of living index in 1914. This was very much a measure of the cost of staying alive and therefore concentrated on the essentials. It was thus of relevance only to those on low incomes. The present RPI is specifically not a cost of living index but a method of measuring changes in all retail prices.

Each set of weights totals 1000. The size of the weight given to each group reflects its relative importance. In the case of the present RPI, the weighting is based on the family expenditure survey (FES) and is revised each January. Thus in 1987 the food groups had a weight of 167; we could therefore consider it as being of 16.7 per cent importance in the index.

As incomes have increased one might have expected to see a decline in the importance of essentials. This is indeed reflected in the decline of the food weight from 350 in 1956 to 158 in 1990. However, when we look at some of the other categories such as housing, we see that they have increased. This is because of the disproportionate rise in the price of these commodities. You will see that the weight for motoring costs has also increased. In this case it is due to the vastly increased car ownership over the period.

Despite the increase in the weights in some categories, the general tendency has been for the range of products included in the index to increase. It was this expanding pattern of household expenditure which prompted the 1987 revision. Several new categories of expenditure were added such as leisure goods and leisure services.

***Table 36.8* Weights used in calculating the UK retail prices index 1914–96**

	1914	*1947*	*1956*	*1974*	*1987*	*1996*
Food	600	348	350	253	167	143
Catering	–		–	51	46	48
Alcoholic drink	–	217	71	70	76	78
Tobacco	–		80	43	38	35
Housing [(a)]	160	88	87	124	157	190
Fuel and light	80	65	55	52	61	43
Household goods [(b)]	40	71	66	64	73	72
Household services	–	79	58	54	44	48
Clothing and footwear	120	97	106	91	74	54
Personal goods and services	–	35	59	63	38	38
Motoring expenditure	–	–			127	124
Fares and other travel costs	–	–	68	135	22	17
Leisure goods	–	–			47	45
Leisure services	–	–			30	65
Total of weights	1000	1000	1000	1000	1000	1000

[(a)] 1914 and 1947 figures refer only to rent and rates.
[(b)] 1914 figure refers to all other categories of goods.
Source: British Labour Statistics: Historical Abstract/Employment Gazette, Labour Market Trends

Alternative measures of inflation

The criticisms that have been levelled at the RPI mean that a range of alternative measures have been developed over the years. While they may have their advantages, they have not succeeded in supplanting the RPI for most uses.

The consumers' expenditure deflator

The consumers' expenditure deflator (CED) is arrived at by comparing the national account estimates of total 'consumers' expenditure' at current prices with these revalued at constant prices. The CED is thus a by-product of the national account calculations. It aims to cover the personal expenditure of the whole population and this includes those sections of the population where expenditure is excluded from the RPI calculations. These categories are expenditure by those in institutions (hotels, army barracks, etc.), those on national insurance pensions and those on over two and a half times the national average income. All business and government expenditure is excluded. This therefore produces an index which does not reflect price change in precisely the same way as the RPI. The RPI and the CED are compared in Fig. 36.6.

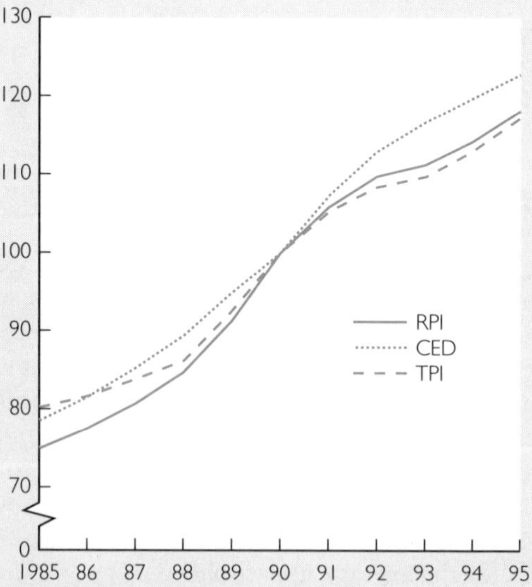

***Fig. 36.6* A comparison of different price indices, 1985–95 (1990 = 100)**
Source: Datastream

The tax and prices index (TPI)

In 1979 the government introduced the TPI. It did this because it believed that changes in the RPI would not give an accurate view of changes in purchasing power because of the government reduction of direct taxes. The TPI is designed to show the increase in gross income (before tax) needed in order to maintain the same level of real net income after taking account of changes in both prices and tax rates and allowances. Alternatively we might describe it as the index formed by averaging changes in taxes including social security contributions and changes in the prices of goods and services.

Table 36.9 compares RPI and TPI increases over recent years. These are each presented as year-on-year changes.The two indices can also be compared as in Fig. 36.6.

Table 36.9 **A comparison of TPI and RPI (taken at December of each year; January 1987 = 100)**

	TPI	*RPI*
1987	101.4	103.3
1988	106.3	110.3
1989	113.1	118.8
1990	123.3	129.9
1991	128.2	135.7
1992	130.1	139.2
1993	132.7	141.9
1994	137.2	146.0
1995	142.1	150.7
1996	143.6	154.4

Source: ONS *Economic Trends*

While it is true that the RPI treats changes in direct and indirect taxes differently, the TPI has problems of its own. Are taxes really prices? There are problems in thinking of them as prices of public sector production. Taxes can go up because the price or cost of public sector production has risen, but they can also rise to fund an increased quantity of public sector production (more hospitals, schools, etc.). Alternatively public sector costs can rise, but taxes remain the same if the government chooses to fund its expenditure by borrowing. It is partly for these reasons that the TPI has never replaced the RPI as the principal measure of inflation. An additional reason may be that in the years immediately after its introduction in 1979 it consistently rose faster than the RPI. It also has a tendency to dip just before elections!

STUDENT ACTIVITY 36.6

Assess how well the RPI would perform in the following situations:

a) Calculating the wage increase needed to allow workers earning average income to buy the same products as they did last last year.
b) Working out the increase needed for pensions in order to maintain their real standard of living.
c) Making a similar calculation for a consultant in the NHS.
d) Calculating how much of the increase in nominal GDP is due to inflation and how much is due to increased output.

International comparisons

The previous section of this chapter has shown that inflation in the UK has sometimes been high, although Table 36.7 shows that inflation has been fairly modest since 1992. Inflation, however, is an international phenomenon. Figure 36.7 traces the purchasing power of the UK, German and US currencies over this century. In each case it can be seen that the decline in value is comparable. The German mark, however, has had a remarkable history. The hyperinflation of 1923 ended with an exchange rate of 534 910 marks to $1. At this time the price of a loaf of bread in Berlin was 201 000 000 000 marks. The currency was re-established in November 1923 but collapsed again after the Second World War. Although there was not the hyperinflation of 1923, marks became almost totally unacceptable and cigarettes and coffee became the money of the country. In 1947 the currency was re-established as the Deutschmark, since when it has been one of the world's soundest currencies.

Table 36.10 shows the average rates of inflation for selected countries from the 1960s to the

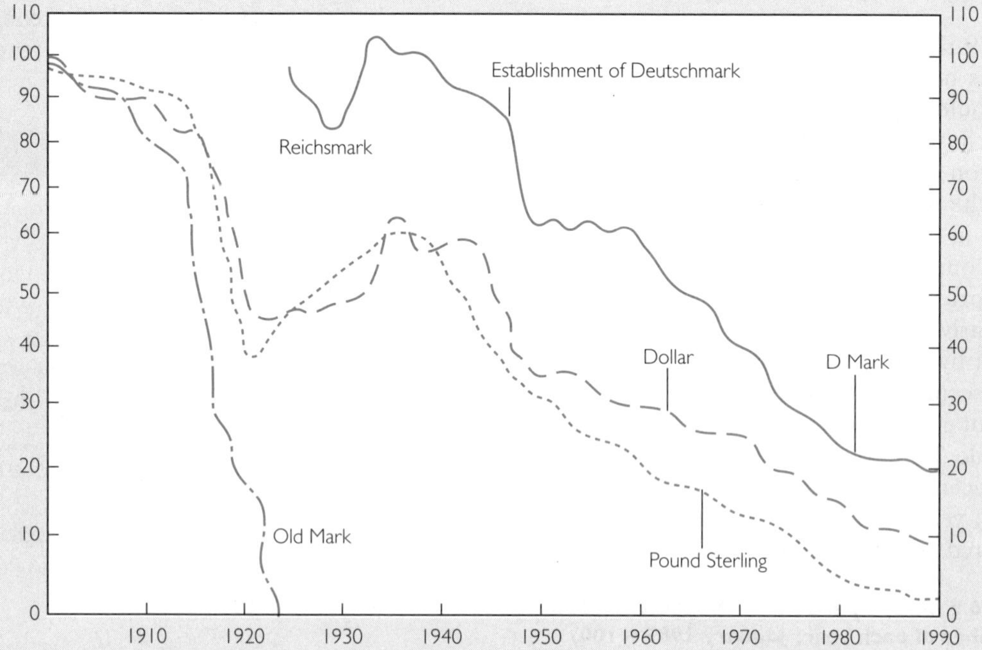

Fig. 36.7 **The purchasing power of various currencies in the twentieth century compared**

Table 36.10 **Rates of inflation for selected countries**

Country	Average annual rate of inflation 1965–80	1980–93
Malaysia	4.9	2.2
Singapore	4.9	2.5
Germany	5.1	2.8
Switzerland	5.3	3.8
USA	6.1	3.8
Canada	7.4	3.9
France	8.0	5.1
UK	11.2	5.6
Australia	8.8	6.1
Sweden	8.0	6.9
India	7.4	8.7
Italy	11.2	8.8
Nigeria	14.5	20.6
Israel	25.2	70.4
Argentina	78.5	374.3

Source: *World Development Report*, IBRD, 1995

1990s. The general pattern during the 1970s was of a rising trend of inflation world-wide. During the 1980s many nations strove to reduce their rates of inflation. In this the UK was moderately successful as you can see from the table. Some countries such as Argentina continued to experience runaway rates of inflation.

Summary

1 Monetary economics is concerned with the nature and functions of money, as well as with how the supply and price of money can influence the main macroeconomic variables.

2 Modern money can be traced back to the goldsmiths of the late Middle Ages.

3 The majority of the money supply is made up of bank deposits. Banks are able to create credit. The limit on their ability to do so is the prudent cash (or reserve assets) ratio.

4 Money has four main functions: medium of exchange; unit of account; store of value; standard of deferred payment. In order to function as money an asset must have a number of characteristics, or attributes, such as acceptability, divisibility, homogeneity and portability.

5 There are several different measures of the money stock such as M_0 and M_4.

6 The equation of exchange $M \times V = P \times T$ demonstrates that the size of the money stock and the velocity of circulation must be considered when thinking about money.

7 As money values goods and services, so the prices of goods and services are used to give a value to money. Changes in the value of money can be seen as changes in its purchasing power or the converse, which is changes in the price level.

8 The price level is measured with index numbers, the most well known of which is the RPI. There are many problems associated with the compilation of the RPI. Other measures exist such as the CED and the TPI but these also have their problems.

9 Inflation is world-wide. Over the last two decades the UK's rate of inflation has been among the highest of developed nations, but much higher rates of inflation have been experienced in some other economies, e.g. Argentina.

Questions

1 Discuss the suitability of the following to function as money:
a) gold b) caviar c) diamonds d) copper e) cattle.

2 Examine the extent to which bank deposits possess the attributes of money.

3 Explain how inflation will affect the functions of money.

4 A monopoly bank has deposits of £1000, cash of £250 and loans to customers of £750. It is obliged not to let its cash ratio fall below 10 per cent.
   a) If the bank wishes to do as much business as possible, illustrate the effect this will have on the balance sheet.
   b) How would the answer to (a) differ if the cash ratio were $12\frac{1}{2}$ per cent?

5 Distinguish between a change in relative prices and an inflationary change in prices.

6 Assuming that there is to be continuing inflation, what measures might people take to protect themselves from its effects?

7 Explain the difficulties which are associated with the interpretation of changes in the RPI.

8 Describe what is meant by the weighting of an index.

9 The information shown in Table 36.11 about four married couples was obtained in December 1997. Give possible reasons why the change in the cost of living varied so much between those families.

10 'If the GDP rises by $8\frac{1}{2}$ per cent and the general price level by $4\frac{3}{4}$ per cent while V is constant, then M must grow by $13\frac{1}{4}$ per cent.' Explain.

11 Consider the following information about a hypothetical economy: the money stock (M) = £30 million; the velocity of circulation (V) = 4; and the number of transactions is 20 million per year.
   a) What is the general price level (P)?
   b) If the stock of money were to increase to £40 million but the velocity of circulation (V) and the number of transactions (T) were to

Table 36.11

	Family			
	A	B	C	D
Ages of parents	35 and 32	36 and 28	60 and 58	45 and 43
Total income	£10 000	£22 000	£25 000	£60 000
Ages of children	2, 5 and 10	–	32 and 28	8, 12 and 15
Residence	Rented	Owner–occupiers	Owner–occupiers	Owner–occupiers
Change in cost of living over previous 12 months	9%	2%	5%	0%

remain constant, what would be the new price level (P)?

c) If in the original situation the velocity of circulation were to rise to $V = 6$ and the number of transactions were to rise to $T = 25$ million, what would be the new general level of prices?

Data response A
The UK inflation rate

Figure 36.8 gives the information relating to the index of retail prices (RPI) in the UK in June 1991. The figures in brackets give the weights. The figures in the boxes are the annual change in price in that particular category. Given that the RPI stood at 126.7 in June 1990, attempt the following questions:

1 What was the value of the RPI in June 1991? Demonstrate how you arrived at your answer. What was the annual rate of inflation between June 1990 and June 1991? Distinguish between the annual rate of inflation and an annualised rate of inflation.
2 What difficulties are encountered in interpreting RPI figures?
3 It was argued by the Chancellor of the Exchequer that it would be better to take mortgage payments out of the index. Why did he say this? Do you agree with him? Explain your answer.

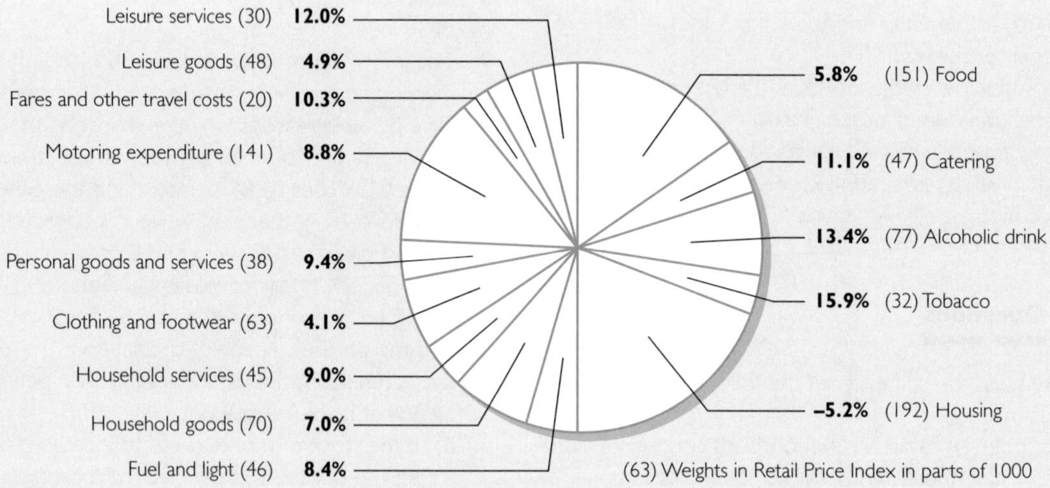

Fig. 36.8

37 Financial systems and monetary policy

Learning outcomes

At the end of this chapter you will be able to:

- Distinguish between the main types of financial institution.
- Describe the main functions of commercial banks.
- Understand the operations of the clearing banks.
- Explain the limitations on the banks' ability to create credit.
- Discuss the functions and significance of the money and capital markets.
- Outline the functions of central banks.
- Appreciate the operations of the Bank of England.
- Explain the development of monetary policy.
- Identify the main weapons of monetary policy.
- Appreciate the problems involved in effecting monetary policy.
- Identify the relative merits of an independent central bank.

Introduction

In the first part of this chapter we will examine the operation of those institutions which make up the monetary sector of the economy. We will also examine the money markets and the capital market.

All the institutions involved may be termed financial intermediaries: these are the institutions which channel funds from lenders to borrowers.

Among such institutions are banks, building societies, finance houses (hire purchase companies), insurance companies, pension funds and investment trusts.

In the second half of the chapter we shall deal with the role and functions of ***central banks***, such as the Bank of England, and with the operation of ***monetary policy*** or the direction of the economy through the supply of and price of money.

Types of financial institution

When we look around the UK and the world we discover many different types of financial institution. In the UK commercial banking is still dominated by the 'big four', although this situation may change as other institutions such as building societies are now able to offer services which have traditionally been the preserve of the banks. Banks themselves can be divided by the type of business they undertake. ***Primary banks*** are those which are mainly concerned with the transmission of money, i.e. clearing cheques, paying standing orders and so on. This obviously includes the high street banks such as Barclays and Lloyds; less obviously it also includes the discount houses (see below). ***Secondary banks*** are those which are mainly involved in dealing with other financial intermediaries and providing services other than the transmission of money. A good example is the merchant banks.

a) *Central banks*. These are usually owned and operated by governments and their most significant functions are in controlling the currency and in implementing monetary policy. They do not generally trade with individuals. Their operations are considered later in the chapter.
b) *Commercial banks*. These are the profit-motivated banks involved in high street banking activities. In the UK this means the London clearing banks and the Scottish and Northern Irish banks. Many foreign

commercial banks now have offices in the UK but they are usually concerned with major commercial types of lending. UK banks also operate extensively overseas; the Barclays Group, for example, operates in over a hundred countries. The Banking Act 1987 provides for the regulation and supervision of banks in the UK.

c) *Savings banks*. Originally designed to encourage the small saver, and often non-profit making, these banks have become very significant in some countries. In Germany, for example, the Sparkassen now account for 35 per cent of all deposits and have their own clearing system. In the UK savings banks are represented by the National Savings Bank (NSB), which is fairly insignificant in terms of its total deposits although, via the Post Office network, it has more branches than the rest of the banks put together (about 20 000).
d) *Cooperative banks and credit unions*. These institutions are much more important in the USA and Europe than in the UK. They are generally small and usually have been established by a group of individuals with a common interest, such as farmers. In France, however, a union of these cooperatives, Crédit Agricole, is now one of the largest banks in the world. The Cooperative Bank in the UK, although established by the cooperative movement, operates more like an ordinary commercial bank.
e) *Foreign banks*. All industrialised countries have foreign banks operating within them. London, being an important international centre, has many. Some of the foreign banks now compete for the business of domestic commercial banks. The Bank of England issues information on foreign banks which are part of the monetary sector. It issues separate information on American and Japanese banks.
f) *Building societies*. Many countries possess specialist institutions to assist home buyers and they often enjoy special privileges from the state. Building societies in the UK and savings and loan associations (S&Ls) in the USA have developed to such an extent as to rival the commercial banks. In the UK the Building Societies Act 1986 lifted some of the restrictions on their activities and allowed them to operate more like banks. In fact, a number of the largest societies, such as Abbey National, Halifax and Leeds, have recently legally converted into banks. In Germany, on the other hand, the Hypothekenbanken and Bausparkassen are relatively small.

We have spoken of financial intermediaries as transforming short-term deposits into long-term loans. In the case of building societies we have reached the extreme of this situation as they may grant mortgages for up to 30 years while accepting deposits for as little as seven days or less.

Common misunderstanding

Commercial banks and building societies nowadays offer a very similar range of services, such as current accounts, credit cards, mortgages and pensions. However, there is an important distinction between them: banks are public limited companies, whereas building societies are not; they accept 'shares' in the form of deposits made by their investors.

---

g) *Merchant banks*. With merchant banks we have reached the wholesalers in banking. It is often said that commercial banks live on their deposits while merchant banks live on their wits. They act more like banking brokers putting those with large sums of money to lend in touch with borrowers and by offering a wide range of financial advice to companies and even to governments.
h) *Discount houses*. Peculiar to UK banking, the discount houses make their living by discounting bills of exchange with funds mainly borrowed from the commercial banks.

STUDENT ACTIVITY 37.1

List the financial intermediaries that may be found in a typical high street. What types of service do they offer?

We will now consider the operation of these various institutions in more detail.

Commercial banks

The functions of commercial banks

The most significant function which the commercial bank fulfils is that of ***credit creation***, as described in the previous chapter. The bank itself, however, would not see it in this light as it is not able to distinguish £1 within its deposits from another. It would see its role as accepting money on deposit and then loaning the money out at interest. The commercial banks must compete with other financial intermediaries such as building societies, both in attracting deposits and in making loans.

The ***transmission of money*** is also a vital function of banks. Customers with current accounts may write ***cheques*** to pay their creditors. In the UK and the USA payment by cheque is the most common form of payment after cash. In other European countries, cheques are less significant because the 'giro' system of payment, run by the banks and post offices, is more popular. Banks also offer other methods of transmitting money such as ***standing orders*** and ***direct debits***. In the UK the major ***credit cards*** are also run by the banks; they are not only a method of making a payment but also a method of obtaining credit. More recently, banks have introduced ***debit cards***, whereby a user's account is directly debited with the amount of the transaction. We can also include ***travellers' cheques*** as a method of transmitting money.

Banks also offer ***advisory services*** to their customers, usually charging for these services. The sort of advisory services which are offered are trusteeship, foreign exchange, broking, investment management and taxation. Since the Big Bang the banks are also now able to offer their customers stockbroking services.

Commercial banks may also offer other ***financial products*** to customers such as mortgages and insurance. In this they will be competing with the more usual suppliers of these services. In the provision of financial products and services the banks are regulated by the Financial Services Act 1986.

Clearing

For payments to be made by cheque it is necessary to have some system of ***clearing*** the cheques. There used to be separate clearing for Scotland but since 1985 all clearing in the UK has been handled by the Committee of London and Scottish Banks. Clearing takes place at the Clearing House, which is at 10 Lombard Street in London and includes the following bank groups: Abbey National, Bank of Scotland, Barclays, Cooperative Bank, Lloyds, Midland, National Westminster, Royal Bank of Scotland and Standard Chartered.

If a person draws a cheque on their bank and pays it to someone who has an account at the same bank then the clearing can be accomplished without going through the Clearing House. This is known as ***interbank*** or ***head office clearing***. If, on the other hand, a payment by cheque involves two different banks then the Clearing House becomes involved. This is perhaps best explained by following a cheque through the system. Suppose that Ms Smith draws a cheque on her account with Barclays at its Sheffield branch and gives it to Mr Jones who has an account with the Midland at its Nottingham branch. When Mr Jones has paid in the cheque at the Nottingham branch of the Midland, it is sent with all their similar cheques to the Midland's clearing department at head office. Midland then total all the cheques drawn on Barclays and the other banks. The cheques are then taken to the Clearing House where they are handed to representatives of the other clearing banks, who in turn hand bundles of cheques to the Midland. It is then possible to arrive at a figure for the net indebtedness of one clearing bank with the other. This means that instead of hundreds of thousands of separate payments being made by Barclays to Midland, and vice versa, one payment will settle their accounts. The banks settle their indebtedness to one another by transferring money which they keep in their accounts with the Banking Department of the Bank of England.

Thus, at the end of each day their debts have been settled by changes in the book-keeping entries at the Bank of England.

Meanwhile Ms Smith's cheque has been returned to Barclays' head office along with all the others that have been exchanged. Details are then fed into the bank's computer so that the accounts may be debited the next day. Provided that Ms Smith's account is in order her account at the Sheffield branch will then be debited. This process will normally take about three working days.

The balance sheet of the clearing banks

One of the best ways to understand the business of a commercial bank is to study its balance sheet. Table 37.1 gives the combined balance sheet for the London and Scottish clearing banks.

One difference which we observe from a normal balance sheet is that there is no sign of the banks' capital or of their real physical assets such as premises. This balance sheet concentrates on the business of the banks in accepting deposits and making loans. (Numbers after the following headings refer to items in Table 37.1.)

The banks' liabilities (1)

The banks' liabilities are the deposits which they have accepted. These are held in a number of different types of account. Banks also raise substantial deposits on the money markets.

Common misunderstanding

Banks used to distinguish between current (cheque) accounts and deposit accounts, current accounts offering instant access to funds but not earning interest, deposit accounts having the opposite characteristics. Nowadays things are a little more complicated. In recent years there has been a decline in the importance of traditional current accounts. In order to attract business away from building societies the banks have introduced such things as instant-access, yet interest-earning, cheque accounts. Other accounts, now mainly referred to as savings accounts, usually earn higher rates of interest although some of these may also be instant access.

***Table 37.1* Balances of UK banks, March 1996**

	£m
LIABILITIES (1):	
Sterling deposits of which:	
Notes outstanding	2 307
Sight	240 333
Time	351 806
Certificates of deposit (CDs)	79 547
Foreign currency deposits	1 021 080
Other liabilities	169 180
TOTAL LIABILITIES	1 864 253
of which eligible liabilities (2)	523 007
ASSETS (3):	
Sterling assets of which:	
Notes and coin (4)	4 087
Balances with Bank of England:	
Cash ratio deposits (5)	1 683
Other balances (6)	–421
Market loans (7):	
Discount houses (8)	8 013
Other UK banks (9)	106 784
UK bank CDs (10)	31 070
Building society CDs	4 700
Local authorities (11)	1 430
Overseas	41 685
Bills:	
Treasury bills (12)	7 467
Other bills (13)	13 007
Investments:	
British government stocks (14)	19 476
Other	54 575
Advances (15)	443 365
Other sterling assets	55 992
Foreign currency assets	1 071 340
TOTAL ASSETS	1 864 253

Source: Adapted from *Bank of England Quarterly Bulletin*, November 1996

The important distinction these days is between ***sight deposits*** and ***time deposits***. A sight deposit is any deposit which can be withdrawn on demand without interest penalty. With time deposits notice of withdrawal (e.g. 7 days) is necessary if depositors wish to receive all the interest they are entitled to. The greater the period of notice that is needed the greater the interest a depositor is likely to receive. Large depositors, such as companies, may place money on deposit for periods of three months or more. When this happens it is likely to be by way of special arrangements such as certificates of deposit (CDs). (See below, item (10).) In 1996 the clearing banks had over £79 billion of deposits in the form of CDs. You can also see in Table 37.1 that deposits of foreign currency are very important to UK banks.

Eligible liabilities (2)

Since the banks' liabilities (deposits) form a major portion of the money supply it is understandable that the monetary authorities will wish to supervise them. Since 1981 the Bank of England's supervision has applied not only to banks but to the whole of the ***monetary sector***. The portions of the banks' liabilities which form the basis of control are termed ***eligible liabilities*** and are those which are of most relevance to the size of the money stock. They comprise, in broad terms, sterling deposit liabilities, excluding deposits having an original maturity over two years, plus any sterling resources obtained by switching foreign currencies into sterling. The banks are then allowed to offset certain of their interbank and money market transactions against their eligible liabilities. Having been defined, these liabilities then form the basis of the various ratios of assets which the banks may be required to maintain.

The clearing banks' assets (3)

In the previous chapter we spoke of a cash ratio which banks maintain. In fact the situation is more complex, with banks possessing a whole spectrum of assets from cash, which is the most liquid, to highly illiquid assets such as mortgages that they have made. In Table 37.1 we divide the banks' assets into those which are primarily designed to protect liquidity, i.e. those in the balance sheet down to ***bills***, and those which are primarily earning assets, i.e. all the items from ***investments*** onwards. Banking business is a conflict between ***profitability*** and ***liquidity***. To earn profits, banks would like to lend as much money as possible at as high a rate of interest as possible. On the other hand they must always be able to meet a depositor's demand for money. Although most business these days is carried out by cheque and credit card, the bank must always be prepared to meet depositors' demands for notes and coins.

When we examine the banks' assets we find that they have different maturity dates; for example, a bank may have loaned money to another bank overnight, while, at the other extreme, it may have granted mortgages which are repayable over 25 years. These days, therefore, the Bank of England, rather than laying down a simple ratio, insists (by a combination of information and persuasion) that the banks hold ratios of assets which are appropriate to the type of liabilities they have accepted. Thus, for example, if a bank has accepted overnight deposits of cash from the money market which are likely to be entirely withdrawn the next day, it is appropriate that these should be 100 per cent covered by highly liquid assets. If, on the other hand, banks have accepted deposits which they will not have to repay for one year a 5 per cent cover might be appropriate.

The assets cover which a bank requires will therefore depend upon the type of deposits it has accepted. It is no longer possible to state it as a simple ratio; it will differ from bank to bank and from time to time. The clearing banks whose activities are relatively stable might well have a predictable ratio but this will differ from other members of the monetary sector.

a) *Coins and notes* (4). These are reserves of cash kept by the banks, sometimes referred to as Till Money. Since 1971 there has been no requirement to keep a specific percentage. In the case of the clearing banks the amount of cash they require is predictable and is a very small portion of their assets. All banks will wish to keep their holdings of cash to a minimum since they earn no interest. The banks' holdings of cash are not included in the Bank of England's calculations of banks' liquidity.
b) *Cash ratio deposits* (5). All members of the monetary sector are required to keep 0.35 per cent of their eligible liabilities in cash at the

Bank of England. These deposits are kept in non-operational, non-interest-bearing accounts, i.e. the banks and other members of the monetary sector may not use this money, its purpose being to supply the Bank of England with funds rather than for control purposes or for liquidity.

c) *Other balances* (6). In addition to the cash ratio deposits the banks keep operational deposits at the Bank of England for the purpose of clearing their debts to one another, as described above. No ratio is laid down by the Bank of England for these deposits.
d) *Market loans* (7). The market referred to is the ***London money market***, which is discussed in detail later in this chapter. The loans consist of money lent for periods from one day up to three months. All banks must agree to keep an average of 5 per cent of their eligible liabilities with certain sectors of the money market and never less than 2.5 per cent of their eligible liabilities with the discount houses.
e) *Discount market* (8). This is money lent to members of the London Discount Market Association (LDMA) at ***call or short notice***. Money lent at call is lent for a day at a time while money lent at short notice is lent for periods up to 14 days. Money lent overnight usually commands a lower rate of interest than that lent for a week, but overnight rates can be very high if the whole market is short of money. After cash these loans are the banks' most liquid assets and will be called in if the banks are short of cash. These loans also form a vital part of the system of money control.
f) *Other UK banks* (9). Banks will make and receive short-term loans from other banks and members of the monetary sector to even out their cash flows.
g) *Certificates of deposit (CDs)* (10). If a customer is prepared to make a deposit of cash for a fixed period of time, say three months, the customer will receive a higher rate of interest than in a normal savings account. However, the holder may want the money back before then. The best of both worlds can be enjoyed if the customer accepts a ***certificate of deposit***. This is a written promise by the bank to repay the loan at a stated date. The certificate is negotiable, i.e. it can be sold on the money market should the customer require the cash before that date. CDs issued by a bank will, of course, form part of its liabilities, but banks also hold CDs issued by other banks as investments and it is these we see on the assets side of the balance sheet. They are available only for very large deposits.
h) *Local authority loans* (11). These are loans made through the money market to local authorities, who are now major borrowers. In addition to local authorities, banks may also make short-term loans to companies.
i) *UK Treasury bills* (12). The Bank of England sells Treasury bills weekly. These are bought in the first instance by the discount houses. The bills usually have a life of 91 days and they are often acquired by banks from the discount houses when they have five or six weeks left to maturity.
j) *Other bills* (13). These are commercial ***bills of exchange*** issued by companies to finance trade and acquired by the banks on the money market. In the early 1960s commercial bills were almost extinct and it was Treasury bills that were important in the bills section of the banks' balance sheet. You can see that commercial bills are now more important; they have staged a comeback in the rapid expansion of the money markets over the last two decades.

The primary function of the assets so far discussed is to give liquidity; the remaining items fulfil different functions.

k) *UK government stocks* (14). When the term investment is used in banks' balance sheets it refers to their ownership of government stock. The government borrows money by issuing interest-bearing bonds such as Exchequer stock or Treasury stock. These are mainly fixed-interest-bearing, although there are now some which are index linked. Government stocks are termed 'gilts' (gilt edged). As you can see the banks hold a considerable amount of UK and other government stocks. The banks will always ensure that they maintain a ***maturing portfolio*** of bills, stocks, loans, etc., i.e. that a quantity of these mature each week so that the bank has the option of liquidating its asset or reinvesting.

l) *Advances* (15). The chief earning assets of the banks are the advances they make to customers. These take the form of overdrafts and loans. The lowest rate at which a bank is willing to make loans (prime rate) could be as little as 1 per cent above base rate, but this is offered only to favoured customers; others may pay 8 or 10 per cent above base. In recent years the clearing banks have made big inroads in the mortgage market; the rate of interest on mortgages usually stays close to base rate.

STUDENT ACTIVITY 37.2

Describe the arrangement of a typical commercial bank's balance sheet. If a bank lends money, it opens an account in the name of the borrower. Should the borrower then draw out all the money, show the effect of this on the bank's balance sheet.

Liquidity ratios

In the previous chapter we saw that it was necessary for banks to maintain a cash ratio. Today, instead of a cash ratio, the Bank of England requires that banks and other institutions in the monetary sector keep a certain proportion of their assets in a prescribed form. There are two main reasons for this:

a) In order to ensure the stability of the system. The failure of the Bank of Credit and Commerce International (BCCI) in 1991 and the merchant bank Barings in 1995 emphasised the point that it is still possible for banks to go 'bust'.
b) It allows the Bank of England to control the credit creation of banks and thus the money supply.

Until 1971 the clearing banks were required to keep a ***cash ratio*** of 8 per cent and a 28 per cent ***liquid assets ratio***. In 1971, as part of the Competition and Credit Control regulations, these were replaced by the 12.5 per cent ***reserve assets ratio***. Since 1981 there has been no stated ratio and the liquidity ratio which is required of a bank will depend upon the type of business it undertakes. The Bank of England nevertheless still expects banks to maintain appropriate ratios and its control now extends to all institutions in the monetary sector.

The present ***integrated*** approach to banks' balance sheets does not closely define which assets are acceptable, as the old ratios did. However, the assets which the Bank of England is willing to accept as providing adequate liquidity for banks are very similar to the old reserve assets. These are:

a) balances with the Bank of England;
b) money at call with the LDMA;
c) UK Treasury bills;
d) local authority and other bills eligible for rediscount at the Bank of England;
e) UK government stocks with less than one year to maturity.

The cash which banks require is now a very small and predictable proportion of their assets and it is therefore today of little significance. However, banks must always have an adequate proportion of their assets in highly liquid form. Under the old reserve assets ratio, the items above had to be at least 12.5 per cent of the banks' eligible liabilities, but for prudential reasons banks may require more liquidity than this. At present typical ratios for clearing banks are in the range of 9–12 per cent.

Limits to credit creation by banks

The limits to banks' ability to create credit may be summarised as follows:

a) *Liquidity ratios*. As we have seen above, the Bank of England lays down liquidity requirements, in addition to which banks will have their own prudential reasons for maintaining ratios.
b) *Other banks*. If one clearing bank pursued a significantly more expansionist policy of credit creation than all the others, it follows that it would quickly come to grief. This is because a majority of the extra deposits it

created would be redeposited with other clearers. The expansionist bank would therefore find itself continually in debt to the other clearers, thus rapidly exhausting its balances at the Bank of England. It would then be forced to reduce its lending to replenish its reserves. Conversely, an overcautious policy of credit creation would decrease the profitability of the bank.

c) *The supply of collateral security*. A majority of bank lending is in the form of ***secured loans***, i.e. the bank has to take something in return, such as a mortgage on a property, an assurance policy or a bill of exchange, as security in case the loan is not repaid. The supply of such assets will therefore influence a bank's ability to make loans. In particular the supply of money market instruments such as Treasury bills and CDs will greatly influence banks' liquidity. The Bank of England is able to manipulate the supply of such instruments as Treasury bills and government stocks to control banks' credit creation. During the 1980s there was a rapid rise in house prices. Many home owners found themselves in charge of an asset with a rapidly escalating value. A significant number of these used their houses as collateral security to borrow from banks. This money was spent on, for example, buying a holiday home or a new car. This borrowing of money and its use added significantly to inflation.
d) *The monetary authorities*. Central banks and governments have a variety of weapons at their disposal for influencing bank lending. These are discussed in detail later in the chapter.

STUDENT ACTIVITY 37.3

Suppose a person borrows £1000 from Lloyds bank and thereafter draws a cheque for this sum to buy goods from Cosmic Discount who bank with Barclays. Describe how the money will be paid to Cosmic. If Barclays maintains a liquidity ratio of 20 per cent, how much new lending or investment will it be able to finance as a result of this transaction?

Money markets

The classical and parallel markets

The expression 'money markets' is used to refer to those institutions and arrangements that are engaged in the borrowing and lending of large sums of money for short periods of time.

Most money market transactions are concerned with the sale and purchase of ***near money*** assets such as bills of exchange and certificates of deposit. Most advanced countries have a money market, but they are most developed in the major banking capitals of the world such as London, New York, Tokyo and Zurich.

In London the money market is geographically very concentrated, all the participants being within a short distance of Lombard Street, although the scope of the market is world-wide through its telephone and telex links.

The ***classical money market*** is the expression used to describe dealings between the Bank of England, the clearing banks and the discount houses. Traditionally the banks have lent money at call or short notice to the discount houses which they, in turn, have lent out by buying Treasury bills from the Bank of England or by purchasing other first-class bills of exchange. In recent years many new activities have been undertaken on the money market and these are referred to as the ***parallel markets***. These include the following:

a) *The local authorities market*. Local authorities borrow money by issuing bills and bonds which are traded on the money market. They may also place funds when they have a surplus.
b) *Finance houses*. These institutions, which are involved in hire purchase, obtain some of the funds from the money market.
c) *Companies*. Large industrial and commercial companies both borrow and place money on the market. If a company lends money to another through the market this is known as an ***intercompany deposit***. Companies will also make large deposits with banks in return for ***a certificate of deposit***, and these are also traded on the market.

d) *Interbank market*. This is the borrowing and lending which goes on between banks. It is of great significance in allowing banks to manage their liquidity. It is also important in the determination of interest rates.
e) *The certificates of deposit market*. As its name implies, this deals with the sale and purchase of CDs in both pounds and other currencies.
f) *Eurocurrencies*. The market began as the eurodollar market, which referred to the holding of US dollars in European banks. Today a eurocurrency is any holding of currency in a financial institution which is not denominated in the national currency; for example, if a UK bank has holdings of Deutschmarks, this becomes a eurocurrency. The market extends beyond Europe to take in other financial centres such as Tokyo. The main centre of the eurocurrency market is London. Today this market is huge and extremely important. The very large sums held on short-term deposit are a potential source of disequilibrium to a nation, because this so-called 'hot money' may move quickly from nation to nation in search of better interest rates or in anticipation of the change in value of a currency.

Significance of the money markets

The money markets are the place where money is 'wholesaled'. As such the supply of money and the interest rate are of significance to the whole economy. They are also used by the central bank to make its monetary policy effective. Since the abandonment of MLR in 1981, money market indicators have acquired a new significance; for example, the three-month interbank interest rate (the rate at which banks are willing to lend to each other) is now carefully monitored.

Discount houses and discounting

A group of institutions make up the London Discount Market Association (LDMA). They are termed discount houses because their original business was concerned with the discounting of bills of exchange and Treasury bills. Discounting a bill is a method of lending money. We can illustrate the process by considering Treasury bills.

Each week the Bank of England, on behalf of the government, offers Treasury bills for sale. They are a method of borrowing and constitute part of the National Debt. A Treasury bill is a promise by the government to pay a specific sum, e.g. £100 000, 91 days (three months) after the date it is issued.

A discount house might offer to buy the £100 000 bill for, say, £97 500, in which case it will cost the government £2500 to borrow £97 500 for 91 days. This is equivalent to an annual rate of interest of just over 10 per cent. However, the rate on bills of exchange is expressed not as an interest rate but as a ***discount rate***. Using the figures above the calculation of a discount rate can be illustrated as:

$$\frac{£2500}{£100\,000} \times \frac{100}{1} \times \frac{365}{91} = 10 \text{ per cent}$$

Thus we have arrived at a discount rate of 10 per cent, whereas the true interest rate, or yield, will be higher, in this case 10.28 per cent. If interest rates are falling this will cause discount houses to tender at a higher price. Conversely, if interest rates rise the price the government can expect will obviously fall since the price of the bill and the rate of interest are inversely proportional to each other.

Commercial bills of exchange are discounted in a similar manner. Commercial bills are a method by which a business can borrow money for a short period at advantageous rates. Often they will be to finance a particular transaction. Once a bill has been ***accepted***, i.e. guaranteed by a ***recognised*** bank, it is therefore eligible for discount at the Bank of England. Such ***first-class bills of exchange*** command the ***finest*** rates of interest on the money market.

STUDENT ACTIVITY 37.4

Assume that a Treasury bill has a redemption value of £250 000. Suppose that on 8 May, when it still had the full 91 days to run, £222 500 was offered for it. What is the discount rate?

The discount houses and the banks

The discount houses obtain their funds by borrowing money from banks at call or short notice. The rate of interest which they pay is a slightly lower rate than they charge for discounting bills, and in this manner they make their profits. Traditionally the banks have been pleased with this arrangement and have ensured the continued existence of discount houses by not tendering for Treasury bills themselves. The advantage to the banks is that they are lending money for only 24 hours at a time instead of 91 days, thereby giving them an asset almost as liquid as cash but earning some interest. If a bank calls in money from a discount house it is usually to settle an inter-bank debt. The discount house is then usually able to reborrow the money from the creditor bank.

If the Bank of England is restricting the supply of money it is possible that all the banks will be calling in money from the discount houses. In this situation, if the discount houses cannot find the money anywhere else, they can in the ***last resort*** borrow from the Bank of England. The Bank does this by ***rediscounting*** the eligible bills of exchange which the discount houses have. The rate at which the Bank is willing to rediscount is very important, because all other rates move in sympathy with it. The rate is always higher than the Treasury bill rate; the discount houses will, therefore, lose money if they are forced to rediscount with the Bank. Thus, in the event of the Bank restricting the money supply, it is the discount houses which get into difficulties first, therefore providing the banks with a shield, or cushion, against government monetary policy. This is another reason why the banks support the discount houses.

Merchant banks

Merchant banks are so called because they were originally merchants. However, over the course of time they found it more profitable to become involved in the financial aspects of trade rather than the trade itself. Many institutions claim the title of merchant bank; indeed some of the clearing banks have set up merchant banking subsidiaries. Traditionally the term 'merchant bank' was linked to the 16 members of the ***Accepting Houses Committee***. This includes such institutions as Hambros, Schroders, Lazards and Morgan Grenfell.

Accepting is a process whereby the accepting house guarantees the redemption of a commercial bill of exchange in the case of default by the company which issued the bill. For this it charges a commission. A bill which has been accepted by a London accepting house becomes a ***fine*** bill or ***first-class bill of exchange***. This makes it much easier to sell on the money market, where it will also command the lowest, or 'finest', discount rate. The bill will also be eligible for rediscount at the Bank of England. In order to be able to guarantee bills in this way, accepting houses have to make it their business to know everyone else's business. A merchant banker will therefore specialise in certain areas of business or in particular areas of the world (companies from all over the world raise money on the London money market); Hambros, for example, specialises in Scandinavian and Canadian business. The regional specialisations often reflect the merchant origins of the bank.

In addition to accepting, merchant banks undertake many other functions. They might undertake to raise capital for their clients or invest in the company themselves. They act as agents in takeover bids and in the issue of new shares. In recent years many merchant banks have become involved in unit trusts and investment trusts. However, merchant banks do not involve themselves in high-street banking activities.

The capital market

The capital market is concerned with the provision of longer-term finance – anything from bank loans to investment in permanent capital in the form of the purchase of shares. Unlike the money market, the capital market is very widespread. Some of the participants in this market are as follows:

a) *Commercial banks*. These are important in providing short- and medium-term loans to industry. In the UK, however, it is unusual for commercial banks to invest in industry by taking shares or debentures, unlike the USA and Germany where this is common practice.

b) *Merchant banks*. These banks participate in the capital market by assisting companies in the issue of new shares and also by direct investment in industry.
c) *Insurance companies and pension funds*. Over recent years the institutional investors have become more and more important, so that today the insurance companies and pension funds own well over half the shares in public companies.
d) *Investment trusts*. There are joint stock companies whose business is investment in other companies. Shares are bought in the normal way and the funds thus raised are used to buy shares in other companies.
e) *Unit trusts*. Although unit trusts also invest in other companies they are not normal companies. Unit trusts are supervised by the Department of Trade and Industry and are controlled by boards of trustees. They attract small investors who buy units in the trust which can be redeemed if the investor so wishes.
f) *Government-sponsored institutions*. Two government-sponsored organisations were created in 1945, the Industrial and Commerical Finance Corporation and the Finance Corporation for Industry. In 1973 a merger of the two corporations was proposed and in 1975 Finance for Industry Ltd (FFI) was formed; this is now called Investors in Industry (3i). Its shareholders are the clearing banks (85 per cent) and the Bank of England. Investors in Industry has access to funds of over £3 billion and is intended to give medium-term assistance to industry.
g) *Consortium banks*. A relative newcomer to the money and capital markets, consortium banks may be defined as banks which are owned by other banks but in which no one bank has a shareholding of more than 50 per cent and in which at least one bank is an overseas bank. The first consortium bank, which was called the Midland and International Bank Ltd, was formed in 1964. The multinational nature of most of these banks stresses the international nature of finance these days.
h) *Private individuals*. The trend for many years has been the decline in the importance of the private individual as an investor. The privatisations of the 1980s did not significantly alter this trend. There are, of course, a few, very wealthy private individuals who are important investors.
i) *Self-finance*. One of the most important sources of finance to industry is ploughed-back profits. (See also the discussion in Chapter 22.)

Central banking

Introduction

Every country in the world has a central bank, and it may be that we shall soon see an international central bank for the EU. The oldest central bank is that of Sweden (1668). The Bank of England was founded in 1694, while in the USA the Federal Reserve did not come into existence until 1913. The Bank of England was founded by a group of businessmen headed by a Scotsman, William Paterson. In return for a loan to the Crown of £1.2 million the Bank of England acquired several privileges. This began its close association with the UK government which culminated in its nationalisation in 1946.

However, in May 1997 the new Labour government, in a historic step, granted the Bank of England 'operational independence' in the determination of interest rates and hence, in large part, for the operation of monetary policy.

This placed the Bank of England more on a par with the Federal Reserve of the USA and the German Bundesbank, two of the more independent central banks.

An important step in the development of the Bank of England was the Bank Charter Act of 1844. This divided the Bank into two departments, the Issue Department, responsible for the issue of notes, and the Banking Department, which is responsible for all the Bank's other activities. The Act also set in motion the process by which the Bank was to become the sole issuer of notes in England and Wales.

Functions of central banks

Central banks are important to the working of the monetary system. Among their most important functions are the following:

a) *Government's banker*. Governments pay their revenues into the central bank and pay their bills with cheques drawn on it. The fees which the bank charges for this are an important source of revenue to the bank.
b) *Banker's bank*. As explained in the previous chapter, commercial banks keep balances with the central bank. This is both a method of controlling banks and also the way by which interbank indebtedness can be settled.
c) *Lender of last resort*. The central bank stands ready to support commercial banks should they get into difficulties.
d) *Banking supervision*. Central banks usually have a major role to play in the policing of the banking system. In some countries this responsibility is shared with other authorities; for example, in the USA the Federal Reserve is supported by the Comptroller of Currency and by the Federal Deposit Insurance Corporation (FDIC).
e) *Note issue*. In most countries of the world the central bank is responsible for the issue of banknotes. This is not so everywhere. In the USA, for example, the currency is issued by the government.
f) *Operating monetary policy*. It is usually the central bank which operates government monetary policy.

It is a matter of debate what the structure and operation of a central bank for the EU would be like. Germany is used to having a strong and independent central bank and its record of combating inflation is second only to that of Switzerland. It is possible that a pattern like that of the USA may emerge: the Federal Reserve Board is the head of the system, but there are 13 regional Federal Reserve Banks. It is almost impossible for the President to control the Board because the system of appointments is beyond his jurisdiction. The Secretary of the Federal Reserve is arguably the second most powerful man in the USA after the President.

We will now turn and examine in more detail the operations of the Bank of England.

The balance sheet of the Bank of England

In the same manner that the operations of commercial banks can be understood through their balance sheet, so can those of a central bank. Table 37.2 shows the balance sheet of the Bank of England as at 25 September 1996. The Bank ***return***, as it is termed, has been published weekly since 1844. Since this date the balance sheet has been in two portions, the Issue Department and the Banking Department. (Numbers after the following headings refer to items in Table 37.2.)

Table 37.2 **Balance sheet of the Bank of England as at 25 September 1996**

Liabilities	*£m*	*Assets*	*£m*
		Issue Department	
Notes in circulation (1)	20 817	Government securities (3)	16 692
Notes in banking department (2)	12	Other securities (4)	4 137
	20 829		20 829
		Banking Department	
Public deposits (5)	937	Government securities (9)	1 256
Special deposits (6)	–	Advances and other accounts (10)	2 010
Bankers' deposits (7)	1 954	Premises, equipment, etc. (11)	2 964
Reserves and other accounts (8)	3 351	Notes and coins (12)	12
	6 242		6 242

Source: Adapted from *Bank of England Quarterly Bulletin*, November 1996

The Issue Department

a) *Notes in circulation* (1). This item illustrates the Bank's function as the sole ***issuer of notes*** in England and Wales. There are two monetary authorities in the UK, since coins are issued by the Crown through the Royal Mint, now based at Llantrisant in Wales. Although coins are very important, until 1983 they formed only a minor proportion of the cash in circulation; however, at this date the Royal Mint began to issue £1 coins, thus modifying the Bank's role.

The Scottish and Northern Irish banks also issue notes, but beyond a relatively small amount these must all be fully backed by Bank of England notes and they, therefore, have little effect on the volume of notes in circulation.

b) *Notes in Banking Department* (2). These are notes which have been printed by the Issue Department and sold to the Banking Department where they are kept ready for distribution to the banks. Thus we also find this item in the balance sheet of the Banking Department. Since the two departments are separate, Bank of England notes are a liability to the Issue Department but an asset to the Banking Department.

c) *Government securities* (3). All banknotes these days are fiduciary issue and the backing for the currency is government securities. Effectively the backing for the currency is that it is both readily acceptable and legal tender.

d) *Other securities* (4). These consist of securities other than those issued by the UK government. This item also includes the government debt dating back to the foundation of the Bank in 1694. Coins bought from the Royal Mint, but not yet put into circulation, are also included in this item. Also in this item are the eligible bills purchased by the Bank in order to even out the flows in the money markets.

The liabilities of the Banking Department

a) *Public deposits* (5). These are the UK government's deposits at the Bank and represent the Bank's function as the ***government's banker***. This item also includes the dividend accounts of the Commissioners of the National Debt, illustrating the Bank's function as the ***manager of the national debt***.

b) *Special deposits* (6). The existence of this item illustrates one aspect of the Bank's function as the ***operator of government monetary policy***.

c) *Bankers' deposits* (7). These are the deposits of the monetary sector, which are equivalent to 0.35 per cent of their eligible liabilities plus the balances they keep for operating the clearing system. This item demonstrates the Bank's role as the ***bankers' bank***.

d) *Reserves and other accounts* (8). This item consists of undistributed profits and the accounts of persons and institutions with the Bank. These fall into three categories: the Bank's employees; private customers who had accounts at the Bank in 1946; and institutions having special need to bank with the Bank, e.g. foreign banks.

Common misunderstanding

Besides acting as the government's banker and as the operator of monetary policy, the Bank of England also functions as an ordinary bank, as evinced by the previous item in its liabilities, reserves and other accounts. Most central banks do not operate as commercial banks; some, however, such as the Banque de France, compete for ordinary business in the high street with commercial banks.

The assets of the Banking Department

a) *Government securities* (9). Like the Issue Department, the main assets of the Banking Department are UK government securities.

b) *Advances and other accounts* (10). This item consists mainly of loans which the Bank has made to institutions such as discount houses. This illustrates the Bank's function as ***lender of last resort***. By always being prepared to lend money, the Bank ensures that the banking system never becomes insolvent. This was described earlier in the chapter.

c) *Premises, equipment and other securities* (11). Like any other business the Bank possesses real assets. As well as its well-known Threadneedle Street site in London, the Bank also has seven branches in other cities, e.g. Birmingham and Bristol.
d) *Notes and coins* (12). The Bank is responsible for supplying the banks with the new banknotes and coins which they require.

Other functions of the Bank of England

There are several functions of the Bank which are not apparent from its balance sheet. First, since 1946 it has had the responsibility for 'disposing of the means of foreign payment in the national interest', i.e. all ***foreign exchange transactions*** are monitored by the Bank. This function is not so important since the abolition of exchange controls in 1979. However, the Bank operates the ***Exchange Equalisation Account***. This is a fund, established in 1932, the purpose of which is to buy and sell currency on the foreign exchange market with the object of stabilising the exchange rate. This function is equally important whether there is a fixed or floating exchange rate. The Bank also ***sells stock*** on behalf of the government. It advises the government on the issue of new securities, it converts and funds existing government debt, it publishes prospectuses for any new government issues and it deals with the applications for them and apportions the issue. It also ***manages the servicing of the National Debt***, i.e. the payment of interest on behalf of the government. The Bank is also responsible for giving the government general ***advice on the monetary system***; it publishes large quantities of statistical information on the monetary system, along with studies of various sectors of the economy. (Conscientious students should acquaint themselves with the ***Bank of England Quarterly Bulletin*** and the accompanying ***Monetary and Financial Statistics***, in which much of this information is contained.) Finally, an important function of the Bank is to ***represent the government*** in relations with foreign central banks and also in various international institutions such as the Bank for International Settlement (BIS) and the International Monetary Fund (IMF).

The development of monetary policy

Monetary policy is the direction of the economy through the supply of and price of money.

In most countries, as in the UK, the operation of monetary policy is undertaken by the central bank.

Early changes

It used to be believed that changes in the rate of interest (the price of money) determined the volume of investment in the economy. Thus, lowering the rate of interest would stimulate the economy while raising it would contract the economy. Up to the time of the First World War, monetary policy consisted of little more than minor changes in bank rate. The question of variations of the money supply hardly arose since the UK was on the gold standard.

During the 1930s the relationship between investment and interest was challenged by Keynes. Certainly, events seemed to support him as interest rates were very low but investment was also very low. This Keynes explained as the *liquidity trap*.

Thus, when Keynes's view became the economic orthodoxy after 1945 it was believed that the connection between interest rates and the level of economic activity was weak and the government relied upon fiscal policy as the principal method of directing the economy.

(See discussion in Chapter 38.) Thus, in the immediate post-war years, active monetary policy was severely curtailed and interest rates were held at a low level.

Monetary policy in the 1950s and 1960s

Monetary policy was revived in the 1950s, as evinced by the rise in bank rates over the decade. It came to be believed that raising interest rates would 'lock up' investment funds in financial institutions. This was because a large proportion of their assets were in government securities and a rise in interest rates would decrease their value, thus making institutions unwilling to sell them because they would make a loss. Thus the orthodox view at this time was that putting up rates would 'choke off' investment and was therefore useful in restricting the economy. However, lowering interest rates would not, of itself, be sufficient to stimulate the economy.

The Radcliffe Report (Committee on the Working of the Monetary System, 1959) endorsed the view that the control of overall liquidity was more important than control of the money supply. The Report was subsequently criticised for its lack of attention to control of the money supply. The Report argued that any contrived changes in the money supply (M) were as likely as not to be offset by changes in the velocity of circulation (V). The view was also challenged by monetarists in later years. The Radcliffe Report's conclusions formed the basis of government monetary policy until the early 1970s. In particular it was believed that monetary policy should be concerned with the ***fine tuning*** of the economy, while its overall direction was a matter for fiscal policy.

The rise of monetarist ideas

The Competition and Credit Control (CCC) regulations of 1971 were an important change in policy. From this date interest rates were supposed to be left free to be determined by market forces. Competition was to be encouraged by such measures as the abolition of the syndicated bid for Treasury bills and the abandonment of the clearing banks' cartel on interest rates. The CCC changes also abandoned the old 28 per cent liquid assets ratio in favour of a 12.5 per cent reserve assets ratio (itself abandoned in 1981). This resulted in an unprecedented rise in the money supply, which was one of the major causes of inflation in subsequent years.

Economists in the UK and the USA, especially the leader of the monetarist school, Milton Friedman, were convinced that the only way to control inflation was through control of the money supply (*M*).

The increasing severity of inflation and the apparent inability of traditional fiscal and incomes policy methods to deal with it won many people over to the monetarist school. In particular the IMF was convinced of the need to control M. Thus, when the UK was forced to apply for a major loan in 1976 it was granted it only on the condition that the money supply be controlled. The accession of monetarist ideas to dominance in monetary policy can be seen to date from 1976.

In 1979 a Conservative government was elected which placed control of the money supply at the centre of its policies. In 1980 the government adopted a ***Medium Term Financial Strategy*** (MTFS). This set down diminishing targets for the growth of the money supply so as to squeeze inflation out of the system. In most years the target rates were exceeded while, at the same time, measures of the money supply were changed and redefined. In October 1985 the MTFS was largely abandoned when the most favoured target, M_3, was suspended. By 1988 the only measure of money supply for which targets remained was M_0.

Despite these changes the Conservative government continued to see control of the money supply and of interest rates as central to its policies, although there was also an increased tendency to use interest rates to avoid fluctuations in exchange rates (see Chapter 41). In 1990 the UK joined the Exchange Rate Mechanism (ERM) and interest rates were primarily used to maintain the value of the pound within the requisite limits. However, the fact that the UK had entered the ERM at what many regarded as too high a level meant that interest rates were also kept high. In 1992 the UK left the ERM and interest rates fell. From 1993 the prime focus of government policy has been to use interest rates to keep inflation within certain 'target bands', the targeting of the money supply *per se* having been long since abandoned.

STUDENT ACTIVITY 37.5

Why do you think that interest rates needed to be kept at a high level when the UK was in the ERM? What impact could such a policy have on the money supply and the level of spending in the economy?

The stages of monetary policy

The five stages of policy

The Bank of England has a number of ***weapons*** or ***instruments*** of monetary policy at its disposal; for example, it may lower interest rates in order to stimulate the economy.

Common misunderstanding

It is sometimes thought that it is possible to use policy weapons to influence the economy and economic variables immediately. However, in most cases, policies do not take effect straight away. For example, there are several steps, or stages, along the monetary policy road.

These steps we may list as follows:

a) *Instruments (or weapons) of policy*, which include, for example, open market operations, which are used to implement policy. It will take some time for these to act upon:
b) *Operating policy targets* such as the liquidity of banks. These in turn will affect such things as the growth of money stock, which are termed:
c) *Intermediate targets*. They are termed 'intermediate' because they are not the actual objective of policy but are important steps along the way. For example, restricting the money supply may be seen as essential in achieving the overall policy objective of controlling inflation. To do this the intermediate targets must affect:
d) *Aggregate demand*. This is the actual level of national income as measured by GDP, NNP, etc., the control of which leads directly to:
e) *Overall policy objectives*. This is the ultimate goal of policy such as the promotion of economic growth or the control of inflation.

Intermediate targets

The central link in the chain is intermediate targets. In choosing the best or most appropriate target, the monetary authorities are constrained by two major considerations: first, which target it is *possible* to control, i.e. it is no good selecting a target which is impossible to influence (perhaps we should say that some targets are more influenceable than others!); second, which intermediate target is thought to influence most the desired ultimate policy objective. Here there is considerable disagreement. Monetarists, for example, would argue that changes in interest rates have a significant influence on economic growth, while Keynesians would argue that the effect would be slight.

These are the main intermediate targets:

a) the money stock;
b) the volume of credit;
c) interest rates;
d) the exchange rate;
e) the level of expenditure in the economy (or PSBR as a percentage of the level of expenditure, as was used in the early 1980s).

It is possible for expenditure to be considered an intermediate target as well as the fourth stage of monetary policy.

The weapons of monetary policy

Monetary policy is aimed at controlling the supply and price of money. However, elementary economics tells us that government cannot do both simultaneously, i.e. it can fix the interest rate but it will then be committed to creating a money supply which is appropriate to that rate, or it can control the money supply and leave market forces to determine the interest rate.

With the exception of M_0, whichever definition of the money supply we take (M_2, M_4, etc.), the major component of it is bank deposits. Thus monetary policy must be aimed at influencing the volume of bank deposits. The ability of banks to create deposits is determined by the ratio of liquid assets which they maintain. If, for example, banks keep to a 12.5 per cent liquid (or reserve) asset ratio, whether statutory or not, then because we have a bank multiplier of 8, each reduction of £1 in banks' liquid assets would cause a further reduction of £7 in their deposits. Much of monetary policy is therefore aimed at influencing the supply of liquid assets.

In order to effect its monetary policy the Bank of England uses a number of methods. These weapons of policy are considered below.

The issue of notes and coins

Theoretically the Bank could influence the volume of money by expanding or contracting the supply of cash. In practice it is very difficult for the Bank not to supply the cash which banks are demanding, so that it is not a viable method of restricting supply. The reverse may not be true, however, for expanding the issue of cash could conceivably expand the money supply. Indeed, many people would argue that the over-printing of banknotes, i.e. sale of government securities to the Bank's Issue Department, was one of the causes of inflation in the mid 1970s.

Table 37.3 traces the growth of the supply of notes and coins (this used to be called the fiduciary issue) in recent years; this is now modified by the introduction of £1 coins.

Table 37.3 **The growth of the value of notes and coins in the UK**

Year to end	Notes and coins outside the Bank of England (£m)	Percentage increase over preceding year
1979	9225	–
1980	10075	9.2
1981	10600	5.2
1982	10775	1.7
1983	11300	4.9
1984	11900	5.3
1985	12190	2.4
1986	12370	1.5
1987	12970	4.9
1988	14020	8.1
1989	14750	5.2
1990	15680	6.3
1991	15910	1.5
1992	16770	5.4
1993	17795	6.1
1994	18752	5.3
1995	18557	–0.1

Source: Bank of England

The quantity of cash is now such a small proportion of the money supply that we might, in the words of the Radcliffe Report, regard it as the 'small change' of the monetary system. However, the fact that by 1988 M_0 (consisting of notes and coins in circulation plus banks' balances with the Bank of England) was the only money supply figure targeted suggests that the supply of cash had assumed some importance as a monetary weapon. You can see from Table 37.3 that the growth of the supply of cash (and hence of M_0) has been relatively stable. This stability was one of the reasons which recommended it to the government as a target for control. However, credit booms, such as the one of the late 1980s, demonstrated that controlling the monetary base does not necessarily control spending in the economy. Besides, as noted above, money supply targeting had been effectively abandoned from about this time.

Liquidity ratios

In 1981 the Bank abandoned the reserve assets ratio. The only stated ratios now are the 0.35 per cent of eligible liabilities which the monetary sector must keep with the Bank and the 5 per cent which has to be kept with the money market. However, as we have seen above, although there is no overall liquid assets ratio, banks are still required to order their assets in particular ways. Since the Bank is able to influence the supply of liquid assets, it is therefore still able to influence bank lending. The Bank has stated that it regards these funds and, in addition, money which the banks voluntarily retain with it for clearing purposes as 'the fulcrum for money market management'.

Interest rates

Interest rate determination has dominated much of monetary policy since the Second World War; variations in interest rates were important means of helping to secure money supply targets when these were first introduced in the late 1970s. In this sense, a key technique for controlling monetary growth has been to influence money demand rather than money supply.
(See also Chapter 38.)

By lowering interest rates the Bank could hope to encourage economic activity by decreasing the cost of borrowing and hence increasing the demand for loans, while, conversely, raising interest rates should discourage borrowing. Most of the weapons of monetary policy will indirectly affect interest rates, but the Bank has a direct influence upon interest rates because, as lender of last resort, it guarantees the solvency of the financial system. Thus the rate at which the Bank is willing to lend is crucial. Great importance used to be attached to the bank rate but this was abandoned in 1972 in favour of the minimum lending rate (MLR) which was supposed to be determined by a formula geared to the Treasury bill rate, thus placing greater reliance on market forces. The announcement (or 'posting') of MLR was suspended in 1981. The Bank now works within an unpublished band of rates. Important money market rates such as the Treasury bill rate will stay close to the Bank's lending rate. This is because the Bank's rate is kept above Treasury bill rate, so that discount houses would lose money if they are forced to borrow. Thus all market rates tend to move in sympathy with the Bank's rates; the clearing banks' base rate, for example, is always at, or near, the Bank's rate.

Open-market operations

These are the sale or purchase of securities by the Bank of England on the open market with the intention of influencing the volume of money in circulation and the rate of interest. The selling of bills or bonds should reduce the volume of money and increase interest rates, while the repurchase of, or reduction in sales of, government securities should increase the volume of money and decrease interest rates.

In order to explain the effects of open-market operations it is necessary to explain their effect upon the balance sheets of commercial banks. Let us consider a bank whose assets and liabilities are arranged in the following manner:

Bank X before open-market sales

Liabilities (£)		*Assets (£)*	
Deposits	100 000	Liquid assets (10% ratio)	10 000
		Securities	40 000
		Advances	50 000
	100 000		100 000

You will note that bank X has a liquid asset ratio of 10 per cent. Let us now assume that the Bank of England *sells* securities, £1000 of which are bought by the depositors of bank X. The customers pay for these by cheques drawn on bank X and the Bank of England collects this money by deducting it from bank X's balance at the Bank. Thus after open-market sales, bank X's balance sheet will be as follows:

Bank X after open-market sales

Liabilities (£)		*Assets (£)*	
Deposits	99 000	Liquid assets (9.09% ratio)	9 000
		Securities	40 000
		Advances	50 000
	99 000		99 000

The Bank of England's actions will have immediate (or primary) effects by reducing the amount of money in circulation by the amount of open-market sales and may also increase the interest rate if increased sales depress the price of securities. However, the most important effects of open-market operations are the secondary effects which come about as a result of bank X's need to maintain its liquidity ratio. In order to restore its ratio the bank is forced to sell off securities, thus further reducing their price and thereby raising the rate of interest, and reduce its advances, which may involve both making advances harder to obtain and more expensive.

Common misunderstanding

Students are often puzzled as to why selling securities does not increase the banks' reserves of cash. The supply of cash is effectively under the control of the monetary authorities so that as the banks sell securities these are paid for by customers running down their deposits.

And after all, banks cannot deposit money in themselves!

Final position of bank X

Liabilities (£)		*Assets (£)*	
Deposits	90 000	Liquid assets (10% ratio)	9 000
		Securities	36 000
		Advances	45 000
	90 000		90 000

The final position of bank X's balance sheet shows that in order to restore its liquidity ratio it has been forced to reduce its balance sheet to £90 000. Thus £1000 of open-market operations have reduced the volume of money in circulation by £10 000. We have demonstrated here the effect of open-market sales. If the bank were to buy securities it would have exactly the opposite effect.

STUDENT ACTIVITY 37.6

The magnitude of open-market operations is determined by the bank multiplier. If, in the above example, bank X worked to a 20 per cent ratio, what would be the effect on its balance sheet of the Bank of England selling £1000 of securities?

Funding

This is the conversion of short-term government debt into longer-term debt. Not only will this reduce liquidity but also, if the Bank of England is replacing securities which could be counted as liquid assets by securities which cannot, it could bring about the multiple contraction of deposits described above. In the mid 1980s the government was concerned to borrow money in a way which would not increase banks' supplies of liquid assets and therefore created more longer-term non-negotiable securities such as 'granny bonds'.

Special directives and special deposits

Since its nationalisation in 1946 the Bank of England has had the power to call for special deposits and to make special directives. However, these powers were not used until after the Radcliffe Report. If the Bank calls upon the members of the monetary sector to make a deposit of a certain percentage of their liabilities in cash at the Bank, and stipulates that these may not be counted as liquid assets, this brings about a multiple contraction of their lending in the same way as open-market operations, the difference being that it is more certain and less expensive. The power to call for special deposits was specifically retained in the Monetary Control Provisions of 1981, although they have not been used since then.

The Bank has issued special directives on both how much banks should lend (quantitative) and to whom they should lend (qualitative). However, since the competition and credit control changes of 1971 it ceased to make quantitative directives and has since only made qualitative ones (and these only rarely).

In 1973 a new scheme came into operation termed special supplementary deposits, which was nicknamed 'the corset'. By this scheme, if banks expanded their interest-bearing eligible liabilities (IBELs) too quickly they automatically had to make special deposits of cash with the Bank. This scheme was abandoned in 1980.

Problems of monetary policy

We have discussed the weapons of monetary policy but there are many doubts about their efficacy. These can be broadly classified into two groups. First, there are conceptual problems concerning the ability of monetary policy to influence the economy, as for instance the doubts about the ability of lower interest rates to stimulate investment (see also Chapter 38). Second, there are the more mechanistic problems which may prevent the weapons from being effective, as for example the existence of excess liquidity in the system preventing open-market operations from being effective. Some of these problems are discussed below.

Interest rate policy

It has already been suggested that decreasing the interest rate may not encourage investment but that raising the interest rate tends to lock up liquidity in the financial system. Businesses, however, might still be willing to borrow at a relatively high rate of interest if they are sufficiently confident: some investment decisions may be considered ***non-marginal***, i.e. the entrepreneur will be anticipating a sufficiently large return on investment that small changes in the interest rate are unlikely to make a potentially profitable scheme unprofitable.

In considering the effect of interest rates we must also take account of the effect of time on investment decisions; the longer the term of an investment project the greater the proportion of total cost interest will represent.

STUDENT ACTIVITY 37.7

We can illustrate the latter point by an analogy with the individual consumer: which borrowing would be most influenced by a rise in the interest rate – borrowing to buy a car or borrowing over the longer term to buy a house?

Having mentioned house purchase we have touched on another problem and that is that governments may be unwilling to put up interest rates because, as so many voters are home buyers, this is extremely unpopular.

There are other factors which make governments unwilling to face high interest rates. With a large National Debt to service, raising interest rates increases the government's own expenditure. Furthermore, higher interest rates may attract inflows of funds from overseas, thus making it more difficult to control the money supply. In addition, the inflow of funds from abroad increases the demand for the currency and pushes up its value; the rise in the exchange rate makes imports cheaper, but means that exports become more expensive, thus creating or enhancing a current account deficit on the balance of payments.

Governments from the 1980s onwards believed in using market forces as much as possible. Therefore, they came to view restriction of the money supply as unhelpful. The money supply is principally bank deposits, and in turning away from trying to control the size of banks' balance sheets, the Bank of England said that it was abandoning 'portfolio constraints'.

By the end of the 1980s the monetary authorities were relying almost entirely on interest rates to control the economy, a process which has continued ever since.

Liquidity and the multiple contraction of deposits

Many of the weapons of monetary policy depend upon limiting liquidity, which has a multiple effect upon banks' deposits through their liquidity ratios. If, however, banks keep surplus liquidity this will protect them against such measures as open-market operations and special deposits. Furthermore, if not all financial institutions were subject to some kind of restriction on their lending (through, say, the imposition of a statutory liquidity ratio), then lending activity would simply shift from the banks to these other institutions, a process known as ***disintermediation***.

The efficacy of open-market sales is also affected by who purchases the securities. For open-market sales to be effective it is necessary that sales be to the general public. If the securities are bought by the banks they will have little effect upon their liquidity since most of the securities count as liquid assets. This problem was especially acute when governments were forced to borrow large amounts in the late 1970s and early 1980s. As banks acquired government securities they used them as a base to expand deposits. Thus, rather than controlling the money supply, sales of securities provided the springboard for its expansion. To counter this effect the monetary authorities adopted the practice of selling more government long-term debt to UK non-bank holders than was necessary to cover the PSBR. The object of doing so was to moderate the effects of rising bank lending on the M_3 definition of money supply, a practice known as ***overfunding***. By creating more long-term debt than was actually needed the authorities hoped to reduce the rate of growth of 'broad' money.

Other problems

Funding may be effective in controlling liquidity and we have already mentioned the government's attempts to increase the sale of non-negotiable securities. However, it is expensive, since the rate of interest on long-term debt is usually much higher than on short-term debt. Considerable funding of the debt might therefore have the undesirable consequence of increasing long-term interest rates.

When we consider special deposits and special directives we discover that these can be simple, cheap, effective and quick acting. However, since the early 1980s governments have avoided using them because they tend to damage the relationship between the central bank and the commercial banks. They also have the effect of distorting market forces; government policy has tended to concentrate upon manipulating market forces rather than imposing its will directly on the system. The distorting effect of direct controls was well illustrated when the 'corset' was abolished in 1980. The immediate result was a surge in the money supply as banks, which had been keeping assets in eurocurrencies, switched them back to sterling.

The European dimension

As has been noted above, the UK belonged to the Exchange Rate Mechanism (ERM) of the European Monetary System (EMS) from 1990 to 1992. As part of European Monetary Union (EMU), we are seen to be faced with a single European currency (the ECU); assuming this comes about it will be accompanied by a European central bank and a common monetary policy for the EU. (These topics are discussed in Chapter 42.)

The independence of the Bank of England

Earlier in the chapter it was noted that the Labour administration elected in 1997 had granted the Bank of England 'operational independence' in the setting of interest rates; previously this function was the preserve of the government in the form of the Treasury. From May 1997 decisions on interest rates have been taken by a ***monetary policy committee***, comprising the governor of the Bank of England, two deputy governors and six others, four of whom are appointed by the Chancellor of the Exchequer.

The main perceived advantage of central bank independence is that it is free from political control; it can thus concentrate on long-term economic objectives and targets rather than being under the influence of politicians who may have at least one eye on the potential short-term electoral impact of any policy change. Often interest rates have to be changed some months before they have an effect on inflation. Politicians may be reluctant to raise interest rates when there is no apparent short-term advantage of so doing, especially when close to an election. An independent central bank may be able to pre-empt higher inflation by raising interest rates immediately, thereby reducing the need for a higher interest rate rise later.

On the other hand, central bank independence means that democratic accountability for managing the economy is reduced. This can be particularly significant given the potential trade-off between inflation and unemployment. An independent central bank in charge of monetary policy is more likely to be committed to a regime of low and stable prices than to policies that result in creating more jobs; thus, it may increase interest rates in order to satisfy the former policy objective, even though such a strategy may adversely affect future employment prospects.

At both the national and international level the role of monetary policy has been the subject of much controversy in recent years. People have often expected monetary policy to accomplish tasks which it was never designed to do. In the best of all possible worlds the job of a central bank would be simply to maintain the system with small adjustments here and there. Monetary policy, however, has often been viewed as a way in which overall management of the economy could be achieved. For the UK there is also an extra dimension to the problem, for London is a world banking centre and the central bank must therefore contend not only with domestic economic problems but also with those of much of the world as well. It remains to be seen whether an independent Bank of England can successfully cope with the additional demands that have been placed upon it. (See also Data response B at the end of the chapter).

Summary

1 Financial intermediaries are institutions which channel funds between different sectors of the economy.

2 The many different types of bank can be grouped under the two headings, primary and secondary banks. Primary banks operate in the high street and deal with the general public, whilst secondary banks deal in very large amounts of money with other banking institutions.

3 The main functions of commercial banks are the creation of credit, the transmission of money and the provision of advisory services to customers.

4 The study of commercial banks' balance sheets explains how their business is conducted.

5 Money markets are those institutions and arrangements which are concerned with the borrowing and lending of money on a very large scale for very short periods of time (overnight to three months).

6 The capital market is concerned with the provision of capital for industry, commerce and the government. The market is very widespread and provides capital for periods over three months to permanent.

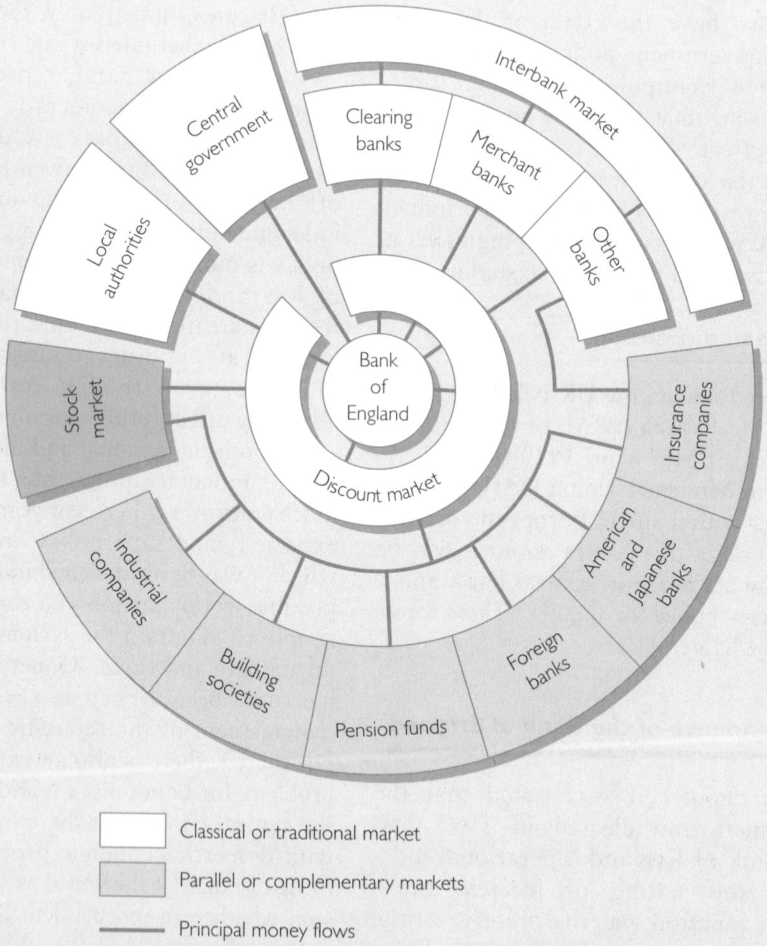

Fig. 37.1 The main participants in the UK financial markets

7 Most central banks act as the government's banker, the banks' bank, lender of last resort and issuer of notes as well as supervising the banking system and operating monetary policy.

8 The Bank of England's balance sheet illustrates most of its major functions. It is divided into two sections, Issue Department and Banking Department.

9 The Bank of England has other functions such as managing the National Debt and running the Exchange Equalisation Account.

10 The weapons of monetary policy may be listed as the issue of notes, changing liquidity ratios, variations in interest rates, open-market operations, funding and special deposits and directives.

11 Interest rate variations have tended to dominate monetary policy since the Second World War; it continued to be an important weapon even when money supply targets were first introduced in the late 1970s.

12 There are many problems associated with the operating of monetary policy. In particular, interest rates do not appear to have a strong correlation with investment, and excess liquidity in the system may frustrate the Bank of England's ability to influence the money supply.

13 An independent central bank is free from political influence, although democratic accountability is reduced. Monetary policy is now at the centre of government policy and economic debate.

Questions

1 What is meant by financial intermediation? How do a bank's activities in transmitting money differ from its role as a financial intermediary?

2 A banker might say: 'My bank's books always balance. We simply lend a proportion of my depositors' savings to investors. We do not create money.' To what extent is this true?

3 'Since banks themselves can now determine their own liquidity ratios, there is no effective constraint on their ability to create credit.' Explain and discuss.

4 Assess the advantages and disadvantages of the capital market being dominated by large institutions.

5 What is meant by the terms 'the discount market' and 'the parallel money markets'? To what extent is it possible or meaningful to distinguish between the two?

6 List the functions of central banks. Discuss the relative merits of an independent central bank.

7 Examine the weapons of monetary policy. Comment on the view that the main thrust of monetary policy has been on controlling money demand rather than money supply.

8 What factors may limit the efficacy of variations in interest rates as a weapon of policy?

9 What conditions are necessary for open-market operations to be effective?

10 Explain how the monetary authorities might seek to influence the quantity of money in the economy. Describe how the monetary authorities have gone about this task since 1979.

Data response A Balancing the books

Table 37.4 gives all the figures which are necessary for the presentation of Midwest Bank PLC's balance sheet. Midwest is a recognised bank and its business is in sterling. The distribution of its assets is in accordance with Monetary Control Provisions of 1981.

Table 37.4 **Midwest Bank PLC**
[Recognised as a bank by the Bank of England]
Items in the balance sheet as at April 1996

	£m
Advances	14 367
Other bills*	602
Coins and notes	451
Money at call and short notice*	650
Certificates of deposit*	729
Loans to UK banks*	531
Investments	3 372
Operational balances with the Bank of England*	563
Government stocks with less than one year to maturity*	206
UK Treasury bills*	326
Sight deposits	9 922
Local authority bills*	279
Time deposits	12 628
Non-operational deposits with the Bank of England	114

1 Present these figures as a balance sheet laid out in the conventional manner for a bank and determine the overall balance for Midwest PLC.
2 If the whole of the items marked * in Table 37.4 are regarded as liquid assets for control purposes, determine the liquidity ratio on which Midwest is operating.
3 Outline the factors which determine the distribution of a bank's assets and liabilities.
4 Examine the consequences of there being a significant decrease in the required liquidity ratio.
5 To what extent does the balance sheet of Midwest differ from that of a typical clearing bank?

Data response B
A good start

Read the article taken from *The Economist* of 10 May 1997 and answer the following questions:

1 Why do you think the government granted the Bank of England 'operational independence' in monetary policy?
2 To what extent is this a 'historic' move?
3 To what extent do the new arrangements in the UK counter the objections that an independent Bank of England reduces democratic accountability?
4 Discuss whether the arrangements for an independent Bank of England may increase the significance of some economic policy objectives at the expense of others. Comment on the potential drawbacks of such a situation.

A good start

GORDON BROWN'S decision to grant the Bank of England "operational independence" in monetary policy is an astonishingly bold start for the new chancellor. Henceforth the Bank, not the Treasury, will set British interest rates. After waiting 18 years for power, Labour's first step is to hand the larger part of its ability to steer the economy to somebody else. As a constitutional innovation it ranks alongside devolution, reform of the House of Lords, voting reform and the other measures on Labour's agenda for constitutional change.

The move is welcome and long overdue. Yet even enthusiasts cannot but be disconcerted by the manner of its coming. Unlike those other proposals, the idea was not in the party's manifesto. There are principled objections to it. One might have expected consultations, debate. But the City, which the chancellor was chiefly aiming to please, didn't mind: shares soared and long-term interest rates fell. Mr Brown has declared himself a bold reformer, dedicated to the long term and determined to get his way, all before his first budget.

The case for central-bank independence is much as Mr Brown described it. The essential difficulty of monetary policy is that interest rates need to be changed many months before they have any effect on inflation. Politics frowns on this. An independent central bank can anticipate higher inflation by raising interest rates promptly – and by less, therefore, than would be needed if the remedy were delayed. The result is smaller swings in inflation and interest rates, and a lower rate of inflation over the medium term. All this should foster investment and growth.

The main argument against is that democratic accountability is undermined. Britain's new arrangements, modelled on those of many other countries, meet this objection halfway. The chancellor will set the target for inflation (to begin with, $2\frac{1}{2}$%), so the Bank will not have to decide for itself what "stable prices" means. In addition, decisions on interest rates will be taken by a monetary-policy committee within the Bank, with members appointed by the government. Policy will be subject to review by both a committee of Parliament and the Bank's Court. In "exceptional" circumstances the Treasury can take charge.

In all these ways, the Bank will be held accountable. But it is wrong to say that no "democratic deficit" remains. The government may set the inflation target, but the Bank's committee will be left to decide how quickly the target should be pursued. It may be true that, in the long term, it is impossible to reduce unemployment by tolerating high inflation, that the power to make such a choice was always illusory, and that nothing is lost by giving it up. But such a trade-off undoubtedly exists in the short term. Much as the chancellor and Eddie George, the Bank's governor, might deny it, the Bank will be engaged in the highly political task of choosing how many jobs to sacrifice in order to hit the inflation target quickly rather than slowly. The true case for independence is not that there is no such democratic loss, but that the loss is more than matched by the economic gain.

In our view, it will be – provided the Bank is given space. It must be allowed to have its way even when, especially when, the Treasury sincerely believes it is wrong: otherwise, independence means nothing, and the benefits will not flow. Mr Brown cannot be so naive as to suppose that such a time will never come, but when it does he may find it a sterner test than he suspects.

Whatever next?

Apart from its other virtues, the chancellor's first measure is a political masterstroke. It deflects blame for the coming increases in interest rates (this week's rise from 6% to $6\frac{1}{4}$% will not be enough). And it lends credibility to a promise Tony Blair made during his campaign, when he said that Labour would be more radical than many supposed – or, indeed, than his manifesto entitled anybody to think. What other startling initiatives, one cannot help but wonder, lie ahead?

It is easy to see where they are most needed. Success or failure for this administration is likely to turn on control of public spending. In some ways, the new approach to monetary policy already serves this cause. It frees the Treasury to concentrate its efforts on fiscal control. Also, the chancellor has armed himself with a potent new reason to resist demands from spending departments: if he gives way, the Bank will raise interest rates whether he likes it or not. So a kind of hell beckons for Labour's spending ministers, crushed on one side by expectations of more and better public services and on the other by a would-be iron chancellor and a newly independent Bank. Perhaps anticipating the protests that may ensue, the prime minis-

Continued on page 510

ter's first announcements have concentrated on strengthening the controls that his office and the Treasury will exert on the rest of the government.

But immovability will not suffice. The only hope of reconciling post-election expectations of better public services with low taxes and low interest rates is to embark on far-reaching reform of the biggest spending programmes: education, health and social security. There was no sign of such a reform in the manifesto – but, you may well ask, what does that prove? If four days is all it takes Gordon Brown to transform Britain's monetary-policy regime, think what Harriet Harman could do to pensions in, say, a week.

Source: *The Economist*, 10 May 1997

38 Monetary analysis and income analysis

Learning outcomes

At the end of this chapter you will be able to:

- Distinguish between monetarist and Keynesian economic thinking.
- Understand the arguments about the effectiveness of fiscal and monetary policy.
- Recognise that the real argument is about whether markets work well at the macro level.
- Make the link between money, aggregate demand and the the labour market.

Monetarists and Keynesians

In Sections V and VI of the book we have examined the determination of national income and monetary economics. We have treated them in a fairly neutral manner. However, we have been considering an area of economics over which there are fundamental theoretical disagreements. In this chapter we will review some of these disagreements. There are, of course, as many views on economics as there are economists. As Bernard Shaw said, 'If all the economists in the world were laid from end to end, they would not reach a conclusion!' It is therefore necessary for us to generalise. We will look on the one hand at those views which we may term ***Keynesian*** (and ***neo-Keynesian***) and on the other at the views of monetarists and other neo-classicists.

What are monetarists?

One thing that ***monetarists*** are not is new; they are simply a modern variation of the neo-classical school which dominated economics from the 1870s to the Keynesian revolution of the late 1930s and 1940s. Monetarists share the same essential 'vision' as the ***neo-classical school***, i.e. they reject theories of macro demand deficiencies and emphasise the efficiency of free markets; for instance, they believe that market forces act quickly to eliminate unemployment. Monetarists are new only in the sense that their theory is more sophisticated than that of their ancestors and that their doctrine has reasserted itself after a long period following 1945 in which Keynesians dominated both economics and economic policy. The modern term monetarist derives from the debate of the 1960s and 1970s concerning the role of money in determining aggregate demand.

Keynesian views of money

Keynes had argued that, in times of deep depression, monetary policy might be totally ineffective as a means of stimulating aggregate demand. By the time of the Radcliffe Report in 1959, most Keynesian economists held the view that there was no causal link between the quantity of money and aggregate demand. They argued, for example, that if an attempt was made to expand the money supply at a time when people in general did not want to spend, then either the money would be held in 'idle' money balances or banks would find it impossible to create new loans. Equally the Radcliffe Report had stated:

> We cannot find any reason for supposing or any experience in monetary history indicating that there is any limit to the velocity of circulation.

Hence, it seemed that a given quantity of mo could support almost any level of aggregate dem

Some Keynesians, such as Kaldor, accepted that there might be a correlation between nominal national income and the money supply but argued this merely reflected the fact that the money supply adjusted ***passively*** to people's desire to spend, i.e. that the money supply adjusted to national income and not vice versa. In short, Keynesian economists, for one reason or another, had come to the conclusion that manipulating the money supply was ineffective as a means of demand management and hence monetary policy should be set in relation to other objectives (see Chapter 43). Keynesian economists therefore emphasised ***fiscal*** policy rather than ***monetary*** policy as the means of implementing the demand management they believed necessary; for this reason they were known as 'Fiscalists' in the USA.

The rise of monetarism

The rise (or re-emergence) of monetarism within mainstream economics dates largely from Milton Friedman's 1956 restatement of the 'quantity theory of money'. Friedman argued that the demand for money depended in a stable and predictable manner on several major economic variables. Thus, if the money supply was expanded people would not simply wish to hold the extra money in 'idle' money balances, if they were in equilibrium before the increase they were already holding money balances to suit their requirements, and thus after the increase they would have money balances surplus to their requirements. These excess money balances would therefore be spent and hence aggregate demand rise. Similarly, if the money supply were reduced people would want to replenish their holdings of money by reducing their spending. Thus Friedman challenged the Keynesian assertion that 'money does not matter'; he argued at the supply of money does affect the amount in an economy, and thus the word 'mone-as coined.

se of monetarism in political circles as Keynesian economics seemed ain or cure the seemingly contra-s of simultaneously rising inflation. On the one hand t seemed to call for Keynesian reflation, but on the other hand rising inflation seemed to call for Keynesian deflation. The resulting disillusionment with Keynesian demand management was summed up in the now famous words of James Callaghan, the Labour party Prime Minister, in 1976:

> We used to think that you could just spend your way out of a recession and increase employment by cutting taxes and boosting government spending. I tell you, in all candour, that that option no longer exists; and insofar as it ever did exist, it only worked by injecting bigger doses of inflation into the economy followed by higher levels of unemployment as the next step. That is the history of the past twenty years.

Not only did monetarists seek to explain contemporary problems; they reinterpreted historical ones. Milton Friedman and Anna Schwartz in their book *A Monetary History of the United States, 1867–1960* argued that the depression of 1930 was caused by a massive contraction of the money supply and not by lack of investment as Keynes had argued. They also maintained that post-war inflation was caused by overexpansion of the money supply. They coined the famous assertion of monetarism that

> inflation is always and everywhere a monetary phenomenon.

At first, to many economists whose perceptions had been set by Keynesian ideas, it seemed that the Keynesian/monetarist debate was merely about whether fiscal or monetary policy was the more effective tool of demand management. But by the mid 1970s the debate had moved on to more profound matters as monetarists presented a more fundamental challenge to Keynesian orthodoxy.

Keynesianism v. monetarism

Keynes had argued that the ***volatility of expectations*** meant that aggregate demand was subject to large fluctuations, and this in turn caused large fluctuations in the level of output and employment. The central political belief of Keynesians is therefore that it is necessary for governments to intervene and manage the level of demand in the economy in order to maintain full employment. As the Keynesian/monetarist debate progressed, monetarists sought to resurrect the pre-Keynesian orthodoxy that market economies are inherently stable (in the absence of major unexpected fluctuations in the money supply). Because of this belief in the stability of free market economies they asserted that active demand management is unnecessary and indeed likely to be harmful. The political right then adopted monetarism as an intellectual underpinning for its wish to return to a *laissez-faire* approach to economic policy in which economic outcomes are left to be determined by the free play of market forces. This was especially attractive to those on the right, such as Margaret Thatcher and Keith Joseph, who interpreted the expansion of the role of government as ***back door socialism***.

There have been several developments in the debate since the 1970s, many of which (such as the ***adaptive*** versus ***rational*** expectations debate and the role of supply side economics) are examined in this book (see Chapter 44). But the central questions at the core of the debate, and which dominate the political discussion of economic policy, remain unchanged.

The first question is the extent to which market forces in a free market economy do, or do not, ensure desirable outcomes (see also Section IV). The second question is the extent to which any government is able to correct for any failings of free market capitalism.

Money and national income

The Classical Dichotomy

The Classical Dichotomy provides a useful starting point for examining the technicalities of the Keynesian/monetarist debate. There is a problem, however, with the term classical. Keynes had lumped together all previous economists (with the exception of Malthus) under the title 'classical'. But many economists see the neo-classical or marginalist revolution of the 1870s as a watershed in the development of economic thought. Whether we wish to use the term classical or neoclassical the dichotomy referred to is central to the perspective of monetarists:

The Classical Dichotomy states that nominal prices are determined by the quantity of money but that the quantity of money has no effect on real things.

Nominal prices are prices in terms of the number of units of money that goods and services sell for, or factors of production are bought for. Hence we can speak of nominal (or money) prices, nominal wage rates and nominal income. Movements in the price 'level' record changes in these nominal prices. In contrast, ***relative*** prices are the price of one thing in terms of another. For example, if an egg costs 10p and a loaf 20p then the relative price of a loaf in terms of eggs is 2. If the price level were to rise by 100 per cent (i.e. if all nominal prices doubled) then relative prices would remain unchanged. The nominal price of an egg would now be 20p, and the nominal price of a loaf would be 40p, but the relative price of a loaf in terms of eggs would still be 2.

It should now be clear that if all prices were to increase by the same proportion then all relative prices would be unchanged. For example, suppose your money wage (the nominal price of your labour) has doubled, but at the same time the nominal price of everything that you buy has also doubled. You would soon realise that you are no better off than before. In this situation the money wage has doubled but the real wage, i.e. the price of labour relative to goods and services, has remained unchanged. Indeed, put like this, it is not apparent that anything real has changed. This is indeed the gist of the Classical Dichotomy: if an increase in the money supply merely increases all nominal prices proportionately, then all real variables such as relative prices, output, the goods and services earned in return for work, the level of employment/unemployment, the level of investment, etc., would be unaffected. It is in this sense that Geoffrey Crowther described money as a 'veil' thrown over the workings of the real economy.

To develop further our understanding of the debate we must now turn to the technicalities involved. First, we shall examine the debate concerning the link between the money supply and aggregate demand. Second, we shall examine th debate concerning what actually determines the le of real variables, such as output and employm and how stable these variables are likely to be.

Money as a determinant of aggregate demand

The effectiveness of monetary policy as a determinant of the level of aggregate demand in the economy depends upon the nature of both the demand for and the supply of money. Most attention and research, however, has focused on the demand for money. Before we turn to this relatively modern concept, however, it is instructive to trace its development, starting with Irving Fisher's 'quantity equation' which was introduced in Chapter 36.

You will recall that Fisher's equation of exchange is:

$$M \times V \equiv P \times T$$

The symbol ≡ denotes that this is an ***identity***, i.e. something which is true by definition. For example, the statement 'All men who have never married are bachelors' is hardly the basis for further research! Similarly, Fisher's equation simply says that 'the amount spent is equal to the amount received'. The early quantity theorists, however, made three assumptions which turned the identity into a theory of the determination of the price level. They argued that the quantity of money (M) is 'exogenously' set (e.g. by the amount of gold mined or the quantity of notes printed) and that V and T are constant. If these assumptions are made it follows mechanically that, say, a doubling of the money supply must be associated with a doubling of the price level. Therefore we are back to the Classical Dichotomy and the assertion of the quantity theorists that the price level varies in direct proportion to changes in the quantity of money leaving real variables unchanged.

The velocity of circulation

…ow concentrate on what determines V, …ocity of circulation of money. Later we … to the question of whether M is …termined and also to the question …nstant.

…y the monetary authorities … then it is easy to calculate the level of expenditure that would be 'caused' by any level of M. For example, if V is fixed at 3 a money stock of £50m would be associated with a total level of spending of £150m, whereas a money stock of £100m would give rise to expenditure of £300m, and so on. The early quantity theorists saw the determination of V in rather mechanical terms. They argued that any given level of spending in the economy would require a certain amount of money to finance it.

In much the same way as an engine running at a higher speed requires the oil within it to circulate at a faster rate to avoid friction reducing its speed, so a higher level of spending in the economy would require a given money stock to circulate faster so that money is always at hand for those desiring to make transactions. But the quantity theorists argued that the rate at which money can circulate around the economy is determined by the payment practices which prevail and the current structure of the economy. For example, if people are paid monthly rather than weekly they must keep more money 'idle', to be spent later in the month, and hence the rate at which the money stock can circulate is reduced. It was argued that factors such as payment practices and the degree of vertical integration changed only slowly. Hence, at any one time the ***velocity of circulation*** of money could be considered a ***constant*** and thus a higher level of spending would require a larger money stock to sustain it.

STUDENT ACTIVITY 38.1

1. If M is £10 billion, T is £50 billion and P is £5, what is the value of V?
2. Using the same figures, what would be the effect of increasing the money supply by a factor of two, assuming T and V are constant?
3. Using the same numbers as in 1, what would happen to V if aggregate demand (T) rose by 10 per cent, but the money stock and the price level remained the same? Why would monetarists find this unlikely?

The number of transactions

If V is a constant then the money value of transactions ($P \times T$) will vary in direct proportion to the quantity of money in the economy (M). We have explained earlier that T refers to all transactions in the economy and thus includes the purchases of ***intermediate*** goods and purely ***financial*** transactions. We are more interested, however, in the level of ***output*** of the economy. Hence it is more convenient to confine our definition of transactions only to those involving the sale of final goods and services. For direct proportionality of the money value of output to the quantity of money we thus require the further assumption that the number of transactions is directly related to the volume of output. We can thus write the quantity equation as:

$$M \times V = P \times Y$$

where Y is the level of output (real income) and P is the price level of final goods and services. In this equation V becomes the ***income velocity of circulation***. If, therefore, V and Y are constants the nominal level of income ($P \times Y$; or money GDP) will vary in direct proportion to M.

The Cambridge approach and the demand for money

In the crude manner in which the quantity theory was formulated by Fisher, money appears as a technical input to spending, i.e. a certain quantity is required per unit of spending. There is no indication that the velocity of circulation might be affected by the decisions of people themselves to hold money. But the more people tend to want to keep their wealth in ***liquid*** form (e.g. cash and cheque/current/sight accounts) rather than time deposits or longer-term loans, the smaller the proportion of the existing stock of money that can be lent out by the financial institutions to be spent by borrowers.

Thus the more people wish to hold reserves of liquidity in money balances the lower will tend to be the velocity of circulation of money.

In the 1920s the notion of the demand for money was reintroduced as an explicit argument in the quantity theory. This approach was developed by the Cambridge economists Pigou and Marshall; hence their formulation became known as the Cambridge equation. In their formulation the demand for money was written as:

$$M_d = k \times P \times Y$$

This states that the demand for money (M_d) is some proportion (k) of money income ($P \times Y$). Once we introduce the notion of a demand for money we can write the equilibrium condition for the economy as:

$$M = M_d$$

This states that for equilibrium the quantity of money demanded (M_d) must be equal to the quantity of money in the economy (M). For example, if M exceeded M_d there would be more money in existence than people wish to hold in their money balances. This would cause people with excess money balances to attempt to reduce them. For the economy as a whole, of course, the total level of money balances cannot be reduced. But the attempts to reduce excess money balances will lead to an increase in expenditure. This increase in expenditure will in turn increase the level of money income. Now, if the demand for money is some fraction of money income, the rise in money income will cause the increase in the demand for money that is required to restore equilibrium.

From the above we can now see that in equilibrium:

$$M = k \times P \times Y$$

By a simple rearrangement of this equilibrium result we have the Cambridge equation:

$$M \times 1/k = P \times Y$$

This looks very much like Fisher's crude representation of the quantity theory except that $1/k$ has taken the place of V. Indeed, if k is constant (i.e. the demand for money is a constant fraction of money income) it produces exactly the same proportionate relation between M and money income as Fisher's equation of exchange. That is, if k is constant and

$$V = 1/k$$

then V is also constant. For example, if $k = 1/5$ then $V = 5$; thus a money stock of £100m would imply an equilibrium level of money income of:

£100m × 5 = £500m

If k were to change to, say, $k = 1/3$, then $V = 3$ and the same money stock would imply an equilibrium level of money income of only:

£100m × 3 = £300m

This result also makes intuitive sense; it says that the velocity of circulation of money is inversely related to the demand for money. Hence if (*ceteris paribus*) the demand for money should rise, people will attempt to increase their holding of money balances. As more money is held rather than passed on, the rate at which money circulates in the economy falls. The fall in V in turn is seen in a fall in money income, until the fall in the level of money income reduces the demand for money back in line with the existing stock of money.

The Cambridge equation thus differs from the crude quantity theory in that it allows for the velocity of circulation to be affected by people's desire for money.

By introducing a role for human behaviour it is less mechanical than Fisher's version. Indeed, the early Cambridge school did explore the possibility that the demand for money (and hence the velocity of circulation) might be influenced by factors other than purely the level of money income. If this is the case, then a change in these other factors could 'disturb' the relationship between a given money stock and the level of money income making the level of money income for any quantity of money less predictable.

For example, perhaps a fall in interest rates reduces the opportunity cost of holding money *vis-à-vis* investing it in, say, a building society to be lent out and spent on property. Such a change in interest rates might have explained the rise in the proportion of money income that people wanted to hold in 'idle' money balances in our example above when k rose from 1/5 to 1/3. If, then, an increase in the quantity of money is accompanied by a fall in interest rates the resulting rise in the demand for money as a proportion of money income might cause the velocity of circulation to fall. This could offset the rise in the quantity of money, thereby leaving money income unaltered. In short, ***a rise in* M *might cause* V *to fall*** such that there is no increase in aggregate demand and hence no increase in money income ($P \times Y$).

In fact the early Cambridge school, as with the earlier quantity theorists, placed most emphasis on money as a means of making transactions. Thus the role of other factors was usually ignored and k was treated as more or less constant. As we have seen, if k is constant the Cambridge equation simply reproduces the crude quantity theory assertion that the price level is directly proportionate to the stock of money. It was left for Keynes, the most famous of all Cambridge economists, to develop the notion of a demand for money other than as a means of making transactions.

Liquidity preference

Belief in the quantity theory of money and the Classical Dichotomy was challenged by the traumatic depression of the interwar years. As unemployment soared it no longer seemed possible to argue that free market capitalist economies are inherently stable; the failure of financial institutions cast doubt on the monetary authority's ability to control the money supply and large fluctuations in aggregate demand suggested that the velocity of circulation of money was highly volatile. We have yet to examine the exogeneity of the money supply (M) and the stability of output (Y), but here we are concerned with the possible ***instability of* V**. Keynes argued in *The General Theory of Employment, Interest and Money* (1936) that V can be unstable as money shifts in and out of 'idle' money balances reflecting changes in people's ***liquidity preference***.

Unlike his predecessors, who focused upon money as a medium of exchange held only for transactions purposes, Keynes emphasised money as a store of wealth. Holding one's wealth in bonds, shares or real assets can be risky as the value of such assets can fluctuate widely, but this risk can be avoided by holding money instead. Thus in addition to money's usefulness for transactions purposes its quality of relatively certain purchasing power means that money will also be held for its own sake. Thus, Keynes argued that a wave of pessimism concerning real-world prospects could precipitate a ***retreat into liquidity*** as people sought to increase their holdings of money. This increase in money holding would lower the velocity of circulation of money and thus aggregate demand would fall bringing about the recession which everyone had feared!

Portfolio balance

If we examine the wealth (or assets) of a person or society in general, we could arrange them in a spectrum of liquidity from most liquid to least liquid, the most liquid being cash and the least liquid being real physical assets such as buildings. People will attempt to find a balance in their holding of assets which they think most advantageous. Holding of money (cash and bank deposits) gives certainty and convenience. On the other hand, the person holding money is forgoing the earning or interest that could be gained by putting this money into bonds and equities. If money is put into earning assets then, although income is gained, certainty and convenience are sacrificed and risk is increased. This is illustrated in Fig. 38.1.

Every individual will try to structure their assets to give maximum satisfaction. A selection of financial assets can be termed a ***portfolio*** and hence the distribution of assets within the portfolio is called a portfolio balance.

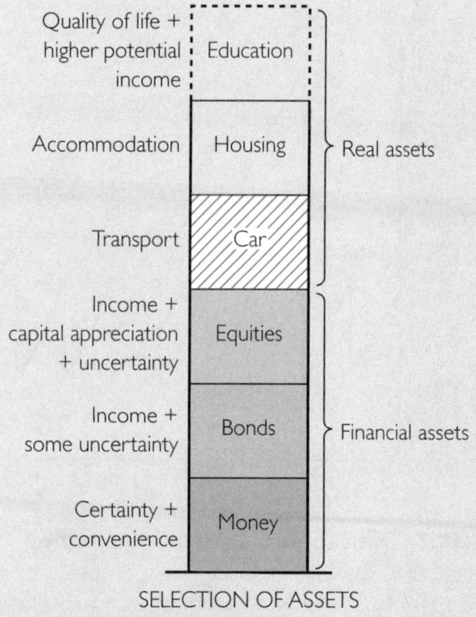

***Fig. 38.1* Portfolio balance**
People distribute their assets between money, financial assets such as bonds and real assets such as housing in a way which they consider maximises their utility. Friedman included in the portfolio investment in human capital such as education.

Keynesian theory of the demand for money

Keynes argued that there are three motives for holding money: the transactions, precautionary and speculative motives.

a) *The transactions motive*. This motive closely corresponds to the notion of money held by the quantity theorists. People hold cash and money in bank accounts simply to carry on the everyday business of life – to pay the gas bill, to buy petrol, to spend on groceries, and so on. Since people are usually paid weekly or monthly but spend money daily (i.e. their monetary receipts and expenditures are not perfectly synchronised) they therefore have to hold a proportion of their income as money rather than in more liquid assets. This gives a pattern as shown in Fig. 38.2, where the peaks in the money balance are caused by monthly salary inputs and the downward slope of the curve shows money being spent over the month.

   If the troughs are above zero there is an amount of idle money held in hand.

   The lower jagged line shows what happens if a person is paid weekly. We can see there is a quicker turnover of money but the overall demand for money is smaller. There is thus a higher velocity of circulation. This type of regular pattern of income and payments is one of the reasons why the quantity theorists believed that the velocity of circulation of money is stable.

   What determines the size of transactions demand for money? Keynes thought that it would be determined by the level of money

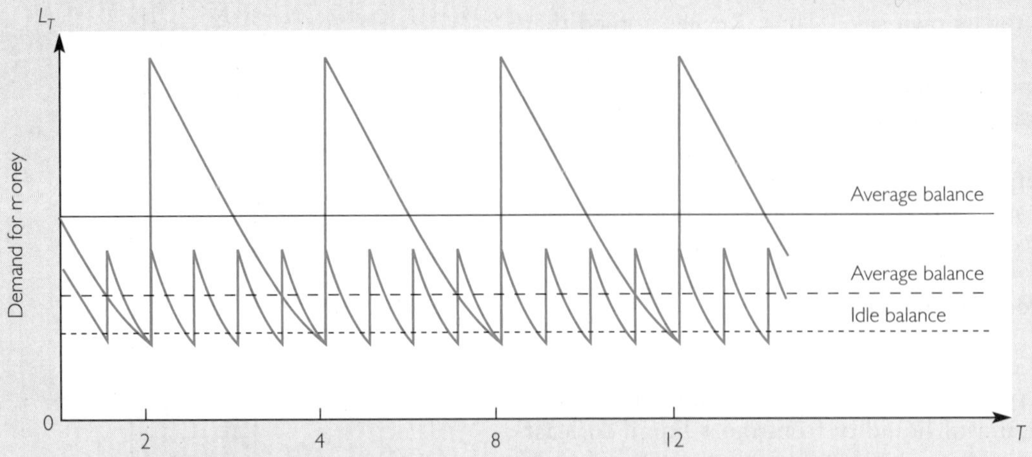

Fig. 38.2 **Transactions demand for money**
Every fourth week there is an injection of salary. This runs out over the month as bills are paid. This gives an average balance (demand for money). If not all of the salary is spent, but is retained in the bank account, then this gives a level for the idle balance. The dotted line shows what would happen if a person was paid weekly instead of monthly. The demand for money is smaller but the velocity of circulation is greater.

income. Indeed, it is clear from our discussion of the transactions motive that this will tend to be the case. It has been demonstrated since (from stock control theory) that such transactions balances are also likely to be economised on when interest rates rise.

STUDENT ACTIVITY 38.2

What would be the effects of increasing numbers of employees being switched from weekly to monthly payment upon the demand for money and the velocity of circulation?

b) *The precautionary motive*. People hold money to guard against unexpected eventualities – the car breaking down, a period of illness, a large electricity bill, and so on. It seems reasonable to suppose that the higher the level of income the larger will be the size of precautionary balances. The reason for this is that the rich need higher precautionary balances; if, for example, you are running several cars and a large house, the unexpected bills are likely to be larger, thus demanding a larger precautionary stock of money. Again it is likely that a rise in interest rates might cause people to economise somewhat on precautionary balances. But because of the similarity with the transactions motive the two are often lumped together.

c) *The speculative motive*. By emphasising this motive Keynes broke with the quantity theorists' view of money. The quantity theorists did not think that people will want to hold money for itself, but only for transactions purposes. Keynes, however, believed that people might speculate by holding money, just as they might speculate with other assets. The speculative demand for money is that money which is held in the hope of making a speculative gain, or to avoid a possible loss, as a result of the change in interest rates and the price of financial assets.

Keynes illustrated the speculative motive in terms of the decision to hold one's wealth in the form of cash or in fixed income bonds. To understand his argument it is necessary to appreciate that the price of bonds and the rate of interest are **inversely proportional** to each other. To make the argument simpler, we will assume that the bond is an eternal bond that will never be repaid by the government (such bonds are only usually issued in wartime). Consider, for example, a fixed income bond which yields an income of £5 per year. If the market rate of interest is 10 per cent the price of the bond will be £50. This is because the rate of interest on the bond must equal what savers could earn by investing their money elsewhere. If the market rate of interest were to fall to $2\frac{1}{2}$ per cent, the price of that same bond would rise to £200.

STUDENT ACTIVITY 38.3

1 How will a fixed income bond which originally cost £100 and has a fixed return of 10% (£10) be revalued when there are the following interest rates obtaining in the market?
a) 10 per cent b) 5 per cent
c) 20 per cent d) $2\frac{1}{2}$ per cent
2 How would the value of the bond be affected in each case if you knew the bond was to be repaid next year?
3 How would the value of the bond be affected in each case if the investors believed that the next movement in interest rates would be upwards?

Keynes believed that investors had some notion of the normal rate of interest. If the current rate of interest was below this then people would speculate by holding cash, anticipating that interest rates would rise and hence bond prices fall. Hence, the lower the interest rates the more people would expect the prices of bonds to fall and thus the more people would hold cash rather than bonds in their wealth portfolios. Thus, low interest rates are associated with a high speculative demand for money. Conversely, if the rate of interest was high, people would buy bonds because their price would be low and the chance of capital gains when interest rates came down would be high. Thus a high rate of interest is associated with a low speculative demand for money.

Later Keynesians, such as J. Tobin, tend to generalise risk to a wider range of assets than just bonds. Basically they argue that holding money is an insurance against the risk associated with other financial assets. If the interest rate increases then the cost of this insurance, i.e. the opportunity cost of holding money, is increased. Thus an increase in interest rates will cause a portfolio readjustment away from liquidity. Therefore they too arrive at the conclusion that the demand for money will be inversely related to the interest rate. Indeed, for the purpose of holding wealth, Keynesians regard money and many other financial assets as ***close substitutes***. As with any commodity with close substitutes, the demand for money is expected to be sensitive to price changes, i.e. Keynesians hold that the demand for money is ***elastic*** with respect to changes in interest rates.
We can summarise the above discussion as follows:

The demand for money is positively related to income and negatively related to the interest rate.

Thus we have arrived at the result that the demand for money is rather like the demand for any normal good; if we put the price of holding money (i.e. the interest rate) on the vertical axis we have a demand curve that slopes downward and which shifts to the right as income increases. What we should emphasise, however, is that in Keynesian theory ***expectations*** play a large part. This means that the relationship between the demand for money and observable variables such as income and the interest rate is likely at any time to become unstable. For example, pessimistic views on the future prices of financial assets and the yield to investment in general could cause a large increase in the demand for money associated with previous levels of income and the interest rate.

Monetarist theory of the demand for money

In common with modern Keynesians, monetarists also take a portfolio adjustment approach to money. Again, individuals are seen to have a choice of different ways in which to hold their wealth. Again, these assets will have varying liquidity as well as other advantages and disadvantages. Thus individuals weigh up the various costs and benefits associated with each asset and arrange their portfolios such that their utility is maximised. But the monetarist concept of a wealth portfolio is much broader than that of Keynesians. Monetarists hold that the relevant portfolio includes not just financial assets but also physical goods. Thus an increase in the money supply which disturbs the equilibrium of wealth holders by making their portfolios 'too liquid' is just as likely to spill over into physical investment assets and ***durable consumption goods*** as into financial assets, as illustrated in Fig. 38.3.

Monetarists, as did the earlier quantity theorists, concentrate on the convenience of money as a medium of exchange. Thus, unlike Keynesians, they believe that there is a dividing line in the portfolio between money and all other assets. Therefore they do not regard money and other financial assets as close substitutes. Monetarists would state this condition in the following form:

Money is a substitute for all assets alike, real and financial, rather than a close substitute for only a small range of financial assets.

As money is not regarded as having close financial substitutes, the demand for money is expected, in contrast to the Keynesian view, to be inelastic with respect to the rate of interest. In addition, monetarists do not include as a determinant of money demand any variable which is likely to be volatile. Thus, again in contrast to the Keynesian view, the demand for money has a fairly stable and predictable relationship to its determinants.

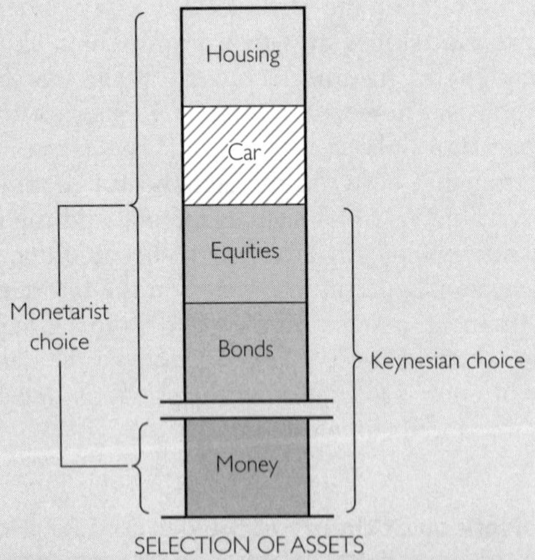

Fig. 38.3 **Different views of portfolio balance**
Monetarists see portfolio balance as choice between money and all other assets, but Keynesians see money and financial assets as close substitutes.

Monetary transmission mechanisms

The transmission mechanisms in a car transmit the power of the engine to the wheels. But how is an increase in the money supply transmitted into increased aggregate demand? We have already touched upon this in our discussion of portfolio adjustments. As would be expected from that discussion monetarists and Keynesians differ as to the mechanisms involved and the strength of the links between variables.

What makes it more difficult for the author of a textbook is that there is not complete unanimity within each school of thought and that there are many complex 'feedback' effects to consider. The presentation here seeks to elucidate the differences which have generated most debate and also serves as a useful introduction to more 'advanced' *IS*/*LM* presentations (e.g. see *Modern Macroeconomics* by Parkin and Bade.)

The Keynesian transmission mechanism

Common misunderstanding

Because of the way in which the difference between Keynesians and monetarists is stressed in textbooks, students often believe them to be complete opposites and therefore conclude that Keynesians believe there is no consequence of an increase in the money supply. Except in the extreme case detailed below, this is not the case, although it is true that Keynesians believe that the responses will be much less dramatic.

Figure 38.4 represents in diagrammatic form the stages in the Keynesian view of the transmission mechanism. In part (a) of Fig. 38.4 we see that there has been an increase in the supply of money (M_{S1} to M_{S2}). At the previous equilibrium rate of interest (r_1) there is now an excess supply of money. Banks thus seek to expand their loans by offering lower rates of interest, or people with excess liquidity in their wealth portfolios will seek to purchase other financial assets and in so doing drive up the price of these assets thus reducing interest rates. In short, interest rates will fall to the new equilibrium indicated by r_2. In part (b) we can see that the fall in the rate of interest will cause an extension of the demand for investment, i.e. the level of the investment will increase by ΔI. Part (c) is the familiar 45° diagram. The increase in the level of investment has increased income by ΔY, i.e. the increase in the money supply has finally led to an increase in aggregate demand.

There are several important points to note about this transmission mechanism:

a) The link between changes in the money supply and aggregate demand is ***indirect*** as it operates only through the effect of money on the interest rates prevailing in financial markets.
b) Keynesians believe the demand for money to be interest elastic. Thus much of the impact of an increased money supply is absorbed because falls in the interest rate cause people readily to increase their holdings of 'idle' money balances.
c) To the extent that interest rates do fall a little, the effect on investment and hence aggregate demand is slight. This is because Keynesians believe the interest elasticity of the demand for investment to be low.
d) Both the demand for money and the demand for investment are likely to be highly ***volatile*** in the face of changes in expectations.

In short, Keynesians believe that the links between changes in the money supply and changes in aggregate demand are extremely tenuous; not only are the links weak, they are unstable. Therefore Keynesians prefer the more direct manipulation of spending and hence aggregate demand through fiscal measures.

An extreme Keynesian view

Some so-called 'extreme Keynesians', notably Kaldor, take a somewhat different tack. They deny money any causal role as a determinant of aggregate demand. Instead they argue that the money supply responds in an entirely ***passive*** manner to accommodate any increase in the desire to spend, i.e. the direction of causation flows from an autonomous increase in the desire to consume or invest to an increase in the money supply. Kaldor's famous example was the sharp increase in the money supply which occurs in the months of November and December. He teased those that ascribed a causal role to money by asking whether it was this increase in the money supply that caused increased consumer spending in the run-up to Christmas! Of course what actually happens is that the monetary authorities anticipate the increase in spending and therefore expand the

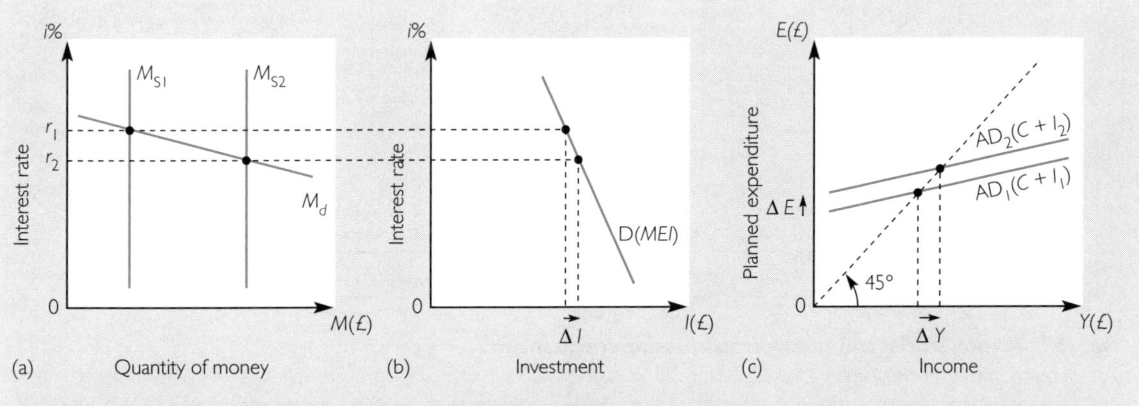

Fig. 38.4 **A Keynesian monetary transmission mechanism**
An increase in the money supply in (a) causes a relatively small fall in the rate of interest. This causes a relatively small increase in investment (ΔI) in (b). This increase in investment leads to a small increase in income (Y) in (c).

money supply so that consumers and traders will have sufficient cash for their transactions.

Kaldor's point should not be dismissed lightly. We have seen that quasi- and near money can perform to some extent the functions of money. It is also the case that attempts since 1976 to control the money supply within pre-set target bands of growth were often unsuccessful and have now been largely abandoned (see Section VIII). Part of the argument is that banks have access to reserve assets that cannot be directly controlled by central banks and that restrictions on such banks tend merely to cause ***disintermediation*** or the diversion of business to ***fringe*** banks or eurocurrency markets not covered by such regulations. Others stress that, historically, central banks have acted to accommodate the stock of money to changes in the needs for trade by giving their supportive responsibilities priority over their control duties. This latter argument explains why many Keynesians are not impressed by the historical evidence presented by Friedman and Schwartz of a correlation between nominal income and the money supply.

But the nature of money itself might make it difficult to control. Essentially, money is based on faith, e.g. we accept bank deposits as payment because it is believed that we could exchange them for cash. But equally any promissory note that one has faith in might be accepted as payment. The granting of credit is often extremely informal between regular trading partners. Credit arrangements can be extended by any large business that feels the advantages in attracting custom outweigh occasional defaults.

Whether they take the view that expansion of the money supply has a weak and unpredictable effect on aggregate demand, or that money is an entirely passive variable which is for practical purposes impossible to control, it is clear that such Keynesians would not emphasise monetary policy as a means of demand management.

The monetarist transmission mechanism

Figure 38.5 represents in diagrammatic form the monetarist view of the transmission mechanism. Again there are several important points to note:

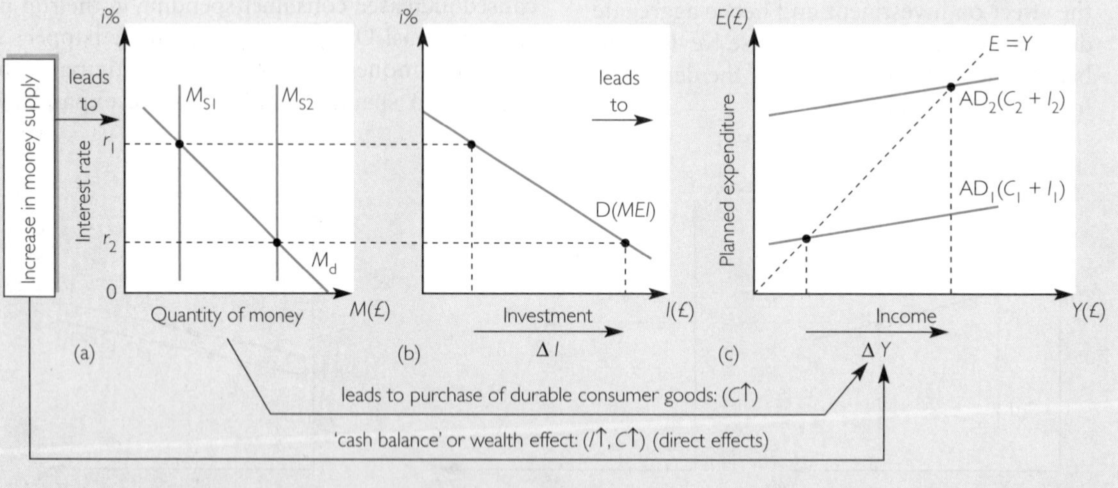

***Fig. 38.5* A monetarist monetary transmission mechanism**
An increase in the money supply causes a large fall in interest rates in (a). This turn causes a large increase in investment (ΔI) in diagram (b)). This increase in investment brings about a large increase in money national income (ΔY) in diagram (c). Money national income is also boosted by the fall in interest rates causing people to buy more consumer durables. Aggregate demand is also boosted by the 'cash balance' effect. Notice the difference in slopes of demand for money and investment schedules compared with the Keynesian view in Fig. 36.4.

a) The links between the money supply and aggregate demand include not only indirect effects but also, through the cash balance effect of portfolio adjustment, direct effects. Moreover, not only does the fall in interest rates prevailing in financial markets cause an increase in business investment, it also causes consumers to increase their 'investment' in durable goods.
b) The demand for money is interest inelastic. Thus large reductions in the interest rate can occur before excess money balances become absorbed by an extension of people's desire to hold money. (Indeed, most of the increase in the demand for money will come from the resulting increase in income. For simplicity such feedback effects are ignored.)
c) Not only is the fall in interest rates from r_1 to r_2 likely to be substantial, it is also assumed that the interest elasticity of investment is high.
d) There will also be a relatively high and stable interest elasticity of consumption, particularly consumer durables.

In short, then, monetarists believe that the link between changes in the money supply and changes in aggregate demand is very strong and relatively stable.

Crowding out

Monetarists believe that Keynesians have overlooked the interest effects of fiscal policy. Expansionary fiscal policy involves an increase in the public sector borrowing requirement (PSBR). How will the government persuade people to buy this increased debt without an increase in interest rates? The increase in aggregate demand implied by fiscal policy will also create an upward pressure in the demand for money which will also increase interest rates. The only way to avoid interest rate rises is to increase the money supply, but monetarists believe that this would increase inflation and is therefore unwise.

Monetarists thus believe that an increase in government spending will raise interest rates which will in turn ***crowd out*** private spending on investment and consumption goods. This will render the fiscal policy ineffective.

Keynesians retort that a little increase in the money supply to finance the expansionary fiscal policy will just help to finance the increase in output, unless the whole economy is close to full employment.

Fine tuning

The crowding out effect is part of the argument against using fiscal policy to 'fine-tune' the economy. Modern monetarists would also accept that fine tuning is not possible in monetary policy either. Instead, monetarists argue that the lags and the strength of links in the transmission mechanisms are uncertain in the short run.

However, monetarists argue that there is a fairly stable demand for money function which will be deviated from in the processes of adjustment but which will tend to re-establish itself as a new equilibrium is reached. Thus, despite significant short-term fluctuations, the velocity of circulation will tend to change only slowly over the long term. Hence monetarists argue that active or 'discretionary' stabilisation policies should not be attempted but, rather, a 'fixed throttle' non-discretionary monetary expansion regime should be adopted and then observed by all governments.

Ideally, the money supply should be set to grow roughly in line with the normal rate of growth of the economy, providing the extra money to absorb increases in output without causing inflation.

STUDENT ACTIVITY 38.4

Which of the following pieces of evidence (if they were correct) would tend to support a Keynesian viewpoint and which a monetarist viewpoint?

a) Statistical evidence suggests the demand for money is inelastic.
b) Statistical evidence suggests that investment is interest inelastic.
c) The government increases public spending but unemployment remains stubbornly high.

The determination of aggregate real income

The debate concerning the monetary transmission mechanism has proceeded with each side conceding partial defeats. In terms of the view as to whether aggregate demand can be affected by fiscal or monetary policy it is now much more difficult to divide economists neatly into Keynesians and monetarists. Today the debate is between monetarists who hold that the level of output in the economy is self-adjusting to the level at which there is no involuntary unemployment, and Keynesians who believe that the level of aggregate demand must be managed by governments so as to produce full employment. It is to this more profound distinction that we now turn.

The nature of the debate

If the only difference between Keynesians and monetarists were that the former advocated fiscal policy to iron out fluctuations while the latter advocated monetary policy, then the debate would concern mere ***technicalities*** of policy rather than a fundamental difference of political vision. But it is this difference of vision concerning the nature of capitalist economies and the proper role of government that is at the heart of mainstream political debate today.

To use a medical analogy, Keynesians (except radical post-Keynesians; see Chapter 43) view the free market capitalist economy as an organism which works well when healthy but, from time to time, is prone to chronic illness. But it is believed that these illnesses can be cured if governments apply the correct treatments. Monetarists/neo-classicists especially admire the workings of free markets but they differ from Keynesians in that they believe the organism seldom suffers from malfunctions. From time to time capitalism might catch a chill but this will be cured by the system's own strong recuperative powers. Indeed, the only thing which is likely to turn a chill into serious ill health is the misguided prescription of Keynesian doctors! (For example, when attempts are made to preserve declining industries instead of allowing market forces to replace them in time with the growth industries of the future.)

As we have seen, Keynesians take the view that, when left unattended, fluctuations in aggregate demand are likely to destabilise the economy. Monetarists differ in that they believe that if the money supply is not allowed to fluctuate, fluctuations in aggregate demand will be slight.

Monetarists believe the economy is always, more or less, at an equilibrium at which there is no ***involuntary unemployment***; the level of employment and hence the supply of output are determined more or less independently of aggregate demand. Hence, in the monetarist's view increases in aggregate demand are not met by an increased supply as all those who wish to work are already working as much as they wish to. It follows that increasing aggregate demand will result only in inflation:

> **Keynesians believe that aggregate output and thus employment are demand determined; monetarists believe that such 'real' aggregate variables are supply determined.**

Aggregate supply

The notion that real variables are supply determined is easy to explain to anyone who has understood the microeconomic sections of this book. This is because monetarists believe that aggregate output and employment are determined by the same market forces that operate in individual competitive markets. Indeed, in such neo-classical analysis there is no clear distinction between micro- and macro-economics. Whereas Keynes warned that those who extended micro analysis to analyse macro variables were guilty of a ***fallacy of composition***, monetarists tend to view aggregate variables as only the sum of many millions of individually made 'micro' decisions. They make the assumption that the whole is the sum of the parts.

To understand how the level of employment, and hence output, is determined in the monetarist view we need only refer back to the neo-classical 'marginal distribution theory' of Chapter 19. In that chapter we saw how a firm in perfect competition in both its product and factor markets would be maximising its profits when:

Wage = Marginal revenue product

Before moving on we should remind ourselves that both sides of this equality are in money terms, i.e. 'wage' refers to money (nominal) wage and 'marginal revenue product' refers to marginal physical product multiplied by money (nominal) price:

$$W = MPP \times P$$

As we have seen, monetarists emphasise that real things are determined by real things. The above equality can be interpreted in real terms simply by dividing through by nominal price:

$$W/P = MPP$$

W/P can be thought of as the real wage, i.e. the actual purchasing power of the worker's money wage. There is an aggregation problem here in that *P* refers to a particular product's price whereas the wage of the worker will be spent on many products. Thus, to see how much the money wage could purchase in general terms we would have to divide it by some composite index of the price level (see for example the construction of the RPI in Chapter 34). It makes it easier to 'strip away the veil of money to reveal the real workings of the economy' if we assume that there is only one product which we will simply call 'output'. Thus, we assume that workers are paid in output and that firms employ workers to produce output. Therefore if the money wage is divided by the price of output we have the real wage in terms of units of output.

We can now interpret the equilibrium of the firm in real terms. In Fig. 38.6 we represent the equilibrium of a perfectly competitive firm in monetary terms in part (a), and in real terms in part (b). In part (a) the employer will employ all workers up to L_E as each of these workers adds more money to revenue ($MPP \times P$) than they add to costs (W). In part (b) the same level of employment results as each worker up to L_E adds more to output (MPP) than the output they receive (W/P).

A numerical example will demonstrate the equivalence of part (a) and part (b) in Fig. 38.6. Recall that in the short run the *MPP* depends only upon the number of workers employed by the firm and that, as employment increases, *MPP* falls owing to the law of diminishing marginal returns. Let us suppose that at L_E $MPP = 5$ units of output. If $W = £10$ and $P = £2$ then at L_E we have:

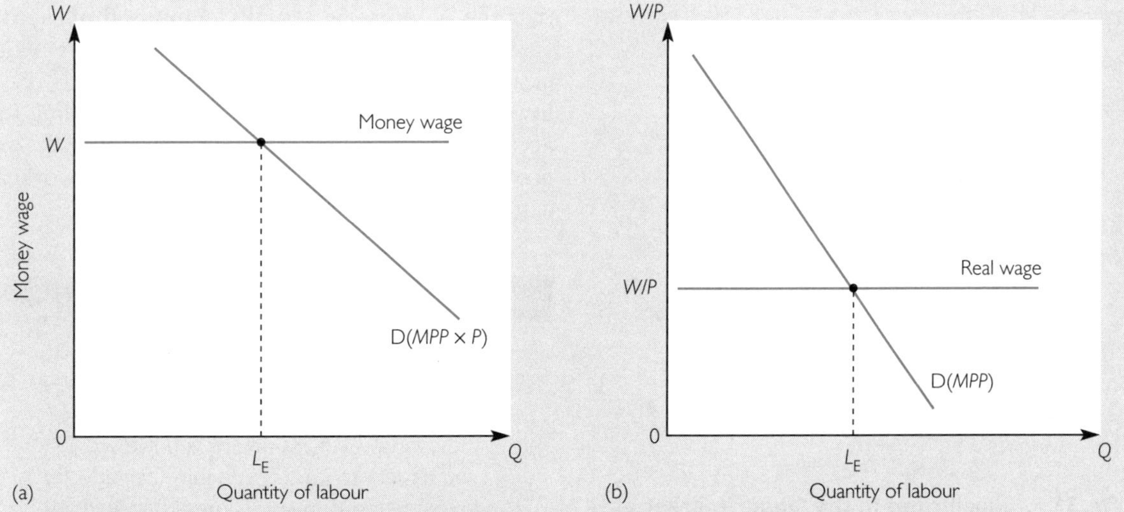

***Fig. 38.6* The same equilibrium (*LE*) expressed in monetary and real terms**
Diagram (a) shows the equilibrium of the perfectly competitive firm in money terms. This occurs where the *MRP* (*MPP* × *P*) is equal to the wage rate. This equates with a quantity of labour employed of L_E. By dividing through by the price (*P*) we see the same equilibrium expressed in real terms.

$$W = MPP \times P = 5 \times £2 = £10$$

or:

$$W/P = MPP = 5 \text{ units of output}$$

Hence the same profit-maximising equilibrium condition can be expressed in both real and monetary terms. Monetarists extend this micro analysis of equilibrium to the economy as a whole. In doing this they make use of the notion of an ***aggregate production function***. Thus it is assumed that at any one time there is a fixed stock of capital in the economy as a whole. As total employment increases the *MPP* of labour therefore falls according to some aggregate version of the law of diminishing returns. It has to be said that the idea of a capital stock and aggregate production function raises logical problems that are complex but which cast doubt on the consistency of neo-classical theory. Nevertheless, as with other schools of thought, we brush aside these problems to present the monetarist/neo-classical view as simply as possible.

In Fig. 38.7 we have extended marginal distribution theory to the economy as a whole.

The demand curve for labour is the *MPP* of labour and slopes downward according to the law of diminishing returns. As we are now looking at the economy as a whole the supply of labour is upward sloping, indicating that higher wages will attract more people into the labour force (in fact the analysis is not significantly altered if the supply of labour is vertical or even slightly backward bending). We should note that everything in the diagram is in real terms, i.e. *MPP* is measured in units of output and the supply of labour is determined by the real wage. The equilibrium of the labour market occurs at the level of employment L_E where the real wage $(W/P)_E$ is equal to *MPP*.

It is instructive to examine the nature of the equilibrium in Fig. 38.7. First, we can note that if the nominal prices *W* and *P* are increased by the same proportion, the real wage, and hence the equilibrium, is unchanged, i.e. $W/P = 2 \times W/2 \times P = 3 \times W/3 \times P = \ldots$. This assumes that workers are not fooled by increasing money wages into offering more labour than before even though the real wage has not changed; in short there is no ***money illusion***. Second, we should note that at L_E the demand for labour equals the supply of labour, i.e. anyone who wants to work at the equilibrium wage rate is able to find a job and thus there is no involuntary unemployment. Third, we should note that the economy is actually composed of many such labour markets each of which has its own clearing real wage. Thus if a worker's *MPP* is very low they will only find work if they are willing to accept a very low real wage; no employer will (or is obliged) to pay a worker more than that worker can actually contribute to output.

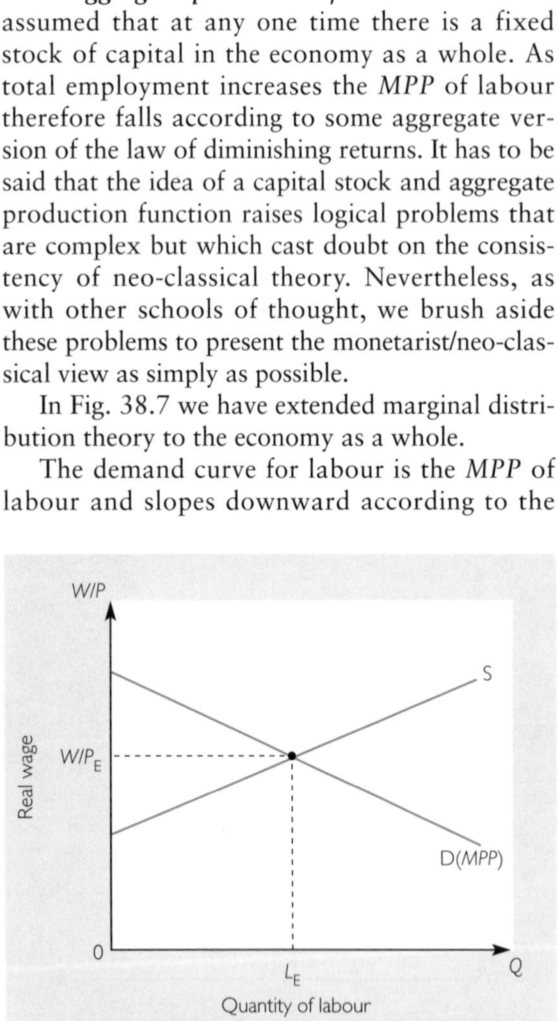

***Fig. 38.7* Equilibrium in the labour market as a whole**

The demand curve for labour is the *MPP* curve. The supply curve represents the supply of labour for the whole economy. Equilibrium occurs where the real wage $(W/P)_E$ is equal to *MPP*.

STUDENT ACTIVITY 38.5

1. What do you think is a reasonable period of time to look for a job before accepting one at a lower than expected wage rate?
2. How far away from where you live would you expect to go to get a job? Can anyone be expected to move some distance in order to get a job?
3. If you have a job, do you think you are paid the value of what you do?
4. Are all people who are unemployed choosing not to work?

Recession or the natural rate of unemployment?

The neo-classical view: the natural rate of employment and output

We can now see more clearly what monetarists mean when they say that 'real things are determined by real things'. As we noted in Fig. 38.7 the supply and demand functions that determine the level of employment are in real, not monetary, terms. The demand function reflects the productivity of labour when combined with the existing capital stock. The supply of labour reflects 'human nature', i.e. the amount of labour that people are willing to offer in return for any given real wage. Hence, far from the level of employment being the government's responsibility as is the implication of Keynesian theory, in monetarism the level of employment is not within the government's control to increase. The government cannot wave a magic wand to make people willing to work longer at the same real wage, nor would it be meaningful for the government to pass laws stating that the *MPP* of labour when combined with the actual capital stock is higher than it actually is. In short, within monetarist/neo-classical theory, insisting that the government should 'do something about unemployment' is rather like demanding that the government should increase the amount of rainfall in the UK.

Indeed, it is in their use of the term 'natural' that the political vision of the monetarists is most evident:

> **Monetarists use the term the natural rate of employment to summarise their belief that the operation of market forces, if not obstructed by government or powerful institutions, will quickly produce an equilibrium in which everybody is doing the best they can without infringing the rights of others.**

This equilibrium is thus brought about by contracts between employers and employees which are voluntarily entered into because they confer mutual benefit. Monetarists believe that, in the short run, the equilibrium in the labour market also sets the level of output or aggregate supply.

Because the natural rate of employment is the result of mutually beneficial agreements, there will be a strong tendency for it to reassert itself if disturbed. For example, if (for some unspecified reason) the real wage is above $(W/P)_E$ in Fig. 38.7, there will be an excess supply of labour. As long as the real wage is above $(W/P)_E$ there will be more people looking for work than employers wish to employ. But such involuntary unemployment will be only transitory. Monetarists argue that, as in any other market, an excess supply will cause a downward pressure on price. In this case it will be unemployed labour competing with the employed that will lower real wages. Hence involuntary unemployment is eradicated when the real wage falls to $(W/P)_E$ and the supply of labour once again matches the demand. Equally, a real wage below $(W/P)_E$ would cause an excess demand for labour and hence a rise in the real wage back to $(W/P)_E$.

The neutrality of money

We are now in a position to present the classical dichotomy in diagrammatic form. In Fig. 38.8 the lower part of the diagram represents equilibrium in the labour market where L_N is the natural rate of employment. The initial money wage is W_1 and the initial price level is P_1. Thus the real wage which clears the labour market is W_1/P_1. The upper part of Fig. 38.8 represents equilibrium in the goods or product market. Although the composition of aggregate output is determined by the interaction of demand and supply in individual markets, the arrow indicates that the level of aggregate output is set by the equilibrium of the labour market.

AD_1 represents the initial level of aggregate demand in the goods sector or product market(s). Note that, in accordance with monetarist views of the monetary transmission mechanism, AD_1 corresponds to a specific supply of money, i.e. M_1. According to monetarist theory the aggregate demand curve is downward sloping as lower levels of nominal prices mean a larger real money

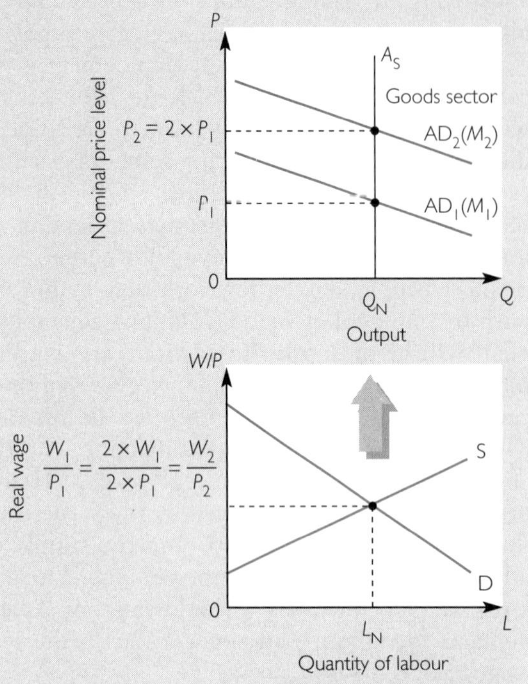

Fig. 38.8 **The Classical Dichotomy and the neutrality of money**
A doubling of the money supply causes the money wage and the price level to double but leaves the equilibrium in the real economy unchanged.

supply. We can see that a nominal money supply of M_1 implies an equilibrium nominal price level in the product market of P_1. Hence, initially the real money supply is M_1/P_1. As the nominal money supply is exogenously set by the monetary authorities and the demand for money is stable there will be no change to the economy's equilibrium unless something real changes, e.g. if changes in the capital stock increase *MPP* or people's willingness to work somehow alters.

Now let us suppose that, perhaps in an attempt to increase employment and output, the government doubles the money supply. At the original price level of P_1 the real money supply will thus have also doubled. The effect, as shown in Fig. 38.8, will be to shift aggregate demand from AD_1 to AD_2. This will cause excess demand which in turn will cause product prices to rise. If money wages were to remain at W_1 these increases in product prices would cause a decrease in the real wage. But this will not happen for the supply and demand conditions in the labour market are in real terms. As long as the people's willingness to work at any real wage is unchanged and there is no change in the capital stock or technology to change the *MPP* of labour, then the equilibrium in the labour market must remain at L_N.

A decrease in the real wage would therefore cause an excess demand for labour. This excess demand for labour would cause the money wage to increase so as to compensate for any increase in product prices. Therefore despite the increase in nominal prices the real wage would remain unchanged.

As the equilibrium in the labour market is undisturbed by the increase in aggregate demand in the product market(s) the number of hours worked and hence the output of the economy is also unaltered. Hence aggregate supply remains at Q_N despite the increase in aggregate demand. How then is equilibrium in the goods sector restored? The answer is that as nominal prices increase so the real money supply (i.e. its purchasing power) is reduced. This in turn, through the monetary transmission mechanism, causes the aggregate demand for products to contract until it is again equal to aggregate supply at Q_N.

It should be clear that once nominal prices have doubled the real money supply is the same as it was before; that is:

$$\frac{M_1}{P_1} = \frac{2 \times M_1}{2 \times P_1} = \frac{M_2}{P_2}$$

Equally, if product prices and money wages have doubled the real wage will be as it was before. Thus once nominal prices have doubled all things real are as they were before. The only difference is that the nominal price level has doubled. In short, attempts to increase employment and output through increasing aggregate demand will only result in inflation. Readers should now check their understanding by working back through the analysis on the assumption that the money supply is reduced once again to M_1.

The above analysis provides a theoretical underpinning for the Classical Dichotomy:

The Classical Dichotomy states that real and monetary things are separate; hence money plays a 'neutral' role in the economy in that an increase in the money supply merely causes an equiproportionate increase in the price level leaving real things unaltered.

A Keynesian recession or the natural rate of unemployment?

Monetarist theory implies that involuntary unemployment can exist only so long as it takes for the labour market to clear. As monetarism is based on the assumption of strong competitive forces this should not take too long. Indeed, for many Keynesians (often called 'neo-Keynesians') and monetarists the supposed speed of this adjustment is what distinguishes the two schools of thought.

Neo-Keynesians believe that persistent unemployment can be caused by the real wage being too high. If this were so there would be more people looking for jobs than there were jobs being offered. Thus some people would be voluntarily unemployed. Unlike monetarists these Keynesians believe that money wages are 'downwardly sticky' for institutional reasons. For example, workers are likely to resist a cut in money wages for fear of losing ground relative to other workers (erosion of 'relativities' or 'differentials' as union leaders often put it). Nevertheless, a decrease in the real wage brought about by product price inflation might be acceptable in that all workers are affected equally. Neo-Keynesians thus recommend that the necessary reduction in real wages can be speeded up by increasing aggregate demand in the economy until full employment is reached. Monetarists reject this account of things as it smacks of 'money illusion' and hence 'irrationality'.

Some 'extreme' Keynesians believe that the adjustment of prices plays a very minor role in the overall operation of the economy. They point out that the implicit assumption of perfect competition is hard to reconcile with the widespread existence of monopoly and oligopolistic power of both firms and organised labour. They argue that in such a world quantities rather than prices are likely to adjust to changes in aggregate demand. Thus, if there is a shortage of demand firms will cut back on output and labour without lowering prices or attempting to offer lower money wages. Thus although nominal prices and the real wage might be consistent with that needed for full employment the economy becomes 'stuck' in recession.

Figure 38.9 demonstrates a Keynesian recession brought about by lack of demand rather than incorrect prices. The top part of the diagram illustrates the equilibrium of aggregate demand in the economy. As can be seen from the lower part of the diagram this level of demand is insufficient to purchase the volume of output that would be produced at full employment. The arrow pointing downwards from Y_E indicates that this level of aggregate demand imposes a quantity constraint on the labour market. The nominal demand for labour as shown is again the *MPP* of labour. This shows how much labour it would be profitable to employ if it were possible to sell all the output so produced. It can be seen that at a real wage of $(W/P)_E$ the level of employment that would occur if the labour market cleared could be reached were there sufficient demand in the economy. But it would not be profitable to employ all this labour, at whatever real wage, if the output cannot be sold. Thus the ***effective demand*** for labour is constrained by the level of demand for products. Therefore *WX* amount of labour remains unemployed even though these people wish to work at the going wage rate and it would be profitable to employ them at this wage if their output could be sold. It should be clear that a cut in wages will not decrease unemployment in Fig. 38.9. It will never be profitable for firms to employ more labour unless the level of demand for products is expanded. Indeed, if a reduction in wages acts to decrease the demand for products it will shift the quantity constraint in the labour market further away from L_N.

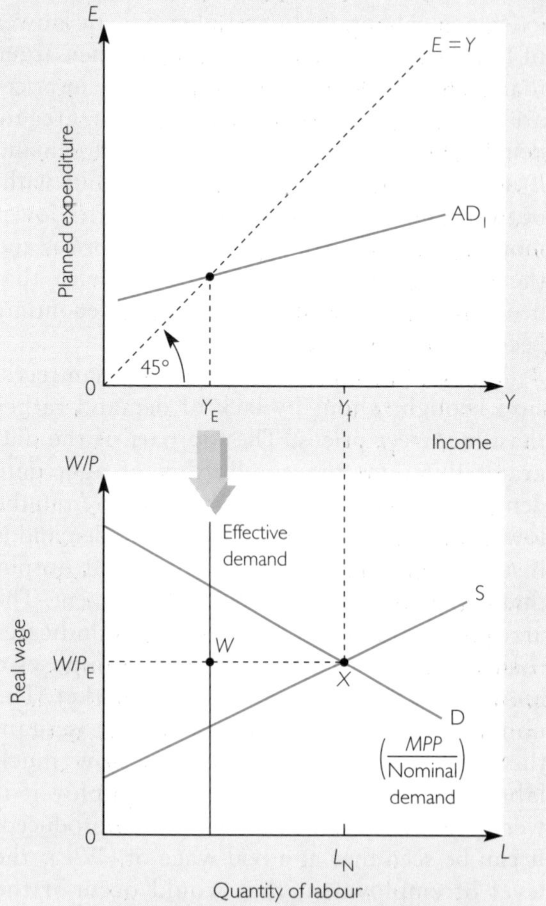

***Fig. 38.9* Keynesian recession: demand deficiency**
In the upper part of the diagram a demand deficiency causes the equilibrium level of national income (Y_E) to be below the full employment equilibrium (Y_f). In the lower part of the diagram this imposes a quantity constraint on the labour market. At wage level $(W/P)_E$ WX amount of labour remains unemployed.

Thus such a recession, if it existed, would not go away by itself. Rather, such Keynesian theorists argue, government intervention to increase aggregate demand is essential.

Keynesian economists can thus account for persistent unemployment in terms of real wages being stuck too high or a general lack of demand in the economy. To this they can add frictional unemployment caused by people moving from one job to another and structural unemployment caused by a mismatch of labour and jobs in terms of either location or skills (see also Chapter 45).

Voluntary and involuntary unemployment

How then can monetarists account for the persistent high unemployment of the 1980s and early 1990s? As we have seen, in terms of involuntary unemployment this is difficult. Some monetarists do emphasise the role of unions in preventing real wage adjustment and lowering labour productivity. But more purist monetarists do not accept that unions can so bend market forces as to contribute significantly to unemployment. Thus such monetarists make much of the distinction between involuntary and voluntary unemployment. In short they believe that persistent unemployment must be voluntary.

Monetarists thus argue that even at the natural rate of employment, where there is overall equilibrium in the labour market, there will be those that remain voluntarily unemployed. For example, at any one time there will be a flow of people through the unemployment register who are searching for better jobs. These people will search until the marginal cost of their search is equal to their expected marginal gain. They are voluntarily unemployed in that they are refusing the job offers already found in order to search for better jobs.

Monetarists point out that unemployed persons might not see themselves as voluntarily unemployed. For example, unskilled workers, or those whose skills are no longer in demand, can expect to be offered only jobs where low pay reflects their low market value. Such persons may well curse 'the system' or their own bad luck, but the monetarist argues that they are worth only a low wage and must thus accept the charity of the state or move house and/or retrain. Keynesians would argue that this is a harsh attitude but the monetarist would reply that attempting to eliminate such unemployment by demand measures will only result in inflation.

For the monetarist the only way to reduce the 'natural rate of unemployment' in an economy is through supply side measures such as skills training, reducing social security payments, lessening the disincentives present by taxation, facilitating the easier flow of finance to firms, removing restrictive practices, etc.

The natural rate of unemployment is defined by monetarists to be that level of unemployment which is consistent with overall equilibrium in the labour market. It cannot be reduced by increasing aggregate demand but only by making markets work better.

Conclusion

Monetarism appeared in the 1950s as a part of a technical debate concerning the importance of money to the functioning of the economy. It soon developed into a revival of the neo-classical school of 'macroeconomics' which Keynes had all but beaten into submission. By the 1980s it had gained (regained) political ascendancy. This had led to a profound shift in economic policy from measures designed to influence demand to measures designed to improve the functioning of the supply side of the economy. These policies are examined in greater length in Section VIII. The return of a Labour government in 1997 has seen no headlong rush into fiscal expansion. Indeed the new Chancellor's first act was to give control of interest rates to a committee of the Bank of England. However, they may be thought of Keynesian in the sense that they do not believe that the market can be trusted to provide an adequate solution. Their policies are, however, as much supply side as demand side.

Summary

1 Keynesian and post-Keynesian economics had downgraded the importance of money in the determination of national income. Monetarism represents a return to the pre-Keynesian orthodoxy of the (neo-)classicists.

2 The Classical Dichotomy states that nominal prices are determined by the quantity of money but the quantity of money has no effect on real things.

3 In the quantity equation of money ($MV = PT$) monetarists argue for the stability of both V and T. This therefore establishes a firm link between the money supply (M) and the general price level (P).

4 In the Cambridge equation ($M \times 1/k = P \times Y$) the expression $1/k$ replaces the velocity of circulation. The symbol k is the proportion of nominal income which is demanded in money.

5 The theory of portfolio balance is concerned with the way in which people distribute their assets between money, financial assets and real assets.

6 The Keynesian view of the demand for money distinguishes three motives for demanding money:

a) transactions;
b) precautionary;
c) speculative.

The first two are directly linked to income while the third is inversely proportionate to the rate of interest.

7 Monetarists argue that there is a dividing line in the portfolio between money and other assets; thus there is only a weak line between the demand for money and the rate of interest.

8 The Keynesian view of the transmission mechanism is that increases in the money supply have weak indirect effects upon national income as falls in the interest rate lead to small increases in investment because the demand for money is interest elastic and the demand for investment is interest inelastic.

9 Monetarists argue for strong links between the money supply and national income through both direct and strong indirect effects. However, such effects act only upon nominal (or money) national income and not real national income.

10 Monetarists argue that the economy is essentially self-regulating while Keynesians maintain that periodic periods of imbalance are possible.

11 Keynesians have tended to focus on the demand side of the economy while monetarists and neo-classicists have stressed the importance of the supply side.

12 Neo-classicists have argued for the existence of a natural level of employment in the economy. It follows from this that such unemployment as exists is either temporary or voluntary.

13 Keynesian economists account for unemployment in terms of lack of demand or real wages being 'stuck' too high. To this can be added frictional and structural unemployment.

14 The political ascendancy of neo-classical views has led to profound shifts in policy designed to improve the functioning of the supply side of the economy.

Questions

1 What factors determine the demand for money in a modern society?

2 Contrast the effect of an increase in the money supply upon a Keynesian and a monetarist model of the economy:

a) in the short run;

b) in the long run.

3 What is meant by the theory of portfolio balance?

4 What effect upon the equilibrium level of national income would there be if the government were to lower interest rates?

5 Contrast Fisher's quantity equation of money with the Cambridge equation.

6 Describe the mechanism by which Keynes said increasing the money supply would lead to an increase in real GDP.

7 What is meant by 'money illusion'?

8 Evaluate the importance of the concept of the 'natural level of unemployment' in the neo-classical view of the economy.

9 Nobody doubts that monetarism will stop inflation if it is practised long enough and hard enough. At some point high interest rates stop all economic activity as well as inflation. But the price is very high, not equally distributed across the population and not endurable in a democracy.

Lester Thurow, ***The Economist***, 23 January 1982

Critically evaluate Thurow's statement in the light of the Conservatives' performance while in government.

10 'Real things are determined by real things.' What is meant by this statement when monetarists use it to refer to the determination of the level of employment?

Data response A
Equilibrium and the labour market

Figure 38.10 represents the equilibrium in the whole labour market of an economy. Answer the questions which follow.

1 Carefully explain what is being shown in Fig. 38.10. Make sure that you make clear all the terms used in the construction of the graph.

2 Describe what assumptions are implicit in Fig. 38.10.

3 What problems might a government have if it was faced with the situation shown in Fig. 38.10? Suggest two measures that a government might take to deal with the situation.

4 Under what circumstances would the demand curve for labour shift to the right?

5 Suppose that there was a considerable increase in the money supply. How would the situation in the labour market be changed? In your answer make clear the difference in viewpoint between Keynesians and monetarists.

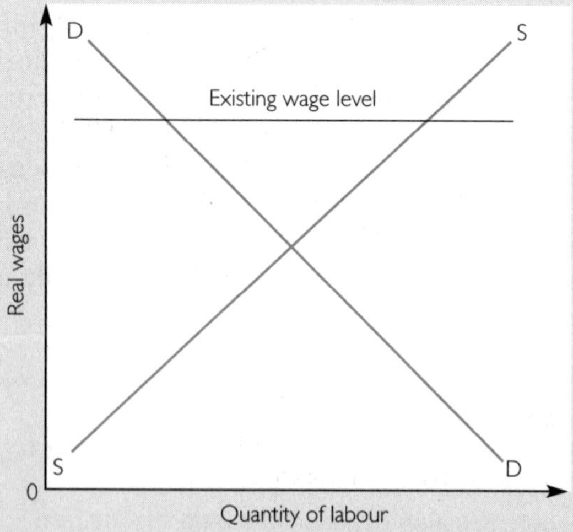

Fig. 38.10 **Equilibrium in the labour market**

Data response B
Monetarism, Keynesianism and recent economic experience

Study the following passage and then answer the questions below.

Monetarism came onto the political stage with great promise. It was to eliminate inflation and create the conditions for growth and reduced unemployment. Coming as it did after the decade of the seventies with unemployment rising above one million and inflation out of control, it seemed like a breath of fresh air. Looking back on the decade of the eighties, its fortunes seem a little more mixed. The massive recession of the early eighties must in part have been due to the excessively tight monetary policy that was introduced from 1979 onwards. There is no doubt, however, that inflation was squeezed out of the economy, so in that sense monetarism was a highly successful, if somewhat costly policy.

It is important to recognise the role which oil played in that period of economic history. We tend to forget in this period of relative calm in the oil market, what a pivotal role it played. The quadrupling of oil prices in 1973-4 undoubtedly had a major impact on the inflation of the seventies, and through its effect on plunging all but Japan and Germany into severe balance of payments deficit, created unemployment and generated world-wide deflationary policies. The impact of oil on Mrs Thatcher's first monetary experiment must also be remembered. As North Sea oil came on stream the oil prices doubled once again in 1979. The balance of payments in the UK moved into strong surplus, in contrast with most other industrial economies. It is not possible to blame all the strength of the pound, as it surged up from $1.50 to $2.40, on high interest rates. Oil seemed to be on our side in 1979. By 1982, we were not quite so sure as the strong pound decimated our manufacturing exports.

The mid eighties were a period of relatively successful monetary policy with inflation falling and employment growing. Mrs Thatcher did not need a Falklands war to get re-elected in 1987 – the economy was doing well. For a brief period it seemed as though monetarism was going to deliver. Optimism on the stock exchange had never been so buoyant. Alas a contradiction of government policy was to undo this promising state of affairs. The control of the money supply and free competition in the financial markets both seemed to accord with conservative principles. Deregulation of the financial markets led to a massive expansion of credit which led to a consumer boom so large that consumer spending was actually growing faster than income.

The party had to end, and the recession of the early nineties was the price we paid. As inflation hit 10% again in 1990, it was clear that interest rates had to rise. It was the early eighties all over again but without the benefit of a balance of payments surplus. Monetary targets for the control of the money supply were no longer the main government policy. A tendency for the financial markets to get around any monetary target by cleverly inventing new kinds of money meant there had been a subtle shift in monetary policy. It was now the demand for money that had to be controlled (via interest rates) rather than the supply.

A second major recession with unemployment over three million in just over 10 years dented faith in monetarism. In managing the recovery from 1992 onwards, the Conservatives allowed themselves a little passive Keynesianism. They allowed the PSBR to rise rather than trying to balance the government's finances as had been the case in the earlier recession.

The experience of these two major recessions has also dented belief in the market's ability to regulate itself. The new Labour administration is not ready to go back to the full blooded Keynesianism of its predecessors, and indeed has promised to hold to the previous government's spending targets for the first two years. One suspects this has more to do with meeting the criteria for a single currency than dogmatic belief. They also had to convince the electorate that they were a prudent 'new' Labour party. The final convincing argument for fiscal restraint is the demutualisation of the building societies and some insurance companies. The consumers are receiving about £35 billion in new wealth which could create a consumer boom every bit as damaging as that in 1987.

By giving control of interest rates to a committee of the Bank of England, the Labour party has more or less forced itself to take fiscal policy decisions that will convince the City that the economy is in good hands. Paradoxically, conditions of boom mean a little fiscal restraint is now called for. Cutting spending is never an easy option for the Labour party, so it would appear increased taxes are the only option. Unfortunately they made all kinds of pledges not to increase taxes during the election campaign. The alternative to taxes increases is high interest rates and a punishingly strong pound for our manufacturing exporters. Surely we have been down that road before. Lets try a little Keynesian policy for a change this time.

1 What were the problems of monetarist policies in the 1980s?
2 What kind of fiscal policy did the Conservative government use in the 1990s?
3 Why does giving interest rate control to the Bank of England mean that prudent fiscal policy is necessary?
4 What are the parallels between 1987 and 1997?
5 Does the record of monetarism under the Conservative government suggest that, left to themselves, markets will work? In which periods was this closest to being the case?

SECTION VII International economics

'Our interest will be to throw open the doors of commerce, and to knock off its shackles, giving freedom to all persons for the rent of whatever they may choose to bring into our ports, and asking the same in theirs.'

Thomas Jefferson

39 The gains of international trade

Learning outcomes

At the end of this chapter you will be able to:

- Understand the theory of comparative advantage.
- Explain why countries may benefit from international trade.
- Appreciate the importance of economies of scale in determining the pattern of trade in differentiated products.
- Identify the major reasons why countries adopt protectionist measures.

We have so far limited ourselves to an examination of economics at a national level. However, we live in an increasingly international world. Nations trade more and more with one another; in the words of Marshall McLuhan, 'interdependence recreates the world in the image of a global village'.

In this section of the book we examine the economics of international trade, the accounting of international trade which is summarised in the balance of payments, and the monetary aspects of trade which determine exchange rates. Finally, we need to consider the major world institutions which are concerned with trade, such as the International Monetary Fund.

One of the major problems we have to deal with in studying international trade is the bias of nationalism. 'The notion dies hard', said Lord Harlech, 'that in some sort of way exports are patriotic but imports are immoral.' Many people believe it is best to buy the products of their own country; we are all familiar with slogans like 'buy British'. However, it makes no more sense to 'buy British' than it does to 'buy Lancastrian'. It does not occur to us in our private lives to feel threatened because we are dependent upon others for our food and clothing, but many people feel threatened by imports.

The bias of economic nationalism often obscures the benefits of specialisation which appear self-evident within the national economy. It is necessary, therefore, to examine the theory of the gains from trade – ***the theory of comparative advantage*** – and to see how international trade leads to what John Stuart Mill described as 'a more efficient employment of the productive forces of the world'.

The theory of comparative advantage

David Ricardo (1772–1823)

People and nations have traded since the time of the Phoenicians, but for most of this time they provided for most of their needs out of the local economy. Trade was for such things as spices, wines and precious metals. However, by the nineteenth century the UK had embarked upon the course which would see it export its products all over the world in return, not for luxuries, but for basic food and raw materials. It was at this time (1817) that, in his book *Principles of Political Economy*, David Ricardo explained his theory of comparative advantage (sometimes called the theory of comparative costs). It is this theory, as subsequently modified by another great classical economist, John Stuart Mill, which is still the foundation of our theory of international trade today.

Absolute advantage and comparative advantage

One of the most fundamental reasons for trade is the diversity of conditions between different countries. For example, the UK can produce cars more cheaply than West African countries, but West African countries produce cocoa more cheaply than the UK. In these circumstances the UK is said to have an ***absolute advantage*** in cars and West African countries an absolute advantage in cocoa. If the West Africans want cars and the UK wants cocoa it is obviously to their mutual advantage to trade. However, trade depends not upon absolute advantage but upon ***comparative advantage***; as Professor Samuelson says, 'it is not so immediately obvious, but it is no less true that international trade is mutually profitable even when one of the two can produce every commodity more cheaply'.

Consider the example of a town which has only one doctor but the doctor is also the best typist in town. Should this person be a doctor or a typist? Obviously the comparative advantage is great in the medical field and the fortunate individual should concentrate on that. If a typist has to be employed, the doctor will be better off because of concentrating on supplying a relatively rarer skill, the town will be better off because it gets more services of the doctor and a job will be created for the typist that is employed. So it is with international trade; a country should specialise not at what it is absolutely best at but at what it is relatively best at.

Common misunderstanding

It is sometimes argued that some of the less developed countries are harmed by international trade because they do not have advantage in the production of any commodity. This argument is wrong because its advocates do not seem to understand that the basis for international trade is comparative and not absolute advantage. Thus whilst it may be possible to come up with a country that has no absolute advantage in the production of any one commodity it is bound to have comparative advantage in some commodities.

Comparative advantage: a model

Production possibilities

Ricardo illustrated his theory by considering trade between two countries, the UK and Portugal, and two products, wine and cloth. We will use two hypothetical countries, Richland and Poorland.

Richland has a population of 10 million and Poorland of 20 million. In Richland a day's labour will produce either 20 units of food or 18 units of clothing, whereas in Poorland a day's labour will only produce either 10 units of food or 4 units of clothing. It is apparent, therefore, that Richland has an absolute advantage in the production of both commodities.

If the two countries do not trade, they must produce both food and clothing for themselves, dividing their labour between the two commodities. Poorland's production possibilities are summarised in Table 39.1. Thus, if all resources were devoted to producing food, 200 million units could be produced, but no clothing. At the other extreme, 80 million units of clothing could be produced but no food. The Poorlanders must therefore choose some combination between those extremes. Say, for example, that the Poorlanders choose possibility D, producing 50 million units of food and 60 million units of clothing. These production possibilities can be represented graphically. Figure 39.1 shows that Poorland can obtain any combination of food or clothing along line AE, such as point D, or any combination within it such as U.

Table 39.1 **Poorland's production possibilities**

Possibility	*Food (million units)*	*Clothing (million units)*
A	200	0
B	150	20
C	100	40
D	50	60
E	0	80

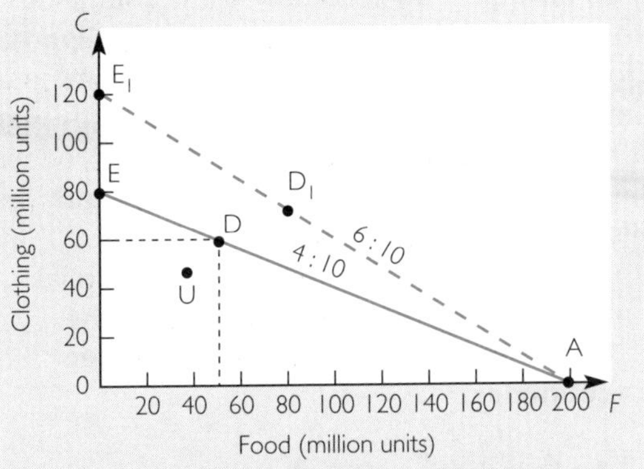

***Fig. 39.1* Poorland's production possibilities**
The line AE shows Poorland's production possibilities before trade, i.e. any combination of food and clothing along line AE or within it. This represents a domestic ratio of 4 : 10. Line AE_1 shows possibilities not attainable at present and a better trading ratio of 6 : 10.

The slope of the line shows the opportunity cost of food in terms of clothing; each 4 units of clothing given up will secure 10 units of food or vice versa. Thus we have a ***domestic trading ratio*** of 4:10. Position D_1 shows a better situation for Poorland, where it would be consuming both more food and clothing, but this is unattainable at the moment.

We can now construct a similar table and graph to show Richland's production possibilities. As you can see in Table 39.2, if Richland devoted all its resources to producing food

***Table 39.2* Richland's production possibilities**

Possibility	*Food (million units)*	*Clothing (million units)*
A	200	0
B	180	18
C	160	36
D	140	54
E	120	72
F	100	90
G	80	108
H	60	126
I	40	144
J	20	162
K	0	180

200 million units could be produced (possibility A) while, at the other extreme, if all resources were devoted to clothing production 180 million units could be produced (possibility K). If there is no international trade, Richland must produce all its own food and clothing. One of the possible combinations must be chosen, e.g. possibility F which is 100 million units of food and 90 million units of clothing. This is illustrated in Fig. 39.2. You can see from Table 39.2 and Fig. 39.2 that the domestic trading ratio of food for clothing is 20 units of food given up gains 18 units of clothing. To make comparison with Poorland easier, instead of writing this as 20:18 we could express it as 10:9.

The opening up of trade

It might appear that there is little possibility of trade between the two nations.

In Richland
one day's labour will produce
either

20 units of food	or	18 units of clothing

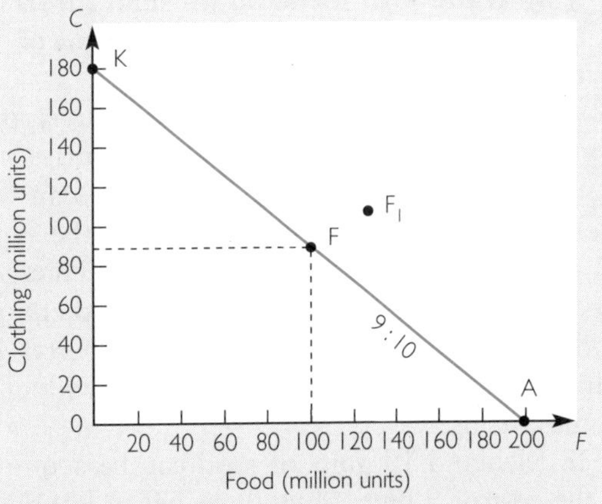

***Fig. 39.2* Richland's production possibilities**
AK is the production possibility line. At point F Richland is producing and consuming 90 million units of clothing and 100 million units of food. Point F_1 shows a position where both more food and clothing would be consumed but which is at present unattainable.

In Poorland
one day's labour will produce
either

10	or	4
units of food		units of clothing

Also, when we examine the production possibilities which each has chosen, i.e. possibility D for Poorland and F for Richland, and divide it by the respective populations we see that their per capita consumption of food and clothing is even more disproportionate.

	Per capita consumption of:	
	Food	*Clothing*
Richland	10.0	9.0
Poorland	2.5	3.0

If the possibility of trade between the two countries arises we can imagine the arguments which might be advanced against it in the two countries. In Richland it would be:

It is highly dangerous for us to trade with Poorland because the low wages of people there will enable producers to undercut our products by using cheap labour.

And in Poorland they would say:

If we trade with Richland we shall surely be swamped by the productive might of that country.

However, let us examine what is likely to happen if trade does begin between the two countries.

In Poorland 10 units of food can be exchanged for 4 units of clothing, but the same 10 units of food in Richland can be exchanged for 9 units of clothing. The Poorlanders therefore find that they can clothe themselves better by selling food to Richland rather than producing clothes themselves.

In Richland 10 units of food can be acquired at the cost of 9 units of clothing but in Poorland 10 units of food cost only 4 units of clothing. The Richlanders therefore find it more advantageous to produce clothing and export it to Poorland in exchange for food.

Thus it can be seen that although Richland has an absolute advantage in both commodities, it is to its advantage to specialise in the commodity in which it has the greater comparative advantage (clothing) and trade this for the other commodity. Similarly, Poorland has a comparative advantage in food and is better off specialising in producing this and trading it for clothing. We can draw from this the general principle that:

International trade is always beneficial whenever there is a difference in the opportunity cost ratios between two countries.

An international trading ratio

If trading is opened up between the two countries the two domestic trading ratios will be replaced by one international ratio. In our example, since the domestic ratios are 10:9 and 10:4, the international ratio must be somewhere between them. When Ricardo explained the theory he did not say how the ratio could be determined; he merely stated that any ratio which lay between the two domestic ratios could be beneficial to both countries involved. Followers of Ricardo argued, wrongly, that the international ratio would lie half-way between the domestic ratios. It was John Stuart Mill who explained that the ratio would be determined by the forces of demand and supply in international markets. This is known as the ***law of reciprocal demand***.

We cannot determine the ratio unless we have all the demand and supply information for both countries. Therefore, in order to proceed with an example we will simply assume an international ratio of 10:6. With the ratio of 10:6 we can demonstrate the advantage of trade to both countries. In Richland, 10 units of food previously cost 9 units of clothing but now they cost only 6 units, whereas in Poorland, 10 units of food bought only 4 units of clothing but with international trade they now buy 6. It is therefore to Richland's advantage to specialise in clothing and trade for food and for Poorland to specialise in food and trade for clothing.

The position after specialisation and trade

Let us assume that, once trade has begun, Richland specialises completely in the production of clothing and so produces 180 million units but no food at all. Similarly, Poorland specialises entirely in food production and therefore produces 200 million units. If you turn back to Fig. 39.1 you can see how Poorland's prospects have changed. It is now at A and if it were to trade all its food for clothing at the improved ratio of 10:6 it could obtain 120 million units instead of 80 million.

In order to complete the example we must make some assumption about the quantity of exports and imports. Let us suppose that Poorland exports 120 million units of food. If each 10 units of food buys 6 units of clothing then Poorland will be able to exchange its exports for 72 million units of clothing. Thus, before specialisation and trade Poorland consumed 50 million units of food and 60 million units of clothing. After specialisation and trade it is now able to consume 80 million units of food and 72 million units of clothing. Thus its position has clearly improved. Figure 39.3 illustrates Poorland's position after trade.

Richland's position has similarly improved. It has specialised in clothing, producing 180 million units. Of these, 72 million have been exported, leaving it with 108 million units. The 72 million units of exports have earned it 120 million units of food, whereas before it consumed only 100 million units. Its position has therefore clearly improved. If you turn back to Fig. 39.2 you will see that Richland is now at point F_1, a previously unattainable position.

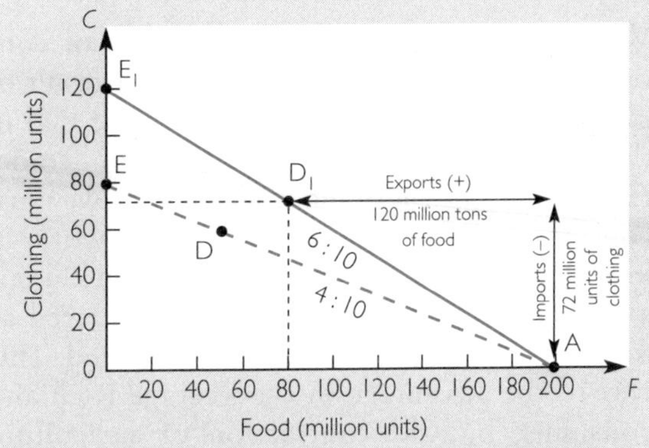

Fig. 39.3 **Poorland after specialisation and trade**
By exporting food and importing clothing Poorland is able to attain position D_1 previously unattainable.

Thus it can be seen that as a result of specialisation and trade both Richland and Poorland are better off. Not only that, but the total world production of both commodities has risen. These findings are summarised in Table 39.3.

Look again at the table on page 540 showing you the consumption per capita of both products in the two countries. You should now be able to determine that, after trade, the per capita consumption of both products in both countries has risen. For example, in Poorland consumption of food rises to 4 units per capita and clothing to 3.6. What are the figures for Richland?

Table 39.3 **Richland and Poorland before and after trade**

Country	*Trading ratio, food/clothing*	*Clothing output*	*Clothing consumption*	*Clothing exports (+) or imports (–)*	*Food output*	*Food consumption*	*Food exports (+) or import (–)*
Situation before specialisation and trade:							
Richland	10:9	90	90	0	100	100	0
Poorland	10:4	60	60	0	50	50	0
Situation after specialisation and trade:							
Richland	10:6	180	108	+72	0	120	–120
Poorland	10:6	0	72	–72	200	80	+120
World gain from specialisation and trade:							
Total	–	30	30	–	50	50	–

Long-term versus short-term benefits

We have demonstrated that the levels of consumption and production increase as a result of international trade, so that we can argue that in the long run everyone benefits from trade. However, in the short and medium term we must consider the fortunes of those who work in industries without comparative advantage. In our example agriculture in Richland contracted as food was bought more cheaply in Poorland. This was to the advantage of the average Richland consumer, but the contraction of agriculture involved farmers going bankrupt and agricultural labourers losing their jobs.

This was indeed what happened in the UK in the late nineteenth century as the UK imported cheap food from the USA, Australia and Europe. As a result of this, agriculture in the UK experienced the 'Great Depression'. In the long term, however, it was also to the advantage of those in agriculture since it was better to enjoy high wages in a factory than low wages on a farm. At the present time the UK is going through great changes and many industries which traditionally had an advantage find that they have lost this advantage to new producers in the Far East. Many arguments have been put forward in favour of protecting the UK's traditional industries against foreign competition. In the short term this may protect some jobs but in the long term protecting such industries will depress the living standard of everyone.

Comparative advantage and exchange rates

The overall theory of exchange rates is considered in a subsequent chapter, but we will here briefly consider the relationship between comparative advantage and exchange rates. Most international trade is not the swapping of one lot of goods for another but buying and selling through the medium of money and the exchange rate. Let us return to our Richland/Poorland example and assume that in Poorland food costs \$2.00 a unit and clothing \$5.00 a unit. These prices maintain the original domestic trading ratio of 10:4. Similarly we will assume that in Richland, food costs £1.00 a unit and clothing £1.11, thus retaining the ratio of 10:9.

If the exchange rate is such that in Richland imported goods are cheaper than domestically produced ones, then the Richlanders will buy them. Consider Fig. 39.4. Here it can be seen that if the exchange rate is \$1 = £1 no trade will take place because in Richland the price of imported goods is higher than that of domestically produced ones. Conversely, if the exchange rate were \$5 = £1 then although imports would be cheap in Richland no trade would be possible because Richland's exports are too expensive for Poorlanders. However, if the exchange rate is \$3 = £1 Richlanders will buy Poorland food, because it is cheaper than the domestic price, and, similarly, Poorlanders will buy Richland clothing because it is cheaper. Trade is therefore possible. In our example trade is possible so long as the exchange lies between the limits \$2 = £1 and \$4.50 = £1.

Domestic price of food and clothing (assuming the same domestic trading ratios as in the text)	*Import prices at various exchange rates*		
	Exchange rate 1 \$1 = £1	*Exchange rate 2 \$3 = £1*	*Exchange rate 3 \$5 = £1*
Price of clothing in Richland = £1.11	£5.00	£1.67	£1.00
Price of food in Richland = £1.00	£2.00	£0.66	£0.40
Price of clothing in Poorland = \$5.00	\$1.11	\$3.33	\$5.55
Price of food in Poorland = \$2.00	\$1.00	\$3.00	\$5.00

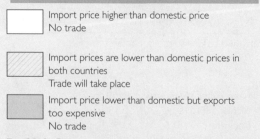

Import price higher than domestic price
No trade

Import prices are lower than domestic prices in both countries
Trade will take place

Import price lower than domestic but exports too expensive
No trade

Fig. 39.4 **Comparative advantage and exchange rates**

It is disadvantageous to a country to have its exchange rate set incorrectly. An exchange rate set too high (overvalued) will cause a trade deficit, while if the rate is fixed too low (undervalued) consumers at home suffer although exporters may benefit. Governments are often tempted to manipulate exchange rates in the hope of benefiting trade. Although this may bring some short-term benefit it cannot alter the basic opportunity cost ratios on which international trade is based.

STUDENT ACTIVITY 39.1

a) In discussing our model of comparative advantage we have assumed constant opportunity costs. How realistic is this assumption?
b) If the production possibilities in both Richland and Poorland were identical what would this imply for the opportunity cost ratios in both countries? Would international trade take place according to the principle of comparative advantage?

Extending the theory

In explaining the theory we have used a model with only two countries and two commodities. In practice the pattern of trade is much more complex than this. We must therefore consider a number of factors which bring about this complexity.

Many countries

The theory of comparative advantage will work better as more countries are brought into the example. This is because international trade not only requires a comparative advantage, but also depends upon countries wanting the goods which another country produces. In Fig. 39.5 you can see that trade is possible between the four countries but would not be possible between two or even three. The UK wishes to import from Canada but Canada does not want the UK's exports, and so on. Multilateral trade allows for the international offsetting of debts from one country to another and so makes greater trade possible. In effect the UK pays for Canadian wheat with exports of machinery to Nigeria which in turn pays for these with exports of oil to the West Indies.

The greater the number of countries involved in trade the greater will be the opportunities for trade. It is for this reason that economists tend to favour multilateral trade agreements but oppose bilateral ones.

Many commodities

G. Harberler in his book *Theory of International Trade* demonstrated that when many commodities are introduced into the theory they can be arranged in order of comparative advantage. Figure 39.6 gives an illustration of this. The UK will tend to specialise in the commodities in the right-hand side of the diagram. As we move to the left so comparative advantage passes to the UK's trading partners. The extent to which a country is able to specialise in producing a commodity in which it has a comparative advantage will depend upon the strength of international demand for that commodity. For example, the greater the demand for, say, chemicals, the more the UK will be able to specialise in producing these and the less it will need to produce other products in which it lacks advantage, such as wheat.

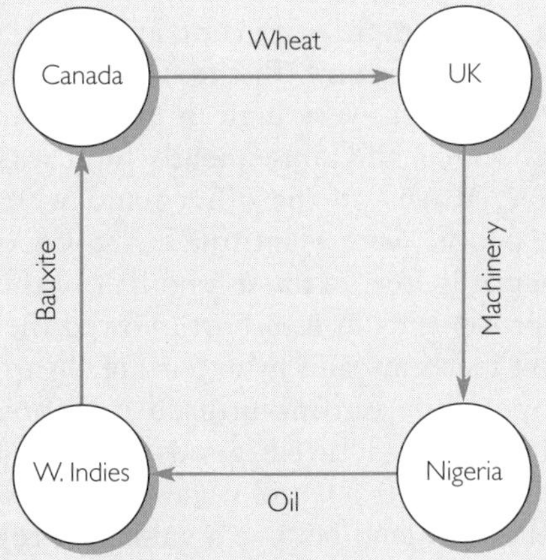

***Fig. 39.5* Multilateral trade**

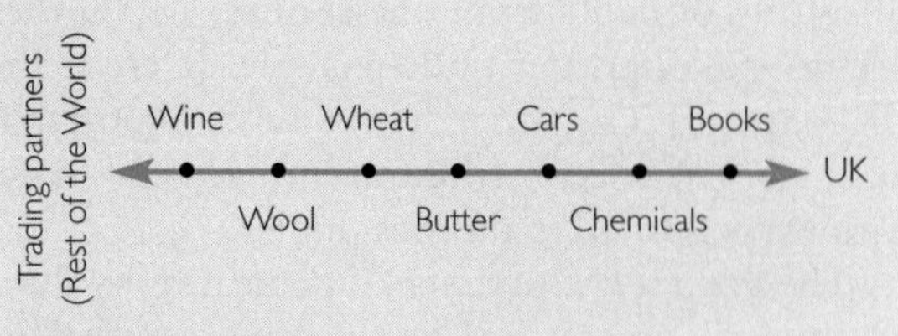

***Fig. 39.6* International trade and comparative advantage**

It will be obvious to the reader that although the UK has no comparative advantage in wheat, it is still produced in the UK. This leads us to an important modification of the theory of comparative cost:

Specialisation is never complete.

Some wheat, and even wine, can be produced in the UK because there are some resources that are uniquely well suited to that product. Thus some of a product can be produced even though the country as a whole has no comparative advantage in it. Total specialisation may also be prevented by the ***principle of increasing costs*** (see page 547).

Factor price equalisation

The idea was put forward by the economist Eli Hekscher, later refined by Bertil Ohlin, that international trade would bring the prices of factors of production closer together. We might illustrate this factor price equalisation hypothesis by considering the example of Europe and the USA in the nineteenth century. In the early nineteenth century rents were very high in Europe because land was scarce, and consequently food was also expensive. Wages on the other hand were low because people were plentiful. In the USA land was practically free. In the second half of the century improvements in transport allowed the USA to exploit its cheap land by exporting cheap food to Europe while Europe utilised its labour by exporting manufactured goods to the USA. Consequently rents fell and wages rose in Europe and in the USA land became a valuable property. Thus the effect of international trade was to bring factor prices and commodity prices closer to each other. The effect of moving goods from country to country is a substitute for moving the factors of production themselves.

Again, we might note that international trade does not benefit every single person. Those that own the factors which are in very short supply have their incomes diminished as international trade lowers high factor prices and raises low ones. However, factor prices never completely equalise because factors of production are not homogeneous; national markets are protected by such things as transport costs and tariffs (see pages 546–7).

Economies of scale: decreasing costs

As a country specialises in the production of a particular commodity it could benefit from economies of scale. In our model so far we have assumed a constant cost case, i.e. the production possibility line is a straight line, indicating that the rate of exchange (food for clothing) is the same at all levels of output. Thus in Richland each time resources are switched from food to clothing production 9 units of clothing are gained for 10 of food. It could be, however, that, as Richland specialises in clothing production, economies of scale reduce the cost of a unit of clothing. This is illustrated in Fig. 39.7. Here the production possibility line is convex to the origin, illustrating decreasing costs. Originally Richland produced 90 million units of clothing at point F. It then specialises in clothing production and plans to move to position I (144 million units) but because of economies of scale it is able to produce more with the same amount of resources. Thus, it arrives at point I_1 (200 million units).

If an industry does experience decreasing costs as it specialises, this will increase the benefits of international trade. This was said to be one of the main reasons why the UK joined the EC. The possibilities of achieving economies of scale could be a reason for specialisation and trade even when no comparative advantage exists.

To appreciate this consider the situation where Richland's and Poorland's production possibility frontiers are identical but both the food and clothing industries are characterised by economies of

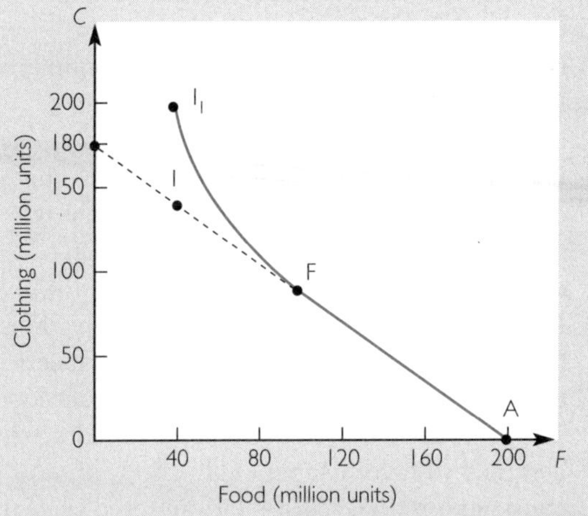

***Fig. 39.7* Decreasing costs**
Richland starts from F and specialises in clothing, but experiences economies of scale so that instead of producing at point I (144 million units) it produces at point I_1 (200 million units).

scale. Under the circumstances, at the pre-trade level, no country has comparative advantage, and thus there is no basis for mutually beneficial trade. However, even though neither country has comparative advantage, international trade will be beneficial for both countries if one country specialises in the production of food and the other in the production of clothing and trade with each other for the good they do not produce. Thus, economies of scale whilst increasing the benefits of trade when comparative advantage exists as illustrated in Fig. 39.7 may also be a separate argument for international trade.

Differences in tastes: a reason for trade

Let us assume that Richland and Poorland can produce fish and meat equally successfully. Let us also assume that the Richlanders have no taste for fish but like meat, whereas the situation is the reverse in Poorland. The result will be that, if there is no trade, the fishing industry in Richland will languish, fish will be very cheap and meat expensive. The converse will be the case in Poorland. However, if trade takes place between them, Poorland will buy fish cheaply from Richland and Richland cheap meat from Poorland. This will reduce the cost of meat in Richland and of fish in Poorland, while the income of fishermen in Richland and of farmers in Poorland will go up. Thus trade will have proved beneficial to both countries even though no comparative advantage existed. (Note: we are here witnessing another example of factor price equalisation.)

The UK fishing industry has benefited from this principle for many years, catching herrings which are not at all popular in the UK and selling them at a good price in Scandinavia.

Increased competition

By bringing more producers into the market, international trade increases competition and, thereby, economic efficiency, and domestic monopolies may be broken down by foreign competition. The greater efficiency encouraged by competition also benefits consumers by offering them a wider choice.

Inter- versus intra–industry trade

The theory of comparative advantage is best at explaining international trade in goods that belong to different industries. For example, the UK exports cars to India and imports tea and leather goods from India. Such trade is referred to as interindustry trade. Yet, since the Second World War the dominant pattern of trade amongst the industrialised countries has been in the form of intra-industry trade – trade in goods that belong to the same/similar industry. For example, the EU exports cars and televisions to Japan and it also imports cars and televisions from Japan.

Whilst it is true that differences in tastes amongst people living in different countries and within a single country explain why the overwhelming par of intra-industry trade is in differentiated products, economies of scale determine intra-industry specialisation. It would not be economically feasible for any one firm to specialise in the production of all possible types/brands of a particular product because of the enormous cost involved. For example, research and development costs in the pharmaceutical industry are huge. Thus, firms specialise in producing a small range of brands in order to benefit from economies of scale.

STUDENT ACTIVITY 39.2

a) List the major trading partners of the UK and the major types of goods that are traded. Identify those countries where trade is overwhelmingly inter/intra-industry.
b) Outline the reasons why you believe consumers demand differentiated as opposed to homogeneous products.
c) List the types of industries where economies of scale are of particular importance.
d) Are the gains from trade likely to be greater when the production possibility frontiers for each country are characterised by increasing or decreasing opportunity costs?

Limitations of comparative advantage

There are a number of factors which prevent us from benefiting fully from comparative advantage. Some arise 'naturally' out of the economic situation, e.g. transport costs; others, however, are artificially imposed, e.g. customs duties. We will consider the more important of these limitations.

Obstacles to trade

There are a great many obstacles to trade which arise out of political considerations.

a) *Tariffs and quotas*. Tariffs are taxes placed on imports. They may have the objective of either raising revenue or protecting industries. Which they accomplish will be determined by the elasticity of demand for imports. Quotas are a quantitative restriction on the amount of imports. Where restrictions successfully keep out imports they have the effect of protecting inefficient home producers. This means that although people employed in that industry may benefit, consumers generally are condemned to paying higher prices for goods.
b) *Political frontiers*. Political frontiers can also be economic frontiers, as used to be the case between the Western world and the Communist Bloc. Trade is further hindered by language differences and differing legal systems.
c) *Currencies*. Foreign trade involves exchanging currency. This in itself is a barrier, but it is often added to by restrictions placed on currency exchange by governments.
d) *Disguised barriers*. Governments may be able to discriminate in favour of home producers by such things as health and safety regulations. The Japanese safety requirements for cars are designed to favour Japanese methods of construction. In 1982 the UK imposed special health regulations on poultry, which had the effect of keeping out European imports. In the same year the French insisted that all video recorders entering France had to be processed by an obscure customs post in the centre of France, thus effectively limiting imports.
e) *Trade diversion*. Before leaving obstacles to trade we must consider the phenomenon of trade diversion. This refers to the distortion of the pattern of world trade by tariffs and other artificial obstacles to trade. Suppose, for example, we consider three countries, Germany, France and Japan. The first two have free trade because they are in the EU but have a common external tariff to keep out non-EU electrical goods. Both Germany and Japan produce video recorders but the German ones are more expensive. Without tariffs both Germany and France would import from Japan, but the effect of the tariff is that France now buys German video recorders even though they are more expensive to make. Thus the pattern of trade is distorted and French consumers suffer, as do Japanese exporters.

The creation of large trading blocks such as the EU introduces considerable trade diversion into the pattern of world trade. The effects of the abolition of tariff barriers between countries can be observed from the application of the Single European Act after 1992.

Transport costs

Although a country may have a comparative advantage, this will be of little use if it is offset by high transport costs. Transport costs have a great influence upon the pattern of UK farming. UK farmers tend to produce products, such as milk or fresh vegetables, in which they are naturally protected by high transport costs.

Factor immobility

For a country to benefit from comparative advantage it is necessary for it to contract those industries in which it is at a disadvantage and expand those in which it has an advantage. This will involve wages, prices and employment falling in the declining industry. The fact that prices seem to go up easily but are very difficult to bring down is referred to as the downward inflexibility of prices or, more memorably, the 'sticky-upwardness' of prices. This will form part of a general resistance to change from those in the declining industry. We need only look at the recent problems in some UK industries such as coal to appreciate this. Such inflexibility may prevent an economy from benefiting fully from comparative advantage.

Increasing costs

Earlier in the chapter we considered the possibility that specialisation might produce decreasing costs. There is, on the other hand, the possibility that specialisation could lead to increasing costs. This could come about as the expansion of an industry drove up the price of labour and other factors, or it could occur as an industry expanded into less and less appropriate resources. This is illustrated in Fig. 39.8. Here, starting from point F, forgoing the production of 60 million units of food at the constant cost ratio of 10:9 should have been expected to gain Richland a further 54 million units of clothing, thus moving it to point I. However, because of increasing costs, it has arrived at point I_1, a much lower level of production.

The principle of increasing costs also helps to explain why specialisation is not complete in international trade. If a country experiences increasing costs as it specialises then its domestic trading ratio is worsening. It would therefore stop specialising at the point where its domestic ratio became worse than the international ratio, since at that point it would become more advantageous to import the product in which it was specialising. For example, in Fig. 39.8, as Richland specialises in clothing production and moves from point F towards point I, it expects that each 10 units of food given up will gain it 9 units of clothing, but, because the production possibility line bends inwards, the rate deteriorates. Thus 10 units of food gain it only 8 of clothing and then 7 and so on. Once the rate has deteriorated to 10:6 (the international trading ratio) it would then be better to trade for clothing rather than produce more.

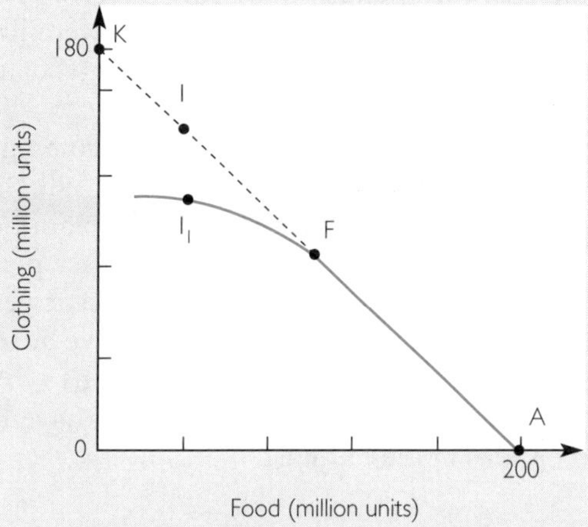

***Fig. 39.8* Increasing costs**
As Richland moves from point F it arrives not at point I but at point I_1. If point I_1 is less than an output of 126 million units of clothing it would not be in Richland's interest to specialise this far because, at 126 million units of clothing 60 million units of food given up have gained only 36 million units of clothing, a rate equal to the international trading ratio of 10 : 6.

Other problems

Specialisation itself can create problems if there is a change in demand. For example, it could be argued that in the UK Lancashire overspecialised in cotton production so that when demand changed the whole area was plunged into depression. In recent years the dangers of overspecialisation were illustrated by the overdependence of the West Midlands in the UK on car production.

This problem also points to a shortcoming of the theory of comparative advantage, which is that it is static. The theory does not explain how comparative advantage arises in the first place, nor how it changes. The history of recent years illustrates only too well that comparative advantage can change; many Western nations which enjoyed an advantage in manufacturing have lost it to nations in the Far East.

Protectionism considered

Adam Smith's *The Wealth of Nations* was designed to show the adverse effects of restrictions on trade. The majority of economists since his time have favoured free trade. However, the depression in the world economy in the late 1970s and early 1980s led to the revival of the protection lobby. Many prominent economists such as Professor Wynne Godley of Cambridge have argued the need to protect the home market. The UK, however, has remained one of the most free markets in the world. Elsewhere protectionism is rife, not only through the use of tariffs but also through the subtler forms of economic nationalism. The UK has entered the EU which, while freeing trade between members, has erected tariff barriers to the rest of the world.

Many arguments are advanced in favour of protectionism. Some of the arguments are sounder than others, but all forms of protection suffer from the disadvantage that they may invite retaliation from trading partners. We will consider the more significant arguments more fully.

Cheap labour

It is often argued that the economy must be protected from imports which are produced with cheap, or 'sweated', labour (see page 540). This argument is basically unsound because it is contrary to the whole principle of comparative advantage. It would not only ensure that wages are kept low in the exporting country but also protect inefficient practices at home, in the long run depressing domestic living standards.

Dumping

If goods are sold on a foreign market below their cost of production this is referred to as dumping. This may be undertaken either by a foreign monopolist, using high profits at home to subsidise exports, or by foreign governments subsiding exports for political or strategic reasons. (Dumping is also discussed in Chapter 18.) It is quite legitimate and necessary for a country to protect its industries from this type of unfair competition.

Infant industries

If a country is establishing an industry it may be necessary to protect it from competition temporarily until it reaches levels of production and costs which will allow it to compete with established industries elsewhere. This argument was advanced to support the protection of the European video cassette recorder industry. The problem is that protected industries tend to become dependent upon the protection.

Unemployment and immobile factors

Imports may aggravate domestic unemployment and protection could be a way of alleviating this. As we have already noted, factors are immobile and protection could allow a country time to reallocate factors of production in a more efficient manner. However, in the long run such protection cannot be justified since it will protect inefficiency and ultimately depress the living standards of a nation.

Balance of payments

Perhaps the most immediate reason for bringing in protection is a balance of payments deficit. A package of measures was brought in by the UK government in 1966 for this reason. They included exchange controls, an import surcharge and an import deposit scheme. Again this argument can be justified only in the short run, especially as it also invites retaliation from other countries.

Strategic reasons

Two world wars taught the UK the danger of being overreliant on imports. For political or strategic reasons a country may not wish to be dependent upon imports and so may protect a home industry even if it is inefficient. Many countries maintain munitions industries for strategic reasons. In the UK, for example, the aerospace industry has received substantial 'protection' in the form of government money. Similarly, the EU is committed to protecting agriculture.

Bargaining

Even when a country can see no economic benefit in protection it may find it useful to have tariffs and restrictions as bargaining gambits in negotiating better terms with other nations.

Revenue

Customs duties are one of the oldest sources of government revenue. It should be remembered, however, that a tax on imports cannot both keep out imports and at the same time raise money. The effect of customs duties will depend upon the elasticity of demand for imports. If the demand is inelastic the tax will indeed make money for the government but will also add to domestic inflation. Where demand is elastic the government could increase its revenues by cutting the tax; this was confirmed as long ago as 1844 when Sir Robert Peel cut import duties. (The analysis of this is the same as that for any other indirect tax; see Chapter 11.)

The optimum tariff case

Where the country is a 'large' country in the sense that it has purchasing power regarding a particular commodity (referred to in textbooks as monopsony power) the government by imposing a tariff on that commodity may succeed in forcing the foreign supplier to lower the price to such an extent that the country as a whole is better off than before the imposition of the tariff. The problem with this case is that in deciding on the optimum tariff very detailed information is needed about the supply and demand elasticities of the product.

Theory of second best

The case for free trade is based on the assumption that the world is characterised by perfect competition. Needless to say this is not the case. For example, most governments in the world provide support for their agricultural industry. Let us take a situation where the government of a country is guaranteeing a price for wheat for its farmers at £2 a kilo whereas the world stands by to provide us with as much wheat as we want for £1.50 a kilo. Under these circumstances if the UK government adopted a free trade policy it would be economic madness. No one in their right minds will produce wheat in the UK; they will simply import it and deliver it to the government at a profit. Thus, the UK government has to impede trade.

Externalities

It is argued that certain industries have important beneficial spill-over effects on the rest of the economy and thus they must be encouraged to grow. A major problem here is that given the nature of the world economy the benefits are often international and not merely national.

Strategic trade policy argument

This is a 'new argument' for protectionism and is based on the observation that the most common form of market structure is oligopoly and not perfect competition. This argument is based on the premise that since abnormal profits are often being earned under oligopoly or monopoly, the government should intervene in order to obtain some or all of these abnormal profits from the foreign firm(s) either for itself by imposing a tariff or for the benefit of its domestic producers by providing them with subsidies. The problem with strategic trade policy is that a tremendous amount of information is needed in order to establish whether or not foreign forms are earning abnormal profits, never mind the magnitude. Furthermore, one needs to know how the rest of the economy will be affected by such a course of action.

Cultural reasons

A country may impose protectionist measures in order to safeguard the culture of its citizens. For example, the French government refused to remove the subsidies to its film industry on the ground that if it were to do so, it would have been destroyed, with dire consequences for French culture.

Conclusion

We have endeavoured to show that the economic arguments are overwhelmingly in favour of a pattern of free world trade. However, in conclusion, we might note three qualifications upon this. First, the pattern of world trade which has grown up has not always reflected comparative advantage; it has all so often depended upon historical accident or upon the possession of surplus resources. Second, tariffs and other forms of protection have significantly modified the pattern of trade. Third, even where the country is committed to free trade and it has comparative advantage, it may be unwise to follow such a policy in a world of protectionism.

Summary

1 The bias of nationalism often prejudices our views on international trade.
2 The theory of comparative advantage explains that international trade is worthwhile and beneficial to both parties wherever there is any difference in their respective opportunity cost ratios.
3 The theory may be extended to include many countries and many commodities and comparative advantage may be improved by such things as decreasing costs.
4 There are many obstacles to free trade such as tariffs, quotas, exchange control and economic nationalism.
5 Comparative advantage is diminished by such things as transport costs, increasing costs and factor immobility.
6 Comparative cost ratios help to explain the determination of exchange rates.
7 Many arguments are advanced to support protectionism but few are valid in the long run.

Questions

1 Explain the difference between absolute and comparative advantage.
2 Explain why every single country in the world is likely to have comparative advantage in the production of some commodity even though it may have no absolute advantage in the production of any one commodity.
3 Suppose that the production of olive oil and wine per unit of labour in Spain and the United States of America (USA) is as follows:

	Olive oil (litres)	*Wine (litres)*
Spain	50	30
USA	40	20

a) Which country has absolute advantage in the production of both commodities?
b) Which country has comparative advantage in the production of olive oil?
c) Define the limits of possible international trading ratios within which the two countries may trade. (Hint: What are the domestic trading ratios in each country?)
d) Explain how the international trading ratio will be determined.
e) Wine costs 16.67 euros a litre and olive oil 6 euros in Spain whereas in the USA wine costs $4 and olive oil $2. Determine the limits of the exchange rate of the euro with the US dollars between which trade will be worthwhile for the two countries.

4 In your view, are there any valid arguments for protectionism?
5 Explain why business people often believe that protectionism will benefit the country whereas most economists believe the opposite?
6 With hindsight, can you think of any industries which should have been supported by the UK government owing to their beneficial externalities?

7 To what extent are exchange rates a result of the differing opportunity cost ratios between nations?

8 In an essay, evaluate the arguments for and against free trade.

Data response A
Putting trade in its place

Based on Larry Elliot's article which appeared in the *Guardian* on 27 May 1996.

1 Outline the case for and against the proposal that 'trade should be linked to basic labour standards'.

2 Some commentators believe that globalisation keeps workers in their place and wages down. Do you agree with this view?

3 'Only around 5% of exports to the west – Europe, North America and Japan – come from outside, and that percentage has actually fallen in recent years'. Is this indicative of inter- or intra-industry trade and what explanations can you offer for this phenomenon?

4 Do you share the author's belief that growth and rising incomes lead to trade rather than the reverse?

Putting trade in its place

Globalisation is to the world economy what monetarism is to the domestic economy. It represents the final triumph of capital over labour, since the corollary of the deregulation of finance is the shackling of trade unions. It means that national governments are left powerless in the face of multinationals who will relocate at the first whiff of interventionist policies.

Last week the OECD summed up current thinking when it said globalisation "gives all countries the possibility of participating in world development and all consumers the assurance of benefiting from increasingly vigorous competition between producers".

Yet these "consumers" are also workers, and here the Panglossian view of globalisation starts to break down. The UK government strained every sinew to prevent the OECD calling for the link between trade and labour standards to be discussed at the first ministerial meeting of the World Trade Organisation in Singapore later this year.

Britain argued that the International Labour Organisation – a body anathema to ministers these past 17 years – should investigate. The intention, of course, is to ensure that the issue is buried.

America thinks otherwise. It is Insistent that trade should be linked to basic labour standards, and what the US wants it usually gets. Nobody should kid themselves that Washington's actions are determined by altruism: rather the US's approach is an amalgam of Bill Clinton's political expediency in the face of Pat Buchanan's blue-collar protectionism and the naked self-interest of big business. The US likes global rules and regulations in areas where it perceives that it is at threat from international competition, but wants all barriers removed where it is the dominant player.

For all that, the American stance is welcome, because it offers some hope that a human dimension can be added to the trade debate. In an election year, Clinton needs organised labour on his side, and the unions are rightly outraged when they see US companies being wooed to Bangladesh by adverts boasting that unions are outlawed and strikes illegal in special low-cost economic development zones.

Further, the debate over labour standards raises the question of whether the cut-throat, lowest common denominator approach has a long-run future. Trade was certainly one of the three pillars of the Golden Age of 1945-73 – along with Keynesianism and postwar reconstruction – but it was ordered trade developed within framework of rules and capital controls.

The way in which US agribusiness pushed through key parts of the Uruguay Round is indicative of a brutal new order in which powerful countries decide what should be liberalised and what shouldn't. This is the route to anarchy and, ironically protectionism as well.

Any challenge to globalisation requires an understanding of what we are dealing with. The theory is that liberalisation and deregulated capital flows allow countries to specialise in what they are good (or least bad) at, and this international division of labour raises global income. Free movement of capital leads to higher foreign investment and the diffusion of best practice. As a result, the developing countries that do best are those with the least state intervention and the freest trade and these new "tiger economies" pose a massive competitive threat to living standards in the developed world.

This last point is one of the keys to the whole debate. Globalisation is an important weapon for international capital because it keeps workers in their place and wages down.

In fact, as the American economist Paul Krugman has pointed out, the idea of global competition bearing down on Western living standards is a myth. Only around 5 per cent of exports to the West – Europe, North America and Japan – come from outside, and that percentage has actually fallen in recent years.

Professor Ajit Singh, of Cambridge University, goes further. He finds no evidence that globalisation has been good for us and, to the extent that it is symbiotically linked to deflationary macro-economic policies, it is positively harmful.

Prof Singh compares the past 15 years with the Golden Age of 1945-73 and concludes: "Under the market supremacy model of the 1980s and 1990s, liberalisation and globalisation in industrial countries have not resulted in increased long-term economic growth, nor are these likely to do so in the foreseeable future under the present policy regime".

This is a valid criticism. On almost any measure that real people could relate to – growth, unemployment, living standards, investment – the record of the past 20 years has been far poorer than in the Golden Age.

Prof Singh does not advocate protectionism. Rather, he argues that the current euphoria for liberalism is potentially dangerous precisely because it could lead to a descent into the beggar-my-neighbour policies of the 1930s. On his reckoning, the Golden Age was not a fluke, but the consequence of the right policy choices and the creation of an appropriate institutional framework.

An Unctad paper by Paul Bairoch and Richard Kozul-Wright, argues that the pre-first world war era was not one of trade liberalisation, nor of diminished expectations for the role of the state. Rather, just as with Japan in the 1960s and Korea in the 1980s, countries grew more rapidly after they became more protectionist. Countries that experienced huge capital inflows – such as Argentina – were often destabilised,

The paper's thrust is that pre-1914 was not a golden age of economic growth and rapid convergence. Instead the internationalisation of finance capital was associated with uneven development, often reinforcing existing differences in the world economy rather than bringing about convergence.

This revisionism is long, long overdue. Internationalism and trade are grand ideals, much to be preferred to nationalism and protectionism, but history suggests that growth and rising incomes lead to trade rather than the reverse.

Source: *The Guardian*, 27 May 1996

40 The balance of payments

Learning outcomes

At the end of this chapter you will be able to:

- Understand the pattern of the UK's trade.
- Describe a country's balance of payments accounts.
- Appreciate the concept of balance of payments equilibrium.
- Analyse the major problems involved in dealing with a fundamental balance of payments disequilibrium.

The pattern of the UK's overseas trade

The importance of international trade

There are few other nations in the world as dependent upon foreign trade as the UK. The UK depends upon imports for almost half its food requirements and for most of the raw materials needed by its industries. Equally, the continued well-being of the economy depends upon exporting a large proportion of the national product each year. The growth of exports and imports is closely linked to the growth of GDP, as Table 40.1 shows. This tendency for an economy to become more international as it becomes wealthier is not confined to the UK; there is a similar pattern in most industrial countries.

International trade is a vital component of national income, as we can see from the identity:

$$Y = C + I + G + (X - M)$$

A trade deficit has a depressing effect upon the level of income and employment whereas a surplus will boost income. The UK economy suffers from the structural problem that, as the economy expands, it tends to draw in raw materials which are necessary for manufacturing industries. However, it often happens that, before these can be turned into exports, the flow of imports has caused a balance of payments crisis which necessitates contractionary policies to rectify the imbalance.

Table 40.1 **GDP and international trade in the UK**

	Index of GDP (1990 = 100)	*Exports as % of GDP*	*Imports as % of GDP*
1971	65.1	23.8	25.9
1975	70.6	27.3	30.13
1980	76.9	29.7	28.65
1985	85.2	31.9	32.15
1990	100.0	26.5	31.0
1997	106.2	31.3	33.6

Source: National Accounts, HMSO

In recent years a disturbing trend has been the tendency for the expanding economy to draw in manufactured goods which the domestic economy is failing to produce. In 1983, for the first time since the industrial revolution, the UK imported more manufactured goods than it exported. The traditional situation is thus changed so that expansion of the domestic economy causes the balance of trade to deteriorate as consumers buy imported manufactured goods. By the late 1980s and early 1990s massive trade imbalances were recorded (see Table 40.2).

The components of trade

The pattern of the types of goods which the UK exports and imports can be seen in Table 40.2. You can see that there is some sort of correspondence between the types of goods which are exported and

Table 40.2 **UK exports and imports by value, 1995**

	Value of exports £m	Value of exports %	Value of imports £m	Value of imports %
Food, beverages and tobacco	11 161	7.3	15 237	9.3
Basic materials	2 932	1.9	6 441	3.9
Oil	8 687	5.7	4 457	2.7
Other fuels and lubricants	563	0.4	1 102	0.7
Semi-manufactured goods	43 437	28.5	45 035	27.5
Finished manufactured goods	83 783	55.0	90 180	55.0
Miscellaneous	1 783	1.2	1 522	0.9
Total	152 346	100.0	163 974	100.0

imported. For example, the UK both exports and imports large amounts of manufactured goods: cars to and from Germany, for instance! This is a developing tendency among industrialised nations, and would seem to fly in the face of the principle of comparative costs discussed in the previous chapter. It can be explained, at least partly, by the growing sophistication and fragmentation of consumer demand. Increasingly, consumers do not want just a car, they want a particular model; if it happens to be imported this does not concern them. This also means that, in many consumer markets, price is not as great a determinant of demand as simple economic theory would suggest.

In addition to trade in goods, which is termed 'visible' trade, there is trade in 'invisibles', i.e. services. For most of the last 100 years or so, the UK has had a deficit on visible trade which has been made up by a surplus on invisible earnings. However, while invisibles have become increasingly important, the UK has also enjoyed an improved position on visible trade due to North Sea oil, which has both added to exports and reduced the need for imports. The years 1980–2 saw surpluses on visible trade which were due both to the impact of North Sea oil and the depressed state of the economy which restrained imports. However, after 1982 visible trade swung back into deficit. A record visible trade deficit of £23 840 million was recorded in 1989. This was due principally to the increasing imbalance in the export and import of manufactured goods.

The changing nature of the UK's trade

The traditional view of the UK is as 'the workshop of the world', i.e. importing raw materials and exporting manufactured goods. This picture is changing rapidly because of: a) exports of North Sea oil which have once more turned the UK into an exporter of primary products; b) growing reliance on tertiary industries such as tourism. The growing tendency is for the UK to import dear and export cheap, i.e. to import high-value, low-bulk products but to export low-value, high-bulk products.

We might express this relationship as a trade value–weight coefficient thus:

$$\text{Trade value} - \text{weight coefficient} = \frac{\text{Average value of 1 tonne of exports}}{\text{Average value of 1 tonne of imports}}$$

If the value were to be 10 the average value of a tonne of exports would be equal to a tonne of imports. A value less than 10 would mean that exports were, in general, less valuable per tonne than imports. In the early 1970s the UK's coefficient stood at just over 0.6, but by 1989 it had decreased to 0.5. Meanwhile West Germany's coefficient had risen from 1.0 to 1.2.

The direction of trade

In Table 40.3 you can see that 65–70 per cent of the UK's overseas trade is with 10 countries. Despite the growing concentration of trade illustrated by these figures, the UK continues to have a more world-wide pattern of trade than most other nations. Traditionally, the UK drew its imports of raw materials from the Commonwealth and Empire to whom, in return, it exported its manufactures. Since 1945 there has been a growing dependence on North America and Europe. This trend was quite apparent before the UK joined the EU and, indeed, was one of the reasons it was essential for the UK to join. Since joining the EU, the UK has become much more dependent upon EU trade. In the year before the UK entered the EU around 27 per cent of visible trade was with the Community but by 1995 this had increased to 57 per cent. This is well illustrated by considering

Table 40.3 The UK's 10 leading trading partners (by value) 1995 and 1985

Country position (in order of importance in UK's trade)	International trade 1995 Imports (CIF) £m	%	Exports (FOB) £m	%	Trade 1985 Imports %	Exports %	Position
1. Germany*	26 106	15.5	20 154	13.1	15.0	11.3	1
2. USA	20 280	12.1	18 023	11.8	11.6	14.4	2
3. France*	16 256	9.7	15 192	9.9	7.7	9.7	3
4. Netherlands*	11 371	6.8	12 256	8.0	7.6	9.2	4
5. Belgium/Luxembourg*	7975	4.7	8 295	5.4	4.7	4.1	6
6. Italy*	8 189	4.9	7853	5.1	5.0	4.3	5
7. Ireland	6994	4.2	7724	5.0	3.3	4.5	7
8. Japan	9 630	5.7	3784	2.5	4.8	1.3	9
9. Spain*	4315	2.6	6064	4.0	2.1	1.9	11
10. Sweden*	4497	2.7	4 113	2.7	2.9	3.8	8
Total of these 10	115 613	68.9	103 458	67.5	64.7	64.5	
Total of all visible trade	167 933	100.0	153 276	100.0	85 657	80 073	

* EU members
Source: Annual Abstract of Statistics, HMSO

the position of one of the UK's traditional trading partners, Canada. In 1967 Canada was the second most important nation in the UK's overseas trade; by 1976 it was ninth, in 1989 it was 14th and by 1995 it was 17th. Japan joined the list of the UK's top 10 trading partners only in 1985. This may seem a little surprising considering the vast quantities of cars and electronic equipment imported from there. However, the list measures both imports and exports and, as you can see from Table 40.3, there is a large deficit in the UK's balance of trade with Japan. Japan sells almost three times as much to the UK as it buys from it. This imbalance is due, at least in part, to the excessive protective measures the Japanese use to guard their home market.

You will see in Table 40.3 the abbreviations FOB after exports and CIF after imports. These stand for ***free on board*** and ***cost, insurance and freight***. The figures are valued in this way because it gives the value of exports and imports at the point they enter or leave the country.

Table 40.4 illustrates the proportion of UK exports and imports going to different parts of the world. Between 1985 and 1995 export and import volumes both increased by 61 per cent. These rises were spread fairly evenly over the years.

Table 40.4 Geographical analysis of UK's visible trade 1985 and 1995

Area	1985 Exports £m	%	Imports £m	%	1995 Exports £m	%	Imports £m	%
European Community*	43 329	54.1	46 059	53.8	89 066	58.1	93 165	55.5
Other Western Europe	3 128	3.9	7544	8.8	6 399	4.2	10 686	6.4
North America	13 515	16.9	11 931	13.9	20 577	13.4	32 050	13.7
Other developed countries	3789	4.7	6 352	7.4	6 460	4.2	11 428	6.8
Oil-exporting countries	5950	7.4	2 810	3.3	6 330	4.1	3 252	1.9
Rest of world	10 362	12.9	10 961	12.8	24 444	15.9	26 350	15.7
Total	80 073	100.0	85 657	100.0	153 276	100.0	167 931	100.0

* Figures relate to all 11 countries
Source: Balance of Payments, HMSO

The terms of trade

The 'terms of trade' is a measure of the relative prices of imports and exports. It is calculated by taking the index of export prices and dividing it by the index of import prices. The import index is compiled from a sample of the prices of 200 commodities while the export index samples 250.

The present index of the terms of trade is based on 1990 (see Table 40.5). If we discover that in 1988 the index of export prices was 92.4 while that of imports was 93.7 then we can calculate the terms of trade as:

$$\text{Terms of trade index} = \frac{\text{Index of export prices}}{\text{Index of import prices}} \times \frac{100}{1}$$

$$= \frac{92.4}{93.7} \times \frac{100}{1}$$

$$= 98.6$$

If the index increases this is said to be a favourable movement in the terms of trade, while when it falls it is termed unfavourable. A favourable movement in the terms of trade means that a given quantity of exports will buy more imports. The word favourable may, however, be misleading: a relative rise in the price of exports will be beneficial only if the demand for exports is inelastic (see below, page 562).

In the mid 1970s the index was low because of the rise in oil and other commodity prices and because of the fall in the value of sterling. It recovered in the late 1970s owing to the recovery in the exchange rate of sterling. During the 1980s and early to mid 1990s, despite great changes in the volume and direction of trade, the terms of trade remained relatively stable.

STUDENT ACTIVITY 40.1

a) Define the expressions terms of trade and balance of trade. Discuss the possible relationship between the two.
b) Over the 10-year period 1985–95 both exports to and imports from the European Union have increased. What possible reasons can you suggest for this?
c) (i) Explain why the terms of trade for the UK remained stable over the period 1985–95.
   (ii) In 1997 the value of sterling against the major European currencies increased dramatically. What effect, if any, would you expect this to have on the terms of trade?

The balance of payments

We have so far considered the export and import of goods and services. However, there are many other international transactions. These are brought together in the balance of payments.

The balance of payments is an account of all the transactions of everyone living and working in the UK with the rest of the world.

If a person normally resident in the UK sells goods or services to someone abroad, this creates an inflow (+) of pounds, while anyone in the UK buying goods or services abroad creates an outflow (–), but if a foreigner invests in the UK, e.g. if a US company takes over a UK company, then an inflow (+) of currency is created. Not so obviously, if the UK reduces its reserves of foreign currency, this is recorded as a credit (+), as is the

Table 40.5 **The UK's terms of trade**

	1985	*1986*	*1987*	*1988*	*1989*	*1990*	*1991*	*1992*	*1993*	*1994*	*1995*
Exports (FOB)	98.1	88.3	91.4	92.4	96.5	100.0	101.4	103.5	116.2	118.6	126.4
Imports (FOB)	96.3	91.9	94.5	93.7	97.7	100.0	101.2	102.1	112.3	116.1	127.8
Terms of trade	101.9	96.9	96.7	98.6	98.8	100.0	100.2	101.4	103.5	102.2	98.9

Source: OBRD

receipt of loans from abroad, while, conversely, increasing the reserves of foreign currency or making a loan is shown as a debit (–). When all these transactions are recorded we arrive at a balance of payments statement as in Table 40.6.

Items in the account

The format of the balance of payments account was revised in 1986, eliminating the section of the account which was termed official financing. We will follow the new format. The numbers against the following headings refer to items in Table 40.6.

a) *Current account* (1). This has two main components: ***visible trade***, which is the export and import of goods (from which we get the balance of trade); and ***invisible trade***, which is chiefly the sale and purchase of services. The balance of trade is often confused with the balance of payments. In Table 40.6 you can see that the balance of trade is only a part of the balance of payments, albeit an impor-

***Table 40.6* Balance of payments of the UK, 1995**

Current account (1)	*£m*
Visible trade:	
Exports (FOB)	152 346
Imports (FOB)	163 974
Visible balance ('balance of trade')	–11 628
Invisibles:	
Services	
General government	–2 020
Private sector and public corporations:	
Sea transport	–165
Civil aviation	–341
Travel	–3 703
Financial and other services	12 371
Investment income	
General government	–2 719
Private sector and public corporations	12 291
Transfers	
General government	15 714
Private sector	–7 180
Invisibles balance	202
Current balance	–2 892
Transactions in external assets and liabilities	
Investment overseas by UK residents	–65 872
Investment in the UK by overseas residents	+37 339
Net foreign currency transactions by UK banks	+4 652
Net sterling transactions of UK banks	+4 809
Official reserves (addition to (–), drawings on (+))	+200
Other	+19 318
Net transactions in assets and liabilities (2)	+446
Balancing item (3)	+2 446

Source: CSO, *Balance of Payments*, HMSO

tant part. It is therefore possible to have a deficit on the balance of trade but a surplus on the balance of payments, or vice versa. The traditional pattern for the UK is to have a deficit on the balance of trade made up by a surplus on invisibles. One of the disturbing trends in the current account involves the growing propensity to import manufactured goods discussed above and the decline in the relative size of the invisible surplus.

b) *Transactions in external assets and liabilities* (2). This involves the movement of capital (money) rather than goods and services, i.e. it is concerned with international loans and investment. It includes such items as:
   (i) UK investment overseas;
   (ii) overseas investment in the UK;
   (iii) borrowing and lending overseas by UK banks;
   (iv) changes in official reserves;
   (v) other items such as government loans to foreign countries.

   Item (iv), the changes in official reserves, refers to the increases or decreases in the reserves of gold and foreign currency held by the Bank of England. Increases in the reserves are shown as a minus (–) and drawings on (running down the reserves) as a plus (+). If this point is not clear remember that the balance of payments is recorded in pounds, and, therefore, if the reserves of foreign currency increase this must be because foreigners have bought pounds. This being the case, pounds must have left the country and hence we show this as a minus (–). Conversely, if the Bank of England runs down the reserves (sells foreign currency) it will be obtaining pounds in return and hence there is a flow of pounds into the country (+).

   The transactions in external assets and liabilities part of the account is often a deficit. Its importance has grown in recent years, as has its instability. This instability is caused by large movements of short-term capital. This so-called 'hot money' tends to move about in search of better interest rates or expectations of changes in the value of currencies. It should also be remembered that the UK is the major exporter of capital. By this we mean that Britons invest in companies and property overseas to a greater extent than foreigners invest in the UK. In the short term, therefore, this creates an outflow. However, we should recall that, in the longer term, money will flow back into the country by way of interest, profits and dividends on the current account. The UK is, in fact, one of the world's largest creditor nations (see page 565).

   Prior to the 1986 changes in format there used to be a separate section of the account termed official financing. In this section were the changes in official reserves and borrowing and lending to such official bodies as the International Monetary Fund. It used to be said that the overall deficit or surplus on this section was needed to balance the overall deficit or surplus on the rest of the account. The reason for discontinuing this section was that it had become dwarfed by the transactions in the private sector so that it was unrealistic to speak of official financing balancing the books. There is, of course, still massive government intervention from time to time but other measures are needed such as changes in interest rates.

c) *The balancing item* (3). This item is necessary to allow for statistical errors in the compilation of the account. It can be either positive or negative. Old accounts are often adjusted in the light of better information and, for this reason, the size of the balancing item may be made smaller.

Common misunderstanding

'The balance of payments always balances, thus there is no need to worry about a country's external equilibrium position.' It is true that in an accounting sense the balance of payments always balances because for every debit there is a corresponding credit. However, from an economic policy view we need to look at the individual balances on the current and capital accounts.

Types of imbalance

It is often said that 'the balance of payments always balances'. This is indeed true, both in the short term and the long term. In the short term a balance is achieved through changes in official reserves. In the long term we can also demonstrate that a balance will be arrived at because, if there is any deficit on current account, this must be matched by a surplus on investment and other capital transactions or else by a surplus in future years. The fact that a balance must eventually be achieved may, however, obscure the fact that a disequilibrium exists in the short term. A short-term disequilibrium need not cause major problems as it may be conveniently dealt with by a change in reserves or by borrowing or lending. A long-term or fundamental disequilibrium exists when there is a persistent tendency for outflows of trade and capital to be significantly greater or smaller than the corresponding inflows.

The correct policy for a fundamental disequilibrium will depend upon its size, cause and upon the exchange rate policy which the government is pursuing. Obviously the size of a deficit or surplus will affect its significance, but it will also be influenced by which items in the account are affected; for example, a persistent deficit on capital items might be expected to cause inflows of interest, profits and dividends in future years and, therefore, pose little problem. Even with the current account, imbalances with different items may call for different remedies. In this connection we must also consider the state of the domestic economy. Table 40.7 summarises some of the possible combinations of problems. A deficit on the balance of payments might be accompanied by either a high or a low level of domestic activity. The required solutions would obviously be very different; for example, if an external deficit was accompanied by heavy unemployment domestically, a solution which aimed at further depressing the level of economic activity would hardly be ideal. Similarly, when we consider the possibility of a surplus on the balance of payments, this too could be accompanied by either a high or low level of domestic economic activity.

Table 40.7 **Problems and solutions with balance of payments**

Causes of problem	*Suggested remedies*
Deficit problems:	
Problem 1:	
a) Inflationary pressures, exports low because prices too high, e.g. UK 1989	a) Increase productivity to lower prices and increase exports.
b) Interest rates low and therefore 'hot' money flows out to earn high interest elsewhere.	b) Tight fiscal policy and dear money policy to deflate economy; also higher interest rates attract 'hot money'.
Problem 2:	
a) Currency overvalued, therefore exports low despite unemployment in the domestic economy, e.g. UK 1981 and 1992.	a) Depreciate or devaluate the currency if import/export elasticities are favourable.
b) Capital outflow because of investment overseas or too much government expenditure overseas.	b) Stop or reduce drain, e.g. by exchange control regulations on investment.
Sulplus problems:	
Problem 3:	
a) Spare capacity in the economy, prices relatively low, exports high, e.g. West Germany 1982.	a) Easy fiscal and cheap money policies, with low taxes and higher government expenditure, boost internal economy while lower interest rates reduce inflow of 'hot money'.
b) Interest rates high, 'hot' money flows in to earn high interest.	
Problem 4:	
a) Currency overvalued, embarrassment to trading partners, exports artificially cheap while imports dear, domestic living standards restricted, e.g. Japan 1983.	a) Appreciate or revalue currency; this will reduce exports and increase imports if Marshall–Lerner conditions fulfilled.
	b) Increase capital expenditure overseas or increase foreign aid.

The type of exchange rate policy to which a country is committed will also influence the situation. When, as was the case with the UK up to 1972, and more recently when sterling was in the ERM over the period October 1990 to September 1992, a country is committed to fixed exchange rates, this limits the options. Under these circumstances the UK was often obliged to subordinate internal policy, such as the pursuit of economic growth, to the external objective of maintaining the exchange rate. However, the adoption of a floating exchange rate has still not entirely freed internal policy from external constraints.

Common misunderstanding

Whenever the UK balance of payments figures are announced, journalists often concentrate exclusively on the current account balance and present it as the balance of payments figure. As our discussion above indicates, this is wrong. Whilst undoubtedly the state of the current account gives a very important insight as to whether or not a country is living within its means, we must add to it the transactions in external assets and liabilities to gain a true picture of the balance of payments position.

The problems of a surplus

Why worry?

It might not be immediately obvious that a surplus presents problems. However, there are a number of reasons why it might.

a) *De-industrialisation.* The UK's experience of surplus in the late 1970s and early 1980s has demonstrated that a surplus can lead to undesirable domestic consequences. The oil surpluses were used to finance industrial imports, thus leading to a rundown of the economy. The surpluses also attracted 'hot' money which led to an overvaluation of the currency, which in turn decreased the competitiveness of exports. This syndrome is sometimes known as the 'Dutch disease' after the experience of the Netherlands following the exploitation of North Sea gas in the 1950s.
b) *Feedback effects.* Since it is the case that overall the international payments of all nations must balance, it must also be the case that while one economy is in surplus, others must be in deficit. A persistent surplus may, therefore, embarrass one's trading partners and force them to place restrictions on imports which are to the detriment of world trade. The activities of a country's trading partners in getting rid of their deficits may well decrease the demand for the surplus country's exports, thus 'feeding back' the effect of a deficit to the surplus country.
c) *Inflationary consequences.* Both Keynesian and monetarist analysis of a balance of payments surplus points to possible inflationary consequences. In Keynesian analysis demand pull inflation will be caused if the economy is at, or near, full employment since a surplus is an injection into the economy. Monetarists argue that a surplus increases the money supply unless exchange rates are freely floating. This argument is considered in more detail below (see page 564).
d) *Depression of domestic living standards.* A country running a considerable balance of payments surplus is, in fact, keeping down the standard of living of its citizens. This is because the reserves of foreign currency built up by the surplus could be turned into goods and services for the population without any cost in resources to the economy.

Curing a surplus

A surplus might be reduced or eliminated by inflating the economy and/or revaluing the currency. Inflating the economy will tend to increase the demand for imports especially if the economy is at full employment. Revaluing the currency will reduce the price of imports and increase the price of exports, thus tending to eliminate the surplus.

Japan had huge current account surpluses during the 1980s. This was partly a result of the superb productivity of Japanese industry but it was also due to protective measures. Under these circumstances the surplus could be reduced by getting rid of the protectionist measures.

A current account surplus is often eliminated by an outflow of funds on the capital account. This balances the books but, of course, creates further inflow of funds on the current account in future years.

It would also be possible for a nation to reduce its surplus by increasing overseas aid.

Deficit problems

Types of policy

The correct measures to remedy a deficit will depend upon its cause and also upon the exchange rate regime. A short-term deficit might be dealt with by running down reserves or by borrowing. Another short-term measure might be to raise interest rates to encourage the inflow of money. When there is a more fundamental payments deficit other measures will have to be taken.

We can divide measures to rectify a deficit into two main categories:

a) *Expenditure reducing*. These are measures such as domestic deflation which aim to rectify the deficit by cutting expenditure.
b) *Expenditure switching*. This refers to measures such as import controls, designed to switch expenditure from imports to domestically produced goods.

The two types of measures need not be regarded as alternatives but rather as complements; for example, a government might reduce expenditure to create spare capacity in the economy prior to creating extra demand through expenditure-switching policies.

Deflation

The demand for imports could be restrained (expenditure reducing) by restricting the total level of demand in the country through fiscal and monetary policies. It might appear that this is a very indirect method. However, there are three reasons it might be adopted. First, the country may wish to maintain a fixed exchange rate policy. Second, protective measures such as import controls may conflict with a nation's treaty obligations such as GATT and the Treaty of Rome. Third, protective measures also invite retaliation. These reasons explain why in the period 1947–72 deflation was the UK's chief method of rectifying a payment deficit. The recurring need to deflate the economy formed part of the so-called 'stop–go cycle'.

Using deflation to rectify a deficit is subordinating the needs of the domestic economy to the external need to maintain exchange rates. The cost of such a policy may be high in terms of unemployment.

Deflation might have a secondary expenditure-switching effect if domestic rates of inflation are reduced below those of the nation's trading partners, thus giving it a price advantage.

Protection

The various methods of protecting the home market from foreign competition were discussed on page 548. We may note here that they are aimed at expenditure switching. It should also be remembered that protective measures do little or nothing about the underlying causes of the deficit but attempt to cure it by simply cutting off imports. Although recent years have seen a rising tide of protectionism in world trade, the succesful completion of the Uruguay round of GATT and the establishment of the World Trade Organisation should hopefully reverse this trend.

If tariffs are used to restrict imports, their efficacy will be determined by the elasticity of demand for imports. For tariffs to reduce expenditure, it is necessary for demand to be elastic.

Devaluation or depreciation

If a nation operating a fixed exchange rate drops the external price of its currency, as the UK did in 1967 when the exchange rate changed from £1 = \$2.80 to £1 = \$2.40, this is referred to as devaluation. If a country has a 'floating' exchange rate and it allows the external value of its currency to decrease, this is referred to as depreciation. The UK allowed its currency to float when it left the ERM in September 1992 and sterling settled at a significantly lower level than its central par value under the ERM. Both of these actions have the same effect, i.e. exports will now appear cheaper to foreigners while imports will appear more expensive to domestic consumers. These measures are thus expenditure switching. In order to assess devaluation or depreciation as a method, we need to consider the elasticities of demand for imports and exports.

The Marshall–Lerner criterion

A. P. Lerner in his book *Economics of Control* applied Alfred Marshall's ideas on elasticity to foreign trade. It is clear that devaluation will increase total earnings from exports only if demand for exports is elastic and, similarly, expenditure on imports will be reduced by devaluation only if demand for imports is elastic. However, the question arises as to how the relative elasticities of demand affect the balance of payments position. The Marshall–Lerner criterion states that devaluation will improve the balance of trade only if the sum of the elasticities of demand for exports and imports is greater than unity. Conversely, a payment surplus would be reduced by revaluation if the same criterion was fulfilled.

We can offer an intuitive proof of the Marshall–Lerner condition as follows. If the UK has a trade deficit, the supply of sterling on the foreign exchange markets is greater than the demand for sterling. If sterling is devalued, the price of exports expressed in sterling will remain constant in the short term and demand for exports will increase because the price of exports expressed in terms of the foreign currencies has fallen. Thus, the demand for sterling on the foreign exchange markets will increase unless demand for exports is perfectly inelastic. Similarly, the sterling price of imports has increased, demand for imports will decrease but total expenditure on imports will only decrease (increase) if the price elasticity of demand for imports is elastic (inelastic).

We can prove the Marshall–Lerner condition by taking the extreme position that the price elasticity of demand for a country's exports is perfectly inelastic (= 0). Given this assumption, devaluation will improve the balance of trade if, and only if, the price elasticity of demand for imports is elastic, i.e. greater than one.

Prior to the 1950s most empirical studies concluded that the Marshall–Lerner condition was barely satisfied. These studies were criticised on the grounds that the estimation techniques used could not distinguish between a movement and a shift of the demand curves (so-called identification problem) and therefore they underestimated the true values of the elasticities. Second, these studies calculated the elasticities over the short run, but as every student of economics knows, the longer the time period the higher the elasticities.

Having corrected for the above weaknesses, the post 1950s empirical studies strongly suggest that the Marshall–Lerner condition is satisfied.

The J-curve

It has frequently been observed that measures taken to rectify a balance of payments deficit have often led to an immediate deterioration in the payments position followed by a subsequent recovery. If we plot this on a graph we obtain the J-curve effect illustrated in Fig. 40.1. A most recent example of the J- curve effect is provided by the UK trade figures following sterling's exit from the ERM. Why should this occur?

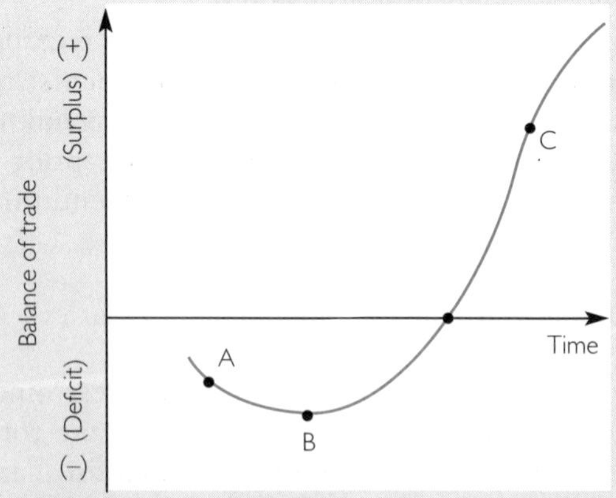

***Fig. 40.1* J-curve effect**
In response to a trade deficit at point A the government depreciates the currency. Initially this causes a further deterioration to point B before moving the balance of trade into surplus (point C).

a) *Crisis of confidence*. Measures taken to rectify a deficit may have the initial effect of creating anxiety, thus leading to an outflow of money which initially leads to a deterioration in the payments position before the (hoped for) recovery.
b) *Insufficient capacity*. If the economy is at, or near, capacity then expenditure-switching policies are unlikely to be successful immediately until capacity can be increased.
c) *Time lags*. Most of the beneficial effects of devaluation are quantitative effects. On the import side we are waiting for the domestic residents to reduce their demand for foreign commodities whilst on the export side we are waiting for foreigners to increase their demand for the devaluing country's commodities. Such quantity effects will take time to materialise. It is estimated that it could take up to three years for 50 per cent and as much as five years for 90 per cent of the benefits of devaluation to come through.

    The disadvantages of devaluation are price effects. The price of imports in terms of the domestic currency will increase whilst the price of exports in terms of the domestic currency will either stay constant in the short run or rise in the long run. These inflationary effects will be immediate. Thus a country that has devalued is likely to see its total expenditure on imports increase at a faster rate than the increase in its total receipts from exports. Thus the balance of trade deteriorates in the short run.

The existence of the J-curve effect is an argument for taking expenditure-reducing measures preparatory to taking expenditure-switching measures.

STUDENT ACTIVITY 40.2

a) What relationship would you expect to see between a country's exchange rate, unemployment rate and balance of payments?
b) Does the recent history of the UK (post September 1992) support your prediction?
c) What explanations can you offer as to why the devaluation of sterling on leaving the ERM did not prove to be inflationary?

The absorption approach

The Keynesian approach to the balance of payments would look on it in terms of whether aggregate demand is sufficient to absorb national output. We write the equilibrium condition for the economy as:

$$Y = C + I + G + (X - M)$$

We can rewrite this as:

$$X - M = Y - C\,(C + I + G)$$

The left-hand side of the equation $(X - M)$ shows the overall payments deficit or surplus. On the other side the expression $C + I + G$ may be recognisable to the reader as the figure for total domestic expenditure (TDE) (see pages 83–4), and we have also identified Y with GDP. Thus we could say that the balance of payments will be in deficit if total domestic expenditure (TDE) is greater than national income (GDP).

From this we can argue that devaluation or depreciation of the currency will be successful only if TDE does not absorb the whole of GDP. For this condition to be fulfilled there must be spare capacity in the economy, otherwise output will not be able to rise to meet the increased demand for exports.

We must now consider the income effect that any depreciation of the currency might have. Any increase in value of exports which is induced will, via the multiplier, create an increase in national income which will in turn create more demand for imports. Thus, even if there is space capacity in the economy, absorption will reduce the effect of any depreciation.

The absorption approach underlines the necessity to have spare capacity in the economy before attempting a depreciation of the currency, demonstrating that it may be necessary to undertake expenditure-reducing policies before expenditure-switching depreciation. The need to combat inflationary pressure created by rising import prices may also argue for the necessity to control factor incomes, e.g. by incomes policy.

This Keynesian approach to the balance of payments concentrates on the current account.

Capital problems

Where the deficit problems occur on the capital account different policy measures may be called for. The government needs to take action to stem the outflow of capital and/or to stimulate the inflow of capital. In the short term capital inflows can be encouraged by raising interest rates. However, this is expensive and is also potentially dangerous if inflation is depreciating the external value of the currency and calling forth even higher interest rates.

Exchange control is a method by which capital flows may be regulated. Many countries have restrictions on the exchange of currency for investment purposes. The UK, however, abolished all exchange controls in 1979 and thereby considerably increased the outflow of capital. The outflow of capital creates inflows on current account in future years. However, if it occurs at a time when the economy is depressed, as it did in the UK during the early 1980s, it can be argued that it has very bad effects. First, it may starve the domestic economy of funds and, second, it is being used to develop the economies of competitors. Thus in future years the economy may have a deficit from importing goods which its own capital has produced.

A monetarist view

The effect of a payments deficit or surplus will depend upon the type of exchange rate policy being pursued. If a country is on a fixed exchange rate, a surplus will cause an expansion of the money supply because the government will be forced to buy up its currency on foreign exchange markets to prevent the exchange rate rising. A deficit would have the opposite effect. However, with a floating exchange rate any imbalance would be adjusted by appreciation or depreciation of the currency. Since monetarists place great emphasis on the control of the money supply, it is easy to see why they favour floating exchange rates.

However, it would be more strictly monetarist if we approach the payments position from the point of view of how changes in the money supply affect the balance of payments. The monetarist view is that the balance of payments is a monetary problem. The economy will be in equilibrium if the total demand for money (L) is equal to the total supply (M). The supply of money, however, is the result of that which is created domestically plus any net inflow resulting from a payments surplus or minus any outflow resulting from a deficit. According to this view, a too-rapid increase of the money supply will cause a payments deficit because the supply of money will exceed the demand because some of this money will be used to buy imports. Thus, if a country wishes to maintain its payments in equilibrium it must control its money supply. Therefore a monetarist prescription for a stable balance of payments situation would be one in which there is a regime of floating exchange rates coupled with tight control of the money supply.

Summary

1 The traditional pattern of the UK's overseas trade is to import raw materials and to export manufactures. This has changed; on the export side the UK is now an exporter of oil and also relies upon tertiary exports such as banking, while on the import side there is an increasing tendency to import manufactured goods.
2 The terms of trade measures the relative prices of exports and imports.
3 The balance of payments is a summary of all a nation's dealings with the rest of the world.
4 Both deficits and surpluses on the balance of payments create problems.
5 Cures for a deficit can be categorised as expenditure reducing and expenditure switching.
6 The effect of a depreciation in the external value of a currency upon a country's balance of payments depends upon the combined elasticities of demand for exports and imports.
7 The Keynesian view of the balance of payments is termed the absorption approach.
8 Monetarists believe that the origins of balance of payments problems are monetary and stress the need for floating exchange rates and control of the money supply.

Questions

1 The last Conservative government was very reluctant to devalue sterling in the summer of 1992, claiming that 'devaluation was fool's gold'. Explain why devaluation may be harmful to the balance of trade in the short run.

2 With reference to the absorption approach explain why the conditions prevailing in the UK economy in September 1992 were favourable to devaluation.

3 According to the absorption approach what are the effects of the following on the balance of trade?

a) The country's marginal propensity to save increases.

b) The government increases public expenditure on domestic goods and services.

4 Compare and contrast Keynesian and monetarist ideas of the balance of payments.

5 Assume that a country is in balance of payments equilibrium on current account such that total current debits are \$40 000 million and total current credits are \$40 000 million. Demonstrate that, as a result of the Marshall–Lerner criterion, a depreciation of 10 per cent in the country's exchange rate, *ceteris paribus*, will improve the balance of payments condition to a surplus of \$4800 million if the combined elasticities of demand for exports and imports is 12($E_X + E_M = 12$).

6 In your view, which is worse: a balance of payments surplus or a deficit?

Data response A
Atlantica's balance of payments

The figures in Table 40.8 are taken from the annual balance of payments statement of Atlantica. Prepare Atlantica's balance of payments to show:

a) the balance of visible trade;
b) the invisible balance;
c) the balance on current account;
d) transactions in external assets and liabilities;
e) the balancing item.

Table 40.8

Items	*\$m*
Capital transactions	+750
Banking earnings	+1 200
Insurance earnings	+500
Interest paid abroad	–300
Interest received from abroad	+900
Exports of manufactures (FOB)	+18 000
Exports of raw materials and fuel (FOB)	+8 000
Imports of manufactures (FOB)	–15 000
Imports of raw materials and fuel (FOB)	–14 000
Shipping earnings (net)	+250
Tourist earnings	+500
Change in reserves	–1 200

Data response B
The invisible men

Read carefully the following article, by Sir Hugh Bidwell, which appeared in the *Financial Times* in July 1991 and study the information in Table 40.9. Having done this attempt the questions which follow.

It is a curious fact that economic commentators, in reviewing a country's trade performance, generally do so solely in terms of trade in goods.

It is even odder that a sector of the economy that provides more than half of Britain's foreign earnings, and has consistently produced a balance of payments surplus for nearly 200 years, does so largely unnoticed by the general public.

The term 'invisible exports' has been in use for more than 100 years and yet is still a source of mystery.

Invisibles include not only straightforward services such as banking, or insurance transactions conducted for foreigners, but also spending in Britain by tourists and businessmen, their use of British ships and aircraft, the fees and commissions paid to British intermediaries or consultants and the return on loans and investments in foreign enterprises.

Invisible exports are many, varied and growing. In 10 years they have risen from 23 per cent to 28 per cent of total world trade, and the Group of Seven countries in 1988 accounted for 65.2 per cent of world invisible exports and 62.8 per cent of invisible imports.

It is big business. As [Table 40.9] shows, Britain's invisible trade represents by far the largest percentage of gross national product within the G7 countries.

A growing awareness of the importance of services to the world economy led to their inclusion, for the first time, in the current Uruguay round of GATT trade talks that began in 1986 and – given sufficient political stimulus – are hopefully nearing completion.

Many believe that a multilateral accord with legally binding rules, covering all service trading activities around the world, is a cornerstone for future development. It will encourage more investment in overseas markets and expand the range of services and innovative products offered.

A modern services sector is the key to national competitiveness and to economic growth and development. This is no less so for the European Community, which is rapidly moving towards its goal of a single market in goods and services.

London's markets and Britain's financial and technical skills are readily available, and all the more valuable for the length of time over which they have been developed and the breadth of international experience acquired.

London dealers and experts are at work as Tokyo, Hong Kong and Singapore prepare to close, and they bridge the two time zones through a multitude of contacts.

After lunch in London, the other key time zone is bridged, first with North America's eastern seaboard (principally New York), later with Chicago and the Midwest, and later still with the Pacific coast centres such as Los Angeles, San Francisco and Vancouver.

Britain's reliance on invisible earnings and London's position as an international financial centre demand strong leadership, and this is what British Invisibles seeks to provide. The Economic Summit is an opportunity for strong leadership on the world stage and, as a former Lord Mayor, I welcome it to London.

***Table 40.9* Invisible trade as a percentage of GNP and total receipts in 1988 for G7 countries**

Country	*% GNP*	*% Total receipts*
Canada	4.5	15.7
France	8.7	34.2
Germany	5.6	17.9
Italy	5.1	24.9
Japan	2.9	27.9
UK	17.3	50.0
USA	3.9	37.3

Source: IMF

Now answer the following questions.

1 Describe as fully as possible what is meant by 'invisibles' and state which items are significant as far as the UK is concerned.
2 Contrast the significance of invisibles to the UK with that of another nation at a different stage of economic development.
3 Trace the development of the invisibles sector in the UK's balance of payments.
4 Assess the role of the exchange rate and interest rates in the determination of the UK's balance of payments.
5 How is the role of the City of London likely to change as the Single European Market develops?

41 Exchange rates

Learning outcomes

After reading this chapter you will be able to:

- Explain the relationship between a country's trade flows and its exchange rate.
- Analyse the strengths and weaknesses of different exchange rate regimes.
- Appreciate the importance of non-trade factors in determining the exchange rate.
- Understand the UK's current exchange rate position.

The subject of international trade is complicated by the existence of different currencies. Money is a complicating factor in studying national economies but in the international sphere we have to contend with different types of exchange rate, exchange control and different units of currency. In this chapter we will examine the different regimes which exist and the problems associated with them.

Exchange rates and nationalism

The problem of exchange rates is often complicated by national pride. Many countries have wasted vast sums of money supporting unrealistic rates. Consider the vocabulary which is used if the exchange rate is high: we are said to have 'a strong pound'; conversely, a low rate is described as 'weak' and the newspapers often speak of 'defending the pound'. These are very emotive words. However, what is important is not that the exchange rate is high or low but that it should be correct for the circumstances.

The theory of exchange rates

Although exchange rates are often complicated by government interference, we will first examine how exchange rates are set in a free market situation. This is normally termed a floating, or freely fluctuating, exchange rate.

An exchange rate is simply the price at which one currency can be traded for another. For example, if the exchange rate is £1 = DM4 then one pound will exchange for four Deutschmarks or one Deutschmark costs 25 pence.

For our purposes we will define the exchange rate as the amount of the foreign currency that may be bought for 1 unit of the domestic currency.

In a world where there is no government interference, no international capital flows, and no trade in services, if people from the UK wish to buy foreign goods they must obtain the foreign currency with which to effect the purchase. It is no good, for example, offering French vintners pounds sterling for wine; they will demand francs. Similarly, if foreigners wish to buy UK goods UK manufacturers will demand pounds in return for them. The exchange rate will be determined by the demand and supply for exports and imports.

The exchange rate for any particular country is the result of the interaction of export demand and import supply.

In Fig. 41.1 we have measured all foreign currencies in dollars. Thus, foreigners wishing to buy UK goods offer dollars for them; this, therefore, constitutes the demand for sterling. Conversely, UK people offer pounds in order to purchase foreign goods. Thus the demand for imports constitutes the supply of pounds to the foreign exchange market.

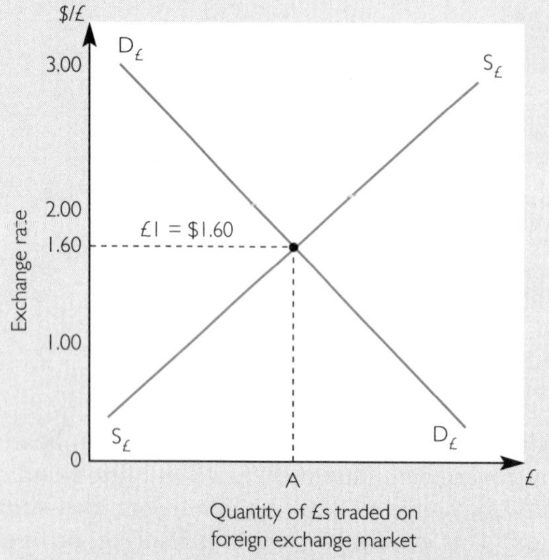

***Fig. 41.1* An exchange rate of £1 = $1.60**
Behind the demand curve lies the USA's desire to buy UK exports, while behind the supply curve is the UK's desire to buy the USA's exports.

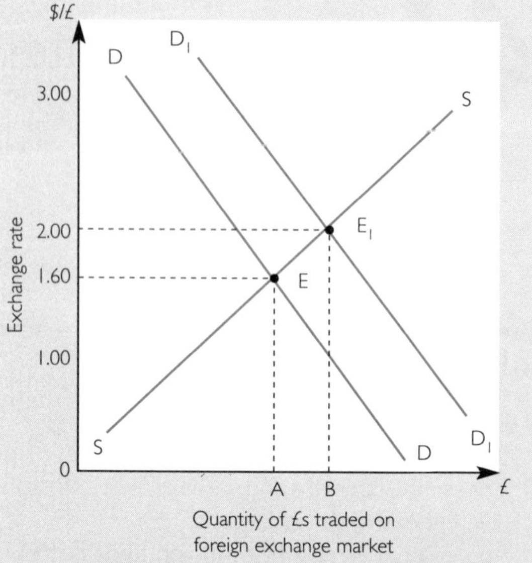

***Fig. 41.2* Effect of an increase in demand on the exchange rate**
The effect of the shift of the demand curve from DD to D_1D_1 increases the exchange rate from £1 = $1.60 to £1 = $2. $1 now only costs 50p.

The exchange rate is now determined like any other price. In Fig. 41.1 we can see that the exchange rate is £1 = $1.60 or that $1 costs 62.5 pence. It is, therefore, possible for us to analyse changes in exchange rates in the same manner as other prices.

Simple changes

If we consider any one factor then we can illustrate it as a shift rightwards or leftwards of either the demand curve or the supply curve. Figure 41.2 shows the effect of an increase in demand for UK exports; foreigners are therefore offering more money so that demand for sterling increases. Thus the price of foreign currency has declined and the pound is said to have appreciated. If foreign currency becomes more expensive the pound is said to have depreciated.

An appreciation in the rate of exchange could therefore be caused by either:
a) an increased demand for UK exports; or
b) a decreased UK demand for imports.
Alternatively a depreciation in the rate of exchange could be caused by:
a) an increased UK demand for imports;
b) a reduced foreign demand for UK exports.

Complex changes

Many factors may change simultaneously and, therefore, the effect upon the exchange rate may be complex. For example, the advent of North Sea oil had at least two major effects upon the UK exchange rate. First, oil reduced the need for imports, thus moving the supply curve to the left, while, second, it became an export, thus moving the demand curve to the right. This is illustrated in Fig. 41.3.

The effect of inflation

Let us assume the UK has inflation but Germany has not. This will mean that the sterling price of UK goods will rise. Thus, other things being equal, the demand for UK goods will decrease, while German goods will now appear cheaper to Britons who will, therefore, buy more. Thus the

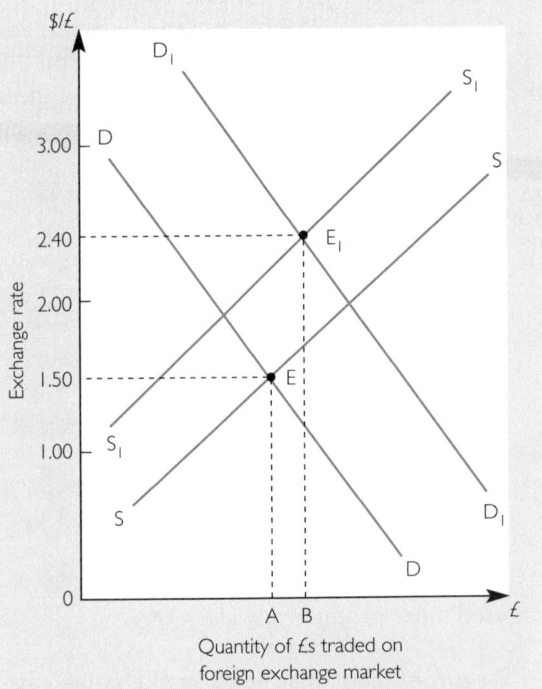

***Fig. 41.3* Effect of North Sea oil**
The exploitation of North Sea oil both increased the demand for £s as oil was exported and decreased the supply of £s as the UK imported less oil. Thus the exchanged rate increased from £1 = \$1.50 to £1 = \$2.40.

demand for sterling will decrease while the demand for Deutschmarks will increase, and both the factors will cause a depreciation in the external value of sterling. If, on the other hand, the domestic rate of inflation is lower than that abroad, these factors may be expected to work in reverse. (See also page 561)

STUDENT ACTIVITY 41.1

Explain what, if anything, will happen to sterling's exchange rate if the following events occur:

a) The Bank of England raises interest rates.
b) Foreign tastes change adversely towards UK goods and services.
c) The productivity of UK workers rises at a faster rate than our major competitors.
d) The Labour government announces its intention to join the Single European Currency by 1 January 1999.

Non-trade influences

We have, so far, discussed exchange rates as being determined by the demand for imports and exports. However, exchange rates are influenced by many other things such as invisible trade, interest rates, capital movements, speculation and government activities.

Confidence

A vital factor in determining exchange rates is confidence. This is especially so because most large companies 'buy forward', i.e. they purchase foreign currency ahead of their needs. They are therefore very sensitive to factors which may influence future rates. Key indicators are such things as inflation and government policy. Thus the exchange rate at any particular moment is more likely to reflect the anticipated situation in a country rather than the present one.

STUDENT ACTIVITY 41.2

a) If the current £/DM exchange rate is DM2.9, whilst the one-month forward rate is DM2.85, which currency should speculators buy/sell forward if they expect the £/DM exchange rate one month from now to be DM2.80?
b) Explain why the value of sterling appreciated dramatically during the first eight months of 1997.
c) On 7 August 1997 the Bank of England lowered UK interest rates by one-quarter of 1 per cent. The £/DM exchange rate fell to its lowest level for a month. How do you account for this?

The exchange rate debate

It is only since the early 1970s that floating exchange rates have become common. We will here consider the advantages and disadvantages of them.

Arguments in favour of floating exchange rates

a) *Automatic stabilisation.* Any balance of payments disequilibrium should be rectified by a change in the exchange rate; for example, if a country has a balance of payments deficit then, other things being equal, the country's currency should depreciate. This would make the country's exports cheaper, thus increasing demand, while making imports dearer and decreasing demand. The balance of payments therefore will be brought back into equilibrium. Conversely, a balance of payments surplus should be eliminated by an appreciation of the currency.

b) *Freeing internal policy.* Where a country has a floating exchange rate a balance of payments deficit can be rectified by a change in the external price of the currency. However, if a fixed exchange rate is adopted, then reducing a deficit could involve a general deflationary policy for the whole economy, resulting in unpleasant consequences such as increased unemployment. Thus a floating exchange rate allows a government to pursue internal policy objectives such as growth and full employment without external constraints. It was these latter reasons which caused the Heath government to float the pound in 1972.

c) *Absence of crisis.* The periods of fixed exchange rates were frequently characterised by crisis as pressure was put on a currency to devalue or revalue. The fact that with floating exchange rates such changes occur automatically has removed the element of crisis from international relations.

d) *Management.* Floating exchange rates have still left governments considerable freedom to manipulate the external value of their currency to their own advantage.

e) *Flexibility.* Changes in world trade since the first oil crisis of 1973 have been immense and have caused great changes in the value of currencies. It is difficult to imagine how these could have been dealt with under a system of fixed exchange rates.

f) *Avoiding inflation.* A floating exchange rate helps to insulate a country from inflation elsewhere. In the first place, if a country were on a fixed exchange rate it would 'import' inflation by way of higher import prices. Second, a country with a payments surplus and a fixed exchange rate would tend to 'import' inflation from deficit countries (see page 560).

g) *Lower reserves.* Floating exchange rates should mean that there is a smaller need to maintain large reserves to defend the currency. These reserves can, therefore, be used more productively elsewhere.

Arguments against floating exchange rates

a) *Uncertainty.* The fact that currencies change in value from day to day introduces a large element of uncertainty into trade. Sellers may be unsure of how much money they will receive when they sell goods abroad. Some of this uncertainty may be reduced by companies buying currency ahead in forward exchange contracts. However, the fact remains that this is costly and only short-term exchange rate risks can be hedged in this way.

b) *Lack of investment.* The uncertainty induced by floating exchange rates may discourage foreign investment.

c) *Speculation.* The day-to-day changes in exchange rates may encourage speculative movements of 'hot money' from country to country, thereby making changes in exchange rates greater.

d) *Lack of discipline.* The need to maintain an exchange rate imposes a discipline upon an economy. It is possible that with a floating exchange rate such problems as inflation may be ignored until they have reached crisis proportions.

Research by the Group of 30 in 1980 concluded that as far as large business was concerned, the system of floating exchange rates had not proved a major obstacle to the development of trade.

Fixed exchange rates

The gold standard

A gold standard occurs when a unit of a country's currency is valued in terms of a specific amount of gold. The Gold Standard Act of 1870 fixed the value of the pound sterling such that 1 ounce of gold cost £3.17s.1½d. This remained constant until 1914.

There are several types of gold standard. A full gold standard is where gold coins circulate freely in the economy and paper money is fully convertible into gold. Such was the case in the UK until 1914. A gold bullion standard is when gold is available in bullion from (bars) for foreign trade only. The UK adopted such a standard in 1925 which lasted until 1931. A gold exchange standard occurs when a country fixes the value of its currency, not in gold, but in terms of another currency which is on the gold standard. For example, from 1925 to 1931 most Commonwealth and Empire countries fixed their exchange rates by quoting their currency against sterling.

After the Second World War the USA maintained the price of gold at \$35 = 1 ounce of gold. However, in 1971 the USA was forced to abandon this and it is unlikely that a gold standard of any type will be readopted in the near future.

The gold standard and the balance of payments

One of the most notable features of the gold standard is that a country operating it will experience automatic rectification of any balance of payments disequilibrium.

Consider what would happen if a country had a payments deficit. In order to pay for the deficit, gold would be exported, for gold was, and is, almost universally accepted. However, this would reduce the money supply in the country because the money supply is tied to gold. The result of this would be deflation. Deflation would contract the economy and, therefore, mean rising unemployment which would reduce consumers' ability to buy goods, including imports. Deflation would depress the domestic price of goods. Thus consumers would tend to buy more home-produced goods. Imports would stay the same absolute price but would appear relatively dearer. For these reasons consumers would buy less imports whereas foreigners would buy more of the country's exports because they are cheaper. Other things being equal, this should bring the country's payments back into equilibrium. The effect of a surplus would be eliminated by this process working in reverse through inflation.

The reader will recall that floating exchange rates also automatically regulate the balance of payments. However, there is an important difference from the gold standard. With the gold standard an imbalance is rectified by changes in the internal level of economic activity and prices. With floating exchange rates the balance is brought about by a change in the external value of the currency.

Pegged exchange rates

When a country is not on a gold standard but wishes to have a fixed exchange rate this can be done by the government 'pegging' the exchange rate, i.e. a rate is fixed and then guaranteed by the government. For example, after the UK left the gold standard in 1931 the government fixed the price of sterling against the dollar, in 1932, and made the rate of £1 = \$4.03 effective by agreeing to buy or sell any amount of currency at this price.

Exchange control

One of the methods by which a government can attempt to make the stated exchange rate effective is through exchange control. Exchange control refers to restrictions placed upon the ability of citizens to exchange foreign currency freely; for example, in 1966 the UK government would allow Britons to convert only £50 into foreign currency for holidays abroad. The Mitterrand government in France imposed similar restrictions in 1983. A more serious restriction in the UK was the dollar premium. Under this arrangement any Briton wishing to change money into foreign currency for investment overseas had to pay a premium of 25 per cent. The Conservative government abolished all forms of exchange control in 1979. It was agreed in 1988 that, as part of the unification of EC markets, in 1992 there would be free movement of capital between EC nations. However, people may still find themselves subject to restrictions by other countries.

The adjustable peg

This was the system of fixed exchange rates operated by the members of the International Monetary Fund from 1947 to 1971. Members agreed not to let the value of their currencies vary by more than 1 per cent either side of a parity. Thus, for example, the UK's exchange rate in 1949 was £1 = $2.80 and sterling was allowed to appreciate to £1 = $2.82 or depreciate to £1 = $2.78. The system was termed 'adjustable' because it was possible for a country to devalue or revalue in the event of serious disequilibrium.

Some countries operated a so-called 'crawling peg'. Under this system a currency was allowed to depreciate (or appreciate) by a small percentage each year. Thus if, for example, a limit of 2 per cent was set and the currency devalued by this amount in year 1, it would be allowed to devalue by another 2 per cent in year 2, and so on.

Since the break-up of the adjustable peg system various other attempts have been made to fix exchange rates. These are discussed later in the chapter.

Fixed rates evaluated

The chief advantage of fixed exchange rates is that they give certainty to international trade and investors. Price signals therefore become easier to interpret by all economic agents promoting greater economic efficiency both in consumption and production. It is also said that they reduce speculation. Fixed exchange rates also impose discipline on domestic economic policies because, in the event of an adverse balance of payments, deflationary measures will have to be taken to restore the situation.

On the other hand, if an exchange rate is fixed incorrectly then this will cause intense speculation against the currency. It can often be an expensive job defending a fixed exchange rate, requiring large reserves of foreign exchange. Defending a currency may also involve raising interest rates, and this can be both costly and damaging to the domestic economy. In September 1992 the Bank of England is reputed to have spent £20 billion in its futile attempts to stem the speculative flow against sterling and raised interest rates from 10 per cent to 15 per cent. It is possible, therefore, that a fixed exchange rate may result in domestic policy being subordinated to the external situation.

The equilibrium exchange rate

We have considered some of the factors which can influence exchange rates. However, there is no completely satisfactory theory which explains how the equilibrium rate of exchange is established. In Fig. 41.1 we might make the assumption that the exchange rate is in equilibrium and that imbalances will cause shifts to new equilibriums. However, we still would like to explain why the exchange rate occurs at the level it does, i.e. why is it £1 = $2 and not £1 = $3 and so on? The Swedish economist Gustav Cassell, building on the idea of the classical economists and mercantilists, attempted to explain this in terms of purchasing power parity.

The theory of purchasing power parity

This theory suggests, for example, that the exchange rate would be in equilibrium if a situation existed where the same 'basket' of goods which costs £100 in the UK cost DM310 in Germany and the exchange rate were £1 = DM3.10. In order to do this we would have to discount transport costs and tariffs. Thus a measure we might use could appear as:

$$\text{Purchasing power parity} = \frac{\text{German consumer price index}}{\text{UK consumer price index}}$$

From this we might deduce that a doubling of the general price level in the UK while prices in Germany remained constant would lead to the exchange rate being cut by one-half. However, no such strict proportionality exists. There are a number of reasons for this:

a) The 'basket' of goods which determines domestic price levels is different from those which are traded internationally. Items which are important domestically, such as housing, bread, rail fares, etc., do not influence foreign trade significantly.
b) Exchange rates are influenced by many other factors such as capital movements, speculation and interest rates.
c) Confidence is also a very significant factor in determining exchange rates.

Thus, we may conclude that although domestic price levels do influence exchange rates, there is no strict proportionality.

Exchange rate stability

The possibility exists that an exchange rate can be inherently unstable. To explain this we must consider the effect of the elasticity of demand for imports upon the supply of sterling to the foreign exchange market. Consider the situation of a German wine producer who sells wine in Germany at DM8 per bottle. The same wine is sold in the UK at £2 per bottle when the exchange rate is £1 = DM4. However, if the exchange rate were to change to £1 = DM2 then, in order to recover the same DM8 per bottle, the UK price must now increase to £4 per bottle.

The effect of this price change upon the supply of sterling to the foreign exchange market is determined by the elasticity of demand for wine in the UK. If demand is elastic people reduce wine consumption substantially and the supply of sterling falls. This is shown in Fig. 41.4 (a). If demand is unitary the amount of sterling offered remains constant and thus the supply curve is vertical. This is shown in Fig. 41.4 (b). However, if demand is inelastic then, despite the price rise, people go on drinking and, therefore, in response to a price rise the supply of pounds increases and we thus have a perverse supply curve. In Fig. 41.4 (c) you can see that, as the exchange rate has fallen from £1 = DM4 to £1 = DM2, i.e. the price of wine in the UK has increased, the supply of sterling has expanded from OA to OB.

In Fig. 41.5 we examine the possible effect of such a perverse supply curve upon the equilibrium rate of exchange. Here, as the result of a trade surplus, there has been an increase in the demand for sterling from foreigners. You can see that the result of this increased demand is a fall in the exchange rate. Such a perverse result is likely to bring instability to the foreign exchange market. For stability to be achieved it is neces-

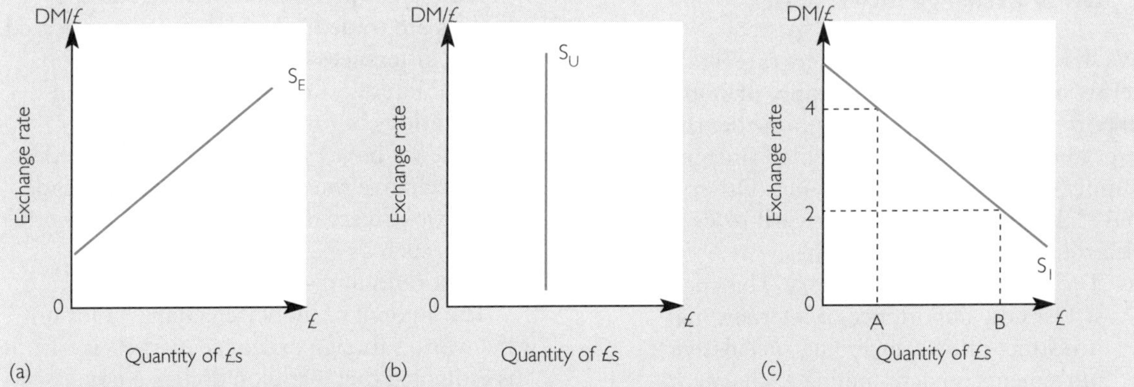

Fig. 41.4 Elasticity of demand for imports and the supply of £s
(a) When demand for imported is elastic this gives a normal supply curve. (b) When demand is unitary the supply of £s remains constant. (c) When demand is inelastic this results in a downward-sloping supply curve. This means that as the £ depreciates from £1 = DM4 to £1 = DM2 the supply of £s on the foreign exchange market increases.

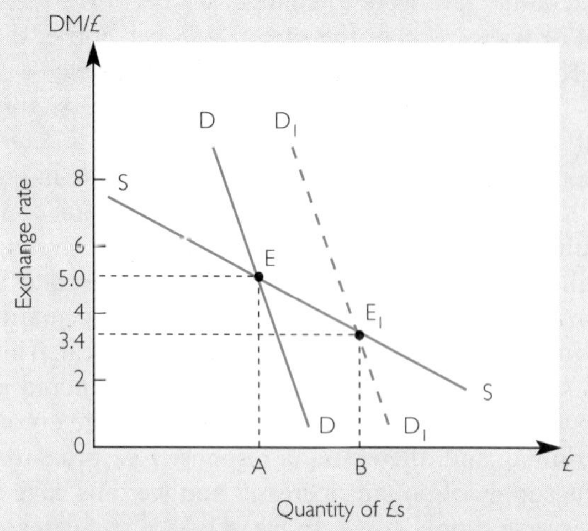

***Fig. 41.5* Effect of an increase in demand with a perverse supply curve**

Despite the fact that the demand for £s has increased from DD to D_1D_1 the exchange rate has fallen from £1 = DM5 to £1 = DM3.4.

sary for the Marshall–Lerner criterion to be fulfilled, i.e. the combined elasticities of demand of foreigners' demand for UK exports and UK demand for imports is greater than unity (see page 562). Under such circumstances a floating exchange rate should correct a balance of payments disequilibrium.

Other exchange rate theories

We have discussed exchange rate stability in terms of the demand and supply of imports and exports. However, as we mentioned earlier, there are many other factors which influence the supply and demand for sterling. Other theories have, therefore, been put forward to explain the determination of exchange rates.

a) *The portfolio balance theory.* This theory stresses the importance of international investment flows, including speculative movements, in determining exchange rates. It assumes that large investors are aware of investment opportunities world-wide. They therefore diversify their portfolios to gain higher yield in different countries. For example, if the yield on, say, Treasury bills in London were to increase then we might expect funds to flow in from other countries. *Ceteris paribus*, this would cause sterling to appreciate until such a time that there was no advantage to be gained from switching funds into pounds. (See also the discussion of portfolio balance in Chapter 38.)

   The huge amount of highly liquid funds in international markets makes interest rates a key factor in determining exchange rates. However, expectations of future interest rates and/or exchange rates may be more important than existing rates. This leads us to the theory of interest rate parity.

b) *The theory of interest rate parity.* In the era of floating exchange rates much currency is bought 'forward'. For example, a company which may need large quantities of Deutschmarks in six months' time may place an order for them now and both buyer and seller agree to exchange the currency in six months' time at the rate agreed today. This rate may be higher or lower than today's 'spot' rate depending upon expectations of the future. Needless to say, there is a very large speculative market in currency futures.

   The interest rate parity theory gets its name from the idea that differences in interest rates between countries will be reflected in the 'discount' or 'premium' at which currency futures are traded. The picture is complicated by the differences between real and nominal rates of interest, i.e. rates of inflation and expectations of rates of inflation.

   Once we have progressed beyond the idea that exchange rates are determined by trade flows we can see the vital importance of other factors such as expectations, confidence, interest rates and speculation.

   The amount of money changing hands on the world's foreign exchange markets is vast. It is estimated that 1 trillion dollars a day ($1 000 000 000 000) is exchanged by dealers, selling dollars for pounds, francs for Deutchmarks, etc. Furthermore, only 5 per cent of the deals struck are for trade reasons. Another 15 per cent are due to foreign direct investment, and 80 per cent are purely speculative. People are simply gambling on whether currencies will go up or down.

Thus we can see that the determination and explanation of the equilibrium exchange rate is a complex topic. It is very difficult to give a simple answer to the straightforward question, 'What is the correct exchange rate?'

STUDENT ACTIVITY 41.3

A UK exporter has won a major contract to supply a firm in the USA with equipment to the value of $3 million. When the equipment is dispatched and the invoice raised for $3 million, the sterling/dollar exchange rate is $1.60. By the time payment is made the sterling/dollar exchange rate is $1.70.

a) How much has the UK firm lost as a result of the exchange rate movement?
b) What, if anything, could the UK firm have done to avoid this exchange rate risk?
c) What factors should a firm take into consideration in deciding whether or not to hedge a foreign exchange risk?

Recent developments

The operation of the International Monetary Fund is discussed in detail in the next chapter. We will here consider how developments since the early 1970s have influenced the UK economy.

Dirty floating

Following the USA's abandonment of the gold standard in 1971 and the failure of the Smithsonian Agreement, the UK floated the pound in 1972. The objective of the government was that the development of the economy should be free to continue without the constraint of having to maintain a fixed exchange rate. Although ostensibly the government allowed the exchange rate to find its own level, it in fact interfered to manipulate the exchange rate. This is termed managed flexibility, or, more memorably, a 'dirty float'.

Figure 41.6 illustrates government intervention in the foreign exchange market. Left to itself the exchange rate would be £1 = $1 but the government forces the rate up to £1 = $1.90 by buying sterling on the foreign exchange market, thus shifting the demand curve to the right.

The government agency responsible for intervention in the foreign exchange market is the Exchange Equalisation Account. This was set up in 1932 following the UK's abandonment of the gold standard. It is controlled by the Treasury and managed by the Bank of England. Its object is to buy and sell sterling for gold or foreign exchange in order to stabilise the exchange rate. In times of fixed exchange rates the Account has sometimes lost large sums of money defending an unrealistic rate. Since the float of 1972 the operation of the Account has been more muted, but it is its actions which give rise to the term 'dirty float'. Nearly all governments operate a similar system. The Account's operations should not be

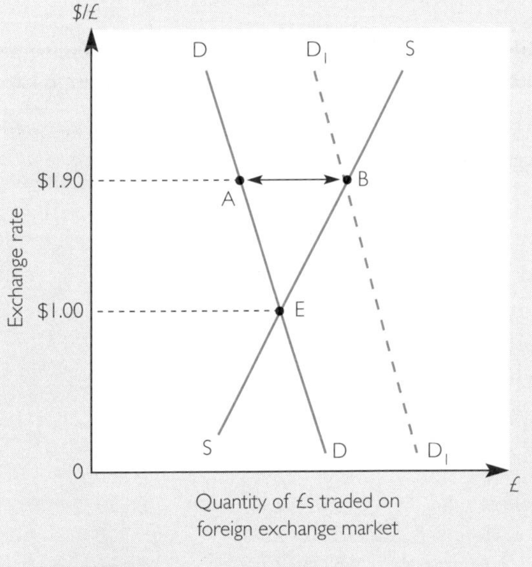

***Fig. 41.6* Dirty floating**
The government forces up the exchange rate from £1 = $1 to £1 = $1.90 by purchasing AB £s on the foreign exchange market.

confused with the official financing of the balance of payments.

Trade-weighted indices

When countries are on a gold standard there is a simple way to show the value of their currencies. However, with floating exchange rates it becomes difficult. The most widely known measure of the UK exchange rate is that against the dollar, but the dollar itself is floating. It is possible, therefore, for the pound to be rising against the value of the dollar while falling against other currencies such as the yen. Trade-weighted indices are an attempt to overcome this problem by providing a measure of a currency in terms of a number of currencies which are weighted in accordance with their importance in trade to the country whose currency is being measured. Table 41.1 shows the Bank of England trade-weighted index, known as the sterling effective exchange rate, based on 1990. Also in Table 41.1 is the dollar and deutchmark exchange rate. You can see that the two do not always move together. Additionally, Table 41.1 shows the considerable change in the fortunes of sterling in recent years.

Table 41.1 **Sterling/US dollar, sterling/deutschmark exchange rate and sterling's effective exchange rate**

Annual average	*US$ to £*	*DM to £*	*Sterling's effective exchange rate (1990 = 100)*
1985	1.2962	3.7829	111.2
1986	1.4671	3.1845	101.4
1987	1.6391	2.9403	99.3
1988	1.7812	3.1235	105.3
1989	1.6397	3.0795	102.3
1990	1.785	2.8742	100.0
1991	1.7698	2.925	100.75
1992	1.7661	2.878*	96.9
		2.5042**	
1993	1.50	2.483	88.9
1994	1.5321	2.483	89.2
1995	1.5782	2.261	84.8
1996 (September)	1.5366	2.299	84.6

*Average for the eight months prior to sterling's exit from the ERM
**Average for the four months following sterling's exit from the ERM
Source: Bank of England

Attempts at stabilisation

After the turbulence in currency markets during the 1970s various attempts were made in the 1980s to bring stability to exchange rates. These were mainly confined to the Western industrialised nations. The EU established the European Monetary System (EMS) which effectively fixes the rates of exchange between Common Market countries. The Plaza Agreement (1985) and the Louvre Accord (1987) attempted to limit the fluctuation in exchange rates between the G5 and G7 nations, respectively. (These systems are discussed more fully in the next chapter.)

The cooperation between the leading industrial nations limited fluctuations. The growing importance of Germany and Japan meant that exchange rates of currencies against the yen and the Deutschmark became significant indicators as well as rates against the dollar. At the end of the 1980s the UK became a full member of the EMS, which limited the fluctuations of the pound against other EC currencies.

The UK: floating experience 1972–90 and 1992–7

How well has the floating rate worked for the UK? When the UK floated sterling in 1972 the exchange rate was £1 = $2.60; it reached a low of £1 = $1.55 in October 1976, an effective devaluation of 40.4 per cent. This massive drop was not altogether unwelcome to the UK government, who believed it would make exports more competitive. It should be remembered, however, that increasing the price of imports will also increase inflation. It is reckoned that a 4 per cent rise in import prices causes 1 per cent domestic inflation. The UK government, however, seemed happy to settle for a rate of about £1 = $1.70, but no sooner had the rate stabilised around this level than the prospects of North Sea oil brought money flooding into London and the exchange rate soared, much to the displeasure of the government. It appeared that a pound that floated upwards was almost as difficult to live with as a sinking one.

The end of the 1970s saw the UK with a large balance of payments surplus and an exchange rate almost back to the 1971 level. The 'overvalued' pound had UK industry screaming for relief. The pound then collapsed, despite a sound balance of payments, and in 1983 dropped below £1 = $1.50 for the first time.

This fall continued until in February 1985 the pound dipped briefly below £1 = $1.10. It was during this crisis that the Bank of England reintroduced MLR for one day in an attempt to stop the fall. This crisis for the pound was caused both by the weakness of the UK economy and by the strength of the dollar.

The recovery of the pound over the period 1985–8 was due both to increased confidence in the UK economy and to the weakness of the dollar. However, at the same time that the pound was rising in value against the dollar the balance of payments was moving into record deficits. The prospect for the pound was, therefore, uncertain. In addition, the UK inflation rate was increasing at a much faster rate than our major competitors. It had reached double figures by the time the UK joined the ERM in October 1990 (10.9 per cent). Sterling's membership of the ERM was short-lived and in September 1992 it was forced out of the ERM (see Chapter 42).

When the UK allowed sterling to float in September 1992, its value against the Deutschmark declined significantly. It stabilised at a rate of DM2.483 for 1993 and 1994 and then reached an all-time low in 1995 of DM2.261. It stayed at this level for 1996 but its fortunes reversed in 1997 when it rose to DM3.07 in July 1997. Sterling's dramatic rise against the other EU currencies is to a large extent due to the belief on the foreign exchange markets that attempts to establish a European single currency by 1 January 1999 are likely to end in failure and thus sterling is seen as a 'safe haven'. Against the dollar sterling declined in 1993 from its 1992 average level of $1.7661 to $1.5. Since then it has remained relatively stable and in August 1997 stands at $1.58.

We may conclude our discussion of floating exchange rates by saying that there have undoubtedly been unprecedented fluctuations in value, but there have also been unprecedented circumstances and it is doubtful if fixed exchange rates could have coped better with the situation. For the UK, as for the rest of the members of the EU, the question of the single currency is upmost on their minds right now.

Summary

1. The problem of exchange rates is complicated by national pride.
2. A floating exchange rate is the result of the interaction of export demand and import supply.
3. Exchange rates are also influenced by many non-trade factors such as interest rates.
4. The chief advantage of floating rates is that they free internal policy from external constraints; however, this also increases uncertainty.
5. There are many types of fixed exchange rate. Fixed rates increase certainty in trade but can be expensive to defend.
6. The equilibrium exchange rate may be unstable.
7. The theory of purchasing power parity attempts to explain the exchange rate in terms of the relative values of currencies.
8. The UK now operates a system of managed flexibility or a 'dirty float'.
9. The problems of floating have brought new measures such as trade-weighted indices and the EMU.
10. Since floating there have been great changes in the value of sterling but there have also been big changes in international circumstances.

Questions

1. The behaviour of sterling against the dollar has been at variance with the behaviour of sterling against the Deutschmark over the period 1993 till August 1997. What explanations can you offer for this?
2. What have been the effects of a floating pound since September 1992 on the UK economy?
3. Discuss the arguments for and against floating exchange rates.

4 A host of currency strategists were claiming in early August 1997 that sterling was overvalued and that some correction to the pound's overvaluation was inevitable. How can one attempt to establish whether or not a currency is at its equilibrium value?

5 Assess the weaknesses of the theory of purchasing power parity.

Data response A
Interest rate parity

The rate of return on a three-month UK Treasury bond is 10 per cent whereas the rate of return on a similar US bond is 5 per cent. The £/$ spot rate stands at $1.60. The three-month forward rate is $ 1.55.

1 Which bond is the most attractive one to a potential investor?
2 As investors attempt to take advantage of this opportunity what will happen to:
   a) The £/$ spot rate?
   b) The UK and US rate of interest?
   c) The £/$ forward rate?
3 When will investors stop switching funds from one money centre to another?

Data response B
The sterling exchange rate

This is based on an article by Robert Chote which appeared in the *Financial Times* on 7 August 1997. Answer the following questions:

1 Which group of people are likely to benefit the most as a result of the upsurge in the value of sterling on the foreign exchange markets?
2 Explain why, according to the author, the actions of the Chancellor are unlikely to dampen the increase in the value of sterling.
3 The rise in the value of sterling affects the service and manufacturing sectors differently. Why is this?
4 Why have the trade figures not yet been affected by sterling's rise?
5 What, if anything, should the UK government do to lower the value of sterling?

Britain's curious boom

Sterling's strength (despite yesterday's softening) may be good news for Britons abroad, it is less welcome to the Bank of England's monetary policy committee which concludes a two-day meeting in London today. The same factors that are making foreign holidays so popular this year – surging consumer confidence and an overvalued exchange rate – present the central bank's committee with an unenviable dilemma: how can it cool down Britain's gathering consumer boom without pushing manufacturing off a cliff?

Elsewhere in Europe the dilemma – and indeed the growth in consumer spending – may seem unfamiliar. In Britain, boom-bust cycles are all too common. The committee is wrestling with the problem now because of the reluctance of Mr Gordon Brown, the chancellor, to impose big tax increases on consumers in last month's Budget. The chancellor's unwillingness to reduce consumption through taxes meant that interest rates were the only instruments left.

"The chancellor's political impotence meant sacrificing exporters and manufacturers to consumers looking to spend their windfall gains," says Mr Geoffrey Dicks at NatWest Markets, the investment banking arm of National Westminster Bank.

Consumers seem to love it Rising take-home pay, rapid increases in house prices and a staggering £35bn or more in windfalls from building society and insurance company flotations have propelled consumer confidence sharply higher in recent months. According to a survey for the European Commission, optimism is at levels unmatched since the late 1980s.

Mr Richard Iley at Hoare Govett says this survey provides a reliable guide to the strength of consumer spending three to six months ahead. Consumer spending grew at a rate equivalent to 3.6 per cent a year in the first quarter of 1997 and Mr Iley calculates that the present level of confidence means annualised growth could be as much as 6.5 per cent by the fourth quarter.

This is a little less than the 8 per cent growth recorded briefly in the late 1970s and late 1980s, but the monetary policy committee knows it is well above the rates that have proved sustainable in the past without fuelling inflation – especially at a time when the Treasury estimates that the economy is already running at full capacity.

But the outlook for spending is more uncertain than consumer confidence suggests. People's willingness to make large purchases has rocketed, but their confidence in the outlook for the economy has dipped. Their view seems to be: buy now, worry later.

This dichotomy underlines the importance of the windfalls. This year, three building societies and one insurance company have produced windfalls. Economists at Nikko Europe estimate this has benefited four in 10 UK households, to the tune of about £31bn.

Mr Chris Wright, economist at Barclays Bank, estimates the windfalls could add between 0.75 and 1 per cent to consumer spending this year and next. "The evidence does, however, still fall short of unequivocally pointing to a strengthening consumer boom," he adds.

Mr Wright notes, for example, that while the Nationwide building society's measure of house price inflation has climbed steadily to 11 per cent, the Halifax measure has been stable at about 7 per cent since last autumn. New housebuilding has slowed and property transactions have been flat since the turn of the year. This casts doubt on the underlying strength of spending on consumer durables once the windfalls have been absorbed. Part of the consumer "boom" may come from a windfall blip.

Estimates of money supply growth may be equally ambiguous. On the face of it, large increases in the measure might suggest a consumer boom is being stoked up. Growth in the broad measure M4 – cash plus bank and building society accounts – has been above the ceiling of the Treasury's 3-9 per cent "monitoring range" for more than a year. But Mr Peter Warburton, at Robert Fleming investment bank and fund management group, says this is less threatening than it looks. Wholesale deposits may be growing at 21 per cent a year, but this reflects takeover activity and changes in the gilts market. Retail deposits have a much closer relationship to consumer spending and they are rising at less than 7 per cent a year.

The boom in consumer spending is in sharp contrast to the weakness in export orders brought about by sterling's strength. Fresh evidence of this emerged on Tuesday, with official figures showing that output in manufacturing – which is relatively exposed to international competition – was lower in the second quarter of the year than in the first.

The Chartered Institute of Purchasing and Supply reported that the service sector continued to grow and that "buoyant consumer confidence was again reported to have played a key role in boosting demand". One in five service sector companies took on permanent staff, with salaries forced higher as businesses had to compete for scarce skilled labour. But, even in this relatively sheltered sector, sterling's strength slowed the rate of growth of new business.

Driven by expectations of higher interest rates and fears of a weak euro, sterling has risen by about 40 per cent from its record low against the D-Mark in November 1995, its longest rally for 17 years. Adjusting its tradeweighted exchange rate for differences in inflation at home and abroad, British companies are less price competitive against overseas rivals than at any time since 1982 – much more so than when sterling was trapped in the European exchange rate mechanism. Mr Tim Congdon, at Lombard Street Research, believes sterling is 20 per cent above what is justified by international price differentials.

But in spite of survey evidence that export orders are collapsing, sterling's strength has not yet hit the trade figures. This has raised hopes that exporters might take all the pain by reducing their profit margins to maintain market share. But Mr Michael Saunders, at Salomon Brothers, says that, after sterling's depreciation on Black Wednesday, exporters increased profit margins and market share. He suggests margins and volumes will both eventually suffer from sterling's rise.

"Indeed, one of the channels by which the high pound will slow exports is by cutting export profitability so far that firms either go bust or retreat to the domestic market," Mr Saunders says.

Against this backdrop, the chancellor's refusal to tax consumers more heavily in the Budget has made the monetary policy committee's job more difficult. Its task is clear: it must set interest rates to deliver underlying inflation of 2.5 per cent in two years' time. But whatever action it takes now, the committee can be confident of booming domestic demand this year and a probable collapse in exports next year. Where inflation will lie at the end of this rollercoaster is anybody's guess.

One strategy would be to ignore the pound's strength or to assume that its fall yesterday will continue, perhaps because of an unexpectedly early tightening in German monetary policy. Base interest rates might then be raised to 8 per cent or so, risking recession if sterling remains strong. The other strategy might be to leave rates at their current 6.75 per cent, relying on sterling's strength to slow the economy, albeit at the cost of a ballooning current account deficit.

Mr Saunders expects the Bank to tread a middle path, raising rates half a point or so. He says that "would risk overkill next year if sterling stays very high, but would allow for the risk that sterling reverses some of its recent gains".

With luck, the Bank will get the balance right and achieve its golden scenario – reducing consumer demand without inflicting too much damage on exporters. But Mr Saunders adds that if sterling either falls sharply or resumes its recent rise, the authorities might end up having to take more dramatic action.

Today's vote on interest rates and next week's quarterly Inflation Report will provide a clue to the Bank's thinking. But it is worth remembering that while independent central banks tend to produce lower inflation than those subordinate to their finance ministries, they also tend to preside over deeper recessions.

The Treasury's latest monthly survey shows that independent economists on average expect the economy to grow by an above trend 2.7 per cent next year – but the mood may be on the turn. More analysts are talking about the threat of a hard landing next year, as exports collapse, consumer spending slows and as the government keeps the screws on public spending. If the pessimists are right, it remains to be seen whether the Bank or Mr Brown will get the blame.

Source: Financial Times, 7 August 1997

42 International institutions

Learning outcomes

After reading this chapter you will be able to:

- Understand the role of the IMF, WTO, and other international institutions in promoting trade and development.
- Recognise the importance of eurocurrency markets in providing international liquidity.
- Identify the benefits and dangers involved in setting up a single European currency.
- Appreciate the latest developments taking place in the European Union.

Introduction

In July 1944 a conference took place at Bretton Woods in New Hampshire to try to establish the pattern of post-war international monetary transactions. The aim was to try to achieve freer convertibility, improve international liquidity and avoid the economic nationalism which had characterised the interwar years. The conference was chaired by the Secretary of the US Treasury, Henry Morgenthau. The conference was dominated, however, by Keynes and the American Harry Dexter-White.

Keynes had a plan for an international unit of currency. This he called the bancor. It was to be a hypothetical unit of account against which all other currencies would be measured. This would be administered by a world bank with which all countries would have an account. In effect this bank would perform the tasks of an ordinary bank, except its customers would be nations: cheques would be written out to settle international indebtedness; money would be created to finance trade; and overdrafts could be given to those countries which required them. It was essential to the concept of the bank, however, that it be allowed to determine each country's exchange rate and adjust it to ensure that nations did not fall hopelessly into debt or run gigantic surpluses. The plan foundered because nations, none more so than the UK, were unwilling to allow an international institution to determine the value of their currency.

The result was that two compromise institutions were established: in 1947 the International Monetary Fund (IMF); and in 1946 the International Bank for Reconstruction and Development (IBRD). The latter is usually called the World Bank, which is misleading, for it is the IMF which contains the remains of Keynes's idea for the bancor, not the IBRD.

The International Monetary Fund

It was the IMF system which dominated the pattern of international monetary payments from 1945 to 1972. The objectives of the IMF were to achieve free convertibility of all currencies and to promote stability in international money markets. Although there is now greater convertibility, there is still much to do. However, until 1972 the IMF system was reasonably stable. The IMF also attempts to give assistance to less developed countries.

In 1995 the IMF had 179 members. Since 1985, 33 new members have joined. Many of these new members were former planned economies, including the countries which emerged from the collapse of the Soviet Union and Yugoslavia.

Quotas

Each of the members of the IMF is required to contribute a quota to the fund. The size of the quota will depend upon the national income of the country concerned and upon its share in world trade. The quota used to be made up of 75 per cent in the country's own currency and 25 per cent in gold. Since the demonetisation of gold the 25 per cent is now subscribed in reserve assets. In this way it was hoped that there would be enough of any currency in the pool for any members to draw on should they get into balance of payments difficulties. Members' quotas are now supplemented by an allocation of SDRs (see below). Table 42.1 shows the size of members' quotas as they were in 1991.

Voting power in the IMF is related to the size of the quota. Each member is allocated 250 votes plus one vote for every 1 000 000 SDRs of its quota. In this way the USA and the other industrialised nations have managed to dominate the IMF for most of its life. It has been necessary to revise the quotas nine times, first to increase the overall size of quotas to take account of the growth of world trade and of inflation, and second, to revise the relative size of members' quotas; for example, the UK's quota was originally 14.9 per cent but now stands at 5.1 per cent of the total.

***Table 42.1* IMF quotas, December 1991**

Country	*Amount (SDR million)*	*%*
USA	26 526.50	19.1
Germany	8 241.50	5.9
Japan	8 241.50	5.9
UK	7 141.60	5.1
France	7 141.60	5.1
Italy	4 590.70	3.3
Canada	4 320.30	3.1
Netherlands	3 442.00	2.5
Belgium	3 103.00	2.3
Australia	2 333.00	1.7
Others	63 920.38	46.0
Total	139 002.08	100.0

Source: Bank of England

Borrowing

Originally each member of the IMF could borrow in ***tranches*** (slices) equivalent to 25 per cent of their quota, taking up to five consecutive tranches, i.e. it was possible to borrow the equivalent of 125 per cent of one's quota. Today a member country with serious balance of payments problems can obtain loans of more than six times the value of its quota over a three-year period. This is not, however, an unconditional right to borrow, for the IMF may, and usually does, impose conditions of increasing severity upon a member as it increases its borrowing.

The methods of borrowing from the IMF have received several modifications.

a) *Standby arrangements*. Devised in 1952, this method of borrowing has become the most usual form of assistance rendered by the IMF. Resources are made available to members which they may draw on if they wish. Attaining a stand-by facility is often enough to stabilise a member's balance of payments without the member actually drawing it, in the same way that the guarantee of a bank overdraft will often stabilise a company's finances. It is still necessary for a member to agree to conditions for each tranche. Drawings are made over a three-year period after which they can be repaid after six years.
b) *General agreement to borrow (GAB)*. In 1962 the leading 10 industrialised nations – the Group of 10 – agreed to make a pool of \$6 billion available to one another. Although channelled through the IMF, the Group of 10 would decide itself upon whether or not to give assistance, and it also restricted its help to the Group. Since 1984 the size of the pool has been increased to SDR17 billion and the GAB has agreed to help less developed countries. Switzerland joined the GAB in 1984. Also in 1984 the Saudi Arabian Monetary Agency agreed with the IMF that it would be prepared to consider supplementary lending under the GAB of up to SDR1.5 billion.
c) *Compensatory finance scheme*. Started in 1963, this was a system to give loans with fewer conditions to members experiencing

temporary difficulties because of delays in the receipt of their export credits. By the early 1980s this accounted for almost one-third of all IMF lending.

d) *Buffer stock facility.* This was a scheme, introduced in 1969, to give loans to members to allow them to pay their subscriptions to buffer stock schemes. It was principally used by members of the international tin agreement and the international sugar agreement.
e) *The extended fund facility.* This was a scheme introduced in 1974 to give longer-term assistance to members experiencing more protracted balance of payments difficulties.
f) *Systematic transformation facility.* This scheme was introduced in 1993. This is a temporary form of IMF credit intended for Russia and other economies in transition from a centrally planned economy to a market economy.
g) *Structural adjustment facility (SAF) and enhanced structural adjustment facility (ESAF).* Developed in 1986 for low-income countries, these are loans on easy terms for countries with permanent balance of payments problems.

The stand-by and extended arrangements represent the bulk of the IMF credits. It was not until the outbreak of the debt crisis in 1982 that the IMF really began to make loans on a large scale. In 1985, the outstanding loans reached a peak of almost SDR40 billion. They declined in subsequent years as repayments became due.

Special drawing rights (SDRs)

In 1967 it was decided to create international liquidity for the first time. This was done by giving members an allocation of ***special drawing rights.*** These do not exist as notes but merely as booking entries. When they were introduced in 1970 they were linked to the dollar and thus to gold (SDR1 = $1) and became known as 'paper gold'. However, since 1974 the value of a unit of SDR has been calculated by combining the value of leading currencies. Originally based on 16 currencies, this was reduced to five in 1981. Table 42.2 shows the weights within the basket in 1995.

Table 42.2 **Weight and percentage weights in SDR currency 'basket', 1995**

Currency	*Weight*	*%*
US dollar	0.572	40
Deutschmark	0.453	21
Japanese yen	31.8	17
French franc	0.800	11
Pound sterling	0.0812	11

Source: Bank of England

SDRs are the nearest equilvalent so far to Keynes's idea of the bancor. (Other hypothetical units of account exist, such as the European currency unit.) The functions of SDRs can be summarised as follows:

a) *A means of exchange.* SDRs can be used to settle indebtedness between nations, but only with the consent of the IMF. However, they cannot be used commercially.
b) *A unit of account.* All IMF transactions are now denominated in SDRs. Several other institutions use the SDR as the unit of account, including the Asian Clearing Union, the Economic Community of West Africa and the Suez Canal Company.
c) *A store of value.* In 1976 at the Jamaica conference it was decided to reduce the role of gold and make the SDR the principal asset of the IMF.

It can therefore be seen that the SDR fulfils the most important functions of money but only to a limited extent. We could therefore best describe it as quasi-money (see Chapter 36). If world trade is not to be limited by lack of international liquidity, further development of SDRs is required.

The adjustable peg

At the heart of the IMF system was the regime of fixed exchange rates known as the ***adjustable peg.*** This was described in Chapter 41 (see page 572). When the UK joined the IMF in 1947 its exchange rate was £1 = $4.03. In 1949 the UK, along with most other countries, devalued against the dollar so that the rate became £1 = $2.80. This rate lasted until 1967 when the UK devalued to £1 = $2.40. The Smithsonian Agreement of 1971 was an attempt to patch up the adjustable peg system and saw the pound revalued to £1 = $2.60. The 1970s, however, saw a collapse of the adjustable peg. We will now have a look at the break-up of this system.

The break-up of the IMF adjustable peg system

The 1967 crisis

Although it was not realised at the time, the UK's 1967 devaluation marked the beginning of the end for the adjustable peg system. The basis of economic power in the world had changed greatly since 1947 when the IMF was set up. At that time the economies of West Germany and Japan lay in ruins, but no changes came about in the IMF system to take account of their subsequent recovery. The UK and the USA solidly refused to devalue their currencies while West Germany and Japan refused to revalue theirs. In 1967 the UK could resist the pressure no longer and devalued.

This precipitated world-wide uncertainty. Speculators realised that gold was undervalued at $35 an ounce and there was, therefore, great pressure on the USA to devalue. The final attempt to save the gold standard occurred in 1968 when a two-tier rate was established. This meant that the price of gold for monetary purposes was maintained at $35 while the price of gold for commercial purposes was allowed to float upwards.

The USA leaves the gold standard (1971)

The announcement by President Nixon in August 1971 that the USA would no longer exchange dollars for gold at the official price ended the gold standard. This was forced upon the USA by a massive balance of payments deficit. The fundamental reason for this was realignment of the economic power in the world which had led to massive and continuing surpluses and the accumulation of vast reserves by West Germany and Japan. However, the situation was made worse for the USA by more immediate circumstances:

a) *Inflation.* This made the price of gold ever more unrealistic.
b) *Speculative pressure.* The vast US deficit meant that there was a large amount of dollars on the foreign exchange market which could be used to speculate upon a rise in the price of gold.
c) *The Vietnam War.* One of the consequences of the unpopularity of this war was that the US government was not able to increase taxation to pay for it. The war was, therefore, partly financed by running up a deficit on the balance of payments.
d) *The 'Watergate' election.* President Nixon desperately needed to reflate the economy to win the election of autumn 1971. This was fatal for the external position of the dollar.

The Smithsonian Agreement 1971

The abandonment of the gold standard swept away the adjustable peg system since the world reference point for currencies had disappeared. The Smithsonian Agreement of December 1971 was an attempt to re-establish the adjustable peg. This agreement put the value of gold at $38 per ounce, an effective devaluation of the dollar of 8.9 per cent. The new rate for the pound was therefore £1 = $2.60.

The Smithsonian peg allowed a $2\frac{1}{4}$ per cent variation in the value of a currency (as opposed to the 1 per cent of the 1947 system). This meant that the maximum possible variation between three currencies (cross-parities) was 9 per cent. The variation was unacceptable to the EC countries and therefore, on 24 April 1972, they established a variation between their own currencies of half that of the Smithsonian variation. The Smithsonian variation was said to provide the tunnel within which the smaller European snake moved. The UK joined the snake on 1 June 1972 but left 54 days later when Anthony Barber, the then Chancellor of the Exchequer, announced that the pound was to float.

The Smithsonian Agreement was short-lived, as most countries were obliged to float their currencies in 1972 and 1973. However, two legacies remain. As it was the last time when most currencies were fixed against one another it is a reference point, and one still finds many references to the Smithsonian parities. The other legacy is the European currency snake. Although abandoned in the mid 1970s it became the EMS in 1979 (see page 595).

The oil crises

The instability which was started in 1971 was made much worse by the oil crises. As a result of the Yom Kippur War of 1973, oil supplies were cut off. When they were resumed the OPEC countries contrived a four-fold rise in price. It is possible to argue that the resulting transfer of money from the developed countries to OPEC nations brought about one of the most fundamental shifts in economic power of all time. It is estimated that this cost the oil-importing countries an extra $100 billion per year.

Then in 1978 oil prices were again raised dramatically, this time doubling, and causing a liquidity problem even greater than that of 1973. This price rise was a major factor in the subsequent world depression. This hit the industrialised countries hard but was disastrous for non-oil-exporting developing countries (NOEDCs). The subsequent slump in oil prices left some less developed oil exporters such as Mexico saddled with large debts which they found it impossible to service.

The Plaza Agreement 1985 and the Louvre Accord 1987

In the mid 1980s there was a consensus of opinion among the leading industrial nations that they would prefer to see a more stable system of exchange rates. The Plaza Agreement (so called after the Plaza Hotel, New York) was an agreement by the monetary authorities of the G5 nations (see below) to bring about an orderly decline in the value of the dollar which was then considered overvalued.

The Louvre Accord (so called because it was arrived at in Paris) was an agreement among the G7 nations to stabilise variations in their exchange rates within certain limits. These limits were not published. However, they could be deduced, at least partly, from the actions of central banks. For example, in March 1988 it became obvious that the Bank of England was committed to holding the pound below the level of £1 = DM3. In the event this was not possible.

These agreements illustrate the urge to return to a more orderly pattern of exchange rates. The fact that they were not arrived at through the IMF also illustrates its decline in importance.

The terms G5 and G7 may be in need of some explanation. The GAB (1962) was said to have been founded by 'the Group of 10'. This was abbreviated by journalists to G10. Subsequently the Group of Five leading industrialised nations – the USA, Japan, West Germany, France and the UK – became G5. When, by the addition of Canada and Italy, the Group of Five became the Group of Seven, this was abbreviated to G7.

The problem of international liquidity

When we speak of the problem of international liquidity we are referring to the lack of universally acceptable means of payment. Since the Second World War the dollar and, to a lesser extent, the pound have attempted to fulfil this role. The regime of floating exchange rates has worsened the problem. Today we can summarise the stock of official international liquidity as being the gold and foreign currency reserves held by nations, plus their quotas at the IMF and their allocation of SDRs. It could be argued that there has been an excess of unofficial liquidity. The expansion of eurocurrency business in the 1970s left many developing nations hopelessly in debt. By the end of the 1980s many of the debtor nations found it impossible to borrow money on the commercial market. However, the scale of the debt problem was so great that the reserves of the IMF and other international agencies were totally inadequate to deal with it. Put more bluntly, the IMF did not have enough funds to help the debtor nations even if it wanted to.

The role of the IMF

In this section we have examined how the orderly arrangements of the IMF broke down in the turbulent times of the 1970s. In 1976 the annual conference of the IMF came to the Jamaica Agreement. This agreement officially recognised the end of the system of fixed exchange rates. It also 'demonetised' gold, i.e. the official price of gold was abolished. Member countries were no longer allowed to use gold as part of their quota subscriptions to the IMF. In addition to this the IMF agreed to get rid of one third of its stocks of gold. This it did by sales and by transfers to members.

The role of the IMF declined significantly during the 1980s. Many developing nations were considered uncreditworthy by the IMF. In addition, some nations were unwilling to borrow from the IMF because of the strict austerity programme which the IMF laid down when giving loans. Debtor nations turned to private sources. The *Financial Times* commented in 1987:

> More and more debtors have been winning concessions from their private creditors (i.e. international lending banks) while the IMF has been relegated to a subordinate role. In January [1987] Brazil became the first country without an IMF programme to negotiate a scheduling of its government-to-government debt.

In 1995 the IMF made the biggest loan to a single nation ever when it bailed out Mexico. In August 1997, the IMF agreed a credit package to Thailand (see Data response A at the end of this chapter).

The role of the IMF with more advanced nations was also reduced. The regime of floating exchange rates lessened the need to borrow foreign currency for official purposes. In addition to this the drop in oil prices got rid of the current deficits of many nations.

Despite its apparent decline in significance the IMF remains important. This is because it is the main economic forum for discussions and agreements about currency and debt. (The international debt crisis is also discussed in Chapter 46.)

STUDENT ACTIVITY 42.1

a) Why did West Germany and Japan refuse to revalue their currencies under the Bretton Woods system of exchange rates?
b) Why is it easy for speculators to make massive profits under a system of stable but not fixed exchange rate systems?
c) What similarities, if any, are there between the Bretton Woods system of exchange rates and the ERM?

Eurocurrencies

There is no one institution which is concerned with eurocurrencies. However, it is convenient to consider them in this chapter since they have such an enormous impact on world trade. For example, the amount of transactions in eurocurrencies is far greater than all IMF business.

Defining a eurocurrency

Eurocurrencies were referred to in Chapter 37. We may formalise our definition thus:

A eurocurrency is any deposit in a financial institution which is not denominated in the national currency.

For example, deposits of sterling in a French bank which continue to be denominated as sterling and not as francs are eurocurrency – in this case eurosterling. A glance at the balance sheet of any commercial bank will show just how much such business they do. Most eurocurrency deposits are in dollars.

The origins and growth of the markets

The original market was the eurodollar market. This emerged in London in the 1950s to handle the supply of US dollars in Europe. The dollar, you will remember, was then (as now) the most important international unit of account. Therefore companies, not necessarily dealing with the USA, demanded dollars for the purposes of international trade.

Up to 1957 sterling also fulfilled a similar role but in that year the government restricted its use in third-party deals outside the sterling area. Merchant banks and others who had specialised in this trade switched to dollars. (Sterling deals in London would not be eurocurrency but dollar deals in London are – see the definition.)

a) *Growth in the 1950s and 1960s.* In addition to the demand from traders for dollars the growth of the eurodollar market was further accelerated by the following factors:
   (i) US balance of payments deficits which created a supply of dollars outside the USA.
   (ii) COMECON countries preferring to hold their dollar reserves in London rather than the USA.
   (iii) Relaxation of exchange controls elsewhere in Europe allowing the holding of foreign currency reserves in London by individuals and institutions.
   (iv) Regulation Q, which restricted the interest rates which US banks could pay and therefore encouraged Americans to place deposits in London to gain higher rates.

   The 1960s also saw the introduction of new financial instruments such as certificates of deposit which encouraged dealing. In this period we also saw the beginning of trade in other eurocurrencies, notably the eurodeutschmark. These forces combined to make London the world centre of eurocurrency dealing.

b) *The 1970s.* There was a spectacular growth of the eurocurrency markets in the 1970s. Towards the end of the decade business was expanding at the rate of 30 per cent per year! There were two main reasons for the growth. First, the huge rise in oil prices in 1973 and again in 1978 left the oil-exporting countries with huge dollar surpluses (all oil transactions are in dollars). A very large proportion of these surpluses were placed on short-term deposit in Europe. Second, the regime of floating exchange rates encouraged speculation and freed many currencies from exchange restrictions.

c) *The 1980s.* This period saw a drastic slowing down in the expansion of the markets. This was partly a result of the world-wide recession but more especially of the world debt crisis. Many developing countries who had been borrowers in the 1970s found it impossible to service their debts in the 1980s when real interest rates were much higher. Despite this slow-down, by the end of the decade the total gross lending in eurocurrencies was over £3000 billion, an amount almost equal to the GDP of the USA and six times that of the UK.

What and where are the eurocurrency markets?

The leading eurocurrency is the dollar, accounting for something like 74 per cent of the market. The second most important is the Deutschmark; other eurocurrencies are the Swiss franc, the yen and sterling. One reason the pound is a relatively unimportant eurocurrency, while London is the leading market, may be obvious to you, i.e. deals in sterling in London would not (by definition) be eurocurrency deals. In addition to this there is only a limited demand for sterling because of the UK's relatively small share of world trade.

We have just mentioned that the yen is a eurocurrency; we have also seen that the leading eurocurrency is the dollar and some of the largest depositors are Arabic. Thus, there is nothing exclusively European about eurocurrencies. This is also reflected in the geographical location of the leading dealing centres. London is the pre-eminent centre. Other centres include Zurich, Hong Kong, Luxembourg, Paris, Tokyo, Singapore, Bahrain and Nassau. (Why isn't New York in the list?)

The importance of the eurocurrency markets

The sheer size of the markets makes them important but activities in the markets have important effects nationally and internationally. The markets are a source of finance for both companies and countries. In particular developing nations such as Brazil and Mexico have borrowed heavily on the eurocurrency markets. The level of interest rates in the markets influences interest rates world-wide. Many loans are at variable interest and are often tied to a key rate such as LIBOR (London InterBank Offered Rate).

The eurocurrency markets are largely beyond the effective control of government but they impinge upon the operation of domestic monetary policy. The fact that banks can switch easily into and out of eurocurrencies makes it very difficult for direct controls (e.g. special deposits) on banks to be effective. This was well illustrated in 1980 when the government abolished the 'corset' (see Chapter 37). The immediate effect of this was a surge in £M_3 as banks switched liquidity they had been 'hiding' in eurocurrencies back into sterling. Because of these problems the monetary authorities have to rely to a much greater extent on the control of interest rates as a method of monetary policy.

The mobility of eurocurrency deposits is a source of instability bringing unwelcome changes in the exchange rate. For example, if interest rates were raised in the UK this could lead to a switch from eurodollars to sterling and hence to an appreciation of the pound and/or a growth in the money supply in the UK. Both of these consequences may be unwelcome.

The existence of the eurocurrency markets may, therefore, be another argument for the return to a more stable regime of exchange rates.

Other international institutions

The World Bank (IBRD)

The International Bank for Reconstruction and Development, or World Bank, was set up in 1947 as the sister organisation to the IMF. Its original aim was to make loans to develop the war-shattered economies of Europe. Subsequently its activities shifted towards financing projects and programmes in developing countries on a long-term basis (ranging up to 35 years). The IMF's purpose is not to give loans to finance development projects; this is the job of the IBRD. Most World Bank loans are used to finance infrastructure investment in transportation, electric power, agriculture, water supply and education. One of the chief problems facing the IBRD is its lack of funds. Funds come from three sources.

a) *Quotas*. The membership of the IBRD is the same as that of the IMF. Members make contributions in relation to their IMF quota. Of the quota, 10 per cent is subscribed while the other 90 per cent is promised as a guarantee for the World Bank's loans.
b) *Bonds*. The World Bank sells bonds on the capital markets of the world.
c) *Income*. A very small proportion of the World Bank's funds come from its earnings. As it developed the World Bank turned its attention from Europe to the poorer countries of the world. Today it is almost wholly concerned with helping LDCs. It is a valuable source of advice and information, besides making loans.

The World Bank has also increased its operations by forming new organisations.

a) *The International Finance Corporation (IFC)*. This was set up in 1956 to enable the World Bank to give loans to private companies as well as governments.
b) *The International Development Association (IDA)*. The object of this organisation, set up in 1960, was to make loans for longer periods and on preferential terms to the LDCs. The IDA has become known as the 'soft loan window'.
c) *The Multilateral Investment Guarantee Agency (MIGA)*. This agency was set up by the G7 nations in 1988 and is operated by the World Bank. The object of the agency is to guarantee long-term private investment in developing countries. The political instability in many nations makes it difficult and expensive for them to borrow. The agency guarantees investors' funds against such things as expropriation by dictators but it does not, however, guarantee them against normal commercial risks. The effect of the agency's guarantee is to level the degree of risk in investments with that in other, more advanced or stable, nations.

As with the IMF, we may conclude that although there is a great need for the services of the IBRD its role is limited. The limitation comes both from lack of funds and from political disagreements. Increasingly the work of the World Bank is overshadowed by that of commercial lending to developing nations.

OECD (the Organisation for Economic Cooperation and Development)

In 1947 the Organisation for European Economic Cooperation (OEEC) came into existence to administer the European recovery programme ('Marshall aid'). This was an important institution and, among other things, helped to establish the European Payments Union (EPU). By 1961 it was thought that the OEEC had succeeded in the task of redeveloping Europe and it became the OECD, a more widely based organisation. Its objectives are:

a) to encourage growth, high employment and financial stability amongst members;
b) to aid the economic development of less developed non-member countries.

The OECD now has 25 members, including most of the European countries, the USA, Canada, Australia, and Japan who joined in 1965.

One of the most important functions of the OECD is to provide information and statistics. In fact all the international organisations we have discussed in this chapter are important sources of information; the reader may like to consult the OECD *Economic Outlook*, the IMF's *Annual Report* and the IBRD's *World Development Report*.

The Bank for International Settlements (BIS)

This institution is based in Basle, Switzerland. It was set up after a proposal by the Young Committee in 1930. Its original purpose was to enable central banks to coordinate their international payments and receipts. Originally it arose out of the need to regulate German reparations. It is one of the oldest surviving and most successful of the international institutions.

Since the Second World War, the BIS has acted like a central bank for central banks. The board of the BIS is made up of representatives of the central banks of the UK, France, Germany, Belgium, Italy, Switzerland, the Netherlands and Sweden. Other countries such as the USA and Japan regularly attend meetings.

The chief functions of the BIS are as follows:

a) the promotion of cooperation between central banks;
b) organising finance for nations in payments difficulties;
c) monitoring eurocurrency markets;
d) provision of expert advice for the OECD and the EMS;
e) administration of the EU's credit scheme.

Not only is the BIS one of the oldest and most successful of international institutions, but also it is a self-supporting and profit-making institution.

The European Bank for Reconstruction and Development (EBRD)

The stated aim of the EBRD is 'to foster the transition towards open market-orientated economies and to promote private and entrepreneurial initiative of Central and Eastern Europe'. We have just mentioned the OECD's origins in the Marshall Plan after the Second World War. The aim of the EBRD is to be a kind of Marshall Plan for the former communist states.

The EBRD is the first international financial institution of the peiod following the Cold War. The agreement establishing it is a response to the changes and challenges in Central and Eastern Europe, as the region moves from centrally planned command systems to free democratic institutions and market economies.

The range of structural transformation required in this process is enormous. It will involve changes as drastic as creating an appropriate legal framework for property rights, contracts and financial transactions; the establishment of commercial codes and accounting systems; reform of the banking system; liberalisation of prices; changes in managerial behaviour; and the fostering of competition throughout each economy.

This radical set of reforms must be supported by sound advice, training and technical expertise and supplemented by major investments in the private and public sectors to ensure an effective supply response. Domestic capital will not be enough: external capital is therefore needed from both private and public sources.

The idea of the European Bank was put forward by President Mitterrand in 1989 and came to fruition in May 1990 with the signature of its agreement by 40 countries, the Commission of the EC and the European Investment Bank.

The EBRD is the first institution where East and West can meet to build a future together. The Bank has its headquarters in London and began operations in April 1991. It remains to be seen whether it is able to live up to its lofty aims. It also remains to be seen if it is able to supply sufficient capital to make any significant difference to Eastern Europe.

The General Agreement on Tariffs and Trade (GATT) and its successor, the World Trade Organisation (WTO)

At the same time as the negotiations on international payments were taking place at Bretton Woods, other negotiations were under way to set up a sort of world-wide common market to be named the International Trading Organisation (ITO). However, the talks foundered and all that was achieved was the General Agreement on Tariffs and Trade (GATT). It is a chapter of 38 articles organised in four parts. Nonetheless GATT has been the most important organisation for the promotion of free trade.

Impediments to free trade such as export subsidies and quotas were outlawed by GATT and if a country wished to impose a new tariff it had to offset it by offering compensatory reductions in other tariffs that affected the exporting countries.

In reality, exemptions were granted. Thus, quantitative restrictions can be used to safeguard a balance of payments and to provide temporary relief for domestic industries. Developing countries can use quantitative restrictions to further development goals. Similarly, agriculture was not affected by the restriction on export subsidies.

GATT attempted to achieve its objective of trade liberalisation by organising 'rounds of negotiations'. There have been eight such rounds. The most important rounds of negotiation were the last three, namely the Kennedy round, which took five years to complete (1962–7), the Tokyo round, which took seven years to complete (1973–9) and the Uruguay round, which took eight years to succeed (1986–93) and has been held by many to be the most important round ever completed.

GATT is guided in its actions by two fundamental principles:

a) *'Non-discrimination'*, also referred to as the 'most favoured nation' (MFN). Every signatory was to be treated as 'a most favoured nation', i.e. trading privileges could not be extended to one member without extending them to all. Existing systems of preference were allowed to continue but could not be increased.
b) *'Reciprocity'*. If a country granted a trade concession to another country then the latter must reciprocate by granting an equivalent trade concession.

Trading blocks such as the EU and NAFTA (North America Free Trade Area) were allowed even though they contravene the MFN principle, and developing countries were not bound by the 'reciprocity' principle.

Leaving aside the Uruguay round for the moment, significant reductions in tariffs in industrial goods were achieved by the Kennedy and Tokyo rounds. By the end of the Tokyo round average tariff levels on industrial goods were on average about 5 per cent in the main industrialised countries. This is a major achievement given that at the start of the first round average tariffs exceeded 40 per cent.

However, before we get carried away with GATT's successes, we need to remind ourselves that neither trade in agricultural goods nor trade in services was covered by these rounds. Furthermore, some sectors such as the steel and textile industries had very high rates of protectionism and non-tariff barriers such as voluntary export restraints, dumping, government procurement policies, etc., were addressed by these rounds. For example, the World Bank, in a study on the extent of non-tariff barriers in industrialised countries, found that whilst 25 per cent of the imports of the industrialised countries, were affected by non-tariff protection, this had grown to 48 per cent by 1986.

No wonder then that the Uruguay round took eight years to complete. The most 'conflict-ridden' areas were on the menu for discussion. Chief amongst them were agriculture, trade in services, trade in intellectual property rights (TRIPS), dumping, and non-tariff barriers.

After a long and difficult round of negotiation, the round was finally concluded in 1993. The main results of the Uruguay round were as follows:

a) Average reductions in tariff barriers by 50 per cent.
b) Non-tariff barriers to be phased out.
c) On agriculture, European farm export subsidies to be reduced by 21 per cent over the next six years. Also the value of export subsidies to be reduced by 36 per cent.
d) Agreement to deregulate trade in services but the audio visual sector to be left out completely. No change in maritime transport. Financial services will not be subject to the MFN/non-discrimination principle.
e) Provision to standardise patents.
f) On textiles, the multifibre arrangements to be phased out and quotas to be replaced by tariffs.
g) GATT to be disbanded and to be replaced by the World Trade Organisation (WTO).

The World Trade Organisation

Established in January 1995, the WTO is responsible for administering multilateral trade agreements negotiated by its members such as the General Agreement on Tariffs and Trade (GATT), the General Agreement on Trade in Services (GATS) and the agreement on Trade in Intellectual Property Rights (TRIPS). Just like GATT, the WTO is to provide a forum for further negotiating rounds. It differs from GATT in that it has a much tighter dispute settlement procedure and a new trade policy review mechanism.

The dispute settlement procedure of the WTO

Under GATT it was possible for one of the parties to a dispute to block the establishment of a panel or the adoption of panel reports. Under the WTO, the adoption of panel reports can only be blocked by a consensus, which is extremely unlikely. The parties to a dispute must initially attempt to solve it themselves. If they fail to find a solution to their dispute within 60 days, the Dispute Settlement Body (DSB) will establish a panel to investigate and make a report to the parties involved and to the DSB. Creation of the panel is automatic. The report must be accepted by the DSB within 60 days. An appeal can be made on legal grounds only. Appeal proceedings should not exceed 60 days and must be completed within 90 days.

The offending party is expected to comply immediately. If this is not possible it will be given a reasonable time to do so. If the offending party fails to act within this period it must offer mutually acceptable compensation. Failure to do so may result in the complainant requesting authorisation from the DSB to retaliate against the offending party. Such authorisation is virtually automatic for a consensus is required to refuse it.

The trade policy review mechanism (TPRM) of the WTO

The TPRM is responsible for reporting on the trading policies of member countries and examining their impact on the trading system. Each member is requested to provide periodic reports as to its trading policies. The frequency of review is dependent upon the member's share of world trade. The four largest players (the EU, the USA, Japan and Canada) are subject to a review every two years.

STUDENT ACTIVITY 42.2

a) What, in your view, are the outstanding problems confronting the world trading system today? How successful do you think the WTO will be in resolving them?
b) Was the French government right in refusing to give in to American pressures to liberate trade in the audio visual industry?
c) Which countries (trading blocs) stand to gain the most from the implementation of the Uruguay round?

The European Union

The origins of the EU

The beginnings of the EU can be traced back to the foundation of the European Coal and Steel Community (ECSC) which was set up in 1952 by France, Italy, Belgium, Holland and Luxembourg. The UK participated in the negotiations but declined to join. West Germany later joined the ECSC, the object of which was to abolish trade restrictions on coal and steel between member countries and to coordinate production and pricing policies. The outcome of further negotiations was the Treaty of Rome in 1957 and on 1 January 1958 the EEC (usually referred to as the Common Market) came into existence. Once again the UK participated in early negotiations but then withdrew.

After two later abortive attempts to join the EC the UK finally became a member in 1972, together with Ireland and Denmark. Norway decided, by a referendum, not to become a member. Greece became a member in 1981 and Spain and Portugal in 1986. Sweden, Austria and Finland became members in January 1995. The introduction of the Single European Act in 1987 aimed to complete the process by which the members economies function as one.

The main features of the EU

There are two main features of the EU:

a) *Customs union*. The establishment of a full customs union involves both the abolition of tariffs between members and the erection of a common external tariff to the rest of the world; if each country did not have the same external tariff then imports would simply flood into the Community through the member state with the lowest tariffs. To arrive at the common external tariff the general policy has been to take the arithmetic mean of the previous six tariffs. In some cases, e.g. the imports of produce from France's tropical ex-colonies, the lowest duty was adopted since there was no conflict with domestic production. Several of the old colonial states have associated status with the EU. The original arrangements for these states were superseded by the Lomé Convention in 1975. Under this, 46 developing nations in Africa, the Caribbean and the Pacific (ACP states) are allowed to send all their industrial exports and most of their agricultural exports to the EU duty free.

   When the UK joined the EU it was particularly difficult for the UK to agree to the common external tariff because it enjoyed duty-free imports from Australia, Canada and New Zealand. The agricultural products of the highly efficient farmers in these temperate countries were in direct competition with European farmers. The UK was not allowed to join until she agreed to erect considerable tariff barriers against her Commonwealth partners.

b) *Common market*. The EU is colloquially known as the Common Market, but this is only one aspect of its organisation, although potentially the most important. The term refers to the running of the economies of the members as if they were one, i.e. the common prices and production policy of the ECSC was to be extended to all industries. A common market agreement implies the free movement of labour, capital and enterprise within the EU. So far it is only in the Common Agricultural Policy (CAP) that there is a truly common policy (see Chapter 12). Despite the fact that the EU has been in existence since 1957 many non-tariff barriers remained in existence during the 1970s and

1980s. The Single European Act sought to establish a truly common market by the end of 1992.

The structure of the EU

The Treaty of Rome envisaged that the EU would eventually lead to economic and political unity. Although at present this has become more unlikely than it seemed some years ago, it is possible to discern the four essential components of state organisation.

a) *The Council of Ministers*. This could be described as the executive or cabinet of the EU. It consists of one minister from each state; which minister it is depends on what is being discussed. If, for instance, the issue were agriculture then it would be the ministers of agriculture who would attend. Voting in the Council is weighted; the UK, for example, has 10 votes while Luxembourg has only two. The Council is assisted by a committee of permanent representatives (Coreper).
b) *The European Commission*. This consists of 20 permanent commissioners (two from each of the five largest countries and one from each of the other 10). The Commission is the secretariat of the EU. Behind the Commission there is a staff of about 2500 people working in the Commission's headquarters in Brussels. The Commission is responsible for the day-to-day running of the Community. It is also responsible for the development of EU policy. It is proposals by the Commission on such things as food hygiene which provoke outbursts in the UK press about 'the European sausage' or 'the European chicken'. More seriously, things such as the introduction of tachographs into lorry cabs have provoked great opposition from many people in the UK.
c) *The European Parliament*. The institution which meets in Strasbourg is the embryonic legislature of the EU. Originally it consisted of MPs nominated by national parliaments. However, since 1979, members have been elected directly to the European Parliament. At present there are 626 members of the European Parliament (MEPs), of which the UK elects 87. As yet the Parliament has little authority or power. Its main function is to monitor the activities of other Community institutions.
d) *The European Court of Justice*. Not to be confused with the European Court of Human Rights, the function of the European Court of Justice is to 'ensure that the law is observed in the interpretation of the Treaty of Rome'. It is the final arbiter on all questions involving interpretation of the EU treaties and it deals with disputes between member states and the Commission and between the Commission and business organisations, individuals or EU officials. It is, thus, the judiciary of the EU.

The UK and the EU

In 1972 the UK Parliament passed the European Communities Act and in 1973 the UK, together with Ireland and Denmark, joined the EU. In joining the EU the UK became part of a community of 260 million people (370 million since the accession of Sweden, Finland and Austria). The economic advantages which the UK gained were enormous and fundamental – those of increased specialisation and comparative advantage (see Chapter 39), i.e. the potential market for UK goods increased six-fold. In many ways it was impossible for the UK to stay out of the EU since, among other things, UK industry had already joined by exporting capital to Europe. The gains from joining are not, however, readily appreciated by the average citizen. Real advantages such as an increased rate of growth in GDP may seem abstract whereas minor changes such as those in driving licences and passports cause disproportionate annoyance.

More seriously the common tariff of the EU prevents us from benefiting from comparative advantage world-wide. The most obvious example is foodstuffs, whereby the UK is condemned to eat expensive European food when it could be imported more cheaply from elsewhere.

1992 and all that

By signing the Single European Act in February 1986 the EU member states committed themselves to progressively completing the single 'common' market, envisaged in 1957, by the end of 1992. The Act, which came into force in July 1987, defines the single market as 'an area without internal frontiers in which the free movement of goods, persons, services and capital is ensured in accordance with the provisions of this Treaty'. At present, for example:

a) the free movement of goods is impeded by technical barriers, such as differing product standards;
b) a free and competitive market for services is blocked by a range of national restrictions;
c) competition in the market as a whole can be distorted by national public purchasing and subsidy policies; and
d) substantial differences in indirect taxes such as excise duty distort the pattern of trade.

Eliminating trade restrictions

The completion of the Single European Market means that people and goods can move freely anywhere in the EU. In theory you should be able to drive from Glasgow to Rome without having to stop at customs, produce documents, etc. The UK, however, insists that border controls should remain as protection against terrorism, drug trafficking and rabies.

In more detail, the elimination of trade restrictions to achieve the Single European Market will cover the following specific areas:

a) European regulations and standards will mean that products approved in any one Community country can be freely marketed throughout the Community.
b) The progressive opening up of government and other public body contracts to all Community contractors on an equal basis.
c) More competitive and efficient services in telecommunications and information technology.
d) Greater competition of air routes, shipping services between member countries on equal terms and the elimination of most red tape on road haulage.
e) All restrictions on the movement of capital to be removed. Banks and securities houses authorised in their home country should be free to provide banking and investment services anywhere in the Community. Insurers will have greater freedom to cover risks in other member states.
f) Protection of industrial property will become easier through harmonisation of national laws on patents and trade marks.
g) Professional qualifications obtained in one country will be acceptable in all other countries.

It should be clear to you that the removal of such barriers to trade presents both opportunities and threats.

The benefits of the Single European Market

Most economists advocate the benefit of free trade. It is argued that, in the long run, everyone will be better off. This is based on the theory of comparative advantage. What follows in this section is a 'commensense' approach; those wanting a more detailed or mathematical treatment should consult Chapter 39.

It is obvious that if the product you wish to buy is cheaper in another country it is to your advantage to buy it from there. You will obtain the product more cheaply, which will leave you with money left to spend on other things. However, you may be prevented from doing this by taxes which make the product seem more expensive or by transport costs. The abolition of tariffs is an attempt to increase the trade and wealth of the members.

But not everyone benefits in the short run. Suppose the product we are considering is cars and they are more cheaply produced in Spain and Germany. The result of free trade will be unemployment for British car workers.

To illustrate the long-term advantages let us consider a historical example. In the late nineteenth century British agriculture experienced what became known as the Great Depression. This was brought about by the import of cheap food from the USA and Australia which was made possible by the development of rail transport and improvements in shipping and refrigeration. If this cheap food had been kept out by barring imports or by placing huge taxes on it, consider what might have happened. Today, instead of working in an office, driving a car, living in a centrally heated house, etc., the average Briton could still be working 15 hours a day in the fields, earning a wage of £15 a week, living off a diet of bread and cheese, etc. The resources freed by the decline of agriculture gave the UK the ability to staff industry, to build roads and schools and to construct our modern economy.

It is salutary to consider the present state of British manufacturing industries. Their present situation may not be unlike that of agriculture in the Great Depression. This has become known as 'deindustrialistation' and some commentators maintain that the UK may be likely to experience a prolonged period of heavy unemployment. On the other hand, taking the optimistic view, we may be evolving into a richer, high-tech economy.

Either way, for those made unemployed, life will indeed be hard, but this seems to be an argument for making adequate transitional arrangements and giving compensation rather than saying to our European partners 'No! We don't want your products – and certainly not those from Korea and Taiwan – because they're much better value than ours!'

Trade diversion

There is free trade only within the EU. To the rest of the world the EU presents a common external tariff, in many cases quite high. Because of this tax Europeans may prefer to buy, say, German goods rather than American and Japanese even though these are produced more cheaply. Thus, we deny ourselves the benefit of free trade. This distortion of the pattern of trading through the imposition of taxes is known as trade diversion.

Fiscal harmonisation

Although 1992 should see the end of tariffs it still leaves the problem of other taxes. The EU believes that VAT and excise duty must be brought more into line throughout the Community. If everyone charges the same rates of excise duty and VAT, there will be no need for elaborate calculations of tax payable on goods moving between countries.

The EU proposes two VAT bands – a high and a low band – and the same goods will be in the same band throughout the EU. The UK objects strongly to this. There has been some progress towards narrowing the range of VAT rates. There is now a lower rate of 15 per cent on the standard rate of VAT and the member states have agreed to abolish higher rates of VAT on luxury items, and to restrict the lower rates of at least 5 per cent on necessary goods to no more than two. Excise duty presents an even bigger problem. To average out duty, the UK would have to reduce the duty on spirits by a significant amount. This would be a massive loss of revenue to the Exchequer and is also firmly opposed on health grounds. The Greeks, meanwhile, would have to multiply their duty by more than 30 times!

Indirect taxes such as VAT and excise duty are an obvious problem. No less so is the problem of direct taxes. If there are large differences between income tax or the taxes on companies, the people or companies will move to minimise their tax burdens. Imagine, for example, that income tax is 40 per cent in Denmark but only 25 per cent in Germany. Those living in southern Denmark might well move to northern Germany and commute to their jobs in Denmark. It is also quite possible that companies might move their main offices to those countries with the most favourable tax regimes.

Thus, we can see that a truly single market must have taxes that are roughly in line with one another. This is called fiscal harmonisation. Without it there can be no true Single European Market.

Other implications of harmonisation

Employment problems

In many industries there is excess capacity in the EU. The Community, for example, is capable of producing much more steel and many more cars than it needs. Rationalisation of output could lead to the loss of millions of jobs. As you can see, if you remember the section above on the benefits of the Single European Market, putting these people back to work depends upon there being other expanding industries.

Industrial combination

In terms of its purchasing power, the Single European Market is the largest market in the world. This is why so many companies are keen on it. It also means, however, that companies will have to be suitably large to compete with other world giants. It is inevitable, therefore, that there will be many takeovers and amalgamations. For example, Siemens and GEC pooled their defence electronics businesses in 1989 to compete with their American rivals. The existence of large monopolistic or oligopolistic companies has implications for EU law on competition. An example of the operation of this was the case of the Distillers Company Ltd who, in 1977, were ordered to stop selling the same brand of whisky at different prices in the Community. (See discussion in Chapter 18.)

The Social Charter

In May 1989 the Commission put forward its proposals for a 'Community Charter of Fundamental Social Rights', usually referred to as the 'Social Charter'. The proposals cover the rights to:

a) improvements in living and working conditions;
b) freedom of movement;
c) fair remuneration in employment;
d) social protection;
e) freedom of association and collective bargaining;
f) vocational training;
g) equal treatment for men and women;
h) information, consultation and worker participation;
i) health protection and safety at the workplace;
j) protection for children and adolescents;
k) protection of elderly and disabled persons.

Most of these 'rights' are not controversial and are necessary if a true common market is to emerge. For example, a higher level of social protection in one country increases its costs and therefore distorts the market to its disadvantage. It may also be a factor in attracting movement of labour to that country. Conversely, a lower level of social protection could present a barrier to the movement of labour to that country. Others, e.g. e) and h), were seen by the Conservative party as 'socialism by the back door'. The Labour government elected in 1997 has now accepted the 'Social Charter'.

The Exchange Rate Mechanism (ERM) of the European Monetary System (EMS)

The Exchange Rate Mechanism (ERM) came into being in March 1979 with the overriding objective of attaining monetary stability within the EU. The attainment of monetary stability was viewed in terms of both exchange rate and price stability.

The creation of the EMS was to a large extent determined by the experience of the member nations during the 1970s. Following the demise of the Bretton Woods system of fixed but adjustable exchange rates, the first attempt at European monetary integration as represented by the 'snake' arrangements ended in failure as each country pursued its own independent monetary and fiscal policies. Needless to say, such independence in policy formulation resulted in widely divergent inflation rates within the member states. For example, over the period 1975–8, Italy, Ireland and the UK recorded the highest levels of inflation, in excess of 15 per cent per annum, whereas West Germany averaged a mere 4.2 per cent rate of inflation over the same period.

The pursuance of independent monetary and fiscal policies also resulted in wide fluctuations in exchange rate movements. For example, over the five-year period 1974–8, the average monthly fluctuation of the pound against the currencies of the ERM was 1.22 per cent, whilst for the Italian lira it was 1.56 per cent and for the Irish punt and French franc it was 1.29 per cent and 1.08 per cent respectively. At the other extreme, the monthly variation of the Dutch guilder in relation to all the other ERM currencies was 0.52 per cent, whilst for the Danish kroner it was 0.6 per cent.

The mechanics and performance of the ERM over the period 1979–92

In order to understand the workings of the ERM, it is important that we appreciate the central role played by the European Currency Unit (ECU). The ECU consists of a basket of specified amounts of each EU country's currency. The proportions of each currency are weighted according to the economic strengths of each member country, taking into account each country's share in EU GNP and intra-European trade. The composition of the ECU was reviewed every five years but has been frozen since November 1993.

All the EU currencies are assigned an ECU-related central rate. Thus the central rate of sterling was 0.696 904 whereas for the Deutschmark it was 2.055 86. Thus the central rate of exchange of sterling against the Deutschmark was DM2.95.

Each currency was allowed to fluctuate around the central bilateral rates. The permissible band of fluctuation was 2.25 per cent on either side for all participating currencies, with the exception of the UK, Spain and Portugal (Portugal became a member of the ERM in April 1992) which were allowed a wider band of fluctuation of 6 per cent on either side.

Intervention is compulsory whenever a currency attains its limit against another. For example, if sterling appreciates/depreciates against the Deutschmark by its full amount (DM3.13/DM2.78) the Bank of England buys/sells Deutschmarks and the Bundesbank sells/buys sterling on the foreign exchange markets to maintain the permitted band of fluctuation. Although the permitted band of fluctuation for any one ERM currency against another is 2.25 per cent or 6 per cent on either side, the maximum band of fluctuation (maximum divergence spread) of any one currency against the ECU is less than 2.25 per cent or 6 per cent on either side. This must be so for the ECU is a composite currency which consists of specified amounts of all EU currencies.

When a currency reaches 75 per cent of its maximum divergence spread, the currency is said to be at its divergence threshold. If it crosses its divergence threshold, the country concerned is 'presumed to act'. Such unilateral action may take the form of:

a) diversified intervention on the foreign exchange markets;
b) change in interest rates;
c) change of central rate devaluation/revaluation if all members agree.

How well did the ERM perform over the period 1979–92? No one doubts that governments everywhere during the 1980s and early 1990s pursued tight monetary policies to fight inflation. Nowhere is this more evident than in the UK where over the period 1981–4 it outperformed the ERM area. Starting from a similar rate of inflation, 11.2 per cent for the UK as opposed to 11.5 per cent for the eight countries that constituted the ERM area, the UK's inflation rate fell for each of the three years to 4.5 per cent in 1984 as opposed to 5.6 per cent for the ERM area. Indeed, over the period 1982–4 only Germany and the Netherlands had a better record on inflation than the UK.

The second primary objective of the ERM was the attainment of stable exchange rates. Over the period from 1979 to August 1992 there were 12 realignments (the last one occuring when Italy joined the narrow band of fluctuation in January 1990). During the early years 1979–83 there were seven such realignments and a further four over the period 1984–7. Until the crisis in September 1992, there had been no significant realignment since January 1987. Thus what started out as a stable but flexible exchange rate system became 'fixed' in the late 1980s and early 1990s.

In the summer of 1992 the ERM came under strong speculative pressure which forced a number of currencies to abandon the system. Chief amongst those currencies were UK sterling and the Italian lira. Indeed the speculative pressures against other ERM currencies continued until the summer of 1993 when the band of fluctuation was increased to 15 per cent on either side.

The reasons as to why the ERM faced such a crisis include the following:

a) *The state of the German economy.* Following the reunification of the two Germanies in 1990, the German government pursued loose monetary policies which resulted in high inflation. The economy was out of step with the rest of the member states. The latter were suffering from recession whilst Germany was suffering from inflation. The Bundesbank pushed up interest rates in its attempts to control inflation. Because of the role of the Deutschmark in determining the value of the ECU, the other member states could either devalue their currencies or push up interest rates in order to maintain their par values within the ERM but at the same time inflicting great pain to already depressed economies. They chose the former course of action, partly because of the requirements of the Maastricht Treaty.
b) *The Maastricht Treaty.* One of the conditions of this treaty for the attainment of a single currency is that the currency of each aspiring country must have been a member of the ERM and had been stable for two years at the narrow band of fluctuation. Individual governments were therefore reluctant to realign their currencies. Furthermore, in September 1992, the French government held a referendum on ratification of the treaty. The referendum was too 'close to call', adding further fuel to the speculative fire that was now engulfing certain currencies within the ERM.
c) *Speculators.* Just like the situation that existed under the Bretton Woods system in 1971, so it was with the ERM system now. Certain currencies, most notably the UK sterling, Italian lira, Spanish peseta and Irish punt, were overvalued. Speculators were once again being offered a 'one way bet'. They could not lose. They picked on each currency in turn forcing them to exit the ERM whilst making huge profits in the process.
d) *National governments.* They refused to devalue their currencies within the ERM, most notably the UK government.

It should be noted that with the exception of UK sterling and the Greek drachma (which never joined the ERM) all other members' currencies have rejoined the ERM and are once again experiencing stable exchange rates, virtually at the old narrow band of fluctuation.

European Monetary Union

One of the objectives of the EU is European Monetary Union (EMU) by 1 January 1999, according to the Maastricht timetable. This would mean a single currency for all members who satisfy the convergence criteria.

The Maastricht convergence criteria that must be satisfied by all countries who wish to join the single currency area are:

a) *Average inflation rate.* For the 12 months prior to the assessment date this must not exceed the average of the three best-performing member states by more than 1.5 per cent
b) *Average nominal interest rate on long-term government bond yields: lowest rate of interest.* This may not be more than 2 per cent above the average of the three countries with the lowest rate of interest.
c) *ERM membership.* Each country's currency must be a member of the ERM and the exchange rate has to be kept within the normal ERM band two years before the assessment date.
d) *General public sector budget deficit.* This must not be greater than 3 per cent of a country's GDP.
e) *Total public sector debt.* This must not exceed 60 per cent of the country's GDP.

At this particular time (August 1997), the overwhelming majority of countries satisfy the first three criteria mentioned above. The major problem concerns the requirement on the general public sector budget deficit which as many as two-thirds of the member states are unlikely to meet, including France and Germany. Faced with this obstacle, some supporters of the single currency have argued for a delay in the timetable. Others argue that such a delay would send the wrong signals to the foreign exchange markets and thus cause speculation to mount against those currencies which aspire to join such a monetary arrangement.

Some commentators are arguing that even if the convergence criteria were met, the establishment of a single currency would prove to be a disaster because the members of the EU do not constitute an optimum currency area. An optimum currency area refers to regions whose economies are closely linked by trade and by factor mobility. Although the extent of intra-European trade as yet is not sufficiently large to enable us to conclude that it is an optimum currency area (most member states currently export between 10 and 20 per cent of their GDP to other EU states) it is to be expected that this will increase as the 1992 measures take full effect.

The biggest problem for the single currency is that the labour force of the EU is relatively immobile owing mostly to language and cultural differences. This aspect is of particular importance for the costs of a single currency increase the less mobile labour is within the area. For example, if the UK experiences balance of payments problems, it cannot use its exchange rate to achieve external equilibrium. It can only use fiscal policies to achieve this. Since prices are rigid downwards, the level of unemployment will have to increase in order to curtail expenditure on imports. If labour is mobile, the unemployed will move on to the more prosperous regions within the EU thus lessening the pain of unemployment.

STUDENT ACTIVITY 42.3

Consider Table 42.3 which appeared in the *Sunday Times* on 21 July 1996 and answer the following questions:

1 Which arguments, if any, are valid from an economic point of view.
2 What has happened since July 1996 that might lead you to believe that EMU is now more/less likely to occur by 1 January 1999?

***Table 42.3* Ten arguments in favour of Britain taking part in Emu and ten arguments against**

For

- Interest rates and transaction costs will fall.
- By joining Emu, Britain will be able to use its muscle to obtain wider reform of Europe.
- It is going to happen, despite what the sceptics say.
- From the inside, Britain could push Europe in a more pro-growth direction.
- 'Wait and see' will widen the gulf between Britain and Europe.
- Sterling could obtain a highly competitive entry rate by joining early.
- Britain can no longer pursue an independent monetary policy anyway.
- The single market needs a single currency.
- The British people want a strong currency.
- By staying out, Britain would be in Europe's second division.

Against

- Britain has never had a monetary arrangement with Europe that has worked.
- Emu does not guarantee anything about the level of interest rates.
- There is little labour mobility between Britain and the rest of Europe to ease unemployment tensions.
- The Emu timetable has no economic logic, has slipped once and could again.
- Europe has huge structural budget deficits which need properly tackling before Emu.
- The single market is imperfect but already operates without a single currency.
- The British people are against the replacement of sterling by the euro.
- You can't have a flexible economy with an inflexible currency.
- Britain, by staying out and maintaining monetary policy freedom, will be better able to forge economic relations with the rest of the world.
- Emu will be dominated by Germany.

Conclusion

The debate on EMU continues to dominate the agenda as the decision time fast approaches. The election of a Labour government in the UK has not really seen a change of the official attitude regarding the single currency.

The state of the European economies, particularly in Germany, is giving cause for concern. In July 1997, the seasonally adjusted total of people out of work stood at 4.396 million (12 per cent unemployment rate), a post-war record. The situation in France and Spain is no better.

The voices of those who want to delay the movement towards the establishment of a single currency are beginning to become louder. However, there are still people who argue that the creation of a Single European Currency must occur by the Maastricht deadline, not so much because they are convinced of the economic validity of their position but because of political reasons.

On the wider front former communist states are likely to become members of the EU in the very near future. At the front of the queue are the Czech Republic, Hungary and Poland.

Summary

1 The IMF and the IBRD were set up as a result of the Bretton Woods conference and were aimed at regulating international payments and helping economic development.
2 The IMF system is based on a system of quotas; members may borrow in relation to the size of their quotas.
3 The adjustable peg was central to the IMF system.
4 The 1970s saw a breakdown of the system of fixed exchange rates.
5 The SDR is a hypothetical unit of account, similar to Keynes's idea of a bancor, and is now the basis of all IMF transactions.
6 Both the IMF and the IBRD are hampered by lack of funds.
7 There has been a decline in the importance of the IMF and the IBRD.
8 The eurocurrency markets are an important source both of finance and of instability in the international system.
9 The EU is both a customs union and a common market.
10 The present EU policy is to achieve 'harmonisation' of members' economies.
11 EU membership, while benefiting the UK, has caused problems because the UK's previous trading relationships differed significantly from those of other members.
12 The 1992 changes present enormous potential for change in European markets.
13 The drive towards EMU presents both opportunities and threats to all EU member states.

Questions

1 Explain the reason for the abandonment of the adjustable peg system.
2 What is the problem of international liquidity and how does the IMF help to overcome it?
3 Describe the main functions of the IMF.
4 Trace the reasons for the variations in the level of economic cooperation in the 1970s and 1980s.
5 Why was the UK forced out of the ERM in September 1992?
6 Outline the activities of the Bank for International Settlement (BIS).
7 Trace the origins and growth of the eurocurrency markets.
8 What is meant by the problem of international liquidity and how does the IMF help to overcome it?
9 Explain why the WTO is thought to be an improvement on GATT.
10 What did the UK achieve by leaving the ERM?
11 Why has progress towards establishing a Single European Market been slow?

Data response A
The IMF and Thailand

The questions below should be answered after reading the article by Ted Bardacke which appeared in the *Financial Times* on 7 August 1997.

1 Why did Thailand turn to the IMF for help?
2 What will the effect of the package be on the baht?
3 Will the IMF be successful in establishing control over Thailand's economy?
4 Was the IMF right to intervene in the internal economic affairs of Thailand?
5 Could and should the IMF have acted earlier to help Thailand?

A hole of its own making

Holes are a common sight in Thailand.

Now, suddenly, comes the biggest hole yet – one in the public accounts. This has so far cost $20bn and shows signs of getting bigger.

On Tuesday, the Bank of Thailand detailed parts of an economic reform package designed to obtain between $12bn and $15bn in emergency credits from the International Monetary Fund. Simultaneously, it announced it had lent nearly $16bn to the finance companies it has now declared insolvent. Another $3bn in public money has been spent to bail out the fraud-ridden Bangkok Bank of Commerce over the past 18 months.

In addition to all that came yesterday's guarantee – worth at least $7bn and perhaps as much as $31bn – to protect all depositors and creditors at both the suspended and operating finance companies. In all, the size of Thailand's financial system bailout is comparable to the US Savings & Loan debacle.

It is little wonder then that the country was forced to turn to the IMF. But after botching last month's flotation of the baht, the fact that the government had to be dragged to the negotiating table must cast doubts on its real commitment to reform.

"I have never seen Thailand in such a serious crisis," Mr Anand Panyarachun told reporters this week. And he should know: twice this decade he was appointed prime minister after bloody military coups.

He added: "There is nowhere else in this world where people have lost all faith in their own government and prefer their financial and monetary affairs to be managed by the IMF."

The frustration of influential intellectuals and economists was, in large part, due to the belief that the Thai government could have forestalled the crisis on its own. The belief is that it should not have waited so long to float the baht and then to announce measures to deal with the aftermath of its 20 per cent fall.

By most economists' reckoning, at the start of the year the country faced no imminent balance of payments crisis. The currency was not seriously overvalued, the first budget deficit in a decade was going to be manageable and international financial markets were giving Thailand some breathing space. If at that point the government had taken some tough decisions – by introducing more flexibility to the baht, cutting government spending and being tough with insolvent financial institutions – it would have rescued the economy on its own with less pain.

Some in Thailand are worried that by, in effect, farming out the difficult economic decisions to the IMF, the government will never learn to tackle difficult issues on its own. There is a fear that, once the economy gets back on its feet, the government will fall into past patterns. This would risk turning Thailand into a boom-and-bust country more akin to Latin America in the 1970s than other south-east Asian tigers.

Most analysts agree that it will be at least two years before Thailand, one of the world's fastest growing economies between 1986 and 1996, can rejoin the ranks of the tiger cubs. Corporate Tliailand has borrowed more money, both in absolute terms and as a percentage of gross domestic product, than its south-east Asian neighbours. Its domestic interest payments as a percentage of GDP are three times those of Mexico's at the time of the peso devaluation, according to Morgan Stanley and Goldman Sachs.

When Thailand's non-performing loans rise as a result of IMF-approved belt-tightening, the pressure on the government's balance sheet is going to grow further. This is not lost on other south-east Asian countries trying both to learn from Thailand and distance themselves from it at the same time.

"Long-term prospects for Thailand are good. But . . . we must never let this happen to us," Mr Lee Hsien Loong, Singapore's deputy prime minister, told a gathering on Sunday to commemorate that country's National Day.

Yesterday, some commercial banks experienced a run on their deposits prompting a return of rumours, categorically denied by the central bank, that a number of small banks could also be shut.

But even if the Bank of Thailand's assurances are to be believed – difficult for some who have seen the institution reverse course with tidal regularity – brokerage W.I. Carr estimates that by closing down half of the financial institutions the central bank has locked up 10 per cent of the financial system's deposits and 15 per cent of its assets. This will deprive the already cash-strapped manufacturing companies of much needed liquidity.

"The impact on the real economy is going to be very, very large," says Mr Warut Siwasariyanon, head of research at ING Barings in Bangkok.

"Companies and financial institutions are just hoarding cash right now. There isn't much scope for interest rates to come down for the next six to nine months," he says.

Thai officials say this is now the IMF's problem. They have declared victory and retreated. Believing he has won the economic battle by calling up reinforcements, Mr Chavalit Yongchaiyudh, the prime minister, is now moving on to the even trickier problem of political reform.

Source: *Financial Times*, 7 August 1997

SECTION VIII Problems and policies

'Economics is a subject that does not greatly respect one's wishes.'

Nikita Khruschev

43 Schools of thought and policy

Learning outcomes

After reading this chapter you will be able to:

- Identify the main objectives of macroeconomic policy.
- Recognise the link between schools of thought and policy preferences.
- Use fiscal and monetary policy examples of how schools of thought differ.
- Understand why some schools of thought reject key assumptions of neo-classical economics.

Introduction

Having completed our survey of economics we can now proceed to bring the various strands together. In this chapter we will survey the general nature of problems facing the government and the policy options available. In subsequent chapters in this final section we will examine some of the problems, such as inflation, growth and unemployment, in more detail.

Problems and policies

The major objectives of government policy

Even within political parties, opinions differ as to the correct objectives of policy, but in general terms all governments pursue similar objectives. These we can summarise as follows.

a) *The control of unemployment.* From 1945 until the 1970s, UK governments were successful in achieving near full employment. However, in the mid 1970s and early 1980s unemployment rose to very high levels, peaking at 3.4 million or 12.3 per cent in the early part of 1986. In the late 1980s unemployment fell to under 2 million. However, with the recession in the early 1990s it rose above 3 million once again. Recovery in the mid 1990s meant that unemployment had fallen below 1.5 million by mid 1997, but this is still high by the standards of the 1950s and 1960s, when rising above half a million was cause for concern. Recent unemployment figures can be seen in Table 43.1.

b) *The control of inflation.* Since the Second World War inflation has proved a continuous problem, reaching a record rate of 26 per cent in 1975. The Conservative government made the control of inflation its main objective. After rising sharply at first, inflation fell in the later 1980s to around 3 per cent. The boom in the economy after 1988 set inflation rising briefly above 10 per cent in the middle of 1990. High interest rates and recession had the effect of decreasing inflation in the early 1990s, bringing the rate down to around the 3 per cent mark by the mid 1990s. Recent inflation figures can be seen in Table 43.1.

c) *A favourable balance of payments.* This is usually taken to mean a surplus on the current account of the balance of payments. Current account deficits were one of the UK's toughest problems in the first 30 years after the Second World War. North Sea oil transformed the balance of payments situation. In the early 1980s this resulted in large current account surpluses, but the revenues from North Sea oil disguised the massive import penetration of many of the

Table 43.1

Year	1986	1987	1988	1989	1990	1991	1992	1993	1994	1995	1996
Unemployment quarter 4 (million)	3.2	2.8	2.1	1.6	1.7	2.4	2.8	2.8	2.4	2.2	2.0
Workforce (million)	28.2	28.5	28.7	28.9	28.8	28.6	28.3	28.3	28.2	28.1	28.0
GDP at market prices (1990 prices) (£billion)	488.1	511.6	537.2	548.9	551.1	540.3	537.4	548.6	572.3	587.9	601.7
PSBR (£billion) (– minus means PSDR)	2.4	−1.3	−11.9	−9.3	−2.3	7.7	28.6	42.5	37.9	35.1	24.9
Current a/c balance of payments deficit (£bn)	0.9	4.8	16.5	22.4	18.7	8.0	10.1	10.3	1.6	3.7	0.4
RPI	3.4	4.2	4.9	7.8	9.5	5.9	3.7	1.6	2.4	3.5	2.4

Sources: ONS *National Income 'Blue Book' and expenditure* and *Economic Trends* August 1997

'UK's markets. Together with a high exchange rate and rapid expansion of the economy, this was to result in balance of payments deficits of over £20 billion by 1990. This situation recovered only after a painful recession in the early 1990s and a period of low exchange rates in the mid 1990s. Recent balance of payments figures can be seen in Table 43.1.

d) *Economic growth.* We can regard the first three objectives of policy simply as 'good housekeeping'. Economic growth, i.e. an increase in real national income, is the true objective of economic policy because it allows everyone to enjoy a better standard of living. The steady, if unspectacular, growth of the 1950s and early 1960s gave way to stagnation in the 1970s. Growth has been uneven in more recent times with two major recessions (negative growth) in the early 1980s and early 1990s followed by surges of growth in the late 1980s and mid 1990s as can be seen in Table 43.1.

STUDENT ACTIVITY 43.1

a) Calculate the annual growth rate of GDP from Table 43.1.
b) Use the data in Table 43.1 to see which economic indicators usually move in the same direction and which ones tend to move in opposite directions. Is there sometimes a lag in these relationships? What additional information about economic variables would you select in order to have a better idea of what is going on?

Some alternative objectives

The list of main objectives above covers the mainstream of UK politics but other objectives can be put forward which may, to some extent, conflict with the main objectives.

e) *Improvements to the environment.* This is partly in conflict with the objective of economic growth because resources have to be diverted to minimise damage to the environment from industrial activity. The extent to which there is a conflict here will depend on whether a 'deep green' or 'light green' approach is taken. Environmentalists would argue they are substituting the goal of 'sustainable development' for economic growth (see Chapter 27).

f) *Aid to less developed countries.* All Western governments pay lip service to aiding the poorer countries of the world. The Brandt Report of 1981 suggested that each country should aim to contribute the equivalent of 0.7 per cent of its GDP to overseas aid, although in practice few countries attain this. The new Labour government of 1997 has made promises to increase its aid donations but has also pledged to retain public spending targets inherited from the outgoing Conservative administration for the first two years. While the government waits to see what it can afford, it has promised to target aid more effectively.

g) *Income distribution.* The development of the welfare state in the twentieth century involves the government in considerable expenditure on benefits for those who are less well-off, whether unemployed, sick or elderly. Certain services, such as education and health, also have the effect of redistributing income because they are provided free to everyone, but are paid for through the tax system. Although governments have introduced reforms to prevent welfare expenditure from growing, no serious political party is suggesting the abolition of the welfare state, and so expenditure in this area is a constraint on fiscal policy.

h) *Correcting market failure.* Although the government may wish to control public expenditure, it is constrained in this objective by the existence of market failure (see Chapters 25 and 29). The provision of public goods such as defence, quasi-public goods such as roads (Chapter 28), and goods with externalities and merit good characteristics such as health and education (Chapter 29) will limit the government's room for manoeuvre in fiscal policy as long as these services have to be funded.

Policy options

In Chapter 6 we reviewed the various types of policy which are available to a government, and we have since established various attributes of these policies. We will review the broad policy options before proceeding further.

a) *Fiscal policy.* This is the direction of the economy through taxation and government expenditure. Increases in government expenditure work through the multiplier effect, discussed in Chapter 34 to increase national income. Reductions in taxation will have a similar effect via an increase in disposable income. If government expenditure increases and/or taxes are reduced to a sufficient extent then there will be a budget deficit. This should have the effect of expanding the level of national income and, therefore, might be deemed to be an appropriate policy in times of unemployment. Conversely, a budget surplus should have a contractionary effect upon national income and therefore could be considered to be the correct policy in times of inflation. The conflict of ideas between the Keynesians and the monetarists that has been the subject of several chapters (e.g. Chapters 31, 35, 38) indicates that not all economists are in agreement about the effects of fiscal policy.

b) *Monetary policy.* This is the direction of the economy through the supply and price of money. Expanding the supply of money and lowering the rate of interest should have the effect of stimulating the economy, while contracting the money supply and raising the rate of interest should have a restraining effect upon the economy. These issues have already been raised in Chapters 36–38.

c) *Direct intervention.* Both monetary and fiscal policies aim at inducing the economy to conform to the government's wishes. The government could, however, intervene directly in the economy to see that its wishes are carried out. Perhaps the most obvious example of this is a prices and incomes policy to restrain inflation. The failure of incomes policies demonstrates that direct intervention is as fraught with difficulties as are other methods of policy; we cannot, for example, easily legislate against inflation without stopping the operation of the market economy.

d) *Supply side measures.* Keynesian economics led to an emphasis on the demand side of the economy. Measures to stimulate the supply side of the economy became fashionable in the early 1980s.

The choice of policy

Different policies will obviously be suitable in different situations but Keynesians will have a natural preference for fiscal policy, and monetarists for monetary policy. Chancellors of the Exchequer are frequently pragmatic men (we're still waiting for our first female Chancellor!) and often choose a blend of monetary and fiscal policy, usually supplemented these days by a few supply side measures. Direct intervention is usually limited to public sector pay.

STUDENT ACTIVITY 43.2

Identify what kind of policy each of the following changes represents (it may be more than one in each case) and what the likely objectives are.

a) A cut in interest rates.
b) A decision to go into the EMU.
c) A decision to build a new hospital.
d) A cut in income tax rates.
e) A decision not to allow planning permission for a factory which is likely to create pollution near to a residential area.

Fiscal policy

Discretionary and automatic changes

Discretionary changes are those which come about as a result of some conscious decision taken by the government, e.g. changes in tax rates or a change in the pattern of expenditure. ***Automatic changes*** come about as a result of some change in the economy, e.g. an increase in unemployment automatically increases government expenditure on unemployment benefits. In fact it is the case that deficits tend to increase automatically in times of recession and decrease in times of recovery. These fiscal weapons which automatically boost the economy during recession and dampen it in times of recovery are referred to as ***automatic stabilisers***. It is possible for a government to compound the effects of a recession by raising taxes in order to recover lost revenues. This, according to Keynesians, would cause a contractionary multiplier effect reducing the level of economic activity.

Fiscal drag

Where progressive taxes are concerned, inflation will mean that the Chancellor of the Exchequer takes a bigger and bigger portion of a person's income as increased money wages raise them from a lower to a higher tax bracket. This tendency is known as ***fiscal drag*** and it is to offset this that the Chancellor frequently raises the tax threshold. There is also a principle known as fiscal boost. This refers to the fact that inflation will reduce the real burden of specific taxes such as excise duty.

Borrowing

If there is any shortfall between the government's expenditure and income this is made up by borrowing, i.e. the government increases the size of the National Debt. If we consider the borrowing both by central and local government, this gives us the public sector borrowing requirement (PSBR). The PSBR forms the subject of a separate section in this chapter.

Common misunderstanding

It should be borne in mind that a government must have a fiscal policy. It is easy in the fiscal policy/monetary policy debate to assume that if the government adopts monetary policy as the chief weapon of policy it can abandon fiscal policy. This can never be so because in an economy where the government collects and spends over 40 per cent of the national income, how this is done must have profound effects upon the economy.

Theoretical problems of fiscal policy

There are disagreements between monetarists and neo-Keynesians about the efficacy of fiscal policy. The monetarists claim that budget deficits (or surpluses) will have little or no effect upon real national income while having adverse effects upon the rate of interest and upon prices. The criticisms of fiscal policy are considered below.

a) *The inflexibility of government finance.* Adjusting the government's level of economic activity to suit changing circumstances is not as straightforward as it may seem. Much of the government's finance is inflexible. One of the reasons for this is that the major portion of almost any department's budget is wages and salaries, and it is not possible to play around with these to suit the short-run needs of the economy. In addition to this, it would be a strange way of ordering priorities if a government were to stop the construction of a half-built motorway, hospital or school because less expenditure was needed. Much of the government's expenditure involves long-run planning.

Another problem contributing to the inflexibility of government finance is the political problems associated with cuts in expenditure. It would not be easy, for example, to cut old-age pensions, and cuts in health and education often bring unwelcome political criticism.

b) *Information.* It is very difficult to assemble accurate information about the economy sufficiently quickly for it to be of use in the short-run management of the economy. There have been numerous occasions when, for example, the balance of payments has been declared to be in deficit in one quarter but a few months later, when more information is available, it has been discovered that the quarter was in fact in surplus. It is difficult, therefore, for a government to be sure about the accuracy of the information. Even if the figures are accurate, the government still has to decide what they mean. For example, if the balance of payments is still in deficit, is this the beginning of a long-run trend or just a freak result of that month or quarter? The same can be said for unemployment and inflation figures which sometimes suffer from temporary blips due to special circumstances.

c) *Time lags.* One of the chief objectives of fiscal policy is stability, i.e. the government tries to avoid violent fluctuations in the level of economic activity. One way to do this is for the government to have a counter-cyclical policy so that if, for example, the level of economic activity were low, government activity would be high, i.e. it would have a budget deficit. Conversely, if there were a high level of activity then the government would budget for a surplus. This ideal policy approach is illustrated in Fig. 43.1.

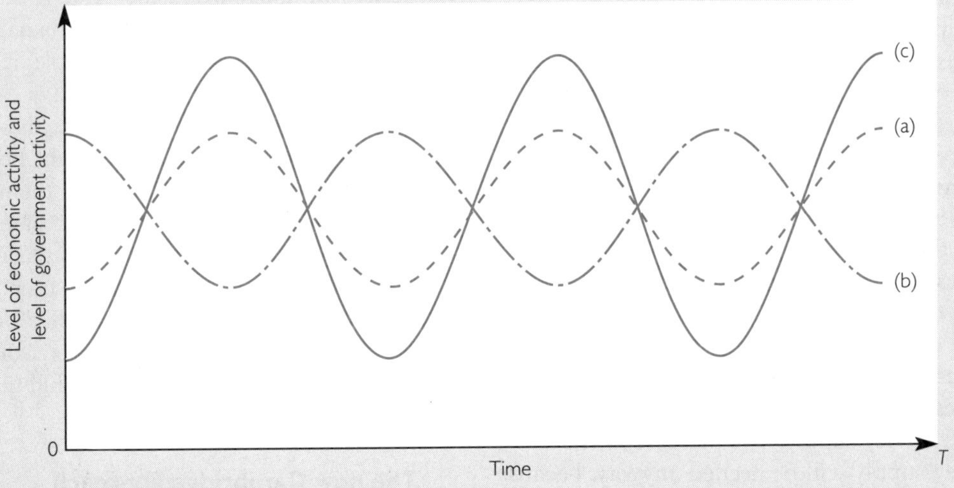

Fig. 43.1 **Counter-cyclical policy**
(a) Fluctuations in the level of economic activity without government intervention. (b) Proposed pattern of government counter-cyclical activity. (c) Worsened fluctuations in the level of economic activity due to government policy acting at the wrong time.

Unfortunately, it takes time for a government to appreciate the economic situation, to formulate a policy and then to implement it. This may mean that the government's policy works at the wrong time. For example, if the government decides to reflate the economy during a recession, it could be that by the time the policy works the economy would have recovered anyway. The government's actions therefore have the effect of boosting the economy beyond that which is desirable. When this happens the government decides to clamp down on the economy but, by the time the policy acts, the economy has naturally returned to recession. The government's action therefore makes the slump worse, and so on. This pattern will be familiar to anyone who lived through the stop–go policies of the 1950s and 1960s (see Chapter 47).

d) *Crowding-out.* It is argued that government borrowing may starve industry of funds and force up interest rates. This argument is put forward by monetarists and neo-classicists. The argument runs something like this: an increase in government expenditure or a decrease in taxes means that the government must borrow more. It cannot borrow from the increased income generated by the multiplier, because that hasn't happened yet. It must therefore borrow from the existing pool of savings, thus pushing up interest rates. This increase in interest rates will reduce private sector expenditure on both investment and consumption. It may also push up the exchange rate, which will also have the effect of reducing expenditure on domestically produced goods. Any benefit from fiscal policy will be cancelled out by these ***crowding out effects***.

The Keynesians reply that this increase in interest rates can be prevented by an increase in the money supply. The increase in the money supply will be needed anyway, because the economy is going to expand as a result of the multiplier effects of the fiscal policy. The monetarists cannot allow this escape from their argument, since they believe that an increase in the money supply will always be inflationary, while Keynesians argue that this will only be true for very sudden increases, or increases near to full employment levels.

The public sector borrowing requirement (PSBR)

The PSBR defined

The PSBR is the difference between the income and expenditure of the whole of the public sector. The pattern of the PSBR over recent years is set against unemployment rates in Fig. 43.2. This should be compared with ideal ***counter-cyclical policy*** depicted in Fig. 43.1. In the late 1980s, for the first time in many years there was actually a surplus in the public sector. Thus the borrowing was negative, i.e. repayment of the National Debt was taking place. The Chancellor therefore suggested that we refer to public sector debt repayment (PSDR) rather than PSBR. Since that time we have returned to the more familiar situation of a PSBR.

Keynesian views on the PSBR

The Keynesian view of the economy closely equates the PSBR with the budget deficit and, as such, forms part of the overall strategy of fiscal management of the economy. At one time, for example, it was considered that households tended to save 'too much' while firms invested 'too little'; under these circumstances the central government might borrow the savings of households and reinject them into the economy to increase the level of aggregate demand. This deficit financing had a central place in fiscal policy for many years. It has recently been suggested by the new Labour government that borrowing should be related to the amount of investment spending by the government, but should not be used to finance current consumption.

The new Cambridge approach

The traditional Keynesian view paid very little attention to the monetary aspects of the PSBR. The most important effect was always thought to

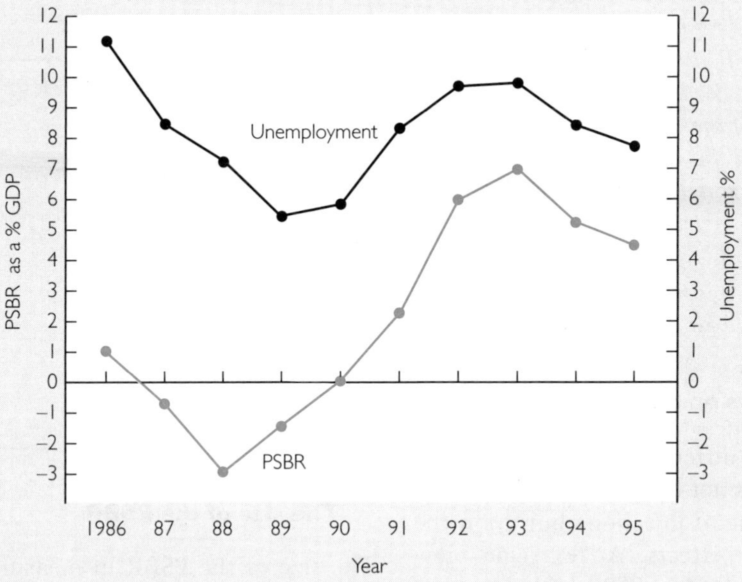

Fig. 43.2 **Fiscal policy and unemployment**
Source: ONS *National Income and Expenditure 'Blue Book'* and *Economic Trends*
Notes: unemployment at year end; PSBR for financial year (1986 is for 1986/7)

be the effect of the overall deficit or surplus; the monetary effects were felt only indirectly through changes in the interest rate. The 'new Cambridge' school of economists, associated with the Cambridge Economic Policy Group led by Wynne Godley, has concentrated upon the ***net acquisition of financial assets*** (NAFA) by each sector of the economy. Overall the deficits and surpluses of each sector must balance out. This can be demonstrated using the identity that withdrawals equal injections:

$$J = W$$

or:

$$G + I + X = T + S + M$$

Therefore:

$$(G - T) + (I - S) + (X - M) = 0$$

In verbal terms this means that the public sector borrowing requirement $(G - T)$ plus the private sector deficit $(I - S)$ plus the balance of payments on current account $(X - M)$ must sum to zero and therefore cancel each other out. It can be argued that the distribution of these deficits and surpluses can have adverse effects. The Cambridge group, for example, argued that if the private sector is broadly in balance $(I = S)$ then a deficit on the government's budget $(G > T)$ will result in a deficit on the balance of payments current account $(M > X)$. Thus, it could be argued that, *ceteris paribus*, increasing the PSBR would increase the balance of payments deficit. This effect could be observed in the early 1980s in the USA, when an attempt to expand the economy by cutting taxes resulted in a large balance of payments deficit on current account which had to be balanced by a large inflow on the capital account. The overall effect of this was to transfer ownership of many US assets to the Japanese.

Common misunderstanding

Many people have difficulty in understanding how one deficit (the PSBR) can balance out another deficit (the current account of the balance of payments). In fact, it is even stranger than that: one deficit is financing the other deficit. This is easier to understand if it is remembered from the international section that there is in fact no such thing as an overall deficit or surplus on the balance of payments. By definition the balance of payments balances. If there is a deficit on the current account, then this must be balanced out by a surplus on the capital account. It is this inflow of capital which actually finances the PSBR. In the real world, if savings are greater than investment (S > I) some of the PSBR may also be financed by the domestic private sector.

Monetarist views on the PSBR

Monetarists take a different view of the PSBR, placing the emphasis not upon the direct effect of changing the volume of injections but upon the 'indirect' monetary effects. An extreme view would argue that each £1 of PSBR adds £1 to the money supply. However, even if this argument is valid it is mitigated by who buys the financial assets sold. If financial assets are bought by the non-bank sector then the effects upon the money supply are neutral or even negative. On the other hand, if a bank acquires financial assets such as Treasury bills as a result of the expansion of the PSBR, this will have an expansionary effect upon the money supply since the banks can use these as liquid assets (see Chapter 37).

Monetarists on the other hand have stressed the adverse effects of the PSBR upon inflation. It is argued that the extra supply of Treasury bills and bonds in the banking system provides a basis on which banks can extend their lending.

It has also been claimed that public borrowing 'crowds out' private sector investment, as explained above. Great stress was therefore laid upon reducing the PSBR in the 1980s, but it was allowed to rise again in the 1990s to assist in the recovery from the recession. There is the fundmental disagreement about the PSBR: neo-Keynesians regard it as a fiscal instrument whilst monetarists concentrate on its monetary effects.

***Table 43.2* The PSBR 1986–95 (calendar year)**

Year	£ bn	% GDP
1986	2.4	0.6
1987	−1.3	−0.3
1988	−11.9	−2.5
1989	−9.3	−1.8
1990	−2.3	−0.4
1991	7.7	1.3
1992	28.6	4.8
1993	42.5	6.7
1994	37.9	5.7
1995	35.1	5.0
1996	24.9	3.4

Source: Adapted from ONS *National Income and Expenditure 'Blue Book'*, August, 1997.

The size of the PSBR

The size of the PSBR in measured in £ billion. However, it is probably more useful to think of it as a percentage of GDP as in Fig. 43.2. Both these methods of measurement are shown in Table 43.2. The table shows the PSBR becoming negative in the late 1980s. It should be remembered that at this time government revenues were being boosted by North Sea oil and also by the proceeds from privatisation. The recession of the early 1990s saw the PSBR rising again leading to cautious fiscal policy in the mid 1990s to try and get the PSBR under control again.

Is the National Debt too large?

If the government borrows money this increases the size of the National Debt. Most of the National Debt is owed to people within the country; only a small proportion is owed overseas. Figure 43.3 shows how the size of the National Debt as a percentage of GDP declined in the 1980s but rose again in the 1990s in line with the rising PSBR. There is much debate as to whether the National Debt is a burden to the country. The National Debt can be said to be a burden in two ways:

a) *Interest payments.* Government must raise revenue to pay interest on the debt. This is

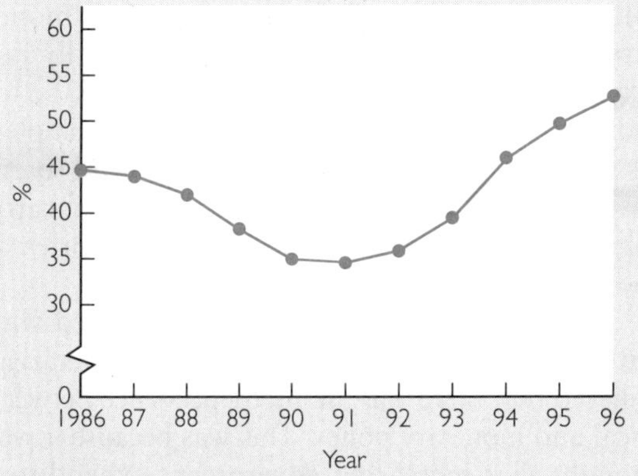

***Fig. 43.3* The National Debt as a percentage of GDP**

Sources: ONS National Income and Expenditure 'Blue Book' Financial Statistics

affected both by the size of the debt and the level of interest rates.

b) *Overseas payments.* The extent to which the debt is owned overseas presents a real burden to the economy. Surpluses must be generated on the balance of payments to repay the debt and to pay interest on it.

Cash limits

A feature of modern fiscal policies has been the imposition of cash limits. These were first introduced in the UK in 1976. They consisted simply of laying down aggregate levels of expenditure which could not be exceeded. This reversed the traditional pattern of fiscal policy in that previously it had been usual to draw up expenditure plans first and then raise revenue to meet them. Cash limits were a way of stating how much money is going to be raised before expenditure plans are formulated. It should be stressed that cash limits cannot apply to such things as social security payments.

The net effects of the budget

The simple Keynesian view is that a budget deficit stimulates the economy, a surplus contracts the economy and a balanced budget has a neutral effect. However, increases in government expenditure will all be spent, while increases in taxation will reduce expenditure by a smaller amount, depending on the marginal propensity to consume. A balanced budget increase will therefore have a slightly expansionary effect on the economy.

The effect of a budget deficit or surplus is also affected by the type of taxes and the type of expenditure undertaken. If, for example, we imagine a very simple budget in which all the taxes are raised by taxing high incomes while all the expenditure is on unemployment benefits, the amount paid might be equal to taxes collected, leaving a balanced budget. However, the money that is collected in taxes is the money that would not have been spent, i.e. people with high incomes would probably have saved a good deal of it. On the other hand, we can be reasonably certain that all the unemployment benefit will be spent. Thus the government has moved the money from non-spenders to spenders and as a result there will be an expansionary effect on the economy, although the budget will be balanced.

This would also work the other way round. If, for example, a government's budget is balanced but its revenue has been raised mainly from taxes on expenditure, such as VAT, and the money thus raised spent mainly on paying interest on the National Debt, the effect of the budget would be deflationary. This is because the government has, effectively, transferred money from spenders to non-spenders. Thus, when the government announces a deficit or a surplus a much more careful examination of its plans will be necessary before we can decide what the net effect on the economy will be. Put in more general terms we can conclude that:

The net effects of taxes and government expenditure are influenced by the marginal propensities to consume of those receiving the government's expenditure.

The different propensities to consume of different sectors of the economy will therefore influence the size of the multiplier effect of any budget deficit or surplus.

Monetary policy

We have already examined the operation of monetary policy and the problems associated with it

(Chapter 37) and discussed theoretical differences between Keynesians and monetarists (Chapter 38). In this section we will look at some of the major policy disagreements over monetary policy.

For most of the period since the Second World War, Keynesian orthodoxy ruled and this placed monetary policy as secondary in importance to fiscal policy. Nevertheless governments did use monetary policy to back up fiscal policy, it being seen as part of the overall policy of managing aggregate demand. This Keynesian view of monetary policy is enshrined in the ***Radcliffe Report*** (The Report of the Committee on the Working of the Monetary System, 1959). This continued to be the viewpoint into the 1960s. However, increasingly, monetary policy became part of the 'stop–go' cycle, when high interest rates and tight credit control were used in attempts to restrain demand and to protect the exchange rate. It is essential to the Keynesian view that the real impact of monetary policy is thought to be through interest rates.

The 1970s saw a transformation in government policies, Keynesian ideas being gradually replaced by monetarist ones. Two features are relevant to our discussion here. First, monetary policy came to be regarded as more important and effective than fiscal policy and, second, the control of inflation came to be the central concern of economic policy.

The acceptance of monetarist ideas meant that control of the money supply rather than interest rates came to be regarded as the premier object of policy. This is because, as was explained above (see Chapter 38), monetarists believed that this and this alone could control inflation.

However, it should not be thought that monetarism simply replaced Keynesian demand management. Monetarists do not see monetary policy as a method of stabilising and directing aggregate demand; rather, they see sound money management as a pre-condition for creating the correct climate for improving the economic environment. Thus, emphasis switched from short- to medium-term management of the economy. A most important part of government policy became the medium-term financial strategy (MTFS). This consisted of making firm announcements for the growth of the money supply. It was believed that this in itself would reduce inflation by reducing inflationary ***expectations***. However, such monetary targets as were announced were usually not achieved, which led the government to seek better indications of the money supply. Thus the emphasis was switched from M_3 to M_1 to M_0, and so on, as the government sought to find an indicator which would accord with monetarist theories of the money supply.

Monetarist policies came to be associated with cutting public expenditure because monetarists believed that there was an interdependence between fiscal and monetary policy. This was because it was thought that increasing government expenditure lead to an increase in the PSBR and therefore to an expansion of the money supply. However, in a time of severe recession it proved very difficult to cut public expenditure in real terms. It was only in the late 1980s, with the economy relatively prosperous again, that the PSBR was brought under control. The recession of the early 1990s again resulted in a high PSBR, but this time controls on public expenditure were less stringent, and the government allowed automatic fiscal stabilisers to assist in the recovery of the economy.

The evolution of monetary policy since 1979 has seen a shift away from controlling money supply and towards controlling the demand for money via interest rates. This change represents a shift back towards Keynesian beliefs that it is the interest rate, not the money supply, which is important. It is an elementary principle of economics that we cannot determine both the supply and the price of a commodity simultaneously. Thus emphasis on the control of money supply tends to leave its price (the rate of interest) to look after itself.

In the later 1980s the government all but abandoned targeting the money supply, by abandoning portfolio constraints upon banks, and instead came to rely almost entirely on interest rates. This accorded with the neo-classical idea that it is difficult to interfere with supply but, rather, that it is better to allow price (i.e. the rate of interest) to regulate the system.

Almost the first act of the new Labour government elected in 1997 was to give independence to the Bank of England in setting interest rates. The Bank is given responsibility for meeting inflation targets. This represents a departure from the normal Keynesian bias of previous Labour governments, but is not a purely monetarist move. There is still room for fiscal policy, although the initial position was largely to accept the targets on public expenditure of the outgoing Conservative government for the first two years.

Supply side economics

Alongside the monetarist revolution came the switch of emphasis to the supply side of the economy. In its earliest phase this consisted mainly of the argument that the problems of the economy could be solved by cutting taxes. Later, other government policies which were thought to constrain supply were included such as planning laws and red tape. The position of the ***supply siders*** starts to resemble that of the Austrians (see later in this chapter) the further down this line of argument the supply siders go. There is even a concern about the supply side from Keynesians about education and training of the workforce. As you might expect, this supply side argument requires an increase in government spending.

The Laffer curve

There is the possibility, pointed out by Professor Art Laffer of the USA, that increasing tax rates might, because of the disincentive effect, actually lower tax revenue. Laffer based his argument on the logic that tax revenue would be zero if tax rates were either zero or 100 per cent. If they were zero, obviously no tax would be collected. If they were 100 per cent, all one's income would be taken in tax and then there would be no incentive to work and therefore no income to tax. As real-world tax rates are positioned between zero and 100 per cent, Laffer concluded that there must be a tax rate at which the revenue is maximised. As tax rates rise, initially revenue would also rise as shown in Fig. 43.4. At some point A, tax revenue would reach a maximum and start to fall.

Michael Beenstock made an early estimate of the effects of the Laffer curve for the UK which suggested that a 5 per cent reduction in taxation would result in a 15 per cent increase in GDP.

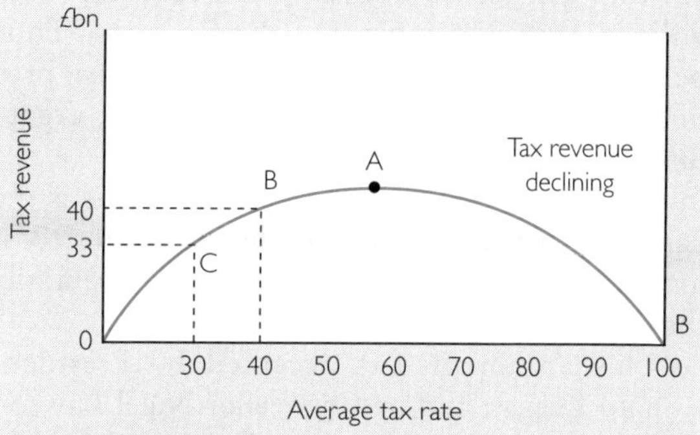

Fig. 43.4 **The Laffer curve**

Beenstock's estimates suggest that a peak in the revenue would be reached at an average tax rate of around 60 per cent; only those with an overriding passion for equality would be prepared to squeeze out the last drops of potential revenue. This is because, due to the rounded top of the Laffer curve, these last drops are at the expense of comparatively large increases in the average tax rate.

Tax revenue and GDP

There is a simple mathematical relationship between average tax rates, national income and tax revenue:

$$T = Y \times t$$

where T is tax revenue and t is the average tax rate. Therefore:

$$Y = T/t$$

We can use this relationship to explain the effects Laffer was predicting. In Fig. 43.4 at point B an average tax rate of 40 per cent (or 0.4) generates tax revenue of £40bn. National income (Y) is therefore equal to £40bn/0.4 or £100bn. A reduction of tax rates to 30 per cent generates a tax revenue of £33bn so national income has risen to £110bn. These numbers are illustrative only and do not reflect any real economy.

Direct taxes: a disincentive to work?

Supply side economists argue that taxes are a disincentive to effort. It is argued that if taxes are cut this will increase incentives because people will be receiving more for their efforts. Thus people will work harder. This will increase productivity and, as the economy expands, create more employment. There will, therefore, be a rise in the level of real national income. If this is the case then it is even possible that a greater total amount of tax may be paid. This was essentially the argument put forward by Laffer.

This argument was accepted by President Ronald Reagan and by Chancellor Nigel Lawson and was the basis of their tax-cutting budgets. (In the USA, at the same time as tax cuts there were massive budget deficits. Logically, therefore, it would be difficult to separate the supply side effects from those of a conventional Keynesian fiscal boost.)

The evidence put forward by Laffer and Beenstock conflicts with much of the evidence considered in Chapter 30, which found only weak evidence that the substitution effect outweighed the income effect. There are criticisms of the Laffer curve approach, mainly from a Keynesian direction. First, there is criticism of the use of the average tax rate when it is remembered that it is the marginal tax rate which is associated with the substitution effect (see Chapter 30). Second, as noted above, where government spending is not reduced, then cutting taxes will have a fiscal expansionary effect. Supply siders reject the idea that the cut in taxes works because it stimulates demand for commodities, and consequently for workers because they believe in the crowding out effect (see above). They argue that it must therefore be a supply side effect. As you can see, we are back to the argument between Keynesians and monetarists.

Other supply side policies

The supply siders started with tax reduction, but moved on to all kinds of government intervention which prevents entrepreneurial activity, ranging from bureaucratic rules, planning permission, legal support for trade unions. The reform of the welfare state to get rid of the culture of welfare dependency and replace it with one of entrepreneurial activity is also high on their list. The introduction of 'workfare' schemes which tie the receipt of benefit to undertaking some work is the major policy innovation in this area.

STUDENT ACTIVITY 43.3

Explain the effects of a cut in taxes from the viewpoint of

a) a supply sider
b) a monetarist
c) a Keynesian.

Radical political economy

A critique of neo-classical economics

Neo-classical economics has been the subject matter of most of this book and is regarded as ***mainstream*** economics. In this section we consider more controversial viewpoints from both the right and left of the political spectrum. On the right are to be found the ***Austrian*** economists who believe in pure capitalism with as little government intervention as possible. On the left are the ***post-Keynesians*** who stress problems of income distribution and unemployment. Further to the left are ***Marxists*** who believe in the violent overthrow of capitalism by the working class. The newly developing ***communitarian*** school of thought is more difficult to classify since it emphasises the importance of the community as an important mediator between the individual and society. It can be thought of as left wing because it claims that the market often damages communities, but it can also be thought of as right wing as it suggests a more authoritarian approach when the actions of individuals conflict with the interests of the community. Although these alternative ***schools of thought*** differ enormously in their views of the economy and economic policy, they share some common misgivings about neo-classical economics which are summarised below.

a) *Microfoundations*. Neo-classical macroeconomics is based on the assumption of perfect competition. Although it is recognised that there are some market imperfections in the real world, neo-classical economists assume that the model of supply and demand is adequate to discuss problems of the whole economy. Post-Keynesians argue that this is no longer a realistic model of the economy in the late twentieth century because they believe the core of the economy is essentially ***oligopolistic***. A more realistic pricing model to underpin macroeconomics would in their view be the mark-up model (see Chapter 17). Marxists also agree that the trend in capitalist economies is towards increasing monopoly power. Austrian economists also believe this to be the case, but they stress the benefit that monopoly power can bring in terms of the accumulation of capital, and innovation. Communitarians criticise the individualism of market processes.

b) *Equilibrium*. The emphasis in neo-classical economics is towards equilibrium, not just in individual markets but in the economy as a whole. This idea of general equilibrium is rejected by Austrian economists who argue that it is the dynamic creative powers of capitalism which make it the best system, and the price of this is some instability. Indeed they see a recession as an ***opportunity*** to reconstruct the economy in new creative ways. Post-Keynesian economists regard equilibrium of the neo-classical kind in which markets clear as unlikely, but emphasise that equilibrium in which the economy gets stuck at low levels of output is more likely. Marxists also treat the economy as a dynamic rather than as a static system, but one which goes through periodic 'crises' which they believe will ultimately be fatal to the system.

c) *Uncertainty*. Post-Keynesians emphasise the idea of uncertainty which was introduced in Keynes's *General Theory*. Sudden shifts in business confidence or expectations about interest rates will divert the economy from its predicted path. It is markets which are the uncertain element in the economy, so Post-Keynesians generally favour an interventionist role for government. For Austrians it is this very uncertainty which leads them to argue against intervention since it may backfire on the government.

d) *Pareto optimality*. Austrians argue that choice is a subjective process which cannot be simulated by the state. Wherever there is market failure, the state can only guess at consumers' preferences. Instead of government intervention, it is better to create actual market processes, however imperfect, so that individuals can exercise their own choices directly. For post-Keynesians the manipulation of consumers by oligopolies, and the absence of full employment, mean that Pareto optimality is a pipe-dream. Marxists also argue that the working class is deluded by capitalist ideology into believing that markets operate in their interests. The removal of this 'false consciousness' is seen as one of their most important tasks in the preparation for socialist revolution. Marx regarded the classical economics of Adam Smith as an ideological justification of capitalism. His followers today believe that neo-classical economics performs a similar function. Communitarians deny that the welfare of society can be thought of as merely the sum of the individuals that comprise it. Antisocial behaviour is likely to follow if the preferences of the individual are stressed to the exclusion of the interests of the community.

The Austrian school

It is easier to understand the Conservative government of the 1980s from the viewpoint of the Austrian school than by using neo-classical economic analysis. The term 'Austrian' refers to the school's beginnings in Vienna rather than the nationality of its modern followers. The Austrian school of thought differs in important respects from the modern 'neo-classical' economics. We are using the term 'neo-classical' here as referring to that economic analysis which is based on utility- or profit-maximising equilibriums under perfectly competitive conditions. The two schools both stem from the 'marginalist' revolution in economic theory in the 1870s, and thus they have much in common. An example of this is that both place an emphasis on explaining economic phenomena in terms of the choices made by utility-maximising individuals. However, the Austrian school has come to be distinguished by its insistence that markets can work effectively only in the complete absence of government 'interference' or of restrictions on the choices of buyers and sellers. Indeed, Friedrich Hayek, this century's leading champion of the Austrian school, believes that even the best intentioned intervention into the market is likely to have unforeseen side effects which result in a loss of overall welfare. For example, Austrian economists have argued that state intervention in education has caused a demand for educational certificates by employers which has adverse effects on the employment opportunities of young people.

Austrian economics is also distinguished from neo-classical economics in that it gives far less stress to the concept of equilibrium. The neo-classical welfare economics which we have looked at is based on the conditions which hold in equilibrium, whereas the Austrian school stresses the desirable welfare effects produced by the ***dynamic*** competitive processes which are generated by market forces within free market capitalism. For Austrian economists it is the process of learning and discovery which is made possible by free market systems that is the major source of economic welfare. Indeed, for many Austrian economists economic welfare is increased through time by allowing firms to compete for monopoly power. According to this perspective, prospective monopoly profit is the spur necessary to induce firms to undertake risky and expensive innovations designed to capture or maintain a monopoly position. The welfare gains to consumers from the 'gales of ***creative destruction***', generated as firms compete for tenuous monopoly positions, are seen as far outweighing any static welfare losses arising from deviations of price from cost at the margin.

Austrian policy prescriptions

The role of government for Austrian economists is to reduce its activity to an absolute minimum. Fiscal policy therefore consists of reducing government expenditure and taxation, privatising nationalised industries and balancing budgets. Monetary policy suggestions from Austrian economists have included the introduction of competitive currencies, with the most successful being the one which is used most. Austrian attitudes to market failure usually suggest ignoring it, since the imperfections of the market will be less than the imperfections of state intervention. Where intervention cannot be avoided, their preferred policy would be to create property rights over the environment as in the case of tradable permits (see Chapter 27) so that the market can be made to deliver on the policy.

Criticisms of the Austrian school

Market failure and income distribution are the Austrians' two weak points with committed environmentalists or socialists unlikely to find their approach attractive. Charitable giving is the basis for income redistribution and so if rich people don't feel like giving, too bad. Neo-classical economists' major complaint about the Austrians is their rejection of statistical testing of their hypotheses.

Post-Keynesian economics

This title is now used to refer to a broad group of economists who regard neo-classical economics as misleading and largely irrelevant to an analysis of actual economies. In particular they feel that the contributions of Keynes are misrepresented by the neo-classical synthesis. In the synthesis Keynes's arguments are reduced to the neo-Keynesian arguments that there are price rigidities or restricted elasticities in an otherwise neo-classical (perfectly competitive) world. Thus, in the synthesis, unemployment is caused by wages being stuck above the labour market equilibrium, but real wages may be reduced by increasing aggregate demand, thereby restoring full employment. Post-Keynesians, in contrast, reject the notion that the economy would achieve full employment even in the absence of wage stickiness or other price rigidities.

Post-Keynesians emphasise quantity adjustments rather than the more familiar price adjustments of neo-classical analysis. In contrast to the notion of Pareto-efficient full employment equilibrium, post-Keynesians emphasise the

dynamic instability of capitalism. There is no presumption that market forces create stability or that their outcome is necessarily desirable.

Many post-Keynesians follow Keynes's emphasis on ***uncertainty***. They identify the assumption of perfect knowledge (or known probabilities) as an additional major flaw of mainstream (i.e. neo-classical and neo-classical synthesis) economics. In the timeless equilibriums of neo-classical economics the problem of uncertainty does not arise. But in the real world where fluctuations in economic activity are frequent and where fortunes ebb and flow, uncertainty is a ubiquitous problem. The same investment project can make or break an entrepreneur, depending on the future course of the economy. The stable relationship between economic variables assumed by neo-classical economists does not capture this uncertainty and instability.

To this is often added the assertion that smooth substitutions between goods and production techniques in response to changing relative prices are another fallacy of mainstream economics. Cambridge University has a tradition of great economists who dissent from the traditional textbook portrayal of the price mechanism as 'a marvellous computer' which efficiently balances the unlimited wants of consumers against the use of scarce resources. One such economist is Joan Robinson, who wrote in her book *A Guide to Post-Keynesian Economics*:

> The slogan that the free play of market forces allocates scarce resources between alternative uses is incomprehensible. At any moment the stocks of means of production in existence are more or less specific. The level of output may be higher or lower with the state of demand but there is very little play in the composition of output. Changes in the adaptation of resources to demand can come about only through the process of investment; but plans for investment are made in the light of expectations about the future which are rarely perfectly fulfilled, and therefore have to be drawn up with a wide margin of error.

For these writers economics cannot be separated from the wider analysis of society as a whole. The allocation of resources between competing uses is seen as interesting, but only a very small part of the wider economic and social dynamics that shape the evolution of societies. Of more importance to the political economist is the analysis of power and its interaction with political, social and economic life.

Criticisms of post-Keynesian economics

The main problem with post-Keynesian economists is that, because of their emphasis on uncertainty, they are less likely to make predictions that can be checked against historical events. This not to say that they reject statistical evidence, but rather that they expect it to be inherently unstable.

Marxist economics

Common misunderstanding

The recent dramatic collapse of communist regimes in Eastern Europe has often been associated in the popular media with a failure of Marx's economics. Such an association is misleading because Marx offered a critique of capitalism rather than a detailed description of the system that would replace it. Moreover, given Marx's concern with human freedom, it seems unlikely that he would have approved of the oppressive totalitarian regimes which operated in his name.

Stages in the evolution of society

Marx identified four stages through which the relations of production and society had passed, namely primitive communism, slavery, feudalism and capitalism. He argued that under feudalism the produce of labour was expropriated (by the lords from the serfs), through a complex social system based on hierarchies of land ownership. In Western Europe by the mid nineteenth century this system of expropriation had been overthrown by the emerging capital-owning class and replaced by a social system which served its interests instead, i.e. capitalism. Just as feudalism had generated its own ideology, 'obligation' and 'divine right', so the ideology of the great liberal thinkers such as Adam Smith and John Stuart Mill was used to justify this new mode of production and social structure. Just as serfs had largely accepted their lot as inevitable and ordained by God so workers typically are not aware of capitalist exploitation.

Exploitation

The ideology of the liberal thinkers emphasised the right to equality under the law. Marx agreed that workers are equal to capitalists in the sense that they can exchange their labour power in the market place in exchange for its market value. They can thus withhold their services from an employer who does not pay this rate. Indeed, for Marx the distinguishing feature of capitalism is that labour power is sold in the market in exactly the same way as any other commodity, in contrast, say, to the ownership of a slave or the feudal obligation of a serf.

This equality in exchange, however, hides the inequality in production. If workers exercise their freedom to refuse to sell their labour power they have no other means of providing for their subsistence. This is because workers have no other access to the prevailing means of production, i.e. capital. In the extreme workers can exercise their freedom to refuse to work until starvation, in which sense slaves are equal to their masters! Thus the capitalist's monopoly of the means of production enforces wage slavery on the working class.

The idea of exploitation in Marx's economics is explained by the labour theory of value. Not only Marx, but also Smith, Ricardo and the other early classical economists argued that value of a commodity was based on the amount of labour that had gone into it. Not until the marginalist revolution of the 1870s was utility used as the basis of value theory. Marx used the idea to emphasise the worker as the source of value. He pointed out that machinery used in production was itself a commodity that had been produced by labour. If the worker is the source of all value, it follows that profit (or ***surplus value*** as he called it) is value that has been taken from the worker by excessive workload, low wages, or replacement by machinery (capital labour substitution). Marx argued that it was in the interests of the capitalists to have a ***reserve army of the unemployed*** in order to keep wages low.

Overproduction

Marx was very complimentary about the productive potential of the capitalist system, but argued that it had a tendency to ***overproduce***. As capitalists increase their profits by reducing wages, making workers work harder so that some of the workforce can be made redundant etc., so the income in the economy to buy their products will be reduced. The capitalist system will produce more than it can consume. This is an example of what Marx calls an ***internal contradiction*** of the capitalist system. The astute reader will recognise that overproduction is essentially the same as the Keynesian idea of underconsumption – when the level of aggregate demand is too low to keep people in employment. There is no multiplier or consumption function in Marx's theory, but the results are much the same. Unlike Keynes, Marx does not suggest fiscal policy to remedy the situation, but sees it as part of the logic of capitalist development and eventual self-destruction

Concentration of capital

An important theme in Marx's work is his stress on 'competitive capital accumulation'. Capitalists compete with one another through time by accumulating capital and applying labour-saving technology. All capitalists seek to defend themselves against competitors or steal an advantage by reducing their costs of production. This capital accumulation reduces the costs of the capitalists by reducing the labour time necessary for the production of their commodities. As each capitalist adopts the more capital-intensive production technique the labour time for the production of commodities is reduced. Thus the value of the commodity falls and the profits of all capitalists producing that commodity fall with it. Those smaller capitalists left behind in the accumulation race are competed out of business by those who have accumulated more capital or adopted a more advanced labour-saving technology. The rule is 'accumulate or die', as the control of capital is concentrated more and more into the hands of fewer and larger centralisations of capital. Concentration of capital is increased during the periodic crises as certain companies become bankrupt and are taken over by the surviving companies.

Marx argued that the constant tendency of competition to expel labour from the production process would cause a continuous flow of workers into unemployment. As output expands the total level of employment might expand, but even while this is happening capitalist competition and accumulation will condemn workers in many regions and industries to unemployment. Workers in depressed regions or with redundant skills will become surplus to the requirements of capitalists. These are the reserve army of the unemployed referred to above. Within this army there will develop a core of the permanently unemployed who will be condemned to relative poverty and misery.

Revolution

Marx believed that as the extent of this misery grew, and as capitalism appeared increasingly unable to provide for workers, the class consciousness of the working class (or 'proletariat') would develop, even among workers whose material conditions were being improved by the capitalists' development of the means of material production. When the proletariat recognised its class interest it would use the economic and political strength that capitalism had unwittingly bestowed upon it through the concentration of workers into places of mass production. The ensuing revolution would overthrow the capitalist order and replace it with a 'dictatorship of the proletariat' whereby the productive power developed through capitalist accumulation would be 'socialised' and coordinated to provide for the good of all. Ultimately, since the state was no longer necessary for oppressing the workers, it would 'wither away'. This is where Marx gets seriously utopian and is at his least believable.

Criticisms of Marx's analysis

Marx is often criticised for his use of the labour theory of value, but this is hardly fair since most other economists of his time, including Adam Smith, also used it. He is also criticised for not coming up with an internally consistent theory of how prices are formed in a capitalist economy. This is a more serious criticism which is too technical to discuss in this introductory text. However, criticisms have also been made of the neo-classical theory of pricing, partly because it depends on the assumption of perfect competition. Perhaps the most effective criticism from a scientific point of view is the absence of testable hypotheses. The types of predictions made by Marx can always be put off into the future. The absence of a revolution in an advanced capitalist economy can be put down to its not having yet reached the right level of development. It should be noted that so-called communist revolutions have all taken place in countries which were not industrialised, such as China (feudal) and Russia (just out of feudalism). Those countries which had some degree of industrialisation, such as Czechoslovakia, had the communist system forced upon them by the advancing Red Army at the end of the Second World War.

In support of Marx, capitalist crises of overproduction are still occurring regularly, with unemployment going above 3 million in both the early 1980s and the early 1990s. Perhaps the whole world has to industrialise before we can be sure that his ideas were not correct. In the meantime the idea of the reserve army of the unemployed forcing down wages has real meaning in the present world. As capitalism becomes more international, enormous reserves of very cheap labour are becoming available in the Indian subcontinent, China and elsewhere, which should create downward pressure on wages in the more industrialised nations.

Summary

1. All governments have to deal with similar problems. We may summarise these as the control of unemployment, the control of inflation, the attainment of a satisfactory balance of payments and promoting economic growth.
2. Four main methods of policy are available to governments, i.e. fiscal policy, monetary policy, direct intervention and supply side policy.

3 The difference between public expenditure and income is the PSBR.
4 The problems associated with fiscal policy are the inflexibility of government finance, conflicts of policy, information, time lags and crowding out.
5 Neo-Keynesians see public borrowing as part of demand management, i.e. borrowing to finance a deficit is an injection to the circular flow. Monetarists, however, see the chief effect of borrowing as being upon the money supply.
6 Having concentrated on control of the money supply, monetary policy turned instead to control of interest rates.
7 Post-Keynesian economists criticise mainstream economics by building on the more fundamentally challenging elements in Keynes's thought such as instability, income/output adjustments, changes through time and uncertainty.
8 Austrian economists reject equilibrium approaches but claim that it is the dynamic properties of capitalism that make it so attractive.
9 Marxists are complimentary about the productive performance of capitalism but believe it will eventually destroy itself and be replaced by a socialist society.

Questions

1 Discuss the problems involved in formulating a policy to achieve full employment, low inflation and a favourable balance of payments simultaneously.
2 Explain why any fiscal policy has consequences for monetary policy and why even a monetarist has to have a fiscal policy.
3 Examine the evidence relating to the Laffer curve from the viewpoint of a Keynesian and from the viewpoint of a monetarist.

Data response A
How do different schools of thought interpret data?

Study the data in Table 43.1 and try to explain what was happening to the economy from the viewpoint of

a) a monetarist
b) a Marxist
c) a Keynesian
d) a post-Keynesian
e) an Austrian.

Data response B
Budget interpretation

Using newspaper reports or official accounts of the latest budget:

1 Work out if the government is using fiscal policy to expand or contract the economy at present.
2 Try to work out which objectives are most important at present.
3 What are currently the greatest problems facing the government in trying to increase employment?
4 Are there any measures which could be described as direct intervention or supply side?

Data response C
Guess which school of thought . . .

Study the following passage and try to work out which school of thought the writer has the greatest sympathy with:

> The recession of the early 90s has provided the UK economy with an opportunity to restructure and develop in new industries. The increasing PSBR of this period resulted largely from falling tax revenues as national income fell, while government expenditure was maintained at its former level. This must be regarded as a missed opportunity to reform the welfare state in such a way as to reduce this expenditure and at the same time provide an incentive for the poorer people in society to find employment. The development of flexible labour markets in this period and our refusal to sign up to the social chapter of the Maastricht Treaty, mean that we have come out of this period in better shape than most of our European rivals, however. The election of the Labour government means that some of these policies may go into retreat, although flexible labour markets look safe in the short term. The most damaging policy is the introduction of a minimum wage which seems certain to result in higher unemployment. The control of public expenditure is also only guaranteed for two years, after which the Labour government may go back to their bad old ways of excessive social spending.

44 The control of inflation

Learning outcomes

At the end of this chapter you will be able to:

- Distinguish between those costs of inflation where inflation has been perfectly anticipated and the costs resulting from imperfectly anticipated inflation.
- Refer to the relationship between inflation and unemployment as shown by the Phillips curve.
- Discuss the adaptive expectations school account of the relationship between inflation and unemployment.
- Restate the rational expectations (neo-classical) view of the relationship between inflation and unemployment.
- Outline the main causes of inflation.
- Explain the policies available to control inflation.

In Chapter 36 we defined inflation as a rise in the general level of prices and a fall in the value of money. We examined various measures of inflation such as the RPI. In this chapter we look at the control of inflation as an object of government policy. Since the mid 1970s control of inflation has become the chief objective of government policy. We will first examine the main costs of inflation for the economy.

The costs of inflation

There are various *costs of inflation* for the economy, although they are often difficult to quantify.

They can be divided into those costs where the rate of inflation has been perfectly anticipated and is fully taken into account in prices and incomes and the ostensibly much larger costs that result from imperfectly anticipated inflation which is not fully allowed for in economic transactions.

Anticipated inflation costs

If inflation is progressing at a steady and fully anticipated rate, then the main cost stems from the fact that interest is not paid on cash in circulation but is paid on bank and building society deposits. Hence, there is an opportunity cost of holding cash, which is the interest that could be gained from placing the money in an interest-bearing account; the higher the rate of anticpated inflation, generally the higher the likely rate of interest and the greater the prospective opportunity cost of holding cash. As a result, there are likely to be 'shoe-leather costs' involved in placing cash in an interest-bearing account or in transferring funds from one account to another that pays a higher rate. Additional costs of anticipated inflation, known as *menu costs*, are incurred in the need to change prices: restaurants have to change their menus, firms have to issue new price lists and cash tills and vending machines have to be altered, all of which takes time and money.

Unanticipated inflation costs

A significant cost of unanticipated inflation is that it *redistributes income and wealth*. A fall in the value of money will remove purchasing power from those living on fixed incomes, such as pensioners, and redistribute it towards those who draw their living from prices. This is illustrated in Fig. 44.1. Wages are seen as being in

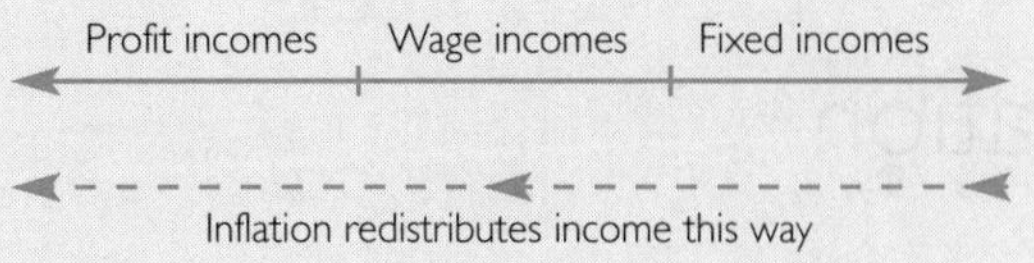

***Fig. 44.1* Inflation and distribution of income in the UK**

the middle of the spectrum, and the ability of wage earners to keep up with or ahead of inflation will depend upon the wage earners' bargaining power. This will tend to mean that those whose skills are in demand or who have strong and well-organised trade unions, such as doctors and computer programmers, succeed in keeping ahead of inflation while those lacking the correct skills and/or who are poorly unionised, such as shopworkers, agricultural workers and bank workers, lag behind.

Furthermore, if inflation is not fully anticipated (i.e. if real interest rates should fall), there will be a redistribution of income from lenders to borrowers; borrowers will gain while savers will lose.

STUDENT ACTIVITY 44.1

If the rate of inflation is 8 per cent per annum and nominal interest rates currently lie at 5 percent, who benefits – savers or borrowers?

It is argued by monetarists that inflation has a bad effect upon ***economic growth***; this is because it ***increases uncertainty*** and ***discourages investment***. If inflation is also accompanied by high nominal rates of interest, this will have a further detrimental effect on investment. A lower level of investment is usually associated with a reduced rate of economic growth.

While it is undoubtedly true that high rates of inflation are damaging to the economy, the evidence at lower rates of inflation is by no means convincing. Indeed it may be argued that some inflation is conducive to growth. This is because inflation may stimulate profits by reducing some costs of business but increasing their revenues. Certain business costs are usually incurred at a rate which is fixed for a period of time. For example, a business may lease premises at, say, £30 000 p.a. for 10 years. Inflation has the effect of reducing this rent in real terms while the price of the business's product (and therefore its revenues) goes up with inflation. Inflation is generally supposed to have an adverse effect upon the ***balance of payments***, especially if exchange rates do not fully adjust in purchasing power parity terms (see Chapter 41), because it makes imports cheaper and exports dearer. Theoretically this situation may be modified by a reversal of the Marshall–Lerner criterion (see page 562).

Common misunderstanding

It should be remembered that, as far as the balance of payments is concerned, it is not the absolute but the relative rate of inflation which is important, i.e. the rate of inflation in the UK compared with that of its trading partners.
If, for example, the domestic rate of inflation is 5 per cent but that of a trading partner is 10 per cent, then as far as foreign trade is concerned the price of exports will be falling and that of imports rising. Until fairly recently, however, the UK experienced constantly higher rates of inflation than those of its major trading partners.

Inflation and unemployment

A topic of great controversy is the relationship between the level of inflation and the ***level of unemployment***. For many years it was claimed that there was a trade-off between the two, i.e. reducing inflation would cause more unemployment and vice versa. Monetarists and neo-classicists, however, claimed that such an inverse relationship between inflation and unemployment only held in the short run; eventually employment would return to its previous level, but at a higher rate of inflation. The controversy surrounds one of the best-known hypotheses of recent years - the ***Phillips curve***. Since this is such an important topic we will now consider this controversy in more detail.

The Phillips curve

The original curve

Professor A. W. H. Phillips (1914–75) published research in 1962 which purported to show the relationship between unemployment, inflation and wage rises in the UK economy, 1862–1958. The research appeared to show that the nearer the economy was to full employment the greater would be the rate of inflation. A diagram based upon the original Phillips curve is shown in Fig. 44.2. It appeared that if unemployment were at 5.5 per cent then inflation would be zero.

The empirical evidence

Phillips's evidence seemed good for the period he investigated. However, since the mid 1960s the relationship seems to have broken down. Figure 44.6 below shows the actual relationship between inflation and unemployment. You can see that on a scatter diagram it offers poor evidence for a Phillips curve. Three possible explanations therefore present themselves:

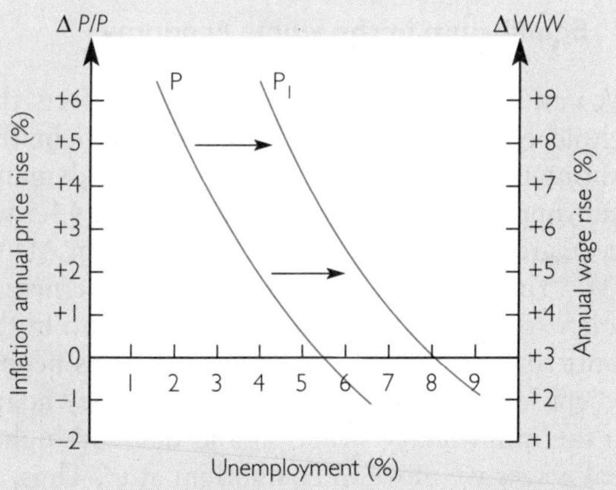

***Fig. 44.2* The Phillips curve**
This shows the relationship between inflation and unemployment. A rate of wage increase of 3 per cent p.a. is consistent with zero inflation if 3 per cent represents the annual rate of increase of productivity.

a) No discernible relationship exists between prices and unemployment.
b) A relationship exists, as described in the Phillips curve, but events have caused it to shift rightwards. This is illustrated in Fig. 44.2. As you can see this could also be made to fit reasonably well with the evidence in Fig. 44.6.
c) M. Sherman, a radical American economist, has suggested that the relationship is the other way round, i.e. increasing inflation is associated with increasing unemployment. The shaded area in Fig. 44.6 suggests the possible trend line of the ***Sherman curve.***

The adaptive expectations school

Milton Friedman put forward the view that there is a short-run trade-off between unemployment and inflation. That is to say, it is possible for the government, in the short run, to reduce unemployment by, for example, increasing the money supply. However, in the long run the jobs market will return to the previous level of employment but with a higher rate of inflation. This phenomenon is caused by the time it takes for people's ***expectations*** to adjust to the changes in prices and money wages.

The money illusion

This is the tendency of people to be fooled by changes in prices or wages when no real change has taken place.

Common misunderstanding
If wages double but prices do as well, some people may still believe that they are better off because they are earning £25 000 a year instead of £12 500. In fact, of course, real wages have remained unchanged.

The effect of the money illusion

Suppose that the government, in an attempt to reduce unemployment, increases the money supply. This has the effect of increasing prices but has no immediate effect upon wages. This, therefore, means that prices have gone up but ***real wages*** have gone down.

We can illustrate the situation using the analysis which we developed in Chapter 38 (see pages 524–6). In Fig. 44.3 real wages are on the vertical axis and the quantity of labour demanded and supplied is on the horizontal axis. The fall in real wages is shown as the shift of the supply curve from SS to S_1S_1. This is to say that people are offering their labour at a lower real wage because they do not appreciate that rising prices have devalued their wages.

In Fig. 44.4 we examine the effect which this has upon the employment situation. There is now a situation of excess demand for labour. This is because real wages are lower and businesses therefore find it profitable to employ more people. The excess demand for labour is shown as distance ab in Fig. 44.4. This excess demand draws more people into the labour market and also begins to increase money wages. We reach a short-run equilibrium at e^1. Thus a rise in prices has caused the level of employment to rise. This is because the rise in money wages has fooled unemployed people into accepting jobs which they refused before.

You will note in Fig. 44.4 that at the new equilibrium the real wage is still lower than the original one. The adaptive expectations school argues that this situation can persist only so long as the money illusion continues. In time expectations adapt and people realise that prices have risen; they therefore demand more wages and, thus, the supply curve of labour returns to its original position. When this happens money wages rise further to restore the level of real wages to what it was before the increase in the money supply.

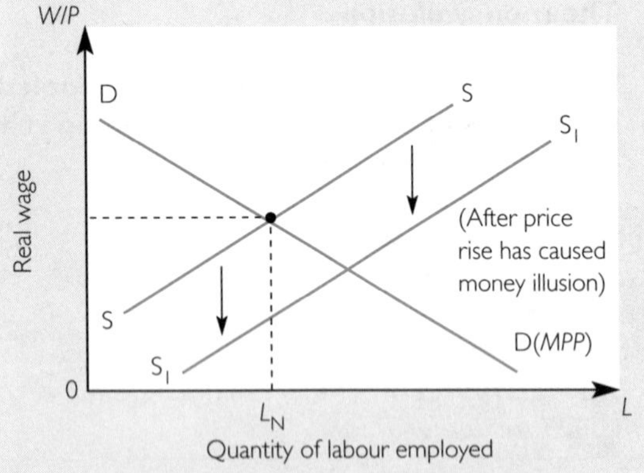

***Fig. 44.3* The effect of inflation with the money illusion**
The real wage is *W*/*P* If prices increase but wages do not, then the real wage declines. We can show this as a fall in the supply curve from SS to S_1S_1, because people are offering their labour at a lower real price not realising that inflation has devalued their wages.

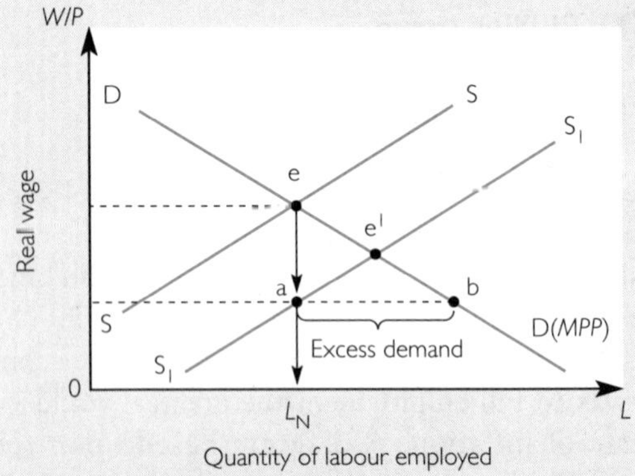

***Fig. 44.4* The money illusion disappears**
Rise in prices shifts supply curve S_1S_1. This creates an excess demand for labour because people are prepared to work for a lower real wage. Short-run equilibrium is e^1. As people demand higher real wage equilibrium returns to e with the original level of employment of L_N.

Equilibrium in the whole economy

We can now have a look at how this affects the whole economy. Instead of equilibrium in the labour market(s) we look at aggregate demand and supply in the whole economy. In Fig. 44.5 we see aggregate demand being increased from AD to AD_1. This is as a result of deliberate government policy to reduce the level of unemployment. In the short run the equilibrium changes to e^1 as people accept lower real wages. However, as they adapt to the inflationary situation and demand higher real wages we move to equilibrium at e^2. Thus, in the long run, we have higher prices but only the same amount of employment. It is argued that this is because there is a ***natural level of unemployment*** for the economy and any attempts to reduce unemployment below this level end in inflation rather than more employment.

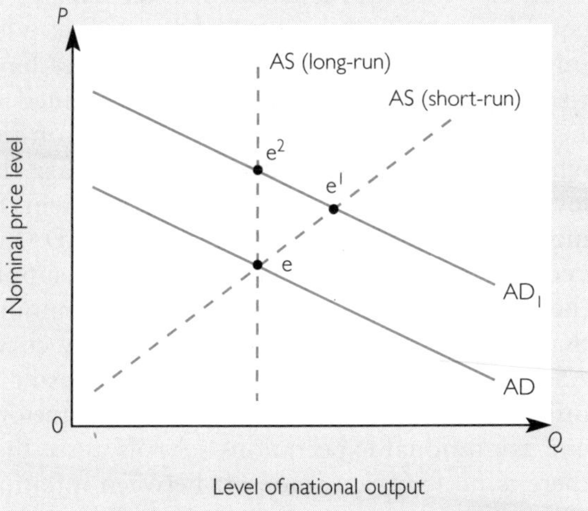

Fig. 44.5 **Equilibrium in the whole economy**
Government policy increases aggregate demand from AD to AD_1. This creates a short-run equilibrium of e^1 at a high level of output and employment. As people adapt to the new level or prices and demand higher wages, the long-run equilibrium becomes e^2 – i.e. the same level of output and employment but a higher level of prices. Thus the short-run aggregate supply curve appears to slope but in the long-run is vertical.

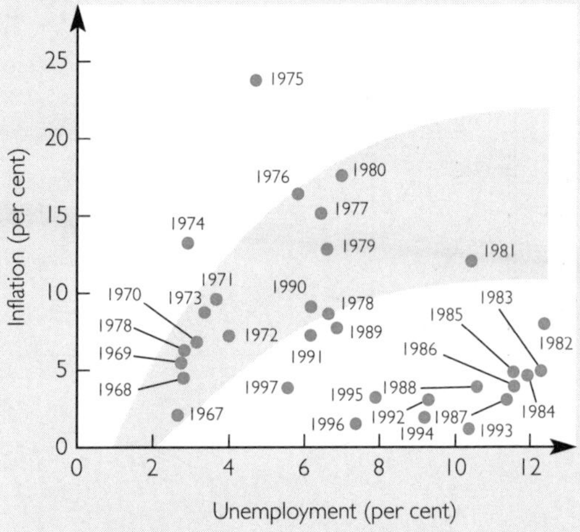

Fig. 44.6 **Inflation and unemployment in the UK**
This shows the relationship between inflation and employment for the years 1967–97. This presents very poor evidence for the Phillips curve. The shaded area, which takes in most of the points of the scattergraph, is possible evidence that unemployment and inflation are positively correlated.

STUDENT ACTIVITY 44.2

Adopting the same sort of reasoning as above, what would be the short-run and long-run effects of a fall in aggregate demand?

The expectations-augmented Phillips curve

Friedman has suggested that there is a vertical long-run Phillips curve (you can see in Fig. 44.6 that the years 1967–75 give reasonable support to this view). The different results are caused by short-run Phillips curves crossing the long-run curve. This possibility is illustrated in Fig. 44.7. The solid vertical line is situated at the 'natural level of unemployment'.

It is argued that at the natural rate inflation is zero. This being the case, workers expect the future inflation rate also to be zero. However, if the government considers that OU unemployment is too much it may try to trade off unemployment against inflation along the Phillips curve P_0, to reach point V, where there is 4 per cent inflation. Employers and unions are willing to settle for this situation because they are under the mistaken belief that their real incomes have risen. But when 4 per cent inflation comes to be anticipated we shift to a new Phillips curve P_4. To maintain unemployment at a reduced level of OZ and to meet expectations of higher real incomes it is necessary to increase aggregate demand by increasing the money supply. Thus the Phillips curve is shifted outwards again to P_8 which is consistent with the level of inflation of 8 per cent at the natural level of unemployment.

This rightward shift of the Phillips curve due to increased expectations produces the expectations-augmented Phillips curve.

In order to get rid of this type of inflation Friedman argued that a period of unemployment *above* the natural rate is necessary.

The explanation is as follows. Suppose we are at point V and the government refuses to expand the money supply. Inflation has now been stabilised at 4 per cent. However, employ-

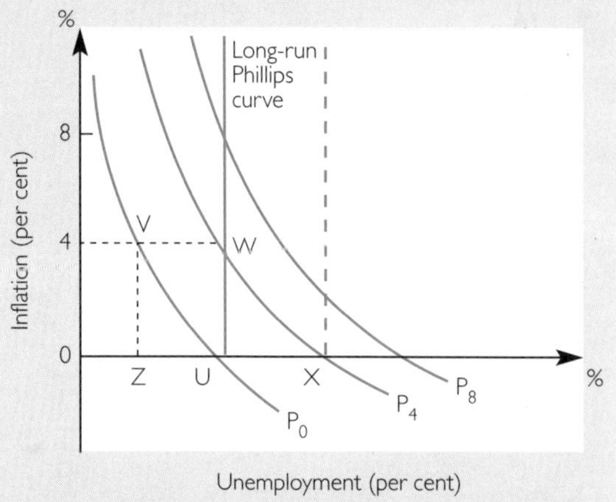

***Fig. 44.7* The effect of expectations upon the Phillips curve**

The natural rate of unemployment is OU P_0. P_4 and P_8 represents short-run Phillips curves based upon various expectations of inflation. If government decreases unemployment to OZ this causes 4 per cent inflation (point V). If inflation stabilises at 4 per cent employers reduce employment back to point W. However, getting rid of inflation altogether now involves increasing unemployment to OX because the economy has shifted to the expectations-augmented Phillips curve P_4. The blue dashed vertical line at OX represents an increase in the natural level of unemployment.

ers now realise that they have ZU more workers than they need; thus they move to point W, at the natural rate of unemployment but at 4 per cent inflation. In order to return to zero inflation it is necessary to move to point X, which is a level of unemployment well above the natural rate. This will rid people of their expectations of inflation and the economy can gradually move back to point U.

The rational expectations (neo-classical) school

According to this school of thought people are not fooled by changes in the price level. If there is an expansion of the money supply people correctly anticipate the effect on inflation and money wages adjust to keep the real wage the same, i.e. there is no money illusion.

In Fig. 44.8 (a) the labour market remains in equilibrium because wages adjust in line with inflation. Thus although prices and wages have risen the level of employment has remained at L_N. In Fig. 44.8 (b) we see the effect upon the whole economy. Here attempts to increase the level of employment lead the government to increase aggregate demand from AD to AD_1 but because there is no change in aggregate supply (because people are working the same amount that they did before) the aggregate supply curve AS is vertical and, therefore, the only result is inflation. Thus, both the adaptive expectations and the rational expectations schools agree that there is no long-run trade-off between inflation and unemployment.

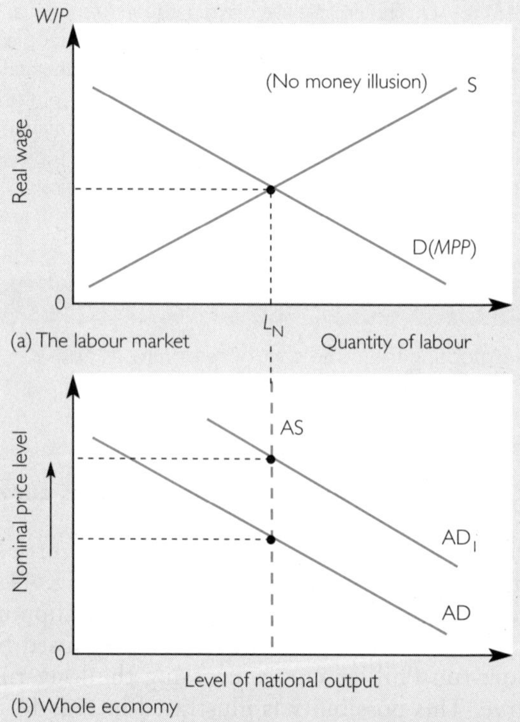

***Fig. 44.8* The rational expectations school**

The labour market remains in equilibrium because wages adjust in line with inflation. In (b) we see that attempts to increase employment by increasing aggregate demand from AD to AD_1 only result in inflation. (See also page 528.)

For those who like logical puzzles the rational expectations school presents a nice example of circular logic. For the theory to work people must be able correctly to predict the effect of increases in the money stock upon inflation. This is possible only if the rational expectations model is correct. Thus the model can be correct only if it is correct and is believed to be correct!

The causes of inflation

With the causes of inflation we have reached one of the key areas of disagreement in modern economics. However, since inflation is one of the central problems of our day we should not be surprised that conflicting views are held. At present three explanations are put forward: ***cost-push; demand-pull;*** and ***monetary.*** We will now consider these.

Cost-push inflation

Cost-push inflation occurs when the increasing costs of production push up the general level of prices.

This, therefore, is inflation from the supply side of the economy. Evidence for this point of view includes the following.

a) *Wage costs.* It is a widely held view (although perhaps rather less so than it used to be) that powerful trade unions have pushed up wage costs without corresponding increases in productivity. Since wages are usually one of the most important costs of production, this has an important effect upon prices. Figure 44.9 demonstrates that there is indeed a correlation between earnings and the level of inflation. We should remember, however, that correlation does not imply causation. The precise nature of the connection between wages and prices remains unclear.
b) *Import prices.* Whatever one's view of inflation, it must be admitted that import costs play some part in it. The huge rise in commodity prices, especially oil, in the 1970s undoubtedly contributed to inflation. It should also be remembered that inflation is a world-wide phenomenon and it is not possible for a nation to cut itself off completely from rising prices in the rest of the world. A fall in the value of the pound relative to other currencies, such as occurred when the UK left the Exchange Rate Mechanism in 1992, makes imports more expensive and can fuel inflation.
c) *Mark-up pricing and profits.* Many large firms fix their prices on a unit cost plus profit basis (see page 218). This makes prices more sensitive to supply than to demand influences and can mean that they tend to go up automatically with rising costs, whatever the state of the economy. In fact, some firms may use their monopoly power to raise prices

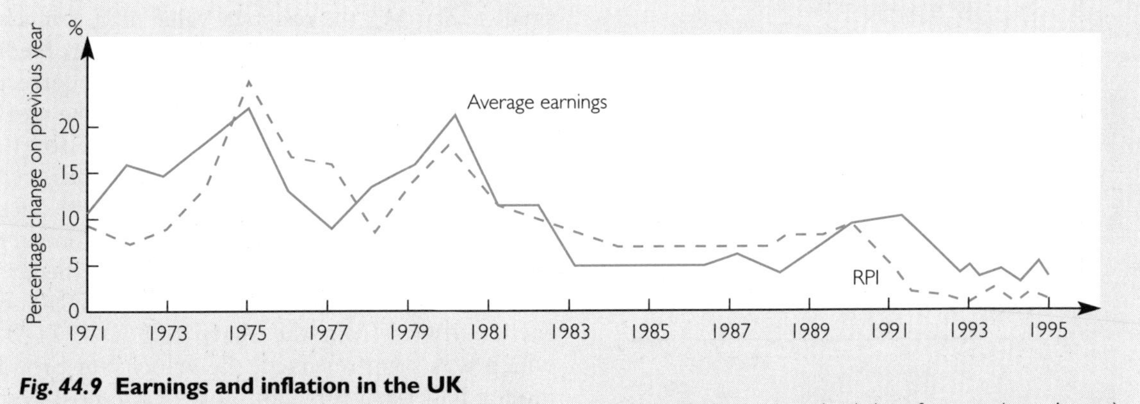

Fig. 44.9 **Earnings and inflation in the UK**
The graph shows a reasonable correlation between the increase in weekly earnings (and therefore employers' costs) and prices.

independently of any other influences, simply to increase profits.

Demand-pull inflation

Demand-pull inflation is when aggregate demand exceeds the value of output (measured in constant prices) at full employment.

The excess demand for goods and services cannot be met in real terms and therefore it is met by rises in the price of goods. Figure 44.10 recapitulates the idea of the inflationary gap introduced in Chapter 33. The aggregate demand line $C + I + G + (X - M)$ crosses the 45° line at point E, which is to the right of the full employment line. Thus at full employment there is excess demand of AB. It is this excess demand which ***pulls up*** prices.

Those who support the demand-pull theory of inflation argue that it is the result of the pursuit of full employment policies since the Second World War. These policies meant that workers felt free to press for increases in wages in excess of productivity without fear of unemployment. In addition to this there was the political demand for high levels of public expenditure which were financed by budget deficits. Both these factors, therefore, put excess demand into the economy.

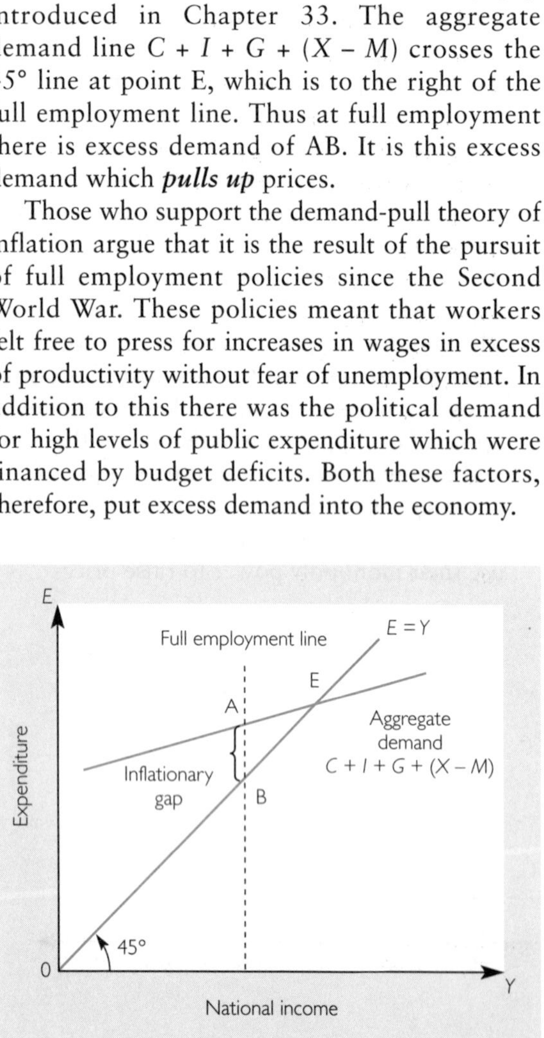

***Fig. 44.10* The inflationary gap**

Common misunderstanding

According to the point made above there may appear to be agreement between Keynesians and monetarists. However, in the demand-pull school it is the demand which brings about the expansion in the money supply and inflation, whereas monetarists see the causality reversed, with the release in the money stock occurring first.

Monetary inflation

'Inflation is always and anywhere a monetary phenomenon in the sense that it can *only* be produced by a more rapid increase in the quantity of money than in output' (our italics). Thus wrote Friedman in 1970. This note contains the core of monetary thinking, which is that inflation is *entirely* caused by a too-rapid increase in the money stock and by *nothing else*. We saw in Chapters 36 and 38 that the monetarist theory is based upon the identity:

$$M \times V \equiv P \times T$$

and that this was turned into a theory by assuming that V and T are constant. Thus, we would obtain the formula:

$$M \times V = P \times T$$

We will briefly examine these two assumptions. Figure 44.11 shows the actual value of V for the UK M_0 and M_4 money stocks from 1970 to 1995. The velocity is worked out by dividing GDP by the money stock. Naturally, as M_0 is considerably smaller than M_4, the resultant value of V is much higher. This also emphasises another problem associated with monetarism: what is the correct measure of money stock? As you can see, the measures give quite different rates of change for V, sometimes even moving in opposite directions.

As regards M_4 the slow-down in velocity since 1980 is a feature common to all broad monetary aggregates and contrasts sharply with the behaviour of velocity through much of the 1970s and earlier. Apart from the sharp fall in 1971–3, which was soon reversed, the velocity of broad money had risen through most of the post-war period up to 1979. When, after this date, the velocity slowed down, it was important for the

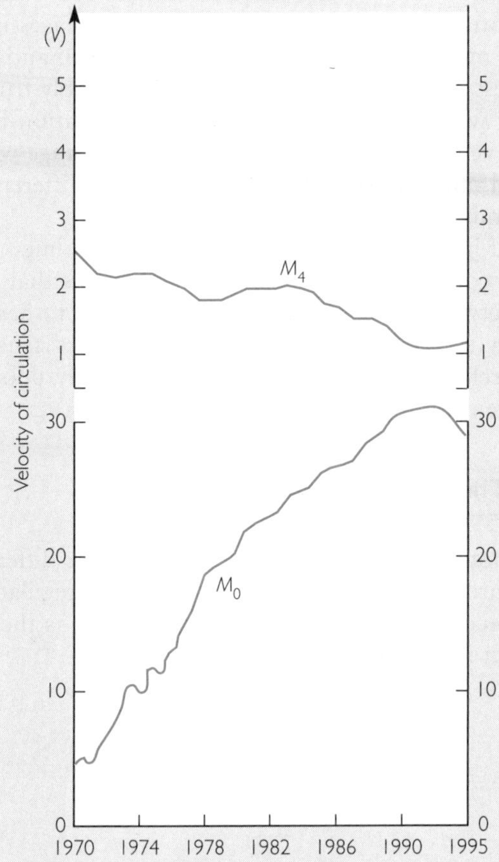

Fig. 44.11 Velocity of money aggregates
Source: BEQB

then authorities to establish why this was so. Did it mean that there was not a reliable connection between the growth of the money supply and inflation which the monetarists said there was?

The reasons for the fall of the velocity were varied, but in general terms they were due to a change in savings behaviour. This in turn may be attributed to greater competition between financial intermediaries for depositors, resulting in more attractive ways for investors to keep money with a bank or building society. It may also be attributed to high real interest rates in the 1980s. The stabilisation in velocity after 1990 can be associated with a decline in the pace of change in the financial markets, accompanied by lower rates of both inflation and nominal interest rates.

As you can see from Fig. 44.11 there was a steady and continuous rise in the velocity of M_0. In 1970 it was just over 10 but by 1990 it was approaching 30.

Bear in mind that a relatively small change in V could cause large changes in money national income; for example, if GDP were £525 billion and M were £150 billion this would give us the value $V = 3.5$. Under these circumstances a rise in V to 3.6 would cause an increase in money GDP by £15 billion whilst an increase to 4.0 would increase GDP by £75 billion. *Ceteris paribus*, this is equal to a rate of inflation of over 14 per cent.

STUDENT ACTIVITY 44.3

If GDP equals £400 billion and M is £100 billion, calculate V. What would be the effect on GDP if V then increased to 4.5?

The fall in velocity of M_0 after 1991 has been the result of a fall in the growth of credit and debit cards; the growth in the use of these cards prior to this meant that people had less need to hold cash, which thus circulated faster.

Thus, as you can see, the idea that V is constant, or even stable, is dubious. Important criticisms of Friedman's views were raised in the *Bank of England Quarterly Bulletin* in December 1983 by Hendry and Ericsson. In the event the Bank did not publish the article as it was too much at variance with the authorities' views at the time. The most devastating claim made was that Friedman adjusted the figures for the money supply and the price levels to produce a constant V. Without a constant V there will be no predictable relationship between money, national income and prices.

The second assumption of monetarism is that T is constant. Put another way, it is the belief that the economy will tend towards a full employment equilibrium. This being the case, any increase in M can result only in price changes and not real changes in national income. Unemployment is caused by a temporary lack of adjustment in the economy when there is confusion between real national income and money national income – the ***money illusion***. The unemployment of the 1980s and 1990s is perhaps stretching the word 'temporary' to its limits.

Figure 44.12 shows the relationship between sterling M_3, M_2, M_0 and inflation. It is Friedman's contention that an increase in the money stock will cause a rise in inflation 18 months to two years later. As you can see the graph shows conflicting evidence. There does seem to be a close correlation between M_0 and the RPI during the 1980s. The period considered in the graph is too brief for a fair appraisal of Friedman's proposition. He obtained very good results for a whole century in the USA. However, even if there is a good fit it does not prove that one thing *causes* the other. Also, we have just seen above that the empirical basis of Friedman's research has been subject to criticism.

Multicausal inflation

Having worked through the chapter the student might now legitimately ask, 'What does cause inflation then?' The answer is probably that inflation has a number of causes – increases in the money supply, excessive wage demands, excess demand and so on. It is also probably true that what may be the chief cause of inflation in one year may not be in the next. At this stage we need more research to separate out the different strands of inflation.

If inflation does have many causes, an important conclusion stems from this and that is that a variety of policy measures will be needed to deal with it. Thus a policy which places its trust entirely upon monetary control or entirely upon wage restraint is unlikely to be successful.

The control of inflation

As noted in Chapter 43 governments have different areas of policy which they can use to regulate the economy. We will now look at these as they affect inflation.

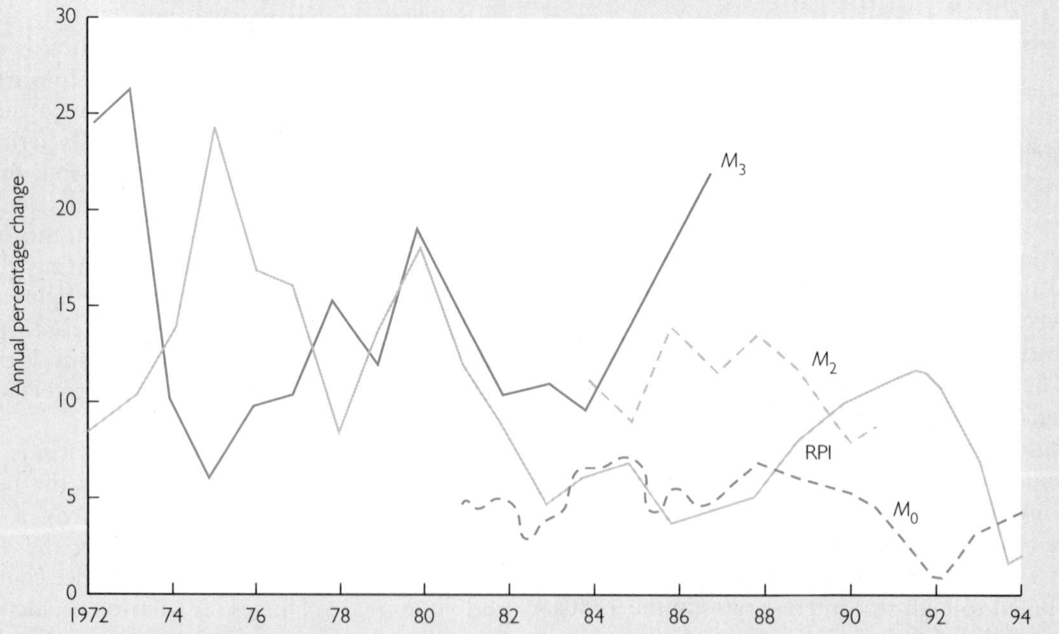

Fig. 44.12 **The money stock and inflation in the UK**
The graphs trace the annual percentage change in M_3, M_2, M_0 and the index of retail prices.

Fiscal policy

Fiscal policy is based upon demand management, i.e. raising or lowering the level of aggregate demand. In Fig. 44.10 you can see that the government could attempt to act upon any of the components in the $C + I + G + (X - M)$ line. The most obvious policy is that the government should reduce government expenditure and raise taxes. It should be stated here that this policy will be successful only against demand inflation. Fiscal policy was the chief counter-inflationary measure in the 1950s and 1960s. One of the reasons for its failure then was the clash of objectives. Governments were usually prone to put full employment higher on their list of priorities than control of inflation. Thus, after a short period of fiscal stringency, unemployment was likely to mount and this repeatedly caused governments to abandon tight fiscal policy and go over to expansion of the economy before inflation had been controlled.

The rise of monetarist ideas has meant that fiscal policy is seen as important only in so far as it affects the money supply. Thus in recent years emphasis has been placed upon reducing the size of the PSBR. This was discussed in the previous chapter.

Monetary policy

For many years monetary policy was seen as only supplementary to fiscal policy. The Radcliffe Report's conclusion, that 'money is not important', was widened into 'money does not matter'. Clearly this was an overstatement and we can see, for example, that the rapid expansion of the money supply in the 1970s was undoubtedly one of the causes of inflation.

If monetary policy had a role, Keynesians saw it as being through the rate of interest. The monetarist prescription is to control the supply of money. This, as we have seen, was believed to be the only way in which inflation could be controlled. In the 1980s great emphasis was placed upon the ***medium-term financial strategy*** (MTFS), i.e. setting targets for monetary growth for the next few years. Not only would reducing the supply of money in itself reduce inflation but the setting of ***firm*** targets would reduce ***expectations***. As we saw earlier in this chapter Friedman argued that increased expectations of inflation are a reason for the rightward shift of the Phillips curve. The policy was aimed at gradually reducing the growth of the money supply until it was in line with the growth of the real economy.

STUDENT ACTIVITY 44.4

What are the main monetary weapons that the government has at its disposal in order to control inflation?

Figure 44.13 shows the targets set for growth in the money supply in the 1980s, together with the actual growth of M_3. You can see from the diagram that MTFS targets were generally greatly exceeded and it was this which, in the end, led to the abandonment of M_3 as a monetary target. As we mentioned earlier, one of the problems in controlling the money supply is choosing the correct measure of it. Should it be M_1, M_2, M_3 or what? The danger is that once policy is aimed at controlling one of these variables it may tend to distort it. A Bank of England official, Charles Goodhart, formulated a principle based upon this difficulty.

Goodhart's law states that any statistical regularity will tend to collapse once pressure is placed upon it for control purposes.

In other words a measure such as M_3 is a good guide so long as we do not make its control the object of policy.

At the end of the 1980s the government had fixed on M_0 as the measure to control in its MTFS (see Fig. 44.14). M_0 proved to be a stable and predictable measure of the money supply but, as you can see from Fig. 44.11, the value of V for M_0 was increasing rapidly at this time. Thus, using the $MV = PT$ formula, it was still possible to have large increases in the nominal level of national income whilst keeping a strict control on M_0.

In the later years of the 1980s inflation dropped to below 5 per cent. However, following a drop in interest rates, inflation then escalated to over 10 per cent but then fell again in 1991 to around 5 per

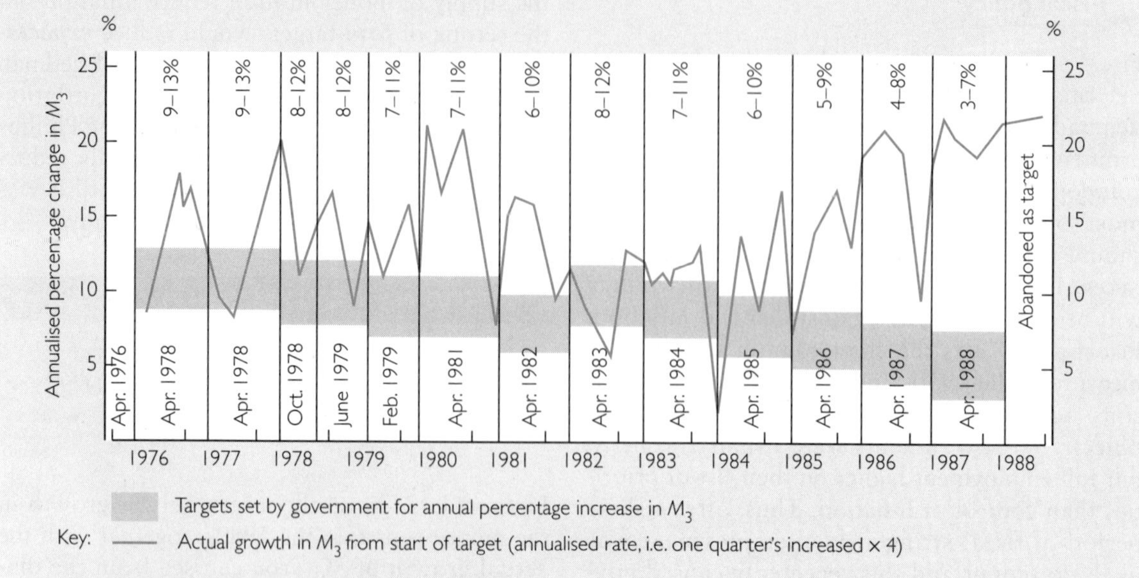

***Fig. 44.13* Monetary targets and money growth in the UK**

cent. Is it possible that we can attribute this to control of the money supply, whichever measure we take? The work of Hendry and Ericsson suggests that this is not so. They argue that the excessive growth of money supply such as that of the 1980s can even be restrictive! If this conclusion is correct it would make it virtually impossible for governments to formulate money supply targets. Their findings also tend to repudiate the idea of the exogeneity of the money supply which is vital to Friedman's arguments (see page 520). Professor Hendry concluded: 'We have not been able to find any evidence that money supply creates either income growth or inflation.' If this were the case then the decrease in the rate of inflation must be due to some other factor, perhaps unemployment moderating wage demands. The government itself was disinclined to accept such a neo-Keynesian conclusion. Despite disillusionment with monetary targets it remained convinced of the primacy of monetary policy. Speaking in 1988 Nigel Lawson said:

> Experience in the '80s has demonstrated that ... monetary policy is the only weapon for bearing down on inflation. The abolition of various controls within the financial system, which has brought enormous benefits, has made it difficult to rely solely on monetary targets.
>
> At the same time, the ending of controls inevitably places more weight on short-term interest rates as the essential weapon of monetary policy. Short-term interest rates are the market route to the defeat of inflation.

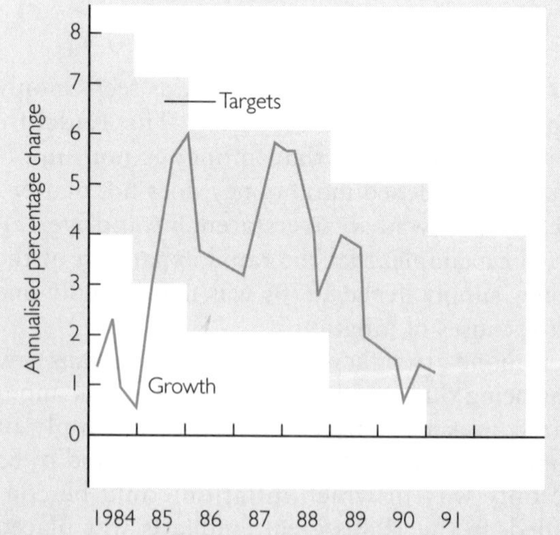

***Fig. 44.14* Monetary targets and monetary growth of M_0 in the UK**

Thus we can conclude that a Conservative government committed to market forces had, by the end of the early 1990s, largely abandoned monetary targets in its fight against inflation and instead placed its faith in the ability of rising interest rates to control spending and hence inflation.

Following the decision by the government to leave the ERM in 1992, it was able to concentrate more on domestic issues rather than having to worry so much about the value of the pound. Since then, following the general dissatisfaction of employing monetary targets as a means for controlling inflation, the authorities have instead opted for explicit ***inflation targets*** in order to ensure price stability. Currently, the inflation target is that the RPI should, over the medium term, average 2.5 per cent or less. The advantage of such a policy is its apparent simplicity: a clear commitment is given by the monetary authorities, one that can be fairly easily understood by the public. Such a commitment is backed up by greater openness. The Bank of England now publishes monthly inflation forecasts and, should it miss its target, has to explain why it did so. The newly independent Bank of England has to account for itself to the Chancellor of the Exchequer if inflation dips blow 1.5 per cent or rises above 3.5 per cent.

On the other hand, such a monetary policy is based on inflation ***forecasts*** (of up to two years ahead given the time lags in the operation of monetary policy) rather than on inflation itself. If a target is set too tightly or if it is pursued too rigorously (i.e. by raising interest rates more than is necessary), then this could result in higher unemployment and lower growth.

So far the policy has been successful in keeping inflation inside its target range, although this was partly due to the existence of tight monetary conditions before targeting began. It remains to be seen whether the new system, in which the independent Bank of England has overall responsibility for setting interest rates, will continue to keep inflation within the target bands.

Direct intervention: prices and incomes policy

A prices and incomes policy is where the government takes measures to restrict the increase in wages (incomes) and prices.

Like other counter-inflationary measures, a prices and incomes policy tries to ensure that wages and other incomes do not rise faster than the improvement in productivity in the economy. If incomes can be kept below that level there is the added bonus of extra resources which are freed for investment. There are two main types of incomes policy.

a) *Statutory*. This occurs when the government passes legislation to limit or to freeze wages and prices. Such policies were used in the UK at various times in the 1960s and 1970s, although they have not been formally employed since then.
b) *Voluntary*. This is where the government tries through argument and persuasion to impose a wages and prices policy. Features of such a policy may include the setting up of a prices and incomes board to examine wage and price increases, exhortations to firms and unions to restrict increases and securing the cooperation of bodies such as the TUC and CBI.

Common misunderstanding

A prices and incomes policy need not be legally enforced by the government; in fact it usually is not. Since 1979 a form of voluntary pay restraint has existed for much of the time in the form of cash limits for the public sector that restrict levels of pay increases.

An incomes policy is thought to be effective as a method of counteracting cost-push inflation caused by increasing wages. The rationale behind the Phillips curve is that it is wage costs which push up prices. Incomes policy could therefore be seen as a way to move the Phillips curve leftwards, achieving lower inflation without causing more unemployment. If inflation results from excess demand an incomes policy is only likely to lead to employers finding disguised ways of paying higher rewards to labour in order to attract people to jobs. Nowadays an incomes policy is more likely to be used in conjunction with other supply side measures, such as reducing the activities of trade unions, deregulation, monopoly legislation, tax incentives and training schemes, in order to attempt to lower the rate of increase in costs in general (see also Chapter 45).

Incomes policies often tend to be more effective in the public sector, thus restricting incomes there more than in the private sector. In addition, if all workers receive similar increases this will tend to distort market forces in the labour market. Expanding sectors will find it hard to attract labour while contracting sectors will hang on to labour for too long.

The UK experience of prices and incomes policies seems to have been that, although they may be successful for a short period, they tend to store up trouble for the future, i.e. incomes policies may restrain inflation and wage claims for a short time but the moment the policy is relaxed a flood of price rises and wage increases is unleashed. It has been suggested that this is at least partly caused because producers and unions see prices and incomes policies as temporary and that if they are permanent, as they have been in Austria and Sweden, this problem would not occur. It could also be argued that prices and incomes policy may fail, as may fiscal policy and monetary policy, if it is relied upon as the only method of controlling inflation, and that what is needed is a combination of policies.

STUDENT ACTIVITY 44.5

What effect do you think incomes polices may have on wage differentials?

Conclusion

We have demonstrated in this chapter that inflation can have a number of causes. The failure adequately to contain inflation except at the cost of other objectives of policy such as full employment may be at least partly attributable to treating inflation as if it were mono-causal, i.e. inflation is entirely caused by excess demand or entirely caused by expansion of the money supply. If inflation has a number of causes it seems likely that we need a 'package' of measures, namely fiscal, monetary and direct, to deal with it.

We must also consider the problem of inflation in the broader sphere. Inflation is a world-wide problem. Whatever measures have been taken domestically, it has been impossible to isolate the domestic economy. This points to the obvious conclusion, that inflation must also be cured on a world-wide basis. Furthermore, we may see the problem of inflation alongside our desire to achieve other objectives of policy such as full employment or economic growth. By the end of the 1980s the problem of inflation seemed to have been at least contained not only in the UK but also in other industrialised nations. However, there were at the same time levels of unemployment which a decade previously would have been considered unthinkable. There still remain fundamental differences of opinion about the causes of inflation.

Summary

1 The costs of inflation are much greater when inflation is imperfectly anticipated than if it is perfectly anticipated.
2 The Phillips curve shows the relationship between inflation and unemployment. Monetarist theory suggests that expectations of inflation shift the Phillips curve rightwards.
3 The adaptive expectations school maintains that, because of the money illusion, there may be a short-term trade-off between inflation and unemployment. But in the long run attempts to reduce unemployment below the natural level result in inflation rather than jobs.
4 The rational expectations school argues that there is no money illusion and hence no trade-off between inflation and unemployment.
5 There are three concurrent explanations of inflation: demand-pull, cost-push and monetary inflation.
6 Fiscal policy has been used to control inflation by regulating aggregate demand. Policy in the 1980s came to regard fiscal policy as important only as a part of monetary policy.

7 The monetarist approach to monetary policy was based upon strict control of monetary aggregates. By the end of the 1980s monetary policy became almost entirely reliant upon control through interest rates. It has remained so despite a move towards inflation targeting.
8 Incomes policies can be either voluntary or statutory.
9 If inflation has a number of causes it is likely that a 'package deal' of various policy measures is necessary to deal with it.

Questions

1 Distinguish between cost-push and demand-pull inflation and discuss the policies that may be used to counteract each.
2 Discuss the usefulness of the Phillips curve as a guide to economic policy.
3 To what extent are the consequences of inflation undesirable?
4 What part do expectations play in the determination of the rate of inflation?
5 Explain the monetarist theory of inflation and state its prescription for the cure.
6 Explain what is meant by prices and incomes policies and assess their effectiveness.
7 Distinguish between the adaptive expectations and the rational expectations views of inflation.
8 'Inflation is always and everywhere a monetary phenomenon.' Critically assess Milton Friedman's statement.
9 Examine the relationship between public borrowing and inflation.
10 In what ways may the control of interest rates be used to control inflation?

Data response A
The determinants of inflation

Study the following data and then answer the questions:

	Increase in M_4	*Inflation rate*	*Increase in average earnings*	*Growth rate*	*Unemployment rate (%)*
1985	13.1	6.1	7.5	3.8	11.4
1986	15.9	3.4	8.0	4.3	11.5
1987	14.7	4.1	7.8	4.8	10.3
1988	17.2	4.9	8.8	5.0	8.3
1989	18.2	7.8	9.3	2.2	6.1
1990	17.6	9.5	9.9	0.4	5.4
1991	8.0	5.9	8.0	–2.2	7.8
1992	4.4	3.7	6.6	–0.6	9.4
1993	5.7	1.6	4.9	2.0	10.1
1994	4.1	2.5	4.5	4.5	9.2
1995	10.0	3.2	2.9	2.8	8.1

1 Outline the main theories of inflation.
2 To what extent, if any, do the above figures support any, or all, of the theories?

Data response B
Dedicated followers of fashion

Read the following article taken from the *Guardian* of 18 August 1997 and then answer these questions:
1 What does the Phillips curve purport to show?
2 Outline the 'expectations' view of inflation.
3 Explain the significance of the natural rate of unemployment for inflation.
4 Outline the reasons for the possible shifts in the Phillips curve according to the evidence of the last 30 years.

Dedicated followers of fashion

Richard Thomas

Economists are unlikely victims of fashion. The closest most get to the catwalk designs of Alexander McQueen is a subtle but daring contrast between the colour of their cords and elbow patches.

But intellectually, for all its seriousness, the profession has developed a butterfly tendency to flit between theoretical fads. Fundamental rules and equations are passé.

Ecomomists are being prodded further in this direction by their common room philosophy colleagues, who espouse postmodernism – a world in which everything is relative, nothing is sacred, and every idea can be dismissed as "socially constructed" (whatever that means).

Politicians, too are enamoured of an accelerating, unpredictable world where trade is exploding, capital flows like water, workers jump between portfolio jobs and national governments are enfeebled by sweeping world-wide shifts.

Not that economists have given up on theories altogether – there is still too much of the scientist in their hearts – simply on the last one, whatever it happens to be. The half-life of theories is diminishing fast. Just look at monetarism. Economics, in short, has lost its confidence.

The process started in the 1970s when the old models appeared to have broken down and forecasting became a mug's game. The spectacular economic policy mistakes of that decade, and of the 1980s – most notably in the British boom and bust – finally snuffed out any remaining self-esteem.

This is a great shame. Partly because economics is more fun when it tries to provide answers as well as questions, but mostly because the profession may have given up its traditional tools of diligent analysis, correlation and prediction just when they are coming back into their own.

One of the quintessentially Old Economist approaches was the Phillips Curve, which shows a stable, inverse relationship between unemployment and wage inflation. It is learned religiously by every economics student and then put safely into the historical, do-not-touch file.

Bill Phillips himself personified the old approach, which assumed that economies could be tracked, graphed and controlled. His other contribution to intellectual progress was a machine which used water to represent money sluicing round the economy.

Ian Shepherdson offers an alternative with a notion that is very simple but heretical: exhume the Bill Phillips Curve. In fact, Mr Shepherdson argues, the Phillips Curve never really died – it simply moved position

He was a practical man – his preparation for economic greatness included stints as a crocodile catcher, cinema manager and rebellious PoW in a Japanese camp. And his curve, unveiled in 1958, took a straightforward approach. Phillips used UK data on pay and unemployment between 1861–1957, and showed a robust predictable relationship between the two variables. Policy-makers had a choice between the two, and could decide where to strike the balance.

Unfortunately, most economies went pear-shaped about a decade after the curve was let loose on the world. Unemployment rose in parallel with inflation, in apparent contradiction of the Phillips hypothesis. A new, ugly word – stagflation – was born.

A new theory, needless to say, had popped up just in time. Milton Friedman, a decade after Phillips' breakthrough, delivered a powerful counter-blast which seemed to undercut fatally the elegant original theory. Friedman said that because workers *knew* that lower unemployment would cause higher inflation, they would build in the expected inflation to their current pay demands – and inflation would take off.

In the Friedman world, wages and prices could only be contained while unemployment remained above a "natural" rate, later refined as the awkward Non-Accelerating Inflation Rate of Unemployment (Nairu).

The 1970s certainly looked a Nairuish sort of place, so Phillips and his near-century of data, were consigned to an early grave. (He died himself in the late 1970s.) Now, of course, the Nairu thesis is in trouble, not least in the United States. Unemployment keeps falling: wages have not gone into orbit.

The hunt is now on for another model to explain the economy – is there a "new economy" based on IT and invisible goods?

There are still some diehard economists trying, like truffle-hunters, to sniff out the "true" Nairu so that it can be avoided. It isn't working. Every time they claim to have isolated it – say at a 5 per cent jobless rate – unemployment falls below it and still wages fail to lift off.

A paper to be published this week by Ian Shepherdson, chief US economist for HSBC* offers an alternative to sticking blindly to the Nairu or dashing off yet again to another theory. His notion is simple but heretical: exhume the Phillips Curve.

In fact, Mr Shepherdson argues, the Phillips Curve never really died – it simply moved position. At the end of the 1960s and early 1970s, the US Federal Reserve significantly loosened monetary policy, even though inflation was rising. From a peak of 9.25 per cent in 1969 the Federal funds rate was cut to 3.75 per cent by the spring of 1971. This took the real cost of borrowing (the Fed funds rate minus inflation) into negative territory for the first time in post-war history.

By cutting rates as prices rose, the Fed signalled to workers and firms that it was prepared to tolerate inflation. Workers therefore asked for more money (as Friedman predicted) while companies figured that they could accomodate the demands by passing the costs on to consumers through higher price tags.

The result was to significantly weaken, and worsen, the unemployment–price trade-off. And so it remained until Paul Volcker came along. The tough new Fed governor performed the opposite trick in 1979–1981, aggressively tightening monetary policy even as inflation eased.

Workers and bosses quickly got the new message, that inflation would not be tolerated, and curbed pay demands.

Mr Shepherdson argues that Mr Volcker – a "visionary" – managed to re-establish a stable Phillips-style relationship to the economy, albeit at a high price. For the last decade, inflation has been a minor features in US pay rounds.

So, Mr Shepherdson argues, it was the 1970s that were the abberation: "the basic association – lower unemployment with greater pressure on earnings – did not disappear into a nightmare Nairu world of ever-accelerating inflation. Instead, the curve simply shifted once, upwards and to the right in the 1970s. It has since moved more or less back to where it was in the 1950s and 1960s." The policy significance of this is profound. The Nairu school contends that once a certain point is reached inflation will suddenly become unstoppable. One more step and we might all be off the cliff into the inflationary abyss. By contrast, a Phillips world means we are on a clearly-marked slope, and that *we* control the descent.

This does not mean that unemployment can simply keep on falling. Indeed the curve gets steeper as the dole queue shrinks: HSBC estimates that while a 0.5 percentage point rise in the US unemployment rate would knock 0.5 percentage points off wage growth, a 0.5 percentage point *fall* in unemployment would add closer to 0.7 percentage points to wage growth.

But it does mean there is no need to panic. Policy-makers are in control, and have models to guide them. The US economy is not about to spiral out of control.

It is not clear whether the Phillips-curvy world extends beyond the US borders but, given the convergence of many labour and product markets towards American lines it seems likely that, if it doesn't yet, it will.

And on top of the greater leverage this implies for policy-makers, it should give economists pause for thought too. In their rush to be the next to produce a new theory, the boffins shouldn't forget there are some sharp tools available already, including Bill's curve. If economics is to thrive, it must tend to its roots.

**Why wage inflation will stay low, HSBC Markets, 140 Broadway, New York, NY 10055.*

Source: *The Guardian*, 18 August 1997

45 Unemployment and government policy

Learning outcomes

At the end of this chapter you will be able to:

- Understand the meanings of the terms employment and unemployment.
- Distinguish between the main methods of measuring unemployment.
- Appreciate the main costs of unemployment.
- Describe the relationship between job vacancies and unemployment.
- Distinguish between unemployment when the economy is in equilibrium and disequilibrium.
- Discuss the main reasons for regional policy and assess the efficacy of regional policy.
- Account for the rise of large-scale unemployment in the 1980s and 1990s.
- Explain the supply siders' view of the control of unemployment.
- Identify the key features of a flexible labour market.
- Explain the neo-Keynesian policy prescriptions for the control of unemployment.

Employment and unemployment

In many ways the control of unemployment is at the core of modern macroeconomics; it was the concern with unemployment which gave rise to the new economics of Keynes and his contemporaries during the 1930s. The pursuit of ***full employment*** (i.e. where all those who wish to work at the current wage are able to do so) as the prime objective of policy was specifically adopted by Western governments at the end of the Second World War and they adopted Keynesian demand management policies as the means of achieving it. Compared with all previous eras this policy was successful, unemployment remaining at very low levels throughout the 1950s and 1960s, so much so that other objectives of policy such as the control of inflation came to be regarded as more important. Many people thought that mass unemployment was a problem which had been banished for ever. However, by the early 1980s the UK had a greater number of people unemployed than in the 1930s and the control of unemployment was once more at the centre of the stage.

Obviously not everyone in the economy works; the young, the old, some housewives, students, the sick and disabled, etc., may not be in employment.

> **Thus when we speak of employment we are speaking of those who are in some form of paid work and when we say the unemployed we are speaking of those who are actively seeking jobs.**

As we saw in Chapter 4, the ***working population*** comprises all those who are working or who are seeking work. The ***unemployment rate*** is the number of unemployed expressed as a percentage of the working population. In July 1997 the working population in the UK was a little over 28 million and of those 5.5 per cent (about 1 550 000 people) were registered as unemployed and seeking work; the number of unemployed people has been falling quite sharply since late 1993, although much of the growth of employment has been in part-time jobs, especially among women, and in self-employment. The post-war high in unemployment was hit in December 1986, with a total of 3.4 million registered without a job.

Common misunderstanding

The unemployed, although not actually officially working, are said to be economically active because they are actively seeking work. The employed and the unemployed are economically active, whereas other groups, such as the young, the old, housewives, students, the sick and disabled, etc., are defined as economically inactive.

STUDENT ACTIVITY 45.1

If the working population comprised 25 million people and of these 2.2 million were registered as unemployed, what is the unemployment rate?

There are two main methods of measuring unemployment: the first, from which the above figures are taken and which has formed the basis of the UK's official statistics since 1982, is based on the ***claimant count***, i.e. those people receiving unemployment-related benefits. The figures are published monthly. However, they may be slightly deceptive in that the figure for unemployment includes only those who have to register as available for work at employment offices. Many people such as married women lose their jobs but do not register as unemployed. In addition to this the government excluded certain categories of unemployed from the figures; for example, those over 60 were not required to register as available for work, even though they were still able to draw unemployment benefit.

The history of unemployment since 1979 has become hard to follow because of the frequent changes in the way the statistics are compiled, there having been a total of 32 changes (see also Table 45.1). Each change may have been defensible on the grounds of greater accuracy or practicality, yet all the changes, except one minor one, have had the effect of reducing published unemployment totals! The inclusion of HM Forces and the self-employed in the size of the working population knocked 1.4 per cent off subsequent figures for unemployment.

The second method of measuring unemployment is by conducting ***surveys*** of the unemployed. In the UK the Labour Force Survey (LFS), based on the International Labour Office (ILO) definition of unemployment, is undertaken quarterly; people are defined as unemployed if they are without a job, available for work and have been actively seeking employment or are waiting to start a job. This definition of unemployment gives a higher figure than the claimant count by including people looking for work but not entitled to benefits (e.g. married women); on the other hand, it yields a lower figure by excluding those people claiming benefits but not actively seeking work.

Table 45.1 **Major changes in the unemployment statistics**

Date	*Change*	*Effect*
Oct. 79	Fortnightly payment of benefits	+20 000
Nov. 81	Men over 60 offered higher supplementary benefit to leave working population	−37 000
Oct. 82	Registration at Job Centres made voluntary. Computer count of benefit claimants substituted for clerical count of registrants	−190 000
Mar. 83	Men aged 60 and over given national insurance credits or higher supplementary benefit without claiming unemployment benefit	−162 000
July 85	Correction of Northern Ireland discrepancies	−5 000
Mar. 86	Two-week delay in compilation of figures to reduce overrecording	−50 000
July 86	Inclusion of self-employed and HM Forces in denominator of unemployed percentage	−1.4%
Sept. 86	Nobody under 18 allowed to register as all 16 and 17 year olds guaranteed a Youth Training Scheme (YTS) place	−50 000
Oct. 96	Introduction of Jobseeker's Allowance (JSA) replacing unemployment-related benefits; new allowance for six months only	−100 000 (estimate, by June 1997)

Figure 45.1 compares the two measures over time for the UK. The broad trends in the two statistics are pretty similar, although the ILO measure fluctuates less. Since the ILO is an international organisation it (and the Organisation for Economic Cooperation and Development, the OECD, which also uses survey data) is able to make international comparisons of unemployment rates using similar, or ***standardised***, definitions. Some of these are shown in Table 45.2.

Table 45.2 **Percentage rates of unemployment in the leading OECD countries**

Country	*1967*	*1975*	*1985*	*1990*	*1992*	*1994*	*1996*
UK	3.3	4.3	11.2	6.9	10.1	9.5	7.9
USA	3.7	8.3	7.1	5.4	7.3	6.0	5.5
Japan	1.3	1.9	2.6	2.1	2.2	2.9	3.3
Germany*	1.3	3.6	7.1	4.8	4.6	8.4	10.3
France	9.1	4.0	10.2	8.9	10.4	12.3	12.1
Italy	5.3	5.8	9.6	10.3	10.5	11.1	11.4
Canada	3.8	6.9	10.5	8.1	11.3	10.3	9.2

*Until end 1990 West Germany, from then all Germany
Source: OECD *Economic Outlook*, June 1997

Unemployment rates were high in most countries in the 1980s, a legacy of the oil price hikes in the 1970s combined with the pursuit of deflationary policies to combat inflation. The rise in unemployment in the UK in the early 1980s was particularly steep. Unemployment rates rose again in the early 1990s owing to a world-wide and severe recession. Unemployment has traditionally tended to be much lower in Japan than elsewhere, the result of its policy of 'lifetime employment' in its largest companies. The success of the USA and to a lesser extent the UK in reducing unemployment in recent years has been noticeable, yet controversial. Supporters of supply side economics claim that it is a result of tax-cutting and other supply side measures, leading to a more 'flexible' labour market. Against this it is argued that many of the new jobs created have been either part-time or temporary appointments, mainly among women; as a result, there is greater anxiety about job insecurity. However, there has also been a rise in male full-time unemployment since 1996.

A feature of the high levels of unemployment since the early 1980s in many countries has been the rise in the relative significance of ***long-term unemployment***, although this has been more true of events in the EU than in, say, the USA. It has been estimated that in the early 1990s over 40 per cent of the unemployed within the EU had been jobless for more than a year, while the equivalent figure for the USA was only about 10 per cent. The reason for this may be the 'open-ended' nature of unemployment benefit payments in many European countries.

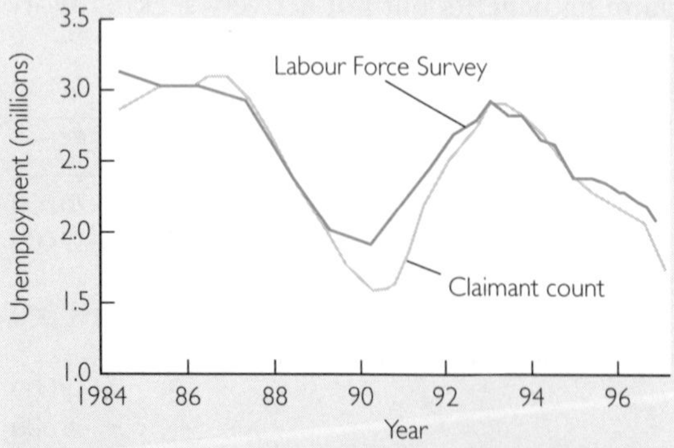

Fig. 45.1 **Claimant count and Labour Force Survey (ILO) measures of unemployment for the UK**
The broad trends in the two measures are similar, although the Labour Force Survey shows less fluctuations.
Source: Barclays Economic Review Second Quarter 1997

The costs of unemployment

There are many costs of unemployment and all sections of society are affected, but naturally the prime costs fall on the ***unemployed themselves and their families***. These comprise not just the net drop in income (lost earnings minus unemployment benefit), but also the loss of self-esteem from not working and the resulting stresses that are placed upon family relationships. Many studies have reported a close association between unemployment and ill-health. The longer the extent of the unemployment, the greater the problems become; workers are increasingly distanced from the job market as skill-needs change and so they find it more and more difficult to find a job. Some short-term unemployment as people change jobs may be indicative of a dynamic economy and a flexible workforce. In general, however, unemployment can produce widespread costs for the ***economy as a whole***. If some people are not working they are not producing anything (although some may be working in the 'hidden' or 'black economy'); hence, total output is less than it otherwise would be. In addition, there is the loss in tax revenue to the government to consider: the unemployed pay no income tax or national insurance contributions and also pay less in VAT and excise duties because they have less money to spend. Finally, there are the possible social costs of unemployment: there is some evidence that joblessness, particularly amongst the young, leads to increased crime, violence and alienation from society at large.

STUDENT ACTIVITY 45.2

Should unemployment benefits be considered a cost of unemployment for society at large?

Vacancies and unemployment

Figure 45.2 shows the trend in job vacancies in the UK from 1980 to 1996. It should come as no great surprise that, comparing this figure with

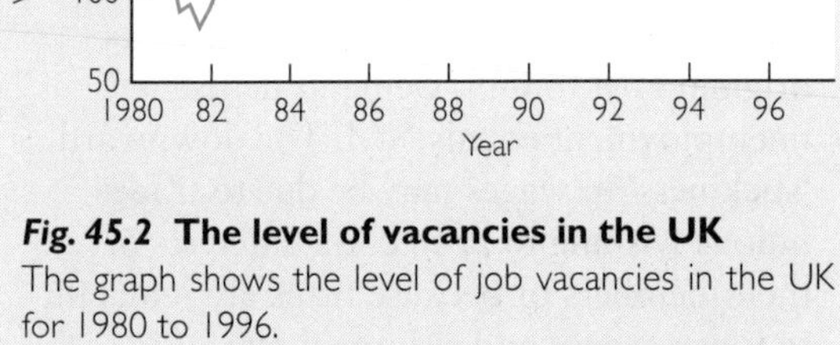

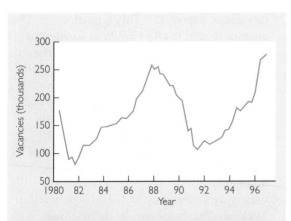

***Fig. 45.2* The level of vacancies in the UK**

The graph shows the level of job vacancies in the UK for 1980 to 1996.

Source: Barclays Economic Review Third Quarter 1997

Fig. 45.1, some kind of inverse relationship can be seen, i.e. the level of vacancies tends to be higher when unemployment is lower and vice versa. When the economy emerges from recession and the demand for goods and services increases, then there is a tendency for the number of job vacancies to rise and the level of unemployment to fall; on the other hand, as demand falls vacancies decline and unemployment rises.

However, this relationship is not nearly as stable as it once was. In the last 30 years or so there has been a steady rise in the number of people unemployed at any particular level of vacancies; the unemployment rate today is four times higher than in 1971, but the number of vacancies is about the same. Furthermore, those people who are unemployed may not possess the right skills for the vacancies that are available; a newly redundant coal-miner is not likely to be able to take a job as a computer programmer.

People often receive a financial payoff if made redundant and so can spend some time searching for a new job. Employers also engage in search activities: looking for the right workers to fill vacant positions. Of course, information is not perfect about what jobs or workers are available; people may have to search for some time before finding the right job, just as employers may have to search for the right workers to take up vacancies. However, once people become unemployed for a long period they tend to lose not just the requisite skills for the workplace but also the heart to continue searching for a job. The main reason for the coexistence of both high unemployment and vacancies in the UK has been the growth in relative importance of long-term unemployment.

Types of unemployment

Unemployment is not a uniform phenomenon, it exists for a number of reasons. When we list those reasons we are therefore considering the ***causes of unemployment***. A distinction can be made between unemployment when the economy is in ***equilibrium*** (i.e. when the aggregate or total demand for labour in the economy equals the aggregate or total supply of labour in the economy) and unemployment when the economy is in ***disequilibrium*** (i.e. when the wage rate is above the equilibrium level). Thus, in Fig. 45.3, which shows the aggregate demand for and supply of labour curves, the equilibrium level of employment for the economy as a whole is OM at a wage rate of O*W*.

Disequilibrium unemployment

The main reasons for disequilibrium unemployment are as follows:

a) *Classical or real wage unemployment* occurs when the real wage is above the equilibrium level and remains there. This may be because trade unions have secured wages above the market-clearing level or it could be due to minimum wage legislation. In Fig. 45.4, for example, if wage levels are established at OW_1, then the demand for labour is OL while the supply of labour is ON; hence, unemployment is represented by the distance LN.

The so-called 'classical' economists pre-Keynes argued that the main reason for unemployment was that real wages were too high. In more recent times such arguments have been revived by supply side economists and have become popular within governments in both the UK and the USA.

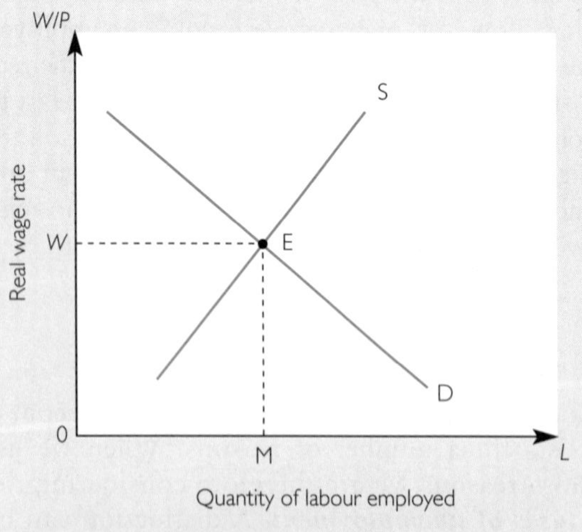

Fig. 45.3 **The equilibrium level of employment**
Equilibrium occurs at point E, giving a level of employment of OM and a wage rate OW.

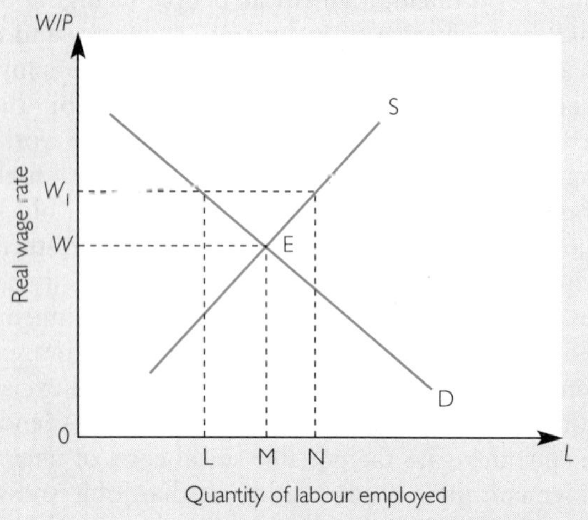

Fig. 45.4 **Classical or real wage unemployment**
If the real wage settles at OW_1, unemployment of LN results

b) *Demand-deficient or cyclical unemployment* exists when an economy is in recession and there is a fall in the aggregate demand for goods and services. As a result, firms reduce their levels of output and eventually lay off workers. This is unemployment which we have traditionally associated with the ***trade cycle*** – hence the term cyclical unemployment. (See also Chapter 35.) This type of unemployment is also known as ***Keynesian unemployment***, since Keynes was the first to postulate that the high unemployment of the 1930s was not associated with too high real wages but with a general decline in demand.

In Fig. 45.5 the demand for labour falls from D to D_1 owing to a recession in the economy. Assuming that wages remain at O*W*, the level of employment declines from its original OM to ON. Demand-deficient unemployment equals NM. The downward 'stickiness' in wages may be due to trade unions wishing to protect the interests of their members or because firms are reluctant to lower wages and risk the wrath of their workers.

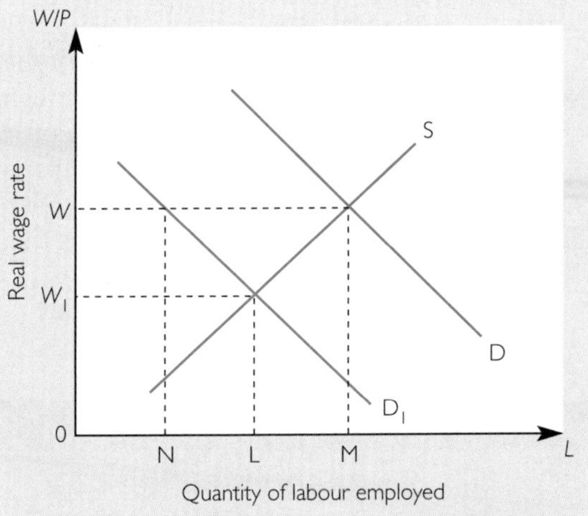

Fig. 45.5 **Demand-deficient unemployment**
The demand for labour falls from D to D_1. As a result, demand-deficient unemployment equals NM.

c) *An increase in aggregate labour supply* due, say, to an increase in the numbers of women who wish to work. Should there be no corresponding increase in the demand for labour and assuming that wages are sticky downwards, then this can lead to unemployment.

Equilibrium unemployment

Common misunderstanding
Unemployment may still occur even though there is equilibrium in the economy as a whole. This is because of a mismatch of labour supply and demand in particular markets or regions rather than at the aggregate level; there may be vacancies for hotel workers in London, while there are unemployed steelworkers in the north of England.

Such equilibrium unemployment is referred to by some economists as ***natural unemployment*** or ***the natural rate of unemployment*** because it is consistent with overall equilibrium in the labour market. (See Chapter 38.)

There are various types of equilibrium unemployment:

a) *Frictional unemployment* refers to people displaced by the normal working of the economy. It is inevitable in a growing economy that people will, from time to time, change or lose their jobs and may perhaps be unemployed for some weeks as they wait to take up the next job or look for a new job. Since this procedure may take some time it is also referred to as ***search unemployment.***
b) *Seasonal unemployment* occurs because some jobs are dependent upon the weather and the season. Facetiously, we might say that this refers to deck-chair attendants being unemployed in the winter or hot-chestnut sales people being unemployed in the summer. However, on a more serious level the construction industry is the most badly hit by seasonal unemployment, with tens or even hundreds of thousands of workers laid off in the winter when the bad weather makes work difficult.
c) *Structural unemployment* results from a change in the structure of the economy; for example, it could be the result of the imbalance caused by the decline of one industry and (hopefully) the rise of another. Unemployment results when new industries do not create enough jobs to employ those made redundant, or because the new industry is in a different area or requires different skills.

Structural unemployment has plagued the UK economy for most of this century. For most of the period it has been caused by the decline of the ***old staple industries*** such as coal-mining, iron and steel and textiles. These industries tended to be concentrated in the coalfields and thus, because of this heavy regional specialisation, structural unemployment manifested itself as ***regional unemployment*** (and see below).

In the 1970s and 1980s new forms of structural unemployment came about as previously prosperous industries such as motor vehicles were hit by foreign competition. This has made the incidence of unemployment more widespread; the West Midlands, which beforehand was one of the most prosperous areas of the country, became one of the most profoundly depressed. In the early 1990s unemployment even hit the service industries in the previously prosperous south-east region.

d) *Technological unemployment*, which occurs when improvements in technology reduce the demand for labour, is often regarded as a form of structural unemployment. There is nothing new about technological unemployment; the spinning jenny, for instance, allowed one person to do the work previously done by 100. What is new at the moment is the speed and breadth of technological change. Microchip technology has affected almost all industries and jobs. It affects unemployment in two ways, first by doing away with jobs and skills and, second, by creating new jobs which many of the unemployed are incapable of doing.

Let us consider the new technology as it affects one industry – banking. We have already seen computerised accounting, electronic transfer of funds, cash dispensers and so on. Now we have EFTPOS (Electronic Funds Transfer at Point of Sale), whereby people's bank accounts are automatically debited from a terminal in the shop. Another development is speaking computers which customers are able to telephone for statements of their accounts etc. All these developments save on labour so that, although banking is one of the UK's fastest growing industries, its total workforce is not increasing; indeed there have been many redundancies. The new technology also produces a division in the workforce, creating a new managerial class of those able to comprehend and to control the technology on the one hand and, on the other, a class of semi-skilled people whose job is to feed the machines. Whole areas of intermediate skills such as book-keeping are being swept away. This pattern is being repeated throughout whole sectors of UK industry and the potential for development seems to be showing no signs of slowing down.

Job prospects have also been adversely affected in the UK by microtechnology because we have failed to keep pace with the manufacturing side of the industry (although we are better placed in the manufacture of software). The manufacture of microchips, for example, is effectively dominated by just two countries, the USA and Japan. Thus the UK and many other traditional manufacturing countries such as Germany and France are placed at a disadvantage.

STUDENT ACTIVITY 45.3

Consider the impact of microchip technology on unemployment – and employment – for the economy as a whole.

Regional unemployment

There are considerable differences in the rates of unemployment in the various different regions of the UK (see Table 45.3). These figures may also disguise much worse conditions in particular places. In Corby, for example, adult unemployment was greater than 50 per cent in the mid 1980s. This was not an untypical figure for the worst-hit towns at the time. In a time of general unemployment, then,

***Table 45.3* Percentage rates of unemployment in the UK**

Region	*1974*	*1982*	*1996*
North	4.6	16.5	10.8
Yorkshire and Humberside	2.5	13.4	8.0
East Midlands	2.2	11.0	7.0
East Anglia	1.9	9.9	6.2
South-east	1.5	8.7	5.5
South-west	2.6	10.8	6.3
West Midlands	2.1	14.9	7.5
North-west	3.4	14.7	6.9
Wales	3.7	15.6	8.3
Scotland	3.8	14.2	7.9
Northern Ireland	5.4	19.4	11.1
UK	2.6	12.2	7.6

Source: CSO *Annual Abstract of Statistics*, HMSO, and *Economic Trends*

we must first consider whether there is a case for a special regional policy.

Arguments for regional policy

a) *The failure of market forces.* Advocates of free market economics argue that the price mechanism will eventually abolish these disparities. Unemployment will reduce wage and other costs in the regions and this will eventually attract industry. However, it appears that, over any reasonable period of time, market forces are as likely to accentuate regional disparities as to remove them.

   Neo-classical economists would also argue that the movement of workers should lessen regional differences, i.e. people will move out of the depressed regions thereby reducing the supply in that area and increasing it in other areas. Unfortunately, to the extent to which this is true, it tends to be the young and vigorous workers who move out of the depressed regions. This therefore leaves an older and less adaptable workforce. This may further add to the reluctance of firms to move to the region.

b) *Cumulative decline.* The depressed areas have tended to have a legacy of labour troubles, a result of the decline of the old staple industries. This problem has diminished in recent years as the power of the unions has dwindled (see Chapter 20), but in the past the history of trade union disputes may have discouraged firms from moving to these areas. In addition to this the social capital of these areas, e.g. housing, transport and communications, tended to be run down. These factors may have further discouraged firms from moving to there. From this point of view there is therefore a need for positive government policy to encourage firms to move to these regions.

c) *Inflationary pressures.* If national measures are taken to stimulate the economy in order to reduce unemployment it is quite likely that they will have an inflationary effect. Consider the following situation:

Area	*Percentage employment of capacity in industry* X	Y
A	100	–
B	–	70

   Industrial capacity in industry X is fully employed in area A but area B is dependent upon another industry (Y) and in this there is considerable unemployment. If the government tries to cure this by stimulating the general level of demand, it may well cause inflationary pressure in industry X before it cures the unemployment in industry Y.

d) *Social costs.* A firm in choosing its location is likely to consider only its private costs. Socially, however, it must be considered that there is already enormous pressure upon resources in congested areas. Roads, schools, hospitals and housing are all much more expensive to provide in the prosperous areas, while in the depressed areas of the country there is often spare capacity. It may be worthwhile, therefore, encouraging firms to go to these regions in order that society may benefit from these lower social costs.

Government policy

The main choice which confronts the government is that of taking 'workers to the work' or 'work to the workers'. Methods of taking workers to the work include removal and relocation grants, retraining schemes and Job Centres. Since the Special Areas Act of 1935 the majority of government regional policy has been aimed at encouraging firms to locate in the less prosperous regions. Over the course of the 1980s and 1990s governments have reduced the scale of regional aid until it could be said that it was virtually relying on the market forces approach. The details of government regional policy are to be found on pages 174–6.

The efficacy of regional policy

There is little evidence to show that government policy had much success up until 1963. After that date there was a more aggressive regional policy. This policy succeeded for some time in reducing regional disparities but it was overtaken by the large-scale recession in the economy in the early 1980s and then by the government's effective abandonment of regional policy. (A map of the regions appears on page 175. See also comments on the north–south divide below.)

Common misunderstanding

It may appear from Table 45.3 that, comparing unemployment in the regions in 1982 and 1996, the disparities between the regions have diminished. However, this has to be seen against the background of lower rates of unemployment nationally in 1996 than in 1982. While the figure for Wales was 27.8 per cent above the national average in 1982, it was only 0.9 per cent above the average in 1996. On the other hand, despite a lower rate of unemployment in the North in 1996 (10.8 per cent) compared with 1982 (16.5 per cent), the 1996 figure was 42.1 per cent above the national average, while the 1982 figure was 35.2 per cent above the average for the country as a whole.

STUDENT ACTIVITY 45.4

Calculate the deviations from the national average level of unemployment for the other regions in the UK shown in Table 45.3 and comment on the implications for the efficacy of regional policy.

The north–south divide

The debate about whether the discrepancies between different regions have become more pronounced continues unabated. (See Data response A in Chapter 13). The prosperous areas tend to be in the south of the country and the depressed ones in the north – hence the name. The existence of the north–south divide is vigorously denied by many politicians. However, we observed in Table 45.3 that there are considerable differences in rates of unemployment between the regions. You can also see from Table 45.4 that there are considerable differences in earnings and, if anything, that these have become more pronounced. We have already mentioned that the decline of the northern regions began with the decline of the old staple industries. In some cases this situation was compounded by the decline of newer industries such as motor vehicles, although in more recent times multinational car firms, notably Japanese, have set up in these areas.

In the 1980s there were rapid improvements in productivity which also caused industries to shed labour. It is certainly true that the depressed areas are attracting new industry but they may not be doing it fast enough to offset the other trends. These trends tend to exacerbate, and be exacerbated by, other factors such as house prices which are much higher in the south than in the north. This in turn makes it more difficult for the people in the north to move south in search of work. This is not just a UK trend. Prosperity in the EU has tended to be concentrated in the 'golden triangle' which takes in northern Germany and France, the Benelux countries and the south-east of England.

***Table 45.4* Average weekly household incomes (£) in the UK**

Region	*1980-1*	*1994-5*
North	136.0	304.0
Yorkshire and Humberside	130.3	343.4
East Midlands	141.8	365.8
East Anglia	143.8	345.6
South-east	173.3	435.4
South-west	140.9	378.9
West Midlands	146.7	321.8
North-west	148.0	340.9
Wales	138.6	282.7
Scotland	144.2	363.0
Northern Ireland	119.2	326.3
UK	150.5	369.3

Source: Regional Trends 1996, Office for National Statistics

The unemployment of the 1980s and 1990s

A study of Table 45.5 reveals that unemployment in the 1980s reached unprecedented levels. (Note that the unemployment percentages differ slightly from those for the UK shown in Table 45.2

***Table 45.5* Unemployment and employment in the UK**

Year	*Total unemployed (thousand)*	*Percentage unemployed (%)*	*Employed labour force (thousand)*
1976	1266	5.5	24 844
1977	1359	5.8	24 865
1978	1343	5.7	25 014
1979	1234	5.3	25 393
1980	1513	6.8	25 327
1981	2394	10.5	24 344
1982	2770	11.6	23 908
1983	2984	11.7	23 610
1984	3030	11.7	24 060
1985	3179	11.9	24 445
1986	3229	11.9	24 542
1987	2953	10.6	25 142
1988	2370	8.4	26 413
1989	1798	6.3	26 725
1990	1664	5.9	26 800
1991	2241	7.8	26 305
1992	2678	9.4	25 775
1993	2865	10.1	25 391
1994	2586	9.2	25 400
1995	2255	8.1	25 741
1996	2104	7.5	25 865

Sources: CSO *Annual Abstract of Statistics*, *Barclay's Economic Review, Second Quarter 1997*

because the figures in Table 45.5 are based on the claimant count.) Levels declined at the end of the 1980s, only for them to rise again in the early 1990s, since when unemployment has fallen quite sharply once again.

The table also shows the figures for all those working. By comparing the unemployed and the employed figures between 1976 and 1988 you can see that although unemployment rose by 1 270 000, the employed total rose by 367 000. We were apparently faced with the curious paradox of employment and unemployment growing simultaneously.

Common misunderstanding

It need not be the case that an increase in unemployment is always accompanied by a decrease in those employed. The growth in employment during the 1980s was caused by the growth of the relative size of the working population and was due to such factors as the changing age distribution of the population and the increased proportion of women working, often in part-time positions. Much of the increase in unemployment at the time comprised men in full-time jobs.

The rise of large-scale unemployment

We must now turn to consider the reasons for this rise in general unemployment. No single explanation is satisfactory but the following factors are significant.

a) *Deficiency of aggregate demand.* The Keynesian explanation of unemployment attributes it to lack of aggregate demand. While it must be true that unemployment is due to lack of demand, this begs the questions of what causes the depression of demand and also whether deficit financing to raise the level of aggregate demand would alleviate it.

b) *Increase in structural and frictional unemployment.* Commentators have pointed to several factors in labour markets which have increased unemployment. In the early 1970s the rise in the ***replacement ratio*** (social security benefits relative to average wages) made unemployment more tolerable for some. The increase in unemployment has also made firms less willing to retrain employees or take on older ones, while employment protection legislation and redundancy payments may have made them more cautious about taking on labour.

   We have already mentioned the decline in some UK industries which has increased unemployment. This was particularly noticeable in the manufacturing sector in the 1970s and early 1980s. The unemployment caused by these structural changes has been made worse by the difficulty that many people have when attempting to move to the south-east in search of jobs because of high housing prices.

c) *International aspects.* Unemployment in the UK cannot be considered in isolation. Rates of unemployment have also been significantly higher in most of the UK's trading partners. This therefore contributed to the general depression of demand. Another international aspect is the import penetration of the UK's manufacturing industries such as iron and steel, motor vehicles and electronics. Exports on the other hand have often been hindered by a too-high exchange rate for the pound. This caused producers to cut prices, even though real wages were rising at the same time, so that profits were often squeezed to the point where firms closed down.

d) *Oil prices*. The OPEC price rise in 1973 played a significant part in the rise in inflation and unemployment in the mid 1970s. The 1978 oil price rises had even more dramatic effects, increasing costs dramatically and thus squeezing profits still further. The 1978 oil price rise was a major factor in precipitating the world-wide recession of the early 1980s. The subsequent collapse in oil prices helped some of the UK's main trading rivals such as Japan and Germany who are major oil importers but further damaged the UK, which is an oil exporter.

e) *Technology*. We have already seen that improvements in technology have reduced the demand for labour (see also the discussion on page 642). However, we may hope that in the long run improvements in technology and the resultant increases in productivity will create jobs by leading to an expansion of the economy.

f) *Government policy*. Until the mid 1970s government policy was aimed at reducing unemployment by expansionary fiscal and monetary policies. However, at this time governments began to adopt contractionary policies, with the aim of squeezing inflation out of the economy. These policies therefore contributed to unemployment. Further, we saw in Chapter 44 that monetary thinking points to the necessity of raising unemployment as a method of eliminating inflation. The then Chancellor of the Exchequer, Norman Lamont, said in the Commons in 1991 that he was 'happy to pay the price of higher unemployment if it cures inflation'. Government policies must therefore be seen as a major factor in the rise of unemployment.

Changes in measurement and population

We discussed earlier in the chapter the many changes in measurement during the 1980s which made it difficult to say precisely what was happening to unemployment. Estimates by Christopher Johnson of Lloyds Bank suggest that unemployment was reduced by at least 400 000 by statistical redefinitions and that special employment measures such as YTS accounted for a further 400 000.

It is also the case that many of the new jobs created have been part-time jobs. Also, some of these part-time jobs were in fact second jobs for those already employed. There was a growing tendency for newly created jobs to go to women. This could be, at least in part, because the jobs were part-time and/or low paid. However, while there were 2 548 000 less men employed in 1994 than in 1979 there were, in fact, 903 000 more women employed.

Because of demographic changes the population of working age was rising by about half a per cent a year, i.e. a figure of about 1.7 million for the period 1979–91. (It has since declined slightly.) The unemployment figures have also been distorted by changes in the ***activity*** or ***participation rate***, i.e. the percentage of those of working age who are working or seeking work. In the early 1980s the activity rate dropped to below 73 per cent but rose again to reach nearly 77 per cent in 1990, since when it has declined slightly. This made the unemployment figures worse. On the other hand, the official policy of discouraging benefit claims kept the activity rate below that which it would otherwise have been.

STUDENT ACTIVITY 45.5

During the 1980s the population of working age increased, as did the activity rate. What do you think were the implications of these trends for a) unemployment and b) employment?

Hysteresis

This is a term for the tendency for equilibrium levels of a variable to gravitate towards actual values. For example, a prolonged increase in unemployment may actually cause an increase in the equilibrium level of unemployment. Economists have put forward several explanations for this phenomenon. These include:

a) the likelihood of workers becoming discouraged in their search for a job and thus decreasing the intensity of their search;
b) a rise in unemployment will decrease the numbers of insider employees (i.e. the tried and trusted employees) and thus the displaced workers find it difficult to obtain work when they attempt to return as outsiders;
c) a prolonged recession is likely to decrease the capital stock and investment;
d) a long period of unemployment will also ~~decrease the skill that~~ a worker possesses.

Hysteresis might be used to explain the change in the equilibrium of variables other than unemployment, such as inflation.

The control of unemployment: the supply side view

Introduction

For most of the period since the Second World War attempts to alleviate unemployment have centred on neo-Keynesian demand side management policies. For example, running a budget deficit was supposed to boost demand and reduce unemployment. During the late 1970s and 1980s various supply side schools of economics gained acceptance in government, not only in the UK but in the USA and most major Western economies. They argued that, not only were demand side policies ineffective but they made matters worse. Budget deficits created inflation and, in the end, created more unemployment, not less.

There are various supply side schools: monetarist, neo-classical, new classical and so on. While there are significant differences between them (see discussion on the ***adaptive expectations*** and the ***rational expectations*** schools on pages 623 and 626) there are common features and policy prescriptions and it is on these that we will concentrate in this section.

Supply side economics emphasises the 'natural' competitive forces in the economy. It is believed that the economy is essentially self-regulating. (See page 527–8.) Problems arise because these 'natural' competitive forces are thwarted by government interference and by restrictive practices by firms and by unions. In short, we need to concentrate on the costs of production (hence supply side). This will reduce costs, control inflation and, in the long run, promote employment.

One central idea of the supply side schools is that there is a natural level of unemployment and that it is the vain attempts to reduce this level that have been a key element in creating inflation. Only when the natural level has been achieved can we expect the economy to be operating efficiently and achieving the economic growth which will create more jobs. (See discussion of this in Chapters 38 and 44.) Common supply side policy prescriptions are:

a) reduced welfare payments, such as unemployment benefits;
b) lower levels of direct taxation;
c) reduction of employee and trade union rights;
d) abolition of wage floors;
e) the promotion of training and retraining schemes.

We have already discussed the argument on lowering tax rates (see page 527). We will now consider the other points listed above.

Reducing welfare payments to the unemployed

It is argued that welfare benefits may be pitched at a level which is above the equilibrium wage rate in the lower-paid labour markets. This being the case, some people will not work since they would be worse off if they did so. Thus, welfare payments have artificially increased the level of unemployment.

In Fig. 45.6 the 'benefits floor' is set at a level of OW_1 which is above the equilibrium wage in that labour market of OW. This being the case only OL will be employed instead of OM. Thus welfare benefits have created LN registered unemployed. The idea of making the level of welfare benefits less than the lowest standard of

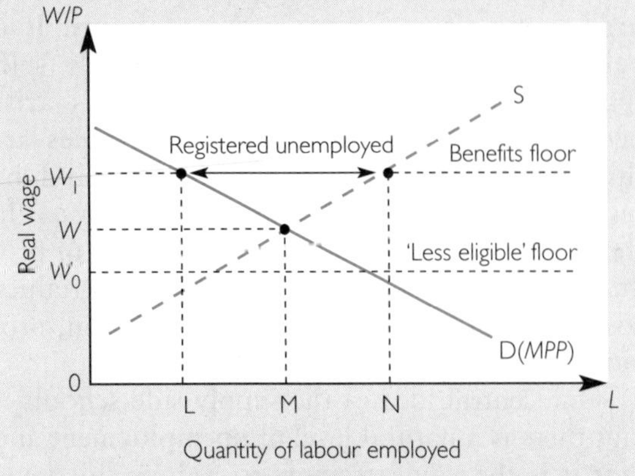

Fig. 45.6 **Effects of welfare benefits on unemployment**

A benefits floor set a OW which is above the equilibrium wage rate results in only OL being employed instead of OM. However, LN claim benefits thus there is less employment and a number of registered unemployed are created. Lowering the benefits floor to the 'less eligible' level eliminates the unemployment.

living achievable by those in work is not new, it is the principle of 'less eligibility' on which the Poor Law of 1834 was founded.

In order to eliminate the unemployment it is necessary to reduce the welfare benefits below the level of the lowest wage available in the labour market. In our example this could be OW_0. This argument contrasts with the Beveridge unemployment insurance argument that welfare insurance should sustain a person at or near their working standard of living whilst they are (temporarily) out of work.

Common misunderstanding

The replacement ratio has fallen since the 1970s as unemployment regulations have hardened. It might be expected, therefore, that unemployment would also fall as people find it increasingly 'costly' to remain out of work. In fact, as has been seen, unemployment has increased sharply since this time, suggesting that other factors must also be responsible for the rise in the number of jobless people.

Reducing trade union rights

Many supply siders believe that overstrong trade unions through such things as closed-shop agreements hold the wage rate above the equilibrium. In Fig. 45.7 union power has lifted the wage rate to OW_1. This is above the equilibrium rate OW. As a result of this employers now only wish to employ OL workers rather than OM at the equilibrium. (See discussion of this point on page 263.)

Supply side policies also aim at increasing productivity by reducing union power. For example, the ending of demarcation agreements and overmanning is said to have a positive effect on both wages and employment. This is illustrated in Fig. 45.8, where you can see that improvements in productivity have shifted the demand curve for labour to the right. Thus, before the ending of restrictive practices the equilibrium wage was OW and the quantity of labour employed was OM. After the resultant rises in productivity the wage rate has risen to OW_1 and the quantity of labour employed to ON.

There were substantial improvements in productivity during the 1980s; often, however, the highest rates of increase occurred in unionised firms compared with their non-unionised counterparts.

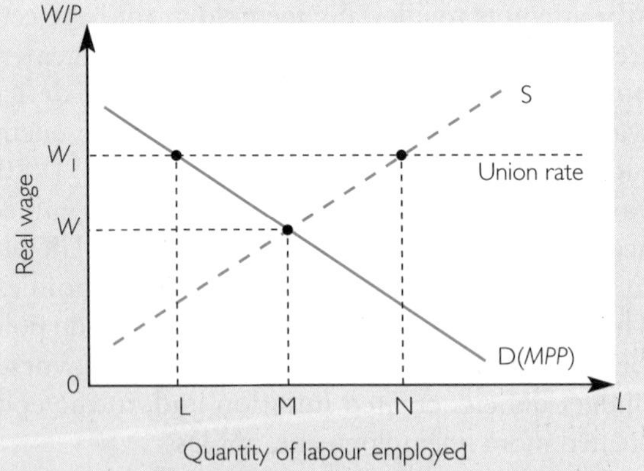

Fig. 45.7 **Wages and union power**

Over-strong unions impose a wage rate at OW_1 which is above the equilibrium OW. Legislation to weaken unions allows the wage rate to return to the equilibrium and more employment to be created.

Training schemes

It is an obvious supply side point that improving the quality of factor inputs should improve productivity and output. Thus schemes to train and retrain labour must have beneficial effects upon the economy. We can illustrate this point by reference to Fig. 45.8. The result of better trained labour should be to shift the demand curve for labour to the right as it becomes more productive.

Governments during the 1980s introduced many training schemes such as TOPs (Training Opportunities Programme), YOPs (Youth Opportunities Programme) as well as YTS. These were politically controversial with many left-wingers claiming that real training was not being given and that the schemes were a method of keeping people off the unemployment register.

It is worth noting that most of the measures described above are designed to improve ***labour market flexibility***, i.e. the ability for workers to move easily and speedily between different tasks and jobs. (See also Data response B at the end of the chapter.) However, labour flexibility has a number of different facets:

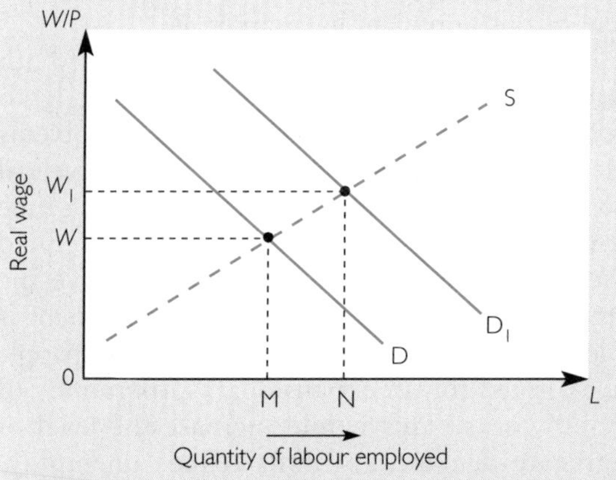

Fig. 45.8 **The effect of increased productivity**
Productivity increases resulting from the reduction of restrictive practices such as demarcation, and/or improvement of the quality of the labour force through improved training shifts the demand curve for labour to the right. This results in both higher wages and increased employment.

a) *Numerical flexibility* refers to the number of jobs; part-time and temporary or short-term appointments create a greater number of individual jobs. Such posts are both cheaper for firms to fill and easier for them to do without, should they need to reduce their number of staff. On the other hand, they may fit the employment needs of some workers, especially working mothers. Part-time workers comprised 16 per cent of the UK working population in 1973, but over 24 per cent in 1995.
b) *Functional flexibility* denotes the extent to which workers possess a variety of skills or are able to undertake a range of tasks within a firm. This aspect of flexibility has, until recently, probably been the least developed within British firms, although the introduction of ***lean production techniques***, traditionally associated with Japanese firms and that rely upon an increased level of automation and reduced levels of stockholding, has hastened a greater flexibility in British industry.
c) *Flexibility of time* can be viewed in terms of greater variability of working hours for staff; having employees adopt variable work patterns (i.e. starting or finishing at different times) is increasingly common among firms, although people are actually working longer hours on average than a decade ago. Flexibility of time can also be defined in terms of job tenure, i.e. how long people remain in their jobs. Average job tenure in the UK has fallen for men in the last 20 years, although not for women.
d) *Wage flexibility* indicates the process by which pay is more closely related to the performance of a firm, e.g. through profit-sharing and productivity-bargaining schemes. Tax concessions have meant that these schemes have become more popular in a number of countries, although the 1996 budget in the UK began the process of phasing out tax relief on them.

STUDENT ACTIVITY 45.6

There are more people working part-time in the UK than ever before. Is this a good thing?

It need hardly be said that the policy prescriptions proposed by the supply siders are hotly disputed by neo-Keynesians. They would see measures such as cutting wages as more likely to increase unemployment by creating a deficiency in demand. However, we may accept all the measures described above as effective and still be left with a problem. You will recall from our definition of labour as a factor of production that it has the unique characteristic of being 'the human factor'. Thus we may find that we have policy measures which are economically sound but which are politically or morally indefensible. This insight was one of the key starting points for Keynes. Below we will go on to look at the more traditional neo-Keynesian prescriptions for the control of unemployment.

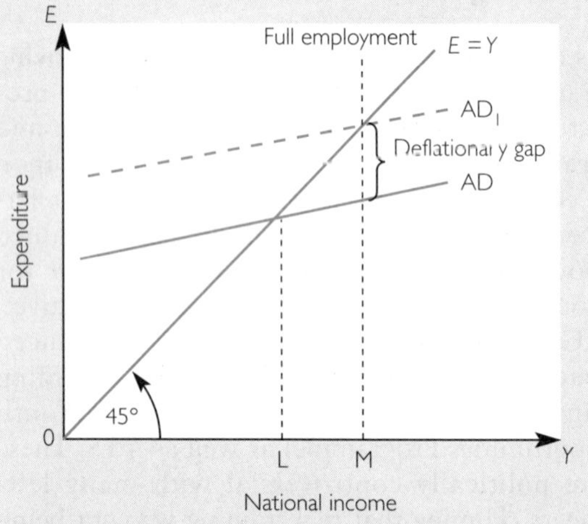

***Fig. 45.9* A deflationary gap**
Unemployment occurs when the equilibrium level of national income (OL) is below the full employment level (OM). Unemployment could be eliminated by increasing the level of aggregate demand from AD to AD_1 ($AD = C + I + G + (X - M)$).

The control of unemployment: neo-Keynesian views

Fiscal policy

Keynesian and neo-Keynesian policies emphasise the primacy of fiscal policy in the direction of the economy. The fiscal prescription for the cure of unemployment is to raise the level of aggregate demand and so to close the deflationary gap. This is illustrated in Fig. 45.9. Most usually this would be done by running a budget deficit. However, two sets of problems are associated with this. First, there are the problems of forecasting and implementation which were discussed on pages 606–8. These problems raise the possibility that fiscal policy may actually make the problem worse rather than better. Second, there is the problem that deficits in times of full or near-full employment tend to cause inflation. It is for these reasons that fiscal policy fell out of favour and monetary policy gained the ascendancy. We are here drawing together many threads of the argument. Assiduous readers should make sure that they are familiar with the contents of Chapter 38 and also with the discussion of the Phillips curve in Chapter 44. You will also find an aggregate supply and demand treatment of this argument in Chapter 34.

It should be remembered, however, that both problems considered above are most likely to occur at or near full employment. The problems associated with a finely balanced counter-cyclical fiscal policy can hardly be said to exist at a time of mass unemployment. It is also to be doubted whether expansionary policies would have the same inflationary effects when unemployment is at levels in the 2 to 3 million area. Many people have argued for an expansionary programme of public works. This would increase the level of aggregate demand and thus reduce unemployment. The cost of such schemes would be at least partly offset by the decrease in social security payments and the increase in tax revenues. It is also pointed out that public works programmes would not greatly stimulate the demand for imports since projects such as road building must mainly call upon domestic resources. Governments since 1979, both Conservative and Labour, have remained concerned about the inflationary aspects of such schemes.

Monetary policy

The conventional monetary policy response to unemployment is to lower interest rates and expand the money supply. As we have seen in previous chapters, the efficacy of monetary policy is a topic of fierce debate. Keynesians argue that reducing the rate of interest eventually causes some rise in national income by stimulating investment. You will recall from Chapters 38 and 44 that monetarists and neo-classicists reject the idea that employment can be created either by expanding the money supply or through budget deficits.

Incomes policy

The term neo-Keynesian embraces a wide spectrum of views and certainly not all would favour incomes policy. Incomes policy is usually regarded as an anti-inflationary device. We can see, however, from the arguments above concerning fiscal and monetary policies that the main reason for not stimulating the economy by such measures is fear of the inflationary consequences. If, therefore, inflation could be restrained by incomes policy while fiscal and monetary policies stimulated demand this could be a major contribution to the cure of unemployment. Incomes policies, however, have other drawbacks, as noted in Chapter 44.

Protection

In the 1970s and 1980s the Cambridge Economic Policy Group argued for protectionist measures to reduce unemployment in the UK, i.e. aggregate demand could be boosted without causing a severe current account deficit on the balance of payments. Conventionally, economists oppose calls for protection since these limit the benefits to be gained from comparative advantage. Some justification for the protectionist argument may be found in the fact that countries such as Japan have for long taken measures to prevent the UK's exports (and those of other countries) entering their country. Given that the UK is now part of the Single European Market, an independent protectionist stance is less likely as a policy weapon.

The political dimension

For 30 years after the Second World War positive economics was concerned with making statements which were scientifically verifiable. Increasingly it came to be recognised that major economic questions have a political dimension to them. If, for example, there is a trade-off between unemployment and inflation, as suggested by the Phillips curve, then whether it is more desirable to have 3 per cent inflation and 10 per cent unemployment or 5 per cent unemployment and 10 per cent inflation is a question which cannot be definitively answered by economics.

Conclusion

Having considered the problem of unemployment we may note that it has a national and international aspect. Whatever its causes, unemployment can be cured only if there is a significant increase in the growth of real national income. This forms one of the prime features of Chapter 46 of the book.

Summary

1. There are different methods of measuring unemployment; the two most common ones are the claimant count and the survey technique.
2. The costs of unemployment fall mainly on the unemployed themselves and their families, but there are other costs for the economy as a whole.
3. There has been a steady increase in the number of unemployed at any level of vacancies, mainly because those who are long-term unemployed have grown in relative significance.
4. There are many different types, or causes, of unemployment, which can be divided into those when the economy is in equilibrium or when it is in disequilibrium.

5 There are a number of valid reasons why governments should have a policy specifically designed to deal with regional unemployment. The efficacy of these policies, however, is open to debate.
6 There are many causes of the high level of unemployment in the 1980s and 1990s. The cure for it, however, is a matter of great controversy. The main concern is that attempts to expand the economy might fuel inflation.
7 The supply side school places great emphasis on the promotion of competitive forces in the economy as the way to reduce unemployment, thereby aiming to make the labour market more flexible.
8 Neo-Keynesians favour demand management and other interventionist measures to reduce unemployment.
9 Unemployment is an international as well as a national problem. It is unlikely, therefore, that a purely national solution can be found to the problem.

Questions

1 Comment on the different methods of measuring unemployment and describe the changes that have taken place in the UK's measurement techniques during the last 20 years.
2 Discuss the view that regional unemployment would be best solved by the price mechanism.
3 Explain why, at any time, job vacancies may coexist alongside unemployment.
4 In the 1930s Keynes advocated that the government should 'spend its way' out of depression. Do you think that this view is still valid today, and if not, why not?
5 Study the figures in Table 45.4 (page 646) and then suggest reasons for the observed differences.
6 There was a considerable economic recovery in the UK in the late 1980s but the number of unemployed remained high in historical terms. What are the implications of this for government policy?
7 In 1996 there were 2.1 million people unemployed in the UK. Attempt to assess the magnitude of the various types of unemployment involved, i.e. frictional, structural, etc.
8 Describe what measures supply side economists might favour to reduce unemployment. To what extent do they have empirical support?
9 During the 1980s employment was rising and so was unemployment. Explain how this was possible.
10 Examine the view that unemployment figures are not facts but, rather, they reflect economic theory.

Data response A
Labour gains job bonus

Read the following article which was taken from the *Guardian* of 15 May 1997 and answer the following questions:

1 Discuss the relative merits of the different methods of measuring unemployment.
2 Outline the trend in unemployment in the UK in the last two to three years.
3 To what extent can this trend be accounted for by changes in the method of measuring unemployment?
4 Discuss the reasons for the growth of the long-term unemployed in the UK and outline the policies that the government can adopt to try to reduce their numbers.

Data response B
Statistics belie benefits of flexible labour market

The article was taken from the *Guardian* of 11 September 1997. Read it through and then answer the following questions:

1 Explain what is meant by the term 'the flexible labour market'.
2 Outline the supply side measures that can be taken to foster such a labour market.
3 There are various facets of a flexible labour market. What are they?
4 Supporters of the idea of a flexible labour market say that it reduces unemployment and can lead to faster growth. Discuss any potential disadvantages.

Labour gains job bonus

Larry Elliot
Economics Editor

THE Government received a boost yesterday when its first set of joblessness figures stifled demands for higher base rates by delivering a combination of rapidly declining unemployment and a surprise easing of wages pressure.

Data from the Office for National Statistics showed the number of people out of work and claiming benefit fell by 59,400 in April, bringing the total down to 1,642,900, the lowest since August 1990.

The trends suggests that, after falling by 420,000 since the introduction seven months ago of tougher measures for claimants of the Job-Seekers Allowance, employment is set to drop to a 17-year low this summer and may soon be below 1,500,000 for the first time since 1980.

It is now 58,000 higher than at the low point reached in the Lawson boom – 1,593,900 in April 1990 – but has fallen by 62,300 a month on average over the past six months.

Shadow employment secretary Gillian Shephard said the fall in unemployment was "entirely down to the successful policies pursued by the last government".

City analysts believe that the downward trend is set to continue even after the Job-Seekers Allowance effects fade.

But even better news for the Blair administration came from yesterday's figures for average earnings. In March, the annual rate of growth slipped from 5 per cent to 4.5 per cent after fresh information on bonuses and revisions to previous data.

The Bank of England – which now has operational control over interest rates – highlighted the pick-up in earnings growth in its Quarterly Inflation Report on Tuesday as a warning sign of price pressure in the pipeline. This was taken as a portent that borrowing costs could rise again next month.

Unemployment

Total, seasonally adjusted, millions

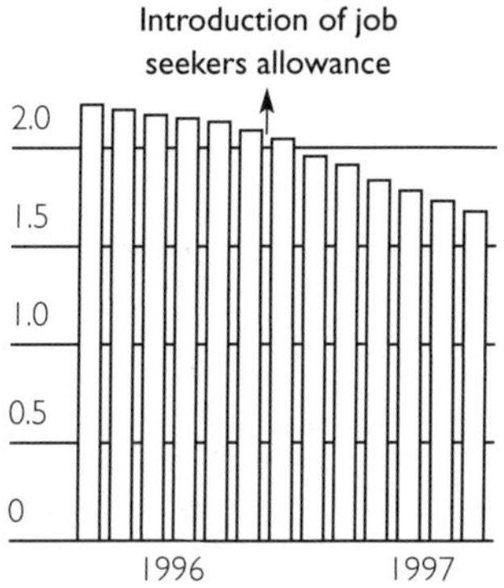

Source: ONS

Keith Davies, UK economist with City firm 4Cast, said the figures suggested that "recent fears of labour market overheating may have been exaggerated".

Simon Briscoe of Nikko said: "Given the weakness in some other parts of the economy, the inflationary threat is easing."

Officials admit that the recent jobless figures have been flattered by the introduction of the allowance, but say the underlying fall is still higher that the 15,000–20,000 drops seen in mid-1996.

Unemployment in April fell in all regions and age groups, and among men and women, the ONS said.

The overall unemployment rate dipped by 0.2 percentage points to 5.9 per cent, while female joblessness is 3.1 per cent, its lowest level since 1980.

Other encouraging news for the Government was that vacancies at Jobcentres are at their highest level since records began, while the number of claimants under 25 – a group targeted by the Government for special help – has declined by 136,000 over the past year.

Long-term youth unemployment – under-25s on the dole for more than a year – has dropped by 39,000 to 90,000.

Employment Minister Andrew Smith welcomed the figures but added that Labour's plan to take 250,000 young people off the dole was crucial. There were "still far too many people without jobs and skills".

John Monks, TUC general secretary, said the jobless fall "should not obscure the considerable level of long-term and youth unemployment. The Government is right to target these groups in its Welfare to Work programme."

Hunt for 'credible' method of counting claimants

The Government is looking urgently at a low-cost way of restoring credibility to the unemployment figures after spending 18 years in opposition lambasting the way joblessness is measured.

A consultation exercise by the Office for National Statistics explores the possibility of using a scaled-down monthly version of the Labour Force Survey as an alternative to the much-abused claimant count.

The previous government rejected plans to replace the claimant count with the LFS on the grounds that a monthly survey would cost an extra £10 million, despite calls from the Royal Statistics Society and the Commons employment select committee.

However, the rejigged proposal would involve a monthly estimate of unemployment based on averages of the past three months' data. This idea had a lukewarm reception but offers the advantage for a cash-strapped government of costing only an extra £250,000.

Andrew Smith, employment minister, said he welcomed the public consultation. "If new policies aimed at helping unemployed people are to succeed, they must be based on accurate statistics.

"Credibility must be restored to the official unemployment statistics."

Source: *The Guardian*, 15 May 1997

Analysis

Larry Elliott studies the figures behind the latest buzz word, which too often means 'You're sacked'

JOHN Edmonds, leader of one of Britain's biggest unions said yesterday that flexibility in the labour market often meant "You're sacked".

But although the GMB general secretary said the use of the phrase made him shiver, flexibility was the new buzz word among policy makers. Germany, once admired for its economic strength, is pitied because its employees lack flexibility. The US, spiritual home of flexibility, is seen as a role model for the rest of the world.

On Monday the Prime Minister told the TUC he had no intention of abandoning the "flexibility of the present labour market". Mr Blair's theme was echoed at the same forum yesterday by Adair Turner, director general of the CBI.

Supporters of flexible labour markets believe they lead to more rapid growth, but there is no evidence of this. Growth in the UK and the US in the 1990s is slower than in the 1980s, which in turn was slower than in the "inflexible" 1970s.

The Government's estimate of the average pace at which the economy can grow without running into difficulties with the balance of payments or inflation is the same now as 20 years ago – 2.25 per cent a year.

A second main argument is that flexible labour markets have delivered lower levels of unemployment. Employers in Britain and America have been more willing to hire workers than those in Germany and France because it is fairly easy to fire them if times get tough.

Recent figures seem to bear out this thesis. Unemployment in America is 4.8 per cent, only fractionally higher than in the last decade of the post-war boom which ended in 1973 while Britain's jobless rate is 5.5 per cent, less than half that in Germany and France.

But these figures rely on statistical sleight of hand. Two per cent of American men of working age are in prison, and the UK figure has been flattered by more than 30 changes since 1979 in the way unemployment is measured, all but one having had the effect of cutting the unemployment total.

Lord Eatwell, the economist who was once economic adviser to Neil Kinnock, also believes that the US and Britain suffer from heavy "disguised unemployment", where a lack of demand for labour and ungenerous benefit regimes force people to take low-productivity jobs. Once these are included, jobless rates in the Anglo-Saxon economies look no better than those in continental Europe.

The Eatwell thesis is supported by a study of downsizing in the US showing that 29 per cent of those affected either left the workforce altogether or were jobless for two years or more, and that two-thirds of the remainder took a pay cut in their new job.

Ministers are keen to point out that the emphasis in flexible labour markets should be on training and education to make workers more employable. However, Alison Booth, of Essex university, will argue at the British Association for the Advancement of Science conference today that flexibility is incompatible with a "learning society", because the low-paid jobs fostered by deregulation offer less training.

Further doubts about flexibility have been raised by the Organisation for Economic Co-operation and Development. Its research found that degregulated labour markets did not make workers more mobile, nor did they make it more likely that the low paid would move up the earnings ladder.

It said workers in the flexible labour markets of the US and the UK tended to be stuck in low pay jobs for much longer than employees in more regulated economies, tending to fluctuate between low pay and no pay.

Source: The Guardian, 11 September 1997

46 Growth and development

Learning outcomes

After reading this chapter you will be able to:

- Distinguish betweeen the concepts of economic growth and economic development.
- Understand the concept of sustainable development.
- Describe those factors that indicate a country's potential for development.
- Distinguish between the main stages of economic development.
- Identify the causes of economic growth.
- Understand the particular problems and characteristics of developing countries.
- Describe the key elements of development.

Growth and development

What is economic growth?

When we speak of ***economic growth*** we mean an increase in the GDP of a nation.

Common misunderstanding

When calculating economic growth, it is important to distinguish between real and nominal increases in GDP. For example, between 1965 and 1995 the GDP of the UK increased from £31.7 billion to £603.2 billion, an increase of 1802 per cent. However, when the effect of inflation is taken into account this amounts to an increase of only 88 per cent. It is the real increase that is important here.

We must also consider the effect of ***population growth***. Consider the case of a nation whose GDP is growing at 5 per cent per year but whose population is growing at 10 per cent. In this case, in real terms the average GDP per capita is declining. Thus the usual definition of economic growth is:

An increase in the real GDP per capita of a nation.

STUDENT ACTIVITY 46.1

A country has a GDP of £100 billion and a population of 10 million. At the end of the year GDP has risen by 10 per cent, but inflation was 5 per cent over the year. Population has risen by 1 per cent. What is the change in real GDP per capita to the nearest pound? Express this as a percentage change. How fast would this economy have to grow in real terms, in order to keep per capita real income at the same level?

The World Bank classifies countries by their GDP per capita. In 1994 there were 45 countries classified as low income, with GDP per capita less than $700. The poorest was Mozambique with a per capita income of $90.

Categorising countries in terms of development

In fact, there are a number of different ways in which the nations of the world are categorised. These categories sometimes cut across one another and categorisations are often rejected by nations. For example, many years ago economists spoke of ***backward countries*** or of ***underdeveloped nations***. These terms were considered pejorative and are not now used.

One of the broadest classifications is that of the ***three worlds***. The ***First World*** is the advanced industrial economies including most of those of Europe, Canada, the USA, Australia, New Zealand and Japan. The ***Second World*** is the communist and former communist countries of Eastern Europe, the old USSR and China. This leaves the ***Third World*** as all the remaining countries of Africa, Asia and Latin America. However, the collapse of communism in Russia and Eastern Europe has made this terminology somewhat obsolete.

Another expression which is used is that of the ***north–south divide***. This refers to the fact that the rich countries tend to be in the Northern Hemisphere while the poor are in the Southern. To be accurate the Southern Hemisphere would have to start well north of the equator in Africa and Asia to include some of the world's poorest nations. Australia and New Zealand, obviously, do not fit into this classification, since they are both relatively rich and yet are situated in the Southern Hemisphere.

An expression which is still in wide use is that of ***less developed country*** (LDC). This term is now also slipping from use and nowadays we tend to use the expression ***developing countries*** to describe the poorer nations.

A developing country is one where real per capita income is low when compared with that of industrialised nations.

Within this term there are distinctions. The very poorest such as Ethiopia and Bangladesh are, in fact, not developing at all and for them the term must be a bitter irony. To those which have experienced rapid economic development in recent years, such as South Korea and Singapore, we give the name ***newly industrialising countries*** (NICs).

The distribution of income

Our simple GDP per capita definition of economic growth is modified by the ***distribution of income*** within a country. If the increase in GDP is concentrated mainly among the rich, this will obviously have very little effect upon the average living standard. Income tends to be more unevenly distributed in poor countries and this therefore further exacerbates the problems of underdevelopment.

Environmental considerations

We too often assume in economics that more is better. As we saw in Chapter 7, economists are becoming increasingly concerned with the fact that the production of ***economic goods*** also involves the production of ***economic bads*** such as pollution. If we turn to the very poor nations of the world it is understandable that they tend to downgrade environmental considerations in their fight against the extreme poverty which exists in their countries.

Even in these countries, however, it is being recognised that the environment cannot be ignored. In 1997 uncontrolled forest fires used to clear land for development in Indonesia caused pollution across the whole region, especially when mixed with traffic fumes and other pollutants among Indonesia's more affluent neighbours. The resulting 'haze' made people in South-East Asia think more carefully about the environment as asthmatic and other respiratory conditions spread. A similar event in London in the 1950s resulted in the banning of domestic coal burning in the capital (unless special smokeless fuels were used) after 'smog' killed thousands of elderly people suffering with respiratory complaints.

Such human calamities are the reason why the idea of ***sustainable development*** (see Chapter 27) is increasingly being put forward by economists as an alternative objective to economic growth. This refers to the aim of meeting the needs of the present generation without harming the needs of future generations by reducing the stock of ecological and socio-cultural assets.

The importance of economic growth

Why worry about economic growth? The answer is that it is this very economic growth that enables us to enjoy a better ***standard of living***. (The relationship between growth and the standard of living is explored further below.) As we saw in the early chapters of the book, we assume that people are acquisitive, wishing to acquire more goods, more leisure, more entertainment, etc. All of these acquisitions are made possible by economic growth, as are better education, health care, and so on. Thus, while there are many who condemn the materialistic society, there are few who would deny that they would like a better standard of life.

Growth, power and influence

Economic growth has important political and military dimensions. It is often the wealthy nations of the world which dictate policies. When a country is wealthy it often develops substantial economic interests around the world. It will naturally be interested in the ***stability*** of countries supplying key raw materials or where multinational businesses have set up production. It may even become concerned about political events in countries neighbouring these countries!

For the European powers in the nineteenth and early twentieth centuries this interest led to ***colonisation*** of many of the poorer countries of the world. The USA, having itself begun as a group of colonies, was opposed to colonisation, but has intervened politically and militarily in many countries it considers to be in its sphere of influence, particularly in South and Central America and South-East Asia. The USSR intervened with military force in Hungary and Czechoslovakia when these East European states attempted to reject communism and leave the Eastern Bloc. Economic power often leads to political power, but it should be remembered that this political power involves money and resources, which could be used for other activities.

STUDENT ACTIVITY 46.2

Resources used in military intervention have opportunity costs. What are they?

Growth and the UK

Between 1967 and 1979 the UK economy grew by 32.7 per cent in real terms. Historically, this compares well with growth in the nineteenth century. However, when we compare it with the growth of our main trading partners it is very poor indeed. This is illustrated in Table 46.1. As you can see, the UK's performance overall is disappointing – although marginally better more recently. (In fact, since 1994 the UK's annual average growth rate has been above most of its major competitors.)

Table 46.1 **Percentage growth of real GDP for selected countries**

Country	*1967–79 (%)*	*1980–95 (%)*
Japan	83.1	50.8
Canada	63.1	42.6
Spain	59.3	38.4
Italy	55.8	29.2
Australia	54.7	47.5
France	52.8	31.5
Netherlands	51.2	31.5
Germany	48.0	34.6
USA	37.8	38.2
UK	32.7	31.0

Source: OECD

Common misunderstanding

It is important to realise that relatively small differences in rates of growth can have very significant differences upon GDP when considered over the medium or long term. This point is often forgotten or ignored, especially by politicians. Over the period 1967–79 the average annual growth in real GDP per capita of the UK was 2.5 per cent while that of Japan was 6.4 per cent. Now consider the information in Table 46.2. Let us assume that the UK is represented by the 2 per cent column, and Japan by the 7 per cent column. If 1990 is the last year we can see how quickly the GDPs begin to diverge. In 10 years' time the UK's GDP increases by 22 per cent but Japan's doubles. After 30 years the UK's GDP is 82 per cent higher but Japan has increased by a factor of eight. After a century the differences are staggering, with all the implications this has for standards of living and political and military power.

Table 46.2 is also useful in explaining the vast differences which exist between the rich and the poor nations. While the UK, the USA and Germany have experienced more than two centuries of continuous economic growth, many of the poor nations have experienced very little. It is small wonder therefore that if, for example, we examine the GDP per capita of the USA in 1995

Table 46.2 How growth rates affect incomes

Year	Index of national income based upon growth rate (%) per year of (1980 = 100)			
	2%	3%	5%	7%
1990	100	100	100	100
2000	122	135	165	201
2020	182	246	448	817
2040	272	448	1 218	3 312
2050	406	817	3 312	13 429
2080	739	2009	14 841	109 660

we find that it is 79 times greater than that of India (see pages 87–92 for discussion of the difficulties of international comparisons).

Growth and the standard of living

It was noted above that growth allows us all to enjoy an improved standard of living. However, there is not an exact correlation between the standard of living and the GDP per capita, although the fact that in 1995 it was only $100 in Ethiopia whilst in Switzerland it was $40 630 tells us something pretty fundamental about the two nations. The World Bank puts out a wealth of statistical information which is significant in assessing the present standard of living of a country and its potential for development. Thus, besides information on the growth of per capita GDP there is data on the debt owed by a country, the relative significance of agriculture in an economy, birth rates and death rates, life expectancy, infant mortality rates, literacy rates, the number of doctors per capita and the numbers enrolled in secondary education as a percentage of the relevant age group. (See also Data response A at the end of the chapter.)

Comparison of some of these other indicators confirms the huge discrepancy between the rich and the poor. In Ethiopia, for example, a newborn baby has a one in six chance of not making it to the age of 1 and a further 4 per cent chance of being dead before reaching the age of 5. This gives an overall infant mortality figure (age 0–4) for Ethiopia of 206 per thousand compared with a figure of 8 for the UK.

It should be noted that the economic and social organisation of the nation can significantly modify the picture presented by the GDP per capita figures. Thus, some countries classified as developing may, using the above indicators, achieve results similar to much richer nations. In terms of life expectancy, infant mortality, calorie intake and the number of doctors communist countries such as China and Cuba have figures achieved only by nations with significantly higher GDPs per capita. This evidence conflicts with the World Bank's own conclusions (*World Development Report,* 1987) that development is linked to the degree of free enterprise in the organisation of the economy, although it should be remembered that free enterprise is now an important force in the Chinese economy.

We may, thus, conclude this section of the chapter by saying that economic development and improvements in the standard of living are influenced by social organisation, choices made and goals set as well as by growth in the real GDP per head.

STUDENT ACTIVITY 46.3

Which factors are able to provide some indication of a country's standard of living and potential for development? Make a list of countries that you would classify as developing economies.

Factors influencing growth

Stages and theories of economic growth

Many attempts have been made to classify the pattern of economic growth as a passage through a number of definable ***stages.*** The most famous of these is Marx's classification. He saw societies as passing through the following stages: primitive communism; slavery; feudalism; capitalism; and, finally, socialism and communism. Recent historical experience suggests this sequence does not apply and countries may go from feudalism to socialism and then on to capitalism.

Another famous classification is that which appears in W. W. Rostow's *Stages of Economic Growth*, which envisages a development of an economy up to the time when there is a 'takeoff into self-sustaining growth'.

Common misunderstanding

In fact, it is now regarded as fallacious by all but hard-line Marxists to view economies as passing through definite stages. It could even be argued that the idea that economies must pass through certain stages has been harmful when such a philosophy has been rigorously applied by governments.

There have also been a number of different ***theories*** of economic growth, which attempt to explain the causes and rates of economic growth: the Harrod–Domar model, that of Smith and Malthus, the Ricardo–Marx–Solow model, and that of Leontieff. However, none of them gives an all-embracing account of the growth problems of developed or developing economies and the mathematics involved is beyond the scope of this book. What we can say is that there are a number of factors that are known to influence the growth rate and we shall now proceed to examine these.

Investment

It is undoubtedly true that investment has an influence on the rate of growth. We can see in Fig. 22.1 (see page 281) that increasing the rate of investment (capitalisation) should increase the rate of growth. However, there appears to be no simple relationship between the rate of investment and the rate of growth. It is obvious that the rates of investment in Singapore, Malaysia and Japan in the 1965–80 period must have been important reasons for their being at the top of Table 46.3. It is also apparent that their average rate of investment was significantly higher than the rest of the nations in the table. The lower figures for the 1980–93 period reflect the world-wide recessions in the early 1980s and 1990s. Nevertheless, Japan still achieved a relatively high annual growth rate of investment over the period.

It is clear from the figures in Table 46.3 that, as far as the UK is concerned, the low rate of investment over much of the period has been matched by poor performance in the growth league. Whether the higher rate of investment since 1980 will lead to a significantly improved growth performance in the long term remains to be seen. There are many imponderables on the horizon. For example, what will be the long-term effect on investment of the Single European Market? As yet it is too soon to say.

Table 46.3 **Growth and investment in selected countries**

	Average annual growth (%) in real GDP per capita		*Average annual growth (%) in investment*	
	1965–80	*1980–93*	*1965–80*	*1980–93*
Singapore	10.1	6.1	13.3	2.8
Malaysia	7.3	3.5	10.4	0.5
Japan	6.5	3.4	6.7	3.7
Canada	5.1	1.4	5.1	3.4
Ireland	5.0	3.6	6.3	−1.0
Spain	4.6	2.7	3.7	3.0
Norway	4.4	2.2	4.2	0.6
Sweden	2.9	1.3	0.9	0.1
USA	2.7	1.7	2.6	3.2
Denmark	2.7	2.0	1.2	−0.5
UK	2.4	2.3	0.6	2.0
Switzerland	2.0	1.1	0.8	3.1

Source: OECD

Difficulties of comparison

The relationship between investment and growth will also be affected by our old friend ***the law of diminishing returns.*** Other things being equal, the principle of ***marginal productivity*** tells us that as we apply more and more investment to an already large stock of capital, the extra output achieved should diminish. This might partly explain why a wealthy country such as Switzerland sees a relatively poor return on its investment while a relatively poorer country such as Malaysia sees a much better return for less investment.

We can also point out that a low rate of growth may appear less burdensome to a rich country than to a poor country. Let us consider an analogy with individual incomes. Suppose we consider two individuals, one with an income of £10 000 per year and the other with £100 000. If both their incomes increase by 10 per cent the first individual has an extra £1000 to spend while the second's will increase by £10 000. Thus rich countries with low growth rates may be able to sustain much higher increases in their real living standards than those of poor nations with high growth rates. In 1995, for example, the GDP per capita in Malaysia was $3890 but that of Switzerland was over 10 times this amount.

It is also possible to consider that geographical conditions may have an effect upon investment. Countries with inhospitable climates or terrains may find that the physical problems of development are disproportionately high. Among the advanced countries, this may affect nations such as Austria, Switzerland and Finland.

Gross and net investment

A major factor influencing the relationship between investment and growth is that of the difference between ***gross*** and ***net investment***. Much investment may simply be to replace obsolete equipment and, thus, will therefore have no effect upon the rate of growth; it is only net investment which increases the wealth of a nation. This is a problem which particularly affects a mature industrial nation such as the UK, since much investment must be to replace out-of-date equipment. This, therefore, has compounded the problem associated with the UK's low rate of investment in the earlier period.

The quality of investment

Units of investment are not homogeneous and it does not follow that there is a constant capital/output ratio even within one industry. We must therefore consider the ***quality of investment.*** An often repeated argument is that at the end of the Second World War the UK was left with much obsolete and worn-out equipment and investment consisted of patching and infilling. On the other hand, in the then West Germany and Japan, where the destruction of capital had been almost total, investment was in all-new integrated plant. There is no point in blaming more recent poor performance on such distant historical events. The point is that investment has to be of the right kind to contribute strongly to economic growth.

Defence expenditure

All economics is a question of allocating scarce resources in the optimal manner. A significant factor when we come to compare growth rates is defence expenditure. If a nation is devoting a proportion of its precious GDP to defence this must consist of resources which could be used for investment to increase the living standard directly. Table 46.4 shows the proportion of government expenditure devoted to defence expenditure in various countries.

Table 46.4 **Defence expenditure of selected countries 1993**

Country	*Defence expenditure as percentage of government total expenditure*
Austria	2.3
Brazil	2.6
New Zealand	3.3
Netherlands	4.2
France	6.0
Germany	6.4
Australia	7.9
UK	9.9
USA	19.3
Israel	20.3
Jordon	22.1
Singapore	24.5

Source: OECD

Again it is impossible to draw any simple relationships between defence expenditure and growth. As regards the UK it may have been one more factor restricting economic growth, especially when comparing its position with its European neighbours. Of course it is impossible to estimate the value of defence expenditure to the community in terms of the security it offers. There are also spin-offs in terms of arms sales etc. On the other hand, the burden of defence expenditure can be disproportionately high because it ties up highly trained personnel as well as some of the most young and vigorous of the workforce.

Two of the most successful economies of the second half of the twentieth century, Japan and West Germany (as was), were prevented from being involved in military activity because of fears they might repeat their aggressive behaviour of the Second World War. It has been suggested that these countries have been able to concentrate their best brains on commercial rather than military activities. Some of the world's poorest countries have spent large amounts on defence, particularly in war-torn areas like the Middle East.

The performance of many developing countries is obstructed by high defence expenditure. Much of their precious foreign exchange goes on importing military hardware. One of the most celebrated cases in recent years must be that of Ethiopia, one of the poorest countries on earth, which, while Bob Geldof was raising money for it, was involved in a bloody and expensive civil war.

Governments are naturally a little coy about disclosing their expenditure on defence. However, for Pakistan in 1993 we find that defence accounted for 27 per cent of the budget. At the same time it had to spend 25 per cent of its exports just to pay the service of its loans. You will realise that it does not leave a lot of latitude for other programmes. In fact less than 1 per cent of government expenditure went on health care in that year.

People and growth

Population growth

As far as advanced economies are concerned it may be debated whether population growth is a spur to economic development or whether increased standards of living have increased population. Figure 4.7 on page 48 shows that, theoretically, there is an optimal size for a population, although the discussion also showed how difficult it is to define this in practical terms. We could argue, for example, that at the moment the stagnation in population growth in Western Europe has some connection with the lack of economic growth, but a similar stagnation in Japan does not seem to have had the same effect.

If on the other hand we turn to developing countries, there can be little doubt that population growth is one of the main inhibiting factors in increasing GDP per capita. It would appear that any major advance in living standards will, for many countries, depend upon limiting the size of families. In recent years the country to take this most seriously has been China, the most populous nation on earth, where draconian measures have been taken to limit population growth.

Population structure

As we learned in Chapter 4, it is not just the size of the population which is important but also its age, sex and geographic distribution. These factors all have important considerations for economic growth. If, as is the case in most advanced countries, there is an increasing proportion of dependent population (the old, the young, etc.), resources will have to be devoted to caring for them. Thus, valuable investment resources will be channelled into projects of very low productivity such as old people's homes. It could be argued that extra investment put into education will pay dividends in the long run, but such projects will not be conducive to high rates of growth in the short and medium term. When we examine the nations with low growth rates in Table 46.3 we see that some, such as Sweden and the UK, have placed a high priority on welfare projects, while others, like the USA, have not.

In considering the effect of population upon growth, we must also consider ***participation rates***, i.e. the proportion of the population which is economically active. In this respect the UK has one of the highest participation rates of any advanced country. Participation rates are governed by such things as school-leaving age, the attitude towards working women, the facilities which exist for child care, the age of retirement, and so on.

The average age of the population may also affect economic growth. By and large, an ageing population tends to inhibit economic growth since older people tend to be more conservative and less inclined to take risks. Again it is possible to argue that the ageing of the UK's population over this century has inhibited growth, although other developed countries have faced a similar situation.

Population and developing countries

The developing nations account for 80 per cent of the population of the world but only 54 per cent of the land area and just 16 per cent of total world output. This situation is bound to get worse as the century draws to its close. If, as predicted, world population reaches 6 billion by the year 2001 the developing nations are likely to account for 84 per cent of the population and an even smaller share of total world output.

By far the greatest rates of population growth occur in the developing world. Advances in science have reduced infant mortality and increased lifespan but, as yet, birth rates remain high. (See discussion of this and population momentum on page 40–2.)

The predictions of Malthus seem to be upon us once again (see page 38–9). It seems unlikely that there will be a drastic slow-down in population growth until 20 years or so into the next century. If, therefore, we are to avoid being overtaken by the law of diminishing returns it is vital that productivity be drastically improved in developing nations.

Childen – investment goods or consumption goods?

It may seem bizarre to regard children as goods, but parents make decisions about whether or not to have children partly on economic criteria. If you live in a developing country without a welfare state, children can be regarded as an ***investment*** in your future. They will be cheap labour when they are young and they will look after you when you are no longer able to work. There is thus an inbuilt bias towards overpopulation which is no longer checked by such high levels of infant mortality. There is also a strong belief in many developing countries that you have to have a reasonably large number of children in order to ensure that at least some survive, although as medical standards rise, this belief will slowly disappear.

Decision making about family size is quite different in developed countries where children are considered more as ***consumption goods*** to whom the law of diminishng marginal utility applies. The welfare state and private pensions provide for old age, and children, far from being a source of income, are considered to be a major expense. With the expansion of higher education, many do not join the workforce until they are in their twenties and must be supported through a lengthy period of education. It may be a case of one child, probably; two, perhaps; while three is often an accident!

Migration

Migration also has an effect upon economic growth. The effects of overall immigration and emigration upon the UK were discussed in Chapter 4, where we noted that immigrants tend to be of working age and therefore beneficial to the economy, whereas the UK has tended to lose highly trained personnel such as doctors through emigration. If we make comparisons between the UK and its immediate neighbours such as France, Germany and Italy in the early and middle parts of the twentieth century, a fact which is apparent is that each of these countries had a large reservoir of labour to draw on, i.e. a drift of the agricultural population to the towns, and in the case of the then West Germany there was for a time the defection of people from East Germany. Thus, each of these countries had a pool of relatively cheap, easily assimilable labour which could be drawn upon. The immigration which the UK has experienced from overseas has been small by comparison but has posed problems of cultural and social differences. These problems have also been experienced by France and, to a lesser extent, by Germany. Reduced job opportunities during the 1980s and 1990s may have exacerbated these problems.

Education and training

It is often said that the wealth of a country lies in the skill of its population. This being the case, the education, training and attitude of a country's population must be a significant factor in determining its rate of growth. While it may appear unpleasant to speak of investment in people as if they were machines, nonetheless it is important that a nation makes sure that it has the adequate skills it needs to advance its economy. That is why an investment in people, or more precisely an investment in ***human capital***, is considered a priority for the economic well-being of a country. Such investment, whether it takes the form of both formal education or on-the-job training, enhances the skills of the population, raises levels of productivity and ensures a faster rate of economic growth, or so it is often claimed.

Despite the large increase in the numbers receiving higher (or university) education in the UK in the last 10 years, the participation rate (i.e. the percentage of people in the age group receiving such education) is still only just over 30 per cent. This is a lower rate than in most other major OECD economies, such as the USA, Canada, Japan, France and Germany. This discrepancy may have had an adverse effect upon growth when compared with these other countries. We might also regard education, as opposed to training, as a component in the quality of life (i.e. it can be regarded as a consumption good rather than as an investment good). Thus those receiving higher education are consuming an economic product which will improve their standard of living by improving their quality of life.

Common misunderstanding

While it is often claimed that increased investment by a country in its human capital will automatically lead to improved levels of productivity and economic growth, in fact there is not a great deal of supportive evidence. Countries with a greater percentage of the relevant age group in further and higher education tend to have higher levels of per capita GDP, but this does not necessarily prove that the one causes the other. In fact, there may be a two-way relationship between per capita GDP and educational standards: higher GDP may require higher levels of education, but higher standards of living may make it easier to afford better education and a better quality of life.

If you are just embarking upon higher education it will doubtless come as a great comfort to know that there is also a marked correlation between higher education and higher earnings later in life!

STUDENT ACTIVITY 46.4

Is a large population beneficial for economic growth?

Is there a British disease?

There can be little doubt that in the years since the Second World War the UK has possessed many of the advantages which were desirable for economic growth and yet, although it has done well compared with many developing countries, it has not done particularly well compared with its peers such as France and Germany. The reasons for this are not to be found in complex mathematical models of growth, but rather in a combination of socio-economic factors which together have probably inhibited the growth of the economy.

These factors include government ***'stop–go' policies*** and the variation in the objectives of government policies, which have had adverse effects upon growth. Government preoccupation with control of the money supply and, more recently, inflation targets, is just the latest in a long line of different policy objectives. This problem is discussed in more detail in Chapter 47.

It has often been the case, especially in the past, that all the problems of UK industry have been blamed on ***trade unions***. While this is an exaggeration, restrictive practices and excessive wage demands, when they occurred, may well have had adverse effects upon growth.

It is probably also the case that UK ***management*** has been too uninventive and unadventurous. In particular, there has been an unwillingness to invest in the future. As indicated in Table 46.5, the UK's spending on research and development

(R&D) is lower than most of its main competitors, although not excessively so.

Table 46.5 Spending on R&D as a percentage of GDP: selected OECD nations

	1987	1992
UK	2.22	2.12
USA	2.84	2.68
Germany	2.88	2.53
France	2.27	2.36
Italy	1.19	1.38
Japan	2.63	2.80

Source: CSO *Economic Trends* No 490, August 1994, and 502, August 1995

In addition, while there is no definitive proof of this, it has often been suggested that there has been a tendency for ***scientific and technical skills*** to be underplayed, while those with qualifications in the arts have often tended to be promoted. It is certainly true that there has been a lack of coordination of research and development programmes by successive governments.

The UK has tended to be a ***net exporter of capital***. It can be argued that this flow of funds abroad starves the domestic economy of investment. There is little evidence to demonstrate that this is so. Rather, it may be the case that the other factors discussed combine to limit investment opportunities.

There is some evidence to show that the performance of the economy is damaged by the fact that investment managers go for quick returns on their funds and that, as a result, firms become more concerned with their short-term share values than with more long-term research and development plans. The Bank of England has expressed concern about this. The shares of the majority of large UK companies are traded on the Stock Exchange and it is argued that this situation results in 'casino capitalism'. Contrasts are often made with Germany which has a larger number of private companies which are more likely to be financed through long-term relationships with regional banks rather than by the flotation of shares on the Stock Exchange.

Recent experience

In the middle years of the 1980s growth in the UK economy exceeded that of most of its trading partners and there was some evidence of a ***catch-up*** process occurring. As you can see from Table 46.6, by the early 1990s the UK had once more slipped down the growth league, although by the mid 1990s it was once again achieving growth rates that compared favourably with its main competitors.

Table 46.6 Average annual growth in real GDP

Country	1980–8 (%)	1986 (%)	1989 (%)	1990 (%)	1992 (%)	1996 (%)
UK	2.8	3.3	1.9	0.6	–0.5	2.4
Italy	2.2	2.7	3.0	2.0	0.7	2.7
France	1.8	2.0	3.9	2.8	1.3	2.2
Canada	3.3	3.3	3.0	0.9	0.8	3.0
Germany	1.8	2.5	3.8	4.5	2.2	2.4
USA	3.3	2.9	2.5	0.9	2.3	2.7
Japan	3.9	2.4	4.7	5.6	1.1	2.0

Source: IBRD and OECD

The success of the mid 1980s was, at least in part, due to government supply side measures although we should not forget our enormous good fortune in North Sea oil. The government would doubtless claim credit for reducing the power of trade unions and for reintroducing a spirit of competition into the economy.

There were also significant increases in productivity at the time. From 1979 to 1993 output per person in UK manufacturing increased by 2.2 per cent p.a., compared with an average figure of 1.6 per cent for OECD countries as a whole during the period. This was due, at least in part, to the elimination of large amounts of capacity, leaving the economy with the most efficient lump of the sector. Productivity gains elsewhere in the economy were less spectacular, although there were significant gains in some service industries such as telecommunications and financial services, due to a combination of a rapid rate of technical progress and a shake-out of labour in the respective industries. There was also huge import penetration of manufacturing industries.

In the 1980s the economy was recovering from the worst recession for 50 years when we ought to have expected rapid growth. Another large recession in the early 1990s accounted for the lower growth rates at this time and for the higher growth rates subsequently, especially since the UK emerged from the recession earlier than its main European competitors, having also entered it earlier. As noted in Chapter 43 the more rapid growth rates of the middle years of the 1990s have been accompanied by a fairly dramatic fall in the level of unemployment, although many of the newly employed are in part-time positions. Furthermore, there are still many other problems, e.g. greater participation in higher education, a lack of coordination in research and development and poor management, that remain to be tackled.

Development economics

What's special about development economics?

We have looked at many branches of economics in this book such as monetary economics, foreign trade, and so on. It should come as no surprise, therefore, that there is a ***specialised branch of economics concerned with development.*** There is also here, as elsewhere, controversy. The argument is concerned with whether or not the principles and policies which apply to advanced economies also apply to relatively poor ones.

It is argued that the problems of developing economies are different from those of developed economies: first, because poor economies are starting out in a world in which there are already rich countries. Thus, for example, models based on the experience of the UK in the industrial revolution, when it was already the richest country in the world, are unlikely to be of use. Second, many people argue that there is a special case for state intervention and coordination in the economies of poor nations, the arguments for which are considered below.

On the other hand, there has, in recent years, been a tendency to absorb development economics back into mainstream economics and argue that the principles are no different. This, for example, has been the point of view of the World Bank. This accords with the neo-classical movement back towards market orientation seen elsewhere in the subject of economics.

A full treatment of development economics is beyond the scope of this book and the syllabus. We will, however, mention some of the main points. (One or two of them, such as population and developing countries and environmental considerations, were considered earlier in the chapter.) We will also consider why it is argued that development economics is a special discipline demanding different theory.

Pioneers and latecomers

In order to advance the developing countries must adopt new technologies, especially in agriculture. What they require, however, is technology which is *appropriate* to their situation. In many cases the adoption of modern techniques has been rejected by the population or else has created jobs for the few and unemployment for the many.

Common misunderstanding

It can be argued that developing countries have the advantage of 'free' access to the ideas and inventions which the advanced nations pioneered. There is, as it were, a 'book of blueprints' which they can draw on. However, it may be doubted whether this access is free and whether the 'book of blueprints' is appropriate to developing nations. For example, the adoption of industrial techniques often throws thousands of skilled workers out of jobs.

Improvements in technology in the advanced nations also cause problems for the developing countries. New processes replace old products as, for example, when synthetic fibre replaced jute in carpets. Additionally, better technology facilitates economies in the use of materials as, for example, with the introduction of much thinner tin cans. Such developments have the effect of depressing the demand and therefore the price of primary products.

Rather than copy the technology of the developed world, it is argued that countries just starting out on the development road should use ***intermediate technology***. This is capital which is cheap to purchase and easy to use – which is appropriate in countries with low levels of savings and low educational levels.

Some nations, however, have made a spectacular success of borrowing the blueprints, e.g. Japan and, later, South Korea and the other Pacific rim countries known as the ***Asian tigers***.

STUDENT ACTIVITY 46.5

Choose an example of a newly industrialising country and discuss the reasons for its success.

The dual economy

Attention has been focused on the fact that development can create a ***dual economy***. In one section there is the subsistence economy where wages are very low, and the other section is the newly industrialising one utilising capital. The existence of the first is important to the second in that it provides a pool of labour. In effect the industrialising sector can operate with a perfectly elastic supply of labour.

As the industrialising sector expands so it draws in a greater and greater percentage of the population. This process will be hindered if the expansion significantly increases wages. The successful expansion of the industrial sector increases the dualism. Dualism existed in economies such as the UK during the industrial revolution. (Some argue that it still exists now in some low-paid service sector jobs.) However, the relatively slow introduction of labour-saving technology kept the process in check. With a developing economy the ability to adopt the latest technology at once may dramatically increase dualism.

The problem of agriculture

We might expect in a simple economic model that developing countries would produce food to sell to the industrialised nations. This, however, is not the case: rather, it is the industrialised world which sells food to the developing world.

In the days of peasant agriculture people produced much of what they required themselves. In the push for development they have been encouraged to produce cash crops. Their livelihood then becomes subject to the variations in market price of the crop. However, this market price is not freely determined. Massive intervention by governments in the developed world effectively precludes many producers in developing countries from the rich markets. Consider, for example, the variable import levy of the CAP which ensures that imported agricultural products are at least the same price as those produced domestically. Worse than this, the CAP produces food surpluses which further depress world prices if they are released.

Trade issues

Early thinking on development economics argued that the ***terms of trade*** (see Chapter 40) tended to move against latecomers especially where they are producers of primary products. This stems from a combination of low price and income elasticities of demand for primary products and a tendency towards the saving of raw material as technology improves in industrialised countries. To this we may add the 'learning by doing argument' which says that, whatever the level of technology a latecomer adopts, it becomes good at producing the goods only through the experience of doing so. By the time the latecomer has learnt the developed countries are likely to have moved on. For both these reasons, therefore, the latecomer (developing country) is likely to be at a disadvantage when trading.

The debate is thus whether, on the one hand, a developing country is at an advantage in the terms of trade by being able to adopt the latest technology and benefit from low wage costs or, on the other hand, the terms of trade are likely to move against it for the reasons stated above. If evidence did support the view that the terms of trade do move against the latecomer this could be an argument for (temporary) protection of ***infant industries*** in the 'learning by doing case'. On a non-theoretical basis it could be an argument for better organisation of primary procedures.

Many developing countries are 'one-horse' economies; that is to say, they are very dependent for their export earnings on one or two products. For example, virtually all of Uganda's export earnings comes from one crop, coffee, while Zambia is very heavily dependent on copper for its export earnings. This can be fortunate for the country if the price of the product goes up and very unfortunate if it comes down. Either way it makes life unstable and unpredictable.

STUDENT ACTIVITY 46.6

Can you think of any examples of a country (or countries) that is dependent on the revenue from a narrow range of primary good exports (or even from the exports of a single product) that have proved to be very lucrative?

In Fig. 46.1 you can see that after a dip in the early 1970s, the terms of trade of developing countries took a dramatic plunge following the OPEC oil price rise in 1973. A swift recovery followed after

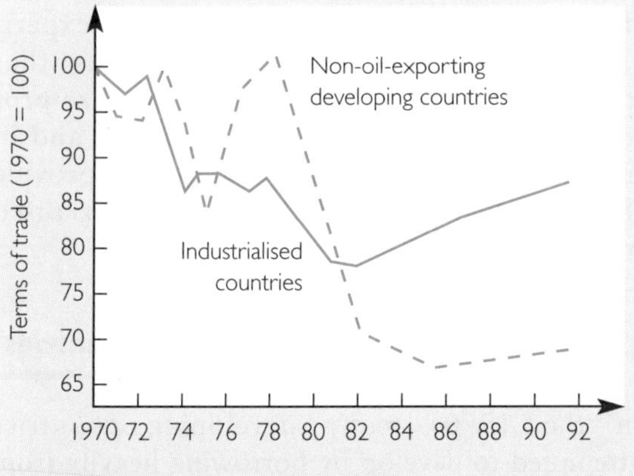

***Fig. 46.1* The terms of trade**
The rise in oil prices in 1973 caused the terms of trade to deteriorate for all oil-importing nations. After recovering in the late 1970s, the terms of trade for developing nations plunged following the oil price rise of 1978 and the depression of the early 1980s.
Source: IBRD

1975 and then the second oil price rise in 1978 sent the terms of trade for non-oil exporters plunging. This drop was compounded by the world depression of the early 1980s, which depressed the demand for primary products. The collapse of oil prices was good news for the developed nations and brought some relief to developing nations, but the continued depression in commodity prices kept the terms of trade against them.

Protectionism

In those developing economies which have grown significantly since the Second World War we find that both the pace and the pattern of industrial growth have been influenced by a plethora of protective tariffs, subsidies, rebates, quotas and licences as well as direct investments by activist states. These interventions attracted the attention of development economists from the 1960s onwards. Many focused on the effects of intervention on incentives and resource allocation. The pattern revealed was higgledy-piggledy. The only discernible regularity was the taxation of agriculture and the subsidisation of some industries, especially those producing consumer goods. However, while a country is free to subsidise or protect an industry, it is still important for it to be able to assess its true opportunity cost. This is especially true for an economy attempting a balanced growth scenario, in which all real variables are assumed to grow at the same constant rate. Thus, it becomes necessary to undertake cost–benefit analyses based on world market prices. The difficulties of such an analysis (see pages 387–8) may be another reason for the reversion to the market forces viewpoint.

Cartelisation

The success of the OPEC oil price rise in 1973 dramatically demonstrated the effects of a successful cartel upon the price of a product. Never has there been a swifter redistribution of wealth from one group of countries to another. This lesson was well learned by the producers of other primary products but they have so far been unsuccessful in organising similar cartels.

A factor which works against the developing nations is that the buyers of primary products are frequently more organised than the sellers. The price of jute, for example, can effectively be set by a small group of people on the London Commodity Exchange. The position of the peasant producing the crop is often undermined by being heavily in debt and having sold the crop a year in advance.

When it comes to imports the developing nation is likely to find the situation reversed with the oligopolistic producers of manufactured goods much better organised. Consider the case of motor vehicles. It is the marketing requirements of the industrialised nations which determine the design and price of cars and these often bear little relation to the needs (or income) of developing nations.

Sacred cows

It is a familiar theme in developed economies that advancement in the developing world is hindered by the people clinging to the practices of their forebears. A recent case cited is where resettled peasants in Ethiopia left their purpose-built houses and hundreds of new tractors to return to their traditional ways and practices.

Common misunderstanding

Economic development is not just measured in terms of material success. It is about increasing the quality of life. This is made up not only of the consumption of material goods but also of social well-being, including a respect for traditional ways of life.

The state and development

In many of the points made in this section, you can see that a key question for governments is whether or not they should intervene. Furthermore, if they intervene, does this mean wholesale direction of the economy or more discreet manipulation of markets?

Those arguing for some kind of ***balanced growth*** say that there is a need for central coordination and state control. The experience of the USSR before its break-up is often quoted. With all its disasters central coordination lifted this country from feudalism to superpower within a lifetime. Central control can direct scarce capital resources to where they are most needed, ensure that education is appropriate, restrict wasteful consumption and so on.

On the other hand those arguing for ***unbalanced growth*** urge the use of market forces in directing the economy. It is said that market forces will maximise the rate of growth. Some infrastructure projects may be neglected but in the long run the benefits created by a high, if unbalanced, rate of growth will 'trickle down' to the rest of the economy.

Until the late 1980s there were two competing models of development, capitalist and socialist. The collapse of the communist bloc in Eastern Europe and the adoption of market processes by the world's remaining communist countries, notably China, have resolved this dispute in favour of the market. Since its adoption of market mechanisms within a communist framework, the Chinese economy has been growing strongly at about 10 per cent a year. It has started to develop some of the problems of capitalist economies as well with soaring unemployment and widening income distribution. Does this mean that the state has no role in development? The experience of developed countries suggests that its main role should be in ***infrastructure*** projects, such as transport and irrigation, and in improving ***health*** and ***education***; these provide the basis for development of an industrialised market economy.

The debt problem of developing countries

In the 1970s many developing countries attempted to develop by borrowing heavily from abroad in order to industrialise. The argument in favour of such a policy was that a lack of internal savings meant that these countries were unable to build up the critical mass of capital needed to industrialise. The sudden massive surplus on the balance of payments of the oil-exporting countries in the middle of the

1970s meant that there was plenty of international capital looking for a home.

Unfortunately the two large oil price rises in 1973 and again in the late 1970s also depressed the economies of the developed economies. This meant that the promised export markets of many of the developing countries failed to live up to expectations and as a result these countries found themselves unable to repay the debt. Much of the money that was borrowed was not used for development purposes but simply to balance the books for the nations' overseas payments. Little found its way into the sort of projects which development economics would suggest.

This situation developed into a full-blown debt crisis in the 1980s with, in many developing countries, debt representing a high percentage of one year's national income.

For instance, in 1995, the value of foreign debt was equivalent to 62.3 per cent of the national income of the African countries. The total debt of developing countries in that year was $1749 billion. Banks that had previously been keen to lend were no longer willing to do so. International agencies either had insufficient funds substantially to affect the situation or imposed very stringent conditions on loans.

Solutions to the debt crisis

For some countries the burden of debt payments is so great that it is difficult to see how they will ever get out of the situation. For instance, in 1993, 44.5 per cent of Peru's export earnings went on debt interest (never mind the repayments). It is said in banking that if you owe the bank £100, you have a problem, but if you owe the bank £1 million, the bank has a problem. This is the situation faced by the bankers who have lent to developing countries. Many imaginative solutions have been put forward ranging from the straightforward ***write-off*** or ***write-down***, to ***debt-for-equity*** swaps, whereby the debt is sold at a discount and the purchaser buys shares in a country's companies, or ***debt-for-nature*** swaps. In the latter case debt is written off in return for a commitment for environmental policies such as preserving the rainforests. Some countries that have attempted to repay have had to introduce (often at the request of the IMF) such stringent budgetary and financial policies as to damage growth seriously. Developing countries are strongly discouraged from using protectionism to improve their balance of payments, so austerity measures are the only alternative. This often results in internal political problems and severe problems of poverty for the unemployed.

Common misunderstanding

The debt crisis is not nearly as bad for some developing countries as it used to be. The debt problem has been relieved for many of the better-off developing countries through the ***rescheduling*** *of the debt: both the governments of developed countries and banks have agreed to delay the repayment date for loans and/or to spread the repayments over a longer period.*

However, for other developing countries, especially the poorest, the problem remains as acute as it ever did, with no obvious solution in sight. Often policy prescriptions only seem to make a bad situation far worse.

STUDENT ACTIVITY 46.7

Explain why a solution to a country's debt crisis is beneficial to both parties in the arrangement.

What is necessary for development

The four elements of development

Despite the disagreements on both theory and practice most people are agreed that there are four wheels to the development vehicle:

a) *Human resources.* We must be concerned with the health, nutrition and education of the workforce. There is a growing recognition that investment in people is a key to development.
b) *Natural resources.* The discovery of gold is doubtless a great boon but natural resources are not the key to development. Switzerland is

an extremely rich nation which is almost devoid of mineral resources, has a terrible climate (unless you are a skier) and an impossible terrain. On the other hand there are oil-rich nations with money gushing out of the ground but which are still, to all intents and purposes, undeveloped with poor schools, health, roads and so on.

Perhaps for the underdeveloped country the key resource is agricultural land. Moreover, land ownership patterns are a key to providing farmers with strong incentives to invest in capital and technologies that will increase their land's yield.

c) *Capital formation*. It is perhaps an obvious tautology that the rich are rich because they have wealth. Again we may turn to Switzerland as an example: it lacks almost everything except that it has enormous stocks of capital. The problem for a developing nation is how to accumulate capital. If possible the best way is the savings of its own people; Singapore and South Korea provide excellent examples of this. But for the poorest nations of the world this is impossible. If a nation is already reduced to the bare minimum of existence, depressing current consumption to accumulate capital is inviting mass starvation.

We can say that the poorest nations of the world are caught in a ***vicious circle of poverty***. Low incomes lead to low saving; low saving retards the growth of capital; inadequate capital prevents rapid growth in productivity; low productivity leads to low incomes, and so on. Other elements in poverty are self-reinforcing. Poverty is accompanied by low levels of skill, literacy and health; these in turn prevent the adoption of new processes and technologies. (See Fig. 46.2.)

The alternative therefore is the importation of capital from abroad. This in turn is beset with problems as we saw above in the section on debt.

d) *Technology*. The adoption of the appropriate technology is a difficult and controversial topic. (See the earlier discussion on pioneers and latecomers.)

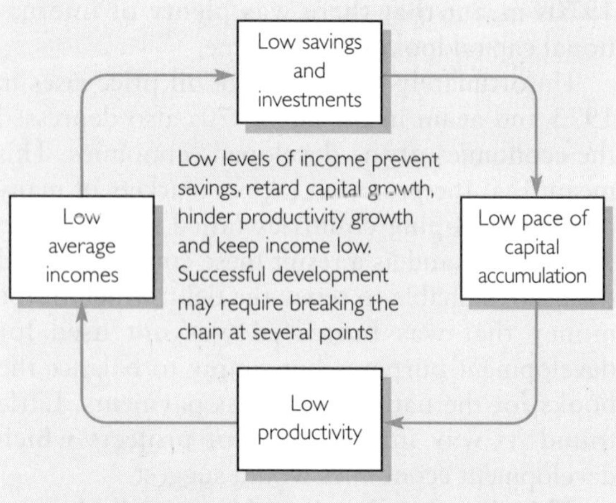

***Fig. 46.2* The vicious circle of poverty**

World Bank policy

As we said in the section on the World Bank (see page 586–6), it is not itself big enough to make a significant contribution to the problems of developing nations. However, we may take its attitude as being generally symptomatic of the approach of the developed nations towards the developing world.

In the early years of its development the World Bank concentrated on projects to improve the infrastructure of developing countries – irrigation projects, transport, power and similar projects. The emphasis has now changed. In the 1980s the World Bank became more concerned with the significance of improved health, nutrition and education in bringing about economic growth. It regards them not only as important for economic development but also as desirable in themselves.

Whether the World Bank has achieved anything in this direction is another question. Despite its stated objectives the World Bank has been obsessed with the debt of developing countries and imposing sound financial packages on them in accordance with the policies of monetarist and neo-classical policies in the advanced world. Other international organisations such as the IMF have followed a similar line. The commercial banks which have lent billions to the developing world have also pressed financial stringency on developing nations. Thus, desperately poor nations have been constrained to deflate their economies, devalue their currencies, rein in government spending – in short, to apply classical supply side economics to their problems.

Does aid help?

There are two questions to be addressed when aid is considered: 'How much is given?' and 'Does it do any good?'

The targets are not ambitious. UNCTAD had suggested that the developed nations should give 0.7 per cent of their GDP in aid, although even this modest target has long since been abandoned. In the past 20 years OECD countries have spent a steady 0.35 per cent of their combined GDP on aid.

On the second point several doubts have been cast on the efficacy of aid. First, aid is usually given to governments or government agencies and thus may be perverted into the political aims of that regime. For example, if the government is buying millions of dollars' worth of arms from overseas, is not aid just aiding the finance of these purchases in a roundabout way? Second, there is a tendency for aid to be spent on prestigious projects rather than the more mundane developments in the economy which may yield better results. Finally, there is concern as to whether aid really furthers development or whether it undermines the self-reliance of a nation.

STUDENT ACTIVITY 46.8

Is there any type of aid that you think may do any good?

Conclusion

Economic growth refers to an increase in a country's real per capita GDP. A developing country has low relative per capita income, although the term developing country covers a wide variety of situations, from very poor economies to those that are growing rapidly.

Growth facilitates a better standard of living. The distribution of income and environmental considerations also need to be taken into account in the development process. Information on factors such as educational achievements, health matters and debt levels can provide further evidence of a country's standard of living.

The emphasis on the market process as the main means for development has had its successes, particularly among the Asian tiger economies, but there are still many very poor countries which are caught in a vicious circle of debt repayment and financial stringency which prevents the growth needed to pay off the debt. Imaginative solutions, so far generally unforthcoming, to the problems of such countries are needed if they are to develop at all.

Summary

1 Economic growth is an increase in the real per capita GDP of a nation.
2 Many different terms are used to describe the poorer nations of the world. Whatever terms are used the poor are those with a low GDP per capita.
3 The standard of living is not just the income per head but also all the other things which are important to the quality of life, such as health care and literacy.
4 An increase in economic growth may not be the same thing as an increase in economic welfare. We must also consider such factors as the distribution of income and the exploitation of the environment.
5 Whatever its relative merits, economic growth is vital to the improvement of the real standard of living of a nation, in terms of either material wealth or other considerations such as leisure and the general state of well-being.
6 Since the Second World War the UK's economic growth has been rapid but it has nevertheless been much slower than that of its main trading partners, at least until quite recently.
7 Investment is crucial to economic growth but there is no simple relationship between the rate of investment and the rate of economic growth.
8 The efficacy of investment is affected not only by its quantity but also by its quality and type.
9 Economic growth is affected by the size and structure of a population.

10 Although the roots of economic growth are difficult to define, when we examine the UK experience we find that, despite some recent improvements, the economy still seems to be lacking in a number of key areas fundamental to the growth process.

11 Some of the major areas of controversy in development economics and those that need special review when considering developing economies are population growth, the appopriate level of technology, trade issues, environmental considerations, the position of agriculture and the role of the state.

12 The four elements of development are: human resources; natural resources; capital formation; and technology.

13 Despite recent improvements in the situation, the world debt crisis still threatens to overwhelm some debtors and creditors.

Questions

1 What factors are significant in influencing the growth rate of a nation?

2 What is meant by the term 'a developing nation'?

3 Discuss the view that economic growth is the sole indicator of a country's standard of living.

4 What is the relationship between investment in a country and the rate of growth?

5 Explain what is meant by the term 'sustainable development' and account for its significance.

6 How would you account for the UK's relatively poor growth performance since the Second World War?

7 The sources of social welfare are not to be found in economic growth per se, but in a far more selective form of development which must include a radical reshaping of our physical environment with the needs of pleasant living and not the needs of traffic or industry foremost in mind.

E. J. Mishan, ***The Costs of Economic Growth***

The anti-growth movement and its accompanying excessive concern with the environment not merely leads to a regressive change in the distribution of resources in the community, it also distracts attention from the real issues of choice which society has to face.

Wilfred Beckerman, ***In Defence of Economic Growth***

Compare and contrast these views of economic growth, stating what role the economist should play in attempting to answer the opposing views of the problems they pose.

8 Discuss those factors considered to be most important in aiding the development process.

9 'Trade not aid'. Evaluate this slogan as a prescription for development.

10 Is there a solution to the debt crisis of developing nations?

Data response A
The potential for development

Study the information in Table 46.7 (based on 1993 data unless otherwise stated) and answer the questions that follow.

1 Developing economies can be classified as low income (≤$700 GNP per capita), middle income ($700 to about $2800) and upper middle income ($2800 to about $8000). How else might they be characterised and categorised?

2 Do you think the information given here provides a sufficient overall indicator of the potential for development for each country? What other information may be useful?

3 How would you now classify Singapore?

4 Given this information, to what extent do you think a uniform programme of development for all developing countries would be a useful strategy?

Table 46.7 The characteristics of development

	Population (millions)	*Population growth (% p.a.) (1980–93)*	*GNP per capita ($)*	*GNP per capita growth (% p.a.) (1980–93)*	*Debt service as percentage of exports*
Mozambique (Mo)	15.1	1.7	90	–1.5	20.6
Ethiopia (E)	51.9	2.7	100	–	9.0
Kenya (K)	25.3	3.3	270	0.3	28.0
Mali (Ma)	10.1	3.0	270	–1.0	4.5
India (I)	898.2	2.0	300	3.0	28.0
Nigeria (Ni)	105.3	2.9	300	–0.1	–
Pakistan (Pa)	122.8	2.8	430	3.1	24.7
China (Ch)	1178.4	1.4	490	8.2	11.1
Sri Lanka (SL)	17.9	1.5	600	2.7	10.1
Indonesia (Io)	187.2	1.7	740	4.2	31.8
Senegal (Se)	7.9	2.7	750	0.0	8.4
Jamaica (J)	2.4	0.9	1 440	–0.3	20.1
Thailand (Th)	58.1	1.7	2 110	6.4	18.7
Brazil (Br)	156.5	2.0	2 930	0.3	24.4
Malaysia (My)	19.0	2.5	3 140	3.5	7.9
Mexico (Me)	90.0	2.3	3 610	–0.5	31.5
Korea, Rep. (Ko)	44.1	1.1	7 660	8.2	9.2
UK	57.9	0.2	18 060	2.3	–
Singapore (Si)	2.8	1.1	19 850	6.1	–
USA	257.8	1.0	24 740	1.7	–

	Life expectancy at birth (years)	*Adult illiteracy 1990 (%)*	*Under 5 mortality rate (per 1000 live births)*
Mo	46	67	282
E	48	–	206
K	58	31	94
Ma	46	68	217
I	61	52	122
Ni	51	49	191
Pa	62	65	137
Ch	69	27	54
SL	72	12	19
Io	63	23	111
Se	50	62	120
J	74	2	17
Th	69	7	45
Br	67	19	63
My	71	22	17
Me	71	13	43
Ko	71	<5	12
UK	76	<5	8
Si	75	<5	7
USA	76	<5	10

Source: World Development Report (WDR) 1995

47 Conflicts between objectives

Learning outcomes

At the end of this chapter you will be able to:

- Recognise conflicts between objectives.
- Suggest policy combinations to deal with the conflict.
- Relate the discussion to current events.

The lessons of history

The approach in this chapter is similar to that adopted in Chapters 26–30. There is a student activity at the end of each section but no further data response at the end of the chapter.

At different periods of history different objectives may be in conflict with each other. For instance, during the 1960s, the balance of payments was an obstacle to the achievement of full employment. The policy adopted in the 1960s and early 1970s was called the 'stop–go' policy, because governments repeatedly tried to expand the economy but were then forced back by the balance of payments constraint. Deficits on the current account created speculation against the pound, which had to be met by higher interest rates and fiscal restraint. The balance of payments constraint disappeared in the the 1980s with the exploitation of North Sea oil. Unemployment and inflation then became the two conflicting objectives. To some extent this conflict existed during the earlier historical period, but in the 1980s the conflict became more apparent. New situations are confronting governments as history unfolds, but a return to consider historical examples is often instructive.

Unemployment and the balance of payments

The conflict between the balance of payments and reductions in unemployment discussed above resurfaced in the early 1990s. The advantage on the balance of payments current account that had been conferred by North Sea oil had finally been eroded by a combination of factors:

a) High interest rates and exchange rates in the early 1980s had resulted in widespread loss of jobs and output in manufacturing industry.
b) Deregulation of the financial sector in the 1980s resulted in an explosion of consumer credit. As house prices also shot up, people felt wealthier and therefore able to borrow against this wealth.
c) The economy was suddenly growing fast after the deep recession of the early 1980s. People believed that the Conservatives had finally solved the long-standing problems of the UK economy and that the expansion of the economy would last.
d) Although the UK was not actually in the ERM, the Chancellor followed a policy of 'tracking the mark', which resulted in high exchange rates.
e) Partly as a result of the above factors, inflation took off again, making British products less competitive.

It is widely recognised that the economy expanded too fast in the late 1980s, fuelled by a consumption boom rather than an investment boom. The Labour government faced similar problems with the expanding economy and high exchange rate that they inherited from the Conservative administration. Its response was to employ fairly restrictive fiscal and monetary policy to prevent a boom resulting in renewed inflation and balance of payments deficits.

STUDENT ACTIVITY 47.1

Use economic statistics from 1997 onwards to see if the Labour government was successful in its objective of avoiding a repeat of 1990.

Unemployment and inflation

The trade-off between inflation and unemployment, and the arguments about the Phillips curve, were discussed in great detail in Chapter 44. After the expansion of the late 1980s resulted in a return of inflation, the ***speed*** of reduction in unemployment became an issue in the argument. If the economy was not given time to expand capacity and retrain workers in the expanding industries, it was argued that bottlenecks would develop in the fastest expanding industries, bidding up prices and wages and raising inflationary expectations in the economy as a whole. This process would also affect the balance of payments case considered above, since consumer demand would suck in imports from abroad if there were insufficient capacity in the UK.

Whether there is a genuine trade-off between unemployment and inflation has been difficult to test in the UK in recent years because unemployment has been so high. In 1997 unemployment fell below 1.5 million for the first time in almost two decades. It will be interesting to see whether inflation starts to rise again if unemployment falls further.

STUDENT ACTIVITY 47.2

Trace the combinations of unemployment and inflation from 1990 to see whether there appears to be any relationship. Include data available after the publication date of this book.

Inflation and growth

There is no conflict between low inflation and growth; indeed it is often argued that low inflation is a prerequisite for sustained growth because of the stability it gives to the economy. However, getting there is another matter. Most policies designed to reduce inflation are also damaging for growth. High interest rates have the effect of reducing investment. High interest rates often have the effect of increasing the value of the currency, thus reducing the demand for domestically produced output. Restrictive fiscal and monetary policy reduce aggregate demand, which in turn results in a reduction in investment in new capacity.

If this kind of anti-inflationary policy had the effect of permanently reducing inflation, then governments could use it, and then get on with the business of achieving economic growth. Unfortunately, when economies are reflated, eventually inflation tends to reappear. Some economies have been more successful in avoiding a return to inflation (e.g. Japan, Germany), but the UK has regularly been revisited with rising prices. After inflation was more or less squeezed out of the economy in the early 1980s, a period of growth in the mid to late 1980s resulted in the return to inflation rates above 10 per cent in 1990. This was squeezed out of the economy during the early 1990s and then the economy began to expand again in the mid 1990s.

STUDENT ACTIVITY 47.3

Using recent data, assess whether the recovery of the economy in the mid 1990s led to substantial rises in inflation.

Income redistribution and growth

The effects of taxation on work effort and, by implication, on economic growth have been discussed in Chapters 30 and 43. If high rates of taxation are imposed on richer people in society, in order to finance those who are less well-off, we have to consider whether there is a cost in terms of reduced growth. Much of the tax policy of the Conservative government from 1979 onwards was based on the idea that there was such a trade-off, resulting in one of the lowest top rates of income tax in the developed world, at 40 per cent. It is fairly clear that the very high rates of tax which existed in 1979 were likely to create disincentives. Charging 98 per cent on marginal income will not encourage people to work hard or to invest. Furthermore such people will normally be able to employ the best tax accountants to help them avoid paying such rates of tax. There is less evidence that reducing top tax rates to as low as 40 per cent creates substantial incentives. The student is referred back to Chapters 30 and 43 for student activities on this topic.

Economic freedom and other objectives

A balance of payments deficit can be resolved by import controls or tariff barriers (as all countries do to a greater or lesser extent). Inflation can be apparently cured by putting a freeze on wages or prices or both (as happened in the UK in the 1960s and 1970s). If growth is not occurring because of a lack of savings, then the government can require people to save (as has happened in Malaysia and Singapore). Unemployment can be 'solved' by requiring those without a job to undertake work in return for their benefit (the workfare system as used in the USA).

As can be seen, where the market has not succeeded in solving a problem, then compulsion can often do the job. There is a cost in terms of a loss of the economic freedom to choose. Sometimes this cost may be considered worthwhile because of the benefits it creates. Ideological arguments about the alleged superiority of the market will always arise when issues of this kind come up, and it will be difficult to separate value judgements from facts.

STUDENT ACTIVITY 47.4

Identify areas of current government policy which represent a restriction of economic freedom. Is it possible to justify these restrictions in each case?

Vicious circles and virtuous circles

The best hope for economic growth will occur when the conflicts discussed above are at a minimum. Some countries seem to have been more successful than others at achieving this state of affairs. When things go wrong, an economy is said to be in a vicious circle. A good example of an economy in a vicious circle would go something like this: a country suffering from a balance of payments deficit on current account and inflation above the average experiences speculation against its currency because of these problems. It deals with this situation by raising interest rates. This has the effect of supporting the currency and reducing domestic demand. Unemployment starts to rise and business confidence falls, resulting in a decline in investment. This policy eventually works, reducing both inflation and the balance of payments problem in the short term. Political pressure then turns the government's attention to unemployment. The government attempts to stimulate the economy using fiscal or monetary means, but the lack of investment means that there is little spare capacity in the economy, particularly in high-tech areas where demand is strong and new techniques have been introduced. Where there is sufficient capacity, new workers cannot be trained quickly enough to meet demand. The economy sucks in imports, the currency speculation returns, and as the currency falls in value so higher import prices start to push up inflation.

A country in a vicious circle can solve one or more of its problems, but each solution brings a new problem into view. An economy with a virtuous circle can deal with one problem at a time and meet more of its objectives. An economy like this would develop something like this: starting from a position of unemployment, the government decides to expand the economy. This reduces the surplus on the balance of payments, but since this was large to begin with, this is not a problem. The increased demand for labour pushes up the wage rate, but prices do not have to rise as much because of the rising productivity of the workforce. The high cost of labour forces firms to continue to think of labour-saving inventions to raise productivity further. Inflation rates are modest and the currency is strong, so interest rates are low. This is a further incentive for businesses to invest, raising productivity and growth further. The low interest rates are a disincentive to savings, but firms are very profitable and able to generate funds internally for investment.

STUDENT ACTIVITY 47.5

Is the UK economy currently in a virtuous circle or a vicious circle?

Conclusion

We have ended the book with a discussion of the dilemmas facing governments. Economics does not always provide straightforward answers, and economists do not always agree with each other. Whenever there are policies there will also be politics about the correct priorities. Although history can provide us with precedents, each new situation facing policy makers will be in some way unique. Economics provides us with a way of thinking about the world, whether it be a government making decisions about the course of the economy, a business person making decisions about investment or pricing, or an individual making decisions about personal finance. There is, thank goodness, room for a wide range of opinions about the economy and politics. Now that you have read this book (or most of it), we would like to welcome you to the unfolding argument of just what humankind should do next.

Summary

1. Expanding employment may run into balance of payments constraints.
2. Inflation and unemployment may be conflicting goals.
3. Policies designed to reduce inflation may also reduce growth.
4. Although very high levels of taxation are likely to have effects on growth, current tax rates may not have significant effects.
5. Economies that can deal with one problem at a time are more likely to achieve a virtuous circle.

Questions

1. Explain why there has been a problem of stop–go policies in the past in the UK. Assess whether the UK has now solved this long-standing problem.
2. Is unemployment soluble without inflationary consequences?
3. Is it possible to have a fairer distribution of income without adversely affecting economic growth?

Select bibliography

General works

Anderton, A., *Economics*, Causeway
Bannock, G., Baxter, R. E. and Rees, R., *The Penguin Dictionary of Economics*, Penguin
Begg, D., Fischer, S., and Dornbusch, R., *Economics*, McGraw-Hill
Core Economics: The Economics 16-19 Project, Heinemann
Curwen, P., (Ed), *Understanding the UK Economy*, Macmillan
Dunnett, A., *Understanding the Economy*, Longman
Dunnett, A., *Understanding the Market*, Longman
Economist (The), *Economist Briefs: Money and Finance; Britain's Economy under Strain; The EEC; The World Economy; European Economies*
Freedman. R (ed.), *Marx on Economics*, Penguin
Friedman, M. and Schwartz, A., *A Monetary History of the US, 1867-1960*, Princeton University Press
Gordon, R J. (ed.), *Milton Friedman's Monetary Framework*, University of Chicago Press
Griffiths, A. and Wall, S. (eds), *Applied Economics: An Introductory Course*, 7th edition, Longman
Hardwick, P., Khan, B. and Longmead, J., *An Introduction to Modern Economics*, Longman
Heilbroner, L. and Thurow, L., *The Economic Problem*, Prentice-Hall
Heilbroner, L. and Thurow, L., *Economics Explained*, Prentice-Hall
Hunt and Sherman, Economics: An Introduction to Traditional and Radical Views, Harper and Row
Keynes, J. M., *The General Theory of Employment, Interest and Money*, Macmillan
Lipsey, R. G., *An Introduction to Positive Economics*, Weidenfeld & Nicolson
Lipsey and Harbury, *First Principles of Economics*, Weidenfeld and Nicolson
Mackintosh, M. *et al., Economics and Changing Economics*, Open University and ITP
Manchester Economics Project, *Understanding Economics*, Ginn
Marx, K. *Theories of Surplus Value*, Parts 1 and 2, Lawrence & Wisehart.
Maunder, P. *et al.*, *Economics Explained*, Collins
McCormick, B. J. *et al.*, *Introducing Economics*, Penguin
Mullard, M., *Understanding Economic Policy*, Routledge
Pennant, R., and Emmott, B., *The Pocket Economist*, Martin Robertson and *The Economist*
Powell, R., *'A' Level Economics: Course Companion*, Letts
Samuelson, P. A., and Nordhaus, W. D., *Economics*, McGraw-Hill
Sloman, J., *Economics*, Harvester-Wheatsheaf/Prentice-Hall
Stanlake, G.F., *Introductory Economics*, Longman
Wonnacott, P. and Wonnacott, R., *Economics*, McGraw-Hill KogaKusha

Journals

Developments in Economics, Causeway Press
Economic Review, Philip Alan
Teaching Business and Economics, EBEA
Sweezy, P. M., 1939, Demand under conditions of oligopoly, *Journal of Political Economy*, 47, August, 568–73
Hall, R. L. and Mitch, C. J., 1939, Price theory and business behaviour, *Oxford Economic Papers*, 2, May, 12–45

Official statistics and publications

UK Economy

Annual Abstract of Statistics, HMSO
Bank of England Quarterly Bulletin, Bank of England

ONS, *Economic Trends*, HMSO
ONS, *Financial Statistics*, HMSO
ONS, *Monthly Digest of Statistics*, HMSO
Department of Trade and Industry, *Employment Gazette*, HMSO
HM Treasury, *Financial Statement and Budget Report*, HMSO
United Kingdom Balance of Payments, HMSO
United Kingdom National Accounts 'The Blue Book', ONS

International

Basic Statistics of the (European) Community, Eurostat
OECD *Economic Outlook*, OECD
World Development Report, Oxford

More specialised and/or advanced texts

Ackley, G., *Macroeconomics: Theory and Policy*, Collier Macmillan
Arestis, P., *The Post-Keynesian Revolution in Economics: An alternative analysis of economic theory and policy*, Edward Elgar
Atkinson, A. B., *The Economics of Inequality*, Oxford University Press
Bailey, S., *Public Sector Economics*, Macmillan
Baumol, W. J., *Business Behaviour, Value and Growth*, Macmillan
Baumol, W. J., *Economic Theory and Operations Analysis*, Prentice-Hall
Beckerman, W., *National Income Analysis*, Weidenfeld & Nicolson
Blaug, M., *The Cambridge Revolution: Success or Failure?* Hobart Paperback No.6, I.E.A.
Black, J., *The Economics of Modern Britain*, Martin Robertson
Brandt Commission, *North-South: A Programme for Survival*, Pan
Brooman, F. S., *Macroeconomics*, Allen & Unwin
Brown, C. V. and Jackson, P. M., *Public Sector Economics*, Martin Robertson
Callinicos, A., *The Revenge of History: Marxism and the East European Revolutions*, Polity Press
Carter, H. and Partington, I., *Applied Economics in Banking and Finance*, Oxford University Press
Chamberlain, E. H., *The Theory of Monopolistic Competition*, Harvard University Press
Cole, C. L., *Microeconomics*, Harcourt Brace Jovanovich
Cole, S., *Applied Transport Economics*, Kogan Page
Copeman, H., *The National Accounts: A Short Guide*, HMSO
Crockett, A., *Money: Theory, Policy and Institutions*, Nelson
Cullis and Jones, *Microeconomics and the Public Economy: A Defence of Leviathan*, Blackwell
Donaldson, P., *Economics: A Simple Guide to the Economics of the Early Eighties*, Pelican
Dunnett, A., *Understanding the Market*, Longman
Fine, Ben, *Marx's Capital*, Macmillan
Friedman, M. and Schwartz, A., *A Monetary History of the United States 1867–1960*, Princeton University Press
Galbraith, J. K., *The Affluent Society*, Pelican
Galbraith, J. K., *Economics and the Public Purpose*, Pelican
Galbraith, J. K., *The New Industrial State*, Pelican
Glennerster, H., *British Social Policy since 1945*, Blackwell
Grant, R. M. and Shaw, G. K. (eds), *Current Issues in Economic Policy*, Philip Allan
Green W., and Clough, D., *Regional Problems and Policies*, Holt, Rinehart & Wilson
Hartley, K., *Problems of Economic Policy*, Allen & Unwin
Haverman, R. H., *The Economics of the Public Sector*, Wiley
Jones, H., *An Introduction to Modern Theories of Economic Growth*, Nelson
Kerry Turner, R., Pearce, D. and Bateman, I., *Environmental Economics*, Harvester Wheatsheaf
Kindleberger, C. P. and Lindert, P. H., *International Economics*, Homewood
Knight, F. H., *Risk, Uncertainty and Profit*, Chicago University Press
Koplin, H. T., *Microeconomic Analysis*, Harper & Row
Laidler, D., *Microeconomics*, Philip Allan
Levacić , Rosalind, *Economic Policy Making*, Wheatsheaf Books
Levacić and Rebmann, *Macroeconomics: An Introduction to Keynesian and Neoclassical Economics*, Macmillan
Lewls, D. E. S., *Britain and the European Economic Community*, Heinemann
Lancaster, K., *An Introduction to Modern Microeconomics*, Rand McNally
Leijonhufvud, A., *On Keynesian Economics and the Economics of Keynes*, Oxford University Press
Mair, D. and Miller, A.G., *A Modern Guide to Economic Thought*, Edward Elgar
Marris, R., *Reconstructing Keynesian Economics with Imperfect Competition*, Edward Elgar

Mishan, E. J., *The Economic Growth Debate: An Assessment*, Allen & Unwin
Milner, C. and Greenaway, D., *An Introduction to International Economics*, Longman
Morgan, B., *Monetarists and Keynesians - Their Contributions to Monetary Theory*, Macmillan
Morris, R., *The Economic Theory of Managerial Capitalism*, Macmillan
Mulvey, C., *The Economic Analysis of Trade Unions*, Martin Robertson
The New Palgrave Dictionary of Economics, Macmillan
Parkin and Bade, *Modern Macro-economics*, Philip Allen
Pearce, D. W. (ed.) *Blueprint 2*, Earthscan Publications
Pearce, D. W., *Cost-Benefit Analysis*, Macmillan
Pearce, D. W., *Environmental Economics*, Longman
Peston, M. H., *The British Economy*, Philip Allen
Prest, A. R. and Coppock, D. J. (eds.) *The UK Economy: A Manual of Applied Economics*, Weidenfeld & Nicolson
Prest, A. R. and Barr, N. A., *Public Finance in Theory and Practice*, Weidenfeld & Nicolson
Price, C. M., *Welfare Economics in Theory and Practice*, Macmillan
Robbins, L. C., *Nature and Significance of Economic Science*, Macmillan
Ryan, W. J. L. and Pearce, D. W., *Price Theory*, Macmillan
Sawyer, M., *The Challenge of Radical Political Economy: An introduction to the alternatives to neoclassical economics*, Harvester-Wheatsheaf
Schumpeter, J. A., Capitalism, Socialism and Democracy, Unwin University Press
Shand, A., *The Capitalist Alternative: An introduction to neo-Austrian economics*, Harvester
Simon, H. A., *Administrative Behaviour*, Macmillan
Smith, A., *An Inquiry into the Nature and Causes of the Wealth of Nations*, Penguin
Stewart, J., *Understanding Economics*, Hutchinson
Thurow, L., *The Zero-Sum Society: Distribution and the Possibilities for Economic Change*, Penguin
Trevithick, J. A., *Inflation: A Guide to the Crisis in Economics*, Penguin
Vane, H. R. and Thompson, J. L., *Monetarism*, Martin Robertson
Veljanowski, C. (ed.) *Privatisation and Competition*, I.E.A. Hobart Paperback 28
Weeks, J., *A Critique of Neoclassical Macroeconomics*, Macmillan
Westaway, A. J. and Weyman-Jones, T. G., *Macroeconomics: Theory, Evidence and Policy*, Longman
Williamson, O. E, *The Economics of Discretionary Behaviour: Managerial Objectives in a Theory of the Firm*, Prentice-Hall

FINANCIAL TIMES

Supplement

How to read the Financial Times

Philip Coggan, Markets Editor, Financial Times

The Financial Times was founded in 1888 and has been known for a century for its distinctive pink paper (an early marketing technique that stuck).

The paper is split into two, with the first section broadly covering politics, economics, social developments and industrial trends and the second section covering individual companies and stock, currency, bond and commodity market movements.

Pages covering UK and international companies

The UK results coverage includes an important feature in the form of comments on the figures. The aim is to guide investors through the morass; for example, to point out when profits have been boosted by one-off factors such as asset sales; when the trend in profits growth is slowing; when a healthy profits figure masks a weak cash position; when the performance is strong, but the shares already reflect all the good news.

Valuing shares

There are a number of techniques for valuing shares, based on the assets, profits, dividends or cash flow of a company. *Net asset value (NAV) per share* is calculated by adding up the value of the tangible assets of a company, deducting the debts, and dividing by the number of shares in issue. It can be a good way of assessing the value of some companies; if the share price is 80p and the NAV per share is 100p, it would in theory be possible for a predator to buy up the company and sell off the assets at a profit. However, many modern companies are in the service sector and have few tangible assets, so NAV is of only limited use in valuing shares.

The *price–earnings ratio* (P/E) is a method of comparing a company's share price with its profits. The first step is to work out a company's profits, after tax and other deductions. These are known as the *earnings*, which are then divided by the number of shares in issue, to get the *earnings per share*. The last step is to divide the *share price* by the earnings per share to get the P/E ratio. Roughly speaking, this figure represents the number of years' earnings an investor is paying for a share; buying a company on a P/E ratio of 10 means one is paying 10 times current earnings. In theory, the lower the P/E the better. However, the markets are always looking ahead. Companies with a high P/E tend to be ones where investors are expecting earnings to grow quickly; companies with a low P/E are expected to show modest, if any, profits growth.

Another popular valuation measure is *dividend yield*, which shows the annual dividend as a percentage of the share price. Many investors own shares for their dividends, which over the long term make up a significant proportion of stock market returns. An advantage of dividends is that they are real, in the sense that they have to be paid in cash; assets and profits can sometimes be accounting illusions. It would be a mistake, however, to assume that the company with the highest yield is the most attractive. Since the yield represents the dividend divided by the share price, as the price falls the yield rises. Sometimes shares offer a high yield because investors expect the company to cut the dividend, or not pay it at all; in other cases, they expect little in the way of growth. If a share has a low dividend yield, it may be that the company is currently paying only a small proportion of its profits out as dividends, so it can reinvest the money to help its business grow. Fast-growing companies tend to have low dividends; investors hope that eventually both profits and dividends will grow at an above average rate and they are prepared to accept a low yield for now.

The London share service pages, give the P/E and the dividend yield (headed **yld gr s**) for most quoted companies.

Sometimes investors prefer to look at *cash flow*, rather than profits or dividends. In some cases, this may be because it is harder to manipulate cash flow than it is to fiddle the earnings or profits figure. In other cases, a company might look better value on cash flow than on an earnings basis; for example, if the company takes a heavy charge against its profits for depreciation of its assets.

Shares are divided by industrial sectors

so that ratios can be easily compared between, say, Sainsbury and Tesco, or Guinness and Allied Domecq. Other information shown includes the share price, the day's change, the 52-week high and low, and the market capitalization (the value placed by the stock market on the company, calculated by multiplying the share price by the number of shares in issue). Symbols direct the reader to footnotes which show where special circumstances apply.

The stock market

The back page of the UK edition contains coverage of the London stock market. The aim is to explain both why shares in individual companies rise and fall and why the overall market goes up or down. This is a difficult area; shares in, say, Acme Construction may rise on hopes of a bid from Megacorp. Even if the rumour turns out to be untrue, it is still the case that the story lifted the shares and it is our job to report it. One way of assessing the credibility of rumours is to look at the volume of shares traded. If it is greater than normal for that stock, it may indicate that the story has some substance; if volume is low, the chances are that few believe the rumours.

Individual shares may move for a whole host of reasons: stockbrokers' reports; bid rumours; executive departures; adverse press reports; results which beat, or fall short of, market expectations. This last factor is one of the most important. Outsiders are often puzzled when a company which reports a 30% rise in profits sees its shares fall. Markets indulge in what one might call the White Queen syndrome, after the character in Through the Looking Glass. The White Queen screamed before she pricked her finger and when the injury actually occurred, made only a small sigh, as she had got all her screaming over with in advance. Similarly, stock markets are forever looking to the future and anticipating what will happen. Expectations are built into the market; thus if a company is expected to increase profits by 40% and only reports a rise of 30%, its shares will fall.

FTSE

Because there are so many quoted shares, investors use 'benchmarks', in the form of baskets of representative stocks, to track the market's overall movements. The most commonly used in the UK is the *FTSE 100*, which stands for the Financial Times/Stock Exchange 100 index and is designed to show the UK's 100 largest companies. Broader indices, such as the *FTSE All-Share* which includes around 800 stocks and the *FTSE SmallCap* which covers shares in smaller companies, are also used. Companies drop in and out of these indices as their shares rise and fall, or are subject to takeover.

The indices are also used to monitor the performance of fund managers who look after other people's money, whether it be pension funds, charities, or the portfolios of private investors. Experience has found that it is very difficult to beat these benchmarks. In part, this is because the index will inevitably represent the average performance of all shares, and thus all investors; by definition, therefore, half of all investors should not beat the index. On top of that factor is the burden of administrative and dealing costs, which investors have to pay, but the index does not reflect. More fundamentally, it seems as if very few people have the ability to pick successful shares. Academics have argued that this is because markets are efficient; share prices reflect all the available knowledge about a company. What will affect the price, therefore, is future news, which by definition cannot be known.

If picking the best shares is difficult, so is predicting the moves of the overall market. Over the long run, at least, it tends to go up. BZW's Equity–Gilt Study shows that £1,000 invested in equities at the end of 1945 would have grown, with net dividends reinvested, into £218,140 by the end of 1995. The same amount in a building society would have risen to just £10,400. But in the short term, it can fall very sharply. On Black Monday, 19 October 1987, the FTSE 100 index fell by 10.8%, and it then dropped another 12.2% on the following day.

The main factors which cause the market to rise and fall include the following:

Interest rates. Broadly speaking, rising interest rates are bad news for share prices and falling rates are good. Rising rates increase the cost of corporate borrowing and thereby reduce profits. Higher interest rates also increase the attraction of selling shares to hold funds on deposit. Factors which are likely to lead the government to raise interest rates – rising inflation, strong economic growth – are therefore often bad news for the markets.

Profits growth. Equities represent a share of the assets and profits of a company. The faster profits grow, therefore, the better for the markets. Tax changes which eat into profits hit the market.

Supply and demand. Flotations and rights issues increase the supply of shares in the market and drive prices down (other things being equal); dividends, share buy-backs and takeovers for cash increase the funds available for investment and push prices up.

International influences. Increasingly, stock markets are being dominated by global influences as investors move money round in search of the most attractive havens. There is a tendency for share prices to move up and down together; London, in particular, is heavily influenced by Wall Street and a sharp fall in the US market usually has a knock-on effect in the UK.

The global picture

For those who are interested in more than just the UK market, the *world stock markets page* covers the rest of the globe. The aim is to explain why each market rose and fell on the day and to give details of a few substantial movements of individual stocks. As with the UK, Wall Street often sets the tone, although Tokyo follows its own agenda. Having been amazingly strong in the 1980s, the Japanese stock market has been in a slump throughout the 1990s in the face of a sluggish economy and weakened financial system.

Investors are becoming increasingly interested in the so-called *emerging markets* of Latin America and Asia, which have faster rates of economic growth, and thus the potential for greater increase in corporate profits, than the developed world. Liberalization of these markets has also encouraged foreign investors to buy shares.

Bond markets

Daily coverage of the *bond markets* appears on the International Capital Markets page.

Government bond market

The market in government bonds is huge; at the end of 1995, there was some $22 trillion of outstanding debt or around $3,500 for every individual on the planet. Bond markets are curmudgeonly and rather misanthropic sorts; they tend to dislike news that pleases the rest of the population. A fall in unemployment, a pick-up in wages or a strengthening of economic growth will tend to cause the bond markets to fall. This is because the biggest enemy of bond markets is inflation. Even at 5% inflation, prices double every 14 years or so, so the real value of a 15-year bond will halve between issue and repayment. Bond investors tend to believe that strong economic growth (which in developed countries tends to be an annual rate of 2.5% or more) leads to inflation.

Apart from inflation, the other important factor in influencing bond markets tends to be supply. The supply of government bonds depends on the size of the country's budget deficit, so a larger-than-expected deficit tends to depress bond prices. In some countries, particularly the developing world, the debts become so large that countries have little hope of repaying the capital, or even the interest; such was the case during the debt crisis of the early 1980s, which centred on Latin America.

An important note for anyone reading the paper's bond market coverage is the relationship between the *yield* and the *price*. The yield is calculated by dividing the interest rate payable on the bond by the market price; as the price rises, therefore, the yield falls and vice versa.

Primary bond markets

The coverage of primary bond issues on the same page looks at how companies and governments are raising money, how much, at what rate, and in which currency. Trends change as borrowers seek to get the best terms available; it may, for example, be advantageous for a UK borrower to raise money in Australian dollars and convert back into sterling.

Foreign exchange markets

Coverage of the *foreign exchange markets* immediately follows the capital markets page. Here again, the market is huge with daily turnover of around $500bn in London, and can be turbulent, as when the UK and other currencies were forced out of the Exchange Rate Mechanism in 1992. The main factors affecting a currency are economic; low inflation, a trade surplus, high real (after inflation) interest rates, tend to cause it to rise; high inflation, a trade deficit and low real rates tend to cause it to fall. But on a day-to-day or week-to-week basis, currencies can often move in a contrary direction to that implied by the economic fundamentals.

Commodites

Financial assets have tended to be good investments in the 1980s and 1990s but back in the 1970s, the smart money was in *commodities*. The era of high inflation saw price booms in most commodities, with the most obvious example being oil. Falling inflation, new sources of supply and improved production techniques combined to bring down commodity prices in the 1980s. Interest in the area has recently revived, however, and our commodities page covers the most important developments; the ups and downs of raw material prices can have important effects in individual sectors of the economy. A poor coffee harvest in Brazil, a cold winter in the US, political unrest in the Middle East; all can have knock-on effects which eventually become apparent to the consumer.

Index